The Computer Music Tutorial

Curtis Roads

The Computer Music Tutorial

SECOND EDITION

The MIT Press
Cambridge, Massachusetts
London, England

The MIT Press would like to thank the anonymous peer reviewers who provided comments on drafts of this book. The generous work of academic experts is essential for establishing the authority and quality of our publications. We acknowledge with gratitude the contributions of these otherwise uncredited readers.

This book was set in Times New Roman by Westchester Publishing Services. Printed and bound in the United States of America.

Library of Congress Cataloging-in-Publication Data

Names: Roads, Curtis, author.
Title: The computer music tutorial / Curtis Roads.
Description: Second edition. | Cambridge, Massachusetts :
    The MIT Press, 2023. | Includes bibliographical references and index.
Identifiers: LCCN 2022003353 (print) | LCCN 2022003354 (ebook) |
    ISBN 9780262044912 (hardcover) | ISBN 9780262361545 (epub) |
    ISBN 9780262361538 (pdf)
Subjects: LCSH: Computer music—Instruction and study. | Computer sound
    processing. | Software synthesizers. | Computer composition (Music)
Classification: LCC MT56 .R6 2023 (print) | LCC MT56 (ebook) |
    DDC 780.285—dc23
LC record available at https://lccn.loc.gov/2022003353
LC ebook record available at https://lccn.loc.gov/2022003354

10 9 8 7 6 5 4 3 2 1

publication supported by a grant from
The Community Foundation for Greater New Haven
as part of the **Urban Haven Project**

Contents

Foreword: New Music and Science

With the use of computers and digital devices, the processes of music composition and its production have become intertwined with the scientific and technical resources of society to a greater extent than ever before. Through extensive application of computers in the generation and processing of sound and the composition of music from levels of the microformal to the macroformal, composers, from creative necessity, have provoked a robust interdependence between domains of scientific and musical thought. Not only have science and technology enriched contemporary music, but the converse is also true: problems of particular musical importance in some cases suggest or pose directly problems of scientific and technological importance, as well. Each having its own motivations, music and science depend on one another and in so doing define a unique relationship to their mutual benefit.

The use of technology in music is not new; however, it has reached a new level of pertinence with the rapid development of computer systems. Modern computer systems encompass concepts that extend far beyond those that are intrinsic to the physical machines themselves. One of the distinctive attributes of computing is programmability and hence programming languages. High-level programming languages, representing centuries of thought about thinking, are the means by which computers become accessible to diverse disciplines.

Programming involves mental processes and rigorous attention to detail not unlike those involved in composition. Thus, it is not surprising that composers were the first artists to make substantive use of computers. There were compelling reasons to integrate some essential scientific knowledge and concepts into the musical consciousness and to gain competence in areas which are seemingly foreign to music. Two reasons were (and are) particularly compelling: (1) the generality of sound synthesis by computer, and (2) the power of programming in relation to the musical structure and the process of composition.

Sound Synthesis

Although the traditional musical instruments constitute a rich sound space indeed, it has been many decades since composers' imaginations have conjured up sounds based on the interpolation and extrapolation of those found in nature but that are not realizable with acoustical or analog electronic instruments. A loudspeaker controlled by a computer is the most general synthesis medium in existence. Any sound, from the simplest to the most complex, that can be produced through a loudspeaker can be synthesized with this medium. This generality of computer synthesis implies an extraordinarily larger sound space, which has an obvious attraction to composers. The reason is that computer sound synthesis is the bridge between that which can be imagined and that which can be heard.

With the elimination of constraints imposed by the medium on sound production, there nonetheless remains an enormous barrier that the composer must overcome in order to make use of this potential. That barrier is the lack of knowledge—the knowledge required for the composer to be able to effectively instruct the computer in the synthesis process. To some extent this technical knowledge relates to computers; this is rather easily acquired. But it mostly has to do with the physical description and perceptual correlates of sound. Curiously, the knowledge required does not exist, for the most part, in those areas of scientific inquiry where one would most expect to find it, that is, physical acoustics and psychobiology; these disciplines tend to provide either inexact or no data at those levels of detail with which a composer is ultimately most concerned. In the past, scientific data and conclusions were used in attempts to replicate natural sounds as a way of gaining information about sound in general. Musicians and musician-scientists were quick to point out that most of the conclusions and data were insufficient. The synthesis of sounds that approach in aural complexity the simplest natural sound demands detailed knowledge about the temporal evolution of the various components of the sound.

Physics, psychology, computer science, and mathematics have, however, provided powerful tools and concepts. When these concepts are integrated with musical knowledge and aural sensitivity, they allow musicians, scientists, and technicians, working together, to carve out new concepts and physical and psychophysical descriptions of sound at levels of detail that are of use to the composer in meeting the exacting requirements of the ear and imagination.

As this book shows, some results have emerged: there is a much deeper understanding of timbre, and composers have a much richer sound palette with which to work; new efficient synthesis techniques have been discovered and developed that are based on modeling the perceptual attributes of sound rather than the physical attributes; powerful programs have been developed for the purposes of editing and mixing synthesized and/or digitally recorded sound; experiments in perceptual fusion have led to novel and musically useful research in sound source identification and auditory images; and finally, special-purpose computer-synthesizers are being designed and built. These real-time performance systems incorporate many advances in knowledge and technique.

Programming and Composition

Because one of the fundamental assumptions in designing a computer programming language is generality, the range of practical applications of any given high-level language is enormous and obviously includes music. Programs have been written in a variety of programming languages for various musical purposes. Those that have been most useful and with which composers have gained the most experience are programs for the synthesis and processing of sound and programs that translate musical specifications of a piece of music into physical specifications required by the synthesis program.

The gaining of some competence at programming can be rewarding to a composer because it is the key to a general understanding of computer systems. Although systems are composed of programs of great complexity and written using techniques not easily learned by nonspecialists, programming ability enables the composer to understand the overall workings of a system to the extent required for its effective use. Programming ability also gives the composer a certain independence at those levels of computing in which independence is most desirable: synthesis. Similar to the case in traditional orchestration, the choices made in the synthesis of tones, having to do with timbre and microarticulation, are often highly subjective. The process is greatly enhanced by the ability of the composer to alter synthesis algorithms freely.

The programming of musical structure is another opportunity that programming competence can provide. To the extent that compositional processes can be formulated in a more or less precise manner, they may be implemented in the form of a program. A musical structure that is based upon some iterative process, for example, might be appropriately realized by means of programming.

But there is a less tangible effect of programming competence that results from the contact of the composer with the concepts of a programming language. Whereas the function that a program is to perform can influence the choice of language in which the program is written, it is also true that a programming language can influence the conception of a program's function. In a more general sense, programming concepts can suggest functions that might not occur to one outside of the context of programming. This is of signal importance in music composition, because the integration of programming concepts into the musical imagination can extend the boundaries of the imagination itself. That is, the language is not simply a tool with which some preconceived task or function can be accomplished; it is an extensive basis of structure with which the imagination can interact, as well. Although computer synthesis of sound involves physical and psychophysical concepts derived from the analysis of natural sounds, when joined with higher-level programming of musical structure the implications extend far beyond timbre. Unlike the condition that exists in composition for traditional instruments under which the relation of vibrational modes of an instrument is largely beyond compositional influence, computer synthesis allows for the composition of music's microstructure.

In the context of computing, then, the microstructure of music is not necessarily of predetermined form, that is, associated with a specific articulation of a particular instrument. Rather, it can be subjected to the same thought processes and be as freely determined in the imagination of the composer as every other aspect of the work.

John Chowning

Preface to the Second Edition

Here is *The Computer Music Tutorial, Second Edition*. When we first submitted a book proposal for *The Computer Music Tutorial* to the MIT Press in 1979, I was editor of *Computer Music Journal*. Three previous editors joined me in this proposal. John Snell was a music hardware engineer, and Curtis Abbott and John M. Strawn were digital signal processing mavens. My research interests at the time revolved around algorithmic composition and granular synthesis. Our general plan had been to divide up the subject matter according to each author's interests and expertise. However, the project went slower than expected, and by 1983, my partners had dropped out due to better opportunities. I was faced with learning about areas of research that were unfamiliar to me. After a sustained period during which I was also working full time, I finished the manuscript in Paris in 1993.

The production process was long, and the book did not appear until 1996. I planned the original as a three-volume set; however, The MIT Press favored a single volume. The size and weight of the book was a practical problem, although it did not deter sales. The scope reflected my insistence on breadth. I felt it important to represent many directions of the field and not just a select few, as favored by certain people and institutions.

I have always been interested in the legacy of electronic and computer music, so a strong thread of the first edition was the history of the field. This historical scholarship was a major endeavor in itself and runs throughout the text.

Later, for the French edition published by Dunod, my colleague Jean de Reydellet suggested a more logical organization into many short chapters (Roads 1998). We used this organization in the second and third French editions (Roads 2007, 2016). I have adopted a similar organization here.

Many chapters can be read independently of one another. However, in certain cases it is helpful to read one before another. This is mentioned in the relevant chapters.

Publishing Context

In this revised edition, the reader will find new chapters and also extensive updates based on recent research. In certain cases, it was necessary to reframe the discussion in the light of all that has transpired since the original edition was published.

Electronic and computer music is developing rapidly. The field rides waves of technological innovation. Faster processors and networks, better displays, and clever controllers have all made their mark. Improvements in audio equipment advance the field. These create a hardware foundation for innovations in software. Today, thousands of companies compete to deliver products to musicians.

Many fundamentals, however, have not changed. Vintage gear and carefully preserved software from decades past can sound wonderful today. The laws of physics that govern digital signal processing are immutable. Many new products are clever reworkings of ancient principles dressed up in fresh interfaces. Yet the power of an interface is not to be underestimated. A novel design can completely transform the method of working. The digital audio workstation (DAW) with its graphical time line interface for editing and mixing was one such innovation. Graphical patching of modules was another (e.g., Max), as was the integration of real-time spectral displays. The modular Eurorack format inspired a giant wave of creativity in synthesis and control. In each of these cases, a novel step quickly propagated and changed the field.

When it was published, *The Computer Music Tutorial* was one of only a handful of books devoted to the subject. Many more books have since been published. If we look solely at the catalog of MIT Press books published since 1996 and narrow it to technical books on computer music, we see a range of texts that expand on subtopics introduced in this volume: *Composing Interactive Music, Microsound, The Audio Programming Book, The Csound Book, The SuperCollider Book, Designing Sound, Sonic Interaction Design, Virtual Music, Music Cognition and Computerized Sound, Computer Models of Musical Creativity, Musimathics 1 and 2, Beyond MIDI, Music Query, Music and Probability,* and *Musical Networks.* Dozens of other books are available from different publishers.

Publishing has been profoundly transformed by the internet. The internet is an extraordinary resource if you know what to look for. A goal of this text is to foster this curiosity. Some 2,000 references support the descriptions.

What Is New in the Second Edition?

To begin, this edition incorporates corrections. Second, after an extensive review of the literature, the content has been thoroughly updated and rewritten for greater clarity. This includes hundreds of new figures and hundreds of new references.

New chapters include virtual analog, pulsar synthesis, concatenative synthesis, spectrum analysis by atomic decomposition, Open Sound Control, spectrum editors, instrument and patch editors, and an appendix on machine learning.

New sections cover MIDI 2.0, piano models, single-sideband modulation, wavefolding, dynamic convolution, immersive sound (VBAP, ambisonics, and wave field synthesis), sidechain control and adaptive effects, additive synthesis based on machine learning, transmission formats for multichannel sound, filter banks and vocoders, fractal interpolation synthesis, scanned synthesis, digital audio workstations and audio middleware, live coding and live notation, and telematic music.

Topics Deleted or Omitted

The original edition had an introductory chapter on computer programming as a general topic. Although it was well-intended, programming is hard to summarize in a chapter. Many tomes cover programming in depth and detail. Identical considerations came into play when I considered a chapter specifically on audio programming. By now many books focus specifically on this topic. For example, *The Audio Programming Book* (Boulanger and Lazzarini 2011) contains over 3,000 pages of text and thousands of lines of code, including code listings for Csound, cmusic, and Music V. Each audio language has its own reference text. Among these are *The Csound Book* (Boulanger 2000), *The SuperCollider Book* (Wilson, Cottle, and Collins 2011), *Programming for Musicians and Digital Artists: Creating Music with ChucK* (Kapur et al. 2015), *Electronic Music and Sound Design, Volumes 1 and 2* (Max) (Cipriani and Giri 2010a, b), *The Theory and Technique of Electronic Music* (PureData) (Puckette 2007), *Designing Audio Objects for Max/MSP and Pd* (Lyon 2012), *Hack Audio* (MATLAB) (Tarr 2019), and *Nyquist Reference Manual* (Dannenberg 2018), among others. Languages such as Faust and AudioKit are documented online. Practical how-to texts such as *Linux Sound Programming* (Newmarch 2017), *Designing Audio Effects Plugins in C++* (Pirkle 2019) and *Designing Software Synthesizer Plugins in C++* (Pirkle 2015) are available. See also *Generating Sound & Organizing Time: Thinking with gen~* (Wakefield and

Taylor 2022). The Audio Developer Conference is another resource, as is the Audio Programmer video channel on YouTube.

Thus our presentation of audio programming in chapter 8 is merely a pointer to a large domain.

The original edition had an appendix on psychoacoustics, a topic that is not specific to computer music. Other texts offer a more comprehensive treatment of this area (Loy 2006; Howard and Angus 2017; Bader 2018).

The old appendix on the mathematics of Fourier analysis is gone, but I merged the essential information into chapter 37, "Spectrum Analysis by Fourier Methods." For those who want a more extended treatment, Loy (2007) devotes over one hundred pages to the same subject; Smith (2011) offers nearly six hundred pages.

I excised the dated chapter "Internals of Digital Signal Processors" with regret, especially the historical section. The pioneers of *digital signal processing* (DSP) hardware in the 1970s and 1980s, such as Sydney Alonso, Harold Alles, Peter Samson, and Giuseppe Di Giugno, were heroes of synthesizer engineering. Fortunately, many of these stories are told elsewhere. Joel Chadabe (1997) tells the saga of the Synclavier and several other pioneering systems. Mark Vail (2000a, b) recounts the early days of analog and digital synthesis. Bjørn and Meyer (2018) interview several modular synthesizer developers. Loy (2013a, b) tells the story of the Samson Box from an historical perspective. Giordano (2020) documents the colorful career of Di Giugno.

The situation of digital audio hardware today is quite different. DSP chips can be found in audio effects hardware, synthesizers from Yamaha, Roland, and other companies, digital Eurorack modules, and unique products such as the Kyma/Pacarana and the Universal Audio Apollo interfaces. However, most audio software today runs on standard microprocessors without DSP hardware support. Thus the topic of DSP architecture per se did not seem as central to this book as it did in the 1990s, when many personal computers had a dedicated DSP circuit board for audio processing.

Ironically, present-day audio computing faces a challenge, as *central processing unit* (CPU) clock speeds stalled years ago (Asanovíc et al. 2006). The short-term solution, adding more cores to the CPU chip, does not benefit real-time audio processing, which is not ideally suited to multicore architectures (Thall 2019). As a solution, some have predicted that audio DSP chips could make a comeback even as *graphical programming units* (GPUs) and *tensor processing units* (TPUs) are also being deployed for audio (Storer 2018; Anderson 2020). However, if these chips do not become standard, their impact will be limited. Time will tell.

At one point I thought it would be useful to have a survey chapter on the broad area of *music information retrieval* (MIR). Fortunately, a textbook called

Fundamentals of Music Processing (Müller 2015) appeared, which covers this topic in a tutorial manner. Müller's book describes specific methods for analysis-based applications, discussed in part V of this book. These include score following, parsing music structure, chord recognition, tempo and beat tracking, content-based audio retrieval, harmonic-percussive separation, and melody tracking. An associated website provides example code in Python (https://www.audiolabs-erlangen.de/news/articles/FMP), and Lerch (2012) covers related subjects. Also refer to Polotti and Rocchesso (2008).

Certain chapters of the book mention mechanical automation, but a full-bore treatment of the topic of musical robots was not possible. Mechanical automation has a deep history dating to the age of eighteenth-century *androids* built by Jacques de Vaucanson (Sousa 1906; Leichtentritt 1934; Ord-Hume 1973, 1984; Buchner 1978; Kapur 2005). Although some musical robots are little more than mechanical sequencers (such as player pianos), others are capable of human interaction by means of machine listening. Specialized conferences and books such as those by Solis and Ng (2011) focus entirely on this area of experimentation.

In the original edition, I did not specifically focus on composition. Neither do I here. It is a topic that demands its own platform, and to this end I have devoted a part of my book *Microsound* (Roads 2001a) and all of *Composing Electronic Music: A New Aesthetic* (Roads 2015) to this end.

Intended Audience

The intended audience of *The Computer Music Tutorial, Second Edition* is the same as the original: music students, but also engineers and scientists seeking orientation to computer music. The word *orientation* is key, as is the word *tutorial* in the title.

Many of the topics discussed in the fifty-two chapters herein could be expanded into book-length treatises. The goal of this book was the opposite: to sift through the research literature, sort out the most fundamental facts, and craft a clear and concise technical narrative that would be understandable by a novice. This tutorial is not intended as a comprehensive resource for advanced developers of computer music algorithms. We aim to introduce the field, explain its motivations, put topics into context, and provide references for further study.

For more than twenty-five years I have used *The Computer Music Tutorial* in my year-long introductory course on electronic and computer music. Judging from this experience, I can testify that the pace and the level of this book are well matched to an introductory course.

Generic versus Specific

In the first edition of the book I was careful to make the explanations generic and not tied to specific hardware and software, which can become obsolete. The field is more stable now. Thus in this revised edition, I still keep the theory generic, but I decided to cite more products as examples in order to make the descriptions more concrete. Many of these products have been around for more than two decades. Of course, although certain products are mentioned as examples, this text is not meant to be a product survey.

Diversity

One of the reviewers of the manuscript brought up the thorny issue of diversity in computer music. This has long been a concern in the field, as pointed by Mary Simoni's 1995 survey of gender issues in electronic and computer music. These concerns echo in more recent studies such as Xambó (2018) and Sofer (2022). Similar issues can be raised concerning other underrepresented groups. *The Computer Music Tutorial, Second Edition* is focused primarily on technical research. It reflects the scholarly literature, which historically has not been as diverse as one would hope. Thus I have made an explicit effort to mention and cite diverse contributors when possible.

Acknowledgments

The Computer Music Tutorial was published immediately before I started teaching at the University of California, Santa Barbara. I would like to thank my UCSB colleagues at the Center for Research in Electronic Art Technology (CREATE). I also greatly appreciate the support from my colleagues in the Media Arts and Technology (MAT) Graduate Program and the Department of Music at UCSB.

For this edition, my former student and research colleague, Professor Bob L. T. Sturm (KTH Royal Institute of Technology, Stockholm) kindly agreed to assist with revisions. Specifically, he revised several chapters and contributed two new chapters.

I would also like to thank my former CREATE colleague Dr. Mathew J. Wright (Center for Computer Research in Music and Acoustics, Stanford) for his collaboration on chapter 52, "Open Sound Control."

Chapter reviewers included Aaron Anderson, Clarence Barlow, Stefan Bilbao, Thom Blum, Ludger Brümmer, Nick Collins, Jean de Reydellet, Rodney Duplessis, Kramer Elwell, Stewart Engart, Tom Erbe, Yuan-Yi Fan, Susan Frykberg, Stefanie Ku, JoAnn Kuchera-Morin, Elizabeth Hambleton, Michael Hetrick, Francisco Iovino, Christopher Jette, Garry Kling, Lawrence Kolasa, Ryan McGee, João Pedro Oliveira, Brian O'Reilly, Robert Owens, Chris Ozley, Brandon Rolle, David Romblom, Giorgio Sancristoforo, Ron Sedgwick, Atau Tanaka, Bruce Wiggins, Michael Winter, and Karl Yerkes. Dr. Tim Wood wrote scripts to verify the citations and references. Thanks to Federico Llach for his consultation on the Max example in chapter 45.

This book includes corrections to the original edition kindly supplied by Keiji Hirata, Takafumi Hikichi, James McCartney, and Graham Hadfield.

I am grateful to Professor Keiji Hirata of the University of Tokyo for organizing the Japanese edition, which appeared in 2001. Alongside Professor Hirata were translators Tatsuya Aoyagi, Naotoshi Osaka, Masataka Goto, Takefumi Hikichi, Saburo Hirano, Yasuo Horiuti, and Toshiaki Matsushima.

I thank Dr. Ken Fields, Adjunct Professor in Media Arts and Technology at UCSB and Professor at the Central Conservatory of Music in Beijing for organizing the Chinese edition, which appeared in 2011. I thank the translators of the Chinese edition, Chang Wei, Chen Yang, Cheng Yibing, Hu Ze, Huang Zhipeng, Jiang Hao, Li Sixin, Li Yueling, Qi Gang, Yang Renying, Zhang Ruibo (Mungo), and the proofreaders, Jin Ping, Li Sixin, and Qi Gang.

Finally, I would like to thank the teams at MIT Press and Westchester Publishing Services for their assistance with the production of this book.

Preface to the Original Edition (1996)

Music changes: new forms appear in infinite variety, and reinterpretations infuse freshness into old genres. Waves of musical cultures overlap, diffusing new stylistic resonances. Techniques for playing and composing music meander with these waves. Bound with the incessant redevelopment in music making is an ongoing evolution in music technology. For every music there is a family of instruments, so that today we have hundreds of instruments to choose from, even if we restrict ourselves to the acoustic ones.

In the twentieth century, electronics turned the stream of instrument design into a boiling rapids. Electrification transformed the guitar, bass, piano, organ, and drum (machine) into the folk instruments of industrial society. Analog synthesizers expanded the musical sound palette and launched a round of experimentation with sound materials. But analog synthesizers were limited by a lack of programmability, precision, memory, and intelligence. By virtue of these capabilities, the digital computer provides an expanded set of brushes and implements for manipulating sound color. It can listen, analyze, and respond to musical gestures in sophisticated ways. It lets musicians edit music or compose according to logical rules and print the results in music notation. It can teach interactively and demonstrate all aspects of music with sound and images. New musical applications continue to spin out of computer music research.

In the wake of ongoing change, musicians confront the challenge of understanding the possibilities of the medium and keeping up with new developments. *The Computer Music Tutorial* addresses the need for a standard and comprehensive text of basic information on the theory and practice of computer music. As a complement to the reference volumes *Foundations of Computer Music,* (edited with John M. Strawn, MIT Press, 1985) and *The Music Machine* (MIT Press, 1989), this book provides the essential background necessary for advanced exploration of the computer music field. While *Foundations of Computer Music* and *The Music Machine* are anthologies, this textbook contains all new material directed toward teaching purposes.

Intended Audience

The intended audience for this book is not only music students but also engineers and scientists seeking an orientation to computer music. Many sections of this volume open technical "black boxes," revealing the inner workings of software and hardware mechanisms. Why is technical information relevant to the musician? Our goal is not to turn musicians into engineers but to make them better informed and more skillful users of music technology. Technically naive musicians sometimes have unduly narrow concepts of the possibilities of this rapidly evolving medium; they may import conceptual limitations of bygone epochs into a domain where such restrictions no longer apply. For want of basic information, they may waste time dabbling, not knowing how to translate intuitions into practical results. Thus one aim of this book is to impart a sense of independence to the many musicians who will eventually set up and manage a home or institutional computer music studio.

For some musicians, the descriptions herein will serve as an introduction to specialized technical study. A few will push the field forward with new technical advances. This should not surprise anyone who has followed the evolution of this field. History shows time and again that some of the most significant advances in music technology have been conceived by technically informed musicians.

Interdisciplinary Spirit

The knowledge base of computer music draws from composition, acoustics, psychoacoustics, physics, signal processing, synthesis, performance, computer science, and electrical engineering. Thus, a well-rounded pedagogy in computer music must reflect an interdisciplinary spirit. In this book, musical applications motivate the presentation of technical concepts, and the discussion of technical procedures is interspersed with commentary on their musical significance.

Heritage

One goal of our work has been to convey an awareness of the heritage of computer music. Overview and background sections place the current picture into historical context. Myriad references to the literature point to sources for further study and also highlight the pioneers behind the concepts.

Concepts and Terms

Every music device and software package uses a different set of protocols—terminology, notation system, command syntax, button layout, and so on. These differing protocols are built on the fundamental concepts explained in this volume. Given the myriad incompatibilities and the constantly changing technical environment, it seems more appropriate for a book to teach fundamental concepts than to spell out the idiosyncrasies of a specific language, software application, or synthesizer. Hence, this volume is not intended to teach the reader how to operate a specific device or software package—that is the goal of the documentation supplied with each system. But it will make this kind of learning much easier.

Use of This Book in Teaching

The Computer Music Tutorial has been written as a general textbook, aimed at presenting a balanced view the field in its current state. It is designed to serve as a core text and should be easily adaptable to a variety of teaching situations. In the ideal situation, this book should be assigned as a reader in conjunction with a studio environment where students have ample time to try out the various ideas within. Every studio favors particular tools (such as computers, software, synthesizers, etc.), so the manuals for those tools, along with studio-based practical instruction, should round out the educational equation.

Composition

Notwithstanding the broad scope of this book, it was impossible to compress the art of composition into a single part. Instead, readers will find many citations to composers and musical practices interwoven with technical discussions. Chapters 18 and 19 present the technical principles behind algorithmic composition, but this is only one facet of a vast—indeed open-ended—discipline, and is not necessarily meant to typify computer music composition as a whole.

We have surveyed composition practices in other publications. *Composers and the Computer* focuses on several musicians (Roads1985a). During my tenure as the editor of *Computer Music Journal* (1978–1989), we published many reviews of compositions as well as interviews with and articles by composers. These include a "Symposium on composition," with fourteen composers participating (Roads 1986b), and a special issue on composition, 5(4) 1981. Some of these articles are available in a widely available text, *The Music Machine* (MIT Press 1989). Issue 11(1) 1987 featured microtonality in computer music composition. Many other periodicals and books contain informative articles on compositional issues in electronic and computer music.

References and Index

In a tutorial volume that covers many topics, it is essential to supply pointers for further study. This book contains extensive citations and a reference list of more than 1,400 entries compiled at the back of the volume. As a further service to readers, we have invested much time to ensure that both the name and subject indexes are comprehensive.

Mathematics and Coding Style

Since this *Tutorial* is addressed primarily to a musical audience, we chose to present technical ideas in an informal style. The book uses as little mathematical notation as possible. It keeps code examples brief. When mathematical notation is needed, it is presented with operators, precedence relations, and groupings specified explicitly for readability. This is important because the idioms of traditional mathematical notation are sometimes cryptic at first glance or are incomplete as algorithmic descriptions. For the same reasons, the book usually uses long variable names instead of the single-character variables favored in proofs. With the exception of a few simple Lisp examples, code examples are presented in a Pascal-like pseudocode.

Corrections and Comments Invited

In a large book covering a new field, there will inevitably be errors. We welcome corrections and comments, and we are always seeking further historical information. Please send comments and corrections via email to the author at clangtint@gmail.com.

Acknowledgments

This book was written over a period of many years. I wrote the first draft from 1980 to 1986, while serving as a research associate in computer music at the Massachusetts Institute of Technology and as editor of *Computer Music Journal* for The MIT Press. I am grateful to many friends for their assistance during the period of revisions that followed.

Major sections of part IV ("Mixing and Signal Processing") and part V ("Sound Analysis") were added during a 1988 stay as visiting professor in the Department of Physics at the Università di Napoli Federico II, thanks to an invitation by Professor Aldo Piccialli. I am deeply grateful to Professor Piccialli for his detailed comments and generous counsel on the theory of signal processing.

Valuable feedback on part III ("Sound Synthesis") came from composition students in the Department of Music at Harvard University, where I taught in 1989, thanks to Professor Ivan Tcherepnin. I thank Professors Conrad Cummings and Gary Nelson for the opportunity to teach at the Oberlin Conservatory of Music in 1990, where I presented much of the book in lecture form, which led to clarifications in the writing.

During spare moments I worked on part VI ("The Musician's Interface") in Tokyo at the Center for Computer Music and Music Technology, Kunitachi College of Music, in 1991, thanks to the center's director Cornelia Colyer, Kunitachi chairman Bin Ebisawa, and a commission for a composition from the Japan Ministry of Culture. Final refinements to the book were carried out in Paris. I presented the first courses based on the completed text in 1993 and 1994 at Les Ateliers UPIC, thanks to Gerard Pape and Iannis Xenakis, and the Music Department of the University of Paris 8, thanks to Professor Horacio Vaggione.

John M. Strawn, formerly my editorial colleague at *Computer Music Journal,* contributed substantially to this project for several years. In between his duties as a doctoral student at Stanford University, he contributed much to part I ("Digital Audio"). Later, he reviewed drafts of most chapters with characteristic thoroughness. Throughout this marathon effort, John consulted on myriad details via electronic mail. I am grateful to him for sharing his wide musical and technical knowledge and sharp wit.

Many kind individuals helped by supplying information, documentation, and photographs or by reading chapter drafts. I am profoundly indebted to these generous people for their myriad suggestions, criticisms, and contributions to this book: Jean-Marie Adrien, Jim Aiken, Clarence Barlow, François Bayle, James Beauchamp, Paul Berg, Nicola Bernardini, Peter Beyls, Jack

Biswell, Thom Blum, Richard Boulanger, David Bristow, William Buxton, Wendy Carlos, René Caussé, Xavier Chabot, John Chowning, Cornelia Colyer, K. Conklin, Conrad Cummings, James Dashow, Philippe Depalle, Mark Dolson, Giovanni De Poli, Gerhard Eckel, William Eldridge, Gianpaolo Evangelista, Ayshe Farman-Farmaian, Adrian Freed, Christopher Fry, Guy Garnett, John W. Gordon, Philip Greenspun, Kurt Hebel, Henkjan Honing, Gottfried Michael Koenig, Paul Lansky, Otto Laske, David Lewin, D. Gareth Loy, Max V. Mathews, Stephen McAdams, Dennis Miller, Diego Minciacchi, Bernard Mont-Reynaud, Robert Moog, F. R. Moore, James A. Moorer, Peter Nye, Robert J. Owens, Alan Peevers, Aldo Piccialli, Stephen Pope, Edward L. Poulin, Miller Puckette, Thomas Rhea, Jean-Claude Risset, Craig Roads, Xavier Rodet, Joseph Rothstein, William Schottstaedt, Marie-Hélène Serra, John Snell, John Stautner, Morton Subotnick, Martha Swetzoff, Karen Tanaka, Stan Tempelaars, Daniel Teruggi, Irène Thanos, Barry Truax, Alvise Vidolin, Dean Wallraff, David Waxman, Erling Wold, and Iannis Xenakis.

I would also like to express my thanks to the staff of The MIT Press Journals—Janet Fisher, manager—publishers of *Computer Music Journal*. This work would have been nigh impossible without their backing over the past fourteen years.

I will always be grateful to Frank Urbanowski, director of The MIT Press, and executive editor Terry Ehling for their extraordinarily patient and kind support of this project.

I am also indebted to Sandra Minkkinen and the production staff of The MIT Press for their fine editing and production labors.

This book is dedicated to my mother, Marjorie Roads.

I   Digital Audio

1 *History of Digital Audio*

History of Analog Audio Recording

Experimental Digital Audio Recording

Digital Sound for the Public

> **Digital Audio Discs**
> **Downloadable Audio File Formats**

Digital Sound for Musicians

Origins of Digital Multitrack Recording

The Art of Recording

This chapter presents a basic introduction to the history and technology of digital audio recording and playback.

History of Analog Audio Recording

Sound recording has a rich history, beginning with Léon Scott's phonautograph of 1857, which could record a sound waveform but not play it back. Thomas Edison's experiments in the 1870s combined sound recording with playback on wax cylinders. Emile Berliner's gramophone (1887) recorded on rotating discs, the precursor to the long-play (LP) vinyl discs still being made (Read and Welch 1976). Early audio recording was a mechanical process (figure 1.1). Air vibrations caused a membrane to vibrate, and these vibrations were traced in a soft medium such as a rotating wax cylinder by a stylus attached to the membrane.

Although the invention of the triode vacuum tube in 1906 launched the era of electronics, electronically produced recordings did not become practical until 1924 (Keller 1981). Figure 1.2 depicts one of the horn-loaded loudspeakers that were common in the 1920s.

Optical sound recording on film was first demonstrated in 1922 (Ristow 1993). Sound recording on tape coated with powdered magnetized material was developed in the 1930s in Germany (figure 1.3) but did not reach the rest of the world until after World War II. The German

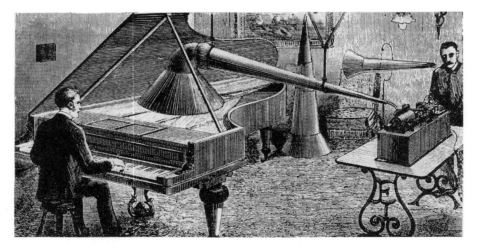

Figure 1.1   Mechanical recording session before 1900. Sound vibrations picked up by the large cone over the piano were transduced into vibrations of a cutting stylus piercing a rotating wax cylinder.

Figure 1.2   Amplion loudspeaker, as advertised in 1925.

magnetophon tape recorders were a great advance over previous wire and steel band recorders, which required hard soldering or welding to make a splice.

The magnetophons and their descendants were *analog* recorders, so called because the waveform encoded on tape is a close *analogy* to the original sound waveform picked up by a microphone. If we could view the magnetized particles on the tape, they would form a pattern resembling the sound waveform. Analog recording is still favored by some for its special quality of sound. However, analog recording faces fundamental physical limits. These limits are most apparent in copying from one analog medium to another—additional noise is inescapable.

For more on the history of analog recording, see chapter 26 on mixing.

Figure 1.3   Prototype of a portable *magnetophon* tape recorder from 1935, made by AEG. (Photograph courtesy of BASF Aktiengesellschaft.)

Experimental Digital Audio Recording

The core concept in digital audio recording is *sampling*, that is, converting continuous analog signals (such as those coming from a microphone) into discrete *time-sampled* signals (*samples*). Each sample is nothing more than a number—a snapshot of a sound waveform (figure 1.4).

The theoretical underpinning of sampling is the *sampling theorem*, which specifies the relation between the sampling rate and the audio bandwidth. It is also called the *Nyquist theorem* after the work of Harold Nyquist of Bell Telephone Laboratories (Nyquist 1928), but another form of this theorem was first stated in 1841 by the French mathematician Augustin Louis Cauchy (1789–1857). The British researcher A. Reeves developed the first patented *pulse-code-modulation* (PCM) system for transmission of messages in *amplitude-dichotomized, time-quantized* (digital) form (Reeves 1938; Licklider 1950; Black 1953). Even today, digital recording is sometimes called *PCM recording*. The development of *information theory* contributed to the understanding of digital audio transmission (Shannon 1948). Solving the difficult problems of converting between analog signals and digital signals took decades and is still being improved. Chapters 3 and 4 describe the conversion processes.

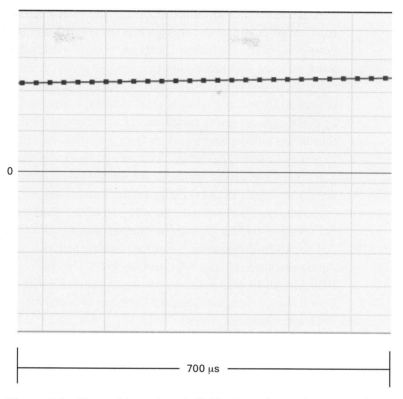

700 μs

Figure 1.4   Zoomed in to show individual samples as they appear in a sound editor. The sound editor drew a line through them to enhance the display. The samples are all positive in amplitude; the line in the center represents 0 amplitude. The time span shown is about 700 μs (less than a thousandth of a second).

Primitive methods of generating sounds, such as placing a radio next to a computer and running programs that loop at audio frequencies to create melodies, date to the early days of electronic computing (Doornbusch 2005). These experiments were very limited in their sound quality.

In the late 1950s, Max Mathews and his group at Bell Telephone Laboratories generated the first sample-based sounds from a digital computer (David, Mathews, and McDonald 1959). Using samples to represent waveforms allowed generating any possible waveshape. The samples were written by the computer to expensive and bulky reel-to-reel computer tape storage drives. The production of sound from the numbers was a separate process of playing back the tape through a custom-built 12-bit vacuum tube *digital-to-sound converter* developed the Epsco Corporation (Roads 1980). Today we call a playback device that translates from digital numbers into analog voltages a *digital-to-analog converter* (DAC). By contrast, an *analog-to-digital converter* (ADC) encodes an analog waveform into digital numbers.

A practical digital audio recording medium needs to be robust, that is, resilient when errors occur. Methods for *error detection and correction* were developed in the 1950s and 1960s and widely used in communications. Later, Sato, Blesser, Stockham, and Doi applied error correction in the first practical digital audio recorders and players. The first dedicated one-channel digital audio recorder (based on a videotape mechanism) was demonstrated by NHK, the Japanese broadcasting company (Nakajima et al. 1983). Soon thereafter, Denon developed an improved version (figure 1.5), and the race began to bring digital audio recorders to market (Iwamura et al. 1973).

By 1977 the first commercial recording system appeared, the Sony PCM-1, designed to encode 13-bit digital audio signals onto Sony videocassette recorders. Within a year this was displaced by 16-bit PCM encoders such as the $40,000 Sony PCM-1600 for the professional recording market (Nakajima et al. 1978).

The Audio Engineering Society established two standard sampling frequencies in the 1980s: 44.1 and 48 kHz. This became known as the AES/EBU or AES3 standard after it was endorsed by the European Broadcast Union. Since then, the standard has been successively revised to incorporate the higher sampling rates of 88.2, 96, 176.4, and 192 kHz, and so on (Audio Engineering Society 2008). A variety of high-resolution recorders are now available, including hand-held *field recorders* with built-in microphones.

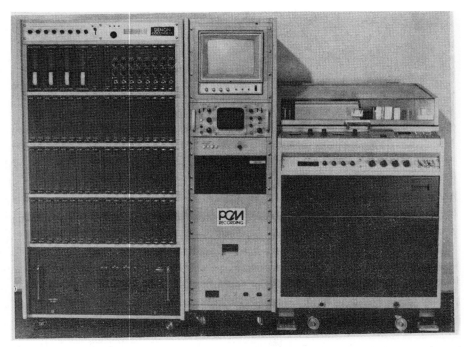

Figure 1.5 Nippon Columbia (Denon) digital audio recorder made in 1973, based on a 1-inch videotape recorder (right).

Digital Sound for the Public

In 1980, computer sound research was still in its infancy, and the standard consumer format for recorded music was the vinyl long-play (LP) record, introduced in 1948. Apart from a small number of audiophile-quality LPs, the majority of LPs manufactured by record companies in the 1970s and 1980s were not of outstanding quality, due to compromised mastering and manufacturing practices. Thus, the market was ripe for an improved format.

Digital Audio Discs

Digital sound first reached the general public in 1982 by means of the *compact disc* (CD) format, a 12 cm optical disc read by a laser. The CD format was developed jointly by the Philips and Sony corporations after years of development. It was a tremendous commercial success, selling over 1.35 million players and tens of millions of discs within two years (Pohlman 1989a). Part of the success of the CD can be traced to its adoption by the computer industry as a general means of distributing software and storing data, the CD read-only memory (CD-ROM).

Introduced in 2000, the specialized DVD-audio (DVD-A) and super audio compact disc (SACD) optical disc formats offered improved sound quality, but neither format gained a foothold in the market. The Blu-ray disc format, first introduced in 2002, is same physical size as the CD and DVD. Blu-ray supports high-definition 3D video, up to 128 gigabytes of data and up to eight channels of high-resolution digital audio (up to 24 bits per sample at a 96 kHz sampling rate). Blu-ray as an audio-only format was announced in 2013 but was not successful.

Downloadable Audio File Formats

The rise of the internet fostered the evolution of downloadable audio file formats. Throughout the 1990s, most internet users relied on slow connections based on telephone modems with sluggish transmission speeds. As a response to these limitations, the popular MP3 medium was developed under the official moniker MPEG Audio Layer III, an international standard. MP3 uses a *lossy compression* algorithm to drastically reduce the size of a sound file (Pohlmann 2005). To reduce the amount of data, audio information is discarded in the encoding phase. This results in a loss of audio fidelity.

By contrast, *lossless compression* reduces the size of the file for the purpose of storage and transmission while allowing the original file to be reconstructed exactly. The free lossless audio codec (FLAC) is an example of a lossless compression format. Digital audio files compressed by FLAC's algorithm can be reduced in size by around 50 percent (Xiph 2015).

New media formats are constantly appearing, partly because there are commercial incentives to introduce proprietary systems. See chapter 4 for more on audio file formats.

Digital Sound for Musicians

High-quality DACs attached to personal computers came on the scene around 1988. At the same time, standard formats for audio files appeared, including Sound Designer II (SDII), audio interchange file format (AIFF), and waveform audio format (WAVE). These developments heralded a major new era for computer music. In a short period, sound synthesis, recording, and processing by personal computer became widespread. Many different *digital audio workstations* (DAWs) reached the musical marketplace, including Pro Tools, Cubase, Digital Performer, Logic, and others. DAWs let musicians record music onto a hard disk connected to a personal computer. This music could be precisely edited using a timeline display on the computer screen with playback from the hard disk.

Origins of Digital Multitrack Recording

Multitrack recorders have a number of discrete channels or *tracks* that can be recorded at different times. Each track can record, for example, a separate instrument, which allows flexibility when the tracks are later mixed together. Another advantage of multitrack machines is that they let musicians build recordings in several layers; each new layer is an accompaniment to previously recorded layers.

The British Broadcasting Company (BBC) developed an experimental 10-channel digital tape recorder in 1976. Two years later, the 3M company introduced the first commercial 32-track digital recorder (figure 1.6) as well as a rudimentary digital tape editor (Duffy 1982). The first computer disk–based random-access sound editor and mixer was developed by the Soundstream company in Salt Lake City, Utah (see figure 16.38). Their pioneering system allowed mixing of up to eight tracks or *sound files* stored on computer disk at a time (Ingebretsen and Stockham 1984).

Early digital multitrack recording was a very expensive enterprise. The Studer digital recorder (figure 1.7) sold for $270,000 in 1991. Then within a

Figure 1.6 3M 32-track digital tape recorder, introduced in 1978.

Figure 1.7 Studer D820-48 DASH digital multitrack recorder, introduced in 1991 with a retail price of about $270,000. To make a backup copy of the tape required the use of two machines.

Figure 1.8   Sony PCM-D100 field recorder.

short time, software DAWs replaced tape recorders in most studios. It became possible to record, edit, and mix on portable laptop computers.

High-quality digital field recorders with built-in microphones became popular (figure 1.8).

To some extent, the functionality of portable field recorders can be achieved on mobile phones with accessories for an audio interface and high-quality stereo microphones. The downside of mobile devices is rapid obsolescence, which afflicts anything connected to them.

The Art of Recording

The art of recording requires more than proper equipment. Serious students of recording have much to learn through apprenticeship. A number of schools offer four-year Tonmeister degrees in recording engineering. Tonmeisters study music as well as applied physics. They learn about the acoustics of rooms (reflection, absorption, and diffraction of sound waves) and instruments, microphone types, microphone techniques, and audio media production methods.

2 *Basics of Sound Signals*

Frequency and Amplitude

>   **Time-Domain Representation**
>   **Frequency-Domain Representation**

Phase

>   **Importance of Phase**

Sound Magnitude

Dynamic Range

This chapter introduces basic concepts and terminology for describing sound signals, including frequency, amplitude, and phase.

Frequency and Amplitude

Sound reaches listeners' ears after being transmitted through air from a source. We hear sound because the air pressure is changing slightly in our ears, causing the eardrum to vibrate. If the pressure varies according to a repeating pattern, we say that the sound has a *periodic waveform*. If there is no discernible pattern it is called *noise*. In between these two extremes is a vast domain of quasiperiodic and quasinoisy sounds.

One repetition of a periodic waveform is called a *cycle,* and the *fundamental frequency* of the waveform is the number of cycles that occur per second. In the rest of this book we substitute *Hz* for *cycles per second* in accordance with standard acoustical terminology. (Hz is an abbreviation for *hertz*, the unit of measurement named after the German acoustician Heinrich Hertz.)

As the length of the cycle (called the *period*) decreases, the frequency in cycles per second increases, and vice versa. Table 2.1 shows the relationship between frequency and period.

Another descriptive term is *wavelength*, which is the measure of the physical distance between periods. Because sound travels at about 343 m/s at 20° Celsius, a wave at 1 Hz unfolds over about 343 m, whereas a wave at 20 kHz unfolds over about 0.017 m or about 1.7 cm.

Time-Domain Representation

A simple method of depicting sound waveforms is to draw them in the form of a graph of air pressure versus time (figure 2.1). This pressure graph is called a *time-domain* representation. When the curved line is near the bottom of the graph, the air pressure is lower; when the curve is near the top of the

Table 2.1   Relationship of frequency to period

Frequency	Period
1 Hz	1 second (s)
10 Hz	0.1 s or 100 milliseconds (ms)
100 Hz	0.01 s or 10 ms
1000 Hz	0.001 s or 1 ms
10000 Hz	0.0001 s or 100 microseconds (μs)

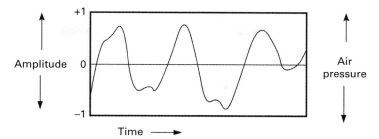

Figure 2.1   Time-domain representation of a signal. The vertical dimension shows the air pressure. When the curved line is near the top of the graph, the air pressure is greater. Below the solid horizontal line, the air pressure is reduced. Atmospheric pressure variations heard as sound can occur quickly; for musical sounds, this entire graph might last no more than one-thousandth of a second (1 ms).

graph, the air pressure has increased. The *amplitude* of the waveform is the amount of air pressure change; we can measure amplitude as the vertical distance from the zero pressure point to the highest (or lowest) points of a given waveform segment.

An acoustic instrument creates sound by emitting vibrations that change the air pressure around the instrument. A loudspeaker creates sound by moving back and forth according to voltage changes in an electronic signal. When the loudspeaker moves *in* from its position at rest, then the air pressure decreases. As the loudspeaker moves *out*, the air pressure near the loudspeaker is raised. To create an audible sound, these in/out vibrations must occur at a frequency in the range of about 20 to 20,000 Hz.

Frequency-Domain Representation

Besides the fundamental frequency, there can be many frequencies present in a waveform. A *frequency-domain* or *spectrum* representation shows the frequency content of a sound. The individual frequency components of the spectrum can be referred to as *harmonics* or *partials*. Harmonic frequencies are simple integer multiples of the fundamental frequency. Assuming a fundamental or *first harmonic* of 100 Hz, its second harmonic is 200 Hz, its third harmonic is 300 Hz, and so on. More generally, any frequency component can be called a partial, whether or not it is an integer multiple of a fundamental. Indeed, many sounds have no particular fundamental frequency.

The frequency content of a waveform can be displayed in many ways. A standard way is to plot each partial as a line along an *x*-axis. The height of each line indicates the strength (or amplitude) of each frequency component. The purest signal is a *sine* waveform, so named because it can be calculated using trigonometric formulae for the sine of an angle. A pure sine wave represents just one frequency component or one line in a spectrum. Figure 2.2 depicts the time-domain and frequency-domain representations of several waveforms. Notice that the spectrum plots are labeled *harmonics* on their horizontal axis because the analysis algorithm assumes that its input is exactly one period of the fundamental of a periodic waveform. In the case of the noise signal in figure 2.2g, this assumption is not valid, so we relabel the partials as *frequency components*.

As we discuss in chapters 36–39, there are many ways to plot the spectrum of a sound.

Phase

The starting point of a periodic waveform on the *y* or amplitude axis is its *initial phase*. For example, a typical sine wave starts at the amplitude point 0 and completes its cycle at 0. If we displace the starting point by $\pi/2$ radians or 90° on the horizontal axis then the sinusoidal wave starts and ends at 1 on the amplitude axis. By convention this is called a *cosine wave*. In effect, a cosine is equivalent to a sine wave that is *phase shifted* by 90° (figure 2.3).

When two signals start at the same point, they are said to be *in phase* or *phase aligned*. This contrasts to a signal that is slightly delayed with respect to another signal, in which the two signals are *out of phase*. When a signal A is the exact opposite phase of another signal B (i.e., it is 180° out of phase, so that for every positive value in signal A there is a corresponding negative value for signal B), we say that B has *reversed polarity* with respect to A. We could also say that B is a *phase-inverted* copy of A. Figure 2.4 portrays the effect when two signals in inverse phase relationship sum: they cancel out each other.

Importance of Phase

It is sometimes said that phase is insignificant to the human ear, because two signals that are exactly the same except for their initial phase are difficult to distinguish. However, research indicates that 180° differences in absolute phase or *polarity* can be distinguished by some people under laboratory conditions (Greiner and Melton 1991). For more on phase perception, refer to Laitinen, Disch, and Pulkki (2013).

Even apart from special cases, phase is an important concept for several reasons. Every filter uses phase shifts to alter signals. A filter shifts the phase

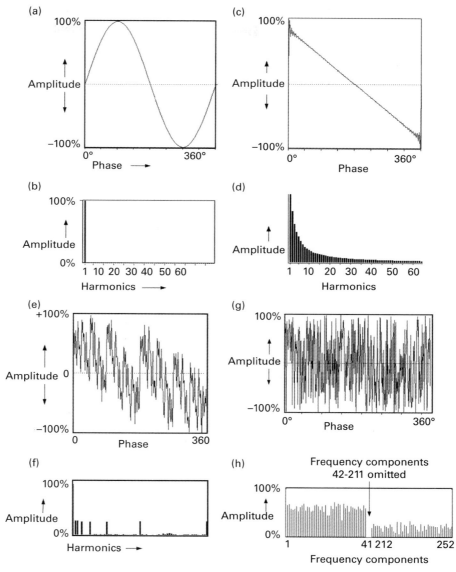

Figure 2.2   Time-domain and frequency-domain representations of four signals. (a) Time-domain view of one cycle of a sine wave. (b) Spectrum of the one frequency component in a sine wave. (c) Time-domain view of one cycle of a sawtooth waveform. (d) Spectrum showing the exponentially decreasing frequency content of a sawtooth wave. (e) Time-domain view of one cycle of a complex waveform. Although the waveform looks complex, when it is repeated over and over its sound is actually simple—like a thin reed organ sound. (f) The spectrum of waveform (e) shows that it is dominated by a few frequencies. (g) A random noise waveform. (h) If the waveform is constantly changing (each cycle is different from the last cycle), then we hear noise. The frequency content of noise is very complex. In this case the analysis extracted 252 frequencies. This snapshot does not reveal how their amplitudes are constantly changing over time.

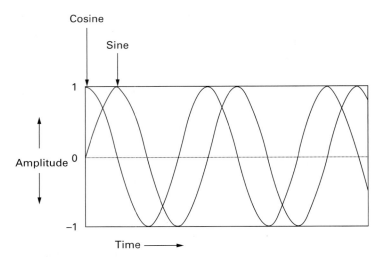

Figure 2.3   A sine waveform is equivalent to a cosine waveform that has been delayed and hence phase shifted slightly.

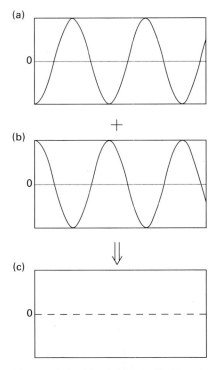

Figure 2.4   The effects of phase inversion. (b) is a phase-inverted copy of (a). If the two waveforms are added together, (c) they sum to zero.

of a signal by delaying its input for a short time and then combines the phase-shift version with the original signal. This creates *frequency-dependent phase cancelation* to attenuate certain frequencies and *phase reinforcement* to boost certain frequencies. By *frequency-dependent* we mean that not all frequency components are affected equally. When the phase shift is time varying, the affected frequency bands also vary, creating the sweeping sound effect called *phasing* or *flanging* (see chapter 30).

Phase is also important in systems that resynthesize sound on the basis of an analysis of an existing sound. In particular, these systems need to know the starting phase of each frequency component in order to assemble the different components in the right order (M.-H. Serra 1997; X. Serra 1997). Phase data is particularly critical in reproducing short, rapidly changing *transient* sounds, such as the onset of a percussive tone.

Finally, much attention has been invested in audio components that shift the phases of their input signals as little as possible, because frequency-dependent phase shifts distort musical signals audibly and interfere with loudspeaker *imaging*. (Imaging is the ability of a set of loudspeakers to create a stable *audio picture* in which each audio source is localized to a specific place within the picture.) Unwanted phase shifting is called *phase distortion*. To make a visual analogy, a phase-distorted signal is *out of focus*.

Sound Magnitude

We all have an intuitive notion of *sound level* or *sound magnitude*. Even a small child understands the function of a volume knob. The *decibel* is a unit of measurement for relationships of magnitude, including voltage levels, intensity, or power, particularly in audio systems. In acoustic measurements, the decibel scale indicates the ratio of one level to a *reference level,* according to the relation

number of decibels = $10 \times \log_{10}$ (*level/reference level*)

where the *reference level* is usually the threshold of hearing (10^{-12} watts per square meter). The logarithmic basis of decibels means that if two notes sound together and each note is 60 dB, the increase in level is just 3 dB. A millionfold increase in intensity results in only a 60 dB boost.

Figure 2.5 shows the decibel scale and some estimated acoustic power levels relative to 0 dB.

Chapter 4 contains a more thorough discussion of sound magnitude and decibels.

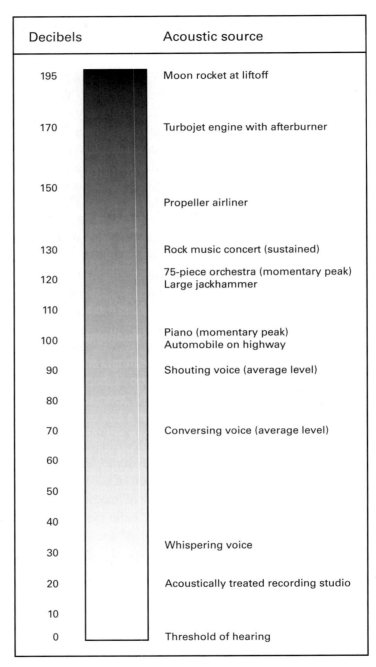

Decibels	Acoustic source
195	Moon rocket at liftoff
170	Turbojet engine with afterburner
150	
	Propeller airliner
130	Rock music concert (sustained)
120	75-piece orchestra (momentary peak) Large jackhammer
110	
100	Piano (momentary peak) Automobile on highway
90	Shouting voice (average level)
80	
70	Conversing voice (average level)
60	
50	
40	
30	Whispering voice
20	Acoustically treated recording studio
10	
0	Threshold of hearing

Figure 2.5   Typical acoustic power levels for various acoustic sources. All values are relative to 0 dB.

Dynamic Range

Dynamic range is the ratio between the loudest and the softest sound that can be handled by a system without distortion. Two important facts describe the dynamic range requirements of a digital audio system:

- The range of human hearing extends from approximately 0 dB, roughly the level at which the softest sound can be heard, to around 125 dB, which is roughly the threshold of pain for sustained sounds.
- A difference of somewhat less than one dB between the amplitude levels of two sounds corresponds to the smallest difference in amplitude that can be heard.

In recording music, we want to reproduce the full expressive power of the music. Thus it is important to capture the widest possible dynamic range. In a live orchestra concert, for example, the dynamic range can vary from silence to a tutti (full orchestra) section exceeding 110 dB.

Every recording device (such as a microphone, mic preamplifier, mixer, or recorder) can handle only a certain dynamic range before it distorts. For example, the dynamic range of analog tape equipment is dictated by the physics of the analog recording process. That range is around 80 dB for a 1 kHz tone using professional reel-to-reel tape recorders without noise-reduction devices. By contrast, a high-quality digital audio recorder can have a dynamic range of around 120 dB.

Chapter 4 goes into more detail about dynamic range in digital audio systems.

3 *Theory of Sampling*

Curtis Roads with John M. Strawn

Analog Representations of Sound

Digital Representations for Sound

      Analog-to-Digital Conversion
      Binary Numbers
      Digital-to-Analog Conversion
      Digital Audio Samples Are Not MIDI Data

Sampling

      Reconstruction of the Analog Signal

Aliasing

The Sampling Theorem

Antialiasing and Anti-imaging Filters

Audio Interfaces

Ideal Sampling Frequency

Jitter

This chapter begins by explaining differences between analog and digital audio systems. We then step through the basics of the digital audio recording and playback chain. For further technical study, consult Pohlmann (2010).

Analog Representations of Sound

Just as air pressure varies according to sound waves, so can the electrical property called *voltage* in a wire connecting an amplifier with a loudspeaker. We do not need to define voltage here. For the purposes of this chapter, we simply assume that it is possible to modify an electrical property in a fashion that closely matches changes in air pressure. We can say that air pressure and voltage are analogous to each other. That is, a graph of the air pressure variations picked up by a microphone looks similar to a graph of the variations in the loudspeaker position when that sound is played back. The term *analog* means that these properties can vary in a similar manner.

Figure 3.1 shows an analog audio playback chain. The curve of an audio waveform can be inscribed along the groove of a traditional phonograph record. The walls of the grooves on a phonograph record contain a *continuous-time* representation of the sound stored in the record. As the needle glides through the groove, it moves back and forth in lateral motion. This lateral motion is then changed into voltage, which is amplified and eventually reaches the loudspeaker.

Analog recording and reproduction of sound has been taken to a high level, but it faces fundamental physical limits. Specifically, when one copies an analog recording onto another analog recorder, the copy is never as good as the original. The reason is that the analog recording process always adds noise. On a *first-generation* or original recording made with a high-quality tape recorder, this noise is not objectionable. But if we copy the first-generation tape onto another tape and then copy the copy, the noise increases noticeably. In contrast, digital technology can create any number of generations of perfect (noise-free) clones of an original digital recording, as we show further on.

Digital Representations for Sound

This section introduces the most basic concepts associated with digital signals, including the conversion of audio signals into binary numbers, and comparison of audio data with MIDI data.

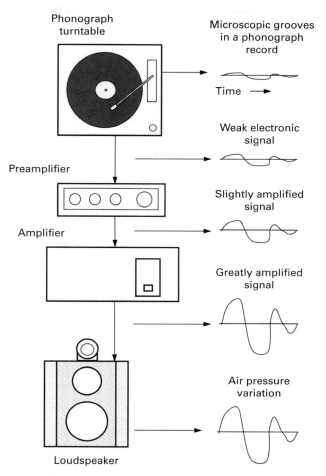

Figure 3.1   The analog audio playback chain, starting from an analog waveform transduced from the grooves of a phonograph record to a voltage sent to a preamplifier, amplifier, and loudspeaker and projected into the air.

Analog-to-Digital Conversion

Let us look at the process of digitally recording sound and then playing it back. Rather than the continuous-time signals of the analog world, a digital recorder handles *discrete-time* signals. Figure 3.2 shows a diagram of the digital audio recording and playback process. In this diagram, a microphone transduces air pressure variations into electrical voltage variations, which are then passed through an *antialiasing filter* and then to an *analog-to-digital converter* (ADC). (We discuss the function of the antialiasing filter in a subsequent section.) The ADC samples and converts the voltage variations into a string of *binary numbers* at each uniform period of the sample

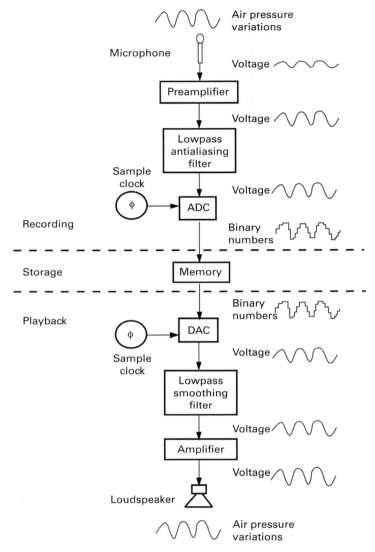

Figure 3.2   Overview of digital recording and playback.

clock. The binary numbers are then stored in a digital recording medium—a type of memory.

Binary Numbers

In contrast to decimal (or *base ten*) numbers, which use the ten digits 0–9, binary (or *base two*) numbers use only two digits: 0 and 1. The term *bit* is an abbreviation of *binary digit*. Table 3.1 lists binary numbers and their

Table 3.1 Binary numbers and their decimal equivalents

Binary	Decimal
0	0
1	1
10	2
11	3
100	4
1000	8
10000	16
100000	32
1111111111111111	65,535

decimal equivalents. In many digital systems the leftmost bit is interpreted as a sign indicator, with a 1 indicating a positive integer and a 0 indicating a negative integer. (Real decimal numbers such as 8.476 can also be represented in binary as *floating-point numbers*, but we will not explain this scheme here.)

The way a bit is physically encoded in a recording medium depends on the properties of that medium. On a magnetic disc, for example, a 1 might be represented by a positive magnetic charge, whereas a 0 is indicated by the absence of such a charge. This is different from an analog magnetic tape recording, in which the signal is represented as a continuously varying magnetic charge. On an optical medium such as a compact disc, binary data might be encoded as variations in the reflectance at a particular location. *Solid-state* or *flash memory* encodes a bit as an electrical charge in a memory cell made out of transistors.

Digital-to-Analog Conversion

Figure 3.3 depicts the result of converting an audio signal (a) into a digital signal (b). When the listener wants to hear the sound again, the binary numbers are read one by one from the digital storage and passed through a *digital-to-analog converter* (DAC). This device, driven by a sample clock, changes the stream of numbers into a series of voltage levels. From there, the process is the same as shown in figure 3.2; that is, the series of voltage levels are lowpass filtered into a continuous-time waveform (figure 3.3c), amplified, and routed to a loudspeaker, whose vibration causes the air pressure to change. Voilà—the signal sounds again.

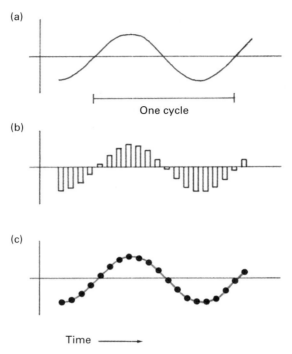

Figure 3.3   Analog and digital representations of a signal. (a) Analog sine waveform. The horizontal bar below the wave indicates one period or cycle. (b) Sampled version of the sine waveform in (a), as it might appear at the output of an ADC. Each vertical bar represents one sample. Each sample is stored in memory as a number that represents the height of the vertical bar. (c) Reconstruction of the sampled version of the waveform in (b). In effect, the samples are connected by the lowpass smoothing filter to form the waveform that eventually reaches the listener's ear.

In summary, we can change a sound in the air into a string of binary numbers that can be stored digitally. The central component in this conversion process is the ADC. When we want to hear the sound again, a DAC can change those numbers back into sound.

Digital Audio Samples Are Not MIDI Data

This section may clear up confusion. The string of numbers generated by the ADC is not related to Musical Instrument Digital Interface (MIDI) data. (For more information on MIDI, see chapter 52.) Digital audio recording samples the sound waveform whereas MIDI recording captures the data played on a controller, such as a keyboard. MIDI note information includes only the start and ending time, pitch (a number), and amplitude at the beginning of the note (a number). If a MIDI note is transmitted back to the synthesizer on which it was originally played, this causes the synthesizer to play the sound as it did originally, similarly to a piano roll recording. If the musician plays four quarter notes at a tempo of sixty beats per minute on a MIDI synthesizer, just sixteen pieces of information capture this four-second sound (four starts, ends, pitches, and amplitudes).

By contrast, if we record the same sound with a microphone connected to a digital audio recorder set to a sampling frequency of 44.1 kHz, 352,800 pieces of information (in the form of audio samples) are recorded for the same sound (44,100 × 2 channels × 4 seconds). The storage requirements of digital audio recording are large. Using 16-bit samples, it takes over 700,000 bytes to store a four-second sound. This is 44,100 times more data than is stored by MIDI.

The advantage of a digital audio recording is that it can capture any sound that can be recorded by a microphone, including the human voice. By contrast, MIDI sequence recording is limited to recording control signals that indicate the start, end, pitch, and amplitude of a series of note events.

Sampling

The digital signal shown in figure 3.3b is significantly different from the original analog signal shown in figure 3.3a. First, the digital signal is defined only at certain points in time. This happens because the signal has been *sampled* at certain times. Each vertical bar in figure 3.3b represents one *sample* of the original signal. The samples are stored as binary numbers; the higher the bar in figure 3.3b, the larger the number.

The number of bits used to represent each sample is called the *quantization* of the system. Quantization determines both the noise level and the amplitude range that can be handled by the system. For example, a compact disc has a quantization of 16 bits. That is, every sample is represented by a 16-bit number. More bits of quantization mean better amplitude resolution. This translates into lower noise and more dynamic range. Fewer bits result in the opposite. We return to this subject in chapter 4 when we discuss quantization at greater length.

The rate at which samples are taken—the *sampling frequency*—is expressed in terms of samples per second. This is an important specification of digital audio systems. It is often called the *sampling rate* and is expressed in terms of hertz (Hz). Simplifying the measurement 1,000 Hz to 1 kHz, we say, "The sampling rate of a compact disc recording is 44.1 kHz," where the *k* is derived from the metric term *kilo*, which means thousand.

Reconstruction of the Analog Signal

Sampling frequencies around 50 kHz are common in digital audio systems, although both lower and higher frequencies can also be found. In any case, 50,000 numbers per second is a rapid stream of numbers; it means there are 6,000,000 samples for one minute of stereo sound.

The digital signal in figure 3.3b does not show the value between the bars. The duration of a bar is extremely narrow, perhaps lasting only 0.00002 s (two hundred-thousandths of a second). This means that if the original signal changes between the bars, the change is not reflected in the height of a bar until the next sample is taken. In technical terms, we say that the signal in figure 3.3b is defined at *discrete* times, each such time represented by one sample (vertical bar).

Part of the magic of digital audio is that if the signal is *bandlimited,* the DAC and associated hardware can exactly reconstruct the original signal from these samples. We call a signal bandlimited if it has frequencies only within a finite range. This means that, given certain conditions, the missing part of the signal between the samples can be restored. This happens when the numbers are passed through the DAC, which includes the lowpass smoothing filter. The lowpass smoothing filter is designed precisely to re-create the missing part of the signal between the discrete samples (see the dotted line in figure 3.3c). Thus, the signal sent to the loudspeaker looks and sounds like the original signal.

Aliasing

The process of sampling is not quite as straightforward as it might seem. Just as an audio amplifier can introduce distortion, sampling can play tricks with sound. Figure 3.4 gives an example. Using the input waveform shown in figure 3.4a, suppose that a sample of this waveform is taken at each point in time shown by the vertical bars in figure 3.4b (each vertical bar creates one sample). As before, the resulting samples of figure 3.4c are stored as numbers in digital memory. However, when we attempt to reconstruct the original waveform, as shown in figure 3.4d, the result is something completely different.

In order to understand better the problems that can occur with sampling, we look at what happens when we change the *wavelength* (the length of one cycle) of the original signal without changing the length of time between samples. Figure 3.5a shows a signal with a cycle eight samples long, figure 3.5d shows a cycle two samples long, and figure 3.5g shows a waveform with eleven cycles per ten samples.

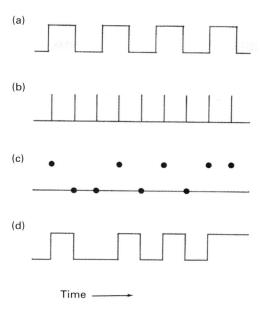

Figure 3.4   Problems in sampling. (a) Waveform to be recorded. (b) The sampling pulses; whenever a sampling pulse occurs, one sample is taken. (c) The waveform as sampled and stored in memory. (d) When the waveform from (c) is sent to the DAC, the output might appear as shown here (after Mathews 1969).

Again, as each of the sets of samples is passed through the DAC and associated hardware, a signal is reconstructed (figures 3.5c, f, and i) and sent to the loudspeaker. The signal shown by the dotted line in figure 3.5c is reconstructed more or less accurately. The results of the sampling in figure 3.5f are potentially less satisfactory; one possible reconstruction is shown there. But in figure 3.5i, the resynthesized waveform is completely different from the original in one important respect. Namely, the wavelength (length of the cycle) of the resynthesized waveform is different from that of the original. In the real world, this means that the reconstructed signal sounds at a pitch different from that of the original signal. This kind of distortion is called *aliasing*.

The frequencies at which this aliasing occurs can be predicted. Suppose, just to keep the numbers simple, that the sampling rate is 1,000 Hz. Then the signal in figure 3.5a has a frequency of 125 Hz (because there are eight samples per cycle, and $1,000/8 = 125$). In figure 3.5d, the signal has a frequency of 500 Hz (because $1,000/2 = 500$). The frequency of the input signal in figure 3.5g is 1,100 Hz.

Notice how the frequency of the output signal is different. In figure 3.5i you can count ten samples per cycle of the output waveform. In actuality, the output waveform occurs at a frequency of $1,000/10 = 100$ Hz. Thus the

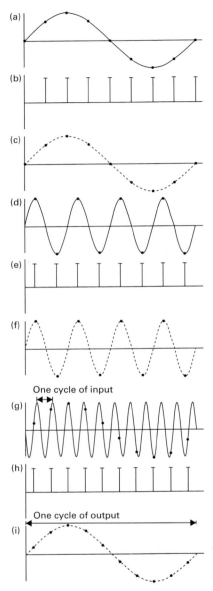

Figure 3.5 Aliasing effects. At the bottom of each set of three graphs, the thick black dots represent samples, and the dotted line shows the signal as reconstructed by the DAC. Every cycle of the sine waveform (a) is sampled eight times in (b). Using the same sampling frequency, each cycle of (d) is sampled only twice in (e). If the sampling pulses in (e) were moved to the right, the output waveform in (f) might be phase-shifted, although the frequency of the output would still be the same. In (h), there are ten samples for the eleven cycles in (g). When the DAC tries to reconstruct a signal, as shown by the dashed lines in (i), a sine waveform results, but the frequency has been completely changed due to the foldover effect. Notice the horizontal double arrow above (g), indicating one cycle of the input waveform, and the arrow above (i), indicating one cycle of the output waveform.

frequency of the original signal in figure 3.5g has been changed by the *sample rate conversion* process. This represents an unacceptable change to a musical signal that must be avoided if possible.

The Sampling Theorem

We can generalize from figure 3.5 to say that as long as there are at least two samples per period of the original waveform, we can assume that the resynthesized waveform will have the same frequency. But when there are fewer than two samples per period, the frequency of the original signal is lost. If the original frequency is higher than half the sampling frequency, then

new frequency = sampling frequency – original frequency

This formula is not mathematically complete, but it is sufficient for our discussion here. It means the following. Suppose that we have chosen a fixed sampling frequency. We start with a signal at a low frequency, sample it, and resynthesize the signal after sampling. As we raise the pitch of the input signal (but still keep the sampling frequency constant), the pitch of the resynthesized signal is the same as the pitch of the input signal until we reach a pitch that corresponds to one-half the sampling frequency. As we raise the pitch of the input signal even higher, the pitch of the output signal starts to descend to the lowest frequencies!

The process is depicted in figure 3.6, which shows why aliasing was sometimes called *foldover*.

To give a concrete example, suppose that we introduce an analog frequency at 30 kHz into an ADC operating at a 48 kHz sampling rate. When reconstructed by a DAC, it will produce a tone at 18 kHz, because $48 - 30 = 18$.

The *sampling theorem* (or *Nyquist theorem*) describes the relationship between the sampling rate and the bandwidth of the signal being transmitted. It was expressed by Harold Nyquist (1928) as follows:

For any given deformation of the received signal, the transmitted frequency range must be increased in direct proportion to the signaling speed. . . . The conclusion is that the frequency band is directly proportional to the speed.

The essential point of the sampling theorem can be stated precisely as follows:

In order to be able to reconstruct a continuous signal from its samples, the frequency at which we sample must be at least twice the highest frequency in the signal.

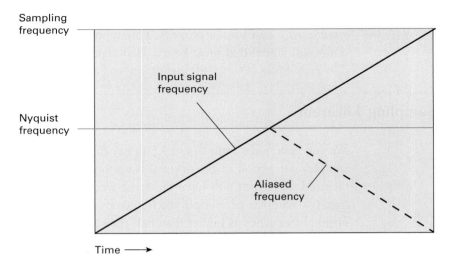

Figure 3.6   When the input frequency exceeds the Nyquist frequency, the recorded signal *folds over* and proceeds downward.

The highest frequency that can be reproduced in a digital audio system (i.e., half the sampling rate) is called the *Nyquist frequency.* In digital musical systems, the Nyquist frequency is usually above the upper range of human hearing, that is, above 20 kHz. Then the sampling frequency can be specified as being at least twice as much, or above 40 kHz. For example, in a recording system that samples at 44.1 kHz (the sampling frequency of compact discs), the Nyquist frequency is 22.05 kHz.

Antialiasing and Anti-imaging Filters

In order to make sure that a digital sound system works properly, two important filters are included. Recall figure 3.2. One filter is placed before the ADC, to make sure that nothing in the input signal occurs at a frequency higher than half the sampling frequency. As long as this filter does the proper work, aliasing should not occur during the recording process. Logically enough, such a filter is called an *antialiasing filter.*

The other filter is placed after the DAC. Its main function is to change the samples stored digitally into a smooth, continuous representation of the signal. In effect, this *lowpass anti-imaging* or *smoothing filter* creates the dotted line in figure 3.3c by connecting the solid black dots in the figure.

Audio Interfaces

The ADCs and DACs built into computers and mobile devices are inexpensive to manufacture. They perform adequately for daily use. However, the standard audio input and output of a computer, tablet, or phone is inadequate for high-quality audio recording and playback.

An *audio interface* provides a high-quality audio solution (figure 3.7). It connects to the computer or mobile device using a protocol that the device supports (such as USB, Thunderbolt, or Ethernet). It includes high-quality DACs and ADCs and microphone/line preamplifiers. Many have traditional MIDI input/output connectors.

The cost of audio interfaces ranges from inexpensive units (< $100) designed for home recording to professional units (> $10,000) that support multiple channels at high sampling rates.

Ideal Sampling Frequency

The Audio Engineering Society has recommended a set of standard sampling rates for audio, including 32, 44.1, 48, and 96 kHz (Audio Engineering Society 2008). It also recognizes that multiples of these basic rates are in use, such as 88.2. 176.4, 192, 352.8, 384, and even 768 kHz.

What sampling frequency is ideal for high-quality music recording and reproduction? Experts disagree.

We all want cameras with high resolution. Should we not also want high-resolution audio recordings? Higher sampling rates increase the bandwidth of recording, which means better audio quality. However, they also produce

Figure 3.7   Front and back panel of the RME Fireface UFX+ audio interface. The front panel shows four mic/line preamplifiers and MIDI jacks. Twelve analog inputs and outputs are supported. The rear panel bristles with connectors, including optical MADI multichannel jacks. The interface processes a total of ninety-six inputs and outputs and connects to a computer via USB 3 or Thunderbolt.

much larger file sizes. The more samples in a file, the greater the processing load. Transmitting a high sample rate file over a network takes more time. A file recorded at 192 kHz/24 bits is about nine times larger than one recorded at 44.1 kHz/16 bits.

One way to view resolution is to see the effect of the sampling process on an analog impulse. Figure 3.8 plots these effects. See how recording at 48 kHz blurs in time the original analog transient, as though it is out of focus.

One justification that has been given for higher sampling rates is that some people hear information (referred to as *air*) in the region around the 20 kHz limit of human hearing (Neve 1992). Many analog systems can reproduce ultrahigh frequencies. Microphones like the Sanken CO-100K can record sounds up to 100 kHz. Some microphone preamplifiers have a bandwidth that extends far beyond 200 kHz.

Scientific experiments confirm the effects of sounds above 22 kHz from both physiological and subjective viewpoints (Oohashi et al. 1991; Oohashi et al. 1993). Melchior (2019), however, points out how the improved quality of high-resolution recordings can be heard by people without extraordinary high-frequency hearing. She observes that the *temporal blur, pre-echo,* and *ringing* inherent in brick-wall filters associated with sampling rates below 50 kHz are contributing factors, and she lists several high-resolution schemes that alleviate these symptoms.

Another argument for high resolution is the more focused spatial imaging that accrues due to the presence of more high-frequency spatial information.

In sound synthesis applications, the lack of *frequency headroom* in standard sampling rates of 44.1 and 48 kHz is a source of serious prob-

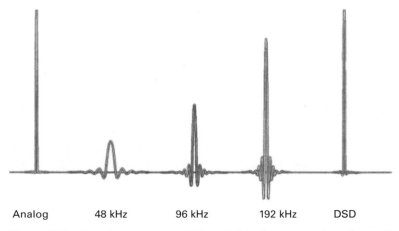

Analog   48 kHz   96 kHz   192 kHz   DSD

Figure 3.8   Impulse responses (*left to right*) of an analog impulse (*left*) as recorded by 48 kHz, 96 kHz, 192 kHz, and direct digital stream (DSD) recording systems. DSD is discussed in chapter 4.

lems. It requires that synthesis algorithms generate nothing other than sine waves above 11.025 kHz (44.1 kHz sampling rate) or 12 kHz (48 kHz sampling rate) in order to avoid aliasing. The reason is that any nonsinusoidal periodic waveform can have partials that exceed the Nyquist rate.

In sampling and *pitch-shifting* applications (see chapter 3.1), the lack of frequency headroom requires that sampled sounds be lowpass filtered before they are pitch-shifted upward to avoid aliasing. When tones recorded at 44.1 or 48 kHz are pitch-shifted downward, they become muffled and lose their high-frequency content because everything above the Nyquist frequency has already been eliminated by the antialiasing filter. In a recording made at a high sampling rate, pitch-shifting downward does not necessarily mean a loss of high frequency content, because ultrasonic energy is transposed into the high-frequency audio range.

High sampling rate recordings are preferable from an audio standpoint, but one needs a high-quality playback system to make the effort worthwhile. Many people listen to music on low-quality ear buds connected to mobile devices, where the luxury of high-resolution recordings is wasted.

Jitter

Jitter is time-based error in sampling. If the clock driving the ADC or DAC is not stable, then the conversions will not happen at the correct times. A typical audible effect of jitter is a high-frequency clicking noise added to the signal.

In a home studio, jitter is not likely to be an issue. The possibility of jitter increases when multiple physical devices are interconnected. Jitter can be a product of multiple factors: clock instability, poor cable/connector quality, impedance mismatches, or software issues. Thus jitter is a practical issue in complex digital audio systems. The general solution to jitter problems is to rely on a *master wordclock generator* device that is interconnected to all other devices via high-quality cables and connectors.

The sampling rate determines how often a digital system measures a continuous signal in time. The next chapter presents the topic of quantization, that is, how precisely a digital system measures a signal in amplitude. Taken together, these two processes, sampling and quantization, constitute the core of digital audio theory.

4 *Sample Quantization, Conversion, and Audio Formats*

More on Sound Magnitude
>   **Decibels**

Quantization
>   **Signal-to-Noise Ratio and Dynamic Range**
>   **Quantization Noise**
>   **Low-Level Quantization Noise and Dither**
>   **Converter Linearity**

Oversampling Converters
>   **1-Bit Converters**
>   **Noise Shaping**

Digital Audio Media and Formats
>   **Lossless versus Lossy File Formats**

This chapter examines the notion of sound magnitude as it pertains to digital audio recording. We then look at the technical issues surrounding dynamic range, quantization, oversampling, and digital audio media and formats.

More on Sound Magnitude

As pointed out in chapter 2, everyone has an intuitive notion of sound level or magnitude. Dozens of terms have been devised by scientists to describe the magnitude of a sound. Among many are the following:

- Peak-to-peak amplitude
- RMS amplitude
- Gain
- Sound energy
- Sound power
- Sound intensity
- Sound pressure level
- Loudness

From a scientific point of view, these terms are all different. From a common sense point of view, the terms are all correlated and proportional to one another: a significant boost in one corresponds to a boost in all. Our ears are sharply attuned to sound magnitude, so the concept is physical and directly perceivable.

From a musical point of view, the most useful scientific terms are peak-to-peak and RMS amplitude (as seen in a sound editor), gain (a standard term for boosting or attenuating a sound), sound pressure level (what a sound-level meter measures in the air), and loudness (perceived magnitude). Sound energy, power, and intensity are terms used by physicists to describe measures of sound magnitude relative to the amount of work done, that is, how much energy it takes to vibrate a medium.

Table 4.1 summarizes the formal definitions of these terms. Figure 4.1 illustrates three of the most important measures: peak, peak-to-peak, and RMS amplitude. The rest of this section explains the useful concept of decibels.

Decibels

The ear is an extremely sensitive organ. Suppose that we sit three meters in front of a loudspeaker that is generating a sine tone at 1,000 Hz that we

Table 4.1   Units for measuring sound magnitude

Peak-to-peak amplitude	A measure of the peak-to-peak difference in waveform values expressed as a percentage or as decibels (dB). Useful for describing the magnitude of periodic waveforms in particular.
RMS amplitude	For complex signals such as noise, root mean squared (RMS) amplitude describes the average power of the waveform. RMS amplitude is the square root of the mean over time of the square of the vertical distance of the waveform from the rest position.
Gain	A measure of the ratio of the input and the output amplitude (or power) of a process, usually measured in decibels. A gain of greater than 1 dB is a boost, and a gain of less than 1 dB corresponds to attenuation.
Sound energy	A measure of work, sound energy is the ability to vibrate a medium, expressed in joules. A joule is a unit of energy corresponding to the work done by a force of 1 newton traveling through a distance of 1 meter. A newton is equal to the amount of force required to give a mass of 1 kilogram an acceleration of 1 meter per second squared
Sound power	The rate at which work is done or energy is used. The standard unit of power is the watt, corresponding to 1 joule per second. 1 watt is the rate at which work is done when an object is moving at 1 meter per second against a force of 1 newton.
Sound intensity	Sound power per unit area, measured in watts per square meter.
Sound pressure level (SPL)	Air pressure at a particular point, given in decibels as a ratio of sound pressure to a reference sound pressure of 20 micropascals. A pascal is a unit of pressure equivalent to the force of 1 newton per square meter.
Loudness	A psychoacoustic measure based on queries of human subjects, measured in phons. 1 phon equals 1 dB SPL at 1 kHz.

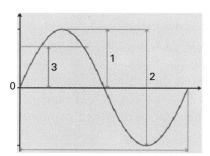

Figure 4.1   Measures of amplitude. (1) Peak amplitude. (2) Peak-to-peak amplitude. (3) RMS amplitude.

perceive as being very loud. Amazingly, one can reduce the power by a factor of one million and the tone is still audible. In an anechoic chamber where all external sounds are eliminated, the reduction extends to a factor of more than one billion (Backus 1977).

Sound transports energy generated by the vibration of a source. The range of sound energy encompasses everything from the subsonic flutterings of a butterfly to massive explosions. A whisper produces only a few billionths of a watt. By contrast, a large rocket launch generates about 10 million watts of power.

The decibel (dB) unit compresses these huge exponential variations into a smaller range by means of logarithms. The dB unit can be applied to myriad physical phenomena; however, the definition changes according to the phenomenon being measured. A standard unit in audio is dB SPL. This compares a given sound pressure level (SPL) with a standard reference level. The logarithm (base 10) of this ratio is the level in decibels, hence

SPL in decibels $= 20 \log_{10} (W/W_0)$

where W is the actual SPL of the signal being measured, and W_0 is a standard reference level of 20 micropascals of air pressure. This corresponds to the quietest sound that a human being can hear.

Describing sound levels in terms of dB enables a wide range. Table 4.2 shows how the decibel unit compresses large changes in percentage amplitude into relatively small changes in the number of dB.

As we move away from a sound source, its SPL diminishes according to the distance. Specifically, each doubling of distance decreases SPL by about 6 dB, which represents a 50% decrease in its amplitude. This is the famous *inverse square law*: intensity diminishes as the square of the distance.

So far we have been talking in terms of amplitude and SPL. Another pair of terms—*volume* and *loudness*—are intuitive. Technically, loudness refers to perceived subjective intensity measured through psychoacoustic tests on human beings and not to sound pressure level measured by laboratory instruments. For example, the ear is especially sensitive to frequencies between 1,000 Hz and 4,000 Hz. Tones in this region sound louder than tones of equal intensity in other frequencies. Thus the measurement of loudness falls into the realm of psychoacoustics. In order to differentiate loudness level (a perceptual characteristic) from sound pressure level (a physical characteristic), the unit *phon* (rhymes with *John*) is used. For example, to sound equally loud (60 phons), a tone at about 30 Hz needs to be boosted 40 dB more than a 1,000 Hz tone.

Table 4.2 Amplitude as a percentage versus as decibels

100%	0 dB
70%	−3 dB
50%	−6 dB
25%	−12 dB
12.5%	−18 dB
6.25%	−24 dB
3.125%	−30 dB
1.562%	−36 dB
0.781%	−42 dB
0.39%	−48 dB
0.195%	−54 dB
0.097%	−60 dB
0.048%	−66 dB
0.024%	−72 dB
0.012%	−78 dB
0.006%	−84 dB
0.003%	−90 dB

Quantization

Sampling at discrete time intervals constitutes one of the major differences between digital and analog signals. Another difference is *quantization,* which is sampling at discrete amplitude intervals. Digital numbers do not have infinite precision. They can be represented only within a certain range and with a certain accuracy, which varies with the hardware used.

Signal-to-Noise Ratio and Dynamic Range

Quantization is an important factor in digital audio quality. Specifically, the number of bits per sample (also called the *sample width*, *bit depth,* or *quantization level*) is important in calculating the *signal-to-noise ratio* (SNR). SNR is a measure of the noisiness of a system: a high SNR means low noise; a low SNR means high noise.

   SNR measures the ratio of the strength of an audio signal to the strength of noise. In an audio system, the SNR is specified as the difference in level between the standard operating level (usually 0 on a VU meter) and the average level of the noise floor, expressed in decibels. In general, each additional bit in the analog-to-digital converter will contribute about 6 dB to the SNR.

Another measurement is the *dynamic range* (DR) of a digital sound system. In simple terms, this is the difference in dB between the loudest and softest sounds that the system can produce. Clearly, SNR and DR are correlated; when the DR is high, so is the SNR. In theory, this is straightforward. It becomes more complicated when stipulating exactly how and in what units of measurement SNR and DR are calculated. As mentioned, the SNR is the difference between the standard operating level of 0 VU and the noise floor. The DR is the difference between the noise floor and the point of distortion. Thus the DR depends on a method of measuring distortion, which people define in different ways.

For our purposes, a simple formula for the dynamic range of a digital audio system is

$$\text{Dynamic range in decibels} = \text{Number of bits} \times 6.11$$

The number 6.11 is a close approximation to the theoretical maximum (van de Plaasche 1983; van de Plaasche and Dijkmans 1983; Hauser 1991); in practice, 6.0 is a more realistic figure. A derivation of this formula is given in Mathews (1969) and Blesser (1978).

Thus, if we record sound with an 8-bit system, then the upper limit on the DR is approximately 48 dB. This is correlated with a low SNR and is audibly noisy. But if we record 16 bits per sample, the dynamic range increases to a maximum of 96 dB—a major improvement. 16-bit audio became the standard of the compact disc. A 20-bit converter offers a potential DR of 120 dB, which corresponds roughly to the range of the human ear.

This discussion assumes that we are using a *linear PCM* scheme that stores each sample as an integer representing the value of each sample. Blesser (1978), Moorer (1979b), and Pohlmann (2010) have reviewed the implications of other encoding schemes. Some encoding schemes (e.g., MP3, discussed later) have the goal of reducing the total number of bits that the system stores or transmits.

Quantization Noise

Samples are often represented as integers. If the input signal has a voltage corresponding to a sample value between 53 and 54, for example, then the converter might round it off and assign a value of 53. In general, for each sample taken, the value of the sample usually differs slightly from the value of the original signal. This problem in digital signals is known as *quantization error* or *quantization noise* (Blesser 1978; Maher 1992; Lipshitz, Wannamaker, and Vanderkooy 1992; Pohlmann 2010).

Figure 4.2 shows the kinds of quantization errors that can occur. When the input signal is something complicated like a symphony, and we listen to just the errors, shown at the bottom of figure 4.2, it sounds like noise. If the errors are large, then one might notice something similar to analog tape hiss at the output of a system.

The quantization noise is dependent on two factors: the input signal itself, and the accuracy with which the signal is represented in digital form. We can explain the sensitivity to noise in the input signal by noting that on an analog tape recorder, tape imposes a soft halo of noise that continues even through periods of recorded silence. But in a digital system there is no quantization noise when nothing (or silence) is recorded. In other words, if the

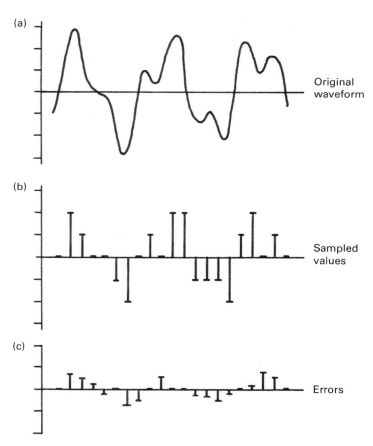

Figure 4.2 Effects of quantization. (a) Analog waveform. (b) Sampled version of the waveform in (a). Each sample can be assigned only certain values, which are indicated by the short horizontal dashes at the left. The difference between each sample and the original signal is shown in (c), where the height of each bar represents the quantization error.

input signal is silence, then the signal is represented by a series of samples, each of which is exactly zero. The small differences shown in figure 4.2c disappear for such a signal, which means that the quantization noise disappears. If the input signal is a pure sinusoid, however, then the quantization error is not a random function but a deterministic truncation effect that can be audibly gritty at low levels (Maher 1992; Stuart and Craven 2019). We discuss this further in the section on dithering.

The second factor in quantization noise is the accuracy of the digital representation. In a linear PCM system that represents each sample value by an integer, quantization noise is directly tied to the number of bits that are used to represent a sample. As previously noted, this is the *quantization level* of a system. Figure 4.3 illustrates the effects of different quantization levels, comparing the resolution of 1-bit versus 4-bit quantization. In a linear PCM system generally, the more bits used to represent a sample, the less the quantization noise.

Figure 4.4 shows the improvement in sine wave accuracy achieved by adding more bits of resolution, going from 2^4 (sixteen possible values) to 2^8 (256 possible values). Consider the improvement in precision accrued by using a 24-bit sample with 2^{24} or more than 16.7 million possible values.

The process of sampling can be viewed as fitting a waveform to a grid of time versus amplitude, as shown in figure 4.5. In general, the finer the grid, the better the approximation to the original waveform. More specifically, the finer the time grid (or sampling rate), the greater the bandwidth. The finer the amplitude grid (or quantization level), the greater the dynamic range and the smaller the amount of noise.

Low-Level Quantization Noise and Dither

Although a digital system exhibits no noise when there is no input signal, at very low (but nonzero) signal levels, quantization noise takes a pernicious form. This gritty sound, called *granulation noise* or *modulation noise*, can be heard when low-level tones decay to silence. A very low-level signal triggers variations only in the lowest bit. These 1-bit variations look like a square wave, which is rich in odd harmonics. Consider the decay of a piano tone, which smoothly attenuates with high partials rolling off—right until the lowest level when it changes character and becomes a harsh-sounding square wave. The harmonics of the square wave can extend even beyond the Nyquist frequency, causing aliasing and introducing new frequency components that were not in the original signal. These artifacts may be possible to ignore if the signal is kept at a low monitoring level, but if the signal is heard at a high level or if it is rescaled to a higher level (a common practice in

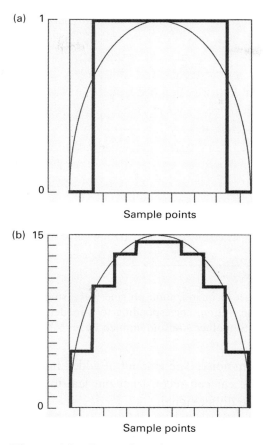

Figure 4.3 Comparing the accuracy of 4-bit quantization with that of 1-bit quantization. The thin rounded curve is the input waveform. (a) 1-bit quantization provides two levels of amplitude resolution. (b) 4-bit quantization provides sixteen different levels of amplitude resolution.

electronic music), it becomes more obvious. Hence it is important that the signal be quantized as accurately as possible at the input stage.

To confront low-level quantization problems, some digital recording systems take a seemingly strange action. They introduce a small amount of uncorrelated noise—called *dither*—to the signal prior to analog-to-digital conversion (Vanderkooy and Lipshitz 1984; Lipshitz et al. 1992; Stuart and Craven 2019). This causes the ADC to make random variations around the low-level signal, which smooths out the pernicious effects of square wave harmonics (figure 4.6). With dither, the quantization error, which is usually signal-dependent, is turned into a wideband noise that is uncorrelated with the signal. For decrescendos like the piano tone mentioned previously, the effect is that of a soft landing as the tone fades smoothly into a bed of

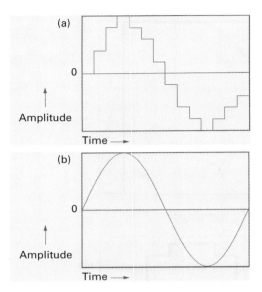

Figure 4.4   Effect of quantization on sine wave smoothness. (a) Sine wave with ten levels of quantization, corresponding to a moderately loud tone emitted by a 4-bit system. (b) Smoother sinusoid emitted by an 8-bit system.

low-level random noise. The amount of added noise is usually on the order of 3 dB, but the ear can reconstruct musical tones whose amplitudes fall below that of the dither signal.

Dithering is recommended in recording at a 16-bit quantization level. Adding dither may not be necessary in recording with a 24-bit converter because the low bit represents an extremely soft signal. But in requantizing signals from a 24-bit to a 16-bit format, for example, dithering is recommended to preserve signal fidelity (Stuart and Craven 2019). Many dithering algorithms exist, so sound editors and mastering plug-ins often provide a variety of options.

Converter Linearity

Audio converters can cause a variety of distortions (Blesser 1978; McGill 1985; Talambiras 1985; Pohlmann 2010). One such problem is that an *n*-bit converter is not necessarily accurate to the full dynamic range implied by its *n*-bit input or output. Although the *resolution* of an *n*-bit converter is one part in $2n$, a converter's *linearity* is the degree to which the analog and digital input and output signals match in terms of their magnitudes. That is, some converters use $2n$ steps, but these steps are not linearly spaced, which causes distortion. Hence it is not unusual to encounter a 24-bit converter, for example, that is actually 19 bits linear. Refer to Pohlmann (2010) for a discussion of these issues.

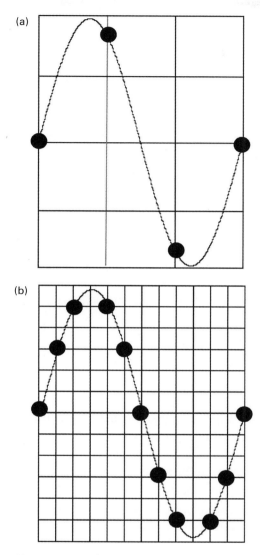

Figure 4.5   The sampling grid. The horizontal axis is time. The vertical axis is amplitude. (a) Crude approximation of a sine waveform caused by low sampling rate and low quantization. (b) Increasing grid resolution results in a better approximation to the waveform. Greater increases in grid resolution would closely approximate the original waveform.

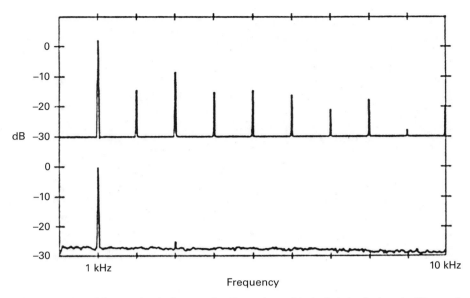

Figure 4.6   Dither reduces harmonic distortion. (*Top*) Original signal. (*Bottom*) Postdithered signal.

Oversampling Converters

In the digital audio systems that we have described, *multibit linear DACs* transform a binary sample value into an analog voltage in one step. That is, they convert a sample of 16 to 24 bits at each sample period. Correspondingly, multibit linear ADCs perform the inverse operation: converting an analog voltage into a multibit sample.

By contrast, *oversampling converters* use more samples in the conversion stage than are actually stored in the recording medium. For our purposes it is sufficient to present the basic ideas, leaving references for those who wish to investigate the topic further.

Oversampling is a family of methods for increasing the accuracy of converters. Most methods rely on 1-bit oversampling (Adams 1990; Hauser 1991; Reiss 2008). These methods convert just one bit at a time at a high sampling frequency.

1-Bit Converters

The theory of 1-bit oversampling converters goes back to the 1950s (Cutler 1960), but it took years for this technology to become incorporated into digital audio systems. The 1-bit oversampling converters constitute a family of different techniques that are variously called *sigma-delta, delta-sigma, noise shaping, bitstream, MASH,* or *direct stream digital (DSD),* depending on the manufacturer. Class D amplifiers, popular in mobile phones and high-power sound reinforcement systems, incorporate this technology (Reiss 2008).

They have the common thread that they sample one bit at a time at high sampling frequencies. That is, rather than trying to represent the entire waveform in a single sample, these converters measure differences between successive samples. They need to measure only whether the waveform has made a positive or negative excursion since it was last sampled, but they do this so frequently that the waveform does not have time to make a large excursion, and so 1 bit of information per sample period is sufficient.

1-bit converters take advantage of a fundamental law of information theory (Shannon and Weaver 1949), which says that one can trade off sample width for sample rate and still convert at the same resolution. That is, a 1-bit converter that oversamples at sixteen times the stored sample rate is equivalent to a 16-bit converter with no oversampling. They both process the same number of bits. The benefits of oversampling accrue when the sampling rate is much higher, meaning that the number of bits being processed is greater than the number of input bits.

One way to describe a sampling system is to determine the total number of bits being processed, according to the relation

Oversampling factor × Width of converter

For example, a 128-times oversampling system that uses a 1-bit converter is processing 128×1 bits each sample period. This compares to a traditional 16-bit linear converter that handles 1×16 bits, or one-eighth the data. In theory, the oversampling 1-bit converter should be much cleaner sounding.

In any case, all the benefits of oversampling accrue to 1-bit converters, including increased resolution and phase linearity due to digital filtering. High sampling rates that are difficult to achieve with the technology of multibit converters are much easier to implement with 1-bit converters. Oversampling rates in the 2.8224 MHz and greater range permit highly accurate quantization per sample (Moorer 1996). The Swiss-based Pyramix digital audio workstation supports high-resolution DSD recording. DSD has evolved into a high-resolution download and streaming format for audiophiles, with some converters supporting oversampling rates in excess of 22 MHz (Melchior 2019).

Noise Shaping

Another technique commonly used in 1-bit oversampling converters is *noise shaping,* which can take many forms (Hauser 1991; Reiss 2008). The basic idea is that the *requantization error* that occurs in the oversampling process is shifted into a high-frequency range, either to a less noticeable frequency band or out of the audio bandwidth, by a highpass filter in a feedback loop with the input sign/al. This *noise-shaping loop* sends only the requantization error through the highpass filter and not the audio signal.

The final stage of any oversampling converter is a decimator that reduces the sampling rate of the signal to that required for storage (for an ADC) or playback (for a DAC) and also lowpass filters the signal. In the case of a noise shaping converter this also removes the requantization noise, resulting in dramatic improvements in signal-to-noise ratio. With *second-order noise shaping* (so called because of the second-order highpass filter used in the feedback loop), the maximum signal-to-noise level of a 1-bit converter is approximately equivalent to 15 dB (2.5 bits) per octave of oversampling, minus a fixed 12.9 dB penalty (Hauser 1991). By running a 20-bit converter at 256 times the target sampling rate, one achieves 24-bit resolution, in theory. In practice, a host of issues in 1-bit oversampling are caused by feedback around a nonlinear quantizer. These include limits cycles, idle tones, distortion, dead zones, instability, and other scary phenomena (Reiss 2008).

Chapter 9 presents the basics on the related issue of *sample-rate conversion,* which is discussed in engineering texts in the context of *multirate signal processing* (Mitra 2006).

Digital Audio Media and Formats

Audio samples can be stored on any digital medium, typically optical or magnetic disks, solid-state drives, and memory chips. On a given storage medium, data files can be stored in a variety of *audio file formats*. The software that performs the encoding and decoding of the audio data is called a *codec* (coder-decoder).

An audio file format like AIFF or WAVE is a data structure that divides the file into subsections, each of which contains a specific type of data. For example, one section stipulates the sample rate, bit resolution, and how many channels of digital audio are stored in the file. Another section contains the raw sample data. Other sections can contain pointers to markers, loop points, and other kinds of information such as file name, author, copyright, and so on.

New media, codecs, and formats are constantly being developed. Scientific advances push these technologies, but just as often the introduction of a new medium, codec, or format is driven by a commercial strategy.

Lossless Versus Lossy File Formats

Three types of file formats are common:

1. Uncompressed
2. Compressed lossless
3. Compressed lossy

An *uncompressed* format (e.g., AIFF or WAV) stores full resolution PCM digital audio waveforms without any data reduction. This includes 16-bit and 24-bit formats at sample rates from 22.05 to 384 kHz. A special uncompressed format is 32-bit *floating-point* (FP), based on the IEEE 754 standard. This format encodes audio as a 24-bit mantissa that can be scaled by an 8-bit exponent, resulting in an effective dynamic range of about 1,500 dB. FP recording is provided in field recorders made by companies such as Zoom and Sound Devices. Audio editors such as Audacity, Adobe Audition, and Reaper also support the FP format.

An advantage of lossless formats is that one can transfer the bits from one medium to another in real time through *digital input/output connectors* (hardware jacks on the playback and recording systems) and *standard digital audio transmission formats* such as AES3 (two channels), S/PDIF (two channels), AES10 or MADI (56 channels), Ethernet 802.1 audio visual bridging (AVB) (200 channels), and Dante (1024 channels). Johns (2017) explains the proliferation of Ethernet audio formats.

A *compressed lossless* format, such as free lossless audio codec (FLAC) or Apple lossless (ALAC), takes advantage of redundancies in the data to pack it more efficiently without losing data. However, the file needs to be unpacked before it can be played. The original waveform can be perfectly reconstructed after it is unpacked. The ubiquitous ZIP and RAR file formats are examples of compressed lossless formats, but because they are not optimized for audio they typically achieve a 20 percent reduction in file size. By contrast, an audio-specific format like FLAC can achieve as much as a 50 percent reduction in file size.

A *compressed lossy* format, such as MP3, Vorbis, advanced audio codec (AAC), ATRAC, or Windows Media Audio), analyzes the input file to determine what information can be thrown away in order to meet a desired minimum bit rate. The goal is not only small file size but also minimum downloading time. The audio quality of these formats tends to be mediocre.

A 128 kbit/s MP3 file is about eleven times smaller than an uncompressed 16-bit 44.1 kHz compact disc track of the same song. The codecs associated with these formats usually let users choose the degree of data reduction or loss when the file is encoded. The term *lossy* refers to the fact that as MP3 encodes audio signals, it discards parts of sound that are deemed less audible in order to compress the size of a sound file. Specifically, MP3 throws away frequency components that are *spectrally masked* by neighboring frequencies, as well as tones that are *temporally masked* by loud events that occur less than about 5 ms before them (Hacker 2000).

Basing audio compression on psychoacoustic factors is called *perceptual coding* (Gibson, et al. 1998). The amount of lossy compression is controlled by the *bit rate* parameter, which for MP3 typically varies from 32 to 320 kbits/s and the sampling rate (from 32 to 48 kHz). The bit rate has a direct impact on both file size and audio quality; a low bit rate means lower audio resolution. One encoding option is *variable bit rate* (VBR) that uses a low bit rate for simple passages (e.g., sustained tones) and a high bit rate for more complex passages, such as transient or noisy events.

In essence, an MP3 encoder subdivides the input signal into thirty-two spectral bands and measures the energy in each of these bands over time. Applying perceptual coding techniques, it then greatly reduces the analyzed data. For example, if the content in any given band falls below a threshold of audition (varying according to frequency), the encoder discards that band.

MP3 playback is performed by what is basically an additive synthesizer. Designed for mass distribution, MP3 files are often played back on cheap loudspeakers and earbuds where high audio quality is not a consideration. For an analysis of the myriad problems of sound quality in MP3 files, read Corbett (2012).

Formats like MP3 and AAC (used in YouTube audio) were conceived when data storage was expensive and network speeds were measured in hundreds of bits per second. Today storage is cheap and network speeds are measured in gigabits per second. Thus the need for music distribution via lossy formats is diminished, much to the relief of recording engineers (Faulkner 2011). The audiophile market has largely moved to high-resolution lossless download and streaming formats such as FLAC, ALAC, and DSD (Melchior 2019).

II Introduction to Sound Synthesis

5   *History of Digital Sound Synthesis*

Earliest Computer Sounds

Experiments at Bell Telephone Laboratories

Music I and Music II

Music III: The Modular Unit Generator Concept

Music *N* Languages

This chapter ambles through the rich history of computer-generated sound, leading to the sophisticated concept of modular unit generators.

Earliest Computer Sounds

Early digital computers did not have visual displays. In order to better understand their operation, programmers sought to sonify computational processes. For example, when a computer was properly operating, it produced audible radio interference. Technicians found it useful to put a radio near the computer to monitor its operation. When the sound stopped, it indicated that the computer had halted. Programmers soon figured out that the sound of the radio interference correlated with the logic of the program. Specifically, when a program executed a repeating loop at an audio rate, the sound was a sustained pitch. For amusement, they wrote programs containing loops of varying lengths that corresponded to the melodies of popular songs.

Some computers had a loudspeaker that could be used as an output device to signal that a particular event had occurred in a program, such as program termination. On these machines, raw 1-bit pulses on the serial output bus could be sent to a speaker. A periodic loop of pulses interspersed with delays produced a pitched tone that was called a "blurt" or "hoot."

In 1949, Frances E. "Betty" Holberton programmed the BINAC computer to play "For He's a Jolly Good Fellow" to the team who built the machine at the Eckert-Mauchly Computer Corporation in Philadelphia (Irrlichtproject 2015). In 1951, both the Australian CSIRAC and the British Manchester Mark II played popular tunes via this method (Doornbusch 2005; Link 2007). These efforts were never intended as formal research, and no scientific papers were published.

The technology of digital-to-analog converters (DACs) for sound samples did not exist at this time. This meant that there was no possibility for generalized waveform synthesis.

Experiments at Bell Telephone Laboratories

The most general way to control all aspects of a computer-generated waveform is to synthesize it according to the 1928 *theory of sampling* devised by Harold Nyquist, a communications researcher at Bell Telephone Laboratories. The first experiments in the synthesis of sound samples by computer began in 1957 by researchers at Bell Telephone Laboratories in Murray Hill,

New Jersey (David, Mathews, and McDonald 1958; Roads 1980; Wood 1991).

With a doctorate in electrical engineering from MIT, Max V. Mathews (figure 5.1) worked at Bell Labs under the direction of J. R. Pierce. Mathews set out to use a computer to produce musical tones. He wrote a program that would make a computer generate a sequence of binary numbers representing successive amplitudes of a musical sound wave (i.e., samples) (Mathews and Guttman 1959). In their experiments, Mathews and his colleagues proved that a computer could synthesize sounds according to any pitch scale or waveform, including time-varying frequency and amplitude envelopes and polyphony.

Their first programs were written for a giant IBM 704 computer (figure 5.2).

Computers were so rare at that time that the computation had to be carried out at IBM World Headquarters on Madison Avenue and 57th Street in Manhattan. Use of the 704 computer was billed at $600 per hour in 1957 dollars (Johnstone 1994). The logic circuits of the computer were made using vacuum tubes (figure 5.3) The 704 was a powerful machine for its day, with a 36-bit word length and a built-in floating-point processor for fast numerical

Figure 5.1   Max V. Mathews, 1981.

Figure 5.2   IBM 704 computer, 1957.

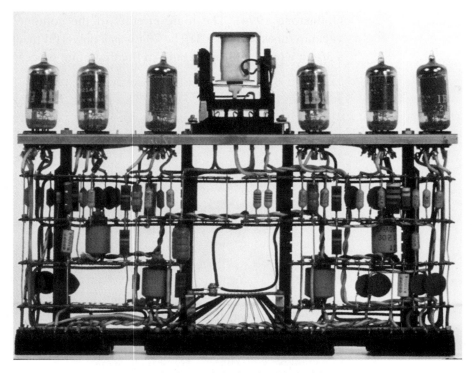

Figure 5.3   Vacuum tube logic module for the IBM 704 computer.

operations. It could be loaded with up to 32 kwords of magnetic core memory and execute up to 4,000 multiplications per second. Sound synthesis calculations took hours. The samples were written to a digital magnetic tape. A 12-bit vacuum tube DAC transformed the samples into sound. This converter, designed by Bernard Gordon, was at that time the only one in the world capable of sound production (Roads 1980).

Music I and Music II

The Music I program developed by Mathews generated a single waveform: an equilateral triangle. A user could specify notes only in terms of pitch and duration (Roads 1980). A perceptual psychology researcher named Newman Guttman made one composition with Music I, a monophonic etude called *In a Silver Scale* written on May 17, 1957 (Guttman 1980). This was the first composition synthesized by the process of digital-to-analog conversion. Recognizing the potential of the computer to generate any frequency precisely, Guttman used the piece as an experiment to contrast two microtonal scales, an equal-beating chromatic scale described by Silver (1957) and just intonation.

Mathews completed Music II in 1958. It was written in assembly language for the IBM 7090 computer, an improved computer along the lines of the IBM 704. The 7090 ran several times faster than the older machines. It was thus possible to implement more ambitious synthesis algorithms. Four independent voices of sound were available, with a choice of sixteen waveforms stored in memory. Music II was used by several researchers at Bell Telephone Laboratories, including Max Mathews, John Pierce, and Newman Guttman.

A concert of the new *computer music* was organized in 1958 in New York City, followed by a discussion panel moderated by John Cage. Later that year Guttman played his computer-synthesized composition *Pitch Variations* at Hermann Scherchen's villa in Gravesano, Switzerland, where composer Iannis Xenakis was in the audience (Guttman 1980). (We encounter Xenakis in chapters 24, 25, and 50.)

Music III: The Modular Unit Generator Concept

The most important development in the design of sound synthesis software was the concept of modular *unit generators* (UGs). UGs are signal processing modules like oscillators, filters, and amplifiers that can be interconnected to form synthesis *instruments* or *patches* that generate and process sound signals. (In subsequent chapters we discuss UGs in more detail.)

The first synthesis language to make use of the modular unit generator concept was Music III, programmed by Mathews and his colleague Joan E. Miller in 1960. Music III let users design their own synthesis networks out of UGs. By passing the sound signal through a series of such unit generators, a large variety of synthesis algorithms could be implemented relatively easily. The flexible design of Music III also enabled multivoice composition (polyphony), albeit with a corresponding increase in computation time.

Bell Labs published the historic recording *Music From Mathematics* in 1961 (figure 5.4). It featured studies in computer-generated sound by Pierce, Mathews, Guttman, and David Lewin, along with an excerpt of the *Illiac Suite*

Figure 5.4 Cover of the author's copy of *Music from Mathematics* vinyl record published by Bell Telephone Laboratories in 1961.

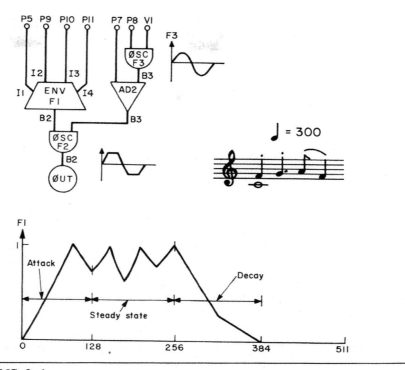

1 INS 0 4
2 ENV P5 F1 B2 P9 P10 P11 P30 ;
3 ØSC P8 V1 B3 F3 P29 ;
4 AD2 P7 B3 B3 ;
5 ØSC B2 B3 B2 F2 P28 ;
6 ØUT B2 B1 ;
7 END ;
8 GEN 0 1 1 0 0 96 1 128 .7 150 1 175 .6 200 1 225 .7 256 1
       320 .3 384 0 511 0 ;
9 SV2 0 50 .050 .100 ;
10 SV3 0 1 .15 ;
11 NØT 0 4 .1 54 349 ;
12 NØT .2 4 .1 54 392 ;
13 NØT .5 4 .13 54 440 ;
14 NØT .6 4 .2 54 349 ;
15 NØT 0 4 .8 54 262 ;

Figure 5.5 Music V synthesis patch. Lines 1–7 define the instrument, which features an envelope generator. The envelope F1 is defined in the GEN statement in line 8. A low-frequency sine wave oscillator modulates vibrato on another oscillator (Mathews 1969).

for String Quartet, an algorithmic composition by Lejaren Hiller (Hiller and Isaacson 1959). Chapter 50 has more on Hiller and algorithmic composition.

Music *N* Languages

Since the time of Music III, a family of software synthesis systems—all based on the unit generator concept—have been developed by various researchers. Music IV was a re-coding of Music III in a new macro assembly language developed at Bell Laboratories called BEFAP (Tenney 1963, 1969).

Music V (figure 5.5), developed in 1968, was the culmination of Max Mathews's efforts in software synthesis (Mathews 1969). Written almost exclusively in FORTRAN IV—a standard computer language at the time—Music V was exported to universities and laboratories around the world in the early 1970s. For many musicians, including the author of this book, it opened a door to the art of digital sound synthesis.

Taking Music IV or Music V as a model, others have developed synthesis programs such as Music 4BF, Music 360, Music 7, Music 11, Csound, MUS10, Cmusic, Common Lisp Music, SuperCollider, ChucK, Synthesis ToolKit, Nyquist, and Max. As a general category these programs are often referred to under the rubric *Music N languages* (see chapter 48).

As the inventor of the modular unit generator synthesis paradigm for generalized waveform synthesis, the late Max V. Mathews (1926–2011) can rightly be called the father of computer-generated sound. Synthesis based on modular graphs of unit generators remains to this day the standard for flexible and experimental synthesis. Music *N* languages deliver this capability to anyone willing to learn to program.

6 *Wavetable Lookup Synthesis*

Wavetable Lookup Synthesis

Changing Waveform Frequency

Algorithm for a Digital Oscillator

Wavetable Lookup Noise and Interpolating Oscillators

Alternatives to Wavetable Lookup

Digital synthesis generates a stream of numbers representing the samples of an arbitrary audio waveform. We can hear these synthetic sounds by sending the samples through a digital-to-analog converter (DAC), which converts the numbers to a continuously varying voltage that can be amplified and sent to a loudspeaker.

Wavetable Lookup Synthesis

A flexible method of waveform synthesis is to scan a prestored wavetable in memory. This process is called *wavetable lookup synthesis.* Wavetable lookup synthesis is the core operation of a *digital oscillator*—a fundamental sound generator.

Let us now walk through the process of table lookup. Suppose that the value of the first sample is given by the first number in the wavetable (shown in figure 6.1 at index location 0). For each new sample to be produced by this simple synthesizer, take the next sample from the wavetable. At the end of the wavetable, simply go back to the beginning and start reading out the samples again. The process is also called *fixed-waveform synthesis* because the waveform does not change over the course of a sound event.

For example, let us assume that the table contains $N = 1,000$ entries, each of which is a 16-bit number. The entries are indexed from 0 to 999. We call

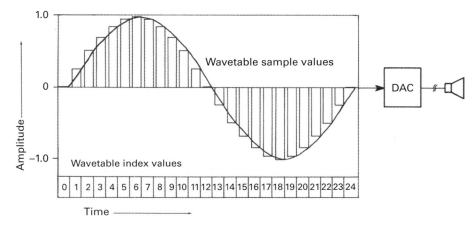

Figure 6.1   Graphical depiction of wavetable lookup synthesis. The list 0–24 in the lower portion contains numbered locations or *table index values.* An audio sample value is stored in memory for each index point. The samples are depicted as the rectangles outlining a sine wave in the top portion. For example, Wavetable[0] = 0, and Wavetable[6] = 1. To synthesize the sine wave, the computer looks up the sample values stored in successive index locations and sends them to a DAC, looping through the table repetitively.

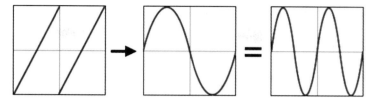

Figure 6.2   The phase increment or *phasor* (a ramp function) goes from 0 to *N* two times, creating two cycles of the sine wave.

the current location in the table the *phase_index* value, with reference to the phase of the waveform. To read through the table the oscillator starts at the first entry in the table (*phase_index* = 0) and moves by an *increment* to the end of the table (*phase_index* = 999). At this point the phase index wraps around the ending point to the beginning of the wavetable and starts again (figure 6.2).

Changing Waveform Frequency

What is the frequency of the sound produced by table-lookup synthesis? It depends on the length of the wavetable and the sampling frequency. Logically, it should be obvious that if one reads through the entire wavetable (no matter its length) in one second, the result is a wave at 1 Hz; reading through it 100 times a second makes a tone at 100 Hz, and so on.

Let us now be more specific about wavetable length and sampling frequency. If the sampling frequency is 50,000 samples per second and there are 1,000 numbers in the table, the result is 50,000 / 1,000: a low tone at 50 Hz. Likewise, if the sampling frequency is 100,000 Hz and the table contains 1,000 entries, then the output frequency is 100 Hz, because 100,000 / 1,000 = 100.

How is it possible to change the frequency of the output signal? As we have just seen, one simple way is to change the sampling frequency. But this strategy has problems, particularly when one wants to process or mix signals with different sampling rates. A better solution is to scan the wavetable at different rates by skipping samples (to shift pitch up) or repeating samples (to shift pitch down). These processes, in effect, resize the wavetable in order to generate different frequencies.

For example, if we take only the even-numbered samples, then we go through the table twice as fast. This raises the pitch of the output signal by an octave. If we skip two samples, then the pitch is raised further (by an octave and a fifth, to be exact). To shift the pitch down we repeat samples. For example, to shift the pitch down an octave, we play each sample twice.

In the table-lookup algorithm, the *phase increment* determines the number of samples to be skipped or repeated. The increment is added to the current phase location in order to find the next location for reading the value of the sample. In the simplest example, where we read every sample from the table, the increment is 1. If we read only the odd- or even-numbered samples in the table, then the increment is 2.

Algorithm for a Digital Oscillator

We could say that the oscillator *resamples* the wavetable in order to generate different frequencies. That is, it skips or repeats values in the table by an increment added to the current phase location in the wavetable. Thus the most basic oscillator algorithm can be explained as the following two-step program:

1. $phase\_index = \text{mod}_L \ (previous\_phase + increment)$

2. $output = amplitude \times wavetable[phase\_index]$

Step 1 of the algorithm contains an addition and a modulo operation (denoted mod_L). The modulo operation divides the sum by the table length L and keeps only the remainder, which is always less than or equal to L. Step 2 contains a table lookup and a multiplication. This is relatively little computation, but it assumes that the wavetables are already filled with waveform values.

If the table length and the sampling frequency are fixed, as is usually the case, then the frequency of the sound emitted by the oscillator depends on the value of the increment. The relationship between a given frequency and an increment is given by the following equation, which is the most important equation in table lookup synthesis:

$$increment = \frac{L \times frequency}{samplingFrequency} \tag{1}$$

For example, if tablelength L is 1,000, the sampling frequency is 40,000, and the specified *frequency* of the oscillator is 2,000 Hz, then the *increment* is 50.

This implies the following equation for frequency:

$$frequency = \frac{increment \times samplingFrequency}{L} \tag{2}$$

So much for the theory of digital oscillators. Now we confront the computational realities.

Wavetable Lookup Noise and Interpolating Oscillators

All the variables in the previous example were multiples of 1,000, which led to a neat integer result for the value of the phase index increment. However, for most values of the table length, frequency, and sampling frequency in equation 1, the resulting increment is not an integer but rather a real number with a fractional part after the decimal point. However, the way we look up a value in the wavetable is to locate it by its index, which is an integer. Thus we need to somehow derive an integer value from the real-valued increment.

The real value can be *truncated* to yield an integer value for the table index. This means to delete the part of the number to the right of the decimal point, so, for example, 6.99 becomes 6 when it is truncated.

Suppose that we use an increment of 1.125. Table 6.1 compares the calculated versus the truncated increments. The imprecision caused by the truncation means that we obtain a waveform value near, but not precisely the same as, the one that we actually need. As a result, small amounts of waveform distortion are introduced, called *table lookup noise* (Moore 1977; Snell 1977b). Various remedies can reduce this noise. A larger wavetable is one prescription, because a fine-grain table reduces lookup error. Another

Table 6.1 Phase index, table lookup list

Calculated	Truncated
1.000	1
2.125	2
3.250	3
4.375	4
5.500	5
6.625	6
7.750	7
8.875	8
10.000	10
11.125	11
12.250	12
13.375	13
14.500	14
15.625	15
16.750	16
17.875	17
19.000	19

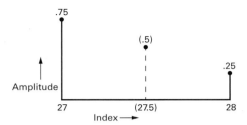

Figure 6.3   Action of an interpolating oscillator. The graph shows two *x* points in a wavetable, at positions 27 and 28. The oscillator phase increment indicates that the value should be 27.5. The interpolating oscillator generates a *y* value between 27 and 28 using a linear interpolation algorithm.

way is to *round* the value of increment up or down to the nearest integer instead of simply truncating it; in this case, an increment of 6.99 becomes 7, which is more accurate than 6. But the best performance is achieved by an *interpolating oscillator.* This is more costly from a computational standpoint, but it generates very clean signals.

An interpolating oscillator calculates what the value of the wavetable would have been, if it were possible to reference the wavetable at the exact phase specified by the increment. In other words, it interpolates between the entries in the wavetable to find the one that exactly corresponds to the specified phase index increment (figure 6.3).

With interpolating oscillators, smaller wavetables can yield the same audio quality as a larger noninterpolating oscillator. Consider that for a 1024-entry wavetable used by an interpolating oscillator, the signal-to-noise ratio for a sine wave is an excellent 109 dB (worst case), as compared with the abysmal 48 dB for a noninterpolating oscillator using the same size wavetable (Moore 1977). These figures pertain to the case of linear interpolation; even better results are possible with more elaborate interpolation schemes (Chamberlin 1985; Crochiere and Rabiner 1983; Moore 1977; Snell 1977a; Dannenberg 1998).

Alternatives to Wavetable Lookup

In certain cases, numerical operations are much faster than memory table lookups. Memories tend to be slower than microprocessor instructions. Modern microprocessors have native hardware instructions for sine and cosine generation, exponentials, square roots, and dot products. Thus, as pointed out by James McCartney (1997), waveforms like sine waves, exponentiated sine waves, formant oscillators, and chaotic oscillators can be generated much more efficiently by direct evaluation of their equation. Smith and Cook (1992) described a highly efficient sinusoidal oscillator based on digital waveguides (see also Smith 2010). Laroche (1998) showed how using resonant filters to synthesize time-varying sinusoids could be an efficient strategy for additive synthesis.

This concludes our introduction to fixed-waveform table-lookup synthesis. The next chapter shows how aspects of synthesis can be varied over time with envelopes.

7 *Time-Varying Waveform Synthesis*

Envelopes, Unit Generators, and Patches

Graphic Notation for Synthesis Instruments

Using Envelopes in Patches

The previous chapter showed how to generate a sine wave at a fixed frequency. Because the maximum value of the sine wave does not change in time, the signal has a constant loudness. This is not terribly useful for musical purposes, because it allows control over only pitch and duration and no control over other sound parameters. Even if the oscillator reads from other wavetables, they repeat ad infinitum. The key to more interesting sounds is *time-varying* waveforms, achieved by changing one or more synthesis parameters over the duration of a sound event.

Envelopes, Unit Generators, and Patches

To create a time-varying waveform, we need a synthesis *instrument* that can be controlled by *envelopes*—functions of time. For example, if the amplitude of the sound changes over its duration, the curve that the amplitude follows is called the *amplitude envelope*. A general way of designing a synthesis instrument is to imagine it as a modular system, containing a number of specialized signal-processing units that together create a time-varying sound.

As chapter 5 pointed out, the unit generator (UG) is a fundamental concept in digital synthesis. A UG is either a signal generator or a signal modifier. A signal generator (such as an oscillator) synthesizes signals such as musical waveforms and envelopes. A signal modifier, such as a filter, takes a signal as its input and transforms that input signal in some way.

To construct an instrument for sound synthesis, one interconnects UGs into a *patch*. The term patch derives from modular synthesizers in which sound modules are connected via *patch cords*. Of course, when the connections are done in software, no physical wires or cables are connected. When a UG produces a number at its output, that number can become the input to another UG.

Graphic Notation for Synthesis Instruments

Now we introduce the graphic notation often used in publications on digital sound synthesis to illustrate patches. This notation was invented to explain the operation of the first modular languages for digital sound synthesis, such as Music 4BF (Howe 1975) and Music V (Mathews 1969) and is still useful.

The symbol for each unit generator has a unique shape. Figure 7.1 shows the graphic notation for a *table-lookup oscillator* called *osc*, a basic signal generator. It accepts three inputs: amplitude, frequency, and a waveform stored in wavetable $f1$. It produces an output signal that is $f1$ repeated at the stipulated frequency and amplitude.

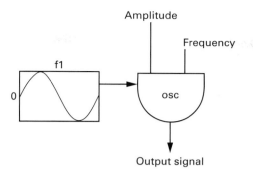

Figure 7.1 Oscillator with sound waveform input *f*1 and fixed parameters for amplitude and frequency.

Using Envelopes in Patches

If we supply a constant number (for example, 1.0) to the amplitude input of an oscillator, then the overall amplitude of the output waveform is constant over the duration of each event. By contrast, most interesting sounds have an amplitude envelope that varies as a function of time. Typically, a note starts with an amplitude of 0, works its way up to some maximum value (usually *normalized* to be no greater than 1.0), and dies down again more or less slowly to 0. (A normalized wave has been scaled to fall within standard boundaries such as 0 to 1 for amplitude envelopes, or −1 to +1 for other waves.) The beginning part of the envelope is called the *attack* portion, and the end of the envelope is called the *release*.

Many synthesizers define amplitude envelopes in the following four stages:

Attack (initial increase from zero to peak)

Decay (transition down to a sustained level)

Sustain (constant level)

Release (time taken for level to return to zero).

The usual acronym for such a four-stage envelope is ADSR (figure 7.2). The ADSR concept is useful for describing verbally the overall shape of an envelope; for example, "Make the attack sharper." However, for specifying a musical envelope, four stages is limiting. More flexible envelope editors allow musicians to trace arbitrary curves.

The instrument of figure 7.1 can be easily adapted to generate a time-varying amplitude by hooking up an envelope to the amplitude input of the oscillator. We are now closer to controlling the oscillator in musical terms. If we set the duration and the curve of the envelope, then the envelope controls the amplitude of each note.

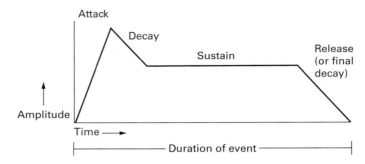

Figure 7.2   Attack, decay, sustain, release (ADSR) amplitude envelope.

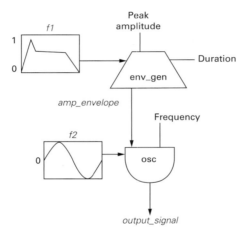

Figure 7.3   Oscillator with amplitude envelope $f1$ and sound waveform $f2$.

Designing an envelope for every event in a composition is tedious. What we seek is a simple procedure for generating an envelope that can scale itself to the duration of diverse events. Figure 7.3 shows an *envelope generator, env_gen*. This UG env_gen takes in a duration, a peak amplitude, and a wavetable. It reads through the wavetable $f1$ over the specified duration, scaling it by the peak amplitude. It is adaptable to tones of any duration. The sound waveform is $f2$ in this case.

As the reader might guess, we could also attach an envelope generator to the frequency input of osc to obtain a pitch change such as vibrato or glissando. Indeed, we can interconnect envelopes, oscillators, and other unit generators in a wide variety of ways in order to make different sounds. This is the modular approach to sound synthesis.

Human beings are naturally sensitive to undulation, so it is not surprising that time-varying envelopes are the key to interesting sounds. Envelopes are profiles of gestures. As analogies of human body movements, they infuse life into otherwise lifeless electronic signals.

8 *Software Synthesis*

What Is Software Synthesis?

Early Software Synthesis

Types of Software Synthesizers

Closed Apps
Patchable Apps
Virtual Modular Synthesizers
Graphical Instrument Patch Editors
Textual Synthesis Languages
Custom Apps Made Using General-Purpose Programming Languages

Real-Time and Non-Real-Time Synthesis

Non-Real-Time Synthesis
Sound Files
Real-Time Digital Synthesis

Audio Programming

This chapter begins by comparing hardware versus software synthesis. We briefly review the history of software synthesis, review various types of software synthesizers, look at real-time and non-real-time synthesis, and introduce resources for audio programming.

What Is Software Synthesis?

In the early days of digital synthesis, computers were too slow for *real-time* operation. What do we mean by *real time*? In this context, real time means that we can complete all calculations for a sample within the duration of one sample period. If a system takes ten seconds to compute one second of sound, it must operate as a *non-real-time system*. This means that the sound output must be written to a file to be auditioned later. Early computer music systems could not be played interactively in the presence of sound—a huge liability from a musical standpoint.

Thus there was a strong motivation to design specialized digital hardware to synthesize sound in real time (Markowitz 1989; Alonso 1973; Alles and Di Giugno 1977; Snell 1977a, 1977b; Samson 1980, 1985; Asta, et al. 1980; Wallraff 1979a; Loy 2013a, 2013b). Early hardware synthesizers were rare and expensive. A breakthrough product was the Yamaha DX7 (1983), a mass-produced keyboard instrument based on specialized chips for *frequency modulation* (FM) synthesis (chapter 16). Selling for less than $2,000, over 200,000 units were sold. Much pop music of the 1980s was infused with the Yamaha FM sound.

Specialized hardware can be efficient but is limited in its flexibility. For example, the chips in the DX7 were designed for FM; they could not realize other synthesis methods. Thus, the most flexible approach to sound generation is a *software synthesis* program running on a computer. In software synthesis, all the calculations involved in computing a stream of samples are carried out by a computer without additional hardware.

Early Software Synthesis

An early example of software synthesis was the venerable Music V language (Mathews 1969), shown in figure 8.1. To create sound, one would write a program in the Music V language and then execute the program. This non-real-time process could take hours (Roads 2001a).

Figure 8.2 is a simple example of a Music V program. Figure 8.2(a) shows a conventional score of the notes to be synthesized. Figure 8.2(b) shows the

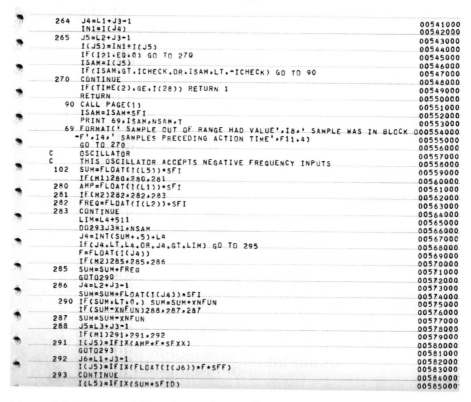

Figure 8.1   Excerpt of the author's printout of the source code of Music V from 1974. The code is classic FORTRAN IV, with program control flow by GOTO statements. The first 16 lines are the end of the OUT unit generator. The rest is the beginning of the OSCIL unit generator. The code for a more modern version of Music V for GFortran and Linux is printed in Boulanger and Lazzarini (2011). GFortran continues to be maintained.

patch for a simple instrument that will play the score. It consists solely of an oscillator and an output box. The oscillator has two inputs: the amplitude of the output is set by the fifth element in the note statement, designated P5. The waveform to be played is determined by the function F2, which is sketched in figure 8.2c.

By the mid-1970s, music synthesis languages could be run on minicomputers. Waiting times for synthesis jobs were reduced to minutes for most short-duration experiments and hours for intensive tasks like synthesizing entire pieces involving reverberation.

By the late 1980s, we began to see the first real-time synthesis software such as Csound (1990), SuperCollider (1996), Seer Reality (1997), and Max/MSP (1997) running on home computers.

Today a multitude of real-time software synthesizers are available. To cite one example, any user of the Native Instruments REAKTOR modular system

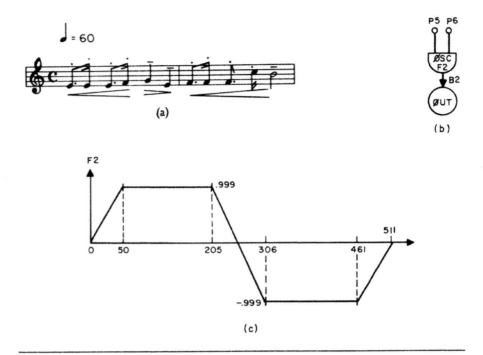

$$\text{(a)}$$

$$\text{(b)}$$

$$\text{(c)}$$

```
 1    INS 0 1 ;
 2    ØSC P5 P6 B2 F2 P30 ;
 3    ØUT B2 B1 ;
 4    END ;
 5    GEN 0 1 2 0 0 .999 50 .999 205  − .999 306  − .999 461 0 511 ;
 6    NØT 0 1 .50 125 8.45 ;
 7    NØT .75 1 .17 250 8.45 ;
 8    NØT 1.00 1 .50 500 8.45 ;
 9    NØT 1.75 1 .17 1000 8.93 ;
10    NØT 2.00 1 .95 2000 10.04 ;
11    NØT 3.00 1 .95 1000 8.45 ;
12    NØT 4.00 1 .50 500 8.93 ;
13    NØT 4.75 1 .17 500 8.93 ;
14    NØT 5.00 1 .50 700 8.93 ;
15    NØT 5.75 1 .17 1000 13.39 ;
16    NØT 6.00 1 1.95 2000 12.65 ;
17    TER 8.00 ;
```

Figure 8.2   A simple orchestra and score in Music V (after Mathews 1969). Line numbers 1–17 have been added to simplify the explanation. Lines 1–4 in the code define instrument number 1 (an oscillator and an output). Line 5 generates the function F2. Lines 6–16 list note statements defining the score. Each note statement gives starting time, instrument number, duration, amplitude, and pitch (encoded in this case). Line 17 terminates the program.

can design and publish a synthesizer, so that thousands of synthesizers are available for this platform alone.

Types of Software Synthesizers

Contemporary software synthesis can be divided into six general categories:

- Closed apps
- Patchable apps
- Virtual modular synthesizers
- Graphical instrument patch editors
- Textual synthesis languages
- Custom apps made using general-purpose programming languages

Chapter 19 looks at virtual modular synthesizers. Chapter 47 surveys graphical instrument patch editors. Chapter 48 addresses textual synthesis languages.

Closed Apps

Closed apps are designed to do one thing very well. They are optimized to realize a single synthesis technique or only a few variations. Their graphical interface reflects this specialization. They cannot be freely reprogrammed to realize any synthesis technique. Figure 8.3 shows the Native Instruments FM8, which emulates a Yamaha DX7 synthesizer. Even a closed app like FM8 provides some flexibility in patching. Its Expert page lets users design their own FM patches.

Many commercial software synthesizers can run either in *standalone* mode (i.e., with no other apps running), or as a *plug-in* extension to a *digital audio workstation* (DAW) or sound editor. The plug-in implementation has the advantage that multiple copies or *instances* of the plug-ins can run simultaneously, and they can be recorded by the DAW as they play.

Patchable Apps

Patchable apps offer a limited set of modules with the possibility of patching the modules to realize different synthesis techniques.

An example of a patchable app is Native Instruments Absynth, which features a *semimodular* design with twelve module slots (figure 8.4). One can choose among various types of oscillators, filters, and modulators to fill in the open slots.

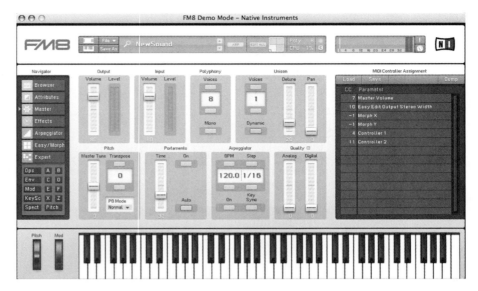

Figure 8.3 Native Instruments FM8. This software synthesizer is optimized for frequency modulation synthesis.

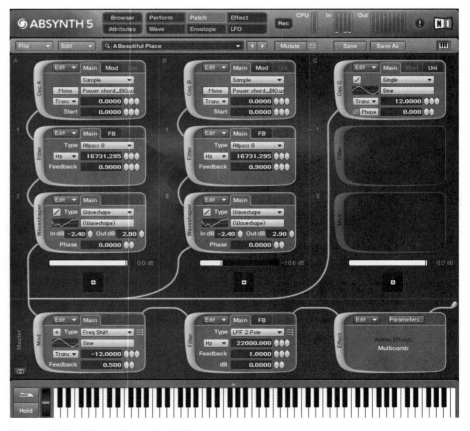

Figure 8.4 Absynth patch window.

Another is Madrona Labs Aalto, a self-styled West Coast synthesizer following the example of the late Don Buchla. Like a Buchla system, it couples a complex oscillator with a lowpass gate. It also features two envelope generators, a waveguide delay, a filter, and a sequencer. Although its collection of modules is fixed, it offers more than two dozen patch points for interconnecting the modules (figure 8.5). According to the developer, it is by playing with the interconnections that unexpected sounds emerge (Jones 2020).

Unfiltered Audio's versatile LION synthesizer (figure 8.6) goes further to offer an expandable number of virtual modulation sources that can be patched to control synthesis parameters.

Virtual Modular Synthesizers

The first wave of virtual modular software synthesizers were simulations of vintage analog synths. Arturia worked with Robert Moog to introduce the Modular V synthesizer in 2003. Since that time, emulations of vintage synths by Arp, EMS, and Buchla have appeared. Figure 8.7 shows the screen of Arturia's EMS Synthi V software synthesizer.

New virtual modular synthesizers include Native Instruments REAKTOR Blocks, VCV Rack, SoftTube Modular, and Cherry Audio's Voltage Modular (see chapter 19).

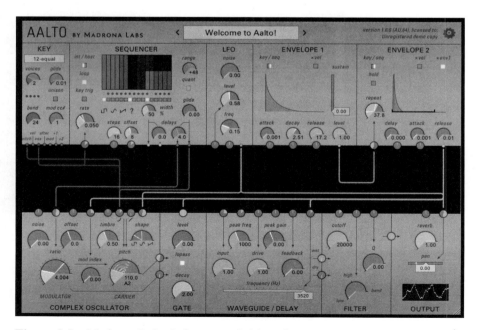

Figure 8.5   Madrona Labs Aalto, a patchable software synthesizer.

Figure 8.6   Unfiltered Audio LION, a patchable software synthesizer.

Figure 8.7   Arturia EMS Synthi V software synthesizer.

Graphical Instrument Patch Editors

A graphical instrument editor such as Max, PureData (PD), or AudioMulch lets one build synthesis patches by interconnecting icons on a screen (figure 8.8). The icons represent unit generators. The difference between what we have called a patchable app and a graphical instrument editor is that in the editor one can add any number of modules into a patch. Moreover, in a system like Max, there are hundreds of modules from which to choose. Once the editing is done, the result can be compiled to make a self-contained app.

Textual Synthesis Languages

Using a language designed for synthesis, a musician can specify sounds by writing a text that is interpreted by a synthesis engine. This category is represented by languages such as Csound, Nyquist, ChucK, Faust, and SuperCollider. Figure 8.9 shows a simple FM synthesis instrument written in SuperCollider 3.

Using a programming language like SuperCollider, one can compile new fully-functioning apps. For example, PulsarGenerator (Roads 2001a, 2001b) was compiled in SuperCollider. Our granulation app EmissionControl was originally coded in a combination of SuperCollider and C (Thall 2005).

Custom Apps Made Using General-Purpose Programming Languages

For the ultimate in customization and efficiency, one can program in a general-purpose language like C++. Most of the software synthesizers on the

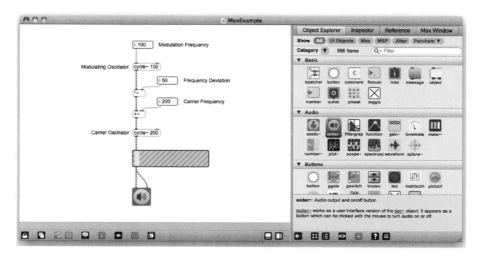

Figure 8.8   Max patch for frequency modulation.

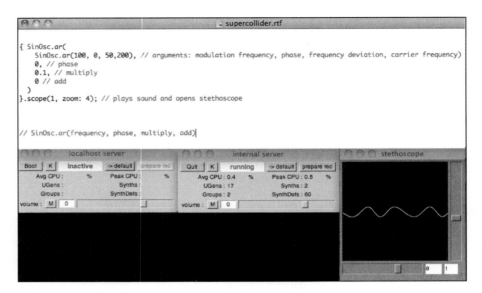

Figure 8.9   SuperCollider code for frequency modulation synthesis.

market are coded in C++. *Code libraries* are vital to programming audio applications because they provide solutions to many basic tasks that are common to these applications. Code libraries facilitate graphical user interface (GUI) design (e.g., ImGui and JUCE), audio input and output (e.g., PortAudio and RtAudio), MIDI control (e.g., RtMidi), signal processing algorithms (e.g., Pedal and STK), and music information retrieval using machine learning (e.g., FluCoMa Project). Our EmissionControl2 granular synthesis app was coded in C++ using the Allolib code library, which was designed to support immersive 3D audio and visuals.

Real-Time and Non-Real-Time Synthesis

For decades, Moore's law (1965) predicted that transistor density would double each year, with a followup effect on clock speed. By 2012, this law began to lose relevance as the clock speed of microprocessors stalled at less than 4 GHz. Chip companies responded by manufacturing *multicore* processors, so that multiple processes could run in parallel, theoretically speeding up operations. However, many real-time interactive audio algorithms do not benefit from *multithreaded* (parallel) processing.

Every step in a sound synthesis algorithm takes a certain amount of time to execute. For a complicated algorithm, a computer cannot always complete the calculations necessary for a sample in the interval of one sample period.

Moreover, the audio thread is competing with other operating system processes.

To understand this point more concretely, consider the following steps required to calculate one sample of sound by the table-lookup method of synthesis:

1. Add increment to current wavetable lookup location to obtain new location.
2. If the new location is past the end of the wavetable, subtract the wavetable length. (In other words, perform a modulo operation.)
3. Store the new location for use in calculating the next sample. (See step 1.)
4. Look up the value in the wavetable at the new location
5. Multiply that value by the amplitude input.
6. Send the product to the output.

The important point here is that each step takes time. For example, let us say it takes a computer one microsecond (one millionth of a second) to perform the six calculations in the preceding list. (This is intentionally slow in order to make the explanation simple; modern computers are faster than this.) If we use a sampling rate of 50 kHz, the time available per sample is 1 / 50,000th of a second or 20 microseconds. This means that in an ideal world, the computer could complete the calculations necessary for about twenty simple oscillators in real time.

In the real world, the process is made more complicated by using interpolation in the table lookup; increasing the sampling rate; adding filters, delays, modulating oscillators, random functions, more channels, reverberation, and spatial processing; updating the graphical user interface; and allowing the time needed to interact with a musician. Here the calculations can become impossible to realize in real time. This is the domain of non-real-time synthesis.

Non-Real-Time Synthesis

Non-real-time operation means that there is a substantial delay between the time we start computing a sound and the time that we can listen to it. Non-real-time (or *offline*) synthesis was the only option in the primordial days of computer music. For example, a two-minute portion of J. K. Randall's *Lyric Variations for Violin and Computer*, realized between 1965 and 1968 at Princeton University (Cardinal Records VCS 10057), took nine hours to compute. If a small adjustment was desired, the entire process would have to be repeated. Even though this was a laborious process, a handful of dedicated composers were able to create computer-synthesized works of music (Tenney 1969; Von Foerster and Beauchamp 1969; Dodge 1985; Risset 1985a).

For a more modern example, the method of atomic decomposition analysis, described in chapter 39, is currently a non-real-time technique. However, it is possible that someone with a powerful multicore computer could substantially increase the speed of this technique by programming it as a multithreaded process.

Many audio computations operate faster than real time. For example, a complex multitrack mix of a piece lasting several minutes can be rendered to a sound file in seconds using a digital audio workstation like Pro Tools, Logic, or Ableton Live.

Sound Files

Whether or not it takes longer than one sample period to compute each sample, software synthesis programs can generate a *sound file* as their output. Common sound file formats include Waveform Audio File Format (WAVE) and Audio Interchange File Format (AIFF), among many others. A sound file is simply an audio data file stored on a digital storage medium. A sound file contains a *header text* and numbers representing sound samples. The header contains the name of the file and relevant information about the samples in the file (sampling rate, number of bits per sample, number of channels, etc.).

As in other computer applications, many different audio file formats coexist. The need to convert between formats is a practical fact of life in computer music studios. Sound editors and utilities like SoundHack (Erbe 1992) perform these conversions. Lazzarini (2011c) teaches how to read and write sound files.

Real-Time Digital Synthesis

The 1970s saw the introduction of the first real-time digital synthesizers based on custom hardware (Markowitz 1989; Alonso 1973; Alles and Di Giugno 1977; Snell 1977a, 1977b; Samson 1980, 1985; Asta, et al. 1980; Wallraff 1979a; Loy 1981, 2013a, 2013b; Alles 1977; Buxton et al. 1978; Strawn 1985c; Roads and Strawn 1985; Roads 1989).

By the 1980s, large circuit boards inside digital synthesizers were being replaced by tiny chips that could realize multivoice synthesis algorithms in real time. These chips could be fabricated en masse and embedded in inexpensive synthesizers made by manufacturers such as Yamaha. In the 1990s, similar chips were embedded in *sound cards* inserted into computers. As processors became faster, for a while it looked as if software synthesis would rule forever. Then the Eurorack phenomenon happened, and hardware synthesis (both analog and digital) made a return alongside software synthesis.

Figure 8.10 shows an overview of a real-time computer music synthesis system. This system has three ways of generating digital sound:

1. Non-real-time software synthesis using a language like Csound. The sounds are calculated on the computer and written to a sound file.
2. Real-time software synthesis calculated on the computer (e.g., Max), possibly controlled by an input device that speaks MIDI or OSC.
3. Real-time synthesis using a synthesizer controlled by an input device that speaks MIDI or OSC.

The obvious advantage of real-time operation is that musical input devices or controllers can be played by the musician as sound is heard. Gestural control leads to more expressive performances. Moreover, the parameter space of a synthesis method can be explored and tested rapidly. *Sequencers* and *score editors* make it possible to record and edit performances. Chapters 40 and 41 present performance controllers and performance software, and chapters 51 and 52 cover the MIDI and OSC communication protocols.

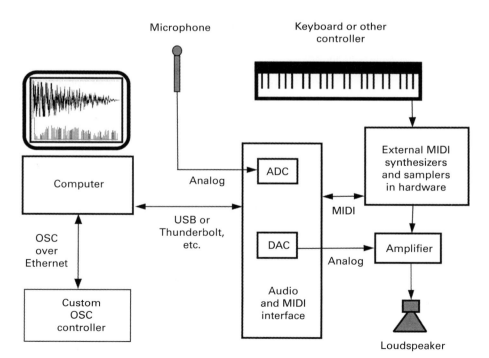

Figure 8.10   Overview of a real-time synthesis system.

Audio Programming

This section provides a brief orientation to audio programming. Many tomes address audio programming in depth and detail. For example, *The Audio Programming Book* (Boulanger and Lazzarini 2011) contains over 3,000 pages of text and thousands of lines of code. Specific books describe each audio programming language (SuperCollider, Csound, Max, Pd, ChucK, FAUST, etc.). Neukom's text (2013) uses Csound, Max, Mathematica, C/C++, and Processing. Another resource is The Audio Programmer video channel on YouTube.

A crucial element of audio programming is the management of audio I/O. Music-specific environments like SuperCollider and Max handle this automatically. By contrast, when coding in a language like C or C++, the programmer has more responsibility for ensuring the smooth stream of audio samples without stuttering. Fortunately, audio libraries such as libsndfile, Portaudio, and JUCE handle many of the low-level details of real-time input and output. In the audio software industry, ROLI's JUCE is favored by many professional developers (Jones 2020).

Real-time synthesis generates a *block* of samples at a time. Typical block sizes range from 32 samples to 2,048 samples. Large buffers provide the most protection against glitches, but they introduce *latency*: a delay from the time that the sound is recorded or synthesized to the time that it is heard.

```
# Set up variables and arrays when the program starts
ON INITIALIZE:
CREATE ARRAY "Wavetable" and FILL with [arbitrary waveform]
CREATE INTEGER "TableIndex" and SET to 0
CREATE INTEGER "BufferSize" and SET to 1024
CREATE ARRAY "BufferOut" and SET size to BufferSize
CREATE ARRAY "BufferHolding" and SET size to BufferSize
END INITIALIZE

# Audio Callback
IF (DAC is asking for a new Buffer) THEN:
     COPY BufferHolding to BufferOut
     SEND BufferOut to DAC
     # fill HoldingBuffer with samples from the wavetable
     FOR BufferIndex = 0 to BufferSize:
          INCREMENT TableIndex by 1
          # Wrap around to the beginning of the wavetable
          IF TableIndex >= Wavetable.Length THEN:
                SUBTRACT Wavetable.Length from TableIndex
          ENDIF
          SET BufferHolding(BufferIndex) to Wavetable(TableIndex)
     ENDFOR
ENDF
```

Figure 8.11   Audio callback loop that reads a wavetable and outputs audio to the DAC. Credit to Rodney Duplessis.

The mechanism for implementing low-latency audio is the *audio callback loop,* which repeats as long as sound is being recorded or synthesized. The audio callback loop takes a block of samples from a synthesizer and puts them into a memory buffer. The block of samples plays by sending the contents of the buffer to the real-time output. However, synthesizing or applying effects to a block of samples may take longer than one sample period. Moreover, the processing speed of a software routine is not constant because it runs concurrently with operating system processes that can start at any time. Hence a scheme using a single output buffer is prone to audio dropouts. Thus it is common practice to use a *double-* or *quad-buffering* scheme in the audio callback loop. One might break a 2,048-sample buffer into two or four buffer sections. One buffer plays while the other buffer is being filled with new samples by the synthesis algorithm. In some cases buffering can be automatically managed by the sound library. Maldonado (2011) walks readers through the steps of the process. The developer of AudioMulch, Ross Bencina (2011) warns of problems in the audio callback loop and provides a list of do's and don'ts to avoid audio glitches. Figure 8.11 shows an example of an audio callback loop written in pseudocode.

Lazzarini (2011d) presents the C++ code for the basic building blocks of a synthesizer engine: interpolating oscillators, envelope generators, filters, delay lines, flangers, convolution, and pitch shifters. The same author has written a two-volume set, *Computer Music Instruments I* and *II*, with detailed examples in Python, Csound, and Faust (Lazzarini 2017, 2019)

The spread of software synthesizers has been fostered by plug-in standards. Steinberg's Virtual Studio Technology (VST) format, introduced in 1996, continues as a broadly supported protocol. Other formats include Apple's Audio Units (AU) and LV2 for Linux, among others. For tutorials on developing audio plugins, refer to Goudard and Muller (2003), Dobson (2011), and Pirkle (2019).

III   **Sound Synthesis**

9 *Sampling*

In popular parlance, *sampling* means making a digital recording of a short sound object like a one-bar drum pattern. The sample is then triggered by a MIDI note statement played on a controller or a sequencer. In the past, samples had to be short because of extremely limited memory space. Today, for all practical purposes, these limitations are gone.

The term *sampling* derives from established notions of digital *samples* and *sampling rate* explained in chapter 3. Sampling instruments are widely available in both hardware and software. All samplers are designed around the basic notion of playing back prerecorded sounds, shifted to a desired pitch.

Because they can mimic the sounds of acoustic instruments, samplers are among the most popular electronic instruments available. But emulation of a known instrument only scratches the surface of the potential of sampling, which can manipulate any sound. The prospect of live sampling onstage introduces another set of possibilities. The California artist Pamela Z samples and loops her voice in complex layers. For the musician Earl Howard, who has played with the New York Philharmonic, a sampler can be used in real time to record the sounds of other instrumentalists in an ensemble and play them back in radically transformed ways. Ultimately, the extraordinary power of a sampler to play back and pitch shift any sound in real time, whether real or synthetic, makes it an essential tool in any electronic music studio (figure 9.1).

Figure 9.1 Native Instrument Kontakt, a popular software sampler. In this simple setup, six sound files are loaded in the sampler (right side). All six are triggered simultaneously by a MIDI keyboard.

Sampling is different from the classical technique of fixed-waveform synthesis explained in chapter 6. Instead of scanning a small, fixed wavetable containing one cycle of a waveform, a sampler scans a large wavetable that contains thousands of individual cycles—usually a second or more of pre-recorded sound. Because the sampled waveform changes over the attack, sustain, and decay portion of the event, the result is a rich and time-varying sound.

Sampling: Background

Composed manipulation of recorded sounds dates back to the 1920s. (See Davies [1996] for a colorful historical account.) Composers such as Darius Milhaud, Paul Hindemith, and Ernst Toch experimented with variable-speed phonographs in concert (Ernst 1977). The 1920s saw the invention of sound recording on optical film (sound photography) and the possibility of creating *sound libraries*. The musical potential of sample libraries was recognized by the Mexican composer Carlos Chavez in 1937 (89–103):

Sound photography . . . has an enormous interest for composers in that it offers new and very ample musical resource . . . Libraries of sound, in which thousands and thousands of noises, murmurings of nature and man in thousands of different places and times, have been preserved . . . Here at hand, ready to be used in our creations, are all the sound elements possible or imaginable.

The composer Halim El-Dabh created *Expressions of Zaar* (1944) from samples of an Egyptian ceremony recorded on a wire recorder, a primitive recording device. El-Dabh recognized that the low fidelity of the original recordings could be exploited artistically. He processed the sounds through echo chambers and other devices to catapult them beyond the literal and into the realm of sonic abstraction—like much electronic music today.

Magnetic tape recording, originally developed in Germany in the 1930s, is a high-fidelity recording medium when a number of technical requirements are met. Moreover, the tape medium permits cutting and splicing and therefore flexible editing and rearrangement of sequences of recorded sounds. Tape recorders became available to musicians only after World War II.

Pierre Schaeffer and Musique Concrète

After experiments with variable-speed phonographs in the late 1940s, Pierre Schaeffer founded the Studio de Musique Concrète at Paris in 1950 (figure 9.2).

Figure 9.2   Pierre Schaeffer's studio for musique concrète at rue de l'Université, Paris, 1960. The studio features three tape recorders (left) along with a disk turntable. On the right is another tape recorder and the multiple-head Phonogène device (see figure 9.3). (Photograph courtesy of the Groupe de Recherches Musicales, Paris.)

He and Pierre Henry began to use tape recorders to record and manipulate *concrète* sounds. *Musique concrète* refers to the use of microphone-recorded sounds or samples, rather than synthetically generated tones-as in pure electronic music.

The musique concrète aesthetic also refers to the manner of working directly in the presence of sound, as opposed to silently writing notes in common music notation (Schaeffer and Moles 1952; Schaeffer 1977, 2017; Chion 1982). In order to describe the vastly expanded range of sonic materials Schaeffer introduced the notion of *sound objects*. A sound object is a generalization of the note concept. It refers to any sound of a duration between about one-tenth of a second and eight seconds (i.e., on the same time scale as musical notes) that can be used as a unit of composition (Roads 2001b).

An outstanding example of musique concrète is *De Natura Sonorum* (1975) by Bernard Parmegiani. Luc Ferrari took the concept of musique concrète in the direction of what is now called *ambient, soundscape,* or *environmental* music with his groundbreaking 1970 composition *Presque rien, no. 1* (Caux 2013). Horacio Vaggione combined musique concrète sources with sophisticated micromontage techniques in works such as *Mécanique des fluides* (2014).

Early Sampling Instruments

Modern sampling instruments are based on a principle of sample playback used earlier in photoelectric and tape devices (table 9.1). These devices played either optical discs (encoded with photographic images of waveforms), or magnetic tapes of sound. Depending on the disc or tape selected and the key pressed on the musical keyboard, a playback head inside these instruments would play the sound on the disc or tape that matched the pitch specified by the depressed key (figure 9.3).

The designer of the Singing Keyboard, Frederick Sammis, described the potential of such an instrument as early as 1936 (quoted in Rhea 1977):

Let us suppose that we are to use this machine as a special-purpose instrument for making "talkie" cartoons. At once it will be evident that we have a machine with which the composer may try out various combinations of words and music and learn at once just how they will sound in the finished work. The instrument will probably have ten or more sound tracks recorded side by side on a strip of film and featuring such words as "quack" for a duck, "meow" for a cat, "moo" for a cow . . . It could as well be the bark of a dog or the hum of a human voice at the proper pitch.

Table 9.1   Early sampling instruments

Instrument	Inventor	Year of invention	City of invention
Light-Tone Organ	E. Welte	1936	Berlin
Singing Keyboard	F. Sammis	1936	Hollywood
Phonogène	J. Poullin	1953 first version	Paris
Special-Purpose tape Recorder	H. LeCaine	1955	Ottawa
Chamberlin	H. Chamberlin	1956	Los Angeles
Mellotron	Streetly Electronics	1963	Birmingham, UK

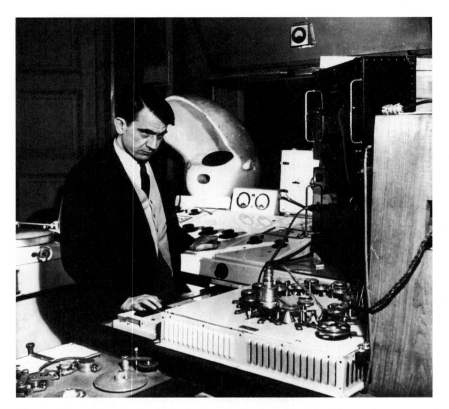

Figure 9.3   Pierre Schaeffer playing the keyboard of the Phonogène, a tape-based transposer and time stretcher, 1953, Paris. (Photograph by Lido, supplied by the courtesy of the Groupe de Recherches Musicales.)

The most famous predigital sampler was the Mellotron, an expensive and heavy instrument containing dozens of strips of tape (figure 9.4). The Mellotron enjoyed popular success with English rock groups such as the Beatles (*Strawberry Fields Forever*) and the Moody Blues (*Nights in White Satin*) in the 1960s and 1970s. They created orchestral and choral backings on popular songs. But the electromechanical design of the Mellotron made it temperamental. Tapes wore out due to head abrasion, and there were inevitable failures in the tricky mechanics for selecting and running multiple tapes. Nonetheless, the Mellotron had a signature sound that was stamped on a number of major hits. The sound of the Mellotron is alive today, as Mellotron remakes, plug-ins, and sample libraries still go strong.

By the 1980s, the rise of digital electronics made it feasible to record and store sound in digital memory chips. As digital memory chips became cheaper it was possible to store several seconds of sound for playback on a musical keyboard–based digital sampling instrument. The Fairlight

Figure 9.4   The Mellotron model 400 (1970).

Figure 9.5   The E-mu Emulator sampling keyboard instrument (1981).

Computer Music Instrument (CMI) was the first commercial keyboard sampler (1979, Australia). The CMI had a resolution of 8 bits per sample and cost over $25,000. Taking advantage of declining costs for digital hardware, the E-mu Emulator (figure 9.5), introduced in 1981, lowered the cost of 8-bit monophonic sampling (Vail 1993). For $9,000, the Emulator offered a total of 128 Kbytes of sample memory or about 10 seconds of sample time.

In order to create a commercial sampling instrument, three basic issues must be addressed: looping, pitch shifting, and data reduction, which we discuss in the next three sections.

Looping

Looping extends the duration of sampled sounds played by a musical keyboard. If the musician holds down a key, the sampler should scan seamlessly through the note until the musician releases the key. This is accomplished by specifying beginning and ending *loop points* in the sampled sound. After the attack of the note is finished, the sampler reads repeatedly through the looped part of the wavetable until the key is released; then it plays the note's final portion of the wavetable.

Commercial sample libraries are often prelooped at the factory. But for newly sampled sounds, the responsibility of specifying the begin and end loop points is usually left to the musician who sampled them. Creating a seamless loop out of a traditional instrument tone requires care. The loop should begin after the attack of the note and should end before the decay (figure 9.6).

Some samplers provide automatic methods for finding prospective loop points. One method is to perform *pitch detection* on the sampled sound (Massie 1986). (See chapter 34 for a discussion of pitch detection methods.) The pitch detection algorithm searches for repeating patterns in the wavetable that indicate a fundamental *pitch period*. The pitch period is the time interval that spans one cycle of a periodic waveform (figure 9.7). Once the pitch has been estimated, the sampler suggests a pair of loop points that match some number of pitch periods in the waveform. This kind of looping algorithm tends to generate smooth loops that are constant in pitch. If the

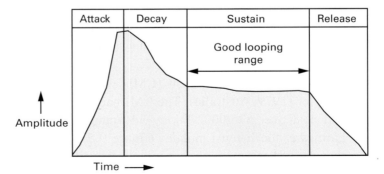

Figure 9.6 Amplitude profile of a sound with a characteristic ADSR amplitude envelope. The best area for a smooth loop is the sustained portion.

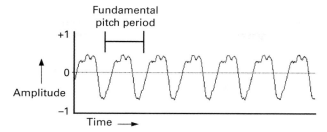

Figure 9.7   The fundamental pitch period is equal to one cycle of a periodic waveform, in this case, a waveform emitted by an alto saxophone.

body of the loop is too short, however, the result is similar to the sterile tones of fixed-waveform synthesis. For example, a loop of one or two periods of a violin note negates the time-varying qualities of a bowed string, which unfolds over hundreds of periods per second. Such a short loop yields an artificial tone that has lost its source identity.

The beginning and ending points of a loop can either be *spliced* together at a common sample point or *crossfaded.* A splice is a cut from one sound to the next. Splicing waveforms results in a click, pop, or thump at the splice point, unless the beginning and ending points are well matched. Crossfading means that the end part of each looped event gradually fades out while the beginning part slowly fades in again; the crossfade looping process repeats over and over as the note is sustained (figure 9.8). Typical crossfade times range from 10 to 100 ms but can also be longer.

When none of these techniques create a smooth loop, due to vibrato or other variations in the signal, more elaborate methods can be brought to bear, such as *bidirectional looping.* A bidirectional loop alternates between forward and backward playback (figure 9.9a). Forward and backward loops can be layered on top of one another to mask discontinuities in either direction (figure 9.9b). Even more elaborate looping techniques based on spectrum analysis are available in some looping plug-ins. For example, one can analyze the sound, randomize the phase of each spectral component in the loop, and resynthesize (Collins 1993).

Pitch Shifting

In an inexpensive sampler it may not be possible to store every note played by an acoustic instrument. These samplers store only every third or fourth semitone and obtain intermediate notes by shifting the pitch of a nearby stored note. Similarly, if one records a single sound into a sampler memory and plays it back by pressing different keys, the sampler carries out the same pitch-shifting

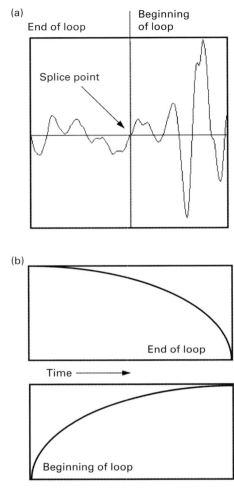

Figure 9.8   Splicing versus crossfading loops. (a) A butt splice of two parts of a waveform at a common zero point. The ending point of the loop splices to the beginning of the same wavetable loop. (b) Crossfade looping can be viewed as a fade out of the end of the loop overlapped by a fade in of the beginning of the loop.

technique. A side effect of simple pitch shifting is that the sound's duration increases or decreases, depending on the key pressed. Looping over a sustained portion of a sound compensates for the duration change.

Two methods of simple pitch shifting exist:

1. Varying the clock frequency of the output digital-to analog converter (DAC) changes the playback sampling rate; this shifts the pitch up or down.

2. *Sample-rate conversion* (*resampling* the signal in the digital domain) shifts the pitch inside the sampler and allows playback at a constant sampling rate for all pitches.

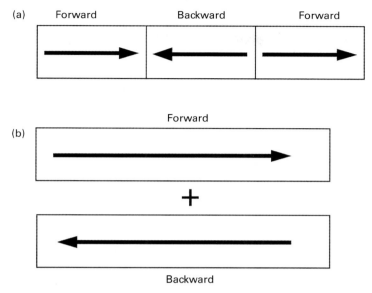

Figure 9.9   Looping methods for smoothing out variations. (a) Three cycles of a bidirectional loop. (b) In a layered forward/backward loop the two versions are added together.

Method 1 was used in early samplers like the original Emulator. Method 2 is the way that it is done today. Both these methods are called *time-domain* techniques because they operate directly on the time-domain waveform. This is different from the *frequency-domain* pitch-shifting techniques discussed in chapter 31. Next, we compare these two time-domain methods.

Because method 1 changed the playback sampling rate, it required a separate DAC for each note that can be played simultaneously on the musical keyboard (typically up to ten DACs). Each DAC had a variable clock rate and a variable-frequency smoothing filter. For full transposability, the DAC and the filter had to work over extremely wide operating ranges. To give an example, if a tone with a pitch of 250 Hz sampled at 44.1 kHz is shifted up six octaves to 16 kHz, the clock frequency of the output DAC would have to shift up six octaves to 2.82 MHz. In practice, this was not feasible. Thus the designers imposed limitations on the audio performance of the system. For example, one sampler that employed this pitch-shifting method allowed only a single semitone of transposition (less than a 6 percent change of clock frequency) for sounds recorded at its highest sampling rate of 41.67 kHz. The DAC and the filter are never forced to work at a sampling rate higher than 44.1 kHz. Other samplers did not permit any transposition above an arbitrary limit.

Pitch-shifting method 2 performs sample-rate conversion. This is essentially the same technique as used in wavetable-lookup synthesis, described in chapter 3. Sample-rate conversion, in effect, resamples the signal in the digital domain. The output DAC's sampling frequency remains constant. Speeding up a sound and increasing its pitch is achieved by resampling the waveform at a lower sampling rate. This is analogous to time-lapse photography in which the frame rate is slowed down to achieve a speed-up on playback. In a digital audio system, samples are skipped in resampling. The number of samples that are skipped is proportional to the amount of pitch shifting that is desired (just as in wavetable-lookup synthesis). The process of skipping samples in resampling is called *decimation* (figure 9.10a). Resampling with decimation is also called *downsampling*. For example, to shift the pitch upward by three octaves, the signal is downsampled by reading every third sample in playback.

To lower the pitch of a sound and slow it down, the sound is resampled at a higher frequency to stretch it out. This is analogous to the operation of a slow-motion camera that speeds up the frame rate to achieve a slow-down effect upon playback. In a digital audio system, new intermediate samples are inserted between existing samples by means of *interpolation* (figure 9.10b). Resampling with interpolation is also called *upsampling*.

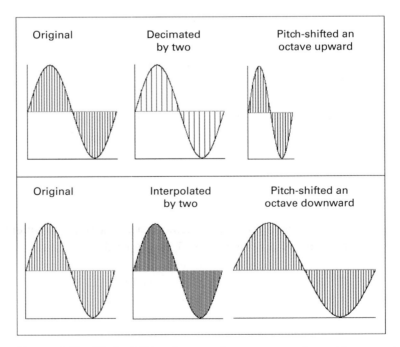

Figure 9.10 Pitch-shifting by sample-rate conversion with a constant playback sampling frequency. Top: If every other sample is skipped on playback, the signal is decimated, and the pitch is shifted up an octave. Bottom: If twice the number of samples are used by means of interpolation on playback, the signal is shifted down an octave.

The relationship between the various resampling rates and pitch shifting can be confusing at first, because pitch-shifting method 1 and method 2 seem to go in opposite directions to achieve the same aim. Method 1 raises pitch by increasing the sampling rate on playback. Method 2, however, raises pitch by decreasing the resampling rate with decimation, even though the playback sampling frequency is constant.

So far, we have seen how to shift pitch by octave intervals. To shift pitch by any integer ratio, a combination of interpolation and decimation are used (Schafer and Rabiner 1973a; Moorer 1977; Rabiner 1983; Lagadec 1983; Crochiere and Rabiner 1983; Hutchins 1986a; Duncan and Rossum 1988; Mitra 2006). In particular, to pitch shift by a ratio N/M, we first interpolate by M and then decimate by N. For example, to shift a sound down by an interval of 3/4 (a perfect fourth) we upsample and interpolate by a factor of 4 and then downsample and decimate by a factor of 3. To shift up by a factor of 4/3 we first interpolate by 3 and then decimate by 4.

Sample-Rate Conversion without Pitch Shifting

Many digital audio recorders operate at the standard sampling rates of 44.1 or 48 kHz and their multiples. How can we resample a recording at one of these frequencies so as to play it back at the other frequency with no pitch shift? In this case the resampling rate is the same as the new output DAC sampling rate.

To convert a signal between the standard sampling rates of 44.1 and 48 kHz without a pitch change, a rather elaborate conversion process is required. First the rates are factored as follows:

$$\frac{48{,}000 = 2^5 \times 5}{44{,}100 = 3 \times 7^2} = (4/3 \times 4/7 \times 10/7)$$

These ratios can be implemented as six stages of interpolations and decimations by factors of 2, 3, 5, and 7, as follows:

1. Interpolate by 4 from 44,100 to 176,400 Hz

2. Decimate by 3 from 176,400 to 58,800 Hz

3. Interpolate by 4 from 58,800 to 235,200 Hz

4. Decimate by 7 from 235,200 to 33,600 Hz

5. Interpolate by 10 from 33,600 to 336,000 Hz

6. Decimate by 7 from 336,000 to 48,000 Hz

The signal can then be played back at a sampling rate of 48 kHz with no change of pitch.

As long as the input and output sampling rates can be written as a simple fraction, then the conversion process is straightforward. If the rates do not have an integer ratio or they are changing, then more sophisticated mathematical techniques must be used, which we will not venture into here (see Crochiere and Rabiner 1983; Rabiner 1983; Lagadec 1983; Mitra 2006). A variable resampling rate applies in the case with *flanging effects* (chapter 30) and audio *scrubbing* (simulating the manual back-and-forth motion of a magnetic tape rocking across a playback head to locate a splice point).

Problems in Resampling

The audio fidelity of resampling is limited by the numerical precision used in the conversion. When there are many intermediate resampling stages, a slight loss in fidelity in the form of added noise is to be expected. Aliasing can also be a problem because, as in the original sampling process, resampling can generate unwanted spectral artifacts due to aliasing. When a sampler skips samples in decimation, it is throwing away intermediate samples. These intermediate samples may have smoothed the waveform's transition between two disjoint points. Thus a decimated signal can contain jagged discontinuities (figure 9.11). At the same time, all frequencies are shifted up, meaning that aliasing can occur on playback. This problem can be reduced to a minimal

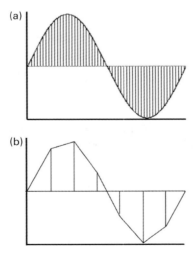

Figure 9.11   With enough decimation, even a sine wave can be turned into a jagged waveform. (a) Original sinusoidal waveform. (b) Decimation of (a) by a factor of 8.

effect by lowpass filtering the signal after decimation. Filtering smooths the jagged edges of the decimated waveform (Pohlmann 2010).

Filtering is also needed in interpolation because simple linear interpolation creates aliased components. Rather than devising a more complicated interpolation scheme, the usual approach in sample-rate conversion is to combine linear interpolation with filtering to shift the frequency content and also minimize aliasing.

Sample and Wavetable Libraries

Because a sampler is a type of recording system, the quality of the samples depends on the recording process. Making high-quality samples requires good players and instruments, excellent microphones, and favorable recording environments. Arranging all these elements for a library of sounds requires serious investment and effort. Thus most users of samplers prefer to supplement their personal collection of samples with libraries prepared by professionals—or by other amateurs, as in https://www.freesound.org (de Jong 2005).

Sample libraries are widely used in the entertainment industry, not only for music but also routinely for ambience and sound effects. Almost every radio and television show, movie, commercial, game, and pop song uses samples to create mood. Responding to commercial demand, a vast palette of sample libraries is available, ranging from orchestral instruments, choirs, and electric instruments (guitars, organs, etc.), to world instruments and sounds from natural habitats and industrial facilities. Well-known professional sound designers create and curate custom sound libraries (Devine 2008).

Some sample libraries are packaged in proprietary formats that can be read exclusively by authorized sample players. An example is the East-West product line with its PLAY sample engine. Other libraries are distributed in standard formats such as 24-bit .wav files or Apple Loops. They can be copied into folders linked with sample players like Apple Logic Pro, Reason, Native Instruments Kontakt, and Steinberg HALion. Free and open formats like SoundFonts (chapter 51) and SFZ (SFZ 2019) are royalty-free. Utilities like Translator by Chicken Systems can convert between many different sample formats.

Wavetable libraries contain thousands of single-cycle waveforms. They function as expansion packs for popular wavetable-based synthesizers like Native Instruments Absynth, Camel Audio Alchemy, U&I Software Meta-Synth, and Cakewalk Rapture. An example library is Galbanum Architecture Waveforms, which offers over 25,000 waveforms.

Emulating Traditional Instruments

A sampler can play back and pitch shift any sound. However, most users are looking for emulations of traditional instruments. Thus the dream of a "symphony orchestra in a box" remains a holy grail for the creators of sample libraries. Unfortunately, sampled sound often has an artificial quality that makes it easily distinguishable from the animated sounds produced by good human performers. Most percussionists, for example, would not mistake the frozen sound of a sampled drum solo from that of a human drummer. In a live performance on acoustic drums, each drum stroke is unique, and there are major differences in the sound depending on the musical context in which the stroke is played. This is not to say that robotic performance is invalid. The commercial success of electronic drum machines like the Roland TR-808 (and myriad sampled versions of it) proves that lock-step rhythms and unvarying percussion sounds have a major audience. Original TR-808s sell for thousands of dollars.

Still, it is understandable that the naturalness or realism of a sampler or sample library should be held up as a criterion for judging between different products. Differences in sample quality are not subtle. Certain instruments, such as organs, can be simulated more or less realistically by most samplers. Other instruments such as voices, strings, woodwinds, brass, and plucked or strummed instruments are intrinsically more difficult to capture with existing sampling technology. Individual notes can be captured well, but when we string the notes together into melodies and phrases, it is apparent that major chunks of acoustic and performance information have been left out.

Factory-supplied samples model the generic singer, the generic saxophone played by the generic saxophonist, the generic orchestra played in the generic concert hall, and so on. Yet most knowledgeable listeners can tell the difference between two vocalists, saxophonists, and conductors with orchestras. It would be difficult to mistake a MIDI sequencer + sampler rendition of a saxophone solo with the signature style of the John Coltrane original. This points out a fundamental limitation in many existing samplers. Beyond a certain point, it is impossible to increase the realism of samplers without understanding the relationship between sound structure and musical performance.

In expressive instruments like voices, saxophones, strings, brass, guitars, and others, each note is created in a musical context. Within a phrase, a note is reached from another note (or from silence) and leads into the successive note (or leads to silence). In addition to these contextual cues, transitional sounds like breathing, tonguing, key clicks, and sliding fingers along strings punctuate the phrasing. Constraints of style and taste determine when context-sensitive effects such as rubato, legato, staccato, portamento, vibrato, crescendi and diminuendi, and other nuances are applied.

How can we model the sound microstructure of note-to-note transitions? This question is the subject of the next section.

Modeling Note-to-Note Transitions

The problem of what happens in note-to-note transitions was the subject of the doctoral research of John Strawn at Stanford University (1985c). He analyzed the transitions in nine nonpercussive orchestral instruments. The time-domain and frequency-domain plots that emerged from this research graphically depicted the context-sensitive nature of tone successions.

In wind instruments, one of the ways to articulate a transition is by *tonguing*–a momentary interruption of the windstream by an action of the tongue, as if the player were pronouncing the letter *t* or *k*. Figure 9.12 shows a time-domain plot of transitions of a trumpet played tongued (a) and untongued (b). The contrast between the two types of transitions is clear.

Figure 9.13 plots the spectrum of this transition. Strawn's research demonstrated that some transitions are stamped with strong transitional cues in amplitude and spectrum changes that articulate the attack of the second note (figure 9.13a). Other transitions are very smooth, with a dip of as little as 10 dB of amplitude between notes (figure 9.13b).

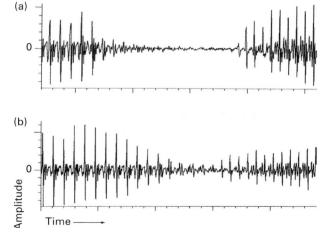

Figure 9.12 Time-domain plot of note-to-note transition of an ascending major third interval for a trumpet played tongued (a) and untongued (b). The time span for the plots is 120 ms.

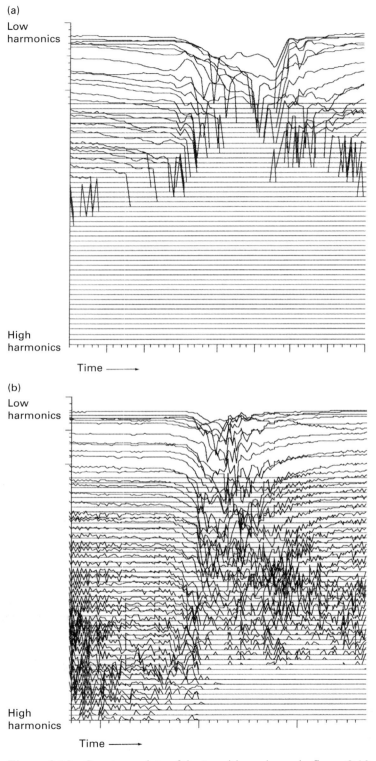

Figure 9.13 Spectrum plots of the transitions shown in figure 9.10. The plots show fifty harmonics plotted over a time span of 300 ms, with lower harmonics at the back. (a) Tongued. (b) Untongued. Notice how the "hole" in the middle of (a) is filled in when the note transition is untongued (more continuous).

Similar issues have been studied in speech, where the issue of phoneme transitions is called the *coarticulation problem*. Certain consonants, for example, are pronounced differently depending on where they are in a word. Consider the *n* in *tenth*. It is pronounced with the tongue against the teeth because the *th* that follows it is also dental, whereas the *n* in *now* is pronounced differently.

Synthesis Methods That Model Note-to-Note Transitions

Several synthesis techniques aim directly at modeling realistic note-to-note transitions. These include physical models (chapter 18 and Smith 2010), spectral models (chapter 37 and Bonada and Serra 2007), and additive synthesis (chapter 10 and Lindemann 2007, 2009).

One of the earliest methods, *diphone synthesis,* addressed the problem of phoneme transitions in speech (Peterson and Barney 1952; Peterson, Wang, and Sivertsen 1958; Olive 1977; Schwartz et al. 1979). The basic theory of diphone synthesis assumes that speech consists of a series of stable sounds separated by transition sounds. Modern speech synthesizers such as Amazon Alexa and Apple Siri use this method to create quasi-natural-sounding speech. Today we would call this *concatenative synthesis* (chapter 23 and Maestre 2009). By generalizing the concept from the limited domain of speech to the open universe of musical sounds, one can build up dictionaries of stable and transition sounds to cover a specific class of sounds, such as bowed cello tones. Researchers have developed dictionaries of transition rules for instruments that smooth the concatenation of adjacent diphones (Rodet et al. 1988; Depalle 1991).

Another way to model the microstructure of note-to-note transitions in instrumental sounds is a "brute force" calculation: capture every possible note-to-note transition as a sample. Then trigger the appropriate transition sample when going from a note to any other note.

In recent years, companies including Yamaha and Roland have introduced expressive samplers that take into account not only the instrument being emulated but also which notes follow which when they are played on a keyboard. These samplers implement *controller-switched transitions* between notes as the musician plays the keyboard. These transitions make the performance sound like a more realistic brass, woodwind, or stringed instrument. For example, the Yamaha MOTIF XF synthesizer combines sampling with physical modeling and real-time analysis of the keyboard in order to replicate the performance nuances of the selected instrument, such as flamenco strumming, plucked-string harmonics, string slides, fret noises, double-bass legato, and marimba trills.

In the same vein, NotePerformer is a sound playback engine for orchestral score editing programs like Sibelius, Finale, and Dorico, among others. Through analysis of the score, NotePerformer offers improved musical phrasing using a variety of articulations and note-to-note transition (mutes, harmonics, pizzicato, sul tasto, staccato and slur, tremolo, flutter tonguing, marcato, tenuto, etc.) on strings, brass, and woodwinds.

Finally, several companies offer sample libraries that play back entire prerecorded phrases so that note-to-note transitions are already baked into the sound. The Sonokinetic product line is a prime example. They supply libraries of hundreds of continuous phrases (beds, textures, ostinato rhythms, arpeggios, runs, rises, drops, etc.) played by orchestra in the style of composers such as Bernard Herrmann, Jerry Goldsmith, Karlheinz Stockhausen, and Krzysztof Penderecki, among others.

10 *Additive Synthesis*

Additive Synthesis: Background

Fixed-Waveform Additive Synthesis
The Phase Factor
Addition of Partials

Time-Varying Additive Synthesis

Demands of Additive Synthesis

Sources of Control Data for Additive Synthesis

Additive Analysis/Resynthesis
Musical Applications of Additive Analysis/Resynthesis
Methods of Sound Analysis for Additive Synthesis
Data Reduction Models in Additive Analysis/Resynthesis
Line-segment approximation
Principal components analysis
Spectral interpolation synthesis
Spectral modeling synthesis
ATS: Analysis, transformation, synthesis
Reconstructive phrase modeling

Additive Synthesis Based on Machine Learning

Walsh Function Synthesis

Additive synthesis is based on the summation of elementary waveforms to create a complex audio signal. Additive synthesis is one of the oldest synthesis techniques, yet it continues to evolve.

Additive synthesis can simulate existing sounds or create new, previously unheard textures. However, the power of additive synthesis is that it is possible to precisely approximate any complicated waveform as a sum of elementary waveforms, a theory that can be traced back to Jean-Baptiste Joseph Fourier (1768–1830).

When coupled with a sound analysis stage, additive synthesis becomes a powerful means of simulating natural sounds and cloning variations of them. Because it is based on a sinusoidal model, sounds such as slowly varying sine waves are well modeled by additive synthesis, which means that they can be described relatively simply. Other sounds such as modulations and noise textures are not so well modeled, so that they require more complicated analysis schemes, as we explain further on.

Two other chapters cover related topics: chapter 37 deals with spectrum analysis by Fourier methods, and chapter 44 surveys spectrum editors.

Additive Synthesis: Background

The concept of additive synthesis is ancient, first applied in pipe organs by means of their multiple *register stops* (figure 10.1). By pulling on a register stop, the organist could route air to a set of pipes. The air was released into the pipe—creating sound—by pressing a key on the organ keyboard. By pulling several register stops, the organist could add together the sound of several pipes. According to one scholar, "The Middle Ages particularly favored the mixture in which every note was accompanied by several fifths and octaves based upon it" (Geiringer 1945). This idea of frequency mixtures is the essence of additive synthesis.

Additive synthesis has been used since the earliest days of electronic music (Cahill 1897; Douglas 1968; *die Reihe* 1955; Stockhausen 1964). The massive Telharmonium synthesizer unveiled in 1906 summed the signal of dozens of electrical tone generators to create additive sound complexes (Weidenaar 1991). Figure 10.2 depicts the additive scheme.

The famous Hammond organ (figure 10.3) manufactured between 1935 and 1972 was a pure additive synthesis instrument that incorporated a miniature version of the Telharmonium's electromechanical rotating tone generators.

All organs, whether mechanical, electromechanical, or purely electronic in technology, do not produce particularly realistic simulations of traditional instruments. The reason is that they produce a fixed waveform that does not

Figure 10.1 Pipe organ console with register stops on either side of the keyboards.

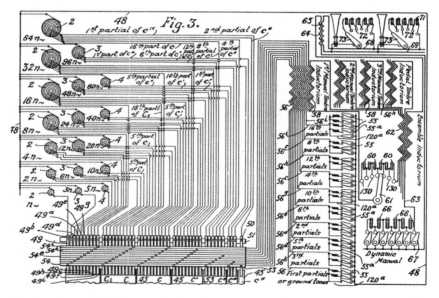

Figure 10.2 Additive synthesis of a complex tone in the Telharmonium. Sine wave harmonics from the tone-generating alternator are fed to bus bars (54). Pressing a key (C in this case) connects each harmonic to a multicoil transformer (56 Inductorium) where they mix. Each harmonic is attenuated to the desired level by the inductors in series with each winding (56a, b, etc.). The tap-switch inductors (60) regulate the amplitude of the mixing transformer output, as do the inductors near the loudspeakers (72, 73) at the listener's end of the transmission line. (Cahill patent drawing, reproduced in Johnson et al. [1970].)

Figure 10.3   The author's Hammond T422 organ, an additive synthesis instrument based on electromechanical tone-wheels. Different mixtures of the various harmonics can be adjusted by pulling drawbars above the musical keys. The instrument contains a built-in Leslie rotating speaker.

vary at the micro time scale. As we show further on, in order to produce a realistic simulation, the mixture of sine waves needs to constantly vary in detail over time.

Fixed-Waveform Additive Synthesis

Some synthesizers let musicians create waveforms by *harmonic addition.* In order to make a waveform with a given spectrum, the user adjusts the relative strengths of a set of *harmonics* of a given fundamental. (The term *harmonic* as an integer multiple of a fundamental frequency was first used by Sauveur in 1701.) For example, 400 Hz is the second harmonic of 200 Hz, because two times two hundred equals four hundred. The harmonics can be displayed as a *bar graph* or *histogram,* with the height of each bar representing the relative strength of a given harmonic. This *spectrum template* aligns to different fundamental frequencies and their harmonics when one changes the pitch of the oscillator. Figure 10.4 shows a harmonic spectrum and the corresponding waveform.

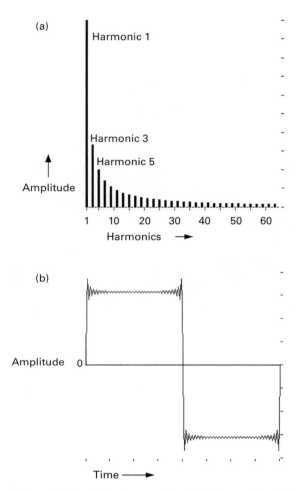

Figure 10.4   Waveform synthesis by harmonic addition. (a) Histogram plot showing the relative strength of the harmonics on a linear scale. In this case, the histogram has energy only in the odd harmonics. The amplitude of the third harmonic is one-third that of the fundamental, the amplitude of the fifth harmonic is one-fifth that of the fundamental, and so on. (b) Approximation to a square wave synthesized by harmonic addition in (a).

Once a desirable spectrum is tuned, a digital oscillator adds together the various harmonics. Figure 10.5 shows successive stages of waveform addition used to create a quasi-square wave.

The Phase Factor

Phase (presented in chapter 2) is a trickster. Depending on the context, it may or may not be a significant factor in additive synthesis. For example, if one changes the starting phases of the frequency components of a fixed

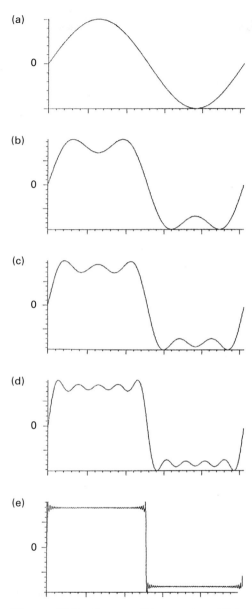

Figure 10.5   Stages of harmonic addition as seen in a series of time domain waveforms. (a) Fundamental only. (b) First and third harmonics. (c) Sum of odd harmonics through the fifth. (d) Sum of odd harmonics through the ninth. (e) Quasi-square wave created by summing odd harmonics up to the 101st.

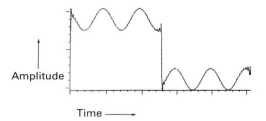

Amplitude

Time ———▶

Figure 10.6 Effect of phase in additive synthesis. This waveform is the result of the same mixture of sine waves as in figure 10.5e except that the starting phase of the fifth harmonic is 90° instead of 0°.

waveform and resynthesizes the tone, this makes no difference to the listener. Yet, such a change may have a radical effect on the visual appearance of the waveform, as shown in figure 10.6.

Phase relationships become apparent in the perception of the brilliant but short life of attacks, grains, and transients. The ear is also sensitive to phase relationships in complex sounds in which the phases of certain components are shifting over time. As we show in the section on sound analysis and resynthesis, proper phase alignment is essential in reconstructing an analyzed sound.

Addition of Partials

We can generalize from addition of harmonics to addition of *partials*. In acoustics, a *partial* refers to an arbitrary frequency component in a spectrum (Benade 1990). The partial may or may not be a harmonic (integer multiple) of a fundamental frequency f. Figure 10.7a shows a spectrum containing four partials: two harmonic and two *inharmonic*. An *inharmonic partial* is not in an integer ratio to the fundamental frequency. Figure 10.7b is the waveform that results from the sum of the four arbitrary partials.

At the level of synthesizing a single waveform, adding partials is limited from a musical point of view. Because the spectrum in fixed-waveform synthesis is constant over the course of a note, partial addition can never reproduce accurately the sound of an acoustic instrument. It approximates only the *steady-state* portion of an instrumental tone. A time-varying timbre is more tantalizing to the ear than a constant spectrum (Grey 1975).

Time-Varying Additive Synthesis

One of the pioneers of computer music, Jean-Claude Risset (1938–2016) analyzed instrumental tones to determine the evolution of their harmonics over

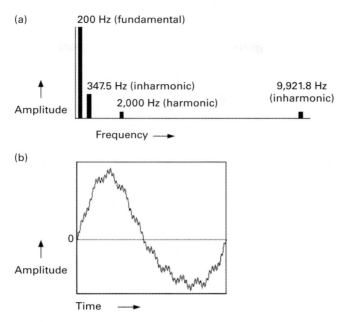

Figure 10.7 Partial addition with four components, both harmonic and inharmonic. The percentage contribution of each component is 73, 18, 5, and 4 percent, respectively. (a) Frequency-domain view. (b) Time-domain waveform.

time (figure 10.8). He discovered that variations in amplitude of each harmonic on a micro time scale was the secret to a tone's identity (Risset 1966, 1969, 1985a, 1985b, 1991; Risset and Mathews 1969; Risset and Wessel 1982). A composer as well as a scientist, Risset explored time-varying additive synthesis in many compositions, notably *Inharmonique* (1977), which charted a course through the vast space of inharmonic sine waves.

By changing the mixture of sine waves over time, one obtains more interesting synthetic timbres and more realistic instrumental tones. In the trumpet note in figure 10.9, it takes twelve sine waves to reproduce the initial attack portion of the event. After 300 ms, only three or four sine waves are needed.

We can view the process of partial addition graphically in several ways. Figure 10.10 shows additive synthesis in the analog domain, as it was originally practiced in the 1950s by composers such as Karlheinz Stockhausen (Stockhausen 1964). The figure shows several oscillator hardware modules, each with a manually controlled frequency knob. The outputs of the oscillators are routed to a mixer. To precisely realize a time-varying mixture took two people working together (Morawska-Büngler 1988). The composer and the assistant adjusted the balance of the oscillators in real time to determine the time-varying spectrum. With this equipment, manual control was the only option.

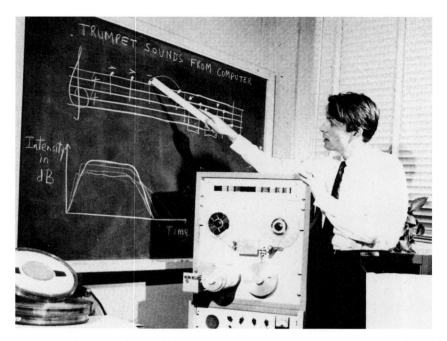

Figure 10.8   Jean-Claude Risset demonstrates a trumpet tone created by additive synthesis at Bell Telephone Laboratories, 1965. (Photograph courtesy of AT&T.)

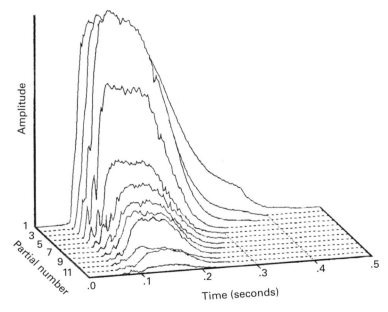

Figure 10.9   Time-varying spectrum plot of twelve partials of a trumpet tone, with the highest partials in the foreground. Time goes from left to right. Notice that the fundamental (back) is not the highest amplitude, but it lasts the longest.

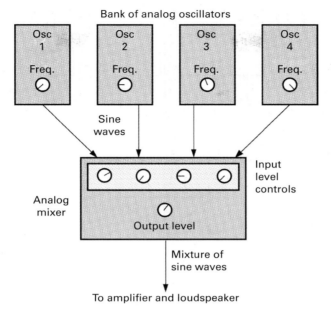

Figure 10.10   Additive synthesis in the analog domain. Oscillators feed a mixer (bottom).

Figure 10.11 shows digital additive synthesis. An audio oscillator is represented as a half-circle with a pair of inputs—one for amplitude and one for frequency. To generate a time-varying spectrum, each frequency and amplitude input to the oscillators is not a constant but a time-varying envelope function read over the duration of the event. The sine wave audio oscillators feed into a module that sums the signals. The sum module then passes the additive result to a DAC for conversion to sound.

David Wessel's *Antony* (1977) was a landmark in additive synthesis because it was the first composition to feature 256 time-varying oscillators (MacCallum, Goodheart, and Freed 2015).

Demands of Additive Synthesis

Time-varying additive synthesis imposes significant computational demands. First, it requires large numbers of oscillators. If we make the musically reasonable assumptions that each sound event in a piece can have up to sixteen partials (each generated by a separate sine wave oscillator) and that up to twenty-four events can be playing simultaneously, we need up to 384 oscillators at any given time. If the system is running at a sampling rate of 48 kHz,

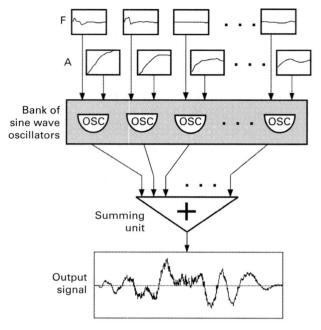

Figure 10.11   Digital time-varying additive synthesis with separate frequency (F) and amplitude (A) envelopes.

it must be capable of computing $48{,}000 \times 384 = 18{,}432{,}000$ samples/second. This is a huge amount of computation compared to twenty-four voices of frequency modulation, for example. (See chapter 16 on frequency modulation.) It is, however, within the range of today's laptop computers. Savioja et al. (2011) describes additive synthesis using *graphics processing units* (GPUs), which can run many operations in parallel. However, computation is not the only demand.

Additive synthesis has a voracious appetite for control data. If a piece contains 10,000 events (such as a typical orchestral score), each with up to sixteen partials, one needs to compute 160,000 frequency envelopes and 160,000 amplitude envelopes. Where does the control data come from? This is the subject of the next section.

Sources of Control Data for Additive Synthesis

Effective use of any digital synthesis technique, including additive synthesis, depends on having good control data for the synthesis instrument. To create animated sounds with a rich internal development, one drives the synthesizer with time-varying control data; hence, the control data are also referred to as the *driving functions* of the synthesis instrument. Control data can be obtained from several sources:

1. An interactive app with intuitive *graphical user interface* (GUI). For example, Native Instruments Razor can generate up to 320 partials in real time. It provides both a detailed studio view that presents dozens of knobs (figure 10.12), and a simplified performance view that maps to eight knobs on any MIDI controller. These *macros* enable control of multiple partials using a single knob. Air's Loom additive synthesizer allows GUI control of up to 512 partials.

2. Imported data from another domain that is mapped to the range of synthesis parameters. For example, some composers have taken data describing the shape of mountains or urban skylines and used these curves as control functions. In essence the composer sonifies a data set or a formula. An example is the early computer music piece *Earth's Magnetic Field* (1970) by Charles Dodge.

3. Generation by an algorithmic composition program that embodies composer-specified constraints on musical microstructure.

4. Manual indication in text by a composer using intuitive, theoretical, or empirical knowledge of psychoacoustics.

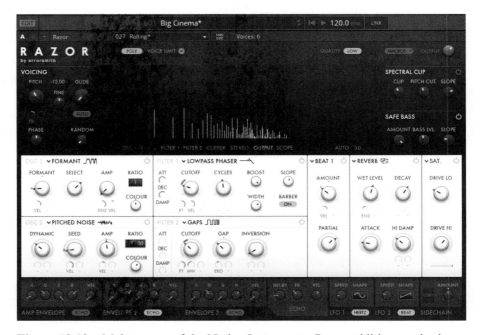

Figure 10.12   Main screen of the Native Instruments Razor additive synthesizer.

5. Output of an analysis subsystem that analyzes a sampled sound and produces the control data needed to resynthesize it. The data can be edited in order to create transformations of the original sounds. Pioneers of this approach include Trevor Wishart (1988), who used sound analysis as an intermediate stage in transforming vocal sounds for his piece *Vox-5*.

The fifth method requires a subsystem for sound analysis; this is the subject of the next section.

Additive Analysis/Resynthesis

Analysis/resynthesis encompasses different techniques that have a three-step process in common (figure 10.13):

1. A recorded sound is analyzed.
2. The musician modifies the analysis data.
3. The modified data is used in resynthesizing the transformed sound.

The concept of analysis/resynthesis is not predicated solely on additive synthesis. It can also be based on subtractive synthesis, combinations of additive and subtractive synthesis, or other methods. See chapters 36 through 39.

Early experiments in additive analysis/resynthesis were carried out by Harvey Fletcher (of the famous Fletcher-Munson loudness curves) and his associates at Bell Telephone Laboratories (Fletcher, Blackham, and Stratton 1962; Fletcher, Blackham, and Christensen 1963). They used analog equipment. When digital additive methods are used for resynthesis, the system resembles that shown in figure 10.14. The analysis is carried out successively on short segments of the input signal. The process of segmenting the input signal is called *windowing* (discussed in chapter 37). We can think of each windowed segment as being sent through a bank of narrow bandpass filters, in which every filter is tuned to a specific center frequency.

In *oscillator bank resynthesis* (chapter 37), the amplitude of the signal coming out of each filter is measured, and this time-varying value becomes the *amplitude control function* for that frequency range. At the same time, the system calculates control functions corresponding to small frequency deviations by looking at the output of adjacent filters (or *analysis bins*). The frequency and amplitude envelope control functions drive a set of oscillators in the resynthesis stage. In other words, we are using the infor-

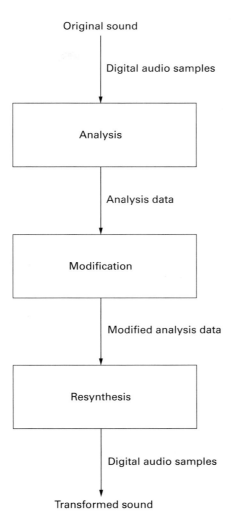

Figure 10.13   General overview of analysis/resynthesis. The modification stage may involve manual edits to the analysis data or modifications via *cross-synthesis* where the analysis data of one sound scales the analysis data from another sound.

mation gleaned from the analysis of an existing sound to create the set of control functions needed to resynthesize that sound additively with sine waves. If the input sound is well modeled as a sum of sine waves, the summed signal generated by the oscillators should sound the same as the original input signal.

Of course, analysis and resynthesis of a sound is not by itself interesting from a musical standpoint; it merely recreates the original sound. In order to create musically interesting effects, we modify the data generated by the analysis. This is the subject of the next section.

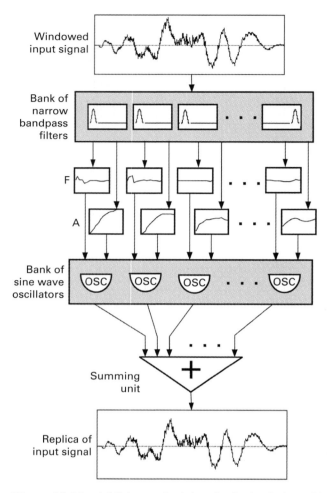

Figure 10.14   Additive analysis/synthesis. A windowed input signal is analyzed by a filter bank into a set of frequency (F) and amplitude (A) envelopes or *control functions* that drive a set of oscillators. If the analysis data is not changed, the output signal should be almost the same as the input signal.

Musical Applications of Additive Analysis/Resynthesis

After the analysis has been performed, musicians can edit the control functions to create variations of the original input signal. Many different effects are possible with this technique, as shown in table 10.1. Three compositions produced in the 1980s stand as pioneering examples of compositional manipulation of analysis data: *Mortuos Plango, Vivos Voco* (1981) by Jonathan Harvey, *Désintegrations* (1983) by Tristan Murail, and *Digital Moonscapes* (1985) by Wendy Carlos.

Table 10.1   Musical transformations using additive analysis/resynthesis

Musical effect	Technique
Variations of recorded sounds	Modify selected frequency and/or amplitude envelopes by editing or multiplication by arbitrary functions.
Spectrum scaling (without time scaling)	Multiply the frequency of all the partials (possibly excepting the fundamental) by a factor n or by arbitrary functions. Because multiplication does not preserve formant structures, vocal and instrumental sounds may lose their characteristic identity.
Spectrum shifting (without time scaling)	Add a factor n or an arbitrary function (without time scaling) to all partials (possibly excepting the fundamental). For small values this preserves formant structures.
Hybrid timbres	Replace some envelopes from one sound with selected envelopes from another sound
Time stretching and shrinking (without pitch shifting)	Adjust the duration of the frequency and amplitude envelopes, or change the *hop size* on playback (see chapter 37).
Timbral interpolation from one sound to another (morphing)	Interpolate over time between the envelopes of two tones.
Spectral filtering	Adjust the amplitudes of selected frequency partials.
Cross-synthesis	Method 1: Use the amplitude envelopes of the partials of one sound to scale the amplitude envelopes of another sound.
	Method 2: Apply the amplitude envelopes from one sound to the frequency (or phase) functions of another sound.
	Method 3: Apply the noise residual from one sound to the quasiharmonic part of another sound (see chapter 37).

In the Harvey piece, the composer analyzed the sound of a large bell. For each sinusoidal component in the resynthesis, the composer substituted the sound of a sampled boy's voice at the appropriate frequency. The voice samples followed the analyzed frequency and amplitude control functions of the chiming bells, creating an eerie effect of a boy/bell chorus. In the composition by Murail, the composer analyzed traditional instrument tones and created synthetic complements to these tones that blend seamlessly with the sounding instruments yet weave out dramatically when the instruments stop.

Désintegrations is a classic example of spectral composition techniques in which the harmonic structure of the work is based on an analysis of instrumental tones (Murail 1991). In *Digital Moonscapes,* Wendy Carlos used analysis data as the inspiration for creating a synthetic orchestra of percussion, string, woodwind, and brasslike timbres, used in an idiomatic orchestral style.

The next section briefly discusses current techniques of sound analysis with additive resynthesis with an emphasis on the data reduction problem. It serves as a prelude to the more detailed treatment in chapter 37.

Methods of Sound Analysis for Additive Synthesis

Many spectrum analysis methods are variations on the basic technique of Fourier analysis of component frequencies. These include *pitch-synchronous* analysis (Risset and Mathews 1969), the *phase vocoder* (PV) (Dolson 1983, 1986, 1989b; X. Serra 1997), *constant-Q* analysis (Petersen 1980; Schwede 1983; Stautner 1983; Loy 2007), and *frequency warping over a Bark scale* (Smith 2011) among others. The practical form of Fourier analysis is the *short-time Fourier transform* (STFT) described in chapter 37. This method can be thought of as analyzing a sampled sound by extracting successive short-duration overlapping segments (shaped by a window function) and applying a bank of filters to the selected segment. The output of each filter is measured, indicating the amplitude and the phase of the spectrum at that particular frequency. A series of these short-time analyses (akin to the frames of a film) constitute a time-varying spectrum. At the core of the STFT is the famous *fast Fourier transform* (FFT), a computationally efficient implementation of Fourier analysis (Cooley and Tukey 1965; Singleton 1967; Moore 1978a, 1978b; Rabiner and Gold 1975).

The PV (Flanagan and Golden 1966; Portnoff 1978; Holtzman 1980; Moorer 1978; Dolson 1983; Gordon and Strawn 1985; Strawn 1985b; X. Serra 1997; Loy 2007; Smith 2011; Lazzarini 2011d; Sethares 2019) deserves special mention here, as it is a popular method of sound analysis/resynthesis that has been distributed with several music software packages. The PV converts a sampled input signal into a time-varying spectral format. In particular, it generates a set of time-varying frequency and amplitude curves. Interesting sound transformations can be achieved by editing and resynthesizing PV data. For example, the PV can be used for *time stretching* or *time shrinking* without pitch change. In this effect, a sound is made longer or shorter without significantly affecting its pitch or timbre. (See chapter 31 for a discussion of various approaches to pitch-time changing.)

Contrary to the expectations of the researchers who invented them (who were searching for efficient coding techniques), sound analysis can generate an "information explosion" (Risset and Wessel 1982). That is, the analysis data (the control functions) can take up many times more memory space than the original input signal. The amount of data depends partly on the complexity of the input sound, that is, how many sine wave functions are needed to resynthesize it, and partly on the internal data representation used in the analysis program. Using the tracking phase vocoder, for example, a short sound file containing noise that takes up two Mbytes may generate tens of Mbytes of analysis data. This situation mandates some form of data reduction of the control data, the subject of the next section.

Data Reduction Models in Additive Analysis/Resynthesis

Data reduction is important to efficient analysis/resynthesis. Data reduction takes two steps. First, the data—a set of amplitude and frequency control functions—are analyzed. Second, an algorithm transforms the original data into a more compact representation. An important goal of data reduction is to reduce data without eliminating perceptually salient features of the input signal. Another goal in computer music work can be to leave the analysis data in a form that can be edited by a composer. The aim is not simply to save bits; rather, one wants to make it easy to manipulate the data-reduced amplitude and frequency envelopes of the partials.

A large body of research work on data reduction of analysis data is recorded in the literature, including studies by Risset (1966), Freedman (1967), Beauchamp (1969, 1975), Grey (1975), Grey and Gordon (1978), Charbonneau (1981), Strawn (1980, 1985b, 1985c), Stautner (1983), Kleczkowski (1989), Serra (1989), Serra and Smith (1990), Holloway and Haken (1992), and Horner, Beauchamp, and Haken (1993). Because real-time work is so important to musicians, one goal of analysis/resynthesis research is to speed up data reduction processing and facilitate real-time synthesis from reduced data.

Many volumes explore data reduction methods. Here we glance at several techniques that have been applied in computer music: line-segment approximation, principal components analysis, spectral interpolation synthesis, spectral modeling synthesis, and reconstructive phrase modeling. (Also see Goldberg 1989 for a description of the genetic algorithm approach, which has also been applied to synthesis data reduction [Horner, Beauchamp, and Haken 1993].)

Line-segment approximation

Line-segment approximation of the amplitude and frequency control functions eliminates the need to store a distinct value for every sample analyzed.

Instead, the analysis system stores only a set of *breakpoint pairs,* which are time (*x*-axis) and amplitude (*y*-axis) points where the waveform changes significantly. Line-segment approximation represents the overall outline of a waveform by storing only the points of maximum inflection (change). In the resynthesis stage the system connects the points, usually by means of straight lines interpolated between the breakpoint pairs.

Initial work with line-segment approximation was done by hand, using an interactive graphics editor to construct functions with four to eight segments each (Grey 1975). A data reduction of a hundredfold was achieved. This manual editing work can also be partially automated, as demonstrated by Strawn (1985b, 1985c). Figure 10.15a shows a perspective plot of the sixteen harmonics of a violin tone, sampled at 25 kHz. Figure 10.15b shows a plot of an approximation to (a) using just three line segments.

Going beyond the storage of line-segment approximations, Beauchamp (1975) developed a heuristic technique for inferring the approximate amplitude curve of all harmonics of a tone from the curve of the first harmonic. For simple periodic tones, Charbonneau (1981) found that even more radical data reduction could be achieved. He used simple variations of a single envelope for all amplitude functions of a given tone. (See Kleczkowski [1989] and Eaglestone and Oates [1990] for refinements of these proposals.)

Principal components analysis

The technique of *principle components analysis* (PCA) has been applied in several analysis/resynthesis systems (Stautner 1983; Sandell and Martens 1992; Horner, Beauchamp, and Haken 1993). PCA breaks down a waveform using the mathematical technique of *covariance matrix* calculation. This results in a set of basic waveforms (the principal components) and a set of weighting coefficients for these basic waveforms. When the components are summed according to their weights, the result is a close approximation of the original waveform.

PCA analysis summarizes the underlying relationships between samples so that the fewest number of components account for the maximum possible variance in the signal. The first principal component is a fit of a single waveform to the entire data set. The second principal component is a fit to the *residual* (the difference, sometimes called the *residue*) between the original and first approximation. The third component is a fit to the residual of the second component, and so on. For further details on PCA, refer to Glaser and Ruchkin (1976).

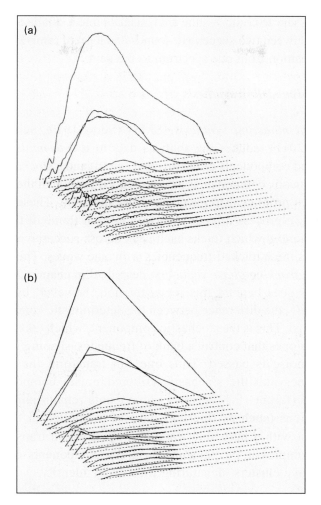

Figure 10.15 Drastic data reduction of analysis data for additive synthesis. Amplitude is plotted vertically, frequency goes from back to front, and time goes left to right. (a) Original spectrum plot of a violin tone. (b) The same violin tone as in (a), approximated with only three line segments per partial.

Spectral interpolation synthesis

Spectral interpolation synthesis (SIS) (Serra, Rubine, and Dannenberg 1990) generates time-varying sounds by interpolating between analyzed spectra. Rather than crossfading between sampled sounds in the time domain (as in multiple wavetable synthesis discussed), SIS starts from analyses of recorded sounds and uses additive synthesis to crossfade between the analyses of successive spectra in the frequency domain. An automatic data reduction algorithm is necessary to compress the analysis data into a small set of common spectral paths between two successive sounds and a set of ramp functions that describe the transition from one spectrum to the next.

Spectral modeling synthesis

Spectral modeling synthesis (SMS) (Serra 1989; Serra and Smith 1990; Smith 2011) reduces the analysis data to a *deterministic* component (narrowband components of the original sound) and a *stochastic* component. The deterministic component is a data-reduced version of the analysis that models the most prominent frequencies in the spectrum. These frequencies are isolated by a process of *peak detection* in each frame of the analysis and *peak continuation,* which tracks each peak across successive frames. SMS resynthesizes these tracked frequencies with sine waves. This is the same method used in *tracking phase vocoders,* described in chapter 37 (see figure 10.16).

SMS goes beyond this representation, however, by also analyzing the *residual*—the difference between the deterministic component and the original signal. This is the stochastic component, which takes the form of a series of envelopes that control a bank of frequency-shaping filters through which white noise is passed. Thus one can transform the deterministic (sine) envelopes and the stochastic (filtered noise) components separately, if desired (figure 10.17). Noisy components remain noisy, even after transformations (such as filtering) have been applied to them. This stands in contrast with a pure sine wave model, in which transformations (such as time compression/expansion) on noisy components often turn them into sine wave clusters, denaturing their noisy identity.

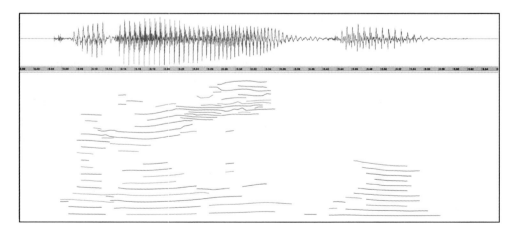

Figure 10.16 Display showing a time-domain waveform (top) of the Italian word *prego* and its tracked partials (*bottom*) in a range to 4 kHz.

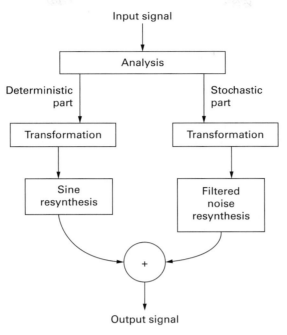

Figure 10.17   Overview of spectrum modeling synthesis. The input signal is divided into a deterministic part and a stochastic part. Each part can be modified separately before resynthesis. (See figure 37.17 for a more detailed view of the analysis stage.)

Efficient algorithms for generating *pseudorandom noise* are well known (Knuth 1973; Rabiner and Gold 1975; Wolfram 2002). Thus using filtered noise results in a tremendous data reduction. Without data reduction, noisy components must be approximated with dozens or hundreds of sine waves. The control functions for these sine waves take up significant storage space, and resynthesis of noise using sine waves is inefficient computationally.

A problem of accuracy left open by SMS is that the filtered pseudorandom noise it uses to reconstruct the stochastic component is generic and not necessarily the same quality of noise as the original source. In the real world, "noise" is the result of complicated turbulences that have an audible character and identity. For some sounds, the approximation by uniform noise leaves room for improvement. The next section addresses this issue.

ATS: Analysis, transformation, synthesis

Analysis, transformation, synthesis (ATS) is based on SMS (Pampin 2004). It goes beyond SMS through its use of psychoacoustic processing both in the sinusoid tracking and in the noise model. In particular, ATS uses perceptual audio coding methods such as the *signal-to-mask ratio* for each spectral band. (*Masking* occurs when sound A *covers* sound B such that B is inaudible.) The model uses the Bark scale for frequency, in which successive intervals are perceptually equal. The twenty-four steps of the Bark scale correspond to the critical bands of hearing, which are used for the noise analysis phase. (A *critical band* is the range of audio frequencies within which a second tone interferes with the perception of the first tone by auditory masking.) ATS's perceptual model analyzes whether a given sinusoidal peak component masks other components. This information informs the peak continuation process. The residual is determined as in SMS. ATS divides the residual into critical bands. At each analysis frame, the algorithm detects partials in each critical band and distributes the band's noise energy among them. The result is a data-reduced model that is capable of many transformations by the manipulation of a small number of perceptually meaningful parameters. A graphical interface has been developed called ATSH (Pampin et al. 2004). ATS has been implemented in Common Lisp Music, C, Csound, SuperCollider, and Pure Data (Di Liscia 2013).

Reconstructive phrase modeling

Realistic instrument simulations depend on the transitions between notes—the connective tissue of musical expression. These transitions include slurs with varying amounts of portamento, lightly tongued or bowed note transitions, fast runs, and detached hard attacks. Eric Lindemann (2001, 2007, 2009) created an application called Synful Orchestra based on *reconstructive phrase modeling* (RPM) to produce realistic simulations of winds, horns, and strings. The technique relies on a relatively compact database of recorded fragments and phrases of orchestral instruments. These represent many types of articulation and phrasing, encoded in terms of an additive synthesis model data reduced by the method of *vector quantization* (Gersho and Grey 1992). Vector quantization encodes values from a multidimensional vector space (the time-frequency analysis data) into a finite set of values from a discrete subspace of lower dimension. This usually takes the form of a dictionary of elements that can be combined to closely approximate the original data.

   The techniques used in Synful Orchestra can be seen as a combination of additive and concatenative synthesis (chapter 23). When Synful Orchestra receives MIDI input it looks at the pitch, velocity, amount of separation or overlap between notes, note duration, volume, pitch, and modulation controls to determine what kind of phrase is being played. The program uses search algorithms to scan a database of musical phrases in real time for fragments that can be concatenated to form this phrase. These fragments represent transitions between notes, slurs with portamento, lightly tongued transitions, aggressive fast bowing, rapid runs, long sustain regions with graceful vibrato, and noise elements like flute chiffs and bow scratches.

The emphasis is on the connection between notes and the ways that performers move from one note to the next. Notes do not stand alone. The timbre and contour of a note is directly affected by notes that precede and succeed it. As previously discussed, in speech this is referred to as *coarticulation* in that the pronunciation of a syllable depends on the syllables that precede and follow it. In this sense, RPM captures the coarticulation of musical sounds.

Thus a single note can be built from multiple rapidly spliced phrase fragments concatenated in time. Splicing ordinary sampled sounds in this way would create clicks and other artifacts, so Synful Orchestra uses a form of additive synthesis in which samples are resynthesized from combinations of pure sine waves and noise elements. This gives it the ability to stretch, shift, and splice phrase fragments while preserving phrase continuity. Users can control the quality of the resynthesis by adjusting parameters like harmonic parity (emphasis on even or odd harmonics), harmonic tilt (emphasis on higher or lower harmonics), bow noise (for strings), breath noise (for winds), *sforzando* strength (strength of attack), tremolo rate spread (tremolo rate variation among different instruments in a string section), and so on.

Additive Synthesis Based on Machine Learning

Around 2015, Google's Magenta research group started publishing papers on projects based on *machine learning* (ML) methods trained using musical sound examples. (See appendix A for an introduction to machine learning.) The ostensible goal of Magenta research is to advance ML methods in the audio domain. The sonic results validate (or not) the methods.

Early experiments in sound synthesis appended fragments of sounds to form larger units of music (Kalchbrenner et al. 2018; Engel et al. 2019). These methods do not, however, fit neatly into the categories of additive, concatenative, or granular synthesis as defined in this book.

Recent Google work labeled *Differentiable Digital Signal Processing* (DDSP) uses *neural networks* (NNs) to analyze recorded sounds (Engel et al. 2020). The analyzed control functions drive a synthesizer based on the harmonics-plus-noise or SMS model presented earlier in this chapter (Serra 1989; Serra and Smith 1990; Smith 2011). Such a model combines an additive harmonic synthesizer with a subtractive filter for synthesizing noisy parts of the spectrum.

In this work, a NN analyzer extracts the synthesizer parameters (fundamental frequency, amplitude, harmonic distribution) from a training data set of violin performances. Pitch is estimated using the *convolutional representation for pitch estimation* (CREPE) model (Kim et al. 2018; chapter 34). Harmonics follow the contours of the fundamental, loudness is controlled by the amplitude envelope, and spectral structure is determined by the harmonic distribution. Violin performances are reconstructed with good fidelity.

DDSP exists as a code library that integrates neural tools with sound modules based on traditional synthesizer functions. Because the system is modular, it is possible to tap the audio output from each module to find various "decompositions" of the original audio signals. The decomposed parts can be modified and combined with other outputs to create transformations of the original sound. Transformations include loudness and pitch changes, a form of cross-synthesis that converts a singing voice into a violin timbre, and extracting reverberation from a violin performance and applying it to a singing voice.

Colonel, Curro, and Keene (2018) describes an *autoencoding neural network* that drives an additive synthesizer. The system is trained to compress and reconstruct magnitude STFT frames. The *variational autoencoder* (VAE) produces a spectrogram by activating its smallest hidden layer, and a phase response is calculated using real-time phase gradient integration. Performing an inverse STFT produces the audio signal. The algorithm is said to be lightweight in comparison with other audio-producing machine learning algorithms.

Walsh Function Synthesis

Thus far we have discussed analysis/resynthesis as a process based mainly on Fourier analysis with resynthesis based on sine wave summation. The Fourier sine wave approach has a long tradition of research and application stemming from the original theorem that states that for periodic signals, a combination of sine waves of various frequencies can be created that approximate arbitrarily closely the original signal. Mathematical research has shown that unnumerable other waveforms besides sine waves can be used to approximate signals, the so-called wavelet bases.

One such basis is the *Walsh functions,* a family of square waves that can be used to approximate a signal after it has been analyzed by means of the *Walsh-Hadamard transform.* Walsh functions, being rectangular waves, are a kind of *digital domain series* because they take on only two values, +1 and −1 (Walsh 1923).

Figure 10.18 presents the first eight Walsh functions. Just as with the Fourier series and its sine waves, an arbitrary periodic waveform can be approximated as an additive sum of a finite series of Walsh functions. Whereas the Fourier series builds up waveforms out of component frequencies, Walsh synthesis builds up waveforms using functions of different *sequencies. Sequency* is defined as one-half the average number of zero crossings per second (zps) (Hutchins 1973).

Figure 10.19 shows a composite waveform derived by summing several Walsh functions. It suggests how sine wave additive synthesis and Walsh

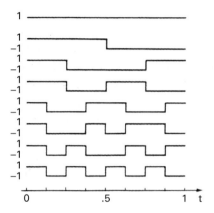

Figure 10.18 The first eight Walsh functions, 0 (*top*) to 7 (*bottom*).

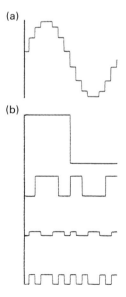

Figure 10.19 Walsh function summation. (a) A simple sine wave approximation built by adding the Walsh functions shown in (b). (After Tempelaars [1977].)

function synthesis are conceptual opposites. That is, the hardest waveform to synthesize in Walsh function synthesis is a pure sine wave. The Walsh approximation to a sine will stay jagged until a very high number of sequency terms are used. Any jaggedness gives an unsinusoidal and generally objectionable quality. By contrast, in sine wave synthesis, the hardest waveforms to synthesize are those with a rectangular corner, such as a square wave. Recall that figure 10.5e depicts a quasi–square wave constructed by summing 101 sine waves.

The main advantage of Walsh functions in digital sound synthesis is their rectangular shape, which can be computed at high speed by inexpensive digital circuits. A conceptual disadvantage of Walsh function synthesis as against sine wave synthesis is that individual Walsh functions are not associated with specific harmonics as they are in sine wave additive synthesis. One can, however, pass mathematically from the Fourier (frequency) domain to the Walsh domain (Tadokoro and Higishi 1978). Thus, one can specify a sound in terms of the addition of various frequency components (partials) and then transform this specification into a set of parameter values for a Walsh function synthesizer. Moreover, natural sounds can be sampled and transformed into the Walsh domain using the Walsh-Hadamard transform and resynthesized using the *fast Walsh transform* (FWT) (Hutchins 1973, 1975).

A number of music synthesis operations have been redesigned for Walsh signal processing circuits. For example, Hutchins (1973) designed an envelope generator using Walsh function circuits. Rozenberg (1979) and Hutchins (1975) showed how to realize amplitude modulation, subtractive synthesis, frequency modulation, frequency shifting, and reverberation—all in the Walsh domain.

Despite the potential of Walsh function synthesis, only a few experimental devices based on this technique have been built (Hutchins 1973, 1975; Insam 1974). None are commercially available. This is probably due to the fact that sine additive synthesis is now cheap (any laptop can easily handle it), so the economic advantage of Walsh function circuits has diminished. The weight of accumulated research in sine wave methods has also contributed to their continuing presence.

11 *Multiple Wavetable Synthesis*

Wavetable Cross-Fading or Vector Synthesis

Wavestacking

Multiple wavetable synthesis encompasses two simple yet sonically effective methods: *wavetable cross-fading* and *wavestacking.* These are not the only synthesis methods that can use multiple wavetables; indeed other methods (FM, for example) can be configured to do so. We distinguish the techniques discussed here because the use of multiple wavetables is the sine qua non of multiple wavetable synthesis.

Multiple wavetable synthesis is a central technique in popular synthesizers. It creates lively and animated cross-faded and stacked hybrids. Blends of sampled and synthetic waveforms can be combined to create exotic time-varying sounds.

Horner, Beauchamp, and Hakken (1993) developed the technique they called *multiple wavetable synthesis.* It is perhaps best classified as a variant of additive analysis/resynthesis (presented in chapter 37). It also can be viewed as an instance of the wavestacking method presented here, in which the wavetables are sums of sinusoids derived from an analysis and data reduction stage.

Wavetable Cross-Fading or Vector Synthesis

As chapter 6 explains, in fixed-waveform synthesis, a digital oscillator scans repeatedly through a wavetable that has been previously filled with a single waveform. This creates a static timbre because the waveform repeats without variance over time. By contrast, wavetable cross-fading is a direct way to generate time-varying timbres. Instead of scanning a single wavetable repeatedly, the oscillator *cross-fades* between two or more wavetables over the course of an event. That is, the event begins with waveform 1, and as 1 begins to fade away, waveform 2 fades in, and so on. Figure 11.1 portrays the cross-fading process. Wavetable cross-fading is the core of the technique called *vector synthesis* or *wave sequencing* (by Sequential Circuits, Korg, and Yamaha), *L/A* or *linear arithmetic* synthesis (Roland), *dynamic spectral wavetable synthesis* (Waldorf PPG Wave), or *wavetable morphing* (XferRecords Serum).

Wavetable cross-fading creates sounds that mutate or morph from one source to another over time. Figure 11.2 depicts an instrument for wavetable cross-fading that scans through four wavetables.

The first commercial synthesizer to implement wavetable cross-fading was the eight-voice Sequential Circuits Prophet VS, introduced in 1985, which could cross-fade between four waveforms. The Korg Wavestation, designed by some of the same team who made the Prophet VS, reached the market in 1990. It was reintroduced as a software synth in 2010 (figure 11.3). Rob Papen Vecto (2019) provides vector synthesis as a software plug-in with over a thousand presets. Waldorf PPG Wave 3.V is a software plug-in that realizes a variant of vector synthesis.

Time span of each waveform

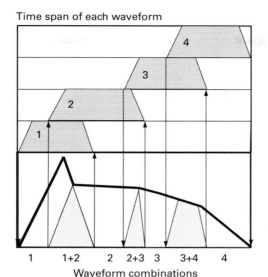

Figure 11.1   Wavetable cross-fading. The bold outline traces the amplitude of a note event. Four waveforms cross-fade over the span of the event. The numbers at the bottom indicate the sequence of waveforms alone and in combination. Each region indicated at the bottom represents a separate timbre; thus the event cross-fades through seven timbres.

In 2020, Korg introduced the 64-voice Wavestate synthesizer, its latest incarnation of vector synthesis technology (figure 11.4).

Wavetable cross-fading can be automatic (triggered by a note event and modulated by a cross-fade function), or it can be manually controlled by rotating a joystick. Some synthesizers let users specify an arbitrary number of waveforms (e.g., 128) to cross-fade during a single event, a process called *wave sequencing*. This creates lively animated sweeps of electronic sound, with radical changes in timbre but also shifts in perceived pitch because the content of the waveform is open. This type of sonic behavior is unlike any acoustic instrument.

A variant of wavetable cross-fading—linear arithmetic, also called L/A synthesis—was introduced in 1987 in the Roland D-50 and became one of the defining sounds of its era, starring in many hit records and soundtracks. L/A synthesis made a comeback in 2017 in the Roland D-05 synthesizer. L/A synthesis grafts sampled attack transients onto the front of a composite sound consisting of a subtractive synthesis waveform (sawtooth or pulse wave through a filter) mixed with a sampled waveform that can be continuously looped.

An extreme example of wavetable cross-fading is the Piston Honda morphing wavetable oscillator, a Eurorack module by Industrial Music Electronics (figure 11.5). The Piston Honda provides a bank of 512 wavetables organized as an 8-by-8-by-8 cube (*X, Y, Z*). The indices *X, Y,* and *Z* can be selected manually with three faders or, as is more typical, modulated using low-frequency

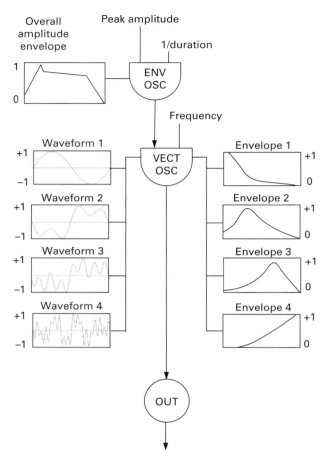

Figure 11.2 Wavetable cross-fading (vector synthesis) instrument using four wavetables. Each envelope on the right applies to a wavetable on the left.

Figure 11.3 Korg Wavestation vector synthesizer in its software incarnation.

Figure 11.4   Korg Wavestate synthesizer.

Figure 11.5   Piston Honda morphing wavetable oscillator.

oscillators (LFOs). Depending on user settings, the oscillator either morphs smoothly from one wavetable to another or steps abruptly between wavetables. Highly animated contrasts in timbre are typical of its sound.

Wavestacking

Wavetable stacking or *wavestacking* is a simple and effective variation on additive synthesis. It was implemented in the hugely successful Korg M1 synthesizer (over 250,000 sold from 1988 to 1995). The M1 was re-released as the iM1 software synthesizer for iPad in 2015 with a sound library of more than 3,000 sounds.

In wavestacking, each sound event results from the addition of several waveforms (typically four to eight). Wavestacking is done differently from

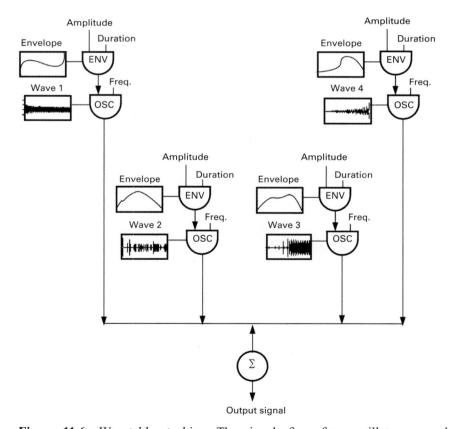

Figure 11.6 Wavetable stacking. The signals from four oscillators are added together. Notice that the wavetables contain not simple periodic functions but long sampled sounds.

classical additive synthesis, which sums sine waves. In wavestacking, each waveform can be a complicated signal, such as a sampled sound (figure 11 6). By layering several sampled sounds, one can create hybrid timbres like saxophone/flute or violin/clarinet. Each waveform in the stack has its own amplitude envelope, so sounds fade in and out of the stack in the course of a sound event. When four to eight complex waveforms are stacked, deep and rich hybrid textures can be created for each sound event.

Wavestacking is implemented by storing a library of waveforms and using table-lookup oscillators to scan them. Each waveform's envelope must be scaled by a factor of $1/n$, where n is equal to the number of stacked waveforms, to avoid numerical overflow. That is, the sum of all the waveforms should be within the quantization range of the synthesizer.

12 *Wave Terrain Synthesis*

Terrains and Trajectories

Generating Predictable Waveforms from Wave Terrains

> **Periodic Trajectories**
> **Time-Varying Trajectories**
> **Time-Varying Wave Terrain**

Extensions of Wave Terrain Synthesis

Implementations of WT Synthesis

Many synthesis techniques start from the fundamental principle of wavetable lookup, explained in chapter 6: a pointer scans a two-dimensional wavetable plotting amplitude on the *x*-axis versus time on the *y*-axis. The index to the position in the table is incremented at each sample period. What happens if we extend the principle of wavetable lookup to the scanning of a three-dimensional (x, y, z) surface, such as the undulations of mountains and valleys in an Alpine landscape? As the wave surface is scanned, the height at a given *x, y* position is captured as samples, in *z* values, for the waveform.

We call such a surface a *wave terrain* (WT). In the rest of this chapter we refer to wave terrain synthesis as WT. Several researchers, including Rich Gold in consultation with Leonard Cottrell (Bischoff, Gold, and Horton 1978), Mitsuhashi (1982a), and Borgonovo and Haus (1984, 1986) were the first to explore the possibilities of techniques that scan a wave terrain using two indexes. Comajuncosas (2000) and Mikelson (2000b) have described the technique in the context of Csound. The most comprehensive documents on wave terrain synthesis are the masters and doctoral theses by Stuart James (2005, 2015).

In general, the sounds WT produces are synthetic in character. Initial musical experimentation with WT focused on drones with continuously mutating timbres. James (2005) showed how WT could—under certain conditions—generate equivalent results to additive synthesis, vector synthesis, amplitude and ring modulation, phase distortion, frequency modulation, and waveshaping synthesis.

Terrains and Trajectories

A wave terrain can be plotted as a function *wave*(*x*,*y*) etched on a three-dimensional surface (figure 12.1). In this case, the *z*-point, which is the height of the surface at each point, represents a waveform amplitude value for a given pair (x, y). The surface stored in such a table can be a *closed-form function of two variables*, and thus the technique has also been called *two-variable function* synthesis (Borgonovo and Haus 1986).

Unlike a traditional wavetable, where the pointer scans from left to right and then repeats, a scan over a wave terrain can take an arbitrary path over the surface. It may repeat or not. A scan over the terrain is called a *trajectory* (James 2005). Early literature called this an *orbit,* but this connotes an elliptical function, when in fact the trajectory can consist of any sequence of points on the wave terrain, including a random walk.

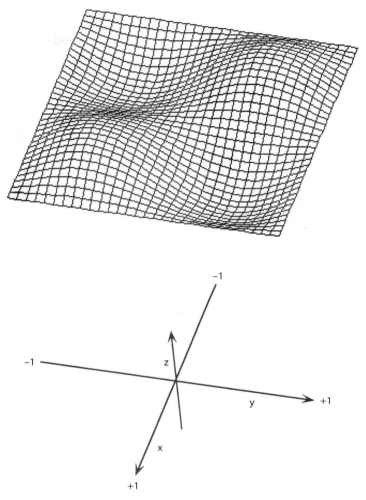

Figure 12.1   A waveform terrain is a three-dimensional surface. The height (z-axis) of the terrain represents the waveform value.

Pitched tones are generated by periodic repetition of trajectories. The frequency of repetition correlates to a fundamental frequency. Amplitude is correlated with the evolution of maxima and minima in the waveform.

No movement or a flat terrain will result in silence. On an undulating terrain, the frequency of the undulations determines the spectral content, and the depth of the undulations determines amplitude. The more jagged the angles of the wave terrain, regardless of amplitude, the more high frequencies will be generated. In contrast, smooth terrain features correlate with a lack of high-frequency content. However, the precise spectral content of a terrain depends on the frequencies at which the terrain is scanned.

Generating Predictable Waveforms from Wave Terrains

For musical purposes, any three-dimensional surface can serve as a wave terrain, from a tightly constrained mathematical function to an arbitrary topographical projection. Indeed one musical project used the Earth's global Digital Elevation Model database as a terrain (Thibault and Gresham-Lancaster 1992, 1997).

James (2005) distinguished between *discrete* and *continuous* terrain functions. Discrete terrains are stored in a table that contains values sampled at discrete points on the surface of the terrain. Continuous terrains can be computed on the fly by mathematical functions to an arbitrary precision. In practice, most terrains are discrete.

Scientific investigations have focused on wave terrains generated by simple mathematical functions. As in techniques like frequency modulation and waveshaping, the advantage of using simple functions is that it is possible to analytically predict exactly the output waveform and spectrum generated by a given wave terrain and trajectory. Mitsuhashi (1982c) and Borgonovo and Haus (1986) devised smooth mathematical wave terrain functions in the range $[-1 \leq x \leq 1, -1 \leq y \leq 1]$. The following conditions must be met in order to predict the output waveform:

1. Both the x and y functions and their first-order partial derivatives are mathematically continuous over the terrain.
2. Both the x and y functions are zero on the boundaries of the terrain.

The second property ensures that the functions and their derivatives are continuous when the trajectory skips from one edge of the wave terrain to another edge. Such a skip is analogous to the right-to-left wraparound that occurs in one-index wavetable scanning.

Of course, if the trajectory is kept within the edges of the wave terrain, condition 2 can be ignored.

The terrain depicted in figure 12.1 satisfies conditions 1 and 2 and is defined by the following equation:

$$\text{wave}(x, y) = \sin(\pi/2 \times x) \times \sin(\pi/2 \times y)$$

Other mathematical functions investigated include piecewise functions (Mitsuhashi 1982c), polynomials (Borgonovo and Haus 1984, 1986; Mikelson 2000a), fractal and iterative maps (Mikelson 2000a), additive and Chebyshev functions (Nelson 2000), elliptic functions (Cafagna and Vicinanza 2002) and dynamical systems of equations (Boulanger et al. 2000; Mikelson 2000a).

James (2005) devoted an appendix to a catalog of mathematically derived WTs. These include the following:

- curves that are periodic within the range $-1 \leq z \leq 1$ and continuous (figure 12.2a)
- curves that are periodic within the range $-1 \leq z \leq 1$ but are discontinuous (figure 12.2b)
- curves that include undefined values (figure 12.2c)
- curves that generally exhibit natural tendencies toward infinity (figure 12.2d)
- wavetable and tiled forms (figure 12.2e)
- other mathematical curves (figure 12.2f)

Figure 12.2 shows examples of each type in the catalog.

Periodic Trajectories

The output signal generated by WT depends on both the terrain and the trajectory. The trajectory can be any sequence of points, such as a straight or curved line across the surface, a zig-zag pattern, a random walk, a sinusoidal function, or an elliptical function generated by sinusoidal terms in both the x and y dimensions. If the trajectory repeats itself (i.e., is periodic), so will the output signal. Figure 12.3 shows a periodic elliptical trajectory defined by the functions:

$$x = 0.5 \times \sin(8\pi t + \pi/5)$$

$$y = \sin(8\pi t)$$

Figure 12.4 shows an example of another periodic trajectory that loops around the terrain.

Time-Varying Trajectories

When the trajectory is fixed, the resulting sound is a fixed waveform characterized by a static spectrum. By changing the trajectory over time one can generate a time-varying waveform (figure 12.5). Trajectories can be controlled in real time using input devices or programmed using automation (James 2005).

Time-Varying Wave Terrain

One can imagine an implementation in which the trajectory is fixed but the wave terrain is time-varying. In this case the wave-scanning process is

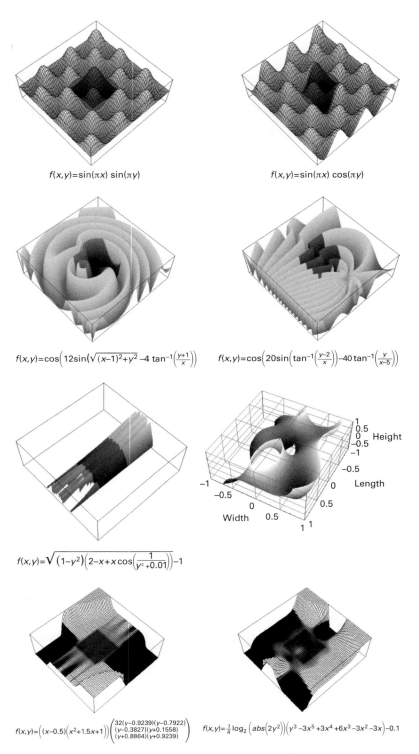

$f(x,y)=\sin(\pi x)\,\sin(\pi y)$

$f(x,y)=\sin(\pi x)\,\cos(\pi y)$

$f(x,y)=\cos\!\left(12\sin\!\left(\sqrt{(x-1)^2+y^2}\,-4\tan^{-1}\!\left(\tfrac{y+1}{x}\right)\right)\right)$

$f(x,y)=\cos\!\left(20\sin\!\left(\tan^{-1}\!\left(\tfrac{y-2}{x}\right)\right)-40\tan^{-1}\!\left(\tfrac{y}{x-5}\right)\right)$

$f(x,y)=\sqrt{\left(1-y^2\right)\left(2-x+x\cos\!\left(\tfrac{1}{y^2+0.01}\right)\right)}-1$

$f(x,y)=\left((x-0.5)\left(x^2+1.5x+1\right)\right)^{\left(\frac{32(y-0.9239)(y-0.7922)}{(y-0.3827)(y+0.1558)}\right)}_{(y+0.8864)(y+0.9239)}$

$f(x,y)=\tfrac{1}{4}\log_2\!\left(abs\!\left(2y^2\right)\right)\left(y^3-3x^5+3x^4+6x^3-3x^2-3x\right)-0.1$

Figure 12.2   Wave terrains defined by mathematical functions. After James (2005).

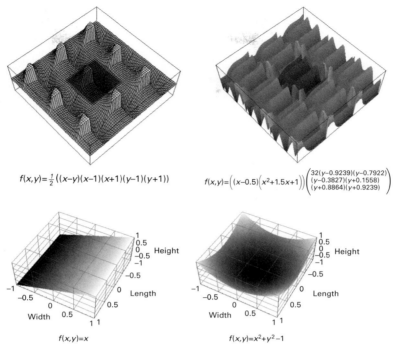

$$f(x,y)=\tfrac{1}{2}\big((x-y)(x-1)(x+1)(y-1)(y+1)\big)$$

$$f(x,y)=\Big((x-0.5)\big(x^2+1.5x+1\big)\Big)\begin{pmatrix}32(y-0.9239)(y-0.7922)\\(y-0.3827)(y+0.1558)\\(y+0.8864)(y+0.9239)\end{pmatrix}$$

$$f(x,y)=x$$

$$f(x,y)=x^2+y^2-1$$

Figure 12.2   (continued)

equivalent to tracing the curves of an undulating surface, like undulations on the surface of the sea. In essence, this is the idea behind *scanned synthesis,* covered in chapter 18.

Extensions of Wave Terrain Synthesis

Basic WT synthesis is conceptually simple. However, it can be extended in many ways. The most intrepid researcher, James (2005), explored a panoply of methods to generate wave terrains: video capture, noise functions, recurrence plots, and spline surfaces. He also explored matrix operations including mappings from colored terrain surfaces, convolution processing (blurring, sharpening, and embossing), mapping sounds to different spatial locations, and video feedback. For his PhD research, the same author turned the interface of WT synthesis into a generator of control data for a spatialization scheme in which different spectral bands follow independent spatial paths (James 2015).

Zabetian (2018) created a WT synthesis instrument with interactive MIDI polyphonic expression (MPE) using a ROLI Seaboard to enhance expressivity.

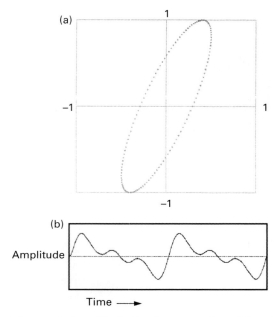

Figure 12.3   Elliptical trajectory and resulting signal. (a) Plot of the trajectory. Both the *x* and *y* dimensions vary from −1 to +1. (After Borgonovo and Haus [1986].) (b) Waveform generated by the elliptical trajectory over the wave terrain defined in equation 1. (Note: This waveform is an approximation redrawn from Borgonovo and Haus [1986].)

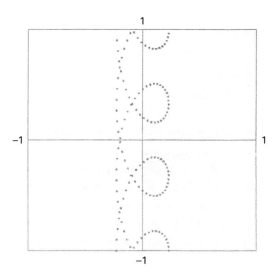

Figure 12.4   Looping trajectory. (After Borgonovo and Haus [1986].)

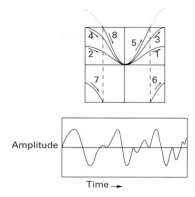

Figure 12.5 Aperiodic trajectory and resulting signal. (Top) Plot of trajectory trajectories in eight passes through the wave terrain. (Bottom) Notice the time-varying waveform. (After Mitsuhashi [1982a].)

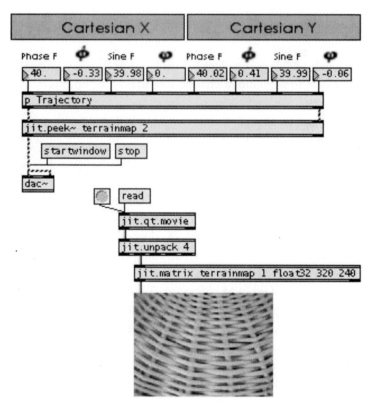

Figure 12.6 A simple WT synthesizer using the Jitter library in Max (after James [2005]). In this case, the WT used is the woven basket pictured at the bottom. All that is required is a table lookup with an interpolation routine, procedures that are performed by the jit.peek~ object.

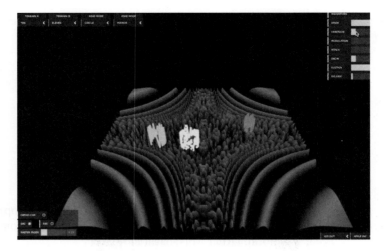

Figure 12.7   WaveTerrain Synth by Aaron Anderson. Here three small trajectories scan the surface of a complex terrain.

(See chapter 51 for more on MPE.) Combined with graphic displays, this enabled interactive control and manipulation of trajectories and terrains. Other extensions included chaotic modulation of both terrains and trajectories.

Implementations of WT Synthesis

Some implementations of WT synthesis do not provide a display. One can, for example, explore WT using Csound code. However, the advantages of visualizations became clear in searching for a "sweet spot" or a particularly smooth or jagged terrain. A user study by Zabetian (2018) showed that graphical visualization greatly helped users to understand the technique.

WT synthesis is represented by the wterrain opcode in Csound and the terrain~ object in Max and Pd. Figure 12.6 shows an implementation in Jitter using the jit.peek~ object (James 2005).

Aaron Anderson (2017) developed the Wave Terrain Synth (figure 12.7), which allowed for multiple simultaneous trajectories (Anderson 2018). Wave Terrain Synth features a large set of terrains and reading methods. It can also convert both images and sounds into terrains. The app is controllable by MIDI, with note velocity tied to trajectory size.

13 *Granular Synthesis*

Theory of Granular Synthesis

Granular Synthesis: Background

Simple Grain Generator Instrument

Parameters of Granular Synthesis

> **Per-Grain Parameters**
> > Envelope
> > Duration
> > Effect of grain duration
> > Waveform
> > Granulation of sampled sounds
> > Frequency (pitch shift for samples)
> > Spatial position
> > Synchronicity (degree of periodicity)
> > Intermittency (degree of irregular emission)
>
> **Density and Fill Factor**

High-Level Granular Organizations

> Time-Frequency Projections
> Clouds
> Streams
> Pitch-Synchronous Granular Synthesis

Sprays
Scrubbing
Micromontage
Physical and Biological Models
Abstract Generative Models
Summary of Higher-Level Organization

Granular synthesis builds up acoustic events from combinations of brief sound particles or *grains*. A single grain serves as a building block for sound objects. By combining thousands of grains over time, we can create animated sonic textures. This chapter introduces the theory, history, and parameters of the technique. A critical factor in synthesis is the choice of how to model the high-level organization of the grains. This model has a strong influence on the types of musical structures that can be produced by granular synthesis.

Theory of Granular Synthesis

A grain of sound is an acoustic event with a duration near the threshold of human auditory perception (figure 13.1) This threshold is typically between one-thousandth of a second and one-tenth of a second (from 1 to 100 ms). These are the shortest durations in which differences in duration, frequency, spectrum, amplitude, amplitude envelope, and spatial position can be perceived (Whitfield 1978; Meyer-Eppler 1959; Winckel 1967; Buser and Imbert 1992). Below 1 ms in duration, no matter how they are varied, sonic events are sensed as sub-symbolic clicks. On a granular time scale, however, we can still perceive differences in sound properties. Thus, if desired, each grain can be unique.

Granular representations are a general and useful way of viewing complex sound phenomena—as constellations of elementary units of energy, each unit bounded in time and frequency. Such *microsonic* representations are common

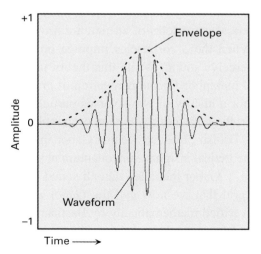

Figure 13.1 Portrait of a grain. An audio waveform is shaped by a short-duration amplitude envelope. The envelope is bell shaped with a smooth attack and decay.

inside synthesis and signal processing algorithms, although there are many different terms for similar phenomena, including *quantum* (Gabor 1946, 1947), *Gaussian elementary signal* (Helstrom 1966; Bastiaans 1980), *short-time segment* (Schroeder and Atal 1962), *short-time weighting function* (Flanagan 1972), *windowed segment* (Arfib 1991; Harris 1978; Nuttall 1981), *sliding window* (Bastiaans 1985), *window function pulse* (Bass and Goeddel 1981), *wavelet* (Kronland-Martinet and Grossmann 1991), *formant wave function* (FOF) (Rodet 1980), *VOSIM pulse* (Kaegi and Tempelaars 1978), *wave packet* (Crawford 1968), *toneburst* (Blauert 1983; Pierce 1990), *tone pulse* (Whitfield 1978), *pulsar* (Roads 2001b), *grainlet* and *trainlet* (Roads 2001a), *tone pip* (Buser and Imbert 1992), and even the *timbron* (Chen 2018). All can be described as granular representations of musical signals, operating at the micro time scale.

The grain is an apt representation for sonic microstructure because it combines time-domain information (starting time, duration, envelope shape, and waveform shape) with frequency-domain information (the frequency of the waveform inside the grain and the spectrum of the waveform inside the grain).

Granular Synthesis: Background

Atomistic views of sound as particles can be traced to antiquity (Lucretius [55] 1951). In 1616 the Dutch scholar Isaac Beekman (1588–1637) proposed a *corpuscular* theory of sound (Beeckman [1604–1634] 1953; Cohen 1984). Beeckman believed that any vibrating object, like a string, cuts the surrounding air into spherical corpuscles of air that are projected in all directions by the vibration. When these corpuscles impinge on the eardrum, Beeckman theorized, we perceive sound. While this theory is not true scientifically, it paints a colorful metaphor for the perception of granular synthesis. Refer to Roads (2001a) for a history of wave versus particle theories of sound.

Centuries later, the notion of a *quantum* or granular approach to sound was proposed by the British physicist Dennis Gabor in a pair of brilliant papers that combined theoretical insights from quantum physics with practical experiments (1946, 1947). Gabor theorized that all sound could be represented by a time-frequency grid that we now call the *Gabor matrix* (figure 13.2). This hypothesis was verified mathematically by Bastiaans (1980, 1985).

In the 1940s Gabor constructed a sound granulator based on an optical recording system adapted from a film projector. He used this to make experiments in *time stretching* and *time shrinking* with *pitch shifting*—changing the pitch of a sound without changing its duration and vice versa. (See chapter 31 for a discussion of pitch-time changing.)

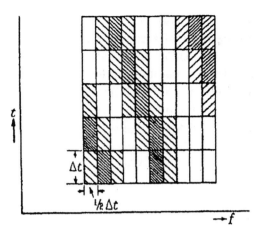

Figure 13.2   Gabor matrix. A detail of a small portion of a time-frequency grid (from Gabor [1946]). Inside each rectangle on the matrix is an elementary grain of time-frequency energy. Shading indicates intensity. Unlike in a traditional sonogram, time is plotted vertically, and frequency is plotted horizontally.

A granular representation is implicit in the *windowing* technique applied in the *short-time Fourier transform,* conceived by Gabor and extended in the 1960s (Schroeder and Atal 1962; Mallat 2009; see chapter 37). Inspired by Gabor, the MIT cybernetician Norbert Wiener (1964) and the information theorist Abraham Moles (1968) also proposed granular representations for sound. *Atomic decomposition,* described in chapter 39, can be seen as an analytical counterpart to granular synthesis. Starting from any sound as input, atomic decomposition generates a reconstruction of that sound based on a granular model (Sturm et al. 2009).

The composer Iannis Xenakis read Gabor's scientific papers and was the first to explicate a compositional theory for grains of sound (Xenakis 1960). He began by adopting the following lemma: "All sound, even continuous musical variation, is conceived as an assemblage of a large number of elementary sounds adequately disposed in time. In the attack, body, and decline of a complex sound, thousands of pure sounds appear in a more or less short interval of time Δt." Xenakis created granular sounds using analog tone generators and tape splicing. These appear in the composition *Analogique A-B* for string orchestra and tape (1959). The composition is described in Xenakis (1992) and analyzed by Di Scipio (1998). The score and tape part are available from Éditions Salabert.

Following an encounter with Xenakis, the author developed a computer-based implementation of granular synthesis using sine waves in 1974 at the University of California, San Diego (Roads 1978b). In 1981 the author made the first experiments in granulation of sampled sounds spatialized to four loudspeakers at the Massachusetts Institute of Technology (Roads 1985c). We created the CloudGenerator app at Les Ateliers UPIC in 1995 (Roads and Alexander 1995; Roads 2001a). Later we developed the Creatovox instrument (2000), the ConstantQGranulator (2001), and EmissionControl at the University of California, Santa Barbara (Thill 2005). This was followed by the EmissionControl2 app (Roads, Kilgore, and Duplessis 2020).

Granular synthesis appears in many compositions, including the author's sets *POINT LINE CLOUD* (2004, reissued in 2019 on Presto!? Records) and *FLICKER TONE PULSE* (2019, Wergo).

Granular synthesis has been implemented in many ways. The Canadian composer Barry Truax (1987, 1988, 1990a, 1990b) developed the first real-time implementations. The book *Microsound* describes other implementations known at that time and includes sixty-eight sound examples (Roads 2001a). Alberto de Campo (2011) provides annotated code for his implementations in SuperCollider. Brandtsegg, Saue, and Johansen (2011) provides a Csound opcode for granular and other methods of particle synthesis.

In the past, granular synthesis was sometimes viewed as an exotic method, as it was not available in a commercial synthesizer. It is now mainstream. Dozens of software and hardware systems incorporate granular synthesis and processing. There are many choices in designing the synthesis engine and the user interface, thus implementations vary greatly.

Simple Grain Generator Instrument

At its most basic, granular synthesis can be implemented with a simple instrument: a sine wave oscillator controlled by an envelope generator (figure 13.3). The early theories of Gabor and Xenakis proposed this model. In the rest of this chapter, we call this model *classical granular synthesis*. By contrast, in place of the oscillator we can substitute a sample player module. In this way any sound can be granulated, from sound files or from live input. This is the prevalent model today.

Despite the simplicity of the instrument, to generate even a plain, uncomplicated sound requires a massive amount of microsonic control data—potentially thousands of parameter updates per second of sound.

Parameters of Granular Synthesis

Most parameters of granular synthesis apply to individual grains. These are the *per-grain* parameters. By contrast, the density parameter provides global control.

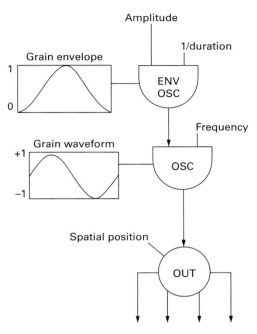

Figure 13.3 Simple granular synthesis instrument built from an envelope generator and an oscillator with four-channel spatial output.

All parameters can be modulated. Indeed, modulation is central to the animated textures produced by granular methods. The modulation sources can be traditional *low-frequency oscillators* (LFOs), random noise sources, or envelopes derived from gestural controllers. This provides another layer of control.

Per-Grain Parameters

Per-grain processing is key to the heterogeneous sonorities produced by granular synthesis. The basic per-grain parameters are the following:

- Envelope
- Duration
- Waveform (sample read pointer)
- Frequency (pitch shift for samples)
- Spatial position
- Synchronicity (degree of periodicity)
- Intermittency (degree of irregular emission)

To this can be added implementation-specific per-grain effects such as filtering, which add another layer of complexity (Roads 2001a, 2012; Roads, Kilgore, and Duplessis 2020).

Envelope

An amplitude envelope shapes each grain. Various envelopes can be used; each has its own effect on the spectrum (figure 13.4). Gabor's theory posited a Gaussian bell-shaped curve. The following equation defines a *normal* or *Gaussian* distribution $P(x)$:

$$P(x) = \frac{1}{\sigma\sqrt{2\pi}} e^{-(x-\mu)^2/2\sigma^2}$$

where σ determines the *standard deviation* (the spread of the bell) and μ is the *mean* or center peak.

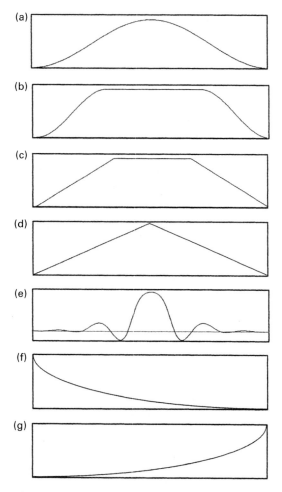

Figure 13.4　Grain envelopes. (a) Gaussian. (b) Tukey. (c) Three-stage linear. (d) Two-stage triangle. (e) Band-limited impulse. (f) Exponentially decaying (expodec). (g) Reverse exponentially decaying (rexpodec).

Figure 13.4b shows a *quasi-Gaussian* or *Tukey window* (Harris 1978), where the peak is extended over 30 to 50 percent of the duration of the grain. This shape has proved sonically effective (Roads 1985c). Simple line-segment envelopes (figure 13.4c and d) were used in the early experiments of Truax (1987, 1988).

Complicated envelopes such as a band-limited pulse (figure 13.4e) create resonant grains that sound like woodblock taps in sparse textures when the grain duration is less than 100 ms. The expodec (exponentially delaying) and rexpodec (reverse expodec) envelopes produce percussive and backward-sounding sound grains, respectively. As one would expect, sharp angles in any envelope cause strong side effects in the spectrum due to convolution. (See chapter 29.)

Duration

The duration of successive grains can be constant, variable according to some function (e.g., an envelope), or random within stipulated limits.

Another possibility is to vary duration according to a property of the grains. For example, we could link short durations to high-frequency grains. A correspondence between grain frequency and grain duration is characteristic of *wavelet* (chapter 38) and *grainlet* paradigms (Roads 2001a).

We should note that the previously mentioned upper boundary of 100 ms for duration concerning classical granular synthesis is not a hard limit. Larger grain sizes using sampled sound can be musically effective. Granular processing over a second or more spawns cascades of pitch-shifted and filtered echoes (possibly reversed) of recognizable material such as voices or fragments of music. Here grain scheduling algorithms that normally operate on the micro level scale up to the level of sound objects.

Effect of grain duration

A profound law of signal processing comes into play in setting the grain duration: the shorter the duration of an event, the greater its bandwidth. Thus short grain durations lead to crackling, explosive sonorities, whereas longer grain durations create a much smoother impression. Figure 13.5 demonstrates this important law for three elementary signals. As the duration of a signal shrinks, its spectrum broadens.

Figure 13.6 displays the dramatic spectral effects of lowering the grain duration and the resulting broadband noise.

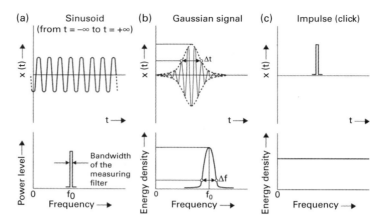

Figure 13.5 Time-domain functions (top) and spectra (bottom) of three elementary signals (after Blauert [1983]). (a) Sine wave of infinite duration corresponding to a single line in the spectrum. (b) Gaussian grain and corresponding formant spectrum. (c) Ideal impulse and corresponding infinite spectrum.

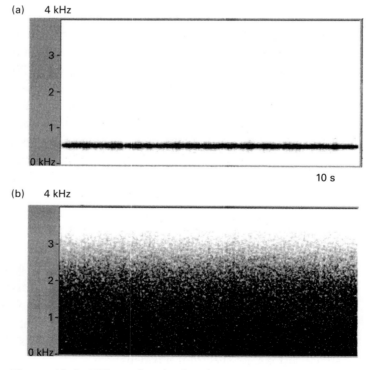

Figure 13.6 Effect of grain duration on spectrum. (a) Sonogram of a granular stream of 100 ms sinusoidal grains with a frequency of 500 Hz. (b) If we shrink the grain duration to 1 ms, the spectrum explodes dramatically into broadband noise.

Waveform

A fundamental principle of granular synthesis is that the waveform within the grain can be derived from any source: synthetic, sampled, or live. In the classical theory of granular synthesis, the waveform of each grain is a sinusoid at a specific frequency. By allowing the grain waveform to vary on a per-grain basis, we can produce colorful polychrome emissions. This enables us to choose among a number of different stored wavetables. Going further to allow sampled sound and live sources opens up a universe of possibilities.

Granulation of sampled sounds

Granulation of sampled sounds feeds acoustic material into a kind of logical threshing machine—delivering grains in a new order with a new micro-rhythm. The granulator reads in a brief segment of a sampled sound (from a sound file or directly from live input) and applies an envelope or *window* to the segment, transforming it into a grain. Listen to Roads (2004) and the CD included with Roads (2001a) for examples of sample granulation.

In sample granulation, a key parameter is the *sample read pointer* (sometimes called *file pointer, file position,* or *scan head*). This is the point in the file (or memory buffer, in the case of real-time granulation) that the granulator starts reading a sample. Once an initial pointer position is set, there are many ways to manipulate it. For example, it can scan forward smoothly to the end of the file. Or it can stutter, looping back repeatedly to its starting position. It may stagger forward slowly, time-stretching the sound. The pointer can move backward, causing the scan to play a sound in reverse. With random modulation it may jump around, causing a "scrambled sound" effect. The manipulation of this pointer is at the core of any granulation algorithm. Figure 13.7 shows three possibilities out of many.

Note that changing the position of the pointer slowly or quickly does not change the pitch. The playback sampling rate is independent of the rate of change of the sample read pointer, which merely sets the starting point. The next parameter discussed, frequency or pitch shift, changes the playback sampling rate.

Frequency (pitch shift for samples)

In classical granular synthesis, the grain waveform is a sinusoid. In this case, the frequency parameter stipulates the number of cycles per second (Hz). For a constant tone, the frequency is the same for a series of grains. In most cases,

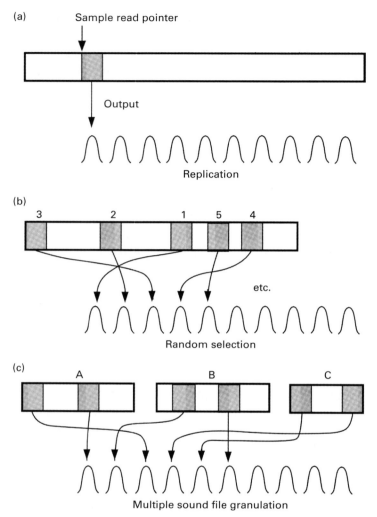

Figure 13.7   Granulation of sampled sound. The sample read pointer is the location in the file where the granulator starts reading a sample. (a) If the position does not change, a single grain is replicated. (b) If the pointer jumps around randomly, the output is scrambled. (c) In a multifile granulator, a texture can emerge from a combination of three different sound files, A, B, and C.

however, we want to be able to vary the frequency on a per-grain basis. To allow for variation in grain frequency we can stipulate a range, called a *band*. Within the upper and lower boundaries of the band, the grain generator scatters grains. This model allows for many possibilities. For example, the grains can follow narrow bands that ascend or descend in the manner of glissandi. The grains can be aligned to a pitch scale or scattered to random frequencies. When the frequency distribution is random and the band is greater than a small interval, the result is a texture in which pitch is ambiguous or uniden-tifiable. The combined effects induced by the envelope and grain density also strongly influence the impression of pitch.

In the case of sampled grains the frequency parameter is a per-grain pitch shift. The pitch shift can be aligned to a scale and modulated by an LFO.

Spatial position

If the texture rendered by the granulator is monaural—every grain in the same spatial position—the impression is flat. By contrast, when each grain scatters to a unique location, the texture manifests a vivid spatial morphol-ogy. This is evident even in stereo. The grains can be scattered randomly in space, pan across two or more channels, or follow an arbitrary 3D spatial path in an immersive environment. Barrett (2016) explored the projection of grains in ambisonic systems (see chapter 32). Deleflie and Schiemer (2009) used a granular representation to render existing ambisonic encodings. Wan Rosli (2016) used spatial information extracted from the spherical harmonics of ambisonics in order to granulate space.

Selective reverberation means setting the depth of reverberation of each grain individually. Per-grain reverberation is most striking at low densities in a multiloudspeaker setup. At high densities in a stereo playback system, the individual reverberation halos fuse into a continuous background cloud, which is not much different from global wave reverberation.

Synchronicity (degree of periodicity)

Synchronicity is the degree of periodicity of the grain emissions. Thus *synchronous granular synthesis* (SGS) emits one or more streams of grains in which the grains follow each other at regular intervals (Roads 2001a). In SGS, grain density determines the frequency of grain emission. For example, a density of two grains per second means that a grain is produced every half second—a repeating tone. Synchronous densities in the range of about 0.1 to 20 grains per second generate metrical rhythms. When the densities change over time, we experience precise accelerandi/rallentandi effects. At higher densities, long grains fuse into continuous tones and textures.

Asynchronous granular synthesis (AGS) breaks the periodicity of per-fectly sequential streams of grains. Instead, it randomizes the grain emission times (Roads 1991). Some implementations call this parameter *jitter.* Notice that randomizing the onset time does not change the overall density.

Intermittency (degree of irregular emission)

The amount of *intermittency* is the degree to which the regular flow of grains is interrupted. Thus intermittency is not the same as asynchronicity. As figure 13.8 shows, in an intermittent emission, grains are lost. Thus intermittency overrides the stipulated grain density, as explained next.

Density and Fill Factor

Now that we have covered the per-grain parameters, we look at a higher-level control. This is *density*—the number of grains generated per second. Density serves as a global control of texture in granular synthesis. When density is low, only a few grains are heard, resulting in a sparse rhythmic pattern. At a critical point (determined by the *fill factor*, explained further on) the individual grains fuse into a continuous texture. High densities spawn massive clouds of sound.

Density, however, is not the only determinant of texture. Density and grain duration combine to make texture. For example, a one-second cloud containing twenty 100 ms grains is continuous and opaque, whereas a one-second cloud containing twenty 1 ms grains is sparse and transparent. The difference between these two cases is their fill factor (FF). FF is the product of density and the grain duration. In the cases just cited, the fill factor of the first cloud is $20 \times 0.1 = 2$, whereas in the second cloud the fill factor is $20 \times 0.01 = 0.2$. In general, when FF < 0.5 the texture is sparse. When it is 1.0 or above the

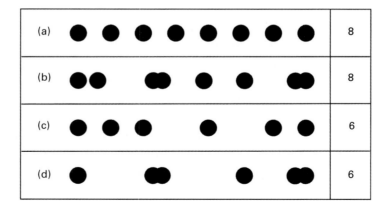

Figure 13.8 Comparison of four granular streams on a time line. In the left-hand column, a circle represents a grain. Density is the same for all four streams. (a) Synchronous. (b) Asynchronous. (c) Synchronous with intermittency. (d) Asynchronous with intermittency. The right-hand column indicates the number of grains. Intermittency results in a loss of grains.

texture is continuous. Other factors can affect continuity, such as density variations in time, asynchronous and/or intermittent grain emissions, and others.

For a grain duration of 25 ms, we can make the following observations concerning grain density as it crosses perceptual thresholds:

< 15 grains/second—Rhythmic sequences

15–25 grains/second—Fluttering, sensation of rhythm disappears. If the cloud is asynchronous, we hear intermittencies.

25–50 grains/second—We no longer perceive an acceleration of tempo in grain emissions, but we feel an increase in granular flow.

50—100 grains/second—Texture band.

> 100 grains/second—Continuous sound mass. No space between grains. Resembles reverberation in some cases.

Density and frequency band or pitch-shift effects are also synergistic, as follow:

- Narrow bands and high densities create pitched streams with formant spectra.
- Medium bands (e.g., intervals of several semitones) and high densities generate turgid colored noises.
- Wide bands (e.g., an octave or more) and high densities form massive clouds of sound.

As we have seen in the section on grain duration effects, another way to modify the bandwidth of the cloud is by changing the grain duration parameter.

High-Level Granular Organizations

The complexity of the sound generated by granular synthesis derives from the amount of control data fed to it. If n is the number of parameters for each grain and d is the average grain density per second of sound, it takes $d \times n$ parameter values to specify one second. Because d can range into the hundreds or thousands, it is clear that for the purposes of compositional control, a higher-level unit of organization for the grains is needed. These units function on the meso time scale of several seconds or more. The purpose of such a unit is to let composers stipulate massive quantities of grains using just a few global parameters.

In products that implement granular synthesis, MIDI control is an essential capability. Most synthesis instruments respond to note-on messages, for example, as well as knobs or faders for other parameters. MIDI control is not essential to all implementations of granular synthesis, however.

Table 13.1 lists various models of granular organization. Next, we look at each model in turn. A brief summary concludes the discussion.

Time-Frequency Projections

These approaches project grains onto the plane of frequency versus time. In this category we include grid-like projections such as the Gabor matrix (Gabor 1946, 1947) and screens (Xenakis 1960, 1992), as well as the short-time Fourier transform (chapter 37) and wavelet transform (Mallat 2009). Another category of time-frequency projection is atomic decompositions (chapter 39), in which there is no fixed grid in frequency or time.

We have already presented the concept of the Gabor matrix. Another grid-oriented conception is Xenakis's (1960, 1971, 1992) notion of *screens*. A screen is an amplitude-frequency grid on which grains are scattered. A

Table 13.1 High-level granular organization

Time-frequency projections	Gabor matrix (Gabor 1946, 1947); screens (Xenakis 1960, 1992); short-time Fourier transform (chapter 37); wavelet transform (Mallat 2009); atomic decompositions (chapter 39)
Clouds	Roads (1978b); CloudGenerator (Roads and Alexander 1995)
Streams	Synchronous and asynchronous (Truax 1987, 1988, 1990a, 1990b), EmissionControl (Thall 2004), EmissionControl2 (Roads, Kilgore, and Duplessis 2020); Monolake Granulator (Robert Henke); Instruo Abhar; AudioMulch; The Mangle; many others
Pitch-synchronous granular synthesis	De Poli and Piccialli (1991); Piccialli et al. (1992); Dutilleux, De Poli, et al. (2011)
Sprays	MetaSynth (Wenger and Spiegel 2010)
Scrubbing	Borderlands Granular (Carlson and Wang 2012; Carlson 2019)
Micromontage	Music of Horacio Vaggione; IRIN app (Caires 2004, 2019)
Physical/biological models	Cook (1996, 1997, 2007); Keller and Truax (1998); Norris (2013); Fischman (2003)
Abstract generative models	Di Scipio (1996, 1999); de Campo (2011); Rhys (2016)

synchronous sequence of screens (called a *book*) constitutes the evolution of a complex sound. Rather than starting from an analyzed sound, Xenakis's proposals use generative algorithms to fill the screen with grains. He proposed scattering grains randomly into screens and then deriving new screens from set-theory operations: intersections, unions, complements, and differences, among others. A basic problem with this screen paradigm is its regular 25 Hz frame rate, which introduces a periodic modulation.

Two related spectrum analysis techniques, the *short-time Fourier transform* (STFT) and the wavelet transform, take in a time-domain sound signal and measure its frequency content versus time (see chapters 37 and 38). In effect, these methods associate each point in the analysis grid with a unit of time-frequency energy—a grain or a wavelet.

The STFT is well known and can be computed using the fast Fourier transform (Rabiner and Gold 1975). The grain in this case is a set of overlapping windows within each of the N frequency bins of the Fourier analyzer. The resulting time-frequency grid can be seen by zooming in on a sonogram (figure 13.9).

The wavelet transform (Kronland-Martinet and Grossmann 1991; Mallat 2009) performs a similar operation, but the spacing of the analysis channels and the duration of the window (called the *analyzing wavelet*) is different from the STFT. In the STFT, the spacing between the channels on the frequency axis is linear, whereas in the wavelet transform it is usually logarithmic. That is, in the wavelet transform, the channel frequency interval (bandwidth) Df/f is constant. In the STFT, the window duration is fixed, whereas in the wavelet transform it can vary as a function of frequency.

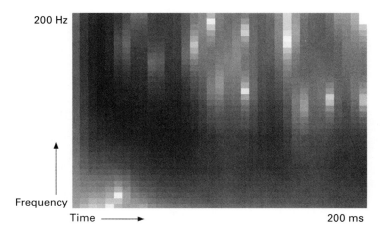

Figure 13.9   Detail of a time-frequency grid produced by the STFT. Snare drum hit, 0–200 ms, 0–200 Hz. The zoomed-in sonogram displays the rectangular cells of energy at each time frame and frequency bin.

Both the STFT and the wavelet transform permit analysis, transformation, and resynthesis, which make them potentially powerful musical tools for the manipulation of sampled sounds. However, these tools are designed to give users an illusion of sonic continuity. Their internal granular structure (quantized in time and frequency) is generally hidden to users and is therefore not controllable as such.

Clouds

The author proposed the concept of generating *clouds* of granular sound (Roads 1978b). A sound cloud can be defined as a region on the time-frequency plane, similar to what G. M. Koenig called *tendency masks* (Koenig 1970b). The region has a precise duration and adjustable frequency boundaries within which grains can be scattered at various densities (figure 13.10). This model requires a specification for each cloud and is thus a non-real-time

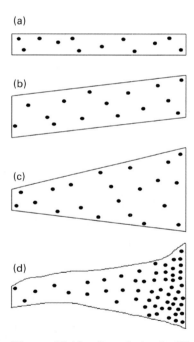

Figure 13.10   Sound clouds filled sparsely using an asynchronous algorithm that scatters the grains randomly in time. The horizontal axis is time, and the vertical axis is frequency. (a) Basic cloud with fixed upper and lower frequency bandwidth. (b) Cloud with linearly varying upper and lower bandwidth, both with positive slope. (c) Cloud with linearly varying upper (positive slope) and lower bandwidth (negative slope). (d) Cloud with continuously varying upper and lower bandwidth. Notice also that the grain density is increasing over time.

approach. In the original implementation, the author provided a script for generating multiple overlapping clouds in a sequence.

The Cloud Generator app (Roads and Alexander 1995) shown in figure 13.11 rendered a single cloud as a sound file. A composer could then arrange multiple sound files on the timeline of a DAW.

Streams

Streaming generation is a real-time process pioneered by Barry Truax (1986). In his initial system, the grain waveform was fixed. Later implementations read the grain waveform from a sound file or live input. A streaming granulator can spawn a large amount of derived sound material from a given sound

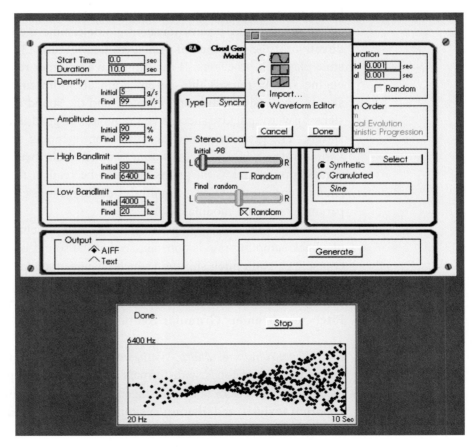

Figure 13.11 Cloud Generator app in action. The main panel sets the parameters of a cloud. The Synthetic waveform option is selected, which brings up a menu of options for the waveform. The Waveform Editor option is selected. Below these windows is another window showing the cloud generated from this specification. Individual grains are visible.

file by manipulating a sample read pointer. As explained previously, this pointer indicates where in the file to get the next grain for playback. An example of live input to streaming granulation is the music of Agostino Di Scipio (1996, 1999), who granulated a soloist on an acoustic instrument in order to produce polyphonic textures.

Figure 13.12 shows the screen of EmissionControl2, a streaming granulator (Roads, Kilgore, and Duplessis 2020). EmissionControl2 can granulate multiple sound files simultaneously, with low-frequency oscillator (LFO) control of grain parameters, including sound file selection. The third panel down shows the sound file being read. The sample read pointer is shown as a vertical line at the beginning of the shaded area. The shaded area is the current scan region.

Instruo Arbhar is an example in Eurorack hardware (figure 13.13). Twistable knobs and voltage control provide direct access to granulation processes.

In any streaming granulator, controls determine the position, speed, and direction of the sequence of grains emitted. Figure 13.14 shows some possible playback processes. If the sample read pointer remains stationary, the engine simply repeats the current grain ad infinitum. If it steps forward slowly, successive grains are repeated, and the sound is time stretched. If it steps forward quickly, successive grains are skipped, and the sound is time shrunk. The grain sequence can also loop: stepping forward and back by various ratios while also continuing forward or backward through the sound file. Stepping backward, grains can also be read in reverse. Simultaneous streams can be triggered as multiples of the first stream's clock. All these parameters can be modulated.

Manipulations of the sample read pointer simply change its position. The playback sampling rate is constant so that the sound is not pitch shifted. Of course, per-grain pitch shifting (which changes the playback sampling rate) can be another parameter of the granular engine.

Pitch-Synchronous Granular Synthesis

Pitch-synchronous granular synthesis (PSGS) is a technique designed for the generation of tones with formant regions in their spectra (De Poli and Piccialli 1991). PSGS is a multistaged operation involving pitch estimation, spectrum analysis, and filtering. A similar method is called *pitch-synchronous overlap and add* (PSOLA) (Dutilleux, De Poli, et al. 2011).

The first stage is pitch estimation of a voice or instrument (see chapter 34). Each pitch period is considered as a separate grain. Then spectrum analysis is performed on each grain. The system derives its impulse response and uses this to set the parameters for a filter. (Chapters 28 and 29 discuss impulse response measurements.)

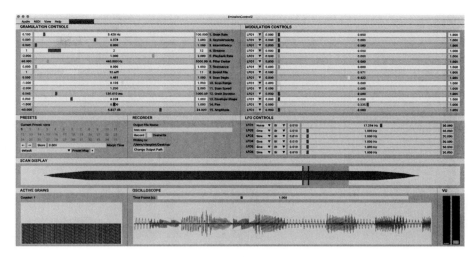

Figure 13.12 Screen of the EmissionControl2 app. Multiple sound files can be granulated simultaneously. The granulation parameter faders are on the top left. Each granulation parameter can be modulated by an LFO source. The faders at top right control the amount of modulation. The six LFOs are in the middle panel. Below it is a display of the current sound file being granulated. The bottom waveform display shows the output.

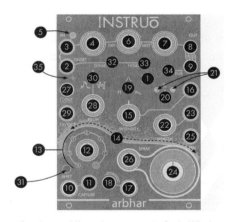

1. Condenser Microphone	19. Grain Window
2. Onset Input	20. Grain Direction
3. Input	21. Grain Direction
4. Input Level	Indicators
5. Input Indicator	22. Length
6. Dry/Wet Mix	23. Length CV Input
7. Output Level	24. Scan
8. Output 1	25. Scan CV Input
9. Output 2	26. Spray
10. Capture Button	27. Gate Output
11. Capture Gate Input	28. Pitch
12. Layer	29. 1V/Octave Input
13. Layer Indicators	30. Pitch Deviation
14. Granular Stream	31. Shift Button
15. Intensity	32. Sensitivity
16. Intensity CV Input	33. Hold
17. Strike Button	34. Dub
18. Strike Input	35. Onset Indicator

Figure 13.13 Instruo Arbhar module with legend of controls and indicators.

abcdef	Orginal (*Scan Speed* = 1; *playback Rate* = 1)
aaaaaa	Frozen (*Scan Speed* = 0; *playback Rate* = 1)
_____	Silence (*Scan Speed* = 1; *playback Rate* = 0)
ɟǝbɔdɐ	Time-reversed (*Scan Speed* = 1; *playback Rate* = 1)
fedcba	Time-reversed with forward grains (*Scan Speed* = 1; *playback Rate* = 1)
ɐdɔbǝɟ	Time-forward with reversed grains (*Scan Speed* = 1; *playback Rate* = 1)
aabbccddeeff	Time-stretched (*Scan Speed* = 0.5; *playback Rate* = 1)
ace	Time-shrunk (*Scan Speed* = 2; *playback Rate* = 1)
a b c d e f	Pitch-shifted down (*Scan Speed* = 1; *playback Rate* = 0.5)
abcdef	Pitch-shifted up (*Scan Speed* = 1; *playback Rate* = 2)

Figure 13.14   Some grain playback possibilities. See the text for an explanation. $\{a, \ldots f\}$ is a set of ordered grains.

In synthesis, a pulse train at the detected pitch period drives a bank of *finite impulse response* (FIR) filters. (FIR filters are discussed in chapter 28.) The output signal results from the excitation of the pulse train on the weighted sum of the impulse responses of all the filters. At each time frame, the system emits a grain that is overlapped and added with the previous grain to create a smoothly varying speech or instrument signal. The PSGS representation enables several transformations to create variations of the original sound. The includes separation of the harmonic part of the sound from the residual inharmonic part (Piccialli et al. 1992).

Sprays

Certain software-based granulators implement a flowing spray jet of sound particles. This is made visually explicit in programs like Metasynth (Wenger and Spiegel 2010) where the user literally sprays grains onto a time-frequency grid onscreen (figure 13.15). In this sense, the cloud, stream, and spray models align with the spirit of Xenakis's UPIC paradigm, in which users directly draw sounds in the time-frequency plane (Xenakis 1992; Weibel, Kanach, and Brümmer 2020).

Scrubbing

Multitouch interfaces enable a graphical *scrubbing* model, after the tape scrubbing methods of the analog era (figure 13.16). Internally, these granulators use streaming. However, they provide manual scrubbing controls for manipulation of the sample read pointer. Borderlands Granular is a prime

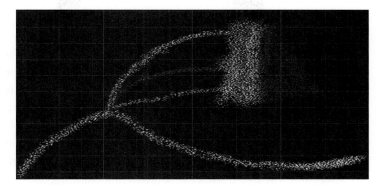

Figure 13.15 MetaSynth granular clouds painted with a spray can tool. Time is the horizontal axis and frequency is the vertical axis.

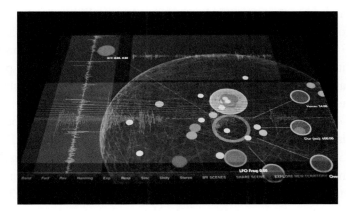

Figure 13.16 Borderlands app for iPad. The user slides or *scrubs* a circle along the waveform to select segments to granulate. The attached satellite circles function as faders for control of synthesis parameters.

example (Carlson and Wang 2012; Carlson 2019). Users begin by placing any number of sound files in a directory. When launched, the software displays waveforms (corresponding to the sound files) on the screen. Each waveform is within a rectangle and is oriented either vertically or horizontally. These rectangles can be selected, moved, and resized using one's fingers. A *grain cloud* with a set of graphic faders can be added to the screen. When the user moves a cloud over a rectangle it begins to play. The position of the cloud can be moved back and forth across the waveform. This is analogous to scrubbing audio tape across a tape head. The user can control the density of voices, their overlap, duration, pitch, envelope, and degree of random motion. The instrument is performed by creating and destroying new clouds and moving them around the landscape.

Micromontage

The technique of micromontage, as developed by the Paris-based composer Horacio Vaggione, involves arranging microsounds manually in the time line of a DAW (Vaggione 2003). The composer loaded a catalog of pre-edited sounds into the app's library. Then the composer selected clips in the library and pasted them onto a track at specific points on the time line running from left to right across the screen. By pasting a single grain multiple times, it became a sound object of a higher temporal order—a *microfigure.* Each paste operation was like a stroke of a brush in a painting, adding a touch more color over the blank space of the canvas. In this case, the collection of microsounds in the library can be thought of as a palette. Because a DAW lets users zoom in and out, the composer could paste and edit on different time scales. Grains and microfigures could be positioned on multiple simultaneous tracks, permitting a rich interplay of microevents.

This approach is extremely free in terms of compositional options, considering that material at any time scale can be processed by plug-ins and placed anywhere in the time line. Detached from real-time constraints, ideas can be tested, edited, submixed, or deleted at will.

One of the strategies that this enables is a thematic approach, that is, manipulating sound material to create repetitions and variations. For example, a copy of a given sonic entity can be pitch shifted, time scaled, ring modulated, filtered, reversed, and so on. Parts of the piece, if not the entire work, can be organized as a montage of variations of a finite number of elements. This approach forms the basis of my compositions *Never* (2010) and *Always* (2013) and all the electroacoustic works of Horacio Vaggione (Roads 2005). It was crystallized by the IRIN app developed by Vaggione's student Carlos Caires (2004, 2019).

Physical and Biological Models

A recurrent theme in computer music is setting up a mapping between a scientific equation and parameters of sound synthesis. For example, Fischman (2003) mapped the Schrödinger wave equation to parameters of granular synthesis. This kind of *sonification* project can have several aims: better scientific understanding, a purely artistic experience, or something in between.

Another approach comes from physical modeling synthesis, in which the goal is to simulate the sound of an acoustic instrument (chapter 18). An early example involving granular synthesis was a simulation of the sounds of shaken and scraped percussion: maracas, sekere, cabasa, bamboo windchime, tambourines, sleighbells, and guiro (Cook 1996, 1997, 2007). Keller and Truax

(1998) created granular models of physical processes such as liquid streams and a bouncing metallic ball. Natasha Barrett modeled processes of self-organized critical systems such as grain avalanches in her work *The Utility of Space* (2000), which was just one facet of a multilayered design.

A potentially compelling paradigm derives from the physics of granular processes (Norris 2013). A large body of scientific literature centers on modeling the micromechanics of processes such as grain vibration patterns, mixing, flow, and interactions between grains and fluids (Aronson and Tsimring 2009). These models could be repurposed for artistic ends.

Particle systems are the computer graphics counterpart to granular synthesis of sound (Reeves 1983). Fonseca (2013) adapted a particle engine from computer graphics to the control of granular synthesis. A product called Sound Particles brings this to users.

Biological models such as DNA sequences, neuron behavior, and cicadas have also been explored as models for sound synthesis (Smyth and Smith 2001). These simulations can be arbitrarily complex and extend into virtual worlds. Unfortunately, the problem with physical and biological modeling has always been the same: a model is worth little without an expert player, whether real or virtual. Virtuosity demands daily practice over a period of years. Obviously, to develop a software model of an expert player poses a daunting challenge.

Abstract Generative Models

Beyond the physical and biological lies the abstract realm of experimental algorithms that are not related to a model of a real-world phenomenon. They are sometimes derived from mathematical formulae such as recursive substitution, cellular automata, or chaotic functions. These generally low-level algorithms emit granular sound as a byproduct of a formal process from an abstract domain. A problem with such bottom-up approaches is that they do not usually incorporate a multiscale notion of time structure. Like the low-level rules in Wolfram's (2002) generative experiments, whether larger scale structures emerge out of such rules is mainly a matter of guesswork. Fractal generators are inherently multiscale (Rhys 2016). This can be easily seen in images but is more difficult to perceive in sound structures.

Abstract algorithms are not directly tethered to human action or perception. To the detached observer, often these processes tend to sound either predictable or merely random. They lack the meaningful sense of causality and effort that we associate with human gestures, the opposition between tension and resolution to which we are psychologically disposed. Human beings are highly sensitive to the virtuosic play of lively human gestures, whether live on stage or practiced behind the scenes in a studio, and to the unfolding of a sonic narrative played out by recognizable sonic characters or themes.

Summary of Higher-Level Organization

Granular models based on time-frequency projections start from sound analysis. From a creative perspective, we want to manipulate the analysis data as a means of sound transformation. Fourier and wavelet models do not, in general provide access to the granular level. Models based on atomic decomposition do.

Cloud, stream, spray, scrubbing, and micromontage models have been effective in composition because they allow composers to agglomerate grains into multiple levels of musical structure, specifically the *object* (100 ms–8 s), *meso* (> 8 s), and macro time scales (Roads 2001a).

Pitch-synchronous granular synthesis is reminiscent of convolution with pulsars (chapter 21).

Methods derived from scientific models and abstract formulas pose compositional challenges. How can one create coherent multiscale structures with these techniques? The key is finding a mechanism to transfer complex structures generated at lower levels into musically interesting structures at higher levels.

14 *Subtractive Synthesis*

Digital Filters: Background

Introduction to Filters

Filter Response Curves

Filter Types

Filter Q and Gain

Phase Response and Latency in Filtering

Filter Banks and Graphic Equalizers

Comb and Allpass Filters

Time-Varying Subtractive Synthesis
          SYTER and GRM Tools

Subtractive Analysis/Resynthesis

> **The Vocoder**

Linear Predictive Coding

> **What Is Linear Prediction?**
> **LPC Analysis**
>> **Filter estimation**
>> **Pitch and amplitude analysis**
>> **Voiced/unvoiced decision**
>> **Analysis frames**
>
> **LPC Synthesis**
> **Editing LPC Frame Data**
> **Cross-Synthesis: A Musical Extension of LPC**

WaveGAN

Subtractive synthesis uses *filters* to shape the spectrum of a source signal. As the source signal passes through a filter, the filter carves selected regions of the frequency spectrum of the input signal (figure 14.1). The term *subtractive* refers to this carving effect. A filter can either cut or boost a specified region of the spectrum.

Spectrally rich source sounds include impulse trains, sawtooth waves, and white noise. Figure 14.2 shows the dramatic effect of two filters on white noise. Using white noise as the input signal, subtractive synthesis can produce many types of *colored noises*–a staple of electronic music (Roads 2015). Colored noise can be obtained by passing white noise through a filter. Works like *Vision and Prayer* (1961) and *Ensembles for Synthesizer* (1964), composed by Milton Babbitt using the RCA Synthesizer, demonstrated how a palette of colored noises could be deployed effectively in composition.

Besides their use in synthesis, filters are also central to sound editing and mixing and, for that matter, to all sound design. Hence everything we say about filters applies to those domains as well.

This chapter serves as a basic introduction to using filters, describing their main characteristics and parameters. Chapter 28 goes into greater technical

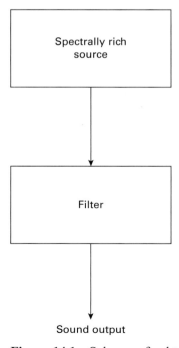

Figure 14.1   Scheme of subtractive synthesis. A spectrally rich source such as noise or pulses is fed into a filter, which shapes the output spectrum.

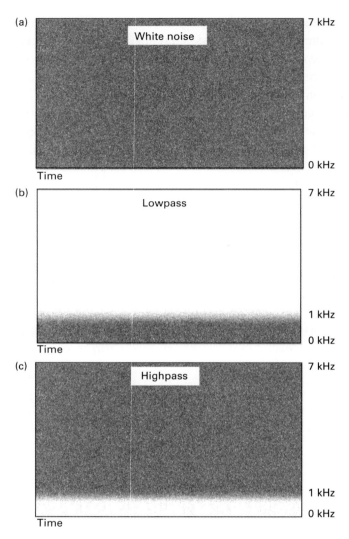

Figure 14.2 Sonogram images show the dramatic effect of two filters on a white noise signal. A sonogram plots the spectrum of a sound over time. The vertical axis is frequency, and the horizontal axis is time. The darker the trace, the more energy there is. (a) White noise lasting several seconds. The uniformly dark grey texture shows that the energy is equal in all audio frequencies. This plot is limited to 7 kHz. (b) A lowpass filter with a cutoff frequency at 1 kHz and a sharp slope eliminates the energy above 1 kHz. (c) A highpass filter with a cutoff frequency of 1 kHz and a sharp slope eliminates all the energy below 1 kHz.

detail about the internal operation of filters. Other technical introductions include Moorer (1977), Moore (1978a, b), McLellan, Schafer, and Yoder (2003), and Loy (2007). Those with an engineering background could also study more advanced texts on filters such as Moore (1990), Smith (1985a, 1985b, 2007b), Oppenheim and Willsky (1983), Rabiner and Gold (1975), and Oppenheim and Schafer (1975), among many others.

Digital Filters: Background

Primordial electronic music instruments used analog filters to shape the raw waveforms emitted by their tone generators, a process dubbed *subtractive tone forming* by Douglas (1968). Among the notable instruments that contained filters were the Mixtur-Trautonium, Solovox, Clavioline, Warbo Formant Organ, Hammond Novachord, RCA Synthesizer, and the Ondioline (Jenny 1958; Rhea 1972; Bode 1984; Roads 1996b).

Standalone analog filters like the Albis Tonfrequenz filter (figure 14.3) were staples in electronic music facilities such as the West German Radio (WDR) studio in which K. Stockhausen, G. M. Koenig, J.-C. Eloy, and other composers worked in the 1950s and 1960s. Later, the development of *voltage-controlled filters* typified the first golden era of modular analog synthesizers (Moog 1965; Chamberlin 1985; Rossum 1992; Bjørn and Meyer 2018).

Experiments with digital filter circuits began in the 1950s. The theory of digital filtering was pushed forward in the 1960s with the general adoption of the *Z-transform calculus* (Kaiser 1963; Rabiner and Gold 1975; Steiglitz 1996). The Z-transform introduced new ideas such as *stability* and *causality* that are essential to filter design (see chapter 28). Rudimentary digital filters appeared in sound synthesis languages such as Music IV, Music 4B, and Music V (Mathews and Miller 1963; Winham 1966; Mathews 1969).

By the early 1980s, engineers built digital synthesizers at several research laboratories. Examples include Stanford's Systems Concepts Digital Synthesizer (Samson 1980, 1985), IRCAM's 4X (Asta et al. 1980), and the Groupe de Recherches Musicales's SYTER (Allouis 1979; Allouis and Bernier 1982). These exotic machines could realize dozens of digital filters in real time. But it was not until a decade later that speed-ups in hardware made it possible to implement real-time digital filters in low-cost synthesizers, plug-in signal-processing cards, effects units, and digital sound mixers.

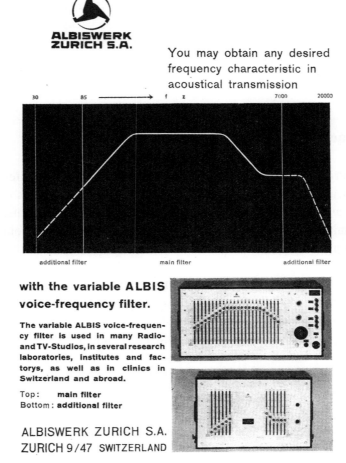

Figure 14.3   The Albis Tonfrequenz filter, a graphic equalizer used in early electronic music compositions.

Introduction to Filters

A filter can be literally any operation on a signal! That is, anything with an input and an output is a filter (Rabiner et al. 1972). But the most common use of the term in audio engineering pertains to devices that boost or attenuate regions of a sound spectrum. This is the meaning we assume here. Filters work according to one or both of the following two methods:

Delaying a copy of an *input signal* by a tiny duration of one or many sample periods and combining the delayed input signal with the new input signal (figure 14.4a).

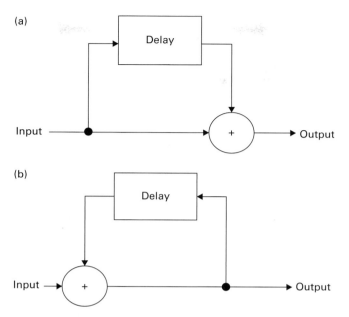

Figure 14.4   Two basic digital filters. (a) Delay the input and add it (feed-forward). (b) Delay the output and add it (feedback).

Delaying a copy of the *output signal* by a short duration and combining it with the input signal (figure 14.4b).

The first case is called a *feed-forward filter.* The second case is a *feedback filter.*

The tiny delays and combinations affect the spectrum by means of *phase cancelation* and *phase reinforcement* effects. Phase cancelation results in attenuation of selected frequencies, and phase reinforcement results in boosting of selected frequencies. Consider a signal with a frequency of 100 Hz. It has a period of 10 ms. If we delay it by 10 ms and combine it with the original, we would have two in-phase signals, and the result of adding them would be a boost in amplitude. If we delay the input signal by 5 ms, then the delayed copy is 180 degrees out of phase with respect to the undelayed signal. Now if we add them together, the result will be phase cancelation. Figure 14.5 shows these effects.

Although figures 14.4 and 14.5 show combination by summation (−), the combination can also take place by subtraction (−). In either case, the combination of original and delayed signals creates a new waveform with a different spectrum. By inserting more delays or mixing sums and differences in various combinations, one can construct many different types of filters.

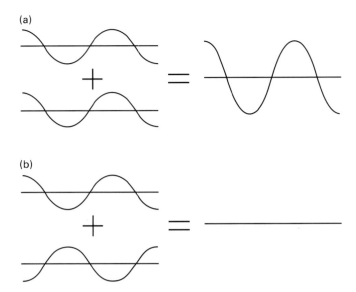

Figure 14.5 Phase effects. (a) Adding two in-phase signals results in a boost at that frequency. (b) Adding two out-of-phase signals results in phase cancelation.

Filter Response Curves

One of the main ways to characterize the various types of filters is to plot their *amplitude-versus-frequency response curve*, also referred to as *magnitude response*. Another common term for the same thing is *frequency response* (FR). The most accurate FR is a straight line, which indicates a *linear* or *flat* amplitude across the frequency spectrum. This means that any frequency within the range of the audio device is passed without any boost or attenuation. Figure 14.6a shows a nearly flat FR, typical of a high-quality audio cable or amplifier. Here we show an arbitrary upper limit of 25 kHz. For high-quality analog audio components such as preamplifiers and amplifiers, the FR may extend beyond 100 kHz. As chapter 3 explains, the frequency limits of digital audio systems depend on their sampling rate.

Many audio devices are not flat. Figure 14.6b shows the FR of a nonlinear system such as a cheap multimedia loudspeaker. We could describe the FR of this loudspeaker as +3.5, −3 dB from 100 Hz to 14 kHz. This means that the loudspeaker boosts some frequencies by as much as 3.5 dB and attenuates other frequencies by as much as 3 dB over the specified range. Below 100 Hz and above 14 kHz, the response falls off sharply. Because it alters the spectrum of a signal fed into it, the loudspeaker acts as a filter.

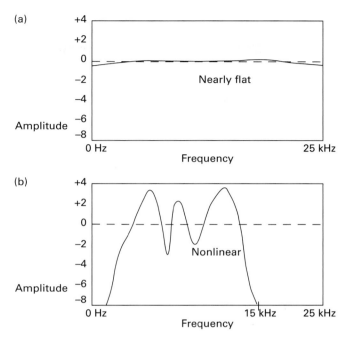

Figure 14.6 Amplitude-versus-frequency response, colloquially called *frequency response*. The vertical axis is amplitude in decibels, and the horizontal axis is frequency. (a) Nearly flat response. (b) Nonlinear response.

Filter Types

We can classify filters on the basis of their characteristic FR curve. Typical FR curves for four basic types of filters are shown in figure 14.7: *lowpass*, *highpass*, *bandpass*, and *bandreject* or *notch*. The names of the filters describe their function. Thus, a lowpass filter passes low frequencies and cuts high frequencies. A highpass filter does the opposite. A bandpass filter passes only a band or range of frequencies, usually in the middle of the spectrum. Finally, a bandreject or notch filter passes every frequency except a specific band

Shelving filters, shown in figure 14.8, boost or cut all frequencies above or below a given threshold. Their names can be confusing, because a *high shelving filter* acts like a lowpass filter when it is set to cut high frequencies, and a *low shelving filter* acts like a highpass filter when it is set to cut low frequencies.

Modern plug-ins let one combine several filters to fine tune the spectrum. Figure 14.9 shows the FabFilter Pro-Q application with its graphical interface for creating filter curves superimposed on a spectral display of the input signal.

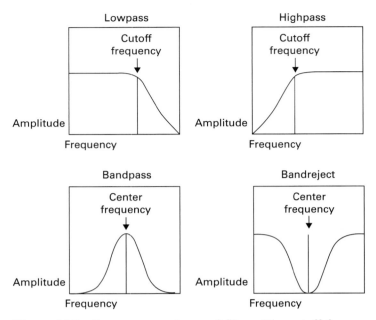

Figure 14.7   Four common types of filters. The cutoff frequency is the point at which the response diminishes. For a bandpass or bandreject filter, a common parameter is a center frequency around which a band of frequencies is affected.

An important property of a filter is its *cutoff frequency*. Figure 14.7 shows the cutoff frequency of lowpass and highpass filters. By convention, this is the point in the frequency range at which the filter reduces the signal to 0.707 of its maximum value. Why 0.707? The *power* of the signal at the cutoff frequency is proportional to the amplitude of the signal squared, because $0.707^2 = 0.5$. Thus, the cutoff frequency is also called the *half-power point*. Yet another term for the cutoff frequency is the *3 dB point* (Tempelaars 1977), so called because 0.707 relative to 1.0 is close to −3 dB.

Spectral components that are attenuated below the half-power point of a filter are said to be in the *stopband* of a filter. Those above the half-power point are said to be in the *passband* of the filter. The difference between the high and low cutoff frequencies in a bandpass filter is the *bandwidth* of the filter. The center frequency of a bandpass filter is the maximum point of amplitude; the center frequency of a bandreject filter is the minimum point of amplitude.

In an ideal sharp filter, the cutoff frequency is an absolute barrier: anything outside it is maximally attenuated, dividing the frequency response neatly into a passband and a stopband (figure 14.10a). In actual filters, the slope of the filter is not linear leading up to the cutoff frequency (there is

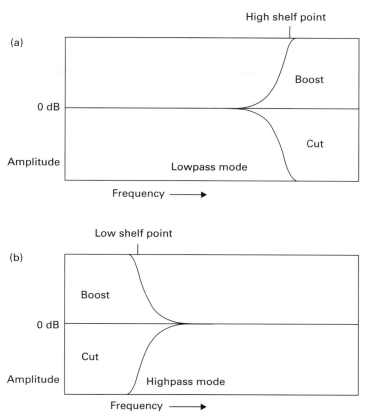

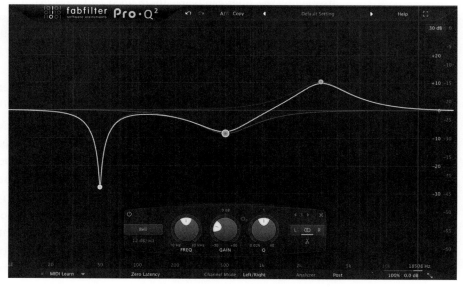

Figure 14.8 Shelving filters. (a) High shelving filter. Above the shelf point, the signal can be either boosted or cut. If the signal is cut, the effect of a high shelf filter is equivalent to a lowpass filter. (b) Low shelving filter. Below the shelf point, the signal can be either boosted or cut.

Figure 14.9 Screen image of FabFilter Pro-Q 2 with multiple filters superimposed.

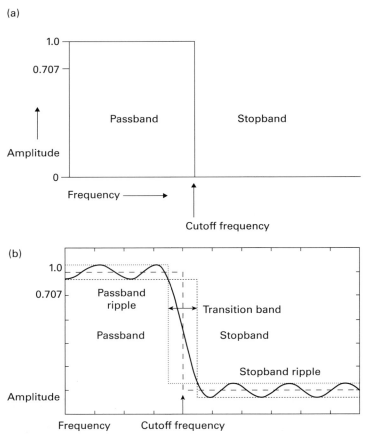

Figure 14.10   Ideal versus nonideal filters. (a) In an ideal filter, the frequencies affected by the filter can be neatly divided into a passband and a stopband, and the cutoff is rectangular. (b) In a nonideal (actual) filter, the response curve shows ripple, and there is a more or less steep transition band between the passband and the stopband.

a *ripple* in the frequency response), and the area between the passband and the stopband is called the *transition band* (figure 14.10b).

The steepness of a filter's slope is usually specified in terms of decibels of attenuation or boost per octave, compactly expressed dB/octave. For example, a 6 dB/octave slope on a lowpass filter makes a smooth attenuation (or *rolloff*), whereas a 24 dB/octave slope makes a sharp cutoff (figure 14.11).

A steep slope of 96 dB/octave is called a *brickwall* filter (figure 14.12). The use of a smooth or sharp slope depends on the musical situation. For example, a sharp notch filter might be needed to eliminate a tone centered on a particular frequency, whereas a gentle lowpass filter could be the most unobtrusive way of attenuating background noise in the high-frequency range.

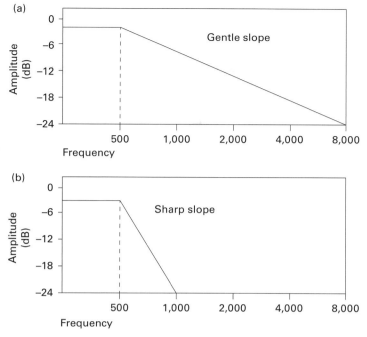

Figure 14.11   Filter slopes. (a) Gentle slope. (b) Steep slope.

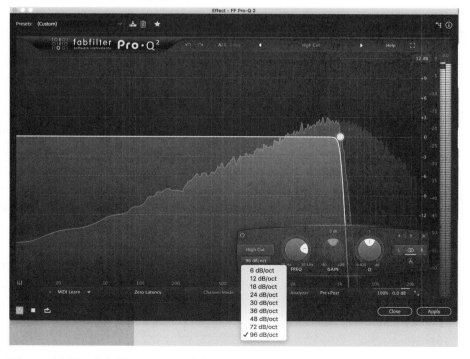

Figure 14.12   FabFilter Pro-Q 2 brickwall lowpass (or high cut) filter with a 96 dB/octave slope applied to a noise signal. The spectrum display shows before (darker) and after (lighter).

Filter Q and Gain

Many bandpass filters have a control knob for Q. An intuitive definition of Q is that it represents the degree of resonance within a bandpass filter. Figure 14.13 shows a filter adjusted to various values of Q. When the Q is high, as in the narrowest inner curve, the frequency response is sharply focused around a peak (resonant) frequency. If a high-Q filter is excited by a signal near its center frequency, the filter *rings* at the resonant frequency, that is, goes into oscillation, for some time after the signal has passed.

Q can be defined precisely for a bandpass filter as the ratio of the center frequency to the spread of its −3 dB point (cutoff point) bandwidth:

$$Q = \frac{center}{highcutoff - lowcutoff}$$

where *center* is the filter's center frequency, *highcutoff* is the upper 3 dB point, and *lowcutoff* is the lower 3 dB point. Notice that when the center frequency is constant, adjusting the Q is the same as adjusting the bandwidth. Here is an example of a calculation of the Q of a filter. We define a bandpass filter with a center frequency of 2,000 Hz and the 3 dB points of 1,800 and 2,200 Hz. This filter has a Q of $2,000/(2,200-1800)=5$. High-Q resonant filters like this are useful in generating percussive sounds. Tuned drums like tablas, wood blocks, claves, and marimba effects can be simulated by exciting a high-Q resonant filter with a pulse train.

Another property of a bandpass or bandreject filter is its *gain*. This is the amount of boost or cut of a frequency band. It shows up as the height (or depth) of the band in a response curve (figure 14.14). When passing a signal through a high-Q filter, care must be taken to ensure that the gain at the resonant frequency (the height at the peak) does not overload the system, causing distortion. Some systems have *gain-compensation* circuits in their filters that prevent this kind of overload.

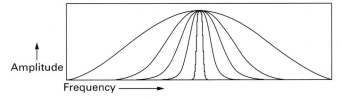

Figure 14.13   A filter set at various values for Q. A high Q corresponds to a narrow response. The gain (height of the peak) is constant.

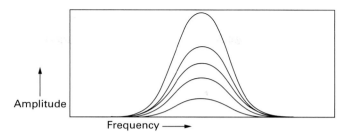

Figure 14.14   Different gain factors applied to the same filter. The bandwidth and Q remain constant.

A special type of bandpass filter is called a *constant Q filter.* To maintain a fixed Q, a constant Q filter must vary its bandwidth as a function of the center frequency. For example, when the center frequency is 30 Hz and the Q is 1.5 (or 3/2), the bandwidth is 20 Hz, because $30/20 = 1.5$. But if we tune the filter to 9 kHz and keep the Q constant at 1.5, then the bandwidth must be equal to 2/3 of the center frequency, or 6,000 Hz. Figure 14.15 shows the curve of two constant Q filters plotted on linear and logarithmic frequency ranges. On a linear scale (figure 14.15a), the filter centered at 30 Hz appears as a very narrow band, whereas the filter centered at 9 kHz appears to have a much broader curve. On a logarithmic scale, the filters have the same shape (figure 14.15b).

A constant-Q filter has the musical quality that the frequency interval it spans does not change as the center frequency changes. For example, a constant Q filter centered at A440 Hz with a Q of 1.222 spans the same musical interval as a filter with a Q of 1.222 centered at A880 Hz (C260 to D620, as compared with C520 to D1240, respectively). An example of a constant Q filter is a *third-octave filter bank,* which is commonly used in sound level meters (Liski and Välimäki 2017).

Phase Response and Latency in Filtering

Audio filtering involves a trade-off between *linear phase response* and *latency.* A filter with linear phase response means that all frequencies are shifted in time by the same constant amount, preserving the waveshape without phase distortion. This time shift or *group delay* is a source of *audio latency*—a delay between the input and the output. A *linear-phase filter* processes signals without phase distortion, but it can introduce a signifi-cant latency (from a few milliseconds to more than 500 ms in the worst

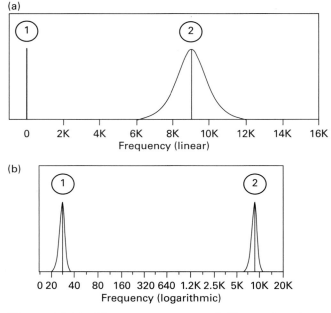

Figure 14.15   The same constant Q filters plotted on linear and logarithmic frequency ranges. Filter 1 has a center frequency of 30 Hz and extends from 20 to 40 Hz in bandwidth. Filter 2 has a center frequency of 9 KHz and extends from 6 to 12 KHz. (a) Linear. (b) Logarithmic.

case) in the sound. A linear-phase filter with a long latency can also introduce pre-echoes that can make low-frequency transients such as bass drums lose their percussive edge.

By contrast, *zero-latency filters* process signals efficiently and without delay, but they introduce *phase distortion*. This is a frequency-dependent time shift that can in some cases audibly blur the audio signal, particularly transients. Zero-latency filters are best used in live performance situations in which latency is unacceptable.

In the studio there is no fixed rule for choosing a linear phase versus a zero-latency filter; it is a matter of testing and listening.

Filter Banks and Graphic Equalizers

A *filter bank* is a group of filters that are fed the same signal in parallel (figure 14.16). The filter bank splits a sound into multiple frequency bands called *subbands* (Cook 2007). Each filter is typically a narrow bandpass filter centered around a specific frequency. The filtered signals are often

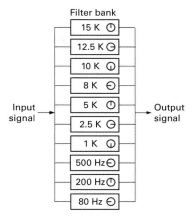

Figure 14.16   A ten-stage filter bank or spectrum shaper with a control knob (boost or attenuate) associated with each frequency band.

combined to form the output sound. When each filter has its own level control, the filter bank is called a *spectrum shaper* because the individual controls can radically modify the spectrum of the input signal. A spectrum shaper can be used to boost certain frequencies or virtually eliminate others.

A *graphic equalizer* (Liski and Välimäki 2017) is a spectrum shaper that has faders that visually mirror the shape of the filter bank's frequency response curve (figure 14.17a). Each filter has a fixed center frequency, a fixed bandwidth, and a fixed Q. (Some units can switch between several Q settings.) The response of each filter can be varied by means of a linear fader to cut or boost specific frequency bands. The potential frequency response of such a filter is shown in figure 14.17b.

A *parametric equalizer* involves a smaller number of filters, but the control of each filter is more flexible. A typical arrangement is to have three or four filters in parallel. Users can adjust independently the center frequency, the Q, and the amount of cut or boost of each filter. A *semiparametric equalizer* has a fixed Q.

Comb and Allpass Filters

Two more filter types merit mention here; they are discussed thoroughly in chapter 28. A filter that has several regularly spaced sharp curves in its frequency response is called a *comb filter*. Figure 14.18 shows the frequency response curves of two types of comb filters. The filter shown in

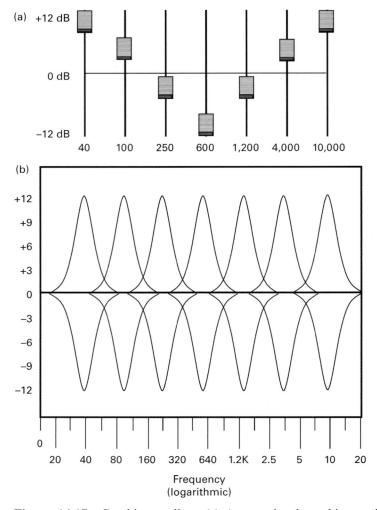

Figure 14.17 Graphic equalizer. (a) A seven-band graphic equalizer with linear potentiometers set to arbitrary levels. (b) The potential frequency response curve of a seven-band graphic equalizer.

figure 14.18a has deep notches in its response, whereas that shown in 14.18b has steep peaks. The derivation of the term *comb* should be clear from these curves.

Whereas low-, high-, band-, and notch filters are implemented with tiny time delays in the range of few microseconds, the delays for a comb filter range up to 10 ms. (See chapter 30 on delay effects.)

The sonic effect of a comb filter is distinct and recognizable. Comb filters can be used to make variations of a sound. For example, a snare drum hit passing through a comb filter will retain the identity of the drum but will

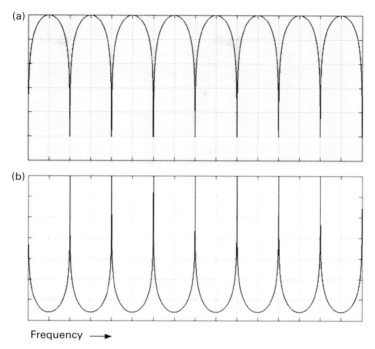

Figure 14.18   Comb filter frequency response curves. The vertical scale is amplitude, and the horizontal scale is frequency plotted linearly. This filter has peaks and troughs every 2,000 Hz. (a) Finite impulse response (FIR) comb. (b) Infinite impulse response (IIR) comb.

have a different timbre due to the comb spectral effect. By nudging the delay time slightly, one can make a variety of different snare drum hits. If we vary the delay time continuously the result is a dramatic *flanging* effect (see chapter 30).

The final filter to mention is an *allpass filter.* For a steady-state (unchanging) sound fed into it, an allpass filter passes all frequencies equally well with unity gain, hence its name. The purpose of an allpass filter is to introduce a frequency-dependent phase shift.

If the input signal varies in time (i.e., is not steady-state), the allpass filter colors the signal, due to frequency-dependent phase-shifting effects. This coloration can be subtle, but it is particularly evident on transient sounds (e.g., cymbals) for which phase relations are so important to sound quality.

A practical application of an allpass filter is to correct for the unwanted phase shift of another filter. A square wave with out-of-phase partials will not look like a square wave. An allpass filter can restore the square shape.

Allpass filters are one of the components of digital reverberators, specifically those based on Schroeder's model (see chapter 33). Allpass filters produce frequency-dependent time shifts. When delay times within the filter are in the range of about 1 to 30 milliseconds, a series of allpass sections vastly increases the echo density or *diffusion* of the reverberated sound. For this reason, allpass filters are sometimes referred to as *impulse diffusers* (Smith 2018).

Time-Varying Subtractive Synthesis

Filters can be *fixed* or *time-varying.* In a fixed filter, the properties of the filter are set and do not change over time. For example, in mixing a pop music track, most of the time the filter settings are tuned in a setup stage and left at a fixed position once the engineer has found the preferred sound color. In the context of mixing, filtering is often referred to as *EQ*. EQ stands for *equalization* and derives from one of the earliest applications of filters, namely, to compensate for irregularities in the frequency response of telephone channels and public address systems. In effect, the filter equalizes the amplitude of all frequencies (Fagen 1975).

In music synthesis, however, we want time-varying filters. Specifically, we want to vary the center or cutoff frequency, bandwidth, gain, and Q in real time. For example, a signature sound of the famous Moog synthesizer featured a sawtooth waveform processed by a high-Q lowpass filter (the Moog 904 filter module) with a sweeping sound as the cutoff frequency moved up and down. A bandpass filter whose Q, center frequency, and bandwidth change over time can impose an enormous variety of sound colorations, particularly if the signal being filtered is also time-varying.

An example of a time-varying filter is a parametric equalizer section in a digital audio workstation or DAW. The mixing engineer can change the Q, center frequency, and amount of cut or boost at any time during the mixing process, or these parameters can all be automated.

Implementing a time-varying filter in the digital domain requires interpolating the filter's internal parameters. As chapter 28 explains, designing an arbitrary time-varying filter is a nontrivial mathematical process, but contemporary filter design tools automate much of this burden.

SYTER and GRM Tools

A notable historical example of a system for time-varying subtractive synthesis was the SYTER audio processor developed in the late 1970s at the Groupe de Recherches Musicale (GRM) studio in Paris (Allouis 1979; Allouis and Bernier 1982; Geslin 2002). SYTER realized several dozen high-Q bandpass filters in real time with dynamic parameter changes. When full-bandwidth sounds such as water and wind were processed through the system, the resonant filters rang in musical chords and clusters. An outstanding example of the use of resonant filters is Jean-Claude Risset's 1985 composition *Sud,* using filter programs by B. Maillard and Y. Geslin. Rich comb filter and phasing effects could also be created. These algorithms have since been ported to the GRM Tools software plug-in package (INA/GRM 2019).

Subtractive Analysis/Resynthesis

As with additive synthesis, the power of subtractive synthesis is enhanced by an initial sound analysis stage. This combination is called *analysis/resynthesis* or just analysis/synthesis. Most of the analysis techniques employed in subtractive analysis/resynthesis are geared toward speech synthesis, because this is where most of research has been concentrated (Flanagan et al. 1970; Flanagan 1972).

Music research using subtractive analysis/resynthesis has focused on extending speech-oriented tools (such as linear predictive coding, discussed subsequently in this chapter), to the domain of musical sound, such as singing and simulation of string ensembles.

The Vocoder

The original subtractive analysis/resynthesis system is the *vocoder* (also called *channel vocoder*) demonstrated by a talking robot at the 1936 World's Fair in New York City (Dudley 1936, 1939a, 1939b, 1955; Dudley and Watkins 1939; Schroeder 1966; Flanagan 1972; Cook 2007; Puckette 2007; Arfib et al. 2011a). We present a different system known as the *phase vocoder* in chapter 37.

A classic analog vocoder consists of two stages. The first stage is a group of fixed-frequency bandpass filters distributed over the audio bandwidth. The output of each filter is connected to an *envelope detector* that generates a voltage proportional to the amount of energy at the frequency tracked by the filter (figure 14.19). The second stage of the vocoder is a bank of bandpass filters, identical to the first stage. All filters are sent the same input signal, and the output of each filter is sent to its own *voltage-controlled amplifier* (VCA). The outputs of all the VCAs combine into an output signal. The filters and detectors in the first stage generate control signals (also called *driving functions*) that determine the amplitude of the audio signal coming from the filters in the second stage of the vocoder. Today vocoders are also implemented with digital technology (Cook 2007). Arfib et al. (2011a) provide code in MATLAB.

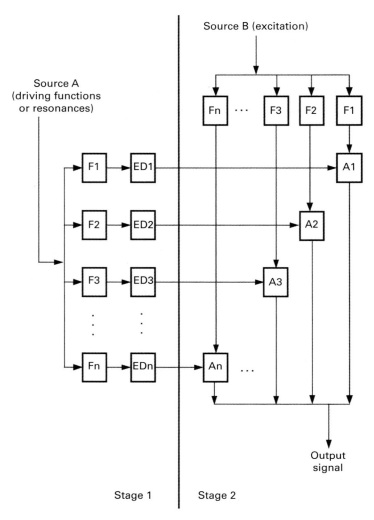

Figure 14.19   Vocoder. Stage 1 is the analysis part, and stage 2 is the synthesis. *F* stands for filter, *ED* stands for envelope detector, and *A* stands for voltage-controlled amplifier—an amplifier whose gain is determined by a control voltage fed into it from the envelope detector. The same structure can also be realized in digital form.

In figure 14.19, source A is the signal from which the formant spectrum is derived, such as a singing voice. If we were to trace an outline of this spectrum it would form the *spectrum envelope*. Source B is the *excitation function* from which the pitch is derived. The excitation function is usually a wide-bandwidth signal such as white noise or a pulse train. The output of this vocoder consists of the excitation function of source B with the time-varying spectral envelope of the singing voice of source A.

Figure 14.20 depicts graphically the process of formant filtering applied to a broadband excitation function.

In musical applications, the separation of the control signals from the excitation signal means that rhythm, pitch, and timbre are independently controllable. For example, a composer can change the pitch of a singing voice (by changing the frequency of the excitation) but retain the original spectral articulation of the voice. By stretching or shrinking the control functions over time, a piece of spoken text can be slowed down or sped up without shifting the pitch or affecting the formant structure. Another common effect is to impose the spectral shape of one sound on another: *cross-synthesis*. The classic example is a *talking orchestra* effect in which the voice provides the driving functions and the orchestra (or a keyboard synthesizer playing chords) is the excitation. Some vocoders have a highpass filter *sibilance band* that passes consonant sounds directly to the output, making for a more intelligible speech effect.

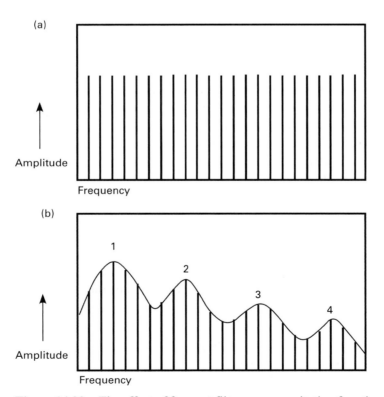

Figure 14.20   The effect of formant filters on an excitation function. (a) Simplified view of an excitation function like the spectrum produced by the open vocal cords; a buzz sound with a number of equal-strength harmonics. (b) Simplified view of the spectrum of a vowel showing four formant peaks labeled 1, 2, 3, and 4.

Linear Predictive Coding

Linear predictive coding (LPC) or *linear prediction* is a subtractive analysis/ resynthesis method that has been used in speech and music applications (Atal and Hanauer 1971; Flanagan 1972; Makhoul 1975; Markel and Gray 1976; Cann 1978, 1979–80; Moorer 1977, 1979c; Dodge 1985; Lansky 1987; Lansky and Steiglitz 1981; Hutchins 1986a; Dodge 1989; Depalle 1991; Arfib et al. 2011a). Bishnu Atal, one of the inventors of LPC, wrote a history of the technique (Atal 2006). LPC can be viewed as a type of vocoder. Unlike the previously described vocoder with its fixed frequency bands, LPC's filters are more flexible.

LPC takes in a sound, such as a speaking voice, analyzes it into a greatly data-reduced form, and resynthesizes an approximation of it. LPC is computationally efficient in the sense that it requires much less data than sampled sound. For example, an integrated circuit for LPC speech was developed and built into speaking toys (Brightman and Crook 1982). From the standpoint of a musician, the power of the LPC technique derives from the fact that one can edit the analysis data and resynthesize variations on the original input signal. Like any vocoder, LPC separates the excitation signal from the resonance or spectrum envelope, making it possible to manipulate rhythm, pitch, and timbre independently and permitting a form of cross-synthesis, explained further on.

The Csound language supports LPC analysis and synthesis (Boulanger 2000), as does MATLAB. The SonicCharge Bitspeek plugin automatically analyzes an input sound such as voice and lets one adjust eight LPC playback parameters in real time using switches and knobs onscreen (figure 14.21).

In speech, the vocal cords generate a buzzy pulsatile excitation waveform. These pitched tones are called *voiced* sounds, such as *ah* and *oh*. *Unvoiced* breaths (with vocal cords silent) produce consonant sounds like *s*, *f*, *t*, and *p*. The rest of the vocal tract filters the sound to create resonances. Because LPC lets users manipulate the excitation independently, one can vary the pitch to transform a talking voice into a singing voice, for example, as the composer Charles Dodge did in his iconic *Speech Songs* (1973).

What Is Linear Prediction?

Linear prediction derives its obscure name from the fact that in the analysis part of the system, output samples are predicted by a linear combination of internal filter parameters or *coefficients* and previous samples. In predicting the next sample, the system already knows the correct result, which comes

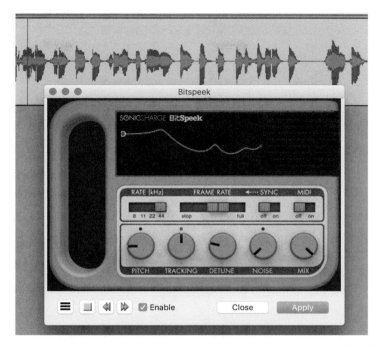

Figure 14.21   BitSpeek plug-in for LPC analysis/resynthesis. The user interface resembles the Speak & Spell toy made by Texas Instruments.

from the input signal. The goal of the analysis is to replace the input signal with a compact LPC model of it. From a musical standpoint, this compact model breaks the input signal into a handful of parameters that enable transformations of pitch, amplitude, duration, and timbre.

A *linear prediction algorithm* based on a difference equation tries to find samples at positions after a region from which one already has samples. Any extrapolation of a set of samples is prediction. Inherent in prediction is the possibility of being wrong; thus prediction algorithms always include an error estimation.

A simple predictor simply continues the slope of difference between the last sample and the sample before it. A simple predictor can be made more sophisticated by taking more samples into account. It can also factor in the error or difference between the sample it predicts and the known value of the input signal.

A key concept to understand is that because the predictor is looking at sums and differences of time-delayed samples in doing its prediction, it can be viewed as a filter that describes the waveform that it is currently processing. We will not go into the prediction algorithm here. Loy (2007) gives a detailed and musically informed description. Also refer to Arfib et al. (2011a).

If we take regular snapshots of these filter coefficients over time, invert them, and then drive the resulting filter with a rich, wide-bandwidth sound, we should have a good approximation of the time-varying spectrum of the original input signal. Thus a side effect of the prediction is to estimate the spectrum of the input signal; this is an important point. However, spectrum estimation is only one stage of LPC analysis. Pitch, amplitude, and the voiced/unvoiced decision are also analyzed. These are briefly described in the next section.

LPC Analysis

Figure 14.22 shows an overview of LPC analysis. LPC analysis branches in the following four directions:

1. Spectrum analysis in terms of formants
2. Pitch analysis
3. Amplitude analysis
4. Decision as to whether the sound was voiced (pitched, like *ah*) or unvoiced (characteristic of noisy consonants like *sh*).

Each stage of analysis is carried out on a frame-by-frame basis, where a frame is like a snapshot of the signal. Frame rates between 50 and 200 frames per second are typical in LPC analysis.

Filter estimation

The next several paragraphs describe the operation of LPC analysis in general terms. First let us state a point about filter terminology used in LPC analysis. Engineers describe bandpass and bandreject filters in terms of the position of their *poles* and *zeros*. Without going into the details of *pole-zero diagrams,* let us just say that a filter pole is a point of resonance—a peak or formant region in a spectrum plot. In contrast, a zero is a null point or notch in the spectrum. (Chapter 28 introduces pole-zero diagrams.) For more on pole-zero diagrams in filter design, refer to Puckette [2007], Loy [2007], and Smith [2007a].)

If a filter has several smooth peaks it is called an *allpole filter.* This type of filter is characteristic of LPC, which models spectra in terms of several formant peaks. Such a model is a reasonable approximation to many sounds uttered by the human voice and certain musical instruments.

Linear prediction—also called *autoregressive* analysis—takes in several input samples at a time, using the most recent sample as a reference. It tries

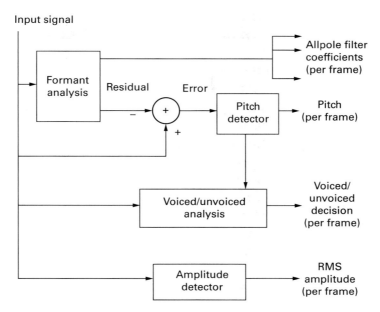

Figure 14.22   Four stages of LPC analysis. Spectrum (formant) analysis, pitch detection, amplitude detection, and voiced/unvoiced analysis.

to predict this sample from a weighted sum of filter coefficients and past samples. As a side effect of this prediction, the algorithm fits an inverse filter to the spectrum of the input signal. The inverse of an allpole filter is an *allzero filter* that creates a number of notches in the spectrum of signals sent through it.

The LPC analyzer approximates the inverse of the filter that one ultimately wants for synthesis. If the approximation is good, the result of linear prediction should be just the excitation signal (figure 14.23). In other words, the inverse filter cancels the effect of the spectrum envelope of the sound. The approximation is never perfect, so there is always a signal called the *residual* that is the excitation function (a series of impulses) plus noise. The goal of LPC spectrum analysis is to minimize the residual.

Once a good fit to the inverse filter has been found, the inverse filter is itself inverted to create a resynthesis filter. Filter inversion is mathematically straightforward. The sign of all the filter coefficients is reversed, and they are applied to past outputs instead of to past inputs (Rabiner and Gold 1975). The filter is thus converted from a FIR filter to an IIR filter (see chapter 28). For an engineering description, refer to Markel (1972), Makhoul (1975), Moore (1990), and Smith (2007a).

The reader may wonder, how does LPC know what is the excitation function of an arbitrary sound put into it? The answer is that it assumes that the

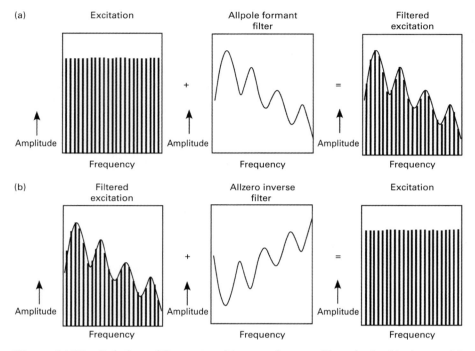

Figure 14.23   Relation of formant and inverse formant filters in the ideal case. (a) Result of formant filter. (b) Result of inverse formant filter.

excitation is either a pitched pulse train or white noise. This assumption works reasonably well in approximating speech and some instruments, but it is not a universal model for all sounds. Thus LPC usually leaves traces of artificiality in the resynthesized sounds.

Improved methods of LPC analysis create a custom pulse train that mixes pitched pulses and noise from segments stored in a codebook or dictionary. This method, called *code-excited linear prediction,* generates a unique excitation signal from analysis of the input signal. It tries to match segments of the input with segments stored in its codebook (Schroeder and Atal 1985). This reduces the artificial quality of LPC resynthesis.

Pitch and amplitude analysis

The pitch detection technique used in LPC can be any of the methods described in chapter 34. Figure 14.22 shows a scheme that tries to estimate the pitch from the residual signal.

Several techniques exist for characterizing the amplitude of each frame. A typical way is to calculate it on a frame-by-frame basis as an average value for the input waveform described by the frame.

Voiced/unvoiced decision

After pitch detection has been carried out, LPC analysis tries to make the voiced/unvoiced decision for each frame. This decision is important because it determines whether the sound will be pitched or not. As previously mentioned, a voiced sound has a pitch, like the vowels created by the buzzing of the vocal cords. An unvoiced sound is like the sibilance of *s* and *sh*, the plosive *t* and *p*, or the fricative *f* consonants. Besides voiced or unvoiced, a third category of excitation is *mixed voice*, combining a pitched tone and noise, like the *z* in *azure*.

In analyzing a wind instrument tone, the voiced/unvoiced data usually indicate the amount of breathiness, and for a violin-like sound they can indicate bow-scraping noise. In resynthesis, voiced sounds are modeled by a pitched pulse train and unvoiced sounds are modeled by white noise. Both are filtered, of course.

The voiced/unvoiced decision is typically based on statistical estimate using various features of the signal. It is hard to fully automate (Hermes 1992). In LPC systems that have been adapted for music, the analysis makes a first pass at the decision, but the composer is expected to make corrections to particular frames (Moorer 1979). The first-pass decision uses various heuristics. Figure 14.22 shows the result of pitch detection feeding into the voiced/unvoiced decision. For example, if the analysis cannot identify a pitch in the input signal, then it generates a large pitch estimation error. When this error—normalized to fall between 0 and 1.0—is greater than a certain value (around 0.2), it is likely that the sound at that moment is a noisy unvoiced sound like a consonant. The average amplitude of the residual is another clue. If the amplitude of the residual is low in comparison to the amplitude of the original input signal, then the signal is probably voiced.

Analysis frames

The result of the analysis stage is a series of frames, representing a greatly data-reduced version of the input signal. Each frame is described by a list of parameters, including the following:

Average amplitude of the residual sound (RMS1)

Average amplitude of the original sound (RMS2)

Ratio of the two amplitudes, which helps to determine whether the frame is voiced or unvoiced (ERR)

Estimated pitch (PITCH)

Frame duration (DUR)

Coefficients for the allpole filter (each pole creates a formant peak in the spectrum).

Figure 14.24 shows an example of the frame data for the word *sit* (Dodge 1985). The filter coefficients are omitted.

The ERR column is a strong clue to whether the frame is voiced or not. A large value for ERR (greater than 0.2) usually indicates an unvoiced frame. However, as mentioned previously, this indicator should be checked because a voiced/unvoiced decision is hard to automate perfectly. Notice how the ERR values change significantly at the boundary of S and I. The RMS1 and RMS2 values are a better indicator of change at the boundary of I and T.

LPC Synthesis

Figure 14.25 depicts the synthesis stage of LPC. The first parameter is the frame duration–the number of output samples generated. The next parameter determines whether the frame is voiced or unvoiced. For voiced frames, the synthesizer uses the pitch parameter to simulate the excitation function (the glottal wave) of the human voice. This is a buzzy bandlimited pulse train used for vowels and diphthongs. (A diphthong is a sequence of vowels such as the *oy* in *toy*.) For unvoiced frames, the synthesizer uses a noise generator to simulate turbulence in the vocal tract.

The output of the appropriate generator, shaped by the amplitude parameter, serves as input to the allpole filter. For speech and singing, the allpole filter simulates the resonances of the vocal tract. Up to twelve poles in the allpole filter are used in speech synthesis, and as many as 250 poles have been used in music synthesis (Moorer 2019).

Editing LPC Frame Data

The LPC technique can be adapted to musical purposes by means of an associated editing and mixing subsystem. Charles Dodge (1985) described an editing command language that performs operations on LPC parameter frames such as the following:

Set the pitch of a frame

Trill on every other frame

Stretch or shrink the duration of a frame

Stretch or shrink the duration of a group of frames

Change parameter values in a frame

Phoneme	Frame	RMS2	RMS1	ERR	PITCH	DUR
S	197	813.27	1618.21	0.252	937.50	0.010
	198	1189.36	2090.14	0.323	937.50	0.010
	199	553.71	838.38	0.436	937.50	0.010
	200	742.59	1183.17	0.393	937.50	0.010
	201	1041.95	1918.33	0.295	123.95	0.010
	202	1449.16	2677.06	0.293	123.95	0.010
	203	1454.84	2920.50	0.248	937.50	0.010
	204	1430.03	2496.88	0.348	937.50	0.010
	205	1570.88	2981.21	0.277	142.84	0.010
	206	1443.27	2665.22	0.293	142.84	0.010
	207	1172.67	2150.50	0.297	150.00	0.010
	208	1200.73	2080.20	0.333	150.00	0.010
	209	1095.51	2055.25	0.284	116.26	0.010
	210	1260.36	2408.14	0.273	116.26	0.010
	211	1105.17	2293.05	0.232	937.50	0.010
	212	809.10	1659.80	0.237	937.50	0.010
	213	428.20	784.93	0.297	250.00	0.010
I	214	419.45	3886.15	0.011	250.00	0.010
	215	925.86	6366.20	0.021	208.32	0.010
	216	746.28	8046.81	0.008	208.32	0.010
	217	829.82	8277.42	0.010	192.29	0.010
	218	754.64	8049.50	0.008	192.29	0.010
	219	771.84	8001.70	0.009	197.35	0.010
	220	726.81	7955.17	0.008	202.69	0.010
	221	807.63	7835.20	0.010	202.69	0.010
	222	874.27	7732.59	0.012	205.42	0.010
	223	776.87	7491.86	0.010	205.42	0.010
	224	684.64	7317.04	0.008	205.42	0.010
	225	560.87	6297.36	0.007	102.03	0.010
	226	175.63	1842.81	0.009	102.03	0.010
	227	46.53	1329.09	0.001	197.85	0.010
T	228	38.25	793.00	0.002	197.85	0.010
	229	39.26	316.92	0.032	202.69	0.010

Figure 14.24   A sequence of LPC frames as they might be displayed for editing purposes (after Dodge [1985]). The Phoneme column is added for clarity. The RMS2 column indicates the residual amplitude, RMS1 is the original signal amplitude. ERR is an approximation to the ratio between the two and indicates an unvoiced signal if the ratio is high. PITCH is the estimated pitch in Hz, and DUR is the frame duration in seconds.

Interpolate values between a group of frames (e.g., create a pitch glissando)

Move frames from point A to point B

Boost or diminish the amplitude of a frame

Boost or diminish the amplitude of a group of frames (crescendo/diminuendo)

One of the main applications of these operations on LPC frames is to transform a plain spoken utterance into singing. Using LPC, a word can be expanded in time, and the original spoken pitch curve can be replaced with a flowing melody. Words and phrases can be repeated or rearranged at will. Sentences can also be compressed in time without affecting their original pitch.

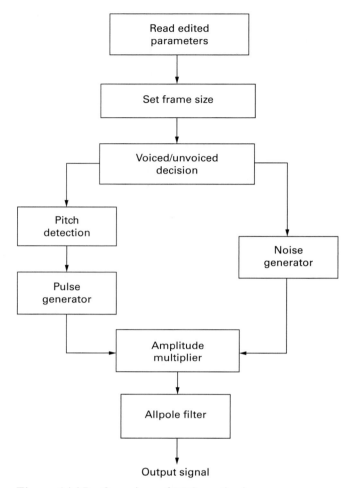

Figure 14.25 Overview of LPC synthesis.

Composers such as Charles Dodge, Paul Lansky, and James A. Moorer have used LPC to achieve all these effects. Examples include Dodge's *Speech Songs* (1973), Lansky's *Six Fantasies on a Poem by Thomas Campion* (1979), and *The Man in the Mangrove Counts to Sleep* (2019) by James A. Moorer.

Cross-Synthesis: A Musical Extension of LPC

LPC can implement a form of cross-synthesis (Mathews, Miller, and David 1961; Petersen 1975; Moorer 1979c; Arfib et al. 2011a). Cross-synthesis refers to techniques that start from an analysis of two sounds and use the characteristics of one sound to modify the characteristics of another sound, often involving a spectrum transformation. LPC cross-synthesis takes the excitation from one source sound (pitch and event timing) to drive the time-varying spectral envelope derived from another source. For example, one can replace the simple pulse train (used for voiced speech) by a complex waveform such as the sound of an orchestra. Because the time-varying spectrum envelope of the original speech remains the same, the resulting effect is that of a "talking orchestra." Figure 14.26 is essentially the same as the vocoder in figure 14.19, except that the simple excitation function normally used in a vocoder is replaced by a wideband musical source (source B) and the internal method of analysis/resynthesis uses the LPC method.

When the desired effect is to make source B "talk," the intelligibility of the speech can be enhanced by using wide-bandwidth sources such as a full orchestra and chorus—as opposed to a narrow-bandwidth source such as a solo violin. If necessary, the excitation function can also be *whitened* to bring all spectral components up to a uniform level (Moorer 1979c; Arfib et al. 2011a).

Another extension of LPC synthesis extrapolates the filter response of a single instrument into a family of like instruments. For example, starting with an analysis of a violin, one can clone a viola, cello, and double bass to make up a string quartet (Lansky and Steiglitz 1981; Moorer 1981b, 1983a). These filter transformations can, in theory, be extended to emulate any instrument's resonances. In Lansky's music, this method called *warped linear prediction* was used to synthesize electronic versions of strings, saxophones, and harmonicas (e.g., *Guy's Harp* [1983]).

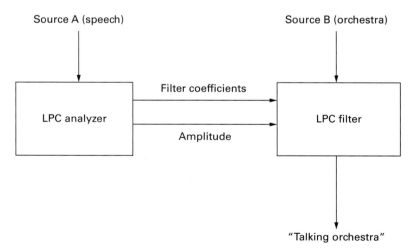

Figure 14.26 LPC cross-synthesis takes the spectral envelope from one sound and maps it onto another sound.

WaveGAN

As a final example of subtractive synthesis we mention experimental research using machine learning techniques, specifically *generative adversarial networks* (GANs). WaveGAN is a project for *adversarial audio synthesis* (Donahue, MacAuley, and Puckette 2019). This involves a neural network that filters a random input (e.g., white Gaussian noise) into a waveform that fools a *discriminator* into deciding that it is real sound, e.g., a fragment of speech. A discriminator in a GAN is simply a classifier. It tries to distinguish real data from data created by the generator using random input.

The WaveGAN algorithm learns to synthesize waveform audio by analyzing many examples of real audio. Its filters learn to reject frequencies corresponding to noise created by a generative procedure. WaveGAN is capable of learning to generate up to four seconds of audio at a 16 kHz sampling rate. It has been tested on words of speech, bird calls, drum hits, and fragments of piano music. (The code in Python and TensorFlow is available at https://github.com/chrisdonahue/wavegan.)

15 *Modulation I: RM, SSM, and AM*

Bipolar and Unipolar Signals

Ring Modulation

Negative Frequencies
Applications of RM
Analog Ring Modulation

Single-Sideband Modulation or Frequency-Shifting

Amplitude Modulation

AM Instruments
Modulation Index
Feedback AM

Modulation is one of the most powerful forces in electronic music. Modulation means that a sound A varies because of the action of *modulation signal* B. The modulation signal is typically an oscillator or a noise generator, but in practice it can be any signal.

On a modular synthesizer, modulation is often implemented by patching the output of one module to the modulation input of another (figure 15.1).

Not having patch cords, many digital synthesizers incorporate a *modulation matrix,* an important concept in electronic sound synthesis. The modulation matrix shows a mapping between a set of modulation sources and the parameters to which they apply. In the modulation matrix shown in figure 15.2, the modulation sources are displayed as columns, and the parameters being modulated are displayed as rows. In the figure, a low-frequency noise source LFNO modulates oscillator frequency, and a low-frequency oscillator LFO3 modulates filter center frequency. LFO1 modulates amplitude, and LFO2 modulates the pan position. A fader or knob (not shown) associated with each connection determines the amount of modulation.

In formal terms, modulation means that some aspect of one signal (the *carrier* C) varies according to an aspect of a second signal (the *modulator* M). When the modulator is in the low frequency range below 20 Hz, we hear

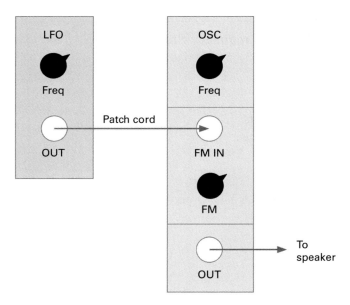

Figure 15.1 Patching the output of a low-frequency oscillator (LFO) to the frequency modulation (FM) input of an oscillator. The white circles are jacks where patch cords can be inserted. The black FM knob determines the amount of modulation.

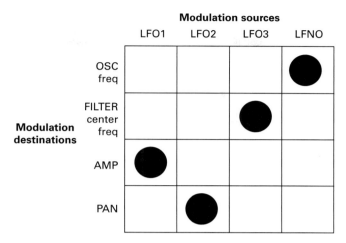

Figure 15.2　Modulation matrix.

the familiar undulations known as *tremolo* (slow amplitude variation) and *vibrato* (slow frequency variation). The carrier is often a pitched tone and the modulator is a slow-varying function in the range 6 to 9 Hz.

Another kind of modulation is musically effective at about twice this frequency. In the acoustical world, we hear this effect in *flutter tongue* flute technique. At the right moment and at the right speed, tremolo and vibrato charge tones with the ineffable feeling of expressivity.

When the frequency of modulation rises into the audio bandwidth (above 20 Hz or so), audible *modulation products* or *sidebands* begin to appear. These are new audible frequencies added to the spectrum of the carrier (typically on either side of the carrier). A technique like frequency modulation can generate a wide range of complex spectra using little computation (chapter 16). Because simple modulation techniques have fewer parameters than additive or subtractive techniques, musicians may find them easier to manipulate. Carefully adjusted modulations generate rich dynamic sounds that can approximate instrumental and even vocal tones. One can also use modulations in a nonimitative way to venture into the universe of unclassified synthetic sounds.

The types of modulations covered in this chapter, *amplitude* (AM), *ring* (RM), and *single-sideband modulation* (SSM), are staples of electronic music. They have a long history due to their applications in radio communications (Black 1953; Nahin 1996). With sinusoidal inputs in the audio band, they generate classic radiosonic sounds, similar to those heard when one adjusts the tuning dial of an analog radio. We can also modulate sampled sounds such as piano and percussion to generate a multitude of interesting variations. The next

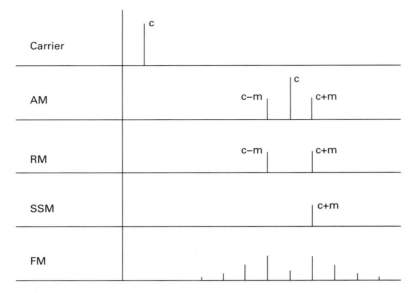

Figure 15.3 Comparison of modulation spectra. Amplitude is the vertical axis and frequency is the horizontal axis. Modulation at audio rates shifts an input signal called the carrier (*c*). Here it is a single sine wave. When *c* is amplitude modulated (AM) this results in *c* being surrounded by the sum and difference of the carrier and the modulating frequencies. In ring modulation (RM) the carrier is suppressed. Single sideband modulation (SSM) results in either sum or difference frequencies, depending on the user's choice. Here we see the sum only. Finally, frequency modulation or FM produces a series of sum and difference frequencies spread out over the spectrum.

chapter deals with frequency modulation (FM). Figure 15.3 is a pictorial comparison of the typical spectra that each type of modulation produces.

A limitation in all modulation techniques is inherent in the modulation formulas. The spectra of sounds generated by these techniques are constrained by mathematical law to fixed kinds of behavior. In practice, this means that each type of modulation has a characteristic sonic signature that can be discerned after a period of exposure to the technique. Depending on the skill of the composer, this signature can either be an annoying cliché or an alluring musical force. In the latter category, Louis and Bebe Barron's electronic music soundtrack to the science-fiction film *Forbidden Planet* (1956) stands as an outstanding example of musical use of modulation. In the future, more elaborate synthesis techniques will be developed, but there will always remain something deeply evocative about artful modulation.

In this tutorial on modulation, we use a minimum of mathematics combined with a liberal dose of instrument diagrams or patches. These diagrams depict synthesis instruments as a configuration of elementary signal-processing unit generators. (See chapter 5 for an introduction to unit generators.)

A special case of modulation occurs when the modulator is a complex noise (see chapter 25).

Bipolar and Unipolar Signals

Two closely related classic modulation effects are ring modulation (RM) and amplitude modulation (AM) (Black 1953). In order to understand the difference between them, it is important to know the different types of signals that they process: *bipolar* and *unipolar.* A bipolar signal is typical of most audio waveforms, in that it has both a negative and a positive excursion around zero when we look at it in the time domain (figure 15.4a). By contrast, the excursions of a unipolar signal remain within one-half of the full range of the system (figure 15.4b). One way to think of a unipolar signal is that it is a bipolar signal to which a constant has been added. This constant shifts all the sample values to the range above zero. Another term for such a constant

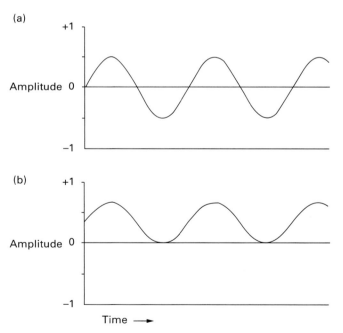

Figure 15.4   Bipolar versus unipolar sine waves. (a) Bipolar sine varies between −1 and 1. (b) Unipolar sine varies between 0 and 1.

is *direct current* (DC) *offset*—a signal at a frequency of 0 Hz. A DC offset is a quasiconstant. It may drift in value over time, but does not repeat periodically.

The unipolar/bipolar distinction is important because the fundamental difference between RM and AM is the following: RM modulates two bipolar signals, and AM modulates a bipolar signal with a unipolar signal.

A standard envelope is generally a positive unipolar signal. However, an *attenuverter* (found in modular synthesizers in both hardware and software) can attenuate and invert the phase of any signal fed into it, including envelopes. If the envelope is controlling pitch, for example, an attenuverter can make a positive envelope go negative so that instead of the pitch going up it goes down.

Ring Modulation

Ring modulation is a trademark sound of electronic music. It is usually used to transform a sound, such as a sampled sound. It has proven effective when applied to piano, drum, and guitar sounds, for example. Taking a snare drum hit, one can make a dozen variations by changing the modulation frequency slightly.

In digital systems, RM is simply the multiplication of two bipolar audio signals by one another. That is, a carrier signal C is multiplied by a modulator signal M. M is classically a sine wave. The formula for determining the value of a simple ring-modulated signal *RingMod* at time t is a straightforward multiplication:

$RingMod_t = C_t \times M_t$

Figure 15.5 portrays two equivalent implementations of an RM instrument. In figure 15.5a it is assumed that the carrier oscillator multiplies the value it reads from the wavetable lookup by the value it takes in from its amplitude input. In figure 15.5b this multiplication is made more explicit. In both cases, the modulator and the carrier vary between −1 and +1; hence they are bipolar.

When the frequency of the modulator M is below 20 Hz, the effect of ring modulation is that the amplitude of C varies at the frequency of M. This is a highly useful tremolo effect. However, when the frequency of M moves up into the audible range, the timbre of C changes. For each sinusoidal component in the carrier, the modulator contributes a pair of *sidebands* to the final spectrum. Given two sine waves as input, RM generates a spectrum

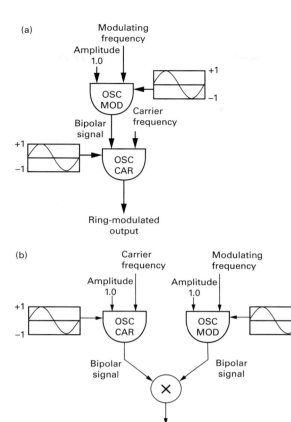

Figure 15.5   Two equivalent implementations of ring modulation or bipolar signal multiplication. The box to the side of each oscillator is its waveform. The top left input of each oscillator is the amplitude, and the top right input is the frequency. (a) RM by implicit multiplication within the carrier oscillator. (b) RM by explicit multiplication of the carrier and the modulator signals.

that contains two sidebands. These sidebands are the sum and the difference of the frequencies C and M. If C and M are in an integer ratio to one another, then the sidebands generated by RM are harmonic; otherwise they are inharmonic. Curiously, the carrier frequency itself disappears.

The sidebands in signal multiplication derive from a standard trigonometric identity:

$$\cos(C) \times \cos(M) = 0.5 \times [\cos(C - M) + \cos(C + M)]$$

Yet another way to understand ring modulation is to consider it as a case of *convolution,* as explained in chapter 29.

To give an example of RM, assume that *C* is a 1,000 Hz sine wave and M is a 400 Hz sine wave. As figure 15.6 shows, their RM spectrum contains components at 1,400 Hz (the sum of *C* and *M*) and 600 Hz (the difference between *C* and *M*).

We can picture this effect at lower frequencies. Figure 15.7 shows the effect of ring modulating (a) carrier of 1 Hz by a modulator (b) of 4 Hz. The result is shown in (c). The component frequencies in (c) are the difference −3 Hz and the sum 5, hence the division into 3 and 5 parts, which is shown graphically in the waveform.

The phases of the output signal components are also the sum and difference of the phases of the two inputs. If *C* and *M* are more complex signals than sine waves or if their frequency changes in time, the resulting output spectrum contains many sum and difference frequencies. A spectral plot would show many lines, indicating a complicated spectrum.

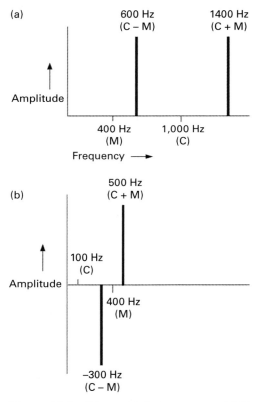

Figure 15.6   Ring modulation spectra. (a) For a carrier of 1,000 Hz and a modulator of 400 Hz, the sum and difference frequencies are 1,400 and 600 Hz, respectively. (b) For a carrier of 100 Hz and a modulator of 400 Hz, the sum and difference frequencies are 500 and −300 Hz, respectively.

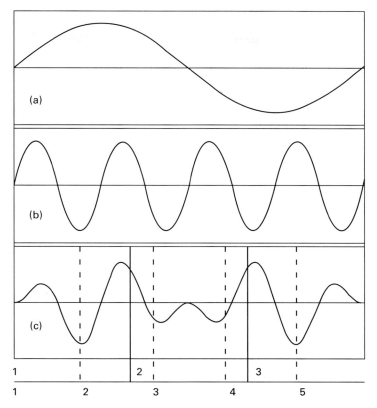

Figure 15.7   Ring modulation waveforms over a 1 s time frame. (a) 1 Hz. (b) 4 Hz. (c) Ring modulation of (a) and (b). The component frequencies in (c) include the difference −3 Hz and the sum +5 Hz, indicated by the division of the waveform into three and five parts (solid line and dashed line, respectively) below.

Negative Frequencies

As figure 15.4b shows, when the modulating frequency is higher than the carrier frequency, *negative frequencies* occur, as in the case of $C = 100$ Hz and $M = 400$ Hz, because $C + M = 500$ whereas $C - M = -300$. In spectral plots, a negative frequency can be shown as a line extending down from the x-axis. The change in sign merely inverts the sign of the phase of the signal. When the sign changes, the waveform flips over the zero or x-axis. Phase is important only in summing components of identical frequencies because out-of-phase components can attenuate or cancel in-phase components.

Applications of RM

Typical musical use of RM involves the modification of sampled carrier signals by sine wave modulators. The German composer Karlheinz Stockhausen was especially fond of ring modulation; he used it in a number of pieces composed in the 1960s, including *Kontake, Mikrophonie I* and *II, Telemusik, Mixtur, Hymnen, Prozession, Kurzwellen,* and *Mantra* (Stockhausen 1968, 1971b). He applied RM to microphone-recorded sounds like percussion and piano.

Another strategy is to create families of pure synthetic sounds starting from sine waves in either harmonic or inharmonic ratios. This is the approach taken by composer James Dashow in pieces such as *Sequence Symbols* (Dashow 1987).

Analog Ring Modulation

Digital ring modulation is bipolar signal multiplication. Basic digital RM should always sound the same. In contrast, analog RM circuits have different characters, depending on the exact circuit and components used. The reason is that implementations of analog RM approximate pure multiplication with a four-diode circuit arranged in a circular ring configuration. Depending on the type of diodes (silicon or germanium) these circuits introduce extraneous frequencies (Bode 1967, 1984; Stockhausen 1968; Duesenberry 1990; Strange 1983; Wells 1981). For example, in an analog ring modulator based on silicon diodes, the diodes in the circuit clip the carrier (turning it into a quasi–square wave) when it reaches the momentary level of the modulator. This creates the effect of several sums and differences on odd harmonics of the carrier, of the form

$$C + M, \; C - M, \; 3C + M, \; 3C - M, \; 5C + M, \; 5C - M, \ldots$$

Figure 15.8 compares the waveforms emitted by multiplying RM and diode-clipping RM.

Single-Sideband Modulation or Frequency-Shifting

Inventor Harald Bode was a pioneer of analog ring modulation. He also implemented an early variation on RM that he called *frequency shifting* (Ussachevsky 1958; Bode 1967, 1972, 1984; Bode and Moog 1972). A frequency shifter adds a value (positive or negative) in hertz to all frequency components of the input signal. This destroys harmonic relations, creating a purely electronic sonority.

Consider a tone with a fundamental of 100 Hz and a second harmonic of 200 Hz. When we frequency shift it by 10 Hz, it becomes a tone at 110 Hz and another component of 210 Hz. However, the second harmonic of 110 Hz is 220 Hz, so the shifted spectrum is no longer harmonic.

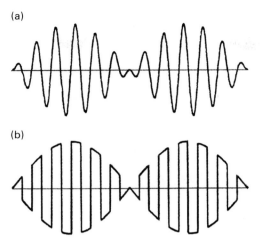

Figure 15.8   Two forms of ring modulation. (a) Multiplication RM. (b) Diode-clipping ("chopper") RM.

Frequency shifting operates by addition and is not the same as *pitch shifting* (discussed in chapter 31). A pitch shifter multiplies all frequencies by a specific factor. A simple pitch shift or speed-up by a factor of two plays everything one octave up and twice as fast. Harmonic relationships remain constant (figure 15.9).

A frequency shifter or *Klangumwandler* has separate outputs for the sum and difference frequencies (figure 15.10). The technical term for this method is *single sideband modulation* (SSM) (Carson 1915; Oppenheim and Willsky 1983; Mitra 2006; Disch and Zölzer 1999; Dutilleux 2011b).

Frequency shifting has a practical use in reducing acoustic feedback in live sound applications. Simply stated, the signal picked up by a microphone or pickup can be slightly frequency shifted before being sent to loudspeakers. This input/output difference reduces acoustic feedback (Schroeder 1959; Thuillier Lähdeoja, and Välimäki 2019).

Multiple technical methods exist for generating an SSM signal. Weaver (1956) outlines three basic techniques. The method described here is called the *Hartley modulation* or *phasing method* because it relies on phase cancelation to extract the upper or lower part of the SSM spectrum. The Hartley method has been used in SSM implementations in Pure Data, Max, Csound, Gamma, and Unfiltered Audio's Fault plug-in (McGee 2018).

The Hartley method uses phase cancelation to null one of the sidebands. It achieves this phase cancelation by means of the *Hilbert transform* (also called a *quadrature filter*). The Hilbert transform is a phase shifter that converts sines into cosines and vice versa. It is defined formally as the convolution

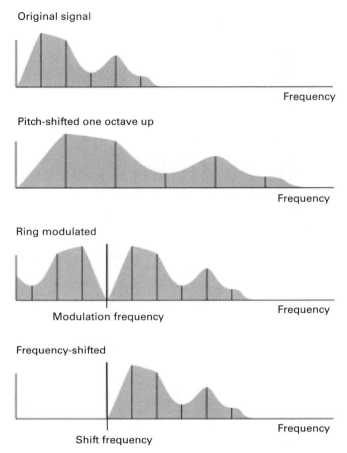

Figure 15.9   Spectrum comparison between the spectra of pitch shifting, ring modulating, and frequency shifting (SSM). (The vertical scale is amplitude and the horizontal scale is frequency.) Pitch shifting scales all the frequencies so that harmonic relations are preserved. Frequency shifting simply adds a constant value to all frequencies, resulting in inharmonic sounds.

of a signal with the curious function $1 / (\pi t)$. In practice the Hilbert transform is usually implemented with a pair of allpass filters, which shift the phase relationships of the original signal (McGee 2018). In particular, it shifts the phase of the negative frequency components of the input by $+90°$ and the phase of the positive frequency components by $-90°$ (figure 15.11).

The output of the Hilbert transform y is then sent to two ring modulators. One ring modulator multiplies its input signal y by a cosine of frequency f, and the other multiplies y by a sine (i.e., a phase-shifted cosine) of frequency f. Depending on whether the user wants to hear the upper or lower sideband, the appropriate signals are mixed together, resulting in phase cancelation of

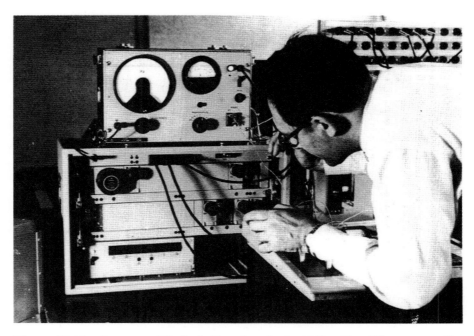

Figure 15.10 Composer Vladimir Ussachevsky in 1958 with a Klangumwandler built by Heck and Burck of the Southwest German Radio in Baden-Baden.

one band. Specifically, when the two signals are subtracted, the upper sideband results. When they are summed, the lower sideband results. In figures 15.3 and 15.9 the lower sideband is suppressed.

Amplitude Modulation

Amplitude modulation is one of the oldest modulation techniques (Black 1953) and has been used extensively in analog electronic music. As in RM, the amplitude of a carrier wave varies in accordance with a modulator wave. The difference between the two techniques is that in AM the modulator is unipolar (the entire waveform is above zero).

Perhaps the most mundane example of infra-audio AM occurs in superposing an envelope onto a sine wave (figure 15.12). The envelope, which is unipolar because it varies between 0 and 1, acts as a modulator. The sine wave, which is bipolar because it varies between −1 and +1, acts as a carrier. To apply an envelope to a signal is to multiply the two waveforms C and M

$$AmpMod_t = C_t \times M_t$$

where $AmpMod_t$ is the value of an amplitude-modulated signal at time t.

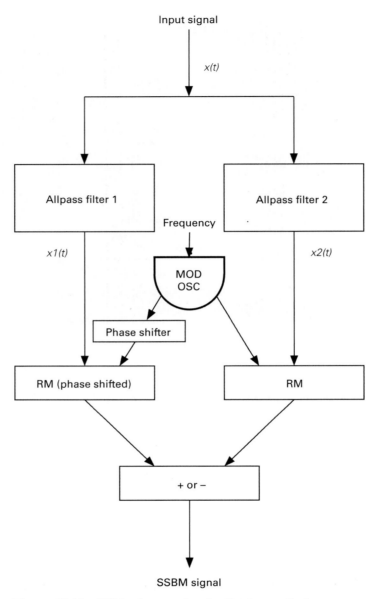

Figure 15.11   SSM scheme using the Hartley method.

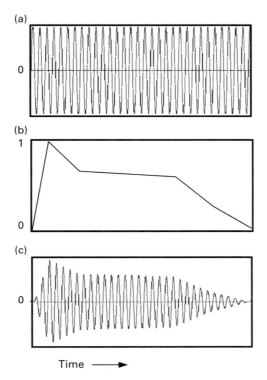

Figure 15.12   Applying an envelope to a signal is a simple case of infra-audio AM. The sine wave signal in (a) is multiplied by the envelope signal in (b) to produce the enveloped signal in (c).

Like RM, AM generates a pair of sidebands for every sinusoidal component in the carrier and the modulator. The sidebands are separated from the carrier by a distance corresponding to the inverse of the period of the modulator. The difference between RM and AM is that the AM spectrum contains the carrier frequency as well (figure 15.13). The amplitude of the two sidebands increases in proportion to the amount of modulation but never exceeds half the level of the carrier.

Figure 15.14 shows a time-domain view of AM created by the modulation of two sine wave signals in the audio band.

Like RM, AM can be described as a convolution, but AM involves the convolution of one signal with another offset by a nonzero constant (Sturm 2018)

AM Instruments

To implement classic AM, one restricts the modulator to a unipolar signal—the positive range between 0 and 1. Figure 15.15a shows a simple instrument for AM for which the modulator is a unipolar signal.

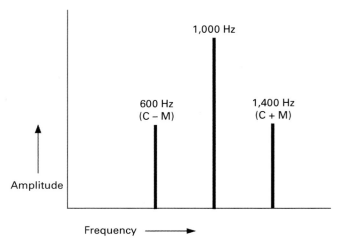

Figure 15.13 Spectrum produced by AM of a 1 KHz sine wave by a 400 Hz sine wave. The two sidebands are at sum and difference frequencies around the carrier frequency. The amplitude of the each of the sidebands is *index* / 2.

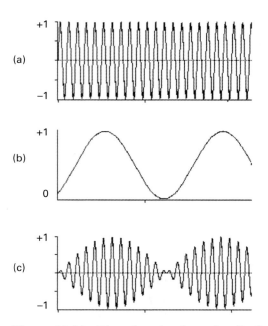

Figure 15.14 Time-domain view of audio frequency AM. The 1 KHz sine wave signal in (a) is modulated by the 40 Hz sine wave signal in (b) to produce the amplitude modulated signal in (c).

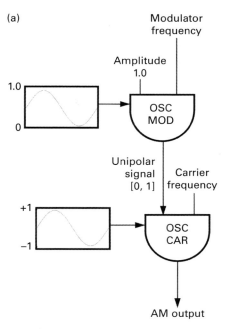

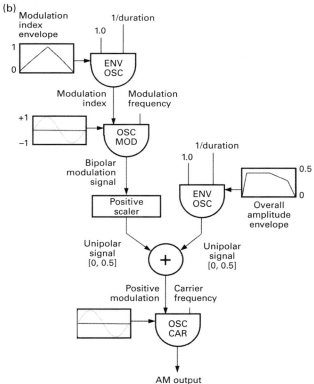

Figure 15.15 Two implementations of AM. (a) A simple instrument for AM where the modulating signal is assumed to be unipolar. (b) A more complicated instrument for AM with controls for the amount of modulation and the overall amplitude over the duration of the note event. The box to the side of each oscillator is its waveform. In the case of the envelope oscillators (denoted ENV OSC), the frequency period is 1 / *note_duration*. This means that they read through their wavetable once over the duration of a note event. The Positive scaler module ensures that the modulation input to the adder varies between 0 and 0.5.

Modulation Index

A slightly more complicated instrument is needed to control the amount of modulation and the overall amplitude envelope. Figure 15.15b depicts an AM instrument that controls the amount of modulation with an envelope (top left of figure). This envelope functions as a *modulation index,* in the parlance of modulation theory (detailed further on). The instrument scales a bipolar modulation signal into a unipolar signal varying between 0 and 1 and then adds this to an overall amplitude envelope over the duration of a sound event. The following equation describes the resulting AM waveform:

$$AmpMod = A_c \times \cos(C) + (I \times A_c) \, / \, 2 \times \cos(C + M)$$

$$+ (I \times A_c) \, / \, 2 \times \cos(C - M)$$

where *AmpMod* is the amplitude-modulated signal, A_c is the amplitude of the carrier, I is the modulation index, C is the carrier frequency, and M is the modulator frequency.

Feedback AM

A feedback oscillator instrument first appeared in Jean-Claude Risset's *Introductory Catalog of Computer Generated Sounds* in 1969. Because this catalog was not publicly distributed until much later (Goebel 1995), the technique first appeared in public in an obscure paper with the cryptic title "Some idiosyncratic aspects of computer synthesized sound" (Layzer 1971). In it, Arthur Layzer described work at Bell Telephone Laboratories in developing a self-modulating oscillator whose output is fed back to its input. This work was a collaboration of Risset, Max Mathews, and F. R. Moore. Moore implemented a feedback oscillator as a unit generator in the Music V language. (Music V is described in Mathews [1969].)

The feedback oscillators developed at Bell Laboratories fed the signal back into the amplitude input. Hence the early feedback oscillators were implementing a form of feedback AM. In chapter 16 we look at feedback FM as developed by Yamaha.

Kleimola et al. (2011) re-examined the potential of feedback AM. On the basis of a theoretical foundation laid by Cherniakov (2003), they construed feedback AM as a kind of *periodically linear time-variant* (PLTV) *filter.* Their research included an analysis of several variations of the algorithm and its sonic possibilities, with implementations in Pure Data and Csound.

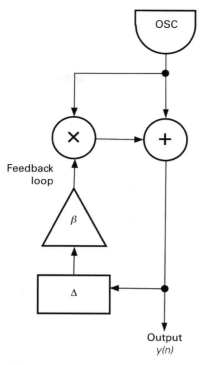

Figure 15.16 Feedback AM patch, after Kleimola et al. (2011). The output of a cosine oscillator is modulated by a feedback loop with a delay Δ and a feedback gain β.

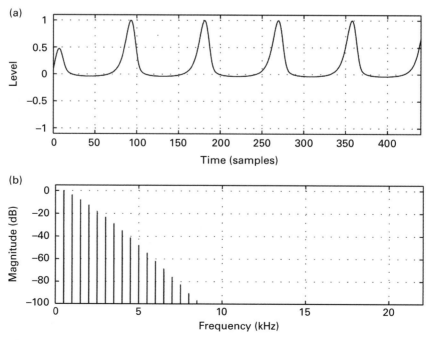

Figure 15.17 Simple feedback AM. (a) Waveform. (b) Spectrum. After Kleimola et al. (2011).

Feedback AM using a one-sample delay feedback can be written

$$y(n) = \cos(\omega_0 n) \times [1 + \beta \times y(n-1)]$$

with the fundamental frequency f_0 and the sampling rate f_s and where $\omega_0 = 2\pi \times f_0/f_s$ and the initial condition $y(n) = 0$ for $n \leq 0$ holds. Spectral brightness is controlled by a parameter β for feedback gain. This parameter acts as the modulation index. Figure 15.16 shows the patch.

The resulting spectrum is composed of various harmonics of the fundamental f_0. The result, shown in figure 15.17a, is a pulsating waveform with a significant DC component, thus no negative amplitude. The spectrum shown in 15.17b has a lowpass profile.

Kleimola et al. (2011) reformulated feedback AM as an equivalent filter with a periodically time-varying impulse response. To make the algorithm more flexible, they made several variations. Using sinusoidal inputs, they produced results similar to subtractive, formant, and physical modeling synthesis methods. Using sampled inputs, they tested feedback AM as an effect. Time will tell whether feedback AM has the same impact as feedback FM.

16   *Modulation II: FM, PM, PD, and GM*

Three-Oscillator Indirect Feedback
FM Parameter Space

Phase Modulation Synthesis

Phase Distortion (PD) Synthesis

General Modulations

Other Approaches to Modulation Synthesis

This chapter examines four techniques: *frequency modulation* (FM), *phase modulation* (PM), *phase distortion* (PD), and a class of methods called *general modulations* (GM).

Frequency Modulation

Frequency modulation is a classic digital synthesis method, used in dozens of compositions beginning in the 1970s. It became world famous after its adoption by the Yamaha corporation in the 1980s, who licensed and developed patents related to the technique and sold hundreds of thousands of FM synthesizers. However, FM is not one technique but a family of methods. Indeed, as it turns out, the FM implementation used by Yamaha is technically phase modulation, which we explain further on (Schottstaedt 2009).

Background: Frequency Modulation

Applications of FM in communications systems date back to the nineteenth century. The theory behind FM of radio band frequencies (in the MHz range) was established early in the twentieth century (Carson 1922; van der Pol 1930; Black 1953). These studies are worth reading today, particularly Black's book, which walks the reader through a guided tour of the hills and dales of waveform modulation.

John Chowning at Stanford University was the first to explore systematically the musical potential of digital FM synthesis (Chowning 1973). Prior to this, most digital sound had been produced by fixed-waveform, fixed-spectrum techniques. Early computer sound is stamped by this brittle sound signature.

In the 1970s, time-varying synthesis (additive or subtractive) was costly from a computational standpoint; users waited hours for a few seconds of sound. Thus there was a strong incentive to develop more efficient techniques for generating time-varying spectra. This motivation was explained by Chowning (1973) as follows:

In natural sounds the frequency components of the spectrum are dynamic, or time variant. The energy of the components often evolves in complicated ways; in particular during the attack and decay portions of the sound (526).

Hence, he sought a way to generate synthetic sounds that had the animated spectra characteristic of natural sounds. The breakthrough came when he was experimenting with extreme vibrato techniques, in which the vibrato becomes so fast that it affects the timbre of the signal:

I found that with two simple sinusoids I could generate a whole range of complex sounds which done by other means demanded much more powerful and extensive tools. If you want to have a sound that has, say 50 harmonics, you have to have 50 oscillators. And I was using two oscillators to get something that was very similar (Chowning 1987).

After careful experiments to explore the potential of the technique, Chowning realized a number of landmark compositions, including *Sabelithe* (1966), *Turenas* (1972), *Stria* (1977), and *Phoné* (1981). Meanwhile, he obtained a patent on FM synthesis (U.S. Patent 4,018,121). Yamaha obtained a license to apply this patent in their products. After several years of development, Yamaha introduced the GS-1 digital synthesizer ($16,000, housed in a wooden piano-like case) in 1980. But it was the introduction of the highly successful DX7 synthesizer ($2,000) in the fall of 1983 that made FM synonymous with digital synthesis to millions of musicians.

Simple FM

In the basic frequency modulation technique (referred to as *simple FM* or *Chowning FM*), a carrier oscillator is varied in frequency by a modulating oscillator (Chowning 1973; Chowning and Bristow 1986). Figure 16.1 diagrams a simple FM instrument.

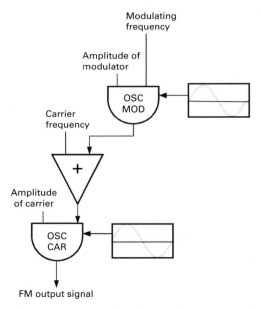

Figure 16.1 A simple FM instrument. The bipolar output of the modulating oscillator is added to the fundamental carrier frequency, causing it to vary up and down. The amplitude of the modulator determines the amount of modulation, which is the frequency deviation from the fundamental carrier frequency.

Looking at the spectrum shown in figure 16.2, we can immediately see the difference between FM and the RM and AM methods presented in chapter 15. Instead of just one sum and one difference sideband, FM of two sinusoids generates a series of sidebands around a carrier frequency *C*. Each sideband spreads out at a distance equal to a multiple of the modulating frequency *M*. Later we investigate the number of sidebands; suffice it to say now that the number of sidebands generated depends on the amount of modulation applied to the carrier.

C:M Ratio

The position of the frequency components generated by FM depends on the ratio of the carrier frequency to the modulating frequency. This is called the *C:M ratio*. When *C:M* is a simple integer ratio, such as 4:1 (as in the case of two signals at 800 and 200 Hz), FM generates harmonic spectra, that is, sidebands that are integer multiples of the carrier and modulating frequencies, as follows:

$C = 800$ Hz   (carrier)

$C + M = 1{,}000$ Hz   (sum)

$C + (2 \times M) = 1{,}200$ Hz   (sum)

$C + (3 \times M) = 1400$ Hz, etc.   (sum)

$C - M = 600$ Hz   (difference)

$C - (2 \times M) = 400$ Hz   (difference)

$C - (3 \times M) = 200$ Hz, etc.   (difference)

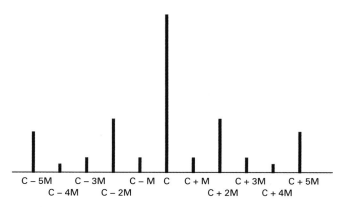

Figure 16.2 FM spectrum showing sidebands equally spaced around the carrier *C* at multiples of the modulator *M*.

When *C:M* is not a simple integer ratio, such as 8:2.1 (as in the case of two signals at 800 and 210 Hz), FM generates inharmonic spectra (noninteger multiples of the carrier and modulator), as follows:

$C = 800$ Hz   (carrier)

$C + M = 1{,}010$ Hz   (sum)

$C + (2 \times M) = 1{,}120$ Hz   (sum)

$C + (3 \times M) = 1{,}230$ Hz, etc.   (sum)

$C - M = 590$ Hz   (difference)

$C - (2 \times M) = 380$ Hz   (difference)

$C - (3 \times M) = 170$ Hz, etc.   (difference)

Modulation Index and Bandwidth

The bandwidth of the FM spectrum (the number of sidebands) is controlled by the *modulation index* or *index of modulation I. I* is defined mathematically according to the following relation:

$I = D/M$

where *D* is the amount of frequency deviation (Hz) from the carrier frequency. Hence, *D* is a way of expressing the *depth* or amount of the modulation. So if *D* is 100 Hz and the modulator *M* is 100 Hz, then the index of modulation is 1.0.

Figure 16.3 plots the effects of increasing the modulation index. When *I* = 0 (figure 16.3a), the frequency deviation is zero, so there is no modulation. When *I* is greater than zero, sideband frequencies occur above and below the carrier *C* at intervals of the modulator *M*. As *I* increases, so does the number of sidebands. Notice that as *I* increases, energy is "stolen" from the carrier and distributed among the increasing number of sidebands.

As a rule of thumb, the number of significant sideband pairs (those that are more than 1/100 the amplitude of the carrier) is approximately *I* + 1 (De Poli 1983). The total bandwidth is approximately equal to twice the sum of the frequency deviation *D* and the modulating frequency *M* (Chowning 1973). In formal terms,

FM bandwidth $\cong 2 \times (D + M)$

Because the bandwidth increases as the index of modulation increases, FM can simulate an important property of instrumental tones. Namely, as

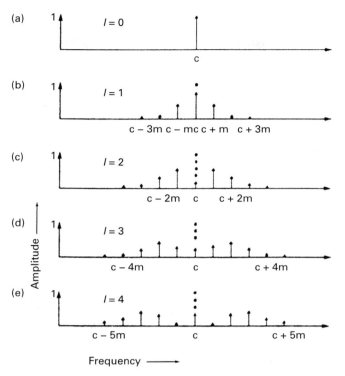

Figure 16.3 FM spectrum with increasing modulation index. (a) Carrier. (b)–(e) Carrier plus sidebands for $I=0$ (see a) to 4 (see e). The sidebands are spaced at intervals of the modulating frequency M and are symmetrical about the carrier C. (After Chowning 1973.)

the amplitude increases, so does the bandwidth. This is typical of many instruments, such as strings, horns, and drums, and is realized in FM by using similar envelope shapes for both the carrier amplitude and index of modulation.

Reflected Sidebands

For certain values of the carrier and modulator frequencies and I, extreme sidebands reflect out of the upper and lower ends of the spectrum, causing audible side effects. An upper partial that is beyond the Nyquist frequency (half the sampling rate) folds over (aliases) and reflects back into the lower portion of the spectrum. (See chapter 3 on aliasing.)

When the lower sidebands extend below 0 Hz, they reflect back into the spectrum in 180-degree *phase-inverted* form. By phase-inverted we mean that the waveform flips over the *x*-axis so that the positive part of a sine wave becomes negative and the negative part becomes positive. Phase-inverted

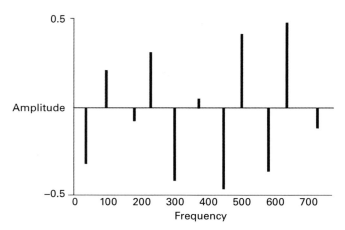

Figure 16.4   Spectral plot showing the effects of reflected low-frequency sidebands. The $C{:}M$ ratio is $1\sqrt{2}$, and the modulation index is 5. The downward lines indicate phase-inverted reflected components. (After Chowning 1973).

partials are drawn as lines extending downward, as in figure 16.4. In general, negative frequency components add richness to the lower-frequency portion of the spectrum, but if negative components overlap exactly with positive components, they can cancel out each other.

The FM Formula

When the carrier and the modulator are both sine waves, the formula for a frequency modulated signal *FM* at time t is as follows:

$$FM_t = A \times \sin(C_t + [I \times \sin(M_t)])$$

where A is the peak amplitude of the carrier; $C_t = 2\pi \times C$; $M_t = 2\pi \times M$; and I is the index of modulation. As this formula shows, simple FM is quite efficient, requiring just two multiplications, an addition, and two table lookups. The table lookups reference sine waves stored in memory.

Holm (1992) and Beauchamp (1992b) analyzed discrepancies between the amplitudes of the spectrum components emitted by the instrument shown in figure 16.1 and the spectra described by the classic FM formula, presented further on. This led to the formulation of phase modulation synthesis, presented in a subsequent section.

Bessel Functions

The amplitudes of the individual sideband components vary according to a class of mathematical functions called *Bessel functions of the first kind and the nth order* $J_n(I)$, where the argument to the function is the modulation index *I*. The FM equation given in the previous section can be re-expressed in an equivalent representation (adapted from De Poli 1983) that incorporates the Bessel function terms directly, as follows:

$$FM_t = \sum_{n=-\infty}^{\infty} J_n(I) \times \sin(2\pi \times [f_c \pm (n \times f_m)]) t$$

Each *n* is an individual partial. So, to calculate the amplitude of, for example, the third partial, we multiply the third Bessel function at point *I*; that is, $J_3(I)$, times two sine waves on either side of the carrier frequency. Odd-order lower-side frequency components are phase inverted.

Figure 16.5 depicts the Bessel functions in a three-dimensional representation for *n* = 1 to 15, with a modulation index range of 0 to 20. The vertical plane (an undulating surface) shows how the amplitudes of the sidebands vary as the modulation index changes. The figure shows that when the number of sidebands is low (at the back of the display) the amplitude variation is striking. As the number of sidebands increases (shown toward the front of the display), the amplitude variations in them (ripples) are small.

From a musical standpoint, the important property is that each Bessel function undulates like a kind of damped sinusoid: wide variations for low

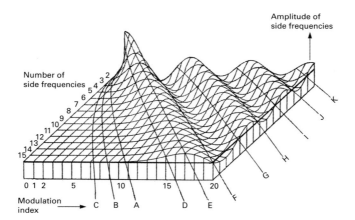

Figure 16.5   Three-dimensional graph of the Bessel functions 1 to 15 (plotted back to front) as a function of modulation index *I* (plotted left to right) showing the number of sidebands generated (after Chowning 1973). Lines A, B, and C show the points at which the amplitude falls off by −40, −60, and −80 dB respectively. Line D indicates the cutoff point for perceptually significant sidebands. Line E is the maximum amplitude for each order. Lines F through K show the zero crossings of the functions and therefore values of the index that produce a null or zero amplitude for various side frequencies.

I and less variation for high I. Simple FM is audibly marked by this undulation as one sweeps the modulation index. Notice also that the $J_n(I)$ for different values of n cross zero at different values of I. So as the modulation index I sweeps, sidebands drop in and out in a quasirandom fashion.

A convenient feature of FM is that the maximum amplitude and signal power do not have to vary with I. This means that as I increases or decreases, the overall amplitude of the tone does not vary excessively. Musically, this means that one can manipulate the amplitude and the index independently by using separate envelopes without worrying about how the value of I will affect the overall amplitude. This is not the case with some other synthesis techniques, notably waveshaping (chapter 17) and the discrete summation formulas. These techniques require *amplitude normalization* because the modulation can drastically affect the output amplitude.

Digital Implementation of FM

Figure 16.1 showed a simple FM instrument in which the depth of modulation is controlled by a constant frequency deviation. However, because the bandwidth is directly related to the modulation index and only indirectly to the frequency deviation, it is usually more convenient to specify an FM sound directly in terms of a modulation index. In this case, the instrument needs to be modified to carry out additional calculation according to the following relation:

$$D = I \times M$$

A musician usually wants dynamic control of the overall amplitude as well as the modulation index. Figure 16.6 provides these envelopes. In Chowning's original paper (1973), he described a variation of this instrument with a modulation index that varies between two values $I1$ and $I2$ according to an envelope. (For another implementation, see Maillard 1976.)

Applications of Simple FM

A straightforward application of simple FM is generating brasslike tones. This family of sounds have a sharp attack on both the amplitude and modulation index envelopes, and maintain a $c{:}M$ ratio of 1. The modulation index should vary between 0 and 7.

When the $C{:}M$ ratio is 1:2, odd harmonics are generated, making possible a crude clarinet simulation. An irrational $C{:}M$ ratio like

$$C : \sqrt{2C}$$

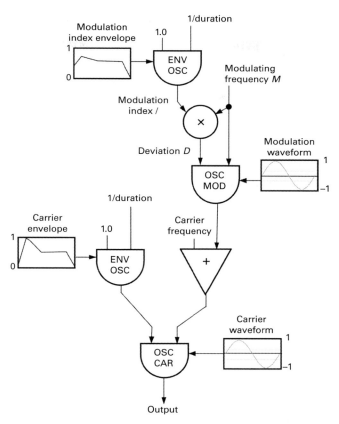

Figure 16.6   Simple FM instrument with envelopes for amplitude and frequency. This instrument also translates a user-specified modulation index envelope into a frequency deviation parameter.

yields an inharmonic complex that can simulate percussive and bell-like sounds (Moorer 1977).

Besides simulations of instrumental tones, another way to compose with FM is to take advantage of its "unnatural" properties and the uniquely synthetic spectra it generates. This is the approach taken by composers James Dashow and Barry Truax. Dashow used FM to harmonize (in an extended sense of *harmony*) pitch dyads (Dashow 1980, 1987; Roads 1985e). Truax systematically mapped out the spectral *families* made possible by various *C:M* ratios (Truax 1977). For example, certain *C:M* ratios generate harmonic spectra, and others generate combinations of harmonic and inharmonic spectra. Each *C:M* ratio is a member of a family of ratios that produce the same spectrum and that vary only in the position of the carrier around which spectral energy is centered. By carefully choosing carrier and modulating frequencies, a composer can generate a progression of related timbres with the same set of sidebands.

Another approach to composition with FM is to set a constant *C* or *M* and generate a set of related timbres with different *C:M* ratios.

Linear, Exponential, and Through-Zero FM

In the usual digital implementation of FM, the sidebands are equally spaced around the carrier frequency. We call this *linear FM.* In FM on some analog synthesizers, however, the spacing of sidebands is asymmetrical around the carrier, creating a different type of sound altogether. We call this *exponential FM.*

Analog synthesizers let a voltage-controlled oscillator (VCO) be frequency modulated by another oscillator. However, in order to allow equal-tempered keyboard control of the VCO, the VCO responds to a given voltage in a frequency-dependent way. In particular, a typical VCO responds to a one-volt-per-octave protocol, corresponding to the protocol of analog keyboards. In such a system, for example, the pitch A880 Hz is obtained by applying one more volt to the control input of the VCO than that needed to obtain A440.

In the case of FM, a modulating signal that varies between −1 volt and +1 volt causes a carrier oscillator set to A440 to vary between A220 and A880. This means that it modulates 220 Hz downward and 440 Hz upward—an asymmetrical modulation. This is fine for vibrato (the musical interval up and down is an octave) but when the modulator is at audio frequencies, other factors come into play. In particular, the average center frequency of the carrier changes, which usually means that the perceived center pitch is detuned by a significant interval. This detuning is caused by the modulation index, which means that the bandwidth and the center frequency are linked. From a musical standpoint, this linkage is not ideal. We want to be able to increase the modulation index without shifting the center frequency. Refer to Hutchins (1975) for an analysis of exponential FM.

In digital modulation, the sidebands are spaced equally around the carrier; hence the term linear FM. As the modulation index increases, the center frequency remains the same. Some analog oscillators also realize linear FM.

Through-zero FM (TZFM) came out of the modular world. It refers to linear FM that inverts the waveform when the frequency passes below zero. The negative-frequency version of a waveform can be thought of as a time-reversed replica of the original waveform. When an oscillator is modulated through zero frequency, the waveform slows down to a stop and then speeds up in the reverse direction. In some implementations, additional nonlinear behavior occurs around 0 Hz that some find interesting. An advantage of TZFM is that pitch material stays in tune regardless of modulation depth.

Analysis and FM

Because FM techniques can create many different families of spectra, it might be useful to have an analysis/resynthesis procedure linked to FM that is similar to those used with additive and subtractive techniques. Such a procedure could take an existing sound and translate it into parameter values for an FM instrument. By plugging those values into the instrument, we could hear an approximation of that sound via FM synthesis. The general name for this type of procedure is *parameter estimation* (see chapter 38).

In decades past, attempts were made to approximate a given steady-state spectrum automatically using FM (Justice 1979; Risberg 1982). The problem of estimating the FM parameters for complex evolving sounds is inherently difficult (Kronland-Martinet and Grossmann 1991; Horner, Beauchamp, and Haken 1992).

Today the motivation for estimating FM parameters has diminished. FM synthesis was originally proposed as a computationally efficient method, which it remains. Early work focused on approximations to traditional instruments like trumpets, drums, gongs, and even singing. Now, however, more accurate synthesis methods such as additive synthesis and physical modeling run in real time.

The aesthetic value of FM techniques is more about their unique possibilities rather than how good they are at simulating known sounds.

Multiple-Carrier FM

By *multiple-carrier frequency modulation* (MC FM), we mean an FM instrument in which one oscillator simultaneously modulates two or more carrier oscillators. The output of the carriers sums to a composite waveform that superposes the modulated spectra. Multiple carriers can create *formant regions* (peaks) in the spectrum, as shown in figure 16.7. The presence of formant regions is characteristic of the spectrum of the human voice and most traditional instruments. Another justification for separate carrier systems is to set different decay times for each formant region. This is useful in simulating brasslike tones in which the upper partials decay more rapidly than the lower partials.

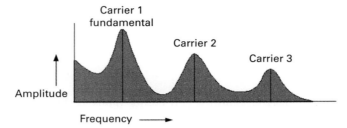

Figure 16.7 A spectrum with three formant regions created with a three-carrier FM instrument.

Figure 16.8 shows a triple-carrier FM instrument. In order to indicate clearly the multiple-carrier structure, the figure omits envelope controls and waveform tables. The amplitudes of the carriers are independent. When the Carrier 2 and Carrier 3 amplitudes are some fraction of Carrier 1, the instrument generates formant regions around the frequencies of the second and third carriers.

The equation for a multiple-carrier FM waveform at time t is simply the addition of n simple FM equations

$$MCFM_t = A^{w1} \times \sin(C1_t + [I1 \times \sin(M)])$$

$$\cdots$$
$$+ A^{wn} \times \sin(Cn_t + [In \times \sin(M)])$$

where A is an amplitude constant, $0 < A \le 1.0$,

$w1$ is the weighting of *Carrier 1*,

wn is the weighting of *Carrier n*,

$C1$ is the fundamental pitch $= 2\pi \times$ carrier frequency 1 (Hz),

and Cn is the formant frequency $= 2\pi \times$ carrier frequency n (Hz)

where Cn is an integer multiple of $C1$,

M is modulating frequency, usually set to be equal to $C1$ (Chowning 1989),

$I1$ is the modulation index of $C1$,

and In is the modulation index of Cn.

The exponents $w1$ and wn determine how the relative contribution of the carriers vary with the overall amplitude A.

Musical Applications of MC FM

Documented applications of MC FM strive to simulate the sounds of traditional instrument tones. The secret of realistic simulation is attention to detail

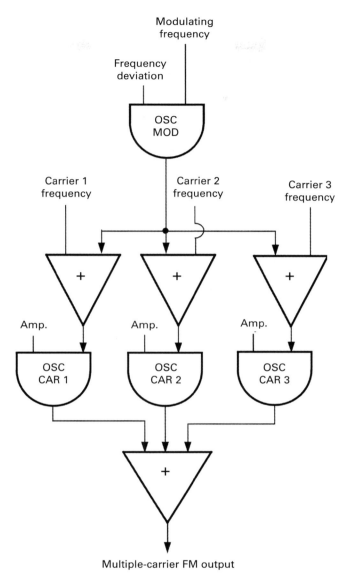

Figure 16.8   Triple-carrier FM instrument driven by a single modulating oscillator (OSC MOD).

in all aspects of the sound: amplitude, frequency, spectral envelopes, vibrato, and musical context.

A straightforward application of MC FM is the synthesis of trumpet-like tones. Risset and Mathews's (1969) analysis of trumpet-like tones showed a nearly harmonic spectrum, a 20–25 ms rise time of the amplitude envelope (with high partials building up more slowly), a small quasirandom frequency fluctuation, and a formant peak in the region of 1,500 Hz. Dexter Morrill

(1977) developed both single-carrier and double-carrier FM instruments for brass tone synthesis on the basis of this data. A double-carrier instrument sounds more realistic because each carrier produces frequencies for different parts of the spectrum. In particular, *C1* generates the fundamental and the first five to seven partials, whereas *C2* is set at 1,500 Hz, the main formant region of the trumpet. Each carrier has its own amplitude envelope for adjusting the balance between the two carrier systems in the composite spectrum. For example, in loud trumpet tones, the upper partials stand out.

Chowning (1980, 1989) applied the MC FM technique to the synthesis of vowel sounds sung by a soprano and by a low bass voice. He determined that a combination of periodic and random vibrato must be applied to all frequency parameters for realistic simulation of the vocal tones. "Without vibrato the synthesized tones are unnatural sounding" (Chowning 1989, 62). A quasiperiodic vibrato makes the frequencies fuse into a vocal-like tone. In Chowning's simulations, the *vibrato percent deviation V* is defined by the relation

$$V = 0.2 \times \log(\text{pitch})$$

Hence, for a pitch of 440 Hz, V is about 1.2 percent or 5.3 Hz in depth. The frequency of the vibrato ranges from 5.0 to 6.5 Hz according to the fundamental frequency range of the pitches F3 to F6.

Sampled Waveforms as Carriers

One way to open up the potential of MC FM is to use a sampled sound as the carrier. Time-varying partials in the sampled sound act as multiple carriers. Yamaha first introduced sampled carriers in its SY77 synthesizer (1989), which combined FM synthesis with their Advanced Waveform Memory (AWM) sample engine. Yamaha continues to sell synthesizers such as the MODX8 (introduced in 2018) that combine FM and sample technologies.

Multiple-Modulator FM

In *multiple-modulator frequency modulation* (MM FM), more than one oscillator modulates a single sine wave carrier oscillator. Two basic configurations are possible: *parallel* and *series* (figure 16.9). MM FM is easiest to understand when the number of modulators is limited to two and their waveforms are sinusoidal.

Important note: in practice, MM FM techniques are implemented by means of phase modulation. This is described in the subsequent section on phase modulation.

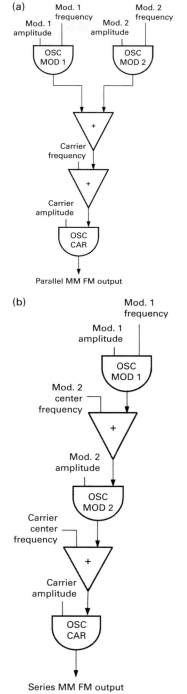

Figure 16.9 MM FM instruments. (a) Parallel MM FM. (b) Series MM FM.

Parallel MM FM

In parallel MM FM, two sine waves simultaneously modulate a single carrier sine wave. The modulation generates sidebands at frequencies of the form

$$C \pm (i \times M1) \pm (k \times M2)$$

where i and k are integers and $M1$ and $M2$ are the modulating frequencies. In parallel MM FM, it is as though each of the sidebands produced by one of the modulators is modulated as a carrier by the other modulator. The explosion in the number of partials is clear in figure 16.10, which lists both the primary and secondary modulation products.

The wave equation of the parallel double-modulator FM signal at time t is as follows:

$$PMMFM_t = A \times \sin \{ C_t + [I1 \times \sin(M1_t)] + [I2 \times \sin(M2_t)] \}$$

For mathematical descriptions of the spectra produced by this class of techniques, refer to Schottstaedt (1977) and LeBrun (1977).

Series MM FM

In series MM FM the modulating sine wave $M1$ is itself modulated by $M2$. This creates a complicated modulating wave with a potentially immense

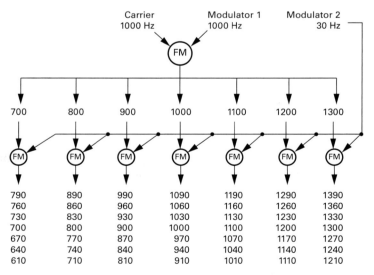

Figure 16.10   Diagram showing the explosion in the number of partials produced by parallel MM FM. Each component emitted by the modulation of the *Carrier* by *Modulator 1* is then modulated by *Modulator 2,* producing the list of spectral components shown at the bottom.

number of sinusoidal sideband components, depending on the index of modulation. The instantaneous amplitude of series double-modulator FM is given in the following equation, adapted from Schottstaedt (1977):

$$SMMFM_t = A \times \sin\{C_t + [I1 \times \sin(M1_t + [I2 \times \sin(M2_t)])]\}$$

The differences between the parallel and series equations reflect the configuration of the oscillators. In practice, *I2* determines the number of significant sidebands in the modulating signal and *I1* determines the number of sidebands in the output signal. Even small values of *I1* and *I2* create complex waveforms. The ratio *M1:C* determines the placement of the carrier's sidebands, each of which has sidebands of its own at intervals determined by *M2:M1*. Hence, each sideband is modulated and is also a modulator.

Musical Applications of MM FM

Schottstaedt (1977) used double-modulator FM to simulate certain characteristics of piano tones. He set the first modulator to approximately the carrier frequency, and the second modulator to approximately four times the carrier frequency. According to Schottstaedt, if the carrier and the first modulator are exactly equal, the purely harmonic result sounds artificial, like the sound of an electric (amplified tuning bar) piano. The need for inharmonicity in piano tones agrees with the findings of acousticians (Blackham 1965; Backus 1977).

Schottstaedt made the amplitudes of the modulating indexes frequency-dependent. That is, as the carrier frequency increases, the modulation index decreases. The result is a spectrum that is rich in the lower register but becomes steadily simpler as the pitch rises. Because the length of decay of a piano tone also varies with pitch (low tones decay longer), he used a pitch-dependent decay time.

Chowning and Schottstaedt also worked on the simulation of string-like tones using triple-modulator FM, in which the *C:M1:M2* ratio was 1:3:4 and the modulation indexes were frequency dependent (Schottstaedt 1977). Chowning also developed a deep bass voice using a combination MC FM and MM FM instrument. Refer to Chowning (1980, 1989) for more details on this instrument.

Feedback FM

Feedback FM is a widely used synthesis technique, due to Yamaha's patented application of the method in its digital synthesizers (Tomisawa 1981; Schottstaedt 2009). In this section we describe three types of feedback FM:

one-oscillator feedback, *two-oscillator feedback*, and *three-oscillator indirect feedback*.

Important note: in practice, feedback FM techniques are implemented by means of phase modulation, described in the section on phase modulation further on.

Feedback FM solves certain problems associated with simple (nonfeedback) FM methods. When the modulation index increases in simple FM, the amplitude of the partials varies unevenly, moving up and down according to the Bessel functions (figure 16.11). This undulation in the amplitude of the partials lends an unnatural "electronic sound" characteristic to the simple FM spectrum, which makes simulations of traditional instruments more difficult.

Feedback FM makes the spectrum more linear in its evolution. Generally, in feedback FM, as the modulation index increases, the number of partials and their amplitude increases relatively linearly.

One-Oscillator Feedback

The basic idea of one-oscillator feedback FM is easy to describe. Figure 16.12 shows an oscillator that feeds its output back into its frequency input through a multiplier and an adder. The adder computes the phase index for the sine table-lookup operation within the oscillator. At each sample period, a value x (the frequency increment) is added to the existing phase. The value in the sine table at this new phase is the output signal $\sin(y)$. In a synthesizer, x is usually obtained by pressing a key on a musical keyboard. This keystroke translates into a large phase increment value for a high-pitched note or a small phase increment value for a low-pitched note.

In feedback FM, the output signal $\sin(y)$ routes back to the adder after being multiplied by the *feedback factor* β. The factor β acts as a kind of scaling function or *modulation index* for the feedback. With the feedback loop, the address of the next sample is $x + [\beta \times \sin(y)]$.

Figure 16.13 plots the spectrum of a one-oscillator feedback FM instrument as β increases. Notice the increase in the number of partials, and the regular, incremental differences in amplitude between the partials, all contributing to a quasilinear spectral buildup. With increasing modulation, the signal evolves from a sine wave to a sawtooth wave in a continuous manner.

The equation for one-oscillator feedback FM can be characterized by reference to the Bessel functions (Tomisawa 1981)

$$FFM_t = \sum_{n-1}^{\infty} \frac{2}{n \times \beta} \times J_n (n \times \beta) \times \sin(n \times x)t$$

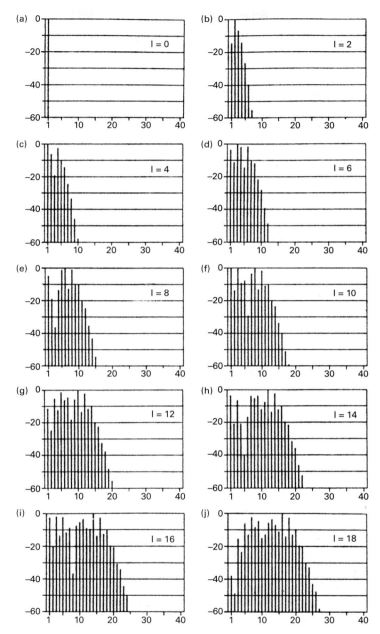

Figure 16.11 A plot of the harmonic spectrum of FM when the frequency of C is equal to that of M, for values of I ranging from $I=0$ to $I=18$ (after Mitsuhashi 1982c). Starting with (a) at the top left, read the graphs from left to right, top to bottom. Note how uneven the spectrum is, with partials going up and then down as the modulation index changes.

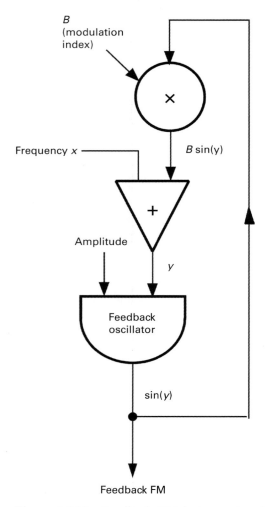

Figure 16.12   Feedback FM instrument. x is a phase increment to a sine wave lookup table. x is added with a signal fed back from the output, multiplied by a feedback factor β.

where $J_n(n)$ is a Bessel function of order n and $n \times \beta$ is the modulation index. The Bessel functions act in different ways in feedback FM as opposed to simple FM. In simple FM, the modulation index I is common for each Bessel component $J_n(I)$. This means that each Bessel function value $J_n(I)$ is represented by a height at a position where the common modulation index crosses. Accordingly, as the modulation index in regular FM increases, the spectral envelope assumes an undulating character. In feedback FM, the order n of the Bessel function $Jn(n \times \beta)$ is included in the modulation index, and the factor $2/(n \times \beta)$ is multiplied as a coefficient to the Bessel equation (Mitsuhashi 1982b).

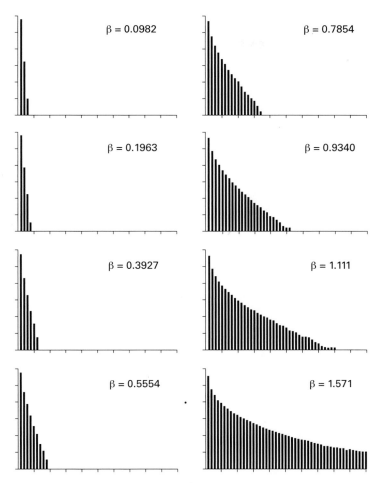

Figure 16.13   Spectrum of a one-oscillator feedback FM instrument as the feedback factor β increases, with the phase increment x set at 200 Hz. The horizontal axis shows frequency plotted from 0 to 10 KHz. The vertical axis shows amplitude on a scale from 0 to 60 dB.

In feedback FM, the modulation index $n \times \beta$ differs for each order n and increases approximately in the manner of a monotone function (i.e., the increase is by a constant factor). The scaling coefficient $2/n \times \beta$ ensures that as the order n of partials increases, their amplitude decreases.

Two-Oscillator Feedback

Another feedback FM patch takes the output of a feedback oscillator and uses it to modulate another oscillator (figure 16.14). The multiplier M in the figure functions as the index of modulation control between the two oscillators.

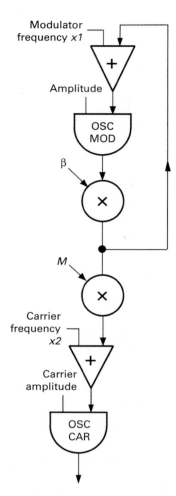

Figure 16.14   Two-oscillator feedback FM instrument. The output of a feedback FM oscillator modulates a second, nonfeedback oscillator.

When M is in the range 0.5 to 2, the spectrum has a monotonically decreasing tendency in which the amplitude of the partials decreases as the number of partials increases (figure 16.15). When the feedback parameter β is greater than 1, the overall amplitude of the high-order partials increases. This creates the effect of a variable filter. It thus has a more strident and shrill sound. However, when M is set to 1, and $x1$ and $x2$ are equal, this instrument generates the same spectrum as the single-oscillator feedback FM instrument shown in figure 16.12.

When the ratio between $x2$ (the carrier) and $x1$ (the modulator) is 2:1, the modulation index M is 1, and β varies between 0.09 and 1.571, the result is a continuous variation between a quasi–sine wave and a quasi–square wave.

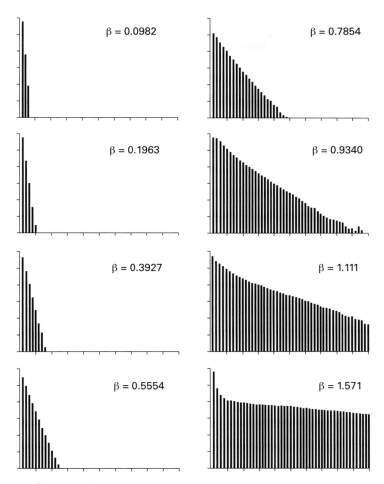

Figure 16.15   Spectrum generated by a two-oscillator feedback FM instrument as the feedback factor β increases from 0.0982 to 1.571. The frequency values for *x1* and *x2* are both set at 200 Hz, and the modulation index *M* is set to the constant value 2. The horizontal axis shows frequency plotted from 0 to 10 KHz. The vertical axis shows amplitude on a scale from 0 to 60 dB.

Three-Oscillator Indirect Feedback

Another variation on feedback FM is a three-oscillator technique with *indirect feedback,* shown in figure 16.16. The feedback parameter is *β1*. Indirect feedback produces a complex form of modulation. When the frequencies *x1, x2,* and *x3* are noninteger multiples, nonpitched sounds are created. A beating chorus effect is produced when these frequencies are very close to being in an integer relationship. According to sound designer David Bristow (1986), who worked for Yamaha in the 1980s, this instrument

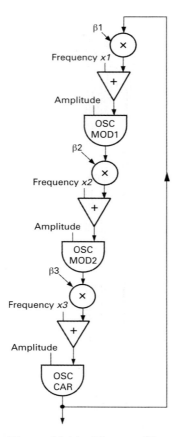

Figure 16.16   Three-oscillator indirect feedback FM instrument. A series of three oscillators modulate each other. Three modulation index factors $\beta 1$, $\beta 2$, and $\beta 3$ determine the amount of modulation. The global output is fed back into the first modulating oscillator.

generates a rich spectrum, and when the feedback is increased the energy tends to focus at the high end of the spectrum, ideal for distorted timbres and metallic sounds.

FM Parameter Space

Commercial implementations of FM synthesis are controlled by a large number of parameters whose interactions can be complicated. As an example, the Jellinghaus DX-Programmer was a hardware controller for professional sound designers with knobs and switches for programming voices on the Yamaha DX7. It provided direct access to the dozens of parameters that were otherwise buried under the submenus of the tiny DX7 display. The Jellinghaus had thirty toggle switches and 148 rotary knobs. This intimidating parameter

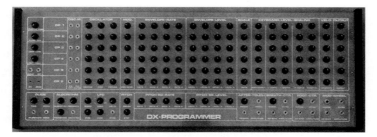

Figure 16.17   Jellinghaus DX-Programmer.

space was in part responsible for the dependence of users on preset libraries delivered by the manufacturer. Few users of Yamaha synthesizers ventured into the realm of FM programming.

Modern FM instruments in hardware and software are supplied with hundreds of presets. Native Instruments FM8, which ships with a library of over 1,200 presets, is a prime example of an easy-to-use FM synthesizer. (See chapter 47 for a look at FM8.)

Phase Modulation Synthesis

FM and the closely related technique called phase modulation represent two similar cases of *angle modulation* (Black 1953, 28–30). The difference can be expressed as follows:

Phase modulation $\quad\quad\quad\quad\quad \cos([phase + increment] + f(t))$
Frequency modulation $\quad \cos(phase + [increment + f(t)])$

where *phase* is the current phase angle, *increment* corresponds to the frequency of the carrier, and $f(t)$ is the modulator (Schottsteadt 2009). PM modulates the phase, whereas FM modulates the phase increment.

In simple cases, the results sound identical. However, for both scientific clarity and support for implementations, it is important to distinguish between FM and PM (Beauchamp 1992b).

Indeed, what is called *FM synthesis* is usually implemented as PM. For example, it has been shown that the method called FM that is described in John Chowning's 1977 patent is actually PM. Similarly, the Yamaha four-operator chip data sheets reveal that Yamaha FM is implemented on the chip as PM.

James McCartney (1997), who created the SuperCollider language, observed that PM was preferable to FM for two reasons:

- The modulation index does not depend on the carrier frequency but is simply equal to the phase deviation induced in radians.

- A DC component in the modulator will not cause a shift in pitch of the carrier. This allows the ability to chain modulators several in a row, which is not always possible in FM due to DC components in the modulators.

The second point is critical. In a simple FM instrument, the current phase is always equal to the sum of all previous increments. When we change the frequency of an oscillator by adding in other functions such as pitch bend, vibrato, or the output of other oscillators, this can introduce undesirable side effects such as DC bias and carrier pitch shifting. PM's immunity from DC offset side effects is important in complex modulation schemes including stacked modulators (MM FM) and feedback FM.

Figure 16.18 shows a basic PM instrument. A phasor at the carrier frequency is added to the modulation signal. This combined signal references a sine wavetable.

SuperCollider provides a PM module called PMOsc that encapsulates the core of this patch. As another example, the FM synthesis instruments in the ChucK programming language emulate the Yamaha PM methods.

For more on the distinction between PM and FM, refer to Bate (1990), Holm (1992), Beauchamp (1992b), Puckette (2007), Schottstaedt (2009), and Lazzarini (2017).

Other FM equivalents include *Doppler FM* (McGee 2015), which pans sounds at audio rates, and *adaptive FM*, which modulates a delay line at audio rates (Lazzarini et al. 2007). Lazzarini (2017) explores other extensions to FM.

Phase Distortion (PD) Synthesis

Phase distortion (PD) synthesis is a term invented by the Casio corporation to describe a simple but sonically effective modulation technique developed for several of its CZ digital synthesizers in the 1980s and described in a patent (Ishibashi 1987).

PD synthesis uses a sine wavetable lookup oscillator in which the rate of scanning through the oscillator varies over the cycle. That is to say, the phase increment of the oscillator is nonlinear. The scanning interval speeds up from 0 to an inflection point d and then slows down from d to 2π (Lazzarini 2017). The overall frequency is constant, according to the pitch of the note, but the output waveform is no longer a sine. By modulating the scan speed over the course of one cycle, PD can be thought of as phase-synchronous phase modulation.

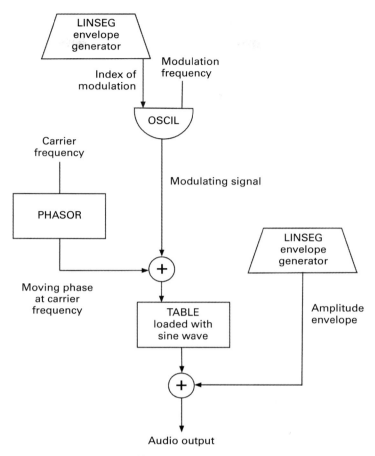

Figure 16.18   A simplified PM synthesis instrument realized with Csound opcodes. The modulating oscillator is shown at the top. The index of modulation is controlled by the LINSEG (line-segment) envelope function. The modulating signal is added to the output of a PHASOR signal. A PHASOR is a periodic sawtooth generator whose value is used to index the sine wave TABLE at the carrier frequency. A LINSEG envelope generator controls the amplitude level.

Figure 16.19 illustrates the effect of the bent (sped up and then slowed down) scanning function on the output waveform. As the amount of speeding up and slowing down increases (bending the scanning function progressively), the original sinusoidal waveform turns into a waveform that is rich in harmonics. Lazzarini and Timoney (2010) analyzed PD and suggested improvements to limit the potential of aliasing.

The PD technique was reintroduced as a commercial product in 2015 with the Oli Larkin Virtual CZ plugin, which added microtonal tuning support. PD is also found in the 2018 MakeNoise Telharmonic module (Eurorack hardware format). Lazzarini (2017) gives a code listing of a phase distortion algorithm in the Python language.

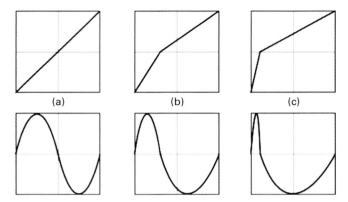

Figure 16.19   Effect of phase distortion on waveform shape. (a) The top image shows a normal linear phasor scanning function for a sine wave shown at the bottom. (b) Slightly distorted scanning function. (c) A greatly distorted scanning function produces a waveform that is spectrally rich.

General Modulations

Certain synthesis techniques can be turned into modulations by substituting a time-varying function for a constant term in the equation of the original technique. If the time-varying function is periodic, the technique is one of a family of synthesis techniques known under the rubric of *waveshape parameter modulation* or *general modulations.* For example, amplitude modulation and frequency modulation can be classified as waveshape parameter modulation techniques. For more on this theory refer to Mitsuhashi (1980) and Lazzarini and Timoney (2010).

James A. Moorer showed that the equation for simple FM is one instance of a general class of equations called *discrete summation formulas* (DSFs) (Moorer 1976, 1977; Moore 1990). DSF refers to a set of formulas that are the *closed-form* solution of the sums of finite and infinite trigonometric series. A closed form is a more compact and efficient representation of a longer summation formula. These formulas are relevant to sound synthesis if we assume that they describe waveforms that are sums of sinusoidal waves. For example, the right-hand side of the following equation is the closed-form solution to the summation shown in the left-hand side:

$$\sum_{k=1}^{n} \sin(k\theta) = \sin[1/2(n+1)\theta]\sin[n\theta/2]\csc(\theta/2)$$

This equation shows that we can represent the sum of *n* sine waves with just five multiplications, three divides, and three table-lookup operations.

As closed-form equations, DSFs have only a few parameters to manipulate and can be realized economically in digital form. Moorer's paper describes four DSFs that show promise for sound synthesis. A broader class of DSFs exists, but most of them are not useful in music synthesis (Hansen 1975).

DSFs can generate time-varying tones that sound similar to FM spectra. Moorer also described DSFs that can generate spectra that are impossible with simple FM, such as *one-sided spectra* whose partials extend in just one direction from the carrier frequency. Another family of spectra possible with DSFs are those with partials whose amplitudes increase monotonically (i.e., by a constant factor).

A disadvantage of basic DSF as against a technique like FM is the lack of amplitude normalization. Hence it is necessary to apply some kind of scaling or normalization to the output of a DSF synthesis algorithm. (See the discussion of amplitude normalization in chapter 17 on waveshaping.)

Chan and Horner (1996) applied genetic algorithms to match DSF spectra to instrumental tones. Lazzarini and Timoney (2010) interconnected waveshaping, FM, and DSF methods under a common theoretical framework of nonlinear distortion synthesis.

Other Approaches to Modulation Synthesis

McGee (2015) experimented with spatial modulation incorporating Doppler shift at audio rates and found it to be equivalent to FM in its spectral effects. Described in chapter 32, *Doppler shift* is an increase in pitch heard when sounds are moving toward a listener and a decrease in pitch when sounds move away from a listener. As previously mentioned, Doppler FM is audio rate frequency modulation resulting from high-velocity sound source movement oscillating back and forth in space across a listener.

Researchers have developed methods that produce spectra similar to AM and FM by modulating a chain of allpass filters (Kleimola et al. 2009). Surges, Smyth, and Puckette (2016) casts the method within the framework of a stable generative feedback network.

The Warps module by Mutable Instrument implements a number of exotic operations, including *exclusive-or (XOR) modulation,* in which the carrier and the modulator are converted into 16-bit binary numbers that are XORed bit by bit.

17 *Waveshaping Synthesis*

The fundamental idea behind waveshaping (also known as *nonlinear distortion*) is to pass a sound signal *x* through a distortion unit. In this case, the distortion unit is a function *w* in a stored table (or array) in computer memory. The function *w* maps any sample input value *x* in the range [−1, +1] to an output value *w*(*x*) in the same range. This has the effect of warping the input waveform and enriching its spectrum (Roads 1979).

In the simplest case, the input signal *x* is a sinusoidal wave generated by an oscillator. However, the input *x* can be any signal, including sampled sound. For each output sample to be computed we use the value of *x* to index table *w*. Table *w* contains the *shaping function* (also called the *transfer function*). We then simply take the value in *w* indexed by *x* as our output value *w*(*x*).

Waveshaping is musically interesting because it gives us a simple handle on the time-varying bandwidth and spectrum of a tone in a computationally efficient way.

Jean-Claude Risset carried out the first experiments with waveshaping synthesis at Bell Telephone Laboratories (Risset 1969). Daniel Arfib (1979) and Marc LeBrun (1979) independently developed theoretical and empirical elaborations of the basic method. Waveshaping has passed the test of time and is currently implemented in many sound synthesis languages and commercial applications, often with additional features, e.g., Tracktion Waverazor, Virsyn microTERA, AudioThing WaveBox, Doepfer A-136 Distortion/Waveshaper (Eurorack), Intellijel μFold (Eurorack), etc.

Simple Waveshaping Instrument

At its most basic, waveshaping synthesis is a means of generating a rich spectrum consisting of many frequency components by passing a sine wave through a distortion table. An instrument for simple waveshaping synthesis is shown in figure 17.1. Here an envelope oscillator (or envelope generator) controls the amplitude of a sinusoidal oscillator that is fed into a shaping function table. The amplitude envelope α is important because it has the effect of scaling the input signal, making it reference different regions of the shaping function *w*. Next, we look at the implications of this.

Example Shaping Functions

As figure 17.2 shows, if the shaping function in table *w* is a straight diagonal line from −1 to +1, the output of *w* is an exact replica of its input *x*. The reason is that the table maps an input of −1 (shown at the bottom of the function)

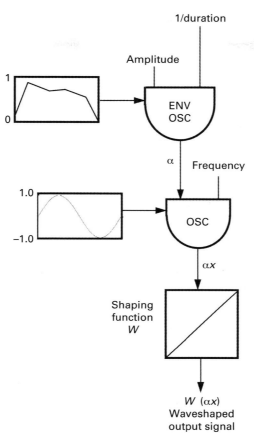

Figure 17.1 Simple waveshaping instrument. A sinusoidal oscillator, whose amplitude is controlled by the amplitude envelope signal α, indexes a value in the shaping function table *w*. As in other example instruments, the input *1 / duration* that is fed into the frequency input of the envelope oscillator indicates that it goes through one cycle over the duration of the note.

to −1 in the output (shown at the right of the function), 0 maps to 0, 1 maps to 1, and so on. Because this simple relationship between the input and the output occurs only when the shaping function is a straight line, we say that in this case the output is a *linear function* of its input.

As Loy (2007) pointed out, one can describe waveshaping as the flip side of wavetable lookup (chapter 6). In wavetable lookup, a ramp function or phasor scans a wavetable. In waveshaping, a waveform scans a ramped shaping function!

If the shaping function *w* contains anything other than a straight diagonal line from −1 to +1, the input waveform *x* is *distorted.* Figure 17.3 shows the effects of several shaping functions on an input sinusoid. Figure 17.3a shows an inverting

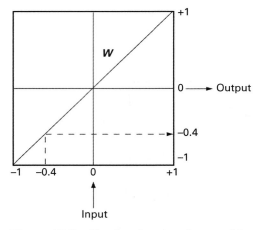

Figure 17.2   Shaping function shown with a linear response. The function maps an input signal scaled over the range shown at the bottom to an output function whose scale is shown at the right. To see how the function maps an input to an output value, read vertically from the bottom and then look to the right to see the corresponding output value. Thus an input value of −0.4 on the bottom maps to an output value of −0.4 on the right. This equivalence between the input and the output is true only for a linear shaping function.

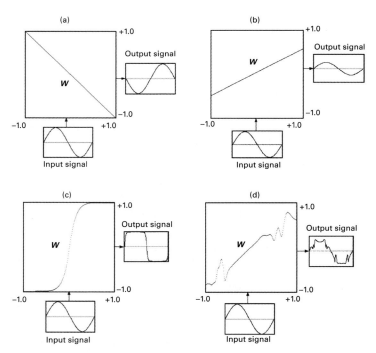

Figure 17.3   Four shaping functions. (a) Inversion of the input signal. (b) Attenuation. (c) Amplification of low-level signals (expansion) and clipping of high-level signals. (d) Complicated amplitude-sensitive distortion.

shaping function. For every positive value of the input amplitude the waveshaper emits a corresponding negative value and vice versa. Figure 17.3b is a straight line but with a narrower angle than the curve in figure 17.2. It maps to a narrower range on the right-hand (output) side of the shaping function, meaning that it attenuates the input signal. Figure 17.3c expands low-level signals and sends high-level signals into clipping distortion. The amplitude-sensitive nature of waveshaping is demonstrated well in figure 17.3d. The shaping function is a straight line around zero, which is the low-amplitude portion of the grid. Such a function passes a low-amplitude input signal with no distortion. When the amplitude of the input signal increases, the extreme ends of the shaping function subject the input signal to a complicated form of distortion.

Lazzarini and Timoney (2010) brought together the theories of waveshaping, FM, phase distortion, and the discrete summation formulae presented in chapter 16. Among other things, they explain how FM can be viewed as waveshaping. Specifically, FM can be seen as a combination of sinusoids ring modulated by sinusoidal waveshaping functions. Kendall, Haworth, and Cadiz (2014) describes another method of distortion synthesis.

Amplitude Sensitivity of Waveshaping Spectra

It is easy to see that the amplitude sensitivity of waveshaping can model a characteristic of acoustic instruments. That is, when one plays an acoustic instrument harder—for example, by strumming a guitar forcefully, blowing a saxophone stridently, or striking a drum intensely—this enriches the spectrum. In waveshaping we can emulate this effect by passing a signal whose overall amplitude varies with time through the shaping function. As the amplitude of the input signal varies, one obtains a correspondingly time-varied spectrum at the output. Put another way, a variation in the time-domain waveform at the input is manifest as a variation in the frequency-domain spectrum at the output. This is an important feature. Given a single shaping function (precomputed and stored in memory), a variety of output waveforms can be obtained simply by varying the amplitude or offset of the input signal in order to apply various regions of the shaping function. Arfib (1979) gives practical examples of the waveshaping technique in specific musical applications.

Chebychev Shaping Functions

Research by LeBrun (1979) and Arfib (1979) demonstrated that it is possible to predict exactly the output spectrum of the waveshaping technique under mathematically controlled conditions. By restricting the input signal x to an unvarying cosine wave and using a family of smooth polynomials called

Chebychev functions, which take values in the range [−1, +1] to construct the shaping function *w,* one can produce any desired combination of harmonics in a steady-state spectrum. This derives from the following identity:

$$T_k \times (\cos[\theta]) = \cos(k \times \theta)$$

where T_k is the kth Chebychev function. In other words, by applying the kth Chebychev polynomial to an input sine wave, we obtain a cosine wave at the kth harmonic. This means that each separate Chebychev polynomial, when used as the shaping function, produces a particular harmonic of *x*. By summing a weighted combination of Chebychev polynomials and putting the result in the shaping table, a corresponding harmonic mixture is obtained as the output. For example, to produce a steady-state waveform with a first harmonic (fundamental), a second harmonic that is 0.3 the amplitude of the first harmonic, and a third harmonic that is 0.17 of the first harmonic, we add the equations

$$T_1 + (0.3 \times T_2) + (0.17 \times T_3)$$

and we put the result into the transfer function wavetable. If a cosine wave is passed through this table, then the output spectrum contains the desired harmonic ratios.

An advantage of using the Chebychev functions is that we can guarantee that the output of the waveshaper is bandlimited. That is, it does not contain frequencies above the Nyquist rate, and therefore it is free of aliasing. Table 17.1 lists the equations for T_0 through T_8 where $x = \cos(\theta)$.

Amplitude Normalization

A drawback of basic waveshaping synthesis is that the output amplitude of the simple waveshaping instrument shown in figure 17.1 varies considerably, even using only one shaping function. This variance is the result of different

Table 17.1 Chebychev functions T0 through T8

$T_0 = 1$

$T_1 = x$

$T_2 = 2x^2 - 1$

$T_3 = 4x^3 - 3x$

$T_4 = 8x^4 - 8x^2 + 1$

$T_5 = 16x^5 - 20x^3 + 5x$

$T_6 = 32x^6 - 48x^4 + 18x^2 - 1$

$T_7 = 64x^7 - 112x^5 + 56x^3 - 7x$

$T_8 = 128x^8 - 256x^6 + 160x^4 - 32x^2 + 1$

---

parts of the shaping function being applied. That is, the output amplitude depends on the amplitude of the input signal to the shaping function.

The point of waveshaping is to use the amplitude of x to control timbre, not the overall loudness of the sound. If we want full independence between timbre and the output amplitude, some form of amplitude normalization is required. At least three kinds of normalization are possible: *loudness normalization, power normalization,* and *peak normalization.*

For musical purposes, the ideal would be loudness normalization, in which the perceived loudness of the instrument is constant for all values of α. Power normalization is based on division by the *root mean square* (RMS) of the harmonic amplitudes generated by a particular shaping function. LeBrun (1979) gives details on this technique. Peak normalization is probably the least complicated and most practical of the three. It is accomplished by scaling the output in relation to the maximum value. Peak normalization ensures that the output amplitude of different tones will at least have the same peak value and will therefore not overload the digital-to-analog converters with a value out of their range.

Figure 17.4 shows a waveshaping instrument with a peak normalization. The easiest way to do this is to prepare a table containing normalization factors for all values of α, because the envelope α determines the amplitude of x. For example, if the value of α input to the normalization table is 0.7, we multiply the output by the entry in the normalization table corresponding to α.

Alternative Shaping Functions

In creative synthesis, we want to be free to use any shaping function generated from any algorithm or even that is hand drawn (Buxton et al. 1982). Sometimes these generate sonic behaviors that venture beyond the limitations of acoustical instruments. In other cases, the goal is to replicate a known waveform or spectrum profile. For this purpose, Lazzarini and Timoney (2010) have pointed out limitations of shaping functions based on Chebychev polynomials. For example, the target spectrum is matched only with a specific distortion index. Thus they propose alternative approaches for shaping function design. For example, hyperbolic tangent transfer functions can generate nearly bandlimited square and sawtooth waves

Variations on Waveshaping

The canonic waveshaping technique—sending a cosine wave through a Chebychev polynomial shaping function—produces a range of harmonic

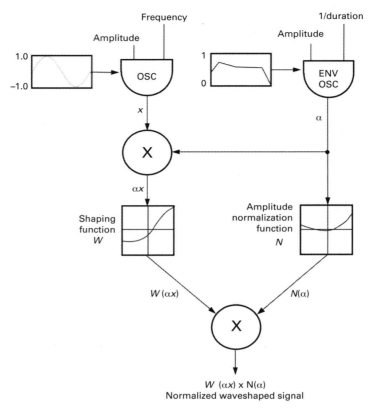

Figure 17.4   Waveshaping instrument with a normalization section. The value of α indexes a value in the normalization table that scales the output of the waveshaper.

spectra. A benefit of using Chebychev polynomials as shaping functions is that the output is bandlimited and is thus not subject to aliasing. Other equations also meet this criterion. Ultimately, *w* can be designed using many possible algorithms or crafted by hand using controllers. (See chapter 25 for an account of waveshaping with a noise modulated shaping function.)

Moreover, the input *x* to the waveshaper can be any signal, not just a cosine wave. The input may be, for example, a sum of two or more cosine waves at different frequencies. Another variation is to use a frequency-modulated signal for the input *x*. The benefit of this is that one can obtain inharmonic combinations of partials and formant structures (Arfib 1979).

The input signal *x* can also be a sampled sound. When the shaping function *w* is a simple and smooth polynomial, the effect is not unlike phasing, because the harmonics of the input undulate in a time-varying way. Hence a waveshaping instrument can generate an interesting hybrid of natural and electronic sound. If *w* contains any straight horizontal or vertical lines, the effect is a strong distortion like the distortion of electric guitar amplifiers turned to maximum volume. Indeed, waveshaping has been used to create distorted guitar sounds.

The rest of this section reviews a number of variations on waveshaping that have been proposed.

Movable Waveshaping

A variation called *movable waveshaping* was invented by Xin Chong at the Beijing Central Music Conservatory (Xin 1987). In this technique the shaping function itself varies with time. This can be accomplished by storing a longer shaping function and moving an index to scan various parts of it at different times. Starting from simple input signals and simple time-varying shaping functions, a multiplicity of results can be obtained.

Fractional Waveshaping

De Poli (1984) analyzed a configuration in which the shaping function is a fraction, specifically a ratio between two polynomials. He calls this *fractional waveshaping*. Fractional waveshaping can generate such effects as exponential spectra and spectra whose shapes resemble a damped cosine wave. The multiple bumps of the damped cosine wave spectrum are heard as formants. Dynamically varying spectra are achieved as in regular waveshaping by varying the amplitude and offset of the input cosine signal.

Postprocessing and Parameter Estimation

The waveshaped signal can be passed through another signal processing device, *postprocessing* the waveshaped signal. This device could be, for example, an AM oscillator, a FM oscillator, or a filter. AM and FM can enrich the waveshaped spectrum by adding, for example, inharmonic partials to a harmonic spectrum (Arfib 1979; Le Brun 1979; De Poli 1984).

De Poli (1984) and Volonnino (1984) developed an experimental filtering method called *frequency-dependent waveshaping*. This was aimed at providing independent control of the phase and amplitude of each harmonic generated by the waveshaping process.

Beauchamp (1979) inserted a highpass filter on the output of his waveshaping model of brass tones in order to mimic the damping effects of brass pipes. Later, Beauchamp and Horner (1992) simulated instrumental tones by a multiple waveshaper + filter model. They first performed a parameter estimation of an instrumental tone and approximated its spectrum with a single waveshaper + filter model. They subtracted this approximation from the original sound to obtain a difference or *residual* signal. They then approximated the residual with another waveshaper + filter model. Using multiple waveshaping models resulted in closer simulations than a single model.

Oversampling with Filtering

Because waveshaping distortion can cause aliasing, the algorithm can be sampled at a higher rate or *oversampled with filtering* to mitigate this effect. Oversampling involves inserting zero-valued samples between existing samples. This increases the Nyquist frequency and facilitates the design of anti-aliasing lowpass filters with a smooth rolloff (Pohlmann 2010).

Wavefolding

A variant of nonlinear distortion synthesis called *wavefolding* came out of the world of modular synthesizers. Originally implemented in the analog Buchla 259 Complex Waveform Generator from 1981 (figure 17.5) and the Serge Wave Multipliers, it has since been incorporated in Eurorack modules by TipTop Audio, Make Noise, Intellijel, Verbos, Befaco, and others. The technique can also be realized in software (e.g., UnfilteredAudio Indent module in VCV Rack and Wavefolder in Reaktor Blocks, among others.).

In wavefolding, when the amplitude of the input signal exceeds a user-specified threshold, (as detected by a comparator), the peaks of the waveform are cut off, similar to digital clipping. The difference is that in wavefolding, the curved amplitude peaks fold over (i.e., they invert at the threshold). Thus

Figure 17.5   Buchla 259 Complex Waveform Generator.

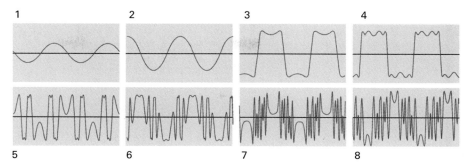

Figure 17.6   A sine wave is folded multiple times as its amplitude is increased from level 1 to level 8. Wavefolding begins at level 3. Courtesy Befaco.

as the signal grows in amplitude it reflects over itself like a mirror image. With simple sine waveforms as input, the folds produce complex spectra (figure 17.6). The sonority of wavefolding with increasing amplitude is reminiscent of time-varying filtering, as different harmonics fade in and out.

Most wavefolders include an additional variable called *offset* or *symmetry* that adds a positive or negative bias. This shifts the center point of the input signal up or down. For example, a positive offset causes the positive sections of the signal to have higher amplitude and the negative sections to have less amplitude. Bipolar bias can make a sonic difference in processing nonsymmetrical waveforms, whether audio or control signals. For even more sonic variation, bias can also be modulated, typically by a bipolar signal (Hetrick 2020).

Esqueda et al. (2017) presented a detailed analysis and model of the Buchla 259 wavefolding circuit. Their Max ~gen model focuses special attention on oversampling strategies for suppression of aliasing caused by the bandwidth-expanding effect of the wavefolder.

18 *Physical Modeling Synthesis*

Status of Physical Modeling Synthesis

Background: Physical Modeling

Excitation and Resonance

Classical Physical Modeling Methodology

Difference Equations
The Mass-Spring Paradigm for Vibrating Strings
The Mass-Spring Paradigm for Vibrating Surfaces and Volumes
The Mass-Spring Paradigm for Excitation
CORDIS-ANIMA and GENESIS
Comparing Classical Methods

Modal Synthesis

Functional Transform Method
Modalys: A Practical Implementation of Modal Synthesis
Modal Synthesis in REAKTOR PRISM
Substantia Modal Synthesizer

Waveguide Synthesis

Waveguide Model of Struck Strings
Generic Waveguide Instrument Model

Waveguide Clarinet
Waveguide Horn
Banded Waveguides for Modeling Solid Objects

Particle-Based Models of Shaken and Scraped Percussion

Models of Pianos

Karplus-Strong Plucked String and Drum Synthesis

Plucked Strings
Drum-like Timbres
Stretching Out the Decay Time
Extensions to KS

Scanned Synthesis

Input Devices for Physical Modeling Synthesis

Source and Parameter Analysis for Physical Modeling

Assessment of Physical Modeling Synthesis

Never, it is believed, since the very first sound of the human voice emanated from the earliest created of mankind, causing the oral mystery of sounded syllables to float upon the balmy airs of Paradise, until now, has aught been perfected which could approximate in any real degree to the Divinely bestowed "music of speech." Many and varied have been the efforts made, from time to time, to accomplish this apparently impossible purpose, but all have proved alike worse than futile. It has been reserved for Mr. Giacopo Saguish, of Constantinople, to become the wonderful and fortunate inventor of the Automaton Head, which (miraculous to relate) he has so contrived, by means of the nicest and most exquisitely constructed mechanism, that it can rival Nature herself in its vocal and elocutionary powers.
—Description of the Anthropoglossos or Mechanical Vocalist, London c. 1835.

Physical modeling synthesis (PhM) starts from mathematical models of the physical acoustics of speech and instrumental sound production. That is, the equations of PhM describe the mechanical and acoustical behavior of a sound production system. This approach has also been called *synthesis by rule* (Ferretti 1965, 1966, 1975), *synthesis from first principles* (Weinreich 1983), or *virtual acoustics* (Yamaha 1993).

PhM technology applies the laws of physics to reproduce the acoustic behavior of an instrument (Vorländer 2008, 2018). Without samples or wavetables, it calculates the sound waveform according to the controls it receives. For example, if one hits a virtual drum head with a virtual stick, a PhM synthesizer simulates (1) the impact of the stick at a particular point, (2) the resulting displacement of the head due to wave motion (taking into account the geometry and properties of the head material), and (3) sound radiation at a particular listening point. Different sounds will be produced by a head of a given geometry and material, depending on the stick velocity, impact point, and listening point. Physical modeling takes all these factors into account naturally because it simulates the behavior of the real object.

The goals of physical modeling synthesis are twofold: one scientific and one artistic. First, PhM investigates the extent to which mathematical equations and algorithmic logic can simulate the sound-producing mechanisms of existing instruments. (For an introduction to the physics of waves in mechanical and acoustic systems, see Pierce [1974], Crawford [1968], or Olson [1991].) This approach is based on the scientific premise that the closer the simulation, the better understood the system is. In this sense, a physical model embodies the Newtonian ideal of a precise mathematical model of a complicated mechanico-acoustic process. An interesting example is the reconstruction using physical models by Stefania Serafin and Amalia De Götzen (2009) of Luigi Russolo's famous Intonarumori instruments, described in his 1916 manifesto *The Art of Noises*.

The second goal of PhM is more artistic. Simulation by physical models can create sounds of fanciful instruments that would otherwise be impossible to build. In this category we include phantasmagorical instruments whose characteristics and geometry can change over time, such as an elastic cello that "expands" and "shrinks" over the course of a phrase, or impossible drums whose heads cannot be broken no matter how intensely they are hit. PhM techniques are often scalable, so that from a description of one gong we can fabricate an ensemble of a dozen gongs, perhaps ranging in diameter from ten centimeters to ten meters. Extrapolating from a specification of a single string, a musician can construct a virtual guitar whose strings are as long and thick as bridge suspension cables. To the delight of musical alchemists, changing the materials of construction—from silver to brass, to exotic woods, to plastic—can be as simple as pressing a button.

PhM excels at simulating transitions between notes and timbres. By dynamically changing the size of certain parts of a virtual instrument (such as elongating a resonating tube), believable sonic transitions often result.

Another characteristic of PhMs is that they capture the accidents that occur in performance, such as squeaks, mode locking, and multiphonics. These sounds are uncontrollable when a novice performer attempts to play, but when used in a controlled manner they inject a dose of realism into the simulation. In PhM synthesis these sounds occur naturally as a side effect of certain gestures and parameter settings. Certain PhMs even let users modify the state of the instrument, "from freshly tuned to completely worn out." Modeling a guitar, for example, it is possible to add interactive gestures like pitch bend, scrapes, slaps, slides, harmonics, pick position, brightness, feedback, and palm muting (Scandalis, Smith, and Porcaro 2015).

Note that in this chapter, when we use the term, *physical modeling* we are referring to computational models of speech and acoustic instruments. Another class of physical models simulate electronic instruments. This involves models of circuit behavior. We discuss these in the next chapter under the rubric of *virtual analog modeling.*

A related area is *procedural audio* (Farnell 2010; Baldan, Monache, and Rocchesso 2017). Procedural audio models natural sound (e.g., wind) and mechanical sound (e.g., helicopters) for use in interactive systems like game audio, computer animations, web browsers, and virtual reality environments. It differs from PhM in that it does not necessarily rely on a physics-based solution but instead adapts efficient methods of sound synthesis (e.g., waveshaping, modulation, or granular) to achieve perceptually similar results on a case-by-case basis.

Status of Physical Modeling Synthesis

PhM synthesis encompasses a family of techniques conceived over many decades. Building a physical model of an acoustic instrument from scratch requires a well-equipped acoustics laboratory with precise measurement tools. Once built, a mathematical model can pose a heavy computational burden. For these reasons, PhM synthesis evolved slowly at first. By the 1990s, the first real-time synthesizers based on PhM began to appear.

Efficient implementations have been developed for some types of PhM synthesis (McIntyre, Schumacher, and Woodhouse 1983; Smith 1986, 1987a, 1987b, 1992, 2010; Keefe 1992; Adrien 1991; Woodhouse 1992; Cook 1991a, 1991b, 1992, 1993; Borin, De Poli, and Sarti 1992; Rabenstein and Petrausch 2008; Scavone 2018; Bader 2018). These efficient algorithms (such as modal synthesis and waveguides) are based on common digital signal processing structures such as delay lines, filters, and table-lookup operations. Sometimes efficiency comes at the expense of drastic simplifications. This can result in instrument-like tones without striking realism. This is not to say that such simulations are uninteresting. From a compositional viewpoint, flexible instrument-like tones can be useful.

A variety of methods of physical modeling coexist. As Trautmann and Rabenstein (2003) observed,

> *There cannot be a single "winner" within the different physical modeling methods. Depending on the instrument and the physical system, one of the simulation methods is superior to the other. . . . Thus it is important to combine the different physical modeling methods to obtain physically meaningful and computationally efficient simulations of musical instruments. (213)*

This chapter describes both the classical or computationally intensive models and efficient strategies such as modal synthesis and waveguides. All three approaches have been tried in designing models of instruments. One trend combines more than one method in a complex model (Avanzini and Marogna 2010). We also present an efficient method called Karplus-Strong synthesis further on in the chapter. The final section deals with a hybrid approach that combines physical modeling with wavetable scanning.

Background: Physical Modeling

The concepts and the terminology, and some of the formulas used in physical modeling synthesis can be traced to late eighteenth- and nineteenth-century scientific treatises on the nature of sound and speech. Wolfgang von Kempelen was a pioneer in the development of a mechanical speech synthesizer. After years of experimentation, he completed a functional model of the human vocal tract (von Kempelen 1791).

Lord Rayleigh's extraordinary volume *The Theory of Sound* ([1894] 1945) detailed the principles of vibrating systems such as membranes, plates, bars, and shells and described the mathematical physics of vibrations in the open air, in tubes, and in boxes. Other nineteenth-century pioneers built mechanical models to simulate the physics of musical instruments (Helmholtz 1885; Poynting and Thomson 1900; Tyndall 1875; Mayer 1878). Following the invention of the vacuum tube, scientists experimented with analog electronic models (Steward 1922; Miller 1935; Stevens and Fant 1953).

As shown in figure 18.1, the developer of the famous RCA Synthesizers, Harry F. Olson, also designed analog circuit models of percussion, lip-reed instruments, air-reed instruments, struck string instruments, and the voice (Olson 1967). But progress in PhM was slow until the computer era.

John Kelly and Carol Lochbaum at Bell Telephone Laboratories were pioneers in adapting a physical model of the human vocal tract to a digital computer (Kelly and Lochbaum 1962). Their rendition of *Bicycle Built for Two,* which appeared on the Bell Telephone Laboratories vinyl record *Music from Mathematics* produced by Max V. Mathews in 1960, became a world-famous symbol of the increasing capabilities of digital computers. (The Stanley Kubrick film *2001: A Space Odyssey* references this achievement when the once-powerful computer HAL regresses to its youth and sings this song. The version in the film is sung by a human actor, however.)

The model used by Kelly and Lochbaum used a pulse generator and a noise source fed into a lowpass filter. Similar methods were used by the PhM pioneer Ercolino Ferretti (1965, 1966, 1975). These *source-filter* models would be considered rough approximations by today's standards. Yet any

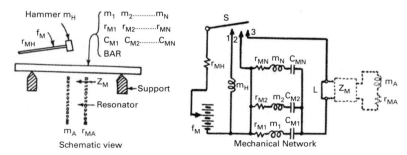

Figure 18.1 Schematic view and mechanical network of a percussion instrument of a bar or rod type (Olson 1967).

computational model is rough compared to the quantum level of ground truth; physical models are always simplifications.

Lejaren Hiller, James Beauchamp, and Pierre Ruiz at the University of Illinois were the first to adapt *finite difference time domain* models (FDTD) to the synthesis of instruments (Hiller and Beauchamp 1967; Ruiz 1970; Hiller and Ruiz 1971). Their work focused on synthesizing the sound of vibrating objects such as strings, bars, plates, and membranes set into motion by plucking and striking. These experiments took hours of computation in the mainframe era.

Fresh interest in physical modeling synthesis was provoked by the discovery of the Karplus-Strong plucked-string algorithm (discussed further on), an efficient waveguide method that could be realized in real time (Karplus and Strong 1983). This method came about more as an accident than as an intentional attempt at physical modeling but was soon refined and generalized (Jaffe and Smith 1983). In 1993 the Yamaha company announced the first commercial real-time synthesizers based on waveguides, the VL1 and VP1.

Since the 1990s, an enormous amount of research has been invested in PhM synthesis, and many instrument simulations have been developed. For detailed historical surveys refer to Fletcher and Rossing (1991), Keefe (1992), Välimäki, Penttinen, et al. (2006), and Bilbao (2009b).

Excitation and Resonance

Question: The resonant modes of a wind instrument are not perfect harmonics, but the tone may be perfectly harmonic. On the other hand, a percussion instrument has non-harmonic resonances and produces a non-harmonic sound. What is the difference?

Answer: The key here is not just to consider the resonant modes and how they are placed, but how the instrument is excited. If you pick up a trumpet and hit it with a hammer, the sound is percussive. If you take a snare drum and excite it with a [vibrator] the sound is harmonic.
—Bernie Hutchins, 1984

A fundamental principle of physical modeling synthesis is the interaction between an *exciter* and a *resonator*. An *excitation* is an action that causes vibration, such as the stroke of a bow, the hit of a stick, or a blow of air. A *resonance* is the response of the body of an instrument to the excitation vibration. From a signal-processing point of view, the body acts as a time-varying filter applied to the excitation signal. For a mathematical analysis of resonance, refer to Loy (2007).

In general, the exciter has a *nonlinear* behavior, and the resonator has a *linear* behavior. By nonlinear we mean a system that has built-in thresholds that, if exceeded, cause the system to respond in a new way, as if a switch had been thrown. By linear acoustical system, we mean a system that responds proportionally to the amount of energy applied to it. If we put two signals into a linear system, we expect that output to be their sum.

As Bilbao, Desvages, et al. (2019) point out, the assumption of linear behavior in a resonator is not always valid. Examples of nonlinear behavior include cymbal crashes and snare drum rattling (Bilbao and Torin 2015).

Exciter/resonator interactions fall into two basic classes: *decoupled* (or *feed-forward*) and *coupled* (or *feedback*). An example of decoupled excitation is subtractive synthesis, where an excitation signal such as noise is sent through a resonant filter. No interaction happens other than a transfer of energy from the exciter to the resonator.

In contrast, the mechanism of tone production in a saxophone is an example of coupled excitation. By coupled, we mean that the vibration of the resonating part feeds back to the excitation part. For example, the frequency of the vibrating reed is strongly influenced by acoustic feedback from the resonating bore (tube) of the instrument after being excited initially by a blast of air from the mouth. Similarly the interaction of a violin bow and a string is mediated by the feedback of friction. Bow force, bow velocity, and the bow-bridge distance strongly affect the sound (Demoucron 2008). Modeling air flow through a flute is a complicated problem of fluid dynamics in a coupled system (Verge 1996).

This interaction between the excitation and the resonance creates the variety and subtlety of sound we hear in performances by instrumental virtuosi. Because PhM techniques model this interaction, they tend to communicate a sense of the gesture behind the sound (Florens and Cadoz 1991; Adrien 1991). This stands in contrast to basic sampling synthesis, which replays the same unvarying sample.

In some implementations of PhM synthesis, the excitation comes from an input device (or controller) played by a performer. This is explained in this chapter's section on input devices. Chapter 40 presents more on musical input devices in general.

Classical Physical Modeling Methodology

The classical approach to physical modeling is represented by the early work of Hiller and Ruiz at the University of Illinois (Ruiz 1970; Hiller and Ruiz 1971). Their models were based on difference equations (explained in the next section). Hiller and Ruiz took the vibrating string as a point of departure in their pioneering research. They solved difference equations for strings plucked and stroked at the center, near the ends, and at the endpoint. The velocity of a bow, the applied pressure, and a friction coefficient were supplied as part of the initial conditions. They also designed difference equations to model air friction, string thickness, movement of the bridge, transmission of energy by the bridge to a resonator, and the radiation of energy from a resonating box. This is an example of the aforementioned FDTD model (Bilbao 2009a, b).

The classical PhM methodology builds a mathematical model according to the following steps:

1. Specify the physical dimensions and constants of vibrating objects, such as their mass and elasticity. This is done because in acoustic instruments, sound is produced by vibrating objects such as strings, reeds, membranes, or flows of air within a tube or body of an instrument.

2. Specify the *boundary conditions* to which the vibrating object is constrained. These are the limiting values of the variables that cannot be exceeded. The boundary conditions also account for the possibility that the system has not fully come to rest or settled following a previous input.

3. Specify the *initial state* in the algorithm, for example, the starting position of a string at rest.

4. Describe the excitation algorithmically as a force impinging on the vibrating object in some way. Typical sources of excitation in acoustic instruments include percussive sources (drumsticks, mallets, and piano actions), wind sources (the flow of air between through a mouthpiece or between reeds), and the bowed sources of stringed instruments. A coupling between exciter and resonator can be specified in this algorithm.

5. Specify the *impedance* effects. Impedance is a resistance to a driving force. In a wave-producing medium with high impedance, a large force is required to produce a small amplitude. As waves pass from one part of an instrument to another, the impedance of the different parts alters the wave propagation. For example, if two strings are joined and the second is much heavier than the first, the wave will hit the heavier string and nearly all the energy will be reflected to the lighter string. If the two strings are of equal impedance, there will be no reflections. Researchers have measured the impedances of various instrument components, and the appropriate equations can be inserted into the physical model (Campbell and Greated 1987).

6. Describe the filtering effects due to factors such as friction and sound radiation patterns as a further restriction on the conditions of vibration.

At this point one has a rather complicated system of equations that represents a physical model of the instrument. The corresponding dynamical system and its wave equation is subjected to the initial conditions and the excitation (Morse 1936; Hiller and Ruiz 1971). The wave equation describes how each point on a vibrating object (line, surface, or volume) changes position over time on the basis of forces in its immediate neighborhood. Refer to Loy (2007) for a derivation of the wave equation. The wave equation is solved by a recursive procedure that tries to find reasonable values for many interdependent variables simultaneously. The solution takes the form of a discrete sample value representing a sound pressure wave at a given instant of time.

The classical methodology uses difference equations as models of vibrating structures in order to generate the sound waveforms. As an example of the classical method, Bilbao (2009a) simulated reed wind instruments using time-space *partial differential equations* (PDEs). Bilbao and Torin (2015) modeled the interactions of strings on a fretboard and finger-stopping effects (figure 18.2).

Difference Equations

Differential equations describe the vibrational behavior of physical objects. A differential equation involves differences and derivatives of functions. These equations are usually invoked when describing how a signal changes over time. Coincidentally, the first application of differential equations, by Joseph Bernoulli in 1732, was the simulation of a vibrating string of finite length—a central technique of physical modeling synthesis. Differential equations usually have an independent variable t of time. The solution to a differential equation is not a number but a function, often a function of time

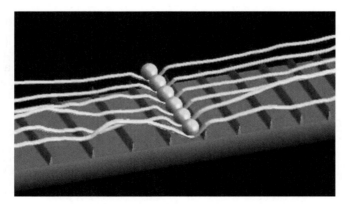

Figure 18.2 Simulation of a barred chord on a fretted guitar neck (Bilbao and Torin 2015).

(waveform or envelope). Refer to Loy (2007) for a tutorial on differential equations in acoustics.

Differential equations describe continuous analog systems. On an analog computer, differential equations can be solved directly. By contrast, in the discrete world of digital signal processing, these equations are called *difference equations*, in which new sample values are derived from combinations of old sample values. Difference equations, for example, describe the operation of digital filters. All the FIR and IIR filter equations in chapter 28 are examples of difference equations.

Physicists use difference equations to describe the laws of change of physical quantities. In modeling a phenomenon this way, the first step is to find the smallest number of variables that can accurately describe the state of the modeled phenomenon. The next step sets up the simplest difference equations that are precise descriptions of the laws governing the changes in these variables. The difference equations can be integrated to obtain estimates of the acoustic wave in response to external forces and boundary conditions (Smith 2004). Certain difference equations have algebraic solutions, and others can be solved only by iterative approximation methods (Press et al. 1988; Bilbao 2009b). In this method, a solution is determined by first guessing at a solution and then improving the solution iteratively. (A recent paper has recast the solution to PDEs in the context of machine learning in the Fourier domain, which can speed up the process greatly. See Li et al. [2020].)

The Mass-Spring Paradigm for Vibrating Strings

Another classical method of PhM synthesis is based on a *mass-spring model* or *lumped mass-spring model* (Bilbao 2009b). The mass-spring model has long been used by physicists to describe vibrating objects and the waves they emit (Crawford 1968; Hutchins 1978; Benade 1990; Cadoz 2002; Cadoz, Luciani, and Florens 1984, 2003; Weinreich 1983; Smith 1982, 1983; Adrien and Rodet 1985; Boutillon 1984; Chafe 1985; Loy 2006, 2007; Villeneuve, Cadoz, and Castagné 2015). In this approach, a plucked or bowed string is modeled as a series of discrete masses connected by springs. Smith (2010) devotes one hundred pages of his book to a detailed analysis of the mass-spring model. He presents results of modeling a guitar bridge and woodwind tone holes by this method.

The mass-spring paradigm captures two essential qualities of vibrating media. First, vibrating media have a *density,* which is the mass per unit amount of the medium. For a string, the density can be measured as its weight. Second, vibrating media are *elastic;* if any part of the medium is displaced from its position of equilibrium, a restoring force immediately appears that tries to push it back. If we create a disturbance in one part of the string by plucking it, the displaced parts of the medium exert forces on adjacent parts, causing them to move away from their equilibrium position. This in turn causes the next portions to move and so on, in a process called *wave propagation*. Because of the mass of the medium, the parts do not move instantly away from their equilibrium positions but instead require a short time. As a result, the pluck impulse propagates through the medium at a specific speed.

Figure 18.3a depicts a string as a number of identical masses connected together by light springs. If the first mass is displaced to the right, the first spring compresses, exerting a force on the second mass (figure 18.3b). The second mass will then move to the right, compressing the second spring and so on, as in figure 18.3c. Because the displacements of the successive masses are in the direction that the disturbance is traveling (that is, horizontally), this is called a *longitudinal wave*.

Figures 18.3d and 18.3e show *transverse wave* propagation that occurs when the initial displacement is perpendicular to the direction that the wave propagates. This is the main type of wave vibration occurring in musical strings that are plucked, hammered, or bowed. Another type of vibration is *rotational,* but this is not usually modeled in sound synthesis.

Separating the string into a set of discrete masses has the computational advantage that the effect of excitation on a given point of the string can be modeled as the application of a force to a single mass that transmits this force to the other masses via the springs. After a string has been struck, the shape of the string at a particular point in time is determined by solving a set of difference equations.

The Mass-Spring Paradigm for Vibrating Surfaces and Volumes

The mass-spring representation can be extended to vibrating surfaces and volumes. Surfaces can be modeled as a fabric of masses connected to by more than one spring (figure 18.4a) or arranged in a circular pattern to model the skin of a drum (figure 18.4b). Volumes take the shape of a lattice (figure 18.4c) with the masses interconnected up to six ways.

The Mass-Spring Paradigm for Excitation

So far, we have described systems of masses and linear springs as models for resonators. If the springs are defined to have a nonlinear behavior, they become good models for excitation. The nonlinear oscillators that are often used as exciters in PhM methods can be viewed in terms of the mass and nonlinear spring model (Rodet 1992). The masses represent the inertial

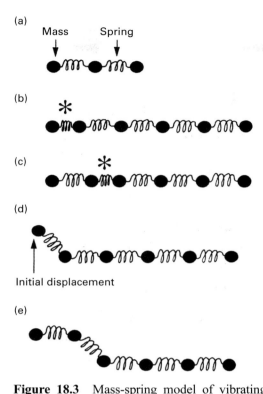

Figure 18.3 Mass-spring model of vibrating strings. (a) The springs model the elasticity of the string. (b) In a longitudinal wave, the disturbance is in the same direction as the wave propagation. The initial displacement (compression of the spring) is marked by an asterisk. (c) Following state. (d) In a transverse wave, the initial disturbance is perpendicular to the direction of wave propagation. (e) Following state.

behavior, while nonlinear springs account for elastic properties of the body of the exciter. A nonlinear friction component accounts for the contact condition between the exciter and the resonator. Such a representation has been applied to a model of the hammer of a piano, for example (Suzuki 1987).

CORDIS-ANIMA and GENESIS

A Grenoble-based team led by Claude Cadoz has long been an exponent of the mass-spring paradigm with a focus on interactivity (Cadoz, Luciani, and Florens 1984, 1993, 2003; Cadoz, Lisowski, and Florens 1990). They developed CORDIS-ANIMA, a modular language with modules that satisfy Newtonian physics. Modules fall into two categories: MAT modules represent "matter," being either moving or fixed; LIA modules mediate interactions and enable interconnections between MAT modules. Modules exchange two kinds of signals through time: positions and forces.

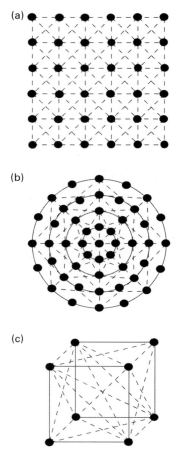

Figure 18.4 Models of vibrating surfaces and volumes as masses connected by springs. The black dots are the masses, and the lines represent springs. (a) Model of a vibrating surface. (b) Model of a drum head as a circular arrangement of springs and masses. (c) A vibrating volume can be modeled as a lattice of masses connected by springs on six sides.

GENESIS is a front-end GUI to CORDIS-ANIMA. Using GENESIS, physical networks can be constructed and tested using graphical representations (Castagné and Cadoz 2002). Thousands of modules can be placed on a virtual bench and interconnected. The Genesis bench is a 3D workspace that displays the acoustical properties of any linear physical network. For example, an impulse response graph displays the amplitude of each vibration mode given a pair of excitation and listening points. One can also visualize nonlinear behavior such as excitation by a hammer on a plate. Figure 18.5 shows wave propagation on a vibrating plate.

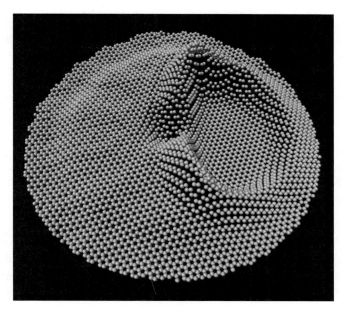

Figure 18.5   GENESIS display shows wave propagation in a plate.

Artists can arrange different models on the bench and interact with them to produce sound. The sound output of GENESIS can be sent to any number of channels for spatialization (Villeneuve, Cadoz, and Castagné 2015).

Comparing Classical Methods

The unifying theme of classical approaches to PhM is their reliance on difference equations. However, Bilbao (2009b) draws a distinction between what he calls *lumped mass-spring* models and *direct simulation* by FDTD models. In his view, mass-spring models are not as flexible as FDTD models. In the FDTD approach, the spatial structure of a sound-producing system (string, plate, membrane, etc.) is described by a model based on PDEs. The FDTD model is computed over a spatial grid composed of a finite set of points. Time is also discretized.

Another classical approach to physical modeling synthesis falls under the rubric of *finite-element methods* (FEM). Like FDTD methods, FEM subdivides an acoustic system into smaller parts, creating a mesh representation with a finite number of points. Each subdomain in the mesh is represented by a set of element equations (called *basis* or *shape functions*) that locally approximate the behavior of the acoustic system. See Bader (2005) for an application of this approach, which he considers an extension of FDTD, to the classical guitar.

As mentioned previously, some practical implementations of PhM synthesis combine classical methods with modal and waveguide techniques, discussed next.

Modal Synthesis

The motion of a complicated system having many moving parts may always be regarded as compounded from simpler motions, called modes, all going on at once. No matter how complicated the system, we will find that each one of its modes has properties very similar to those of a simple harmonic oscillator.
—F. Crawford, *Waves*, 1968

Modal synthesis is an alternative to classical methods (Calvet, Laurens, and Adrien 1990; Adrien 1991). It starts from the premise that a sound-producing object can be represented as a modular collection of vibrating substructures. The number of substructures is usually very small in comparison with those in the classical approach. Typical substructures include strings, violin bridges, violin bodies, acoustic tubes, bells, drum heads, and so on. As in the mass-spring paradigm, the substructures respond to an externally applied excitation (forces, air flows, pressures, or movements). When excited, each substructure has a set of natural *modes of vibration.* These modes are specific to a particular structure; they include geometry, topology (holes and joints), density, and many other physical properties (Benade 1990). The normal modes of a vibrating musical instrument (strings, air pipes, drums, etc.) are its harmonics or overtones.

A modal approach benefits from a well-established methodology for analysis of modes of vibration, due to its many industrial applications (Hurty and Rubinstein 1964; Hou 1969; He and Fu 2001). This analysis methodology can be applied to musical instruments (Bork 1992; Smith 2010; Ban, Zambon, and Fontana 2010). For example, physics software such as Comsol and Autodesk Fusion 360 can analyze vibrations in a given solid made with any material.

Modal synthesis characterizes each substructure as a set of analyzed modal data, consisting of (1) the frequencies and damping coefficients of the substructure's resonating modes, and (2) a set of coordinates representing the vibrating mode's shape. Hence the general instantaneous vibration of an instrument can be expressed as the sum of the contributions of its modes.

In Adrien's implementation, the instantaneous vibration is described by a vector of N coordinates associated with N chosen points over the structure. These coordinates are bound together in such a way that the geometrical and mechanical features are close to the instrument's characteristics. The set of N points is equivalent to the corresponding N sets of modal data. A given vibration mode can be described by the relative displacements of the N points.

For simple vibrating substructures such as an undamped string, modal data can be found in the mechanical engineering literature as equations. For complex vibrating structures, modal data can be obtained through experimentation with actual instruments. Tools for mechanical analysis, such as transducers and analysis software, are readily available because they are extensively used in industrial applications such as aircraft design. Bruyns (2006) showed how to apply modal analysis and synthesis to arbitrarily shaped objects.

Modal synthesis is more flexible than classical approaches, due to the modularity of the modal substructures. It partitions sound-producing mechanisms into vibrating substructures. One can dynamically add or subtract substructures to create time-varying synthesis effects, such as "expanding" or "shrinking" the size of an instrument. Moreover, one can combine modal and FDTD models to create sophisticated simulations of complicated instruments such as pianos (Guillaume 2011).

As Sancristoforo (2020) has noted, exciting a modal synthesizer with real-world microphone-captured sounds—rather than synthetic excitation functions—results in more interesting dynamic and timbral ranges.

Functional Transform Method

We should mention the *functional transform method* (FTM), proposed by Trautman and Rabenstein (2003), which is closely related to modal synthesis. The advantage of the FTM approach is that whereas traditional modal synthesis parameters are bound to a discrete set of measured modal patterns, FTM can more precisely model the system being studied. Thus it allows for a more continuous exploration of the parameter space. Nonlinear interconnections of modules as well as multirate implementations to reduce the computational load have been developed (Rabenstein et al. 2007). Rabenstein, Koch, and Popp (2010) presents an FTM model of tubular bells. A disadvantage of FTM is that it can be more complicated to set up than modal synthesis. Thus one approach is to combine FTM with other methods mentioned in this chapter.

Modalys: A Practical Implementation of Modal Synthesis

The Modalys system, originally developed by Jean-Marie Adrien and Joseph Morrison, is a realization of modal synthesis as a modular software toolkit (Morrison and Waxman 1991; Morrison and Adrien 1991). For this pedagogical reason, we present a full example here.

In the world of Modalys, you sit before a virtual workbench with a collection of *objects* that you assemble into instruments. The objects include strings, air columns, metal plates, membranes, and violin and cello bridges. Other objects excite the instrument, such as bows, hammers, and plectra. Interactions between objects are called *connections*. Connections can be thought of as black boxes that go between objects and specify a relationship between them. For example, two objects can be connected by means of gluing, bowing, plucking, striking, and pushing. On each connection are *controllers*—knobs that stipulate the parameters of the control. A bow connection, for example, has controllers for speed of bowing, amount of rosin, and so on. Finally, a physical location on an object is called an *access*. To connect two objects, for example, we need to specify their accesses.

Modalys allows one to design instruments using one of three interfaces: a textual programming language based on LISP, a patching interface based on IRCAM's OpenMusic environment, or the Max patcher.

Figure 18.6a shows a schematic patch in Modalys. Figure 18.6b shows how the concepts of objects, connections, controllers, and accesses are expressed in LISP code.

The following example is written in Scheme (Abelson and Sussman 1985), a dialect of the LISP programming language. The Scheme language follows a general syntax of the form

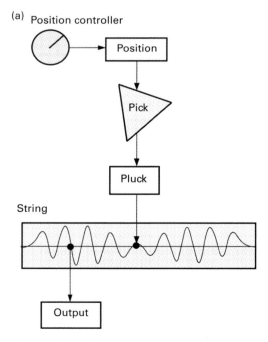

Figure 18.6   Plucked string simulated by the MODALYS program. (a) Graphical representation. (b) MODALYS code in LISP corresponding to (a). Lines beginning with a semicolon are comments.

(b)
```
;;; MOSAIC plucked string example, written in Scheme

;;; Make string and plectrum objects

(define my-string (make-object 'monostring))
(define my-plectrum (make-object 'bi-two-mass))

;;; Make pluck connection between plectrum and string

(define my-string-pluck
      (make-access my-string (const .6) 'trans0))
(define my-plectrum-pluck
      (make-access my-plectrum (const 1) 'trans0))

(make-connection 'pluck my-string-pluck
      my-plectrum-pluck 0 .1 (const 50))

;;; Make position connection to push plectrum

(define my-plectrum-move
      (make-access my-plectrum (const 0) 'trans0))

;;; Move plectrum from .1 meter to -.5 meter in .5 secs

(make-connection 'position my-plectrum-move
      (make-controller 'envelope 1
                       (list (list 0.00  .1)
                             (list 0.50 -.5)))))

;;; Make listening point on string

(define my-string-out
      (make-access my-string (const .3) 'trans0))

(make-point-output my-string-out)

;;; Run the synthesis and play the sound

(run 2) ; Make 2 seconds of sound
(play)
```

Figure 18.6   (continued)

```
(function arguments)
```

This means that the function or operation name is specified first, followed by the specific arguments to that operation. For example, the expression (+ 2 3) says to add 2 and 3. When parenthetical expressions are nested, the inner ones are executed before the outer ones. For example, the command

```
(define my-string (make-object 'mono-string))
```

creates a string object named my-string and places it on the virtual workbench. When Modalys carries out this command, it performs a full modal analysis. The name my-string points to the data generated by this analysis. Besides a string, we need a plectrum, expressed

```
(define my-plectrum (make-object 'bi-two-mass))
```

We want to tell Modalys to use the plectrum to pluck the string, but Modalys requires that we stipulate specific *access points*. These are given by the lines

```
(define my-string-pluck
  (make-access my-string (const .6) 'trans0))
(define my-plectrum-pluck
  (make-access my-plectrum (const 1) 'trans0))
```

The names my-string-pluck and my-plectrum-pluck are just names for the points at which the two objects touch. The next line makes the plucking connection

```
(make-connection 'pluck my-string-pluck
  my-plectrum-pluck 0 .1 (const 50))
```

The first argument after the 'pluck are the access points for the *object plucked* and the *plucker*. The subsequent two arguments say that the position of the object plucked is 0 and that the plucker is 0.1 meter from that point. The third argument directs a controller that determines when to release the string. The number 50 is the force in newtons. (A newton is a unit of force. A force of 1 newton pushes 1 kilogram to accelerate 1 meter per second.) When the plucker is pushing harder than 50 newtons, the pluck connection disengages. The next lines make a second access on the plectrum so that it can be moved by an envelope controller.

```
(define my-plectrum-move
  (make-access my-plectrum (const 0) 'trans0))
(make-connection 'position my-plectrum-move
  (make-controller 'envelope 1
    (list (list 0.00 .1)
      (list 0.50 -.5))))
```

The envelope values are specified in terms of pairs of the form (*time value*). The list functions create a list of two lists out of these pairs. The last line in figure 18.6 makes an access for listening to the string and commands the instrument to play.

Modal Synthesis in REAKTOR PRISM

REAKTOR PRISM is a software synthesizer for modal synthesis (Gover, Jackson, and Schmitt 2010).

PRISM starts with an exciter that generates impulses or noise. The exciter signal is fed into the Modal Bank, which has dozens of resonating bandpass filters per voice (figure 18.7). The narrowband filters of the Modal Bank turn impulse signals into decaying sine oscillations, and with noise signals they create continuous tuned sounds. The filters function like the oscillation modes of a physical object (e.g. membrane, string, and mallet), where each mode has a characteristic frequency, decay time, and amplitude amount. By adding up multiple resonant partials, complex sounds can be produced. Depending on the chosen frequencies, the sound can be a clear harmonic tone or a more inharmonic timbre characteristic of percussion instruments.

Substantia Modal Synthesizer

Substantia by Giorgio Sancristoforo is a modal synthesizer in software (figure 18.8). Users can choose from among sixteen model shapes and also stipulate one of twenty-three materials (aluminum, gold, glass, copper, stone,

Figure 18.7   Detail of REAKTOR PRISM front panel showing Exciter and Modal Bank.

Figure 18.8   Substantia modal synthesizer screenshot.

etc.). Alongside classic shapes like pipes and bowls are unusual shapes such as pyramids and serpentines (Sancristoforo 2020). Each shape resonates at its own particular frequencies.

At the core of Substantia are hundreds of resonant bandpass filters. The tuning of the resonant frequencies and the balance between even and odd harmonics can be changed in real time. Users can play or excite the resonators using a built-in noise generator, their own imported samples, or a pair of *contact microphones* (also called *vibration pickup microphones*) mounted on a plywood square. A contact microphone picks up vibrations from things to which it is attached. Performers can use their hands or small objects to scratch, rub, tap the surface of the square. Users can also play on a keyboard to produce note patterns that can be looped and varied using the probabilistic sequencer/rhythm generator.

Waveguide Synthesis

Waveguides are an efficient implementation of PhM synthesis (Smith 1982, 1983, 1986, 1987a, 1987b, 1991b, 1992, 1993, 2010; Garnett and Mont-Reynaud 1988; Cook 1991a, 1991b, 1992, 1993; Hirschman 1991; Hirschman, Cook, and Smith 1991; Paladin and Rocchesso 1992; Van Duyne and Smith 1993; Mikelson 2000a). Julius O. Smith III's book *Physical Audio Signal Processing* (2010) is a major tome on this topic.

Simply put, a waveguide (or *waveguide filter*) is a computational model of a medium along which waves travel. In musical applications this medium is usually a tube or a string. Waveguides have long been used by physicists to describe the behavior of waves in resonant spaces (Crawford 1968).

A basic waveguide building block is a pair of *digital delay lines* (see chapter 30). Each delay line is injected with an excitation wave propagating in the opposite direction and reflecting back to the center when it reaches the end of the line. A delay line is a good model of this process because wavefronts take a finite amount of time to travel the length of a resonating medium. Traveling waves running up and down the waveguide cause resonances and interferences at frequencies related to its dimensions. When the waveguide network is symmetric in all directions, the sound it produces when excited tends to be harmonic. If the waveguide curves, changes size, or intersects another waveguide, this changes its resonant pattern. As we discuss further on, the voice and instruments such as brass, woodwinds, and strings can be simulated by means of oscillators driving a waveguide network. Garnett (1987) built a simplified model of a piano out of waveguides. Lindroos, Penttinen, and Välimäki (2011) made an electric guitar model. Chapter 33 describes applications of waveguides to reverberation.

An attractive feature of waveguides is that they are largely compatible with the Music N synthesis language paradigm introduced in chapter 5. This means that the building blocks of waveguide networks can be merged with standard unit generators (Link 1992).

The next four sections describe a waveguide model of struck strings, a generic waveguide instrument that can simulate either stringed or wind instruments, and more specific models of a clarinet and a horn.

Waveguide Model of Struck Strings

The simplest waveguide model is a monochord or single-string instrument. The waveguide model can be understood as a picture of what happens when a string is struck at a particular point: two waves travel in opposite directions from the impact point (figure 18.9). When they reach the bridges, some of their energy is absorbed, and some is reflected back in the opposite direction, toward the point of impact and beyond where the two waves interact, causing resonances and interferences. In the parlance of waveguide theory, the bridges act as *scattering junctions* because they disperse energy to all connected waveguides (Loy 2007; Smith 2010). The pitch of the vibrating string is directly related to the length of the two waveguides.

Generic Waveguide Instrument Model

Figure 18.10 shows a generic model of a simple waveguide instrument capable of modeling stringed or wind instruments (Cook 1992). A sharp

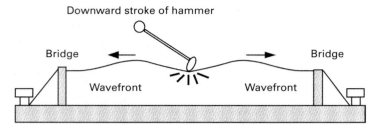

Figure 18.9   A string struck by a hammer at the center generates two waves moving in opposite directions. This behavior is the basis of the delay line paradigm of string vibration.

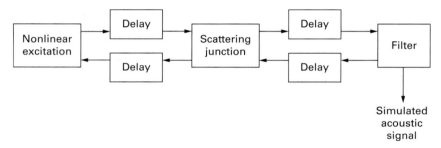

Figure 18.10   Generic waveguide instrument model capable of simulating stringed or wind instruments (after Cook [1992]). A nonlinear excitation injected into the upper delay line travels until it hits the scattering junction, which models the losses and dispersion of energy that occur at junctions in acoustical systems. Some energy returns to the oscillator junction, and some passes on to the output junction, modeled by a filter.

nonlinear excitation wave is injected into a delay line. For a plucked string, the excitation can be modeled as a bandlimited impulse (Smith 2010). The wave travels through the delay line until it hits a scattering junction that passes some energy on and bounces some energy back. The scattering junction is a linear or nonlinear filter that models the effect of a finger or bow pressing on a string or a tone hole on a wind instrument. The filter at the end models the effect of the bridge, body, or bell of the instrument.

In order to approximate a noncylindrical tube such as a horn or the vocal tract, the tube is divided into equal-length sections, each of which is represented by a waveguide filter. This is called *sampling in space,* directly corresponding to *sampling in time*, because it takes a finite amount of time for a wavefront to travel a certain distance in space. The parameters of the scattering junction at the boundary of adjacent waveguides derive from physical dimensions of the tube at that point.

Figure 18.11 shows how a smooth acoustic tube is partitioned into a series of discrete sections, each modeled by a waveguide. Similar approximations can

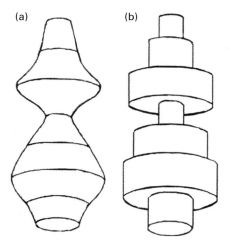

Figure 18.11 Waveguide approximation of noncylindrical tubes. (a) Smooth acoustic tube, such as an exotic horn or a portion of the vocal tract. (b) Approximation by partitioning the tube into sections—in effect, sampling in space.

be fitted to two-dimensional surfaces and three-dimensional spaces (for room reverberation simulation) (Smith 1991b, 2010; Cook 1992, 2007).

In brass and woodwind simulations, a waveguide simulates each section of tube of the instrument. The reed or mouthpiece, which serves as the excitation, is modeled either by a simple table-lookup oscillator or by a more complicated nonlinear oscillator driving the waveguide network. The nonlinear oscillator is modeled as a mass-spring-damper mechanism. This same scheme (nonlinear oscillator driving waveguide network) can also be applied to bowed string synthesis, where the nonlinear oscillator models the interaction between the bow and the string (Chafe 1985).

By adjoining different waveguides via scattering junctions, adding filters at strategic points, and inserting nonlinear junctions that excite the waveguide network, researchers have constructed models of whole families of musical instruments. A generalization that extends to 3D structures is the *digital waveguide mesh* (Van Duyne and Smith 1993), which has been applied to vocal tract modeling and reverberation (Murphy et al. 2007). The next two sections give specific examples of waveguide instrument models.

Waveguide Clarinet

Figure 18.12 shows a waveguide model of a clarinet, after Hirschman, Cook, and Smith (1991) and Hirschman (1991). The clarinet model has five parts:

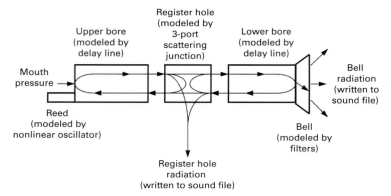

Figure 18.12   Clarinet modeled as a five-part structure using waveguide techniques. Only a single hole is needed because the size of the upper and lower bores changes according to the pitch being played.

1. Reed
2. Upper bore
3. Register hole
4. Lower bore
5. Bell

Only a single hole is needed because the size of the upper and lower bores changes according to the pitch being played. This type of model produces a clarinet-like tone with several realistic features, including the generation of harmonics according to input amplitude, and instrument squeaking, given the appropriate inputs.

Waveguide Horn

Figure 18.13 shows a screen image from TBone, a brass instrument simulation using waveguides controlled by a graphic interface (Cook 1991b). Although this is a historical example, it serves the pedagogical point of exposing a multiplicity of parameters even in a highly simplified model. The display divides into three windows: French Trumbuba Controller, Performer Controller, and Time-Varying Event Controller.

The French Trumbuba Controller at the bottom provides graphical controls for modifying the instrument. Sliders control the position of the trombone slide, the flare of the bell, and individual sections of the mouthpiece. Text fields let users specify the length of the bell, the slide, and each section of tubing associated with the four valves. Clicking the valve buttons causes them to

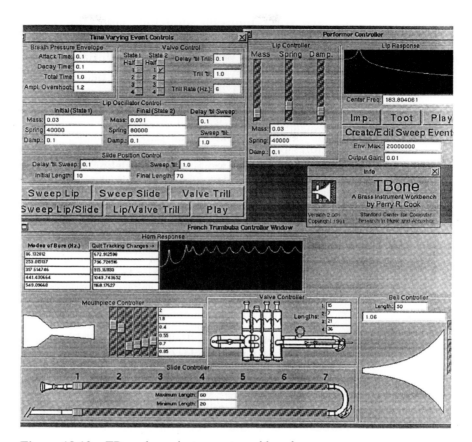

Figure 18.13   TBone brass instrument workbench.

toggle between the up and down positions and causes the appropriate piece of tubing to be placed in or removed from the acoustic circuit. The spectrum display shows the magnitude Fourier transform of the impulse response of the current horn configuration. This is called the *transfer function* and describes the gain each frequency would experience in a trip through the horn system.

The Performer Controller window at the upper right provides controls for modifying the model of the brass player's lip. Simple controls of mass, spring constant, and damping are enough to specify the natural frequency of the lip oscillator. The transfer function of the lip is shown in a spectrum display. When the Toot button is pressed, the instrument synthesizes and plays a short note. The Play button causes the same sound file to be played again.

The Time-Varying Event Controller at the upper left has controls for time-varying sound synthesis. Sweeps of the lip and slide and valve trills can be specified by begin and end times.

Banded Waveguides for Modeling Solid Objects

Essl et al. (2004a, b) presented a theory of *banded waveguides* as a way of synthesizing sounds made by solid objects. Banded waveguide synthesis divides the excitation signal into frequency bands. Each band contains one resonant mode. The bands are centered around the dominant modal frequencies of the instrument being modeled. For each band, separate waveguides model the dynamics of the traveling wave and the resonant frequency of the mode. Banded waveguides are good for modeling instruments such as struck bars in which many modes are excited initially, but only a few inharmonic modes dominate after the attack. This method led to models of bar percussion instruments, a musical saw, bowed wine glasses, bowed cymbals, bowed bowls, and a tabla.

Particle-Based Models of Shaken and Scraped Percussion

Many instruments in the percussion family create sound by the accumulation of microsonic sound particles (Roads 2001a). Shaken and scraped percussion such as maracas, sekere, cabasa, bamboo wind chime, tambourines, sleigh-bells, and guiro can be modeled by sound particles. Perry Cook's *Physically Informed Stochastic Event Modeling* (PhISEM) exemplified this approach. PhISEM was a suite of programs that simulate the sounds of shaken and scraped percussion (figure 18.14) (Cook 1996, 1997, 2007). He also developed a model for water drops based on the same principles and suggested that the technique could synthesize the sound of feet crunching on gravel, or ice cubes in a shaken glass. The PhISEM instruments are now part of the ChucK music programming language (Kapur et al. 2015).

The common thread among instruments modeled by PhISEM is that sound results from discrete microevents. At the core of PhISEM are particle models. Basic Newtonian equations governing the motion and collision of point masses produce the sounds. For shaken percussion instruments such as the maracas, the algorithm assumes that the gourd contains multiple beans. It calculates the probability of bean collisions, which is very high after a shake, but rapidly decays. If a bean collision occurs, it is simulated by a burst of exponentially decaying noise. All collision noises pass through a sharply tuned bandpass filter that simulates the resonance of the gourd. Also refer to Keller and Truax (1998) for more physics-based particle models of sound.

Physical models of particles could go much further. A large body of scientific literature devoted to models of granular processes has not yet been harnessed for sound synthesis (Roads 2001a).

```
/*********************** MARACA ***************************/

#define MARA_SOUND_DECAY 0.95
#define MARA_SYSTEM_DECAY 0.999
#define MARA_NUM_BEANS 25

void maraca_setup() {
  num_objects = MARA_NUM_BEANS;
  gain = log(num_objects) / log(4.0) * 40.0 / (MY_FLOAT) num_objects;
  coeffs[0] = -0.96 * 2.0 * cos(3200.0 * TWO_PI / SRATE);
  coeffs[1] = 0.96*0.96;
  soundDecay = MARA_SOUND_DECAY;
  systemDecay = MARA_SYSTEM_DECAY;
}

MY_FLOAT maraca_tick() {
  MY_FLOAT data;
  shakeEnergy *= systemDecay;                  // Exponential system decay
  if (my_random(1024) < num_objects)           // If collision
    sndLevel += gain * shakeEnergy;            //    add energy
  input = sndLevel * noise_tick();             // Actual Sound is Random
  sndLevel *= soundDecay;                      // Exponential Sound decay
  input -= output[0]*coeffs[0];                // Do gourd
  input -= output[1]*coeffs[1];                //    resonance
  output[1] = output[0];                       //       filter
  output[0] = input;                           //          calculations
  data = output[0] - output[1];                // Extra zero for shape
  return data;
}
```

Figure 18.14   Maracas model coded in C (Cook 1996, 1997, 2007).

Models of Pianos

Digital pianos cater to a large market. Most play recorded samples. But recorded samples cannot reproduce acoustic phenomena that real pianos emit. These include the free vibration of the strings when the sustain pedal is down, the coupling between strings of sounding notes, and the restrike of an already-sounding string (Bank and Chabassier 2019). What if we wanted to alter the physical properties of the piano: the hardness of the hammer, the tuning of a string, or the position of a virtual microphone? For a digital piano based on sampling, this would require different sample sets for every possible configuration, which is not practical. All these phenomena, however, can be faithfully produced by an accurate physical model.

Three competing approaches have preoccupied researchers: modal synthesis, waveguides, and FDTD models. In his doctoral dissertation, Bank (2006) proposed an approach using modal synthesis. Rauhala et al. (2008) proposed a model of a piano based on waveguides. While efficient, this model was criticized for being unrealistic in sound quality because waveguides are not ideal at modeling nonlinear string behavior. Juliette Chabassier, a doctoral student at the École Polytechnique X, created a comprehensive mathematical model of a piano using on a FDTD approach (Chabassier 2012). For each second of sound it produced, her "heavy, accurate" model took 24 hours of computation on a network of three hundred processors (Bank and Chabassier 2019).

Seeking a practical real-time solution, the acoustician Philippe Guillaume (2011) proposed a unique combination of nonlinear exciters, modal algorithms, and finite-element models to create simulations of keyboard instruments. In this work, the hammer is realized by mass and nonlinear spring model. An initial velocity projects it towards the strings before it is repelled. The interacting force is a nonlinear function of the hammer compression (Chabassier 2012; Chabassier, Chaigne, and Joly 2013). The coupled strings are represented as an additive sum of exponentially damped sinusoids—the product of modal synthesis. The reverberant soundboard of the piano, which is coupled to the strings at the bridge, is realized by a finite-difference filter model.

This research resulted in the Modartt Pianoteq software product in 2006. For a few hundred dollars, Pianoteq convincingly models expensive pianos by Steinway, Bösendorfer, Bechstein, and Petrof, among others. As a testament to the quality, these piano manufacturers license their brand names on the software models. Modartt software also models electric pianos, vibraphones and marimbas, clavichords, plucked-string instruments such as harpsichords and concert harps, and pipe organs.

Roland's V-piano PhM was launched in 2009 with a progressive hammer-action eighty-eight-note weighted keyboard. The keyboard features haptic escapement for every key, that is, the feel of a "click" produced by a real piano action.

The venerable instrument maker Viscount introduced the Physis piano in 2012 (figure 18.15). Based on modal synthesis, its technology is detailed in Ban et al. (2010).

Karplus-Strong Plucked String and Drum Synthesis

The Karplus-Strong (KS) algorithm for plucked string and drum synthesis is an efficient technique based on the principle of a delay line or *recirculating wavetable* (Karplus and Strong 1983; Jaffe and Smith 1983). The basic model can be seen as a noise burst fed into a feedback filter.

Plucked Strings

The basic KS algorithm starts with a wavetable of length p filled with random values (noise). As values are read out of the wavetable from the right

Figure 18.15   Viscount Physis G1000 piano.

(figure 18.16), they are modified in some way and the result is reinserted at the left of the wavetable. The simplest modification is an averaging of the current sample with the previous sample—the core operation of a simple lowpass filter. (See chapter 28 for an explanation of averaging lowpass filters.) At each sample interval, the wavetable read and write pointers are incremented. When the pointers reach the end of the wavetable they wrap around and start at the beginning again. The audible result of this simple algorithm is a pitched sound that sounds bright at the outset, but as it decays the timbre rapidly darkens to a single sine tone—much like the sound of a plucked string.

If the wavetable is initially filled with random values, the reader may wonder why the result does not sound like noise, at least at the outset of the tone. The reason it sounds pitched is that the wavetable is being repeated (with a slight modification) at each fundamental cycle. Because these repetitions occur hundreds of times per second, what was initially a random waveform becomes in an instant a quasiperiodic waveform.

In practice, loading the wavetable with a new random values for each note gives each note a slightly different harmonic structure.

Drum-like Timbres

KS generates drum-like timbres by using a slightly more complicated modifier to the fed back sample. The timbre is controlled by setting the value of a probability parameter b called the *blend factor*, where $0 \le b \le 1$. Then the modifier algorithm is as follows:

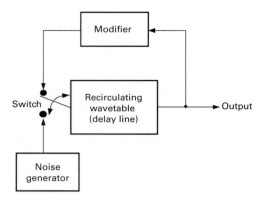

Figure 18.16 Core of the Karplus-Strong recirculating wavetable. The input to the recirculating wavetable switches to the noise source at the beginning of each event and then switches back to the modifier loop for the rest of the event. The modifier averages successive samples, simulating a damping effect.

$$
Signal_t = \begin{cases}
+1/2(Signal_{t-p} + Signal_{t-[p-1]}), \text{ with probability } b \\
-1/2(Signal_{t-p} + Signal_{t-[p-1]}), \text{ with probability } 1-b
\end{cases}
$$

where t is the current sample index, and p is the length of the wavetable.

When b is 1, the modifier is a lowpass filter as before and the sound is like that of a plucked string. When b is 0.5, the sound is no longer string-like. It loses its pitch and sounds more like a drum. When b is set to 0, the signal is negated every $p+0.5$ samples. This cuts the perceived frequency in half and leaves only odd harmonics in the spectrum, creating a harp-like sound in the low registers.

Figure 18.17 depicts a KS instrument for drum synthesis. Notice how samples from the recirculating wavetable are averaged with previous samples and given a positive or negative sign on the basis of the blend factor b. When b is close to 0.5, the wavetable length no longer controls pitch because the waveform is no longer periodic. Instead, the length p determines the decay time of the noise burst at the beginning of the drum tone. When p is relatively large (over 200) the instrument sounds like a noisy snare drum. When p is small, (less than 25) the effect is that of a brushed tom-tom. To make a resonant drum, the wavetable is preloaded with a constant value instead of random values.

Stretching Out the Decay Time

Because the decay time of the sound produced by KS is proportional to the length p of the wavetable, notes using a short wavetable decay rapidly. Ideally, we want to decouple the decay time from the wavetable length. This is done

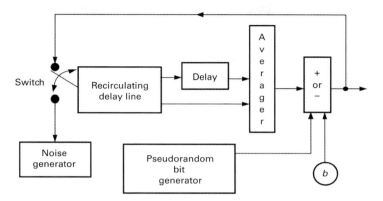

Figure 18.17   The Karplus-Strong drum synthesis algorithm. The quantity b is the blend factor.

by a technique known as *decay stretching*. The algorithm for decay stretching is as follows:

$$Signal_t = \begin{cases} Signal_{t-p}, \text{with probability } 1-(1/s) \\ 1/2(Signal_{t-p} + Signal_{t-[p-1]}), \text{with probability } 1/s \end{cases}$$

where s is the *stretch factor*. With s set to 1, the usual averaging algorithm is applied and the decay time is not stretched. When s is close to zero, the tone is not averaged, so it stretches out its decay time.

Extensions to KS

Jaffe and Smith presented a detailed technical analysis of the KS technique (Jaffe and Smith [1983], reprinted in Roads [1989]). Using this analytical vocabulary, they developed a number of important extensions. In particular, by adding a variety of filters to the basic KS circuit, they obtained the following effects:

Correcting for tuning inaccuracies at high pitches

Decay shortening and decay lengthening

Eliminating the initial plucked sound

Varying the loudness of the tone in relation to its bandwidth

Creating glissandi and slurs

Correcting for clicks on notes followed by rests

Mimicking the effects of sympathetic string vibrations

Simulating the sound of a pick that moves up and down the bridge

Simulating up and down picking

Simulating stiff strings for more inharmonicity

See Kapur et al. (2015) for a description of implementations of these techniques in the ChucK programming language.

Other extensions aim at simulating electric guitar distortion and feedback (Sullivan 1990), and more realistic simulation of the player's touch (Cuzzucoli and Lombardo 1999; Laurson et al. 2001). Karjalainen et al. (1991) even applied a KS model to synthesis of flute-like tones.

Scanned Synthesis

Scanned synthesis implements a dynamic wave table (figure 18.18) controlled by a performer. It can be seen as a combination of physical modeling and wave terrain synthesis (presented in chapter 12). At the core of scanned synthesis is a physical model of a vibrating system whose frequencies of vibration are below about 15 Hz. This model is directly manipulated by motions of a performer. The vibrations of the system are a function of the initial conditions, the forces applied by the performer, and the dynamics of the system. Recall that wave terrain synthesis generalizes the idea of a wavetable to N dimensions and generalizes the trajectory of the read pointer to a scan over an arbitrary N-dimensional surface.

In a similar fashion, scanned synthesis consists of reading audio sample values from a wavetable that is dynamically changing over time (Boulanger, Smaragdis, and Fitch 2000; Verplank, Mathews, and Shaw 2000). The wavetable is vibrating and evolving at low frequencies, like wave motions on the surface of

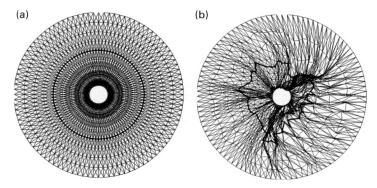

(a)   (b)

Figure 18.18 Graphical interface for scanned synthesis in the Wablet app by Rootnot. In this case, a two-dimensional circular mesh has been selected. (a) The finite-element model at rest, quietly vibrating at a low frequency. (b) The finite-element model after being excited by a touchscreen gesture. When this shape is scanned it produces a specific timbre that can be mapped to an arbitrary pitch with a slider or keyboard.

the sea. The shape of these waves is repeatedly scanned across an arbitrary scanning path or orbit at the frequency of the desired musical note. The process is conceptually similar to a record player needle, which tracks the waveform grooves imprinted on a vinyl disc. Unlike a vinyl disc, where the needle follows an inevitable spiral path, in this case the orbit can follow an arbitrary path across the surface. In this sense it is similar to wave terrain synthesis (chapter 12).

Verplank, Mathews, and Shaw (2000) developed scanned synthesis on the basis of a finite-element model of a generalized string after that of Cadoz, Luciani, and Florens (1984). Whereas the goal of Cadoz's research was the simulation of audio frequency vibrations, the goal in scanned synthesis is the simulation of an infrasonic vibrating wave surface with a goal of producing dynamically changing waveforms. In scanned synthesis, the finite-element models are a collection of masses connected by springs and dampers that can be analyzed with Newton's laws of physics. The performer manipulates the model by pushing or hitting different masses, tracing orbits or scanning paths, and manipulating parameters.

Qu-Bit Electronix built a Eurorack module for scanned synthesis called Scanned, which opened up the technique to voltage control. The sounds it produces are reminiscent of FM, waveshaping, and multiple wavetable synthesis and not of traditional acoustic instruments.

Input Devices for Physical Modeling Synthesis

A typical computer graphical interface with mouse and alphanumeric keyboard can provide an entertaining visual interface for engaging a simple PhM instrument or sound game app. However, with such an interface, it is impossible to control a physical model of an acoustic instrument such as a cello with any hope of attaining realism due to the need to control many parameters simultaneously. Some work can be done to group parameters, but for effective performance the ideal controller is a musical input device with many degrees of freedom. Multitouch interfaces on phones and tablets have been marshaled in support of this task (Scandalis, Smith, and Porcaro 2015).

When synthesis is realized in real time, PhM techniques come almost full circle, from an actual instrument to a virtual instrument that is played using an input device. What is sought is a physical coupling between performer and instrument, restoring *instrumentality* linked to expressiveness. In chapter 40, figure 40.5 shows two examples of input devices for PhM synthesis. The original ACROE keyboard (figure 40.5g) contained motors that modeled the physical action of various mechanical keyboards (Cadoz, Luciani, and Florens 2003). The ACROE-ICA Ergon_X platform has a 20 Hz mechanical bandwidth and 200 newtons of force. It can be fitted with bows, joysticks, styli, or piano keys (Leonard et al. 2013).

The MIKEY keyboard uses force feedback to emulate the actions of a grand piano, harpsichord, and Hammond organ (Oboe 2006). Perry Cook's HIRN combined several different types of controllers (mouth interface, buttons, sliders, and different blowing angles) into one device (Cook 1992).

Expressive E Arché violin, viola, and cello are physical modeling synthesizers that combine a keyboard for note selection with their Touché controller for articulation.

It is clear that in order to produce a virtuoso effect from PhM instruments, one needs to become a virtuoso on a controller. This raises the question: why not just learn to play the acoustic instrument in the first place? Indeed, the best user of a PhM saxophone is likely to be a virtuoso saxophonist playing a saxophone-like controller. What then is the point of the physical model? Presumably, the answer is that the controller+PhM instrument combination enables new modes of performance and synthesis that go beyond the limits of acoustic instruments. Another benefit is realized in low-cost software products that offer a collection of instruments that would be difficult to finance, store, and maintain in physical form. Modartt Pianoteq comes to mind.

Source and Parameter Analysis for Physical Modeling

Given a physical model of an existing instrument, the usual method of determining the proper performance parameters is to perform laborious trial-and-error experiments on individual tones, transitions, and gestures in an acoustics laboratory, in collaboration with accomplished players. This detail work could be greatly sped up by an analysis stage that could listen to a performance of a virtuoso and estimate the characteristic parameters automatically. Maestre et al. (2010) explores this direction.

Another motivation for an analysis stage in physical modeling is *automatic instrument construction.* Existing physical models correspond to only a tiny corner of the universe of sound. What about sounds that are not currently realizable with existing models? One can dream of an automatic compiler that would spawn a virtual instrument corresponding to any input sound. The automatically constructed physical model would give the musician gestural instrumental control over this sound and a family of similar sounds. This is not so far-fetched. Keep in mind that Fourier analysis already acts as a similar sort of compiler, realizing an additive synthesis instrument corresponding to any sound fed into it.

From this point of view, all sound analysis can be seen as a form of *parameter estimation*. That is, analysis tries to characterize an incoming sound in terms of the parameter settings that would be needed to approximate that sound with a given synthesis model (Tenney 1965; Justice 1979; Mian and Tisato 1984). Early experiments with parameter estimation for PhM synthesis showed the difficulties and the potential of this direction (Szilas and Cadoz 1993).

Wold (1987) is an important study in parameter estimation based on a physical model approach to resynthesis. His ultimate goal was not synthesis per se but separation of polyphonic sources. That is, the system was fed a mixed signal of two different instruments. It then tried to estimate what the resynthesis parameters would be for each instrument, with reference to a physical model synthesizer. He began by designing approximate physical models of acoustic instruments such as voices, marimbas, and clarinets. The form of these models was a set of parameterized state equations. For any given input sound, the goal was to compare the input sound with the state-equation model and try to identify a combination of parameter settings that would result in the same sound.

Figure 18.19 shows a diagram of Wold's parameter-estimation system. The first part of the system addressed the problem facing all estimators: making an educated guess of where to start. His system used spectrum analysis and pitch detection to make an initial estimate. On the basis of that estimate, the system refined its analysis using iterative techniques and checked its results against a state-equation model for resynthesis. The part dealing with refinement of an initial estimate was based on a statistical *Kalman filter* approach. (Kalman filter theory is an advanced topic; see Rabiner et al. [1972].) The computational burden of Kalman filter estimation of physical model synthesis parameters is heavy. High-fidelity parameter estimation based on percussion, voice, and clarinet models requires billions of floating-point operations per second of analyzed sound (Wold 1987).

P. Cook's Singer is a waveguide filter physical model of the human vocal tract (Cook (1991a, 1993). Singer contains models of the lips, vocal tract, and nasal tract, allowing it to capture articulatory details more realistically.

The complexity of this model is evident from the patch shown in figure 18.20. Dozens of parameters must be carefully tuned for each utterance. Such a model raises the question: where can one obtain the proper data in order for it to make realistic speaking and singing? Using the Singer model, Cook employed parameter estimation on speech in an effort to match the parameters of the model to the speech signal. A notable aspect of this research was the effort to model the *glottal waveform*, the speech excitation signal emitted by the vocal cords. Cook used deconvolution to derive the glottal waveform and estimated pitch by means of a comb filter method. Vocal tract noise was modeled using a fluid

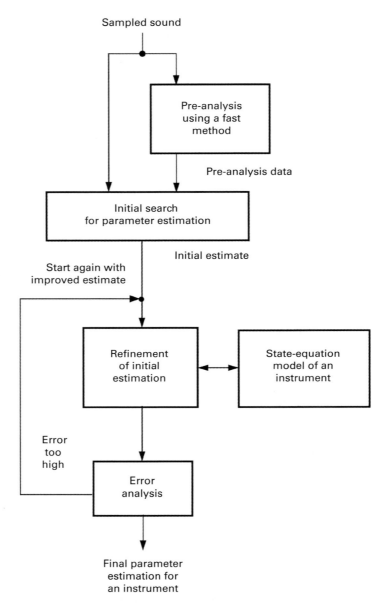

Figure 18.19   Parameter-estimation sound analyzer implemented by Wold (1987).
The goal was to estimate parameters for a physical model–based synthesizer, with
a view toward separation of two mixed signals. If a given estimate was too far from
the approximate state-equation model, the system tried another iteration of estimation.

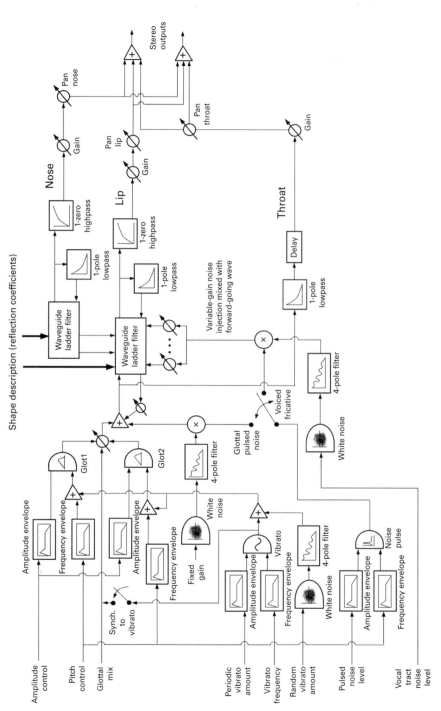

Figure 18.20 Block diagram of Singer, a physical model synthesizer for vocal sounds. The left section of the figure depicts the excitation sources. The center section depicts the waveguide resonators. The right section depicts the output stage. Two glottal wavetable oscillators (Glot1 and Glot2) allow slow, vibrato variations in the excitation signal. The glottal noise source consists of filtered white noise multiplied by a waveshape synchronized to the glottal oscillators. This permits pulsed noise to be mixed into the periodic source. A sine oscillator simulates vibrato, the frequency of which is randomized by noise. Filtered white noise is injected into the forward-moving glottal wave. Noise can be inserted into any number of waveguide sections. The mixed glottal source feeds into the vocal tract filter. Glottal reflections are modeled by a simple reflection coefficient, and a lowpass filter simulates lip and nostril effects. A lowpass filter and delay line model the radiation from the skin in the Throat output path.

dynamics approach. (Refer to Blake [1986] for more on fluid dynamics models of sound and vibration.)

Casey (1996) proposed a multilayer *neural network* (NN) to estimate parameters for physical model instruments. In this research, a NN was trained to estimate parameters to distinguish a modeled trumpet from a saxophone. Gabrielli et al. (2017) developed a supervised convolutional NN paradigm for parameter estimation. The method was applied to a digital waveguide flue pipe organ model.

Assessment of Physical Modeling Synthesis

Massive research has been invested in PhM synthesis over the decades. Despite many technical achievements, success in the marketplace has been mixed. Korg and Yamaha manufactured hardware synthesizers based on waveguide physical models in 1990s with little commercial success. Tassman was a modular software synthesizer with several PhM modules, some of which implemented modal synthesis (Applied Acoustic Systems 2007). Typical modules included: beam, bowed beam/marimba/membrane/plate/ string, flute, mallet, marimba, membrane, plate, pickup, plectrum, recorder, string, and tube resonator. Tassman was discontinued, but the company has bundled the same technology into Chromaphone and other products that model percussion, guitars, strings, and electric piano.

Among other PhM products in the marketplace are Logic's Sculpture, Ableton Collision (figure 18.21), Audio Modeling SWAM, AAS Objeq, Modartt Pianoteq, moForte GeoShred and Guitar, Korg Kronos STR-1 plucked string model, Madrona Labs Kaivo, Reaktor Prism, Spicy Guitar, Intellijel Plonk (Eurorack) and Mutable Instruments Elements (Eurorack). PhM functions are also available in software toolkits such as Faust, Csound, SuperCollider, ChucK, Max, Pd, and REAKTOR.

As mentioned previously, models of pianos are impressive. For a few hundred dollars, one can have a simulation of a Bösendorfer Imperial Concert Grand selling for $500,000, as well as dozens of other exotic pianos. Part of the reason that piano models have been successful is that there are relatively few performance variables. Even a child can strike a key, play a melody, and obtain a perfect tone. The same cannot be said of string and wind instruments.

Sonic realism, however, is not the only criterion for evaluating a PhM synthesizer. It might produce an instrument-like sound with other interesting properties that are possible only in the digital domain. For example, the Hartmann Neuron VS software synthesizer is supplied with a large library

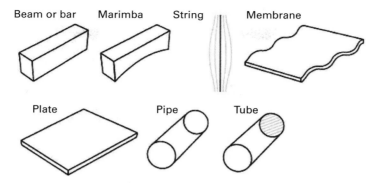

Figure 18.21 Ableton Collision instruments for mallet sounds such as xylophones, marimbas, and glockenspiel and for other percussion.

of exciter and resonator models. The synthesizer makes it possible to pair any exciter (called a *scape*) with any resonator (*sphere*). Exciters can be blended, as can resonators (Hartmann 2013). These possibilities take the synthesizer beyond known acoustic instruments. MoForte's GeoShred and Guitar for mobile devices model electric and acoustic guitar, pedal steel guitar, and a sitar-like instrument. None of these models would fool an expert player, but for the price of few sets of guitar strings, they offer value through multitouch + accelerometer interfaces with added effects. Ableton Collision encourages users to "create instruments that would be physically impossible in the real world" or "go full-on experimental for completely new sounds" (Ableton, n.d.). These trends point toward a virtual universe of new instrumental sounds. Otherworldly possibilities have always been part of the promise of PhM, even if scientists find it hard to evaluate.

Current physical models describe only a fraction of a limitless world of real sounds. Building an accurate physical model of a musical instrument is a serious scientific project. Only a few laboratories have the necessary measurement equipment and applied physics expertise for this undertaking. Pages of acoustics journals are rife with details that scientists have gleaned from decades of patient experimentation and measurement. Thousands of different types of acoustical instruments exist in the world, and yet only a few PhM models have been attempted. Once a model is constructed, the issue remains of determining the proper settings for dozens of parameters for each sound to be played on the instrument.

A fundamental problem of PhM synthesis is that a synthesis algorithm alone is not a complete system of sound production. One also needs a physical interface and a player. Early attempts to play PhM instruments like violin and saxophone sometimes sounded like the painful practice sessions of a novice. Keyboards, thumbwheels, sliders, and foot pedals are not ideal for playing these instruments. The ideal interface for a violin model is a physical controller (resembling a violin) played by an expert violinist. Such a model might someday deliver the tone of a million-dollar Stradivarius for the price of a cheap fiddle interface.

When the instrument is driven purely by software (rather than a manual controller), one must in effect define a physical model of a player as well as the instrument. This player model should be able to realize idiomatic gestures and good playing technique in whatever way these goals are defined for a particular instrument. Initial player models were prototyped in the 1990s (Garton 1992). Progress has been made since then, particularly in the case of bowed string technique (Cadoz 2002; Demoucron 2008; Maestre et al. 2010; Mansour 2016).

19 *Virtual Analog*

Evolution of Analog Synthesis

        Fall and Rise of Analog Synthesis

Digital versus Analog Synthesis

Virtual Analog

Issues in VA Synthesis

        The Philosophy of Emulation
        Waveform Generation and Aliasing
        Analog Filter Emulation
        Control Interfaces
        Interconnection of Modules
        Modulation

Modeling Analog Signal Processing

This chapter presents the topic of virtual analog synthesis and processing. As we explain, this is a broad field with a sizable research literature and close connections to physics and electrical engineering. Our exposition consists of an historical overview followed by an introduction to the major technical issues, accompanied by many citations of the research literature.

Evolution of Analog Synthesis

Analog synthesis of sound began with the invention of the first vacuum tube oscillators around 1912 (Fleming 1919). One of the earliest oscillator instruments was the Theremin, demonstrated in 1920 (Chadabe 1997). Many electronic instruments were invented thereafter, but not all were based on oscillator tone generation. Some amplified an acoustic, electromagnetic, or electrooptical generator such as vibrating metal reed or a rotating tone wheel (Rhea 1972; Roads 1996b). Prior to World War II, however, the majority of electronic music instruments were limited in timbral variety. For example, classic instruments such as the Theremin and the Ondes Martenot did not provide a great deal of timbral variation. Musicians achieved expressivity with these instruments primarily through sensitive variations in pitch and loudness.

The Ondioline instrument invented by Georges Jenny in the 1940s was a breakthrough in timbral variety (figure 19.1). Its sound circuit produced pulse trains passing through a bank of resonant filters. This was combined with an innovative gestural interface—including a spring-mounted keyboard for vibrato—that enabled a wide range of timbral variations (Jenny 1958). In the hands of its foremost exponent, Jean-Jacques Perrey, it could imitate dozens of acoustic instruments and make new sounds that have not been duplicated (Fourier 1994). In recent years, Wally De Backer restored several Ondiolines and brought out a limited-edition vinyl record of Perrey's music with reproductions of vintage manuals (Forgotten Futures 2017). SonicCouture has introduced a virtual analog Ondioline.

The early, classic electronic music studios built after WWII, such as the Westdeutscher Rundfunk (WDR) studios in Cologne, were largely equipped with laboratory test generators powered by vacuum tube circuits. A limitation of this equipment was that the controls were not meant to be freely played or automated. Thus, in order to create a time-varying effect, two or more people had to be in the studio to operate the controls on multiple devices such as impulse generators, filters, and variable-speed tape recorders. Compositions such as *Kontakte* (1960) by Karlheinz Stockhausen required detailed technical planning and teamwork.

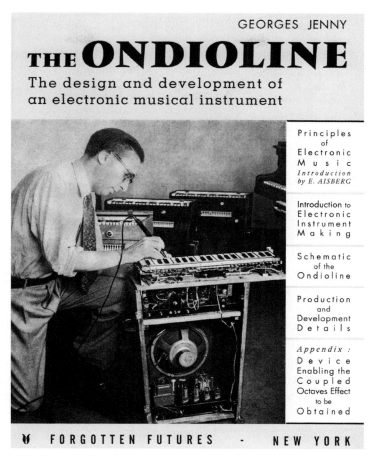

Figure 19.1   Reissue of George Jenny's 1968 article on the Ondioline (Forgotten Futures 2017).

The 1960s saw a breakthrough: *modular voltage-controlled synthesizers* (Moog 1965; Arp 1972; Vail 2000b). *Modular* meant that the different functions of a synthesizer (oscillators, filters, amplifiers, sequencers, etc.) were encapsulated in separate modules but joined by means of a common chassis and interconnection scheme. *Voltage-controlled* meant that one module could control another via patch cords. Modules controlling other modules provided a form of automation. As a simple example, one could connect the output of a low-frequency sine wave oscillator (LFO) to control the center frequency of a bandpass filter, causing it to sweep up and down.

The original analog synthesizers by Moog, Arp, EMS, and Buchla were handmade, and production runs were small. Few musicians could afford a large modular analog synthesizer.

Fall and Rise of Analog Synthesis

Analog synthesis fell out of favor with the introduction of low-cost mass-produced digital synthesizers such as the Yamaha DX7 in the 1980s. By the late 1990s, however, musicians began to rediscover the world of analog (Vail 2000b; Pinch and Trocco 2002). Antique modular synthesizers from the vintage analog era are now prized by collectors.

At the same time, the small-format Eurorack standard introduced by Dieter Doepfer in 1995 led to a revolution in modular synthesis. Addressing the demand for analog modules, a new generation of boutique designers introduced a wave of innovative modules into the marketplace. Today we see a competitive mix of relatively low-cost Eurorack systems alongside high-end modular synths from Moog, Buchla, and others that are more expensive than ever.

There is something special about interacting with the physicality of a modular synthesizer, with its blinking lights, patch cords, and dozens of physical knobs, sliders, switches and joysticks that are touch-accessible at any time. This multisensory experience is impossible to replicate on a computer screen.

However, many aspects of the sound of an analog synthesizer can be simulated accurately in software. Thus we see a strong trend to develop analog-behaving and analog-sounding synthesizers implemented in digital form (Hetrick 2016). The main goal of these techniques is to mimic the voltage-control behavior and sound of analog synthesizers. Digital technology inevitably offers additional features, such as saving patches and graphic displays.

Analog modeling, analog emulation, or *virtual analog* (VA) techniques deliver many of the sonic benefits of expensive hardware at lower cost. However, the quality of the models varies. Just as the signature sound of a saxophonist like Coleman Hawkins is distinct and immediately recognizable, every vintage analog synthesizer (Moog, Arp, EMS, Buchla, Serge, etc.) has a discernable sound. These differences can be traced to many factors: circuit topologies, the component parts within a circuit, and the control regime or user interface to that circuit. Some emulations are impressively accurate and represent serious efforts to reverse-engineer an actual analog circuit. Starting from schematics and working hardware, companies such as Softube, Universal Audio, and Arturia, among others, have invested in accurate circuit emulation.

By contrast, many VA synthesizers are generic; they do not attempt to model a specific circuit or synthesizer. Some VA plug-ins are based on samples rather than physical modeling.

The VA trend goes beyond synthesizers to the emulation of guitar pickups and amplifiers, Rhodes and Wurlitzer electric pianos, tape recorders, and spring and plate reverberators, as we discuss further on.

Digital versus Analog Synthesis

What is the difference between digital synthesis and analog synthesis? Digital synthesis generates discrete sampled and quantized audio signals. *Sampled* means that an audio signal is divided into a stream of tens of thousands of snapshots of a waveform. *Quantized* means that there are a finite number of possible amplitude values that any sample can have. At each tick of the sample-rate clock, the synthesizer emits another quantized sample. Digital synthesizers can be implemented in software—as standalone applications, as plug-ins, or in the form of a hardware unit. Regardless of implementation, the core of any digital synthesizer is an algorithm for sample generation.

By contrast, in an analog synthesizer, there is no microprocessor. Instead, the synthesizer contains hardware circuits built of basic components such as operational amplifiers, resistors, capacitors, diodes, transformers, and inductors (figure 19.2). These circuits generate *continuous* (as opposed to discrete) signals. No sampling clock drives the circuit. Signals in an analog synthesizer circulate at nearly the speed of light. The amplitude of continuous analog signals varies freely and instantaneously within a stipulated voltage range.

Over a century of invention has gone into the design of analog electronic music instruments (Roads 1996b; Rhea 1972, 1977, 1984; Vail 2000b). Before the invention of the digital computer, all electronic circuits were analog in design. The behavior of these circuits could be predicted according

Figure 19.2   Inside an analog audio circuit. The dark cylinders are capacitors. The dark squarish object at left is a transformer. One can also see resistors and op-amps.

to the flow of the continuous quantities of voltage and current in interaction with circuit properties such as resistance, capacitance, and inductance. For those interested in details on the characteristics of analog circuits, refer to Black (1953), Chirlian (1971), Benedict (1976), and Old Colony Sound Labs (2004). Other books explain the principles of analog signal synthesis and voltage control from both a musical and a technical point of view (Strange 1983; Manning 1993; Wells 1981; Chadabe 1967; Bjørn and Meyer 2018).

Virtual Analog

The first generation of VA synthesizers appeared in the 1990s as keyboard instruments in hardware. This includes the Clavia Nord Modular, the Alesis Micron, Korg Prophecy, Walfdorf Q, Roland JP-8000, and Yamaha's AN1x among others. The VA model in these synthesizers is generic. That is, they do not attempt to emulate any specific analog instrument of the past.

The next generation of VA instruments emulated the characteristics and sound palette of classic Moog, Arp, Buchla, and EMS synths from the vintage analog era between 1960 and 1980 (figure 19.3). Arturia's product, Buchla Music Easel, is an example of this approach, even though the hardware version of the Music Easel has also been revived.

Another trend in VA synthesis has been influenced by the flexibility of the Eurorack format to mix modules from different companies into one system. An example is the Softube Modular collection of software modules that model Eurorack hardware modules by Doepfer and Intellijel, among others (figure 19.4)

Native Instruments Reaktor is a combination development system and synthesizer library (figure 19.5). Its Blocks library provides a patching interface with dozens of different blocks (modules), including collections by leading synthesizer designers. For example, Michael Hetrick's Euro Reakt contains over 140 modules.

VCV Rack is another popular software modular synthesizer platform, with software emulations of hardware by Audible Instruments, Befaco, Grayscale, and Synthesis Technology. Cherry Audio's Voltage Modular provides its own modules.

Because genuine analog instruments and devices are widely available, one might ask, what is the point of emulation? The answer is simple: cost and convenience. A polyphonic analog modular synthesizer can easily cost over $10,000 and can be difficult to transport. By contrast, its software homologue sells for a fraction of this price or is free (e.g., VCV Rack) and can be trans-

Figure 19.3   Screen image of the Arturia Moog V, a virtual analog emulation of a Moog Synthesizer. The onscreen control panel mimics the original hardware.

ported on a laptop computer. The same factors apply to models of amplifiers, loudspeakers, microphones, compressors, plate reverberators, tape machines, and other audio devices. The appeal of carrying a modular synthesizer studio in a backpack is understandable.

Software synthesizers can add new features not present on traditional analog synthesizers. This can include precise and stable frequency tuning, hundreds of memorized presets, arbitrary waveforms, increased signal-to-noise ratio, graphical interfaces, spectrum displays, and high-quality effects (Barbour 1998). For example, pulsar synthesis, presented in chapter 21, was conceived with the goal of providing a graphical interface for a digital synthesis engine that emulated an analog synthesis technique.

Figure 19.4   The Softube Modular virtual synthesizer.

Figure 19.5   Native Instruments Reaktor Blocks front panel.

Issues in VA Synthesis

The main issues in VA synthesis are as follows:

- The philosophy of emulation
- Waveform generation and aliasing
- Filter emulation

- Control interfaces
- Interconnection of modules
- Modulation

The next sections discuss these issues in more detail.

The Philosophy of Emulation

Emulation poses philosophical questions. Is the goal to create a model that captures all the flaws as well as all the features of the original? What is the benefit of modeling the quirks of analog systems? Do these define its "personality"? Or is the goal to create an improved and more ideal digital version of the original with lower noise, less distortion, more stable behavior, graphical displays, additional effects, and the advantages of digital storage and retrieval of settings?

In a VA simulation, every analog module is replaced by its software homologue. The analog oscillator for example, is replaced by a digital oscillator algorithm. Beyond this level, however, different teams carry the emulation to different depths. One approach is to study the original analog circuits, including components such as transistors, resistors, capacitors, and diodes to reverse-engineer the design (Civolani and Fontana 2008; Yeh, Abel, and Smith 2010; Yeh 2012; De Sanctis and Sarti 2010; Najnudel, Hélie, and Roze 2019). This approach is called *component-level modeling* (Peavey 2016). Thorny problems such as nonlinear circuit behavior caused by feedback, aliasing, and artifact-free real-time parameter tuning by users must be solved along the way (Fontana and Civolani 2010).

Another approach creates a generic model that is not based on any specific analog device, like the first generation of VA synthesizers mentioned previously. Or the simulation could simply be based on samples of an old instrument. Likewise, convolution-based methods make no attempt to model the actual circuits and components. This approach samples the *impulse response* of the modeled device and convolves it with an input signal in order to impose the sonic signature of the device onto the input sound (chapter 29).

To some, the flaws and unpredictability of analog synthesizers are one aspect of their charm. For example, in certain analog synthesizers of the 1970s, the frequency of the oscillators drifted with changes of temperature. At the time, this was considered a major flaw. In the twenty-first century, frequency drift has been reintroduced as a feature of VA synthesizers!

Every analog device is constructed with specific hardware circuit components. The choice of specific components can have a strong impact on the sonic character of the device. A classic example is the *vactrol,* an electro-optical part used in the Buchla 292 lowpass gate module, which is part of the signature sound of Morton Subotnick (Parker and D'Angelo 2013). (We explain this more in a subsequent section.) Similarly, one can build a family of analog ring modulators all employing the same circuit design but using different diodes. Each will sound different. By contrast, the digital counterpart to ring modulation is simple multiplication, which produces an identical result in every computer.

Waveform Generation and Aliasing

An advantage of digital over analog synthesis is its waveform flexibility. An algorithm can generate any waveform (limited by the given sampling rate). In addition, a digital oscillator can read any waveform loaded into its memory, including prerecorded samples. In both cases, the waveform can be continuously varied.

By contrast, an analog oscillator is restricted by its circuit topology to producing certain types of wave shapes. Volumes are devoted to the art of analog waveform synthesis (Strauss 1960; Dorf 1958; Douglas 1968). The most practical circuits generate sine, sawtooth, triangle, square, and pulse waveforms. Many analog oscillators allow continuous transitions between, for example a sine and a sawtooth, or a sine and a square wave. Such transitions are a characteristic of analog synthesis.

Digital oscillators face difficulty simulating all analog waveforms accurately. This occurs because certain analog waveforms such as impulses, square waves, sawtooths, and noise bands contain frequencies that can extend up to and beyond typical audio sampling rates. We can consider them to be *nonbandlimited.* This is a feature, not a flaw, of an analog synthesizer. By contrast, as noted in chapter 3, a digital synthesizer must be constrained to generate *bandlimited* signals, that is, signals that contain frequencies no greater than the Nyquist frequency (half the sampling rate). If the synthesizer is not so constrained, the output signal will be marred by *aliasing distortion,* in which frequencies greater than the Nyquist frequency are reflected into the audio spectrum.

The first generation of VA synthesizers operated internally at the standard sampling rates of 44.1 and 48 kHz. The lack of frequency headroom in these rates opened the door to aliasing from within the synthesis algorithm. Common waveforms cause aliasing if they are transposed outside a narrow frequency range. For example, in a synthesizer operating at a 44.1 kHz sampling rate, a bandlimited square wave made by summing sixteen odd-harmonic components causes aliasing at fundamental frequencies greater than 760 Hz. Lane et al. (1997) showed aliasing from a digital sawtooth waveform at 1,500 Hz. This kind of internal aliasing cannot be cured by lowpass filtering of the output of the oscillator, because the aliased frequencies are already present in the output signal! Like other forms of nonlinear distortion, once aliasing has occurred it is almost impossible to eliminate it.

As a consequence of these hard limits, digital oscillators require preventative measures in order to eliminate aliasing distortion. At least the following three strategies are possible, which can be used together:

1. *Construct bandlimited approximations of analog waveforms.* Various strategies have been proposed. As a simple example, one can approximate the shape of a square wave by adding together sine waves at odd harmonic frequencies (figure 19.6). Stilson and Smith (1996) proposed using windowed-sinc functions, which are bandlimited. Välimäki (2005) generated a digital sawtooth waveform by differentiating a parabolic waveform. Another approach applies filtering within the oscillator to reduce aliasing

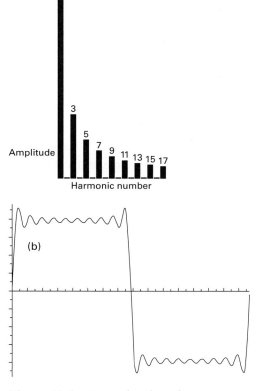

Figure 19.6 Approximation of a square wave by adding nine sinusoidal components at odd harmonic frequencies. (a) Spectrum. (b) Waveform. By adding more odd sine components, the waveform will be made more square-like while still being bandlimited.

(Välimäki and Huovilainen 2006, 2007; Lane et al. 1997; Romblom 2004). Deslauriers and Leider (2009) adapted Laroche's (2000) idea, an efficient *inverse fast Fourier transform* (IFFT) method. Lazzarini and Timoney (2010) proposed a general method of bandlimited waveform synthesis within the framework of waveshaping (chapter 17). Nam et al. (2010) proposed fractional delay filters. Välimäki and Huovilainen (2006, 2007) and Välimäki, Parker, and Abel (2010) generated waveforms using polynomials, with interpolation to correct transition regions.

2. *Run the emulation at a higher internal sampling rate.* For example, assuming that one wants to produce output at a 48 kHz sampling rate, one could run the oscillator at an internal rate of 96 kHz, which would allow for sinusoidal components as high as 48 kHz to be generated without aliasing. Then simply lowpass filter the output of the oscillator with a cutoff frequency of 24 kHz before downsampling (decimating) the signal to a 48 kHz rate. A number of commercial products employ this simple solution, which can be combined with method 1.

3. *As a last resort, limit the frequency range within which the oscillator can operate.* Run tests to determine when aliasing becomes noticeable and set a limit on the oscillator's fundamental frequency. This hack might be used in a situation where one is prototyping a synthesis patch.

Analog Filter Emulation

An analog synthesizer often functions as a source-filter or subtractive synthesizer. That is, its filters sculpt a spectrally rich input signal to form the output signal. Thus a major issue in analog emulation is modeling the behavior of hardware filter circuits.

The design of authentic analog filters is an art that balances theory with practice (Moog 1965). As one audio engineer put it,

> *[After presenting the mathematical equations for the standard filter types] Whilst these are academically correct, it will hardly ever be possible to calculate tone filters by this means since the input and output impedances will not match and the regulation of the filter response is best achieved by ear. (Douglas 1968, 122)*

Analog filters can be complicated to design. Many decades of experimentation have resulted in a variety of filter circuits. A laboratory-grade analog filter such as the Krohn-Hite 3550 has a frequency response beyond 200 kHz. Moreover, every filter is constructed with specific circuit components (resistors, capacitors, vacuum tubes, transistors, etc.), and the choice of these components can have a major impact on its sonic performance. By contrast, only a handful of circuit topologies are accounted for in software.

Techniques exist for converting an analog filter design into a digital filter design, but these work well only in standard cases. As Smith (2007a) observed, it is not easy to preserve all desirable properties of an analog filter (such as frequency response, order, and control structure), when it is translated to digital form by standard means. Another issue in the emulation of time-varying analog filters concerns the discrete nature of sampling. Whereas signals flow instantaneously in an analog filter, changes in digital filters are limited by the sampling clock. As the filter coefficients change, the current filter states reflect what happened with the previous set of coefficients. Higher sampling rates and greater numerical resolution within the filter are helpful.

Rossum (1992) analyzed the characteristics of analog filters in general and deduced that one of their major differences with respect to digital filters was their soft limiting behavior when the filter resonates. By contrast, when basic digital filters overload, they become instantly loud, raspy, and harsh. He came up with a digital filter scheme whereby the distortion is fed back through a lowpass filter so that it never overloads, producing a smoother tone quality. A MATLAB implementation of Rossum's nonlinear resonator is published in Välimäki et al. (2011).

Stilson and Smith (1996) reverse engineered the Moog voltage-controlled filter (figure 19.7). It exhibited a ladder structure consisting of four one-pole filters in series with global feedback for resonance. Välimäki and Huovilainen (2006) proposed improvements to the Moog model, as did Fontana (2007). Välimäki and Huovilainen (2006) listed the following five desirable characteristics of a digital resonant filter:

1. The filter coefficients should be updated on a per-sample basis.
2. The filter cutoff frequency and resonance (Q) parameters should be independent.
3. The filter should remain stable as long as parameters are within allowed ranges.
4. The filter should have a response similar to that of an analog resonant filter.
5. The filter should be capable of self-oscillation.

They describe a model that improves the emulation by introducing nonlinearities inside sections of the filter.

As another example, Civolani and Fontana (2008) designed a nonlinear model of the Electronic Music Studios (EMS) VCS3 voltage-controlled filter, introduced in 1969.

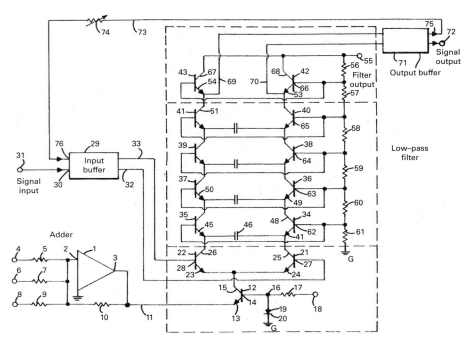

Figure 19.7   The Moog four-stage lowpass filter from the 1969 U.S. Patent 3,475,623, a component of the Moog 904 lowpass/highpass/bandpass/bandreject filter modules.

Parker and D'Angelo (2013) undertook an elaborate study of the characteristics of the iconic Buchla 292 lowpass-gate. A major issue in emulating this filter was to model its response to voltage control. The 292 used vactrols at the heart of its control circuit. The vactrol exhibited a "lazy" response to modulation; that is, it would respond to increasing values quickly but to decreasing values more slowly. Thus the filter's control input could be hit with a trigger impulse and the filter would open quickly before decaying slowly to silence. This quintessential Buchla sound was like that of a struck physical object.

Control Interfaces

A synthesizer's control interface (keys, knobs, buttons, joysticks, switches, display screens, etc.) has great influence on the types of gestures that can be played on it. Analog synthesizers are famous for offering dozens of directly touch-accessible control knobs. Such a direct interface is called *nonmodal*; that is, the meaning of a given control is always the same, and there are no submodes. A consequence of nonmodality is that all controls are available to the user in parallel. Nonmodal interfaces facilitate immediate access.

By contrast, digital synthesizer interfaces are often *modal*: a single controller (slider, knob, button, etc.) can have many modes. For example, each depression of a push-knob accesses a different parameter set. The effect of turning the knob depends on which parameter is selected (the modal context). In other systems, a menu interface serves the sample purpose of selecting the mode. Such schemes reduce costs in hardware synthesizers because knobs and buttons are an expense. In a software synthesizer, additional knobs and buttons take up valuable screen real estate. Modal interfaces cause the user to take extra steps to adjust a parameter. In many cases they make it impossible to control two or more parameters simultaneously and independently.

A characteristic feature of today's hardware-based analog emulation synthesizers is the provision of a control panel of knobs and buttons (figure 19.8). In a purely software implementation, this control panel is onscreen, so the user must either map a physical MIDI controller to the onscreen controls or be content to adjust one parameter at a time with the mouse.

Interconnection of Modules

In VA synthesizers, a patch between two synthesis modules means simply that one module passes data to the other. How this is represented externally to the user varies. For example, figure 19.3 shows a display in which the metaphor of patch cords is taken literally; the cords even jiggle onscreen when they are moved. Other VA software synthesizers offer a more abstract patch editor or just a collection of preset patches.

Figure 19.8   Control panel of the Clavia Nord Lead 4 virtual analog synthesizer with over sixty directly accessible buttons and knobs.

Of course, a great advantage of digital patching is that a given routing, no matter how complicated, can be saved and recalled along with all parameter settings for every module. By contrast, in the world of the modular analog synthesizers, exactly reproducing a previous patch was rare, given that the patch connections and all parameter settings had to be written down and precisely reproduced.

Modulation

Modulation in electronic music means that some aspect of one signal (the *carrier*) varies according to an aspect of a second signal (the *modulator*). Expressive modulation is a staple of analog synthesis, whether low frequency (corresponding to tremolo, vibrato, and pulse-width modulation) or audio rate (corresponding to amplitude, ring, and frequency modulation). Louis and Bebe Barron's electronic music soundtrack to the science-fiction film *Forbidden Planet* (1956) stands as an outstanding example of musical use of analog modulation.

Chapters 15 and 16 explore digital modulation synthesis. Chapter 21 discusses pulse-width modulation (PWM) in the context of pulsar synthesis. The basic principles explained in those expositions apply equally in the domain of analog modulation, with some qualifications. For example, chapter 15 discusses the differences between analog ring modulation and its digital counterpart. Parker (2011) implemented a program for emulation of analog (diode-based) ring modulation. Chapter 15 also describes the differences between *exponential FM* (implemented on many voltage-controlled synthesizers) and *linear FM* (implemented in digital synthesizers). Lest we forget, *spatial modulation,* or *voltage-controlled panning,* was a signature of the analog era, heard in works like Morton Subotnick's quadraphonic *Touch* (1968).

Modeling Analog Signal Processing

The drive to model all things analog extends beyond synthesis to sound processing: loudspeakers, microphones, guitar pickups, electric pianos, vacuum tube instrument amplifiers, microphone preamplifiers, equalizers, tape recorders, spring and plate reverberators, tape echo machines, phasers, distortion boxes, limiters, and compressors. A large research literature is dedicated to this pursuit (Yeh et al. 2008; Yeh, Abel, and Smith 2010; Yeh 2012; Arnardottir, Abel, and Smith 2008; Välimäki et al. 2011; Välimäki, Parker, and Abel (2010); Raffel and Smith 2010; Bilbao 2007; Bilbao and Parker 2010; Dutilleux et al. 2011b; Damskägg et al. 2019; Raffensperger 2012; Paiva, Pakarinen, and Välimäki 2012; Smith 2010; Smith et al. 2002; Pfeifle 2017).

The technology of *convolution* plays a central role in modeling the sound of audio devices. Indeed it has revolutionized the field. See chapter 29 for the story of convolution.

The main goal of analog modeling amplifiers is to emulate the characteristics of classic analog amplifiers and loudspeaker cabinets. Designed originally for keyboards and electric guitars, analog modeling amplifiers take two forms:

- Hardware boxes: analog amplifiers with a digital signal processor input stage. The digital processor contains algorithms that emulate various tube and transistor amplifiers. The box can come with or without loudspeakers, for example, as a pedal effect or *stomp box.*

- Software: a standalone application or plugin that emulates an audio device. The emulation can include microphone models that offer various techniques for capturing the sound in a room.

As is the case with VA synthesis, some analog modeling attempts to replicate measured sonic characteristics of tube amplifiers through techniques such as convolution, rather than the actual circuitry.

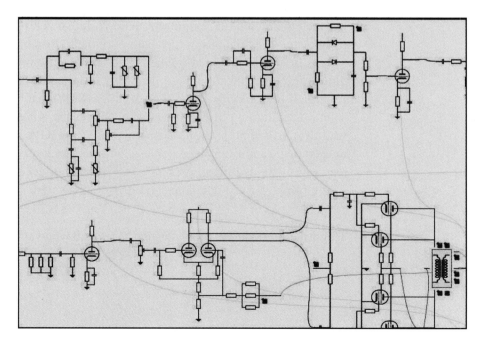

Figure 19.9 Peavey ReValver *Module tweak page* lets users modify the circuit schematic at the component level.

Vacuum tube guitar amplifiers have a highly recognizable sound color, particularly when they are overdriven. Conventional wisdom says that vacuum tube amplifiers emphasize "sweet" even harmonics whereas transistor amplifiers distort by emphasizing "harsh" odd harmonics. Following this line, Lassfolk (1996) described a simple distortion scheme based on the technique of waveshaping (see chapter 17) for the emulation of vacuum tube circuits.

More sophisticated circuit-level emulations take into account that amplifiers have several internal stages, each of which colors the signal in a different way (Dutilleux et al. 2011b; De Sanctis and Sarti 2010; Yeh et al. 2008; Yeh, Abel, and Smith; Yeh 2012; Välimäki et al. 2011; Damskägg et al. 2019). Peavey's ReValver software (figure 19.9) lets circuit designers modify the schematics directly (Peavey 2016).

In order to measure the sonic characteristics of a vacuum tube amplifier, compressor, or equalizer, engineers subject the original device to a battery of tests using a variety of input signals. Using this test data, they develop algorithms that closely emulate the signal processing effects imposed by different amplifier types. They then run difference tests that compare the operation of the original device with that of the emulation. Listening tests are central to the evaluation process, because the schematic describes only the circuit connections of components; it does not describe the behavior of the components when interconnected. In the case of well-engineered emulations, the difference between the digital model and the analog original is less than the unit-to-unit manufacturing variations in the analog originals (Romblom 2004).

Finally, we should mention the recent trend to use machine learning techniques in VA applications. (Appendix A introduces machine learning.) An example is the Kemper Profiling Amplifier (KPA) that learns to replicate the sound of guitar amplifiers. Users can connect the KPA to an amplifier they want to profile and hook up a microphone. The KPA sends a series of test tones into the amplifier and receives them via the microphone. Using machine learning methods, the KPA is able to generate an accurate sonic profile of the amplifier's basic dynamics and drive characteristics.

20 *Formant Synthesis*

Formant synthesis refers to a body of techniques designed to generate resonant peaks in a frequency spectrum. Such techniques can simulate the resonances of the human vocal tract as well as those of traditional and synthetic instruments. Not surprisingly, tones with strong formants have long been a staple timbre of electronic music.

A *formant* is a resonance peak of energy in a spectrum (figure 20.1), which can include both harmonic and inharmonic partials as well as noise. Within the range of 0 to 5,000 Hz, the vocal tract is usually characterized as having five formant regions (including the fundamental).

Formant regions serve as a kind of spectral signature or timbral cue to the source of many sounds. This is not to say that the formants of a voice or an instrument are fixed. Rather, they change relative to the frequency of the fundamental (Luce 1963; Bennett and Rodet 1989). In any case, formants are only one clue the ear uses to identify the source of a tone.

Understanding the formant nature of human speech has long been a scientific research goal. Ingenious methods for synthesizing the formants of vowel-like tones have been developed through the ages, including "singing flames," "singing water jets," and mechanical contraptions designed to emulate the formants of dogs and human beings (Tyndall 1875). Taking the physical modeling approach literally, Dr. Marage in Paris made a vocal tone emulator wherein each vowel was voiced by a pair of rubber lips attached to an artificial mouth. The air flow for the speech was supplied by a pair of electromechanical lungs, which were bellows powered by an electric motor (Miller 1916). Other experimental devices used special combinations of organ pipes to create vowel-like sounds. Recently Howard (2017) mounted 3D-printed models of the vocal tract on loudspeaker drivers in order to synthesize vowels.

Speech research has served as a wellspring of ideas for musical formant synthesis. The rest of this section discusses the following synthesis techniques that generate formants:

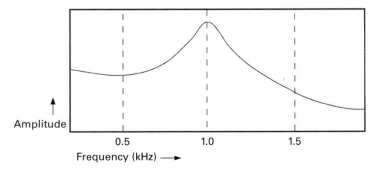

Figure 20.1   A formant region appears as a peak in the spectrum. Here a formant centers at 1 KHz.

- Formant wave-function or FOF synthesis
- VOSIM
- Window-function (WF) synthesis
- Phase-aligned formant synthesis (PAF)
- ModFM

FOF and VOSIM evolved directly out of attempts to simulate human speech sounds, whereas WF was developed to emulate the formants of traditional musical instruments. PAF and ModFM were derived from mathematical analysis of the general problem of formant synthesis.

To be sure, many techniques besides those presented in this chapter can generate formants. These include pulsar synthesis, concatenative synthesis, additive synthesis, subtractive synthesis, granular synthesis, frequency modulation, and physical modeling, and others. We distinguish the methods described here for two reasons: first, because they do not fit neatly into any of the aforementioned synthesis categories, and second, because they were designed primarily for formant synthesis.

Formant Wave-Function Synthesis and CHANT

Formant wave-function synthesis (FOF, abbreviated according to the French translation *fonction d'onde formantique*) is the basis of the CHANT sound synthesis system. (The French word *chant* means *singing* or *song*.) Over the decades since it was first conceived (Rodet and Santamarina 1975; Rodet and Delatre 1979; Rodet and Bennett 1980; Bennett 1981; Rodet, Potard, and Barrière 1984; Iovino 1993), CHANT has been reimplemented on a variety of platforms, ranging from synthesizers like the IRCAM 4X (Asta et al. 1980) to personal computers (Lemouton 1993). FOF generators have been implemented in the Csound synthesis language (Clarke 1990, Clarke 2000). The technique is also supported in IRCAM's OpenMusic library (IRCAM 2018).

CHANT was designed to model a class of natural mechanisms that resonate when excited, but that are eventually damped by physical forces such as friction. Bells resonate for a long time, for example, but a wood block is a damped resonance that cuts off almost immediately. One can excite a resonance of the cheek by tapping on it with one's finger. This single impulse produces a pop. The vocal cords generate a series of fast impulses to continuously excite resonances in the vocal tract, creating a pitched sound. These systems are all analogies for the way that FOF generators operate.

The basic sound production model embedded in CHANT is the voice. However, users can tune the parameters of CHANT to take it beyond vocal synthesis, toward emulations of instruments and synthetic effects. Rodet and colleagues used CHANT to develop models of male and female singers, traditional stringed instruments, woodwinds, horns, and percussion.

Fundamentals of FOF Synthesis

Kelly and Lochbaum (1962) famously synthesized a voice singing *Bicycle Built for Two* (1892) using a subtractive method. *Linear predictive coding* (LPC) is another subtractive method that has been deployed for singing synthesis. (See chapter 14.) In these traditional subtractive approaches, a source signal with a broad spectrum, such as a pulse train or a noise signal, passes through a complicated filter. The filter carves out most frequencies, leaving only a few resonant peak frequencies or formants in the spectrum.

Rodet showed that the complicated filters used in subtractive synthesis can be broken into an equivalent set of parallel bandpass filters excited by pulses. (The filters are *second-order sections,* described in chapter 28.) An FOF realizes one of these parallel bandpass filters; several FOFs in parallel can model a complicated *spectrum envelope* with several formant peaks. The spectrum envelope is a smooth outline that traces the peaks of a spectrum (Depalle 1991), akin to the curve produced by LPC analysis.

An alternative implementation of FOFs replaces the filters with a bank of damped sine wave generators. The signal and spectra of these generators are equivalent to those generated by a pulse-driven filter (figure 20.2). According to Rodet, the advantages of replacing the filters with sine generators are several. The sine generators are efficient and require less numerical precision than their filter counterparts. Also, one or more of the formants can be continuously changed to a sinusoid with controllable amplitude and frequency, making a continuous transition between formant synthesis and additive synthesis (Rodet 1986).

Both the filter and the damped sine wave generator methods can be combined with external sounds to make a compound sound, as depicted in figure 20.3.

Anatomy of an FOF

For synthesis, an FOF generator produces a grain of sound at each pitch period. Thus a single musical note contains a series of grains. To distinguish these grains from those discussed in chapter 13, we call them *FOF grains.* An FOF grain is a damped sine wave with either a steep or a smooth attack and a quasi-exponential decay (figure 20.4a). The envelope of an FOF

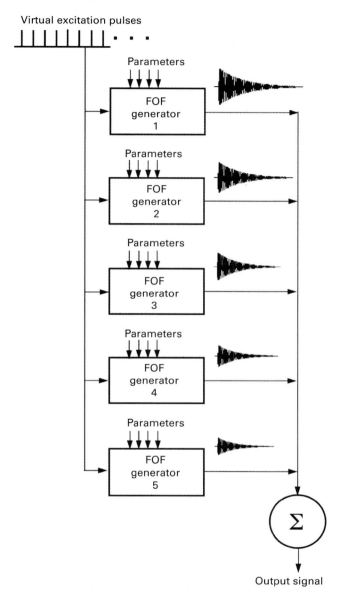

Figure 20.2   A bank of FOF generators driven by input pulses that trigger an FOF *grain* at each pitch period. The output of all FOF generators is summed to generate a composite output signal.

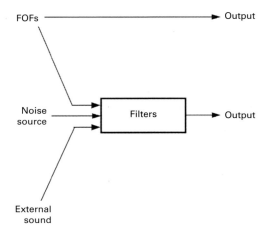

Figure 20.3   FOF synthesis and processing configuration. The output can be sine waves, filtered noise, filtered sampled sounds, or a combination thereof.

grain is called the *local envelope,* as opposed to the global envelope of the note.

The local envelope is formally defined as follows. For $0 \leq t \leq tex$

$$env_t = 1/2 \times [1 - \cos(\pi_t \, / \, tex)] \times \exp(\text{-}atten_t)$$

For $t \geq tex$

$$env_t = \exp(\text{-} \, atten_t)$$

where π_t is the initial phase of the FOF signal, *tex* is the attack time of the local envelope, and *atten* is the decay time (D'Allessandro and Rodet 1989).

Because the duration of each FOF grain lasts just a few milliseconds, the envelope of the FOF grain contributes audible sidebands around the sine wave, creating a formant. (This is caused by the convolution of the envelope with the sinusoid; see chapter 29 for an explanation of convolution.) The spectrum of the damped sine generator is equivalent to the frequency response curve of one of the bandpass filters (figure 20.4b).

The result of summing several FOF generators is a spectrum with several formant peaks (figure 20.5).

FOF Parameters

Each FOF generator is controlled by a number of parameters, including the fundamental frequency and amplitude. Figure 20.6 shows the four formant parameters, which we call *p1* through *p4*:

p1 is the center frequency of the formant.

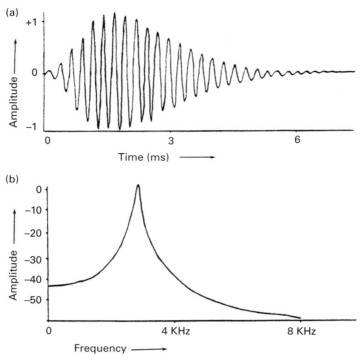

Figure 20.4   FOF grain and spectrum. (a) A single grain or toneburst emitted by an FOF generator. (b) Spectrum of the grain in (a), plotted on a logarithmic amplitude scale. (After d'Allessandro and Rodet 1989.)

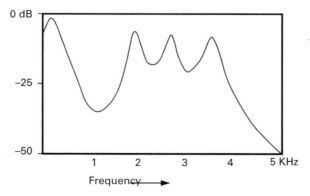

Figure 20.5   Formant spectrum of a vocal tone produced by several FOF generators in parallel.

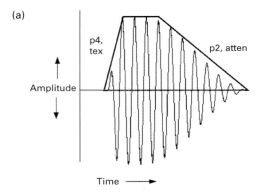

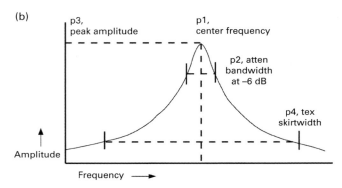

Figure 20.6 FOF parameters. (a) Time-domain view of an FOF. Parameter *p4* represents the attack time (called *tex* in most implementations), and *p2* represents the decay (called *atten*). (b) Frequency-domain view of the four formant parameters. Parameter *p1* is the center frequency of the formant, and *p2* is the formant bandwidth. Parameter *p3* is the peak amplitude of the formant, and *p4* is the width of the formant skirt.

p2 is the formant bandwidth, defined as the width between the points that are attenuated −6dB from the peak of the formant.

p3 is the peak amplitude of the formant.

p4 is the width of the *formant skirt*. The formant skirt is the lower part of the formant peak, about −40 dB below the peak, akin to the foothills of a mountain. The skirt parameter is independent of the formant bandwidth, which specifies the breadth at the peak of the mountain.

The inherent link between time domain and frequency domain operations is exemplified in the way FOF parameters are specified. Two of the main formant (frequency domain) parameters are specified in the time domain as properties of the envelope of the FOF grain. First, the duration of the FOF attack controls parameter *p4,* the width of the formant skirt (around −40 dB).

That is, as the duration of the attack lengthens, the skirt width narrows. Figure 20.7 depicts this relationship.

Second, the duration of the FOF decay determines *p2,* the formant bandwidth at the −6 dB point. Hence a long decay length translates into a sharp resonance peak, and a short decay widens the bandwidth of the signal. (This link between the duration of a sound and its bandwidth also shows up in granular synthesis, which is discussed in more detail in chapter 13.)

Typical applications of FOF synthesis configure several FOF generators in parallel. Beyond the six main parameters per FOF generator, implementations of CHANT offer supplementary parameters for more global control. Table 20.1 lists the main parameters. Some implementations have over sixty parameters. The numerous parameters mandate a database structured into rules for controlling the synthesis engine. This is particularly necessary for the emulation of vocal and instrumental sounds, where parameter settings are critical. Part of the job of CHANT and associated high-level languages like OpenMusic is to provide a rule database.

The CHANT Program

The original CHANT synthesis program (Baisnée 1985) offered three modes of interaction to users. In the first and simplest mode, the user supplies values for a preset list of variables for singing synthesis. These variables translate into the parameters *p1* to *p4* for the individual FOF generators, described previously. The variables can be grouped into the following categories:

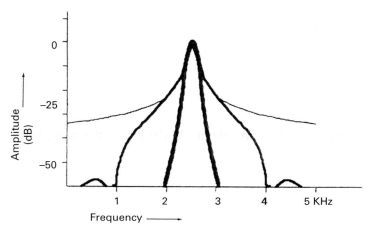

Figure 20.7   Effect of varying the attack time on the formant skirt bandwidth. Thin line, wide formant: *p4* = 0.1 ms. Medium line, medium formant: *p4* = 1 ms. Thick line, narrow formant: *p4* = 10 ms.

Table 20.1   Main FOF Parameters

For each FOF generator
Amplitude
Fundamental frequency
Octaviation—attenuation of alternate grains
Center frequency of the formant (p1)
Formant bandwidth at −6 dB from the peak of the formant (p2)
Peak amplitude of the formant (p3)
Width of the formant skirt (p4)
Grain overlap
Function tables (usually sine)
Initial phase
Spectrum correction for vocal synthesis
Filter Parameters
Center frequency of formant
Amplitude of formant
Bandwidth of formant

- Loudness

- Fundamental frequency

- Vibrato and random variation of the fundamental frequency

- Spectrum shape and formant amplitude

- Local envelope of the formant waveforms

- Overall amplitude curves

In the second mode, FOFs serve as time-varying filters applied to sampled sounds. This mode has been used by composers as a sound transformation technique.

In the third mode of interaction, users write algorithms that describe transitions and interpolations between timbres in OpenMusic (Bresson and Stroppa 2011).

FOF Analysis/Resynthesis

With its formants and sine waves, FOF represents a potentially general method of synthesis. Two efforts have been made to develop analysis systems that generate parameters for FOF resynthesis: *models of resonance* and an approach based on linear predictive coding. At this point, they can be considered to be historical methods.

Models of resonance (MOR) refers to a methodology for capturing the timbre of traditional acoustic instrument tones; the resynthesis uses FOFs (Barrière, Potard, and Baisnée 1985; Potard, Baisnée, and Barrière 1986, 1991). The premise of MOR is the classic excitation-resonance model. That is, sound-producing mechanisms are divided into an excitation stage and a resonance stage. MOR assumes that the excitation is an impulse like a pluck of a plectrum or a tap of a drumstick. The resonance is the acoustical response of the instrument body to the excitation.

MOR analysis captures only the resonance portion. As such, it is not a complete physical or spectral model of an instrument, nor was it designed to exactly replicate its input signal. Its goal, rather, was to extract features that could be used in synthesis (Barrière, Potard, and Baisnée 1985).

According to the developers, the analysis methodology of MOR was somewhat arduous and imperfect (Potard, Baisnée, and Barrière 1986; Baisnée 1988; Potard, Baisnée, and Barrière 1991). Basically, it involves taking a single fast Fourier transform (FFT) of a segment of a tone. (The FFT is explained in chapter 37.) A peak extraction algorithm isolates the most important resonances in this spectrum, eliminating other components. Then another analysis is tried with a larger time window, and the spectrum peaks are merged in a common file. Resynthesis from these peaks can be tried to determine how closely it matches the original. One repeats the analysis with successively larger windows until a satisfactory resynthesis can be obtained. MOR resynthesis used up to several hundred standard FOF generators. Best results were obtained for pitched percussive tones such as marimba, vibraphone, and tubular bells (Baisnée 1988).

D'Allessandro and Rodet (1989) and Depalle (1991) reported on experiments using LPC spectrum analysis. After tracing the outline of the spectrum envelope on a frame-by-frame basis, the process extracted formants corresponding to a bank of FOF generators. The results were not an identity reconstruction but were said to be similar to the original.

VOSIM

The *voice-simulation* (VOSIM) synthesis technique was developed by Werner Kaegi and Stan Tempelaars at the Institute of Sonology in Utrecht during the early 1970s (Kaegi 1973, 1974; Tempelaars 1976; Kaegi and Tempelaars 1978). The core idea is the generation of a repeating tone-burst signal, producing a strong formant component. In this sense, the technique has links to the FOF technique described earlier. VOSIM was originally used to model vowel sounds. Later, it was extended to model vocal fricatives—consonants such as [sh]—and quasi-instrumental tones (Kaegi and Tempelaars 1978).

VOSIM Waveform

The VOSIM waveform was derived by approximating the signal generated by the human voice. This approximation takes the form of a series of pulse trains, where each pulse in the train is the square of a sine function. The amplitude of the highest pulse is set by parameter A. Each of the pulse trains contains $N \sin^2$ pulses in series that decrease in amplitude by a decay factor b (figure 20.8). The width (duration) of each pulse T determines the position of the formant spectrum. A variable-length delay M follows each pulse train, which contributes to the overall period of one pulse train and thus helps to determine the fundamental frequency period. We can calculate the period as $(N \times T) + M$, so that for seven pulses of 300 μsec duration and a delay equal to 900 μsec, the total period is 3 ms and therefore the fundamental frequency is 333.33 Hz. The formant centers at 5,000 Hz.

Two strong percepts emerge from the VOSIM signal: a fundamental corresponding to the repetition frequency of the entire signal and a formant peak in the spectrum corresponding to the pulsewidth of the $\sin^2$ pulses (figure 20.9). One formant is produced by each VOSIM oscillator. In order to create a sound with several formants, it is necessary to mix the outputs of several VOSIM oscillators (as with FOF generators).

A VOSIM oscillator is controlled by varying a set of parameters that affect the generated sound (table 20.2). T, M, N, A, and b are the primary parameters.

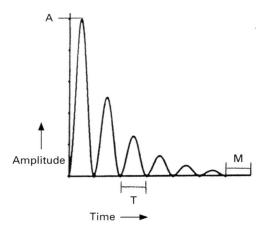

Figure 20.8 A VOSIM pulse train.

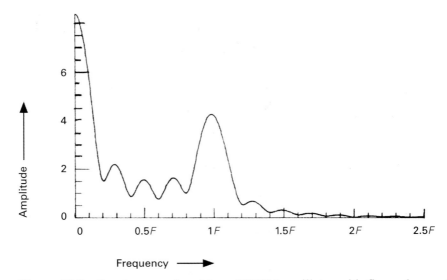

Figure 20.9 Spectrum produced by a VOSIM oscillator with five pulses and an attentuation constant of 0.8. (After De Poli 1983.)

Table 20.2 VOSIM parameters

Name	Description
T	Pulse width
dT	Increment or decrement of T
M	Delay following a series of pulses
dM	Increment or decrement of M
D	Maximum deviation of M
A	Amplitude of the first pulse
dA	Increment or decrement of A
b	Attentuation constant for the series of pulses
N	Number of pulses per period
S	Type of modulation (sine or random)

In order to obtain vibrato, frequency modulation, and noise sounds, one modulates the delay period M. This constraint led Kaegi and Tempelaars to introduce three new variables: S, D, and NM, corresponding to the type of modulation (sine or random), the maximum frequency deviation, and the modulation rate, respectively. They also wanted to be able to provide for transitional sounds, which led to the introduction of the variables NP, dT, dM, and dA. These are the positive and negative increments of T, M, and A, respectively, within the number of periods NP.

By changing the value of the pulse width T, the formant can be made to change in time. The effect is that of *formant shifting*, which sounds like a filter is sweeping up or down.

The unadulterated VOSIM signal is not bandlimited. This can cause aliasing problems in systems with a low sampling rate. Above twice the formant frequency, the amplitudes of the spectral components are at least 30 dB down from the fundamental. Above six times the formant frequency, components are at least 60 dB down (Tempelaars 1976).

J. Scherpenisse at the Institute of Sonology (Utrecht, Netherlands) designed and built a number of VOSIM oscillators in hardware controllable by computer (Tempelaars 1976; Roads 1978a). VOSIM oscillators were also built into the hardware of the SSSP digital synthesizer at the University of Toronto (Buxton et al. 1978a). More recently, VOSIM has been implemented in Csound, Max, SuperCollider, and Native Instruments REAKTOR and in hardware in the Mutable Instruments Braids Eurorack module.

Window Function Synthesis

Window function (WF) synthesis is a multistage technique for formant synthesis using purely harmonic partials (Bass and Goeddel 1981; Goeddel and Bass 1984). The technique begins with the creation of a broadband harmonic signal. Then a weighting stage boosts or cuts different harmonics in this signal to create time-varying formant regions that emulate the spectra of traditional instruments.

The building block of the broadband signal used in the initial stage of WF synthesis is a *window function pulse* (figure 20.10a). Window functions are special envelopes used in a variety of signal-processing tasks such as filter design and sound analysis. Chapters 36 and 37 present more on window functions.

A variety of window functions have been devised (Harris 1978; Nuttall 1981). Plots of window spectra always exhibit a characteristic *center lobe* and *side lobes*. The center lobe is typically much higher in amplitude than the side lobes, meaning that the signal is, in effect, bandlimited. In the Blackman-Harris window function chosen by Bass and Goeddel, the frequencies in the side lobes are attenuated by at least 60 dB (figure 20.10b). Because the audible harmonics are within the center lobe, this ensures that aliasing is not an issue.

The broadband signal is created by linking together a periodic series of WF pulses separated by a period of zero amplitude called *dead time*. For different fundamental frequencies, the duration of the WF pulse stays the same; only

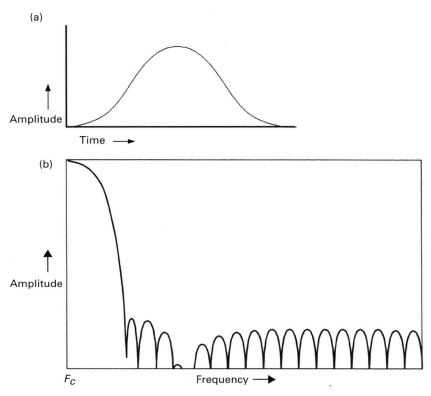

Figure 20.10   Window function pulse. (a) Pulse shown in time domain. (b) One side of the frequency spectrum. The left edge of the figure corresponds to the center frequency of the pulse, and the lobes represent sidebands, all of which are more than 70 dB down from the center frequency peak. (After Nuttall 1981.)

the interpulse dead time varies. Figure 20.11 shows two signals an octave apart; the only difference between them is the dead time interval. In this use of a pulse followed by a period of dead time, the WF technique is not unlike VOSIM and the FOF methods and pulsar synthesis (explained in the next chapter). Like these methods, WF synthesis adds the output of several generators to create complex, time-varying spectra.

In WF synthesis, the number of harmonics increases as the fundamental frequency decreases. This occurs because the higher harmonics fall outside the center lobe of the WF pulse's spectrum. Thus low tones are timbrally rich, and high tones are less so. This is characteristic of some traditional instruments such as pipe organs and pianos, which Bass and Goeddel wanted to simulate. Note that some other instruments, such as harpsichords, do not exhibit this behavior. In addition, some instruments do not have a purely harmonic spectrum and thus are not good models for the WF technique.

(a)

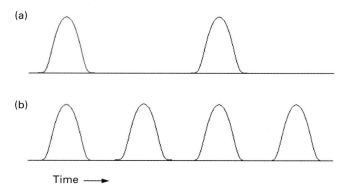

(b)

Time ⟶

Figure 20.11   Time domain view of two WF signals an octave apart. (a) Low-frequency signal. (b) Higher-frequency signal.

So far, we have discussed a scheme in which fixed tones are generated. These tones vary from broadband (at a low fundamental frequency) to narrowband (at a high fundamental frequency). In order to create formant regions in the spectrum, further processing called *slot weighting* is required.

A *time slot* is defined as the duration of a single WF pulse plus a portion of its dead time. By weighting the slots (i.e., multiplying a slot by a value) with a periodic sequence of *N slot weights*, the timbre of the output signal can be manipulated. This weighting is accomplished by feeding a stream of WF pulses as an input signal to a multiplier along with a periodic stream of slot weights. The multiplier computes the product of each input pulse with a specific weight. The result is an output stream containing WF pulses at different amplitudes (figure 20.12). The spectrum of such a stream exhibits peaks and valleys at various frequencies. For time-varying timbres, each slot weight can be specified as a time-varying function.

WF synthesis requires an amplitude compensation scheme, because low frequencies contain few pulses and much zero-amplitude dead time, whereas high frequencies contain many pulses and almost no dead time. A nearly linear scaling function can be applied for scaling amplitude inversely proportional to frequency. That is, low tones are emphasized and high tones are attenuated for equal balance throughout the frequency range.

The basic WF algorithm can be augmented by various means that increase its flexibility. For details, see Bass and Goeddel (1981) and Goeddel and Bass (1984). In a practical implementation, with eight WF oscillators, 256 slots per period (maximum), a sampling rate of 40 kHz, a WF pulse width of 150 μsec, and twenty-eight piecewise linear segments used to model each slot weight as a function of time, reasonable emulations of traditional instrument tones were reported by Bass and Goeddel.

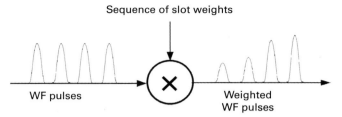

Sequence of slot weights

WF pulses   Weighted
WF pulses

Figure 20.12   A stream of WF pulses multiplied by a periodic sequence of slot weights to obtain a series of weighted WF pulses.

Figure 20.13 shows two plots of an alto saxophone tone, a difficult test for a synthesis method. Figure 20.13a shows the original tone, and figure 20.13b shows a synthetic tone generated by the WF technique.

Phase-Aligned Formant Synthesis and ModFM

Two related techniques called *phase-aligned formant* synthesis (PAF) and ModFM start from mathematical derivations. Invented by Miller Puckette and patented by IRCAM, PAF combines a two-cosine carrier signal with a wave-shaping pulse modulator (Puckette 1995, 2007). (See chapter 17 on waveshaping.) PAF has a well-defined spectrum, including predictable phases, and is computationally efficient. Starting from a desired spectrum, Puckette derived a formal method in the context of FM and waveshaping in which the shaping function sculpts the amplitude of the partials in the spectrum. The basic formula for an output signal $x[n]$ is, using Puckette's notation

$$x[n] = \underbrace{g\left(a\sin(\omega n/2\right)}_{\text{modulator}}\underbrace{\left[p\cos(k\omega n) + q\cos((k+1)\omega n)\right]}_{\text{carrier}}$$

A slight twist in the implementation is that the sinusoid in the modulator is all positive or rectified (Puckette 2007). The waveshaping function g is a Gaussian-like function (a bell-shaped curve), a is a waveshaping index controlling bandwidth of the modulator, ω is the fundamental frequency, and k, p, and q control the formant center frequency. Thus the carrier is a weighted sum of two cosines whose frequencies are increased by multiplication (by k and $k+1$, respectively) and phase wrapping. This means that all the lookup phases are controlled by the same sawtooth oscillator. Indeed, all parameter calculations are synchronized to this phase (hence are phase-aligned).

A bank of six PAF generators has been used to synthesize vocal formants (Puckette 1995). In Puckette (2007), the method is presented as a set of Pure Data patches. Lazzarini (2017) provides PAF code in Python.

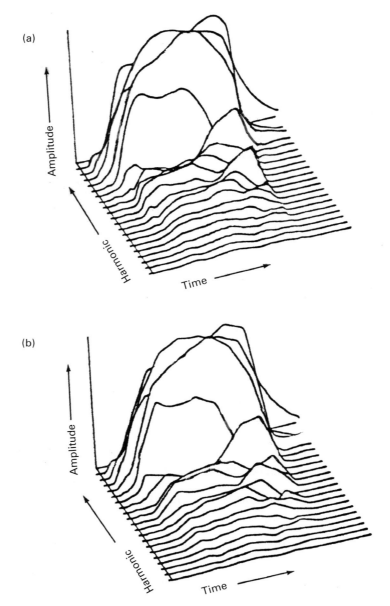

Figure 20.13   Plots of the first twenty harmonics of the time-varying spectrum of an alto saxophone tone. Low harmonics are toward the back of the plot. (a) Original played on alto saxophone. (b) Synthetic tone created with WF synthesis. (After Goeddel and Bass 1984.)

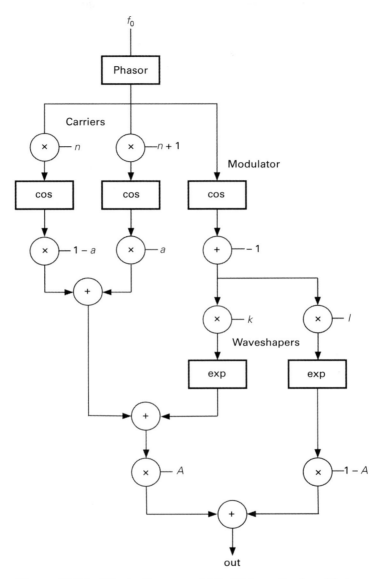

Figure 20.14 Block diagram of ModFM synthesis with two carriers and two waveshapers (after Lazzarini and Timoney [2013]). A single phasor synchronizes all cosine generators. The modulator signal passes through two waveshapers with exponential functions. The spectrum mix is controlled by variable A in the range [0,1].

Lazzarini and Timoney (2013) compared PAF and their method called ModFM. Here we focus specifically on *phase-synchronous ModFM*. It generates an impulse train using a simple heterodyne synthesis model

$$s(n) = M(n) \times \sin(\omega_c \times n)$$

A sinusoidal carrier at the center frequency is amplitude modulated by $M(n)$, which is phase-synchronous to the sinusoid. Here again, waveshaping is applied as a method for dynamically controlling the modulator $M(n)$ spectrum.

Derived from classic FM, ModFM implements a summation formula based on modified Bessel functions (see chapter 16). Unlike the undulating Bessel functions of classic FM, modified Bessel functions are unipolar and decaying: they always produce a decaying spectral envelope. The equation for basic ModFM synthesis is

$$s[n] = e^{(k\cos(\omega_m n) - k)} \cos(\omega_c n)$$

with the modulator and carrier frequencies w_m and w_c, respectively, and

$$w_m = 2\pi f_m / f_s$$

where f_s is the sampling frequency and

$$w_c = 2\pi f_c / f_s$$

One then tunes the modulator as the fundamental frequency and the carrier to the center of a formant. A key parameter is k, which controls the amount of modulation in the output signal. This is the distortion index that controls the bandwidth of the signal.

Figure 20.14 shows a block diagram of ModFM synthesis augmented by the use of two carriers and two exponential waveshapers, summed together to produce an output signal (see Lazzarini and Timoney [2013]).

Csound has a modfm opcode. For code examples using modfm, refer to Lazzarini et al. (2016).

21 *Pulsar Synthesis*

Composing with Pulsars

Musical Applications of Pulsar Synthesis

Assessment

This chapter describes a method of digital sound synthesis with links to past analog techniques. This is *pulsar synthesis* (PS), named after the spinning neutron stars that emit periodic signals in the range of 0.25 Hz to 642 Hz (Roads 2001a, 2001b). By coincidence, this same range of frequencies—between rhythm and tone—is of central interest in pulsar synthesis.

PS melds established principles within a new paradigm. In its basic form, it generates pulses and pitched tones similar to those produced by analog instruments such as the Ondioline (Jenny 1958; Fourier 1994) and the Hohner Elektronium (1950), which were designed around a *source-filter* model of synthesis using filtered pulse trains (Cherry 1949). Pioneering electronic music composers such as Karlheinz Stockhausen (1955, 1957, 1961, 1963) and Gott-fried Michael Koenig (1957, 1959, 1962) used filtered impulse generation as a staple in their studio craft. PS is a digital technique, however, and so it accrues the advantages of programmable control, waveform flexibility, graphical user interface, and extensibility. In its advanced form, pulsar synthesis generates a world of rhythmically structured crossbred sampled sounds.

PS belongs to a larger family of *microsonic* or *particle synthesis* techniques, one example of which is granular synthesis, presented in chapter 13 (Gabor 1946, 1947, 1952; Xenakis 1960; Roads 1978b, 1991, 2001a). These techniques stream or scatter acoustic particles in myriad patterns to produce time-varying sounds.

This chapter presents the basic theory of pulsars and pulsar graphs. We then move on to a more advanced technique using pulsars to transform sampled sounds through cross-synthesis.

Basic Pulsar Synthesis

Basic PS generates a family of classic electronic music timbres that are akin to those produced by an impulse generator connected to a bandpass filter. Unlike the classic technique, however, there is no filter in the basic PS circuit.

Anatomy of a Pulsar

A single pulsar is a particle of sound. It consists of an arbitrary *pulsaret* waveform w with a period d followed by a silent time interval s (figure 21.1a). The total duration of a pulsar is $p = d + s$, where p is the *pulsar period*, d is the *duty cycle,* and s is silent. Repetitions of the pulsar signal form a *pulsar train*. Let us define the frequency corresponding to the repetition period as $f_p = 1/p$ and the frequency corresponding to the duty cycle as $f_d = 1/d$. Typical

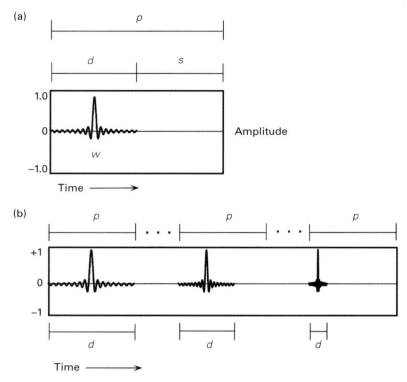

Figure 21.1 Anatomy of a pulsar. (a) A pulsar consists of a brief burst of energy called a *pulsaret w* of a duration *d* followed by a silent interval *s*. The waveform of the pulsaret, here shown as a bandlimited pulse, is arbitrary. It could also be a sine wave or a period of a sampled sound. The total duration is $p = d + s$, where *p* is the fundamental period of the pulsar. (b) Evolution of a pulsar train, time-domain view. Over time, the pulsar period *p* remains constant while the pulsaret period *d* shrinks. The ellipses indicate a gradual transition period containing many pulsars between the three shown.

ranges of f_p are between 1 Hz and 5 kHz, and the typical range of f_d is from 80 Hz to 10 kHz.

In PS, both f_p and f_d are continuously variable quantities. They are controlled by separate envelope curves that span a train of pulsars. The train is the unit of musical organization on the time scale of notes and phrases. A pulsar train can last anywhere from a few hundred milliseconds to a minute or more.

Notice in figure 21.1b that the *duty ratio* or *d:s ratio* varies while *p* remains constant. In effect, one can simultaneously manipulate both fundamental frequency (the rate of pulsar emission) and what we could call a *formant frequency* (corresponding to the duty cycle), each according to separate envelopes. Lowering the fundamental means increasing *s,* and raising the fundamental means decreasing *s.*

So far, the structure that we have described is similar to a standard impulse generator. Pulsar synthesis generalizes this configuration in several ways. First, it allows the pulsaret *w* to be any waveform. Figure 21.2 shows some typical pulsaret waveforms, including those with multiple subperiods within their duty cycle (b, d, and e).

Let us assume that *w* is a single cycle of a sine wave. From a signal processing point of view, this can be seen as a sine wave that has been limited in time by a rectangular function *v*, which we call the *pulsaret envelope*. An important generalization is that *v* can also be any shape. As we discuss further, the envelope *v* has a strong effect on the spectrum of the pulsar train.

Figure 21.3 shows some typical pulsaret envelopes. A rectangular envelope (figure 21.3a) produces a broad spectrum with strong peaks and nulls for any pulsaret. Figure 21.3g depicts a well-known configuration for formant synthesis, an envelope with a sharp attack followed by an exponential decay (Kaegi and Tempelaars 1978; Rodet 1980). (See chapter 20 on formant synthesis.) This configuration can be seen as a special case of pulsar synthesis. As figure 21.3h shows, the envelope can also be a bipolar ring modulator.

Keeping *p* and *w* constant and varying *d* on a continuous basis creates the effect of a resonant filter swept across a tone. There is, of course, no filter in this circuit. Rather, the frequency corresponding to the duty cycle *d* appears in the spectrum as a formant peak. By sweeping the frequency of this peak over time, we obtain the sonic equivalent of a time-varying bandpass filter applied to a basic impulse train.

Pulsaret-Width Modulation

Pulse-width modulation (PWM) is a well-known analog synthesis effect that occurs when the duty cycle of a rectangular pulse varies while the fundamental frequency remains constant (figure 21.4a). This produces an edgy "sawing" quality as the upper odd harmonics increase and decrease over the course of the modulation. At the extremes of PWM, the signal is silent. For example, when $d = 0$, PWM results in a signal of zero amplitude (figure 21.4b). When $d = p$, PWM produces a signal of a constant amplitude of 1 (figure 21.4c).

Pulsaret-width modulation (PulWM) extends and improves this model. First, the pulsaret waveform can be any arbitrary waveform. Second, it allows the duty cycle frequency to pass through and below the fundamental frequency. Here $f_d \leq f_p$. Notice in figure 21.4 how the duty cycle of the sinusoid increases from (d) to (e). In (f), $p = d$. Finally, in (g) $p < d$. That is, the duty cycle is longer than the fundamental period. Only the first quadrant of the sine wave repeats. The fundamental period cuts off the duty cycle of the pulsaret in mid-waveform. In our implementation, we apply a user-controlled crossfade time around this

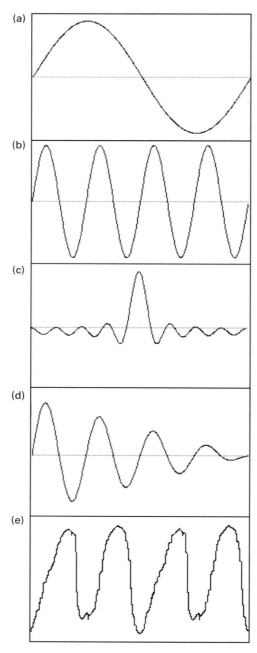

Figure 21.2   Typical pulsaret waveforms. In practice, any waveform can be used. (a) Sine. (b) Multicycle sine. (c) Bandlimited pulse. (d) Decaying multicycle sinusoid. (e) Cosmic pulsar waveform emitted by the neutron star Vela X-1.

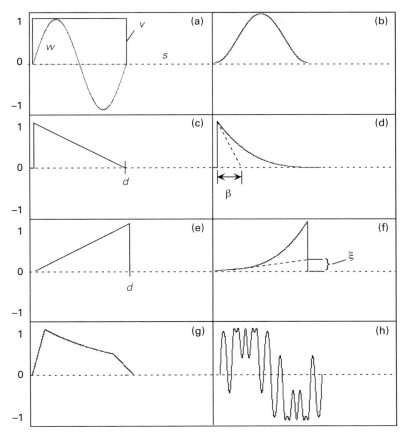

Figure 21.3 Typical pulsaret envelopes *v.* (a) Rectangular. (b) Gaussian. (c) Linear decay. (d) Exponential decay. The term β determines the steepness of the exponential curve. (e) Linear attack, with duty cycle *d.* (f) Exponential attack. The term ξ determines the steepness of the exponential curve. (g) FOF envelope. (h) Bipolar modulator.

cutoff point, which we call the *edge* factor. When there is no crossfade, the edge factor is high.

An alternative approach to pulsar-width modulation produces a different sound. In *overlapped pulsaret-width modulation* or OPulWM, the fundamental frequency is interpreted as the rate of pulsar emission, independent of the pulsaret duty cycle. That is, the duty cycle of an individual pulsar always completes, even when it crosses below the fundamental frequency. Whenever the fundamental period expires, our algorithm spawns a new pulsar. Thus when $d > p,$ several pulsars overlap with others whose duty cycle has not yet completed. As d increases, the generator spawns more and more overlapping pulsars. For practical reasons, then, we stipulate an arbitrary

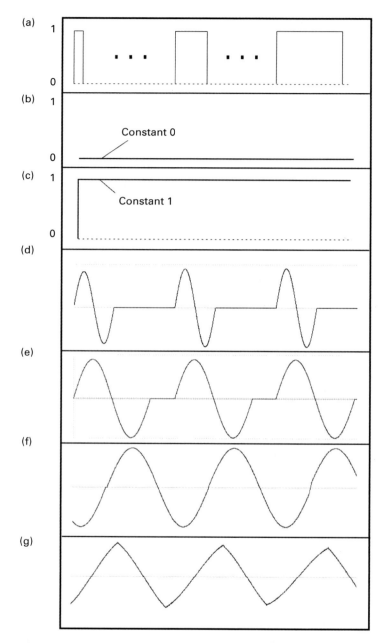

Figure 21.4   PWM and PulWM. (a) Classical PWM with a rectangular pulse shape. The ellipses indicate a gradual transition between the pulses. (b) PWM when the duty cycle $d=0$ results in a signal of zero amplitude. (c) PWM when the duty cycle $d=p$ (the fundamental period), the result is a signal with a constant amplitude of 1. (d) Pulsar train with a sinusoidal pulsaret. (e) Same period as (d), but the duty cycle is increasing. (f) The duty cycle and the period are equal, resulting in a sinusoid. (g) The duty cycle is greater than the fundamental period, which cuts off the final part of the sine waveform.

overlap limit. In general, OPulWM results in a much phase cancelation and thus tends to be a more subtle effect than regular PulWM.

Synthesis across Time Scales

PS operates within and between musical time scales. It generates a stream of microsonic particles at a variable rate across the continuum spanning the infrasonic pulsations and the audio frequencies. When the distance between successive impulses is less than about one twentieth of a second, the human hearing mechanism causes them to fuse into a continuous tone. This is the *forward masking effect* (Buser and Imbert 1992). As Helmholtz (1885) observed, in the range between 20 and 35 Hz, it is difficult to distinguish the precise pitch of a sustained tone; reliable pitch perception takes hold at about 40 Hz, depending on the waveform. Thus for p between approximately 25 ms (corresponding to $f_p = 40$ Hz) and 200 μs (corresponding to $f_p = 5$ kHz), listeners ascribe the characteristic of pitch to a periodic sustained tone.

As the rate of pulsar emission slows down and crosses through the threshold of the infrasonic frequencies ($f_p < 20$ Hz), the sensation of continuous tone evaporates and we can perceive each pulsar separately. When the fundamental f_p falls between 62.5 ms (corresponding to the time span of a thirty-second note at the metronome setting of a quarter note = 60 MM) and 8 s (corresponding to the time span of two tied whole notes at a quarter note = 60 MM), we hear rhythm. The fundamental frequency envelope becomes a graph of rhythm (figure 21.5). Later we present a software application that lets one draw this function onscreen. Such a pulsar graph can serve as an alternative form of notation for one dimension of rhythmic structure, namely, the onset time of events. The correspondence between the musical units of rhythmic structure (note values, tuplets, rests, etc.) can be made clear by plotting note values on the vertical or frequency scale. For example, assuming that a tempo of 60 MM, a frequency of 5 Hz corresponds to a quintuplet figure. Note that the duration of the events is not represented by a two-dimensional pulsar graph but could be represented by adding a third dimension to the plot.

In order to interpret the rhythm generated by a function inscribed on a pulse graph, one has to calculate the duration of the grain emission curve at a given fixed frequency rate. For example, a grain emission at 4 Hz that lasts for 0.75 seconds emits 3 grains. When grain emission switches from one value to the next, the pulsar corresponding to the new duration is immediately played, followed by a silence equal to the period of grain emission. Figure 21.5 shows a rhythm that alternates between fixed-rate pulses, accelerandi, and silence.

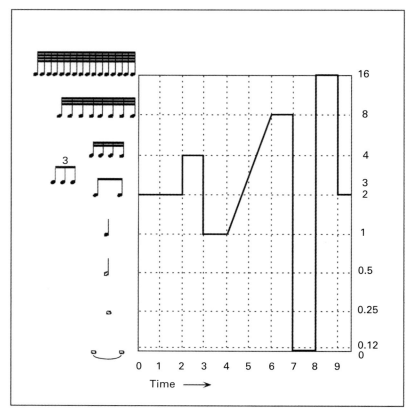

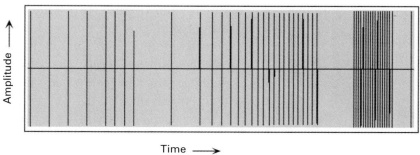

Figure 21.5   Pulsar rhythms. Top: Pulse graph of rhythm showing rate of pulsar emission (vertical scale) plotted against time (horizontal scale). The left-hand scale measures traditional note values, and the right-hand scale measures frequencies. Bottom: Time-domain image of generated pulsar train corresponding to the plot at the top.

Spectra of Basic Pulsar Synthesis

The spectrum of the pulsar stream is the convolution product of w and v, biased in frequency by f_d and f_p. Since w and v can be arbitrary waveforms, and f_d and f_p can vary continuously, the range of spectra produced by PS is quite large.

When the formant frequency is set at a specific frequency, for example 1 kHz, this spreads energy in that region of the spectrum. Precisely how the energy is spread depends on w and v. The pulsaret waveform w can be considered a template of spectrum shape that repeats at the stipulated fundamental frequency f_p and is scaled in time by the duty cycle or formant frequency f_d. If, for example, the ratio of the amplitudes of the first five harmonics of w is 5:4:3:2:1, this ratio is preserved independently of p and d, when $f_p \leq f_d$.

The pulsaret envelope's contribution to the spectrum is significant. Figure 21.6 shows the spectra of individual pulsars where the waveform w is fixed as a sinusoid, and the pulsaret envelope v varies between three basic shapes. In the case of figure 21.6a, v is rectangular. Consequently, the formant spectrum takes the form of a broad sinc function in the frequency domain. The spectrum shows strong peaks at factors of $1.5f_d$, $2.5f_d$, and so on, and nulls at harmonics of f_d. This is characteristic of the sinc function. An exponential decay or *expodec* envelope (such as shown in figure 21.3d) tends to smooth the peaks and valleys in the spectrum (figure 21.6b). The bell-shaped Gaussian envelope conforms the spectral energy around a central formant frequency (figure 21.6c).

Thus by modifying the pulsaret envelope, one can alter the profile of the pulsar spectrum. Refer to Roads (2001b) for a mathematical analysis of the effect of pulsaret envelope on the spectrum.

Advanced Pulsar Synthesis

Basic pulsar synthesis technique is the starting point for advanced pulsar synthesis. The advanced technique adds several features that take the method beyond the realm of vintage electronic sonorities. In particular, advanced pulsar synthesis is built on the following three principles:

1. Multiple pulsar generators sharing a common fundamental frequency but with individual formant and spatial trajectories

2. Pulse masking to shape the rhythm of the pulsar train

3. Convolution of pulsar trains with sampled sounds

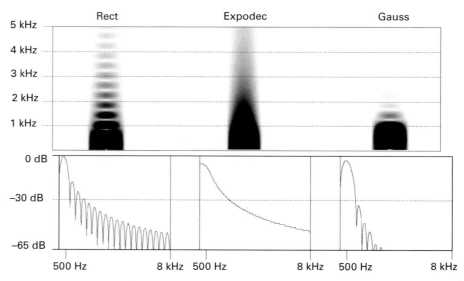

Figure 21.6 Effect of the pulsaret envelope on the spectrum. The top panel presents frequency-versus-time sonograms of an individual pulsar with a sinusoidal pulsaret, a fundamental frequency of 12 Hz, and a formant frequency of 500 Hz. The sonograms are based on 1,024-point fast Fourier transform plots using a Von Hann window and are plotted on a linear frequency scale. Shown left to right are the sonogram produced by a rectangular envelope, an expodec envelope, and a Gaussian envelope. The bottom panel plots the spectra of these pulsars on a dB scale.

Figure 21.7 outlines the schema of advanced pulsar synthesis. The different parts of this schema are explained in the following sections.

Multiple Pulsar Generators

A pulsar generator has the following seven parameters:

1. Pulsar train duration
2. Pulsar train fundamental frequency envelope f_p
3. Pulsaret formant frequency envelope f_d
4. Pulsaret waveform w
5. Pulsaret envelope v
6. Pulsar train amplitude envelope a
7. Pulsar train spatial path s

The individual pulsar train is the simplest case. To synthesize a complex sound with several resonance peaks, we can add several pulsar trains with

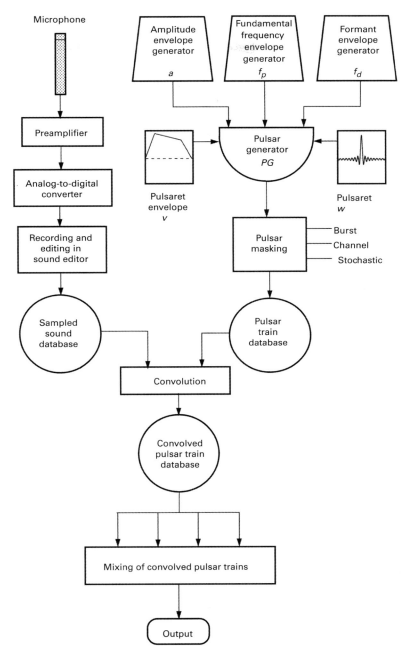

Figure 21.7 Schema of pulsar synthesis. A pulsar generator with separate envelope controls for fundamental frequency, formant frequency, amplitude, stochastic masking, and spatial position. In advanced pulsar synthesis, several generators may be linked with separate formant and spatial envelopes. A pulsar stream may be convolved with a sampled sound.

the same fundamental frequency but with different time-varying formant frequencies f_d. One envelope controls their common fundamental frequency, and two or more separate envelopes control their formant trajectories f_{d1}, f_{d2}, and so on.

One of the unique features of pulsar synthesis is that each formant can follow its own spatial path. This leads to complex spatial interplay within a single tone or rhythmic phrase.

Pulsar Masking

A pulsar generator emits a sequence of pulsars, where the rate of emission can vary over time according to the fundamental frequency envelope function f_p. *Pulsar masking* breaks up the stream by introducing intermittencies (regular or irregular) into the metronomic sequence. It deletes individual pulsarets, leaving an interval of silence in their place. This takes three forms: *burst, channel,* and *stochastic masking.*

Burst masking (figure 21.8a) models the tone burst generators of the classic electronic music studios such as the Krohn-Hite 5300A. It produces a regular pattern of pulsarets that are interrupted at regular intervals. The on-off pattern can be stipulated as the *burst ratio b:r,* where b is the burst length in pulsaret periods and r is a rest length in pulsaret periods. For example, a *b:r* ratio of 4:2 produces an alternating sequence of four pulsarets and two silent periods: 1111__1111__1111__1111__, and so on. If the fundamental frequency is infrasonic, the effect is rhythmic. When the fundamental is in the audio frequency range, burst masking imposes an amplitude modulation effect on the timbre (figure 21.9), dividing the fundamental frequency into a subharmonic frequency $b + r$.

Channel masking (figure 21.8b) deletes pulsars in alternate channels. By selectively masking pulsars in channels 1 and 2, one creates a dialog within a phrase, articulating each channel in turn. Figure 21.8b shows two channels only, but one can generalize this scheme to N channels.

Stochastic masking introduces random intermittency into the regular stream of pulsars. We have implemented stochastic masking as a weighted probability that a pulsar will be emitted at a particular point in a pulsar train. The probability is expressed as an envelope over the duration of the pulsar train. When the value of the envelope is 1, a pulsar is emitted. If the value is less than 1, it has less possibility. A value of 0 results in no emissions. Values between 0.9 and 0.8 produces an interesting analog-like intermittency, as if there were an erratic contact in the synthesis circuit (figure 21.8c).

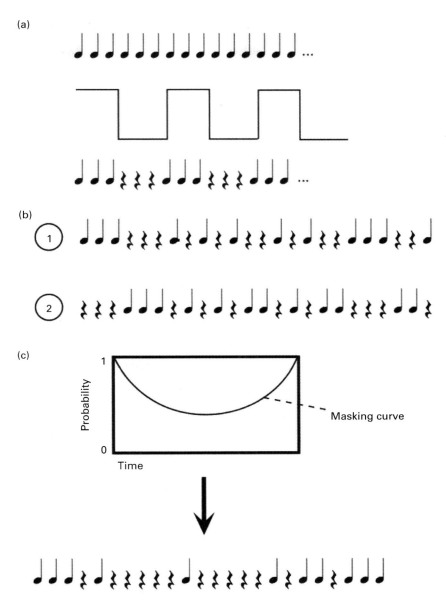

Figure 21.8   Pulsar masking turns a regular train into an irregular train. Pulsars are illustrated as quarter notes, and masked pulsars are indicated as quarter rests. (a) Burst masking. The burst ratio here is 3:3. (b) Channel masking. (c) Stochastic masking according to a probability table. When the probability is 1, there is no masking. When the probability is 0, there are no pulsars. In the middle, the pulsar train is intermittent. Notice the thinning out of the texture as the probability curve dips in the center.

Transformation of Sampled Sounds by Convolution with Pulsars

The technique of pulsar synthesis can be harnessed as a method of sound transformation through the technique of convolution. Convolution is fundamental to the physics of waves (Rabiner and Gold 1975). (See chapter 29 on convolution.) It "crosses" two signals, creating a new signal that combines the time structures and spectra of both inputs. Many transformations emerge from convolution, including exotic filters, spatializers, models of excitation/resonance, and a gamut of temporal transformations such as echoes, reverberation, attack smoothing, and rhythm mapping. Refer to Roads (1992, 1993a, 1997) for applications of convolution in musical sound transformation. Pure convolution has no control parameters. That is, the type of effect achieved depends entirely on the nature of the input signals.

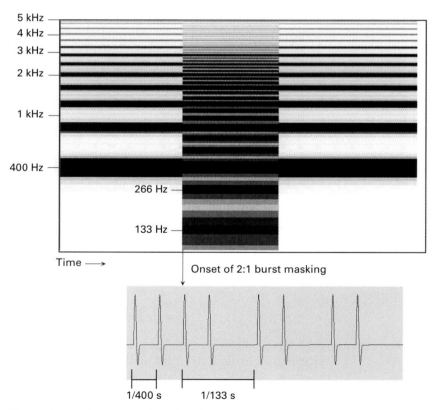

Figure 21.9   Sonogram depicting the effect of burst masking in the audio frequency range. The pulsaret is one cycle of a sinusoid, and the pulsaret envelope is rectangular. The *b:r* ratio is 2:1. The fundamental frequency is 100 Hz, and the formant frequency is 400 Hz. Notice the subharmonics at 133 Hz and 266 Hz caused by the extended periodicity of the pulse masking interval (400 Hz/3).

Sophisticated transformations involving rhythm and spatial mapping can be achieved through convolution. It is well known that any series of impulses convolved with a brief sound maps that sound into the time pattern of the impulses. These impulses can be emitted by a pulsar generator such as the one that we have implemented. If the pulsar train frequency is in the infrasonic range, then each pulsar is replaced by a copy of the sampled sound object, creating a rhythmic pattern. The convolution of a rhythmic pattern with a sound object causes each impulse to be replaced by a filtered copy of the sound object. Each instance of the sampled object is projected in space according to the spatial location of a specific pulsar's position in space.

In convolution, each pulsar represents the impulse response of a filter. Thus timbral variations can derive from two factors: (1) filtering effects imposed by the time-varying pulsar train, and (2) overlapping effects caused by convolution with pulsar trains whose fundamental period is shorter than the duration of the sampled sound.

Figure 21.10 shows the temporal and filtering effects of convolution in the form of sonograms. The input signal (a) is the Italian word *qui* (pronounced *kwee*). It convolves with the pulsar train (b) with a variable infrasonic

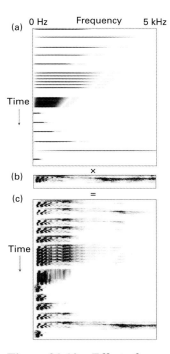

Figure 21.10   Effect of convolution with pulsar train. (a) Sampled sound, the Italian word *qui* (pronounced *kwee*). (b) Infrasonic pulsar train with a variable fundamental and formant frequency. (c) Convolution of (a) and (b).

fundamental frequency and a variable audio formant frequency. The resulting convolution (c) combines the time structure and the spectra of the two signals.

A database of sampled sound objects can be stockpiled for crossing with trains selected from the pulsar database. If the goal of the synthesis is to retain the time structure of the pulsar train (e.g., to maintain a specific rhythm), the sampled sound objects should be of short duration (less than the fundamental period of the pulsar train) and have a sharp attack (a rise time less than 100 ms). These constraints minimize the time smearing effects of convolution (Roads 1992, 1993b, 1997). Thus a good starting point for a sound database is a collection of percussion samples. The constraints can be relaxed if one seeks a smoother and more continuous texture. Samples with long durations superimpose multiple copies of the sampled object, creating a rippling sound stream. Samples with slow attacks blur the onset of each sample copy, smearing the stream into a continuum. Thus by controlling the attack shape of the sample one has a handle on the sonic texture.

Implementations of Pulsar Synthesis

The author of this book developed the first implementation of PS in 1991, using James McCartney's Synth-O-Matic, a programmable sound synthesis environment for Apple Macintosh computers (McCartney 1990, 1994). In 1996, Mr. McCartney replaced Synth-O-Matic with SuperCollider, an object-oriented programming language (McCartney 1995).

PulsarGenerator

On the basis of SuperCollider (McCartney 1998), Alberto de Campo and the author developed a new realization of pulsar synthesis. We presented it in a 1999 summer course at the Center for New Music and Audio Technology (CNMAT) in Berkeley. Further refinement of this prototype led to the Pulsar-Generator application, distributed by the Center for Research in Electronic Art Technology (CREATE) at UCSB. Figure 21.11 presents the graphical interface of PulsarGenerator. Notice the control envelopes for the synthesis variables. These envelopes can be designed in advance of synthesis or manipulated in real time as the instrument plays. Alberto de Campo implemented a scheme for saving and loading these envelopes in groups called *settings*. The program lets one crossfade at a variable rate between multiple settings,

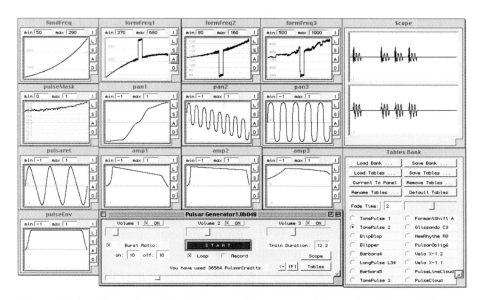

Figure 21.11   Control panel of the PulsarGenerator application by Alberto de Campo and Curtis Roads.

which takes performance with PulsarGenerator to another level of complexity. De Campo (2011) presents annotated code for pulsar synthesis.

In wave-oriented synthesis techniques, an algorithm loops through a wavetable and varies the signal according to relatively slowly updated control functions. Thus the efficiency of synthesis corresponds to the number of simultaneous unit generators (oscillators, filters, etc.). By contrast, particle synthesis is more demanding because the synthesis algorithm must also handle the task of scheduling possibly thousands of events per second, each of which may be unique. The efficiency of pulsar synthesis is thus related to the rate of particle emission. Tests by the developers showed that pulsar emission rates of greater than 6,000 pulsars/second (corresponding to a three-formant instrument at a fundamental frequency of 2 kHz) are easily achievable.

nuPG

nuPG is a more recent implementation of pulsar synthesis (Pietruszweski 2019). The developer, Marcin Pietruszweski, performs with the software in a manner that combines graphic user interaction with live coding. That is, he manipulates waveforms and envelopes onscreen and also launches new code segments in real time. This has the effect of changing the graphical user interface as different control panels are instantiated (figure 21.12).

Written in SuperCollider, nuPG offers several extensions to the original PulsarGenerator including the following:

Sieve-based masking is supported by an editor, allowing definition of sieves and their combination using logical operators (union, intersection, difference, and symmetric difference). The output of the operation is converted to a sequence of 0s and 1s that are used to mask an active pulsar train. A musical theory of sieves was first proposed by Xenakis (1992).

Matrix modulation of synthesis parameters, where modulation oscillators include: sine, saw, chaotic hennon, and latocarfian, and stochastic gendyn (Xenakis 1992). Each synthesis parameter can be modulated by up to four modulators simultaneously

Parameter linkage links synthesis parameters within a pulsar train and across multiple trains. When two parameters *A* and *B* are linked, an increase in parameter *A* will cause an increase in *B*. Parameters can also be inverse linked. Each of these can have added offset.

Per-pulsar modulation means every pulsar can be modulated individually.

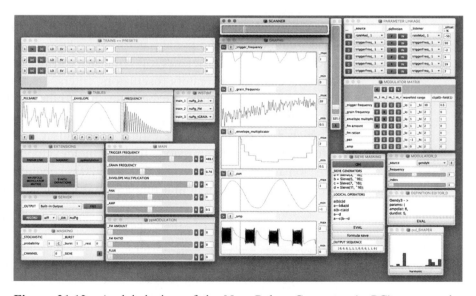

Figure 21.12   A global view of the New Pulsar Generator (nuPG) program by Marcin Pietruszewski (2019). The program emulates functionality of the classic PulsarGenerator by Roads and de Campo and provides a set of extensions such as per-pulsar processes (frequency and amplitude modulation, spatialization), parameter modulation, parameter linking, and sieve-based pulsar masking.

Text based live-coding control of synthesis parameters enables fast prototyping of formalized compositional structures (e.g. dynamic generation of pulsaret waveforms and envelopes, and additional per-pulsar effects such as spatialization and delay).

Nuklear

Hamburg Audio's Nuklear is a pulsar synthesizer in the form of a software plug-in. This implementation changes the interaction paradigm by making the synthesizer playable from a MIDI keyboard (Wilmering, Rehaag, and Dupke 2012). It also adds traditional features such as low-frequency oscillators for modulation and a 16-step sequencer.

Composing with Pulsars

To interact with a pulsar generator in real time is to experiment with sonic ideas. In the course of experimentation, a composer can save settings and plan how these will be used within a composition. Sound produced by a pulsar generator can be recorded in the studio. Material from this recording session can be edited by the composer and possibly convolved or mixed with other material.

A final stage of pulsar composition is to merge multiple trains to form a composite texture. This is a question of montage and is usually best handled

Figure 21.13   Screen image of Hamburg Audio Nuklear pulsar synthesizer.

by editing and mixing software that is designed for this purpose. Each layer of the texture may have its own rhythmic pattern, formant frequency envelope, choice of convolved objects, and spatial path. Working on a variety of time scales, a composer can apply signal processing transformations on individual pulsars, pulsar trains, and pulsar textures. These can include mixing with other sounds, filtering, modulations, reverberation, and so on.

Musical Applications of Pulsar Synthesis

The author developed PS in the course of realizing *Clang-tint* (Roads 1993b), an electronic music composition that was commissioned by the Japanese Ministry of Culture (Bunka-cho) and the Kunitachi College of Music, Tokyo. The second movement of this work, entitled *Organic,* focuses on expressive phrasing. It combines bursts of insect, animal, and bird calls with electronic pulse tones. The electronic sound palette is based on pulsar synthesis in multiple forms: pulsating blips, elongated formant tones, and clouds of asynchronous pulsars. For the last form, the author first generated multiple infrasonic pulsar trains, each one beating at a different frequency in the range of 6 to 18 Hz. He then mixed these together to obtain the asynchronous pulsar cloud.

The raw material of the electronic music composition *Half-life*, composed in 1998 and 1999 by the author, is a one-minute pulsar train that varies wildly. Most sounds in the rest of the work were derived from this source. *Half-life* extends the pulsar material through processes of granulation, microfiltration, granular pitch-shifting, recirculating feedback echo, individual pulsar amplitude shaping, and selective reverberation. Similarly, *Tenth vortex* (2000) and *Eleventh vortex* (2001) by the author, are both granulations of a pulsar train. By contrast, *Pictor alpha* (2003) is pure PS with editing on a micro time scale.

Assessment

Music transpires on multiple time scales, from high-level macrostructure down to a myriad of individual sound objects or notes. Below this level is another hierarchy of time scales. Here are the microsonic particles such as the classical rectangular impulses, grains, wavelets, and pulsars (Roads 1999, 2001a). Impulse generation as an effective means of music synthesis was established decades ago in the analog electronic studio. By comparison, digital pulsar synthesis offers a flexible choice of waveforms and envelopes, increased precision, and graphical programmable control.

Unlike wave-oriented synthesis techniques, the notion of rhythm is built into techniques based on particles. Rhythm, pitch, and timbre are all interrelated but can be controlled separately. Pulsar synthesis offers a seamless link between the time scales of individual particle rhythms, periodic pitches, and the meso or phrase level of composition. Another novel feature of this technique is the generation of multiple independent formant trajectories, each of which follows its own spatial path.

22 *Waveform Segment Synthesis*

Waveform Interpolation

SAWDUST

SSP

Instruction Synthesis

This chapter explores four experimental approaches to sound synthesis. They were all intended for the production of electronic sounds. This stands in contrast to synthesis methods that sometimes try to simulate traditional instrument tones, such as additive synthesis or physical modeling. The experimental techniques described in this chapter were motivated by a conceptual approach to compositional aesthetics, rather than by traditional acoustical theory.

Waveform segment techniques are idiomatic to the computer. They begin with the specification of individual amplitude points and commands to construct simple waveforms segments by connecting the points. The commands link segments into more complex waveforms. One version of this technique creates waveforms automatically, as the side effect of the operation of a virtual machine programmed by the composer.

Waveform segment synthesis techniques were motivated by a desire for a fresh theoretical approach to the problem of synthesis. The ideas are closely related to the goals of sound art, which often hews to a conceptual and experimental line.

A common feature among these techniques is that they easily generate rich, wide-bandwidth, and noisy sounds

Waveform segment synthesis techniques constitute a collection of methods for building up sounds from wave fragments that are stitched together to create larger waveforms, sections, and entire pieces. In effect, digital sounds are created out of their atomic constituents: samples. Waveform segment techniques represent a time-domain approach to synthesis because they construct the sound out of individual amplitude points. Concepts such as frequency, spectrum, and rhythm may not be explicitly represented in the synthesis parameters but instead arise as a by-product of compositional manipulations.

This chapter describes four waveform segment techniques:

Waveform interpolation

SAWDUST

SSP

Instruction synthesis

Waveform interpolation can be related to the frequency domain, because interpolation methods have predictable effects on the spectrum of a signal, as discussed further on. In two of the techniques described here, SAWDUST and SSP, the composer works directly with sample points. Time-varying spectra result from the composer's operations on waveform segments. Instruction synthesis is an abstract approach to synthesis because the composer specifies sounds in terms of logical instructions that have no direct connection to acoustical parameters.

Waveform Interpolation

Interpolation is a mathematical technique for generating a line between two *endpoints* or *breakpoints*, where each breakpoint is a pair (point on *x*-axis, point on *y*-axis). Many interpolation algorithms exist, including *constant, linear, exponential, logarithmic, half-cosine,* and *polynomial,* among others. Each generates a different family of curves between the breakpoints. As figure 22.1 shows, constant interpolation draws a straight line parallel to the abscissa between the two breakpoints. Linear interpolation draws a straight line connecting the breakpoints.

The two points of inflection (curvature) in half-cosine interpolation ensure a smooth curve between the breakpoints. Figure 22.2a shows half-cosine interpolation between two points, and figure 22.2b shows half-cosine interpolation connecting several points. Polynomial interpolation techniques (including cubic splines and Chebychev polynomials) fill the space between two points with arbitrarily smooth or widely varying curves, depending on the polynomial used.

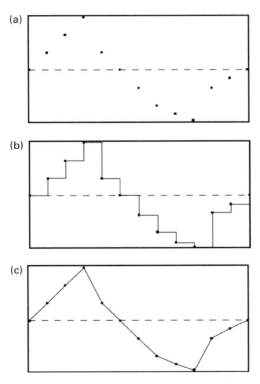

Figure 22.1 Simple interpolation techniques. (a) Original breakpoints. (b) Constant. (c) Linear.

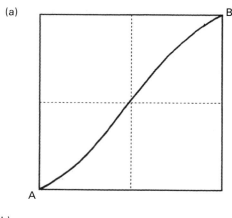

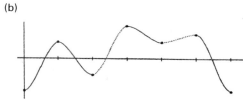

Figure 22.2   Half-cosine interpolation. (a) Half-cosine drawn between two points *A* and *B*. Notice the two points of inflection (bending points). (b) Half-cosine interpolation between several points. (After Mitsuhashi [1982a].)

Linear Interpolation Equation

Linear interpolation is simple and ubiquitous. It tries to find an intermediate point *i* between two known endpoints. An equation to achieve this is

$$f(i) = f(start) + \{([i - start] \:/\: [end - start]) \times [f(end) - f(start)]\}$$

where *f(start)* and *f(end)* are the starting and ending breakpoints, respectively, and *i* is an intermediate point on the abscissa between *start* and *end*. In effect, linear interpolation figures out how far along *i* is between *start* and *end,* multiplies that ratio times the difference between *f(end)* and *f(start),* and adds that to *f(start)*.

Interpolation in oscillators and envelope generators

Computer music systems often use interpolation. We find it inside oscillators and envelope generators, for example (Moore 1977, 1990; Parmenter 2011). Chapter 3 explains how an interpolating oscillator generates a waveform with a dramatically improved signal-to-noise ratio in comparison to a non-interpolating oscillator. In envelope generators, interpolation connects break-point pairs (*x-y* coordinates) that describe the outline of an envelope. This technique is more memory efficient than storing every point of the envelope but requires a bit more computation.

Interpolation can also be used to generate new waveforms from existing waveforms. Some implementations of Music N languages, for example, include unit generators for waveform interpolation (Leibig 1974). These units take two signals as their input and generate a signal that is a weighted interpolation between the two (figure 22.3). By varying the weight over time we obtain a time-varying cross between the two input waveforms.

Interpolation in GEN Functions

Several of the table generation (GEN) functions of the Music N languages like Csound interpolate between composer-specified breakpoints. These GEN functions create envelopes and waveforms that are used in Music N instruments. Typical interpolating GEN functions in Music N languages include line-segment (linear interpolation), exponential, cubic spline (polynomial), and Chebychev (polynomial).

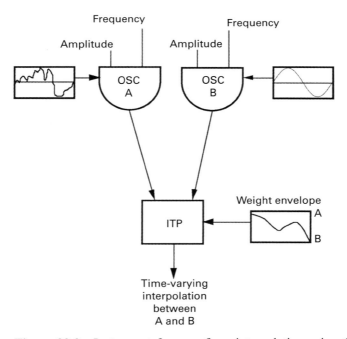

Figure 22.3   Instrument for waveform interpolation using the ITP unit generator found in some Music N software synthesis languages. The weight envelope specifies which waveform will predominate. When the weight envelope is 1, the left oscillator waveform is heard. When it is 0, the right oscillator plays. When it is 0.5, the waveform is the point-by-point average of the two waveforms.

Interpolation Synthesis

Bernstein and Cooper (1976) proposed a method of waveform synthesis based exclusively on linear interpolation. In this method, one period of a waveform is assumed to contain *n* breakpoints spaced at equal intervals of time. The main drawback to linear interpolation for waveform synthesis is that the sharp angles in the waveforms that it generates create harsh-sounding uncontrollable high-frequency partials. Mitsuhashi (1982a) presented several alternatives to the linear interpolation approach, including *constant, half-cosine,* and *polynomial interpolation.* He demonstrated that constant interpolation is similar to Walsh function synthesis (see chapter 10) in terms of the waveforms that it generates (all right angles), and the number of parameters needed to create the waveforms. In contrast to Walsh function synthesis, constant interpolation does away with the additions needed to sum the weighted coefficients in Walsh synthesis. Thus, it has the potential of being more efficient. Unfortunately, like linear interpolation, constant interpolation also suffers from the problem of generating uncontrollable higher partials.

Half-cosine interpolation does not suffer from this problem. By using half-cosine interpolation functions, Mitsuhashi could determine the mixture of harmonics in the waveform, producing results equivalent to those produced by additive synthesis. The advantage is that half-cosine interpolation uses fewer computational resources than an additive synthesis system.

Mitsuhashi also analyzed the case of interpolation by arbitrary polynomial functions. When uniformly spaced breakpoint intervals are used, the polynomial can be evaluated very efficiently using the method of *forward differences.* The mathematical details of polynomial interpolation by the method of forward differences are beyond the scope of this book. For more information refer to Mitsuhashi (1982a, 1982b) and Cerruti and Rodeghiero (1983).

The spectrum of the signal generated by interpolation is a result of two terms: the ordinates of the breakpoints $f(i)$ and the interpolation function chosen. In synthesizing a periodic waveform whose one period incorporates *n* breakpoints, the amplitude of $n/2$ harmonics can be controlled by varying the height (ordinates) of the breakpoints (Mitsuhashi 1982a). Thus, if the number of breakpoints is 20, the zeroth through the tenth harmonics can be controlled.

It follows that time-varying spectra can be generated by changing the ordinates of the breakpoints at each period. Conveniently, linear changes in the ordinates of the breakpoints cause linear changes in the amplitudes of the harmonics.

Up to this point we have considered the case of uniformly spaced breakpoint intervals. Nonuniform breakpoint intervals can also be used. When they are chosen carefully, nonuniform breakpoint intervals can provide a much better approximation to a given waveform than uniform breakpoints. This results in lower distortion. Figure 22.4 indicates how uniformly spaced breakpoints provide a poor approximation to a waveform, whereas nonuniformly spaced breakpoints, positioned at points of greatest change, provide a much better approximation. Bernstein and Cooper (1976) give the Fourier coefficients determining the spectra of waveforms approximated by nonuniformly spaced breakpoint intervals. Further study is needed to determine all the benefits and liabilities of this approach.

Fractal Interpolation Synthesis

Gordon Monro proposed a method called *fractal interpolation synthesis* (FIS) (Monro 1995) for sound waveforms. The basic idea is to generate functions that pass through a set of points (figure 22.5). FIS has the appeal that complicated waveshapes can be synthesized with little information. Figure 22.5 shows an iterative process in which the previous waveform is

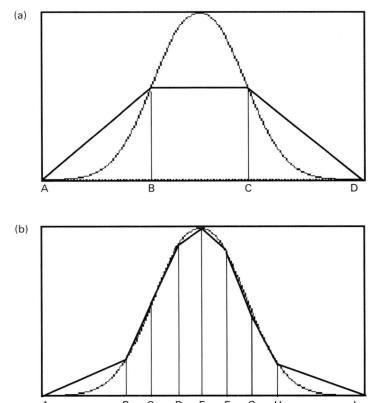

Figure 22.4   Effect of nonuniform breakpoints. (a) Curve drawn with uniform breakpoints. (b) Curve drawn with nonuniform breakpoints, yielding a better fit to the curve.

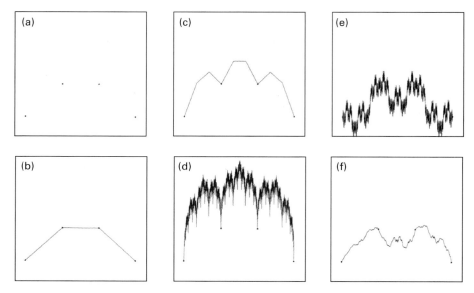

Figure 22.5   Fractal interpolation synthesis. (a) Four points. (b) Linear interpolation through the points in (a). (c) Function (b) is imposed on each point. (d) The result of eight iterations of this process. (e) Eighth iteration using the same points but with negative displacements (i.e., the waveform of the previous generation is inverted). (f) Eighth iteration of the same points but with positive and negative displacements.

superimposed on each point, resulting in fractal self-similarity. The superimposition can also be scaled by a positive or negative displacement factor *d*. As the number of iterations increases, so does the high frequency content. Compare (b) with (d). Plucked sounds can be generated by starting with high *d* and reducing *d* after the initial attack. Due to the ease with which high frequencies can be generated, aliasing can be an issue. To minimize aliasing, Monro proposed rules of thumb such as using small displacements and tailoring the number of iterations to the frequency.

SAWDUST

The SAWDUST system, designed by Herbert Brün and implemented by a team of programmers at the University of Illinois (Blum 1979), represents an original approach to sound synthesis. (Refer to Grossman [1987] for commentary on SAWDUST from the standpoint of implementation.)

The term *sawdust* concatenates two words: *saw*, a tool, and *dust*, tiny particles that are by-products of a process. In Brün's conception, the *saw* is a computer and the *dust* is the data, consisting of minuscule amplitude points (samples). The SAWDUST system is an interactive environment for manipulating amplitude points (which Brün calls *elements*) and combining them hierarchically into pieces of waveforms, sections, and ultimately, complete compositions. As with other waveform segment techniques, the signals produced by the SAWDUST system often exhibit a raw, jagged-edged quality.

The basic operations in SAWDUST include concatenation of elements, cycling (looping), mixing, and varying. The operations are carried out by the subprograms LINK, MINGLE, MERGE, and VARY. LINK is an ordering function that transforms a collection of unordered elements A into a set of ordered elements called a *link*. Formally speaking, LINK$(A) \rightarrow L$, where A is a list of elements or links.

MINGLE is a cycling operation that takes a collection of ordered links and forms a new set in which the original collection is repeated n times. This is one mechanism for creating periodic waveforms in SAWDUST. For example, MINGLE$(2, L3, L4) = \{L3, L4, L3, L4\}$.

MERGE is an ordering operation that alternatively selects successive elements from two links to form a new link. For example, given two links Lj and Lk, with $Lj = \{e1, e2, \ldots e10\}$ and $Lk = \{e21, e22, \ldots e30\}$, then MERGE$(Lj, Lk) = Lm = \{e1, e21, e2, e22, \ldots e10, e30\}$.

VARY transforms one link into another. The composer specifies an initial link, a duration, and a final link. In addition, the composer stipulates the degree of a polynomial. In the resulting operation of VARY, each point in the initial link varies according to a computer-generated polynomial of the degree specified by the composer, until it winds up at its corresponding endpoint in the destination link.

SSP

SSP is a waveform segment synthesis system designed by the composer G. M. Koenig and implemented by Paul Berg at the Institute of Sonology (Utrecht) in the late 1970s (Berg 1978b, 1979, 2009). Like Brün's SAWDUST, SSP is an interactive system for manipulating individual elements into waveforms and large-scale compositional structures.

SSP was designed by a composer with a serial and postserial background. As a result, the system owes more to the post World War II era of composition theory than it does to signal processing theory. In particular, SSP's library of operations can be traced directly to serial and postserial *selection principles* used in Koenig's composition programs Project 1 (Koenig 1970a) and Project

2 (Koenig 1970b). These operations act on *elements* and *segments*. Elements in SSP are time and amplitude points, that is, samples. The SSP system connects sample points in between the elements specified by the composer by linear interpolation. Segments are waveforms constructed from operations on elements.

In working with SSP, the composer prepares a database of time points and a database of amplitude points. By associating a set of time points and amplitude points, the composer can specify such familiar waveform patterns as sine, square, sawtooth, and triangle waveforms, as well as more idiosyncratic patterns, possibly derived from probabilistic procedures. SSP selection principles create or extract parts of the element database and combine these into waveform segments. The composer determines the time order of the segments by using another round of selection principles. Table 22.1 lists the six selection principles in SSP.

Both Brün's SAWDUST and Koenig's SSP are well matched for direct synthesis with a digital-to-analog converter attached to a small computer. The sound material generated by both methods tends toward raw, spectrally rich waveforms that are not derived from any standard acoustical or signal-processing model.

Instruction Synthesis

Instruction synthesis is a conceptual approach to sound synthesis that generates sequences of computer instructions (e.g., binary addition, subtraction, AND, OR, loop, delay, branch) to manipulate binary data. This data is considered to be a sequence of sound samples to be sent to a digital-to-analog converter. All synthesis methods, of course, use computer instructions at the lowest level of software. The point of instruction synthesis is that the sound is specified exclusively in terms of logical instructions, rather than in terms of traditional acoustical or signal processing concepts.

Synthesis by instruction is a conceptual opposite to synthesis by rule or physical modeling synthesis, discussed in chapter 18. Physical modeling starts from a mathematical description of an acoustical mechanism. This model can be complex, requiring a great deal of computation. In contrast, instruction synthesis starts from the idiomatic use of computer instructions with no acoustic model. The technique is efficient and can be run in real time on the most inexpensive computers.

The sounds produced by instruction synthesis are different in character from those produced by rule-based synthesis. In many cases, it would be difficult

Table 22.1   Selection Principles in SSP

Selection Principle	Arguments	Explanation
Alea	A, Z, N	N random numbers are chosen between A and Z.
Series	A, Z, N	N random values are chosen between A and Z. When a value is selected, it is removed from the pool of available values. The pool is refilled when it is empty.
Ratio	Factors	N random values are chosen between A and Z. The probability of occurrence of values A and Z is specified by a list between of probability weightings called Factors.
	A, Z, N	
Tendency	N, M	N random values are chosen for each of M tendency masks. The N values occur between the initial boundaries A1 and A2 and the final boundaries Z1 and Z2.
	A1, A2	
	Z1, Z2 . . .	
Sequence	Count, Chunks	Directly specify a sequence of elements. Count is the number of elements specified; Chunks is a list of their values.
Group	A, Z, N, Type, LA, LZ	A random value between A and Z is chosen. This happens one or more times, forming a group. The size of the group is randomly chosen between LA and LZ.

to produce these sounds using standard digital or analog synthesis techniques, much less mechanical-acoustic means.

Most work in instruction synthesis was carried out by associates of the Institute of Sonology in the Netherlands. One category of instruction synthesis system is an *assembler* for a *virtual machine* (Berg 1975; Berg 1978a, 1979). An assembler is a low-level programming language where each statement corresponds to a hardware instruction. A virtual machine is a program that simulates the operation of an abstract computer with its own instruction set, data types, and so on. These systems require the composer to write fairly long programs that generate the individual samples. The program is the specification for a composition, and so it is also the score.

Paul Berg's PILE language (Berg 1978a, 1979) is a canonical example of instruction synthesis. The motivation for the PILE language springs from an aesthetic belief that "computers produce and manipulate numbers and other symbolic data very quickly. This could be considered the idiom of the computer" (Berg 1979, 30). To implement his idea, Berg designed a virtual machine for numeric and symbolic operations, emulated by a program written for a small computer. The PILE language is the instruction set of the virtual machine. The execution of these programs by the virtual machine causes samples to be generated and sent to a digital-to-analog converter.

The instruction set of PILE consists of operations such as RANDOM (create a random number), INCR (add one to a number), SELECT (assign a random value to a variable), and CONVERT (send a sample to the digital-to-analog converter). Other operations change bit masks and manipulate program control flow by performing various random operations and inserting delays. Although tight control of pitch, duration, and timbre selection is possible in PILE (Berg realized a popular song to prove this point), the language is biased toward interactive experimentation with sound and trial-and-error improvisation. Due to the presence of random variables, the sonic results of a particular set of PILE instructions cannot always be predicted in advance. This is in keeping with the exploratory aesthetic of the language's inventor.

Holtzman's system (1979) was an attempt at controlling instruction synthesis from a higher level. He developed a program generator that produced short sound synthesis programs. Using a high-level notation, the composer could specify the order in which these programs were executed.

It is in the nature of instruction synthesis that the acoustic qualities of the sounds produced are not predictable. Accepting this, the composer who relies on instruction synthesis works in a trial-and-error mode. Because it is easy to produce a wide variety of sounds quickly with these techniques, many possibilities can be tried out in a single studio session. The composer then selects the most useful sounds.

23 *Concatenative Synthesis*

Bob L. T. Sturm with Curtis Roads

To compose a 4 minute 15 second realization of John Cage's *Williams Mix* (1953) took six people nine months of cutting and splicing tape (Kostelanetz 1970). Concatenative synthesis automatically facilitates such practices with an unlimited amount of recorded musical material—beyond the possibilities of manual labor. The aesthetic goals of concatenative synthesis vary. On one hand, concatenative synthesis can create realistic simulations of musical performance: more real than sampling. On the other hand, concatenative synthesis can spawn wild remixes, such as substituting a database of monkey sounds for the sounds of a classical orchestra.

This chapter surveys concatenative synthesis: its design and mechanics, its varieties, and its historical relationship to speech synthesis and *micromontage* composition (Roads 2001a). We can view concatenative synthesis as a form of sampling synthesis (chapter 9), vector synthesis (chapter 11), or granular synthesis (chapter 13), but driven by an engine of sound analysis, description, and comparison (Schwarz 2004, 2006, 2007; Sturm 2006a). We can also see it as a dictionary-based method (chapter 36) in which the corpus acts as a dictionary of atoms and the resulting resynthesis as an approximation of the score. (A dictionary is also called a *codebook*.)

The graphical synthesis program Metasynth can analyze the spectrum of a sound and map it to any other sound tuned to an arbitrary scale on any time scale (Wenger and Spiegel 2010). The resynthesized result can thus be quite distant from the original input sound. Consider, for example, analyzed speech played back by a percussion ensemble. In this capability, Metasynth acts like a concatenative synthesizer that maps a spectrum to an arbitrary corpus of sounds.

Other labels for concatenative synthesis are *audio, sound* or *music mosaicking* (Zils and Pachet 2001), *reconstructive phrase modeling* (Lindemann 2007), *audio analogies* (Basu et al. 2006), and *descriptor-driven transformation* (Lindsay, Parkes, and Fitzgerald; Collins 2007).

Many text-to-speech systems (e.g., Apple's Siri) use a form of concatenative synthesis. They assemble words and sentences using segments extracted from recordings of spoken speech (Taylor 2009). These segments are called *diphones.* Loosely speaking, a diphone is an adjacent pair of phonemes.

Concatenative synthesis can create realistic sound textures, such as crowds of people and rainfall (Schwarz 2011). It can generate also unusual variations of its input sounds (Schwarz 2004, 2006; Sturm 2006a, 2006b) by means of cross-synthesis. Furthermore, one can use concatenative synthesis to navigate libraries of sound recordings (Schwarz 2006, 2007; Schwarz et al. 2006; Janer et al. 2009).

One application of concatenative synthesis creates realistic music performances by incorporating the nuances of professional musicians, such as note-to-note transitions. Some methods are patented and commercially available as tools for performance (Lindemann 2001, 2007; Bonada and Serra 2007; Basu et al. 2006; Jehan 2010; Umbert et al. 2015). For example, Vocaloid (Bonada and Serra 2007) emulates human singing and has been used in pop music production. Synful Orchestra (https://www.synful.com) achieves realistic renditions of instrumental music by concatenating musical segments derived from instruments (Lindemann 2001, 2007). We look briefly at these applications at the end of the chapter.

CataRT is a real-time concatenative synthesizer from the IRCAM Forum. CataRT plays grains from a large corpus of segmented and descriptor-analyzed sounds by moving a target in the descriptor space, controlled by the mouse or by external controllers. This can be seen as a content-based extension to granular synthesis providing direct access to specific sound characteristics. We explain the concept of descriptors later in the chapter. The MuBu Toolbox from IRCAM dissects sounds in support of concatenative synthesis, among other functions.

Free software for concatenative synthesis is also available, including AudioGuide and SuperSampler (Schwarz 2004, 2006; Bernardes 2014; Hackbarth et al. 2013; Wu 2017). Concatenative synthesis has the potential to evolve as researchers make progress in the automatic analysis, modeling, and description of content in audio signals (Casey 2005; Casey et al. 2008).

Although concatenative synthesis has been widely used for speech synthesis, an alternative approach based on machine learning using a massive database of human speech is gaining ground. A prime example is Google Assistant, which uses the company's Wavenet technology (based on neural networks) to offer multiple voices speaking in many languages.

Background

In realistic text-to-speech synthesis, the text serves as a kind of score, directing the algorithm to select and splice together units drawn from an extensive corpus of labeled speech units such as consonants, vowels, diphthongs, phonemes, and even entire words.

The early classification scheme of Pierre Schaeffer (1977, 2017) in sound description resembles the mid- and high-level description of sound units (Casey 2005; Janer et al. 2009). As cited previously, the score for Cage's *Williams Mix* stipulates how to splice together snippets of magnetic tape drawn from different sound classes. Similar applications of tape splicing include Iannis Xenakis's *Analogique B* (1959) and *Concret PH* (1958). Explored in numerous works, the oeuvre of Horacio Vaggione is an outstanding example of manual micromontage (Roads 2005). John Oswald has also assembled works in a similarly detailed manner (Holm-Hudson 1997; Oswald 2001).

Fundamentals of Concatenative Synthesis

Figure 23.1 is an overview of the basic algorithm of concatenative synthesis. Its aim is to create a new sound (the *result*) that resembles in some way a *target* sound, but using sound materials drawn from a *corpus*. The corpus is a collection of sound recordings providing the sonic material for synthesis.

This is the approach is taken by Schwarz (2004, 2006) and Sturm (2006a, 2006b). This algorithm analyzes a target sound and then segments it into units. A *unit* is some segment of audio, for example, a 100 ms windowed segment or an entire musical note. The algorithm then describes each unit using a variety of quantitative values and qualitative labels called *descriptors* or *features*, such as spectral centroid or note name. These describe properties of the content of the unit. The algorithm then searches the corpus to find the

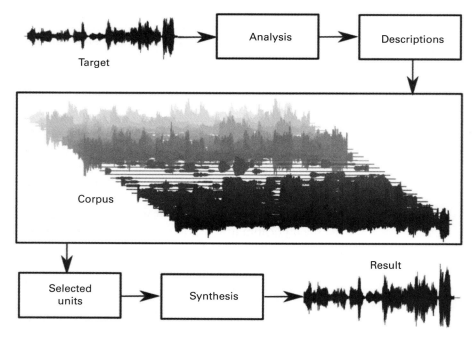

Figure 23.1 A basic algorithm for concatenative synthesis. It analyzes a target sound and transforms it into a set of units described in specific ways, such as time, duration, and pitch. It then compares these units within the corpus, selects the best ones, and finally synthesizes them to create a result.

best unit to replace each target unit using statistical criteria. Finally, it combines the selected units to synthesize the result.

The target need not be a sound; it could instead be a score, MIDI data (Schwarz 2004; Simon et al. 2005; Lindemann 2007; Bonada and Serra 2007; Maestre et al. 2009) or even an interactive control (Aucouturier and Pachet 2006; Collins 2007; Schwarz et al. 2006; Comajuncosas et al. 2011). In this case, the algorithm analyzes the score or gestures and produces a set of descriptions of the target units to guide the selection of units from the corpus.

Segmenting Audio into Units

The simplest approach that we can take to segment digital audio into units is to use a sliding window (similar to windowing in the short-time Fourier analysis mentioned in chapter 37). A more complex approach is to parse meaningful structures in the musical audio, for instance, changes in timbre, locations of onsets, notes and the transitions between them, beats, instruments, and melodies (Lindsay et al. 2003; Schwarz 2004; Jehan 2004; Simon et al. 2005; Aucouturier and Pachet 2006; Lindemann 2007; Maestre et al. 2009; Janer et al. 2009). This approach requires a significant amount of acoustic, perceptual, and musical knowledge to provide meaningful segmentations. Figure 23.2 show a segmentation of a phrase into a lexicon of gesture types. One can do this by hand (Holm-Hudson 1997; Oswald 2001; Simon et al. 2005; Lindemann 2007), but clearly the labor involved precludes using large data sets.

Automated methods of segmentation are scalable, but their success is sensitive to the nature of the digital audio. For instance, it is difficult for an algorithm to reliably find and extract units of single notes from mixtures without additional information to guide the process (Schwarz 2004; Ewert et al. 2014). For clean speech signals, current segmentation approaches are successful in discriminating between speech and silence, as well as particular phonemes (Rabiner and Schafer 2011). However, in the case of general audio and music, this remains an open area of research (SMC 2012; Serra et al. 2013).

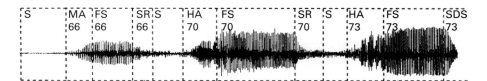

Figure 23.2 Segmenting a musical phrase (jazz trumpet) into gesture types (from Lindemann [2001]). S = silence. MA = medium attack. FS = flat sustain. SR = soft release. HA = medium attack. SDS = small downward slur.

Describing Units

A concatenative synthesis algorithm selects a unit from the corpus on the basis of a comparison of its quantitative and/or qualitative description with respect to the target unit. A variety of descriptors exists at three different levels: low, mid, and high. We call a descriptor *low-level* if it describes specific quantitative information without the imposition of any acoustic or musical model, akin to descriptive statistics like mean and variance. We call a descriptor *mid-level* when it involves some kind of model, for example, fundamental frequency in a harmonic model or voiced/unvoiced in an autoregressive model. Finally, we call a descriptor *high-level* when it exists at a semantic level, for example, a note, duration, dynamic, or instrument. Contrary to low- and mid-level descriptors, high-level descriptors are those that people typically use to talk about music. Schwarz (2004, 2007) provides a large list of descriptors specifically for concatenative synthesis. We now describe specific descriptors from each of these three levels.

Low-level descriptors

One example of a low-level descriptor of a unit is its *mean energy*, which is the sum of the squared sample values of the unit divided by the number of samples. Another low-level descriptor is the *zero-crossings rate*, which is nothing more than the number of consecutive samples in a unit having different signs divided by its duration. We can also create low-level descriptors from a Fourier transform of a unit. For instance, the *spectral centroid* of a unit is the frequency below which half its energy exists. We can further divide its spectrum into finer *spectral quantiles*, for example, the frequency below which lies 10 percent, 25 percent, and so on, of its power. For instance, the *spectral rolloff* of a unit is the frequency above which exists 15 percent of its energy. Many other low-level descriptors are specified in the MPEG-7 standards (Manjunath, Salembier, and Sikora 2002; Lindsay, Parkes, and Fitzgerald 2003).

Mid-level descriptors

One mid-level descriptor is *harmonicity*, which is a measure of the strength of integer relationships between peaks in the magnitude spectrum of a unit. If a unit has strong harmonic content, then another mid-level descriptor is its *fundamental frequency*. A unit could also have several fundamental frequencies. One might also use a perceptual model to a unit to measure its frequency masking properties (Bosi and Goldberg 2003). Other mid-level descriptors are the spectral shape and the location of formants, derived from the autoregressive modeling of the samples in the unit.

High-level descriptors

High-level descriptors are semantically meaningful because they describe what we hear: pitches and harmonies, beats and stress, instruments, loudness, and so on. Due to the time scales of musical events (Roads 2001a), high-level descriptors often make sense to apply only to units of appreciable duration. For instance, there is a minimum duration over which we can perceive a sound with a low pitch. Similarly, we cannot describe a unit as having a slow tempo if does not contain more than one beat.

The automatic high-level description of digital audio continues to be an active research problem because it relies heavily on understanding and modeling the human perception of sound and music (SMC 2012; Serra et al. 2013). Some high-level descriptors can come reliably from the analysis of mid-level descriptors. Techniques for estimating single pitches are relatively mature (chapter 34), and those for estimating multiple pitches are well established (Christensen and Jakobsson 2009). Tempo detection and rhythm recognition is also maturing (chapter 35). Among problems yet to be adequately solved though, are instrument identification in polyphonic textures, separation of sources from mixtures, and genre and emotion recognition (SMC 2012; Serra et al. 2013; Sturm 2014).

Selecting and Sequencing Units

The basic way a concatenative synthesis algorithm selects a sound unit from the corpus is by finding the one with the descriptors closest to that of the target. For instance, if the target specifies the selected unit should exhibit the note C4 played by an oboe, or that a unit should have a spectral centroid of 1,500 Hz, then the algorithm will search the corpus for a unit having such a description. If no such unit exists, then the algorithm might find the next best unit, perhaps the note C4 played by an English horn, or a unit with a spectral centroid of 1,490 Hz. Figure 23.3 shows an example using two low-level descriptors.

The concatenative synthesis algorithm can also transform a unit to better fit the target unit, and/or its previously selected units (Schwarz 2006; Sturm 2006b; Coleman et al. 2010). This can be done, for example, by using envelope shaping, time-stretching, or pitch shifting (chapter 31). To enhance the transformability of a unit, one can decompose the samples into an analytical representation of sinusoids, transients and noise (Lindemann 2007; Bonada and Serra 2007).

For continuity between selected units, a combination of good unit selection and transformation are critical for synthesizing realistic and high-quality

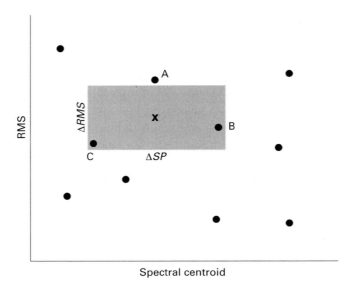

Figure 23.3 Each corpus unit (dots) and the target unit (x) are described by the low-level descriptors *root mean square* (RMS) energy and spectral centroid. The algorithm defines the *best* corpus unit as the one closest to the target unit within the box demarcated by ΔSP and ΔRMS centered on the target unit. In this case, the best corpus unit is that labeled B.

performances (Simon et al. 2005; Lindemann 2007; Bonada and Serra 2007; Maestre et al. 2009). High-quality text-to-speech synthesis takes the same approach (Taylor 2009). Such algorithms select units together so that they require only a small amount of transformation.

With mid- to high-level description of audio units, the concatenative synthesis algorithm moves from working with samples of acoustic pressure signals to working with content (Amatriain et al. 2003; Jehan 2004), *objects* (Schaeffer 1966; Janer et al. 2009), or *lexemes* (Casey 2005). This enables the algorithm to compare and gauge the similarity and compatibility of units at multiple levels, called *specificities*. When the algorithm makes comparisons between low-level descriptors, it is working at a *high specificity*. This means the descriptors are quite specific to the digital samples of a unit and not necessarily to its content. For instance, the difference between the zero crossing rates of two units may be extremely large, but this might not translate to an equally large perceptual difference between the units. By comparing mid-level descriptors, that is, comparing models of units, or comparing high-level descriptors, such as notes, an algorithm is working at *low specificity*. Audio and music similarity at all specificities continues to be an area of active research (SMC 2012; Serra et al. 2013).

Two General Approaches

The naïve approach to concatenative synthesis selects and sequences audio units without regard for their original context, such as mapping an orchestra into the sound of monkeys. This kind of interest is behind the idea of creating an original musical mosaic (Zils and Pachet 2001) and has been applied to micromontage composition (Sturm 2006a; Schwarz et al. 2008; Bernardes 2014), audiovisual concatenative synthesis (Collins 2007), and the navigation of sound libraries (Schwarz 2006, 2007; Schwarz et al. 2006; Janer et al. 2009). One can augment this approach by using different unit durations for analysis and synthesis, incorporating randomness, and specifying rules if the search finds no suitable match (Sturm 2006a). Figure 23.4 shows an example application of concatenative sound synthesis.

A context-aware approach to concatenative synthesis selects, transforms and sequences units in ways sensitive to context (Aucouturier and Pachet

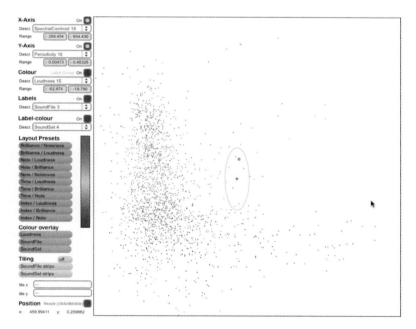

Figure 23.4   Screenshot of the CataRT system, built by Diemo Schwarz in Max (catart.lcd5). On the left side are parameters for changing the display shown in the box at right. Each dot in the display is a sound unit in the corpus. Here, the *x*-axis describes the spectral centroid of a unit, the *y*-axis describes its periodicity, and the color of a dot describes its loudness. Here, the user has selected a set of corpus units by drawing an ellipse. The system plays the selected units randomly. The mouse (pointer) can also be used to explore the units in this space.

2006; Schwarz 2004; Basu et al. 2006; Lindemann 2007; Bonada and Serra 2007; Maestre et al. 2009). Considering context creates a complex problem that involves thinking of several units at the same time, but a problem that can be readily solved with path-following methods (Zils and Pachet 2001; Schwarz 2004, 2007; Aucouturier and Pachet 2006; Lindemann 2007; Bonada and Serra 2007; Maestre et al. 2009; Rabiner and Schafer 2011). Transformation of units can ease such constraints, as done in text-to-speech synthesis and also in the Synful Orchestra product (Lindemann 2007).

Case Studies: Vocaloid and Synful Orchestra

This section presents two case studies involving concatenative synthesis. Both are actually hybrids of concatenative and additive synthesis methods.

Vocaloid Singer Library emulates human singing and has been used in pop music production in Japan. Developed by Yamaha after research by Bonada and Serra (2007), it consists of a database of vocal fragments sampled from human singing (figure 23.5). The database contains all possible combinations

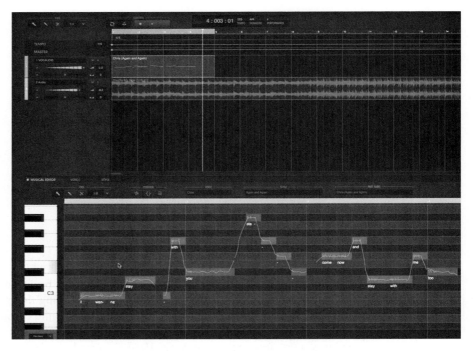

Figure 23.5 Screen interface of the Vocaloid synthesizer.

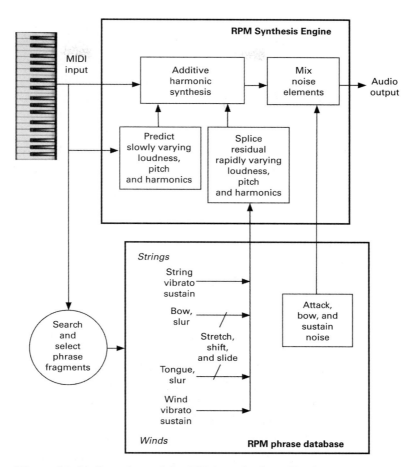

Figure 23.6   Overview of the RPM synthesizer. The input MIDI stream includes note-on and note-off messages with pitch and velocity as well as continuous controller information that determines vibrato intensity, instrument loudness, timbre, and pitch bend. When a performer blows a trumpet harder it is louder and brighter in timbre. RPM uses this correlation to predict a timbre of the instrument based on the slowly varying pitch and loudness derived from the MIDI stream. This timbre is represented as slowly varying amplitudes of the individual harmonics of the instrument sound. The slowly varying pitch and loudness and basic underlying timbre do not have the small rapid fluctuations of instruments. These rapid fluctuations in loudness, pitch, and timbre give an instrument its realism. This is especially true during transitions from note to note when the fluctuations are rapid and unique for each instrument. To generate these rapid fluctuations RPM relies on a database of recorded musical phrases. These are not isolated notes but continuous musical passages that represent articulation and phrasings: detached, slurred, portamento, sharp attacks, soft attacks, and so forth. (Lindemann 2007)

of phonemes of the target language, including diphones and sustained vowels, as well as polyphones with more than two phonemes. For example, the voice corresponding to the word *sing* can be synthesized by concatenating the sequence of diphones #-s, s-I, I-N, N-# (# indicates a voiceless phoneme) with the sustained vowel *I*. Vocaloid changes the pitch of these fragments so that it fits the melody. In order to get more natural sounds, three or four different pitch ranges are stored in the library.

The Synful Orchestra synthesizer aims at expressive solo and ensemble instrument performances from MIDI input by means of *reconstructive phrase modeling* (RPM), which can be viewed as a diphone-like concatenation of sound segments (Lindemann 2001, 2007, 2009). (See the description of RPM in chapter 10 on additive synthesis.) Figure 23.6 depicts the RPM synthesis process.

Synful Orchestra incorporates a sound database derived from instrument recordings segmented into attack, sustain, release, and transition units of varying subtypes. The recorded phrases are not stored as raw audio samples. Rather, they are analyzed and stored in a processed sinusoidal additive synthesis + noise model. Specifically, the recorded phrases are stored using a *residual pitch, loudness, and harmonics + noise* (RPLHN) representation. The RPLHN representation describes fluctuations of the time-varying pitch, loudness, and amplitudes of the harmonic components of the recorded sound. The representation separates noise elements such as breath noise and bow noise from the sound and stores these as sampled signals in the database.

Synful Orchestra converts MIDI data by rules to a synthesis target that is then satisfied by selecting the closest units in a dictionary according to a simple pitch and loudness distance function. The synthesis algorithm uses transformation of pitch, loudness, and duration, favored by the database units.

24 *Graphic Sound Synthesis*

Graphics in Sound Synthesis: Background

Graphic Control of Digital Synthesis

Implementing a Graphic Synthesizer

Drawing is a universal human practice (Bourotte and Kanach 2019). *Graphic sound synthesis* is an interactive approach based on drawing and image transformation. Today's systems provide sophisticated paint boxes for sound images, with a variety of brushes and spray jets for applying sound color as well as a multitude of implements for modifying sound images.

Graphic sound synthesis is a direct and intuitive approach to sound sculpture. At the level of events inscribed on the time-frequency plane, interaction with graphical synthesis can be either precise or imprecise, depending on how the user treats the process. A composer who plans each brush stroke and its mapping into sound can obtain exact results. The composer who improvises on-screen treats the medium as a sketchpad, where initial drawings can be refined into a finished design. In any case, a fundamental fact of graphic synthesis is that a beautiful image does not necessarily make a beautiful sound, and vice versa.

Graphic control of pitch is natural for many composers, making it easy to create melodic shapes and phrases that would be difficult to achieve with other means. Obvious examples include microtonal phrases with multiple glissandi or with a detailed filigree of portamento and vibrato effects. This requires that the drawing surface is clearly labeled at every time scale. Simple graphical transformations change the identity of a sound. Thus it is possible to start from a known sound and rapidly enter unknown sonic territory.

Graphical synthesis offers a distinct paradigm for the manipulation of sound, serving as an alternative to the standard library of synthesis and signal processing techniques based on linear system theory and physical models (Rabiner and Gold 1975; Smith 2010). In contrast to the standard signal processing software library, which considers sound as a function of amplitude and frequency in time, graphic synthesis treats it as a picture. This opens the door to a range of graphical operations and image processing techniques. Even simple operations such as *rotate by 45°* can result in radical audio transformations that would be difficult or impossible to achieve with the standard audio library.

This chapter examines the history of graphic synthesis and surveys recent research. Graphical synthesis overlaps with the domain of sonographic spectrum editors, explained in chapter 44.

Graphics in Sound Synthesis: Background

I am sure that the time will come when the composer, after graphically realizing the score, will see this score automatically put on a machine that will faithfully transmit the musical content to the listener. As frequencies and new rhythms will have to be indicated on the score, our current notation will be inadequate. The new notation will probably be seismographic.
—Edgard Varèse, "Nouveaux instruments et nouvelle musique," 1936

The technology of graphical synthesis has a long history (Rhea 1972). The fundamental principles of optical sound were known as early as 1880 by Alexander Graham Bell, who developed a primitive light-beam telephone called the *photophone* (U.S. Patent 235,199). Andrew Smirnov's book *Sounds in Z* (2013) recounts Evgeny Sholpo's 1918 vision of a "mechanical orchestra" that could be controlled by means of a graphical score, anticipating all of graphic synthesis. Smirnov (2020) is a concise historical survey.

In 1925, R. Michel patented a process for photographic notation of musical tones, similar to the technique used in making optical film soundtracks (Rhea 1972). The Russian artist A. Avraamov experimented with hand-drawn geometric forms on optical film as early as 1929 (Smirnov 2013). Similar efforts by the German experimental animators R. Pfenninger and O. Fischinger followed (Le Grice 1978; Levin 2003).

In the same period, Potter patented a *photoelectric tone generator* instrument (1928, U.S. Patent 1,678,872). Schmalz made an instrument with removable optical discs for greater sonic variety (1929, German patent 536,597). By placing a new *phonogram* into the instrument (an image of a waveform etched on glass), the timbre changed.

These early experiments were followed by instruments based on rotating photoelectric tone generators, such as the Celluophone, the Superpiano, and the Welte Light-Tone Organ (1936), which scanned optical discs with photoetched waveforms (figure 24.1).

The Photona (figure 24.2) was developed by Ivan Eremeef at the WCAU radio broadcasting station in Philadelphia (1936, U.S. Patent 2,033,232). A notable supporter of Eremeef's experiments was the conductor Leopold Stokowski (who also premiered several of Edgard Varèse's compositions in the 1920s). This represented one of the rare collaborations between engineers and prominent musicians prior to the 1950s. Also refer to Clark (1959) for a description of a photoelectric instrument.

Norman McLaren made films in which he drew sound waveforms for printing onto a sprocketed optical soundtrack (figure 24.3), one frame at a time (McLaren 1948).

Another group of instruments could scan graphical notation. Lavallée's *sonothèque* (sound library) read music encoded graphically using conductive ink sensed by a series of electrically charged brushes (Rhea 1972). The Cross-Grainger Free Music Machine (first working version 1944) read a graphic notation inscribed on paper (Bird 1982), and synthesized sound with eight vacuum-tube oscillators. Grainger called his graphical notation Free Music:

Free Music demands a non-human performance. Like most true music, it is an emotional, not cerebral, product, and should pass directly from the imagination of the composer to the ear of the listener by way of delicately controlled musical machines. (Percy Grainger [1938], quoted in Bird [1982])

Figure 24.1   Waveforms etched on an optical disc used in the Welte Light-Tone Organ.

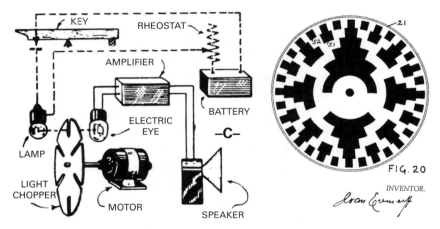

Figure 24.2   Mechanism of the Photona. Pressing a key on the keyboard causes a lamp to light. The light chopper modulates this light at a rate corresponding to the key depressed. An "electric eye" (photocell) picks up the alternating light beam and converts it to alternating voltage that is amplified to drive a loudspeaker.

Figure 24.3 Norman McLaren directly designed waveforms for an optical film soundtrack in the 1950s.

The Coded Music Apparatus (1952) of Hugh LeCaine let composers control sound generation by means of five continuous curves: for pitch, amplitude, and three timbre controls (Young 1985, 1989). His analog Oscillator Bank (1959) was driven by an optical apparatus to scan a sonogram-like score (Young 1985, 1989). (See chapter 36 on sonograms.) The Composer-Tron, developed by O. Kendall in the late 1950s, scanned envelopes drawn by hand on the face of a cathode-ray tube (a display screen). It then used these envelopes to control analog synthesis equipment.

The Nobel Prize–winning physicist Dennis Gabor (1952) reported on experiments in painting speech formants on a sonogram, which was scanned by ten photocells. "The result was a certain degree of intelligibility, not sufficient for communication, but surprisingly high considering that gradations in amplitude had been entirely thrown away." Subsequent experiments with a 30-channel vocoder rendered intelligible, although not natural-sounding speech.

In the remarkable Oramics Graphic System developed 1957–1962 by Daphne Oram in the UK (Oram 1972; Douglas 1973), the composer drew control functions for an analog synthesizer onto transparent film. These control functions determined pitch, vibrato, tremolo, filter setting, and the amplitude level of several voices. The sprocketed film ran by an optical

Figure 24.4   Oramics system.

scanning head, which transformed the image into an electronic control voltage fed into various modules of a synthesizer (figure 24.4).

Yevgeny Murzin developed the ANS synthesizer (1938–1957), named after the Russian composer Alexander Nikolayevich Scriabin. The ANS featured a photo-optical sound generator consisting of multiple rotating glass disks, each containing 144 optical phonograms (graphic representations of sound waves). A composer stipulated the tones by etching the *coding field* (the score), which was a glass plate covered with an opaque black mastic (figure 24.5). The vertical axis of the coding field represented pitch and the horizontal axis was time. The score moved past a reading device that allowed a narrow aperture of light to pass through the etched part of the plate onto a bank of photocells to control sound. The ANS synthesizer was used by composer Edward Artemiev in the score to Tarkovsky's classic science-fiction film *Solaris* (1972). The Virtual ANS software instrument is described further in this chapter.

Graphic Control of Digital Synthesis

Computer technology enabled the next steps forward in graphical synthesis. Interactive light-pen technology enabled early experiments in graphic control of digital sound. These began with the experiments of Mathews and Rosler (1968, 1969) using the Graphic 1 console (figure 24.6).

For the most part, Mathews and his colleagues were interested in graphical control of performance (figure 24.7). However, they also used graphics to control algorithmic compositional processes, such as the degree of interpolation between different melodies (figure 50.8).

Figure 24.5   ANS synthesizer at the Glinka Museum of Musical Culture, Moscow. The black panel at center is the etching surface.

Figure 24.6   Max Mathews (right) and Lawrence Rosler with the Graphic1 console, controlled by a DEC PDP-5 computer, around 1968, Bell Telephone Laboratories.

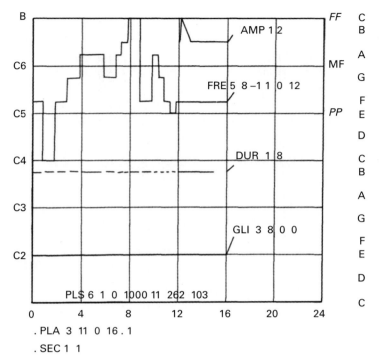

Figure 24.7   Graphic 1 screen. Four envelopes for controlling synthesis, including envelopes for amplitude, frequency, duration, and glissando.

The UPIC System

The UPIC (Unité Polyagogique Informatique de CEMAMu) was a synthesis system conceived by Iannis Xenakis and engineered by Guy Médigue at the Centre d'Etudes de Mathématique et Automatique Musicales (CEMAMu) in Paris (Xenakis 1992). The UPIC system provided a flexible graphical user interface to create a unique approach to sound composition. A 670-page text, *From Xenakis's UPIC to Graphic Notation Today* (Weibel, Kanach, and Brümmer 2020) is available as a free download (https://zkm.de/de/from -xenakiss-upic-to-graphic-notation-today).

  The UPIC system was an especially pliable musical tool because it integrated many levels of composition within a common user interface. Graphic functions created on-screen can be treated equally as envelopes, waveforms, pitch-time scores, tempo curves, or performance trajectories. In this uniform treatment of composition data at every level lies a generality that should be extended to more computer music systems.

The first UPIC

The initial version of the UPIC system dates from 1977 (Lohner 1986; Médigue 2020). In this implementation, which the author used in 1983, interaction was mediated by a large, high-resolution graphics tablet mounted on an architect's drafting table, as well as a computer terminal (figure 24.8).

At the level of creating sound microstructure, waveforms and event envelopes could be drawn directly on the tablet and displayed on a graphics terminal. Alternatively, composers could tap a set of points to be connected by the computer by means of interpolation. With a waveform and an envelope defined, their product could be auditioned.

At a higher level of organization, composers could draw the frequency/ time structure of a score *page*. As the composer moved a pointing device, lines—called *arcs,* in the UPIC terminology—appeared on the display screen. Individual arcs could be moved, stretched or shrunk, cut, copied, or pasted. Figure 24.9 is an example from Iannis Xenakis's *Mycenae-Alpha* (1980), created on the UPIC system.

Musicians also had the option of recording, editing, and scoring sampled sounds. The sampled signals could be used either as waveforms or as envelopes. When samples are used as envelopes, dense amplitude modulation effects occur. Graphic scores could be orchestrated with a combination of synthetic and sampled sounds, if desired.

Figure 24.8   Xenakis with the first UPIC system in 1980.

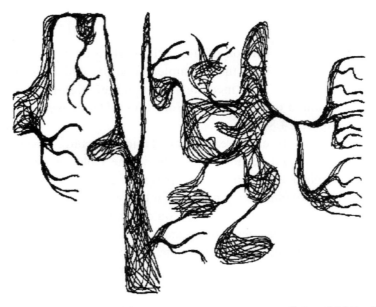

Figure 24.9 Xenakis's UPIC score *Mycenae-Alpha* (1980). The branch-like structures exemplify Xenakis's use of *arborescences* (Harley 2004).

Gestural interaction lets composers easily create score structures that would be cumbersome to specify by any other means. At the level of a page, the UPIC captures both microstructural detail and macrostructural evolution.

Real-time UPIC

The first version of the UPIC system ran on a slow minicomputer. Although designing the graphics was an interactive process, the calculation of sound samples from the composer's graphical score involved a delay. A break-through for the UPIC was the development of a real-time version based on a 64-oscillator synthesis engine (Raczinski and Marino 1988). By 1991 this engine was coupled to a personal computer running the Windows operat-ing system, permitting a sophisticated graphical interface (Marino, Raczin-ski, and Serra 1990; Raczinski, Marino, and Serra 1991; Marino, Serra, and Raczinski 1993; Pape 1992). A software-only version was developed in 2001 (Bourotte and Kanach 2019; Pape 2020).

We should also mention the Phonogramme software, introduced in 1993, which offered an UPIC-like interface with many innovations, such as har-monic pens (Lesbros 1993, 1999).

Figure 24.10 is a page created with the real-time UPIC. In this version, a page could have sixty-four simultaneous arcs, with 4,000 arcs per page. The

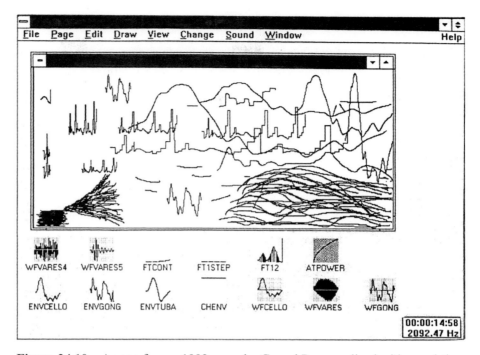

Figure 24.10 A page from a 1992 score by Gerard Pape, realized with a real-time UPIC system at Les Ateliers UPIC, Paris. The icons in the lower part of the screen represent a working set of waveforms and envelopes.

duration of each page could be from 6 ms to more than 2 hours. Editing operations such as cut, copy, and paste rearranged the arcs, which could also be stretched or compressed in time and frequency. These operations could occur while a page was being played. Four different musical scales could be assigned to the same page. When played with a discrete scale, the arcs followed the frequency steps defined in a tuning table.

Real-time synthesis turned the UPIC into a performance instrument. Normally the synthesizer performed the score from left to right, moving at a constant rate defined by the page duration set by the user. However, the rate and direction of score reading could also be controlled in real time by a mouse. This allowed discontinuous jumps from one region of the score to another region, for example. The sequence of control motions could be recorded by the system as it played a score. Later the same performance could be played or edited.

UPISketch

A product of the Centre Iannis Xenakis, UPISketch is the latest incarnation of the UPIC concept (Bourotte and Kanach 2019). One of its principal design goals is to be easier to use than the UPIC, and in this it succeeds. The user manual (version 2) is 675 words in length. UPISketch runs on Windows, OSX, and iOS devices.

Using UPISketch is simple. On the iPhone, one selects the pencil tool, and a default palette of sounds appears (figure 24.11). It is also possible to import one's own sounds. One selects a sound and draws with a finger. Each trace, called a *gesture,* is enclosed in a box. If desired, one can select a box and move it in pitch or time, adjust its amplitude envelope using breakpoints, and change its duration. By drawing with different sounds, one creates a multitimbral composition. Microtonal scales can be defined and zooming allows precise drawing and editing.

Virtual ANS

Virtual ANS (figure 24.12) is a software simulator of the ANS photoelectronic musical instrument. Donation-ware, it runs on many platforms including smartphones. The original ANS made it possible to draw music in the form of a sonographic representation in the 1950s. Virtual ANS extends the capabilities of the original instrument with hundreds of tone generators, limited only by the processor on which it runs. One can convert any sound into an image, load and play pictures, and draw microtonal music using a variety of brushes.

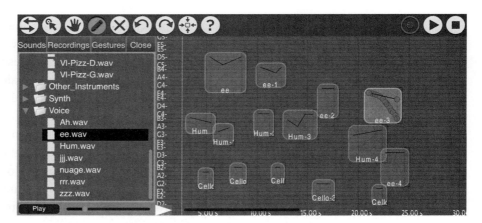

Figure 24.11 UPISketch screen image from iPhone. On the left is the palette of sounds. On the right is the pitch/time drawing area. Although hard to discern in this grayscale image, each gesture box contains two envelopes. At the top of each box is the amplitude envelope. Shown in faint gray (in reality, bright orange) is the pitch envelope. Notice that the gesture box labeled ee-3, at the upper right, has been selected for editing. At the top of the screen are tools for file input/output and settings, select and edit, zoom, draw, delete, undo, redo, and documentation.

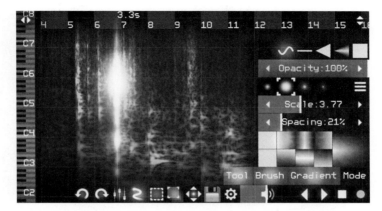

Figure 24.12   Screen image of the Virtual ANS synthesizer.

MetaSynth

MetaSynth, introduced by Eric Wenger in 1997, is an important rethinking of the graphic synthesis model. The program operates with real-time playback. It offers many unique features that take graphical synthesis to an advanced level of power and expressivity.

A given sound can be analyzed into a sonographic image. Moreover, any image file (e.g., a photograph) can be converted into sound. Depending on the color of the image, the sound is distributed spatially; green means left, yellow means center, and red means right. The musician can trace figures with a variable brush and selectively blur, highlight, or erase a sonographical image of sound.

An essential feature of MetaSynth is that the sonographic image can be played back with any sound (i.e., not just with sine waves). Let us call this playback sound *A*. For each trace on the image, a pitch-shifted copy of *A* plays. One can also map the frequency axis onto a bank of samples, so that low tones play sound *A*, a slightly higher tone plays sound *B*, and so on. Moreover, playback can be mapped to an arbitrary scale. Finally, the result can be time scaled. If the original sound lasted 10 seconds, the image can be rescaled to 1 second or 100 seconds. Using this flexible image-to-sound mapping interface, MetaSynth can function like a concatenative synthesizer. (See chapter 23 on concatenative synthesis.) For example, to completely transmogrify the sound of speech, map its sonographic image to a bank of percussion samples.

Kaleidoscope

Kaleidoscope from 2C-Audio has a similar interface to MetaSynth, but the synthesis model is based on a bank of resonating filters. When a broadband

Figure 24.13   MetaSynth's ImageSynth screen.

sound is played through the resonator bank, graphic *image maps* determine which ones play and at what intensity as a cursor scans from left to right. In essence, the image maps function as envelope controls for the resonators. Thus Kaleidoscope can act as an effects processor for a given sound fed into it or as a synthesizer when the input signal is pure noise. The number of resonators (from 64 to 512) can be changed, as can the tuning of the resonators. As in MetaSynth, color controls the position of the sound in the stereo plane.

Implementing a Graphic Synthesizer

Jean-François Charles (2008) wrote a tutorial on spectral sound processing using Max, with Jitter for matrix computations. It serves as a useful guide to manipulating sonographic data in software. Although the implementation details are specific to Max, certain principles are universal.

25 *Noise, Chaotic, and Stochastic Synthesis*

Colored Noises

Noise Modulation

> **Pseudorandom Noise**
> **Sources of Noise**
> **Noise-Modulated AM and FM**
> **Waveshaping with a Random Shaping Function**

Stochastic Waveform Synthesis

> **Chaotic Function Synthesis**
> **Dynamic Stochastic Synthesis**
>> **GENDYN**
> **Real-Time Stochastic Synthesizers**

Writing in 1916, the Futurist composer Luigi Russolo predicted a new world of music based on "the art of noises" (Russolo [1916] 1986). Many of the sound signals that we encounter there have spectral undercurrents that swell and break the crest of a fundamental pitch, scattering its energy along the frequency plane. We call this dispersed energy *noise*, a term that sometimes has unpleasant associations, as in *noise pollution*. Yet noise elements always have been a fundamental ingredient of musical sound, from the sharp punctuation of percussion to the gentle scraping of a bow across a string and the sensual breathy effects of the wind instruments. What these have in common is a *broadband spectrum*—that is, a spectrum containing many frequencies from low to high in constant flux.

The noisy sounds generated by techniques explained in this chapter can serve as structural foils to the smooth and familiar textures generated by periodic waveforms. In the twentieth century, percussive and unpitched noise components of musical sound emerged as a central resource (Varèse 1971). Indeed they form one of the most vital elements of the compositional palette. As John Cage predicted in 1937,

I believe that the use of noise to make music will continue and increase until we reach a music produced through electrical instruments. . . . Whereas in the past, the point of disagreement has been between dissonance and consonance, it will be, in the immediate future, between noise and so-called musical sounds. (Cage [1937] 1961, 3)

Noise elements came to the fore in classic works of early electronic music, such as Karlheinz Stockhausen's *Gesang der Jünglinge* (1956), which features filtered noises mixed with sine waves and boys' voices. Stockhausen's colleague, Gottfried Michael Koenig, realized a series of noisy modulated works using analog generators, including *Klangfiguren* (1956), *Essay* (1958), and *Terminus I and II* (1962 and 1967, respectively). Iannis Xenakis's composition *Bohor* (1962) deploys the sound of a Laotian mouth organ (slowed down), small crotale bells, and hammerings on the inside of a piano to create a hypnotic and monumental sound mass. The last two minutes presents sheets of broadband noise.

Many other synthesis techniques can generate noise: additive, subtractive, modulation, sampling, granular, and others. The waveform segment techniques described in chapter 22 generate signals by stitching together pieces of waveforms, and in this they resemble the GENDYN system described in this chapter.

Colored Noises

White noise contains all frequencies in equal measure. Any noise with a limited frequency bandwidth can be considered a *colored noise*. A common way to obtain a colored noise is to start from a broadband noise such as white noise and send it through a bandpass filter. The filter limits the frequency range of the noise. Colored noises have been a staple of electronic music since the 1950s.

The color analogy derives from light, in which each color represents a certain frequency range in the electromagnetic spectrum. This analogy can be applied to the sound spectrum. Thus scientists have defined certain types of noises according to their spectra, analyzed statistically over time.

Table 25.1 presents a list of noises labeled by color name. Although most have a mathematical description, in two cases the color names are simply those of the scientists Elisha Gray and Robert Brown. It is not claimed that this list of noises is comprehensive or complete.

Noise Modulation

Modulating sine waves with noise is a classic technique of electronic music. This category of techniques includes noise-driven amplitude modulation, frequency modulation, and waveshaping. Noise modulations are ideal for generating sounds that range from aperiodic vibrato and tremolo effects to broad and narrow bands of colored noise.

Pseudorandom Noise

To implement noise modulation on a computer we need a digital source of noise. In the ideal, a source of noise should generate random sample values. To define an algorithm for generating truly random numbers is, however, impossible mathematically (Chaitin 1975, 1998). Any software method for random number generation ultimately rests on a finite deterministic procedure. Hence, an algorithm for generating "random" numbers is actually a *pseudorandom number generator* (PRNG), because the sequence generated by a finite algorithm ultimately repeats after a certain number of iterations. Programming language environments provide PRNGs with different characteristics, such as the frequency range and the length of the sequence before it repeats. Stephen Wolfram (2002) famously developed a PRNG that he called *Rule 30* on the basis of a cellular automata algorithm that is more random (i.e., it has a longer length before repeating) than previous algorithms, depending on its inputs. Most programming languages, however, use another PRNG, the Mersenne Twister, with a period of $2^{19937} - 1$. Marin Mersenne (1588–1648) was an important music theorist and mathematician.

Table 25.1   Colored noises

White noise: If the frequency spectrum is flat (equal energy at all frequencies), then the noise is called white by analogy to the spectrum of white light, in which all colors (frequencies) are present with approximately the same intensity.

Pink noise (1/f-noise or flicker noise): Pink noise also contains energy at all frequencies, but its energy distribution or amplitude curve varies for different frequencies. Pink noise contains equal energy per octave and is often represented as 1/f or *fractal noise*. In terms of perception, pink noise has more bass rumble than white noise, as it falls off in amplitude at a rate of 3 dB per octave with increasing frequency. A 3dB change is equivalent to a halving of power, thus doubling the frequency halves the power, which is equivalent to saying that power is proportional to 1/frequency.

Blue noise (azure noise): According to Federal Standard 1037C, in blue noise, the spectral density or power per hertz is proportional to the frequency. Blue noise power density increases 3 dB per octave with increasing frequency over a finite frequency range. In effect, blue noise is high-pass filtered white noise.

Purple noise (violet noise): Purple noise's power density increases 6 dB per octave with increasing frequency over a finite frequency range.

Green noise: Strange (1983) extended the color analogy to describe *green noise* as a white noise with boosted mid frequencies. There is no mathematical definition, however.

Red noise (brown noise): Continuing with the color analogy, *red noise* means a boost in low frequencies, more extreme than pink noise. It falls off in the high frequencies by a factor of 6 dB per octave. Some definitions construe it to be the same as *brown noise* ($1/f^2$ noise), named after botanist Robert Brown (1773–1858).

Gray noise: Gray noise results from flipping random bits in an integer representation of a sample stream. The spectrum is stronger in the lower frequencies. Like brown noise, it is named not for its relationship to light but due to its relation to the code developed by Elisha Gray.

Grey noise: Random noise subjected to a psychoacoustic equal loudness curve (such as an inverted C-weighting curve) over a given range of frequencies, giving the listener the perception that it is equally loud at all frequencies.

Black noise: Black noise has several different definitions. By one definition, it is "darker" than red or brown noise, characterized by a falloff of about 18 dB per octave (Castine 2002). Federal Standard 1037C states that black noise "has a frequency spectrum of predominantly zero power level over all frequencies except for a few narrow bands or spikes. An example of black noise in a facsimile transmission system is the spectrum that might be obtained when scanning a black area in which there are a few random white spots. Thus, in the time domain, a few random pulses occur while scanning." Another, contrasting definition of black noise is that it is inverted white noise. This is the noise that cancels out white noise, an "antinoise." Informally, the definition of black noise has been broadened to cover the inverse of any noise, for example in reducing the roar in the passenger cabins of airplanes on noise-reducing headphones.

Infrared noise: A random fluctuation or rhythm in the infrasonic frequencies below 20 Hz.

Velvet noise: It consists of sample values −1, 0, and 1 only (Karjailainen and Järväilinen 2007). It can be interpreted as a randomly jittered-in-time impulse train in which the sign of each impulse is random. Velvet noise is used to create reverberation, as explained in chapter 33.

Sources of Noise

As an alternative to pseudorandom digital noise, the sampled sound of natural wind, sea spray, waterfalls, and thunder are outstanding sources of noise. Speech and animal sounds contain many evocative noises, especially the brief fricatives and plosives of speech [s], [z], [sh], [f], [k], [t], [p], [g], and so on. This includes the rich noises of the unpitched percussion instruments. Collections of samples recorded at industrial sites are available. A metal scrapyard is a particularly noise-intensive environment, with sounds of crushing, creaking, scraping, squealing, squeaking, and grinding.

Analog electronic circuits produce the most scientifically complex noises. For example, the quantum noise from a diode is one of the most random phenomena in nature; it can be amplified to make an analog noise generator or a cryptographic-quality random source (Wilber 2013). Analog FM radios emit rich noises in the high region around 108 MHz, where few stations broadcast.

Digital distortions such as aliasing and overload sound noisy but are highly correlated with the input signal. That is, given the same input, they produce exactly the same output, so they are deterministic.

Noise-Modulated AM and FM

The composer who disposes himself to aleatoric modulation will . . . discover that this type of modulation leads directly into a world of phenomena previously described as "noises."
—W. Meyer-Eppler, "Statistic and Psychologic Problems of Sound," 1955

Noise modulation techniques use a pseudorandom signal generator or *noise generator* to control the amplitude or frequency of an oscillator. As figure 25.1 shows, when the noise is filtered down to the infrasonic frequency range (below about 20 Hz), the effect is a kind of aleatoric tremolo (in the case of AM) or vibrato (in the case of FM).

When the noise has a wider bandwidth, the result of modulation is a type of *colored noise,* that is, a noise band centered around the carrier frequency of the oscillator. Figure 25.2 shows the patch diagrams for noise-modulated AM and FM instruments. In both cases, it is a good idea to use a noise source that has been lowpass filtered such that the randomness introduced by the noise is itself near the carrier frequency. If the noise is not filtered, the effect may sound like a high-frequency noise component has been added to the carrier signal.

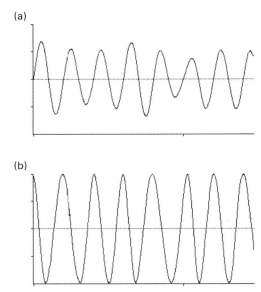

(a)

(b)

Figure 25.1 Random AM (a) and FM (b).

Waveshaping with a Random Shaping Function

Waveshaping, explained in chapter 17, makes possible another kind of noise modulation. In waveshaping, the instantaneous amplitude of a signal is remapped by a *shaping function*. A random shaping function distorts the periodic signal into a more broadband sound. Figure 25.3 depicts four progressively noisy shaping functions.

Figure 25.4 shows the effects of the four shaping functions in figure 25.3 on a sine wave passed through a waveshaper.

A more subtle use of randomness in waveshaping employs a smooth waveshaping function at low amplitudes and introduces increasing randomness at higher amplitudes. Another possibility is to link the degree of randomness in the waveshaping function to the duration of the tone or another parameter of the event.

Stochastic Waveform Synthesis

Musical sound is too limited in its variety of timbres. The most complicated orchestras can be reduced to four or five classes of instruments in different timbres of sound: bowed instruments, brass, woodwinds, and percussion. Modern music flounders within this tiny circle, vainly striving to create new varieties of timbre. We must break out of this limited circle of sounds and conquer the infinite variety of noise-sounds!
—Luigi Russolo, *The Art of Noises*, 1916

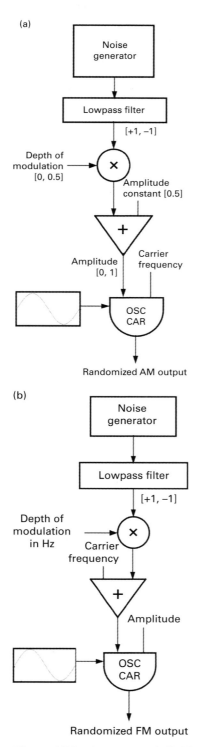

Figure 25.2 Instrument definitions of random AM (a) and FM (b).

(a)   (b)

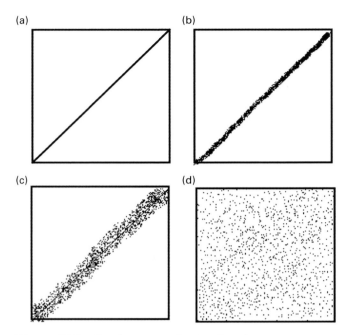

(c)   (d)

Figure 25.3   Random waveshaping functions.

Stochastic waveform synthesis generates sound samples by comparing the value of a pseudorandom number against a *probability distribution*. A probability distribution is a curve (stored in an array in computer memory) that indicates the numerical probability of a range of possible outcomes. In the case of waveform synthesis, the outcomes are the amplitude values of successive samples.

Because algorithms for waveform generation must produce tens of thousands of sample values for each second of sound, small computational efficiencies can add up to large savings in calculation time. For example, one efficiency could be to preload a large table with pseudorandom values rather than call a pseudorandom number generator function for each sample. Then all that is needed to obtain a pseudorandom number is a table lookup.

Devising an appropriate probability distribution for a particular compositional application is a fine art. Many texts on probability theory are available. A good reference with musical examples and program code is Lorrain (1980). Other good references on stochastic techniques in composition include Xenakis (1992), Jones (1981), and Ames (1987a, 1989a). Experiments in fractal waveform generation are reported in Waschka and Kurepa (1989).

Waveform generation by simple probability table lookup generates a fixed-spectrum noise. Thus it is important to impose constraints—additional rules

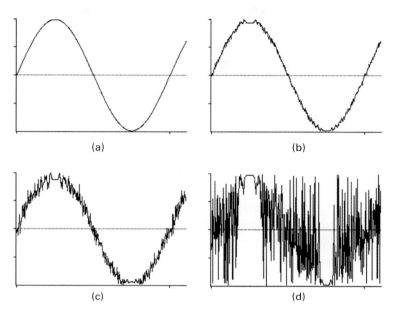

Figure 25.4   Sine waves shaped by the functions shown in figure 25.3.

that vary the probabilities in order to produce interesting time-varying sounds. This is the goal of dynamic stochastic synthesis, described next.

Chaotic Function Synthesis

I sometimes like to suggest the difference between chaos and randomness by comparing the behavior of commuters dashing through a train station at rush hour with the behavior of a large, terrified crowd. The activity of the commuters resembles chaos in that although an observer unfamiliar with train stations might think people were running every which way without reason, order does underlie the surface complexity: everyone is hurrying to catch a specific train. The traffic flow could rapidly be changed simply by announcing a track change. In contrast, mass hysteria is random. No simple announcement would make a large mob become cooperative.
—W. J. Freeman, "The Physiology of Perception," 1991

Chaotic systems are deterministic dynamic systems that have a high sensitivity to initial conditions. That is, with a small change to an input variable, the system output rapidly diverges in an unpredictable manner (Moon 1987). Only dynamic systems that have a nonlinear feedback path can exhibit truly chaotic behavior.

Solutions of chaotic and fractal equations have been harnessed to produce images, sound waveforms, and control functions (Slater 1998; Di Scipio 1990, 1999; Di Scipio and Prignano 1996; Yadegari 2003; Chang 2011; ffitch 2000;

Neukom 2013). Myriad chaotic and fractal equations exist (Lorenz, Chua, Duffing, Henon, frequency modulation, etc.). Here, we focus on just one as an example. The *logistic map* is one of the simplest chaotic systems. It is defined

$$x_{n+1} = \lambda(x_n - x_n^2)$$

This equation states that the next x value will be a coefficient λ times the difference between the current x value and the current x^2 value. The solution to this equation is chaotic when the value of λ is between 3.57 and 4. As figure 25.5 shows, when λ is near 3.6, the plot is noisy and rapidly changing. When λ is in the region of 3.8, however, an *island of stability* appears and remains stationary for many values of λ. A delicate balance between stability and noise is characteristic of chaotic systems.

We can invent strategies for turning a differential equation such as the logistic map into a sound synthesizer. One strategy would be to scan through all values of λ between 3.57000001 and 4.00000001 to produce a range of values that make a chaotic waveform oscillator. A simple additional control would be to vary the step time. Instead of $n+1$, for example, the step time could be $n+20$. This provides a crude pitch control to the chaotic oscillator. Others have used a chaotic function to modulate a sinusoid, which already has a pitch. Another possibility is to take the second- or third-order derivative of the function to use as either a waveform or a control function. Using

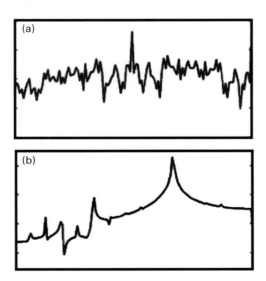

Figure 25.5   Plot of the values produced by the logistic map. (a) Rapidly changing chaotic waveform when λ is near 3.6. (b) An island of stability appears and remains stationary when λ is in the region of 3.8.

similar creative strategies, one can derive chaotic sound from many other nonlinear differential equations.

A notable example of chaotic sound synthesis is the GENDYN program developed by Iannis Xenakis, described next.

Dynamic Stochastic Synthesis

In his book *Formalized Music*, the composer Iannis Xenakis (1971, 1992) proposed an alternative to the usual method of sound synthesis. Instead of starting from simple periodic functions and trying to animate them by injecting disorder (distortions and modulations), why not start with pseudorandom functions and tame them by adding order (i.e., weights, constraints, and barriers)? This proposal takes the form of eight strategies for exploring a *dynamic stochastic* approach to waveform synthesis, listed in table 25.2.

Figure 25.6 shows two waveforms generated using stochastic methods. Figure 25.6a shows the product of a hyperbolic cosine with exponential densities using barriers and nonrandomized time. Figure 25.6b shows the same algorithm with randomized time intervals.

GENDYN

The GENDYN (GENeration DYNamique) program is an implementation of stochastic dynamic synthesis, with conceptual links to the interpolation

Table 25.2 Xenakis's proposals for stochastic waveform synthesis

1. Direct use of probability distributions (such as Poisson, exponential, Gaussian, uniform, Cauchy, arcsine, and logistic) to create waveforms

2. Multiplications of probability functions with themselves

3. Combining probability functions into mixtures through addition, possibly over time

4. Using the random variables of amplitude and time as functions of elastic forces or other random variables

5. Using random variables that bounce back and forth between elastic boundaries

6. Using probability functions to generate the values of parameters of other probability functions (these latter functions used to produce sound waveforms)

7. Assigning probability curves into classes, and considering these classes as elements of higher-order sets and processes (i.e., introducing hierarchical control over waveform generation)

8. Injecting the choice of stochastic sound synthesis techniques into a stochastic composition program (an extension of item 7)

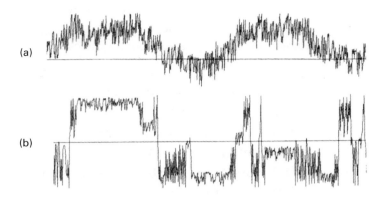

Figure 25.6   Hyperbolic cosine waveforms. From Xenakis (1992).

synthesis and waveform segment techniques described in chapter 22 (Xenakis 1992; Serra 1992; Hoffmann 2000). Like SSP and SAWDUST, described in chapter 22, GENDYN's waveform generation model is based on time- and amplitude-point manipulations that are based on abstract principles that are not directly related to acoustical categories like pitch, timbre, or rhythm. The results of GENDYN synthesis are not predictable. Xenakis likened it to controlling a herd of wild horses.

GENDYN makes sound by repeating an initial waveform and then distorting that waveform in time and amplitude. Thus the synthesis algorithm computes each new waveform by applying stochastic variations to the previous waveform.

In the program, the waveform is represented as a polygon, bounded by sides on the time axis and sides on the amplitude axis. The segments of the polygon are defined by vertices on the time and amplitude axes (figure 25.7). The program interpolates straight line segments between these vertices.

GENDYN synthesizes the vertex points according to various stochastic distributions. If the stochastic variations are not held within a finite interval, the signal tends quickly toward white noise. For this reason the program constrains time and amplitude variations to remain within the boundaries of a *mirror.* The mirror consists of an amplitude barrier and a time barrier. Points that fall outside the mirror are reflected back into the mirror (figure 25.8). In effect, the mirror filters the stochastic variations. By increasing or decreasing the amplitude barrier, the composer controls the number of reflections. Reflections represent discontinuities in the waveform, so this is a timbral control. Because the time barrier sets the interval between time points, it has an influence on the perceived frequency of the sound.

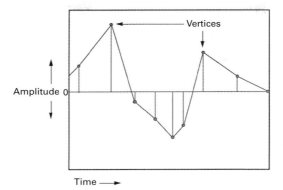

Figure 25.7   GENDYN polygon waveform indicating vertices and interpolation.

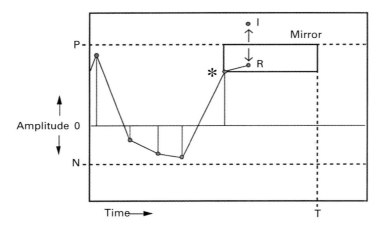

Figure 25.8   GENDYN mirror. The amplitude and time barriers P, N, T (positive, negative, time) defining a mirror constrain the next vertex generated from the vertex labeled with an asterisk. If the next vertex generated stochastically falls outside the barriers of the box (the initial projection I) the barrier P overrides this, reflecting the vertex back into the box (reflection R).

The control parameters of the GENDYN system are thus the number of time segments, the mirror boundaries, and the choice of stochastic distribution for time and for amplitude vertices. These are set on a per-voice basis. Figure 25.9 shows the evolution of a waveform produced by GENDYN. It is quasiperiodic, as determined by small mirror. By adding secondary mirrors, effects such as vibrato and tremolo can also be imposed on the varying waveform.

As Hoffmann (2000) pointed out, the initial conditions and time-varying parameter settings by which the probabilities are tuned are decisive in determining the character of the resulting sound. With only slight adjustments, the results can vary enormously. This is both the difficulty and the opportunity of stochastic synthesis.

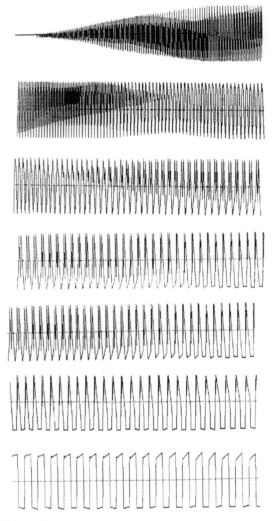

Figure 25.9 Waveform generated by the GENDYN program. The progression starts at the top and proceeds to the bottom.

Brown (2005) extended the original GENDYN by making previously hard-coded constants into variable parameters, adding new parametric controls, and adding support for real-time interaction.

Real-Time Stochastic Synthesizers

Many stochastic synthesizers have been developed. For example, real-time implementations of chaotic GENDYN-type synthesis have appeared with

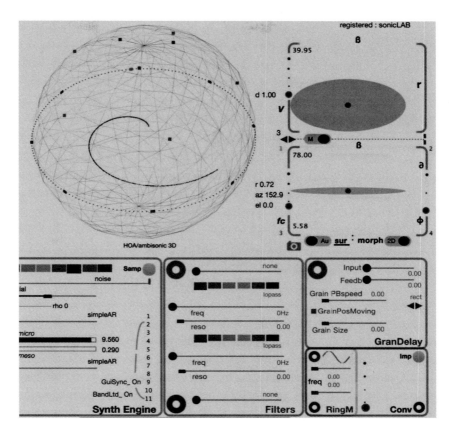

Figure 25.10 Detail of the screen of Soniclab Cosmos*f* FX7 synthesizer. The original has an inverse color scheme, that is, a black background.

additional features within the SuperCollider language (Collins 2008a) and Native Instruments REAKTOR synthesizer (Spek 2009).

The Stochos application used stochastic, chaotic, and deterministic envelopes to control sound synthesis and transformation (Bokesoy and Pape 2003). Stochos evolved into the SonicLab Cosmos*f* family of products (figure 25.10). These real-time apps combine granulation, FM, RM, and waveshaping with stochastic controls that are manipulated via MIDI and a graphical interface.

Finally, the Eurorack marketplace has hundreds of modules (both analog and digital) devoted to noise and chaotic waveform synthesis.

IV   Mixing and Signal Processing

26   *Sound Mixing*

Mixing in the Digital Domain

The Core Aesthetic Problem of Mixing

Non-Real-Time Software Mixing

Mixing by Script
Digital Audio Workstations
Assessment of Software Mixing

Mixing Consoles

Properties of Mixers
Input Section
Output Section
Auxiliary Returns
Talkback Section
Monitor Section
Metering Section
Grouping Facilities

Hybrid Consoles

Playing Back the Mix

Features of Digital Mixing Consoles

Multitrack Recording and Remixing

Multitrack Recording: Background
Advantages of Multitrack Recording
Mix Automation
Problems Posed by Multitrack Remixing
The "Purist" Approach to Recording

Audio Monitoring

Headphones
Loudspeaker Stereo Monitoring
  Near-field monitoring
  Control room monitoring
  Listening room monitoring
Mixing and Monitoring in Performance

Nature mixes sounds acoustically in the air—for example, in the fused orchestral sonority at a symphony concert. In the studio we use a *mixer*—either hardware or software, which sums many signals to a composite signal.

Let us make a distinction between tracks and channels. A *track* is a sound stored on a recording medium. It can be a monophonic (mono) or a stereo track. A colloquial term for track is *lane,* deriving from the highway analogy.

A *channel* is a source or destination for audio. For example, a mono input channel on a mixer takes in sound from a microphone. An output channel can route sound to a loudspeaker or to a recording device.

The act of mixing blends a set of sounds into a finished composition. When this process takes many tracks or channels and blends them into fewer tracks or channels, we call it a *mixdown.* When this process takes a small set of tracks or channels and distributes them to a large set of tracks or channels, we call this *upmixing.* An example of upmixing is taking a stereo track and spatializing it in time over eight loudspeakers.

Mixing in the Digital Domain

In the digital domain, audio signals mix according to the rules of simple addition. To help visualize this process, figures 26.1, 26.2, and 26.3 show mixing at three different time scales. Figure 26.1 depicts the sample time scale. We see a sample from source (a) at time $t1$ with a value of 32,767 is added to another sample from source (b) at time $t1$ of −32,767, and the resulting summed sample value is 0 (c). When two positive signals of 10,000 each are added at time $t2$, the result is 20,000.

Figure 26.2 shows mixing on the micro time scale, where we see waveform addition, combining a low-frequency wave with a high-frequency wave.

Finally, figure 26.3 shows the result of mixing at the sound object time scale; each tone lasts about 2.5 seconds.

The Core Aesthetic Problem of Mixing

In order to grasp the fundamental nature of musical materials, one must understand them as acoustic signals. The artificial division between "composition," "orchestration," and "conducting" need not apply in electronic music. To generate, process, and mix acoustical signals is to compose—more directly than inscribing ink on paper.

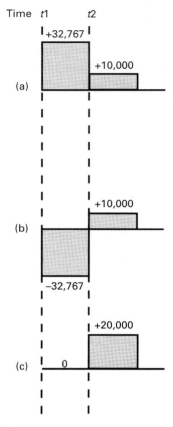

Figure 26.1   Mixing on a sample time scale. Signals (a) and (b) consisting of two samples at time points *t* 1 and *t* 2 mixed, showing the result as signal (c).

To combine sounds is one of the most common tasks of the electronic musician. Yet surprisingly little analysis has focused on the art of mixing outside the context of pop music, where it is a central production technique. Perhaps this is because pop music tends to separate music making into discrete phases of production: song writing, performance, recording, editing, mixdown, and mastering. By contrast, in electronic music practice, all phases tend to be deeply intertwined, and mixing is central to the process.

From an aesthetic point of view, the core problem in mixing is to articulate opposing processes of fusion and fission. Fusion melds several sounds into a gestalt—a composite whole. By contrast, fission comingles sounds while keeping them perceptually distinct. The art of mixing plays with and between these two poles. In this sense, mixing is deeply connected with the articulation of musical structure. Indeed, fusion and fission are basic structural functions of music.

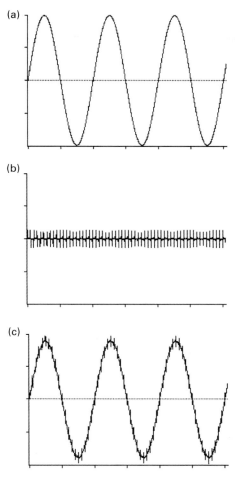

Figure 26.2 Waveform mixing on a micro time scale. (a) Sine tone at 50 Hz. (b) Sine tone at 500 Hz. (c) Mix of (a)+(b).

Non-Real-Time Software Mixing

Digital audio mixing can be performed either in hardware or in software. Software-based mixers generally operate in two steps: the musician plans the mix in some way, and then the software carries out the mix. This is non-real-time mixing, or more specifically, mixing without real-time control.

Even without real-time control, software mixing programs have several advantages over other types of mixers. First, they can automatically carry out precise and complicated mixes that would be impossible to realize by any other means. This includes mixes involving large numbers of tracks that would

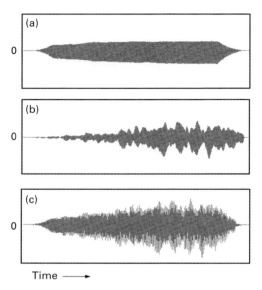

Figure 26.3   Sound object mixing. (a) Alto saxophone tone. (b) Granular synthesis texture. (c) Mix of (a) + (b).

exceed the capabilities of a physical hardware mixing console. A software mixer should have no problem dealing with dozens of tracks and hundreds of sound files over the course of a mix. If desired, signal processing can be applied with microscopic precision on a short time scale. Second, software mixers can be integrated with other tools in the software environment (e.g., a sound file can be transformed by a plug-in as it remains in the mix window). Third, some software mixers are open systems that can be extended in arbitrary ways by programming. An example is Reaper, whose *application programming interface* (API) can be scripted in EEL, Lua, or Python.

Software mixers fit into two main categories: mixing by script and digital audio workstations, the subjects of the next sections.

Mixing by Script

Languages for software synthesis enable mixing by script. In Csound, for example, individual sound files can be read into the program using the *soundin* unit generator, which reads *note* statements that tell it what files to mix and from what time point in the file to read. The level of individual sound files can be scaled using envelopes. All the signal processing facilities of the language are available for additional transformations. The result of the mix is typically a sound file. Other software synthesis languages provide similar functionality.

Mixing by script opens the door to the notion of *algorithmic mixing.* An early example was the author's implementations of automated granular synthesis. In 1974 the author wrote an algorithm that generated thousands of note statements, each of which generated a brief sine wave with a quasi-Gaussian envelope. The note statements were often densely clustered in sound clouds, causing the overlapping grains to be mixed automatically (Roads 1978c). Later the author developed another implementation that algorithmically mixed grains with sampled percussion waveforms (Roads 2001a).

Digital Audio Workstations

A *digital audio workstation* (DAW) provides a graphical timeline interface for audio editing and mixing. The first commercial apps for interactive graphical timeline mixing were SoundEdit by Steve Capps (1986) and MacMix by Adrian Freed (1987). SoundEdit displayed individual tracks to be mixed as sound pressure waveform clips (figure 26.4). The user could select clips and drag them horizontally along the timeline—an essential operation that is impossible with serial media such as multitrack tape recorders. Each track could be faded in or out, with the envelope adjustable on-screen.

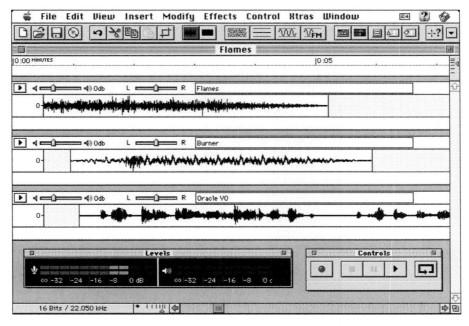

Figure 26.4   Interface of the pioneering SoundEdit app (1986), showing three overlapping sounds. Each waveform clip could be selected by the mouse and freely positioned anywhere on the timeline.

Following the example of SoundEdit, many companies developed multichannel mixing programs with similar graphical timeline controls: Pro Tools, Cubase, Ardour, FL-Studio, Studio One, Nuendo, Logic Pro, ACID Pro, Ableton Live, Bitwig, Digital Performer, Reaper, Reason, Samplitude Pro, Sonar, Garage-Band, and others. Many of these DAWs combine multichannel audio with MIDI sequence data, common music notation, and video (figure 26.5). Chapter 43 has more information on DAWs.

Assessment of Software Mixing

Software mixing has the advantages of flexibility and precision. It involves a preparation stage that gives the user time to plan a precise mix. The mix can be arbitrarily complex in terms of number of channels and mixing operations, far exceeding the capabilities of human beings at a physical mixing console.

For all its flexibility and precision, software mixing has issues. Planning is necessary even in the case of a simple mix. It usually takes several rehearsals to adjust the timings and mix envelopes properly.

A drawback is the lack of "feel" in non-real-time software mixing. When there are no real-time faders to manipulate, it is impossible to respond intuitively as one listens. Some computer-based mixers use a mouse or alphanumeric keys to control the channel amplitudes, but these are not ideal controllers for this delicate task; a set of precision faders is preferable. Hence, a mixing

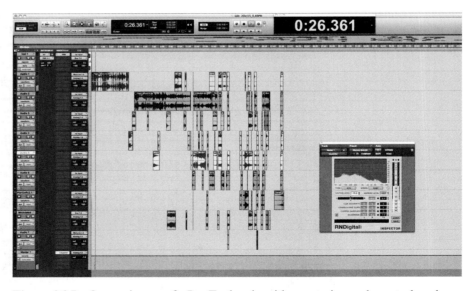

Figure 26.5   Screen image of a Pro Tools mix with a metering and spectral analyzer plug-in on the master track.

console with precision faders can be a valuable complement to software mixing.

Mixing Consoles

A sound mixing console (also called a *mixing desk* or just a *mixer*) combines a number of input channels into some number of output channels in real time. Mixers also perform auxiliary operations such as filtering and signal routing.

Recording studio mixing consoles were originally custom-built exclusively from analog circuits, sometimes to a high sonic standard (figure 26.6).

Fine analog consoles are still being made (figure 26.7). They have the advantage of being standardized in function and straightforward to operate. *Hybrid consoles,* discussed later, combine analog audio circuits with digital control of motorized fader automation. All-digital mixers are increasingly used.

Properties of Mixers

Mixing consoles can be characterized by an input/output ratio that represents the number of input channels they handle versus the number of mixed output channels they produce. For example, a mixer that can handle eight channels of input and mix it down to two channels of output is called an 8/2 ("eight-to-two")

Figure 26.6   Producer George Martin (The Beatles) adjusting a custom-built EMI mixer in the early 1960s at Abbey Road Studios, London.

Figure 26.7   AMS Neve BCM-10 mk2 analog mixing console costing $70,000 in 2020.

mixer. Many mixers have several *output buses* to which signals can be routed simultaneously. To give an example, a mixer with eight inputs, a four-output bus, and a two-output bus can be referred to as an 8/4/2 mixer. On such a mixer one could make simultaneous four-track and two-track recordings, via the four-output bus and the two-output bus, respectively.

A typical recording studio mixer consists of six main sections: an *input* section, an *output* section, an *auxiliary return* section, a *talkback* section, a *monitor* section, and a *metering* section. A simple 8/4/2 mixer is shown in figure 26.8. The eight channels of input are routed to one or more of the six output buses through a set of *output bus assignment buttons* (LR, 1/2, and 3/4) and *pan pots* (abbreviation of *panoramic potentiometer*). When one of the output bus assignment buttons is pressed, the signal is routed to two output buses; turning the pan pot left or right selects one of the two output buses. The pan pots can also be used to position or move a sound in the stereo field.

On this mixer, the input can also be routed to two *auxiliary send* (AUX) buses for outboard signal processing or for *cue mixing* (sending a mix to a musician's headphones). The *auxiliary return* (RET) from an effects unit can be mixed into the output buses by a small rotary potentiometer above the output level fader. Alternatively, the output from the effects unit can be routed into one of the input channels for more control over the sound. The CM and SM potentiometers at the top right set the amplitude of the monitor loudspeakers in the control room (CM) and studio (SM), respectively. They

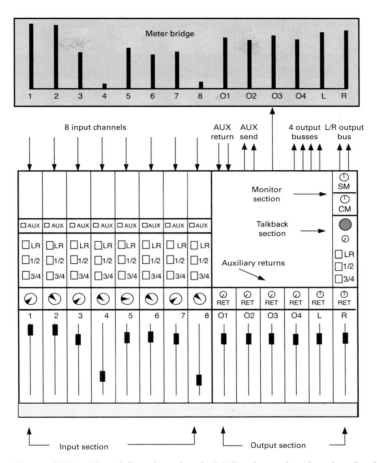

Figure 26.8 Signal flow in a simple 8/4/2 mixer, also showing the different sections of the mixer. The squares represent push-button switches, and the circles represent rotary knobs. 01 through 04 indicate output buses, as do L and R (for *left* and *right*). The indicators CM and SM in the monitor section refer to controls for studio monitor and control room monitoring levels.

take their input from the L/R buses. A *talkback microphone* (right) lets the mixing engineer communicate with musicians or label a recording. The *meter bridge* shows the amplitude levels of the eight input channels and the six output buses.

The next paragraphs discuss the sections of a mixer in more detail.

Input Section

The input section usually consists of a number of identical input modules (figure 26.9). Table 26.1 explains the parts of the input module.

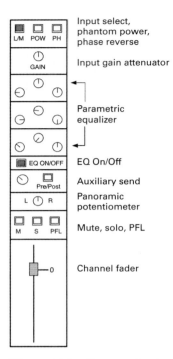

Input select, phantom power, phase reverse

Input gain attenuator

Parametric equalizer

EQ On/Off

Auxiliary send

Panoramic potentiometer

Mute, solo, PFL

Channel fader

Figure 26.9   Stages of a simple input module on a mixer. Table 26.1 explains each stage.

Output Section

Operating the output section of a mixer is usually simple. It consists of a fader to control the output level of a signal sent to an output bus, and a meter display.

Auxiliary Returns

The auxiliary returns can also be called the *effects* or *cue* section. The auxiliary returns allow the mixing engineer to blend sounds processed by effects units into the output signal. Alternatively, they allow the engineer to create special monitor or cue submixes for individual musicians who are listening with headphones (in a recording studio) or through a loudspeaker (onstage).

Talkback Section

The talkback section lets the recording engineer communicate with musicians in the recording studio. Another use of talkback in the computer music studio is to *slate* or *log* a recording with comments for later reference. Technically, the talkback section consists of a microphone, a level control, and various switches to determine where the engineer's voice is routed.

Table 26.1 Functions of a mixer input module

Input select, phantom power, and phase reverse switches	The input select switch chooses either microphone or line-level source. The phantom power switch sends a DC power signal to a condenser microphone. Phase reverse inverts the phase of the incoming signal (useful in multiple microphone setups).
Input attenuator/pad	Attenuates (*buffers*) the level of the incoming signal so that the input channel is not overloaded by a high-level signal. For line-level signals, the input attenuator ensures that the mixer is aligned to the operating level of the external device
Parametric equalizer	Alters the spectrum of the sound by boosting certain bands of frequencies and attenuating others. Shown is a three-band parametric EQ. The three controls for each band adjust the bandwidth, the center frequency, and the amount of boost or cut for each band. A *semiparametric equalizer* omits the bandwidth control.
EQ on/off	Switches the equalization section in or out of the circuit.
Auxiliary send/return	Routes the sound to an effects unit (e.g., a reverberator) or a cue output. A cue output is usually routed to headphones worn by performers in a recording studio or to a monitor loudspeaker onstage. Thus, the cue output constitutes a submix of the music that can be balanced so that each musician can hear their own instrument above the rest. The send knob controls the level of the sound sent to the effects unit or cue. The return knob controls the level of the sound coming back from the effects unit. (See the effects/auxiliary return section.) When the sound is routed to the effects send after the input fader (postfader), if the fader is off, so is the send. Otherwise (prefader) the input sound is always sent to the effects send bus.
Pan pot (panoramic potentiometer)	Controls the spatial location of the sound between two or more channels
Mute, Solo, and PFL	The mute button shuts off a channel. The solo button allows an individual channel to be auditioned. All other channels mute when the solo button is pressed. PFL (prefader listen) is used when an input channel needs to be checked without opening a fader. For example, DJs and radio broadcast engineers push the PFL button to hear the beginning of a track through headphones, but because the fader is down, the audience does not hear it. PFL provides a means to set levels and equalization at a time when a normal sound check might be impossible.
Channel assignment (not shown)	The channel assignment section is usually a set of buttons, with one button per output bus. The signal passing through the input channel is routed to all output channels selected.
Channel fader (or potentiometer)	A linear slider or rotary knob that controls the amplitude (or gain) of the sound.

Monitor Section

This section takes its input from the left/right output bus and routes it to loudspeakers and headphones in the control room (where the sound engineer is) and the studio (where musicians are).

Metering Section

Meters indicate sound levels in the input channels and the output buses. *Peak meters* reflect the instantaneous peak amplitude of the signal. Their *rise time* (the time it takes to reach 99 percent of final value) is a few milliseconds, whereas their *decay time* is longer. (Various peak reading meters have different specifications.) *Volume unit* (VU) meters have a much slower rise time, on the order of 300 ms, so they tend to reflect the average amplitude (akin to perceived loudness) of the signal over a brief time period. Some meters (e.g., Dorrough or RTW) combine both peak and average characteristics of a signal. An entire book has been written on metering (Brixen 2011).

Grouping Facilities

Some mixers have *subgrouping* facilities. These let the engineer assign several input channels to a single fader, called the *submix* or *subgroup fader.* Subsequent movements of the subgroup fader control the level of all the channels assigned to the subgroup simultaneously.

Hybrid Consoles

Digital technology came to mixers in the early 1970s. The first benefit of digital technology was *motorized fader automation*—the ability to recall switch settings and moving fader positions to recreate a particular mix. Some mixers are hybrids of digital and analog technology, combining the automation facilities of digital with the sound quality and wide bandwidth of analog signal processing, which can extend far beyond 100 kHz (figure 26.10).

Playing Back the Mix

Manufacturers implement fader automation by robotic means. That is, as the engineer moves faders, these gestures are recorded digitally. On playback, this data is used to drive the control motors that physically move the faders

Figure 26.10   A large hybrid mixing console with motorized fader automation, the AMEK 9098i, designed by Rupert Neve and Graham Langley.

(and hence the channel level) according to previously recorded motions. Motorized faders can be constructed to high standards, performing top-to-bottom fades in less than 100 ms over 4,096 steps of 0.1 dB. The mixing engineer can see previously recorded mixing levels change over time by watching the fader motions. In order to modify a recorded mix, the engineer can press on a moving fader, overriding computer control and enabling the fader to be adjusted manually.

Features of Digital Mixing Consoles

Digital mixing consoles have capabilities that are not possible with analog and hybrid consoles. Figure 26.11 shows a high-end digital mixer by LAWO. Here are some of these features (not all are available in every digital mixer):

1. Signal processing operations occur in the digital domain, so the artifacts of multiple DAC and ADC conversions are avoided.

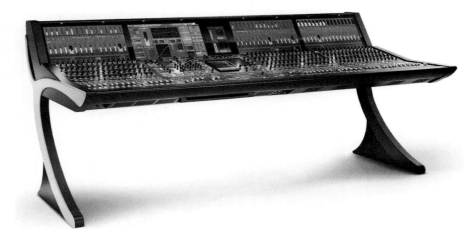

Figure 26.11   LAWO mc² 96 large-format digital mixing console runs at 96 kHz sampling rate with 24-bit quantization using 40-bit floating-point signal processing. This luxury mixer offers touch-screen control, dozens of video displays, and hundreds of physically accessible knobs, buttons, and faders. This stands in contrast to a small digital mixer on which the controls can be accessed only through a labyrinth of menus and submenus.

2. On a small portable digital mixer, control panels can be redesigned to use fewer control knobs. Instead of having one knob for each circuit (up to 4,000 knobs, buttons, and sliders on large consoles), *assignable* control knobs manipulate different things at different times. A centralized control facility can be accessed by any channel (figure 26.12), or one fader can be assigned to control any number of input channels.

3. Control panels and mixing hardware can be separated, so that a digital control panel can take up much less space than an analog mixer would require.

4. Digital effects such as delay, reverberation, equalization, and dynamic range processing can be built into the mixer.

5. Other digital technologies like scene selection, fader automation, storage and recall of signal routing setups, touch-control graphics displays, and multichannel network communications (AVB, Dante, MADI, etc.) can be integrated into the system because all devices "talk digital."

6. To the degree that the system is software-based, it can be updated to provide improvements.

7. It can be reconfigured via software to realize different numbers of input and output channels, equalizers, and so on, to meet the needs of different sessions.

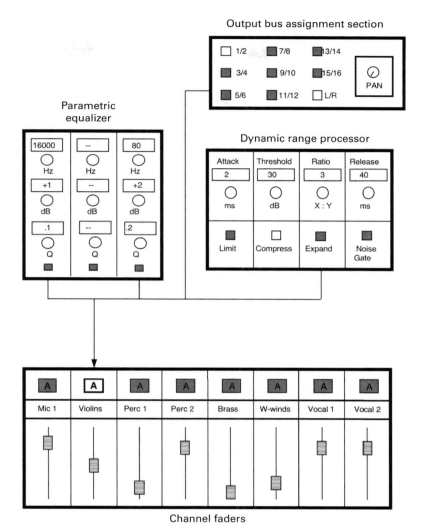

Figure 26.12 In an assignable console, each input channel has a fader, but the console has just one set of controls for equalization, dynamics, output bus assignment, and so forth. Access to a control on any channel is obtained by touching an *assign button* (marked A) above the relevant fader. This switches control to that channel. In this figure, channel 2 accesses two parametric equalization units and a dynamic range expander and routes its output to several output buses. Endless-turn rotary knobs are ideal assignable controls.

Despite these advantages, there are issues to consider. Digital mixers are not as standardized as analog mixers are. Knowing how to operate one type will not necessarily translate into knowing how to operate another type. They can be complicated to set up and operate.

On small digital mixers with a limited number of physical knobs, users must navigate a dense warren of menus to get to a control that would be readily accessible on an analog console.

Multitrack Recording and Remixing

Early audio recording was monophonic—recorded on a single channel. Sound reproduction was correspondingly monophonic through a single loudspeaker. Stereophonic (two-channel) recording was pioneered in the 1930s (Blumlein 1933; Keller 1981), and for years all sound recording was based on either one- or two-channel recording. Performances were recorded live, and the relative balance of the various sound sources was fixed at the time of the recording.

In contrast, *multitrack* recorders have several discrete tracks, and each track can be recorded at a different time. In the rest of this section we look briefly at the history of multitrack recording, describe its advantages, and also consider the remixing problems that it poses.

Multitrack Recording: Background

Working in collaboration with the Ampex Corporation in California, the electric guitarist Les Paul pioneered the concept of overdubbing using multitrack techniques in the 1950s (Bode 1984). The first commercially manufactured multitrack tape recorders came to market in 1960. That year, Karlheinz Stockhausen used a Telefunken T9 four-track recorder at the West German Radio (WDR) studios to realize his electronic music opus *Kontakte* (Stockhausen 1968; Morawska-Büngeler 1988). By 1964, the Swiss-based Studer company produced its first four-track tape recorder, the J37, which was shipped to producer George Martin and sound engineer Geoff Emerick for the production of the famous *Sgt. Pepper's Lonely Hearts Club Band* album by The Beatles (figure 26.13).

Advantages of Multitrack Recording

Multitrack recording media offer flexibility in several stages of recording practice. First, sound engineers can separate each sound source on its own

Figure 26.13   Studer J37 four-track tape recorder from 1964.

track. Instead of trying to balance all the channels when the sound is recorded, they can postpone the level balancing to the remix or mixdown stage.

For synthesized music, the multitrack approach to recording and the possibility of layering tracks is attractive. Digital recording allows the possibility of *track bouncing* (mixing several tracks down to a single track at the same time) otherwise known as *submixing* or *stem mixing.* In digital media there is no *generation loss* (i.e., noise buildup caused by copying). This is a serious constraint with copying analog media.

Mix Automation

Remixing a multitrack recording with dozens of tracks can be complicated, easily exceeding the physical capabilities of a single human being. Before the development of *mix automation,* a complicated multitrack mix (such as a film soundtrack) could involve as many as four people working at a single console.

Automation can be built into either a hardware console or a graphical software mixer. The benefit of mix automation is that a lone engineer can perform a complicated mix in a number of simple steps. For example, the engineer may start by mixing two stereo programs, on tracks 1–2 and 3–4. The automation system built into the mixing system records the control information needed to replicate this mix in real time. Once the first step is complete, another stereo program (5–6) can be blended into the mix. At each stage of mixing, previously entered mix data is recalled as the mix is built up incrementally. Only in the final stage is the entire audio mix recorded.

Full-function automation systems continuously scan all settings on a physical console many times per second. During the scan, the current position of a fader or button is compared to the stored representation of the previous scan. If the position has changed, a burst of data is sent, identifying the control and the new position. On playback, the console computer updates the console controls from memory at the same rate. The engineer can at any time override the stored settings by adjusting the desired control knob manually.

Problems Posed by Multitrack Remixing

Although it makes recording more flexible, multitrack recording is not a universal panacea. In order to take advantage of the independence offered by multiple channels, sounds on one channel must be isolated from the sounds being recorded on other channels simultaneously. In order to approach this ideal, recording engineers use isolation booths, acoustic baffles, directional microphones, and close microphone ranges to achieve maximum isolation. The signals from electric and electronic instruments are fed directly to individual tracks.

When these isolated sources are added together, the result is an unnatural sound perspective. Particularly when heard through headphones, each track sounds as if one's ear was within inches of each different instrument. For music in which the goal is to create a synthetic sound stage (such as much pop and electronic music), this situation is not necessarily a problem. To fuse the individual tracks into a unified sound stage, engineers add global reverberation along with careful balancing and spatial assignment in the stereo plane. If we are not concerned about artificially "unifying" these diverse sources, we can create fantastic and otherworldly artificial spaces by applying spatial effects to individual tracks.

The "Purist" Approach to Recording

At the opposite end of the spectrum, the goal of certain recording projects is to recreate as accurately as possible the sound image that a listener would hear in a concert hall. For this, the standard multimicrophone/multitrack approach is not a panacea. This is the case with much acoustic music (orchestras, ensembles, soloists, and vocalists). As a reaction to multitrack practices, some recording engineers have returned to a "purist" approach to recording, using fewer microphones and fewer channels (Streicher and Dooley 1978). Success with the purist approach requires that the engineer properly position the musicians and the microphones in a good-sounding hall. This puts more pressure on the original recording technique because the mix is essentially determined at the time of recording.

Audio Monitoring

The audio monitoring or listening environment is important in recording and mixing. Various monitoring philosophies coexist.

Headphones

For *location recording* (recording on site, away from the studio), where there is no separate room for listening, headphones are the only option. But headphones are not just for location recording. Listening through good headphones is like viewing a sound under a magnifying glass. Headphones are the best way to check a recording for subtle flaws such as splice points, clicks, noise, distortion, and phase problems. These may not be as obvious on loudspeakers at moderate volume. Headphones can be deceptive, however. A crossfade that sounds perfect on headphones may seem abrupt when heard on loudspeakers. Too much or too little bass is another common outcome.

Loudspeaker Stereo Monitoring

Loudspeakers and rooms work together. In this section we look at three types of stereo loudspeaker monitoring environments: near-field, control room, and listening rooms. Obviously, there are other monitoring environments for more than two speakers: four-channel or *quadraphonic*, 5.1, eight-channel or *octophonic*, and so on. Refer to chapter 32 on spatialization.

Near-field monitoring

In small studios and apartments, *near-field* or *close-field* monitors are popular (figure 26.14a). Near-field monitors are also used in large studios when the sound engineer wants to hear what the music sounds like on loudspeakers that are similar to those in most home music systems. Mounted on top of or near the mixing console at ear level, these small dynamic loudspeakers should be less than two meters away from the mixing engineer. In this setup, the direct sound from the loudspeakers predominates over any room-induced indirect reflected sound. The smallness of the near-field monitor is important because the listener is so close to the unit that the monitor should project a *fused* spatial image; this effect cannot be achieved in close proximity to a large multiple-driver loudspeaker in which the *tweeter* (high-frequency driver) may be a meter away from the *woofer* (low-frequency driver).

A problem with some near-field monitors is inaccurate bass frequency response due to their small size. An octave or more of sound may be missing

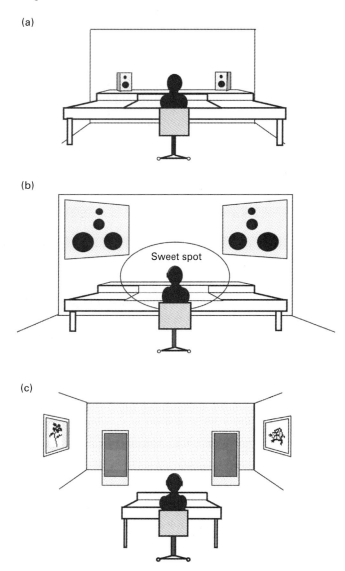

Figure 26.14 Three stereo monitoring environments. (a) Near-field. (b) Control room. (c) Listening room.

or strongly attenuated in reproduction via desktop near-field monitors. In other small monitors, an indistinct bass "boominess" occurs whenever the spectrum moves below 200 Hz.

Control room monitoring

Another approach to audio monitoring derives from the design of traditional recording studios, which are split into two parts: the *studio*, where the musicians perform, and the *control room*, where the recording engineering and the mixing console are. The control room approach to monitoring involves mounting the loudspeakers in the forward wall of an acoustically tuned environment (figure 26.14b). Each loudspeaker driver can be powered by a separate amplifier; this is referred to as *biamplification* or *triamplification,* depending on the number of drivers in the loudspeaker system. The entire system (including the room) is equalized for flat response at a *sweet spot* centered at the engineer's head. The control room approach supports monitoring at high sound pressure levels, which is typical of large pop music studios.

Listening room monitoring

The *listening room* approach places the monitor speakers in a more informal environment as is typical of a living room (figure 26.14c). The room may be acoustically treated but not as radically as a typical studio control room. The loudspeakers are large, full-range models with flat frequency response and accurate spatial imaging. Three-way *dynamic* loudspeakers (tweeter, midrange diaphragm, and low-frequency woofer) or ultrathin *electrostatic* loudspeakers project the sound. The listening room approach is preferred by many mastering engineers and classical music producers for monitoring at moderate levels.

Mixing and Monitoring in Performance

From the standpoint of judging what the audience is hearing, the best position for mixing a performance of music projected over loudspeakers is in the middle of the hall, among the audience. The question of loudspeaker configuration is an open one and is primarily an artistic decision. Another aesthetic question comes up when presenting acoustic instruments in combination with electronic sound. Should they be blended or should they be separated? Refer to Morrill (1981b) for a discussion of these issues by a composer who wrote many works for instruments and computer-generated sound.

27   *Dynamic Range Processing*

Envelope Shapers

Gates

Compressors

        Compressor Parameters

            Peak versus average detector

            Threshold

            Threshold knee

            Compression ratio

            Attack time

            Release time

            Makeup gain

        Multiband Compressors

Expanders

Limiters

Noise Reduction Units and Companders

Sidechain Control and Adaptive Effects

The Loudness War

Parallel Compression
Manual Compression

Dynamic range techniques transform the amplitude of signals. These serve as the foundation of devices such as *envelope shapers*, *gates*, *compressors*, *limiters*, *expanders*, *noise reduction units*, and *companders* (McNally 1984; Katz 2002; Dutilleux, Dempwolf, et al. 2011). The applications of dynamic range processing vary from practical tasks such as cleaning up noisy signals to creative tasks such as reshaping the envelope of an instrument or voice.

Envelope Shapers

Sound editors let musicians rescale the overall amplitude envelope of a sampled sound. This rescaling can involve a simple change in gain (i.e., some number of decibels higher or lower in amplitude) or a redesign of the overall envelope of a sound. The reshaping can apply to an individual sound object or to an entire section of music.

Figure 27.1 shows how the sharp attack of a harpsichord tone has been rounded off by the envelope shown in figure 27.1b. The middle portion of the tone becomes a kind of sustained ringing before it fades out.

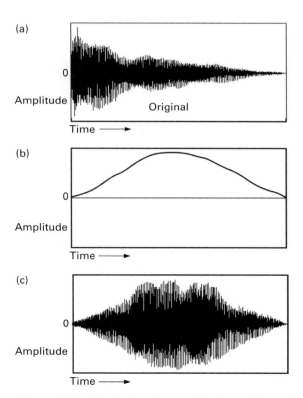

Figure 27.1 Reshaping the amplitude envelope of a harpsichord tone. (a) Original tone. (b) New envelope drawn by hand. (c) Reshaped harpsichord tone that follows the outline of the new envelope.

Gates

A gate is one way to clean up music signals that are obscured by a constant noise, such as hiss or hum. In general, the noise is assumed to be below the level of the music signal. The gate functions as a switch that is open when higher-amplitude music signals pass through it and switches off when the music stops, thereby cutting off any residual system noise. In particular, when the peak amplitude of the input signal to a gate drops below a specific *threshold*, the gate maximally attenuates the input signal, which, ideally, is mere residual system noise. The *attack time* of the gate determines how quickly at reacts, and the *release time* determines how long it will take to ungate the signal after the peak has passed. Figure 27.2 depicts this process. As shown in figure 27.2a, a noisy signal fades until all that is heard is

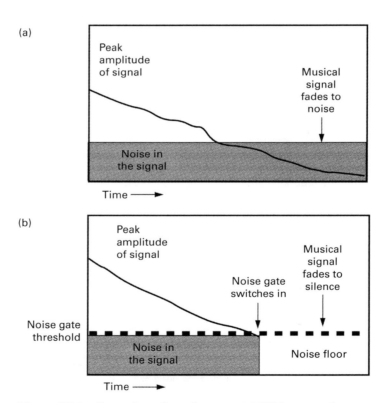

Figure 27.2 Operation of a noise gate. (a) Without a noise gate, a musical signal that contains low-level noise fades to noise. (b) With a noise gate, the fading signal crosses the noise gate threshold so that the noise gate switches in. Hence the signal fades to silence instead of to a mixture of signal and noise.

noise. As shown in figure 27.2b, as soon as the signal drops below the threshold, the noise gate eliminates both the signal and the noise. It should be obvious that a gate cannot eliminate noise when the music signal is playing, so this process works well only when the music signal masks the noise signal.

Beyond the elimination of noise, a gate can serve creative functions in sound processing, particularly in the realm of rhythmic enhancement when a percussion track gates another sound, for example. (See the discussion of *sidechaining* further along in this chapter.) Other applications include transient shaping, drum replacement, and even granulation when the attack and decay times are short (Unfiltered Audio 2016).

Compressors

We first need to distinguish between *audio compression* and *data compression*. An audio compressor reduces the dynamic range or level of input signals fed into it in real time. That is, it tries to keep the output level somewhat constant. An audio compressor can be analog or digital in its implementation. By contrast, data compression is a purely digital process that reduces the size of a file in bits. Data compression can be applied to any type of file, such as text, binary, graphics, and others. For example, a common .zip file is data compressed.

An audio compressor is an amplifier whose gain (i.e., amount of amplification) is controlled by its input signal. A primary use of a compressor is to keep the output signal constant in level. When the input signal rises above a specified upper bound, the compressor attenuates it. The first industry to embrace audio compressors was radio broadcasting, where it was called *automatic gain control.* Compressors ensured that exceptionally loud sounds never overmodulated the radio transmitter, which could cause the signal to become unintelligible.

A good way to characterize a compressor is by its *transfer function,* which shows how a given amplitude value sent into the device is mapped to a given amplitude value at the output. This representation of a transfer function is exactly the same as that used to explain waveshaping synthesis in chapter 17.

Figure 27.3 shows the transfer functions of several dynamic range processors. We can think of the input signal coming into the box from the bottom and exiting to the right. Figure 27.3a shows a perfectly linear transfer function. A value of −1 on the bottom maps to a value of −1 on the right; a value of +1 on the bottom maps to +1 on the right; and so on.

Figure 27.3b shows the transfer function and processed waveform for a relatively soft compression effect. Note how peaks on the input map to lesser values on the output of the transfer function.

We explain the transfer functions in Figures 27.3c and 2.7d further along in this chapter.

Compressor Parameters

Peak versus average detector

Inside a compressor, a *detector* circuit monitors the amplitude envelope of the input signal. The detector can respond to either *peak* or *average* amplitude of the input. A peak detector reacts to amplitude peaks even if these occur for just an instant. In contrast, an average or *root mean square* (RMS) detector responds more slowly to the overall amplitude of the signal, typically over a period of one or two seconds. Peak detectors provide insurance against sudden amplitude overload. On the other hand, average detectors deliver smoother response to input signal changes.

Threshold

The threshold determines the level at which the compressor acts. The input signal is assumed to have a maximum of unity gain or 0 dB. When −10 is selected, only sounds that are above −10 dB from the peak are compressed. Thus a threshold of −40 dB is more drastic than a compressor that has a threshold of −10 dB because it means that much more of the input will be compressed.

Threshold knee

The *knee* sets the inflection of the threshold response curve (figure 27.4). When the inflection is a smooth continuous curve, this is called *soft knee compression*. Here the effect of compression is gradual. When the inflection line is discontinuous, the compression takes effect fully the instant the threshold is exceeded. When the knee is hard and the compression ratio is high, the compressor becomes a limiter (discussed in the next section). A limiter aggressively squashes all sounds above the threshold.

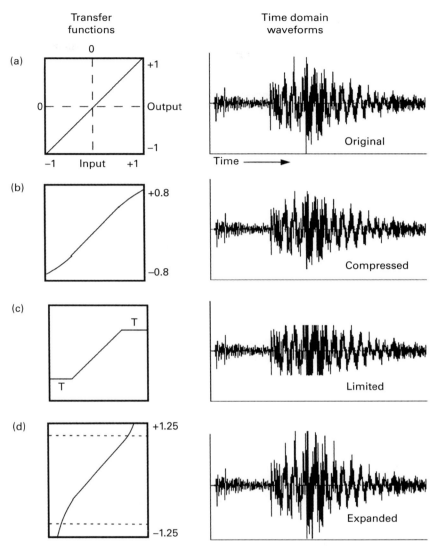

Figure 27.3 Dynamic range processing. The left column shows the transfer functions associated with the various processing methods. (a) Original signal—a cymbal crash—with a linear transfer function. (b) Soft compression of peaks scales them down several decibels. (c) Hard limiting flattens peaks to keep them within the threshold boundaries indicated by T. (d) Expansion exaggerates peaks, creating several new ones.

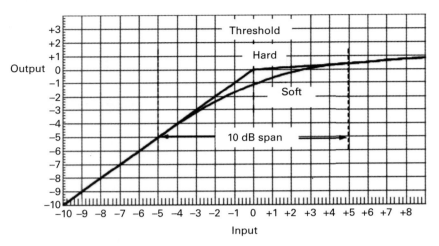

Figure 27.4   Soft versus hard knee compression.

Compression ratio

The *compression ratio* or *input/output ratio* is the ratio of change of the input signal versus the change in the output signal. An ordinary amplifier has a compression ratio of 1:1. A ratio of 3:1 means that a 3 dB change in the input signal causes only a 1 dB change in the output signal. Compression ratios greater than about 8:1 tend to squash the signal audibly, flattening transients and thereby introducing distortion products.

High compression is a common cliché in the production of popular music. Ratios in the range of 10:1 make pop vocals sound "intimate" due to the exaggeration of tongue gesticulations, lip smacking, saliva dripping, and breathing noises that results from scaling all vocalisms to the same amplitude range. With plucked string instruments like electric guitars, extreme compression creates sostenuto effects. That is, the compressor reduces the pluck transient while elevating the overall level by a large factor. When this compressed signal is highly amplified, as with electric guitars, it reinforces sustained oscillation of the string.

Attack time

Usually stipulated in milliseconds, the attack time determines how quickly the compressor reacts to sounds above the threshold. Sometimes a threshold of several milliseconds is best, as it allows percussive hits to pierce through.

Release time

The release time determines how quickly the compressor returns to a non-compressed state when sounds fall below the threshold. If the release time is too long, then quiet sounds following a loud sound will be reduced in amplitude even further.

Makeup gain

Because compression reduces the volume of the peaks in the input, makeup gain boosts the signal upward to compensate for the compression. Makeup gain is a key component in the manufacture of extremely compressed (or *phat*) drum tracks in which the transient peak is squashed and the drum resonance is highly boosted and sustained by makeup gain.

Multiband Compressors

A *multiband compressor* applies the effect in a frequency-dependent way. That is, the input signal is filtered into several frequency bands, each of which is compressed separately—a process called *band-splitting.* By segregating the compression into individual frequency bands, each with its own compression curve, the side effects of compression can be made less audible. Only certain bands need to be compressed; the rest can be left as they are.

Whereas most compressors operate directly on time-domain waveforms, a multiband compressor can be implemented as a frequency-domain device (Zaunschirm et al. 2012). Such a device operates directly on data obtained from spectrum analysis (see chapter 36). An example of a compressor based on spectrum analysis is Pro Audio DSP's Dynamic Spectrum Mapper plug-in, which can also capture the spectral signature of one track and apply it to another.

Multiband compression can be applied as a clever substitute for time-varying equalization (Maserati 2014). In multiband compressor plug-ins such as Waves C4 or FabFilter Pro MB, for example, the frequency bands of compression can be freely tuned by the user. This lets the mixing engineer focus on a harsh region in the spectrum. When energy in this region exceeds a certain threshold, it is automatically diminished in gain without need for equalization.

Expanders

An *expander* is the opposite of a compressor. It exaggerates small changes in its input signal into wide-ranging changes in its output signal. The *expansion ratio* determines the degree of expansion. For example, an expansion ratio of 1:3 means that a 1 dB change in the input signal is converted to a 3 dB change in the output signal. Figure 27.3d shows a peak expansion effect applied to the input signal shown in figure 27.3a.

The multiband compressors explained in the previous section also perform expansion, so that one can focus expansion on a narrow band without affecting the rest of the signal. Noise reduction units often contain compressor-expander pairs, as we explain further in this chapter.

Limiters

Limiting is extreme compression—in which the compression ratios are beyond 10:1 and the threshold knee is flat. As figure 27.3c shows, the relationship between the input and the output is linear up to a certain level. This level is indicated by the positive and negative threshold bounds T. (Note that in practical systems, one specifies a single absolute value for the threshold rather than separate upper and lower bounds.) Beyond the threshold, the output remains constant regardless of the input level.

Limiters are useful in live concert recording when it is imperative not to overload the absolute dynamic range of any component in the recording chain. For example, digital recorders have an absolute input level threshold beyond which harsh numerical clipping distortion occurs. A recording engineer might insert a limiter before the recorder inputs to ensure that the recorder's threshold is never exceeded.

Noise Reduction Units and Companders

Noise reduction (NR) units usually employ a compressor on the input stage of a recorder and an expander on the output stage (figure 27.5). For this reason, they are sometimes called *companders* (a contraction of *compressor* and *expander*). The compressor stage reduces transients and boosts the rest of the input signal to an artificially high level. On playback, the expander stage restores the dynamic range of the original. Because the compressed recording contains little noise (it is all recorded at a moderately high level above the noise floor of the recorder), the result is a low-noise but wide-dynamic-range recording.

Figure 27.6 depicts the process of compansion. The dynamic range of the recording shrinks within the noisy channel (e.g., an analog cassette recorder).

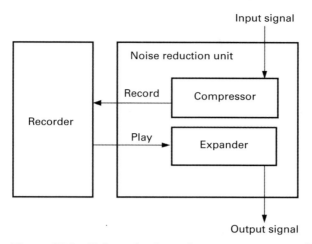

Figure 27.5   Noise reduction units compress on recording and expand on playback.

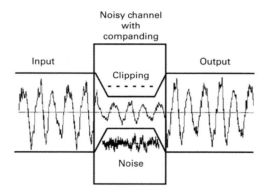

Figure 27.6   Companding noise reduction unit reduces the wide dynamic range going into the noisy channel. It tries to keep the signal above the noise level and below the clipping level. The final stage of the compander expands the dynamic range.

The recording signal remains at a high enough level to avoid some of the noise in the noisy channel but is low enough to avoid clipping or overload distortion.

Certain noise reduction schemes carry out compression and expansion in a frequency-dependent way by using multiband compansion. Sounds that cross frequency bands, such as continuous glissandi, can still pose a problem for such systems because audible artifacts can occur as each band's noise reduction circuits trigger into operation. Moreover, even small irregularities in the amplitude-versus-frequency response of the bands can lead to audible colorations in the overall sound (Lagadec and Pelloni 1983).

Sidechain Control and Adaptive Effects

Gates and compressors with *sidechain* or *key* inputs allow signals other than the one being compressed to modify the behavior of the effect (figure 27.7). For example, the amplitude of a vocal track can be used to control the amount of compression on an instrumental track in order to reduce the gain when the vocalist is singing. This process is known as *ducking*, as the vocal causes the instrument to "duck down" in level to make room for the vocal part (Kadis 2012). Some plug-ins can duck multiple tracks in a mix in response to vocals. Another common effect applies a sidechain percussion signal to gate another track in order to enliven the overall rhythm.

The technique of sidechaining leads to the broader concept of *adaptive effects* or *content-based transformations* (Amatriain et al. 2003; Poepel and Dannenberg 2005; Holfelt et al. 2017). In this approach, an audio track acting as a control function is analyzed and a feature from this analysis is used to control an effect on the same or another audio signal. For example, the amount of bass in track 1 (the control track) could be used to determine the amount of reverberation on track 2. Reiss and Brandtsegg (2018) have surveyed the recent history of this field and its applications in live performance and sound mixing.

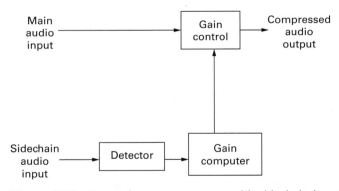

Figure 27.7   Dynamic range processor with sidechain input.

The Loudness War

Mastering engineer Bob Katz (2002) pointed out a phenomenon that has come to be known as The Loudness War. Compressors let sound engineers produce recordings that are maximally loud at all times, thus lacking contrasts in dynamic range. For example, certain pop albums have a dynamic range variation of no more than 3 dB across multiple tracks from beginning to end (DynamicRangeDay.com). In these cases, the crisp transient edges of percussion envelopes are flattened by extreme compression. Confronted with loud distorted recordings, many listeners turn down the volume, which defeats the purpose of engineering maximal loudness (figure 27.8).

In general, to compress the amplitude of a sound is to introduce distortion. This occurs because dynamic range processing modulates the amplitude (AM), which generates sidebands in the spectrum (see chapter 15). Thus dynamic range processing should be used with full knowledge of its effects on the spectrum of the input signal.

Dynamic range processors impose attack and decay envelopes on a global basis, affecting all sounds passed through them, regardless of musical context. They react to the amplitude of the signal passing through them. The reaction delay between the *cause* (an amplitude variation in the signal) and the *effect* (switching on processing) is a well-known problem. Certain devices reduce this effect by delaying the input signal slightly and "looking ahead" to determine whether there are any waveforms that will trigger dynamic range processing. If so, the device can switch in the effect more or less synchronously with these waveforms. Other processors employ no such lookahead. One can change the attack time to cause it to react more quickly, but then

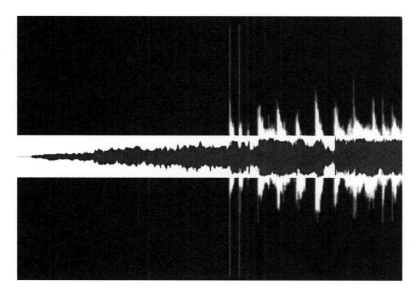

Figure 27.8   The superposition of two waveforms. The center bar shows a compressed version that has been turned down in volume, and the upper and lower parts of the image show the original transients that have been flattened and eliminated by compression. The compressed version in the center bar lacks dynamic range variation (or "punch").

the effect switches in and out too often, leading to a well-known pumping sound.

No single setting of attack time, threshold, compression ratio, and release is optimal for any more than one sound. Thus, adjusting these parameters is usually a compromise between no processing on one hand, and audible distortion on the other hand. In the case of compression, it is precisely distortion that many pop music producers seek. Ultimately, compression, like any effect, is easy to overuse.

Parallel Compression

Parallel compression is a set of audio studio techniques that combine the conventional formula of *downward compression + makeup gain* with other operations (Robjohns 2013). In its simplest form, it mixes an uncompressed track with its highly compressed counterpart. By means of this combination, dynamic transients are retained in the uncompressed signal, whereas in the compressed signal, quiet sounds are boosted and louder sounds are attenuated. The intended result is a thicker mix, particularly for vocal tracks.

Manual Compression

As an alternative to using a compressor, one can manually re-envelope the tracks in a sound editor on an event-by-event basis, as shown in figure 27.1. This means applying makeup gain to passages that are too soft while leaving transients intact. The manual approach to dynamic range optimization is more time consuming than running entire tracks through a compressor, but it represents the ultimate in detailed control of amplitude levels with a minimum of transient distortion (Roads 2015, chapter 12).

28 Digital Filtering

Bob L. T. Sturm with Curtis Roads

Design of Filters

FIR versus IIR Filters
Second-Order Sections

Subjective Perception of Filters

Chapter 14 introduced the basics of digital filters, describing the basic filter types, the concepts of Q and gain, filter banks, comb and allpass filters, vocoders, and linear predictive coding. This chapter takes the discussion to the next technical level.

A committee of signal-processing engineers defined a digital filter as follows:

A digital filter is a computational process or algorithm by which a digital signal or sequence of numbers acting as input) is transformed into a second sequence of numbers termed the output digital signal. (Rabiner et al. 1972, 322)

Thus, we can call any *black box* with a discrete input x and a discrete output y a digital filter, as shown in figure 28.1.

A common use of the term *filter* describes devices that boost or attenuate regions of a sound's spectrum. However, digital mixers, reverberators, compressors, companders, spatializers and other effects are also digital filters. Thus a digital filter can change not only the spectrum of an input signal but also its amplitude and temporal structure.

Presenting Filter Theory to Musicians

The theory of digital filtering is a rarefied specialty, couched in mathematics that are removed from ordinary experience. The equation of a digital filter, for example, does not necessarily reveal the effect that it will have on an audio signal. This is unfortunate, because perception and emotion are sharply attuned to the effects of filters.

The profound subject of the aesthetics of filtering is seldom addressed in the signal processing literature, even though the impact of filters on musical sound can range from the sublime to the horrific. Papers by Gerzon (1990), Rossum (1992), Massie and Stonick (1992), and Välimäki and Huovilainen (2006) are exceptions.

Musicians speak of filters as "harsh" or "warm" or "musical" in an attempt to describe filters' various effects. Perhaps more precise terminology will evolve as the art of digital filtering matures.

Figure 28.1   A filter as a black box with an input x and an output y.

Standing between our subjective experience of filters and their practical implementation is a forest of theory. Electrical engineering texts describe digital filters in a variety of ways, from the time domain to the frequency domain and, most generally, to the *Z domain*. This variety of viewpoints helps one understand the implementation and behavior of digital filters. Our presentation of digital filters takes a similar approach. We use multiple viewpoints to understand how they work and how they affect any input signal *x*. Taken with the basic filter concepts explained in chapter 14 on subtractive synthesis, this presentation covers the essential knowledge needed by musicians using filters in composition and performance.

Adventurous readers who trek the forest of filter theory will find hundreds of papers to wander through. The better musically motivated papers include Moore (1978b, 1990), Cann (1979–1980), Steiglitz (1996), Moorer (1981a, 1983a) and Smith (1985a, b, 2007a). Also refer to the tutorials on filter design by Hutchins (1982–1988), complete with code listings. Dozens of engineering textbooks are devoted to filters, either wholly or in part. A classic engineering reference is Hamming (1989).

Important Properties of Filters

Three important properties of filters guide their design: *stability, time invariance,* and *linearity.* A *stable* filter always outputs bounded values no matter the input. With an *unstable* filter, the output values grow larger and larger, resulting in numerical *overflow* (numbers larger than the audio converters can handle) and a distorted result. A stable filter never "explodes." An example of unstable filters is feedback from a guitar or microphone. By contrast, natural room reverberation is a stable filter: it always decays in intensity.

Another important property of a filter is whether or not it is time-invariant. A filter is *time-invariant* if its effect on an input does not depend on when it has been sent. For instance, if we send a signal through a time-invariant filter now and repeat the send five seconds from now, its output will be the same in both cases, but the second send will be delayed by five seconds.

The filters discussed in this chapter are time-invariant. By contrast, flanging and chorus effects are examples of filters that are not time-invariant.

The third important property of a filter is *linearity.* A filter is *linear* if its output for a sum of two inputs is the same as the sum of its outputs for each individual input. Reverberation is a linear filter, but a dynamic range compressor is not (see chapter 27). The reason is that a compressor will react differently in time to two separate inputs as opposed to the sum of the two inputs.

An important class of digital filters is *linear time-invariant* (LTI) filters (Rabiner and Gold 1975). Because of these properties, we can switch the order of any sequence of LTI filters to achieve the same results. Their order in the signal processing chain does not matter (figure 28.2).

LTI filters consist of only three simple components: adders, scalar multipliers, and delays (figure 28.3). Just using these creates a large variety of possibilities. The figure shows these three components, where labeled arrows indicate signal flow, the plus (+) sign indicates an addition of two inputs, a triangle indicates scalar multiplication by the number shown, and D indicates a delay of one sample.

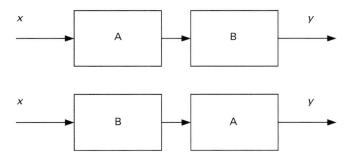

Figure 28.2   Two LTI filters (A and B) can be swapped in sequence and the resulting *y* will be the same.

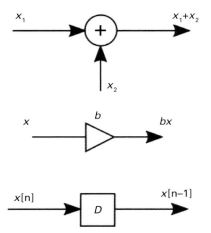

Figure 28.3   LTI filters consist of only three simple components: adders (+ or −), scalar multipliers (triangle), and delays (D).

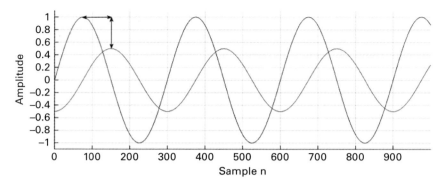

Figure 28.4   LTI filter effect on amplitude and phase. The input signal is the larger amplitude, and the output is the sinusoid with smaller amplitude. Notice the delay between the first peaks, indicated by the arrows.

Finally, if a filter is LTI, then it is easy to understand what its effects will be on any input. In effect, an LTI filters the amplitude and phase of an input sinusoid but not its frequency. This is diagramed in figure 28.4. The input signal is the one with the larger amplitude, and the output is the sinusoid with smaller amplitude. We see the filter has changed its amplitude (vertical double arrow) and shifted its phase (horizontal double arrow).

Understanding Digital Filters in Time

We now look at digital filters in the time domain. The important point is that filters work by splitting the input signal into an original part and a delayed part. Delays can create out-of-phase waveforms (for a filter that attenuates certain frequencies) or in-phase waveforms (for a filter that boosts certain frequencies) with respect to the original part. The delayed part is then added to or subtracted from the original to sculpt the spectrum by means of *phase cancelation* or *phase reinforcement* effects, as explained in chapter 14.

Filters as Equations and Block Diagrams

Any digital filter can be described by an equation that relates the input to the output. The samples of the input and output are numbered or indexed (e.g., the sample at time n, the sample that follows $n+1$, etc.), and the sample number is often enclosed in brackets. So, $x[0]$ is the sample of the input signal at time $n=0$; $y[1]$ is the sample of the output signal at time $n=1$; and so on.

An equation describing one simple filter is $y[n]=2x[n]+x[n-1]$. This says that the nth value of the output signal is twice the nth value of the input signal plus the previous value of the input. Hence, the output will be just double the input plus the input delayed one sample. If the input signal is $x=\{\ldots, 0, \underline{1}, -2, 3, -1, 0, \ldots\}$ (where the underline denotes the value of $x[0]$), then $y=\{\ldots, 0, \underline{2}, -3, 4, 1, -1, 0, \ldots\}$.

Another simple filter is $y[n]=x[n]\times y[n-1]$. This says the nth value of the output is the product of the previous output and the nth value of the input. If the input signal is $x=\{\ldots, 0, \underline{1}, -2, 3, -1, 0, \ldots\}$, and we assume $y[-1]=1$, then $y=\{1, \underline{1}, -2, -6, 6, 0, \ldots\}$. This filter involves *feedback* because its output is computed using other output (y) values.

For any filter, its *order* is the number of delays involved in creating an output sample. A *first-order* filter, for example, has only one delay. Both examples presented previously are first-order filters. A *second-order* filter contains two delays. One example is $y[n]=2x[n]+x[n-2]$.

Another way to express a digital filter is by using a block diagram. This makes explicit the operations of a digital filter in transforming an input into an output. Figure 28.5 shows the block diagrams of two first-order filters. These filters are fundamentally different for three reasons. The first is that in computing the output, the diagram shown in figure 28.5b uses *feedback*, or past values of output, whereas the diagram shown in figure 28.5a uses only *feed-forward*, or past values of the input. The second difference is that the filter shown in

(a)

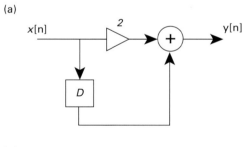

(b)

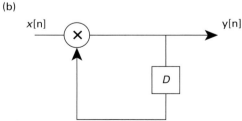

Figure 28.5 Two first-order filters. (a) Finite-impulse response (FIR) feed-forward filter. (b) Infinite-impulse response (IIR) feedback filter.

figure 28.5b is unstable, whereas the other filter (figure 28.5a) is stable. Imagine feeding into the unstable filter an infinite sequence of samples all equal to 2. The output value would then double at each time step without bound. Finally, the last difference is that the figure 28.5a filter is linear whereas the figure 26.5b filter is nonlinear. Although both filters are time-invariant, only the filter shown in figure 28.5a is LTI.

The most general equation of an LTI filter is as follows:

$$y[n] = b_0 \times x[n] + \cdots + b_M \times x[n-M] - a_1 \times y[n-1] - \cdots - a_N \times y[n-N]$$

which can be compactly written as

$$y[n] = \sum_{m=0}^{M} bm \times x[n-m] + \sum_{l=1}^{N} al \times y[n-l]$$

Figure 28.6 shows a block diagram of this filter. This filter is a series of two *tapped delay lines*. The line on the left delays past input values, and after each delay there is a multiplier and a summer. The coefficients $b_0, \ldots, b_M$, control this feed-forward delay line. The line on the right delays past output values, and again, after each delay there is a multiplier and a summer. The coefficients $a_1, \ldots, a_N$, control the feedback delay line. The memory of each

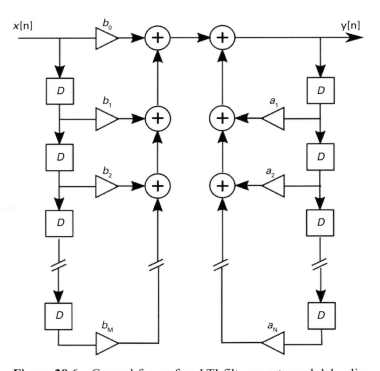

Figure 28.6 General form of an LTI filter as a tapped delay line.

delay line goes back to only a finite number of samples corresponding to the number of delay units.

Impulse Response

For a filter that is LTI there exists a simple way to know exactly how it will change any input. From Fourier's theory (chapter 37), we know that we can represent any input as a sum of sinusoids. We also know that passing a sum of sequences through a linear filter is equivalent to passing those sequences through the filter individually and then summing them all. Hence, we can know exactly what an LTI filter will do to any input by measuring how it changes all possible sinusoids individually.

An elegant way to determine how an LTI filter will affect any frequency is to observe its response to an impulse. This comes from the fact that an impulse contains all frequencies with equal energies. As Fourier showed in the eighteenth century, an inverse relationship exists between the duration of a signal and its frequency content. A sine wave of infinite duration has all its energy in a single frequency. As we shrink the duration of the sine wave, its Fourier spectrum becomes distributed across a broad range of frequencies. Thus, the shorter the signal, the wider its spectrum. In the limit of a single impulse of infinitesimal duration, all frequencies become present with equal amounts. Hence, all characteristics of an LTI filter are revealed by its output response) to a perfect impulse. This gives rise to the following canon in digital signal processing:

Any LTI filter can be completely characterized by its impulse response (IR).

There are two broad classes of digital filters in terms of their IR: *finite impulse response* (FIR) and *infinite impulse response* (IIR). When an FIR filter processes a finite-length input, its output will return samples with a value of zero after some time.

An IIR filter has an IR with an infinite number of non-zero-valued samples. When an IIR filter processes a finite-length input, its output will never return to zero after some time. When an LTI filter has feedback, it is typically an IIR filter. Any LTI filter with only feed-forward operations is an FIR filter.

Figure 28.7 shows the IR of a digital filter created to approximate room reverberation. Each individual spike is a single echo occurring at the time location of the spike. The height of a spike shows the amplitude change of the original signal. If it is negative, then the polarity of the original signal is flipped. We can see that the echoes are somewhat regularly spaced, and their amplitudes decay exponentially with time.

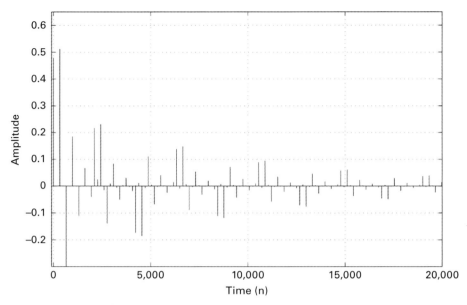

Figure 28.7   Impulse response of a filter that simulates room reverberation.

Understanding Digital Filters in Frequency

We now look at digital filters in the frequency domain. This provides another perspective for understanding the effects of a filter.

Consider figure 28.8. Each plot shows a spectrum, which describes how the amplitude energy in a signal is distributed in frequency. The top plot shows the spectrum $X(f)$ of a time-domain signal $x[n]$. We see a large amount of energy in a band centered around some high frequency. Let us say we want to reduce the energy in that band but keep the rest unchanged. We can create a spectrum $H(f)$ such that when we multiply it by $X(f)$ we produce the spectrum in the lowest plot. We now see $X(f)H(f)$ has lower energy in the specific band we wanted to remove. When we take the inverse Fourier transform of our new spectrum $X(f)H(f)$, we find that we have just convolved $x[n]$ with the time-domain sequence $h[n]$ having a spectrum $H(f)$.

Frequency Response

Whereas the IR of an LTI filter shows how it changes an impulse signal, its *frequency response* (FR) shows how it changes the flat spectrum of the impulse signal. Because an LTI filter changes only the amplitude and phase

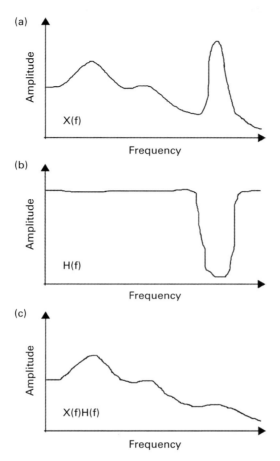

Figure 28.8 The spectra of three signals. (a) Large amount of energy in a band centered around a high frequency. (b) Filter that reduces the peak in (a). (c) Resulting spectrum after filtering (a) by (b).

of a sinusoid, we can plot both of these changes separately as functions of frequency. The *magnitude response* of a filter shows its effect on the amplitude of any input sinusoid; the *phase response* shows its effect on the phase of any input sinusoid.

The top of figure 28.9 shows the magnitude response, and the bottom shows the phase response. The filter has little effect on the amplitudes of sinusoids with frequencies less than about 0.2 π radians/sample but has a major effect on sinusoids with frequencies greater than 0.3 π radians/sample. We can see from the magnitude response that this is a lowpass filter. It attenuates all frequencies above a *cutoff frequency*. Compared with the magnitude response, the phase response is more difficult to interpret in terms of the perceptual effects. We see that the phase response of this filter is linear in

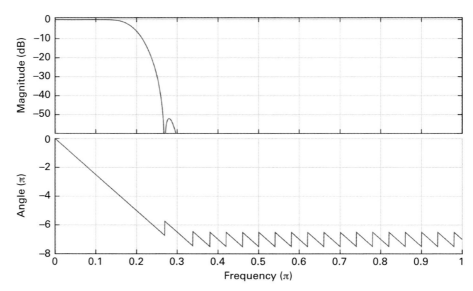

Figure 28.9 Magnitude and phase response of a lowpass filter.

the *passband*. A linear phase response in the passband essentially means that the lowpass envelope of an input signal will be preserved after filtering.

The FR and IR of an LTI stable filter are closely connected. The FR is just the Fourier transform of the IR; and the IR is just the inverse Fourier transform of the FR. Because the Fourier transform is unique, the IR and the FR contain the same information but in different domains. The IR exists in the time domain, and the FR in the frequency domain.

Poles and Zeros

Another way to understand the behavior of a digital filter is in terms of *poles* and *zeros*. This analysis method uses the *Z-transform*—an interpretation of the Fourier transform that correlates to filter stability. The mathematics are obscure without sufficient background, but understanding the results is simple.

The *Z*-transform of a filter shows a pattern of poles and zeroes plotted on the unit circle. The zero frequency (or DC frequency) is at the right-most position on the unit circle, and the Nyquist frequency (half the sampling rate) is at the left-most position on the unit circle. As we sweep around the unit circle counter clockwise from the zero frequency position, we are increasing in frequency until we reach the Nyquist frequency position.

A pole is a resonance or peak in the FR. The closer a pole is to the edge of the unit circle, the sharper its peak in the FR. A zero is a trough in the FR. The closer a zero is to the circle, the deeper the trough in the FR. If any

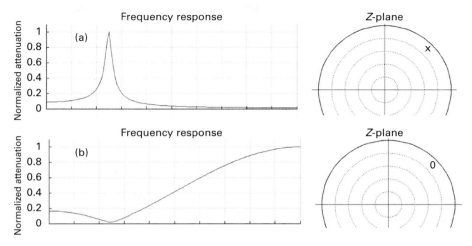

Figure 28.10 Pole and zero of a digital filter. (a) A pole creates a peak in the frequency response. (b) A zero creates a trough.

pole is on or outside this circle, then the filter is not stable. The location of a zero has no effect on the stability of a filter.

Figure 28.10a shows a pole (x) that is close to the unit circle. It produces a peak centered at a particular frequency (in this case, about a quarter of the sampling rate). If we replace that pole with a zero, we see the magnitude response shown in figure 28.10b: the peak has become a trough.

Examples of Filters

We now show several examples of LTI digital filters, in both the time domain and frequency domain, and as equations and block diagrams.

Simple FIR Lowpass Filter

We can create a simple lowpass filter by merely averaging input samples. For instance, let us add the current input sample with the previous input sample and divide by two. The equation for a simple averaging filter is as follows:

$$y[n] = (0.5 \times x[n]) + (0.5 \times x[n-1]).$$

The scaling constants (0.5) in the expression are called the *filter coefficients*. Figure 28.11 shows two equivalent block diagrams of this filter.

Let us now look at the response of this filter. Figure 28.12 depicts the FR of the filter, which looks like the first quadrant of a cosine wave. We can see

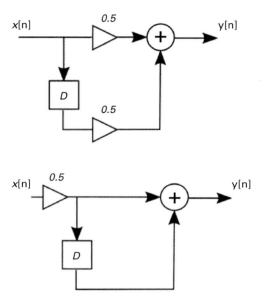

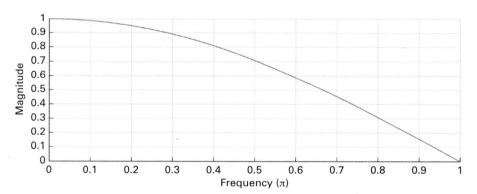

Figure 28.11 Two equivalent diagrams of a simple lowpass filter.

Figure 28.12 Magnitude response of the simple averaging lowpass filter shown in figure 28.11.

that it is a lowpass filter. It will smooth out sudden changes in an input, which is what we see happen when averaging.

What if we average the output of the average? This is just passing the output of this filter into another filter that does the same thing. The FR of that filter is shown in figure 28.13. It has a steeper rolloff in the high frequencies.

What if instead of averaging the output of the averaging filtering, we average four samples instead of two? The equation will then be

$$y[n] = (0.25 \times x[n]) + (0.25 \times x[n-1]) + (0.25 \times x[n-2]) + (0.25 \times x[n-3])$$

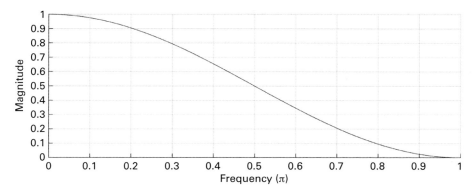

Figure 28.13 Lowpass filter that averages two samples. It has a sharper rolloff than the simple filter in figure 28.12.

The magnitude response of this filter is seen in figure 28.14. We see that it still looks like a lowpass filter, but it is not equivalent to the average of the average. This is because averaging four points along a sequence is not the same as averaging two points along a sequence and then two points along the resulting averaged sequence.

Simple FIR Highpass Filter

Next, we present a *highpass* filter that attenuates low frequencies. This filter subtracts samples instead of adding them. That is, it calculates the differences between successive pairs of samples

$$y[n] = (0.5 \times x[n]) - (0.5 \times x[n-1])$$

Now the output sample $y[n]$ is the current input sample minus the previous input sample, divided by two.

A highpass filter suppresses low frequencies because the differences between samples are small, and it passes high frequencies because the differences between successive samples are large. Figure 28.15 shows the magnitude response.

Passing the difference through a difference results in a filter with the magnitude response shown in figure 28.16. This attenuates more low frequencies.

Simple Bandpass Filter

What if we were to pass the second-order difference through a second-order average, or equivalently, the second-order average through the second-order difference? Figure 28.17 shows the response of the resulting bandpass filter.

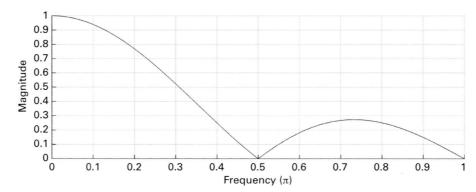

Figure 28.14   Lowpass filter that averages four samples.

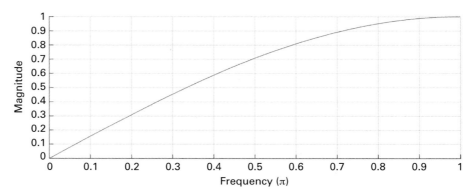

Figure 28.15   Simple highpass filter response.

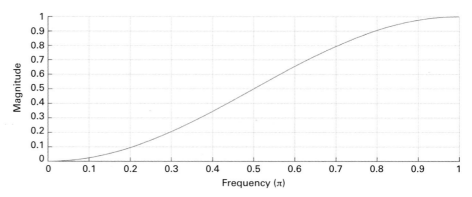

Figure 28.16   Response of a double difference highpass filter.

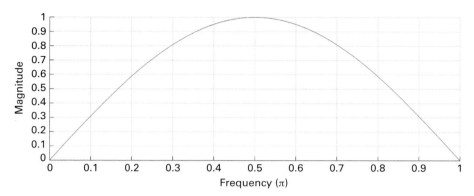

Figure 28.17   Bandpass filter response.

Exponential Smoothing Filter

If we route the filter's output back into its input, the filter blends more of the past history of the signal than a simple FIR filter can. A filter that uses past output samples is said to operate by means of *feedback*, or *recursion*.

An example of a simple IIR filter is the *exponential smoothing* filter. This filter adds the current input $x[n]$ to a multiple of its last output $y[n-1]$ to generate the new output sample

$$y[n] = x[n] + a \times y[n-1]$$

The block diagram of this filter is shown in figure 28.18.

Figure 28.19 plots the magnitude response of the exponential smoothing filter for six different values of the multiplier a. The closer we move a to 1 from the left, the more it attenuates all frequencies above 0 (or *DC*). And the closer we move a to -1 from the right, the more it attenuates all frequencies below the Nyquist rate (1).

We can express this filter as an "infinitely long" tapped feed-forward delay line

$$y[n] = x[n] + a \times x[n-1] + a^2 \times x[n-2] + a^3 \times x[n-3] + \cdots$$

This shows that if $|a| >= 1$, then the output values grow without bound. In this case, the filter is no longer stable. We must keep $|a| < 1$ to guarantee stability.

Comb Filter

A comb filter creates a regular series of peaks and troughs—equally spaced in frequency—in the spectrum of the input signal. It is so named because the peaks and troughs resemble the teeth of a comb. A simple FIR comb filter

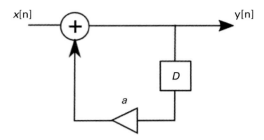

Figure 28.18 Exponential smoothing filter with feedback.

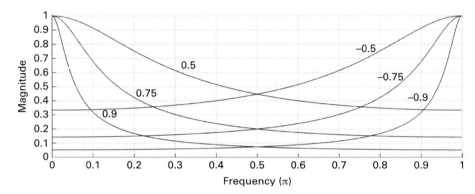

Figure 28.19 Response of an exponential smoothing filter for six different values of the multiplier *a*.

splits an incoming audio signal into two paths and inserts a multiple-sample time delay into one of the paths before summing them. The equation for a simple *M*-order FIR comb filter is as follows:

$$y[n] = x[n] + x[n - M]$$

The structure of an FIR comb filter is similar to that of a FIR lowpass filter. The important difference is that the delay time *M* of a comb filter is longer. At a sampling rate of 48 kHz, a one-sample delay in the circuit creates a mild lowpass filter effect. The reason is that the delay is only 0.00002083 s or about 0.02 ms. Only when the delay is greater than 0.1 ms does the filter begin to create multiple *null points* (points at which the amplitude is zero) in the audible spectrum due to phase cancelation effects, resulting in the audible comb filter effect.

Figure 28.20 shows the magnitude response of the FIR comb filter for three different orders (delays). The comb effect results from phase cancelation and reinforcement between the delayed and undelayed signals. If the original and the delayed signals add together—as in the *positive summing comb filter*—the resultant filter has its first off-DC peak at a frequency of $f = 1/M \times fs$, where

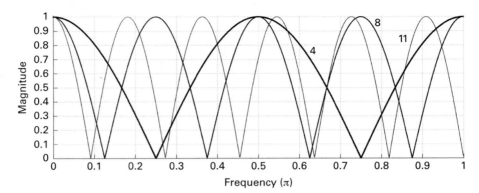

Figure 28.20   Response of a FIR comb filter for three different orders: 4, 8, and 11 samples.

M is the delay in samples and fs is the sampling frequency. Successive peaks occur at $2f$, $3f$, $4f$, up to the Nyquist frequency. Hence, this filter can be used for reinforcing a fundamental at f Hz and all of its harmonics.

For example, if the sampling rate is 48 kHz and the delay is twelve samples (0.25 ms), and the original and delayed signals are positively summed, the first audible peak occurs at $1/12 \times 48,000 = 4$ kHz, with subsequent peaks at 8 kHz, 12 kHz, and so on, up to the Nyquist frequency (24 kHz). The same comb filter has nulls at 2 kHz, 6 kHz, and other 4 kHz intervals up to the Nyquist frequency.

The phase cancelation and reinforcement effect can be explained as follows. At low frequencies the delay has virtually no effect on the phase of the signal, and the two signals (original plus delayed) add together, boosting the output signal. As the delays affect higher frequencies, they become closer and closer to a 180° phase shift. At 2 kHz, a 0.25 ms delay causes precisely a 180° phase shift. When this is added to the original signal, the two signals cancel at that frequency. Beyond 180° the signals add again until the phase shift delay reaches 0° or 360°, which produces a reinforcement peak at 4 kHz. At 6 kHz they are again 180° out of phase, producing a null, and so on.

Longer delays create more closely spaced teeth in the comb. For example, when the delay is 50 ms, the first null appears at 10 Hz with subsequent nulls at 30 Hz, 50 Hz, 70 Hz, and so on. Short delays of less than 5 ms produce the richest comb filter effects because the space between the peaks and nulls increases so that the teeth of the comb become broader in frequency and appear more striking to the ear.

What happens when the two signals (original and delayed) are subtracted rather than added together? This is the *negative summing* case, because the effect is the same as adding together the two signals with one of them 180° out of phase. The equation for this simple subtracting FIR comb filter is

$$y[n]=x[n]-x[n-M]$$

where M is the delay in samples.

If the two signals are subtracted rather than added, the first null appears at 0 Hz, with successive nulls at f, $2f$, $4f$, and so on. In this case the comb filter removes the fundamental and its harmonics. The signal is reinforced at $f/2$, $3f/2$, $5f/2$, and so on. Figure 28.21 shows its response.

An *IIR comb filter* feeds some of its output back into the input. The equation for a simple recursive comb filter is

$$y[n]=x[n]+a\times y[n-N]$$

Figure 28.22 plots the frequency response of this filter for $a=0.9$ and several N. Depending on the value of the coefficient a in particular, the IIR comb filter will have a more pronounced *resonance* effect on the signal than a corresponding FIR filter. If a is set too high, the filter becomes unstable and feeds back excessively, causing numerical overflow and subsequent distortion.

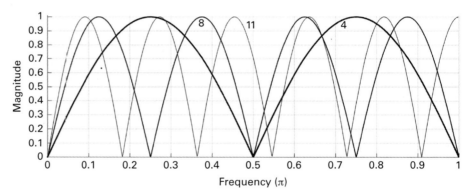

Figure 28.21   Response of a subtracting FIR comb filter.

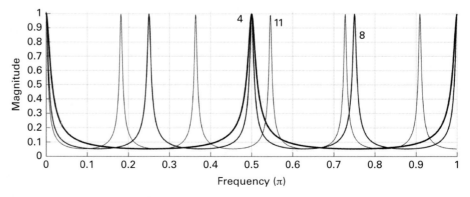

Figure 28.22   IIR comb filter response for three different delays: 4, 8, and 11 samples.

Allpass Filter

An *allpass filter* is a peculiar signal processor. For steady-state tones fed into it, the allpass filter passes all frequencies equally well with no change in amplitude—hence its name. Thus it is said that an allpass filter has a flat magnitude response throughout the audio bandwidth. However, the allpass also imposes a frequency-dependent phase shift on the incoming signal; that is, it delays various frequency regions by different amounts. This type of frequency-dependent delay is also called *dispersion.*

Figure 28.23 displays a frequency-versus-sample delay curve for three allpass filters of different orders. Notice how low frequencies are delayed by 7.5 samples, but higher frequencies are delayed by fewer samples. The audible effects of an allpass filter show up in sharp attacks and decays, when it "colors" the signal through frequency-dependent phase shifting (Preis 1982; Deer, Bloom, and Preis 1985; Chamberlin 1985). Moorer described the allpass filter as follows:

We must remember that the all-pass nature is more a theoretical nature than a perceptual one. We should not assume, simply because the frequency response is absolutely uniform, that the filter is perceptually transparent. In fact the phase response of an allpass can be quite complex. The allpass nature only implies that in the long run, with steady-state sounds, the spectral balance will not be changed. This implies nothing of the sort in the short-term, transient regions. In fact, both the comb and the allpass have very definite and distinct "sounds" that are immediately recognizable to the experienced ear. (Moorer 1979a, 14)

This view was seconded by reverberation designer Barry Blesser (quoted in Dattorro 1997, 666):

White noise passed through an allpass will not sound like real white noise. When passed through many allpass structures it sounds like a machine shop rather than random noise.

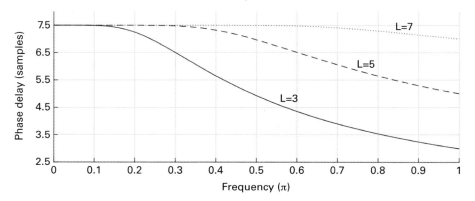

Figure 28.23 Allpass filter response for orders 3, 5, and 7.

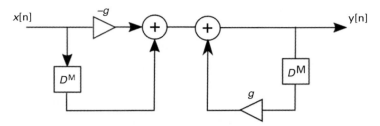

Figure 28.24   Allpass filter.

The next equation describes a simple allpass filter with a flat frequency response (from zero to half the sampling rate) that delays various frequencies by different amounts. When the delay in samples M is in the range 10–30 ms, the allpass generates a series of decaying echoes, an effect used in *Schroeder reverberators* (see chapter 33).

$$y[n] = (-g \times x[n]) + x[n-M] + (g \times y[n-M])$$

Figure 28.24 shows one possible structure of the allpass filter, equivalent to the one presented by Schroeder (1961, 1962; Moorer 1977; Cook 2007). This allpass consists of an IIR comb filter (right) with feedback (controlled by g) in series with a feedforward comb filter. This series cancels out the spectral effect of the comb filter while it creates phase-delay characteristics.

Musical applications of allpass filters are manifold. An allpass filter can help compensate for the phase shift introduced by another filter (Meyer 1984). For example, several audio companies marketed allpass filters as retrofits for early digital audio recorders to compensate for the phase distortion inherent in the unmodified recorders. Another application is found in some synthesizers. Here an allpass filter creates a time-varying, frequency-dependent phase shift, which can lend richness to otherwise static sounds. This is one means of creating a so-called *chorus effect*—a combination of delay and phase shifting. Surges, Smyth, and Puckette (2016) describe an application of allpass filters in a feedback configuration to produce self-sustaining chaotic oscillations. The most widespread application of allpass filters is in so-called algorithmic or Schroeder reverberators, as discussed in chapter 33.

Design of Filters

An important question arises: how does one decide on M, N, and all the filter coefficients? This is the realm of *filter design* (Hamming 1989; Moore 1990;

Smith 2007a; Liski and Välimäki 2017). Given filter specifications, such as a frequency response and type of filter (FIR or IIR), several different methods exist for designing a realizable LTI filter. Figure 28.25 shows some example specifications for the three bands of a lowpass filter: the passband, the stopband, and the transition band (defined in chapter 14). These specifications limit the "ripple" in the passband to avoid distorting the spectrum of the signal in that frequency band. Here, the ripple should not exceed a maximum amount. We see the frequency above which the amplitudes of input sinusoids are at least halved (the *cutoff frequency*) should be 0.3 radians/sample. Our specifications state that the transition band should occur between ω_p and ω_s. Finally, our filter should attenuate all frequencies greater than ω_s by a factor of $1/A$.

In general, realizing a filter from an arbitrary set of specifications is a nontrivial task. Even when the desired specifications do not conflict with one another, a more-or-less complicated algebraic and numerical derivation must be carried out. The result is often an approximation of the desired specification, requiring choices that balance one characteristic against another.

Fortunately, the vexing detail of filter design has been coded into automatic filter design systems (McClellan, Parks, and Rabiner 1973). These are available as code libraries (Smith 1981, 2007a) and as interactive programs such as MATLAB. The FAUST (Functional Audio Stream) programming language by Yann Orlarey and colleagues at the GRAME center in Lyon, France, generates efficient C++ code for interactive real-time filters and other signal processing plug-ins from a high-level specification (GRAME 2017; Gaudrain and Orlarey 2007).

Interactive programs let users specify the design strategy and characteristics of a filter while hiding most of the algebraic and numerical manipulations

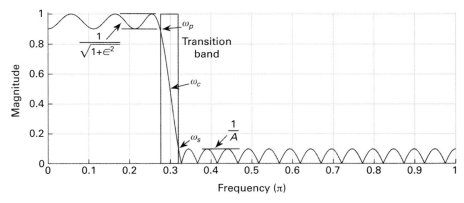

Figure 28.25 Example specifications for the passband, the stopband, and the transition bands of a lowpass filter.

required to implement it. Many of these systems let users test the simulated filter with audio signals.

The theory of filter design is a discipline in its own right, with various competing design strategies. Many engineering textbooks treat the theory of filter design in a rigorous and detailed manner; hence we recommend this literature to technically oriented readers. The texts by Rabiner and Gold (1975) and Hamming (1989), which we have cited numerous times, are classic sources. Smith (2007a) is an excellent reference with a focus on audio applications. Steiglitz (1996) and Cook (2007) are accessible treatments with a focus on audio and computer music.

FIR versus IIR Filters

We must remark briefly on the advantages and disadvantages of each kind of LTI filter. FIR filters are always stable. By contrast, IIR filters can be unstable unless care is taken in their design. FIR filters are simple to implement, but they are limited in how sharp their magnitude responses can be while avoiding excessive delays. For instance, to make an FIR filter with a very narrow transition band requires many coefficients. This requires many delays and multiplications, producing more latency in the output. With the use of feedback, however, IIR filters can have very sharp changes in their magnitude response with only a few delays and multiplications. The feedback, however, can result in instability.

Figure 28.26 shows a comparison of the magnitude and phase response of an FIR and an IIR filter designed using the same specifications. The FIR filter (gray) involves 306 delays; the IIR filter (black) has only 15 delays.

IIR filters can suffer from phase distortion and *ringing* (Preis 1982). Ringing means that transients tend to excite the filter, causing it to oscillate (ring) for some time. This can smear transients, blurring high frequencies such as cymbal crashes. Thus some engineers turn to linear phase FIR filters in critical applications. As its name indicates, a linear phase FIR filter shows no phase distortion around the cutoff or center frequency. However, linear phase filters also have disadvantages. As previously mentioned, they introduce latency: the entire signal is delayed when passing through the filter. Delaying all frequencies by the same amount preserves the waveshape as much as possible. However, the sharper the desired filter response, the longer the delay. Moreover, the impulse response of a linear phase filter is time-symmetric. The pre-impulse response is the mirror image of the postimpulse response (Gerzon 1990). This can introduce

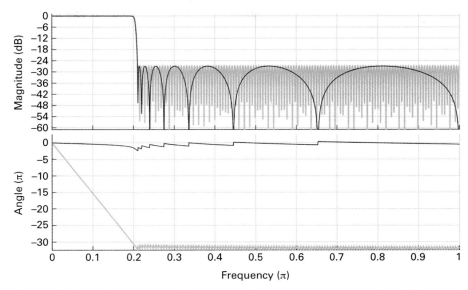

Figure 28.26 Comparison of the magnitude and phase response of an FIR (gray) and an IIR (black) filter designed to the same specifications.

audible pre-echoes that can make transients lose their punch, especially in low-frequency bass tones.

For live applications—in which latency cannot be tolerated—a *zero-latency minimum-phase filter* is preferable to a linear-phase filter. A minimum-phase filter imposes the smallest average phase delay. For this reason, minimum phase is sometimes referred to as *minimum delay* (Smith 2007a). A Butterworth-type filter is a minimum-phase filter.

Second-Order Sections

It is common practice to design complicated filters out of a network of first- and second-order filters, each of which is relatively stable and robust, rather than implementing a large and more delicate structure. See Rabiner and Gold (1975) and Dattorro (1997) for discussion.

A *second-order section* is an IIR structure that is particularly popular in digital audio systems (Shpak 1992). As a second-order IIR filter, it looks back two samples, to the past of its output y. The term *section* means that this filter can be combined with other of like kind to form a more complicated filter. It realizes a bandpass frequency response, so it is often used as a building block for parametric and graphic equalizers. When some of its coefficients are set to zero, it can also realize lowpass and highpass filters, hence its wide application.

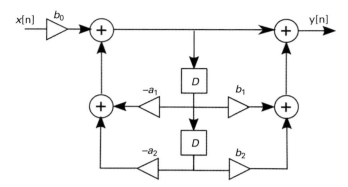

Figure 28.27   Second-order section, or biquad, filter.

The literature presents several forms of second-order sections. Here we present "the most general" form, after Rabiner and Gold (1975, 19–20): The equation is as follows:

$$y[n] = (b_0 \times x[n]) + (b_1 \times x[n-1]) + (b_2 \times x[n-2]) \\ - (a_1 \times y[n-1]) - (a_2 \times y[n-2])$$

Here the b coefficients scale the feedforward paths, and the a coefficients scale the feedback paths. Feedback paths usually contribute peaks to the response, and the feed-forward paths cause notches.

Another term for a second-order section is a *biquadratic* or *biquad* filter, referring to the two quadratic formulas in its equation (one for a and one for b). Figure 28.27 shows a circuit diagram corresponding to the equation just presented. Such a design is so common that the audio processing power of a DSP system is sometimes expressed in terms of the number of second-order sections that it can realize in real time (Moorer 1983a).

Subjective Perception of Filters

When we examine the subjective perception of filters, we are reminded of Gustav Fechner, the nineteenth-century pioneer of the science of *psychophysics*. Psychophysics is the study of relationships between physical stimuli and psychological sensations. One of his main insights was on the role of context in perception, that is, how the same effect is perceived differently in different contexts.

In his famous article "Why do equalisers sound different?" the British audio master Michael Gerzon (1990) pointed out how, in certain cases, tiny nonlinearities in phase (around 1°) and amplitude response (±0.1 dB) could produce audible coloration. Depending on context, ripples in amplitude and phase response can have subjective audible effects, causing obvious colorations. Yet in other situations, large deviations in amplitude or phase response cause no perceived coloration.

Gerzon discouraged the use of filters to compensate for defects in bad recordings:

Equalisation may improve the tonal accuracy in such cases but it can (and often does) increase the audible colouration. If this is right, we may be unable, ever, to 'fix it in the mix' properly, and this re-emphasises the importance of using the best and least-coloured sounding audio equipment at every stage of the audio recording chain. The best equaliser is no equaliser!

Of course, for the creative sound artist, filter coloration is a feature, not a bug! We relish the distinct color of a Moog 904A analog filter versus that of a Buchla 291 or a Krohn-Hite 3550. In the digital domain, we see models of vintage analog filters alongside innovations such as multifilters with independently adjustable parameters, real-time spectrum displays, and full automation of filter parameters.

29 *Convolution*

Curtis Roads with Bob L. T. Sturm

Time Domain versus Frequency Domain

The Operation of Convolution

Mathematical Definition of Convolution

Relationship of Convolution to Linear Time-Invariant Filtering

The Law of Convolution

Fast and Instant Convolution

Real-Time Convolution

Dynamic Convolution

Deconvolution

The Sine-Sweep Method of Measuring Impulse Response

Musical Significance of Convolution

Filtering as Convolution
Temporal Effects of Convolution
Modulation as Convolution
Convolution with Grains and Pulsars

Convolution is a fundamental operation in digital audio signal processing (Rabiner and Gold 1975; Dolson 1985; Oppenheim and Schafer 1975; Oppenheim and Willsky 1983; Steiglitz 1996). As implied by its origin in the French word *convoluer*, it *marries* two signals. Everyone is familiar with its effects, even those who have never heard of convolution. Convolution is often disguised under more familiar terms such as *filtering* or *reverberation*. However, explicit use of convolution is now common.

Convolution combines an input signal with another signal, usually an *impulse response* (IR). As discussed in the previous chapter, a general way to test any system is to measure its response to a brief impulse. In a digital system, the briefest possible signal lasts just one sample. This signal contains energy at all frequencies that can be represented at the given sampling frequency. A single-sample impulse is an approximation to the infinitely brief *unit impulse.*

One can measure the IR of a concert hall with another impulse: popping a large balloon, for example, and recording the result. (Today other methods of measuring the IR are preferred, as discussed further on.) The important point is that by convolving the hall's IR with any sound, we impose the sonic signature of the hall onto the sound.

The magical power of convolution means that the IR of any audio device (microphone, amplifier, loudspeaker, filter, effect, etc.) can be convolved with an arbitrary audio signal to make the signal take on the signature of the device.

Many companies sell convolution-based products. Because the algorithm for convolution is well known, the main value added by these products is a proprietary library of impulse responses, some of which have been recorded at exotic or exclusive locations at high cost. Many free IR libraries are also available for download. Applications such as Voxengo Impulse Modeler let one design one's own virtual hall and extract its IR.

Going even further, one can dispense with the notion of IR and convolve a given sound with any other sound. This is the domain of *cross-synthesis.* For instance, the convolution of two instrumental sounds may sound as if one instrument is "playing" the other (e.g., a chain of bells playing a gong). Cross-synthesis by convolution simultaneously transforms the time-space structure and spectral morphology of its inputs. Its effects range from subtle enhancements to destructive distortions that obliterate the identity of both inputs. Only a knowledgeable user can predict what the outcome of certain convolutions will be. Many convolutions that appear to be interesting musical ideas (such as, "How about convolving a clarinet with a speaking voice?") result in amorphous sound blobs. Thus a thorough exploration of the terrain is necessary before this technique can be applied systematically in composition. Refer to Roads (1997) for a description of specific musical applications of convolution.

Time Domain versus Frequency Domain

A fundamental distinction in digital signal processing is that of *time-domain representation* versus *frequency-domain representation* of a signal.

A direct method of visualizing sound waveforms is to draw them in the form of a graph of positive and negative variations in air pressure versus time. This is called a *time-domain* representation or *pressure graph.* Audio editing programs generally display pressure graphs, which plot the amplitude profile on a vertical scale versus time on a horizontal scale. One can zoom in and out to view the pressure graph at different levels of resolution. The waveform shown in figure 29.1a is a snapshot of a sound lasting around 50 ms.

A *frequency-domain* or *spectrum* representation shows the distribution of frequency energy in a sound. We can view a sound in the frequency domain after transforming it from the time domain to the frequency domain via *spectrum analysis.* Figure 29.1b shows a frequency domain representation of the waveform shown in Figure 29.1a, plotted on a decibel scale.

As chapters 37-39 show, there are many ways to measure the spectrum of a sound. One method, however, has a privileged tie to convolution. This is the *Discrete Fourier Transform* (DFT) as realized by the *Fast Fourier Transform* (FFT) algorithm (Smith 2007b; Braasch 2018). Thus, when we speak of the frequency domain in the context of convolution, we mean the

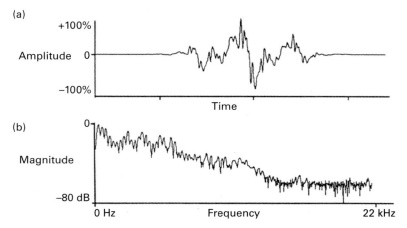

Figure 29.1   Time-domain versus frequency-domain representations of sound. (a) A time-domain waveform of a brief segment of sound lasting around 50 ms. This segment has been scaled by an envelope (or *window*) so that it fades in and fades out. (b) The frequency-domain spectrum of the sound in (a), showing the level or *magnitude* of each frequency from 0 Hz to the Nyquist frequency.

spectrum that is the result of an analysis using the FFT. The DFT assumes that any sound can be analyzed as a collection of sinusoidal waves where the starting phase of each sinusoid is derived from the analysis. In practical terms, the spectrum is represented as a pair of arrays in computer memory: one array contains the magnitude (or amplitude) of every analyzed frequency, whereas another array contains the starting phase for each sinusoidal component.

This representation makes possible the idea of *multiplying spectra,* by taking the arrays associated with one sound and multiplying them point by point with the arrays associated with another sound using complex arithmetic.

The Operation of Convolution

To understand convolution, let us look at the simplest case: convolution of a signal *a* with a unit impulse, which we call *unit*[*n*].

At time $n=0$, $unit[n]=1$, but for all other values of *n, unit*[*n*]=0. The convolution of *a*[*n*] with *unit*[*n*] can be denoted

$$output[n] = a[n] * unit[n] = a[n]$$

Here the asterisk (*) signifies convolution. As figure 29.2a shows, this results in a set of values for *output* that are the same as the original signal *a*[*n*]. Thus, convolution with the unit impulse is said to be an identity operation with respect to convolution, because any function convolved with *unit*[*n*] leaves that function unchanged.

Two other simple cases of convolution tell us enough to predict what will happen at the sample level with any convolution. If one scales the amplitude of *unit*[*n*] by a constant *c,* the operation can be written

$$output[n] = a[n] * (c \times unit[n])$$

The result is simply

$$output[n] = c \times a[n]$$

In other words, we obtain the identity of *a,* scaled by the constant *c,* as shown in figure 29.2b.

In the third case, we convolve signal *a* by a unit impulse that has been time-shifted by *t* samples. Now the impulse appears at sample $n-t$ instead of at $n=0$. This can be expressed

$$output[n] = a[n] * unit[n - t]$$

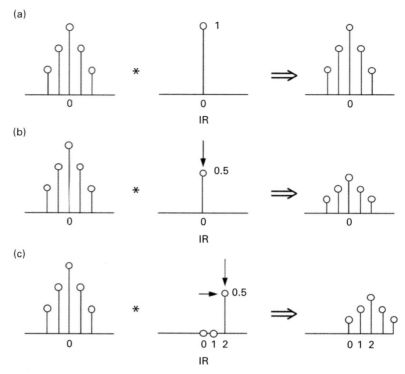

Figure 29.2   Prototypical examples of sample convolution. (a) Convolution of an input signal with the unit impulse is an identity operation. (b) Convolution with a scaled unit impulse of value 0.5 scales the input by 0.5. (c) Convolution with a delayed or time-shifted unit impulse time-shifts the input sequence correspondingly.

The result of this is

$$output[n] = a[n - t]$$

That is, *output* is identical to *a* except that it is time-shifted by the difference between *n* and *t*. Figure 29.2c shows a combination of scaling and time-shifting.

Putting together these three cases, we can view any sampled function as a sequence of scaled and delayed unit impulse functions. They explain the effect of convolution with any IR. For example, the convolution of any signal *a* with another signal *b* that contains two impulses spaced widely apart results in a repetition or echo of *a* starting at the second impulse in *b* (figure 29.3a).

When the impulses in *b* move closer together, the scaled repetitions of *b* start to overlap each other (figure 29.3b). This "time-smearing" is the beginning of reverberation. The IR of a reverberant concert hall can last several

(a)

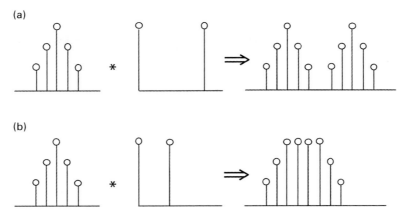

(b)

Figure 29.3 Time-domain effects of convolution. (a) Convolution with two impulses spaced widely apart produces an echo effect. (b) Convolution with two impulses close together produces a time-smearing effect.

seconds. For example, in a hall with a reverberation time of three seconds, sampled at 48 kHz, the IR consists of 144,000 samples.

Thus, to convolve an input sequence $a[n]$ with an arbitrary function $b[n]$, one places a copy of $b[n]$ at each point of $a[n]$, scaled by the value of $a[n]$ at that point (figure 29.4). The convolution of a and b is the sum of these scaled and delayed functions.

Mathematical Definition of Convolution

Here we switch to a more formal presentation. The convolution of two sequences $x[n]$ and $h[n]$, where n represents an index to an array of samples, is defined as follows, where the asterisk ($*$) is the convolution operator:

$$y[n] = (x * h)[n] = \sum_{m=-\infty}^{\infty} x[m]h[n-m]$$

for $-\infty < n < \infty$. An important point is that convolution is commutative. That is, we can swap x and h and the result does not change. Hence, x convolved with h is the same as h convolved with x.

Because real-world sequences are not infinite in length, we need another equation to describe them. Let us say x is of length N_x and h is of length N_h. Then the convolution of x and h is defined

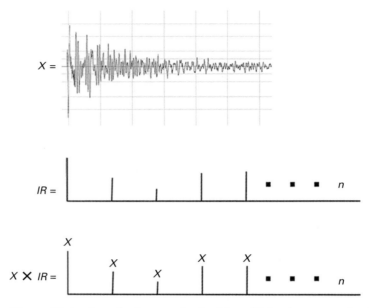

Figure 29.4   Sound x is convolved with an IR lasting n samples. For each sample in the IR, we replace it with a scaled and delayed copy of x.

$$y[n] = (x * h)[n] = \sum_{m=0}^{N_x - 1} x[m]h[n-m] = \sum_{m=0}^{N_h - 1} h[m]x[n-m]$$

for $0 \leq n \leq N_x + N_{h-1}$. Notice that the convolution of these two sequences produces a new sequence longer than both of them. Specifically for two sequences x and h, the convolution product length will be equal to length(x) + length(h) −1 sample.

Relationship of Convolution to Linear Time-Invariant Filtering

To filter is to convolve. Recall from chapter 28 the equation of a general length–N FIR filter:

$$y[n] = b_0\, x[n] + b_1\, x[n-1] + \cdots + b_{N-1}\, x[n-(N-1)]$$

If we define the sequence $b[n] = (b_0, b_1, \ldots, b_{\{N-1\}})$, then we can write this more simply as

$$y[n] = \sum_{m=0}^{N-1} b[m]x[n-m]$$

We now see this is just the convolution of the two sequences, $b[n]$ and $x[n]$. (Note that $b[n]$ and $b[m]$ are the same thing. Only the index into the series has changed in the convolution summation.) The coefficients in $b[n]$ are the multipliers on the taps of a feed-forward delay line or FIR filter. The sequence $b[n]$ is also equivalent to the impulse response of the filter, which has finite length N.

What about an IIR filter? Because an IIR filter has an infinite impulse response, this just means that $b[n]$ has infinite length. Hence, only the limit changes on the previous convolution sum:

$$y[n] = \sum_{m=0}^{\infty} b[m]x[n-m]$$

The convolution expressions above for FIR and IIR filters have two important properties. First, the convolution sum is linear. If our input is $c_1 x_1[n] + c_2 x_2[n]$, then its convolution with a sequence $h[n]$ is the sum of the scaled individual convolutions

$$(h * (c_1 x_1 + c_2 x_2))[n] = c_1(h * x_1)[n] + c_2(h * x_2)[n]$$

The second property is time-invariance. This means that it does not matter if we delay our input; the resulting convolution sum will be the same except for being shifted by the corresponding delay. This shows us that time-domain convolution is just *linear time-invariant* (LTI) filtering. In summary, convolving two signals means we are passing one through an LTI filter with an impulse response that is identical to the other signal.

The Law of Convolution

As we discussed in chapter 28, filtering can be viewed as a multiplication of two spectra in the frequency domain derived by Fourier analysis (see chapter 37). This results in a fundamental law of signal processing:

Convolution in the time domain is equivalent to multiplication in the frequency domain, and vice versa.

This law has profound implications. By virtue of the symmetry of the Fourier transform, multiplying two audio signals (i.e., performing *amplitude modulation* or *ring modulation*) convolves their spectra. Whenever we reshape the amplitude envelope of a sound (e.g., *windowing*), one is convolving the spectra of the new envelope and the original sound. This shows that every linear time-domain transformation entails a corresponding frequency-domain transformation, and vice versa.

Fast and Instant Convolution

Notice that the formula for the convolution sum involves many multiplications and additions. If both sequences are length N, then directly implementing the convolution sum requires something on the order of N^2 operations. For an IR of more than about 4,096 samples, direct or *time-domain convolution* is not practical for real-time use without recourse to a *graphics processing unit* (GPU) (Savioja, Välimäki, and Smith 2011). The reason is that the *central processing unit* (CPU) clock speed on a typical laptop has not increased greatly since 2012.

Fortunately, the law of convolution provides a more efficient solution. Because time-domain convolution is equivalent to frequency-domain multiplication, we can transform the two input sequences to the frequency domain via the FFT, compute their product, and transform that back to the time domain via the *Inverse Fast Fourier Transform* (IFFT). The FFT and the IFFT are explained in chapter 36. This multiplication in the frequency domain entails on the order of N operations.

To give an example, compare the direct convolution of a two-second sound and a two-second IR sampled at 48 kHz. This requires about $96,000^2$ or 9 billion operations. Fast convolution with the same two sounds requires less than 1.5 million operations, a speed-up by a factor of 6,100. Put another way, a fast convolution that takes one second to calculate on a given microprocessor would require more than 100 minutes to calculate via direct convolution.

Direct convolution is rarely used to implement narrow-band filters or reverberators, both of which have long impulse responses. (See the discussion of reverberation by convolution in chapter 32.) Many practical applications of convolution use a frequency-domain method called *block-transform* or *fast convolution* (Stockham 1966, 1969). Figure 29.5 depicts a simple scheme for fast convolution.

A special case of efficient convolution takes place when the IR consists of only of positive and negative unit impulses and zeros:

- When the IR contains a positive unit impulse, the sound to be convolved is added at that point.
- When the IR contains a negative unit impulse, the sound to be convolved is inverted in phase and added at that point.
- When the IR contains a zero value, nothing is done.

Because no multiplication is involved, this can be called *single-pulse* or "instant" convolution. This efficiency has been exploited in pitch-synchronous

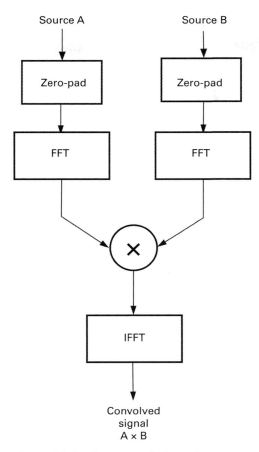

Figure 29.5 Fast convolution scheme.

granular synthesis (Cavaliere and Piccialli 1997) and in *reverberation with velvet noise* (chapter 33).

Real-Time Convolution

In real-time applications, a main goal is to minimize *latency* caused by processing delays. Latency is inevitable in digital systems that process incoming sound in *blocks* of samples, where a block can vary from 32 to 1,024 samples or more. These blocks are called the *input buffer size* in the preference settings of audio programs.

Various methods have been proposed for real-time convolution. The linearity of convolution enables it to be implemented in *sections*. That is, one can convolve a short section of the IR with a short section of the signal and then convolve another short section of the IR and so on. This produces equivalent results to convolution as if one had both sequences in their entirety. Refer to Rabiner and Gold (1975) and Kunt (1981) for an explanation of standard techniques for sectioned convolution.

William Gardner (1995) published a breakthrough paper on real-time convolution without input-output delay. Gardner's method applies the direct method of convolution (an FIR filter) to the first short block of, for example, 128 samples (about 1.3 ms at a 96 kHz sampling rate). It then schedules a sequence of short block FFT transforms that keep up with the incoming signal. As mentioned previously, GPUs can be programmed to realize convolution efficiently in real time (Savioja, Välimäki, and Smith 2011). For a review of fast convolution techniques, refer to Välimäki et al. (2012).

Brandtsegg, Saue, and Lazzarini (2018) confronted the problem of updating the IR in real time without interruption. This is important in varying the parameters of a convolving filter in a concert situation involving real-time cross-synthesis, for example. They provided two solutions that update the filter coefficients at audio rates.

Dynamic Convolution

Simple convolution uses a single "snapshot" IR in its operation. This works in modeling most acoustic spaces because reverberation is a linear effect. In particular, the response will be largely the same whether a soft or loud sound is played.

By contrast, certain effects are *nonlinear*; that is, they have amplitude-dependent thresholds. When the level crosses a given threshold, the device behaves differently. A classic example of a nonlinear processor is a compressor (see chapter 27). A compressor is an amplitude processor that reacts to changes in the level of the input signal. It varies its response according to these changes.

In order to model such systems, *dynamic convolution* (also called *nonlinear convolution*) techniques are needed (Kemp 2000). Dynamic convolution applies unique level-dependent impulse responses to every sample of audio. Dynamic convolution thus requires that there be an array of stored IRs to model every possible input level. In products based on dynamic convolution, these are measured from classic hardware devices.

Focusrite Liquid Channel pioneered this technology in 2004 by modeling forty classic compressors and preamplifiers, measured from devices manufactured by AMEK, API, dbx, Pultec, Fairchild, Millennia, Neve, Solid State Logic,

Trident, UREI, and others (Focusrite 2018). More recently, Acustica Audio offers a family of products based dynamic convolution.

Deconvolution

Just as we can multiply two spectra in the frequency domain, we can divide them as well. If we know the spectrum $H(f)$ of the signal $h[n]$, then we can multiply the convolution of $x[n]$ and $h[n]$, which is the spectrum $X(f)H(f)$ by the inverse of $H(f)$, or $1/H(f)$, to recover the spectrum $X(f)$ (figure 29.6). In the time domain, this is the process of *deconvolution*. The signal with the inverse spectrum $1/H(f)$ is also called the *matched filter* (Vorländer 2018).

Note that the division of frequency-domain spectra is an element-by-element division of a complex polynomial. That is, each complex frequency bin of $X(f)$ is divided by the corresponding complex bin of $H(f)$, to produce the resulting complex spectrum of the IR, which can then be turned into the IR by IFFT (Cabrera 2019).

Importantly, $X(f)H(f) = H(f)X(f)$. Thus convolving $x[n]$ with $h[n]$ is equal to convolving $h[n]$ with $x[n]$. However, $X(f)/H(f) \neq H(f)/X(f)$. For example, if $x[n]$ is a drum sound and $h[n]$ is a voice sound, when we

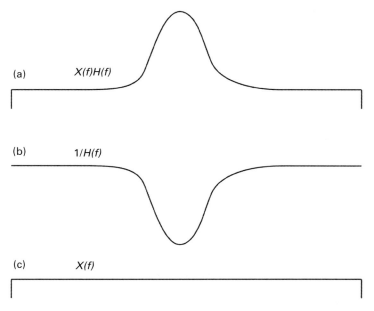

Figure 29.6 Deconvolution. At the top, the original convolved signal. In the center, the divisor. At the bottom, the deconvolved signal.

divide out the voice, we should get a drum, and vice versa. Thus deconvolving $x[n]$ with $h[n]$ is not equal to deconvolving $h[n]$ with $x[n]$. Second, $X(f)/H(f)$ is essentially the product of the spectra of $x[n]$ and the spectra $1/H(f)$ of a different sequence $h'[n]$. So, while the convolution of $x[n]$ and $h[n]$ produces a new signal with spectrum $X(f)H(f)$, to recover $x[n]$ we need to convolve $(x * h)[n]$ with the sequence $h'[n]$ that has spectrum $1/H(f)$, that is, $x[n] = (x * h * h')[n]$.

Just as convolution can be used to produce reverberation, deconvolution can be used to remove reverberation. A deconvolution algorithm divides out the IR of the acoustic environment (assuming that the IR is known).

Statistical estimation techniques are used for deconvolutions in which one is attempting to extract signals about which one has only approximate knowledge. For example, due to the particular nature of speech signals, two categories of deconvolution can achieve approximate separation of the excitation (glottal pulses) and the resonance (vocal tract formants) of vocal sounds. These are *autoregressive* and *homomorphic* deconvolution (Stockham, Cannon, and Ingebretsen 1975; Rabiner and Gold 1975). A method of homomorphic deconvolution is the *cepstrum* analysis technique, described in chapter 34.

The Sine-Sweep Method of Measuring Impulse Response

The traditional method of obtaining an IR in a room is to pop a large balloon or fire a starter pistol and record the result. This approach has disadvantages. First it is difficult to make an undistorted recording of a blast such as a starter pistol shot, due to the loud nature of the initial transient. A further issue is that pistol shots have a nonlinear frequency response.

Several improved methods of IR measurement have been developed; refer to Stan et al. (2002) for a comparative review. One method injects a one-second burst of Gaussian noise into the space (Braasch 2018). Today the most widely adopted approach is the *sine-sweep* method (figure 29.7). This method records a sine wave sweeping from low frequencies (~20 Hz) to the Nyquist frequency over a period of some fifteen seconds, with a segment of silence added at the end (Farina 2000, 2007; Müller and Massarani 2001).

The sine-sweep method has a better signal-to-noise ratio than other techniques (Välimäki et al. 2012). It separates out the nonlinear components of the measured response (such as those produced by the loudspeaker used to play the sweep, which has harmonic distortion) from the linear components of the acoustic space, considered as an undistorted system.

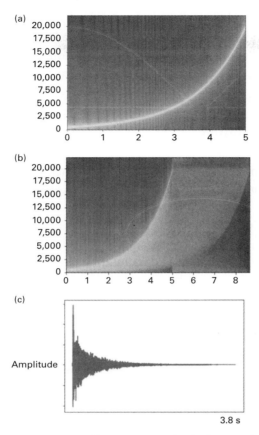

Figure 29.7 Sine-sweep method of measuring the impulse response. (a) Sonogram of a sine sweep plotted as a function of frequency versus time. The duration is 5 seconds. (b) Sonogram of a sine sweep in a reverberant hall. The duration is 8.8 seconds. (c) Time-domain plot of the impulse response of the hall after deconvolving the swept sine out of the signal. The duration is 3.8 seconds. Images courtesy Dr. Shashank Aswathanarayana.

The recording of the sine sweep in the space cannot be used directly as an IR. The recorded file contains all the echoes and reflections of the space stretched out over the length of the sine sweep. To make an IR, one needs to deconvolve the sine-sweep recording. This time-aligns all reflections present over the entire recorded sine sweep to the beginning of the file.

Deconvolution is realized by convolving the output of the measured system with an inverse filter to transform the initial sweep into a delayed impulse. The inverse filter is derived by reversing the swept sine and delaying it. Convolution always reinforces the commonality of two signals. The sweep and its inverse are exactly opposites, so spectrum multiplication nullifies the sweep. Time reversal also causes a sign inversion of the phase spectrum.

Thus the convolution of the two results in a signal with linear phase (corresponding to a delay) with squared magnitude. The magnitude spectrum of this signal is then divided (in the complex domain) by the square of the magnitude spectrum of the initial sine sweep to obtain the IR.

Musical Significance of Convolution

Many sonic transformations can be understood in terms of convolution, including filtering, temporal effects, and modulation, discussed in the next three sections.

Filtering as Convolution

Filtering is a good example of the multiplication of spectra, because we can implement any LTI filter by convolving an input signal with the impulse response of the desired filter. But convolution goes beyond simple filtering to cross-synthesis—filtering one sound by another. Let us call two sources *a* and *b* and their corresponding analyzed spectra *spectrum_a* and *spectrum_b*. If we multiply each point in *spectrum_a* with each corresponding point in *spectrum_b* and then resynthesize the resulting spectrum, we obtain a time-domain waveform that is the convolution of *a* and *b*. For example, the convolution of two saxophone tones, each with a smooth attack, mixes their pitches, sounding like the two tones are being played simultaneously. Unlike simple mixing, however, the filtering effect in convolution accentuates metallic resonances that are common in both tones. Another effect, which is subtle in this case but not in others, is time smearing, discussed next.

Temporal Effects of Convolution

Convolution also induces time-domain effects such as echo, time-smearing, and reverberation (Dolson and Boulanger 1985; Roads 1993a). These effects may be subtle or obvious, depending on the nature of the signals being convolved.

A unit impulse in one of the inputs to the convolution results in a copy of the other signal. Thus if we convolve any sound with an IR consisting of two unit impulses spaced 500 ms apart, the result is a clear echo of the first signal.

The IR of a room may have many impulses, corresponding to reflections from various surfaces of the room—its echo pattern. When such an IR is convolved with an arbitrary sound, the result is as if that sound had been played in that room, because it has been mapped into the room's echo pattern.

If the peaks in the IR are closely spaced, however, the repetitions are time-smeared (refer to figure 29.2b). Time-smearing smooths out sharp transients and blurs the precise onset time of events. Figure 29.8 shows how the convolution of a cowbell sound with itself results in a time-smeared version.

The combination of time-smearing and echo explains why noise signals, which contain thousands of sharp peaks, result in reverberation effects when convolved. If the amplitude envelope of a noise signal has a sharp attack and an exponential decay, the result of convolution will be a kind of naturalistic reverberation envelope. To color this reverberation, one can filter the noise before or after convolving it. If the noise has a slow logarithmic decay, however, the second sound will appear to be suspended in time before the decay.

Modulation as Convolution

Ring modulation calls for multiplication of bipolar time-domain waveforms. The law of convolution states that multiplication of two waveforms convolves

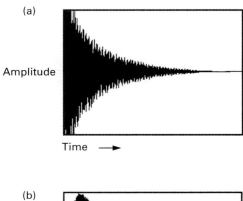

(a)

Amplitude

Time ⟶

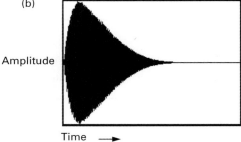

(b)

Amplitude

Time ⟶

Figure 29.8 Example of time-smearing. (a) Original source, a cowbell strike with a sharp attack. (b) Result of convolution of the cowbell with itself. Notice the time-smearing in the attack.

their spectra. Convolution accounts for the sidebands that result from these modulations. Consider the examples shown in figure 29.2 and imagine that instead of impulses in the time domain, the convolution is working on lines in the frequency domain. The same rules apply—with the important difference that the arithmetic of *complex numbers* applies. The FFT, for example, generates a complex number for each spectrum component.

Figure 29.9 is a graphical depiction of the spectrum convolution that occurs in ring modulation. Figure 29.9a shows the spectrum emitted by an FFT for a single sinusoid at 100 Hz. Figure 29.9b shows a sinusoid at 1 kHz. Figure 29.9c depicts their convolution. The two pulses at −100 and +100 are delayed and scaled to the region around 1 kHz and −1 kHz. The frequencies of 900 and 1.1 kHz represent the sum and difference frequencies of the two input signals, which is typical of ring modulation.

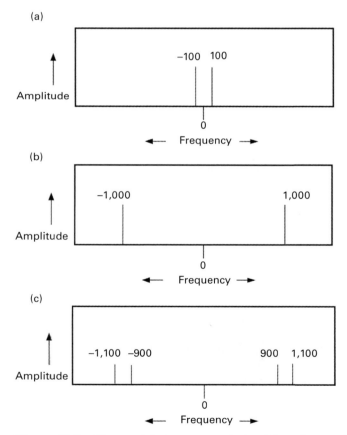

Figure 29.9   Ring modulation as convolution. These images show the representation of spectra inside the FFT, where a symmetrical representation applies. (a) Sinusoid at 100 Hz. (b) Sinusoid at 1 KHz. (c) Convolution of (a) and (b).

Convolution with Grains and Pulsars

A unique class of sound transformations involves convolutions of sounds with clouds of sonic grains. In this application the grains are not heard on their own; rather, they can be thought of as the *virtual impulse response* of an unusual filter or synthetic space (Roads 1992).

The results of convolution with grains vary greatly, depending on the properties of the granular cloud and the input signal. For a sharp-attacked input signal, convolution with a sparse cloud containing a few dozen short grains contributes a statistical distribution of echoes of the input sound (figure 29.10). The denser the cloud, the more the echoes fuse into an irregular reverberation effect. Longer grains accentuate time-smearing and round off sharp attacks. When the input sound has a smooth attack—as in a legato

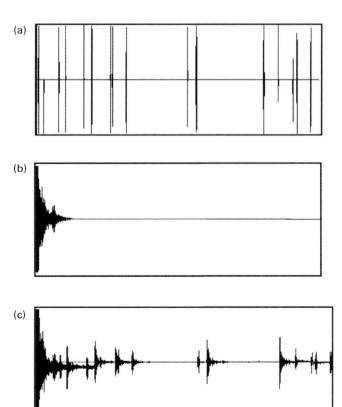

Figure 29.10   Convolution with grains. (a) Sparse cloud of brief grains lasting 0.5 ms each. (b) Tambourine hit. (c) Convolution of (a) and (b) results in multiple tambourine hits, corresponding to the temporal pattern of the cloud. Notice the momentary shift to negative energy caused by the second grain in (a).

saxophone tone—the result is like a time-varying filtering effect on the tone, which depends on the spectrum of the waveform within the grains. Refer to Roads (1993a, 1997) for more details on this technique.

Another class of synthesized sounds arises out of convolution between sampled sounds and trains of variable-waveform impulses called *pulsars* (Roads 2001a, 2001b). The pulsar trains fall into the continuum between the infrasonic and audio frequencies, leading to a range of rhythmic as well as timbral effects. Refer to chapter 21 for more details on this technique.

30   *Time Delay Effects*

Time-delay effects are fundamental to electronic music. The earliest time delay effects were made with tape recorders. An example is the early electronic music of Pauline Oliveros. She deployed tape recorders patched to one another in a feedback loop. The distance between the record head and playback head on a tape recorder produced a delay. If this output signal was routed back to the input it produced an infinitely repeating *tape echo feedback*, a signature sound of electronic music.

The hypnotic effect of repeating echoes has a profound impact on human perception, from the natural echoes of canyons to myriad examples of echo in pop and electronic music. Delay-based effects called *flanging* and *phasing* produce the sound of a comb filter sweeping through the spectrum. Chorus effects turn one voice into a simulation of many.

A *digital delay line* (DDL) takes in a stream of input samples and stores them in its memory for a brief period before sending them out again. Mixing a delayed sound with the original undelayed signal can produce a variety of musical effects. Indeed, DDLs are fundamental components of audio signal processing, in which they are used to implement effects such as filtering, reverberation, and pitch shifting or to model wave propagation in physical models of musical instruments (chapter 18).

Let us distinguish between *fixed* and *variable* delay effects. In a fixed delay unit, the delay time does not change while sound is passed through it. In a variable delay unit, the delay time is constantly changing; this is implemented by varying the delay *tap points* at some control rate. We address the topic of fractional delays along the way.

Fixed Time Delay Effects

A DDL takes an input signal and delays it for one or more sample periods

Figure 30.1 depicts a simple digital delay line circuit. Exactly the same circuit could also describe a simple lowpass filter. The only difference between them is the delay time involved. For a simple lowpass filter, the delay can be as short as one sample, so the circuit has the effect of averaging successive samples. For a comb filter the effective delay times are around 0.1 to 10 ms. For a delay or echo effect, the delay times are greater than 10 ms.

Implementation of a Delay Line

A data structure called a *circular queue* is an efficient means of implementing a delay line (figure 30.2). Such a queue is simply a list of sequential memory

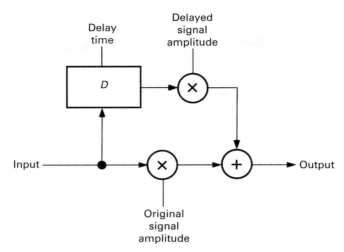

Figure 30.1 Circuit of a digital delay line. Notice the similarity between this structure and the filter structures in figure 28.6.

locations containing audio samples. At every sample period the delay program reads the oldest sample, and replaces it by writing a new incoming sample at the same location. The read/write pointer then goes on to the next position in the queue, which now contains the oldest sample. When the pointer reaches the end of the queue it wraps around (skips) to the first location in the queue—hence the term *circular*.

So far, we have described a delay with a fixed duration proportional to the length of the queue. This delay has one read pointer—*delay tap* in the parlance of signal processing—and the tap always precedes a write into the same location. By allowing the read pointer to tap any point in the queue, we can implement delays that are shorter than the length of the queue, including delays that change over time. These possibilities lead to the variable time delay effects described further on.

Logically, a *multitap delay line* has more than one tap. Figure 30.3 depicts a multitap delay line implemented as a circular queue. At each sample period, a new sample is written into the queue at the position marked *N*. Simultaneously, two samples are read out from the positions marked *Tap*1 (a three-sample delay) and *Tap*2 (a one-sample delay). Then all the pointers increment to the next position to prepare for the next sample period.

Fixed Delay Effects

Fixed audio delays can be grouped into three time spans, corresponding to different perceptual effects they create:

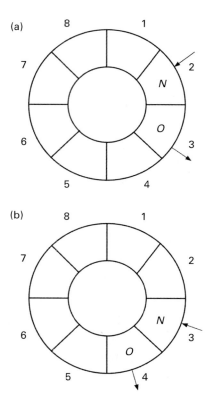

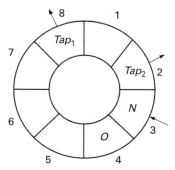

Figure 30.2   Operation of a circular queue to implement a delay line. N is the newest sample. The arrow shows that it is written to the queue. O is the oldest sample. The arrow shows that it is read from the queue. (a) "Before" shows samples in a circular queue at time t. (b) "After" shows samples in the queue at time $t+1$, indicating that the space held by the oldest sample at time t has been read out and replaced by a new incoming sample.

Figure 30.3   A two-tap delay line implemented as a circular queue. The two read taps, *Tap*1 and *Tap*2, circulate around the queue along with pointers O (old) and N (new). Incoming samples are written into the position occupied by N at each sample period.

- Short (less than about 10 ms)
- Medium (about 10 to 50 ms)
- Long (greater than about 50 ms)

Short delays are perceptible primarily in terms of the frequency-domain anomalies that they introduce. For example, a delay of one to several samples, mixed with the original signal, is equivalent to an FIR lowpass filter. When the delay extends over the range [0.1 ms, 10 ms], comb filter effects appear (chapter 28).

Medium delays are used to magnify signals from a perceptual standpoint. Mixing an original sound with one or more delayed versions is extensively used in popular music to magnify vocal, drum, and synthesizer tracks. A medium delay creates an ambience around the signal, giving an illusion of increased loudness without a corresponding increase in measured amplitude. (Note that loudness is a percept whereas amplitude is a physical measurement.) A delay between 15 and 50 ms creates a *doubling* effect, as though more than one person is singing. The doubling effect can be enhanced by applying subtle time-varying pitch shifts and delays to the signal before mixing it with the original.

Long delays (greater than about 50 ms) create discrete echoes—sounds heard as repetitions of the original sound. In nature, echoes occur when sound waves travel away from their source, bounce off a reflective surface, and hit listeners late enough that they hear the reflected sound as a discrete repetition. Because sound travels at about 1,100 feet (344 meters) per second in air at 20° centigrade, a delay of 1 ms corresponds to a total sound path from the source to the listener of about 1 foot (0.3 meters). To create a discrete echo requires a time delay of at least 50 ms. This implies a distance of at least 25 feet (8 meters) from the reflective surface, or about 50 feet (16 meters) for the total distance from the source to the reflective surface to the listener (figure 30.4).

Repeating Echoes

A repeating echo entails a feedback loop in the circuit, as shown in figure 30.5. If we inject a single impulse into this circuit and the feedback amplitude is less than 1.0, we will hear a series of repeating echoes of the impulse with an exponential decay in amplitude. If the feedback amplitude is greater than 1.0, we will hear an exponentially increasing echo that can quickly overload with distortion.

The circuit shown in figure 30.5 is a recursive (feedback) filter. By means of clever filter design, it is possible to shape the pattern of repeating echoes and spatialize them in creative ways. Putnam (2015) proposed a method predicated on complex-valued signals to produce truncated *echo shapes*

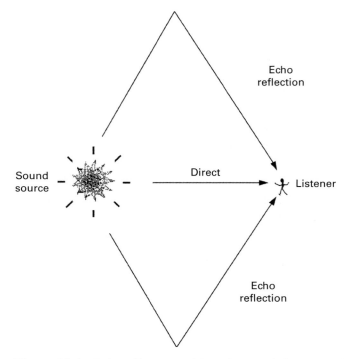

Figure 30.4   Echo effect caused by mixture of direct sound with reflected sound.

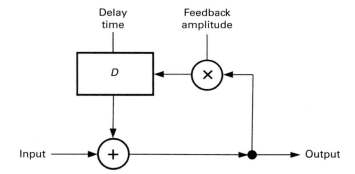

Figure 30.5   A feedback circuit for repeating echoes.

shown in figure 30.6, among other patterns. They simply stop after a certain number of echoes, in the manner of a multitap delay line.

Delays and Sound Localization

Localization refers to the ability of the ear to detect the location from which a sound emanates. Delays are one type of localization cue in a multichannel sound system. To give an example, if a sound is sent at equal amplitude to

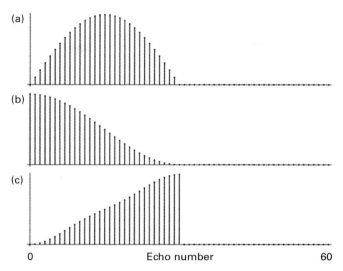

(a)

(b)

(c)

0   Echo number   60

Figure 30.6   Impulse responses of filters with *echo shaping*, in which the repetition is suddenly truncated after a stipulated number of echoes (after Putnam 2015). Amplitude is the vertical axis and time (as echo number) is the horizontal axis. (a) Cosine IR. (b) Cosine decay. (c) Approximation of a linear swell.

two loudspeakers and the listener sits in the middle of the listening area, the *sound image* concentrates in the center of the listening stage. If a short (~0.2 to 10 ms) time delay is applied to the sound emanating from the right loudspeaker, the apparent source of the sound shifts to the left speaker (Blauert 1983). This shows that our ears use delay as a cue to localization.

An acoustic wave reflected by multiple surfaces of a room reaches the listener after multiple delays, each delay corresponding to the length of its path. This delay pattern or *impulse response* (chapter 29) constitutes the room's sonic signature. Thus a specific pattern of delays applied to a sound can conjure the illusion of that sound emanating from a specific space.

Variable Time Delay Effects

Variable time delay effects result from delay lines whose delay times vary as signals pass through them. Another way to describe this technique is *delay modulation.* Delay modulation is central to vibrato, chorus and flanger effects, Doppler shift, and rotating speaker emulation (Dattorro 1997b).

The most basic effect with this method is vibrato, in which the signal being read from the delay line is not mixed with the input signal. Flanging and phasing (or *phase shifting*) first became common in popular music in the 1960s and 1970s. The techniques are similar but offer different sonic effects. Both are caused by mixing the original input signal with a delayed copy of itself.

Flanging

The sweeping sound of electronic flanging derives from a natural acoustic phenomenon that occurs whenever a wideband noise is heard in a mixture of direct and delayed sound. Bilsen and Ritsma (1969) give a history of the effect, beginning with its discovery by Christian Huygens in 1693. The guitarist and recording innovator Les Paul was the first to use flanging as a sound effect in the recording studio. His 1945 flanging system employed two disk recorders, one with a variable speed control (Bode 1984). Flanging was achieved in recording studios with two analog tape recorders and a mixing console. The tape recorders were fed an identical signal. The engineer monitored their combined tape output, while putting occasional pressure on the flange (or rim) of one of the reels to slow it down (figure 30.7), thus delaying it. The use of two recorders was necessary in order to synchronize the overall delay introduced by monitoring from the playback head of the flanging recorder. At a 38 cm/s tape speed, the distance between the record head and the playback head on a

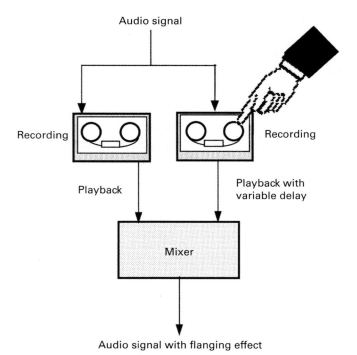

Figure 30.7   Tape flanging using two analog tape recorders. The playback speed of the second tape recorder varies as an operator applies finger pressure to the flange of the reel.

typical recorder introduces a fixed delay of about 35 ms. Thus one could also substitute a fixed delay line for the left tape recorder shown in figure 30.7.

The general principle of flanging is simply:

flanging = *signal* + *delayed signal*

where the delay time is constantly varying.

Electronic flanging uses a continuously varying delay line to achieve the same effect (Factor and Katz 1972). In place of manual pressure on a tape reel, the delay time of an electronic flanger is varied by a low-frequency oscillator (usually emitting a sine or triangle wave) operating in the range of about 0.1 to 20 Hz.

Flanging could be called a *swept comb filter effect*. In flanging, several peaks and nulls sweep up and down the spectrum. (See figure 14.17 for a comb filter spectrum.) Filter peaks are located at frequencies that are integral multiples of $1/D$, where D is the delay time. The depth of flanging is maximum if the amplitudes of the original signal and the delayed version are equal.

The structure described so far is equivalent to a feed-forward or FIR comb filter with a time-varying delay. In practice, most modern implementations of flanging use an IIR or recursive feedback comb structure with time-varying delay, as shown in figure 30.8. Dutilleux et al. (2011a) gives an example of a

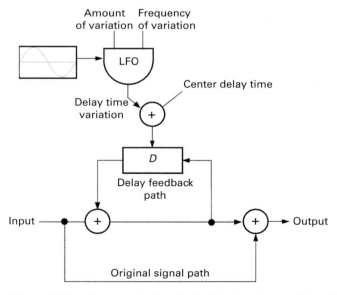

Figure 30.8 Flanger circuit with feedback, mixing a delayed signal with an original signal. A low-frequency oscillator (LFO) supplies the variation in the delay time around a *center* delay time. This circuit could be made more sophisticated by inserting multipliers on the delay feedback path and the original signal path, so that one could adjust the ratio between the two signals or invert the phase of the feedback.

flanger in the MATLAB language. Smith (2010) presents a waveguide interpretation of flanging.

Fractional Delays

A fixed delay unit takes an individual sample as the smallest possible unit
of delay. For a system operating at 48 kHz, the shortest delay period is 20.8
µsec. In a time-varying or *modulated delay line,* we want continuous delay
times in order to avoid signal discontinuities when the delay time is swept or
modulated. Delay-line interpolation is used when delaying a signal by some
number of samples expressible as a whole plus a fractional part of a sample.
The problem is closely related to that of interpolating oscillators (chapter 6)
and falls under the category of *variable-rate sample conversion* (Mitra 2006).

For a delay by M samples plus a fraction of the sample interval $0 < frac < 1$
the problem can be seen as:

$$y(n) = x(n - [M + frac])$$

where *y(n)* is the output signal, *x(n)* is the input signal, M is the delay time
in samples, and *frac* is the amount of fractional delay.

When the delay time is modulated, the relative distance between the waveform reading pointer and the waveform writing pointer is varied sample by
sample. In order to allow for fractional lengths and click-free modulation,
interpolation has to be applied at the waveform reading point (Rocchesso
2000; Smith 2010).

Dattorro (1997b), Rocchesso (2000), and Smith (2010) proposed filter
structures that could implement various fractional delay effects. Dattorro
showed the negative effects of linear interpolation (distortion and loss of high
frequencies) and recommended polynomial interpolation or allpass interpolation in its place. Refer to Lazzarini (2017) for fractional delay code in Csound
and FAUST.

Phasing

Phasing is similar in effect to flanging, but the churning sound produced by
the sweeping comb filter is usually not as pronounced. In phasing, a spectrally rich signal is typically sent through a series of allpass filters (Hartman
1978; Beigel 1979; Smith 1984). The allpass filters have a flat frequency
response (i.e., they do not attenuate any frequencies), but they shift the phase
of the original signal. A low-frequency oscillator can be used to sweep the
amount of phase shift introduced by each allpass filter. The outputs of the
filters are mixed at unity gain with the original signal.

What is the difference between flanging and phasing? Flanging results in complete peaks and nulls in the spectrum, and these are spaced at uniform intervals in frequency. By contrast, the number of peaks and notches in the response of the phase shifter corresponds to the number of filter stages in it. The spacing, depth, and width of the notches can be varied.

Phasing leads to a variety of sonic effects. Chamberlin (1985) gives an example of four allpass filters in series with the same turnover frequency and a broad transition width. A 1 kHz sine tone is fed into the filters. If the turnover frequency is swept from 10 to 100 Hz, the tone undergoes a constantly increasing phase shift. The effect of this is to lower momentarily the frequency of the sine wave. If the turnover sweep is reversed, the sine tone will momentarily shift up in frequency. If the sine wave is replaced by a signal with many harmonics, the temporary frequency shift causes an audible "ripple" through the harmonics as the turnover frequency changes. Smith (2010) presents a waveguide interpretation of phasing.

Chorus Effects

The quest for chorus effects has long fascinated musicians and musical engineers. Given an instrument with one voice (which can be any electronic timbre), is there a way to process this signal so that it sounds as if multiple voices are singing the same thing? Such an effect requires that there be small differences between the various voices of the simulated ensemble, including slight delays, alterations of fundamental frequency (resulting in beating effects), and asynchronous vibrato. There is no single algorithm for chorus effect; various implementations use different means to achieve it.

Note that here we put *harmonizer effects* into a separate category. A harmonizer creates "ghost voices" from the input signal that are pitch-shifted to specific intervals (see chapter 31).

Efforts to build chorus effect generators date back at least as early as the 1940s, when Hanert constructed electromechanical delay lines for electronic music (Hanert 1944, 1945, 1946). These were manufactured in Hammond organs to achieve a *choral tone effect* (Bode 1984). By the 1950s, W. C. Wayne Jr. had constructed a purely electronic *choral tone modulator* for the Baldwin electric organ (Wayne 1961).

In digital systems, one type of chorus effect can be realized by sending a sound through a multitap delay line, in which the time delays are constantly varying over a narrow range. This variation causes detuning and time-varying doubling effects. This is equivalent to putting the signal through a bank of parallel flangers, although the delays in a flanger tend to be shorter than those used for a chorus effect.

These types of techniques can be enriched by using negative feedback (routing back a phase-reversed version of the delayed sound), as in flanging. This means phase reversing the feedback path of the flanger shown in figure 30.6. Negative, rather than positive, feedback minimizes the risk of resonances and system overload.

Another chorus effect technique splits the input signal into several octave-wide bands and applies a separate *spectrum* or *frequency shifter* to each band. The frequency shifter can be thought of as adding a constant to the frequency of every component in the spectrum. With a frequency shift of 10 Hz, 220 Hz becomes 230 Hz, 440 Hz becomes 450 Hz, 880 Hz becomes 890 Hz, and so on. Clearly, this frequency shifter destroys harmonic relationships among the components. The amount of frequency shifting varies randomly over a narrow range. Following the frequency shifter is a time-varying delay line. According to Chamberlin (1985), this type of design is best for simulating the effect of large ensembles. Using several allpass filters in parallel, a type of chorus effect can be achieved by driving the filter turnover frequencies with low-frequency quasirandom signals (Chamberlin 1985). Smith (2010) presents a waveguide interpretation of chorus effect.

Doppler Shift, Vibrato, and Rotary Loudspeaker Effect

Doppler shift is the primary perceptual cue to the radial velocity of sound. It was first described by the Austrian physicist Christian Doppler (1842). The first simulations of Doppler shift to computer music were carried out by John Chowning (1971).

Doppler shift, vibrato, and a rotating speaker or Leslie effect can be implemented with a modulated delay line (Dattorro 1997b; Dutilleux et al. 2011a). Smith (2010) presents a waveguide interpretation. Refer to chapter 32 for more on the Doppler effects and moving sounds in space. Current rotating loudspeaker effects played back on stereo headphones or two loudspeakers are by necessity simplified. They do not compare with the actual effect heard in a physical room, which is an immersive 360° spatial experience. Another generation of research and development is needed to achieve greater realism.

31 *Pitch-Time Changing*

"Duration and frequency alteration," as it was called by Marlen (1966), has a long history. This chapter examines the difference between simple pitch shifting and pitch-time changing. Pitch-time changing can be accomplished using a number of different methods, and we look briefly at each one in turn.

Pitch Shifting versus Pitch-Time Changing

If we change the rotation speed of a vinyl record player, for example, from 78 RPM to 33 RPM, we hear a drastic downward shift in pitch and a lengthening of the duration of the track. The same thing happens if we slow down the playback speed on an analog tape recorder. In these cases, pitch and duration both change. This effect is called *varispeed, speed change,* or *simple pitch shifting.* Varispeed lets users control playback speed with a knob or graphical envelope, so that the speed and pitch can be changed continuously up and down. Varispeed is a staple of electronic music practice.

In contrast to simple pitch shifting, *pitch-time changing* separates pitch and time by means of a pair of related techniques. Pitch-time changing combines *time stretching/shrinking* (also called *time warping*) with *pitch shifting.* In pitch-time changing the duration of a sound can be altered while the pitch remains constant. In effect, we change the *time base* (or *time support*) of a sound. Alternatively, we can keep the duration constant while transposing the pitch.

Applications of pitch-time changing are many: fitting audio cues to video clips, fitting audio clips to a tempo grid (as in Ableton Live's Warp mode), slowing down recordings for musical transcription or practicing, and creative pitch-time effects for sound design and composition.

Pitch editors (also mentioned in chapter 46) combine pitch-time changing with sophisticated pitch-detection algorithms (see chapter 34). These include correcting the pitch of a vocalist (the auto-tune effect), creating harmonies of a given melody, altering portamento/vibrato patterns, manipulating vocal formants (e.g., male to female), and altering melodies and chords (figure 31.1).

The most effective pitch-time changing happens when it is applied in a selective, context-sensitive manner. In order to preserve the identity of the original sound, it is important to preserve the fine structure of attacks and other transients while processing only the steady-state part of the signal. In stretching speech, for example, intelligibility and naturalness can be enhanced by stretching vowels more than consonants. Certain products attempt to do exactly that: performing "intelligent" pitch-time changing by preserving plosive and percussion hits while time-varying the intoned material.

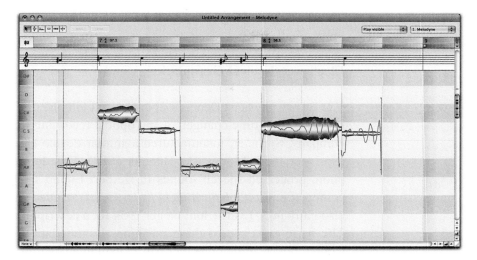

Figure 31.1   Screenshot of the Melodyne pitch editor by Celemony. Musical notes are indicated in a piano-roll style in the left column. The top row displays music notation. The center portion shows note blobs. Superimposed on the blobs are pitch drift lines showing portamento, vibrato, and other pitch deviations.

Time-Domain and Spectrum-Based Methods

How does pitch-time changing work? Techniques for pitch-time changing fall into two broad categories. The first category are *time-domain techniques* that operate directly on the audio waveform. This category comprises granular and harmonizer algorithms. The second category could be broadly character- ized as *spectrum-based methods*. These include such diverse techniques as the phase vocoder, wavelet methods, atomic decomposition, and linear predictive coding. These methods all analyze the spectrum of the sound as a prelude to manipulating it. The rest of this chapter synopsizes these techniques. To avoid repetition of descriptions in other parts of the book, the presentation of each method here is brief.

Pitch-Time Changing by Granulation

Granulation segments an audio waveform into short-duration units called *grains*. The grains can be segments cut at regularly spaced successive inter- vals along the time line, or they can be extracted from overlapping intervals and enveloped so that their sum reconstitutes the original waveform. In time granulation, the duration of each grain can vary from as short as 1 ms to as long as 200 ms or more. Chapter 13 describes granular representations in more detail.

Electromechanical Granulation

The British physicist Dennis Gabor (1946) built one of the earliest electrome-chanical pitch-time changers using optical recording technology. A German company, Springer, manufactured a similar device based on magnetic tape (Springer 1955; Morawaska-Büngler 1988). This device, called the Tempo-phon, processed speech sounds in Herbert Eimert's 1963 electronic music composition *Epitaph für Aikichi Kuboyama* (recorded on Wergo 60014). (See also Fairbanks, Everitt, and Jaeger 1954 for a description of a similar device.) The basic principle of these machines is granulation of recorded sounds. Contemporary digital methods can be explained by reference to the operation of these early tools.

The basic principle of time-base manipulation can be explained by analogy to cinematography. Everyone is familiar with *time-lapse photography* and *slow-motion* effects. In time-lapse photography, we might take a single shot every hour. If the images are played back at a rate of 24 frames per second, an entire day passes by in one second. By contrast, for a slow-motion effect, we need to take more shots per second than the playback frame rate. If the frame rate is 24 frames per second but we take 48 frames per second, when it is played back at 24 frames per second, one second of images is elongated into two seconds in playback.

In an electromechanical pitch-time changer, a rotating head (the sampling head) spins across a recording (on film or tape) of a sound. The sampling head spins in the same direction that the tape is moving. Because the head comes in contact with the tape for only a short period, the effect is that of taking an audio snapshot or sampling the sound on the tape at regular inter-vals. Each of these sampled segments is a grain of sound.

The grains were reassembled into a continuous stream on another recorder. When this second recording was played back, the result was a more-or-less continuous signal with a different time base. For example, shrinking the duration of the original signal was achieved by slowing down the rotation speed of the sampling head. This meant that the resampled recording contained a sequence of grains that had formerly been separated (figure 31.2a). For time expansion, the rotating head spun quickly, sam-pling multiple copies (clones) of the original signal. When these samples were played back as a continuous signal, the effect of the multiple copies was to stretch out the duration of the resampled version (figure 31.2b). The local frequency content of the original signal is preserved in the resampled version.

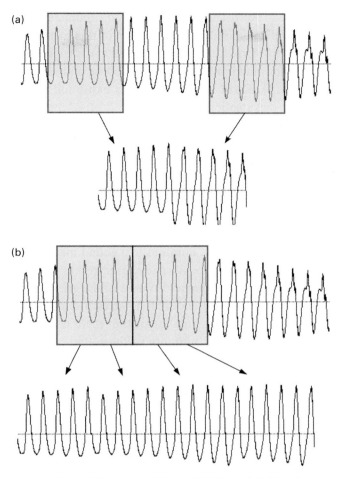

Figure 31.2   Time granulation. (a) Time shrinking by extracting separated grains and combining them into a shorter waveform. (b) Time expansion by cloning two copies of each grain. In both cases the local frequency content of the signal is preserved.

To effect a change in pitch without changing the duration of a sound, one need only to change the playback rate of the original and use the time-scale modification just described to adjust its duration. For example, to shift the pitch up an octave, play back the original at double speed and use time granulation to double the duration of the resampled version. This, in effect, restores the duration to the original length.

Digital Time-Granulation

Pioneering research at the University of Illinois Experimental Music Studio led to an early digital implementation of pitch-time granulation (Otis, Grossman, and Cuomo 1968). This implementation simulated the effect of rotating-head sampling; it also pointed out the flaws of this method in its most basic form. The main problem is that the waveforms at the beginning and end of a sampled grain do not match in level with preceding and successive resampled grains (figure 31.3). Early implementations exhibited a periodic clicking sound caused by these splicing transients.

Lee (1972) developed the Lexicon Varispeech system as a digital time stretcher and shrinker interfaced with an analog cassette recorder. Lee's design featured an electronic circuit for level matching at splice points to reduce the clicking sound. Jones and Parks (1988) showed how a more smooth reconstruction of the signal could be achieved by using smooth grain envelopes that overlap slightly, creating a seamless crossfade between grains.

Figure 31.4 illustrates the basic principles of granular time stretching and shrinking. Doubling the duration of a sound means that each grain is cloned into two (c). To halve the duration, every other grain is deleted before playback (d). The local frequency content of the grains is preserved, whereas the time scale is altered by cloning (to stretch duration) or deleting (to shrink duration) grains. In an actual algorithm there would be overlap between the grains to preserve the continuity of the sound.

To shift the pitch of a sound up an octave but not change its duration, the playback sampling rate is doubled, and every grain is cloned to restore the duration to the original. Notice that in (e) we see the waveform after it has been pitch-shifted up an octave, which halves its duration. To restore the original duration, we granulate it (f) and clone the grains to double its duration (g).

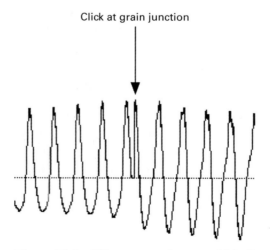

Figure 31.3   When two grains are arbitrarily spliced, the end of one grain may not match the beginning of the next grain. This can cause a transient (a click) at the splice point.

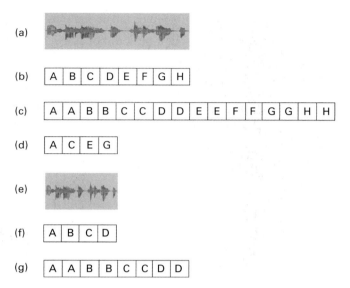

Figure 31.4   Granular time stretching and shrinking. (a) Original speech waveform. (b) Waveform in (a) cut into grain segments A through H. (c) Time stretching by a factor of two repeats every grain in (b). (d) Time shrinking throws away every other grain in (b). (e) Waveform (a) pitch-shifted up by an octave. (f) Granulation of (e). (g) Time stretching by a factor of two restores the original duration of the pitch-shifted speech. Note that in practice the waveform is not usually cut with a rectangular envelope as shown here but rather with a smooth bell-shaped envelope.

To shift the pitch down an octave but not change the duration, the playback sampling rate is halved, and every other grain is deleted to restore the duration to the original.

So far, we have described operations that double or halve pitch or time, but these operations are not limited to products of two. The frequency and time scale can be altered by arbitrary ratios by sample-rate changing with grain cloning or deleting in corresponding ratios.

Formant-Corrected Pitch Shifting

When a sound is pitch-shifted by changing the sampling rate (re-sampling), as previously discussed, its spectral envelope is also shifted. In sounds with prominent *formant* or spectral peaks, such as instruments and vocals, this sounds unnatural.

A granular time-domain method called *pitch-synchronous overlap add* (PSOLA) enables pitch shifting while preserving the formant peaks in their proper frequency position (Hamon et al. 1989; De Poli and Piccialli 1991; Bristow-Johnson 1995; Bastien 2003; Santacruz et al. 2016). The process has the following three steps:

1. A pitch detector (chapter 34) finds the periodic frequency of the input signal.

2. The signal is granulated at a periodic or *pitch-synchronous* rate.

3. Depending on the desired pitch shift, the grains are retriggered at a different rate and added (with overlap) in time.

The magic of this method is that sampled grains contain the entire period, including the partials in the spectrum. Thus they preserve the spectral signature of the input signal. Pitch is changed not by resampling the waveform but by retriggering the grains at a different rate (figure 31.5).

Of course, the process is not perfect. Pitch detection algorithms are fallible, and windowing introduces spectral artifacts due to convolution (chapter 29). The mismatch between the original continuous waveform and the sound of retriggered grains in a new period is heard as a timbral difference. These side effects become prominent with large intervals (e.g., greater than an octave).

Note that PSOLA can be hacked to create the effect of formant shifting while preserving the pitch. The first two steps are the same as those presented previously for PSOLA. Then steps 3 and 4 are the following:

3. Depending on the desired formant shift, the grains are resampled at a different rate, which cause the formants to shift.

4. The grains are retriggered at the original rate, which preserves the fundamental pitch.

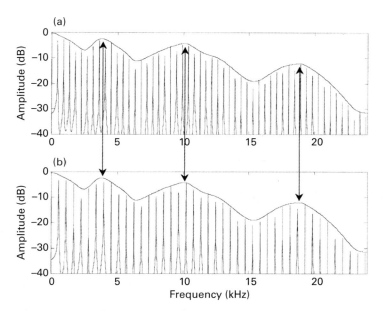

Figure 31.5 The spectrum of (a) is pitch shifted up to (b) while maintaining the formant peaks (indicated by the arrows).

Pitch-Time Changing with a Harmonizer

A *harmonizer* is a real-time transposing device that shifts the pitch of an incoming signal without altering its duration. Purely on the basis of time-domain techniques, the Eventide H910 Harmonizer, released in 1975, was the first commercially available digital device of this type (Bode 1984). Modern harmonizers can pitch-correct a vocal in real time while adding multiple voices of harmony with selectable gender voicing, in which the harmony is guided by a guitar, auxiliary input, or MIDI keyboard (TC Helicon 2018). The sound quality of a harmonizer is based on the nature of the input signal and on the ratio of pitch change it is asked to perform. Small pitch changes tend to generate less audible side effects.

The following description describes the operation of the Publison, a harmonizer and effects processor developed in France (Bloom 1985).

The basic notion of a harmonizer is to load a memory buffer with an incoming signal sampled at a rate of *SRin* and to read out the samples at a rate *SRout*. The ratio *SRin/SRout* determines the pitch change. In figure 31.6(a) the ratio of reading in and playing out is 1:1. Figure 31.6(b) shows the entire file being read in half the normal time, which causes an upward pitch shift. Figure 31.6(c) shows only half the input file being read, reflecting a downward pitch shift.

The main use of a harmonizer is to pitch-shift an input sound while preserving its duration. As the device is operating in real time, to maintain a continuous output signal, input samples must be repeated for upward pitch shifts, as shown in figure 31.7(b), or skipped for downward pitch shifts, as shown in figure 31.7(c). Because the output address pointer repeatedly overtakes the input address pointer (for pitch increases) or is overtaken by the recirculating input address pointer (for pitch decreases), the output address must regularly jump

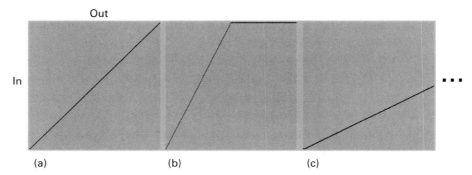

Figure 31.6 Simple pitch shifting. As the pitch increases the duration shrinks, and vice versa. After McMillen (2015).

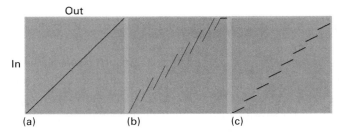

Figure 31.7   Granular pitch-time changing. In this case, the pitch is shifted up (b) and down (c) while maintaining the original duration. After McMillen (2015).

to a new point in memory. In order to make this splice inaudible, the precise jump is calculated on the basis of an estimate of the periodicity (pitch) of the incoming signal. When the decision has been made to splice, a smoothing fade-out envelope ramps the amplitude of the presplice signal to zero, and a corresponding fade-in envelope ramps to postsplice the signal to full amplitude.

Many refinements can be added to this basic scheme to improve sonic performance. One is a noise gate connected to the input so that the device does not shift the ambient noise when the performer is not playing.

Pitch-Time Changing with the Phase Vocoder

The phase vocoder (PV), explained in chapter 37, applies the *fast Fourier transform* (FFT) to short overlapping segments of an incoming sound. The FFTs result in a series of spectrum frames that capture the frequency-domain evolution of the sound over time. On the basis of this data, the original sound can be resynthesized by additive synthesis; each sine wave oscillator's frequency corresponds to an analyzed frequency component. The output of the additive resynthesis is a simulacrum of the original.

Overlap-Add Transformations

The compositional interest of the PV lies in transforming the analysis data prior to resynthesis, producing variations of the original sound. One of the most common transformations is time stretching/shrinking. This can be accomplished in two ways, depending on which version of the PV is used. In the version that uses *overlap-add resynthesis* (explained in chapter 37), time stretching is accomplished by moving the onset times of the overlapping frames farther apart in the resynthesis. Time shrinking moves the onset times closer together. As Dolson (1986) notes, the phase vocoder prefers integer transposition ratios for both time and pitch changing. For smooth transpositions, the PV should multiply the phase values by the same constant used in the time base changing (Arfib 1991).

Pitch transposition is simply a matter of scaling the frequencies of the resynthesis components. For speech signals in particular, however, a constant scale factor changes not only the pitch but also the formant frequencies. For upward shifts of an octave or more, this reduces the intelligibility of the speech. Thus Dolson (1986) suggested a correction to the frequency scaling that reimposes the original spectral envelope on the transposed frequency spectrum. If the original spectrum went only to 5 kHz, for example, the transposed version will also cut off at this point, regardless of how stretched the component frequencies are within this overall envelope.

Laroche and Dolson (1999) observed a "phasiness" or perceived "loss of presence" in material time-stretched with the PV. They proposed an efficient solution that reduces audible artifacts.

Tracking Phase Vocoder Transformations

Another way to alter the time base of analyzed sounds deploys the *tracking phase vocoder* or TPV (see chapter 37). A TPV with a graphical interface is SPEAR (Klingbeil 2005, 2009).

The TPV converts a series of spectrum frames into a set of amplitude and frequency envelope functions for each analyzed frequency component. These functions are typically represented as arrays in computer memory. By editing these amplitude and frequency functions, one can shift the pitch or extend the duration of a sound independently (Portnoff 1978; Holtzman 1980; Gordon and Strawn 1985). For example, to stretch the duration, points are interpolated between existing points in the amplitude and frequency arrays. To shrink the duration by a factor of n, only every nth value is used in reading the amplitude and frequency arrays. In effect, this shifts the sampling rate (figure 31.8). Maher (1990) discussed some of the distortions these simple interpolations may entail and offered remedies for better envelope warping.

To shift the pitch of a sound but not change its duration, one multiplies the frequency values assigned to each of the frequency functions by the desired factor. For example, to shift a sound up by the interval of a major second, each frequency component is multiplied by 11.892 percent; thereby a 1 KHz sine wave becomes 1118.92 Hz. One can also shift pitch selectively, altering only the fundamental frequency and leaving other partials unchanged.

The SPEAR interface lets one use tools of the graphical interface to select a set of tracks and then simply type in the pitch or time-scale effect (figure 31.9).

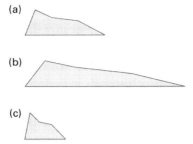

(a)

(b)

(c)

Figure 31.8   Time-scale modification of tracking phase vocoder envelopes. The plots show amplitude on the vertical axis and time on the horizontal axis. (a) Original. (b) Stretched in time. (c) Shrunk in time.

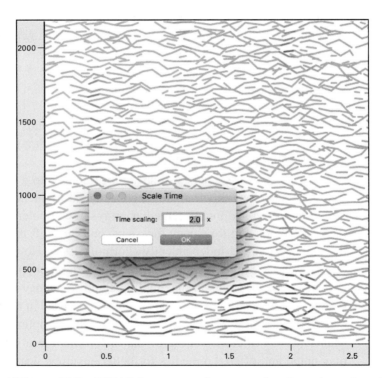

Figure 31.9   SPEAR lets a user select a set of tracks and type in a time-scale factor. The tracks are stretched or shrunk to the new time scale.

Formant-Corrected Pitch Shifting in the Frequency Domain

Another method of pitch shifting is a block-by-block frequency-domain approach using the *cepstrum* to find the strong peaks or formants in the input signal. These peaks define the spectral envelope of the input. (The cepstrum is explained in chapter 34.) Figure 34.12 gives an overview of this process. First the audio signal is converted to the frequency domain via the FFT. Then the spectral envelope of the original signal is derived by the cepstrum operation. The signal is then pitch shifted and the spectral envelope of the transformed signal is computed. The formants of the original signal are imposed by applying a correction factor to the pitch-shifted signal. In essence this moves the formants in the opposite direction of the pitch shift (Arfib et al. 2011a). The pitch-shifted formants are removed, and the original spectral envelope is applied to the pitch-shifted signal via FFT convolution (i.e., filtering by multiplication in the frequency domain). (See chapter 29 on convolution.) Next the signal is transformed back into the audio time domain by means of the inverse fast Fourier transform (IFFT). Refer to Arfib et al. (2011a) for a diagram and MATLAB code of this process.

Pitch-Time Changing with the Wavelet Transform

The first stage in the wavelet pitch-time changing is spectrum analysis (Kronland-Martinet 1988; Kronland-Martinet and Grossmann 1991; Vetterli 1992; Evangelista 1991, 1997; Mallat 2009). Chapter 38 explains the basic concept of wavelets. They are similar to the windowed segments used with the FFT, but the duration of each wavelet is dependent on its frequency content: the higher the frequency, the shorter the wavelet. This means that the temporal resolution of the wavelet transform (i.e., its ability to pinpoint the onset time of events) is greater at high frequencies.

The wavelet transform splits a sampled sound into a collection of individual time-frequency wavelets. These components are characterized by amplitude and phase values gleaned from the analysis. To shift pitch by a constant factor, one multiplies the phase values of the analyzed wavelets by this factor (Kronland-Martinet and Grossmann 1991). To stretch or shrink the time base while keeping the pitch the same, one stretches or shrinks the point of overlap of the wavelets in resynthesis. Livingston (2006) discusses challenges of producing artifact-free pitch-time changing with wavelets.

Pitch-Time Changing with Atomic Decomposition

As chapter 39 explains, *atomic decomposition* can be described as an analytical counterpart to granular synthesis. Just as Fourier analysis shows how one can build a sound using a set of sinusoids, atomic decomposition methods show how one can build it using a set of atoms or grains (Sturm et al. 2009; Kereliuk 2012). If we can describe each atom by meaningful parameters, such as time scale (duration), frequency, and time shift (starting time), we can select specific components of an atomic decomposition for manipulation and resynthesis.

The output of atomic decomposition is a list of atoms and their parameters (start time, amplitude, frequency, duration, and spatial position). Parametric manipulation involves changing the numerical values in this list. For instance, we can pitch-shift or time-stretch a sound recording by scaling durations, frequencies, and time shifts of the atoms of its decomposition. Figure 31.10 shows the SCATTER app, which manipulated atomic decomposition analysis data in real time (Sturm, Daudet, and Roads 2006; Sturm et al. 2009).

Pitch-Time Changing with Linear Predictive Coding

Chapter 14 introduced *linear predictive coding* (LPC), a subtractive analysis/resynthesis method that can generate speech, singing, instrument-like timbres, and resonant synthetic sounds (Cann 1979–1980; Moorer 1979c; Dodge and Jerse 1985; Dodge 1989; Lansky 1987; Lansky and Steiglitz 1981; Arfib et al. 2011a). LPC analysis models an input signal as an *excitation function*

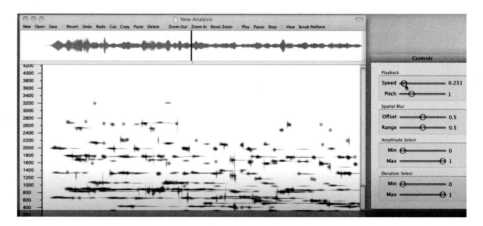

Figure 31.10   The SCATTER app slowing down a playback while preserving pitch.

(such as produced by human vocal cords or the vibrations of a reed or bowed string) and a set of *time-varying resonances* (such as the human vocal tract or the body of a saxophone or violin). The resonances are implemented as a time-varying filter that simulates a response to the excitation.

LPC does not perfectly reconstruct the analyzed signal. Artifacts are present. LPC was originally designed to be an efficient coding for speech, permitting low-bandwidth communication. It has been extended for musical purposes, but the resynthesized sound has an artificial character (Moorer 1979c). This can be mitigated but requires extraordinary effort (Moorer 2019).

LPC encodes the analysis results as a sequence of short-duration *frames,* with each frame capturing the filter coefficients, pitch, and voiced/unvoiced data for a given time slice of sound. Refer to chapter 14 for an explanation of the frame data. For musical purposes, composers edit the frames, transforming the original sound. Figure 14.19 shows a sequence of data in LPC frames.

To realize time/pitch changing, one edits the frames and then uses the edited frames to drive the resynthesis. LPC analysis frames are usually calculated at regular intervals, from 50 to 120 per second. By issuing an editing command the duration of frames can be changed, for example, to extend a single frame from 10 to 100 ms. The pitch column can be edited separately to change only the pitch of the resynthesized version. Thus duration and pitch can be independently transformed. In addition to time/pitch changing, the LPC data can be edited in other ways to create radical variations on the original analyzed sound. (See Cann [1979–1980] and Dodge [1985] for examples of editing LPC data.) Musical applications of time/pitch changing via LPC can be found in compositions by James A. Moorer, Paul Lansky, and Charles Dodge.

32 *Sound Spatialization*

Sound Spatialization

Spatialization: Background

Localization Cues

Rotating Loudspeakers

Superdirectional Sound Beams

Immersive Sound

        Vector Base Amplitude Panning (VBAP)
        Distance Based Amplitude Panning (DBAP)
        Ambisonics
            Spherical harmonics
        Wave Field Synthesis

Spatialization Tools

Transmission Formats for Multichannel Sound

        Software
            Audio definition model (ADM)
            SpatDIF
            MPEG standards for spatial audio
        Hardware
            Multichannel audio digital interface (MADI)
            AES67
            Audio video bridging (AVB)
            Digital audio network through Ethernet (Dante)

To deploy sound in space is to choreograph: positioning sources and animating movement. Immersing sound in reverberation, we bathe listeners in its lush ambience.

Sound spatialization has two aspects: the virtual and the physical. In the virtual reality of the studio, composers spatialize sounds by imposing delays, filters, panning, and reverberation—lending the illusion of sounds emerging from imaginary environments. Sometimes these virtual spaces take on characteristics that would be impossible to realize architecturally, such as a continuously changing echo pattern.

In the physical world of concert halls, sounds can be projected over a multichannel sound system from a variety of positions: around, above, below, and within the audience (figure 32.1).

Sound spatialization has become an important aspect of composition. Portable recording devices make it possible to make *field recordings* of indoor or outdoor spaces. These can be used to paint *soundscapes* to sculpt a virtual immersive 3D sound world (Smalley 1997, 2007). Luc Ferrari's classic *Presque rien no. 1* (1970) defined this genre. *Cinematic* use of space is seen in works that feature dramatic contrasts between sounds that are *close-miked* and those that are distantly reverberated. Some composers use microphone techniques and spatial processing in a manner similar to the cinematic use of camera angle, lens perspective (width), and depth of field. Jean-Claude Risset's pioneering computer music composition *Sud* (1985) comes to

Figure 32.1   The Klangdom at the Hertz-Lab in the Center for Media Technology (ZKM) in Karlsruhe, Germany (c. 2010). Above the audience are 48 Genelec loudspeakers. On the ground are two subwoofers for deep bass.

mind, as do many works of Natasha Barrett. Barrett and Crispino (2018) investigated listeners' perception of *human agency* (intention and action) in immersive sound spatialization.

This chapter opens with a glimpse at the projection of sound in three-dimensional space from a historical perspective. We then examine the perceptual cues that our ears use to localize sound horizontally, in terms of distance, speed of movement, and altitude. We present the idea of binaural sound and the concept of sound radiation or dispersion patterns. This leads to a discussion of rotating loudspeakers and superdirectional sound beams. We then take up the important area of multiloudspeaker immersive sound systems with 360° spatial projection. Finally, we discuss software and hardware transmission formats for multichannel audio.

The next chapter addresses other important aspects of spatialization: reverberation and room simulation.

Sound Spatialization

Reasoning about spatial relationships is fundamental to consciousness and intelligence (Piaget and Inhelder 1967). Spatial perception is tightly integrated with both thought and action (Blauert 1983; Kendall 2010). Our body moves in space and must be aware at all times of its position in accordance with everything around it. Our mind needs to be able to recall through spatial memory the location of innumerable things, whether in physical space (e.g., our home) or virtual space (e.g., the location of a file).

We not only compute space, we feel it. Spatial experiences can be emotionally moving, such as beholding a breathtaking view, looking over a cliff, and playing or watching all manner of sports involving the movement of the body in space. We react to the choreography of moving things. The motion of sound reconnects us to the realm of kinesthetic experience.

Decades of experimentation have proven that spatial choreography of sound is intrinsically interesting and meaningful to audiences. As a result, spatialization in the twenty-first century has assumed a newfound significance. Indeed, the spatial structure of a composition may be of aesthetic importance that is equal to or greater than its organization in terms of pitch, rhythm, and timbre (Barrett 2002; Brümmer 2017; Roads 2015).

The movement of sound through space creates dramatic effects and can serve as an important structural element in composition. Composers can articulate the voices in a contrapuntal texture by giving each a unique spatial location. The virtual and physical *sound stage* around the audience can be treated as a landscape, with its background and foreground and its fixed and moving sources. This sound stage can be fixed in playback or controlled by a sound projectionist's gestures in concert.

Digital simulations of moving sound sources pose special problems. In many concerts the audience is surrounded by a number of loudspeakers. How does one create the illusion of a sound traveling about the hall, moving away from or toward the listener as it goes? In listening situations with only two loudspeakers or with headphones, the illusion of sounds moving freely in space is even more difficult.

The most popular spatial illusions are horizontal *panning*, which uses lateral sound movement from speaker to speaker, and *reverberating*, which adds a dense and diffuse pattern of echoes to a sound to situate it in a larger space. Vertical panning (up and down and overhead) can also create striking effects in electronic music. (See Gerzon 1973 for a pioneering presentation of "sound with height" or *periphonic* recording and playback, which we discuss further on.)

The following five paradigms for spatialization are common in practice:

- *Live diffusion* to multiple loudspeakers performed manually using a mixer in concert, pioneered by the Groupe de Musiques Électroacoustique de Bourges and the Groupe de Recherches Musicales in the 1970s
- *Interactive upmixing*, e.g., from a stereo source to multiple loudspeakers, assisted by generative spatial software, e.g. SpatialChords (Roads 2015)
- *Automated spatial sequencing* to multiple loudspeakers, for example, IRCAM Spat (Carpentier, Noisternig, and Warusfel 2015), ZKM Zirkonium (Ramakrishnan 2009; Miyama, Dipper, and Brümmer 2015), and Space-Control (Oliveira and Radna 2021)
- *Immersive naturalistic spatial imagery* in games and virtual reality heard on headphones
- *Sound art installations with multiple sound sources* distributed around a gallery space, in which audience members are free to wander and create their own spatial experiences

Spatialization: Background

From which side, with how many loudspeakers, whether with rotation to left or right, whether motionless or moving, how the sounds and sound groups should be projected into space: all this is decisive for the understanding of the work.
—Karlheinz Stockhausen, describing his composition *Gesang der Jünglinge* (*Song of the Youths*), 1956

Spatial techniques in music composition have a long history. In the sixteenth century, composers associated with the Basilica San Marco in Venice (notably Adrian Willaert and his pupil Andrea Gabrieli) employed spatial antiphony in their compositions for two or more choirs. In these works, an initial verse was heard from one side of a hall, and a response verse came from another side. This arrangement was facilitated by two facing organs in the basilica. Mozart wrote compositions for two spatially separated orchestras (K. 239 and K. 286), and Hector Berlioz and Gustav Mahler wrote compositions for multiple orchestras and choruses, some of which were offstage. For a survey of spatialization techniques in twentieth-century instrumental music, refer to Maria Harley (1998) (also known as Maja Trochimczyk).

The invention of the loudspeaker could be compared to the invention of the light bulb. Suddenly it was possible to project sonic energy in spaces small and large, at any angle or intensity. However, the use of loudspeakers—in movie theaters, stadiums, railroad stations, and home radios—remained for the most part plain and functional. Only with the dawn of the post-World War II era were the aesthetic possibilities of sound projection via loudspeakers exploited in electronic music.

Historical Examples of Spatialization in Electronic Music

The following famous examples of spatial projection in electronic and computer music deserve mention here:

- Karlheinz Stockhausen's *Gesang der Jünglinge* was projected in a 1956 concert over five groups of loudspeakers in the auditorium of the West German Radio (Stockhausen 1961). His opus *Kontakte,* realized in 1960, was the first electronic music composition performed from a four-channel tape, using the Telefunken T9 tape recorder (Stockhausen 1968).

- In 1958 Edgard Varèse's classic tape music composition *Poème Electronique* and Iannis Xenakis's *Concret PH* were projected over 425 loudspeakers through an eleven-channel sound system installed on the curved walls of the Philips pavilion, designed by Xenakis and Le Corbusier at the Brussels World's Fair (Trieb 1996; Tazelaar 2013; de Heer and Tazelaar 2017; Meyer and Zimmermann 2006).

- Stockhausen played his electronic music over fifty-five loudspeakers distributed on the interior surface of the geodesic dome of the German pavilion at EXPO 70 in Osaka (Stockhausen 1971a).

- At the same exposition, Iannis Xenakis performed his twelve-channel electroacoustic composition *Hibiki Hana Ma* in the Japanese Steel Pavilion on a system of 800 loudspeakers distributed around the audience, over their heads, and under their seats (Matossian 1986). A twelve-channel sound projection system animated his sound-and-light spectacle *Polytope de Cluny* projected on the interior of the ancient Cluny Museum in Paris (Xenakis 1992).

■ Composer Salvatore Martirano built a complex digital apparatus called the Sal-Mar Construction to control a custom analog synthesizer and distribute the sound to 250 thin loudspeakers suspended at various heights from the ceilings of concert halls (Martirano 1971).

■ Christian Clozier, with Françoise Barrière and colleagues at the Groupe de Musique Expérimentale de Bourges (GMEB), developed the idea of projecting sound over an orchestra of dozens of loudspeakers on stage and around the audience (Clozier 1997, 2001). The first GMEBaphone concert was in 1973.

■ The first concert of the Acousmonium, an assemblage of dozens of *sound projectors* conceived by the Groupe de Recherches Musicales (figure 32.2), took place at the Espace Cardin, Paris, in 1974 (Bayle 1989, 1993).

Figure 32.2   The Acousmonium, a multichannel spatializer designed by the Groupe de Recherches Musicales (GRM), installed in Olivier Messiaen concert hall, Maison de Radio France, Paris, in 1980. Projecting sound over eighty loudspeakers played through a 48-channel mixer, the Acousmonium achieves a complexity of sound image rivaling that of an orchestra. It lets a composer reorchestrate an electronic composition for Acousmonium spatial performance. (Photograph by Laszlo Ruszka and supplied courtesy of François Bayle and the Groupe de Recherches Musicales.)

- The steel frame used in the mid-1980s performances of Pierre Boulez's *Répons* held loudspeakers suspended over the heads of the audience. Spatial control was implemented using Di Giugno's 4X synthesizer (Asta et al. 1980; Boulez and Gerzso 1988).

- In 1987 researchers at Luciano Berio's Tempo Reale studio in Florence developed a computer-based sound distribution system called Trails that could distribute sound to up to 32 audio channels, combining preprogrammed and real-time spatial patterns (Bernardini and Otto 1989).

Other pioneering computer-based sound spatialization systems were developed in the 1970s and 1980s, including Edward Kobrin's sixteen-channel HYBRID IV (Kobrin 1977) (figure 32.3). See also (Federkow, Buxton, and Smith 1978; Loy 1985a; Haller 1980).

The twenty-first century has continued this trend, with immersive multichannel or *pluriphonic* spatialization systems installed at institutions around the world. Two issues of *Computer Music Journal* have documented these systems (Lyon 2016, 2017).

Enhancing Spatial Projection in Performance

Even ad hoc concerts of electroacoustic music with simple sound projection systems can take steps to enhance the spatial qualities of the performance. Figure 32.4 illustrates the following five standard configurations:

1. When possible, use at least a *quadraphonic* sound projection system (four channels of amplification with four loudspeaker systems), located around the audience (figure 32.3b). An *octophonic* setup (eight loudspeakers in a ring around the audience) is also common in performances of electronic music. With a subwoofer for deep bass, this is called an 8.1 setup.

2. When two-channel recordings are played on the quadraphonic system, route two channels to the front and two channels to the back with the left-right configuration in the back channels reversed. This way, when a sound pans from left to right in the front, it also pans from right to left in the back, increasing the sense of spatial animation.

3. To add even more spatial articulation, situate the loudspeakers at opposite corners in an elevated position. This is called periphony or *sound with height* playback (Gerzon 1973). In this scheme, when a sound pans from left to right, it also pans vertically (figure 32.3c).

4. When amplified instruments or vocalists are employed, give each performer their own amplifier and loudspeaker unit, along with effects (such

Figure 32.3   Edward Kobrin's HYBRID IV studio set up in Berlin, 1977, featuring a computer-controlled sixteen-channel spatialization system. The loudspeakers are mounted on the walls.

as equalization) that articulate that particular instrument. To root each instrument on the sound stage and mitigate the *disembodied performer* syndrome, the loudspeaker should be near the performer (Morrill 1981b). In the disembodied performer syndrome, the sound of an instrument is fed to a general sound reinforcement system that is far from the performer. Because listeners' image of the source of a sound in dominated by the first sound to reach their ears (this is the *precedence effect* [Durlach and Colburn 1978]), any global amplification of a performer playing an acoustic instrument should be delayed by up to 40 ms to allow the local amplifier to make the first impression as to the source (Vidolin 1993). (Sometimes, of course, the goal is to project the sound of an instrument around a hall, or to merge it with a prerecorded source; this is another case.)

5. A different approach is to assemble a *pluriphonic* or multiloudspeaker "orchestra" of different types of loudspeakers onstage and around the audience (Clozier 1997, 2001). This creates a spatial and spectral diversity usually associated with an orchestra of acoustic instruments.

Precise control of spatial illusions requires knowledge of the *theory of localization*, that is, how human beings perceive a sound's direction, the subject of the next section.

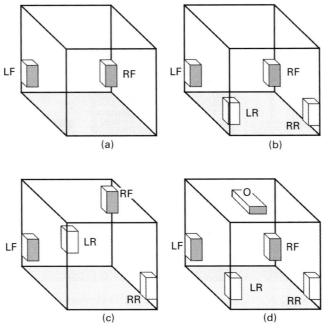

Figure 32.4   Setups for configurations for spatialization of electronic and computer music with a small number of loudspeakers. (a) Basic stereo, LF = left front, RF = right front. (b) Quadraphonic, RR = right rear, LR = left rear. (c) Quadraphonic periphony. The right front and left rear loudspeakers are mounted above ear level, so that when sound pans horizontally it also pans vertically. (d) Five-speaker configuration with vertical loudspeaker projecting downward. If the ceiling is relatively low and reflective, the loudspeaker can be on a stand projected upward so that the sound will be heard reflected from above.

Localization Cues

Before delving into techniques of sound spatialization, it is important to understand basic principles of how listeners pinpoint the locale from which a sound emanates. This subject, an extensively mined area of psychoacoustics, is called *sound localization* (Blauert 1983). Localization is dependent on the following cues for three dimensions (figure 32.5):

Azimuth or horizontal angle

Distance (for static sounds) or *velocity* (for moving sounds)

Zenith or altitude or elevation or vertical angle

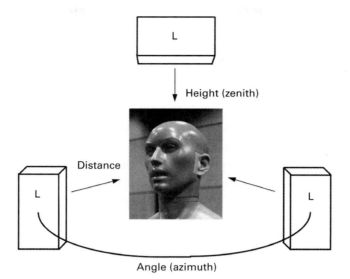

Figure 32.5 The attentive listener can localize a sound source from cues of its horizontal angle, height, and distance. L = loudspeaker.

To determine the azimuth of a sound, listeners use the following three cues:

- The different arrival times of a sound to the two ears when the sound is coming from one side (the maximum difference, approximately 650 μs, is called the *binaural delay*)
- The difference in amplitude of high-frequency sounds heard by two ears, which results from the *shadow effect* of the head
- Spectral cues provided by asymmetrical reflections of sound off the outer ears (pinnae), shoulders, and upper torso

The three cues for distance are

- The ratio of direct signal to reverberated signal, when the direct signal decreases in intensity according to the square of the distance
- The loss of high-frequency components with increasing distance
- The loss of detail (absence of softer sounds) with increasing distance

When the distance between the sound and the listener is changing, the cue to the velocity of the sound is a pitch change called the *Doppler shift effect* (explained further on).

The main cue for zenith is a change in the spectrum caused by sound reflections off the pinnae and shoulders.

Simulating the Azimuth Cue

Listeners can easily localize an intense high-frequency sound coming from a particular direction at ear level. Logically enough, for a sound source to be positioned directly at a loudspeaker position, all of the signal should come from that loudspeaker. As the source pans from one loudspeaker to another, the amplitude in the direction of the target loudspeaker increases, and the amplitude in the direction of the source loudspeaker decreases.

To enhance perceptual salience, the technique of Stockhausen in works such as *Kontakte* (1960) applies low-frequency square-wave (on-off) amplitude modulation to sounds in motion. Just as a blinking light draws the eye, a fluttering sound stands out to the ear.

In performances where a number of loudspeakers are placed equidistantly in a circle around the audience, an algorithm for spatial position needs only to calculate the amplitudes of two adjacent loudspeakers at a time, regardless of the total number of loudspeakers. To position a sound source at a precise point P between the two loudspeakers A and B, first find the angle (θ) of the source measured from the midpoint between A and B (figure 32.6).

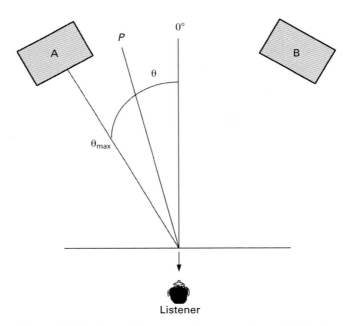

Figure 32.6 To position a sound source at a point P between the two loudspeakers A and B, ascertain the angle θ of the source measured from the midpoint between A and B. In the middle θ equals 0°. The angle θmax is the maximum angle, typically plus or minus 45°.

Many different panning curves are possible, each of which lends a slightly different spatial impression of sound movement. We next discuss two panning curves: *linear* and *constant intensity.* For a symmetrical pan, these curves assume that a listener sits in the exact center between the two loudspeakers. When the listener sits off center there is an azimuth offset in the sound image. For efficiency the curves can be computed in advance, requiring only a table-lookup operation using the index θ.

Linear panning

The most simple formula for positioning is a simple linear relation:

$$A_{amp} = \theta/\theta_{max}$$
$$B_{amp} = 1 - (\theta/\theta_{max})$$

The problem with this type of pan is that it creates a "hole in the middle" effect because the ears tend to hear the signal as being stronger in the end-points (the loudspeakers) than in the middle (figure 32.7). This is due to the *law of sound intensity,* which states that the perceived loudness of a sound is proportional to its intensity. The intensity of the sound can be given

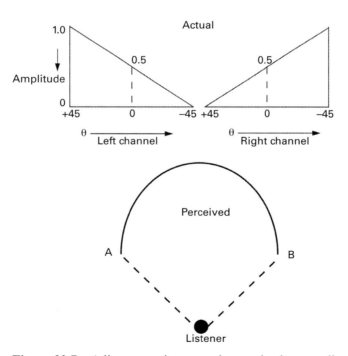

Figure 32.7   A linear panning curve is perceived as receding in the middle due to a diminution of intensity. The amplitude curves for each channel are shown at the top; the perceived trajectory is shown at the bottom.

$$I = \sqrt{A_{amp}^2 + B_{amp}^2}$$

In the middle of the pan (i.e., where $q = 0$), $A_{amp} = B_{amp} = 0.5$, this becomes

$$\sqrt{0.5^2 + 0.5^2} = \sqrt{0.25 + 0.25} = \sqrt{0.5} = 0.707$$

Thus the intensity drops to 0.707 in the middle, from a starting point of 1 at the side. This is a difference of 3 dB. To the ear, the sound appears to be fainter in the center, as if it has moved away from the listener.

Constant power panning

A constant power pan uses sinusoidal curves to control the amplitude emanating from the two loudspeakers (Reveillon 1994). This creates the impression of a pan with a more stable loudness.

$$A_{amp} = \frac{\sqrt{2}}{2} \times [\cos(\theta) + \sin(\theta)]$$

$$B_{amp} = \frac{\sqrt{2}}{2} \times [\cos(\theta) - \sin(\theta)]$$

In the middle of this pan, $A_{amp} = B_{amp} = 0.707$, thus

$$I = \sqrt{0.707^2 + 0.707^2} = \sqrt{0.5 + 0.5} = \sqrt{1} = 1$$

and a constant intensity is preserved.

Figure 32.8 shows the constant intensity pan. The perceived pan is seen as rotating between the two loudspeakers at a constant distance from the listener. Note that a straight line between A and B would not create an equidistant impression because the distance would be shorter in the center.

Spatial image operations

In a stereophonic sound system, the *stereo image* is the perceived spatial resolution of sound when reproduced from a pair of loudspeakers. Traditionally, an image is considered to be good if the location of the performers in a recording of a live concert can be clearly identified. The image is considered poor if the location of the performers is hard to locate.

In creating electronic music, we seek to control the spatial image of each sound: from individual grains to longer passages. Some sounds appear as monophonic. They come out of one loudspeaker only or they come out of both simultaneously. By contrast, sounds recorded in stereo have three components: a pure left side, a center or mono part that is common to both channels, and a pure right side. Several operations let us manipulate the spatial image.

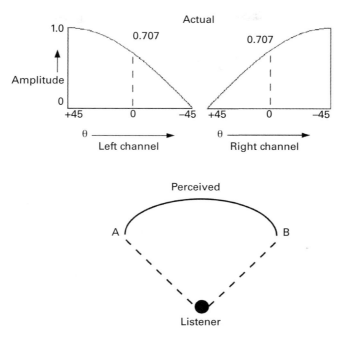

Figure 32.8   A constant-power panning curve maintains the perceived distance and intensity in the middle. The amplitude curves for each channel are shown at the top; the perceived trajectory is shown at the bottom.

Stereo image widening is a well-known technique and is offered in many software plug-ins. One way to widen the image involves minimizing the mono part, pushing the sound to extreme left and extreme right. Figure 32.9 illustrates the process of extracting the three components of the stereo image. Once extracted, the image can be spread or skewed as a function of the ratio of the L, M, and R signals.

Another simple way to manipulate the stereo image is to invert the phase of one channel for a short period of time. This causes a noticeable shift in the stereo image that is content dependent. It can cause the sound to appear outside of one speaker. A short delay of a few milliseconds in one channel will cause the sound to appear to be coming from the opposite speaker. Filtering one channel independently of the other also affects the stereo image.

Gary Kendall and his colleagues studied the effects of *decorrelation* on spatial imagery (Kendall 1995b; Cabrera and Kendall 2013). Decorrelation is any process (delays, filters, modulation, etc.) whereby an audio signal is transformed into multiple output signals whose waveforms appear different from one another. When played back over a multichannel system, these copies produce a sound image that is spatially enlarged.

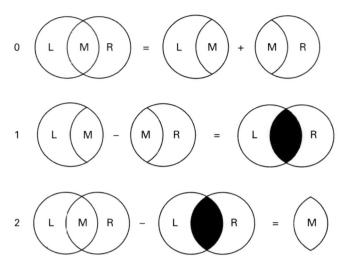

Figure 32.9   Separating the three spatial components L=left, R=right, and M=mono. (0) The original stereo signal LMR can be considered as a sum of LM and MR. (1) to extract the L and R signals, subtract MR from LM. (2) To extract M, subtract LR from LMR. Now we can manipulate L, M, and R independently to vary the stereo image.

Reflections

As sound pans from loudspeaker to loudspeaker in a concert hall, reflections in the hall provide more cues to source position. Thus to enhance the localization effect, the composer can add small delays to the signal coming from the *nondirect* channels (i.e., the channels from which the main source is not being projected). These delays simulate the reflections of a hall; they tell the ear that the source direction is elsewhere. In the ideal, the reflection pattern should change as the sound pans.

To impart an idea of the relationship between the delay time and the perceived distance of a sound, consider table 32.1. This shows the distance sound travels per unit time. The third column in table 32.1 is added for the sake of the curious, showing the wavelength corresponding to a given distance. As the third row down shows, for example, an acoustical tone at 168 Hz (about an E) takes shape in two meters of air.

Simulating Distance Cues

To make a sound recede into the distance, one can lower its amplitude, apply a lowpass filter, add echoes, or blend in reverberation. (Chapter 33 is devoted to reverberation.) The first two cues model what happens outdoors in a large

Table 32.1 Distance traveled by sound waves per unit of
time, with the corresponding wavelength

Time (ms)	Total distance (m)	Wavelength frequency (Hz)
1.0	0.34	1,000
3.4	1	340
6.8	2	168
34	10	34
68	20	16.8
100	34	10
340	100	3.4
680	200	1.68
1,000	340	1

Note: To calculate the delay time of a reflection, use the total
distance from the source to the reflecting surface to the
listener. The speed of sound is assumed to be about 340 m/s
at 19° Celsius, increasing 0.6 m/s for every additional degree.

open field, where we sense the distance of a sound by its intensity and the
filtering effect of air absorption on high frequencies.

Echo and reverberation cues model what happens in an enclosed space such
as a concert hall. To simulate a specific distance within a room, the simplest
method is to keep the level of reverberation (R) constant and scale the direct
(D) signal to be inversely proportional to the desired distance (figure 32.10).
An extension of this technique is to scale the reverberant signal as well, according to a function that decreases less rapidly than the direct signal. As the source
moves away, the total sound emanating from the source diminishes.

The most accurate methods of room simulation capture early reflections
as well as the late reverberation. These involve physical modeling: finite-
difference time-domain, geometric acoustics, and waveguide models. Refer
to chapter 33.

Local and global reverberation

Another distance cue is the relationship of *local* reverberation to *global*
reverberation, which can be demonstrated with a multiple loudspeaker
system. Global reverberation is distributed equally among all loudspeakers,
whereas local reverberation feeds into adjacent pairs of loudspeakers. Thus,
a sound might have a short and weak global reverberation but have a long
and strong local reverberation coming from one pair of loudspeakers in a

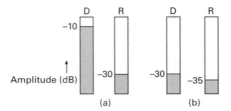

Figure 32.10   Level indicators for simulating a sound that moves away from the listener. D = direct; R = reverberated. (a) Close sound in which the direct sound is much higher in amplitude than the reverberated sound. (b) Distant sound. The overall amplitude is lower, and the ratio of the direct to the reverberated sound has narrowed.

multispeaker setup. This would simulate the case of an opening into a large space between the two loudspeakers.

A distinction between local and global reverberation helps overcome a masking effect that occurs at distances where the amplitudes of the direct and global reverberant signals are equal. This masking eliminates the azimuth cue. One way to negate this effect is to split the reverberation into local and global components and make local reverberation increase with distance according to the relation:

Local_reverberation $\cong 1 - (1/distance)$

As the distance increases, this relation tends toward 1. Thus, when the source is close to the listener, the reverberation is distributed equally well in all channels. As the source moves away, the reverberant signal concentrates in the direction of the source.

The Velocity Cue or Doppler Shift

Basic localization cues for static sounds can be extended to the simulation of moving sound sources. The cue for the *velocity* of a sound source is *Doppler shift,* first described by the Austrian physicist Christian Doppler (1842). Doppler's theory was controversial at the time (Nolte 2020). Today it is regularly applied in physics, astronomy, and medicine as an analytical tool.

In music, the Doppler shift effect is a technique of sound spatialization involving pitch shifting. The first simulations of Doppler shift were carried out by John Chowning (1971). McGee (2015) examined Doppler modulation in detail and compared approximations with true Doppler formulae.

The Doppler shift effect in sound is a continuous change in pitch that results when the source and the listener are moving relative to each other. A common example can be heard next to a train track as a train approaches at high speed and then passes. As the train moves closer, it is compressing the space of sound waves, forcing the wave fronts of the sound to reach us more quickly, causing the pitch to be raised. When the train passes, we hear the inverse effect as a pitch shift downward.

A Doppler shift is a cue to the *radial velocity* of a source relative to a listener. Radial movement is motion with respect to a center–in this case, a listener (figure 32.11a). Radial velocity is different from *angular velocity*. For a sound to have angular velocity, it must move in a circle around a listener (figure 32.11b). In this case the distance from the source to the listener is constant (i.e., the radial velocity is zero), so there is no Doppler effect. If the position of the listener remains fixed, the Doppler shift effect can be expressed as follows:

new_pitch = original_pitch × [vsound / (vsound − vsource)]

where *original_pitch* is the original pitch of the sound source, *vsound* is the velocity of sound (~344 meters/second or 1100 feet/second), and *vsource* is the velocity of the source relative to the listener. If *vsource* is positive, the sound is moving closer to the listener, and the pitch shift is upward. If it is negative, the pitch shifts downward.

The pitch change that occurs in Doppler shifting can be explained as a shrinking of the interval between wave fronts as the source moves closer to

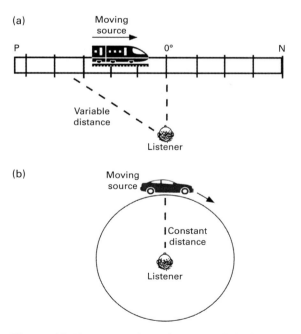

Figure 32.11   A sound moving toward the listener has positive (P) radial velocity. Sound moving away has negative (N) radial velocity. (b) Sound moving in a circle is always the same distance away from the listener and so has zero radial velocity.

the listener. Figure 32.12a depicts a static sound emitting wave fronts at a constant rate or pitch. Figure 32.12b depicts a sound source moving toward the listener. The dots S1, S2, and S3 represent successive positions of a moving sound source. As the sound approaches, the wave fronts become closer, producing an upward pitch shift. The technique is implemented with a *time-varying* or *modulated delay line* (chapter 30; Dattorro 1997b; Dutilleux et al. 2011a)

At a given instant the Doppler effect is shifting all frequencies by the same logarithmic interval. For example, an approaching sound moving at 20 meters/second (about 45 miles/hour) rises by about a minor second (6.15 percent). A shift of 6.15 percent for a component at 10 kHz is 615 Hz, whereas a

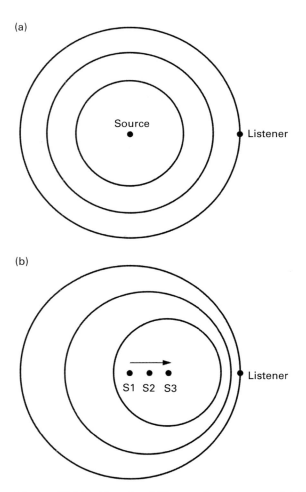

Figure 32.12   Doppler shift wavefront patterns. (a) Static sound, wavefronts arrive at constant intervals so there is no pitch change. (b) S1, S2, and S3 represent successive positions of a moving sound source. Upward pitch shift.

6.15 percent shift for a 100 Hz component is only 6.15 Hz. Thus the Doppler effect preserves the logarithmically scaled harmonic relations within a sound. This is opposed to a linear frequency shift that occurs in modulation. An example of linear frequency shift is the addition of 50 Hz to all components. Shifting a pitch from 100 to 150 Hz constitutes a major fifth interval, whereas at a range of 10 kHz, a 50 Hz shift is barely perceptible. Linear frequency shifting destroys existing harmonic relationships in a sound. (See chapter 15 for an explanation of frequency shifting.)

Simulating Altitude (Zenith) Cues

The effect of sound sources descending from on high can be dramatic. Since the 1970s it has been shown that vertical sound illusions can be achieved with headphones.

In general, three-dimensional (3D) sound systems are based on research that shows that high-frequency sound (greater than about 6 kHz) reflecting off the outer ears (pinnae) and shoulders provides a critical cue to vertical localization. The surfaces of the pinnae and shoulders act as reflectors, creating short time delays that are manifested in the spectrum as a comb filter effect (Bloom 1977; Rodgers 1981; Kendall and Martens 1984; Kendall, Martens, and Decker 1989; Kendall 1995a).

Zenith cues can be simulated electronically, giving the impression that a sound is emanating from high places. This is done by filtering the input signal, imposing the change in spectrum that is normally caused by reflections off the head and shoulders. The filters are set according to the position of the source that one is trying to simulate. The frequency response of this filtration is called the *head-related transfer function* (HRTF) (Begault 1991). Figure 32.13 plots typical HRTFs for sounds above, at, and below ear level.

As all other spatial effects, vertical panning works best on broadband impulsive sounds rather than low-frequency sounds with smooth envelopes.

Problems with vertical sound illusions

Every head, shoulder, and earlobe is different. As a result, no two people have the same HRTF. As figure 32.14 shows, a problem with projecting sound in a simulated vertical plane is the variation in HRTFs for different people (Begault 1991; Kendall, Martens, and Decker 1989; Kendall 1995a). When the wrong HRTF is used for a particular person, the vertical panning effect falls apart.

Virtual reality (VR) and *augmented reality* (AR) systems need 360° audio. This has created renewed interest in HRTFs. Various companies offer services

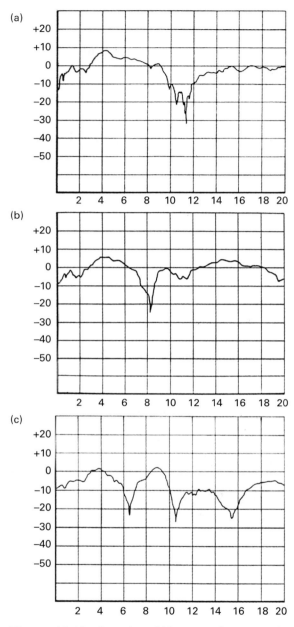

Figure 32.13   Doppler shift wave fronts. HRTF spectra (amplitude *x* versus frequency *y*) for sounds heard at 90° (straight into left ear) at various altitudes. (a) 15° above ear level. (b) Ear level. (c) Below ear level. (After Rodgers 1981; published courtesy of the Audio Engineering Society.)

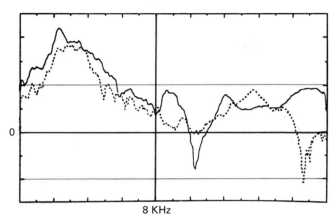

8 KHz

Figure 32.14 HRTF spectra for two different persons. Left ear, with source at ear level. The frequency plot goes from 1 to 18 KHz. The vertical line indicates the 8 KHz mark. The differences between the two HRTFs above 8 KHz are striking. The horizontal lines indicate 20 dB differences.

to deliver customized HRTFs based on an individual's physical anatomy. For example, Genelec's Aural ID service measures the interaural distance as well as shape of the earlobes and torso (AES 2019). Other services measure facial geometry and micromovements of the head (see the reason for this below). Countering this trend toward customization, some argue that generic HRTFs based on publicly available data sets can approximate most people's perceptions. Ghorbal et al. (2017) presents an analysis of this controversial topic.

Listeners instinctively use head motion to disambiguate and fix sound in space, particularly with respect to elevation and front/back differentiation. VR headsets provide the ability to track a listener's head orientation, which can be used to enhance spatial audio perception.

In a concert situation, it is possible to situate actual loudspeakers over the heads of the audience (see figure 32.1), rather than rely on the fragile illusion of virtual vertical sources. Immersive sound environments can have a dozen or more loudspeakers overhead (Lyon 2016, 2017).

In a traditional room, another tactic is to project sound toward the ceiling; if the ceiling is relatively low the sound will be heard reflecting from above.

Binaural Sound

In psychoacoustics research, *binaural* originally referred to a unique listening situation in which subjects are placed in an anechoic chamber with their heads held still by a mechanical restraint and probe tubes inserted into their ear canals. These conditions are designed to analyze a variety of auditory mechanisms in a controlled environment (Durlach and Colburn 1978; Colburn and Durlach 1978; Buser and Imbert 1992). Due to the difficulty of such experiments, many investigations employ headphones. In other experiments, a dummy head with microphones in its ears substitutes for the human subject.

An outgrowth of this research is a genre of *binaural recordings,* made with two microphones in a dummy head or a similar construction, that are meant to be heard through headphones. This genre has been particularly popular in radio productions and has led to the availability of binaural recording systems.

One of the results of binaural research has been the realization that is possible to create an illusion of a sound source at a specific position in a *binaural field* through filtering alone. By *binaural field* we refer to the space perceived through headphones, including above and behind the head. These techniques employ the HRTFs discussed previously. Refer to Blauert (1983), Durlach and Colburn (1978), and Begault (1991) for details.

Sound Radiation

We conclude the discussion of localization with a note on sound radiation. Every sound-producing mechanism has a characteristic *radiation pattern.* This three-dimensional pattern describes the amplitude of sound projected by the device. In traditional acoustical instruments, the radiation pattern is frequency dependent (Fletcher and Rossing 1991). That is, it changes depending on the frequency being radiated. Perceptually, a radiation pattern is one clue to the identity and locale of the source.

Loudspeaker systems exhibit their own radiation patterns, characterized by the technical specification called *dispersion.* The dispersion of a front-projecting loudspeaker indicates the width and height of the region in which the loudspeaker maintains a linear frequency response. A typical studio monitor has a dispersion pattern of 90° in the lateral plane.

The extent to which listeners can detect the difference between a real violin and playback of a violin recording has been attributed to their different radiation patterns. Thus one line of acoustics research has concentrated on modeling the radiation patterns of instruments, projecting them using spherical multiloudspeaker systems (Bloch et al. 1992; Avizienis et al. 2006; Zotter et al 2017). Such systems, under computer control, could also be used for compositional purposes, for example, to give each voice in a piece its own radiation pattern.

Rotating Loudspeakers

The radiation of sound emitted by a spinning loudspeaker creates a striking spatial effect. The physical rotation of a loudspeaker enlivens even dull, stable sounds, animating them with time-varying qualities.

Rotating Loudspeakers: Background

The original rotating loudspeaker mechanism was the Leslie Tone Cabinet (figure 32.15), which routed an incoming signal into two separate rotating mechanisms: a spinning horn for high frequencies and a rotating circular baffle (blocking and unblocking a stationary woofer) for low frequencies (Leslie 1949, 1952). A remote control of motor speed let musicians adjust the speed of rotation. The spinning sound makes the Leslie Tone Cabinet immediately identifiable.

The Leslie Tone Cabinet was designed to enrich the static sound emitted by electric organs such as the famed Hammond B3, with which it was often coupled. But musicians and recording engineers discovered that any sound could be enriched this way, including voice and electric guitar.

In the 1950s, engineers working at Hermann Scherchen's Experimental Studio Gravesano (Switzerland) developed a spherical loudspeaker (figure 32.16) that rotated both horizontally and vertically (Loescher 1959; 1960). Their goal was to reduce the *directional soundbeam* characteristics of normal loudspeakers. According to one of the designers,

A double rotation in the horizontal and vertical plane results in inclined rotational planes of the single speakers and gives best results. The sound field becomes practically homogenous, reproduction takes on an astonishing fullness and smoothness, and the harshness of normal reproduction is completely gone. (Loescher 1959)

Karlheinz Stockhausen manually rotated a loudspeaker affixed to a turntable to create the spinning sounds in his compositions *Kontakte* (1960) and *Hymnen* (1967) (figure 32.17). Later, engineers at the West German Radio (WDR) built a motorized sound rotation system for concert performance of Stockhausen's works (Morawska-Büngler 1988).

Simulation of Rotating Loudspeakers

The simulation of rotating loudspeakers takes two basic approaches. The most common is to apply signal processing techniques to model in software what happens when a rotating loudspeaker spins. For example, many

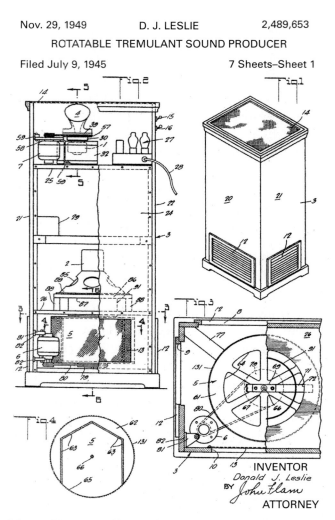

Figure 32.15   Leslie rotating loudspeaker patent, 1949.

commercial plug-ins attempt to simulate a Leslie effect. The second, more experimental approach, is to build a physical system with multiple speakers in a shape like a sphere and route the sound in a spinning pattern to the various speakers. Only a few systems of this type have been made in research laboratories (Smallwood et al. 2017). For example, a team at the Institute of Electronic Music, Graz, Austria, developed a sound projection in the form of an icosahedron with 20 loudspeakers (Zotter et al. 2017; Wendt et al. 2017). The computer-controlled distribution of sound to the speakers creates moving patterns of sound beams.

The simulation of Doppler shift alone is relatively straightforward, as Chowning (1971) demonstrated convincingly with his pioneering demon-

Figure 32.16   Rotating spherical loudspeaker constructed in 1959 at the Experimental Studio Gravesano.

Figure 32.17   Karlheinz Stockhausen with rotating loudspeaker mechanism in 1960. Four microphones are positioned around the loudspeaker turntable, which was manipulated by hand. A later version was controlled by a motorized mechanism. (Photograph copyright WDR, Cologne.)

strations of sound spinning around four loudspeakers in a room. (See also Dattorro [1997b] and Dutilleux et al. [2011a].)

The Leslie effect is another beast entirely (Leslie 1949, 1952). The experience of being in a room with a rotating loudspeaker is immersive, as the sound is being reflected by all three-dimensional surfaces of the room. These complicated acoustical effects are difficult to simulate convincingly. Thus, effects designers try to simulate the sound as it would be heard when recorded closely with a microphone: a much simpler proposition. In simulating a Leslie effect, one must take manifold factors into account. The effects of rotation involve Doppler shift vibrato, time-varying filtering and phase shifts due to sound diffraction, and distortions caused by air turbulence. One must also account for the transfer characteristics of the amplifiers, loudspeakers, and microphones used (Smith et al. 2002). The original Leslie Tone Cabinet, for example, employed vacuum tube electronics with overdrive distortion.

Superdirectional Sound Beams

The directionality or dispersion pattern of a loudspeaker is a design feature and can vary from omnidirectional to superdirectional. Most conventional loudspeakers are broadly directional, that is, they typically project sound forward through a horizontal angle spanning 90°. *Narrow coverage* loudspeakers feature dispersion in the 50° range (Meyer Sound Laboratories 2020).

By contrast, loudspeakers that act as superdirectional sound beams behave like an audio spotlight, focusing sound energy on a narrow spot, typically about 15° in width (figure 32.17). A person in the beam may hear the sound while someone outside the beam does not. Superdirectional sound beams can be constructed using a variety of technologies. Here we look at loudspeaker arrays and ultrasonic devices. We discuss wave field synthesis further on in the context of immersive sound systems.

It has long been known that loudspeaker arrays can form focused directional sound beams. A contemporary incarnation of this approach is found in the Yamaha YSP digital sound projector (figure 32.18). The device works by focusing sound into beams and then projecting them at angles into a room. The resulting sound waves—both direct and reflected—create a soundscape

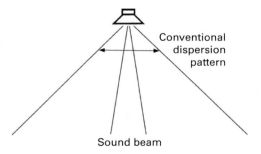

Figure 32.18   The conventional dispersion pattern of a loudspeaker is broad, whereas a superdirectional sound beam is narrow.

that seems to be coming from speakers placed throughout the room, but in reality, all the sound emanates from the sound projector in the front.

An alternative technology for superdirectional sound beams employs ultrasound—the domain of high frequencies above the range of human audibility. Ultrasonic superdirectional loudspeakers are based on the scientific principle of *acoustic heterodyning* (Pompei 1999), first observed by Helmholtz. When two sound sources are positioned relatively closely together and are of sufficiently high amplitude, two new tones appear: one lower than either of the two original ones and a second one that is higher than the original two. The two new combination tones correspond to the sum and the difference of the two original ones. For example, if one were to emit two ultrasonic frequencies 90 kHz and 91 kHz into the air, with sufficient energy, one would produce the sum (181 kHz) and the difference (1 kHz), the latter of which is in the range of human hearing. Helmholtz argued that the phenomenon had to result from a nonlinearity of air molecules, which begin to behave nonlinearly (to heterodyne or intermodulate) at high amplitudes.

Unlike regular loudspeakers, acoustical heterodyning loudspeakers project energy in a collimated sound beam, analogous to the beam of light from a flashlight. One can direct the ultrasonic emitter toward a wall—a listener within the reflected beam perceives the sound as coming from that spot. One could imagine coupling such a loudspeaker with a robot arm to create a spatial choreography of precisely controlled sound beams that are synchronized with a musical structure.

Immersive Sound

A trend in electronic music performance is a move away from the traditional stage-centered experience toward immersive sound environments. Examples include the Klangdom of the Hertz-Lab at ZKM Center for Art and Media Karlsruhe (figure 32.1), the Mumuth auditorium at the Arts University Graz, the Cube at Virginia Tech, and the Sonic Arts Research Centre (SARC) at Queen's University, Belfast, the AlloSphere at UCSB, the GRAIL at Stanford, among others (Barrett 2016; Cabrera, Kuchera-Morin, and Roads 2016; Hollerweger 2006; Lopez-Lezcano 2016; Lyon 2016, 2017; Lyon et al. 2016; Wiggins 2004). In these spaces, the audience is surrounded by dozens of loudspeakers, around, above, and sometimes below them. In the case of the AlloSphere the immersion is also visual, as the audience is surrounded by a spherical screen that is illuminated by many stereo video projectors (figure 32.20).

Immersive sound systems extend the reach of spatialization to a three-dimensional enclosure. Composers such as Ludger Brümmer (2017) and

Figure 32.19   The Yamaha YSP-100 projects sounds from forty-two loudspeakers to create surround sound effects.

Figure 32.20   A 2016 CREATE Ensemble performance on the exterior of the UCSB AlloSphere, a 54.1 Meyer Sound system. The audience can be seen inside the AlloSphere.

Natasha Barrett (2016) have written about the aesthetic possibilities of such systems. Sound can be distributed in space according to its frequency content or duration (Torchia and Lippe 2004; McLeran et al. 2008). Lynch and Sazdov (2017) created an algorithm that maximizes the sense of "engulfment" in immersive sound environments. The algorithm applies a bank of sweeping bandpass filters and delays to each channel. Without amplitude panning, sound energy is perceived to move around the audience in the space.

The realm of immersive sound or *sound field synthesis* is an active area of research and experimentation, with a number of approaches in competition. Among these are several techniques that have fascinating musical potential. These are: *vector base amplitude panning* (VBAP), *distance based amplitude panning* (DBAP), *ambisonics,* and *wave field synthesis* (WFS). Commercial systems like Dolby Atmos and Apple Spatial Audio have also entered the immersive sound marketplace. All combine a physical infrastructure with spatial signal processing. The physical infrastructure consists of a regular array of many loudspeakers surrounding the listener in three dimensions. Spatial signal processing diffuses a potentially unique audio signal to each loudspeaker in the system to create an immersive spatial impression.

As Ahrens, Rabenstein, and Spors (2014), observed, it is possible to mix different spatial techniques, for example to combine WFS with ambisonics and even stereophony to take advantage of the unique features of each type of sound projection. Brümmer (2020) says that using VBAP for point sources and ambisonics for environmental sounds makes an effective combination.

As our previous discussion of localization cues inferred, the perceptual salience of all methods of sound spatialization is partially frequency dependent.

Vector Base Amplitude Panning (VBAP)

VBAP is a three-dimensional extension of stereophonic techniques (Pulkki 1997). Instead of projecting a signal from a stereo field with a phantom source between two loudspeakers, VBAP projects a phantom source from triples of loudspeakers arranged in triangles, allowing for vertical as well as horizontal panning (figure 32.21). A typical VBAP configuration has regularly spaced loudspeakers around and above the audience. VBAP is a highly effective way to pan sound around the inner surface of a dome or sphere of loudspeakers.

Distance Based Amplitude Panning (DBAP)

DBAP takes the physical positions of the speakers in space as the point of departure, while making no assumptions as to where the listeners are. This makes DBAP useful for situations such as stage productions, installations, and museum sound design with irregular speaker layouts. DBAP amplitude panning uses all available speakers simultaneously. The gain applied to each speaker is calculated according to an attenuation model based on the distance between a virtual sound source and each speaker (Lossius, Baltazar, and de la Hogue 2009).

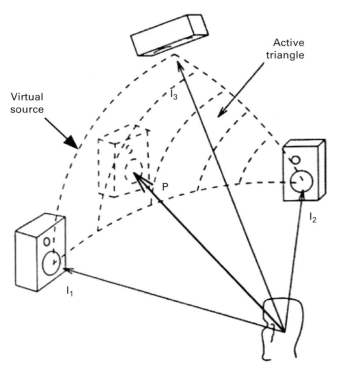

Figure 32.21   Vector base amplitude panning. The three-dimensional unit vectors I_1, I_2, and I_3 define the directions of loudspeakers 1, 2, and 3. The virtual sound source p is a linear combination of the gain factors of I_1, I_2, and I_3. Using these three loudspeakers, virtual sources can be created anywhere within the active triangle shown. This can be generalized to arbitrary spatial configurations of multiple loudspeakers. After Pulkki (1997).

Ambisonics

Ambisonics and wave field synthesis go beyond the positioning of isolated phantom sources in space toward immersive environments. The aim of immersive spatialization is the reconstruction of the acoustic sensations that a listener would perceive around the listener in all directions. This work focusses on the reproduction of coherent *wave fronts* to create an immersive experience (Malham 1998, 2003; Malham and Myatt 1995; Rumsey 2001). A wave front consists of all points in space that are reached at the same instant by a propagating wave.

The original ambisonic products were invented by the British physicist Michael Gerzon, with limited success (Gerzon 1973). In recent times, ambisonics has seen a surge of interest due to the spread of AR and VR systems and games (Zotter and Frank 2019). One reason is that even when the sound field rotates, as when a gamer rotates her head in a VR world, ambisonics maintains a stable continuous sound image. Companies such as Google, Meta, and Amazon (among others) have all invested in ambisonic technologies.

An ambisonic audio stream contains information about which frequencies are radiating in what directions and at which levels. Ambisonics uses all loudspeakers to cooperatively recreate the directional components. Thus speakers to the rear of the listener help locate sounds in front of the listener, and vice versa. This stands in contrast to techniques that use only adjacent speakers such as VBAP.

Ambisonic-encoded signals carry the directional information of an entire periphonic sound field. A decoding and playback system converts a multichannel ambisonic stream into actual speaker signals. Most importantly, the raw ambisonic stream is independent from the loudspeaker layout chosen for decoding the sound field. Thus the same signal can be decoded for mono, or stereo including headphones, or an arbitrary number of loudspeakers (Gerzon 1977). Scalability to multiple playback systems is one of the most attractive features of ambisonics. (Scalability is also a main selling point of Dolby Atmos and Apple Spatial Audio.) With ambisonics, the more loudspeakers, the higher the accuracy of the reconstructed sound field.

An ambisonic microphone has at least four capsules in a tetrahedral configuration (figure 32.22). The four channels they pick up are called the *ambisonics A* or raw format. Through a processing matrix this can be converted to the *first-order ambisonics B-format*. B-format requires only four channels of information (W, X, Y, and Z) to reproduce the sound field emanating from a sphere around the listener. W corresponds to the spherical sound pressure picked up by an omnidirectional microphone. X, Y, and Z all represent the signal picked up by a *bidirectional* or *figure-eight* microphone. In particular, X corresponds to a front-back microphone, Y corresponds to a left-right microphone, and Z corresponds to an up-down microphone.

Figure 32.22   Sennheiser AMBEO VR microphone.

Since there are no bidirectional capsules in the ambisonic microphone, these patterns are derived from mathematical transformations on the A-format signals. In the post-production stage, an ambisonic recording can be decoded to simulate a multitude of microphones using a plug-in such as Soundfield By Røde.

Figure 32.23 shows how one might use an ambisonic B-format system to spatialize two mono input channels to an arbitrary number of loudspeakers. The boxes marked FX indicate the point at which plug-ins for sound field manipulation would be inserted (Wiggins 2004). This would include effects such as panning and reverberation.

The spatial resolution of a first-order ambisonic B system is limited. *Higher-order ambisonics* (HOA) was developed to increase the spatial resolution. (*Higher-order* refers to greater than four channels.) HOA increases the size of the sweet spot of listening in which the sound field is accurately reproduced. It also extends the frequency bandwidth, thus improving the overall quality of localization (Hollerweger 2006). In support of HOA, the ZYLIA ZM-1 multitrack microphone consists of nineteen omnidirectional capsules distributed on a sphere for up to third-order ambisonics. Software provided with the microphone provides a toolbox for manipulating the virtual image in a postproduction stage.

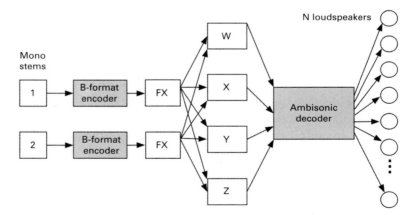

Figure 32.23 Ambisonic B-format configuration to spatialize two mono input channels to an arbitrary number of loudspeakers. The *mono stems* could be generated by a traditional DAW. The boxes marked FX indicate the point at which plug-ins for sound field manipulation would be inserted before being sent to the four channels W, X, Y, and Z of the B format. The effects could include panning, sound field rotations, tilting, and reverberation, for example. The loudspeakers are shown in a vertical line. In reality they need to be in a regular geometrical configuration around the audience.

Spherical harmonics

To reproduce from all directions perfectly, one would need an infinite number of minute speakers on a sphere around the listener, and an infinite number of "delta function" (i.e., infinitely directional) microphones pointing in all directions to record the sounds. In practice, the restricted number of channels will reduce the obtainable directional resolution. In periphony, we aim to record the values on the surface of a sphere (representing the directions around the microphones). . . . In order to discuss directional resolution on the sphere, one needs some analogy to the theory of Fourier transforms on a line. . . .
—Michael Gerzon (1973)

The theoretical foundation of ambisonics is based on *spherical harmonic decomposition of a sound field* (Malham and Myatt 1995; Malham 1998). This decomposes the directionality of the original sound field into spherical harmonic components. Spherical harmonic components represent regions of space using constants, sine, and cosine terms. Their shapes can be compared to different microphone patterns. By analogy, one can liken spherical harmonics to a kind of "Fourier series for spatial position" in that one can synthesize any position on a sphere as a combination of spherical harmonics (Gerzon 1973).

The spherical harmonics form a set of orthogonal base vectors. Thus they can be used to describe any function on the surface of a sphere, where the sphere represents a sound wave front emanating in all directions (figure 32.24).

Ambisonic decoding requires a regularly space loudspeaker configuration: squares and hexagons for horizontal playback and a cube as a minimum for with-height (periphonic) playback (Malham and Myatt 1995). The decoder

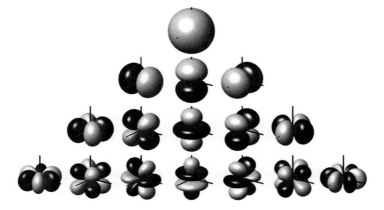

Figure 32.24 Visual representation of the Ambisonic B-format spherical harmonics components up to third order. Dark portions represent regions where the polarity is inverted. Note how the first two rows correspond to omnidirectional and figure-eight microphone polar patterns.

sends each speaker its own weighted sum of all ambisonic channels passed through variable-gain shelf filters. The filters account for the differences in the high- and low-frequency sound localization mechanisms in human hearing (Benjamin, Lee, and Heller 2006).

For synthesized sound, a higher-order ambisonics *encoder* can generate a spatial position for any sound fed into it. It can, for example, take a monaural sound and generate a multichannel signal in order to place the sound at a virtual source position. Scalability to multiple moving sources and multiple loudspeakers is one of the major advantages of the HOA approach, which also enables manipulations of the encoded sound field, such as rotation and zoom (emphasizing sounds in the front). Rotation matrices have been defined for rotation about the *x* axis (*tilt* or *roll*), the *y* axis (*tumble* or *pitch*), the *z* axis (*rotate* or *yaw*), or any combination of these (Malham and Myatt 1995). Such capabilities are clearly of compositional interest.

Malham and Myatt (1995) give examples of ambisonic encoding and decoding in Csound. Blue Ripple Sound offers the free 03A plug-in library that provides the basics of HOA. Waves 360° Ambisonics Tools is designed to support applications in augmented and virtual reality. Table 32.2 lists more ambisonics tools.

Wave Field Synthesis

Wave field synthesis (WFS) enables the construction of a sound field within a listening area using an array of loudspeakers. The term *within* is key. In a conventional loudspeaker setup the closest the sound can get to the listener is the loudspeaker itself. By contrast, in WFS the sound can move into the listening space to directly approach the listener.

WFS is based on the Huygens principle (1678), which states that any wave front can be regarded as a superposition of many elementary spherical waves (Berkhout 1988, Berkhout et al. 1993). By analogy, a rock thrown in the middle of a pond generates a wave front that propagates along the surface. The Huygens principle states that an identical wave front can be generated by simultaneously dropping an infinite number of rocks along any position defined by the passage of the primary wave front.

The mathematical basis of WFS is the Kirchhoff-Helmholtz integral (Pierce 1994). This states that the sound pressure can be determined at any point inside a volume if sound pressure and velocity are known in all points on its surface. The mathematics of WFS can be implemented efficiently in real time. A single common filter is applied to all input signals. Each speaker is delayed and weighted individually. Thus, while ambisonics uses primarily amplitude differences to position virtual sources, WFS uses delays (Pulkki, Lokki, and Rocchesso 2011).

The special feature of WFS is that it can create the impression of a 3D virtual point source located inside the listening area between the loudspeakers and the listener. Sources in front of the speakers can be rendered by concave wave fronts that focus on the virtual source. To achieve this effect, a computer controls a large array of closely spaced loudspeakers and actuates each one in exactly the same instant when the desired virtual wave front would pass through it (figure 32.25).

In theory, the entire surface of a room has to be covered with closely spaced loudspeakers, each driven with its own signal. This could entail thousands of channels. Moreover, the listening area has to be anechoic in order to avoid sound reflections. Such theoretical considerations, however, are not practical. Because acoustic perception is most acute in the horizontal plane, real-world WFS systems reduce the problem to a horizontal line of loudspeakers in front of an audience (Baalman 2008), or a circle or rectangle around the audience. In a typical application, WFS demands hundreds of closely spaced loudspeakers—each with its own amplifier—fed by hundreds of tracks of audio (figure 32.26). All loudspeakers contribute to the reproduction of a single virtual source.

Hundreds of channels, DACs, amplifiers, and loudspeakers translates into high cost. Unfortunately, reducing the number of speakers by increasing their spacing defeats the purpose by introducing *spatial aliasing*, in which the sound's position blurs due to extraneous wave fronts (Ahrens, Rabenstein, and Spors 2014). The theory of WFS assumes that the loudspeakers are a half-wavelength from one another (Pulkki, Lokki, and

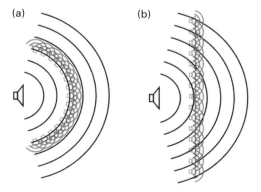

Figure 32.25 Multiple loudspeakers synthesizing a wave front. (a) Huygens principle of 1678. (b) Wave field synthesis with an array of loudspeakers. Each loudspeaker is amplified and delayed to approximate (a).

Figure 32.26 EMPAC wave field synthesis array consisting of 558 independently controllable loudspeakers. Courtesy of Rensselaer Polytechnic Institute.

Rocchesso 2011). In practical systems, typical loudspeaker spacings are between 10 and 15 cm, which limits high-frequency spatial accuracy. (A sine tone at 5 kHz has a wavelength of 6.8 cm.)

Figure 32.27 shows a simulation of the synthesis of a traveling plane (horizontal) wave by a circular configuration of fifty-six loudspeakers. A person inside this ring would hear the plane approach and pass by. As alluded to, it is also possible to synthesize a source at a limited-size region inside the circle.

Recording for a WFS system faces particular challenges and remains an experimental arena. One strategy is to assume no relation between the recording process and the playback system. This means recording dry mono signals for each source and then spatializing them in an arbitrary way later (de Bruijn et al. 1998). This solution works well for electronic music in which there is no attempt to reconstitute a natural sound field. If the recording involves an acoustic space, the impulse response of the space can be recorded separately and later convolved with the dry signal (see chapter 29 on convolution). Another solution is to record using multiple microphones (typically up to 32). Various methods have been proposed. Refer to de Bruijn, Piccolo, and Boone (1998), Braasch, Peters, and Valente (2008), and Braasch et al. (2016).

Support for WFS is provided by IRCAM's SPAT package. WFS Collider is a library of tools in SuperCollider. Also, the MPEG-4 format provides an object-based sound scene description that is compatible with WFS reproduction.

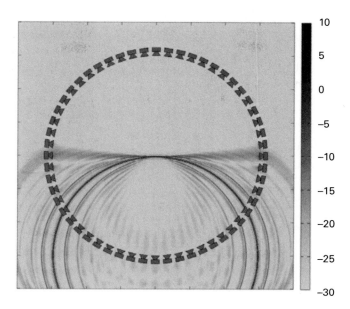

Figure 32.27 Simulation of 56 monopole loudspeakers synthesizing a plane wave that propagates in a positive direction (i.e., toward the top in this overhead diagram). In this simulation all loudspeakers are active. An amplitude scale in dB is shown at the right. After Ahrens, Rabenstein, and Spors (2014).

Spatialization Tools

Spatial audio operators are built into languages like SuperCollider and Csound, as well as patchers such as Max and Pure Data. Using these tools, numerous musicians have made custom spatializers for specific situations. James (2015) surveys these systems in arguing the case for *timbre spatialization,* in which sound is spatialized according to its frequency content. Many other spatializers have appeared in recent years, driven by the rise of virtual reality (VR) systems in which 360° sound is important. Table 32.2 lists some tools for spatialization, ranging from plug-ins to software developments kits or SDKs.

Transmission Formats for Multichannel Sound

Transmission formats for multichannel sound fall into two categories: software and hardware. Many spatialization algorithms use a self-contained syntax and storage format, in which control messages, such as sound

Table 32.2 Tools for Spatialization

Tool name	Source	Comments
Zirkonium	ZKM	Developed for immersive loudspeaker setups. Ramakrishnan (2009)
SpatialChords/ Zirkonium	C. Ramakrishnan	The theory is described in Roads (2015).
Spat	IRCAM	2D and 3D ambisonic spatialization; embedded in Max.
HoloPhon with HoloEdit and HoloSpat	GMEM, Marseille	Graphical editor and algorithmic functions for creating spatial paths in real time.
SpatGris2	Groupe de recherche en immersion spatiale (GRIS), Montréal	Plug-in allows the user to spatialize sound in 2D or in 3D with 128 inputs and outputs.
Resonance Audio	Resonance Audio	Open-source SDK for Unity, Unreal, FMOD
Atmos	Dolby	Surround technology for multiple platforms, from streaming video (e.g., Netflix) to mobile phones. Authoring on Pro Tools and Nuendo.
Spatial Audio	Apple	Surround sound application programming interface (API) for multiple platforms. It tracks the listener's head movement using accelerometers and gyroscopes on Apple devices in order to position sounds accurately.
Virtual:X	DTS	Surround technology for multiple platforms, including cars and Xbox. Authoring tool is DTS:X Creator Suite.
Microsoft Spatializer	Microsoft	Works with Microsoft HoloLens headset and with Unity and Unreal game engines.
Audio Spatializer	Unity	SDK for game development
Oculus Spatializer	Oculus	Unity plugin
Steam Audio	Steam	Supports ambisonics, works with Unity, Unreal, FMOD
Premiere Pro	Adobe	Supports ambisonics
Pro Tools HD	Avid	Supports ambisonics, Atmos, and 360° VR audio
YouTube spatial audio	You Tube	Supports ambisonics using MP4 metadata
Works and VR360 Audio	Gaudio	Plug-ins and SDKs
Facebook Audio 360	Facebook	VST plug-in
DearVR Pro	Dear Reality	Binaural, ambisonics, multichannel, plug-in format
Ambisonic Toolkit	ATK Community	For SuperCollider and Reaper
Chunity	Stanford	ChucK language programming in the Unity game engine

trajectories, programmed for one application are incompatible with any other implementation. This lack of a standardization complicates the portability of compositions and requires manual conversion of control data—a time consuming affair. Incompatible data formats also prevent collaboration between researchers and institutions. SpatDIF and MPEG-H 3D Audio software address these concerns.

Software

Audio definition model (ADM)

ADM is an emerging standard for object-based spatial audio file interchange. ADM is a .wav file with metadata to describe its spatial properties. The International Telecommunications Union (ITU) has a renderer that supports the ADM specification. Avid's ProTools with Dolby Atmos support can handle ADM files.

SpatDIF

SpatDIF is a software format that describes spatial sound information in a structured way. The format enables describing, storing, and sharing spatial audio scenes across audio applications and concert venues (Peters et al. 2013). A website (http://www.spatdif.org) provides the specification and examples. Extensions of Max and OpenMusic support the protocol, but it is not widely used.

MPEG standards for spatial audio

The Moving Picture Experts Group (MPEG) was formed by International Standards Organization (ISO) and International Electrotechnical Commission (IEC) to set standards for audio and video compression and transmission. The MP3 audio format is one of its most well-known specifications. MPEG has defined a number of standards that concern spatial audio. Refer to the MPEG website for details.

The MPEG-4 format provides an object-based sound scene description for spatial audio. It separates sound content (dry audio signals) and the specification of its ultimate spatial rendering.

MPEG-H 3D Audio is a standard developed to support coding audio in terms of audio channels, *audio objects*, or higher-order ambisonics. Audio objects are sounds that have been encoded in an XML format such that they can be scaled to different spatial output formats such as stereo, 5.1 surround, vertical, and others, depending on the playback system available. MPEG-H can support up to sixty-four loudspeaker channels. Binaural rendering for headphone listening is also supported.

Another standard is MPEG-D spatial audio object coding (SAOC). This provides user-controllable rendering of multiple audio objects based on transmission of a mono or stereo downmix of the object signals.

Hardware

A hardware issue that arises in setting up an immersive sound system is figuring out how to transmit the multichannel audio signals from the audio server to the loudspeakers. The old solution is analog audio cables. Analog cable connections are easy to understand. However, analog signals deteriorate over distance and are susceptible to noise. Multichannel analog systems require the use of cable bundles called *snakes* that are heavy and can be difficult to troubleshoot and repair.

By contrast, digital transmission solutions mean that hundreds of channels of audio can be delivered on a single low-cost fiber-optic or standard Ethernet coaxial cable. Thus new immersive spaces are increasingly being designed around an all-digital solution. MADI, AES67, AVB, and Dante are competing formats for multichannel audio transmission. This section glances briefly at each one (AES 2009; Rumsey 2019).

Multichannel audio digital interface (MADI)

Multichannel audio digital interface (MADI) or AES10 is an Audio Engineering Society (AES) standard electronic communications protocol that defines the data format and electrical characteristics of an interface that carries multiple channels of digital audio. Introduced in 1991, it supports serial digital transmission over coaxial cable or fiber-optic lines of 28, 56, or 64 channels and sampling rates of up to 96 kHz with resolution of up to 24 bits per channel. It is a unidirectional interface (one sender and one receiver). A fiber-optic connection can provide a range of up to 2 km. Over forty companies provide interfaces and computer cards for MADI.

AES67

AES67 is a technical standard for audio over internet and audio over Ethernet interoperability. The standard was developed by the Audio Engineering Society and first published in September 2013. AES67 is based on existing standards and is designed to allow interoperability between various audio networking systems such as RAVENNA, Livewire, Q-LAN and Dante. It also provides interoperability with audio video bridging (AVB) (discussed next).

Audio video bridging (AVB)

Audio Video Bridging (AVB) is set of technical standards developed by the Institute of Electrical and Electronics Engineers (IEEE) for transporting audio and video content over Ethernet. Ethernet is inherently scalable and flexible and is in wide use. A critical factor in a real-time audio-video network AV streams is *quality of service*, a term denoting priority in network transmissions. Quality of service allows voice and video traffic to be prioritized over data traffic ensuring timely and reliable delivery. AVB enhances quality of service by adding stream signaling, automatic bandwidth reservation and traffic prioritization, as well as time synchronization. AVB works by reserving up to 75 percent of the available Ethernet bandwidth for audiovisual data. AVB packets are sent regularly in the allocated slots. As bandwidth is reserved, there are no collisions.

AVB streams have a sizeable overhead, limiting the number of streams that an Ethernet cable can carry. A 100 Mbit Ethernet cable can carry nine stereo AVB streams for a total of eighteen channels or a single AVB stream with forty-five channels. Application layer protocols such as Milan have been proposed as an open standard based on an AVB foundation (Rumsey 2019).

Digital audio network through Ethernet (Dante)

Dante is a combination of software, hardware, and network protocols that deliver uncompressed, multichannel, low-latency digital audio over a standard Ethernet network. Developed in 2006 by the Audinate company, Dante supports high-speed, high channel count, low latency, and automatic configuration using the Dante Via app. Up to 1,024 channels can be supported. The maximum sampling rate is 192 kHz, and the maximum bit depth is 32. Audinate has licensed over three hundred companies to integrate Dante technology into their products (Robjohns 2018).

33 *Reverberation*

Feedback Delay Networks

Fictional Reverberation Effects

         Granular Reverberation

De-reverberation

Reverberation is a naturally occurring acoustical effect. We hear it in concert halls and other spaces with high ceilings and reflective surfaces. Sounds emitted in these spaces are reinforced by thousands of closely spaced echoes bouncing off the ceiling, walls, and floors. Due to the relatively slow speed of sound waves, we hear these echoes well after the original sound has reached our ears.

The ear distinguishes between the *direct* (original) sound and the *reflected* sound echoes because the reflected sound is slightly delayed, lower in amplitude, and lowpass filtered due to absorption of high frequencies by the air and surfaces (figure 33.1). Thousands of echo reflections per second fuse in our ear into a lingering cloud trailing the original sound.

A recording made in a concert hall is bathed in natural reverberation, particularly when the recording microphone has an omnidirectional pattern. For recordings made in small studio spaces, it is often desirable to add artificial reverberation because without it a voice or ensemble sounds *dry* and

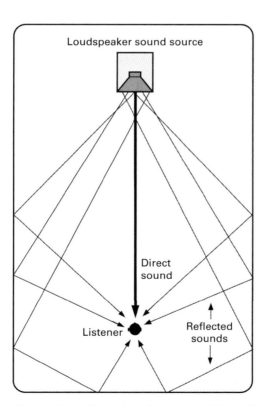

Figure 33.1 Reverberation is caused by reflections of sound by surfaces in a space. The dark line is the path of direct sound; all other lines represent sonic reflections that arrive later than the original because of their longer paths.

lacks *space* or *depth*. Moreover, basic electronic synthesis waveforms have no intrinsic spaciousness. These acoustically dead signals can be enlivened by spatial processing.

Reverberation is not a monolithic effect; myriad colors and qualities of reverberation are available. No single quality of reverberation is ideal for all sounds. Most electronic reverberators offer several types. Some attempt to simulate known concert halls, and others produce fantastic spatial images that would be impossible to duplicate in a real hall. Even "bad" (unrealistic, echoing, ringing, metallic, etc.) reverberators have their place when used expressively on selected sounds. (See the section on fictional reverberation effects.)

The best concert halls have a quality of immersive reverberation. Although this envelopment is best appreciated in the hall, natural reverberation transmits well on recordings played through loudspeakers. Digital reverberation began as an attempt to mimic this lush ambience, which imposes a global spatial halo on an entire composition.

Although global reverberation used to be the ultimate goal, one can now apply spatial processing at any time scale, from the macro down to the micro time scale (Roads 2001a). If desired, each grain of sound can be projected from its own virtual space.

The goal of this chapter is to introduce fundamental concepts and to describe in basic terms the inner workings of digital reverberators. The literature of reverberation algorithms is substantial. Välimäki et al. (2011) surveys over three hundred references. Thus another goal of this chapter has been to cite key publications for further study.

Properties of Reverberation

Glorious-sounding salons and concert spaces have been constructed since antiquity, but their acoustical principles were not well understood from a scientific standpoint until the late nineteenth century. Pioneering work on the analysis of reverberant spaces was carried out by physicist Wallace Sabine (1868–1919), who advised in the construction of Boston's acclaimed Symphony Hall in 1900 (figure 33.2). Symphony Hall was the first performance space designed according to scientific principles of acoustics. Sabine developed a formula for reverberation depending on a room's volume, geometry, and the reflectivity of its surfaces (Sabine 1922). He also observed that humidity affects the reverberation time in large halls, because humid air tends to absorb high frequencies. Natural reverberation darkens over time.

Figure 33.2 Boston Symphony Hall. The statues and niches around the sides of the hall multiply the reflections.

Given that with more reflections there is more reverberation, it is no surprise that large rooms with reflective surfaces have long reverberation times, and small rooms with absorptive surfaces have short reverberation times. Smooth, hard surfaces like glass, chrome, and marble tend to reflect all frequencies well, and absorptive surfaces like curtains, foam, and thick carpeting tend to absorb high frequencies.

The geometry of a room determines the angles of its sound reflections. Walls that are not parallel scatter wave fronts in complicated reflection patterns. Small irregularities such as plaster trimmings, indentations, columns, and statues tend to diffuse reflections, increasing echo density per unit time. The geometry of these irregular features affects some frequencies more than others. Thousands of echoes per second are heard as a fused reverberation effect.

Impulse Response of a Room

One way to measure the reverberation of a room is to trigger an *impulse* (a brief burst of sound) and plot the room's amplitude response over time. This plot shows the *impulse response* (IR) of the room (chapter 29). Natural reverberation typically has an IR structure similar to that shown in figure 33.3. The buildup follows a quasi-exponential curve that reaches a peak within a half second and decays more or less slowly.

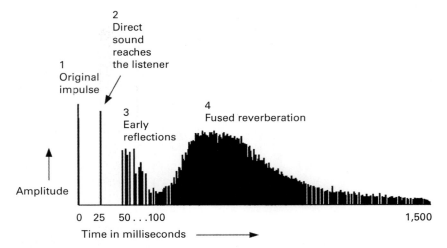

Figure 33.3 Impulse response envelope of a reverberant hall. The components of reverberation are shown as the *predelay* (a 25 ms delay before the direct sound reaches the listener), the early reflections, and the fused late reverberation. Note that the separation between these components is idealized.

In general, an irregular time interval between peaks is desirable in a concert hall. Regularly spaced peaks indicate *ringing*—resonant frequencies in the hall that can be annoying.

Reverberation Time

Another important measurement of reverberation is *reverberation decay time* (RT60). The term RT60 refers to the time it takes the reverberation to decay 60 dB from its peak amplitude (1/1,000 of its peak energy). Typical RT60 times for most concert halls range from 1.5 to 3 seconds. The RT60 point of the plot shown in figure 33.4 is 2.5 seconds.

Artificial Reverberation: Background

The earliest attempts at artificial reverberation of recordings transmitted the sound through an *acoustic echo chamber* and then mixed the reverberated signal with the original. Legendary recording studios, such as Abbey Road (London), Sunset Sound (Hollywood), and Capitol Studios (Hollywood), still have echo chambers. To make an echo chamber, one can place a loudspeaker at one end of a reflective room and put a high-quality microphone

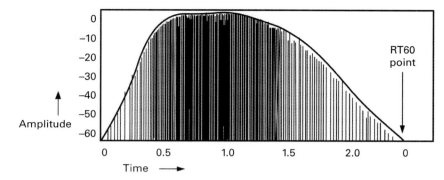

Figure 33.4   The reverberation time or RT60 is measured as the point at which the reverberation decays to −60 dB of its peak level.

at the other end. The sound to be reverberated is played over the loudspeaker and picked up by the microphone (figure 33.5). An echo chambers offers a unique acoustical ambience created by the convolution of a specific room, loudspeaker, and microphone. The quality of reverberation in an echo chamber can be excellent. A drawback to the echo chamber approach (besides the practicalities of allocating and constructing such a space) is that the effect cannot be varied a great deal.

Today it is common to use a reverberator in either hardware or software form. The earliest reverberators were electromechanical, containing two transducers (input and output) and a reverberating medium such as a long metal spring or a metal plate. Hammond organs, for example, incorporated spring reverberation as early as the 1940s, and by the 1960s many guitar amplifiers followed suit. (For digital simulations of spring reverberation, see Parker and Bilbao [2009], Bilbao and Parker [2010], and Välimäki, Parker, and Abel [2010].) In these devices, the sound was transmitted from the input transducer to the reverberating medium. The medium transmitted the sound to the output transducer mixed with myriad echoes caused by vibrations/reflections of the signal within the medium. The result was amplified and mixed with the original signal to create an artificial reverberation effect.

By contrast to spring reverberators, the EMT plate reverberators produced clean and diffuse reverberation, albeit limited in RT60 time. The EMT plate proved to be well suited to electronic music, as these units were installed in the famous West German Radio (WDR) studio in Cologne. There Stockhausen composed *Kontakte* (1960), a quadraphonic piece that remains most compelling spatially. The sound of plate reverberation remains in demand, and software emulations abound (Bilbao 2007).

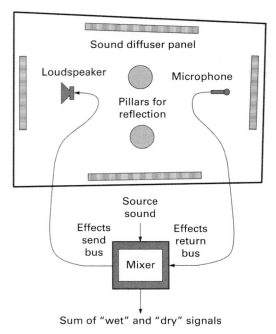

Figure 33.5   To create an acoustic ambience effect, sound can be fed into an echo chamber via a loudspeaker. The reflected, indirect sound is picked up by a microphone at RT60 from the other end of the room. Ideally, the room is irregularly shaped. To maximize and randomize the reflections, the room should be fitted with *sound diffuser panels*, which contain many recesses spaced at different distances. As sound waves strike them, they are reflected at different delay times, depending on which recess they hit. This diffusion effect tends to eliminate *standing waves* (resonant frequencies in the room) caused by parallel walls. Another way to increase reflections is to install reflective sound pillars made of polished marble that will scatter the sound in all directions.

Modern digital reverberators can be divided into several broad classes on the basis of the structure of their filter algorithm, as follows:

- Schroeder algorithms
- Convolution
- Physical models
  Finite-difference time-domain
  Geometric acoustics
  Waveguides
- Feedback delay networks

We discuss each method in subsequent sections.

Algorithmic Reverberation Based on Schroeder's Model

In the primordial days of digital signal processing, Dr. Manfred R. Schroeder of Bell Telephone Laboratories (AT&T) (1961, 1962, 1970) was the first to implement an artificial reverberation algorithm on a computer. The Schroeder design was the earliest *algorithmic reverberator* based on a computational model. It took over twelve hours of computation time to run Schroeder's algorithms on ten seconds of sound. Beltrán and Beltrán (2002) presented a MATLAB implementation of a Schroeder reverberator. Also refer to Erbe (2014) for an implementation in Pure Data. Freeverb is an open-source variant of the classic Schroeder reverberator.

Parts of Reverberation

The effect of reverberation can be broken into the following three parts, shown previously in figure 33.2:

- *Direct (unreflected) sound* travels in a straight path and is the first sound to arrive at the listener's ears.
- *Discrete early reflections* hit the listener just after the direct sound.
- *Late or fused reverberation* contains thousands of closely spaced echoes but takes some time to build up and then fade away exponentially.

Users can manipulate the balance between these parts if they desire. The balance between the reverberation effect and the direct sound is called the *wet/dry* ratio (the reverberated sound is said to be *wet*), and the delay just before the early reflections is called the *predelay*. Table 33.1 lists common parameters provided by many commercial reverberators

The sparse early reflections of a concert hall can be simulated by means of a *tapped delay line* whose effect is heard just before the dense late reverberation. A tapped delay line can be sampled or *tapped* at multiple points to generate several copies of the input signal that are each delayed by a different time. (See chapter 29 for an explanation of tapped delay lines.)

The lush sound of fused late reverberation requires a high echo density. The earliest digital reverberators produced as few as 30 echoes per second, whereas in actual concert halls, an echo density of ten thousand echoes per second is typical (Jot and Chaigne 1991; Smith 2010). However, we do not perceive the full complexity of natural reverberation, so fewer echoes can be tolerated in an artificial reverberator (Smith 2018). Indeed, fewer echoes may be the desired effect. Most reverberators let users adjust the echo density or *diffusion* from discrete echoes to a dense sheet of reverberation.

Table 33.1   Typical parameters of reverberators

Parameter	Description
Type of reverberation	Includes hall, chamber, plate, studio, gated, and so on
Size	Sets the delay times within the unit reverberators
Predelay	Controls the onset time of the effect after the direct sound
Reverberation time	Sets the decay time
Diffusion	Determines echo density
Mix (wet/dry ratio)	Ratio of *wet* effect versus *dry* input sound
Highpass filter	Reverberates only the upper octaves of the sound, creating a *sizzling* reverberation effect
Lowpass filter	Reverberates only the lower octaves of the sound, creating a *muffled* reverberation effect

Unit Reverberators

Schroeder called the algorithmic building blocks *unit reverberators,* which take two forms: *recursive comb filters* and *allpass filters,* both introduced in chapter 28.

As explained in chapter 28, a recursive or *infinite impulse response* (IIR) comb filter contains a feedback loop in which an input signal is delayed by D samples, multiplied by an amplitude or gain factor g, and then routed back to be added to the latest input signal (figure 33.6a). The delay time is also called the *loop time*.

When the delay D is small (less than about 10 ms) the comb filter's effect is primarily a spectral one. That is, it creates peaks and dips in the frequency response of the input signal. When D is larger than about 10 ms, it creates a series of decaying echoes, as shown in figure 33.6b. The echoes decay exponentially, so for the maximum number of echoes (the longest decay time), g is set to nearly 1.0. The time it takes for the output of the comb filter to decay by 60 dB is specified by the following formula (Moore 1990):

decay_time $= (60/-loopGain) \times loopDelay$

where *loopGain* is the gain g expressed in decibels $= 20 \times \log_{10}(g)$, and *loop-Delay* is the delay D expressed in seconds $= D/R$, where R is the sampling rate. Thus if $g = 0.7$, then *loopGain* $= -3$ dB.

Allpass filters transmit all frequencies of steady-state sinusoids equally well. But they color sharp transient signals by introducing frequency-dependent delays. When the delay time is long enough, the allpass filter shown in figure 33.7a has an impulse response as shown in figure 33.7b: a series of

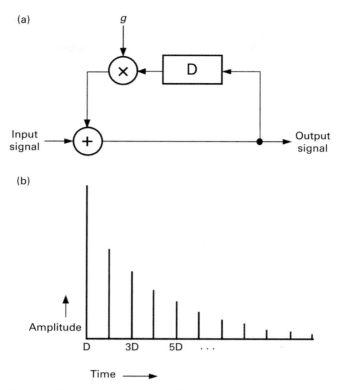

Figure 33.6   A recursive comb filter for reverberation. (a) Circuit of comb filter with coefficients *D* (number of samples to delay) and *g* (amount of feedback). (b) Impulse response, as a series of echoes.

exponentially decaying echo pulses, similar to a comb filter with a long delay. The uniform spacing between the pulses suggests that when a short, transient sound is applied, the filter rings with a period equal to the delay time of the filter. This explains why allpass filters are not "colorless" when they process sounds with sharp attack and decay transients. As we will see later, modern reverberators constantly modulate delay times to greatly reduce such artifacts.

Reverberation Patches

For lush reverberation, it is necessary to interconnect several unit reverberators to create sufficient echo density so that the echoes fuse perceptually. When unit reverberators are connected in parallel, their echoes add together. When they are connected in series, each echo generated by one unit spawns a series of echoes in the next unit, resulting in much greater echo density. The number of echoes produced in series is the product of the number of echoes produced by each unit.

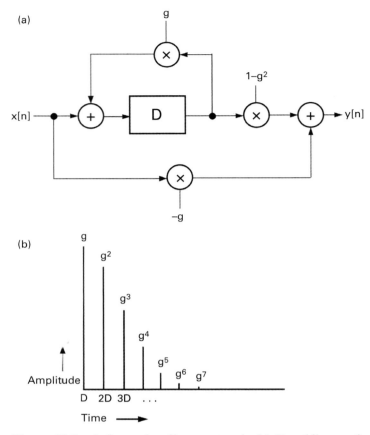

Figure 33.7   A first-order allpass network. (a) By adding −*g* times the input into the output of the delay, a comb filter is changed into an allpass filter. (b) The impulse response of an allpass filter is an exponentially decaying series of echo pulses. This makes the impulse filter useful as a building block of reverberators.

In Schroeder's designs, comb filters with different settings are interconnected in parallel to minimize spectral anomalies. For example, a frequency that passes through one comb filter might be canceled out by another. Allpass filters are usually connected in series. Because of the phase distortion they introduce, connecting allpass filters in parallel can result in a nonuniform amplitude response.

Figure 33.8 shows two reverberators proposed by Schroeder. In figure 33.8a, the parallel comb filters initiate a primary train of echoes that are summed and fed to two allpass filters in series. In figure 33.8b, four allpass filters cause the echo density to be multiplied by each unit. If each allpass generates just four audible echoes, the end result is 1,024 echoes at the output of Allpass 4.

The characteristic sound of a reverberation system of this type is dependent on the choice of the delay times *D* (these determine the spacing of the echoes) and amplitude factors *g* (these determine the decay or reverberation time) for

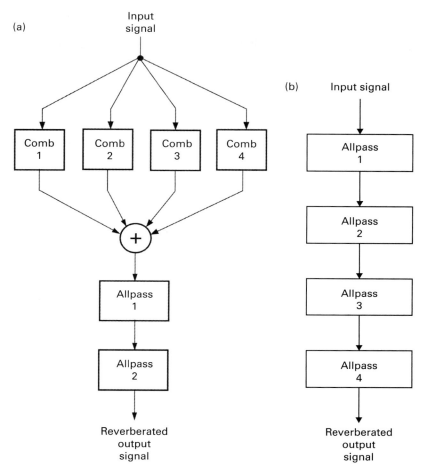

Figure 33.8   Schroeder's original reverberator designs. (a) Parallel comb filters fed into two allpass filter stages. (b) Four allpass filter stages in series.

each of the unit reverberators. A typical value for g is 0.7 (Smith 2010). Delay line lengths are typically mutually prime and span successive orders of magnitude, such as 113, 337, and 1051 samples (Smith 2010). Mutual prime delay times is important for natural-sounding reverberation (Moorer 1977, 1979a). Why is this? Consider two comb filters, where the delay time of the first is 10 ms and that of the second is 12.5 ms. The lengths of their delay lines are 800 samples and 1,000 samples, respectively, at a sampling rate of 40 kHz. Because the lengths of both delay lines are divisible by 200, a reverberator built from these two units does not have a smooth decay. At multiples of 200 ms, the echoes coincide to increase the amplitude at that point, causing a sensation of discrete echoes or regular "bumps" in the decay. When the delay times are adjusted to 10.025 and 24.925 ms, the length of their delay lines are 799 and 997, respectively. Now the first coincidence of echoes does not occur until $(799 \times 997)/40$ KHz $= 19.91$ seconds. Refer to Moorer (1979a) and Smith (2010) for a discussion of how to tune these parameters.

As one would expect, shorter delay times correlate with the sound of smaller spaces. For a large concert hall, the reverberator shown in figure 33.8a uses comb filter delay times around 50 ms with a ratio of *longest:shortest* delay of 1.7:1. For a small tiled room effect, the comb filter delay times can be set in the range of 10 ms. The allpass filters have relatively short loop times of 5 ms or less. The reverberation time of the allpass filters must be short because their purpose is to increase the echo density of the overall reverberation, not its duration.

Extensions to Schroeder Reverberation

Schroeder's reverberation algorithms can be characterized as *tapped recirculating delay* (TRD) models. As explained previously, the reverberator is usually partitioned into comb and allpass sections, which generate sufficient echo density to create a reasonable simulation of global reverberation. The TRD model is efficient, but it simulates only generic global reverberation and not the detailed acoustic properties of an actual performance space.

In 1970 Schroeder extended his original reverberator to incorporate a multi-tap delay line to simulate the early reflections that are heard in a hall before the outset of the fused reverberant sound. This design, which is now common in algorithmic reverberators, is shown in figure 33.9. Thus to simulate a particular concert hall, a simple way to improve the basic TRD model is to graft the measured early reflection signature of the hall onto the generic global reverberator (Moorer 1979a). A further extension is to lowpass filter the global reverberation according to the measured sound absorption characteristics of the hall.

In the standard Schroeder reverberation algorithms, the allpass filters generate a series of echoes with an exponential decay. An extension to the Schroeder model is to substitute an *oscillatory allpass* filter for the allpass filter in the Schroeder design. In this case, the impulse response of the allpass filter is a pulse train with an amplitude of a damped sinusoid (figure 33.10). This models the case of a "good sounding" room with a slightly undulating reverberation pattern (Chowning et al. 1974; Moorer 1979a).

Low-frequency modulation of delay parameters at decorrelated rates was key to the sound of the famous Lexicon reverberation algorithms designed by David Griesinger (Griesinger 2014). Dattorro (1997a) presented a simplified diagram of a reverberator in the style of Griesinger. See also Erbe (2014). The reverberator features four input diffusers followed by four *tank diffusers* that feed back into themselves. Sounds fed into the tank recirculate. Decay coefficients control the recirculation time, which can range from short

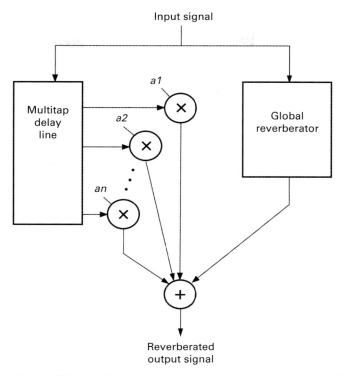

Figure 33.9   In Schroeder's later designs, a multitap delay line simulated the early reflections of sound in a concert hall.

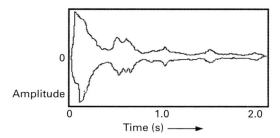

Figure 33.10   The impulse response of an oscillatory allpass unit reverberator.

to infinite. Beltrán and Beltrán (2002) present a MATLAB implementation of Datorro's reverberator.

Multiple-Stream Reverberation

Multiple-stream reverberation can be viewed as a compromise between detailed but computationally intensive approaches to reverberation (such as geometrical modeling discussed later) and the efficient but generic Schroeder or TRD model. Multiple-stream reverberation splits the reverberated signal into several *streams,* each of which models the local reverberation emanating from a small spatial region of the virtual room. Each stream is implemented with a TRD network (comb and allpass filters) tuned for that region of the room.

One spatial reverberator system took the multiple-stream approach and combined it with two other processes: (1) a model of room reflections, and (2) localization cues caused by the reflection of sound off the pinnae, shoulders, and upper torso (Kendall and Martens 1984; Kendall et al. 1986; Kendall, Martens, and Decker 1989). Reflections determine the delay times of each independent reverberation stream. Then, after reverberating each stream separately, a *directionalizer* filtered each stream to impose additional cues as to its position in a virtual three-dimensional space (figure 33.11). To simulate a room's reverberation pattern, each of the main directions of reverberation is processed as a separate stream (Kendall, Martens, and Decker 1989).

The concept of separate reverberation streams was also present in quadraphonic reverberation research carried out at MIT (Stautner and Puckette 1982). In this work the loudspeaker outputs were spatially responsive to the input channel of the source. For example, a direct sound emanating from a left front loudspeaker would be heard to reverberate from two adjacent loudspeakers and finally from the opposite right rear loudspeaker. (Further along in this chapter is a mention of directional reverberation in the context of feedback delay networks.)

Convolving Reverberators

Reverberators based on convolution let users imprint the acoustic signatures of real and imaginary spaces on any sound (Roads 1997). Chapter 28 explains convolution in detail. Whereas Schroeder algorithms tend to model generic spaces, convolution usually starts with a sampled IR. This is the authentic signature of a real acoustic space from the perspective of the microphones used to record it.

The IR of a room is obtained by recording the room's response to a brief impulsive sound, a long noise burst, or a swept sine wave (Farina 2000, 2007; Farina and Ayalon 2005; Braasch 2018). The IR is then convolved with the signal to be reverberated. Convolution replaces every sample of the signal with a scaled and delayed copy of the IR.

The raw output of convolution is 100 percent wet. For realistic reverberation, one blends the wet output of the convolution with the original (dry) input signal, where the convolved wet part is at least 15 dB lower than the original.

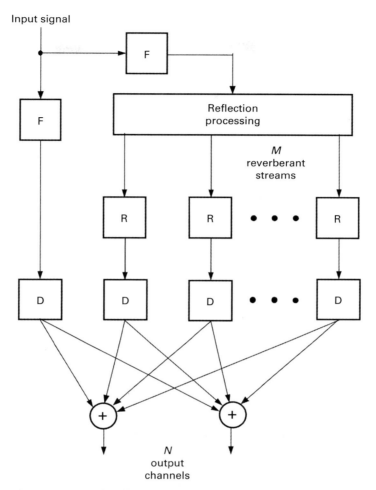

Figure 33.11   Simplified view of a *spatial reverberator* after Kendall, Martens, and Decker (1989). This system models a space by summing the contributions of *M* local reverberators, which ultimately generate *N* output channels. F is a filter that imposes spectrum changes caused by distance and air absorption. R is a local reverberant stream, modeling the reverberation in a subspace of the total room. D is a directionalizer that filters the sound according to its position in the virtual space. The implemented system has two independent reflection processors and some cross-feeding in the reverberant streams.

The first commercial real-time convolving reverberator was the $10,000 Sony DRE-S777, introduced in 1999. Since then, the technique has been implemented by dozens of companies. Because the convolution algorithm is well known, the added value of these products comes in the form of flexible GUIs and libraries of proprietary IRs of exotic spaces, including concert halls, cathedrals, stadiums, theaters, churches, recording studios, rooms, scoring stages, clubs, and tombs, as well as the sampled IRs of vintage artificial reverberators such as the EMT 140 plate and classic Lexicon digital reverberators (figure 33.12).

As chapter 29 points out, direct convolution is sometimes not practical for real-time reverberation because of the enormous amount of computation it entails. Thus a practical approach uses *fast convolution,* taking advantage of enormous speed-ups offered by the *fast Fourier transform* (FFT) for longer impulse responses (Smith 2012). Convolution is performed on successive blocks of samples in the frequency domain. Given the Fourier transform of the IR and the Fourier transform of a block of input signal, the two can be multiplied point by point and the result transformed back to the time domain. However, in real time, a block of samples must be read and then processed while a second block is being read. Therefore, the input-output latency in samples is twice the size of a block. This is not feasible in real-time performance. Thus direct-form and block-processing methods can be mixed, as shown by Gardner (1995). Beltrán and Beltrán (2002) present a MATLAB implementation of Gardner's reverberator. *Graphics processing units* (GPUs) can also be programmed to perform efficient convolution (Savioja et al. 2011). For a review of fast convolution techniques, refer to Välimäki et al. (2012).

Convolution with Velvet Noise

It is well known that a burst of Gaussian white noise with an exponential decay is a reasonable first approximation to the IR of a concert hall's late reverberation (Moorer 1979c; Roads 1993a, 1997). Using this as a starting point, investigations have shown that convolution with *velvet noise* is a computationally efficient method of producing artificial reverberation with a "smooth" response (Karjalainen and Järveläinen 2007; Välimäki et al. 2017). The smoothness can

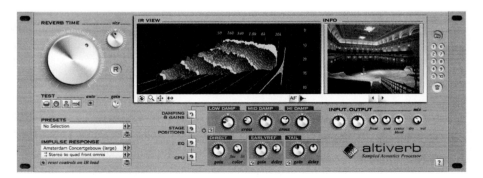

Figure 33.12   Interface of the AudioEase Altiverb convolving reverberator, with the IR of the Amsterdam Concertgebouw selected.

be attributed to the perceived flatness of the time envelope of velvet noise versus the constantly fluctuating envelope of white noise.

Velvet noise was discovered by Karjalainen and Järveläinen (2007). It consists of sample values −1, 0, and 1 only (figure 33.13). It can be interpreted as a randomly jittered-in-time impulse train in which the sign of each impulse is random. The *pulse density* determines the probability of non–zero-valued samples in the noise. A typical pulse density range for reverberation is 600 to 2000 pulses per second. Each pulse corresponds to an echo in a space when convolution is applied.

The samples of the velvet noise sequence serve as *sparse FIR* (SFIR) filter coefficients. (See chapter 28 for FIR filters.) Velvet noise convolution is fast to compute because all multiplications by zero can be skipped. In addition, as the non-zero values are either −1 or 1, multiplications are not needed here either. Thus convolution with velvet noise reduces to a sparse multiplication-free convolution. In practice, the input signal propagates in the delay line of the filter, and only those input samples that coincide with non-zero coefficients of the velvet noise sequence add together to produce the output. Thus the SFIR is much more efficient than a typical direct convolution.

An implementation by Välimäki et al. (2017) divides the IR into short segments of variable length to avoid artifacts of a frame rate. It fills each segment with velvet noise. Each segment is lowpass filtered and adjusted in gain to achieve an exponential decay with high-frequency rolloff. This basic structure can be augmented with a Schroeder-type allpass filter for each segment to increase the echo density and smooth transitions between segments.

Spatial Convolution beyond Reverberation

Going beyond reverberation effects, the IRs of loudspeakers, megaphones, walkie-talkies, microphones, amplifiers, telephones, and any other object with an acoustic response can be sampled and convolved. These can in turn be convolved with room models to position them at a particular location. By this means, sounds can be localized inside tin cans, cardboard boxes, or airplane cockpits, under blankets, or in the trunk of a car.

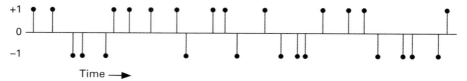

Figure 33.13   A velvet noise sequence consists of zero-valued samples interspersed with +1 and −1.

Physical Models

A physical model represents a scientifically rigorous approach to the problem of reverberation (Moore 1983). In this section we look at three types of physical models: finite-difference time-domain, geometric acoustics, and waveguides.

Finite-Difference Time-Domain Models

In principle, solving the wave equation using *finite-difference time-domain* (FDTD) methods is the most accurate of physical models. (See chapter 18.) For reverberation, the space to be modeled is divided into a 3D grid into which sound waves will be projected. For a given sound projected into the space, its wave equation, including all reflections, is solved by numerical approximation for each point on the grid. As Smith (2018) estimated, for a small hall (30 m × 15 m × 6 m) a fine-grained FDTD model accurate to 0.6 cm requires more than three quadrillion operations per second. Thus recent work in FDTD reverberation has focused on computational acceleration (Webb and Bilbao 2011; Bilbao et al. 2016). In particular, massive wave simulations can be computed in parallel using GPUs. This has made it possible to carry out optimized wave simulations of room acoustics at audio rates.

FDTD methods can be applied not just to physical models but also to *virtual analog* (VA) models (chapter 19). Reverberators based on VA models simulate not physical rooms but electromechanical devices such as spring and plate reverberators. This approach starts by modeling the physics of the mechanical reverberation medium using FDTD methods and incorporating behavior of the analog circuitry to which it is coupled. For example, Bilbao (2007) proposed a scientifically derived VA model of a plate reverberator. Refer to Välimäki et al. (2012) for more VA examples, including tape-based echo effects.

Geometric Acoustics Models

As previously mentioned, wave-based methods can be computationally expensive, so it is sometimes more appropriate to resort to faster but less accurate techniques. This is the domain of *geometric acoustics* (GA) modeling (Välimäki et al. 2012). GA modeling gives an acoustician a way to listen to a hall before it is built, called *auralization* (Vorländer 2008, 2018). Today GA is also driven by the needs of the game and virtual reality industries for realistic acoustic rendering of virtual spaces (Tsingos 2009).

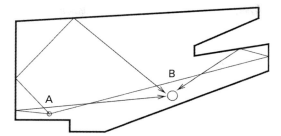

Figure 33.14   Acoustic ray-tracing model of room. Source (A) and receiver (B). After Savioja and Svensson (2015).

In GA modeling, each sound source can be modeled as a vector with an adjustable position, directionality, magnitude, and dispersion. As figure 33.14 shows, starting from the projection of a source vector into the room, an acoustic ray-tracing algorithm traces the path of sound reflections. In a complete geometric model, the reverberation algorithm models the reflection patterns of hundreds of simulated sound rays, beams, cones, or pyramids, depending on the model chosen. Because a detailed GA model can be computationally expensive, in practical applications it is common to use a GA to model only the early *specular* (mirror-like) reflections of a simulated room and then combine this with an efficient algorithmic reverberator if needed. Efficient implementations on GPUs have been demonstrated (Schissler and Manocha 2011).

As Moorer (1979c) pointed out, an overly simplistic GA model fails to account for the scattering sound rays in real halls. This scattering happens because no surface is 100 percent smooth and reflective, so that sound waves reflect, and their energy is partially absorbed at each point of reflection. Thus a number of methods try to improve on the simple ray-tracing model by explicitly modeling the physics of sound propagation. More realistic models take into account both specular and diffuse (scattered) reflections on sound absorbing surfaces, diffraction over the edges of screens, energy passing through panels (sound insulation), holes in large surfaces, and windows and doors made of a material different from the surrounding surface (Vorländer 2008). Savioja and Svensson (2015) present an overview of GA models in general.

Waveguide Models

A *waveguide* is a computational model of a medium in which waves travel. Physicists have long used *waveguide networks* to describe the behavior of waves in resonant spaces (Crawford 1968). The waveguide network approach to reverberation is built out of a set of bidirectional delay lines (Smith 1985c, 1987a, b; Garnett and Mont-Reynaud 1988). The delay line contains a wave propagating in one direction and reflecting back to the center junction when it reaches the end of the line. By interconnecting a number of waveguides together into a network, one can build a model of acoustical media, such as the reflection pattern of a concert hall.

In waveguide reverberation, the lengths of the individual waveguide delay lines are different from one another in order to simulate different echo times within a hall. At the junction of multiple waveguides the energy is scattered among them, causing a diffusion effect that is typical of fused reverberant sound (figure 33.15). In a *closed network,* once a signal is introduced it recirculates freely throughout the network without loss of energy (Rocchesso and Smith 1997, 2003). To obtain a reverberation effect, one introduces small losses of amplitude energy within the network to achieve the desired reverberation time. Signal inputs and outputs can be chosen anywhere in the network.

Waveguide networks make efficient reverberation models. A network with N junctions requires N multiplies and $2N-1$ additions to generate an output sample. The number of junctions N depends on the system being modeled. A model of a resonating box might require eight intersections, whereas a model of a complex room's reverberation response might take hundreds of junctions because any place where a signal might scatter requires a junction.

The structure of a waveguide network ensures that there is never any numerical overflow or oscillation within the network. Moreover, the important property of diffusive scattering of sound rays (Moorer 1979c), which is poorly handled by a Schroeder-type TRD model, is simulated well by a waveguide network. An undulation effect can be obtained by smoothly modulating the delay line lengths.

Murphy et al. (2007) developed a mesh of interconnected waveguides that form a grid to fill the space being modeled, the *Digital Waveguide Mesh.* It can used from two perspectives. The Wave or W-mesh models the delay elements. The Kirchoff or K-mesh models the nodes of this grid and is

● = Junction

Figure 33.15   A three-port waveguide network with six nodes. This waveguide propagates energy out of the outputs, meaning that it is an open network that eventually loses energy, as a reverberant hall does.

equivalent to a FDTD model. Välimäki et al. (2012) discuss its numerical problems and efforts to address them.

Feedback Delay Networks

Jot and Chaigne (1991, 1996) proposed a *feedback delay network* (FDN) approach to algorithmic reverberation, after the theory of Gerzon (1971, 1972) and the prototype of Stautner and Puckette (1982). FDN provides a general framework for reverberators, allowing separate and independent control over the energy (sound intensity), damping (decay time), and diffusion (echo density) of the reverberator. The basic FDN approach models late reverberation.

An FDN can be regarded as a bank of parallel comb filters that route into a feedback matrix, as shown in figure 33.16 for order three. This is a recursive IIR filter bank, which makes it computationally efficient. An FDN can also be described as a waveguide network in which all waveguide endpoints meet at the same scattering junction (Smith 2010, 2013).

The core of the system is the feedback matrix, which interconnects the delay lines, scattering energy among them. Jot and Chaigne (1991) observed that a configuration of delay lines with an interconnection matrix could represent any combination of comb or allpass filters. Thus the design of the matrix strongly affects the quality of the reverberation (Rocchesso 1997; Rocchesso and Smith 1997). The overall goal is maximal diffusion (i.e., more echoes) and decorrelation between channels—in short, a more spacious reverberation cloud. In order to ensure this, the matrix should have no null coefficients. Ideally, all coefficients have the same magnitude. Several families of

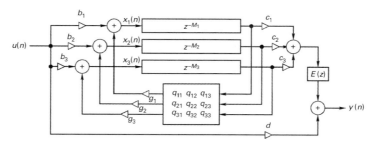

Figure 33.16   A third-order FDN (after Jot and Chaigne 1991 and Smith 2010). The top rectangles are three comb filters. Their output signal is fed back through a feedback matrix shown at the bottom. An additional filter $E(z)$ is applied to the nondirect signal. This filter is called a *tone corrector* by Jot and Chaigne (1991). It serves to equalize the energy regardless of the reverberation time in each band. In other words, if the user adjusts the decay time in a band, $E(z)$ will impose a corresponding alteration in gain in that band so the total energy in the band's impulse-response is unchanged.

unitary matrices can satisfy this criterion (Jot and Chaigne 1991). With such a matrix, eight to sixteen delay units with a length of one to two seconds are sufficient to ensure dense reverberation.

As a unity gain network, an FDN can sustain indefinitely. Thus a useful starting point is a *lossless* FDN with an infinite reverberation time (Smith 2010). One can then work on obtaining the desired reverberation time in each frequency band.

Alary et al. (2019) proposed an FDN with directional properties in the context of Ambisonic spatial projection (see chapter 32). This means that the reverberation can be localized to a given azimuth and elevation in an immersive sound environment.

Free-software implementations of FDN reverberators can be found in the Faust programming language (GRAME 2013; Smith 2013). Pulkki, Lokki, and Rocchesso (2011) presents an overview of reverberators including FDNs with examples in MATLAB. Beltrán and Beltrán (2002) also present a MATLAB implementation of an FDN reverberator. Frenette (2000) is scholarly study on a time-varying FDN reverberator with code listings in C++. Erbe (2014, 2015) documents the design of the FDN-based voltage-controlled Erbe-Verb Eurorack module.

Fictional Reverberation Effects

In the virtual world, the morphology of space is completely malleable. It can be transformed gradually or suddenly. For example, an intimate enclosed space can morph into a reverberant cathedral and back again. We can compose echo patterns that correspond to a fantastic voyage through an imaginary world. Indeed, the central focus of a musical composition can be the evolution of its spatial morphology (Smalley 1991).

Thus the goal of spatialization goes beyond realism to open up a world of fantastic spaces that could never exist in nature. Any of the methods described in this chapter can produce fictional reverberation. As Lexicon's reverberation guru David Griesinger (2000) observed,

I have not tried to generate real rooms but patterns of reflections and reverberations that do what is optimum perceptually, whether a room could do that or not.

Eventide's Blackhole reverberation product is advertised as "allowing you to create virtual spaces that could never exist in reality" (Eventide 2019). A common example of a nonrealistic effect is gated reverberation, which explodes quickly in echo density and then cuts off suddenly. Other effects include a "sizzling" reverberation obtained by applying a highpass filter to the reverberated sound, and its opposite, a muffled reverberation obtained by applying a lowpass filter. By manipulating parameters, one can create weird combinations such as tiny rooms with long reverberation times.

We already mentioned reverberators with indefinite sustain, also called *infinite reverberation* or *freeze effect*. These grab a section of the active reverberation tail in real time and sustain it continuously.

Another fictional effect is pitch-shifted reverberation. *Chordal reverberation* combines several layers of pitch-shifted reverberation to impart a harmonic decay to a noise sound (Roads 2015). This can be realized in non–real time by recording the reverberation signal on a separate track and then pitch-shifting it multiple times on different tracks.

Several reverberators offer pitch-shifting in real time. For example, Valhalla's Shimmer plug-in uses granular pitch-shifted reverberation to add a harmonizing voice to a melody (Valhalla 2011). (See chapter 31 for an explanation of granular pitch shifting.) Zynaptiq's Adaptiverb plug-in uses source separation to eliminate noisy components and adapts its reverberation tail to the tonality of the input or a user-defined set of notes. Another tool of this type is Sonible's smart:reverb that analyzes the input signal and suggests reverberation settings.

We have already mentioned the Erbe-Verb module (Erbe 2015). A principal design goal was interactive control of reverberation parameters. This means that multiple parameters can be varied freely in real time with a knob or a control voltage (Erbe 2014). For example, with a surge of control voltage, the room size can change dramatically.

AcousModules Univerb and ScatterVerb project reverberant fields in up to sixty-four channels with RT60 times extended to 240 seconds. Their FocusVerb places the reverberation effect only in a specific area, which can grow, shrink, or move over time.

An extreme example of a fictional effect was Puckette's "infuriating nonlinear reverberator." It consisted of a contraption in which a contact microphone was attached to ceramic tile (Puckette 2011). A performer tapped the contact microphone on various small objects. After filtering out resonances, the resulting audio signal was fed into a nonlinear reverberator to simulate an assortment of fanciful percussion sounds.

Granular Reverberation

The rolling of thunder has been attributed to echoes among the clouds; and if it is to be considered that a cloud is a collection of particles of water . . . and therefore each capable of reflecting sound, there is no reason why very [loud] sounds should not be reverberated . . . from a cloud.
—Sir John Herschel, quoted in *Sound*, 1875

Particle synthesis methods, as described in chapters 12 and 21, can generate artificial IRs (Roads 2001a). This opens a path to an unlimited territory of

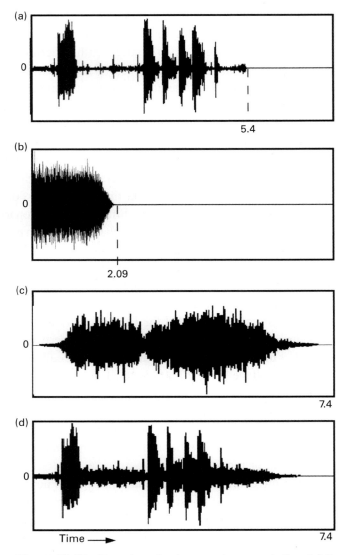

Figure 33.17   Reverberation by granular convolution. (a) Speech input: "Moi, Alpha Soixante." (b) Granular impulse response, consisting of 1,000 9 ms sinusoidal grains centered at 14,000 Hz, with a bandwidth of 5,000 Hz. (c) Convolution of (a) and (b). (d) Mixture of (a) and (c) in a proportion of 5:1, creating reverberation around the speech.

virtual spaces. Many of the spaces created in this manner would be impossible to realize in the physical world, such as spaces with time-varying echo densities or the simultaneous presence of different qualities of ambience. Convolving an arbitrary sound with a cloud of sonic grains can lead to many unusual effects: spatial, temporal, and timbral. The convolution with a cloud of sound particles creates a scattershot *time-splattered* effect. Time-splattering begins with a more-or-less dense cloud of sound grains generated by the technique of *asynchronous granular synthesis* (AGS) (chapter 13). AGS scatters grains statistically within a region defined on the time/frequency plane. The virtual reflection contributed by each grain splatters the input sound in time; that is, it adds an irregularly spaced delay. If each grain were a single-sample pulse, then the echoes would be faithful copies of the original input. Because each grain can contain hundreds of samples, however, each echo is locally time-smeared and filtered.

Time-splattering effects can be divided into two basic categories, which depend mainly on the attack of the input sound. If the input begins with a sharp attack, each grain generates an echo of that attack. If the cloud of grains is not continuous, these echoes are irregularly spaced in time. If the input has a smooth attack, however, the time-splattering itself is smoothed into a kind of strange colored reverberation (figure 33.17). The color of the reverberation and the echoes is determined by the spectrum of the grains, which is a factor of the duration, envelope, and waveform of each grain.

De-reverberation

The complicated process of *de-reverberation* attempts to remove reverberation from a recorded sound. This field has gained new prominence with increasing use of teleconferencing in suboptimal acoustic environments. The main research focus has been on speech, so that voices are perceived as clearer and closer. Naylor and Gaubitch (2010), Habets (2016), and Habets and Naylor (2018) have outlined the main strategies. These involve *beamforming using microphone arrays* (weighting the microphone facing the talker in a multimicrophone setup), *speech enhancement* (based on a model of speech such as linear predictive coding [chapter 14]), and *blind deconvolution*. In this last case, the impulse response of the room is identified using statistical techniques. This information is then used to make an inverse filter that compensates for the reverberation. Made into a commercial product with an intuitive GUI, Zynaptiq's Unveil plug-in uses recurrent neural networks to separate the reverberation from the direct signal, giving users a separate handle on each (Nercessian and Lukin 2019).

V Sound Analysis

34   *Pitch Estimation*

Pitch, Rhythm, and Waveform Analysis: Background

           Early Images of Sound

           Early Sound Recorders

Pitch and Rhythm Recognition in MIDI Systems

The Pitch Estimation Problem

           Applications of Pitch Estimation

                      Melody transcription

                      Real-time pitch recognition

                      Pitch editing

                      Un-mixing

                      Automatic dialog replacement

           Difficulties in Pitch Estimators

                      Attack transients

                      Low frequencies

                      High frequencies

                      Legato notes and melisma

                      Myopic pitch tracking

                      Acoustic ambience

Pitch Estimation Methods

           Time-Domain Fundamental Period Pitch Estimation

           Autocorrelation Pitch Estimation

            Adaptive Filter Pitch Estimation

Frequency Domain Pitch Estimators
    Tracking phase vocoder analysis
    Cepstrum analysis
    Maximum likelihood
Pitch Estimators Based on Models of the Ear
Neural Network Pitch Estimation
Polyphonic Pitch Detection
Analysis of Musical Context

Sound analysis plays a pivotal role in new methods of sound transformation. It is also the foundation of applications in *music information retrieval:* score following, parsing music structure, chord recognition, tempo and beat tracking, content-based audio retrieval (e.g., finding a song by humming), harmonic-percussive separation, voice separation, and melody tracking (Müller 2015). In this broader context, sound analysis has been characterized as *audio content analysis* (Gouyon et al. 2008).

Our goal here is to present the basic issues, survey past strategies, and describe musical applications of these techniques. Before plunging directly into pitch analysis, we prescribe a preliminary dose of history of inquiry into the properties of sound.

Pitch, Rhythm, and Waveform Analysis: Background

Efforts to describe and measure the properties of musical sound date back to antiquity. Ancient Vedantic (orthodox Hindu) texts on music acknowledged the notion of octave equivalence and divided the octave into 22 *shruti* intervals (Framjee 1958; Daniélou 1958). This *shruti* scale, which the Greeks called the *Enarmonikos,* was considered by the Hellenic peoples as the basis of all musical scales. Pythagoras (ca. 580–500 BCE) documented a correspondence between musical pitches and divisions of a length of string, which led him to describe musical intervals and scales in terms of arithmetic ratios. The Greeks also developed a set of rhythmic patterns or *modes* that served as the rhythmic basis for much European medieval music.

Before the invention of electronic devices such as audio amplifiers, oscillators, and oscilloscopes, acoustic measurements were limited to the most basic properties of sound. In 1636, Galileo (1564–1642) and Mersenne (1588–1648) experimentally ascribed pitch to the frequency of a waveform. Around 1700, Sauveur (1653–1716) invented a method to count acoustic vibrations. He coined the term *les harmoniques* to describe higher tones that accompany a fundamental tone.

The tuning fork, which vibrates at a constant pitch, was invented in 1711 by the Englishman John Shore, a trumpeter and lutenist. He humorously referred to the instrument as a "pitch fork." In 1830 Savart developed a pitch measuring technique using rotating serrated wheels. Savart pressed a reed against different wheels to determine the precise frequencies of sounds on the basis of the number of teeth and the speed of rotation (Beranek 1949). Working in a quiet laboratory on the Île Saint Louis in Paris, the German-born acoustician Rudolf Koenig (1842–1914) built a precision *tonometer,* covering the audible range, for measuring the pitch of sounds by resonant beating of 154 tuning forks (Miller 1916; Wood 1940).

The first precision instruments for measuring the intensity of sound waves were the *phonic wheel* of La Cour (1878) and the *Rayleigh disk* (1882), named after the great British acoustician Lord Rayleigh (1842–1919). The first electronic sound level meter did not appear until G. W. Pierce constructed one in 1908, two years after the invention of the triode vacuum tube by Lee DeForest (1873–1961).

Early Images of Sound

One problem that early acousticians faced in studying sound is that waveforms could be heard but not seen. They devised ingenious, though contrived, methods of viewing sound. One method involved modulating a Bunsen burner with sound and observing the effect on the flame. Apparently the first documented attempts at analysis of sound flames was carried out by a Dr. Higgens in 1777 (Tyndall 1875). Rudolf Koenig built precision instruments for generating sound images that he called *manometric flames* (figure 34.1). (For details, see Mayer [1878], Poynting and Thomson [1900], and Beranek [1949].)

By placing a resonant tube around a Bunsen burner, the physicist John Tyndall (1820–1893) made flames "sing." He also described experiments with what he called *sensitive naked flames*—not surrounded by tubes. Tyndall analyzed sound flame patterns according to their "tails," "wings," and "forks." Other media for representing sound waveforms included sound-modulated smoke and high-pressure water jets.

More direct images of sound waveforms appeared in the mid-nineteenth century. The Wheatstone Kaleidaphone (1827) projected vibrating motions onto a screen. This led Lissajous (1857) to develop his Lissajous patterns, which indicate both the frequency interval and the difference of phase between two vibrating signals. The Scott-Koenig Phonautograph (1857) was a diaphragm at the end of an acoustic horn. Attached to the diagram was a stylus that traced its vibration on a smoked paper carried on a rotating cylinder (figure 34.2). The Phonodeik (1916) by D. C. Miller was a great advance in display of time-domain waveforms because it photographed short sounds on an optical film traveling at speeds up to sixteen meters per second.

Early Sound Recorders

The first sound recorders grew out of efforts to capture sound pictorially. Inspired by the Phonautograph, Thomas Alva Edison's Phonograph (1878)

(a)

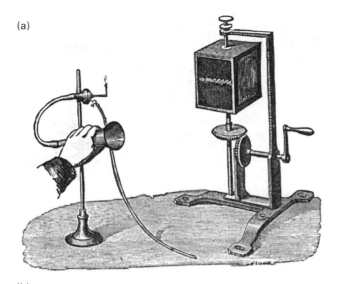

(b)

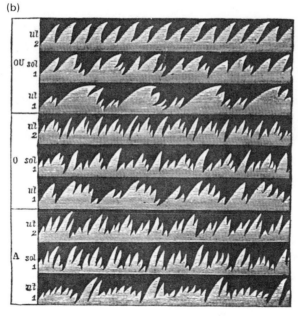

Figure 34.1 Manometric flames for waveform analysis. (a) Apparatus. Sounds picked up by the mouthpiece modulate the Bunsen burner flame within the box. When the box is rotated, mirrors on the outside of the box project the flame as a continuous band with jagged edges or teeth corresponding to the pitch and spectrum of the input sound. (b) Flame pictures of the French vowel sounds [OU], [O], and [A] by R. Koenig, sung at the pitches C1 (bottom of each group), G1 (middle of each group), and C2 (top of each group). (After Tyndall 1875.)

(a)

(b)

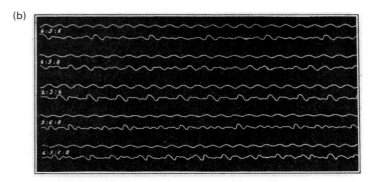

Figure 34.2   Rudolf Koenig's version of the Phonautograph for recording images of sound waveforms. (a) Phonautograph mechanism. (b) Phonoautograph records.

inscribed sound waveforms on tin foil cylinders that permitted subsequent playback of sounds. A year later Edison switched to wax cylinders. A number of researchers concocted methods for photographing the sound waveforms inscribed on phonograph cylinders (Miller 1916). Another recording device, Emile Berliner's Gramophone system (1887), used rotating lacquer disks, which eventually became the medium of choice. The Poulson Telegraphone (1900) was the first audio recording system to use magnetic signals. In the Telegraphone, a wire spun from one rotating spool to another spool while passing across a recording head. By 1924 Stille devised a recording system called the Magnetophon that used magnetic tape as its storage medium. The ability to record acoustical signals led to genuine progress in sound analysis.

We now turn to the topic at hand: pitch estimation.

Pitch and Rhythm Recognition in MIDI Systems

Pitch and rhythm recognition start from either of two points of departure: analysis of raw sound waveforms, or parsing streams of MIDI (or OSC) messages (chapters 51 and 52). Obviously, the latter is the easier approach.

When a musician plays a MIDI input device such as a keyboard, pitch and event detection are taken care of electromechanically by the input device itself. A microprocessor inside the input device is constantly monitoring the state of the keys, buttons, and other control surfaces of the instrument. As the musician plays, the states of these controls change, and the microprocessor detects these events. The microprocessor generates MIDI note messages containing the start and end time of each event and the MIDI pitch that is associated with the controller that was changed. These messages can be routed from the controller to analysis programs running on a computer. These programs have only to parse the MIDI messages to obtain the pitch and timing information. This is a basic task of a music notation editor (chapter 45).

By contrast, detecting the pitch of most acoustic instruments requires a microphone that is connected to pitch detection hardware or software. Analysis starting from sound waveforms is the focus of the rest of this chapter. MIDI systems face this issue only when the data stream derives from a *pitch-to-MIDI converter* (PMC). A PMC attempts to emit MIDI pitch values that correspond to the pitch of sounds fed into it (Fry 1992). Pitch-to-MIDI conversion is common in mobile devices (e.g., the phone app MIDIMorphosis).

The Pitch Estimation Problem

In the width of perception the ear exceedingly transcends the eye; for while the former ranges over eleven octaves, but little more than a single octave is possible to the latter.
—John Tyndall, *Sound,* 1875

We can define a *pitch estimator* (PE), *pitch detector*, or *pitch tracker* as a software algorithm or hardware device that takes a sound signal as its input and attempts to determine the *fundamental pitch period* of that signal. That is, it attempts to find the frequency that a human listener would agree to be the same pitch as the input signal (assuming that there is one such pitch). Partly because the concept of pitch is ambiguous in many sounds and because human pitch perception is not completely understood, PEs can be successful only on a limited corpus of sounds. It makes no sense to attempt to find "the pitch" of a noisy percussive sound such as a cymbal crash, brief impulses, low rumblings, or complex sound masses. Indeed, if we look closely at the frequency traces of traditional instrumental tones, we see that their pitch is never perfectly steady and is full of microvariations. In many musical applications, such as live performance, the job of a PE is to ignore these microvariations and quickly locate a central pitch. So what we ask of a PE is inherently difficult. It should be accurate, but not too accurate—like a human listener.

The difficulties that we face in teaching machines how to hear music reminds us of how sensitive and powerful the human perceptual systems are (Carterette and Friedman 1978; Buser and Imbert 1992). Human listeners can pinpoint the source of an isolated sound (in direction and in timbre); follow complex harmony, counterpoint, and polyrhythms; and recall entire pieces of music from fragments of as few as two or three notes—all more or less instantaneously. Teaching machines these skills is an ongoing experiment.

Machine methods for pitch and rhythm recognition continue to evolve, however. PEs for speech that work in non–real time are "very reliable" (Hermes 1992). Reliable real-time PE is inherently harder, even if we exclude polyphony (i.e., almost all music!). However, great strides have been made in recent years. Commercial pitch correction software operates in real time with latencies below 50 ms. To get the best results from such technology requires fine adjustment of the parameters according to the situation.

Applications of Pitch Estimation

Musical applications of PE are myriad. This section looks briefly at melody transcription, real-time pitch recognition, pitch editing, un-mixing, and automatic dialog replacement.

Melody transcription

An early application of PE derived from ethnomusicologists' needs to capture the florid melodies of world music cultures, such as Indian singing. These elaborate microtonal melodies cannot be properly represented in common music notation. A device called the Seeger Melograph scanned the output of 100 third-octave bandpass filters every four milliseconds and searched for a maximum. The first maximum is assumed to contain the fundamental. After some processing, the Melograph produced a two-tiered chart or *melogram* (figure 34.3) showing fundamental frequency and amplitude versus time (Seeger 1951; Moorer 1975). The technique of the Seeger Melograph was updated using computer technology to provide different views of melodic motion (Gjerdingen 1988).

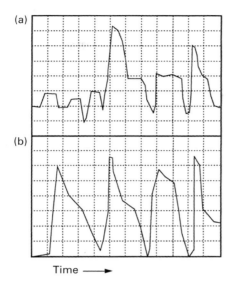

Time ———▶

Figure 34.3 Melodic trace like that of a Melograph for two seconds of an Indian singer. Time moves horizontally. (a) Fundamental pitch trace. (b) Amplitude trace. (After Gjerdingen 1988.)

Melody transcription is a subset of the more general problem of *automatic transcription*—from sound to notated score. Full automatic transcription requires not only pitch estimation but also sophisticated mid-level and high-level analysis of musical context (Scheirer 2000; Klapur and Davy 2006; Benetos et al. 2019). Operations like the separation of two simultaneous voices start from pitch detection (Maher 1990). Refer to chapter 35 for more on automatic transcription.

Real-time pitch recognition

A real-time PE can track the melodic performance of an instrumentalist or a singer. Real-time PE can be applied in an automatic music teaching system in which the student plays with synthetic accompaniment and her performance is tracked and graded. Or it can be part of an interactive improvisation system, such as the Tango[2] software developed over many years by trombonist Henning Berg (Berg 2019). For a PE to work in real time, the pitch decision must be computationally efficient, which limits the complexity of the algorithm (Cuadra, Master, and Sapp 2001).

Real-time voice-processing software using PE running on a *harmonizer* can correct off-key notes, add harmonic voices, change formants to make a man's voice turn into a woman's or vice versa, and transpose performed pitches.

Pitch editing

Sound-editing programs often include pitch estimation routines that are used as a guide for pitch-shifting and time-scaling operations. Some apps are designed expressly to edit pitch. Antares Auto-Tune, introduced in 1997, made *pitch correction* famous. Pitch correction came to be known as the *Cher effect* after it was extensively used on the star's vocals in her 1998 hit song *Believe*. Within a user-specified key signature, Auto-Tune analyzes the singer's vocal line, moving "wrong" notes up or down to what it estimates is the intended pitch. The user can control the time it takes for the program to alter the pitch: slower is more natural, faster makes the pitch jump in a robotic sounding manner.

Going further, applications like Celemony's Melodyne use PE to enable editing individual notes in chords and polyphonic textures (Neubäcker 2011). This work is based on research by Every and Syzmanski (2006). They applied *a priori model-based information*—in the form of prespecified models of harmonic structures of pitched instruments—together with a filtering methodology for separating overlapping spectral peaks, in order to separate the harmonic structure of multiple instruments from a mono recording.

Un-mixing

A prime use for PE is the extraction of the melody (usually a vocal) from a song. This process is also called *un-mixing* (also discussed in chapter 35). Once separated, the melody can be remixed with a different accompaniment.

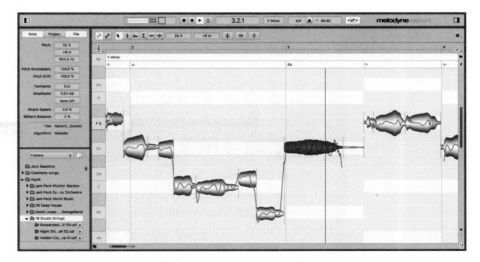

Figure 34.4   Screenshot of Melodyne Assistant. Each blob is a note. The squiggly lines in the center of the note is the detailed pitch curve. If desired, these can be straightened out and the notes can be repositioned to another pitch.

Although it is impossible to perform melody extraction perfectly, tools can do this fairly well automatically, while giving the user spectral editing tools to refine the initial results. In effect, they generate a graphical pitch curve that can be edited with drawing and erasing tools (figure 34.5).

Automatic dialog replacement

Automatic dialog replacement (ADR) for films or ADR on singing substitutes one performance for another while retaining the precise pitch, inflections, and timing of the original. This includes double tracking of vocals.

Commercial programs such as ReVoice Pro, VocALign, Auto-Tune, Melodyne, Trax, Xtrax Stems, and Instant Dialogue Cleaner use pitch estimation but combine it with sophisticated pattern recognition algorithms, statistical methods, dynamic programming, and trained neural networks. They not only track the pitch; they also reduce noise. They isolate notes by amplitude envelope detection and then separate related spectral components, such as vocal formants, that accompany that pitch. Once they have identified these components, the analyzed data can be used to transform and resynthesize individual notes as desired by the user. The developers of Melodyne have filed patents that describe some of their methods (Neubäcker 2011), as have the developers of VocALign (Bloom 2010) and IntelliScore (Kohler 2000).

Difficulties in Pitch Estimation

Human pitch perception is a complex phenomenon (Goldstein 1973; Moorer 1975; Hermes 1992). Our ears sense musical pitch even in the presence of

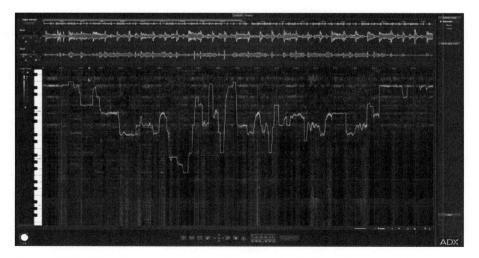

Figure 34.5   Vocal pitch curve derived automatically by Audionamix Trax.

noisy signals. We can follow several pitches simultaneously (otherwise harmony and counterpoint would be indecipherable) and also detect slight but expressive pitch deviations (vibrato, melisma, microtonal intervals). Nonetheless, the ear can be led into hearing pitches that are not there (e.g., fundamental frequencies implied by the presence of their harmonic series—an effect heard from any small loudspeaker), and illusory pitch trajectories (e.g., *Shepard tones*—sounds that appear to be continuously ascending or descending). Many sounds evoke no sense of pitch. The mechanisms by which we detect pitch are not fully understood, because they involve cognitive processing and subjective factors such as training and familiarity, as well as the mechanics of the inner ear.

Some PEs try to emulate a theoretical model of human pitch perception mechanisms, but the majority of practical devices involve simpler techniques chosen primarily for their computational efficiency. Efficiency is especially important in PEs that must work in real time to identify the pitch being played. In any case, no pitch detector is 100 percent accurate in all situations (there may be background noise, for example), although some non-real-time methods are quite reliable when the input signal is constrained in various ways.

Attack transients

The first problem faced by PEs is sorting out the attack transient of a sound. Detailed analysis of the attack of many instruments reveals chaotic and instable waveforms. If a fundamental frequency is present in the attack. It is probably obscured by noise and inharmonic partials. Some instruments may take greater than 100 ms for the instrument to settle into a stable pitch; this period of instability confuses PEs (Fry 1992). Thus many PEs have a delay time or latency before pitch estimation (or correction) starts.

Low frequencies

Pitch detectors that start from spectrum analysis usually have difficulties with very low tones, necessitating the use of time-domain PEs (Lyon and Dyer 1986). Any PE has problems identifying low pitches in real time. In order to determine the fundamental pitch period, at least three cycles of the steady-state waveform should be sampled before the analysis can begin. For a low-frequency pitch, for example, an A at 55 Hz (MIDI note 33), three cycles take 54 ms to sample. If one adds to this the duration of the attack transient and the computation time of the PE algorithm itself, then a perceivable delay is inevitable. The lowest notes that a male bass can sing is in the range of 80 Hz, which reduces the three-cycle lag to 36 ms.

High frequencies

High frequencies can also pose problems to some real-time PEs. As the frequency rises, one pitch period is represented by fewer samples. The resolution with which pitch can be determined in the time domain is directly affected by the length of the pitch period or the number of samples of delay used in comparing a signal with its past (Amuedo 1984).

Legato notes and melisma

Legato note beginnings can consist of mere changes in frequency with no change in volume. By contrast, some legato endings and beginnings can have no change in frequency, yet an automatic transcription is expected to detect two separate note events. Melisma poses similar problems.

Myopic pitch tracking

All PEs start with an analysis of a frame of time that lasts from about 10 to 100 ms. Thus their analysis is based on a narrow time segment. In contrast, human pitch perception is not so time localized. Expectations shape pitch perception; that is, we estimate pitch on the basis of musical context. If PEs work only from local information, they may myopically track irrelevant details that were produced unintentionally, such as unsteadiness at the beginning of a note or excessive vibrato.

Acoustic ambience

The acoustic ambience within which an instrument or voice is heard affects the accuracy of pitch detection. A closely miked and compressed studio recording may exaggerate incidental playing or singing noises, such as bow scraping, key clicking, or breathing sounds, cluttering the signal heard by the PE. By contrast, tones bathed in reverberation and echoes smear early notes over the start of new notes. Provided that the analysis is carried out in non–real time, an attempt at ambience removal may help the PE. (See Beauchamp, Maher, and Brown 1993 and the description in the section on frequency-domain pitch detection.)

Pitch Estimation Methods

The majority of PE algorithms grow out of speech recognition and speech synthesis research. The nontrivial nature of the problem is reflected by the number of methods that have been developed (Gold 1962; Noll 1967; Schafer and Rabiner 1970; Moorer 1973; Rabiner et al. 1976; Hess 1983; Amuedo 1984; Fry 1992; Hermes 1992; Hutchins and Ku 1982; Hutchins, Parola, and Ludwig 1982; Beauchamp, Maher, and Brown 1993; Brown and Puckette 1993; McLeod and Wyvill 2005; Gómez, et al 2003; de Cheveigné and Kawahara 2002; Cuadra et al. 2001; Lerch 2012). We can classify most methods for pitch detection into six general categories: *time-domain, autocorrelation, adaptive filter, frequency-domain, models of the human ear,* and *neural networks,* discussed in the next sections.

The methods presented here are based mainly on low-level signal processing algorithms. In pitch detectors employed in commercial products, additional heuristics are added for more accuracy (Puckette et al. 1998). For a comparative study of several PE algorithms, refer to Gerhard (2003).

Time-Domain Fundamental Period Pitch Detection

Fundamental period methods look at the input signal as a fluctuating amplitude in the time domain, like the signal that appears on the screen of an oscilloscope. They try to find repeating patterns in the waveform that give clues as to its periodicity. Perhaps a more apt term for these types of pitch estimators would be *periodicity detector*.

A simple type of PE tries to find periodicities in the waveform by looking for repeating *zero-crossings*. A zero-crossing is a point where the waveform's amplitude goes from positive to negative or vice versa. For example, a sine wave crosses the zero amplitude threshold at the middle and end of its cycle. By measuring the interval between zero crossings and comparing successive intervals, the PE infers a fundamental frequency (figure 34.6). A variation on zero-crossing detection is measuring the distances between peaks (Hermes 1992). In general, zero-crossing and peak PEs are relatively simple and inexpensive, but they are also less accurate than more elaborate methods (Voelkel 1985; Hutchins and Ku 1982). The reason is that other frequencies that are not the pitch frequency may also generate waveforms that cross the zero point or exhibit peaks. Figure 34.6b shows that, for example, to track the visually obvious fundamental frequency, the PE must ignore the three or four rapid, low-amplitude zero crossings caused by the high-frequency component at every major zero crossing.

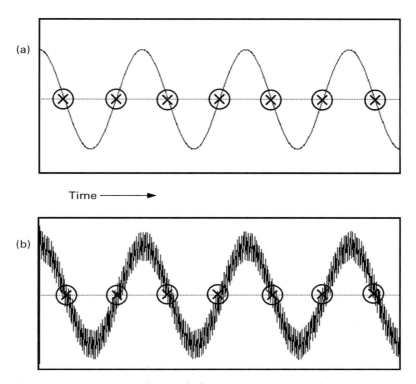

Figure 34.6 Zero-crossing pitch detector. (a) By measuring the interval between the zero crossings (marked Ä), we obtain a clue as to the lowest periodicity of the signal. (b) For signals with a strong fundamental, this works regardless of the presence of high-frequency components superposed on the signal, provided that the PD ignores the rapid low amplitude zero-point variations caused by the high-frequency components.

Zero-crossing PEs have false detection problems (e.g., octave errors), function poorly in the presence of noise, and do not handle polyphonic sounds. These issues are not insurmountable, but they need to be addressed with additional heuristics. For example, preprocessing by filters can improve the accuracy of time domain PEs. Kuhn (1990) proposed an improvement to the basic zero-crossing method that passes the input signal through a bank of filters. The algorithm checks the amplitude of the filter outputs and performs zero-crossing detection only on the output of the lowest two filters that have significant amplitude after filtering.

Finally, for speech and singing signals only, an *electroglottograph* or *laryngograph* has been used with some success. These methods require a vocalist to wear a neckband that senses pulses emitted by the vocal cords. However, the method fails to sense unvoiced (whispered) speech and may generate errors in certain nasal vowels (Hermes 1992). It also has the same problems as any real-time PE in handling note attacks (Fry 1992).

Autocorrelation Pitch Estimation

Correlation functions compare two signals. The goal of correlation routines is to find the *similarity* (in a precise mathematical sense) between the two signals. Correlation functions compare signals on a point-by-point basis; thus the output of a correlation function is itself a signal. If the correlation function has a value of 1, the two signals are exactly correlated at that point. If it is 0, then the two signals are uncorrelated.

Autocorrelation methods compare a signal with versions of itself delayed by successive intervals, whereas *cross-correlation* methods compare two different signals over a range of time delays or *lags.* The point of comparing delayed versions of a signal is to find repeating patterns—indicators of periodicities in the signal. It is this periodicity detection—a clue to pitch—that interests us here.

Autocorrelation pitch detectors hold part of the input signal in a buffer (Moorer 1975; Rabiner 1977; Brown and Puckette 1987). As more of the same signal comes in, the detector tries to match a pattern in the incoming waveform with a part of the stored waveform. If the detector finds a match within a given error criterion, this indicates a periodicity and the detector measures the time interval between the two patterns to estimate the periodicity. Figure 34.7 shows a scheme for an autocorrelation pitch detector.

Various autocorrelation algorithms exist (Moorer 1975). For a given delay or *lag time,* a typical autocorrelation function is

$$autocorrelation[lag] = \sum_{n=0}^{N} signal[n] \times signal[n+lag]$$

where n is the input sample index, and $0 < lag \leq N$. The degree to which the values of *signal* at different times n are the same as the values of the same *signal* delayed by *lag* samples determines the magnitude of *autocorrelation*[*lag*]. The output of an autocorrelation shows the magnitude for different lag times.

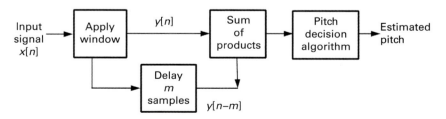

Figure 34.7 Autocorrelation scheme. The input signal is windowed, and the windowed segment is compared with versions of itself delayed by one sample, two samples, and so on, up to m samples. The strongest correlation is estimated as the dominant or fundamental pitch.

The autocorrelation of a sine wave illustrates the principle. In the example shown in figure 34.8a, the lag = 0 and the two functions are identical. Thus the autocorrelation function normalized by the power of the sine wave is 1. The autocorrelation function is shown plotted at the bottom of figure 34.8. Suppose that the sine wave is delayed by one-quarter period. As case (b) shows, the sum of the products of *signal*[n] and *signal*[$n + lag$] over one period is 0. In case (c), the delay is one-half period, and the correlation is −1. In case (d) the delay is three-quarters of a period, and the correlation is 0. Finally, in case (e) the delay is one full period, so the correlation is 1. Thus we see that the autocorrelation of a sine wave is itself a sine wave with maxima at integral multiples of the period of the input sine.

Pitch estimation routines search for recurrent peaks in the autocorrelation, indicating (possibly hidden) periodicities in the input waveform (figure 34.9).

Problems with the autocorrelation method arise in analyzing harmonically complex waveforms. The PE must compare several peaks, including those of subharmonics, and then make a decision, which increases computational complexity.

Pitch detection by autocorrelation is most efficient at mid to low frequencies. Indeed, researchers have used autocorrelation for analysis of periodic rhythms (Wright 2008). It has also been popular in speech recognition applications in which the pitch range is limited. In musical applications, in which the pitch range is broader, direct calculation of the autocorrelation requires several million multiply-add operations per second of sound input.

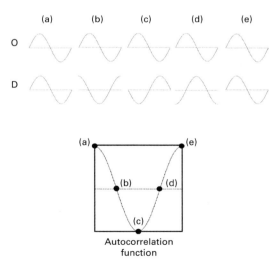

Figure 34.8   Autocorrelation of a sine wave is itself a sinusoidal wave. O indicates original signal; D indicates delayed signal. The text explains cases [a] through [e].) The autocorrelation function is plotted at the bottom.

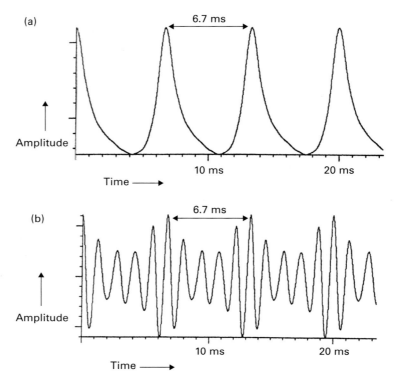

Figure 34.9 Autocorrelation functions of periodic signals are themselves periodic functions of time. (a) Autocorrelation of a signal with five harmonics, including the fundamental with a period of 6.7 ms or 149 Hz (close to D3). The autocorrelation is periodic, but its harmonic amplitudes are different from the input. Notice the peak corresponding to the fundamental. (b) Autocorrelation of a signal with only three harmonics: the fifth, sixth, and seventh. The autocorrelation is periodic with a period of 6.7 ms equal to the missing fundamental (implied pitch) of the waveform. (After Moorer 1975.)

Thus another way to compute the autocorrelation of a signal is to segment it and apply the *fast Fourier transform* (FFT) to each segment. The FFT analyzes the frequency content or *spectrum* of a signal (see chapter 37). After calculating the FFT, we then multiply the analyzed spectrum by its complex conjugate and perform the inverse FFT. Conjugation in the frequency domain is equivalent to reversal in the time domain, so convolving a sound with itself backward is a form of autocorrelation. Refer to Rabiner and Gold (1975) for details.

McLeod and Wyvill (2005) proposed an extension to autocorrelation called the *normalized square difference function* with heuristics for "peak picking" (i.e., estimating the fundamental) that enables PE in real time. By contrast, the YIN method of de Cheveigné and Kawahara (2002) attempts to minimize the difference between the waveform and its delayed duplicate instead of maximizing the product (as in autocorrelation). YIN incorporates a cumulative mean function that de-emphasizes higher-period dips in the difference function, thereby suppressing subharmonic peaks.

Adaptive Filter Pitch Estimators

An adaptive filter operates, as its name implies, in a self-tuning manner, depending on the input signal. One pitch detection strategy based on an *adaptive filter* sends the input signal into a narrow bandpass filter. Both the unfiltered input signal and the filtered signal are routed to a *difference detector* circuit. The output of the difference detector circuit is fed back to control the bandpass filter center frequency (figure 34.10). This control forces the bandpass filter to converge to the frequency of the input signal. The convergence test measures the difference between the filter output $y(n)$ and the filter input $x(n)$. When the difference is close to zero then the system makes a pitch decision.

Another adaptive filter technique is the *optimum comb method* (Moorer 1973). This method seeks to find a comb filter that minimizes its input signal. (Chapter 28 discusses comb filters.) In order to minimize the input signal, the notches of the comb filter must be tuned to the dominant frequency of the input. Thus, by finding the optimum comb filter, one has found the dominant pitch. This method is mainly applicable to sounds with a strong fundamental and regularly spaced harmonics.

See Lane (1990), Hush et al. (1986), and Hutchins (1982–1988) for more on adaptive filter pitch detectors.

Das et al. (2020) presented an accurate real-time pitch tracker based on an extended Kalman filter. A Kalman filter is a statistical estimator. In this application, it predicted a result based on measurement of pitch, amplitude, and phase. It then adaptively updated its prediction as new samples come in, using the minimization of an error factor.

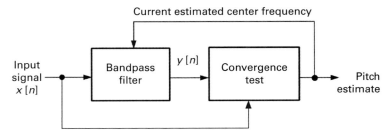

Figure 34.10   Pitch detector based on an adaptive filter scheme. Notice the feedback loop from the estimate back to the filter.

Frequency Domain Pitch Estimators

Frequency domain (FD) PE methods start from an analysis of the spectrum of the input signal. The spectrum shows the strength of the various frequency components contained in the signal. The goal is to isolate the dominant frequency or pitch.

A typical FD approach analyzes successive frames of the input signal using the *short-time Fourier transform* (STFT), which uses the FFT algorithm. (See chapter 37.) FD pitch detectors seek peaks in the spectrum that correspond to prominent frequencies. After finding the peaks, the pitch detector must decide which frequencies are fundamentals (generally perceived as pitches) and which frequencies are merely harmonics or extraneous partials (Kay and Marple 1981; Mitre et al. 2006). A quick real-time FD pitch detector might simply select the strongest frequency as the pitch. A more sophisticated detector might look for harmonic relationships that imply a fundamental frequency. This fundamental may not be the strongest component, but it may be the most prominent perceived pitch due to the reinforcement of multiple harmonics.

A problem with basic STFT-based pitch detectors is that they divide the audio bandwidth into a set of equally spaced frequency *channels* or *bins* where each channel is n Hz apart from its neighbors. Since human pitch perception is basically logarithmic, this means that low pitches are tracked less accurately than high pitches. For example, an analyzer with frequency resolution of 20 Hz can resolve microtones in the octave between 10 and 20 KHz, but offers less than a semitone resolution below middle C.

Brown and Puckette (1993) proposed an alternative PE method based on their *fast constant-Q transform* (Brown and Puckette 1992). The fast constant-Q transform is realized by frequency warping the FFT algorithm (see chapter 38). This analyzes a logarithmically spaced frequency grid using a bank of filters with a constant Q value (see chapter 28). Their PE algorithm compares an initial analysis with an "ideal" harmonic template. Through a combination of PE methods, including those drawn from Smith and Serra (1987), they analyzed microsonic phase changes to isolate pitch with notable accuracy.

In a similar fashion, Ryynänen and Klapuri (2008) set up a bank of bandpass filters on logarithmic critical band boundaries to find the band with the most likely fundamental frequency. Additional analysis derived melody. This analysis was exhaustive across all pitched frequencies so much computation was spent eliminating possible candidates.

Tracking phase vocoder analysis

The *tracking phase vocoder* (TPV) stands in contrast to the fixed-frequency channels of the STFT by allowing the possibility of changing frequencies (McAulay and Quatieri 1986; see also chapter 37). The TPV starts from data generated by the STFT and then generates a set of *tracks,* with each track representing a prominent partial in a spectrum. The tracks can change frequency in time, interpolating across the fixed analysis bands. Implicit in the tracking process is data reduction; because only the most prominent partials are tracked, the TPV generates a "sanitized" version of the input that attenuates extraneous noises and ambience below a stipulated threshold.

Maher (1990) and Beauchamp, Maher, and Brown (1993) developed a FD pitch detector that starts from the output of a TPV. Their system scans the tracked frequencies and compares them in various ways to harmonic frequencies of a hypothetical fundamental. The hypothesis with the least difference overall becomes the estimated fundamental pitch.

Figure 34.11 depicts three plots generated by the system. As shown in figure 34.11a, the system accurately tracks a dry MIDI version of *Partita III* by J. S. Bach. Figure 34.11b shows how the performance degrades when confronted with a studio recording of a violin performance. Glitches between the notes indicate points where the system is confused by bow noises. Figure 34.11c shows a further degradation caused by a *chord effect* (in which previous notes continue to ring in the presence of new notes) in analyzing a violin recording made in a reverberant space.

As a step toward improving the performance of the system, the authors applied the same algorithm to a version of the violin recordings that had been sanitized by the TPV. As part of its data reduction, the TPV removes some noise and grit from the recording, including bow scraping noise and reverberation. When the PE is run on resynthesized versions, its performance becomes more accurate.

Cepstrum analysis

A common frequency-domain pitch detection method is the *cepstrum* technique, having first been used in analysis of speech (Noll 1967; Schafer and Rabiner 1970). Cepstrum analysis has often been applied in conjunction with the technique of *linear predictive coding* (LPC), described in chapter 14. The term *cepstrum* was formed by reversing the first four letters of *spectrum*. A simple way of describing the cepstrum is that it tends to separate a strong pitched component from the rest of the spectrum. This is a reasonable model of many vocal and instrumental sounds whose spectrums can be considered as the sum of an *excitation* (the original vibrational impulses, typically at the

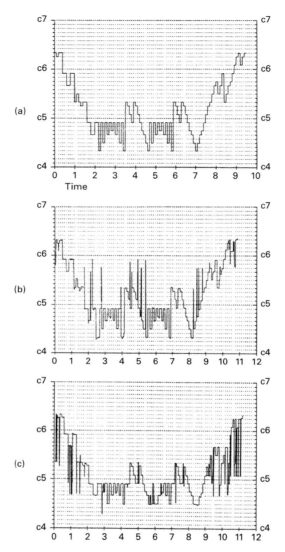

Figure 34.11   Plots generated by frequency-domain pitch tracking of the estimated pitch of the first eight measures of *Partita III* by J. S. Bach. The vertical axis is divided into semitones of the equal-tempered scale, from C4 to C7. The horizontal axis is time. (a) Computer-synthesized pitches. (b) Studio recording. (c) Reverberant recording. (After Beauchamp, Maher, and Brown 1993.)

pitch of the sound) and the *resonances* (the filtered part of a sound created by the body of an instrument or the vocal tract). (Chapter 18 explains the excitation/resonance concept in physical modeling synthesis.)

Technically, the cepstrum is the inverse Fourier transform of the *log-magnitude Fourier spectrum* (figure 34.12). This is the absolute value of the log (base 10) of the output of the *discrete Fourier transform*.

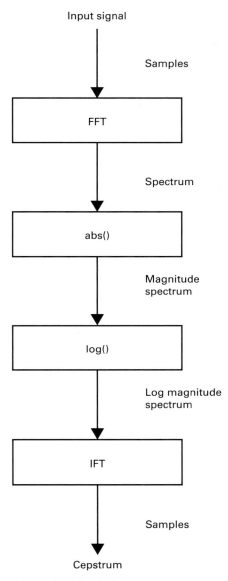

Figure 34.12   Scheme for cepstrum computation.

The result of cepstrum computation is a time sequence, like the input signal itself. If the input signal has a strong fundamental pitch period, this shows up as a peak in the cepstrum. By measuring the time distance from time 0 to the time of the peak, one finds the fundamental period of this pitch (figure 34.13).

How does cepstrum analysis work for speech? The cepstrum serves to separate two superposed spectra: the glottal pulse (vocal cord) excitation, and the vocal tract resonance. The excitation can be viewed as a sequence

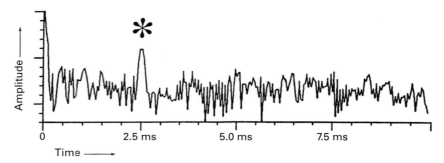

Figure 34.13 Cepstrum plot from a note of a trumpet solo recorded in a large reverberant hall. The note is 396 Hz. The peak marked by an asterisk indicates the period of the signal, about 2.52 ms, which corresponds to the detected pitch. Notice that the cepstrum peak appears clearly even in the presence of reverberation. (After Moorer 1975.)

of quasiperiodic pulses. The Fourier transform of these pulses is a line spectrum where the lines are spaced at harmonics of the original frequency (see the thin wiggly lines shown in figure 34.14). The process of taking the log magnitude does not affect the general form of this spectrum. The inverse Fourier transform yields another quasiperiodic waveform of pulses. By contrast, the spectrum of the response of the vocal tract (acting as a filter) is a slowly varying function of frequency, shown as the thick undulating line in figure 34.14. The process of applying the log magnitude and the inverse Fourier transform yields a waveform that has significant amplitude only for a few samples, generally less than the fundamental pitch period. It can be shown that the impulse response decays as a function of $1/n$, and then its cepstrum decays as $1/n^2$. Thus the cepstrum clusters the impulse response into a short burst at the beginning of the cepstrum wave, and it clusters the pitch into a series of peaks at the period of the fundamental frequency.

Cepstrum computation has many applications because it sorts out the impulse response from the excitation. In other words, the cepstrum tends to *deconvolve* the two *convolved* spectra (Smith 1981). For musical signals, the deconvolution is rarely perfect. The log magnitude operations in the cepstrum procedure tend to cluster these two quasiseparate components of the spectrum. By advanced operations that we do not describe here, either of these features can be filtered out so that cepstrum contains spectrum information associated with either timbre or pitch. (For details, see Noll [1967], Schafer and Rabiner [1970], Rabiner and Gold [1975], and Rabiner et al. [1976].)

Another application of the cepstrum is found in speech analysis/resynthesis. If there is no peak in the cepstrum, this is an indication that the

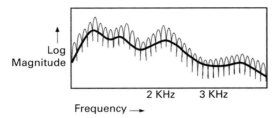

Figure 34.14   Cepstrum separation of vocal cord impulse response from the vocal tract impulse response. Applying the log function separates the thin wiggly lines (corresponding to the excitation) from the thick undulating broad spectrum (corresponding to the impulse response or resonance).

sound being analyzed is *unvoiced*—that is, it is a breathy or consonant sound with no pitch, such as *f* or *s*, as opposed to a voiced vowel such as *ah*.

Maximum likelihood

PE by *maximum likelihood estimation* (MLE) is a statistical approach that attempts to match the frequency domain characteristics of an input signal to known harmonic frequency maps of instruments or voice (Doval and Rodet 1993). MLE attempts to find the parameter values that maximize the likelihood or matching function, given the input signal. The approach starts with a short-time Fourier analysis of the input signal. The method assumes that the strongest partial belongs to the harmonic series of the fundamental. The next step consists of collecting the harmonic series of each pitch frequency candidate. Statistical methods are used to determine the most likely fundamental frequency. Mitre et al. (2006) and Klapuri and Davy (2006) provide details on this approach.

Pitch Estimators Based on Models of the Ear

One trend in sound analysis is to hitch knowledge of the human hearing mechanism to the train of technology with the goal of achieving new insights into sound microstructure (Hermes 1992; Slaney and Lyon 1992; Klapuri 2008). One application of these models is pitch estimation. These PEs combine algorithms based on perception theories with models of known mechanisms of the human auditory system. Licklider's theories of pitch perception anticipated modern implementations of this approach (Licklider 1951, 1959).

Figure 34.15 shows the overall structure of such a PE, which divides into three submodels: outer and middle ear, cochlea, and central nervous system. The first step is a preprocessing stage of filtering based on the responses of

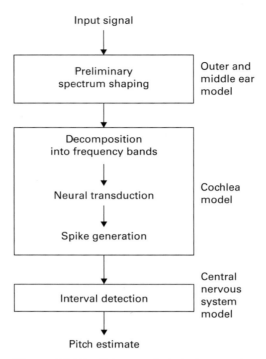

Figure 34.15   Schema of pitch detector based on a model of the human auditory system.

the outer and middle ear. The next stage transforms the input signal into a frequency-domain representation by means of a bank of bandpass filters. Then follows a transduction stage in which the energy of the basilar membrane is transformed into a series of nerve firing probabilities and subsequently a train of spikes in the time domain (Meddis et al. 1990). Up to this point the process is based on well-established, if simplified, scientific data. The next stage is the most speculative part, modeling central nervous system processing of the incoming spikes. The goal is to measure the period between spikes and estimate their most frequent interval. These final stages are akin to the time-domain and autocorrelation PEs. The advantage of combining frequency-domain and time-domain methods in this way is that inharmonic "contamination" is filtered out when the channels of the frequency domain are converted to time-domain spikes. Paiva et al. (2006) and Klapuri (2008) applied auditory models to the estimation of multiple simultaneous pitches.

Neural Network Pitch Estimation

CREPE (Convolutional Representation for Pitch Estimation) is a high-quality pitch estimator based on neural network technology. CREPE operates directly on 64 ms grains of the time-domain waveform (Kim et al. 2018). It was trained with fifteen hours of synthetic and sampled waveforms with labels specifying their precise pitch. In effect, the system learns numerically to associate specific input patterns with specific labels. Sound input to the algorithm is processed through six convolutional neural networks resulting in a representation in 2,048 dimensions. This was then connected to an output layer spanning 360 pitches with 20 cent resolution. The resulting pitch estimate in the form of a Gaussian curve is calculated deterministically. The algorithm was tested in the presence of seven levels of noise. The Python code is available on Github. Refer to appendix A for an introduction to machine learning including neural networks.

Polyphonic Pitch Detection

All the difficulties of pitch detection magnify for a pitched sound in the presence of noise or several pitched sounds. This is the difficult task faced in *polyphonic transcription,* that is, generating a written score from an acoustic signal. Most theories of human pitch perception focus on hearing a single pitch. Much less is known about the mechanisms by which people listen to polyphony.

Attempts at polyphonic pitch detection usually apply frequency-domain analysis techniques within a search-and-decision mechanism. The main task is to sift out a single melodic line or multiple lines from a spectrum containing many amplitude peaks, where the peaks may be either fundamental pitches or strong harmonics. In order to determine which peaks are probably fundamental pitches, the analysis must examine the data from several perspectives and weigh different factors in estimating from the results (Moorer 1975; Maher 1990). Techniques derived from artificial intelligence research are often employed, such as *expectation-driven search* through lists of prominent frequencies. Systems are said to be expectation-driven when they use knowledge about the domain being analyzed to direct the search strategy (Moorer 1975; Terhardt 1982; Chafe et al. 1982, 1985; Foster et al. 1982; Strawn 1980, 1985a, 1985b; Maher 1990; Neubäcker 2009; Bloom, et al. 2010; Kohler 2000).

Paiva, Mendes, and A, Cardoso (2006) tackled the thorny problem of isolating the main melody in polyphonic music. They used rules for *salience* (which pitches were the most intense in amplitude) and *smoothness* (which pitches followed others stepwise in small intervals) to find an initial set of melody note candidates. They then applied rules to eliminate *ghost octaves* (less salient notes of the same pitch class, onset time, and modulation pattern) and *false positives* (notes in pauses between melodic notes played by background instruments). False positives were difficult to eliminate perfectly. They reported an 81 percent average success rate in identifying the main melody using a standard database of polyphonic music.

Not surprisingly, due to the extra data-gathering, searching, and complex decision-making algorithms, computation times for polyphonic pitch detection are much greater than in the monophonic case.

Analysis of Musical Context

For some applications it is necessary to go beyond mere pitch detection to pitch analysis—the examination of melody and harmony in the broad sense. That is, having isolated the pitches that have occurred, what is their musical significance, what do they imply? This task is *analysis of musical context.* An example of analysis of musical context is the identification of the key and clef of a piece of tonal music (Chafe et al. 1982; Holtzman 1977). Proceeding from this analysis, the further goal might be to assign the proper note name (e.g., F-sharp or G-flat) for the purposes of transcription to score in common music notation. For a book devoted to problems of music transcription, refer to Klapuri and Davy (2006).

In interactive performance systems, the computer is expected to respond in real time in an appropriate way to a human performer. Thus it must quickly discern the musical context. Various algorithms for fast chord and melodic analysis have been developed. These are usually customized for the style requirements of the composers who use the system (Chabot et al. 1986; Roads 1985d; Rowe 1992a, b; Berg 2019). Beyond such rapid algorithms lies the vast domain of musical content analysis (style, genre, etc.), a topic in its own right that is outside the scope of this book (Widmer et al. 2008).

35 *Rhythm Recognition and Automatic Transcription*

Applications of Rhythm Recognition

Levels of Rhythm Recognition

Event Detection

          Amplitude Thresholding

Separating Voices in Polyphonic Music

Automatic Transcription

          Automatic Transcription: Background
          Transcribing Rhythmic Structures
               Pulse induction and tempo tracking
               Note duration assignment
               Grouping into patterns
               Estimating meter and measure boundaries
               Recovery from confusion

One of the skills acquired in music lessons is playing rhythms written in common music notation. A related skill is learning to recognize played rhythms and then transcribing them into notation. A long period of practice stands between the beginner and the master of these skills. Likewise, teaching a computer to listen and automatically transcribe musical rhythms is a nontrivial task.

The pedagogy of rhythmic dictation in the European classical tradition is already simplified, because it is based on recognition of metrically related rhythms (Yeston 1976; Lerdahl and Jackendoff 1983). By contrast, many rhythms in electronic music do not align to a regular meter. Furthermore, any type of rhythmical grouping—including those with no simple metrical relation—can occur within a metric. Thus the general problem of rhythmic recognition is quite open.

Machine recognition of rhythm from an acoustic signal turns input waveforms into a list of individual sonic events. It assigns these events to note duration values (half note, quarter note, etc.). It then groups the notes into larger musical units: beamed groups, tuplets (triplets, etc.), measures, and perhaps phrases, while also determining the meter. These tasks are inherently difficult, partly because human performance of musical scores is not perfectly accurate and music notation is ambiguous. That is, the same or similar rhythms can be written in different ways. As in pitch estimation, a rhythm recognizer must ignore "insignificant" variations in order to extract the "essential" rhythm. For example, it must realize that a slightly staccato whole note is not a tied half-quarter-eighth-sixteenth-thirty-second. This is related to the quantization problem in sequencers (chapter 42), but the problem is much harder in starting from an acoustic signal because it is up to the system to find the note list, and the tempo (which may be varying) is not known at the outset. Systems that try to segment music at the phrase level are challenged at the outset by the fact that the concept of "phrase" is dependent on context and style. Expert musicians do not always agree about how to parse the phrase structure of a given piece of music.

Applications of Rhythm Recognition

Rhythm recognition is one of the core problems of *machine listening* to music. It serves *music information retrieval (MIR)*, *audio content analysis*, or what is called *semantic audio* (Orio 2006; Müller, Goto, and Schedl 2012; Müller 2015; Lerch 2012). Machine listening technology is found in many musical applications, including the following:

- Query by humming or singing
- Tempo and beat tracking
- Estimation of meter and time signature
- Correcting tempo fluctuations in recorded performances
- Synchronizing multiple recordings with inexact tempi
- Real-time score following in interactive accompaniment systems
- Software for music instruction that listens to a student player and tracks errors
- Automatic transcription of musical sound into notation
- *Un-mixing* or *de-mixing* a song into drums, instrumental, and vocal tracks so that they can be manipulated independently
- Removing unwanted noise or reverberation from a recording
- Analyzing the beat structure of a song to drive a generative algorithm
- Automatic musical structure segmentation to annotate music recordings, enabling commands such as "Play the chorus" (Goto and Dannenberg 2019)
- Audio fingerprinting in support of digital rights management

Another application of analysis is the visualization of hierarchical rhythmic structure or rhythmic strata (Yeston 1976; Lerdahl and Jackendoff 1983). This has been done with *time-frequency* (TF) analysis methods such as wavelets, atomic decomposition, and Fourier techniques (Smith 1996; Smith and Honing 2008; Cheng, Hart, and Walker 2009; Sturm et al. 2009). Rhythmic analysis reduces a TF representation into a basic time pulse representation. Wavelet scalograms can indicate a hierarchy of grouping structures, with high-frequency components corresponding to individual percussion strikes and low-frequency components corresponding to rhythmic groups. The use of Gabor scalograms for analyzing percussion sequences was introduced by Smith (1996). Sethares (2007) presented a rhythmic analysis method based on the phase vocoder.

Many other tools can be applied to problems of rhythm recognition, including filtering, deconvolution, matching spectral templates of known sounds, and statistical methods.

Recent research emphasizes strategies that deploy *machine learning* (ML) (appendix A). ML systems are based on statistical algorithms. These algorithms are trained to recognize patterns by presenting them with a large number of examples (often labeled by human beings) of a pattern one wishes to recognize in the future. For example, one might train a system by setting up a correlation between images of music notation depicting triplets and spectrograms of thousands of sound files of audio containing triplets. The system learns to associate images of notation with images of sound spectra (Müller et al. 2019). Training algorithms include nearest-neighbor classifiers, hidden Markov models, Bayesian networks, Gaussian mixture models, and nonnegative matrix factorization (Smaragdis and Brown 2003; Benetos et al. 2019), support vector machines, and deep neural networks, among others. An explanation of each of these could merit a chapter of its own. Müller (2015) offers a book-length treatment. For surveys, refer to Widmer et al. (2008), Klapuri and Davy (2006), Gouyon and Dixon (2005), and Müller et al. (2011). Collins (2011) describes machine listening resources in the SuperCollider language. Benetos et al. (2019) presents an overview of recent strategies applied to automatic music transcription. The rest of this chapter outlines issues that must be confronted by any method. Refer to appendix A for a general overview of ML.

Levels of Rhythm Recognition

Analysis of rhythm can take place on three levels:

- Low level: event detection
- Middle level: transcription into notation
- High level: style analysis and beyond

In the low-level case, the input is a raw acoustic signal that must be converted to digital form and then segmented into a list of starting and ending times for discrete musical events. In the middle-level case, the input stream is already segmented and encoded, as is the case with MIDI data emanating from a keyboard. Here the task is to convert the note list into a meaningful musical score from the segmented data. Note assignment and note grouping are the main subtasks at this level. High-level rhythm analysis falls into the domain of genre, style, and mood analysis (Gouyon et al. 2008). We discuss only the first two levels here.

Event Detection

Low-level rhythm analysis centers on event detection—isolating individual events in a stream of audio samples and determining their durations. As discussed further on, myriad methods have been invoked to tackle the problem (Rosao 2012).

One approach that we do not focus on here uses the spatial position of a source; for example, the bass guitar is in the left channel. Obviously, when spatial information is available it should be deployed (Evangelista et al. 2011). This is not the typical case, however. Thus here we assume that the recording being analyzed is already mixed and that spatial location is not a major cue.

Amplitude Thresholding

For simple monophonic music recorded in a nonreverberant room, event detection can be approached with time-domain techniques such as *amplitude thresholding* (Foster, Schloss, and Rockmore 1982; Schloss 1985; Bello et al. 2005; Wright 2008). In this method, the system scans the input waveform looking for obvious attack transients. If it sees an attack envelope that exceeds a given amplitude threshold, this indicates the start of an event. This method can be enhanced by preprocessing with highpass filters to bring out *transients* (points where sharp onsets and decays occur).

Bello et al. (2005) proposed a preprocessing stage of separating the input signal into multiple frequency bands and then combining each band's data to obtain a final decision. The signal can also be reduced to a *detection function* (figure 35.1), which is essentially a set of event triggers. One detection function is the amplitude envelope, obtained by rectifying and lowpass-filtering the signal. An alternative is the *energy envelope*, which squares

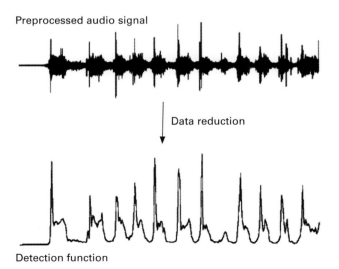

Figure 35.1 Deriving a data-reduced detection function from a preprocessed audio signal.

rather than rectifies the signal. The derivative of the envelope is often used to spot sudden increases in energy.

However, amplitude plots can be misleading as a cue to event onset and duration. Some musical signals are inherently hard to segment by time-domain techniques alone. Examples include slurred bowed string attacks, new notes blurred by sustained notes or reverberation, polyphonic signals such as chords, or any music that has been compressed in dynamic range. In these cases, a continuous amplitude envelope may encapsulate several events, even obscuring accented events that play a significant rhythmic role. For example, when a vibraphone is played with the sustain pedal down, the amplitude plot is not a clear guide to note attack times (figure 35.2). In such cases, pitch and spectrum changes are the best clues to new events.

Following this line, Puckette, Apel, and Zicarelli (1998) observed that rapid changes in the spectral envelope are a better indicator of percussive attacks than changes in power tracked by a classical envelope follower. Hence a combination of time-domain and frequency-domain techniques is most effective (Chafe et al. 1985; Piszczalski and Galler 1977; Piszczalski et al 1981; Klapuri and Davy 2006). For example, a frequency-domain event segmenter based on an *autoregression* (AR) model fit of the input data succeeds where simple amplitude thresholding fails (Makhoul 1975; Foster, Schloss, and Rockmore 1982). Autoregression detects changes in the periodicity of the signal, making it sensitive to changes in pitch. AR and amplitude thresholding work well together because AR is frequency sensitive and thresholding is amplitude sensitive.

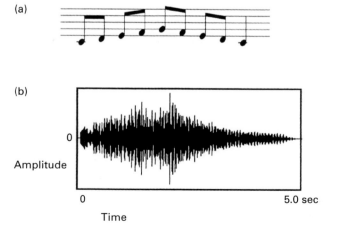

Figure 35.2   A problem case for time-domain event detection. (a) Sequence of notes. (b) Time-domain signal generated by a vibraphone playing these notes with the sustain pedal pushed down.

With the short-time Fourier transform (chapter 37), a simple measure that indicates transients is a large amount of high frequency energy in the signal. This feature is best used with percussive onsets where transients are modeled as bursts of white noise. Refer to Bello et al. (2005) for a survey of probabilistic and model-based methods of deriving detection functions.

More recently, neural networks have been applied to the task of detecting note onsets and note lengths (Benetos et al. 2019).

Separating Voices in Polyphonic Music

The problem of separating voices in polyphonic music is an ongoing topic of research (Vincent, Virtanen, and Gannot 2018). This section offers a glimpse. The ability to separate sources is desirable in applications such as pitch and spectrum editing (chapter 44), automatic transcription (discussed further on), and effects processing (e.g., a reverberator that echoes the harmonic content of the audio signal), among others.

For a small number of distinct instruments, separating the onset times and durations of individual voices in polyphonic music is tractable, as demonstrated by products such as Celemony Melodyne (Neubäcker 2011; Kareer and Basu 2018), Zynaptiq Stem Maker, Audionamix Xtrax Stems (Vaneph et al. 2016), and AudioSourceRE DeMix Pro (Cano et al. 2019).

Music that has a notated score can supply knowledge about pitch and timing that can be exploited by a source separator (Bader 2018; Müller, Goto, and Schedl 2012, Müller et al. 2019; Raphael 2008; Vincent, Virtanen, and Gannot 2018). This has been called *informed source separation* (Ozerov, Liutkus, and Richard 2014). Still, much research has focused on a simple testbed without a score: vocals, drums, bass, and guitar in popular music. In this limited domain, results are good (Cano et al. 2019). Beyond a certain level of complexity, however, source separation becomes impossible (Müller et al. 2019; Cano et al. 2019; Benetos et al. 2019). For example, no one has attempted to segment each note of each instrument in a tutti section played by an orchestra. Nonetheless, ambitious steps toward "universal sound separation" are being taken. This research aims to separate acoustic sources from any sound mixture, not just speech and music (Tzinis et al. 2020).

The following strategies have been used in polyphonic source separation:

- Isolating instruments sounding in different registers by multiple-band filtering
- Using spatial location as a clue if the sources are widely separated in a multichannel recording

- Comparing the input signal with *spectral templates* (a known spectrum pattern) to separate a voice or specific instruments (Wold 1987; Kohler 2000; Bloom 2010; Cano et al. 2019)

- Finding common vibrato and tremolo patterns in a spectrum that indicate which partials were played by a particular instrument. These are called *source coherence criteria* or *common fate* in psychoacoustics research (McAdams and Bregman 1979; Chafe and Jaffe 1986)

- Finding clues in the characteristic attack pattern of individual instruments, even at the start of a chord, because the instruments rarely start exactly synchronously

- Borrowing elements of different recordings of the same music for audio restoration (Vincent et al. 2018)

- Reducing the effects of sounds from one track leaking into another track on a multitrack recording (Präzlich et al. 2015; Pardo, Rafil, and Duan 2018)

- Applying neural nets to estimate and separate sources in a polyphonic music texture (Leglaive, Hennequin, and Badeau 2015; Kareer and Basu 2018; Venkataramani, Subakan, and Smaragdis 2017)

- Leveraging human expertise by having users "paint" on a sonographic image to label separate instruments, which trains an ML algorithm, for example, the ISSE editor (Bryan, Mysore, and Wang 2014)

In practice, the process usually involves several steps in which various techniques and heuristic rules are applied in combination (Hung and Lerch 2020; Wu et al. 2018). Thus a source separation system needs a rule-based decision-making algorithm that weighs the results obtained by different methods.

No standard methodology has emerged. The sigsep website at GitHub provides a collection of free tools for audio source separation. Much research to date focuses on finding spectral templates—the signatures of known sounds—in the mixed signal (figure 35.3). For example, the spectral template of instruments like organ, guitar, and bass consists of mainly stable harmonic components—horizontal lines in a spectrogram. Harmonic components share a common fate: they all start and stop together, and glissandi and vibrato affect them all. By contrast, the spectral template of drums tends to be transient and broadband noise—vertical blocks in a spectrogram. The singing voice has harmonic components in vowels and noise components in consonants, so the model is more complicated. In any case, the basic identity of each component sound is already defined before source separation begins.

The starting point for separation is time-frequency analysis of the mixed signal. The source separation algorithm then tries to match a model of the sound that it is trying to extract from the mixed signal. This is done on each spectral frame, which is typically less than 100 ms. If the goal is to separate

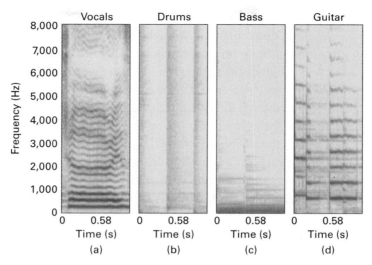

Figure 35.3   Spectral signatures of four source sounds. Left to right: vocals, drums, bass, and guitar. From Cano et al. (2019).

the vocal melody from the instruments, the process discards spectral components that are not part of the vocal line (Durrieu et al. 2010). The process works iteratively, looking for traces that match the source models, homing in to greater detail as it goes (Cano et al. 2019). In some systems, such as spectral editors, the work can be checked by a human operator at various stages.

Another trend is the use of machine learning techniques, especially neural networks (NN). The networks undergo supervised training using data sets where individual sources and mixes of the sources are both available (Leglaive, Hennequin, and Badeau 2015; Nugraha, Liutkus, and Vincent 2016; Venkataramani, Subakan, and Smaragdis 2017). Most supervised NN training models take as inputs spectrograms of the mixed audio. The targets are set to spectrograms of the desired sources. The quantity and quality of the training data is important (Benetos et al 2019). The Jamendo Corpus, for example, is one such data set for sung vocals (https://www.jamendo.com).

Automatic Transcription

> Any given sequence of note values is in principle infinitely ambiguous, but this ambiguity is seldom apparent to the listener.
> —H. C. Longuet-Higgins (1976)

Automatic transcription—the middle level of rhythm recognition—begins once a list of discrete events is assembled. Notation programs that take in MIDI keyboard data commence from this point. Transcription includes the subtasks of pulse induction, tempo tracking, rhythm value assignment, note grouping, determination of meter, setting measure boundaries, and possibly sorting out basic phrase structure.

As a pragmatic step, notation software constrains the problem by requiring a setup stage. For example, as a starting point for keyboard transcription, a notation editor will typically demand that the user fill out a *setup template* that tells the computer more-or-less what to expect. Given a proper setup template, transcribing from MIDI data works well.

In contrast to transcription from MIDI data, the subject of this section is *automatic transcription from audio* (figure 35.4). Commercial apps like Sibelius AutoScore, Akoff Music Composer, ScoreCloud, AnthemScore, and Transcribe! use ML strategies to turn a performed audio performance (e.g., on an acoustic piano) into sheet music.

The goal of transcription is not always to construct a score for printing. The goal may be to parse the sound coming in to a teaching or accompaniment system or interactive composition program. Transcription could also be used to validate a model of musical listening. Because goals differ, methods of parsing the score may vary.

Figure 35.4   Automatic transcription from audio. Top: Audio waveform. Center: Mid-level and parametric representation of pitch, onset, offset, stream, and loudness. Bottom: Music notation using note name, key, rhythm, and instrument in score time. After Duan and Benetos (2015).

Automatic Transcription: Background

Automatic transcription of performed music played on a clavier dates back centuries. A mechanism for recording the time of key depressions and their durations was developed by Père Marie Dominique Joseph Engramelle (1727—1781) and documented in his text *La Tonotechnie ou l'Art de Noter les Cylindres* (1775). Keystrokes were inscribed in real time on paper in a piano-roll form of notation. This recording could be transcribed to common music notation by a musician (Leichtentritt 1934). By 1747, Reverend Creed of London presented a paper to the British Royal Society demonstrating the possibility of automatic music transcription from keyboard improvisation. The German musical engineers J. F. Unger and J. Hohlfeld first implemented such a system, attached to a harpsichord, in 1752 (Boalch 1956; Buchner 1978).

Over two centuries later, a computerized keyboard transcription system at the University of Utah employed a minicomputer to scan an organ manual, capture keystrokes, and display rudimentary music notation (Ashton 1971; Knowlton [1971, 1972]; see also Ben Daniel [1983]). Today most commercial notation programs handle this task well.

Transcription from sound is a much deeper problem. In the field of digital signal processing, it has traditionally been called the *source separation* or *cocktail party problem* (Pollack and Pickett 1957). Can we isolate the voice of a particular person speaking in a room full of talking people? In the context of music, the question becomes, can we follow one line in a polyphonic texture? The first important application to musical sound was J. A. Moorer's landmark doctoral research in computer science at Stanford University to create a "musical scribe" (Moorer 1975). Figure 35.5 outlines the strategy followed by Moorer.

Figure 35.6 compares an original score with the score transcribed by Moorer's system. Another early system developed at Stanford analyzed melodies from eighteenth-century music and attempted to perform automated transcription into music notation typical of that period (Chowning, et al. 1984; Chowning and Mont-Reynaud 1986). Importantly, the goal of the transcription system was to recover the original score, not what was actually played. This required both low-level analytic prowess and high-level knowledge of the idioms of eighteenth-century notation.

A dramatic demonstration of sound and vision understanding was WABOT-2 (figure 35.7), a robot constructed at Waseda University and reimplemented by the Sumitomo Corporation in Japan (Matsushima, et al. 1985; Roads 1986b). The robot performed for millions of visitors to the Tsukuba World Expo in 1985 and 1986. Within constraints, WABOT-2 understood speech, musical sound, and visual score notation. It could respond to song requests spoken in Japanese and could read music notation. While memorizing a score

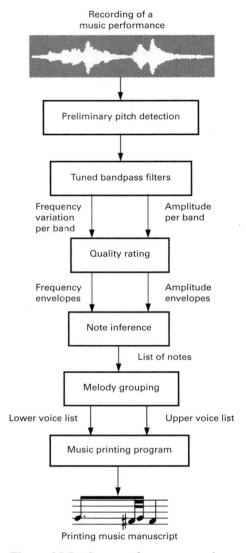

Figure 35.5   Strategy for an automatic music scribe developed by James A. Moorer in 1975.

placed in front of its robot eye, WABOT-2 planned its performance. It could also accompany a human singer. If the singer strayed from the original intonation or rhythm, the robot made adjustments to the pitch of the organ and the rhythm of the accompaniment to try to match the singer.

Transcribing Rhythmic Structures

Since chapter 34 covers the topic of pitch estimation, in the rest of this chapter we look at the transcription problem mainly from the viewpoint of

Figure 35.6 Comparison of the original score (top) with the transcription from acoustic performance accomplished by Moorer's system (bottom). The lengths of longer notes are underestimated, and a note is missing in the penultimate measure. The most conspicuous change, however, is due to the fact that the guitar was mistuned a half step high. The literal-minded computer faithfully reports the score mistuned a semitone high throughout.

rhythm. In order to transcribe into notation, we need to track the pulse and tempo, estimate event durations and assign them to note symbols, group notes into conventional notation patterns, and estimate the meter and measure boundaries. Finally, in particular if the task is attempted in real time, we need a strategy for recovering from confusion.

Much research into automatic transcription today relies on ML in combination with rule-based pattern classifiers (Abesser et al. 2017; Desain and Honing 1989, 1992a, 1992b, 1992c; Linster 1992; Smith and Honing 2008; Ryynänen and Klapuri 2008; Widmer et al. 2008; Müller 2015; Benetos et al. 2019). For example, an approach based on neural networks trains the recognizer to correlate snippets of notation with short clips of audio (Dorfer, Artz, and Widmer 2017). These systems establish correspondences between note heads in a score and their audio onset times in a sonogram (figure 35.8). However, to perform a useful task such as music typesetting, raw symbol recognition is usually combined with high-level knowledge about music in the form of heuristic rules based on precepts of music theory.

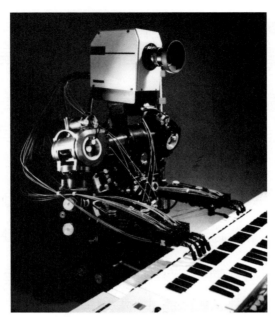

Figure 35.7   WABOT-2, a musical robot developed in 1985 at Waseda University in Japan, with further engineering by Sumitomo Corporation.

(a)   (b)

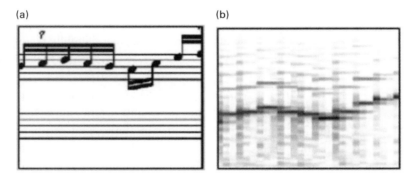

Figure 35.8   A training pair matching two images of music. (a) A snippet of music notation (180 by 280 pixels). (b) An audio clip in the form of a log-frequency spectrogram representation of ninety-two frames and forty-two frequency bins. Pitches stand out as black horizontal lines (Müller et al. 2019).

An exception is the project of Carvalho and Smaragdis (2017), based on a deep learning model. Instead of employing typical processing steps such as spectrum analysis front-ends, harmonicity and scale priors, and temporal pitch smoothing, they showed that a neural network could learn such steps on its own when presented with appropriate training data. Their system accepted unprocessed audio waveforms and directly produced a music score written with the Lilypond notation language.

Pulse induction and tempo tracking

Musical meter is a hierarchical structure. A metrical level (or pulse) is the periodic recurrence of a feature in time. A rhythm recognizer scans for periodic behaviors to identify pulse periods. The process of *pulse induction* aims at highlighting periodicities and is central to rhythm understanding. *Tempo tracking* tries to find the beat—a perceived pulse that marks time intervals of equal duration (Müller 2015). As Scheirer (2000) argued, tempo is a perceptual attribute; its physical correlate is not well defined. Thus there is no standard method. The literature describes a wide variety of heuristic approaches (Gouyon and Dixon 2005). Klapuri (2004) surveyed the art of meter analysis and compared ten different approaches.

In a music notation program, the tempo tracking problem is aided by having the musician enter the music by playing along with a metronome click generated by the program. Although this is expedient, we consider here the more difficult problem of tempo tracking from audio without a metronome reference, which corresponds to the task of tracking actual musical performances (Rowe 1975; Pressing and Lawrence 1993; Scheirer 2000; Laroche 2003; Klapuri, Eronen, and J. Astola 2005).

The first step in tempo tracking is measuring the time distances between events. This measurement can be used to set up a hierarchical *metrical grid*. The beat is usually a common denominator of the measured durations. This process sounds straightforward, but tempo variations can warp the grid and make it difficult to estimate the basic pulse initially. If there is any syncopation in the rhythmic pattern, the tempo tracker must somehow realize that the beat is not changing in the presence of off-beat accented notes.

A musical model is needed to achieve stable meter tracking and to fill in parts where the meter is only faintly implied by the musical surface. One approach is to scan over a finite-duration window, for example, five seconds at a time (Miller et al. 1992). A history mechanism with a decaying memory of past beats captures a similar idea (Dannenberg and Mont-Reynaud 1987; Allen and Dannenberg 1990). A short memory ignores past events, allowing rapid tempo fluctuations, but tends to instability. A long memory steadies the tempo at the expense of ignoring fast tempo changes.

Figure 35.9 demonstrates a tempo tracker that pursues two strategies in parallel. The upper left area shows the procedures that extract "important events" or *phenomenal accents*. Phenomenal accents are events that give emphasis to a moment in music. Among these are especially the onsets of long pitched events, sudden changes in loudness or timbre, and harmonic changes (Lerdahl and Jackendoff 1983; Klapuri et al. 2005). These events serve as structural anchors in the music. The heuristic applied here is that rhythmic or melodic accents normally happen at structurally important points such

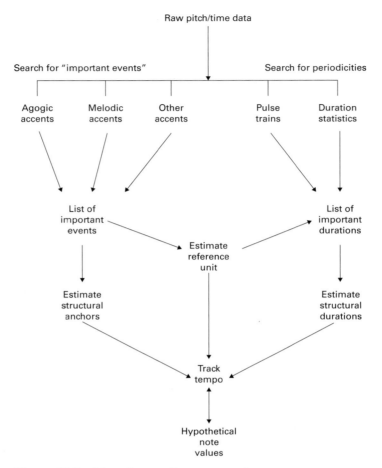

Figure 35.9   Mont-Reynaud's tempo tracker.

as strong beats. Thus the duration from anchor to anchor is often a simple relationship.

Since this is not always true, the upper right area of figure 35.9 shows procedures that use an independent method of tracking tempo fluctuations. These procedures search for repeating patterns in successive durations and keep running statistics on the most common durations. Significant durations are usually in a simple relationship to one another and to the anchor-to-anchor durations. By combining these two approaches, tempo-tracking decisions select a reasonable hypothesis about the current tempo. The flexibility of the approach is demonstrated in the presence of syncopation—the anchors occur off beat, but the significant durations keep track of the tempo. Conversely, when anchors give strong hints, major tempo adjustments are accommodated.

Taking a different approach, Scheirer (2000) demonstrated that pitch data is not necessary to extract rhythm; the temporal envelopes of the filter sub-bands of a musical signal are sufficient to convey the beat of a signal. He used a bank of resonators to phase-lock with the beat of the signal.

Another family of approaches to tempo tracking employ neural net strategies (D'Autilia and Guerra 1991; Rowe 1992a, b). In these systems, a network of nodes representing the time span between events interact with one another. They alter their values to become simpler rational multiples of one another. In the ideal these values define a metrical grid.

Note duration assignment

Given a steady beat, each detected event can be assigned a metrically related duration. This would be simple if the performance were mechanically perfect, but expressive musical performances exhibit considerable variation in the durations of supposedly equal-duration notes (Chafe et al. 1982; Clarke 1987; Clynes and Nettheim 1982; Clynes and Walker 1982). Staccato articulations, which shrink the notated duration, and agogic accents, which stretch the duration of important notes, abound in performed music.

To make the task of deducing the metrically related duration easier, the analysis program may *quantize* the durations of notes, that is, round them off to a metrically related duration such as a sixteenth note. Practical notation programs usually solicit hints from performers before the transcription, such as requiring them to stipulate the smallest note value to be played, which presets the quantization grid. Even so, as Desain and Honing (1992b) show in a comparative study, simple grid-based quantization strategies such as those employed in music notation programs can lead to pathological transcriptions. Figure 35.10 shows what happens when a program quantizes a triplet according to a sixty-fourth-note grid. One problem is that the note labeled *A* is played shorter than note *B,* even though they are notated the

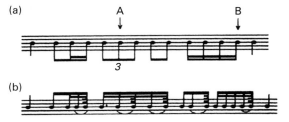

Figure 35.10 Deleterious effects of quantization. (a) Musical input written appropriately. (b) Transcription by music score editor using quantization according to a sixty-fourth-note grid.

other way round. Alternative quantization strategies exist, including those based on neural net models, but each seems to have its own limitations.

Grouping into patterns

The next step in recognition is subdividing the list of notes into groups of notes or rhythm patterns. Figure 35.11a shows the starting point of the grouping process: a list of note durations with no indication with regard to measure boundaries or time signature. How does the program reckon that bar lines should be inserted after notes 1, 7, and 14, as in figure 35.11b? How does it determine that the most musical interpretation of the second, third, and fourth notes of the input is a triplet?

Various music applications may group the notes according to different criteria. A notation system, for example, may look for groups of notes to beam, such as a series of eighth notes. A program that attempts to model human listening may attempt to build a hierarchy of phrases. Grouping notes by measure requires some hypothesis about the meter, so we discuss it in the next section.

Early rhythm pattern recognition was dominated by search-and-compare techniques (Rowe 1975; Mont-Reynaud 1985b; Mont-Reynaud and Goldstein 1985). Quasigrammatical theories of rhythm parsing, such as those in Lerdahl and Jackendoff (1983), Longuet-Higgins (1976, 1987), and Longuet-Higgins and Lee (1983), have served as guides for parsing algorithms. For example, Rosenthal (1988) cited five rules derived from Lerdahl and Jackendoff and presented a step-by-step walkthrough of these rules applied to simple musical rhythms. We list them here as an example of typical grouping rules:

1. Groups begin on accented notes.

2. Do not form groups of a single event.

3. Events of short-duration tend to be grouped together with subsequent events of long duration.

Figure 35.11   A rhythmic grouping problem. (a) Sequence of notes as seen by a rhythmic parser. (b) Plausible interpretation of (a).

4. A grouping boundary separates events of long duration from subsequent events of short duration.

5. Groups at the same hierarchical level should be as equal as possible in duration.

These theories, it should be stressed, derive from written and not necessarily performed music. Thus, in practice, such algorithms are usually embellished by empirical rules derived by experimentation. More complicated heuristics take into account pitch and amplitude patterns in order to resolve two competing rhythmic hypotheses (Katayose and Inokuchi 1990).

Today ML techniques are increasingly used to recognize basic rhythmic patterns, but the assembly of such patterns into a full score still requires a knowledge base of music theory rules (Benetos et al. 2019).

Estimating meter and measure boundaries

Meter is a ratio between two time scales. One is the beat period (e.g., one quarter note equals one second), and the other is a larger period based on a fixed number of beats: the measure. Meter generally imposes an accent structure on beats, a structure that tends to articulate the measure. Determining meter can be divided into two problems. The first is finding the *perceived meter* on the basis of recurring patterns that are divisible by an integer n (e.g., duple, triple, quadruple, and quintuple). This is usually the goal of interactive composition programs and models of listening. The second problem is estimating the exact time signature of a piece (e.g., 2/4 and not 4/4), which is the problem faced in transcription to printed score.

Because of the ambiguities of rhythmic relations, the task of estimating the perceived meter and subdividing the music by measure is not straightforward. Rosenthal's (1992) strategy was to deploy multiple specialized agents, each of which gathered statistics about note placement, note durations, accents, and characteristic pitch and rhythm patterns. Each agent proposed a hypothesis, and a manager program decided among the multiple hypotheses presented to it. It did this by noting that certain agents were more reliable than others (thus had more weight) and that when reliable agents agreed on a hypothesis, it was likely to be the correct one. Miller, Scarborough, and Jones (1992) compared a rule-based versus a neural network (NN) strategy in estimating meter. The rule-based method is somewhat rigid, and its strengths and weaknesses are predictable. The NN strategy, being more flexible, can handle situations that cause the rule-based method to fail, such as estimations in the presence of tempo variations. But sometimes the NN approach made a wild estimate, pointing out the general difficulty of understanding the output of NN analyzers.

Estimating the exact time signature is challenging and few algorithms exist (Gouyon and Dixon 2005). Part of the problem is that many time signatures can sound the same. For example, a given melody can be played in 1/2, 2/2, 2/4, 4/4, 4/8, 8/8, etc., and sound identical, assuming the tempo is adjusted accordingly. Assigning a specific time signature to a given rhythm requires musicological knowledge of the style in which the piece was composed. For example, a piece composed in eighteenth-century Vienna is likely to adhere to conventions that limit the choice of time signature. Generally, the best that current programs can do is make an educated guess, based on the style of the music. For contemporary music compositions with frequently changing time signature the problem is obviously much harder.

Recovery from confusion

Rhythm value estimation can be reliable when a metronome reference beat is provided to the machine and a quantization range is prespecified. In the absence of such strong hints, rhythmic recognition does not always achieve perfect results. Even the most successful systems can account only for conventional rhythmic formulas. Even if we develop new parsing rules, for every rule in music there are exceptions. Thus numerous scores exceed the complexity that can be handled by machine rhythmic analyzers. This includes much of modernist contemporary music.

The problem is compounded if the rhythm recognizer is expected to perform in real time. Many factors can confuse a recognizer: a wild performance, rhythmic ambiguity, octave ambiguity, a low-amplitude passage where note onsets are not clear, missed notes in chords, notes assigned to the wrong voice, or simply a hole in the ability of the recognizer to parse a particular type of passage (Benetos et al. 2019).

Thus any practical rhythm recognizer must try to recover smoothly from a point of confusion, to pick up again as a human musician would. This subject is complicated, and the strategies for recovery depend on the task being performed, so we can only mention it as an issue here. As Allen and Dannenberg (1990) stress, if the system maintains multiple interpretations of the performance, it is less likely to become completely confused in the first place. Understanding more about human perception seems to be the key to progress in this domain.

36 *Introduction to Spectrum Analysis*

Applications of Spectrum Analysis

Spectrum Plots

       Static Spectrum Plots
       Power Spectrum
       Time-Varying Spectrum Plots

Models behind Spectrum Analysis Methods

Spectrum and Timbre

       MPEG-7 Timbre Descriptors

Spectrum Analysis: Historical Background

       Computer-Based Spectrum Analysis
          Heterodyne filter analysis
          The saga of the phase vocoder

Just as an image can be described as a mixture of colors (light frequencies in the visible part of the electromagnetic spectrum), a sound can be described as a blend of elementary acoustic vibrations. As the pioneering acoustician D. C. Miller (1916) wrote a century ago:

Will not the creative musician be a more powerful master if he is also informed in regard to the pure science of the methods and materials of his art? Will he not be able to mix tone colors with greater skill if he understands the nature of the ingredients and the effects which they produce? (269)

One way of dissecting sound is to consider the contribution of various components, each corresponding to a certain rate of variation in air pressure. Gauging the balance among these components is called *spectrum analysis*.

A working definition of spectrum is *a measure of the distribution of signal energy as a function of frequency.* Such a definition may seem simple, but no more general and precise definition of spectrum exists. This is because different analysis techniques measure properties that they each call "spectrum" with more or less diverging results. Except for isolated test cases, the practice of spectrum analysis is not an exact science (see Marple [1987] for a thorough discussion). The results are typically an approximation of the actual spectrum, so that spectrum analysis is more precisely called *spectrum estimation.* We often seek to measure the spectrum as it evolves in time. Thus the term *time-frequency* (TF) *analysis* is often used in the literature to describe a spectrum that is changing in time, and the data the analysis produces is called a *time-frequency* (TF) *representation.*

Musicians seek not only to analyze spectra but to modify the spectral data in order to transform the sound for creative purposes. Wright et al. (2000) compared various techniques for analyzing and resynthesizing sound in terms of their sound model, interpolation model, noise model, analysis parameters, and characteristic artifacts.

Spectrum analysis continues to evolve. The surveys in this book, though broad, cannot account for every possible approach. Our primary goal is to decipher sometimes abstruse concepts in terms of musical practice.

Applications of Spectrum Analysis

Spectrum analysis of sound serves the following applications:

- Acoustics and sound engineering—acoustic measurements
- Restoration of old recordings—reducing noise

- Audio data compression—MP3 files, telephony
- Music information retrieval—genre, song, and artist recognition
- Psychoacoustics—studies of pitch and timbre perception
- Musicology—analysis of performances
- Sound visualization—visually projecting TF energy
- Automatic transcription into notation
- Interactive performance—machine listening to a human player
- Sound transformation—pitch-time changing, spectrum filtering

Acousticians and sound engineers use spectrum analysis to measure the properties of rooms, voices, instruments, sound files, and audio components. Live sound engineers generate test tones and analyze the responses of stadiums and other venues in order to tune their sound reinforcement systems.

Sound engineers use spectrum analysis in restoring old recordings for reissue (Borish 1984; Lagadec and Pelloni 1983; Moorer and Berger 1986). Restoration can be as mundane as eliminating clicks and hum, or as exotic as removing an instrumental background from a vocal performance. This is called *source separation* in the literature. A pioneering example was the restoration of the opera singer Enrico Caruso's singing. In this case, a poorly recorded orchestra sound was separated from the voice. Then a new high-fidelity orchestra was substituted while leaving the voice more-or-less intact (Miller 1973; Stockham, Cannon, and Ingebretson 1975). Today, source separation technologies that un-mix a song into multiple stem tracks are available as products, as discussed in chapter 35.

Spectrum analysis is fundamental to audio data compression algorithms (e.g., MP3 and AAC) (Moorer 1979b; Pohlmann 1989b; Gibson et al. 1998; Sayood 2000).

Much effort has been invested in the creation of sound databases in which sounds can be accessed according to their acoustic properties (called *audio descriptors* in the research literature). These techniques enable *music information retrieval* (MIR) and *automatic music recommendation systems* (Casey et al. 2008; Rumsey 2009; Lerch 2012; Müller 2015). *Adaptive audio effects* use audio descriptors to extract features from a recording and use them to control an audio effect (Campbell et al. 2016; Reiss and Brandstegg 2018). This process is often called *sidechaining* (see chapter 27).

Psychoacousticians correlate physical measurements of spectrum with human perception (Risset and Wessel 1982; Barlow 2012).

Musicologists turn to sound analysis techniques in order to study music performance and the structure of electronic music (Cogan 1984; Licata 2002; Simoni 2006).

Sound analysis can be used to make artistic visualizations. Video jockey (VJ) apps often use spectrum analysis to generate abstract visuals or transform videos in sync with the music.

Automatic transcription of music—from sound to score—starts from spectrum analysis and through elaborate processing generates a score, either in the form of common music notation or in an abstract graphic form (see chapters 35, 42, and 43).

Real-time spectrum analysis is one type of "ear" for interactive music systems that listen to musicians and respond in kind. Spectrum analysis reveals the characteristic frequency energy of instrumental and vocal tones, thus helping to identify timbres and separate multiple sources playing at once (Maher 1990). As previous chapters have shown, the results of spectrum analysis are valuable in pitch and rhythm recognition.

But musicians want not only to analyze sounds; they want to transform sounds. More and more sound transformation techniques begin with an analysis stage, including time compression and expansion, frequency shifting, convolution (filtering and reverberation effects), and many types of cross-synthesis—hybridization between two sounds.

Spectrum Plots

Many strategies exist to measure and plot spectra. This section looks at strategies falling into two basic categories: *static* (like a snapshot of a spectrum), and *time-varying* (like a motion-picture film of a spectrum over time).

Static Spectrum Plots

Static plots capture a still image of sound. These sonic snapshots project a two-dimensional image of amplitude versus frequency. The analysis measures the average energy in each frequency region over the time period of the analyzed segment. This time period or *window* can vary from a brief instant to several seconds or longer. (Later we discuss the trade-offs of various window lengths.)

One type of static plot is a *discrete* or *line spectrum*, in which a vertical line represents each frequency component. For a tone with multiple strong harmonics, the clearest analysis is *pitch synchronous*. Pitch-synchronous analysis measures the amplitude of the harmonics of a tone whose pitch can be determined beforehand. Figure 36.1a shows the line spectrum of the steady-state part of a trumpet tone, measured using a pitch-synchronous

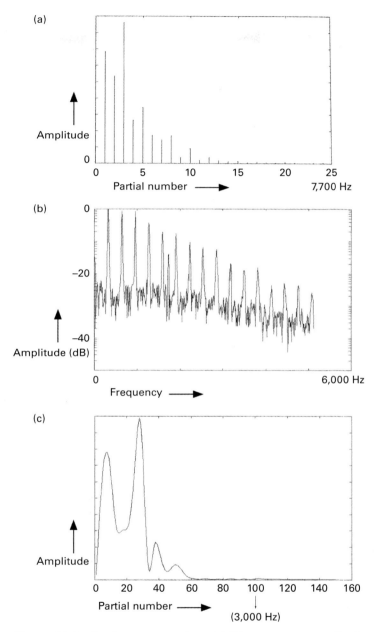

Figure 36.1   Static spectrum plots. (a) Line spectrum amplitude-versus-frequency plot of the sustained portion of a trumpet tone. Each line represents the strength of a harmonic of the fundamental frequency of 309 Hz. Linear amplitude scale. (b) Spectrum of trumpet tone in (a) plotted on a logarithmic (dB) scale, which compresses the plot into a narrower vertical band. (c) Spectrum plot in a continuous form, showing the outline of the formant peaks for a vocal sound *ah*. Linear amplitude scale. (Plots courtesy of Aldo Piccialli, Department of Physics, Federico II University of Naples.)

technique. Notice that at the instant this spectrum was measured, the third harmonic is higher in amplitude than the fundamental.

Figure 36.1b shows another trumpet spectrum plotted on a logarithmic (dB) amplitude scale. The decibel scale compresses large differences in amplitude into small differences in dB. Thus the plot is packed into a narrower vertical band. By tracing the outline of the peaks one can see the overall formant shape.

Figure 36.1c shows a plot of the spectrum of a vocal sound *ah* in a *continuous* form, in which the discrete points measured by the analyzer have been filled in by graphical interpolation. Individual sinusoidal components are hidden, but the overall shape of the spectrum (called *spectral envelope*) is clear.

Each type of static spectrum plot has its advantages, depending on the signal being analyzed and the goal of the analysis.

Power Spectrum

From the amplitude spectrum one can derive the *power spectrum*. Physicists define *power* as the square of the amplitude of a signal. Thus, power spectrum is the square of the amplitude spectrum. Displays of spectrum sometimes show power rather than amplitude, because this correlates better with human perception. Yet another measure is the *power spectrum density* (PSD), which applies to continuous spectra like noise. A simple definition of the PSD is that it is the power spectrum (energy per unit time) within a specified bandwidth (Tempelaars 1977).

Time-Varying Spectrum Plots

Details in the spectrum of even a single instrument tone are constantly changing, so static, timeless plots can represent only a portion of an evolving sound form. A time-varying spectrum depicts the changing blend of frequencies over the duration of an event. It can be plotted as a three-dimensional graph of spectrum versus time (figure 36.2). These plots essentially line up a series of static plots, one after the other.

Figure 36.3 shows two more display formats for time-varying spectrum analysis. Figure 36.3a is a still photograph from a *waterfall display*, a spectrum plot in which the time axis is moving in real time. The term waterfall display comes from the fact that this type of plot shows waves of rising and falling frequency energy in a fluidlike depiction. Figure 36.3b depicts a vocal melody.

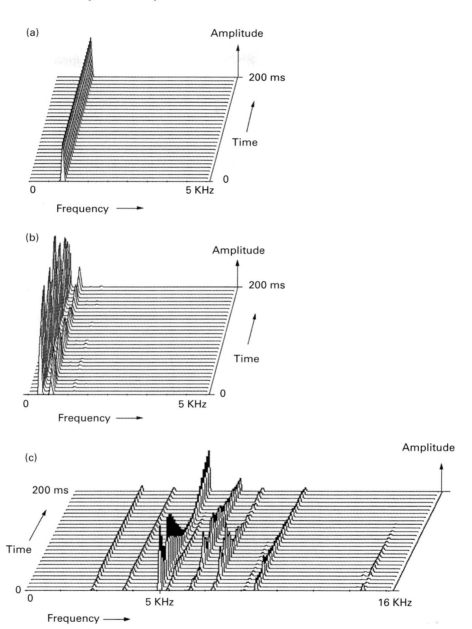

Figure 36.2   Time-varying spectra plotted on a linear amplitude scale. Time moves from front to back. (a) Sine wave at 1 KHz. (b) Flute playing fluttertongue at pitch E4. (c) Triangle, hit once. Notice the beating frequencies as one partial goes high while another goes low.

(a)

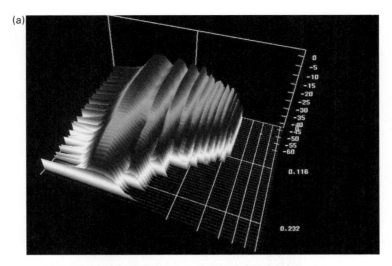

(b)

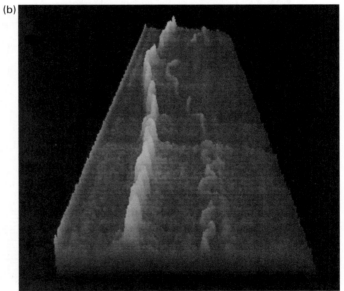

Figure 36.3 images from real-time waterfall displays. (a) Synthetic trumpet tone. The most recent time is at the front. The frequency scale is logarithmic, going from left to right. The fundamental frequency is approximately 1 kHz. Amplitude is plotted vertically on a logarithmic dB scale. (b) Vocal melody. The most recent time is at the front. Low frequencies are at left. (Images courtesy of A. Peevers, Center for New Music and Art Technologies, University of California, Berkeley.)

(a)
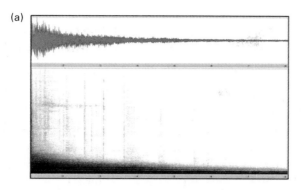

(b)
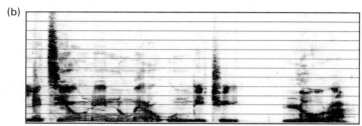

Figure 36.4   Sonogram plots. (a) Struck tam-tam, time-domain waveform on top. In the sonogram below it, the vertical axis is frequency, and the horizontal axis is time. This sonogram uses 1,024 points of input data and a Hamming window. The plot has a frequency resolution of 43 Hz and a time resolution of 1 ms. The analysis bandwidth is 0 to 22 kHz, and the measured dynamic range is −10 to −44.5 dB, plotted on a linear amplitude scale. (b) Sonogram of speech plotted to 12 kHz.

Another way to display a time-varying spectrum is to plot a *sonogram* (also called a *spectrogram*)–a common tool in speech analysis, in which it was originally called *visible speech* (Potter 1946). A sonogram shows the frequency versus time content of a signal, where frequency is plotted vertically, time is plotted horizontally, and the amplitudes of the frequencies in the spectrum are reflected in terms of the darkness of the trace. That is, intense frequency components are plotted darkly, and soft frequency components are plotted lightly (figure 36.4). We discuss the sonogram representation in more detail further on.

Models behind Spectrum Analysis Methods

No single method of spectrum estimation is ideal for all musical applications. Fourier analysis—the most prevalent approach—is actually a family of different techniques that are still evolving. Many non-Fourier methods continue to be developed, as explained in chapters 38 and 39. Indeed, as the computer music pioneer Jean-Claude Risset (1991) observed:

There does not seem to be any general or optimal paradigm to either analyze or synthesize any type of sound. One has to scrutinize the sound—quasi-periodic, sum of inharmonic components, noisy, quickly or slowly evolving—and also investigate which features of the sound are relevant to the ear. (18)

Every sound analysis technique should be viewed as fitting the input data to an assumed model. Methods based on Fourier analysis model the input sound as a sum of harmonically related sinusoids. Other techniques model the input signal as an excitation signal filtered by resonances, as a sum of exponentially damped sinusoids or square waves, as a combination of inharmonically related sinusoids, as a set of formant peaks with added noise, or as a set of equations that represent certain behavior of a traditional instrument. Innumerable other models are conceivable. As we see in detail later, variations in performance among the different methods can often be attributed to how well the assumed model matches the process being analyzed. Hence it is important to choose the appropriate analysis method for a particular musical application.

Spectrum and Timbre

The vague term *timbre* is a catchall for a range of phenomena (Plomp 1976). It may someday be superseded by a more precise vocabulary of sound qualities, of which the MPEG-7 timbre descriptors discussed subsequently represent a starting point (Martinez 2004).

The classification of musical timbre is an ancient science. Early Chinese civilization developed sophisticated written descriptions of timbre, including a taxonomy of instrumental sources (metal, stone, clay, skin, silk threads, wood, gourd, and bamboo), and elaborate accounts of the different *touches* (attack forms, pulls, and vibratos) involved in playing the silk strings of the classical *chhin* instrument. Indeed, the main playing technique of the *chhin* is the production of different timbres at the same pitch (Needham, Ling, and Girdwood-Robinson 1962).

Spectrum and timbre are related concepts, but they are not equivalent. Spectrum is a physical property that can be characterized as a distribution of energy as a function of frequency. How to measure this energy precisely is another question! Psychoacoustics uses the term *timbre* to denote perceptual mechanisms that classify sound into families. By this definition, timbre is at least as concerned with perception as it is with sound signals.

It is certainly easiest to discuss timbre in the realm of traditional instrument and vocal tones, on which almost all past research has focused. Only a few attempts have been made to classify the universe of sound outside this category, the most heroic being the studies of Pierre Schaeffer and his colleagues. Recognizing that the vast range of sound material opened up by musique concrète was largely undefined and unclassified, Schaeffer made a pioneering attempt to describe the correlates of timbre in his *Traité des Objets Musicaux* originally published in 1966 (Schaeffer 1977, 2017; Chion 2009), with accompanying sound disc *Solfège de l'object sonore* (Schaeffer, Reibel, and Ferreyra 1967, 1998). Although the vocabulary he developed is idiosyncratic, there is no question that Schaeffer was a pioneer of timbre research who made many discoveries.

For instrumental sounds, timbre is officially defined as those aspects of a tone that can be varied without affecting pitch, duration, or loudness (Howard and Angus 2017). No matter what notes are played, for example, one can always identify a piano. Nor is it difficult to distinguish a marimba from a violin tone of the same pitch, loudness, and duration. Of course, a single instrument may also emit many timbres, as in the range of sonorities obtained from saxophones.

Numerous factors inform timbre perception. These include the attack morphology, the amplitude envelope of a sound, undulations due to vibrato and tremolo, formant structures, perceived loudness, duration, and the time-varying spectral envelope (frequency content over time) (Schaeffer 1977; Risset 1991; McAdams and Bregman 1979; McAdams 1987; Gordon and Grey 1977; Grey 1975, 1978). Traditional instrument families such as reeds, brass, strings, and percussion each have characteristic attack *signatures* that are important in recognizing tones made by them.

Amplitude and duration have an influence on the perception of timbre. For example, the proportions of the frequencies in the spectrum of a flute tone at 60 dB may be the equivalent to those in a tone amplified to 120 dB, but we hear the latter only as a loud blast. Similarly, a toneburst that lasts 30 ms may have the same periodic waveshape as a tone that lasts 3 seconds, but listeners may find it difficult to say whether they represent the same source.

The point is that spectrum is not the only clue to perceived timbre. By examining the time-domain waveform carefully, one can glean much about the timbre of a sound without subjecting it to a detailed spectrum analysis (Strawn 1985b).

Most scientific research on timbre has focused on traditional instrument and vocal tones. A classic example is the research of John Grey, who made a three-dimensional map of the perceived timbre space for different instrumental tones (Grey 1975, 1978). Tones that sound similar were close together in this space, and dissimilar tones were far apart. Wessel (1979) devised a scheme for navigating timbre space by means of additive synthesis.

MPEG-7 Timbre Descriptors

Until the introduction of the MPEG-7 timbre descriptors in 2002, timbre was a vaguely defined territory described by many incompatible maps. The MPEG-7 multimedia content description standard changed this situation. It provided a set of mathematically defined terms to describe a number of perceptually-relevant aspects of timbre. Thus it represents a significant advance in timbral description. For software resources in support of MPEG-7, refer to Casey (2010).

A media file that conforms to the MPEG-7 format contains *metadata*, that is, descriptors of the contents of the file. One category of descriptors built into this standard concerns timbre. Table 36.1 is a list of these descriptors, with capsule definitions adapted from Martinez (2004).

Although the definitions are described in capsule form here, they are precisely defined mathematically in the standard. This means that they can be used in practical applications. For example, Mintz (2007) developed a software synthesizer that could analyze a sound and synthesize similar sounds based on its MPEG-7 descriptors. Campbell et al. (2016) developed a prototype of a generalized adaptive effects processor that could map arbitrary audio features to arbitrary audio effects. For example, the pitch in one track could control the amount of reverberation in the same track or another track. (See chapter 27 for a brief introduction to adaptive audio effects.)

MPEG-7 descriptors form a scientific beginning for a taxonomy of timbre. It is only a beginning, however, because MPEG-7 is not a complete account. Its focus is specifically on harmonic, coherent, sustained sounds, and nonsustained percussive sounds. The development of a standard set of descriptors to describe the vast world of so-called noises remains to be done.

Table 36.1   MPEG-7 timbral descriptors

Audio waveform	The audio waveform envelope (minimum and maximum), typically for display purposes.
Audio power	Describes the temporally smoothed instantaneous power, which is useful as a quick summary of a signal and in conjunction with the power spectrum.
Log-frequency power spectrum	Logarithmic-frequency spectrum, spaced by a power-of-two divisor or multiple of an octave.
Audio spectral envelope	A vector that describes the short-term power spectrum of an audio signal. It may be used to display a spectrogram, to synthesize a crude *auralization* of the data, or as a general-purpose descriptor for search and comparison.

Table 36.1   (continued)

Audio spectral centroid	Describes the center of gravity of the log-frequency power spectrum. A general indicator of "brightness," this is a concise description of the shape of the power spectrum, indicating whether the spectral content of a signal is dominated by high or low frequencies.
Audio spectral spread	Describes the second moment of the log-frequency power spectrum, indicating whether the power spectrum is centered near the spectral centroid or spread out over the spectrum. This may help distinguish between pure-tone and noise-like sounds.
Audio spectral flatness	Describes the flatness properties of the spectrum of an audio signal for each of a number of frequency bands. When this vector indicates a high deviation from a flat spectral shape for a given band, it may signal the presence of tonal components.
Fundamental frequency	Describes the fundamental frequency of an audio signal. The representation of this descriptor allows for a confidence measure in recognition of the fact that the various extraction methods, commonly called *pitch-tracking*, are not perfectly accurate, and in recognition that there may be sections of a signal (e.g., noise) for which no fundamental frequency may be extracted. Applies chiefly to periodic or quasiperiodic signals.
Harmonicity	Represents the distinction between sounds with a harmonic spectrum (e.g., musical tones or voiced speech [e.g., vowels]), sounds with an inharmonic spectrum (e.g., metallic or bell-like sounds) and sounds with a nonharmonic spectrum (e.g., noise, unvoiced speech [e.g., fricatives like f], or dense mixtures of instruments).
Log attack time	Characterizes the attack of a sound, the time it takes for the signal to rise from silence to the maximum amplitude. This feature signifies the difference between a sudden and a smooth sound.
Temporal centroid	Characterizes the signal envelope, representing where in time the energy of a signal is focused. This descriptor may, for example, distinguish between a decaying piano note and a sustained organ note, when the lengths and the attacks of the two notes are identical.
Harmonic spectral centroid	The amplitude-weighted mean of the harmonic peaks of the spectrum. As such, it is very similar to the audio spectral centroid but is specialized for use in distinguishing musical instrument timbres. It has a high correlation with the perceptual feature of the "sharpness" of a sound.

(continued)

Table 36.1   (continued)

Harmonic spectral deviation	Indicates the spectral deviation of log-amplitude components from a global spectral envelope.
Harmonic spectral spread	Describes the amplitude-weighted standard deviation of the harmonic peaks of the spectrum, normalized by the instantaneous harmonic spectral centroid.
Harmonic spectral variation	The normalized correlation between the amplitude of the harmonic peaks between two subsequent time slices of the signal.
Audio spectrum basis	A series of (potentially time-varying and/or statistically independent) basis functions that are derived from the singular value decomposition of a normalized power spectrum.
Audio spectrum projection	Used together with the audio spectrum basis descriptor, it represents low-dimensional features of a spectrum after projection upon a reduced rank basis.
Silent segment	Indicates a silent segment; may aid further segmentation of the audio stream or hint not to process a segment.

Spectrum Analysis: Historical Background

In the eighteenth century, scientists and musicians were aware that many musical sounds were characterized by harmonic vibrations around a fundamental tone, but they had no technology for analyzing these harmonics in a systematic way. Sir Isaac Newton had already coined the term *spectrum* in 1781 to describe the bands of color showing the different frequencies passing through a glass prism.

In 1822 the French engineer Jean-Baptiste Joseph, Baron de Fourier (1768–1830) published his landmark thesis *Analytical Theory of Heat* (figure 36.5). In this treatise he developed the theory that complicated vibrations could be analyzed as a sum of many simultaneous simple signals. In particular, Fourier proved that any periodic function could be represented as an infinite summation of sine and cosine terms. Due to the integer ratio relationship between the sinusoidal frequencies in Fourier analysis, this became known as *harmonic analysis.* In 1843, Georg Ohm (1789–1854) of the Polytechnic Institute of Nuremberg was the first to apply Fourier's theory to acoustical signals (Miller 1935). Later, the German scientist H. L. F. Helmholtz (1821–1894) surmised that instrumental timbre is largely determined by the harmonic Fourier series of the steady-state portion of instrumental tones

Figure 36.5   The grave of Fourier, Père Lachaise Cemetery, Paris.

(Helmholtz 1885). Helmholtz developed a method of harmonic analysis based on mechanical-acoustic resonators.

Precomputer analyses, such as those of Miller (1916) and Hall (1937), averaged out the time-varying characteristics of instrumental tone. As in the research of Helmholtz, these studies presumed that the steady-state spectrum (corresponding to the sustained part of a note) played a dominant role in timbre perception. It is now recognized that the first half-second of the attack portion of a tone is also important perceptually to the identification of an instrumental source.

Through the middle of the nineteenth century, Fourier analysis was a tedious and error-prone task of manual calculation. Then in the 1870s, the British physicist Lord Kelvin and his brother built the first mechanical harmonic analyzer (Marple 1987). This elaborate gear-and-pulley contraption analyzed hand-traced waveform segments. The analyzer acted as a mechanical integrator, finding the area under the sine and cosine waves for all harmonics of a fundamental period. The Michelson-Stratton harmonic analyzer (1898) was probably the most sophisticated machine of this type. Designed around a spiral spring mechanism, this device could resolve up to eighty harmonics. It could also act as a waveform synthesizer, inverting the analysis mechanically to reconstruct the input signal. (The *inverse Fourier transform* reconstructs a given waveform from its spectrum analysis data.)

Translating Helmholtz's term *Klangfarbe* (sound color), the British physicist John Tyndall coined the term *clang-tint* to describe timbre as "an admixture of two or more tones" and carried out imaginative experiments in order to visualize sound signals, such as "singing flames" and "singing water jets" (Tyndall 1875).

Backhaus (1932) developed an analysis system for a single harmonic at a time. This consisted of a microphone whose signal was sent to the input of a tunable bandpass filter. The output of the filter was routed to an amplifier, whose output was in turn connected to a pen and rotating drum recorder. Backhaus tuned the filter to the frequency of the harmonic of interest and commanded an instrumentalist to play a note. As the musician played, Backhaus cranked a drum while a pen traced the output of the filter for that frequency on a roll of paper. The resulting trace was taken to represent the amplitude of a single harmonic. Meyer and Buchmann (1931) developed a similar system.

Advances in the design of oscilloscopes in the 1940s generated a wave of new research. Scientists photographed waveforms from the oscilloscope screen and then manually traced their outline using mechanical Fourier analyzers.

A theoretical leap forward was described in Norbert Wiener's classic paper on *generalized harmonic analysis* (Wiener 1930), which shifted the emphasis of Fourier analysis from harmonic components to a continuous spectrum. Among other results, Wiener showed, by analogy to white light, that white noise was composed of all frequencies in equal amounts.

Following the development of stored-program computers in the 1940s, programmers created the first digital implementations of the *Fourier transform* (FT), but these consumed enormous amounts of computer time—a scarce commodity in that era. Finally, in the mid-1960s the voluminous calculations required for Fourier analysis were greatly reduced by a set of algorithms known as the *fast Fourier transform* or FFT, described by James Cooley at Princeton University and John Tukey at Bell Telephone Laboratories (Cooley and Tukey 1965). Today's computers can easily analyze sound in real time using the FFT.

Dennis Gabor's (1946, 1947) pioneering contributions to sound analysis had a delayed impact but are now viewed as seminal, particularly because he presented a mathematical method for analysis of time-varying signals. This was the theory of what became known later as the *short-time Fourier transform* or STFT (Loy 2007). See chapter 37. Gabor's theory asserted that any sound could be analyzed simultaneously in the time and frequency domain into units he called *quanta*—now called *grains, wavelets, atoms,* or *frames,* depending on the analysis system being used.

Computer-Based Spectrum Analysis

Early experiments in computer analysis of musical instrument tones required heroic efforts. Analog-to-digital converters were rare, computers were scarce, theory was immature, and analysis programs had to be cobbled from scratch on punched paper cards (figure 36.6). Against these obstacles, computer-based analysis and synthesis developed in the 1960s yielded more detailed results than

Figure 36.6   James Beauchamp performing sound analysis experiments at the University of Illinois around 1966.

previous analog models. At Bell Telephone Laboratories, Max Mathews and Jean-Claude Risset analyzed brass instruments using a pitch-synchronous analysis program (Mathews, Miller, and David 1961; Risset 1966; Risset and Mathews 1969). Pitch-synchronous analysis breaks the input waveform into *pseudoperiodic segments*. It estimates the pitch of each pseudoperiodic segment. The size of the *analysis segment* is adjusted relative to the estimated pitch period. The harmonic Fourier spectrum is then calculated on the analysis segment as though the sound were periodic. This presumes that the pitch be quasiconstant throughout the analysis segment. This program generated time-varying amplitude functions for each harmonic of a given fundamental. Luce's (1963) doctoral research at the Massachusetts Institute of Technology implemented another pitch-synchronous approach to analysis/resynthesis of instrumental tones.

Several years later, Peter Zinovieff and his colleagues at Electronic Music Studios (EMS), London, developed a hybrid (analog-digital) real-time Fourier analyzer/resynthesizer for musical sound (Grogorno 1984).

Heterodyne filter analysis

The next step in computer analysis of musical tones involved *heterodyne filters* (Freedman 1965, 1967; Beauchamp 1969, 1975; Moorer 1973, 1975). The heterodyne filter approach is good for resolving harmonics (or quasiharmonics)

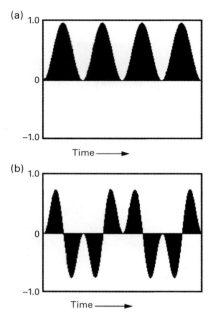

Figure 36.7   Heterodyne filter analysis. (a) Product of an input signal (a 100 Hz sine wave) with an analysis signal (a 100 Hz sine wave). The result is entirely positive, indicating strong energy at 100 Hz. (b) Product of an input signal (a 200 Hz sine wave) with an analysis signal (a 100 Hz sine wave). The result is scattered positive and negative energy, indicating no strong energy at 100 Hz in the input signal.

of a given fundamental frequency. This implies that the fundamental frequency is estimated in a prior stage of analysis. The heterodyne filter multiplies an input waveform by a sine and a cosine wave at harmonic frequencies and then sums the results over a short time period to obtain amplitude and phase data.

Figure 36.7a shows the operation of the heterodyne method. The input signal is multiplied by an analysis sine wave. As shown in figure 36.7a, the frequency of the two signals exactly matches, so the energy is completely positive, indicating strong energy at the analysis frequency. In figure 36.7b, the two frequencies are not the same, so we obtain a waveform that is basically symmetrical about the amplitude axis. When the heterodyne filter sums this waveform over a short time period it cancels itself out due to the equal presence of positive and negative amplitudes.

After a period of experimentation in the 1970s, the limits of the heterodyne method became known. Moorer showed that the heterodyne filter approach is confused by fast attack times (less than 50 ms) and pitch changes (e.g., glissando, portamento, and vibrato) greater than two percent (about a quarter tone). Although Beauchamp (1981) implemented a *tracking* version of the heterodyne filter that could follow changing frequency trajectories (similar in spirit to the tracking phase vocoder discussed later), the heterodyne approach has been supplanted by other methods.

The saga of the phase vocoder

One of the most popular techniques for analysis/resynthesis of spectra is the *phase vocoder* (PV). Flanagan and Golden of Bell Telephone Laboratories developed the first PV in 1966. It was originally intended to be a coding method for reducing the bandwidth of speech signals. Far from compressing audio data, however, the PV causes a data explosion! That is, the raw analysis data is much greater than the original signal data.

The PV can be computationally intensive. Early implementations required so much computing time that the PV was not applied in practical applications for years. Working at MIT, Portnoff (1976, 1978, 1980) developed an efficient PV, proving that it could be implemented using the FFT. He experimented with sound transformations of speech such as time compression and expansion. This led to Moorer's landmark paper on the application of the PV in computer music (Moorer 1978). We go into this topic in more detail in the next chapter.

37 *Spectrum Analysis by Fourier Methods*

Fourier Series

Fourier Transform

Discrete Fourier Transform

Short-Time Fourier Transform

        Windowing the Input Signal

        Window Functions

        Operation of the STFT

        Overlap-Add Resynthesis

            Limits of overlap-add resynthesis

        Why Overlapping Windows?

        Oscillator Bank Resynthesis

        Analysis Frequencies

        Time/Frequency Uncertainty

            Periodicity implies infinitude

            Time/frequency trade-offs

        Frequencies between Analysis Bins

            Significance of clutter

Sonogram Representation

        Sonogram Parameters

Phase Vocoder

> **Phase Vocoder Parameters**
> > Frame size
> > Window type
> > FFT size and zero padding
> > Hop size
>
> **Typical Parameter Values**
> **Window Closing**
> **Phase and Accuracy of Resynthesis**

Tracking Phase Vocoder

> **Operation of the TPV**
> **Peak Tracking**
> **Accuracy of Resynthesis with the TPV**
> **Analysis of Inharmonic and Noisy Sounds**

Deterministic Plus Stochastic: Spectral Modeling Synthesis

> **Application of Spectral Modeling Synthesis: Vocaloid**

Transformation of Sound in the Frequency Domain

> **Cross-Synthesis, Spectral Mutation, and Timbre Morphing**

The survey in this chapter focuses on Fourier-based methods of spectrum analysis. Specifically, this chapter covers the short-time Fourier transform, the sonogram, the phase vocoder, the tracking phase vocoder, and spectral modeling synthesis.

The *Fourier transform* (FT) is a mathematical procedure devised by Jean-Baptiste Joseph, Baron de Fourier (1768–1830) (Grattan-Guinness 1972). The FT maps a continuous-time (analog) waveform to a corresponding infinite Fourier series summation of elementary sinusoidal waves, each at a specific amplitude and phase. In other words, the FT analyzes a time-domain waveform input into a corresponding spectrum output. Once a sound signal is converted into a spectrum representation, we can display the spectrum, estimate the pitch, analyze its rhythm, or perform transformations for the purposes of composition.

Every analysis technique is based on a model of sound, and Fourier's model assumes that all sounds are the sum of harmonically related sinusoids. Thus Fourier methods are the analytical counterpart to additive synthesis (chapter 10). Part of the reason for the ubiquity of Fourier analysis is that its mathematical theory is closely tied to other fundamental concepts such as convolution, filtering, and cross-correlation (Braasch 2018). However, many non-Fourier spectral models of sound have been developed. They are surveyed in chapters 38 and 39.

Chapter 44 is devoted to the related topic of editing spectral data for the purpose of sound transformation.

Fourier Series

Fourier showed that a periodic function $x(t)$ of period T can be represented by the infinite summation series:

$$x(t) = C_0 + \sum_{n=1}^{\infty} C_n \cos(n\omega t + \phi_n)$$

That is, the function $x(t)$ is a sum of harmonically related sinusoidal functions with the frequency $n\omega = n2\pi/T$. C_0 is the 0 Hz offset or DC component; it shifts the waveform up or down. The first sinusoidal component $C1$ is the *fundamental*; it has the same period as T. The variables C_n and ϕ_n give the magnitude and phase of each component.

Figure 37.1 shows the result of a Fourier series summation. A Fourier series summation is a formula for synthesizing a periodic signal. However it does not tell us how to derive the coefficients C_n and ϕ_n from an arbitrary

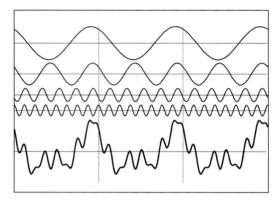

Figure 37.1 Fourier sum. The bottom waveform is the sum of the four periodic sinusoids above it. Each of the four sinusoids has a different starting phase.

input sound. For this, we need the analysis method called the Fourier transform, presented next.

Fourier Transform

Suppose that we wish to analyze a continuous-time analog signal $x(t)$ of infinite extent and bandwidth. Fourier's theory says that $x(t)$ can be accurately reconstructed with an infinite number of pure sinusoidal waves of different amplitudes, frequencies, and initial phases. The *Fourier transform* (FT) spectrum represents all frequencies from 0 Hz (a constant) to infinity (∞) Hz, with a mirror image in the negative frequencies.

The formula for the FT or *Fourier integral* is

$$X(f) = \int_{-\infty}^{\infty} x(t)e^{-j2\pi ft}\, dt$$

This says that the FT at any particular frequency f is the integral of the multiplication of the input signal $x(t)$ by an infinite set of pure sinusoids $e^{-j2\pi ft}$. Intuitively, we can surmise that this integral will be larger when the input signal is high in amplitude and rich in partials. $X(f)$ represents the magnitude of the Fourier transform of the time-domain signal $x(t)$. By *magnitude* we mean the absolute value of the amplitude of the frequencies in the spectrum. The capital letter X denotes a Fourier transform, and the f within parentheses indicates that we are now referring to a frequency-domain signal, as opposed to the time-domain signal $x(t)$. Each value of $X(f)$ is a complex number.

The magnitude is not a complete picture of the Fourier transform. It tells us just the amount of each complex frequency that must be combined to synthesize $x(t)$. It does not indicate the starting phase of each of these components. One can also plot the *phase spectrum,* as it is called, but this is less often shown, as it usually looks random to the eye.

The magnitude of the Fourier transform $X(f)$ is symmetric around 0 Hz. Thus the Fourier representation combines equal amounts of positive and negative frequencies. Negative frequencies are simply inverted in phase. Note that the inverse Fourier transform takes a complex input signal—a spectrum—and generates a real-valued waveform as its output.

Discrete Fourier Transform

The one kind of signal that has a discrete frequency-domain representation (i.e., isolated spectral lines) is a periodic signal. A periodic signal repeats at every interval T. Such a signal has a Fourier transform containing components at a fundamental frequency $(1/T)$ and its harmonics and is zero everywhere else.

A periodic signal, in the precise mathematical sense, must be defined from $t = -\infty$ to $t = \infty$. Colloquially, one speaks of signals as periodic if $x(t) = x(t + T)$ for an amount of time that is long relative to the period t. We can construct this kind of periodic signal by replicating a finite-length signal. Imagine that we infinitely replicate a finite-length signal $x(t)$ backward and forward in time. In the discrete-time (sampled) domain, this produces a periodic signal $x[n]$. The use of brackets rather than parentheses indicates that the signal is discrete rather than continuous.

The frequency-domain representation of this replicated periodic signal $x[n]$ is called its *discrete Fourier transform* (DFT). The DFT provides a sampled look at both the magnitude and phase of the spectrum of $x[n]$. It is a central tool in musical signal processing. In effect, the DFT sets up a one-to-one correspondence between the number of input samples N and the number of frequencies that it resolves. For a book-length treatise on the DFT as applied to sound, refer to Smith (2007b). A related operation is the *discrete cosine transform* (DCT) used in compressed audio formats such as MP3 (Rao and Yip 1990). (MP3 is described in chapter 4.)

Short-Time Fourier Transform

To adapt Fourier's mathematical theory to the practical world of finite-duration time-varying signals, Dennis Gabor (1946) proposed that elementary sonic quanta, bounded in time and in frequency, could be represented as rectangles tiled on a matrix of time-frequency energy. This is the famous *Gabor matrix* (see chapter 13). Years later, this representation was reformulated as the *short-time Fourier transform* (STFT) (Schroeder and Atal 1962; Flanagan 1972; Allen and Rabiner 1977; Schafer and Rabiner 1973a; Steiglitz 1996; Loy 2007; Smith 2007b, 2011).

Windowing the Input Signal

As a preparation for spectrum analysis, the STFT imposes a sequence of *time windows* on the input signal (figure 37.2). That is, it breaks the input signal into "short-time" (i.e., brief) segments bounded in time by a window function. A window is nothing more than a specific type of amplitude envelope designed for spectrum analysis. The duration of the window is usually in the range of 10 ms to 100 ms, and the segments overlap. By analyzing the spectrum of each windowed segment separately, one obtains a sequence of measurements that constitute a time-varying spectrum.

Unfortunately, windowing has the side effect of distorting the spectrum measurement. This is because the spectrum analyzer is measuring not purely the input signal but rather the product of the input signal and the window. The

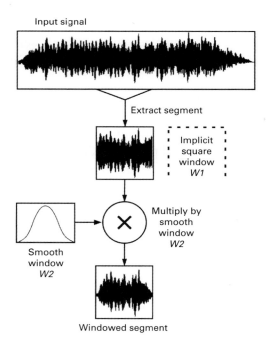

Figure 37.2 Windowing an input signal. The extracted segment has an implicit square window *W1*, which distorts the analysis. The smooth window *W2* reduces the distortion.

spectrum that results is the convolution of the spectra of the input and the window signals. (Chapter 29 explains convolution.)

Window Functions

A window is a function that is nonzero only over a limited time range. Many types of window functions exist. The first criterion for a window is its length or size, that is, its duration-limiting property (Hutchins 1986b). The length of the analysis window has a direct bearing on the frequency resolution of the analysis. For each windowed segment, we can think of the STFT as applying a bank of filters at equally spaced frequency intervals to the windowed input signal. The frequencies are spaced at integer multiples (harmonics) of

$$\frac{\textit{sampling frequency}}{\textit{window length N in samples}}$$

Thus if the sampling frequency is 50 kHz and the window length is 1,000 samples, the analysis frequency *bins* are spaced at intervals 50,000 Hz/1,000 = 50 Hz apart. A bin is a discrete point on the frequency continuum.

The second criterion in the choice of a window function is its shape, because this affects the spectrum measurement. Recall from chapter 15 that the multiplication of two such signals is a case of amplitude modulation, where the input signal serves as the carrier and the window acts as the modulator. The DFT of a windowed signal acts on the product of the signal times the window, that is, $x[n] \times w[n]$. Because multiplication in the time domain results in convolution in the frequency domain (explained in chapter 29), the resulting spectrum is that of $x[n]$ convolved with $w[n]$.

The crudest windowing technique selects a part of an input signal $x[n]$ and sets all other values of $x[n]$ to zero. Such a window is called a *rectangular* or *boxcar* window because it is equivalent to multiplying $x[n]$ by a signal $w[n]$ that looks like a rectangle of length N, starting at 0 with a height of 1 (*W1* in figure 37.2).

When a single sine wave is fed into an analyzer, it might be ideal if the energy showed up exclusively in one frequency bin. However, as previously mentioned, the effects of convolution inherent in the process of windowing distort the analysis and cause "splatter" or "clutter" in the spectrum (Jaffe 1987a, b). That is, any frequency energy present in the windowed signal splatters across all frequency bins of the output spectrum (Harris 1978). The response in any given bin is a function of the distance from the input frequency to the bin center. This can clearly be seen in the spectrum of a sine wave windowed by a rectangle. Here the rectangular window scatters the single input frequency component into energy extending across the band-width of the analyzer (figure 37.3).

In order to reduce clutter, standard windows used in Fourier analysis have a symmetric bell-shape curvature. Their spectral shapes resemble a mathematical sinc function, that is, $\sin(t)/t$. This spectral shape is characterized by a prominent *center lobe* and a series of *side lobes* on either side of the center lobe. The primary properties of the window spectrum are the width of the center lobe—defined as the number of frequency bins it spans—and the highest side lobe level, which measures how many decibels down the highest side lobe is from the center lobe.

One indicator of how well a window suppresses leakage from adjacent frequencies is the peak side lobe level, relative to the center lobe; another is the rate of decay of these levels. A window with a rapid decay is more immune to interference. Figure 37.4 depicts a typical window function, a Gaussian curve. The first side lobe of the spectrum is about 45 dB down from the center lobe.

The convolution of the window spectrum with the signal spectrum means that the most narrow spectral response of the transform is limited to that of the center lobe width of the window transform, independent of the input signal. Generally, the price to be paid for a reduction in the side lobes is a broadening of the center lobe width. In other words, reducing the side lobes

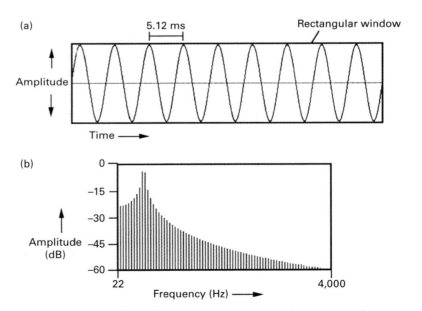

Figure 37.3   The effect of a rectangular window on the spectrum plot. (a) A rectangular window around eight periods of a sinusoid at 177 Hz. (b) Spectrum of (a) indicating energy from 22 Hz to 4,000 Hz. Ideally, the spectrum of a sinusoid should be a single line. Instead, the rectangular window scatters the energy above and below the input frequency.

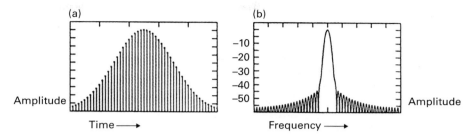

Figure 37.4   Gaussian window function (left) and its spectrum (right).

decreases the resolution of the spectrum estimate. Hence, in selecting an envelope, one has to choose between distortion (high side lobes, which may smother adjacent peaks) and lack of resolution (too broad a center lobe).

From a practical standpoint, there is no universally best window choice for all sounds and all analysis purposes. For musical applications involving sound transformation, a smooth bell-shaped curve such as a Hann window is recommended for stable sounds with low pitches. The Blackman window, with its narrower frequency response, is recommended for unstable and noisy sounds (IRCAM 2011). Other common bell-shaped windows include the Kaiser and Gaussian types.

Operation of the STFT

After windowing, the STFT applies the DFT to each windowed segment. The output is a discrete-frequency spectrum, that is, a measure of energy at a set of specific equally spaced frequencies. The *fast Fourier transform* or FFT shown in figure 37.5 is simply an efficient implementation of the DFT. Each block of data generated by the FFT is called a *frame,* by analogy to the successive frames of a film. Each frame contains two things: (1) a magnitude spectrum that depicts the amplitude of every analyzed frequency component, and (2) a phase spectrum that shows the initial phase value for every frequency component.

We can visualize each of these two spectra as histograms with a vertical line for each frequency component along the abscissa or horizontal axis. The vertical line represents amplitude in the case of the magnitude spectrum, and starting phase (between $-\pi$ and π, or between $-180°$ and $+180°$) in the case of the phase spectrum (figure 37.6). The magnitude spectrum is relatively easy to read. When the phase spectrum normalized to the range of $-\pi$ to π it is called the *wrapped phase* representation. For many signals, it appears to the eye like a random function.

The equation for a DFT of an input signal $x[m]$ multiplied by a time-shifted window $h[n-m]$ is (after Dolson 1986)

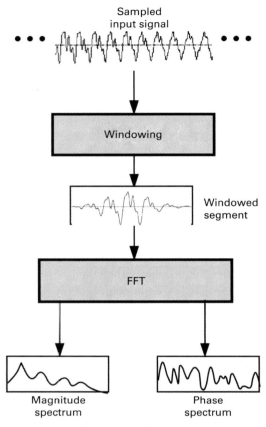

Figure 37.5   Overview of the short-time Fourier transform, with the FFT at its core.

$$X[n, k] = \sum_{m=-\infty}^{\infty} \{x[m]h[n-m]\}e^{-j(2\pi/N)km}$$

Thus the output $X[n, k]$ is the Fourier transform of the windowed input at each discrete time n for each discrete frequency band or bin k. The equation says that m can go from minus to plus infinity; this is a way of saying "for an arbitrary-length input signal." For a specific short-time window, the bounds of m are set to the appropriate length. Here, k is the index for the frequency bins. N is the number of points in the spectrum. The following relation sets the frequency corresponding to each bin k

$$f_k = (k/N) \times f_s$$

where f_s is the sampling rate. So for a sampling rate of 44.1 kHz, an analysis window length N of 1024 samples, and a frequency bin $k = 1$, f_k is 43 Hz.

A discrete STFT formulation indicating the *hop size* (window overlap or time advance of each window) is:

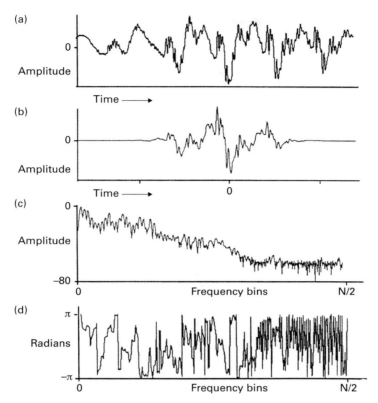

Figure 37.6   STFT signals. (a) Input waveform. (b) Windowed segment. (c) Magnitude spectrum plotted over the range 0 to −80 dB. (d) Phase spectrum plotted over the range −π to π. (After Serra 1989.)

$$X[l,k] = \sum_{M=0}^{M-1} h[m]x[m+(lH)]e^{-j(2\pi/N)km}$$

where M is the number of samples in the input sequence, $h[m]$ is the window that selects a block of data from the input signal $x[m]$, l is the *frame index,* and H is the hop size in samples (Serra 1989). Further on, we discuss the effect of hop size.

To summarize, the application of the STFT to a stream of input samples results in a series of frames that make up a time-varying spectrum.

Overlap-Add Resynthesis

To resynthesize the original time-domain signal, the STFT can reconstruct each windowed waveform segment from its spectrum components by applying the *inverse discrete Fourier transform* (IDFT) to each frame. The IDFT takes each magnitude and phase component and generates a corresponding time-domain signal with the same envelope as the analysis window. Then by overlapping and adding these resynthesized windows, typically at the point where they are −3 dB down from their peak, one obtains a signal that is a close approximation of the original. Figure 37.7 depicts the overlap-add process in schematic form.

Limits of overlap-add resynthesis

Resynthesis with the plain *overlap-add* (OA) method is of limited use from the standpoint of musical transformation. This is because the OA process is designed for the case in which the windows sum perfectly to a constant. As Allen and Rabiner (1977) showed, any transformations that disturb the perfect summation criterion at the final stage of the OA cause side effects that will likely be audible. Time expansion by stretching the distance between windows, for example, can introduce comb filter effects, depending on the number of frequency channels (bins) used in the analysis. Using speech or singing as a source, many OA transformations result in robotic, ringing voices of limited musical use.

One way to lessen these unwanted artifacts is to stipulate a great deal of overlap among successive windows in the analysis stage, as explained in the next section.

Why Overlapping Windows?

Theory says that we can analyze a segment of any length and exactly resynthesize the segment from the analysis data. Thus we can analyze in one pass Stravinsky's *Rite of Spring* using a thirty-minute-long window and reconstruct the entire piece from this analysis. This being the case, why bother to break the analysis into small, overlapping segments?

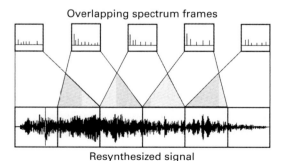

Figure 37.7   Overlap-add resynthesis. The gray areas indicate overlapping spectrum frames. Note that for visual clarity, we show only five frames. In practice it is typical to use more than 100 frames per second of analyzed sound.

The reasons are several. The analysis of a monaural sound sampled at 44.1 kHz and lasting 30 min would result in a spectrum of over 79 million points, with most of them corresponding to infrasonic time scales (below 20 Hz down to frequencies in minutes.)

A visual inspection of this enormous spectrum would eventually tell us all the frequencies that occurred over a thirty-minute duration but would not tell us when they occurred; this temporal information is embedded deep in the mathematical combination of the magnitude and phase spectra, hidden to the eye. Thus the first thing that windowing helps with is the localization of the spectrum evolution in time. That is, by limiting the analysis to a sequence of short snapshots (less than a tenth of a second, typically), each analysis plots fewer points, and we know more accurately when these frequencies occurred.

A second reason for short-time windows is that one obtains results quicker. For *Rite of Spring* one would have to wait up to thirty minutes just to read in the entire input signal plus however long it takes to calculate an FFT on a 79 million point input signal. Windowing the input lets one obtain initial results after a few milliseconds of the input has been read in, opening up the world of real-time spectrum analysis.

These reasons explain the segmentation, but why overlap the windows? As explained earlier, smooth bell-shaped windows minimize the distortion that occurs in windowing. And of course, bell-shaped windows must overlap somewhat in order to capture the signal without gaps. But even greater overlap is often desirable, more than is dictated by the perfect summation criterion. Why is this? Increasing the overlap factor (by shrinking the hop size) is equivalent to *oversampling the spectrum*. This has two effects. First, it increases the frequency resolution. Second, it protects against artifacts that can occur in transformations, such as time-stretching and cross-synthesis (Serra 1997). An overlap factor of eight or more is recommended when the goal is transforming the input signal (IRCAM 2011).

Further on we discuss criteria for selecting a window and setting its length. Next, we present an alternative to the overlap-add resynthesis model.

Oscillator Bank Resynthesis

Sinusoidal additive resynthesis (SAR) (or *oscillator bank resynthesis*) differs from the overlap-add approach. Rather than summing the sine waves at each frame, as in the OA resynthesis model, SAR applies a bank of oscillators driven by amplitude and frequency envelopes that span frame boundaries (figure 37.8). This implies that the analysis data must be converted beforehand into such envelopes. Fortunately, the conversion from analysis data (magnitude

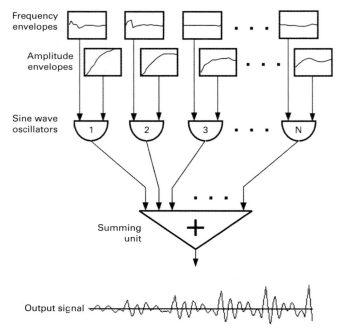

Figure 37.8 Oscillator bank resynthesis. The analysis data has been converted into a set of continuous amplitude and frequency envelopes. The number of oscillators needed for the resynthesis grows and shrinks depending on the complexity of the sound.

and phase) to synthesis data (amplitude and frequency) takes little calculation time.

Figure 37.9 schematizes the process of constructing amplitude envelopes for each analyzed frequency. The magnitude in each bin at each frame is mapped to a breakpoint in an envelope curve. An advantage of the SAR model is that envelopes are more robust under musical transformation than the raw spectrum frames. Within broad limits, one can stretch, shrink, rescale, or shift the envelopes without artifacts in the resynthesis process; the perfect summation criterion of the OA model can be ignored. A disadvantage of SAR is that it is not well adapted to real-time operation, in contrast to OA methods that can run analysis/synthesis in real time.

A tracking phase vocoder can be seen as a SAR method because it also constructs frequency envelopes for additive sine wave synthesis. We discuss this approach in more detail further along in the chapter.

Analysis Frequencies

One can think of the STFT as applying a bank of filters at equally spaced frequency intervals to the windowed input signal. As previously mentioned, the frequencies are spaced at integer multiples (i.e., harmonics) of *sampling*

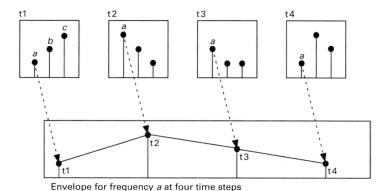

Envelope for frequency *a* at four time steps

Figure 37.9 From frames to amplitude envelopes. The top part shows four successive frames at times t1 to t4. Each frame has three frequency bins. The amplitude of frequency bin *a* is mapped from four different times to breakpoints of an envelope.

frequency/N where N is the size of the analyzed segment. Audio signals are bandlimited to half the sampling rate and so we care about only half the analysis bins. The effective frequency resolution of an STFT is thus $N/2$ bins spread equally across the audio bandwidth, starting at 0 Hz and ending at the Nyquist frequency.

Time/Frequency Uncertainty

As Robinson (1982) observed, all windowed spectrum analyses are hampered by a fundamental *uncertainty principle* between time and frequency resolution, first recognized by quantum physicists such as Werner Heisenberg in the early part of the twentieth century. This principle means that if we want high resolution in the time domain (i.e., we want to know precisely when an event occurs), we sacrifice frequency resolution. In other words, we can tell that an event occurred at a precise time, but we cannot say exactly what frequencies it contained. Conversely, if we want high resolution in the frequency domain (i.e., we want to know the precise frequency of a component), we sacrifice time resolution. That is, we can pinpoint frequency content only over a long time interval. It is important to grasp this relationship in order to interpret the results of Fourier analysis.

Periodicity implies infinitude

Fourier analysis starts from the abstract premise that if a signal contains only one frequency, then that signal must be a sinusoid that is infinite in duration. Purity of frequency—absolute periodicity—implies infinitude. As soon as one limits the duration of this sine wave, the only way that Fourier analysis can account for this is to consider the signal as a sum of many infinite-length sinusoids that just happen to cancel each other out in such a way as to result in a limited-duration sine wave! This abstraction does not jibe with our most basic experiences with sound. As Gabor (1946) pointed out, if the concept of frequency is used only to refer to infinitely long signals, then the concept of changing frequency is impossible!

Still, we can understand one aspect of the abstract Fourier representation by a thought experiment. Suppose that the window of analysis is only one sample in length. Now we know at time *t* precisely when this sample occurred and what its value is (figure 37.10a). However, since the window is so short, we cannot see what waveform it may be a part of; it could be a part of a high frequency waveform (figure 37.10b) or a low frequency waveform (figure 37.10c). Indeed, we cannot confirm the presence of a low-frequency waveform until we have a window big enough to capture its entire period.

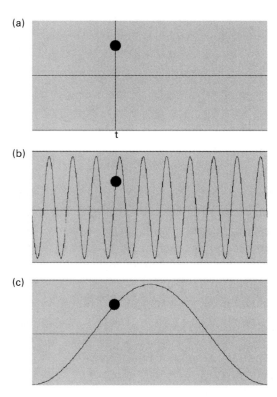

Figure 37.10   Frequency uncertainty. (a) The smallest possible window, consisting of one sample point, reveals nothing about the waveform it could be part of. The sample could be part of a high frequency waveform (b) or a low-frequency waveform (c). Only by expanding the window size can we know with precision what frequencies are in the window.

As we zoom out, we have more samples to analyze, and so the more certain we can be about what possible frequencies they might represent. But since Fourier analysis calculates the spectrum for the entire segment at a time, spectrum displays that use long windows leave uncertainty as to when a particular frequency occurred. All we know is that the analyzed frequencies occurred sometime within the time span of the window. Once again, frequency precision comes at the expense of temporal imprecision.

Filter design provides more clues. Recall from chapter 28 that the number of delay stages influences the sharpness of a filter. In order to isolate a very narrow band, such as a single frequency component, we need extremely sharp edges in the filter response. This implies that one needs to look back into the distant past of the signal in order to extract a pure frequency. Another way of saying this is that such a filter has a long *impulse response.* (See chapters 28 and 29 for an explanation of impulse response.)

Time/frequency trade-offs

The FFT divides the audible frequency space into $N/2$ frequency bins, where N is the length in samples of the analysis window. Hence there is a trade-off between the number of frequency bins and the length of the analysis window (figure 37.13). In other words, there is a trade-off between frequency resolution and time resolution. For example, if N is 512 samples, then the number of frequencies that can be analyzed is limited to 256. Assuming a sampling rate of 44.1 kHz, we obtain 256 bins equally spaced over the bandwidth 0 Hz to the Nyquist frequency 22.05 kHz. Increasing the sampling rate only widens the measurable bandwidth. It does not increase the frequency resolution of the analysis.

If we want extremely high time accuracy (say 1 ms or about 44 samples at a 44.1 kHz sampling rate), we must be satisfied with only 44/2 or 22 frequency bins. Dividing up the audio bandwidth from 0 to 22.05 kHz by 22 frequency bins, we obtain 22,050 / 22 or about 1,000 Hz of frequency resolution. That is, if we want to know exactly when events occur on the scale of 1 ms, then our frequency resolution is limited to the gross scale of 1,000 Hz–wide frequency bands. By sacrificing more time resolution and widening the analysis interval to 30 ms, one can spot frequencies within a 33 Hz bandwidth. For extremely high resolution in frequency (1 Hz), one must stretch the time interval to 1 s (44,100 samples)!

Because of this limitation in windowed STFT analysis, researchers continue to examine alternative methods. For example, *multiresolution analysis* and *atomic decomposition* to try to resolve both dimensions at high resolution (Lukin and Todd 2006; Sturm et al. 2009).

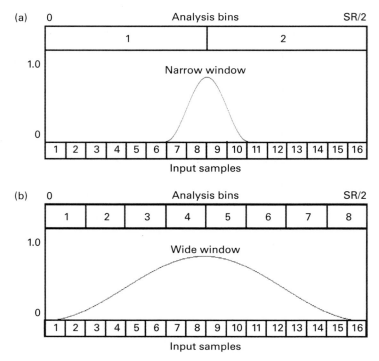

Figure 37.11   Relationship of window size to the number of frequency analysis bins. (a) A narrow window of four samples can resolve only two frequencies. (b) a wider window of sixteen samples divides the spectrum into eight bins.

Frequencies between Analysis Bins

The STFT knows only about a discrete set of frequencies spaced at equal intervals across the audio bandwidth. The spacing of these frequencies depends on the length of the analysis window. This length is effectively the *fundamental period* of the analysis. Such a model works well for sounds that are harmonic or quasiharmonic where the harmonics align closely with the bins of the analysis. But what happens to frequencies that fall between the equally spaced analysis bins of the STFT? This is the case for inharmonic sounds such as gongs or noisy sounds such as snare drums.

Let us call the frequency to be analyzed f. When f coincides with the center of an analysis channel, all its energy is concentrated in that channel and so it is accurately measured. When f is close to but not precisely coincident with the center, energy is scattered into all other analysis channels, but with a concentration remaining close to f. Figure 37.12 shows three snapshots of a frequency sweeping from 2 to 3 Hz, which can be generalized to other frequency ranges. The leakage spilling into all frequency bins from components in between bins is a well-known source of unreliability in the spectrum

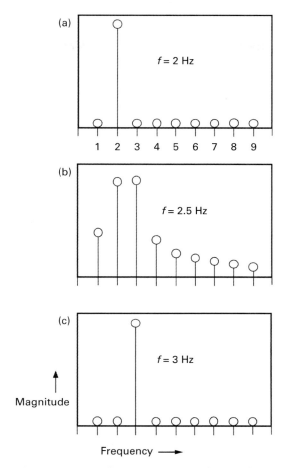

Figure 37.12 Three STFT "snapshots" of a sound changing frequency from 2 to 3 Hz. The STFT in this case has analysis bins spaced at 1 Hz intervals. When the input frequency is 2.5 Hz, it falls between the equally spaced frequency bins of the analyzer, and the energy is spread across the entire spectrum. (After Hutchins 1984.)

estimates produced by the STFT. When more than one component is in between bins, *beating effects* (periodic cancelation and reinforcement) may occur in both the frequency and amplitude traces. The result is that the analysis shows fluctuating energy in frequency components that are not physically present in the input signal.

Significance of clutter

If the signal is resynthesized directly from the analysis data, the extra frequency components and beating effects pose no problem; they are benign artifacts of the STFT analysis that are resolved in resynthesis. Beating effects are merely the way that the STFT represents in the frequency domain a time-varying spectrum. In the resynthesis, some components add constructively and some add destructively (canceling each other out), so that the resynthesized result reconstitutes the original signal.

Beating and other anomalies are harmless when the signal is directly resynthesized, but they obscure attempts to inspect the spectrum visually or to transform it. This is why they are called clutter. Dolson (1983) and Strawn (1985c) assay the significance of clutter in analysis of musical instrument tones. Gerzon (1991) presented a theory of *super-resolving* spectrum analyzers that offer to improve resolution in both time and frequency, at the expense of increased clutter, which, Gerzon argues, has some perceptual significance.

Sonogram Representation

A *sonogram, sonograph*, or *spectrogram* is a well-known spectrum display technique in speech research, having been used for decades to analyze utterances. A sonogram shows an overview of the spectrum of several seconds of sound. This enables the viewer to see general features such as the onset of notes or phonemes, formant peaks, and major transitions. A trained viewer can read a speech sonogram. Refer to Cogan (1984) for an example of using sonograms in the analysis of music. The sonogram representation has also been employed as an interface for spectrum editing (Eckel 1990; IRCAM 2011).

The original sonogram was Backhaus's (1932) system; see also Koenig et al. (1946). In the 1950s the Kay Sonograph was a standard device for making sonograms. It consisted of a number of narrow bandpass analog filters and a recording system that printed dark bars on a roll of paper. The bars grew thicker in proportion to the energy output from each filter. Today sonograms are generally implemented with the STFT.

Figure 37.13b shows a sonogram representing a sound signal as a two-dimensional display of time versus frequency + amplitude. The vertical dimension depicts frequency (higher frequencies are higher up in the diagram) and shades of gray indicate the amplitude, with dark shades indicating greater intensity.

Sonogram Parameters

The parameters of the modern sonogram are the same as those of the STFT, except for certain display parameters. Adjustments to these parameters make a great difference in the output image, as follows:

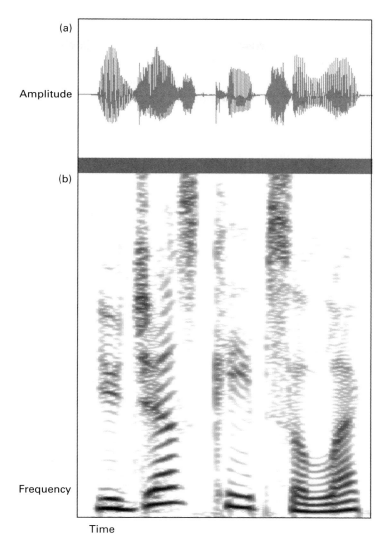

Figure 37.13 (a) Time-domain waveform of a female voice saying: "You just keep selecting." (b) Sonogram of (a). The frequency scale extends to 7 kHz.

1. Range of amplitudes and the type of scale used, whether linear or logarithmic.

2. Range of frequencies and the type of scale used, whether linear or logarithmic.

3. Time advance of the analysis window, also called hop size (in samples) or window overlap factor. This determines the time distance between successive columns in the output display. (We discuss this more in the section on the phase vocoder.)

4. Number of samples to analyze and the size of the FFT analysis window; the resolution of time and frequency depend on these parameters.

5. Number of frequency channels to display, which determines the number of rows in the graphical output and is related to the range and scale of the frequency domain; this cannot exceed the resolution imposed by the window size.

6. Window type—Hann, Hamming, Blackman, and others. (We discuss windows further on.)

Parameter 4 includes two parameters; the FFT window size is usually greater than the actual number of sound samples analyzed, the difference being padded with zero-valued samples. (See the section on phase vocoder analysis parameters.) These parameters have the most dramatic effect on the display. A short window results in a vertically oriented display, indicating the precise onset time of events but blurring the frequency reading (figure 37.14a). A medium length window resolves both time and frequency features fairly well, indicating the presence of formant frequencies (figure 37.14b). A long window generates a horizontally oriented display, as individual frequency bands come into clear view, but their position in time is smeared along the horizontal axis (figure 37.14c).

Phase Vocoder

The phase vocoder (PV) is a popular sound analysis tool, offered in several widely distributed software packages such as SoundHack (Erbe 1992), IRCAM's Audiosculpt and TS2, Csound, Max, and the Nyquist language. Gordon and Strawn (1985), Moore (1990), and Lazzarini (2011d) contain annotated code for phase vocoders. Arfib et al. (2011b) provides a version in MATLAB, as does Sethares (2019).

The PV was originally developed in the 1960s at Bell Laboratories (Flanagan and Golden 1966). Chapter 14 presented the basic *channel vocoder,* which analyzes the amplitude in each frequency band of a bank of filters. The PV is a more precise analyzer. One can view the PV as passing a windowed input signal through a bank of parallel bandpass filters spread out at equal intervals across the audio bandwidth. These filters measure not only the amplitude of a sinusoidal signal in each frequency band but also its phase. This additional phase information results in a highly accurate resynthesis. Resynthesis of the original signal is accomplished by summing the outputs of *n* oscillators modulated in amplitude and phase.

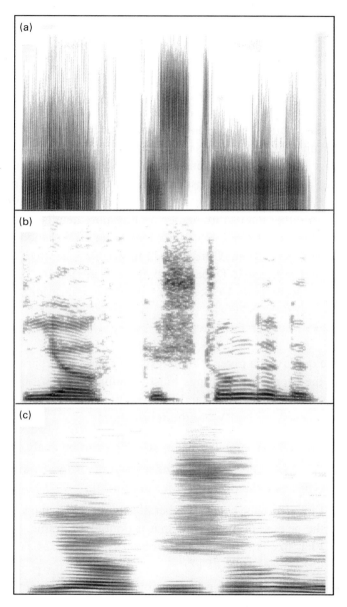

Figure 37.14   Time-versus-frequency trade-offs in sonogram analysis and display. All displays show speech sound sampled at 44.1 KHz. (a) Analysis window is 32 samples long, time resolution is 0.725 ms, and frequency resolution is 1378 Hz. (b) Analysis window is 1,024 samples long, time resolution is 23.22 ms, and frequency resolution is 43.07 Hz. (c) Analysis window is 8,192 samples long, time resolution is 185.8 ms, and frequency resolution is 5.383 Hz. (Sonograms provided by Gerhard Eckel using his SpecDraw program.)

In some implementations, this information can be converted into two envelopes: one for the amplitude of the sine and one for the frequency of the sine. This corresponds to the case of oscillator bank resynthesis previously discussed.

A musician's use of the PV inevitably involves modification of the analysis data before resynthesis. What a composer seeks in the output is a musical transformation that maintains a sense of the identity of the source. That is, if the input signal is a spoken voice, one usually wants it to sound like a spoken voice even after being transformed. This stands in contrast to a transformation such as convolution, whose product may not sound like either of its inputs!

In this tutorial, we focus on the theory of the PV from the perspective of a user rather than an implementer. For more details on implementing the PV see (Portnoff 1976, 1978, 1980; Holtzman 1978; Moorer 1978; Moore 1990; Dolson 1983, 1986; Gordon and Strawn 1985; Strawn 1985b; Strawn 1987a; Serra 1989, 1997; Depalle and Poirot 1991; Erbe 1992; Walker and Fitz 1992; Beauchamp 1993; Arfib et al. 2011b; Lazzarini 2011d; Sethares 2019).

Phase Vocoder Parameters

The quality of a given PV analysis depends on the parameter settings chosen by the user. These settings must be adjusted according to the nature of the sounds being analyzed and the type of results that are expected. The main parameters of the PV are the following:

1. Frame size—number of input samples to be analyzed at a time.
2. Window type—selection of a window shape from among the standard types (see the discussion further on).
3. FFT size—the actual number of samples fed to the FFT algorithm; usually the nearest power of two that is double the frame size, where the unit of FFT size is referred to by *points,* as in a "1,024-point FFT" (equivalent to "1024-sample FFT").
4. Hop size or overlap factor–time advance from one frame to the next.

Now we discuss each parameter in turn. Then in the following section we give rules of thumb for setting these parameters.

Frame size

The frame size (in samples) is important for two reasons. The first is that the frame size determines one aspect of the trade-off in time/frequency resolution. The larger the frame size, the greater the number of frequency bins but the lower the time resolution, and vice versa. If we are trying to analyze sounds in the lower octaves with great frequency accuracy, large frame sizes are unavoidable. Because the FFT computes the average spectrum content within a frame, the onset time of any spectrum changes within a frame is lost when the spectrum is plotted or transformed. (If the signal is simply resynthesized, the temporal information is restored.) For high-frequency sounds, small frames are adequate, which are also more accurate in time resolution.

The second reason frame size is important is that large FFTs are slower to calculate than small FFTs. Following the rule of thumb that the calculation time for an FFT is proportional to $N \log2(N)$, where N is the length of the input signal (Rabiner and Gold 1975), it takes more than a thousand times as long to calculate a 32,768-point FFT, for example, than a 64-point FFT. The latency of a long FFT may be too onerous in a real-time interactive system.

Window type

PVs give the option of using one of a family of standard bell-shaped window types, including Hamming, Hann, Gaussian, Blackman-Harris, and Kaiser (Marple 1987). All of these work fine in generating a basic sonogram display. For analyses where precision is important (such as creating a systematic catalog of spectra for instrumental tones) the choice of analysis window can be more critical. This is because each type of window contorts the analysis plots in a different way (Harris 1978; Nuttall 1981). Refer to Smith (2011), appendix E, for a detailed comparison of window types.

FFT size and zero padding

The choice of FFT size depends on the transformation one plans to apply to the input sound. A safe figure for cross-synthesis is the nearest power of two that is double the frame size. For example, a frame size of 128 samples would mandate an FFT size of 256. The other 128 samples in the FFT are set to zero—a process called *zero padding*. Note that zero padding is a way to increase the frequency resolution of an analysis (Verfaille, Holters, and Zölzer 2011). If we are interested only in computing the spectrum of 64 input samples and would like to increase the frequency resolution, we can add zero-valued samples up to the length 1,024 and then perform a 1,024-point FFT.

Hop size

The hop size (or window overlap factor) is the number of samples that the analyzer jumps along the input waveform each time it takes a new spectrum

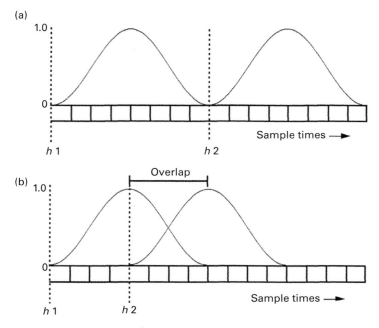

Figure 37.15 Varying hop size for analysis windows that are eight samples long. $h1$ and $h 2$ are the starting times for each window. (a) Nonoverlapping windows when hop size = window size. (b) Overlapping windows when hop size is less than window size. In this case the hop size is four samples.

measurement (figure 37.16). The shorter the hop size, the more successive windows overlap. Thus some PVs specify this parameter as an overlap factor that describes how many analysis windows cover each other. Regardless of how it is specified, the hop size is usually a fraction of the frame size. A certain amount of overlap (e.g., four times) is necessary to ensure an accurate resynthesis. Even more overlap can improve accuracy when the analysis data is going to be transformed, but the computational cost is proportionally greater.

Typical Parameter Values

No parameter settings of the PV are ideal for all sounds. But when the parameters are set within a certain range, a variety of traditional instrumental sounds can be analyzed and resynthesized with reasonable fidelity. Here are some rules of thumb for PV parameter settings that may serve as a starting point for more finely tuned analyses:

1. Frame size—Large enough to capture four periods of the lowest frequency of interest (Depalle and Poirot 1991). This is particularly important if the sound is time stretched; too small a frame size means that

individual pitch bursts are moved apart, changing the pitch, although formants are preserved.

2. Window type—Any standard type except rectangular.

3. FFT size—Double the frame size, in samples.

4. Hop size—If the analysis data is going to be time scaled, the recommended hop size is an eighth of the frame size, in samples (i.e., eight times overlap). In general, the minimum technical criterion is that all windows add to a constant, that is, all data is equally weighted.

Window Closing

Once is not enough.
—S. J. Marple, *Digital Spectral Analysis,* 1987

Any given setting of the window size results in an analysis biased toward harmonics of the period defined by that window size. Frequency components that fall outside the frequency bins associated with a given window size will be estimated incorrectly. Thus some spectrum analysis procedures run the same signal through the analyzer repeatedly with different settings for the window size. A procedure that starts from high time and low frequency resolution and works progressively to low time and high frequency resolution is called *window closing* (Marple 1987).

Some analyzers try to estimate the pitch of the signal in order to determine the optimal window size. As mentioned earlier, pitch-synchronous analysis works well if the sound to be analyzed has a harmonic structure.

Phase and Accuracy of Resynthesis

The accuracy of all Fourier-based resynthesis is limited by the resolution of the analysis procedures. Small distortions introduced by numerical roundoff, windowing, peak-tracking, undersampling of envelope functions, and other aspects of the analysis introduce errors. In a well-implemented system, when the analysis parameters are properly adjusted by a skilled engineer and no modifications are made to the analysis data, the resynthesis error is not perceptible.

For efficiency, some PVs have the option of discarding phase information, saving only the amplitude and frequency data. This results in a data reduction and corresponding savings in computation time, but it degrades the accuracy of the resynthesis. Without proper phase data, a resynthesized waveform, for example, does not accurately recreate the original, although it has the same basic frequency content (Serra 1989). (One can liken this to a jigsaw puzzle where all the pieces are centered in the right location, but they have not been rotated to the proper position where they all fit together perfectly.) In certain steady-state sounds, a rearrangement of phases may not be audible. But for high-fidelity reproduction of transients and quasi-steady-state tones, phase data help reassemble short-lived and changing components in their proper order. In particular, the phase difference of each bin between two successive analysis frames determines that bin's deviation from its mid frequency. This enables a high-quality reconstruction on a different time basis (Bernsee 1999). Laroche and Dolson (1999) demonstrated improved phase calculation techniques that reduce artifacts of PV transformations.

Tracking Phase Vocoder

Some implementations of the PV are called *tracking phase vocoders* (TPVs) because they follow or track the most prominent peaks in the spectrum over time (Dolson 1983; McAulay and Quatieri 1986; Quatieri and McAulay 1986; Serra 1989; Maher and Beauchamp 1990; Bonada et al. 2011; Smith 2011). Another term used for the same process is *sinusoidal modeling* (Klingbeil 2005, 2009). Loris is an example of an open-source software package that implements this model (Walker and Fitz 1992).

Unlike the ordinary phase vocoder, in which the resynthesis frequencies are limited to harmonics of the analysis window, the TPV follows changes in frequencies. The result of peak tracking is a set of amplitude and frequency envelopes that drive a bank of sinusoidal oscillators in the resynthesis stage. The tracking process follows only the most prominent frequency components. For these components, the result is a more accurate analysis than that done with an equally spaced bank of filters (the traditional STFT implementation). The other benefit is that the tracking process creates frequency and amplitude envelopes for these components, which make them more robust under transformation than overlap-add frames.

A disadvantage is that the quality of the TPV analysis depends more heavily on proper analysis and synthesis parameter settings than in the regular STFT. Specifically, STFT analysis and resynthesis with no transformations creates a result that is perceptually indistinguishable from the original input signal. TPV resynthesis using default parameters tends to have an artificial quality.

Operation of the TPV

A TPV carries out the following steps:

1. Compute the STFT using the frame size, window type, FFT size, and hop size specified by the user.

2. Derive the squared magnitude spectrum in dB.

3. Find the bin numbers of the peaks in the spectrum.

4. Calculate the magnitude and phase of each frequency peak.

5. Assign each peak to a *frequency track* by matching the peaks of the previous frame with those of the current frame (peak tracking is described further along).

6. Apply any desired modifications to the analysis parameters.

7. If additive resynthesis is requested, generate a sine wave for each frequency track and sum all sine wave components to create an output signal; the instantaneous amplitude, phase, and frequency of each sinusoidal component is calculated by interpolating values from frame to frame (or use the alternative resynthesis methods described previously).

Peak Tracking

The tracking phase vocoder follows the most prominent frequency trajectories in the spectrum. Like other aspects of sound analysis, the precise method of peak tracking should vary depending on the sound. The tracking algorithm works best when it is tuned to the type of sound being analyzed—speech, harmonic spectrum, smooth inharmonic spectrum, noisy, and so on. This section briefly explains more about the tracking process as a guide to setting the analysis parameters.

The first stage in peak tracking is peak identification. A simple control that sets the *minimum peak height* focuses the identification process on the most significant landmarks in the spectrum (figure 37.16a). The rest of the algorithm tries to apply a set of *frequency guides* that advance in time (figure 37.16b). The guides are hypotheses only; later the algorithm will decide which guides are confirmed frequency tracks. The algorithm continues the guides by finding the peak closest in frequency to its current value. The alternatives are the following:

- If it finds a match, the guide continues.

- If a guide cannot be continued during a frame it is considered to be "sleeping."

- If the guide does not wake up after a certain number of frames specified by the user, then it is deleted. One can switch on *guide hysteresis*, which continues tracking a guide that falls slightly below the specified *amplitude range*. Hysteresis alleviates the audible problem of *switching* guides that repeatedly fade slightly, are cut to zero by the peak tracker, and fade in again (Walker and Fitz 1992). With hysteresis the guide is synthesized at its actual value, which may be less than the amplitude range, instead of with zero amplitude.

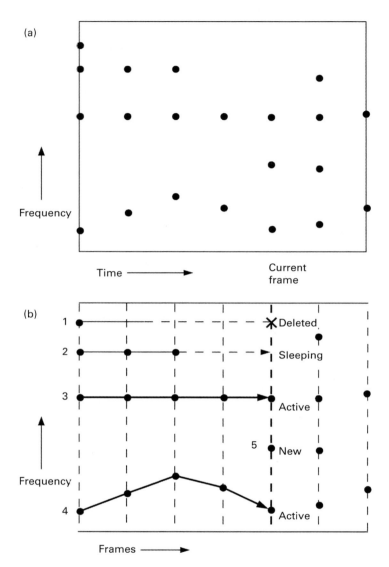

Figure 37.16   Peak identification and tracking. (a) Isolation of a set of spectrum peaks. (b) Fitting frequency guides to peaks. Guide 1 at the top did not wake up after three frame, so it is deleted. Guide 2 is still sleeping. Guides 3 and 4 are active. Guide 5 starts from a new peak.

- If there is a conflict between guides, the closest guide wins and the "loser" looks for another peak within the *maximum peak deviation*, a frequency band specified by the user.

- If there are peaks that are not accounted for by current guides, then a new guide begins.

The process of windowing can compromise the accuracy of the tracking, particularly in rapidly moving waveforms such as attack transients. One strategy to alleviate this is to process sounds with a sharp attack in time-reversed order (Serra 1989). This gives the partial trackers a chance to lock onto their stable frequency trajectories before encountering the chaos of the attack, resulting in less distortion. The data is reversed to its normal order before resynthesis.

Accuracy of Resynthesis with the TPV

The tracking PV interprets the raw analysis data in constructing tracks. It discards all information that does not contribute to a track. This sifting may leave out significant portions of sound energy, particularly noisy, transient energy. This can be demonstrated by subtracting the TPV spectrum from the original spectrum to yield a *residual signal* (Strawn 1987a; Gish 1978, 1992; Serra 1989, 1997; Smith 2011). One can consider this residual or difference to be analysis/resynthesis error. It is common to refer to the resynthesized, quasiharmonic portion as the "clean" part of the signal and the error or noise component as the "dirty" part of the signal. For many sounds (i.e., those with fast transients such as in cymbal crashes), the errors are quite audible. That is, the "clean" signal sounds unnaturally "sanitized" or sinusoidal, and the "dirty" signal, when heard separately, contains the missing grit.

Analysis of Inharmonic and Noisy Sounds

Demonstrations prove that tracking phase vocoders can analyze and resynthesize many inharmonic sounds, including bird songs and tuned percussion tones (gongs, marimba, xylophone, etc.). But because the TPV is based on Fourier analysis, it must translate chaotic, noisy, and inharmonic sounds into combinations of periodic sinusoidal functions. Particularly for noisy signals, this can be costly from a storage and computational standpoint. To synthesize a simple noise band, for example, requires an ever-changing blend of dozens of sine waves. Storing the control functions for these sines takes a great deal of memory. For a noisy sound, the analysis data can be more than ten times the size of the original sound samples.

Resynthesizing the sines demands a large amount of computation. Moreover, since the transformations allowed by the TPV are based on a sinusoidal model, operations on noisy sounds often result in clusters of sinusoids that have lost their noisy quality. Spectral modeling synthesis, discussed next, was developed to address this issue.

Deterministic Plus Stochastic: Spectral Modeling Synthesis

The TPV has been extended to make it more effective in musical applications. Serra (1989) added filtered noise to the inharmonic sinusoidal model in *spectral modeling synthesis* (SMS). (See Serra and Smith [1990] and Smith [2011].) A coded example in MATLAB is given in Bonada et al. (2011).

As figure 37.17 shows, SMS reduces the analysis data into a *deterministic* component (prominent narrowband components of the original sound) and a *stochastic* component. The deterministic component tracks the most prominent frequencies in the spectrum. SMS resynthesizes these tracked frequencies with sine waves. The tracking follows only the most prominent frequency components, discarding other energy in the signal. Thus SMS also analyzes the *residue* (or *residual*), which is the difference between the deterministic component and the original spectrum. This is used to synthesize the stochastic component of the signal. The residual is analyzed and approximated by a collection of simplified spectrum envelopes. One can think of the resynthesis as passing white noise through filters controlled by these envelopes. In the implementation, however, SMS uses sine waves with random phase values, which is equivalent to the filtered noise interpretation. This representation makes it easier to modify the stochastic part in order to transform the sound. Graphical operations on envelopes are intuitive to a musician, whereas changing filter coefficients leads to technical complications. A challenge with SMS is that the perceptual link between the deterministic and stochastic parts is delicate; editing the two parts separately may lead to a loss of perceived fusion between them.

Since SMS was first proposed, research has continued to refine the technique. The *sound description interchange format* (SDIF) serves as a common file format for exchange of SMS data between researchers (Wright et al. 1999). Ding and Qian (1997) proposed refinements to the original SMS model. One focus has been on developing more sophisticated peak-tracking algorithms (Röbel 2008; Zivanovic et al. 2008). Fulop and Fitz (2007) developed methods for pruning a spectrogram to show only sinusoidal components, only impulses, or both. Their methods compute the second-order partial

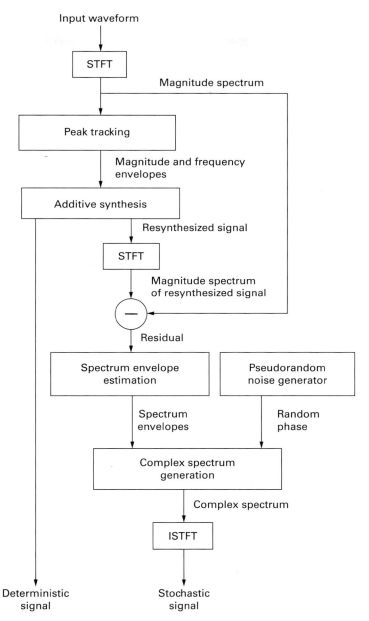

Figure 37.17   Analysis part of Xavier Serra's spectral modeling synthesis technique. The deterministic part takes a sinusoidal additive synthesis approach. The stochastic part of the signal derives from the difference between the resynthesis of the deterministic (quasiharmonic) part and the STFT of the input waveform. The system simplifies each residual component by fitting an envelope to it. The envelope representation makes the stochastic part easier to modify by musicians. The resynthesis of the stochastic part then uses these envelopes with a random phase component— equivalent to filtered white noise.

derivative of the STFT phase, which can distinguish between sinusoids and impulses.

Another extension called analysis, transformation, and synthesis (ATS) uses a sinusoidal plus *critical-band noise model* and psychoacoustic information (Pampin 2004; Pampin et al. 2004). Tracked partials are synthesized using interpolated phase information and subtracted from the analyzed sound in the time domain to obtain a residual signal. The resulting residual is modeled as time-varying critical-band noise. This is performed by warping the frequency spectrum of the residual into a *Bark scale* (Zwicker 1961). This divides the spectrum into twenty-five critical bands and computes the energy in each band at each time frame. Critical-band energy is then re-injected into partials present in those spectral regions as modulated narrow-band noise. Thus sinusoidal and noise information are encapsulated into a single entity. An advantage of this representation is that sinusoidal and noise components are perceptually well integrated when synthesized. If perceptually relevant noise is present within regions where no partials were tracked, a complementary noise model is applied.

Application of Spectral Modeling Synthesis: Vocaloid

Vocaloid is an SMS-based voice synthesis technology originally developed by Xavier Serra's student Kenmochi Hideki at the Pompeu Fabra University in Barcelona in 2000. The ideas were taken under the wing of Yamaha and turned into the commercial product Vocaloid, a singing synthesizer first released in 2004. A collection of voice banks has been released for use with the Vocaloid synthesizer technology. Each is sold as "a singer in a box" with a corresponding avatar.

The voice model behind Vocaloid is a combination of SMS and a subtractive source-filter model (chapter 14). The synthesis engine is a variation on concatenative synthesis (chapter 23) in the frequency domain, which splices and processes the vocal fragments extracted from human singing voices, using a spectral representation. The Vocaloid system can produce quasirealistic voices by adding vocal expressions like vibrato that is given to the system in the form of a score by a sound designer.

Transformation of Sound in the Frequency Domain

Musicians are not only interested in analyzing sound; they want to transform it for creative purposes. Once we have an analyzed spectrum representation, we can change the parameters of the resynthesis to produce mutations in the sound. In the past, this type of work took place only in research laboratories (Moorer 1978; Dolson 1983; Gordon and Strawn 1985).

Today we have many avenues to pursue this approach. The SoundHack app has an easy-to-use phase vocoder, convolver, and spectral mutator (Erbe 1992; Polansky and Erbe 1992). The Csound language has a battery of tools for transforming spectral data (Karpen 2000). Charles (2008) wrote a tutorial on spectral processing using Max and Jitter. Collins (2011) described spectral opcodes in SuperCollider. For a guide to spectral processing in the C programming language, see Lazzarini (2011a and c). Chapter 44 describes a number of interactive tools for spectral editing.

One of the most comprehensive packages for sound transformation is the Composer's Desktop Project (CDP), which contains hundreds of functions. A major component of this package is a suite of spectrum-based transformations developed by the composer Trevor Wishart. Some of these are documented in his book *Audible Design* (Wishart 1994). Inspired by Wishart, Michael Norris developed a set of spectrum operations called SoundMagic Spectral that work as plug-ins in DAWs and sound editors. Table 10.1 (chapter 10) lists basic musical effects made possible by modification of spectrum data.

The phase vocoder handles harmonic and smoothly changing tones best. Thus transformations such as pitch-time changing on these sounds result in natural-sounding effects. Certain sounds, however, are inherently difficult to modify with basic PV techniques. These include noisy sounds such as raspy or breathy voices, motors, room noise, or any sound that is rapidly changing on a timescale of a few milliseconds. PV transformations on these types of sounds may result in echoes, flutter, unwanted resonances, and undesirable colored reverberation effects. Here is where SMS, with its built-in noise model, makes a difference.

Some PVs let one process only the steady-state part of the signal, not the transients. In this way, attacks are kept crisp. Průša and Hollighaus (2017) proposed refinements to the PV for transformations involving transients. Laroche and Dolson (1999) proposed refinements that enable pitch-shifting, chorusing, harmonizing, partial stretching and other effects based on a peak-detection stage, followed by a peak-shifting stage.

The most common application of spectral transformations is *pitch-time changing,* that is, changing the pitch of a sound without changing its duration, or changing the duration without changing its pitch. See chapter 31, "Pitch-Time Changing," and chapter 44, "Spectrum Editors," for more on this topic.

Cross-Synthesis, Spectral Mutation, and Timbre Morphing

Cross-synthesis, a transformation that combines two different sounds, is not one technique; it takes a number of forms. The most well-known form is the channel vocoder, mentioned previously (and also in chapter 14). A vocoder uses a bank of filters to measure the spectral energy in one sound and then uses that data to control the spectral energy in another sound. For example, the sound of a person talking can be used to control the sound of an orchestra, resulting in a "talking orchestra" effect.

Another common method of cross-synthesis uses the magnitude functions from one spectrum to control the magnitude functions of another. That is, the energy of each frequency component in sound *A* scales the energy of the corresponding frequency component in sound *B*. This is implemented by multiplying each point in spectrum *A* by each corresponding point in spectrum *B*. Another term for this type of cross-synthesis is *filtering by convolution*. Musically, cross-synthesis is most effective when one of the sounds being filtered has a broad bandwidth, like a noise source. By using a phase vocoder with two inputs, cross-synthesis is basically automatic (Depalle and Poirot 1991). Another type of cross-synthesis uses the magnitude functions from one sound with the phase functions of another sound to create a hybrid sound effect (Boyer and Kronland-Martinet 1989).

Polansky and Erbe (1996) developed a related method of cross-synthesis over time called *spectral mutation*, implemented in SoundHack. Spectral mutation is the process of combining two sounds *A* and *B* to create a new sound that transitions from timbre *A* to timbre *B* over time. As opposed to a simple crossfade, which mixes two sounds in the time domain, mutation performs the mixture in the frequency domain. That is, it interpolates from *A* to *B* using spectral data. They designed five mutation functions; each produces a different timbral crossfade. A function takes two sound files (source and target) and returns a third sound file (mutant). The functions operate on the phase/amplitude data pair of each frequency band of the source and target spectra. The output of the functions is a phase/amplitude data pair for each frequency band in the mutation sound file. Each mutation function deals with the interval between two frames (time slices) of the frequency band of a spectra. That is, the amplitude in a given band for a specific frame of the mutation is the result of a transformation on the source and target amplitude intervals between the current frame and the previous frame.

By combining the magnitude and phase spectra of two sounds, we produce a hybrid sound. If there is an amplitude envelope that fades from the spectrum of sound *A* to that of sound *B*, we can achieve a *spectral crossfade* (X. Serra 1997).

Morphing based on the tracking phase vocoder has a long history dating back to the Lemur and Loris apps developed at the University of Illinois (Walker and Fitz 1992; Fitz and Haken 1996; Fitz et al. 2003). Morphing is a transformation that begins with sound *A* and over time morphs into sound

B. In this sense it is like spectral mutation, although the underlying analysis and representation methods are different. While Lemur used a model based on the tracking phase vocoder, Loris used a model based on *reassigned bandwidth-enhanced* (RBE) analysis. Unlike the TPV where the partials are strictly sinusoidal, in RBE analysis the partials are "bandwidth enhanced" to incorporate a noise component. The bandwidth component can be used to manipulate both sinusoidal and noisy parts of a sound. The method of reassignment improves the analysis resolution by using a nonuniform grid of time and frequency.

Another morphing strategy using the TPV takes two sampled sounds *A* and *B* and creates a new sound *C* that combines their characteristics. For example, if *A* were long and *B* were short, *C* would be medium in duration (Tellman, Haken, and B. Holloway 1995). Other applications of morphing include transitions over time from *A* to *B*.

38 *Spectrum Analysis by Alternative Methods*

Constant *Q* Filter Bank Analysis

      Constant *Q* versus Traditional Fourier Analysis

      Implementation of Constant *Q* Analysis

Analysis by Wavelets

      Operation of Wavelet Analysis

      Wavelet Display

      Musical Feature Detection Using Wavelets

      Wavelet Resynthesis

      Sound Transformation with Wavelets

      Gabor Transform

      Wavelet Separation of Noise from Harmonic Spectrum

Signal Analysis with the Wigner Distribution

      Interpreting Wigner Distribution Plots

      Limits of the Wigner Distribution

      Wigner-Ville Distribution

Autoregression Spectrum Analysis

      Autoregressive Moving Average Analysis

Source and Parameter Analysis

      Parameter Estimation

Analysis by Walsh and Prony Functions
> **Walsh Functions**
> **Prony's Method**

Auditory Models
> **Mel Frequency Cepstrum**
> **Cochleagrams**
> **Correlograms**

Higher Order Spectrum Analysis

Our attention is clearly attracted by transients and movements as opposed to stationary stimuli, which we soon ignore. Concentrating on transients is probably a strategy for selecting important information from the overwhelming amount of data recorded by our senses. Yet, classical signal processing has devoted most of its efforts to the design of time-invariant and space-invariant operators, that modify stationary signal properties. This has led to the indisputable hegemony of the Fourier transform, but leaves aside many information-processing applications. The world of transients is considerably larger and more complex than the garden of stationary signals. The search for an ideal Fourier-like basis that would simplify most signal processing is therefore a hopeless quest. Instead, a multitude of different transforms and bases have proliferated.
—Stéphane Mallat, *A Wavelet Tour of Signal Processing,* 2009

One of the main stumbling blocks in developing a consistent theory [of time-frequency distributions] is the fact that the behavior of these distributions is dramatically different and each has peculiar properties.
—Leon Cohen, "Time-frequency Distributions—A Review," 1989

The "Fourier Kingdom" rules over linear time-invariant signal processing, the building blocks of which are frequency filtering operations. As long as one is satisfied with linear time-invariant operators or uniformly regular signals, the *short-time Fourier transform* (STFT) provides answers to many questions (Mallat 2009).

In attempting to represent transient phenomena, however, the STFT becomes cumbersome. It requires increasingly many coefficients to represent an increasingly time-specific event. This is because analysis based on the classical approach of the Baron de Fourier has fundamental weaknesses for finite-length signals. First, it has limited frequency resolution (inability to distinguish two close frequencies) over a short time scale. Second, leakage in the spectral domain occurs as a side effect of the windowing that is implicit in the *discrete Fourier transform* (DFT) (Gish 1978; Kay and Marple 1981). Third, Fourier analysis is an inherently inefficient (not sparse) way to analyze noisy sounds, because it assumes that these sounds are combinations of hundreds or thousands of harmonically related sinusoids. In the case of sinusoidal modeling, this can result in a data explosion, with the analysis file size being many times greater than the input file. Finally, the premise of periodicity inherent in Fourier methods blurs the view of the inner structure of complicated aperiodic phenomena.

In an attempt to alleviate these limitations, myriad alternative spectrum analysis methods have been proposed. Figure 38.1 portrays the multiplicity of methods and the diversity of results that can be obtained from an input of three sinusoids and a band of filtered noise, shown as (a). Fourier methods are shown in (b), (c), and (g). They cannot resolve the sinusoids or even separate the sinusoids from noise. A technique like (k) accurately measures

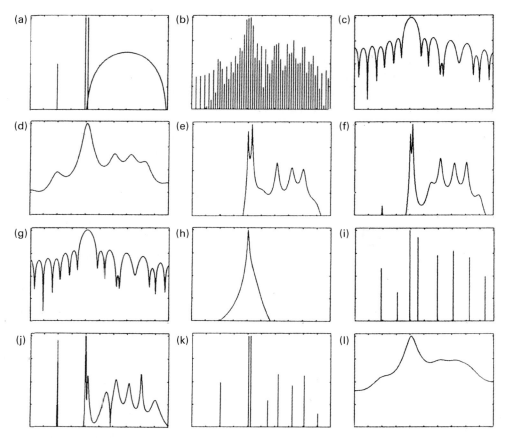

Figure 38.1   Different ways of measuring spectrum for a single input sound, from Kay and Marple (1981). In the descriptions, PSD means *power spectrum density.* The horizontal scale in all cases is frequency, from 0 up to half the sampling rate. The vertical scale is amplitude, from 0 dB at the top to −40 dB at the bottom, plotted linearly. (a) Input source, consisting of three sinusoids and a band of noise. (b) Periodogram with double-zero padding FFT. (c) Blackman-Tukey PSD. (d) Autoregressive PSD via Yule-Walker approach. (e) Autoregressive PSD via Burg approach. (f) Autoregressive PSD via least-squares approach. (g) Moving average PSD. It is identical to (c) because only autocorrelation lag estimates were used. (h) ARMA PSD via extended Yule-Walker approach. (i) Pisarenko spectral line decomposition. (j) Prony PSD. (k) Special Prony via Hildebrand approach. (l) Capon or maximum likelihood.

the three sinusoids but then depicts the noise band as a sum of five sinusoids! Evidently, there is no "best" spectrum measurement technique for all seasons; it depends on what we are looking for.

This chapter looks at alternative methods. In particular, we examine constant Q filter banks, wavelets, the Wigner distribution, auditory models, and higher-order spectra. In the next chapter we look in more detail at another alternative: *atomic decomposition* using a dictionary of sound atoms or grains.

Constant Q Filter Bank Analysis

Various analysis methods can be grouped under the rubric of *constant Q* filter bank techniques (Petersen 1980; Petersen and Boll 1983; Schwede 1983; Musicus et al. 1984; Brown and Puckette 1992, 1993; Schörkhuber and Klapuri 2010). Within this family are the so-called *auditory transform* (Stautner 1983) and the *bounded Q frequency transform* (Mont-Reynaud 1985a; Chafe et al. 1985).

Recall from chapter 28 that Q can be defined for a bandpass filter as the ratio of its center frequency to its bandwidth. In a constant Q filter bank, each filter has a similar or the same Q. Thus the bandwidth of the high-frequency filters is much broader in terms of frequency differences than those of the low-frequency filters. Constant Q analyzers work on a logarithmic frequency scale and thus are aligned to a musical interval. The constant Q filter bank has been a staple of the audio industry for decades in *one-third octave spectrum analyzers* in sound level meters and *one-third octave graphic equalizers* for live sound reinforcement (Liski and Välimäki 2017).

Note that another analysis technique that uses a nonlinear frequency scale is the *Bark frequency scale* (or *critical band*) method described by Smith (2011). See Zwicker (1961) on the Bark scale.

Constant Q versus Traditional Fourier Analysis

The constant Q filter bank's logarithmic frequency analysis is different from regular Fourier analyzers. Fourier analysis divides the spectrum into a set of equally spaced *frequency bins,* where there are half as many bins as there are samples taken as input (for real signals, negative frequency components duplicate the positive frequency components). In Fourier analysis, the width of a bin is a constant equal to the Nyquist rate divided by the number of bins. For example, for a 1,024-point *fast Fourier transform* (FFT) at a sampling rate of 48 kHz, the width of a bin is 24,000 / 1024, or 23.43 Hz.

When the results of the FFT are translated to a logarithmic scale (such as musical octaves) it is clear that the resolution is worst in the lower octaves. To separate two low frequency tones E1 (41.2 Hz) and F1 (43.65 Hz) that are a semitone apart requires a large time window (e.g., 2^{14} or 16,384 samples). But to use the same resolution at higher frequencies is a waste, because human beings cannot distinguish between two tones that are 2.45 Hz apart in the octave between 10 and 20 kHz. Hence there is a mismatch between the logarithmic continuum of frequencies that we hear and the fixed linear frequency scale of FFT analysis. This problem is addressed by methods like the constant Q transform, in which the bandwidth varies proportionally with frequency. That is, the analysis bands are thin for low frequencies and wide for high frequencies (figure 38.2). Thus in constant Q analysis the length of the analysis window varies according to the frequency being analyzed. Long windows analyze low frequencies, and short windows analyze high frequencies.

Constant Q filter banks do not avoid the uncertainty relationship between time and frequency, discussed earlier, but temporal uncertainty is concentrated in the lower octaves, where the analysis bands are narrow, and therefore the windows and the filter impulse responses are long. Since sonic transients (attacks) tend to contain high-frequency components, a constant

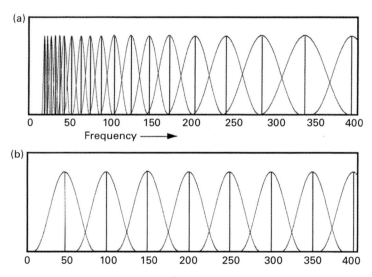

Figure 38.2 Spacing of filters for constant Q versus Fourier techniques. (a) Using only 43 filters (19 are shown), the constant Q method achieves 1/4-octave frequency resolution from 20 Hz to 21 kHz. (b) Fourier filter spacing, with a band every 46 Hz. Using almost 12 times as many filters (512; 8 are shown), Fourier methods still do not have the low-frequency resolution as constant Q methods. The Fourier method will have 46 Hz resolution throughout the audio bandwidth, even in the highest octave where the ear cannot accurately resolve these differences.

Q response has the advantage of time localization in high frequencies with frequency localization in low frequencies.

Another attractive feature of constant Q techniques is that the human ear has a frequency response that resembles constant Q response, particularly above 500 Hz (Scharf 1961, 1970). That is, the auditory system performs a type of filter bank analysis with a frequency dependent bandwidth. These measured auditory bandwidths are of such a fundamental nature that they are called *critical bands* (Whitfield 1978; Buser and Imbert 1992).

Implementation of Constant Q Analysis

The direct method of implementing constant Q analysis uses a bank of filters where the bandwidth of a filter is proportional to its center frequency (Stautner 1983). However, the direct method is computationally inefficient. Thus research focused on constructing a constant Q analysis based on data generated by the more efficient FFT (Nawab, Quatieri and Lim 1983), or on methods such as *frequency warping* a filter implemented with the FFT (Musicus 1984). For an overview of frequency warping methods, see Evangelista (2011, 2017). Constant Q analysis can also be formulated in the context of wavelet theory, explained in the next section. (Mallat 2009).

Constant Q algorithms may not be as efficient as those based on the fast Fourier transform, but the logarithmic spacing of the analysis channels means that the number of channels can be fewer for constant Q methods, while maintaining the same perceptual resolution as the STFT. The number of analysis channels in the STFT typically varies between several hundred and several thousand. The number of constant Q filter channels required to cover the same gamut is often less than 100.

Another issue with constant Q filter banks is invertibility. The existence of a constant Q filter bank does not necessarily imply a method for resynthesis. Some implementations provide this capability, while others do not (Schörkhuber and Klapuri 2010).

Analysis by Wavelets

In the theory of *wavelets,* every input signal can be expressed as a sum of elementary sound particles, each having a precise starting time, duration, frequency, and initial phase. A wavelet is a brief burst of sound energy, similar to a grain in granular synthesis, but with some important differences.

The *wavelet transform* (WT) is a *time-frequency* (TF) spectrum analysis method that was originally developed by scientists at the University of Marseille for applications in physics and acoustics (Dutilleux, Grossmann, and Kronland-Martinet 1988; Kronland-Martinet and Grossmann 1991; Evangelista 1991; Boyer and Kronland-Martinet 1989; Kronland-Martinet 1988; Strang 1989; Kussmaul 1991; Vetterli 1992; Mallat 2009). The term *wavelet* and its French equivalent *ondelette* were used in early-twentieth-century physics to describe the packets of energy emitted by atomic processes (Crawford 1968). Modern wavelet theory brings together a cluster of ideas imported from mathematics, computer vision, image processing, and signal processing. A pioneer in the field, Yves Meyer (1993) traced seven different origins for modern wavelet theory.

The notion of correlation is central to wavelet theory. Mathematically, a wavelet correlates with an unknown signal if that signal contains similar pattern. Wavelets can be designed to correlate with arbitrary features in an input signal. For example, a wavelet can be designed to have a frequency of middle C and a short duration. If this wavelet is used to analyze a song, it highlights instances of a short middle C note. This is discussed in the section on musical feature detection.

This ability to resolve highly specific information derives from the flexibility of the wavelet TF grid. The STFT divides the TF plane by means of a uniform grid. By contrast, wavelet analysis can divide the TF plane into nonuniform regions (figure 38.3). In wavelet analysis, low-frequency regions can be long in time and narrow in frequency range, whereas high-frequency regions can be short in time and wide in frequency range. Thus a cymbal crash remains invisible to a *slow* (low-frequency) wavelet but will be detected by a burst of *fast* wavelets.

As Evangelista (2001, 2011, 2017) has demonstrated, *frequency warping* allows the wavelet grid to be tiled in arbitrary ways (figure 38.4).

Wavelets, scaled in duration and frequency and translated in time, form an analysis *basis* for the analyzed signal. An individual wavelet is a *basis function*. A basis function lets one reconstruct any continuous waveform from a combination of discrete elementary waveforms. To give examples, a sine wave is the basis function of Fourier analysis, and a sample is a basis function of a digital audio waveform.

Musical applications often use the Morlet wavelet, which has a Gaussian envelope. Thus the wavelet is similar to the grains in granular synthesis and to the windowed segments of the STFT. However, an unlimited number of other types of wavelets basis functions can be defined.

A specific property of a wavelet is that no matter what frequency it contains, it always encapsulates a constant number of cycles. This implies that

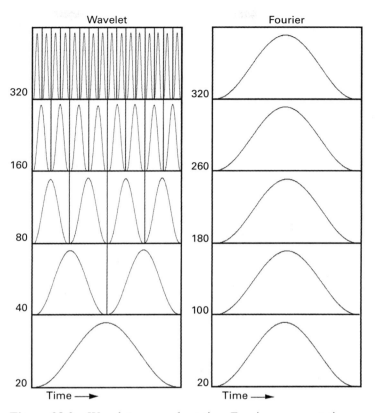

Figure 38.3   Wavelet versus short-time Fourier representation over the same time-versus-frequency area. Frequency is on the vertical axis. On the right, the STFT's time resolution is uniform at every frequency. The wavelet grid on the left has finer time resolution in the upper range of the spectrum. This is a representation of the so-called *dyadic wavelet* with octave resolution. Other grids can be defined to have greater resolution (Evangelista 2001).

the size (duration) of the wavelet window stretches or shrinks according to the frequency being analyzed. This stretching and shrinking is referred to as *dilation* and *contraction*. The implication of the variable window size is that the WT trades frequency resolution for time resolution at high frequencies and trades time resolution for frequency resolution at low frequencies.

Operation of Wavelet Analysis

The WT multiplies the input signal by a grid of analyzing wavelets, where the grid is bounded by frequency on one axis and by time dilation factor on the other. The operation of this multiplication process is equivalent to a bank of filters. Indeed, one way to think of wavelets is that each represents the impulse response of a bandpass filter (Vetterli and Herley 1992). Time dilation

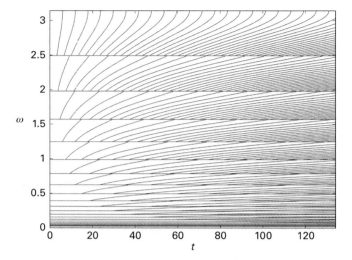

Figure 38.4   Tiling the time-frequency plane by means of frequency warped wavelets. Due to the frequency-dependent delay of each basis element, the time-frequency localization zones are characterized by curved boundaries. From Evangelista (2001).

of this impulse response corresponds to an inverse frequency scaling. Thus, the duration of each wavelet corresponds to the center frequency of a filter; the longer the wavelet, the lower its center frequency.

The WT simultaneously windows the input signal and measures the energy of the input signal at the frequency of each analyzing wavelet. The result is a grid in which the energy at each cell (*kernel*) reflects the time-frequency energy of the original signal. The output of the WT is a two-part spectrum, with one part representing the magnitude at a given frequency and the other part representing phase.

The Grossmann-Morlet equation defining a wavelet (Kronland-Martinet and Grossmann 1991) centered on point b in time is

$$\psi_{a,b}(t) = \frac{1}{\sqrt{a}}\,\psi\left(\frac{t-b}{a}\right),\ a>0,\ b\in \mathrm{R}$$

The variable a is the scale factor. The wavelet function $\psi_{a,b}(t)$ oscillates at the frequency $1/\sqrt{a}$. When the scale is very small, the first factor in the equation, $1/\sqrt{a}$, tends toward 1, and the time interval contracts around b as $(t-b)/a$ tends toward $t-b$.

The wavelet transform is

$$S(a,b) = \int \bar{\psi}_{a,b}(t)s(t)\,dt = \frac{1}{\sqrt{a}}\int \bar{\psi}\left(\frac{t-b}{a}\right)s(t)\,dt$$

where $\overline{\psi}$ represents the complex conjugate. In effect, the WT multiplies the input signal $s(t)$ by a grid of analyzing wavelets, bounded by frequency on one axis and by time scale factor on the other.

The frequency scale of the analysis grid can be logarithmic according to a musical interval such as a perfect fifth or major third, depending on the way the system is set up. In many papers on wavelets, the analyzing grid is assumed to be *dyadic,* which can be interpreted as constant Q filtering with a set of octave-band filters (Vetterli and Herley 1992). The use of a logarithmic scale is not mandatory, however, because the WT can be aligned on an arbitrary frequency scale.

The wavelet transform was a slow operation until 1985, when Mallat and Daubechies presented a recursive algorithm for what is called the *fast wavelet transform* or FWT (Mallat 1989, 2009).

Wavelet Display

A by-product of research in wavelet analysis is a display method originally developed by the Marseille group and shown in figure 38.5. This can be thought of as a traditional spectrum plot projected in time and flipped on its side. Another way to see it is as a kind of sonogram: plotting time horizontally, and frequency from the low frequencies on the bottom to the high frequencies on the top.

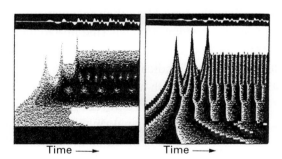

Figure 38.5   Three overlapping sinusoids shown in a wavelet display. The wavelet display has two parts: the *modulus* (or magnitude), shown at left, and the phase display or *phasogram.* Both show time going from left to right. The vertical axis plots frequency on a logarithmic scale. At the top of both parts is a standard time-domain plot of the waveform for reference. In the modulus, darkness indicates energy. Notice the high-frequency "pointers" showing the onset time of each sinusoid. The phasogram (right panel) shows excursions of the waveform directly. The U-shaped "mountains" follow the peaks of the waveform. Any changes show up as chaotic surfaces, again with "pointers" to the instant of change. After Arfib (1991).

The difference between the sonogram plot and this wavelet plot is the pattern of time localization they project. Short wavelets detect brief transients, which are localized in time. These wavelets sit at the apex of a triangle on the frequency-versus-time plane, seen pointing upward in figure 38.5. This triangle is the wavelet's *domain of influence in time*. Long wavelets detect low frequencies; they sit at the bottom of the triangle, spread out (blurred) over time. The *domain of influence for frequencies* is a constant horizontal band, as in the spectrogram. The darker the band, the stronger the magnitude within that frequency range.

Of course, this technique of plotting is just one of many other ways of projecting the data generated by the WT. In the Marseille work, both modulus (magnitude) and phase images are plotted.

Musical Feature Detection Using Wavelets

One application of wavelets is detecting specific features in a given input signal. For example, if the frequency grid is aligned to a musical interval, the display projects a strong dark indicator when the input signal contains that interval. This is shown in figure 38.6 for a WT configured for octave detection. The four instances of octaves show up as dark triangles. In this case, one could say that the analyzing wavelet is the sum of two simpler wavelets an octave apart in frequency.

Figure 38.7 shows transient detection by wavelets. High-frequency wavelets point precisely to the time of a glitch in a waveform (top). The glitch is invisible to the low-frequency wavelets (the horizontal band at the bottom).

Kronland-Martinet and Grossmann (1991) derived points of stationary phase to determine "ridges" indicating the frequency modulation (FM) function of an acoustic signal. Smith and Honing (2008) applied the same technique to the analysis of musical rhythm. They extracted the FM function for the purpose of determining a principal rhythmic partial that corresponds to the tactus or beat. This research is based on the premise that human listeners can distinguish musical rhythms independently of the music's original pitch and timbre, even using short impulse-like clicks. The rhythm is thus perceived from the *inter-onset intervals* between events alone, that is, the pure temporal structure. Figure 38.8 shows a wavelet analysis revealing a changing rhythm based on inter-onset intervals (detailed in the figure caption).

Wavelet Resynthesis

As in the STFT, wavelet resynthesis can be carried out in two ways: overlap-add and additive. Each method lends itself to certain types of transformations.

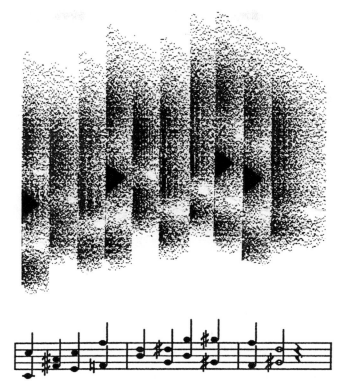

Figure 38.6 Modulus of the wavelet transform corresponding to the music notation written below. Dark triangles indicating maxima occur when octaves play. After Kronland-Martinet and Grossman (1991).

In the case of the overlap-add method, we need as many oscillators as there are overlapping wavelets. In additive resynthesis, the number of oscillators is constant because each frequency component is assigned its own oscillator.

Sound Transformation with Wavelets

Musical transformations based on wavelet analysis/resynthesis include filtering by suppressing certain frequency channels in the resynthesis (Boyer and Kronland-Martinet 1989). Logarithmic spacing of the frequency channels makes it possible to extract musical chords from a sound. When this technique is applied to the speaking voice, for example, it gives the impression of a person talking "harmonically." Another effect is a form of cross-synthesis that uses the amplitude components from one sound and the phase components from another to create a hybrid sound.

One can substitute a different wavelet function for the resynthesis than was used for the analysis. Using Mallat's smooth wavelet for the analysis,

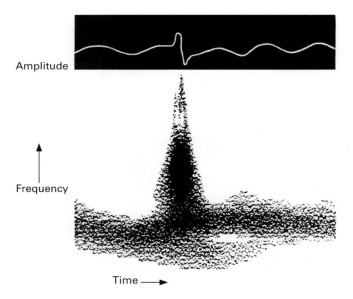

Figure 38.7   Transient detection by wavelets. The top graph shows a glitch in the time-domain signal. The bottom graph shows the wavelet representation. High-frequency wavelets point precisely to the time of the glitch. The glitch is invisible to the low-frequency wavelets (the horizontal band at the bottom). After Kronland-Martinet (1988).

for example, and substituting Haar's boxcar wavelet for the synthesis introduces a noisy distortion effect.

Other transformations include changing the geometry of the frequency grid, such as adding or multiplying a scaling factor to all the frequencies in resynthesis. Time stretching and shrinking effects are also possible (i.e., warping the time grid). In both frequency and time warping, the phase components must be multiplied by the same scale factor as the pitch or time operation (whichever is being modified). This is called *phase unwrapping.* Refer to Arfib (1991) for a discussion of phase unwrapping in the wavelet transform. Martinet (1988) describes a pitch-shifting method based on waveshaping the phase values in resynthesis.

Gabor Transform

The Gabor transform (GT) straddles between the wavelet and short-time Fourier transform (Quian and Chen 1993; Feichtinger and Strohmer 1998). The elementary signal of the GT is a wavelet is called a *gaboret.* The gaboret by another name is a sine wave with a Gaussian window in the STFT, or a *Gaussian atom* in atomic decomposition.

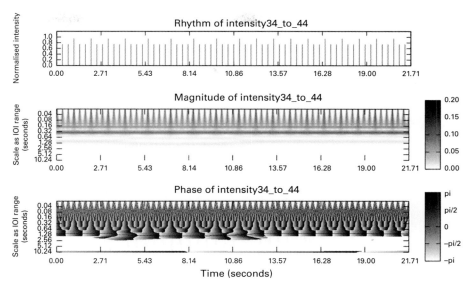

Figure 38.8   A constant frequency rhythm changing in meter by variations in amplitude, after Smith and Honing (2008). The upper plot shows the impulse amplitudes, with the meter changing from 3/4 to 4/4 over the period of 4.2 to 11.2 seconds. The scalogram (center) and phasogram (lower) plots display a continuous wavelet transform of the rhythmic impulse function. The intensity variations of the impulses are discernable in the scalogram at short inter-onset interval scales, and the time-frequency ridge with the most energy is at 0.35 seconds matching the inter-onset interval. A lower energy ridge is visible on the scalogram and more clearly on the phasogram, changing in its period from 1.05 seconds to 1.4 seconds, matching the duration of the bar. It is marked on the phasogram as a black line.

Arfib and Delprat (1992) developed a program called Sound Mutations based on the GT. One of their first results was a robust pitch-time changer. (See chapter 31 for more on pitch-time changing.) They also applied the GT to phase manipulations, cross-synthesis, and modifying the vibrato of a sung vocal tone, among other operations. Arfib et al. (2011b) provides MATLAB code for the GT.

Wavelet Separation of Noise from Harmonic Spectrum

The *comb wavelet transform*, developed at the University of Naples Federico II, sorts out transients, nonpitched sounds, and pitch changes from quasiperiodic signals (Evangelista 1992; Piccialli et al. 1992). The comb WT starts from a windowed segment of sound. The fundamental pitch period is estimated, and a comb filter is fitted to the segment, with peaks aligned on the harmonics of the fundamental. The comb filter sifts out the energy in the harmonic spectrum. A wavelet analysis is then performed on this "clean" harmonic signal. When the inverse WT is subtracted from the original signal, the residual or "dirty" part of the signal remains (figure 38.9). The dirty part includes the attack transient and the details that give the sound its identity and character.

Once the clean and dirty parts are separated, one can perform a kind of cross-synthesis by grafting the dirty part of one sound into the clean part of another. This type of separation is similar in concept, though not in implementation, to the separation of sinusoids from noise in spectral modeling synthesis (X. Serra 1989, 1997; Smith 2011), described in chapter 37. A

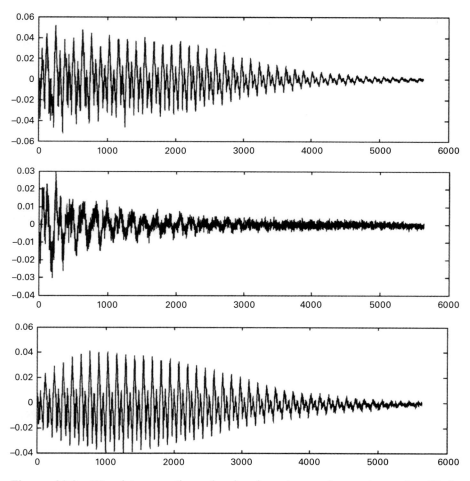

Figure 38.9 Wavelet separation of noise from harmonic spectrum. Amplitude (vertical) versus time (horizontal) plots. The top part is the original guitar tone. The middle part is the noisy residual from the comb wavelet transform, which includes the characteristic attack part of the note. The bottom figure shows the resynthesis from the quasiharmonic part of the comb wavelet method. (Figure courtesy of Gianpaolo Evangelista.)

related technique was demonstrated by Polotti and Evangelista (2001) and Polotti (2003). This used a modified wavelet transform to model the deterministic components of a sound, and $1/f$ noise to model the stochastic components. (In $1/f$ noise, also known as *pink noise,* energy diminishes by 3 dB per octave going upward.)

Signal Analysis with the Wigner Distribution

The *Wigner distribution* (WD) was first applied in the 1930s to problems in quantum physics (Wigner 1932). In acoustics applications, the goal of the WD is not sound analysis per se, but system analysis. In other words, the input to the WD is not necessarily a sound but is the response of a loudspeaker, transducer, circuit or other system to a sound. The WD then characterizes the time-versus-frequency distribution of this system. From a theoretical standpoint, the WD is a direct relative of other Fourier-based methods such as the sonogram. For details on the mathematics of the WD, see Janse and Kaizer (1983, 1984), Preis et al. (1987), Preis and Georgopolous (1999), and Gerzon (1991).

Interpreting Wigner Distribution Plots

The typical input to the WD is either the impulse response or the amplitude-versus-frequency response of the system being measured. (See chapter 14 for a definition of amplitude-versus-frequency response.) The output is a plot of frequency versus time. Engineering measurements such as group delay, instantaneous frequency and power, transient distortion, and spectrum can be derived from a WD plot, which can be displayed in two or three dimensions. For a two-dimensional plot, the area under a horizontal slice of a given frequency gives the value of the frequency response (magnitude squared) at that frequency (figure 38.10a). The *center of gravity* of that horizontal slice (the point at which all the area could be concentrated to produce the same "weight" on the vertical axis) gives the group delay time for that frequency. This is shown as a black dot in figure 38.9a. Similarly, the area under a vertical slice at a given time yields the *instantaneous power* of the signal's envelope at that time (figure 38.10b), whereas the center of gravity of that slice equals the *instantaneous frequency* (black dot shown in figure 38.10b). In this case, the plots are symmetrical in both the *x*- and *y*-axes so that the centers of gravity are both at the center. In real signals they vary as the signal varies. When the instantaneous power and the instantaneous frequency are

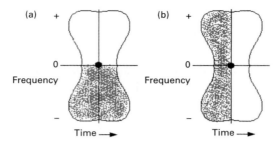

Figure 38.10   Wigner distribution plots.

plotted over time, the effects of amplitude modulation and frequency modulation on the signal can be revealed.

Janse and Kaizer (1983, 1984) presented three-dimensional plots and guidelines for interpreting the WD. In particular, they compared the plots of ideal systems (ideal filters, for example) with real-world devices like loudspeakers.

Limits of the Wigner Distribution

In practice, the WD is based on sampled and windowed data, and is sometimes called the *pseudo-Wigner distribution* (Janse and Kaizer 1983). Known distortions are introduced by sampling and windowing, as in other analysis techniques. These are relatively minor in effect.

A significant problem with the WD is that it is nonlinear. That is, the WD of the sum of two signals is not the sum of their individual WDs. For example, a single sinusoid at 100 Hz run through a WD shows up as an individual frequency component, as does a single sinusoid at 300 Hz. But if we run the sum of two sinusoids at 100 and 300 Hz through the WD, we see a third component at 200 Hz—the difference between the two frequencies. This *interference* or *clutter* represents a frequency that is not present at the input. Clutter makes visual inspection of WD plots difficult for musical signals.

Wigner-Ville Distribution

A related spectrum representation called the *Wigner-Ville distribution* (WVD) has been applied extensively in the time-frequency analysis method called *atomic decomposition* (presented in chapter 39). According to Mallat (2009) the WVD has a time-frequency resolution superior to that provided by the spectrogram. It has the advantage of not spreading the time or frequency support of impulses, sinusoids, or Gaussians thus increasing the clarity and resolution of the analysis.

With this given, it would seem that the WVD would be an ideal tool for analyzing the time-frequency structure of signals. This is not the case, however, because like the WD, the WVD also suffers from interference.

One way around the interference problem is to superpose the WVD of each separate atom into a composite display. Sturm et al. (2009) called this visualization a *wivigram*.

Figure 38.11 compares three spectrum displays. Figure 38.11(a) shows the analyzed waveform. The spectrogram (log magnitude of STFT) is shown in figure 38.11(b) and was created using a Hann window of length 5.8 ms and a constant overlap of 99 percent. It is possible to determine when and where energy exists in both time and frequency but finding and delimiting particular content is difficult. The scalogram in figure 38.11(c) shows the magnitudes of a *dyadic wavelet transform* (DWT) using the Gabor wavelet (Mallat 2009). Precise times of sharp discontinuities in the original signal (e.g., around 22 ms) can be found, in addition to a concentration of energy at wavelets with larger scales. The wivigram shown in figure 38.11(d) is significantly less redundant than both the scalogram and spectrogram and is able to simultaneously resolve various aspects of the signal at high and low frequencies and large and small scales—such as transient and tonal structures.

Autoregression Spectrum Analysis

The *autoregression* (AR), *linear predictive coding* (LPC), and *maximum entropy methods* (MEM) constitute a family of similar techniques for designing a filter that corresponds to the spectrum of the input signal (Makhoul 1975; Burg 1967; Atal and Hanauer 1971; Flanagan 1972; Markel and Gray 1976; Cann 1978, 1979–1980; Moorer 1979c; Dodge 1985; Lansky 1987; Lansky and Steiglitz 1981; Hutchins 1986a). Hence it is possible to apply them as methods of spectrum analysis. Here we treat all three methods under the rubric AR.

An advantage of AR methods over Fourier methods is that they can estimate a spectrum from a small amount of input data; hence they have the potential for improved time/frequency resolution. But the form of spectrum analysis performed by AR is not directly comparable to Fourier analysis. The AR model assumes the spectrum is the result of an excitation signal (such as glottal pulses emitted by the vocal cords) applied to a resonator (like the rest of the vocal tract). The AR estimates the spectrum peaks or resonances. Figure 38.12 shows this effect.

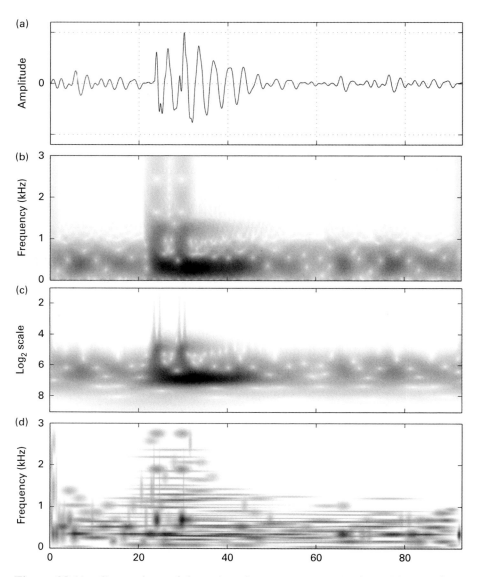

Figure 38.11   Comparison of three time-frequency representations. (a) Waveform of a 100 ms extract from *Pictor alpha* (2003) by Curtis Roads. (b) Spectrogram from short-time Fourier transform. (c) Scalogram from discrete wavelet transform using Gabor wavelet. (d) Wivigram from atomic decomposition using a dictionary of Gabor atoms. From Sturm et al. (2009).

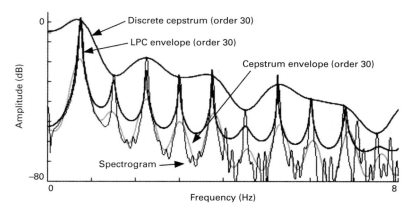

Figure 38.12 Comparing several spectrum estimators. The cepstrum finds the overall spectrum envelope. LPC is best at extracting spectral peaks. (See chapter 34 for an explanation of cepstrum.) From IRCAM (2011).

The AR method takes in several input samples and then uses the most recent sample as a reference. It tries to "predict" this sample from a sum of past samples weighted by filter coefficients. As a side effect of this prediction, the AR algorithm fits an inverse filter to the spectrum of the input signal. It is this side effect that is of musical interest. When the inverse filter is itself inverted—a trivial procedure—the resulting filter response is an estimate of the spectrum of the input signal.

The AR method predicts the tth value of a signal according to the equation

$$signal[t] = \sum_{i=1}^{p} \{coeff[i] \times signal[t - i]\} - noise[t]$$

That is, the predicted value $signal(t)$ is calculated by convolving the p number of prediction filter coefficients with the p known values of *signal*. (Convolution is described in chapter 29.) The choice of p is complicated. Too low a value for p produces an overly smoothed spectrum; too high a choice of p results introduces spurious peaks. So this parameter has to be adjusted depending on the application (Moorer 1979c; Kay and Marple 1981). Iterative methods for choosing p exist. The goodness of fit of the prediction can be measured as p increases from a small value. When there is no further improvement in the fit, the process stops.

Usually $noise(t)$ is assumed to be a white-noise-driven signal that is filtered to yield a spectrum matching the input signal. Several algorithms employ *linear regression*, which models the relationship between two variables, to compute the filter coefficients from a block of data. Hence the term *autoregression*. This process is carried out by matrix operations (Burg 1967; Makhoul 1975; Markle 1972; Markel and Gray 1976; Bowen and Brown 1980). Refer to Kay and Marple (1981) for a comparison of these methods.

Autoregressive Moving Average Analysis

The AR method is an efficient model for smooth, continuous spectra with sharp peaks but no deep nulls. Hence it does not model well sounds such as nasal vowels—where there are holes in the spectrum—or percussive impulses (snare drum, cymbals, etc.) where its prediction error is large. For these types of sounds a better choice may be a generalization of the AR method called the *autoregressive moving average* (ARMA) method. ARMA derives an output sample by a combination of both past input values and past output values. Hence an ARMA filter has both poles and zeros and is potentially more accurate than an AR approach. ARMA filters are much more costly from a computational standpoint than AR, however.

Source and Parameter Analysis

In some types of analysis, notably AR, cepstrum analysis (described in chapter 34), and the *physical model* approach (described in chapter 18), the goal of the analysis is not simply to tally up the frequencies present in a signal, but rather to recover source information, such as the parameters of the excitation and the resonance needed to resynthesize that sound. This approach is useful for certain sounds that have musical interest, such as snare drum hits and cymbal crashes. These types of sounds carry a great deal of information about their source, such as their size, mass, geometry, and the material from which they are made. Another application of source and parameter analysis is the separation of multiple sound sources. Indeed, the scientific motivation for these techniques has been their use in separating a signal from noise or in resolving several mixed signals (Kashino and Tanaka 1993).

Parameter Estimation

All sound analysis is a form of *parameter estimation* that tries to analyze the incoming sound in terms of the parameter settings that would be needed to approximate that sound with a given synthesis method (Tenney 1965; Justice 1979; Mian and Tisato 1984). For example, we can think of Fourier analysis as a kind of parameter estimation method for sine wave resynthesis because it computes all the frequencies, amplitudes, and phases needed to approximate the input sound.

In theory, parameter estimation can be applied to any synthesis technique. In practice, successful simulation of a given input sound by an arbitrary synthesis method is not guaranteed. Numerous attempts to develop parameter estimation analyses for frequency modulation synthesis, for example, resulted in gross approximations of the original input sound. No universal analysis/ resynthesis technique exists that is optimal for all sounds. Certain techniques were not made for specific types of sounds.

In general, parameter estimation employs *adaptive* signal-processing algorithms that try to minimize the error between the input signal and the simulation through adjusting the parameters of the simulation model. In a real-time system the measurements and adjustments must be made with the time period of a single sample, forcing compromises on mathematically ideal solutions.

Analysis by Walsh and Prony Functions

Fourier's method adds together sine waves to reproduce a given input signal. But sine waves are just one instance of a large class of functions that can be used to decompose and then replicate a given input function. *Walsh functions* (square waves) and *complex exponentials* (sinusoids with a decaying amplitude envelope) are just two of these basic units. Innumerable other functions can be conceived, but because these two have special properties and have already been applied to music, we discuss them next.

Walsh Functions

The main advantage of Walsh analysis is that its basic unit—the binary pulse or square wave—seems natural to implementation in digital systems, seemingly more natural than a sinusoidal wave, for example. A disadvantage of Walsh analysis is that it breaks down a signal into a combination of so-called *sequencies* that are not directly related to the frequency domain. Because chapter 10 explains Walsh functions in more detail, we refer the reader to that discussion.

Prony's Method

Damped sinusoids are the basic units in what is called *Prony's method* of analysis (Kay and Marple 1981; Marple 1987; LaRoche and Rodet 1989). *Damped sinusoids* start with a sharp attack but are abruptly attenuated, typically by an exponential decay. The technique is named after Gaspard Riche, Baron de Prony, who originally developed a method for analyzing the expansion of various gases (Prony 1795). The modern version of the technique has evolved from Prony's original method and is similar to the AR methods described previously.

Prony's method is now a family of related techniques that model an input signal as a combination of damped sinusoids plus noise (Kay and Marple 1981). Like AR techniques, Prony's method estimates a set of coefficients based on past input samples. But instead of driving a filter, as in AR methods, the coefficients in Prony's method drive the frequency, damping factor, amplitude, and phase of a set of damped sinusoids that approximate the input signal. Prony's method is turned into a spectrum analysis technique by taking the FFT of the output signal emitted by Prony's method. An advantage of Prony's method over AR techniques is that it yields phase information that makes for more accurate resynthesis. Refer to Marple (1987) for an algorithmic description of the method.

In computer music, Prony's method has been applied in the analysis stage of the CHANT synthesis system (d'Alessandro and Rodet 1989; see chapter 10) and in an experimental analysis/resynthesis system by LaRoche (1989a, b). LaRoche used it to analyze and resynthesize damped percussive sounds, such as glockenspiel, vibraphone, marimba, low piano tones, and gong. According to LaRoche, the results were not promising with high piano tones and cymbals.

In comparing Prony's method to Fourier analysis, LaRoche (1989a) noted that in general, Prony's method is more sensitive to its parameter settings than Fourier analysis. Users must meticulously adjust the analysis parameters; otherwise, the resulting spectrum estimation bears little resemblance to the actual spectrum. In contrast, the primary parameter in Fourier methods is the analysis window. The results of Fourier analysis may be incomplete and imprecise, but they are never totally incoherent.

When the parameters of Prony's method are properly set, it has little problem accounting for inharmonic partials and can resolve multiple closely spaced sinusoids; for example, refer to figure 38.1j. By contrast, Fourier analysis arbitrarily divides up the spectrum into equally spaced harmonic partials and lumps closely spaced sinusoids into an overall formant-like peak in the spectrum. The Prony method is limited to analyzing up to about fifty partials because beyond this point the polynomials used to calculate it do not converge to a solution. Prony's method is more intensive computationally than Fourier analysis.

To summarize, in Prony's method we have an analysis method that is good at resolving accurately a certain class of signals, in particular percussive tones consisting of a few sinusoidal components, provided that it is carefully adjusted beforehand.

Auditory Models

We can cluster sound analysis methods around two poles: those that try to emulate the known behavior of the human hearing system and those that do not. In the former category are *auditory models,* and in the latter category are mathematically inspired techniques like the Wigner distribution. Auditory models usually start from a form of spectrum analysis, but this stage is merely the starting point for elaborate postprocessing according to a computational model of hearing mechanisms (Mellinger 1991; Lyon, Katsiamis, and E. Drakakis 2010).

The goals of auditory modeling are twofold: (1) clearer views of musical signals that are more in accord with what we perceive, and (2) deeper understanding of human hearing mechanisms by using models in simulation experiments. Here we discuss briefly three auditory models, namely, the Mel-frequency cepstrum, cochleagram, and the correlogram.

Mel Frequency Cepstrum

The *Mel frequency cepstrum* (MFC) models audio as a source and filter, on a frequency scale that approximately models the critical bands in the cochlea (Mermelstein 1976). (The concept of cepstrum is presented in chapter 34.) Information about the source appears as low cepstral coefficients, and these are used when attempting to extract information about instrument timbres present in an audio signal.

MFC is commonly used in speech recognition systems, so it has been applied in separating sung vocals in mixed music and other applications in music information retrieval (Leglaive, Hennequin, and R. Badeau 2015). (See chapter 35.) The MFC is derived from a linear cosine transform of a log power spectrum on a nonlinear mel scale of frequency. Cepstral coefficients capture the spectral envelope, extracting primarily the resonances or *formants* (Smith 2011).

The MFC is derived as follows:

1. Apply the Fourier transform of a windowed excerpt of a signal to obtain a spectrum.

2. Map the powers of the spectrum onto the mel scale, using triangular overlapping bands.

3. Compute the logs of the powers at each of the mel frequencies.

4. Apply the discrete cosine transform on the list of mel log powers, as if it were a signal.

The MFC coefficients are the amplitudes of the resulting data set.

Cochleagrams

The *cochlea* is the tiny snail-like organ in the inner ear that maps incoming vibrations into nerve impulses that are transmitted to the brain (Buser and Imbert 1992). Each place along the length of the cochlea responds to vibrations broadly tuned around a center frequency specific to that place. Auditory scientists have measured the average firing rate of the neurons along the length of the cochlea and have determined that they are related to different frequencies perceived by the ear.

A software model of the cochlea's response to incoming signals is called a *cochleagram* (Slaney and Lyon 1992). Rather than mapping frequency to the vertical axis, like the spectrogram, the cochleagram maps *cochlear place* to the vertical axis. That is, it represents the response of different parts of the cochlea to incoming sound. When the cochleagram is plotted at a coarse resolution it looks something like a sonogram representation but with an enhanced representation of onsets. A more important difference between the sonogram and the cochleagram can be seen in figure 38.13. This zoomed-in view on a high-resolution cochleagram image reveals the timing of the individual glottal pulses of a speech signal. Thus the cochleagram provides a way to study both low-level timing (onsets) and spectrum.

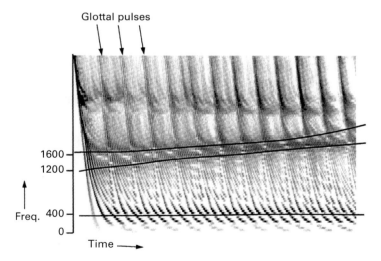

Figure 38.13   Expanded cochleagram of the American diphthong *ree*. The horizontal lines indicate the first three formant tracks. The vertical lines indicate glottal pulses, which are tilted slightly due to the natural delay through the cochlea. From Slaney and Lyon (1992).

Correlograms

Correlograms were proposed in the early 1950s by Licklider (1951, 1959), but it is only in the 1990s that they became practical from a computational standpoint. The correlogram starts with a model of the cochlea and follows this with an autocorrelation of the signals emitted by each channel of the cochleagram (Slaney and Lyon 1992). This autocorrelation is done on a frame-by frame or windowed basis 30 to 120 times per second, depending on the application.

The resulting correlogram is a movie depicting a three-dimensional function of frequency, time, and autocorrelation delay (Slaney and Lyon 1991a, b).

The position along the cochlea is plotted on the vertical axis, with high frequencies corresponding to the upper portion of the image. The horizontal axis shows autocorrelation time delay. As in a conventional sonogram, dark areas represent areas of higher amplitude. Sounds with a strong sense of pitch and harmonic structure show up as vertical lines at autocorrelation lag times where a large number of cochlear cells are firing at the same period. (See Slaney and Lyon 1992 for an application of the correlogram to pitch detection.) When the pitch increases, the dominant vertical line moves to the left to a lag representing the shorter period. Horizontal bands represent large amounts of energy in a frequency band, such as a formant. Noisy, unpitched sounds show up only as horizontal bands, with no vertical pitch lines.

Recall from chapter 32 that the autocorrelation of a sine tone is itself a sine wave, with peaks spaced at subharmonic periods of the fundamental period f, that is, $f, f/2, f/3, \ldots$ Similarly, a single sine tone passed through a correlogram shows up as a series of vertical lines, corresponding to "virtual" subharmonics of the fundamental period, which is in the leftmost position. We do not necessarily hear these subharmonics; they are an artifact of the periodicity-seeking nature of the autocorrelation function.

Figure 38.14 shows three frames of a correlogram movie, taken at 0 seconds, 600 ms, and 2 seconds, respectively. In this case we see the striking of a chime. At first there are many harmonics, and the sound is rich. Different overtones decay at various rates, as shown in the second frame. By the last frame there are only two components left.

The advantage of the correlogram is that it presents a time-sensitive simultaneous display of pitch and formant information. The horizontal or delay dimension represents pitch, and the vertical dimension represents spectrum. Calculating the correlogram is a computationally intensive operation. The correlogram has also been used as a basis for resynthesis (Slaney, Naar, and Lyon 1994).

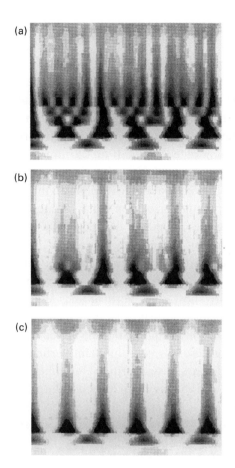

(a)

(b)

(c)

Figure 38.14 Correlogram of the striking of a chime. (a) Onset. (b) 600 ms. (c) 2.0 seconds. The U-shaped curve, particularly evident in (a), results from successive divisions of the grid in time—as if you were looking at the waveform peaks of a band of frequencies, with low frequencies (and therefore longer periods between peaks) at the bottom. From Slaney and Lyon (1992).

Higher Order Spectrum Analysis

Another approach to mention in passing is a family of techniques called *higher order spectra* (HOS) or *polyspectra* analysis. The goal of HOS analysis in general is to characterize nonlinear systems (Nikias and Raghuveer 1987; Mendel 1991). Since many instrument sounds start from a nonlinear excitation, HOS methods can be used as a tool for analyzing this source. The advantage of HOS analysis is that it shows the relationships between components. This is especially important in nonlinear systems, because they always contain intermodulation effects. HOS can show where the behavior of a component derives from other components through a nonlinear process. The method has been used to identify instrumental sources in music information retrieval (Brown, Houix, and McAdams 2001). A software package for signal processing with HOS is the Hi-Spec Toolbox for MATLAB (Swami, Mendel, and Nikias 2001).

39 *Spectrum Analysis by Atomic Decomposition*

Bob L. T. Sturm

Fundamentals

Approximation Theory
Bases and Dictionaries
Sparsity and Error

Methods

Greedy Decomposition
Optimization

Applications

Sound Modeling and Analysis
Sound Visualization
Sound Synthesis

Advanced Topics

Atomic decomposition can be seen as an analytical dual to *granular synthesis* (chapter 13). Just as Fourier analysis shows how one can build a sound using a set of sinusoids, atomic decomposition methods show how one can build it using a set of grains—called *atoms* in this method. This makes atomic decomposition methods powerful tools for the analysis, synthesis, and visualization of sound. We first review the background and fundamentals of approximation theory, which forms a foundation for atomic decomposition. We then discuss two main classes of atomic decomposition methods. We then survey several applications of atomic decomposition methods for sound analysis, visualization, and synthesis.

Fundamentals

We begin by introducing the basics of approximation theory in signal processing. Next, we present the notations of bases and dictionaries. Finally we present the concepts of sparsity and error in the context of atomic decomposition.

Approximation Theory

Computers have limited memory with finite precision, so they cannot acquire or reconstruct real-world signals or data exactly. The success of digital computers thus critically depends upon approximation. *Approximation theory* (Hamming 1987; Christensen and Christensen 2005) provides key methods and guarantees for expressing real-world signals given finite precision. Approximating a signal entails *decomposing* it into a finite number of functions.

For example, Fourier analysis shows how we can express a signal $y(t)$—given that it satisfies particular conditions—using an infinite number of sinusoids:

$$y(t) = \int_{-\infty}^{\infty} Y(f)e^{i2\pi ft}df = \int_{-\infty}^{\infty} Y(f)(\cos 2\pi ft + i \sin 2\pi ft)df$$

where $Y(f)$ is the complex amplitude of the sinusoid with frequency f Hz. Because we cannot evaluate this expression with finite memory, we must make a choice of which sinusoids to keep, among the infinite number of sinusoids. The exact expression of $y(t)$ above thus becomes a decomposition into a finite number N of sinusoids

$$y(t) \approx \sum_{n=1}^{N} a_n \cos(2\pi f_n t + \varphi_n)$$

where a_n is the real amplitude of the sinusoid having frequency f_n Hz and phase φ_n radians. Approximation theory tells us which N sinusoids to keep, guaranteeing that our approximation of $y(t)$ has the precision we desire.

We can decompose, or approximate, our signal $y(t)$ in many other ways. For instance, the previous Fourier decomposition uses sinusoids that exist for all time. Short-time Fourier analysis instead decomposes a signal as a sum of time-localized sinusoids, or sinusoids that exist for a finite duration at a specific time. (See chapter 37.) At the extreme, we can shrink the duration of a sinusoid to become a single impulse at a point in time. When we decompose a signal using a collection of impulses spaced uniformly in time, we are essentially performing uniform time-domain sampling. (See chapter 3.) The Nyquist theorem is then an outcome of approximation theory, enabling the reconstruction of the analog signal from its impulse decomposition. Wavelet analysis provides other decompositions (Mallat 2009).

Bases and Dictionaries

A decomposition of a signal enables it to be stored, analyzed, modeled, and modified. Approximation theory tells us how to build a decomposition from a collection of functions we wish to use, for example, sines, impulses, and wavelets. Hence, a key aspect of approximation and decomposition is how one selects a collection of functions.

An important collection is a *basis*: a collection of functions such that any signal from the space spanned by the collection can be exactly represented by one unique sum of the functions in the collection. For instance, the *Fourier basis* is the infinite set of all complex sinusoids with frequencies from minus to positive infinity. Fourier analysis shows how we can express any signal (satisfying certain conditions) as a unique infinite sum over the Fourier basis. In a discrete domain of dimension N, the discrete Fourier basis (*sine basis*) is a set of N discrete complex sinusoids, each with length N. Fourier analysis shows how we can express any complex sequence of length N as a unique sum of these N functions. This leads to the discrete Fourier transform, which is implemented by the *Fast Fourier Transform* (FFT). Another basis for the same space is the set of N *Kronecker delta* functions (impulses or *spikes*). This is just the set of all unique length-N sequences that are all zeros except a single 1. We can thus decompose any length-N sequence as a unique sum in the sine or spike basis.

When we combine collections of functions, such as the sine basis with the spike basis, we form a larger collection called a *dictionary* (Mallat 1993; Elad 2010). We call each element of the collection an *atom*. The decomposition of a signal over a dictionary is called *atomic decomposition* (Chen,

Donoho, and Saunders 1998; Donoho and Huo 2001). When a dictionary contains more atoms than are necessary to represent any signal in the space spanned by the atoms, we call the dictionary *overcomplete*. A basis is called *complete*. Essentially, an overcomplete dictionary produces an infinite number of possible decompositions of a signal.

A useful metaphor of a dictionary and atomic decomposition is the following (Mallat 1993): each atom of a dictionary can describe a specific structure in a signal. Some atoms have similar meanings, and others are unrelated. When we increase the number of atoms in a dictionary, we enrich the vocabulary with which we can meaningfully describe a signal. The atomic decomposition of a signal over a dictionary thus involves finding those atoms that best describe or explain it for our desired goals.

To make the above more concrete, consider the sine and spike bases above. We can see them as providing completely different information about a signal. A finite-length sequence decomposed over the sine basis tells us about its *frequency content*—what frequencies are present or absent in the signal—but nothing about its *spike content*—what spikes are present or absent in the signal. In contrast, a finite-length sequence decomposed over the spike basis provides information about its spike content but no information about its frequency content. Hence, when we wish to decompose a signal over a basis, we must decide what information it is we want, for example, frequency or time, and then choose the appropriate basis. However, what if our signal has some structures that are sine-like and some structures that are spike-like, as in the top left of figure 39.1? Expressing this signal in only one basis can limit our analysis; however, we can combine the sine and spike bases to form a dictionary, and then decompose the signal over this bigger collection of functions.

When we combine many bases to form a dictionary, we increase the potential richness of our decompositions, but we also destroy uniqueness of the decomposition. With one basis, there exists one and only one decomposition of a signal. If we combine two bases, we have an infinite number of possible decompositions. This can add complexity to the process of decomposition because the problem becomes one of finding the "best" decomposition among an infinite number of possibilities. So, we must define what we mean by "best."

Sparsity and Error

One important qualifier of "best" is *sparsity*, or the number atoms we select from a dictionary to be in the signal decomposition, where fewer is better. Sparsity appears to be natural as well. Evidence supports the hypothesis that

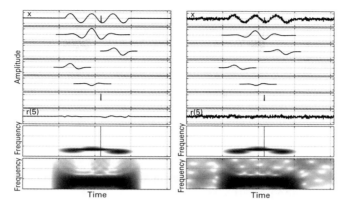

Figure 39.1 The original clean signal (top left), which is then corrupted by noise (top right). The five waveforms below these are the atoms selected by matching pursuit from a dictionary of Gabor atoms (modulated Gaussian windows) and Dirac impulses. The final waveforms $r(5)$ show the resulting residual (the initial signal with the five atoms removed). The two time-frequency plots at the bottom of each figure are the *wivigrams* of the decomposition, which is a superposition of the Wigner-Ville distributions of the individual atoms selected by matching pursuit, and the short-term Fourier transform (STFT). The time-frequency localization of each wivigram is clearly superior to that of the STFT.

the mammalian auditory system itself operates using principles of sparsity (Lewicki 2002; Smith and Lewicki 2005a, b). The second important quality of "best" is *approximation error*, or how close our approximation is to the original signal. We wish to find an approximation that is accurate.

Hence, the best atomic decomposition is the one using the fewest number of atoms but produces the least error. Sparsity and approximation error, however, are at odds with each other. In order to make an accurate approximation of a signal, we may need to use a large number of atoms; but to have a very sparse decomposition, we may need to accept a large amount of error. The number of ways we can handle this trade-off and the computational complexities involved motivate numerous algorithms for the atomic decomposition of signal. In the following section, we present an overview of the two main classes of methods.

Methods

There are two main classes of sparse decomposition methods. First, *greedy decomposition* iteratively decomposes a signal until some pre-specified criterion is met. These methods are computationally simple but can fail to produce "ideal" solutions. The second main class of methods, *optimization*, poses the problem of decomposition as a minimization of some function subject to given constraints. These methods are computationally complex but can produce solutions that are more sparse and precise than greedy methods. Kereliuk and Depalle (2011) provide a deeper review of these methods for the audio domain.

Greedy Decomposition

Greedy decomposition applies a simple iterative approach to decomposition (Tropp 2004; Mallat 2009; Elad 2010). At each step, such an algorithm finds an optimal atom in the dictionary, adds it to the signal model, removes it from the residual (or approximation error), and repeats the process. The algorithm constructs the *residual* by subtracting each atom it selects from the previous residual, starting with the original signal. The algorithm repeats this process until it has selected a prespecified number of atoms or the residual energy is below some prespecified threshold. The most basic algorithm, called *matching pursuit* (Mallat and Zhang 1993), defines the *optimal* atom as the one most correlated with the residual. The matching pursuit algorithm has in fact been "discovered" several times (Friedman and Tukey 1974; Huber 1985). Figure 39.1 shows several steps of the matching pursuit decomposition with a dictionary of Gabor atoms and spikes for a signal with and without noise.

Many varieties of greedy decomposition methods have been developed, including *orthogonal matching pursuit* (Pati, Rezaiifar, and Krishnaprasad 1993; Tropp 2004), *orthogonal least squares* (Blumensath and Davies 2007), *psychoacoustic-adaptive matching pursuit* (Heusdens, Vafin, and Kleijn 2002), and *cyclic matching pursuit* (Christensen and Jensen 2007; Sturm and Christensen 2010). These all take slightly different approaches to selecting atoms and can produce better decompositions, but at an increased computational complexity over the basic matching pursuit algorithm. Approximate greedy methods, such as *gradient pursuit* (Blumensath and Davies 2008) and *stochastic atom selection* (Peel et al. 2012), aim to reduce this complexity yet still produce acceptable decompositions.

Some greedy methods attempt to take advantage of prior knowledge about the signal. For instance, *harmonic matching pursuit* (Gribonval and Bacry 2003) uses a dictionary of atoms that can efficiently model harmonic content. *Molecular matching pursuit* (Daudet 2006) models tonal and transient structures by building "molecules" of atoms during decomposition. *Stereo matching pursuit* (Gribonval 2002) takes advantage of correspondences between audio channels. These provide methods for building representations rich with meaning and ways to access content (described in the "Applications" section further on).

A major advantage of greedy decomposition methods is that they are computationally simple. Dictionaries can have billions of atoms and can even be virtually limitless (Goodwin 1997; Goodwin and Vetterli 1999; Gribonval 1999, 2001). The Matching Pursuit Toolkit (Krstulovic and Gribonval 2006) provides a free software library for the decomposition of recorded audio signals over user-defined dictionaries.

A disadvantage of greedy methods is that they do not consider the global solution. A greedy algorithm selects each atom on the basis of its similarity to the residual, regardless of what has been selected before and what will be selected after. If it selects a poor atom, then it may have to select many other atoms to correct the mistake. These additional atoms do not model anything in the original signal (Sturm et al. 2008; Sturm 2009; Sturm and Shynk 2010). Greedy methods can thus fail to produce the *best* model in terms of both the sparsity and desired approximation error.

Optimization

Optimization methods are important in many domains (Boyd and Vandenberghe 2004). For instance, a company might wish to find a way to maximize profit subject to a finite amount of resources. A delivery service might wish to minimize fuel costs while maximizing the number of deliveries made. For sparse decomposition, we can apply optimization methods to produce solutions by simultaneously balancing requirements for sparsity and approximation error. That is, we can define the problem as trying to find an approximation of a signal using no more than a certain number of atoms but producing the smallest approximation error possible. Or alternatively, we can define the problem as trying to find an approximation of a signal that is within some approximation error but uses the smallest number of atoms. Solving these problems is not computationally feasible (Davis et al. 1997), but it becomes much easier if we relax the sparsity constraint by replacing it with a function that promotes sparse solutions but aids computability. An example is the *solution l1-norm*: the sum of the magnitudes of all atoms selected from a dictionary.

When we pose the optimization problem as minimizing the residual squared error subject to a constraint on the solution l1-norm, we are applying what is called the *principle of basis pursuit denoising* (Chen, Donoho, and Saunders 1998). This principle was previously "discovered" in statistics, where it is known as the regression approach *least absolute shrinkage and selection operator* (LASSO) (Tibshirani 1996). Chen, Donoho, and Saunders (1998) and Tibshirani (1996) present a variety of examples of their application of this principle.

Finding a solution to an optimization problem posed with the principle of basis pursuit denoising involves interior point or simplex methods (Tibshirani 1996; Chen, Donoho, and Saunders 1998; Boyd and Vandenberghe 2004; Figueiredo et al. 2007; Elad 2010). Contrasted with greedy methods, these optimization methods essentially *scale down* or refine a solution rather than build it up (Chen, Donoho, and Saunders 1998). The complexity of solving such optimization problems increases with the size of the dictionary, however, and so it is rare to see such methods applied using dictionaries consisting of billions of atoms.

Applications

We now present some applications of atomic decomposition in the domains of sound and music analysis and modeling, visualization, and synthesis. Broader overviews can be found in Plumbley et al. (2009) and Sturm et al. (2009).

Sound Modeling and Analysis

Atomic decomposition can be applied to sound modeling and analysis to produce concise and/or informative descriptions of the variety of content in audio signals. Ravelli et al. (2008) use greedy atomic decomposition with an eight-times overcomplete modified discrete cosine transform dictionary to produce compressed audio that has better fidelity than standard compression at very low bit rates. Heusdens, Vafin, and Kleijn (2002), Christensen and Jensen (2007) apply greedy approaches to perceptually based audio coding, whereas Christensen and Sturm (2011) apply optimization methods for the same purpose.

Atomic decomposition provides adaptive methods for decomposing or modeling sounds at levels of content that can be higher than basic atoms, such as tonal and transient structures (Daudet 2006), instrument-specific sets of harmonic atoms (Leveau et al. 2008), or multiple pitches (Adalbjörnsson 2014). The molecular matching pursuit of Daudet (2006) breaks a music audio signal into transient structures and tonal structures. This separation allows higher-level processing without interference between the two, for example, visualization and synthesis. The work of Leveau et al. (2008) assembles dictionaries of harmonic atoms (Gribonval and Bacry 2003) specific to particular musical instruments. The atomic decomposition of a music recording with these dictionaries thus results in a mid-level representation that can then be used to identify and transcribe the playing instruments. Atomic decomposition can also be seen as feature extraction used to describe the content of a music recording for indexing and retrieval applications (Lyon, Katsiamis, and Drakakis 2010; Ravelli et al. 2010).

Motivated by the classic work of Lewicki (2002) and Smith and Lewicki (2005a, 2005b), Blumensath and Davies (2006) and Abdallah and Plumbley (2006) apply sparse approximation to *learning* dictionaries from music signals. The resulting atoms are relatable to music note–like content that can be specific to instruments, e.g., piano, guitar and vocals. These results are quite remarkable because they come independent of any musicological information. In other words, this procedure independently finds a concise way to describe music recordings (monophonic recordings of many voices), and arrives at something with musical meaning (notes, timings, and dynamics). Such methods can be used to help separate sources in a recording and to transcribe music recordings.

Sound Visualization

Along with analysis and modeling, the atomic decomposition of a sound provides ways to visualize it. Since an atomic decomposition is a sum of atoms, we can visualize a sound by adding together visualizations of the individual atoms. For instance, if each atom in a dictionary has energy centered about some location in time and frequency, we can create a *spikegram* of a sound by placing a dot in the time-frequency domain for each atom of its decomposition (Smith and Lewicki 2005b; Manzagol, Bertine-Mahieux, and Eck 2008). The top of figure 39.2 shows a spikegram representation of the music composition *Pictor Alpha* (2004) by Curtis Roads, which we decompose with the Matching Pursuit Toolkit (Krstulovic and Gribonval 2006) using a dictionary of over five million Gabor atoms. This dictionary contains Gabor atoms of length 4, 8, 16, 32, 64, 128, 256, 512 and 1,024 samples.

A *Gabor atom* is a time-localized sinusoid or, equivalently, a time-shifted and modulated Gaussian window. Nobel-prize winning physicist Dennis Gabor refers to such an atom as an "acoustic quanta" (1947) because its energy is maximally concentrated in time and frequency. In fact, the short-term Fourier transform can be seen as the magnitudes of the projection of a signal onto a dictionary of Gabor atoms of one duration.

Mallat and Zhang (1993) use a dictionary of Gabor atoms in their decomposition of a speech signal and then visualize the speech by summing together the *Wigner-Ville distributions* of the individual atoms—a visualization we call a *wivigram* (Sturm et al. 2009). The Wigner-Ville distribution has a time-frequency resolution superior to that provided by the spectrogram (Cohen

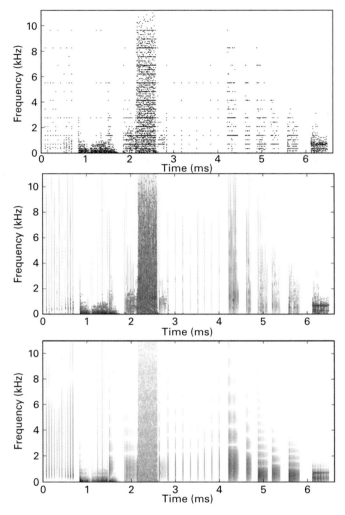

Figure 39.2   Decomposition of the first seven seconds of *Pictor Alpha* (2004) by Curtis Roads with the Matching Pursuit Toolkit (Krstulovic and Gribonval 2006) and a dictionary of 5,825,779 Gabor atoms. Top: Spikegram representation, a pattern of dots that indicate the precise onset of events. Center: Wivigram representation. Bottom: Projection onto short-time Fourier transform dictionary.

1989; Preis and Georgopoulos 1999; Pielemeier et al. 1996; Mallat 2009). The center part of figure 39.2 shows a wivigram of the matching pursuit decomposition, using 5,000 atoms. In comparison with the bottom image, a projection of the same signal but on a dictionary of short-time Fourier transform atoms, we can see greater clarity in time and frequency. Other techniques exploiting sparsity can also enhance visualization of sound in the time-frequency plane (Gardner and Magnasco 2006; Kereliuk and Depalle 2013).

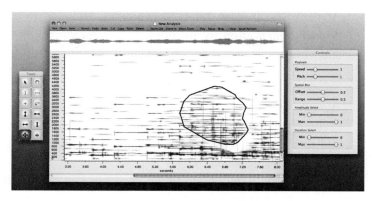

Figure 39.3   Screenshot of the application SCATTER. We loaded the results of a matching pursuit decomposition of a musical signal using a multiscale Gabor dictionary. The center window shows the wivigram representation and the time-domain resynthesis above it. With the tools at the left, we can select specific atoms or regions of atoms to adjust. Here, a group of atoms has been selected with the lasso tool and displaced in time and frequency. The pane at right shows a variety of options for further selection; for example, select only those atoms in our group having a minimum duration or amplitude.

A wivigram can also provide an interface to modify an atomic decomposition, as shown in figure 39.3. With such a display, musicians can perform many operations on atoms in the decomposition, such as selection, deletion, modification, and so on. For instance, after selecting all short atoms in the decomposition of a signal, one can modify its transient content; after selecting the long atoms, one can modify its tonal content. This is one motivation for the molecular matching pursuit (Daudet 2006).

Sound Synthesis

Because sparse approximation can be seen as regression (Huber 1985; Tibshirani 1996), a natural application of atomic decomposition is denoising. In this case, one can define *noise* as any structures in a signal that are not similar to the atoms in a dictionary. We can see this in figure 39.1, in which the atoms selected for the noisy signal are nearly the same as for the clean one. Mallat and Zhang (1993) show a simple example of denoising speech by using a dictionary of Gabor atoms. Dörfler et al. (2010) and Siedenburg and Dörfler (2011) design some advanced approaches to denoising using atomic decomposition. Other possibilities are declipping audio (Adler et al. 2012) and repairing other corruptions (Kereliuk 2012).

Because atomic decomposition is granular synthesis in reverse, it motivates many unique opportunities for sound synthesis and modification

(Bascou and Pottier 2005; Sturm et al. 2009; Kereliuk 2012). If we can describe each atom by meaningful parameters, such as scale, frequency, and time shift, we can select very specific components of an atomic decomposition for resynthesis, as shown in figure 39.3. Removing only the short-scale atoms in a decomposition can remove all of the transients. We can thus see this process as a kind of *atomic filtering*. We can also gradually resynthesize a sound by increasing the atom density (sonic coalescence), or make a sound evaporate by decreasing the density (sonic disintegration).

Parametric manipulation involves changing the parameters of the atoms used in an atomic decomposition. For instance, we can pitch-shift or time-stretch a sound recording by adjusting frequency and/or time shifts of the atoms of its decomposition (Sturm et al. 2006). If short-scale atoms model the transients in a signal, then one might preserve their information by only adjusting the scales of longer atoms. Other unique effects can be achieved, such as randomly changing time shifts of atoms (*jitter*), increasing atom scales (*bleed*). We can create other exotic effects by substituting one dictionary for another or morphing between decompositions (Collins and Sturm 2011).

Although an atomic decomposition makes sound malleable at an atomic level, problems can arise when *dark energy* (Sturm et al. 2008) becomes audible. Transforming the atoms of a decomposition can break fragile relationships between atoms added by a decomposition to correct its "mistakes." This reinforces the fact that atomic decomposition is approximation, which can be at odds with requirements for "high quality" sound transformation. Nonetheless, as with other synthesis techniques, atomic decomposition can have characteristics that favor particular kinds of sound qualities, for example, fire (Kersten and Purwins 2012), water, or other textures.

Advanced Topics

Two advanced topics are (1) how to choose a dictionary (Tosic and Frossard 2011), and (2) how to learn a dictionary. Lewicki (2002), Smith and Lewicki (2005a, 2005b), Blumensath and Davies (2006), and Abdallah and Plumbley (2006) all show how to learn dictionaries for audio coding and music description. Aharon, Elad, and Bruckstein (2006) present a general algorithm for learning overcomplete dictionaries. Which algorithms or dictionaries are best depends on one's specific objectives.

Much is yet to be explored in the atomic decomposition of audio and music signals (Plumbley et al. 2009). These methods are much more computationally intensive and complex than standard analysis techniques based on the Fourier transform. However, with increased computational resources, real-time atomic decomposition is nearing reality. For instance, the Matching Pursuit Toolkit (Krstulovic and Gribonval 2006) can run at four times real time. However, it must be remembered that the latency depends on how the signal is related to the atoms in a dictionary. If there is a strong relationship, then we can produce a good approximation using only a handful of atoms. If the relationship is very weak, then it might take millions of atoms to produce as good an approximation.

VI The Musician's Interface

40   *Musical Input Devices*

Conducting: Remote Control and Remote Sensing

Responsive Input Devices and Haptic Technology

An instrument is the most traditional musician's interface, mediating gesture and sound. Virtuoso musicians are capable of great subtlety and grace in the range of expressions that can be communicated through instruments by means of gestures of the mouth, hands, and feet. These inflections of the human body infuse music with signs of life: breath, body rhythm, a sense of effort, motion, and feeling. Listeners react instinctively to these performance qualities; instrumental virtuosity can lift even a mundane composition onto a higher plane of interest.

This chapter explores the instruments of real-time performance: *musical input devices* (also called *controllers*) played by musicians. Recent years have seen an explosion of development of custom musical input devices (Jensenius and Lyons 2017). This is partly thanks to the advent of low-cost microcontroller circuit boards from Arduino (figure 40.1), Raspberry Pi, and Bela among others. Many types of inexpensive sensors can be connected to these circuit boards. Some sensors capture human gestures, and others sense the environment. This makes it relatively easy to build a custom interactive controller. A worldwide *maker* movement supports this trend (*Make* 2019). Crowd-sourced funding enables niche instrument builders to continue experimentation.

Inexpensive videogame controllers can be repurposed as music controllers. Smart watches, mobile phones, and tablets add to the mix of possibilities. DJ applications such as Serato support dozens of interactive controllers. Software toolkits let programmers quickly make touchscreen interfaces (Roberts and Höllerer 2011). A lively culture of independent instrument designers gathers at the annual New Instruments for Musical Expression (NIME) conferences. An example is the instrument maker known as glui,

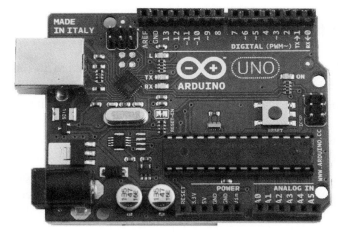

Figure 40.1 Arduino microcontroller board. Sensors can be attached to this board to turn it into a musical input device.

who originally worked at the Dutch center for interactive music STEIM. glui has built dozens of new instruments over the years (glui 2020). The book *PUSH TURN MOVE: Interface Design in Electronic Music* celebrates interfaces and their designers in a colorful coffee-table format (Bjørn 2017). Perry Cook (2017) enumerated principles for designing computer music controllers. O'Modhrain (2011) presented a framework for evaluating the effectiveness of digital musical instruments, taking into account studies in the field of human-computer interaction (HCI). Graham-Knight and Tzanetakis (2015) and Frid (2018) reviewed inclusive and adaptive instruments that are accessible to people with health conditions or impairments.

Following a historical background section, this chapter explores the ergonomics of input devices—their efficiency and ease of use. We examine temporal precision—how fast an instrument can respond to a human gesture. The next section examines the most popular input devices: musical keyboards. Then follows a look at controllers with *remote control* and *remote sensing* capabilities, giving performers more freedom. The final part of the chapter deals with *responsive input devices* that can be programmed to respond physically to a performer's gestures. This chapter also includes two tables and a photocollage that demonstrates the diversity of possible input devices.

To simplify the presentation we focus on control of synthesizers, but virtually everything in this chapter also applies to applications such as interactive sound art installations.

An input device is, of course, only one component of the technology of interactive performance. Other chapters cover performance software (chapter 41), MIDI (chapter 51), and Open Sound Control (chapter 52).

Advantages of Electronic Input Devices

A musician playing a traditional acoustic instrument must supply the energy for both controlling and producing the sound. Even a cleverly designed instrument is constrained by inescapable mechanical limitations. Simply obtaining a good basic sonority on many instruments requires a long period of practice and expert counsel. Some instruments are more physically difficult to play than others. For example, the large instruments of the lower registers (bass and baritone saxophones, double bass, and tuba) require more strength to play and may necessitate stretching to achieve proper note selection. Certain acoustic instruments are hard to play softly, and others are difficult to play loudly. Extremely high or low pitches may require extraordinary effort if they can be played at all. Retuning the instrument to a different scale may be arduous or impossible, and the timbre of the instrument is predetermined by its physical construction. All these constraints can go away with electronic input devices.

Electronics technology has sparked a new wave of instrument design (Bovermann et al. 2017). Input devices transduce human motion into electrical form. This transduction provides two main advantages. First, electronic input devices detach the control of sound from the need to power the sound; any one of dozens of input devices can control the same sound generator (figure 40.2). This translates into musical flexibility. With electronic instruments, a single wind controller can create low bass sounds as easily as high soprano sounds. Creating extremely soft or loud sounds requires minimum effort since the control is electronic. Of course, the detachment of sound control from sound production has a negative side—a reduction of the *feel* associated with producing a certain kind of sound. The section on responsive instruments discusses this problem and its palliatives. Arfib, Couturier, and Kessous (2005) analyzes the general problem of expressiveness in electronic instruments.

A second main advantage of electronic input devices is their tuning and timbral flexibility. Changing the scale on many electronic instruments is a matter of pressing a button; some allow users to create their own scales. Being able to add vibrato to a piano sound gives this familiar timbre a new expressiveness. The musical possibilities of instruments that can sound like a wooden flute one minute and Balinese jecogan the next—or that can play both at the same time—are empowering from a compositional standpoint.

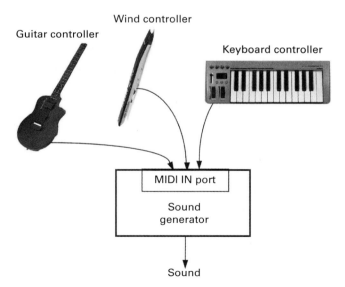

Figure 40.2   Electronic input devices detach the gesture from the sound production mechanism. Any one of a number of input devices can generate the same sound.

Model of an Input Device

A simple model of an input device is a *sensor* connected to an *electronic interface circuit* (figure 40.3). The sensor responds to a physical stimulus, such as:

light

sound

temperature

smell

humidity

electricity

magnetism

radio waves

kinetic energy (pressure, torque, inertia)

biometrics (bio-electricity, heart rate, muscle tension, etc.)

This response is translated by the interface circuit into either a *discrete* (on-off) or a *continuous* control signal. Refer to Paradiso (1997), Bongers (2000), and Tanaka (2009) for surveys of sensors and their applications in interactive music performance.

The sensor is typically a mechanical/analog device. At some point the interface circuit translates its output into digital form—usually a MIDI or OSC message. In commercial input devices, the sensor and the interface are combined in one unit that directly emits MIDI messages.

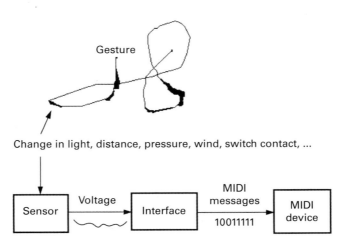

Figure 40.3   Model of an input device as a sensor connected to an electronic interface.

Background: History of Gestural Input to Computers

Decades of performance with analog electronic instruments preceded computer music experiments (Rhea 1972, 1984; Young 1989). Today's digital performance systems grew out of a strong tradition of live electronic music as well as free jazz and improvisation (Mumma 1975; Battier 1981; Bernardini 1986; Valentino 1986). George Lewis (Roads 1985d; Lewis 2000, 2009) and Pamela Z (Lewis 2007) are pioneers of improvisation with digital technology.

Expressive electronic instruments such as the Theremin (1928), Ondes Martenot (1928), Croix Sonore (1934), Ondioline (1941), Electronic Sackbut (1948), and Mixtur-Trautonium (1949), among others, pioneered new performance techniques and electronic sounds decades before MIDI (figure 40.4).

Voltage Control

The modular analog synthesizers introduced in the 1970s operated by the principle of *voltage control*. In a voltage-controlled synthesizer, the pitch, amplitude, filter center frequency and many other parameters can be varied by applying a changing voltage to the *control input* jack on a synthesis module. Modular analog synthesizers were flexible because the musician could manipulate control voltages (scale, invert, smooth, etc.) and repatch interconnections between input devices and the modules they controlled.

An analog synthesizer can respond to a performer's gestures by means of *triggers* (for example, a trigger pulse is emitted when a performer first touches a key on a keyboard), *gates* (for example, a pulse whose duration corresponds to the time a performer holds down a key), faders and knobs, and pressure sensors. One of the more interesting control sources is an *envelope follower* that can track the amplitude envelope of any sound event fed into it and output a corresponding control voltage.

Digital Control

Working at Bell Telephone Laboratories, Mathews and Rosler (1969) pioneered research on the use of gestural input to digital computers. They developed a system in which users could draw line-segment control envelopes on a display screen with a light pen. In this same period, researchers at the National Research Council (Ottawa, Canada) developed a system for graphical interaction with a music notation editor via a mouse-like device. The Dartmouth digital synthesizer (Alonso, Appleton, and Jones 1977) was the first digital synthesizer to incorporate real-time controllers such as a keyboard, an assignable knob, and a bank of buttons and switches.

Figure 40.4   Robert Moog demonstrating the correct position for playing the Theremin, from *Operating Instructions for the Vanguard Theremin Model 505,* 1960.

Traditional versus Novel Input Devices

A main question in designing an input device for a synthesizer is whether to model it after existing instruments.

The advantages of using a traditional instrument as a model are clear. Musicians who are already familiar with a traditional instrument such as a keyboard or violin can adapt more easily (Overholt 2005; Bianchini et al. 2019) (figure 40.5). Thibodeau and Wanderley (2013) analyzed twelve trumpets that were augmented through the attachment of electronics. Using these

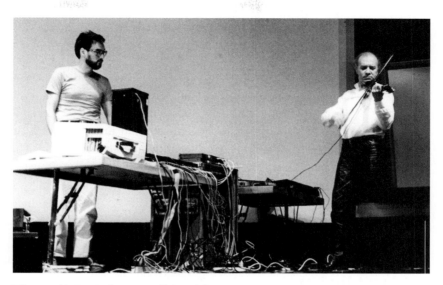

Figure 40.5 Using a traditional instrument as a controller for computer music (Negyesy and Ray 1989). Violinist Janos Negyesy playing a violin equipped with sensors to control electronic music hardware. Left: Lee Ray, system designer.

augmented instruments, trumpeters can immediately apply highly developed performance skills built up over many years. Also, finding virtuosos to play entirely new input devices is difficult, because music education tends to be tradition-bound. From a commercial standpoint, an input device that looks like a familiar instrument stands a better chance in the marketplace than a bizarre-looking appliance.

But the traditional instrument model has disadvantages. The full power of a synthesizer may be limited by a traditional instrument interface. In this case we need special input devices tailored to the synthesizer's capabilities. Open Sound Control (OSC), described in chapter 52, was invented precisely because a custom synthesizer needed a nontraditional controller (Wright and Freed 1997).

The design of traditional instruments reflects considerations that may not be relevant today. For example, the fingering scheme used to produce tones on instruments in the woodwind family is partly dictated by the acoustic properties of the instruments. With an electronic wind instrument, the fingerings can be made simpler and more intuitive (Yunik, Borys, and Swift 1985). Many instruments are designed around an equal-tempered pitch scheme. A musician who would like to explore other tunings might prefer a different design.

New concepts of musical process are also driving interface design. Many of the new input devices control high-level musical processes like timbral evolution, variations in polyphonic density, morphing from one patch to another, multichannel spatial projection, and phrase generation. This type of mesostructural control, enabled by interactive performance software, calls for a different interface from one made to play individual notes. New modes of control mandate custom input devices and interaction styles (Collins 1991a, b; Waisvisz 1985; Ferreira-Lopes 2004; Vail 2014). A prime example is the Lady's Glove of Latitia Sonami but also her new instruments based on machine learning in collaboration with Rebecca Fiebrink (Sonami 2006; Fiebrink and Sonami 2020; Fiebrink 2020).

In a studio situation, flexibility and management of complexity are prime concerns, rather than ease of spontaneous expression. The studio environment favors tools that aid the musician or sound engineer in building planned structures—complex, multilayered productions. Devices such as alphanumeric keyboards, mice, linear faders, rotary knobs, and lighted switches are suited for programming and fine control of digital audio workstations (DAWs).

Types of Input Devices

Musical gestures can be expressed through a wide range of body movements. Dozens of input devices have been developed to capture these gestures. Table 40.1 summarizes the major types of input devices as well as several rare types. Figure 40.6 is a series of photocollages of music input devices.

Mapping the Data from the Input Device

Gestures gathered from an input device produce raw messages of bit streams. A microprocessor inside the receiver must decode these streams before commanding the synthesis engine to emit sound. The separation of the input device from sound generation (figure 40.7) leaves the opportunity to *process* and *map* the information coming from the input device in a myriad of ways. Musical software such as SuperCollider, Max, or Pure Data is often deployed for this purpose.

Processing can shape the data by inversion, compression and expansion, limiting, smoothing, or quantizing (thresholding). The data can be analyzed for rates of change, delayed, convolved, or distorted by linear or nonlinear transforms.

Setting up a mapping between an input device and a synthesizer means setting up a link between a parameter coming from the input device to a parameter on the synthesizer. This is what MIDI and OSC were designed to do (chapters 51 and 52). Depending on the desired setup, the mapping between an input device and a synthesizer can be arbitrarily complex (Hunt

Table 40.1 Input devices

Device	Description	Typical uses; references
Switch	Multiposition switch.	Synthesizers, effects units, mixing consoles.
Pushbuttons	On/off, in/out motion.	Synthesizers, effects units, mixing consoles.
Linear potentiometer or fader	Made of conductive plastic; up means increase, down means decrease.	Synthesizers, effects units, mixing consoles.
Rotary potentiometer or knob	Circular motion, either limited in range or continuous.	Synthesizers, effects units, mixing consoles (EQ section).
Motorized faders	Linear faders that recall physical motions or track envelopes in a DAW.	Digital mixing consoles.
Trackball	Ball or disc housed such that the top half can be rotated.	Mice, older game consoles.
Joystick	Stick that can be rotated and sometimes pulled up and down.	Mixing consoles, synthesizers.
Game paddles and consoles	Detects motion and gestures in 3D, buttons.	Can be repurposed for interactive audiovisual performance.
Alphanumeric keyboard	Numbers and letters, special function keys and modifier keys (shift, option, control).	All computers.
Mouse	Movement of mouse moves the cursor; buttons select items onscreen.	Personal computers.
Graphics tablet and stylus	Used for drawing and graphical interaction.	Personal computers (Wacom tablet); live performance.
Multitouch screen and trackpads	Detects several fingers on its surface.	Mobile devices and personal computers.
Musical keyboard	Keys are switches, but detecting velocity and aftertouch adds expressiveness.	Many synthesizers.
Three-dimensional keyboard	Several forms. Notebender let keys move in and out as well as up and down. In Moog's scheme, position of the finger on the key was detected.	(Moog 1987; U.S. Patent 4,498,365; Moog and Rhea 1990).

(continued)

Table 40.1   (continued)

Device	Description	Typical uses; references
Thumbwheel	Used for pitchbend and vibrato control, typically with 30 degrees of forward or backward rotation.	Many MIDI keyboards.
Footpedal and switch	Can be either a swell pedal for volume or just a push-button to control sustain or effects.	Supported by synthesizers as a MIDI controller.
Organ bass pedals	Keyboard played by the feet	Some digital and electronic organs, also available separately.
Drum pad and other percussion controllers	Detects drum strokes and sends a signal to a drum machine or computer.	Mathews Sequential Drum (Mathews and Abbott 1980); Daton (Mathews 1989) Radio Drum (Boie, Mathews, and Schloss 1989).
Ribbon controller	Thin long strip touched by fingers with sliding or wiggling gestures.	Moog and Buchla modular systems; Kurzweil 2600.
Breath controller	Generates a time-varying function depending on how hard one blows into a mouthpiece.	Supported on Yamaha synthesizers.
Wind controller	Electronic instrument produces no sound unless attached to synthesizer; saxophone or flute fingering.	Yamaha WX5; AKAI EWI 5000' Roland Aerophone.
Flute controller	Flute with sensors to detect key depressions; may also do pitch detection.	IRCAM 4X flute; flute of Yunik et al. (1985).
Guitar controller	Special guitar that detects each string and sends MIDI; sometimes uses touch strip instead of strings; some units come as a special hex pickup to be attached to an existing guitar.	Fender Stratocaster GC-1 and Roland GR-55 Guitar Synthesizers; guitar game controllers.
Violin and cello controllers	Special violin with pickups that transmit MIDI to Roland or Zeta Synthesizer.	MIDI violins by Zeta, Cantini, Fourness, Yamaha, NS Design; Overtone violin (Overholt 2005).

Table 40.1   (continued)

Device	Description	Typical uses; references
Microphone directed at a musical sound source	Acoustic signal can be converted to digital form and analyzed for pitch, time, amplitude, and spectrum cues.	Ubiquitous in recording and sound reinforcement; also used in interactive systems such as Tango (Berg 2016).
Microphone for voice recognition	Speech recognition software.	Execute editing commands in a studio environment or onstage.
Mobile phone and tablet computer	Position and orientation sensors, accelerometer, microphone, GPS tracking; multitouch interaction; BlueTooth, telephone, and WiFi communications.	Phone becomes a musical instrument or a controller for an interactive system, possibly with other performers.
Theremin and capacitance fields	The performer waves her hands in the vicinity of two radio antennas. The circuit generates signals that vary according to hand position.	The original theremin; Moog's MIDI theremin.
Ultrasonic detector (sonar ranger)	Ultrasonic ranger can sense the motion of a conductor's wand or track motions of a dancer.	Chabot (1990)
Video camera	Machine vision. Can read score, do motion tracking, interpret facial gestures, and so on.	WABOT-2 musical robot (Roads 1986b); Morita, Hashimoto, and Ohteru (1991); Matsushima, et al. (1985); Fujinaga, et al. (1989, 1991).
Glove interfaces	Slip-on glove or hand-attached interface senses hand and finger movements.	The Hands (Waisvisz 1985); Lady's Glove (Sonami 2006).
Airdrums	Drum sticks fitted with accelerometers along three dimensions. Motion in air generates drum triggers.	Chabot (1990); Keane, Smecca, and Wood (1990).

and Kirk 2000; Hunt, Wanderley, and Paradis 2003). (A 2014 special issue of *Computer Music Journal* 38(3) is devoted to mapping strategies.) This complexity derives from the following three sources:

1. Programmable input devices

2. Remapping devices or performance software

3. Programmable synthesizers

Figure 40.6a   Photocollage of electronic and computer music input devices (1960–2020), Keyboards.
(i) Yamaha Disklavier MIDI upright piano.
(ii) Lync portable MIDI keyboard controller.
(iii) Excelsior Digisyzer MIDI accordion.
(iv) George Secor's Generalized Keyboard for the Motorola Scalatron synthesizer.
(v) Notebender keyboard by Key Concepts.
(vi) Roland A88 MkII MIDI 2.0 keyboard controller.
(vii) Haken Continuum Fingerboard.
(viii) Hi PI Tonal Plexus keyboard.
(ix) Crumar pedalboard
(x) Nektar MIDI foot controller
(xi) ACROE force-feedback keyboard with motorized keys.

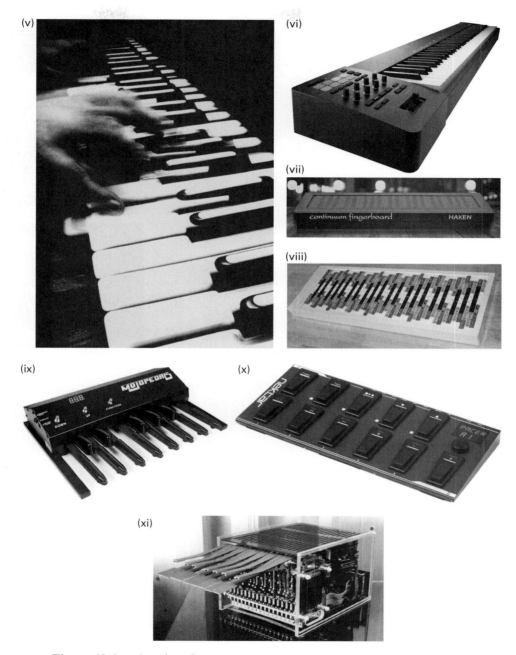

Figure 40.6a   (continued)

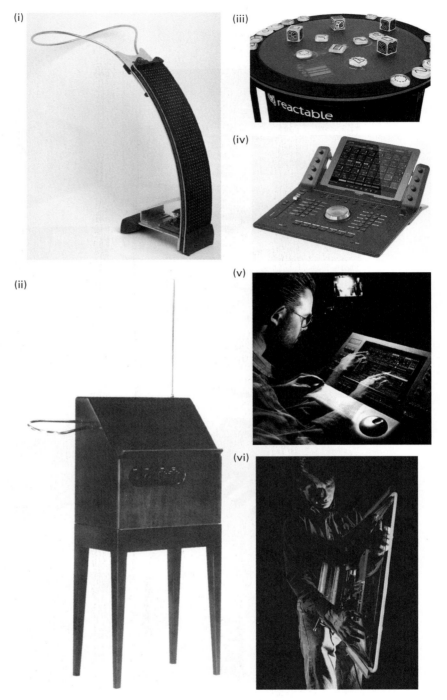

Figure 40.6b Photocollage of electronic and computer music input devices (1960–2020), Miscellaneous.
(i) Arcontinuo controller.
(ii) Theremin.
(iii) Reactable.
(iv) Avid Pro Tools Dock with iPad touchscreen.
(v) Touch display of the Digital Audio Research Sound Station.
(vi) VideoHarp. The surface is divided into a number of different regions, each of which invokes a different timbre or other MIDI message.

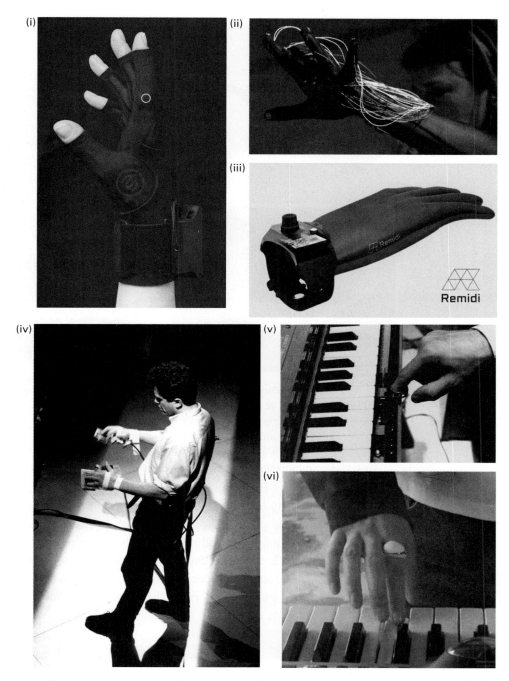

Figure 40.6c Photocollage of electronic and computer music input devices (1960–2020), Gloves & Rings.

(i) Mimu glove controller.

(ii) Laetitia Sonami Lady's Glove.

(iii) Remidi T8 wearable MIDI controller.

(iv) Michel Waisvisz playing The Hands.

(v) Ondes Martenot pitch-shifting ring.

(vi) Neova MIDI Ring.

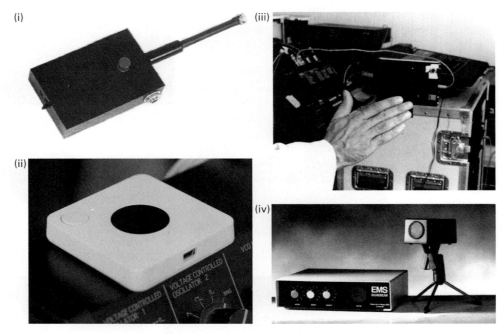

Figure 40.6d   Photocollage of electronic and computer music input devices (1960–2020), Ultrasound & Infrared.
(i) Buchla Lightning infrared controller.
(ii) OWOW Mob motion infrared MIDI controller.
(iii) Xavier Chabot's hand in the path of an ultrasonic detector.
(iv) EMS Soundbeam ultrasonic controller box and secondary beamer.

In case 1, many input devices can be programmed to emit various signals, depending on the gesture. For example, keyboards can be programmed to emit different signals depending on which key is pressed or how fast it is pressed. In case 2, the input data can be remapped and processed. In case 3, synthesizers let users set up correspondences between the signals emitted by an input device and parameters on the synth. A common way to do this is using MIDI Learn (chapter 51).

Ergonomics of Input Devices

Ergonomics refers to the design of objects that are well suited to human proportions and gestures. Good ergonomics ensures that we can exploit the effective precision of an input device. That is, if a device is easy to manipulate, it is easier to use it precisely. Conversely, if a device is hard to manipulate, whatever precision is built into the device is likely to be squandered in practice.

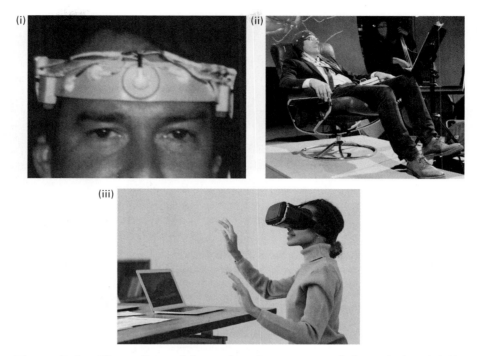

Figure 40.6e   Photocollage of electronic and computer music input devices (1960–2020), Brain & VR.
(i) Hugh Lusted wearing the Biomuse, a brain wave MIDI controller.
(ii) Thomas Deuel performing with the Encephalophone brain wave controller.
(iii) Head-mounted display for virtual reality.

For example, in a cheap guitar, the strings are often too high from the fretboard, making the instrument difficult to play. Precision and *feel* go together. For example, if a potentiometer has mechanical resistance, it is hard to make a precise fade with it.

Another factor in the design of an input device is size. A general rule of thumb is that the larger the device (but within the scale of the human hand), the more precision we can obtain with it. This is why *long-throw linear faders* on mixing consoles are favored by studio professionals (figure 40.8). *Long-throw* refers to 100 to 120 mm faders, as opposed to shorter and inherently less precise faders. Large rotary faders have the same benefit. Because the dynamic range of a channel is mapped to the travel of the fader, a slight nudge of the fader should produce a small increment of change rather than a large change.

Beyond a certain point, size and ergonomics compete with each other. A double bass requires stretching and more physical strength to play than a violin.

For some highly evolved input devices, only one size is optimal, for it bears a uniquely efficient relationship to the human being manipulating it.

Figure 40.6f Photocollage of electronic and computer music input devices (1960–2020), Strings.
(i) Godin MultiAc nylon string left-handed guitar with MIDI electronics.
(ii) Zeta MIDI guitar.
(iii) Max Mathews playing one of his electronic violins. (Photo Ivan Massar.)
(iv) Dan Overholt's Overtone violin.
(v) Yamaha EZ AG MIDI guitar.
(vi) Casio digital guitar.
(vii) Zeta electronic violin (foreground) and cello.

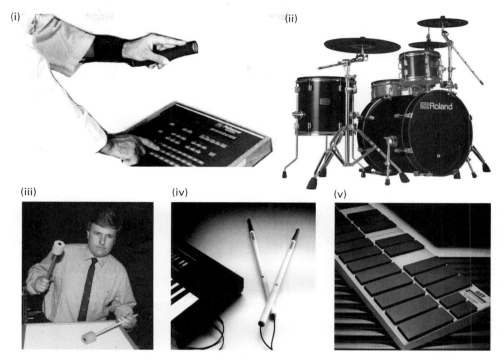

Figure 40.6g   Photocollage of electronic and computer music input devices (1960–2020), Percussion.
(i)   Airdrum controller.
(ii) Roland VAD 503 electronic drums.
(iii) Richard Boulanger playing the Radio Drum (Boie et al. 1989).
(iv) Casio SS-1 Sound Sticks.
(v)   KAT electronic marimba.

For example, the keys of piano keyboards are just the right size for performers with long, thin fingers. If they were any smaller the fingers would be cramped, like on a toy piano. If they were larger, certain wide-spanning chords would be impossible to play.

Musical Keyboards

More instruments have been made with twelve-note equal-tempered (ET) keyboards than with any other type of controller (figure 40.9). This trend shows no sign of changing; virtually all synthesizers developed in the past two decades can be configured with a keyboard, and the widespread MIDI specification was designed with keyboard performance in mind.

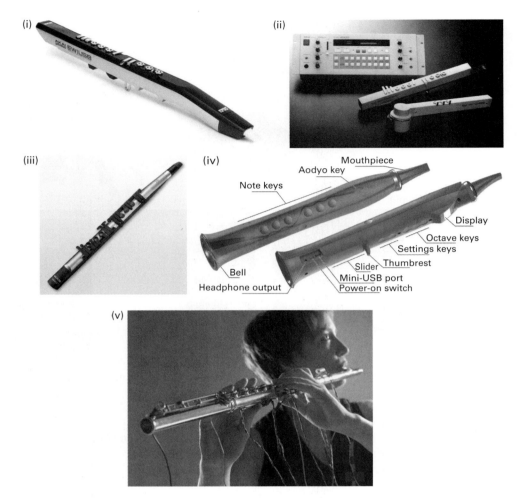

Figure 40.6h   Photocollage of electronic and computer music input devices (1960–2020), Winds.

(i) AKAI EWI-USB electronic wind instrument.

(ii) AKAI EV1000 and EW1000 wind controller (1987).

(iii) Yamaha WX5 horn.

(iv) Aodyio Sylphyo horn.

(v) Hyper-flute played by Cléo Palacio-Quintin.

(vi) Gary Nelson playing the MIDI Horn designed in collaboration with John Talbot. Photograph by John Corriveau.

(vii) Casio DH-100 digital horn.

(viii) Eigenlabs EigenHarp Pico instrument.

(ix) Carnegie-Mellon McBlare robotic bagpipe by Ben Brown, Garth Zeglin, and Roger Dannenberg.

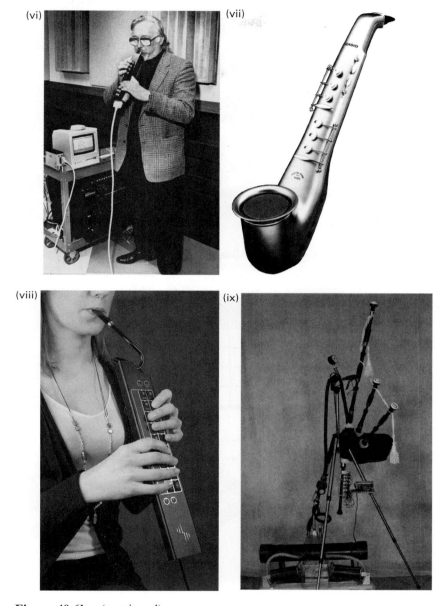

Figure 40.6h   (continued)

Figure 40.6i Photocollage of electronic and computer music input devices (1960–2020), Sliders, Buttons, and Knobs (MIDI fader boxes).

(i) William Buxton at the console of the SSSP synthesizer in Toronto (1978). At left, continuous potentiometers. In the center, traditional alphanumeric terminal. At right, pointing device on tablet.

(ii) Sliders and buttons on the AKG ADR 68K reverberator remote controller (1986).

(iii) Monome ARC knob controller.

(iv) CNTRLCap pressure-sensitive fader cap.

(v) Native Instruments Maschine controller for plug-ins.

(vi) Salvatore Martirono at the all-button control panel of the Sal-Mar Construction (1973).

(vii) Special-Waves modular MIDI controllers.

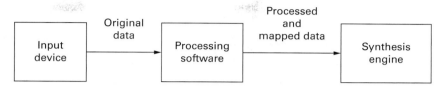

Figure 40.7 Software in between the input device and the synthesizer allows the possibility of interpreting and remapping the instrumentalist's gestures.

Figure 40.8 Professional portable audio mixer with long-throw faders.

In its simplest form, a keyboard is simply an array of on/off switches. The keyboards attached to early analog synthesizers were *monophonic*, meaning that only one key depression (i.e., one note) could be handled by the synthesizer.

Today's digital synthesizer keyboards are *polyphonic,* meaning that several keys (notes) can be played at once. Unlike a piano, however, many synthesizers are not fully 88-note polyphonic, but are limited to a lesser number of simultaneous notes. A synthesizer needs not only to respond to a real-time performer; it needs to be able to playback possibly dozens of tracks from a DAW sequencer. Only a few synthesizers are 128-note or 256-note polyphonic. Polyphony can become an issue when a sustain pedal is depressed, because notes are still playing even if they are not the latest notes.

So far, we have been referring to traditional keyboard designs. The MIDI Polyphonic Expression (MPE) protocol, ratified by the MIDI Manufacturer's Association in 2018, enables MPE-compatible keyboards (e.g., ROLI Seaboard)

Figure 40.9   Digital synthesizer keyboard of the Waldorf Quantum (2019) with display screen, 61 keys, two thumbwheels at the left for pitch bend and vibrato, and dozens of LED-lit rotary knobs and buttons. On the back of the unit are jacks for foot pedal inputs, audio inputs and outputs, and USB and MIDI input and output.

to articulate each note individually with pitch bending and vibrato. (For more on MPE, see chapter 51.)

State of the Keyboard

Within a keyboard instrument, a microprocessor is continually monitoring the state of the keys. The state of the keys can be represented as a sequence of bits, in which 1 signifies that a key is currently depressed, and 0 signifies that the key is not depressed. If the microprocessor scans the key switches a hundred or more times per second, this state information can amount to tens of thousands of bits per second. Clearly, some means of data reduction on all this key state information is desirable. The most straightforward approach is to capture only changes in key states.

In order to determine when a change takes place, the raw binary data is reduced via a logical exclusive-or operation, which takes just one instruction cycle. Exclusive-or compares the current keyboard state with the previous keyboard state: keys that change state take a value of 1; all others take a value of 0. For example, consider the following sequence of keyboard states:

Key number	1	2	3	4	5	6	7	8	9
Previous state	1	0	0	1	1	0	0	0	0
Current state	0	0	0	1	1	1	0	0	0
Changed keys	1	0	0	0	0	1	0	0	0

Here the system has detected that keys 1 and 6 have changed. Thus the exclusive-or acts as a filter that quickly reduces the entire keyboard state to a handful of bits.

Temporal Precision

Expressive gestures are infused with musical meaning and structural significance (Sundberg et al. 1983; Gabrielsson 1986; Wessel, Bristow, and Settel 1987; Goebl et al. 2008). To capture performance subtleties, instruments need to have high temporal precision. This raises the question: how fast must a device track a human gesture in order to capture nuance? A related question is, if a pianist performs on a keyboard, to how many decimal places must we compute the durations of the events played? The problem is more complicated than it appears at first glance, because there is more to a musical event than note-on and note-off. That is, one usually wants to measure more than simply the duration of the notes. To measure the velocity of key depression (a strong clue to the intended amplitude and envelope), one needs much more temporal precision. This is because one measures velocity by comparing the time it takes for the key to travel its downward path.

Keyboards require an especially high degree of precision because the performance techniques are so complicated and subtle, involving ten fingers. The same complexity is not necessarily associated with simpler controls such as the rotary knobs, switches, buttons, and sliders on a synthesizer. These devices can be sampled at low rates, less than 200 Hz (Mathews and Moore 1970; Alles 1980). Even so, a synthesizer can have dozens of manual controls, so the total sample rate for all controllers can be high. This amount of data is often handled by a dedicated microprocessor whose job is to filter or *data-reduce* it into a manageable form for the main microprocessor within the synthesizer. Refer to Kaplan (1981) and the discussion of performance software in chapter 41 for more on this subject.

Keyboard Scan Rate

How fast should a keyboard be scanned for changes? An early investigator, Knowlton (1971), estimated that a scanning time of 20 times per second per key would suffice to capture complex keyboard activity. He drew this conclusion from an examination of mechanical player-piano rolls. For a simple on-off keyboard, this resolution may be adequate for performances of some traditional music. If we intend to build an expressive keyboard, much more resolution is required, with scan rates on the order of several hundred times per second per key (Alles 1980). The next section explains why this is so.

Sensitivity to Velocity, Aftertouch, and Pressure

A *velocity sensing* keyboard measures how hard the musician hits each key by gauging the speed (velocity) with which a key is depressed. If a key takes 5 ms to travel from resting position to the bottom of its travel range, we can deduce that the key was hit harder than a key that took 35 ms to travel the same downward distance. A computer and a synthesizer can make use of velocity information to alter the sound produced. Just as a piano key makes a special sound if we strike it hard (louder and brighter), so a synthesizer can be programmed to respond to key velocity with corresponding loudness and timbre changes.

Various means exist to measure the speed of key depressions. Some keyboards use an optical sensing technique in which key depressions cause a photosensitive switch to trigger (Dworak and Parker 1977; Andersen 1978; Moog and Rhea 1990). The Bösendorfer 290 SE recording piano (which uses optical sensing) measures the velocity of the hammer about to strike the string, and not the velocity of the key (Moog and Rhea 1990). Goebl and Bresin (2003) analyzed the timing accuracy of computer-controlled grand pianos.

The most common way to measure key velocity is to use a switch in the form of a standard two bus-bar keyboard (Alles 1980; Chamberlin 1985). The contacts of the keyboard switch are arranged so that when the key is in the up position, the switch makes contact with the *up bus bar* common to all the key switches. When the key is down, it makes contact with the *down bus bar* (figure 40.10). When the key is going from up to down, there is a period of time during which the key switch makes no contact with either bus. This is called the *transition time* of a keystroke. The transition time is inversely proportional to the key velocity: i.e., the greater the transition time, the less the key velocity.

Practical transition times fall between 5 and 35 ms. Longer transition times delay the start of the note, because the note does not start sounding until it hits the down bus bar. A skilled pianist can use about thirty different velocities in the range 5–35 ms transition times. Many of these velocities are concentrated in the 5–15 ms range, so transition timing needs to be accurate to about 0.5 ms (Alles 1980).

In order to detect velocity information, the keyboard's microprocessor must scan the state of the keyboard much more rapidly than it would for a non-velocity-sensing keyboard. For example, one of the first commercial digital synthesizers, the Digital Keyboards Synergy (Alles 1980; Kaplan 1981) sampled the keyboard at 40 kHz. This speed is necessary because the micropro-

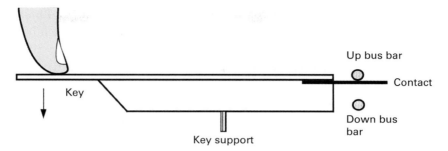

Figure 40.10 Horizontal cutaway view of bus bars in a keyboard. The contact plinth moves from the upper to the lower bus bar when the key is pressed.

cessor must sample each key at more than one point in the keystroke. As an example, a typical organ keyboard has sixty-one keys. If each key is examined every 500 μs (0.5 ms), an examination of a key can take only 500/61 or about 8 μs.

More expressiveness can be obtained by measuring the *release time*—how quickly or slowly the keys are let up by the performer.

Aftertouch is MIDI data sent when pressure is applied after the key has been struck and while it is being held down or sustained. It is often used to control vibrato, for example. Simple aftertouch information can be gleaned by adding another level of sensing to the keyboard (e.g., another bus bar or optical switch). Hard playing on the keyboard causes the key to touch the third level of switches, and this information is sent to the synthesizer for a sonic response (such as vibrato). Most electronic keyboards that have aftertouch have *monophonic aftertouch*. Monophonic aftertouch means that if any key is pressed hard, a global effect is applied to all currently playing notes. Much better is *polyphonic aftertouch,* in which an effect such as vibrato is applied only to those keys held down hard.

True *pressure-sensitive* keyboards can gauge the amount of pressure applied at the bottom of a keystroke, or more specifically, how hard the key is held down. Various means for measuring key pressure exist. Chamberlin (1985) recommends the substitution of a linear transducer instead of a contact switch at the bottom of the keyboard key's travel. One option is to use conductive rubber to detect key pressure (Moog 1987). As the key is pressed harder, more of the conductive rubber is engaged in the pressure-detection circuit.

Pressure information can be used in a number of ways, to control amplitude, timbre change, vibrato, or tremolo. Pressure pads beneath the key have been used to bend pitch, but this can cause problems. First, the pad gives no touch response corresponding to the amount of pitch bend. Second, the amount of arm weight required for a specific pitch bend varies depending on whether the player is seated or standing. Finally, holding a bent pitch this way can be difficult. Pitch bend wheels, or *thumbwheels* (figure 40.11), or three-dimensional keyboards (see table 40.1) are better suited for pitch bending.

Location Sensing

Certain keyboards can sense the location of the finger on the key, including the Roli Seaboard and the Keith McMillan Instruments QuNexus controller (Vail 2014). This can be mapped a timbral control, for example. Refer to McPherson (2015) for a review of continuous-control keyboard instruments.

Keyboard Actions

The *haptic feel* or *action* of a keyboard is important to players. Unweighted organ-type keyboards provide little feedback to the musician. Modifications can improve this. For example, a key of an organ-type keyboard has a return spring that brings the key back to its resting position, so substituting a heavy spring can give the keyboard a more substantial feel.

Weighted wooden keys with heavy springs are another approach. Introducing a rubber barrier at the bottom of a key's path gives the key a more mechanical feel. If the rubber is electrically conductive, pressure information can be gauged as well.

For many performers, the mechanical action of a piano keyboard is the most expressive. Thus the ultimate strategy is to install a mechanical piano

Figure 40.11   Thumbwheels on keyboard for the Bohlen-Pierce scale made by Elaine Walker.

action (minus the strings and soundboard) inside an electronic instrument. The *double escapement* action of a grand piano keyboard involves dozens of components (Topper and Wills 1987; Gillespie 1992; Gillespie and Cutkowsky 1992; Gillespie et al. 2011).

Computer-Controlled Pianos

Automatic player-piano systems with storage on paper rolls go back to the nineteenth century. (See the fascinating volumes by Ord-Hume 1973, 1984 for an historical and technical account.). The earliest attempts to control a player-piano engine by computer date to the late 1970s (Helmers 1979; Stahnke 1981; Moog and Rhea 1990). Yamaha's Disklavier system debuted in 1987 and has been continuously refined. A key feature of their PRO models is greater recording and playback accuracy than previously available. These instruments record not only hammer velocity (as MIDI note-on velocity) but also key-down velocity and key-up velocity (MIDI note-off velocity). Before the PRO, Disklaviers were limited like all MIDI 1.0 instruments to working within a 0–127 range of values for note-on velocity, note-off velocity, and incremental pedal movement. To break this accuracy limit, engineers used additional MIDI controllers to extend the range of values for note-on/note-off to 0–1,023 and for pedal movement to 0–255.

A modern Disklavier contains an embedded Linux operating system connected to the Internet. Thus it can stream performances from remote locations to subscribers of Yamaha's Disklavier Radio. The Disklavier control system can also be installed in handcrafted Bösendorfer pianos, which cost hundreds of thousands of dollars (figure 40.12).

Steinway's Spirio piano automation technology lets users record and playback performances. It has similar specifications to the Yamaha PRO system because both the Yamaha and Steinway automation mechanisms are based on the same patented technologies (Stahnke 1981; 2009).

The superhuman speed of computer-controlled pianos tempts composers to write scores that challenge traditional performance boundaries. However, computer-controlled pianos have mechanical limitations that must be respected, such as the number of notes per second; if its limitations are exceeded, the instrument may overheat. Another issue that appears in any robotic instrument is latency related to key velocity. As MIDI made explicit, key velocity is correlated with note loudness. This means that soft notes are literally slower to sound. The trigger to start a note initiates a mechanical process that results in a sound after a significant delay. To compensate for this, one manufacturer adds a default delay of 500 ms to all notes played back from a performance file in order to allow its scheduling algorithms to compensate for note latencies.

Figure 40.12   Dancers with automatic accompaniment. Advertisement for Bösendorfer Disklavier reproducing piano.

This becomes a problem only when the piano is used in live interaction with other musicians and this delay must be turned off.

Key Layout and Splitting

The design of the key layout has been another area of experimentation. A normal piano key measures 2 cm wide by 14 cm long. This size seems optimal for virtuoso musicians. Keyboard synthesizers aimed at professional musicians use keys of about this size. In inexpensive electronic music instruments and toys, keys can be as small as 1 cm wide by 3 cm long.

Keyboard controllers can be bought with as little as one octave of keys, with an octave switch for transposition. The traditional 88-key piano layout is available only on more expensive keyboard controllers (figure 40.14).

Keyboard splitting divides the span into two or more *zones* divided at *split points,* with each zone assigned to a particular synthesizer voice or patch (figure 40.14). For example, the lower half of the keyboard might be assigned to a low-register bass voice, while the top half of the keyboard is assigned to a high-register melodic voice. This can be accomplished via the MIDI channel mechanism. assigning one zone of the keyboard to MIDI channel *A,* which is routed to synthesizer voice *A,* assigning another zone to MIDI channel *B* routed to synthesizer voice *B,* and so on.

Of course, the equal-tempered black-and-white-key keyboard is not the only possible design; it is merely the most common. The demands of microtonal music call for different key arrangements. Numerous electronic instruments—from the Motorola Scalatron (Secor 1975), to the 31-tone organ (Fokker 1975), to the Egg digital synthesizer (Andersen 1978; Manthey

Figure 40.13   Doepfer LMK4 + 88-key hammer-action keyboard. It weighs 24 kg and costs around $1,800.

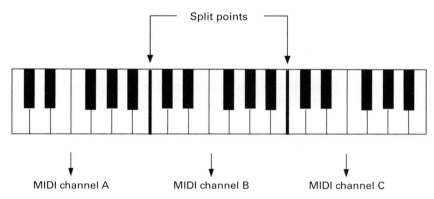

Figure 40.14   A split keyboard is divided into several regions, each of which transmits over a different MIDI channel.

1978, 1979)—incorporate innovative key layouts. (See Keislar 1987 for an illustrated history of microtonal keyboards.)

Expressive MIDI Keyboards

The quest for a more expressive electronic keyboard is ongoing. The Multiply Touch-Sensitive Keyboard designed by Robert Moog (Hybrid Management 1984; Moog 1987; Kramer, Moog, and Peevers 1989) used conductive rubber to detect the position (left-right, front-back) of the performer's finger on the surface of the key. This information could be conveyed to a synthesizer. For example, if the performer's finger is near the front of the key, this could be interpreted as a "smooth timbre," whereas touches near the back of the key could be interpreted as a more "rough" timbre. One could also map finger position to vibrato, pitch bend, or another musical parameter.

A contemporary instance of this concept is the Roli Seaboard (figure 40.15). It senses five dimensions of touch: striking the keys, gliding sideways along

Figure 40.15   Two Roli Seaboards in action. The devices are wireless, communicating via the Bluetooth protocol.

them, sliding up and down the keys, pressing into them, and lifting off. This is enabled by the MIDI protocol MPE mentioned previously, or *Expressive MIDI.* MPE is intended to provide per-note expressivity in hardware and software sound generators by means of a touch-sensitive keyboard interface. Pressure-sensing on newer controllers such as the LinnStrument, Haken Continuum, Roli Seaboard, and Osmose keyboard starts when a musician lightly touches the note, and then continues as they add pressure. This makes it possible to emulate a wind or bowed-string instrument, controlling the intensity of the note from silence to full loudness. To bend a single note, the musician places a finger on one position and slides it up to the other position at the rate and movement desired. On MPE-enabled controllers, a finger continuously controls the speed, shape, and width of vibrato, as a violinist would.

Conducting: Remote Control and Remote Sensing

Certain musical situations call for remote control of devices. In a recording studio, for example, the sound engineer would like to have all controllable devices within arm's length. A handy remote controller near the mixing console is a great convenience for control of hardware in a rack that is out of reach.

Onstage, a musician might prefer the mobility of a portable keyboard in concert as against a bulkier package in which the keyboard is integrated into the synthesizer electronics. Many musicians control an entire rack of synthesis and signal-processing devices from a single onstage MIDI keyboard.

Remote controllers transmit information via one of four means: electrical cable, fiber optic cables, infrared (IR) light, and wireless radio-frequency broadcast (e.g., WiFi and Bluetooth).

This is only one side of the story, however. In these scenarios, the remote control unit is a tactile device within close reach. Another control situation involves *remote sensing,* in which the performer is at some distance from the sensing device. This falls in the realm of *motion tracking* (Miranda and Wanderley 2006).

The original remote controller for music is the conductor's baton. Without touching an instrument, conductors can signal beginnings, endings, changes in tempo, balance, articulation, and expression—primarily through the baton and their other hand, but also by means of facial gestures and body language. Responding to the gestures of a conductor is thus a test case for remote sensing.

The first electromechanical remote controller was also wielded by a conductor. In his 1843 treatise "On Conducting," Hector Berlioz recounted his use of an electrified key (similar to a piano key) installed in a Brussels concert hall (Berlioz and Strauss 1948). This key flashed a light on and off, thereby signaling the musical tempo to an offstage chorus.

In these cases the remote sensing problem is solved by the fact that human beings are trained to watch and follow the conductor's gestures. What if the orchestra is replaced by a computer? In this case, there must be some way for the conductor's gestures to be recognized at a distance. This remains a realm of lively experimentation. Following are some of the sensing means that have been deployed:

- Magnetic trackers
- Ultrasound beams and detectors
- Video cameras
- Infrared (IR) LED light beams and infrared cameras
- Accelerometers (detect physical motion)
- Conducting gloves with multiple sensors

These and other means can be combined to make a more effective remote sensing system.

An example of an early computer-based conducting system was developed at MIT (Haflich and Burns 1983). The conductor held a special wand that reflected ultrasonic signals back to an ultrasonic rangefinder. A computer interpreted this information. Under rigidly controlled conditions, the wand could transmit the performance tempo of a synthesized composition. Since this experiment, various electronic batons have been developed. The conducting system of Morita, Hashimoto, and Ohteru (1991) was simultaneously tracked by a camera (watching the baton in one hand) and an electronic glove (sensing the position of the fingers on the other hand). Buchla's Lightning II used IR technology to track the position of two hand-held wands. The two IR wands transmit location, acceleration, velocity, and direction to photosensors on a receiver. The receiver then translates these actions into corresponding preset sounds. The Leap Motion Controller uses a combination of several IR beams and cameras to track a performer's gestures (Ritter and Aska 2014; Berndt, Waloschek, and Hadjakos 2016). Wearable biometric sensing technology has also been studied (Nakra 2000).

Gesture Recognition

Beyond sensing technologies, the deeper problem in performance is always gesture recognition. Designing a system that can respond to the full range of expression of a conductor's hands, facial gestures, and body language is of equal difficulty to other difficult artificial intelligence problems like understanding spoken language. Human musicians feel the emotional current of the conductor's gestures.

The problem of decoding a conductor's gestures in real time is well matched to a machine learning methods, including neural network pattern-matching system (Rumelhart and McClelland 1986; see appendix A). Neural nets can be trained by demonstration to recognize arbitrary gestures; their output can in turn be translated into control parameters for real-time synthesis A long history of research has explored this realm (Lee, Garnett, and Wessel 1992; Ilmonen and Takala 1999; Nakra 2000; Nakra et al. 2009; De Prisco et al. 2011; Françoise 2013; Leman 2016).

Conductor-level control need not be linked to traditional conducting technique. This was proven in the 1970s by Joel Chadabe (figure 40.16), who—prior to the invention of MIDI—used theremin antennae to assume conductor-like control of a computer-controlled digital synthesizer (Chadabe 1984).

Responsive Input Devices and Haptic Technology

Though the principle of effortlessness may guide good word processor design, it may have no comparable utility in the design of a musical instrument. . . . Effort is closely related to expression in the playing of traditional instruments. It is the element of energy and desire, of attraction and repulsion in the movement of music.
—Joel Ryan 1991

Figure 40.16   Joel Chadabe conducting a New England Digital Synclavier synthesizer using modified theremin antennae designed and built by Robert Moog. Performance at The Kitchen performance space, New York City, 1979. (Photograph by Carlo Carnevali.)

Any mechanical instrument, such as a piano, trumpet, sitar, or glockenspiel, is a naturally responsive input device for music. That is, the physical construction of the device constrains the instrument to a particular action or *feel*. This action varies, depending on the force and the shape of the gesture that the performer attempts to play on the instrument. On a trumpet, for example, high-pitched notes require more physical effort. The strings of a sitar or a guitar require manual force to be bent. The chimes of a glockenspiel move when they are struck, and if they are hit too hard, they bump into one another.

By contrast, a typical electronic instrument involves little, if any, mechanical action to generate sound. Any pitch is as easy to play as any other; pitch bending and loudness controls are simply additional knobs or pedals that demand only minimal effort to manipulate. The controllers attached to many electronic instruments, such as organ keyboards, joysticks, and knobs, have little mechanical *feel* to orient the musician. And yet experience shows that virtuosic performance is greatly aided by mechanical feedback cues from the instrument. This is why manufacturers try to improve the mechanical action of their keyboards and controls.

Computer control of mechanical devices offers another possibility: input devices with a *programmable response* to the touch. This is an application of *haptic feedback* technology. Haptic feedback technology uses the sense of

Table 40.2   Responsive Input Devices

Device	Description	Citation
Piano action	Mechanical action with *feel*.	Pianos and piano controllers.
ACROE joystick	Used in ACROE Cordis system for programmable reaction to gestures; can be stiff, stepped, supple, and so on.	Cadoz, Luciani, and Florens (1984); Cadoz, Lisowski, and Florens (1990).
ACROE key and keyboard	Used in ACROE Cordis system for programmable action; can be stiff, stepped, supple, and so on.	Cadoz, Luciani, and Florens (1984); Cadoz, Lisowski, and Florens (1990).
Atari joystick	Programmable motorized action; could simulate a gear box, a surface, a circular joystick, and so on.	Experimental game research at Atari Cambridge Research Center in the 1980s.
Touchback keyboard	Haptic simulation of piano action.	Gillespie (1992).
vBow	Force-feedback violin bow controller.	Nichols (2002).
MIKEY keyboard	Simulations of the action of a grand piano, harpsichord, and Hammond organ.	Oboe (2006).
University of Michigan haptic key	Adjustable touch response.	Davis et al. (2009).

touch to apply forces, vibrations, and motions to the user. The stimulation of a haptic device allows an artist to have direct contact with an instrument in a virtual world. Haptic feedback informs the musician about the mechanical state of the instrument. Refer to Visell et al. (2013) for a survey that situates responsive instruments within a more general framework of *human-computer interaction* (HCI).

The mobile phone industry put haptic technology in the hands of billions of people with its vibration mode. Cars use haptic vibrations in the steering wheel to convey to the driver when crossing lanes inadvertently. Haptic technology in musical instruments remains in the experimental stage. By using digitally controlled electrical motors, researchers have designed keyboard keys and joysticks with a variable *force-feedback* response (Cadoz, Luciani, and Florens 1984; Cadoz, Lisowski, and Florens 1990; Florens and Cadoz 1990; Gillespie 1992; Oboe 2006). For example, a single keyboard can be made to react like piano, harpsichord, or organ. A key can be made to have a stiff or loose action. It can be programmed to have *steps* that can correspond to steps in amplitude, in timbre, or in both.

Responsive input devices require special electrical motors with a wide bandwidth and strong force (for simulating rigid objects). Cadoz, Lisowski, and Florens (1990) describe a keyboard in which there is one motor per key. This ACROE keyboard and its motors are shown in the photocollage of figure 40.6. The Atari force-feedback joystick could be programmed to feel like a 360° audio panner, an automobile gear box, a spring-loaded joystick, or another mechanical systems. (See Cadoz, Luciani, and Florens [1984] for a description of a similar device.) The benefits of an input device whose action can be tuned for a particular piece are clear. Table 40.2 lists examples of responsive input devices.

41 *Interactive Performance Software*

This chapter examines interactive performance software—the programs that capture gestures and transmit them to sound generators. Performance software is designed for the studio, the concert hall, the gallery, and the interactive media channel. Hence it must be able to respond in real time to human gestures.

Several surveys examine the field. Wessel and Wright (2002) described the problem space of gestural interaction with computers. Paolo Ferreira-Lopes (2004) analyzed musical interactivity from a philosophical point of view. Sergi Jordà (2007), principal developer of the Reactable, pointed out possibilities for new types of music from interactive music. Tahiroğlu (2021) surveyed applications of artificial intelligence in interactive music systems based on mutual cooperation between human and machine.

After a historical review, we introduce the main categories of performance software and describe their internal operation in basic terms. The main categories are

- Sequencers
- Interactive performance systems
- Improvisation systems
- Networked computer bands and live coding

Sequence playback is at the core of most performance software, although the concept of sequencing continues to evolve. Sequencers merge multimedia playback of sound with graphics, animation, and video. Interactive multimedia sequencers are spilling into opera, dance, and theater performance, as well as sound art installations in galleries. An example is the work of the artist Mira Calix (1969–2022), who worked with mixed media pieces, installations, sound design for theater, and concert works. Kaffe Matthews is another prolific sound artist working in the zone between performance and (sometimes mobile) installations.

By their nature, interactive improvisation systems resist standardization and remain an open field of exploration. A central challenge of these systems is managing the powers of automation (precision and complexity) with the gesture and feeling of human performance.

Interactive Performance with Computers: Background

Visionaries such as Presper Eckert (codesigner of the ENIAC computer) imagined real-time interactive systems in the earliest days of electronic data processing (Eckert 1946). But it took decades before this dream became a practical reality. In the early days, few musicians had direct access to the computers on which their music programs ran. They wrote programs on *offline* (not connected to a computer) punch-card machines and submitted boxes of cards to staff that ran one program at a time. To create a minute of sound could take days, due to slow computation times and the multiple steps involved in producing sound (David et al. 1958, 1959; Schroeder and Logan 1961; Tenney 1963, 1969; Mathews and Miller 1963; Mathews 1969; Risset 1966, 1969; Roberts 1966; Von Foerster and Beauchamp 1969; Howe 1975).

Not until the late 1970s did the advance of interactive timesharing terminals and lower-cost minicomputers for digital synthesis improve the situation. Alphanumeric display terminals let musicians edit the input data *online* (directly connected to a computer). They could type commands to launch immediate calculations.

Up until this time, real-time gestural control of music synthesis was possible only with analog instruments. The first digital systems to allow real-time gestural input were the *hybrid* music systems of the 1970s. Hybrid systems combined a digital computer with an analog sound synthesizer.

The pioneering real-time GROOVE hybrid synthesizer at Bell Telephone Laboratories (figure 41.1) let musicians play on a musical keyboard, joysticks, and knobs as well as an interactive computer display (Mathews and Moore 1970). For the first time, a musician could draw curves on a display screen that represented frequency or amplitude envelopes. Higher levels of musical control were also possible. For example, the CONDUCT program

Figure 41.1   Max Mathews playing a musical keyboard (right hand) and controlling a knob (left hand) connected to the GROOVE hybrid synthesizer, which became operational in 1970.

allowed overall control of amplitude, tempo, and instrument balance, analogous to controls exercised by a conductor.

The Sequential Circuits Prophet-5 (1978) was the first mass-produced hybrid polyphonic synthesizer, with over 6,000 instruments sold (Vail 2000a). The Prophet-5 brought interactive computer technology to the musical arena. Today, the revived Sequential company has brought back the Prophet-5 synthesizer.

Sequencers

Memory-based playback of music is often part of an interactive performance system. A sequencer is a type of recording and playback system with a programmable memory. Instead of recording the waveform of a sound, however, a sequencer records only the sequence of *control* or *performance data* needed to regenerate a series of musical events. For example, when a musician performs on a synthesizer keyboard, the times of key-up and key-down events can be recorded by a sequencer. Later, the sequencer can play back this sequence and send the control information to the synthesizer to recreate the musician's performance (figure 41.2).

A digital sequencer can be implemented in multiple forms:

- A software application, for example, part of a digital audio workstation or DAW
- A dedicated hardware box with buttons and knobs (figure 41.3)
- A subsystem of a synthesizer (either software or hardware)
- A robot, more or less in the image of a human performer

We make a distinction between an *analog hardware sequencer*—a component of a modular synthesizer—and a digital sequencer. As we discuss further on, analog sequencers are quite different in design and operation from scheduler-based digital sequencers. For example, although an analog synthesizer operates under the regime of voltage control, the MIDI specification remains a standard protocol for communication between a digital sequencer and the devices it controls. This means that digital sequencers sold today receive and transmit MIDI messages, and the control data they store is MIDI data. (See chapter 51 for more on MIDI.) Open Sound Control (OSC), described in chapter 52, has gained acceptance as a flexible alternative protocol but requires that the user write code to make it work.

The next sections develop the history of sequencing technology and stress the performance features of sequencers. Further on, we discuss the internal operation of a digital sequencer.

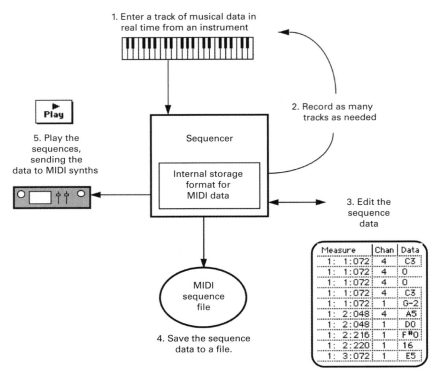

Figure 41.2 Overview of a sequencer, showing (clockwise) the operations of (1) music data entry, (2) multitracking, (3) editing, (4) saving edited data, and (5) performing.

Figure 41.3 Korg SQ-1 hardware sequencer generates both MIDI and control voltages.

Sequencers: Background

The challenge of musical performance inspired some of the earliest experiments in automation. Indeed, sequencing in music was implemented centuries before its industrial applications. The first sequence-controlled loom, which could produce repeating patterns in fabric, operated under the programmed control of a perforated paper roll, did not appear until 1725 (Usher 1954). By contrast, the first description of a sequenced instrument that could play by itself is found in the manuscripts of the famous Banu Masa brothers *Book of Ingenious Devices,* dating to 890 (Ord-Hume 1973). As early as the 1200s, Dutch instrument builders designed and constructed programmable mechanical carillons (chimes or bells). Inside the mechanism of the carillon was a revolving cylinder covered with holes (analogous to the binary digit 0). If a wooden peg (analogous to the binary digit 1) was inserted into a hole, it triggered a bell-ringing mechanism when the cylinder revolved. By placing pegs in various holes, a musician could program different melodies and chords (Buchner 1978). According to Leichtentritt (1934) some Flemish carillons had nine thousand memory locations (holes) for the insertion of note pegs (figure 41.4). Today we would call this type of sequential programming *step mode* recording.

Figure 41.4 Step mode programming an ancient carillon in at Bruges (from Buchner [1978]).

Jacques de Vaucanson (1709–1782) was a celebrated designer of musical robots or *androides*–as he called them. Some of his inventions are on display at the Musée des Art et Métiers in Paris. Performing robots became a popular attraction in the late eighteenth and nineteenth centuries and can be found today at amusement parks.

The first attempt to make a *sequence recorder*—able to register a series of key depressions played on a keyboard for later reproduction—was implemented in the eighteenth century (Leichtentritt 1934; Boalch 1956; Buchner 1978). The term *melography* was coined by J. Charpentier in 1880 to name this process. A *melograph* was a paper roll inscribed with ink lines that a skilled human reader translated into music notation (figure 41.5). Thus the recording process was only half automated.

Figure 41.5   Melograph sequence recording on a continuous roll of paper. Below the keys of instrument lies a brass strip connected to the positive terminal of a battery. If a key is depressed, a spring establishes contact with the corresponding wire of the key. The circuit is closed, and current passes through the paper where the corresponding tooth of a comb lies. A chemical reaction takes place and produces a colored line on the moving paper as long as the key is depressed (Ord-Hume 1973).

In the mid-1800s, the French instrument builder Debain built the first portable sequence players (Ord-Hume 1984). Debain's Antiphonel devices could be fitted on a normal keyboard instrument and operated by moving a lever up and down. The coding of music into an Antiphonel and all early sequence players was a tedious process carried out in a factory. It was not until the early 1900s that pneumatic paper-punching machines were developed to record keyboard performances. These were the first fully automatic *real-time sequence recorders* because the rolls they produced could be used to drive a player piano.

Paper-tape sequencers

All the sequence-controlled music boxes, player pianos, and other musical automata constructed up through the early twentieth century were mechanical devices.

Pioneering research in automation of electronic music was undertaken by the French engineers Givelet and Coupleux, who in 1929 designed and built a synthesizer consisting of four vacuum tube oscillators controlled by a punched paper-tape mechanism (Rhea 1984). In 1945, Hanert built a programmable synthesizer employing punched-card technology to control an oscillator bank (Ernst 1977, U.S. Patent 2,541,051). In the Inge-Schole Stiftung Studio für Elektronische Musik, Munich (which later became the Siemens studio), engineers built an analog synthesis system that was programmable via punched paper tape (Tjepkema 1981; Kaegi 1967).

The RCA Synthesizers were the last grand effort at sequence automation by paper tape. Dubbed the Mark I (1955) and Mark II (1957), these room-sized vacuum tube machines were designed by Harry F. Olsen and Herbert Belar of the RCA Research Laboratories (Olson and Belar 1955; Olson 1967, 1991; Babbitt 1964). Milton Babbitt used the Mark II in a number of electronic music compositions (e.g., *Ensembles, Philomel, Vision and Prayer*) composed at the Columbia-Princeton Electronic Music Center in New York City (figure 41.6).

We would be remiss not to mention the extraordinary player piano music of Conlon Nancarrow (1912–1997). Although no electronics were involved, Nancarrow used a custom paper-punching machine so that he could realize mathematically precise contrapuntal sequences.

As an alternative to the discrete note-oriented paper tape controllers, some inventors, such as Daphne Oram, preferred inscribing continuous graphical envelopes for control of electronic sound. Chapter 24 describes pioneering optoelectrical mechanisms for reading graphic notation.

Figure 41.6   RCA Mark II Synthesizer at the Columbia/Princeton Electronic Music Center in New York City. The typewriters punch holes in paper tape, which is fed into the control mechanism of the synthesizer.

Analog voltage-controlled sequencers

The commercial introduction of *analog voltage-controlled synthesizers,* by companies such as Moog, Arp, Buchla, and EMS in the late 1960s brought new possibilities to musicians worldwide. These transistorized systems contained a dozen or more modules that could be interconnected via patch cords. Voltage control meant that individual parameters of the sound could be controlled either by input devices such as keyboards, or automatically by signals from other modules—opening up a new field of sonic possibilities. Paper tape, foil tape, and optical film were all used to sequence analog synthesizers (Ghent 1967a; Young 1989; Oram 1972).

By the early 1970s, manufacturers of analog synthesizers offered *analog sequencers* as optional modules (figure 41.7). To use such a device, a musician tunes a row of knobs, each corresponding to a voltage that controlled a sonic parameter (such as oscillator pitch). The sequencer then steps through these voltages, sending each voltage in turn to a module such as an oscillator connected to it by a patch cord the rate at which the sequencer steps is set by a clock, which can itself be voltage-controlled.

Figure 41.7   Moog 960 analog sequencer module. The 24 steps of the sequencer are divided into three rows. A clock module is at the left. Lights above each column indicate active steps.

If desired, the sequence can loop, thus realizing, for example, a repeating melody. More generally, the sequence can control any module, such as filter center frequency, the gain of an amplifier, spatial position, and so on.

The demands of *integral serial* composition techniques of the 1950s motivated the development of some early sequencers (Young 1989, pp. 140–146; Scherpenisse 1977). Integral serial composition organizes each musical parameter, such as pitch, duration, and amplitude, as an independent series. (A classic exegesis of integral serialism is Ligeti's 1960 analysis of Boulez's composition *Structure 1a.*) Integral serial patterns can be realized using a sequencer that has several parallel rows—one for each parameter—that can be programmed individually.

Ironically, the logic inherent in sequencing suggested a new direction for music—far from serialism. According to Steve Reich (1974), the repeating patterns generated by looping analog sequencers inspired him to create his repetitive minimalist music style.

A major technical limitation in analog sequencers is the number of different steps that they contain, corresponding to the size of their voltage memory. The Moog 960 sequencer module shown in figure 41.7 offered twenty-four steps, the Arp 1027 module provided thirty, and the Buchla 246 module had forty-eight steps. In these sequencers, when more than one parameter was controlled at each step, then the number of steps was reduced by that factor. For example, a twenty-four-step Moog sequencer could control the pitch, duration, and amplitude of just eight notes (twenty-four divided by three parameters). Moreover, each parameter at every step had to be tuned by hand with a control knob; it was not possible to program the sequencer by playing. For this, digital memory technology was needed.

Digital sequencers

The aforementioned GROOVE system at Bell Telephone Laboratories in the late 1960s was a computer-controlled analog synthesizer (Mathews and Moore 1970). GROOVE stored performance information in its memory in the form of functions of time (envelopes) for each synthesis parameter. Another experimental system at the University of Utah used a computer to scan the state of an organ keyboard and capture sequences of notes played on it. This system also displayed a form of rudimentary music notation (Ashton 1971; Knowlton 1971, 1972).

A major breakthrough for digital sequencing was the Synthi AKS, a portable synthesizer manufactured by Peter Zinoviev and his associates at Electronic Music Studios (EMS), London in 1972. The Synthi AKS was a modular analog synthesizer in a briefcase coupled with a digital sequencer that could record and play up to 256 events, with each event having six parameters, for a total of 1,536 stored values. This was a giant leap over analog sequencer modules, which could store a maximum of forty-eight values.

By the end of the 1970s, digital sequencers were built into more commercial instruments such as the hybrid Sequential Circuits Prophet-5 (Darter 1979). When the MIDI protocol was introduced in 1983, the concept of digital sequencing suddenly became widespread (Tobenfeld 1984). Personal computers had megabytes of storage for sequences.

Digital sequencing suffuses popular music today. Many digital synthesizers have built-in sequencers. Software plug-in synths can be driven by sequencers implemented in DAWs such as Pro Tools, Ableton Live, Logic, Cubase, BitWig, Performer, etc.

Musical robots

The most theatrical form of sequence player has always been a robot–a motorized android with a mechanical or electronic brain. These have a long history. As Ord-Hume (1973) described one 1820 robot,

The Musical Lady could play sixteen tunes and her music was played as by a human performer, by the depression of the piano keys by her fingers. As well as playing the instrument, she moved her head and her breast heaved in a lifelike impression of breathing. (19)

A rich literature awaits those who wish to explore further. (See, for example, Leichtentritt 1934, Chapuis 1955, Bowers 1972, Buchner 1978,

Prieberg 1975, Losano 1990, Ord-Hume 1973, 1984, and Weiss-Stauffacher 1976.)

Musical robots are found in amusement parks such as Disneyland. Research is leading to a more sophisticated breed, able to accompany human performers on keyboards, read music, and carry on conversations (Matsushima et al. 1985; Roads 1985b; Katayose and Inokuchi 1989, 1990; Solis et al. 2006; Solis and Ng 2011).

Musical instruments that integrate electronics, mechanical motion, and acoustics can be called *mechatronic* (Gurevich 2014). Recent years have seen the invention of mechatronic non-keyboard instruments, such as flute, saxophone, recorder, drums, guitar, trumpet, violin, cello, bagpipe, and even Theremin! (Sekiguchi, Amemiya, and Kubota 1993; Ohta et al.1993; Alford et al. 1999; Solis et al. 2006; Solis and Ng 2011; Raes 2012) (figure 41.8). Placencia, Murphy, and Carnegie (2019) surveys mechatronic stringed instruments. Kapur (2005) reviews the history of robot instruments. Kapur et al. (2011) examines the combination of human laptop performers with robotic musical instruments. Bretan and Weinberg (2016) survey robot musicianship.

The Nature of MIDI Performance Data

After this historical look, we turn to the technology of modern digital sequencers. The lingua franca of digital sequencers is the MIDI protocol. What aspects of performance are captured in MIDI data? Four basic types of MIDI data are important in performance:

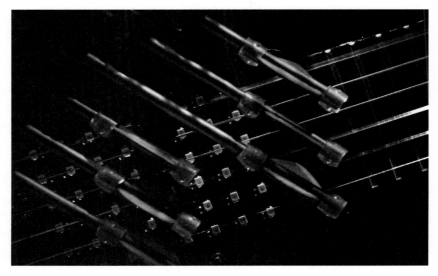

Figure 41.8   Z-Machines robot guitar player, detail of plucking mechanism (Suzuki 2018).

1. *Discrete note data* such as start and stop times, pitch, amplitude (velocity), and channel.

2. *Discrete MIDI program change* messages that select new patches (or instruments) on a synthesizer or signal processor. Program change messages can be entered into the sequencer in real time by pressing *program select* or *voice select* buttons on a MIDI device. They can also be entered through editing operations.

3. *Discrete system exclusive messages* supply parameters to selected synthesizer and effects programs. Consider the example of controlling a synthesizer in performance. After a program change message selects the Program 5: FM Strings program, a system exclusive message might modify the parameters of Program 5, such as the amplitude envelope, modulation depth, and so on.

4. *Continuous controller* data coming from pitch bend and vibrato wheels, volume pedals, and sliders.

Notice the important distinction between discrete and continuous in this list. *Discrete* means that notes and program change messages occur when an on/off button is pushed. A key on a musical keyboard can be thought of as a button. In contrast, continuous data comes from analog controllers such as wheels, pedals, and sliders. A continuous controller transmits discrete messages continually whenever its position changes from a stationary null position.

We have already mentioned that a note event captures the velocity and the channel of the note. If the reader is not familiar with MIDI, the meaning of these terms is not yet clear. Before going on, let us explain these terms, because they are ubiquitous in the sequencing world. For simplicity, we assume the MIDI 1.0 protocol. Refer to chapter 51 for more on MIDI 2.0.

Anatomy of a note

The MIDI system encodes a note in two separate messages: note-on and note-off. The difference in time between the on and the off is the duration of the note. Either type of note message has four main parameters:

1. *On or off*—Indicates whether to start or stop a note.

2. *Pitch*—Encoded as a number from 0 (C0) to 127 (G10).

3. *Key velocity*—On a keyboard, a measure of how fast a key moved in a vertical direction. It has a value between 0 and 127. Because a fast-moving key indicates that the note was played with more force, it is usually interpreted by a synthesizer as the initial amplitude of the note.

4. *Channel*—In traditional MIDI systems, this is a number from 1 to 16; the channel mechanism is one of MIDI's ways of indicating timbre

differences, because one can assign different synthesizer voices to different channels.

Next, we look at practical aspects of sequencers in performance.

Using a Sequencer in Performance

A sequencer is a strange *chien savant*—incapable of performing the simplest of tricks without a spoon-fed diet of musical data, yet once trained, it astonishes with its quickness and agility. This section examines the training phase and the practice of performance.

Quantizing

Preparation for performance—sequence entry, editing, quantizing, and setup for playback—can be a major task. Chapter 42 presents methods of entering and editing sequencer data. Here we focus on the art of quantizing, and the next section deals with performance setup.

Many sequencers offer the option of *quantizing* or rounding off the durations of previously performed events to align them to a timing grid. For example, events might be quantized to sixteenth-note resolution and aligned to a steady metronome beat. Quantization can correct slight timing errors in performances that are played to a metronome accompaniment. It also makes the events easier to transcribe into a readable form of common music notation. Without quantized input data, a notation editor must fabricate weird configurations of tied notes—connected thirty-seconds, sixty-fourths, and one-hundred-twenty-eighths—in order to accurately reflect the duration of performed events that are slightly shorter or longer than sixteenth notes.

However, quantization also lessens the human feel of a performed rhythm, so it should be used carefully. As an antidote to quantization, a *humanize* or *groove quantization* operation is sometimes available to add small timing variations and amplitude changes.

Performance setup and orchestration

Performance setup means establishing a correspondence between sequencer tracks, MIDI channels, devices, and specific patches. The point of the setup process is to map the tracks to specific sounds—to orchestrate the sequence.

In the past, MIDI devices were always external to the computer, so it was necessary to map track data via specified tracks to specific devices (described in the next section). As initially defined, MIDI 1.0 permitted only 16 channels per cable. By the 1990s, *multiport MIDI interfaces* supported several independent 16-channel MIDI lines. A typical multiport interface can support 8 MIDI ports for a total of 128 channels.

Today, however, most musicians rely on software instruments for playback, to which the channel limitations of MIDI need not apply. In Avid's Pro Tools DAW for example, one creates an *instrument track* for a MIDI-controlled software instrument or a *MIDI track* for a MIDI-controlled external hardware synth. There is no limit to the number of instrument tracks. Users need not bother about channel mappings. This is all handled inside the DAW.

The next section looks at the problem of setting up a performance with an external MIDI synthesizer.

Performance setup with external MIDI-controlled devices

For an external hardware synthesizer, several elements must be coordinated in the setup phase (figure 41.9).

1. Tracks in sequencer software—Tracks (or *lanes*) segregate compositional data into streams that can be sent to individual MIDI channels.
2. MIDI channels—The sequencer MIDI OUT channel and the device MIDI IN port must be tuned to receive messages on the proper channels.
3. Physical device interconnections—MIDI or USB cables connect the sequencer to the external MIDI device.

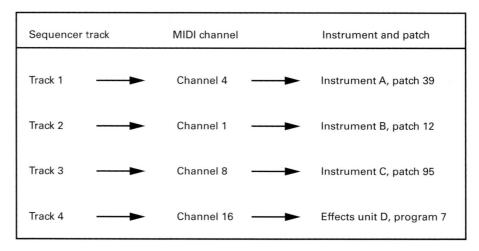

Sequencer track	MIDI channel	Instrument and patch
Track 1 ⟶	Channel 4 ⟶	Instrument A, patch 39
Track 2 ⟶	Channel 1 ⟶	Instrument B, patch 12
Track 3 ⟶	Channel 8 ⟶	Instrument C, patch 95
Track 4 ⟶	Channel 16 ⟶	Effects unit D, program 7

Figure 41.9 Sequencer performance setup in the case of external MIDI hardware instruments and effects units. Mapping of sequencer tracks to channels, instruments, and patches.

4. Program change messages—Program change messages switch from one patch or timbre to another on the MIDI device.

5. System exclusive messages—System exclusive messages pass parameter data to the selected patch. That is, they customize the patch with data prepared in advance (filter settings, oscillator tunings, effects parameters, and so forth).

Apart from the General MIDI mode (chapter 51), which establishes a standard performance configuration, musicians must set up their own correspondences between these elements.

Performing with a sequencer

Performing with a sequencer means playing sequences in a planned or spontaneous manner. Characteristics of the playback can be controlled in real time, such as the tempo, panning, pitch bend, and vibrato among others. DAWs provide onscreen controllers, but performing musicians usually prefer tactile input devices. A *MIDI controller*—an inexpensive box with programmable pads, switches, faders, and knobs—is a common external controller for triggering sequences and samples.

Subsequences and performance logic

Some sequencers let one record many individual sound clips or MIDI *subsequences* that can be assigned as *macros* to the keys of a keyboard or MIDI controller. By pressing various keys, the musician starts various clips or subsequences running in series or concurrently. One can also program a sequencer to trigger subsequences according to external events such as a switch on a foot pedal or a tap on a control pad (figure 41.10).

Another possibility is to chain together sequences in performance according to a subroutine logic of conditional execution. That is, the start of sequence B may be dependent on the start of an event in sequence A. If an event in sequence B occurs before the musician starts sequence C, this may cause sequence D to start. For truly programmable control of sequence playback, designing one's own sequence algorithm using an interactive performance toolkit such as Max, PureData, SuperCollider, or ChucK gives the most flexibility.

Inside a Digital Sequencer

How does a digital sequencer work? This section digs a level deeper into the mechanism of a sequencer.

Figure 41.10   Novation Launchpad Pro, a popular controller designed to launch clips and sequences in Ableton Live.

The core task is to record a performance while simultaneously playing back previously recorded performances stored on multiple tracks. To accomplish this, the sequencer must first determine which new notes have been started or finished. Second, it must find all notes in previously recorded tracks that should start playing soon. Finally, the sequencer must monitor its input controls (knobs, buttons, faders, keyboard, mouse, etc.), and update its displays.

Here is a simple scheme for accomplishing these tasks, adapted from the description in Mauchly (1982). We begin by looking at the software needed for recording sequencer tracks. This software assumes that the note event information from a musical keyboard has been preprocessed into *event packets*. An event packet contains the following information:

- Key number
- Key status—whether the key is pressed or released
- Key velocity
- Time that the key status changed

Within a sequencer, time is typically measured as a count of *MIDI clock ticks* since the sequencer began recording a track. (See the description of MIDI clock in chapter 51.) The sequencer program then assembles the event packets for a track into a *track event array*. A track event array has two parts: a value indicating the number of events packets in the array, and the track event packets themselves.

This sequential array representation has the advantages of simplicity and compactness. However, if the musician wants to edit the track, for example, to insert a note event at a time *t* between other notes, an array representation poses problems. In order to make a slot for the new event, all events after *t* would have to be copied (shifted) one slot down. Hence a sequential array representation is not optimal for editing purposes. The editor program might use a *linked-list* representation for the events. At each edit point, the editor creates a *link* data structure. A link consists of two *pointers* (or memory addresses): one pointer contains the address of a track event array, and the second pointer contains the memory address of the next link.

A practical solution combines the two representations. For unedited note events the sequencer uses the array representation (figure 41.11a). Whenever an array is altered, the sequence editor creates a link to make room for new events or to fill in the gap between deleted events (figure 41.11b). The playback portion of the sequencer can read either type of representation.

When it is time to play back a stored sequence, the software merges event data from several sequencer tracks into a single stream, sorting the events in time order (figure 41.12). It packages the events into MIDI messages and sends them to one or more MIDI synths.

Machine Music

One aesthetic issue that immediately crops up in sequencing is the possibility of *machine music* enabled by *trans-human* performance: playback with super-human speed and precision (Collins 2002). This was already feasible in mechanical music performance. Conlon Nancarrow's amazing *Studies for Player Piano*

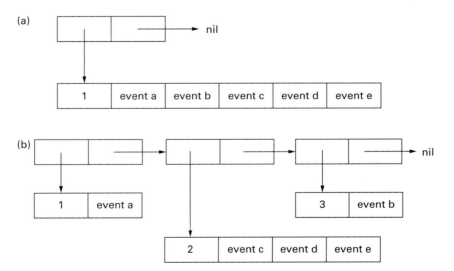

Figure 41.11   Internal representation of a sequencer track. (a) Before editing, the track can be represented as an array. (b) During and after editing the track becomes a linked list, intermingling individual events and subarrays. Here *event b* has been moved from the second element to the last element position.

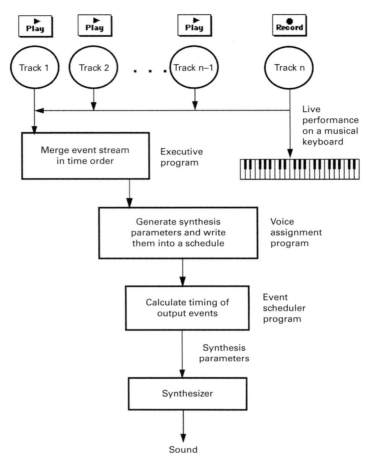

Figure 41.12   Operation of a sequencer program simultaneously recording and playing back. The sequencer merges existing tracks with input from a real-time performance.

(1948–1992) demonstrated multiple simultaneous tempi and irrational tempo ratios (Tenney 1988). The aesthetic of superhuman speed and precision came to the fore in the early days of computer music, when Arthur Roberts composed his dazzling *Sonatina for CDC 3600* (Von Foerster and Beauchamp 1969). Extreme uptempo playback is also characteristic of the genre of *tracker music* and in sequenced electronica by artists such as Squarepusher, for example on the track *Ultravisitor* (2004). His *Music for Robots* (2014) also exploits the high speed and precision possible by machine performance.

Software for Expressive Performance of a Score

One category of performance software reads a score file and attempts to play it in an expressive manner like a virtuoso human musician would. The goal is to interpret the score, using rules derived from analyzing human performances. These studies apply "pronunciation rules" for musical texts—akin to prosodic rules for speech—that correspond to the appropriate style (Sundberg, et al. 1983; Goebl et al. 2008; Friburg and Bresin 2008).

Possibilities of Interactive Performance Software

Technology affords the opportunity to go beyond traditional performance modalities, which are usually limited to supplying pitch and time information for a single instrument (Jordà 2007). This section describes some extended musical possibilities opened up by interactive performance software.

Transmitting Audio or Visual Cues

In one form of interactive performance, the computer transmits visual or sonic cues to musicians. In effect, the computer tells the performer what to do and/or when to do it. One way is to transmit cues via headphones (Ghent 1967b). Another is to project visual cues. This can be organized as a signal-and-response system, where audio cues cause page turns in a score on a screen. The music can be algorithmically composed and notated in performance. (See chapter 49 on live coding and live notation.) More loosely, the performance can include projection of artistic images that performers are expected to respond to in some fashion.

Another trend combines sound structure visualizations with live coding. Figure 41.13 shows a visualization based on analysis of the sounds generated in performance by the Edinburgh-based laptop duo of Jules Rawlinson and Marcin Pietruszewski. The sound is analyzed by a machine listening system designed in the SuperCollider language. Analysis data is sent via Open Sound Control (chapter 52) to the Unity game engine for visualization in real time.

Conducting an Ensemble of Synthetic Instruments

Conducting software offers the possibility to go beyond the kinds of control given to a traditional instrumentalist—such as control of a single voice—to control at the level of a conductor (Kobrin 1977; Chadabe 1984; Dannenberg and Bookstein 1991; Mathews 1989; Morita, Hashimoto, and Ohteru 1991; Keane, Smecca, and Wood 1990; Friburg and Bresin 2008; Nakra 2000; Nakra et al. 2009; Johannsen and Nakra 2009; Malinowski 2015). Such a

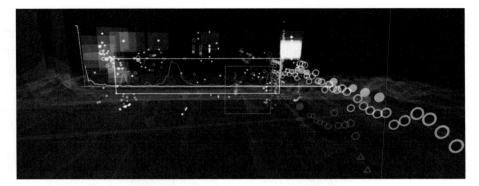

Figure 41.13   Projection of two event streams (one from each player) on multiple time scales. (In the original the streams have different colors.) The circles and triangles on the right of the image indicate frequency (left to right), amplitude (bottom to top), and spectral brightness (symbol) over a five-second time scale. A circle indicates spectral flatness, and a triangle indicates brighter elements. Diamonds, squares, and hatched squares (not shown) appear as the signal becomes noisier/ brighter. Solid circles indicate onsets. At the back of the image is an instantaneous spectrum display plus a partly opaque waterfall plot of previous values. Tiny dots show a histogram of activity on a longer time scale (forty-five seconds). The big solid boxes serve as a short-term view of frequency, amplitude, and timbre and make it easy to see repeating patterns. Image courtesy of Julian Rawlinson.

system must be able to interpret a performer's gestures and translate these into the manipulation of *ensemble parameters.* Ensemble parameters include tempo, overall articulation, stress, balance of voices, and spatial projection.

Accompanying a Human Performer

An *accompaniment system* plays along with a human musician, following the performance of a score by the human, and playing its own score simultaneously (Buxton 1986; Dannenberg 1989b; Dannenberg and Mont-Reynaud 1987; Rowe 1992a,b, 2001; Puckette and Lippe 1992; Raphael 2008, 2009). There can be several aims for an accompaniment system. One application is teaching music instrument performance. Here a computer plays an accompaniment while listening to the student and grading the student's playing (e.g., MakeMusic SmartMusic). Another goal is a time-flexible rendition of a contemporary music score, replacing the fixed-duration "tape recorder mode" of performance in which the instrumentalist plays along with a pre-recorded sound track (Winkler 1998).

The main technical problem in accompaniment is following the human performer (Puckette and Lippe 1992; Winkler 1998; Rowe 2001; Raphael 2009). This problem is many-faceted; there is a tendency for systems to solve one aspect of it while ignoring others. Some try to follow the pitches played by the instrumentalist, some track only the tempo, some merely look for isolated cues without trying to follow every note. In the playback, some alter the tempo according to the instrumentalist's tempo, some try to match dynamics, and some modify only the onset time of the accompaniment sequence. Even when the accompaniment system is performing flawlessly, it is possible for the human instrumentalist to make a mistake; thus in concert situations it has been recommended to keep a backup musician on hand to initiate sequences manually in case synchronization is lost.

Accompaniment systems developed by Dannenberg (1984), Dannenberg and Mukaino (1988), Dannenberg and Mont-Reynaud (1987), Chabot and Beauregard (1984), Vercoe (1984), Horiuchi and Tanaka (1993), Inoue et al. (1993), and Raphael (2009) tracked a live performer and altered the playback tempo of a prepared score for a computer-performed part.

Several works of composer Morton Subotnick involve interaction between one or more performers and a sequenced accompaniment (figure 41.14). To support this work, Subotnick and Coniglio developed the Interactor program, which tracked real-time performance of a precomposed score and triggered the playback of sequences (Coniglio 1992). By looking only for landmarks in the score—unique pitch and rhythmic configurations—the Interactor program allowed a great deal of interpretive leeway on the part of the performer.

Figure 41.14   Morton Subotnick, live in concert at Lincoln Center, New York in 1983. The synthesizer is a computer-controlled Buchla analog system. (Photograph by B. Bial.)

Recognizing musical patterns

Figure 41.15 shows a block diagram of an accompanist system. An input processing subprogram handles data from the soloist. Ideally, this input data is already encoded with timing information (such as MIDI note-on and note-off messages). If the data stream is raw audio samples, the input processor must be capable of converting this into symbolic score data—a major task. The matcher subprogram compares the actual performance of the soloist with the soloist's score. In doing so, it must be able to ignore anomalies played by the human performer and track missing notes to find the best possible correspondence. For complicated polyphonic music, the program may maintain several hypotheses about the current location and discard a hypothesis when evidence points strongly to a single conclusion. The third subprogram is the accompaniment performance, which controls the timing of the accompaniment. In the simplest case, timing is the only aspect of the accompaniment that varies from one performance to another.

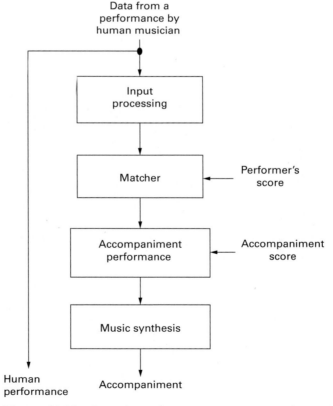

Figure 41.15 Overview of a computer accompaniment system. It listens to a human performer and generates an accompaniment that matches the direction and flow of the human performer.

Based on a Markov model, Pachet's Continuator (2003) was able to learn and generate music in many styles, either in standalone mode, as continuations of a musician's input, or as interactive improvisation. Recent accompaniment systems use dynamic time-warping algorithms or hidden Markov models to match note onset times with a score (Déguernel, Vincent, and Assayag 2018; Goto and Dannenberg 2019).

Control by Gestures

Another class of interactive performance involves a performer whose gestures are recognized by the system, triggering sound responses. The gestures may come from a dancer or from a performer with a custom controller. A popular method of training a system to recognize gestures is neural network algorithms. (See appendix A.)

Shared Control of One Instrument

The flexibility of digital instruments means that they can be controlled by a variety of input devices. We can plug a keyboard, wind, guitar, or exotic controller into the same sound generating instrument. For a complex instrument, we can have all these devices connected simultaneously. Thus another performance situation is having several musicians control one multivoice synthesizer (Weinberg and Gan 2001). A spectacular example was the Soundnet (figure 41.16), an instrument played by the Sensorband (Atau Tanaka, Zbigniew Karkowski, and Edwin van der Heide) crawling and climbing on its tension sensor-loaded cable structure (Bongers and Sensorband 1998; Bongers 2000; Tanaka 2009).

Interactive Virtual Worlds

One class of interactive compositions involves a sonic ecosystem with networks of feedback and interaction, involving a performer, electronics, and a room. The composer Agostino Di Scipio has written extensively about this approach (Di Scipio 2018).

Virtual reality technology has opened up the possibility of making visual, sonic, and haptic worlds that function like interactive instruments. For a survey of this domain, refer to Serafin et al. (2016).

Networked Computer Bands

Networks of computers can be formed to make up a computer band (Bischoff, Gold, and Horton 1978). The musicians may let their systems run autonomously,

Figure 41.16   Artists of the Sensorband playing the Soundnet instrument in 1996.

or they may interact with them and each other in a musical way. Depending on how the rules of interaction are defined, the results can vary from free improvisation to synchronized ensemble performance.

The potential is great. One possibility is to combine multiple interacting musical algorithms with multiple human musicians. A pioneering example of this approach is the work beginning in the 1970s of composers from Mills College and affiliated with the League of Automatic Music Composers and The Hub (figure 41.17) in the San Francisco area (The Hub 1989; Brown and Bischoff 2005).

Today, laptop, tablet, and mobile phone ensembles are widespread, with group experimentation enabled by Ethernet and WiFi communications (Trueman, et al. 2006; Collins 2010).

Telematic Music: Networked Performance via the Internet

With the rise of the internet in the 1990s, the idea of connecting musicians around the world came to the fore. Thorington (2005), Barbosa (2008), Oliveros et al. (2009) and Manning (2013) discuss the early history. Early experiments reported by Atau Tanaka include the use of video conferencing

Figure 41.17   The Hub, a pioneering a computer band, performing in concert at Mills College, Oakland, California. Each musician interacts with a computer that in turn interacts with other computers to create an ensemble performance. From left to right: T. Perkis, P. Stone, C. Brown, S. Gresham-Lancaster, M. Trayle, J. Bischoff. (Photograph copyright Jim Block.)

technology over telephone lines to connect Tokyo and Paris, for example (Tanaka 1999). These were important lessons in dealing with delay, synchronization, and musical congruence.

One pioneering event in 1998 originated from three locations: Mills College in Oakland, California, Harvestworks in Soho, New York City, and the Morton Street Studio in the West Village, New York City. The Morton Street Studio was the hub location, where incoming streams from the other sites were mixed with live and prerecorded music and sound, and the final mix was streamed back to the server and onto participating sites and the broader Internet. An online audience could listen in. As is often the case, the piece was an improvisation including acoustic and electronic instruments as well as sampled sounds. A slide show of video stills by Mary Lucier and a text by Allen Grossman accompanied the work but were not synchronized to the performance.

The multimodal nature of the performance, combining musical improvisation with video images and text, is typical of many internet events. Not just audio, visual, and text data can be streamed but also data from sensors using MIDI and OSC protocols. With control signals streaming from remote locations, the result can be a complex and unpredictable multimedia "happening."

Apart from free-form jam sessions, remote music instruction and auditions are a practical need. These do not usually require precise tempo synchronization between sites, so they are easier to manage.

How can one set up a multisite internet audio performance? The process usually starts with an agreement between the sites on basic parameters. Each network node needs to have sufficient bandwidth to send and receive the performance data. The next step is to stipulate the specific internet protocol (IP) input/output ports to be used. This can be complicated when the computer in question is behind a router's firewall. In this case, it may be necessary to open a router's firewall ports. The audio sample rate and the audio buffer size need to be determined. For transmitting audio to the network, many setups use JackTrip, an open-source low-latency network audio router that is designed for performance over the internet (Cáceres and Chafe 2010). Also refer to QuackTrip (Puckette 2020). Commercial apps like JamKazam, Soundjack, and Jamulus (Fischer 2020) have come on the scene to facilitate the process.

One obstacle faced in connecting remote internet sites is the problem of *latency*, which is the delay it takes for sound (or other data) to travel between countries and continents (Rowe 2005). Even with theoretically ideal communication from Santiago to Moscow (14,000 km) at the speed of light, the delay is 93 ms (Barbosa 2008). In the real world, computer networks introduce additional delays. Driessen et al. (2011) analyzed the effects of network delay on tempo and showed how increasing delays cause musicians to decrease the tempo. Some network musicians set the tempo of their piece to the latency lag so that participants can stay synchronized. Of course, this is a musical limitation. Thus most networked compositions are organized around free improvisation, drones, asynchronous multimedia layering, or other strategies for which synchronicity is not important (Chafe 2009). Another problem is silent gaps or *audio dropouts* (Fischer 2020). Whereas Fischer suggests that band members should not focus on the issue and concentrate on their own playing, Rottondi et al. (2016) suggests strategies for packet loss concealment.

A different set of services is designed to stream high-resolution audio files in real time, in which the issues of interaction and latency are not an issue. Musicians collaborating on a project can exchange tracks. Audio mastering and mixing services can stream audio to clients for approval. A commercial service like Audiomovers ListenTo is an example, but this is an evolving area with many players and with both free and pay options.

Live Coding

Live coding fuses the role of the improviser with that of the computer programmer (figure 41.18). The idea is that the music is created in real time by a computer programmer live on stage. Live coding has a long history dating back to the early microprocessor era, in which musicians such as Ron Kuivila programmed in the Forth language on stage (Roads 1986c). Many live coders project their screen to make clear what they are typing. The inspiration for live

Figure 41.18   Ge Wang, co-inventor of the ChucK music programming language, live coding in performance around 2008. The code is projected on-screen for the audience to see.

coding comes from a conceptual aesthetic that considers code as art and programming as performance (Collins 2003; Collins et al. 2003; Freeman and Troyer 2011; McLean and Wiggins 2010; Roberts, Wakefield, and Wright 2015).

Events called *algoraves* combine live coding with a dance club scene. The website www.toplap.org serves as a hub for the community of interest. Chapters 48 and 49 discuss languages for live coding.

One trend has been the combination of live coding software with interactive MIDI controllers (e.g., Olivia Jack) or EuroRack modular systems (e.g., Richard Devine).

Another trend used by the CREATE Ensemble at UCSB is *network data sharing*. The software JackTrip enables sharing of multiple audio streams with remote players (Cáceres and Chafe 2010). In performance, each player can simultaneously live code a single shared program using software such as ShareDB (Yerkes 2018).

Improvisation Systems Onstage and in Installations

The flexibility inherent in software means that computer-based instruments can respond to a gesture in arbitrarily complex ways (Nelson 1989; Roads 1986a; Pachet 2003). For each gesture of the musician, a procedure might execute an arpeggio or chord or trigger an entire sequence. This interaction is not necessarily based on score following, because the human performer may be improvising. The point is that the system's response is not predetermined but is algorithmically improvised on the spot.

Improvisation Systems: Background

One of the first computer-based interactive improvisation systems was demonstrated in 1968 at London's Institute for Contemporary Art. In the system developed at the Electronic Music Studios company by Peter Zinoviev and his associates, gallery visitors whistled a melody into a microphone connected to a Digital Equipment Corporation PDP-8/s minicomputer. The computer then rearranged the melody and calculated variations, performing them on an attached analog synthesizer (Grogono 1984).

In the 1970s and early 1980s, composers such as the Paris-based Giuseppe Englert with the Groupe Art et Informatique Vincennes (GAIV), Salvatore Martirano, Edward Kobrin, Laurie Spiegel, Joel Chadabe, George Lewis, and David Behrman pioneered the use of real-time algorithmic composition in performance (Chadabe 1997). Activity in this domain expanded rapidly with the spread of MIDI systems, which simplified and standardized the technical aspects of real-time performance (Rowe 1992b).

The aesthetic aims of improvisation systems owe much to the confluence of algorithmic composition, live electronic music, free jazz, the improvisatory tradition, and the tradition of interactive sound sculpture (Mumma 1975; Stockhausen 1971b, 1978; Battier 1981; Bernardini 1986; Roads 1985b; Valentino 1986). Improvisation systems allow a virtuoso soloist to create a dialog onstage. Doug Van Nort, with Pauline Oliveros and Jonas Braasch (2013), described the need for "deeply listening machines."

Autonomous Performance and Installations

Standalone performance systems are evolving into increasingly sophisticated droids. Their sharply focused intellects can recognize patterns in external events and respond according to programmed rules.

We find these systems onstage, improvising with soloists or ensembles, but also in art galleries, where interactive sound art installations respond to environmental cues like light, temperature, sound, and proximity to sensors and capacitance fields. The New York–based sound artist Liz Phillips is a pioneer in this field (figure 41.19). Dance movements can drive music improvisation by attaching electronic sensors to dancers or by placing dancers within the sensory field of the computer.

The necessity for real-time operation places great demands on improvisation software. Only the most efficient recognition algorithms work in the heat of performance. In systems that are expected to respond in an original manner—either to a human performer or to other intelligent instruments—the musical problem is to avoid mechanistic behavior. The computer must have an understanding of specific musical contexts, and it must interpret gestures within such contexts.

The Neurswing system was an early example of using a trained neural network for improvisation including context controls (Baggi 1991). The

Figure 41.19   An interactive installation by Liz Phillips. *Soundtable II,* 1992 installation at the Threadwaxing Space, New York City. The water in the table conducts and transmits a capacitance field. As viewer/listeners move near the table, a loudspeaker under it emits reverberated resonances. Sound formations respond to the gestures of those who approach the table. They can watch as waves of sound energy vibrate the surface of the water, creating a framed image in the pool. (Photograph by R. Winard.)

system took as input a harmonic progression. It then generated a rhythm section accompaniment for piano, bass, and drums. The algorithm was controlled by three context parameters: *hot/cool, dissonance/consonance, as-is-ness/free.* An increase in the *hot* knob favored louder playing, more appoggiaturas, more nervous drum patterns, and more cymbal crashes. An increase in the *dissonance* knob favored the insertion of dissonant harmonic patterns, flattened fifths in dominant seventh chords, inverted piano chords, and half-step appoggiaturas. An increase in the *free* knob caused the program to deviate from the original harmonic progression.

George Lewis's Voyager system listens to his trombone playing through a microphone connected to the computer (Roads 1985d; Lewis 2000, 2009). The computer follows the pitch of the melodic line and responds according to rules of improvisation provided by Lewis. In concert, a synthesizer controlled by a computer improvises with the live performer. The design of the system follows this schema (Lewis 2000, 34–35):

The Voyager program is conceived as a set of 64 asynchronously operating single-voice MIDI-controlled "players," all generating music in real time. Several different (and to some, clashing) sonic behavior groupings, or ensembles, may be active simultaneously, moving in and out of metric synchronicity, with no necessary arithmetic correlation between the strongly discursive layers of multi-rhythm. While this is happening, a lower-level routine parses incoming MIDI data into separate streams for up to two human improvisors, who are either performing on MIDI-equipped keyboards or playing acoustic instruments through "pitch followers," devices that try to parse the sounds of acoustic instruments into MIDI data streams. The aperiodic, asynchronously recurring global "behavior specification" subroutine setphrasebehavior, which runs at intervals of between 5 and 7 seconds, continually recombines the MIDI "players" into new ensemble combinations with defined behaviors.

Inspired by Lewis, Henning Berg developed the Tango software for interactive improvisation over more than two decades (Berg 2019). Tango takes a modular approach, allowing the user to customize its Player, Listener, Modifier, and Harmony modules to interpret the current context and generate unique musical responses.

42 *Sequence Editors*

Tracks and Controller Lanes

Loop-Oriented Sequencers

Modular Step Sequencers

Visual Representations for Editing

> **Piano Roll Notation**
> **Event List**
> **Common Music Notation**
> **Metrical Grid/Drum Editor**
> **Controller Envelopes**
> **Faders**
> **Audio Waveforms**

Sequence Editing Operations

Sharing Sequence Data

A sequencer records the control data needed to play a series of musical events on one or more synthesizers. In computer music this is usually MIDI data. A MIDI sequencer records the time and velocity of notes played on a MIDI input device like a musical keyboard. (Key velocity tells how hard a key was pressed; faster usually signifies louder.) These gestures generate *note-on* and *note-off* messages. The sequencer also records position changes in input devices like vibrato wheels, foot pedals, knobs, and buttons, as well as data entered by clicking and drawing on a screen. This is called *controller data.* Note and controller data can be edited and then played back into sound.

Chapter 41 recounted the history of sequencing and described it from the perspective of performance. Here we introduce the basics of sequence editing. Sequence editing is a core function of *digital audio workstations* (DAWs).

It is easy to learn how to insert, cut, copy, and paste MIDI notes on a graphical time line. For many reasons, however, editing MIDI data can become complicated, requiring detailed knowledge of the MIDI protocol as well as mastery of a sequence editor. The multiple different types of MIDI data have led to many ways to edit, each with its own visual representation. The major sequencers have similar visual representations, but they provide different toolsets to operate on these representations. The user manual for a typical DAW devotes many pages to detailed instructions on sequence editing. Obviously, this chapter cannot replace a manual. Rather, our goal is to present an overview of sequence editing in general.

Basic understanding of MIDI is recommended before reading this chapter; refer to chapter 51.

Tracks and Controller Lanes

Tracks are units of musical organization in a sequencer. One can use them in arbitrary ways to group related data or to segregate unrelated data. For example, one can assign a track to receive and send data on a specific MIDI channel. If desired, however, a single track can also contain many channels of data. Importantly, MIDI 1.0's sixteen-channel limit does not apply in the case of software instruments. In a DAW like Pro Tools, one can set up an arbitrary number of tracks and associated instruments without worrying about channel assignments (figure 42.1).

In general, a track includes all the controller data associated with a plug-in synthesizer. Controller data is of two basic types: (1) generic MIDI controller

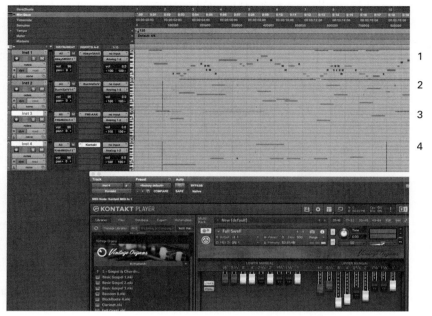

Plug-in instrument

Figure 42.1   Pro Tools screen showing four MIDI tracks (stacked vertically) in piano-roll time line notation played by four different software instruments. Track 4 is selected, so its software instrument is displayed at bottom.

data applies to any plug-in, and (2) specific controller data applies only to the parameters of a particular plug-in. Generic MIDI controller data includes velocity, volume, mute, pan, pitch bend, aftertouch, program change, system exclusive data, and other MIDI controller data. Specific controller data for a plug-in filter might include on/off, filter type, gain, center frequency, and *Q*. For a synthesizer the parameters would be different.

Controller data can be displayed and edited in an *automation* or *controller lane*. Some controller data takes the form of *discrete* values that occur only at isolated points in time. An example is note velocity, which is displayed as a vertical spike in the time line. The greater the velocity, the higher the spike. By contrast, *continuous controller data* is displayed as an envelope. Figure 42.2 shows four tracks with MIDI generic controller lanes superimposed on the piano-roll note display.

Some DAWs can also display and edit controller lanes underneath a track, as shown in figure 42.3.

Another way to use tracks is to keep different versions or *takes* of a musical line in separate tracks. Later one might select a single take for the final mix or use muting to switch between the best parts of multiple

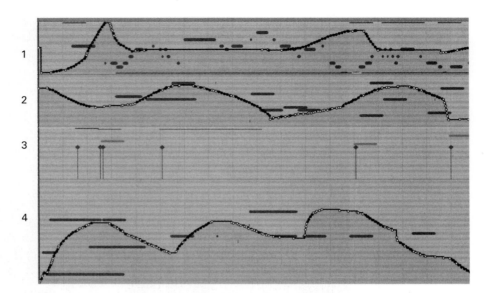

Figure 42.2   Data in controller lanes superimposed over note data in piano roll display. Lanes 1,2, and 4 show continuous envelopes. Lane 3 shows MIDI discrete note velocity values plotted as vertical spikes.

takes. In any case, it is common for a musical sequence to consume dozens of tracks. Some editing operations apply to every event in a track (e.g., "transpose track 38 by a whole tone"). Others apply only to selected events.

Loop-Oriented Sequencers

Pattern or *loop* orientation in a sequencer breaks the data into subsequences within a sequence. A subsequence or pattern can be looped, played back in combination with other patterns, or triggered to play from an external event. Patterns or loops are an alternative unit of organization in many sequencers. This means that one can add, delete, insert, transpose, or operate in other ways on patterns the same as note events.

A classic looping beat and bar sequencer is Ableton Live (figure 42.4). By default, audio clips are *warped* (time stretched or shrunk) to fit the bar lines. Imported MIDI note data is automatically aligned to a metric grid. In the Session view of Ableton Live, clips can be triggered by mouse-clicking on them or using the Push controller box. Clips will not start until the next bar starts, ensuring alignment with the beat. Audio clips loop within the metric

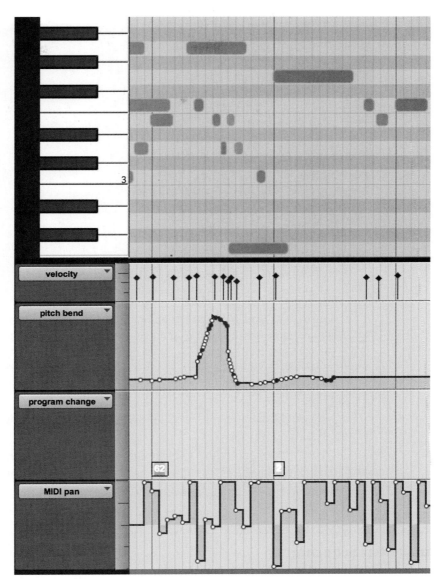

Figure 42.3   Four controller lanes displayed beneath the piano-roll note display at top. Note velocity data is shown as vertical spikes. Pitch bend is an envelope. Program changes are indicated by numbered boxes. MIDI pan is a random envelope swinging between left and bottom right.

Figure 42.4   Ableton Live, a loop-oriented sequencer. In Session view, the columns (Drums, Bass, Synths, etc.) show loops that can be triggered in performance. Arrangement view (not shown) is used for composition on a timeline. Users often compose in arrangement view and then transfer individual clips into session view for live performance. Image thanks to Chris Ozley.

grid structure. If desired, default settings can be overridden, and events can be positioned freely on the time line.

The Studio One DAW lets one insert a MIDI pattern at any point in a time line. The pattern plays at the current tempo. Multiple patterns with different rhythmic schemes can be overlaid for polyphonic effect.

Modular Step Sequencers

A step sequencer has a limited number of stages or steps (see chapter 41). It typically repeats or loops at the end of the sequence. The classic analog step sequencers by Moog and Buchla offered between 8 and 48 steps. Recent Eurorack modules such as the MakeNoise Brains/Pressure Points are analog step sequencers. Many other analog sequencers are available in the EuroRack format.

Digital software sequencers such as Numerology (Five12 2014) emulate analog step sequencers but go far beyond their analog counterparts (figure 42.5).

Figure 42.5   Detail of Numerology step sequencer screen. A polyphonic sequence (top) with per-step gate and velocity controls beneath.

Freed of hardware constraints, software step-based sequencers let one instantiate multiple sequences in parallel, each with an arbitrary number of steps. They share a common clock.

Visual Representations for Editing

A musician can enter MIDI data into a sequencer in several ways:

- Opening a pre-existing MIDI file
- Playing an input device in real time connected to the sequencer
- Entering data in non-real-time with keyboard and mouse
- Generating from another app (e.g., Max) and routing into the sequencer using ReWire (see the section on Sharing Sequence Data further on).

For editing, MIDI information can be displayed in multiple visual representations, each of which highlights a particular view on the data. The main representations include

- Piano roll notation
- Event list
- Common music notation (CMN)
- Metrical grid
- Controller events and envelopes
- Faders
- Audio waveforms (with conversion to MIDI data)

Here we give a brief overview of each type. Chapter 45 discusses CMN editors in more detail.

Piano Roll Notation

Piano roll notation derives from the era of player pianos, when notes were encoded as punched holes in a roll of thick paper. The typical DAW sequencer piano roll display shows note events on a time line from left to right. Individual pitches are laid out vertically, and the start time and duration of note events are encoded as a dot or horizontal line, depending on duration (figure 42.6).

Event List

An *event list* representation lists the recorded MIDI data as text sorted in time order (figure 42.7). The event list is a detailed representation so that one can use it to fine tune a sequence. A typical event list will indicate the event type, channel, and data associated with the event. MIDI events types include note, control change, pitch bend, program change, aftertouch, poly pressure, system exclusive, and meta events. Meta events are specific to the manufacturer of the sequencer.

Common Music Notation

Some DAW sequencers perform transcription of MIDI performance data into a raw form of common music notation (figure 42.7); for example, Digital Performer uses QuickScribe, Pro Tools uses Sibelius, and Cubase and Nuendo provide Score Editor. Manual editing is usually needed to turn the raw notation

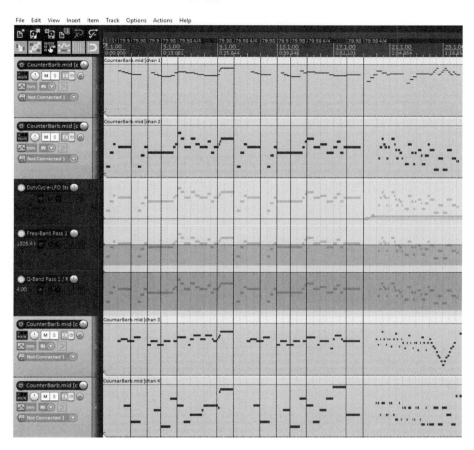

Figure 42.6   Piano roll notation in Reaper.

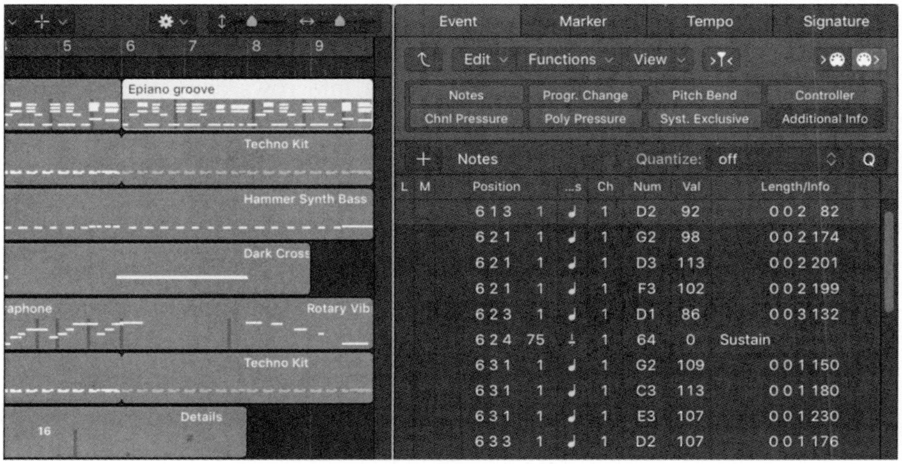

Figure 42.7   MIDI event list in Logic Pro. The event list view (right) displays all MIDI events that have been selected in the track view (left).

Figure 42.8   MIDI and CMN. Bach *Prelude and Fugue in C Major* BWV 846 shown in Pro Tools with the built-in Sibelius notation editor. The corresponding piano-roll display can be seen on the right.

into an aesthetically presented score. Scores can be exported in XML format for additional refinement in a full-featured notation editor such as Dorico, Finale, or MuseScore. (See chapter 45.)

Metrical Grid/Drum Editor

Some sequencers and drum machines use a metrical grid to display rhythmic patterns played by percussion instruments (figure 42.9). The horizontal axis represents time. It is subdivided according to the beat pattern and desired resolution. That is, a 4/4 measure divided by quarter notes shows four divisions; the same measure divided on a sixteenth-note grid would show sixteen divisions. The vertical axis divides into rows according to the number of percussion instruments.

Some sequencers use a similar but coarser *overview grid* to display measures. Each measure is a box; if the box is shaded, it contains an event. This view allows an overview of a large piece. To edit a measure, one can click on its box with the mouse.

Controller Envelopes

Pitch and vibrato wheels, foot pedals, and breath controllers, among other devices, generate continuous controller messages. These are envelopes for different aspects of the sound. They can be applied to one note, a selection of notes, or an entire track (figure 42.10). Sequencers provide a palette of

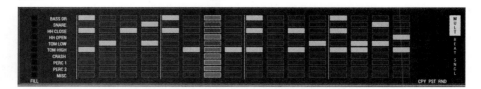

Figure 42.9   Metrical grid in a drum sequence editor.

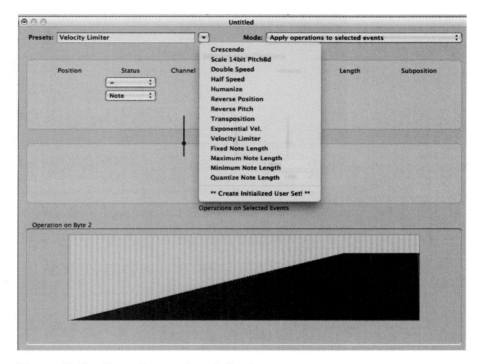

Figure 42.10   Controller envelope in Logic.

tools for drawing these curves, from straight lines to curves to random functions of time.

Faders

Faders allow control of synthesizer parameters such as amplitude. When the sequencer records fader movements, this enables automated mixing (figure 42.10).

Audio Waveforms

In a DAW sequencer, waveform clips can be positioned in audio tracks alongside MIDI tracks (figure 42.11). The clips can be moved around the

Figure 42.11   MIDI volume faders on four instrument (MIDI plug-in) tracks and four external MIDI tracks in Pro Tools.

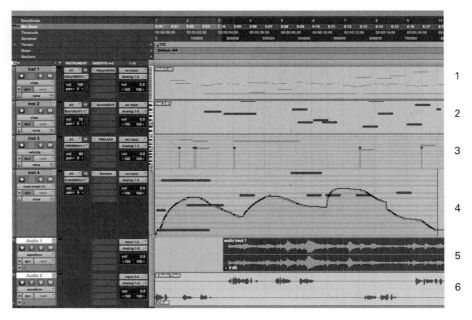

Figure 42.12   DAW session with combination of MIDI and audio tracks. Tracks 1–4 are MIDI. Tracks 3 and 4 show editing in controller lanes. Stereo tracks 5 and 6 are audio. Track 5 starts later than track 6.

time line and edited using audio editing tools (see chapter 43 on audio editing). This graphical representation is ideal for viewing the time correspondence between the MIDI data and the audio waveforms.

Some sequencers can convert audio waveforms to MIDI (using pitch detection) and also convert from MIDI to audio. This is done by rendering the MIDI data into sound by means of a plug-in synthesizer.

Sequence Editing Operations

MIDI sequence editors can operate on individual notes or on groups of notes defined by common properties such as track, channel, pattern, or other selection criteria. Edits can be made as *real-time replacement edits* (called *punch-in/ punch-out*, with reference to editing invoked by the Record button), or in non-real-time step mode, or as *random-access* edits. In step mode editing, musicians go through a composition one note at a time, adding, deleting, or changing notes as they go. This is usually done with a mouse by drawing note lengths graphically (Lehrman and Tully 1993). In random-access editing, musicians can look at a representation of all or part of the sequence (e.g., an event list or a piano roll) and edit material at any point.

Besides the usual insert, delete, copy, and paste operations, typical sequence editing operations can be divided into several groups: time, pitch, amplitude, channel, program change, and continuous controller editing. Refer to table 42.1

Sharing Sequence Data

Sharing sequence data is trivial if both parties have the same sequencer; they simply exchange files in that sequencer's format. When users have different sequencers, this can be done in two ways: via real-time transfer, or in non-real time via the standard MIDI file (.smf or .mid) format.

Real-time transfer from one computer to another is straightforward. An application on machine *A* plays the sequence while an application on machine *B* records it. The connection can be made through a MIDI interface or via a network. On MacOS the Audio MIDI Setup utility shows a Network icon that sets up a MIDI port for computer-to-computer transfers. A Bluetooth icon can also be configured for the same purposes.

A transfer can also be made between two apps on one machine using a virtual MIDI bus like the IAC (interapplication communication) Driver on MacOS or MIDI Yoke on Windows.

Table 42.1 Sequence editing operations

Time and tempo	Besides editing note durations, time editing includes rhythmic *quantization* and *dequantization*. Quantization means rounding off rhythms to align them to a meter, and dequantization ("humanizing") does the opposite.
	Time offsets, such as shifting a track by several milliseconds, can lend a different rhythmic feel to a track.
	Abrupt tempo changes can be inserted at any point, or the tempo can be made to accelerate or decelerate over a specified duration by drawing a tempo curve.
Pitch	Pitch editing can include transposition, pitch bend, or vibrato applied to individual notes or selected regions in a track. Many other note-level transformations are available in some sequencers, including alignment to a selected scale, reflections around a note, arpeggiation of selected notes, randomization of note amplitude or duration, thinning or thickening of note density, and others.
Amplitude	Following the keyboard bias of MIDI, the adjustment of the loudness of individual notes is expressed in terms of note velocity—how fast a key was pressed. Besides note-by-note changes, one can compress or expand the velocities in a track or in a selected region. This is similar to compression/expansion in signal processing but applied to MIDI velocities instead of samples.
	Another option is to apply crescendi and diminuendi to the MIDI volume parameter via a continuous controller envelope from a foot pedal or MIDI fader. MIDI volume affects the overall amplitude regardless of velocity values. One can also edit a MIDI mute on/off envelope to suppress certain parts.
Aftertouch	Many synthesizer voices respond to key pressure on a held note. This is called *aftertouch* in MIDI parlance. Aftertouch data is often used to control vibrato and other parameters. There are two types. *Channel* or *mono aftertouch* looks at all keys being held and transmits only the highest aftertouch value among them. Less commonly implemented is *polyphonic aftertouch*, in which each key being held transmits an independent aftertouch value.
Channel	Channel editing in a traditional setup with MIDI cables means reassigning the channel number associated with a one or more notes or a track. Because each channel is usually assigned to a different voice or instrument, changing channels is akin to reorchestration.
Program change	Program change editing means inserting MIDI *program change messages* into the sequence. Program change messages select the voice or patch to be played on a synthesizer.
Continuous controller data	Continuous controller data can also be used to vary aspects of timbre in a synthesizer. For example, we might assign a filter setting on a synthesizer voice, such as center frequency, to a continuous controller. Then by editing the envelope for this controller we can vary the center frequency of the filter over time.
System exclusive data	In a traditional MIDI setup, system exclusive (*sysex*) data can be sent from a hardware device via a sysex dump command on the device and can be recorded by a sequencer at a specific point in time. This is usually data associated with a particular patch, such as envelope settings.

On Linux systems, virtual and physical MIDI ports are handled by the Advanced Linux Sound Architecture (ALSA). Users can connect virtual MIDI ports through the command line. The JACK Audio Connection Kit provides an alternative when coupled with the graphical interface to the JACK patch bay called Catia.

ReasonStudios ReWire, which is supported by Digital Performer, Logic, Ableton, Pro Tools, Sibelius, Cubase, Reaper, Max, and many other platforms, is designed to transfer MIDI and audio tracks in real time between two programs.

Real-time transfer of MIDI data opens up the possibility of transformation of the data as it is being transferred, using the processing capabilities of the receiving program. For example, interactive performance programs (such as Max) can receive a performed sequence while another musician transforms it in real time. This might be tried in a networked improvisation, for example. If we instead reversed the direction and send MIDI from Max to a DAW via ReWire, we could generate MIDI messages from an intricate algorithmic process and record them in the DAW's sequencer (Elwell 2020).

43 Sound Editors, DAWs, and Audio Middleware

This chapter provides an overview of *sound editors, digital audio workstations* (DAWs), and *audio middleware.* Each serves a different function. A sound editor typically operates on one or two tracks of sound in fine detail. By contrast, a DAW organizes dozens of tracks and potentially hundreds of *audio clips.* An audio clip is a recorded segment of any length stored in its own file. DAWs import clips into a *session* and let users position them independently in time, mixing them with MIDI instrument tracks.

Audio middleware provides an interface for linking sounds to events in an interactive environment. Middleware supports the development of games, *virtual reality* (VR) and *augmented reality* (AR) worlds.

Sound editors, DAWs, and middleware permeate the audio and media industries, and experts in these systems are in high demand. DAWs and middleware in particular demand detailed study to achieve a professional level of expertise. The goal of this chapter is to distill the essential concepts, opening the door to further exploration.

Sound Editors

In the past, sound editing involved physically cutting into a reel of magnetic tape, with the angle of the cut determining the length of the fade into the next piece of tape. One then removed fragments, possibly inserted another fragment, and *spliced* (joined) them back together using adhesive tape. As tedious as this seems today, it was taken to a high art form by composers such as Bernard Parmegiani in his 1975 opus *De Natura Sonorum.*

Today, musicians and sound engineers record and modify sampled sound waveforms using a digital sound editor. These editors work mainly with a time-domain representation of a waveform, that is, a pressure graph. To avoid clicks at splice points, most splices use *crossfading,* a central operation in sound editing. A crossfade imposes a gradual transition from one signal to the next. This makes the splice sound seamless. We discuss this in more detail further along in the chapter.

Some editors incorporate spectrum displays and permit *spectrum editing,* which is covered in chapter 44. A *pitch editor* is another type of sound editor; refer to chapter 34.

Digital sound editors allow *rehearsable* or *nondestructive editing.* With rehearsable editing, a musician can try out an edit before making the definitive version. This is possible because memory buffers in the editor store rehearsal edits along with the original version. Only when the user decides that the splice is right does the editor save the new sample sequence. Rehearsable editing is the same thing as an *undo facility*, which allows one to reverse the effect of an editing operation as if it had never occurred.

Digital Sound Editors: Background

In *random-access media* such as hard disks or semiconductor memory, any piece of sample data can be retrieved as fast as any other piece, regardless of its location in the flow of music. Random-access media enabled the first generation of experimental audio editors with graphical waveform displays. The experimental Edsnd and S editors developed at Stanford University in the 1970s were among the first editors of this type (Moorer 1977; Roads 1982). Other experimental systems included DPYSND (Schottstaedt, c.1983, Stanford), SE (Milne, 1980, MIT), the New York Institute of Technology editor (Kowalski and Glassner 1982), and GCOMP (Banger and Pennycook 1983).

The first company to develop a graphical sound editor was Soundstream (Warnock 1976; Ingebretson and Stockham 1984). With the Soundstream system, a digital tape recorder sampled the original signal. In order to edit the sound, the data on the tape was transferred to a disk attached to a Digital Equipment Corporation PDP-11 minicomputer. Up to eighty-four *track-minutes* of music could be stored on the disk for editing. (A track-minute is a single track or channel of audio.) The eighty-four minutes on the disk could be divided into forty-two minutes of stereo audio, or about ten minutes of eight-track material.

Due to the general unreliability of hard disks in this period, the first commercial digital sound editors were based on *serial media* such as tape, with no graphical waveform displays. To find a sound at any position of the tape one had to fast-forward or rewind the tape to the sound's location. A classic example was the Sony PCM-1610 Compact Disc Mastering System, based on half-inch U-Matic video tape, introduced in 1981.

Later, the Fairlight and Synclavier synthesizers incorporated sample editors with graphical waveform displays. However, the cost of these systems put them out of reach of most musicians.

The cultural change known as the personal computer revolution began in 1981 with the introduction of the IBM PC. Early personal computers by IBM, Apple, and others were driven by floppy disks. Floppy disks allowed random access but were tiny in storage capacity and too slow for audio. Sound recording and editing became practical as faster and larger-capacity hard disks appeared on the market (Griffiths and Bloom 1982; Abbott 1984b; McNally et al. 1985; Freed 1987; Freed and Goldstein 1988). Digidesign's

Sound Designer for Apple Macintosh appeared in 1984. A main function of Sound Designer was to edit sounds for hardware samplers of the day.

It is hard to overstate the importance of graphical sound editors on audio production. Not being able to see waveforms was a major handicap. The simple ability to zoom in and out to any time scale in order to perform an edit—a capability taken for granted today—was a major breakthrough.

Features of Sound Editors

A graphical display of the time domain can be likened to a lens on sound. The lens's aperture can vary from microseconds to minutes, and users can scroll forward or backward through the sound file. The sound can be displayed in different formats (figure 43.1).

Users select portions of the display with a mouse and then choose an operation to apply to the selected portion.

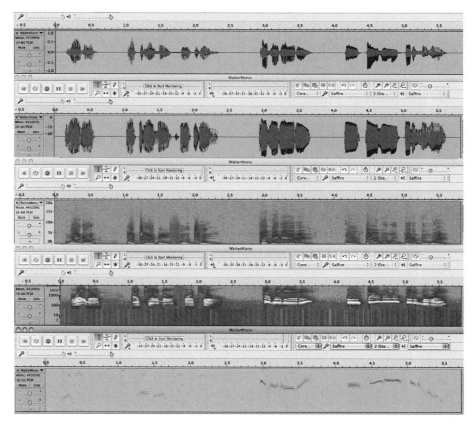

Figure 43.1   Five different displays of the same sound (spoken voice) in the Audacity sound editor. From top to bottom: Amplitude, amplitude in dB, spectrum with linear frequency scale, spectrum with log frequency scale, and pitch curve.

Table 43.1 lists basic operations provided by sound editors.

Zooming in and out in time is essential in order to define the scope of the edit. To find a thirty-second silent gap, for example, requires an overview display that shows a minute of sound. By contrast, to find a transient click in a complex passage requires resolution at the level of individual samples.

One of the fundamental capabilities of an audio editor is the ability to fade and crossfade sounds. Without it, sounds are merely juxtaposed, and artifacts such as clicks, pops, and thuds inevitably appear at the splice point (figure 43.2).

Figure 43.3 dissects a crossfade. Here (a) will be crossfaded into the end of (b). Figures (c) and (d) show the same sounds with their proper fade-in and

Table 43.1 Operations in graphical sound sample editors

Record–Capture a new sound to edit.

Cut—Delete unwanted material.

Splice two audio clips using crossfade functions drawn by hand or selected from a menu, thereby increasing the overall length; with or without crossfade.

Replacement edit—Write over a previously recorded segment.

Assembly edit—Link disparate passages by splicing.

Move a segment from point *A* to point *B* by graphical cut-and-paste methods

Mix numerous tracks into a smaller number of tracks.

Synchronize tracks—Adjust the timing of audio tracks relative to each other or to video.

Shrink or stretch the playing time without pitch change (pitch-time changing).

Pitch shift by a constant interval without changing the duration (pitch-time changing).

Pitch shift by a constant interval (constant speed change), causing the duration to change as well.

Pitch shift according to an envelope drawn by the user (variable speed change), causing the duration to change as well.

Equalize–Emphasize or deemphasize certain frequency regions by filtering.

Convert sample rate from a higher rate to a lower rate or vice versa.

Display samples in various time-domain formats, such as peak, average, and rectified.

Display multiple sound files simultaneously.

Horizontal and vertical zoom.

Find the maximum sample value in a region of a sound file.

Trace the amplitude envelope of a signal (peak or RMS value).

Reshape amplitude envelope—Rescale the amplitude of the samples according to a curve drawn by the user or extracted from another sound.

Play samples at full speed, half speed, double speed, or varispeed.

Perform spectrum analysis on a sound file for graphical editing and resynthesis.

Segment and label musical notes detected in the continuous stream of samples.

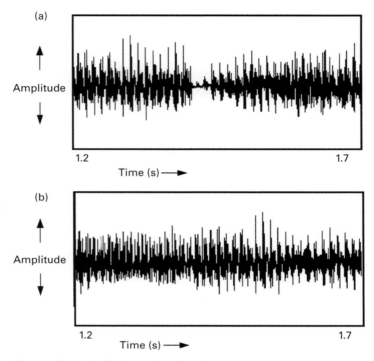

Figure 43.2 Splicing. (a) A simple paste command is equivalent to a hard cut. This juxtaposes the end of one sound with the beginning of another. (b) A crossfade smooths the transition between the two sounds. In this case, the crossfade time is 90 ms, during which the first sound fades down and the second sound fades up.

fade-out envelopes. Figure (e) depicts the result of a smooth crossfade with overlap between them. A sound editor makes this operation quick and easy.

Recognizing the importance of smooth fades and splices, many editors offer several fade curve functions for different musical situations, including linear (straight line), quarter-sine, and logarithmic curves (figure 43.4). As figure 43.4(c) shows clearly, logarithmic fades apply more effective energy than a linear fade or quarter-sine fade, so they are good for crossfades when the goal is to avoid the "hole in the middle" effect, that is, a drop in energy in the middle of the crossfade.

The Problem of DC Offset

Graphical waveform displays let us see problems in the audio waveform. A pernicious problem in audio is *direct current* (DC) offset, also known as *0 Hz*. This is a constant or nearly constant signal that can creep into a signal from many sources, both hardware and software. For example, certain plug-ins produce it as an inadvertent side effect. It is recognizable in a time-domain display as a waveform that is not centered about the zero amplitude

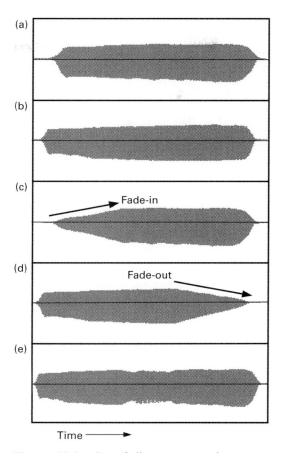

Figure 43.3 Crossfading two saxophone notes. (a) and (b) shows the amplitude envelope of the original two notes, a minor third apart in pitch. (c) and (d) are their faded versions. (e) is the result of crossfading (c) with (d).

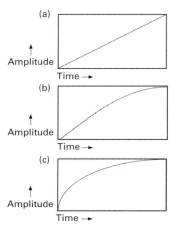

Figure 43.4 Fade-in functions in a sound editor. (a) Linear. (b) Quarter-sine. (c) Logarithmic.

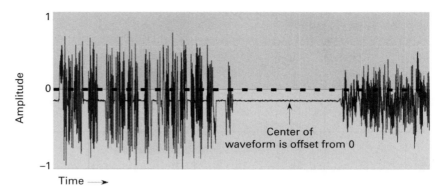

Figure 43.5   DC offset. The center of the waveform is offset from 0.

point (figure 43.5). DC offset can rob a mix of apparent loudness and cause clicks at the beginning and end of tracks. It diminishes the available dynamic range, which is especially damaging to bass frequencies. The most pernicious problem occurs when a track with DC offset is mixed with other tracks. The result contains the sum total of all the DC offsets in any tracks, exacerbating the problem. An effective way to remove DC offset is to apply a highpass filter with a cutoff frequency of 20 Hz.

DAWs

Chapter 26 on mixing introduces the concept of a DAW. A DAW provides a graphical time interface for audio editing and mixing. What is the difference between a sound editor and a DAW? A sound editor typically edits a single sound file and then saves the file when editing is done. By contrast, a DAW can load dozens of sound files as clips on multiple tracks. One can position multiple clips on a time line. The clips can be cut, copied, and pasted at any point in time, or they can be dragged into position using the mouse or key commands. The clips in all the tracks can be rendered to a mixed-down file.

The distinction between editor and DAW is blurred in apps like Audacity and Adobe Audition, which can handle multiple files on multiple tracks. However, as we see in this and the following section, a modern DAW is not just a multitrack audio mixer.

As chapter 26 points out, the first commercial apps for interactive graphical editing and mixing on personal computers were SoundEdit (1986) by Steve Capps and MacMix (1987) by Adrian Freed (Capps 1992; Freed 1987). As figure 26.4 shows, SoundEdit displays individual tracks to be mixed as sound pressure waveform clips.

In 1990, Opcode introduced Studio Vision, the first DAW to integrate MIDI tracks with audio tracks. Over the next decade, other DAWs developed similar capabilities. Since then, DAWs have continued to incorporate more and more features, including

- Multiple automation lanes
- Synchronized video
- Common music notation
- Plug-in synthesizers, samplers, and effects
- Hardware control surfaces
- Network capabilities for work sharing

among many others. Modern DAWs have hundreds of features. Many arcane features are tailored to the needs of specific groups (e.g., field recordists, the postproduction industry, and mixing to Dolby Atmos or Ambisonics), so everyone uses a subset of the overall feature set. Indeed, although modern DAWs have many complicated features, the basic functions of importing sound files, positioning clips on the time line, applying fades, and mixing down to stereo can be learned quickly. Table 43.2 lists typical features of a DAW.

An increasing number of sound editors and DAWs incorporate pitch editing utilities (figure 43.6). (See chapter 34 for more on pitch editing.)

Comparing DAWs

Dozens of DAWs compete in the marketplace, including Pro Tools, Cubase, Ardour, FL-Studio, Studio One, Nuendo, Logic Pro, ACID Pro, Ableton Live, Bitwig Studio, Digital Performer, Reaper, Reason, Samplitude Pro, Cakewalk Sonar, LMMS, Rosegarden, GarageBand, and many others. Figure 43.7 shows the interfaces of four DAWs. Due to the numerous, constantly changing features of DAWs, a detailed comparison is not given here. However, some general observations can be made.

All DAWs offer packages of built-in instruments, effects, and sample libraries. DAWs such as Pro Tools, Cubase, Ableton Live offer multiple versions, with the most expensive versions having extensive add-on packages.

Some DAWs run only under Linux (e.g., Ardour, LMMS, Rosegarden), and some run only on Windows (e.g., FL Studio, and Samplitude Pro). Others run only on Apple's operating system (e.g., Logic Pro and GarageBand).

Some DAWs are beat-, groove-, and loop-oriented, designed principally to support pop song production (e.g., Ableton Live, FL Studio, and ACID Pro). In these apps, by default, clips are "warped" (time-modified) to conform to the bar.

Table 43.2   Typical features of a DAW

Volume and pan automation	Hand-drawn envelopes to control the amplitude and pan (spatial) position of a track.
Groups	Groups enable editing several tracks in exactly the same way or mixing several tracks while keeping them at the same relative volume level.
Auxiliary sends	Auxiliary (aux) sends route a track to an output or bus path for further processing, Sends can be returned to the mix through an auxiliary input, audio track, or instrument.
Track inserts	An insert to tracks can be either a software plug-in insert, a hardware insert, or an instrument plug-in. Plug-ins and hardware inserts route the signal from the track through an effect, and automatically return it to the same track. Some instrument plug-ins accept audio from the track as input
Master Fader	Master Fader tracks control the master output levels of output and bus paths. They provide master level control for a main mix, headphone mix, stems, and effects sends.
VCAs	VCA master tracks emulate the operation of voltage-controlled amplifier channels on analog consoles, where a VCA channel fader controlled the signal levels of other channels on the console.
Render in place	Render in place performs a submix, bouncing a set of MIDI and audio tracks to a new track, including all track settings, inserts, sends, master channel settings, and automation lanes.
Sound to MIDI, MIDI to Sound	Sound to MIDI is useful for automatic transcription. MIDI to sound renders the MIDI instrument as well as any effects applied to it.
Keyboard shortcuts	Single-key commands let a user quickly control recording playback, scrubbing, zooming, undo, nudging, cut, copy, paste, separate, selection, toggling options, etc.
Audio alignment	Synchronizes stacked vocal and other tracks, matching multiple tracks to a reference track.
Drum editor	Provides a MIDI drum machine editor within the DAW.
Chord editor and chord entry	Edit and insert MIDI chords.
Pitch editor	Enables fine adjustment of melody lines in audio tracks.
Mastering tools	Tools for final equalization, dynamics, and imaging, and also analysis tools like spectrum displays, K-System and EBU loudness metering, phase metering, and oscilloscope.

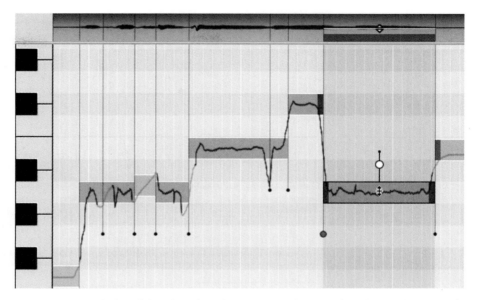

Figure 43.6 Pitch editing interface in Reason. The note handle (dark rectangle above the note) adjusts the amplitude of the selected note. Moving the drift handle (vertical bar with the white circle on top) down reduces vibrato and pitch drift. A double arrow on the center of the note is the pitch shift control.

Other DAWs do not assume by default that the audio content is pop songs. Pro Tools, for example, is commonly used in the television and movie industry for mixing dialog with music that weaves in and out. Nuendo is often used in game sound production due to its native connectivity with audio middleware.

Ableton's Live's Session interface was originally designed for DJ performance. Bitwig Studio has a similar Clip Launcher. It also features an integrated modular synthesizer (called GRID) that can modulate any track.

Max for Live lets users extend and customize Ableton Live by creating unique instruments or effects. For example, users can map Max-created *low-frequency oscillators* (LFOs) to any parameter for modulation. Toward a similar end, Reaper provides an integrated scripting language that allows users to customize and extend its capabilities. This includes hacks such as customizing the look and feel of the app, adding novel MIDI operations, adding a stutter function, and so on.

Certain DAWs are free and open-source (e.g., Ardour, LMMS, and Rosegarden), whereas most others are commercial apps (e.g., ProTools, Cubase, Ableton Live, Logic Pro, and Studio One). The cost of a commercial DAW can vary greatly. Introductory versions for laptop use cost less than $100. Professional DAWs with multichannel audio interfaces and hardware mixing consoles run well beyond $100,000 (figure 43.8).

(a)

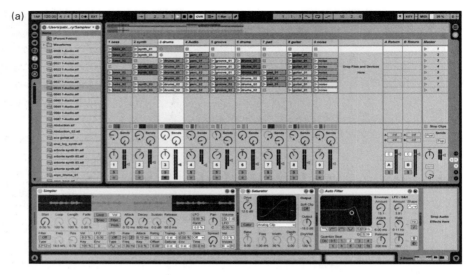

(b)

Figure 43.7   Image of four DAW windows. (a) Ableton Live Session window, in which sounds can be triggered in real-time. (b) Pro Tools mix window. A submixing session for *Always* (2013) by the author, mixing four new tracks into the stereo stem in the top track. (c) Cubase Pro 10.5, showing track time line, mixer, plug-in instruments and effects, and a video with timecode. (d) Ardour for Linux OS, showing *De Rerum Natura* (2020) by Rodney Duplessis.

(c)

(d)

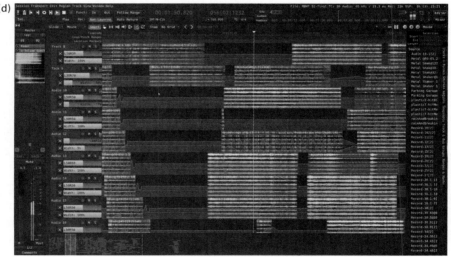

Figure 43.7   (continued)

Audio Middleware

Audio middleware lets composers and sound designers integrate music and sound into interactive environments with minimal text coding. Interactive environments include games and VR/AR such as Oculus and also training systems such as flight simulators.

Middleware provides a *graphical user interface* (GUI) and a library of functions that work with a game or VR development system. This common library

Figure 43.8   Avid S6 console. The S6 supports EUCON, Avid's high-speed Ethernet control protocol that allows its control surfaces to connect to a variety of audio and video software, including Pro Tools, Media Composer, Logic Pro, Cubase, Nuendo, Premiere, Audition, and others.

alleviates the need to have a programmer re-create the wheel for each project. Early examples of middleware for interactive audio were Microsoft's Direct-Sound (1995–2012) and DirectMusic (1996–2008).

Examples of middleware apps include AudioKinetic Wwise, FMOD Studio, Elias Studio, and Fabric (a Unity plugin). These serve sound designers working with game engines such as Unity, Unreal, CryEngine, others. They provide a GUI for editing waveforms and sound parameters along with mechanisms for linking sounds to events in the interactive environment (figure 43.9). They also provide functions (in the language C, C+, etc.) that developers can use in building their interactive system.

The core task of audio middleware is to connect sounds with the logic of the game. How are sounds triggered, with what real-time effects, and in what order? Users typically run a game development system, such as Unity, alongside the middleware to test as they go and ensure that sounds are being triggered appropriately. Developers can also monitor central processor unit (CPU) use and memory as well as the overall audio level.

Another task audio middleware performs is managing a library of *sound assets*. An asset is any file that is built into a project, including sounds, 3D models, backgrounds, animation, and code. Middleware lets sound designers link sound files to named sound events in the game's code that are triggered in real time according to a potentially complex logic. The sound designer can cache sounds that need to play instantaneously. Meanwhile, sounds that can tolerate latency, such as musical accompaniment, can be streamed as needed from disk. Although default sound libraries or *sound banks* can be used, a sound designer usually prepares custom music and sound assets using a standard DAW.

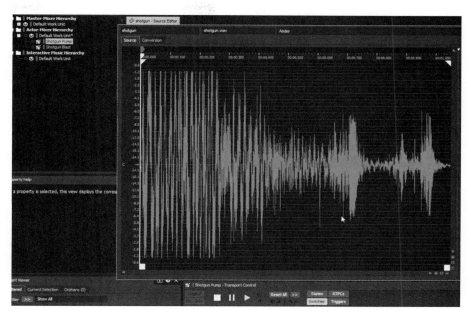

Figure 43.9   View of the waveform editor in Wwise.

As the basic sounds in the library are often untreated mono files, middleware lets users automate real-time effects such as spatial movement, early reflections, reverberation, filtering, pitch shifting, and granulation. This alleviates hand coding.

Since most VR and game environments are set in immersive worlds, support for 3D sound is available. Some middleware provides tools so that users feel the action with haptic feedback.

A common use of audio middleware is for creating *adaptive music*. In adaptive music, the mix can change in response to certain conditionals, such as the position of the player, or it can depend on probabilities. For example, the orchestration can evolve over time by dynamically fading tracks in and out, or it can change in response to a shift in the environment. An adaptive music system can sense that the current music needs to change, wait for the right moment, and then cue a smooth transition that leads into a new section.

44 *Spectrum Editors*

Command-Line Editors and Plug-Ins

Static Spectrum Editors

Envelope Editors

Sonographic Editors

Sample editors operate on waveforms in the time domain, whereas *spectrum editors* operate on partials in the frequency domain. Thus a spectrum editor analyzes a sound file to construct a representation of its frequency content. This analysis is often done with the *fast Fourier transform* (FFT), but other methods can also be used. Chapters 36–39 explain spectrum analysis.

A spectrum editor can serve many purposes. One might use an editor to understand the detailed nature of sound evolution, to declutter a mix, or to remove an unwanted sound. The boundary between pitch editing (discussed in chapter 34) and spectral editing blurs when a pitched tone and all its partials can be manipulated together or separately. Some spectrum editors can decompose a recording into its respective sources (e.g., separating the vocal part), in effect *de-mixing* or *un-mixing* a recording. This capability is also useful in applications such as audio denoising, music transcription, and music remixing. Finally, musicians want to edit spectral data in order to transform sounds for creative purposes. Such work overlaps with drawing sound and is a form of graphic synthesis (chapter 24).

Because of these disparate applications, there is no common paradigm for what a spectrum editor should do. Various editors are designed for different types of users and applications.

Note that the filters described in chapters 14 and 28 also modify spectra, but they operate on waveforms in the time domain. In this chapter, when we talk about *spectrum editing*, we mean editors that operate on frequency-domain data obtained after an analysis of the incoming waveform.

In this chapter we look at four main types of spectrum editors:

- Command-line editors and plug-ins
- Static spectrum editors
- Envelope editors
- Sonogram-like graphical editors

Command-Line Editors and Plug-Ins

The command-line terminal interface has been around for decades. The most famous example is the Unix shell. Command-line interfaces remain common, particularly for users of the Linux operating system. An example of spectral editing using a command-line interface is the Composers Desktop Project (CDP), a software package for sound manipulation. A simple CDP spectral command is

```
spec cut infile outfile starttime endtime
```

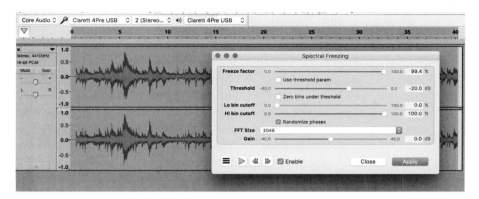

Figure 44.1   SoundMagic Spectral *spectral freeze* plug-in.

This command cuts a section out of a spectrum analysis file between *start time* and *endtime.*

The majority of the CDP software was written by Trevor Wishart. He developed a large number of sound transformations for "surgical work inside sounds" (Composers Desktop Project 2020). Many of these manipulate the analyzed spectra of sounds. These include operations for spectral blurring, freezing, tracing, harmonizing, pitch shifting, stretching, and randomization, interpolation, among others.

Michael Norris implemented many of the CDP spectral processing algorithms as MacOS plugins called SoundMagic Spectral (freeware). These plug-ins work in a *set-then-do* mode, similar to the way the command line interfaces work. That is, users tune parameters and then click Apply (figure 44.1).

Table 44.1 lists the SoundMagic Spectral plug-ins.

Table 44.1   SoundMagic Spectral Plug-ins

Spectral Averaging	Averages the spectral information over *n* windows, similarly to Spectral blurring.
Spectral Bin Shift	Shifts the entire spectrum up or down a set number of bins.
Spectral Blurring	Applies a low-pass filter to the spectral changes from one window to the next, progressively "smearing" the sound. Has similar spurious problems as Spectral Averaging but may still be useful.
Spectral DroneMaker	Turns any sound into a slowly changing drone. Uses large FFTs to smear out detail.
Spectral Emergence	Tracks the partials and applies an amplitude envelope to them to create a pulsating sound.
Spectral Filterbank	A bank of extremely narrow bandpass filters using the FFT.

(continued)

Table 44.1   (continued)

Spectral Freeze	Each bin is watched until its amplitude reaches a peak. It is then held at that peak until it is exceeded by another peak in that bin.
Spectral Gate and Hold	Each bin is watched until its amplitude exceeds a threshold level. A bin is frozen for a specific length of time rather than until it is exceeded by a higher amplitude.
Spectral Gliding Filters	Creates a series of spectral filters that glide in pitch.
Spectral Granulation	Grains of the spectrum of a certain frequency range and duration are taken and delayed by a certain length.
Spectral Harmonizer	The spectrum is transposed up or down by a series of intervals and mixed back into the original.
Spectral Partial Glide	Tracks partials and shifts their pitches by a set amount.
Spectral Pitch Shift	Spectral pitch shifts up or down by a set amount. Spectral peaks are tracked and shifted independently of one another.
Spectral Pulsing	Switches bins on and off across the spectrum in a pulsating fashion.
Spectral Shimmer	Multiple parameters to make a variety of ways to add "shimmer," "jitter," "sparkle," "pulsation," or "sizzle" to a sound.
Spectral Shuffle	Randomly shuffles blocks of bins around within the spectrum.
Spectral Stretch	Spectral peaks are tracked and shifted to create a variety of inharmonic stretches.
Spectral Tracing	Typically used to retain only the loudest bins in a spectrum and remove the others.
Spectral Weave	Waits until the audio crosses a threshold and is sustained above that threshold; then it samples one FFT frame. Keeps this frame in memory for a set length of time while creating sustained *threads* of sound from the frame by sustaining in and applying a fade-in/fade-out envelope. A number of independent threads can be held in memory simultaneously to produce a contrapuntal weaving of spectral sustains.
Chorus	A time-varying chorus/flanger effect.
Grain Streamer	Captures and repeats grains.
Idee Fixer	A granular effect that works by capturing audio from the input into a buffer and then creates granular versions of it.
Super Filterbank	A bank of narrow bandpass filters using time-domain methods.

Static Spectrum Editors

What we call a *static spectrum* display shows a frequency-domain image that plots frequency versus amplitude. The dimension of time is not shown.

The display is "timeless" in the sense that the image in figure 44.2 could correspond to one second or one hour. It tells us all the frequencies that were present, but it does not tell us when they occurred.

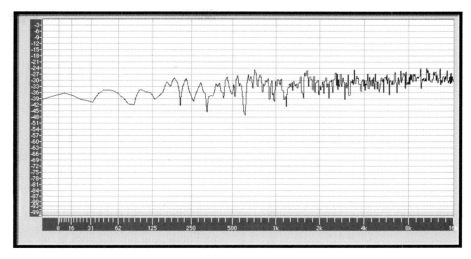

Figure 44.2   2D spectrum display of white noise. Frequency is plotted on the horizontal axis logarithmically. The vertical scale is amplitude in decibels.

The fundamental frequency of such an analysis is the period of the analysis window. Thus when one changes the visual representation in the low frequencies, one is altering both the (hidden) time structure and the frequency structure. The results can alter the time structure and introduce waveform discontinuities. The Passport Designs Alchemy sound editor (1988) included a line spectrum editor. One could select a part of a sound and then edit its spectrum by adjusting the level of individual partials (figure 44.3). One could also cut, copy, and paste spectrum data. It was a useful tool for learning about static spectrum manipulations. However, it was criticized as being of limited use in music production for the reasons stated here (Rich 1988).

It is more common to find harmonic line spectrum editors for waveform synthesis (figure 44.4). Here the vertical lines indicate harmonics of a fundamental period. For example, the raised line at the leftmost position represents a sine wave fundamental, the second line is the second harmonic, and so on.

Envelope Editors

As discussed in chapter 10, one way to represent spectrum information is in the form of control envelopes for each of the partials involved in additive resynthesis (figure 44.5). James Beauchamp, a pioneer of computer-based sound analysis, conducted research at the University of Illinois (Beauchamp 1969, 1975, 1979, 1981). Beauchamp, his former student Andrew Horner, and Lydia Ayres published many papers with plots of data reduction techniques

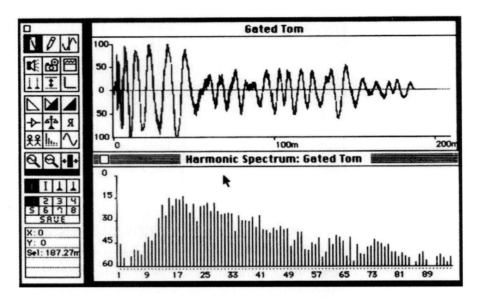

Figure 44.3   Static spectrum editor in Alchemy. The top panel shows the waveform; the bottom shows the spectrum, labeled as sinusoidal partial numbers.

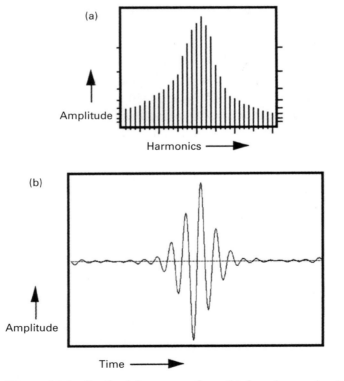

Figure 44.4   Synthesizing a waveform (b) from harmonics (a).

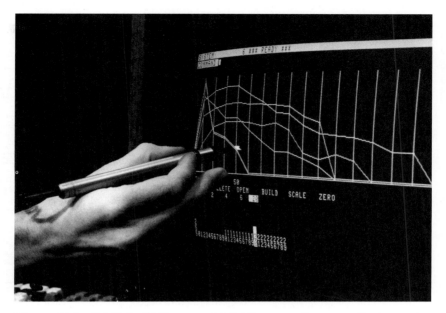

Figure 44.5   Fairlight CMI screen, 1979. The user adjusts amplitude envelopes for each harmonic of an analyzed sound.

for the envelopes of additive resynthesis (e.g., Horner and Beauchamp 1996; Ayers and Horner 1999; Lee et al. 2012).

James A. Moorer's research with phase vocoder analysis produced a time-varying amplitude and frequency function for each channel of the analysis (Moorer 1975, 1977; Moorer et al. 1977a, 1977b, 1978). The resulting analysis data was many times larger than the original sound file. This motivated the development of a spectrum editor in order to reduce the data but also to allow creative transformations of the control envelopes before resynthesis (Strawn 1985a, 1987b).

Figure 44.6 shows plots of the amplitude of the first twenty-four harmonics of a violin tone (Strawn 1987b), created with the eMerge editor. Figure 44.6a shows the partials before editing, and figure 44.6b shows them after editing. An issue with this approach is the labor involved. Manually adjusting the harmonics of each instrumental note is not practical. The data reduction methods described in chapter 10 offer algorithmic solutions.

Sonographic Editors

A *sonogram* or *spectrogram* representation plots frequency on the vertical axis and time on the horizontal axis. Amplitude is projected as darkness in

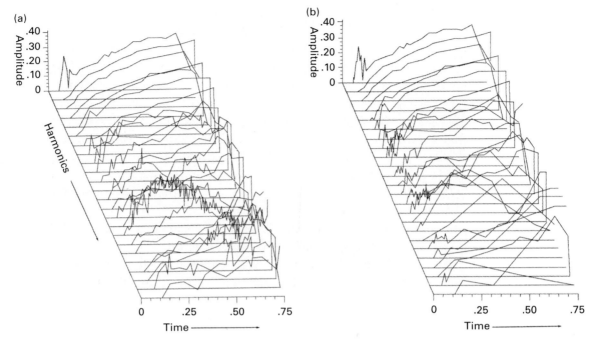

Figure 44.6   Control functions for twenty-four partials of a violin tone, after Strawn (1987b). Most 3D plots of this kind show the amplitudes of the harmonics relative to the maximum of all of them; this plot shows each harmonic scaled to its own maximum, an option that makes it easier to see detail in the higher harmonics. One can add, move, and delete breakpoints. In the example shown in (b), the attacks of the harmonics were cleaned up by manual editing. This is especially easy to see in the fundamental. Also, some detail, especially in the upper harmonics, was removed. This extraneous detail resulted when the line-segment approximation algorithm "worked too hard" in a few cases. Such detail must be removed for more than cosmetic reasons: according to Strawn (1987b), audible artifacts called *breebles* occur if the amplitudes of the upper harmonics change too rapidly relative to each other.

a grayscale sonogram. That is, the darker a frequency component appears, the greater its amplitude. Some sonogram representations plot amplitude in terms of color. Any display that plots frequency versus time can be called a *sonographic representation.*

For pedagogical purposes, we can divide sonographic editors into three categories: *sound transformation editors*, *repair and restoration editors*, and *source separation editors*. These categories are not absolute; one could use a given tool for more than one purpose.

Sound Transformation Editors

Chapter 24 on graphic synthesis presents tools that let one draw sound on a sonographic display. Some tools, such as U&I Software's MetaSynth CTX, can analyze a given sound or image into a sonographic representation that can be manipulated with graphical operations (Wenger and Spiegel 2010; U&I Software 2021). Unlike conventional resynthesis using sine waves, Meta-Synth can play back an analyzed spectrum using any other sound tuned to an arbitrary scale on any time scale. For these reasons, the resynthesized result can be radically different from the original input sound. Consider, for example, a sonographic representation of speech played back by a bank of percussion samples. In this capability, MetaSynth acts like a concatenative synthesizer that maps a representation of spectrum to an arbitrary corpus of sounds. (See chapter 23 on concatenative synthesis.)

Returning to a conventional studio-based spectrum editing paradigm, the pioneering SpecDraw prototype let users directly edit and resynthesize sono-grams using drawing tools (Eckel 1990). This technology was absorbed into IRCAM's AudioSculpt editor, reviewed further on.

Figure 44.7 shows the power of a sonogram-type editor. In this example the wavy lines indicate a vibrato pattern that is characteristic of a vocal tone. The similarity of the vibrato patterns is referred to as following a *common fate* (McAdams and Bregman 1979; Cano et al. 2019). By encircling these lines one can extract the vocal part from the orchestra, resynthesizing either one without the other.

AudioSculpt (Bogards, Röbel, and Rodet 2004; IRCAM 2011) analyzes spectral data. Its interface provides tools to play and manipulate the signal, as well as waveform and sonographic displays. When the mouse is moved over the sound, the app shows the instantaneous spectrum corresponding to the position of the cursor.

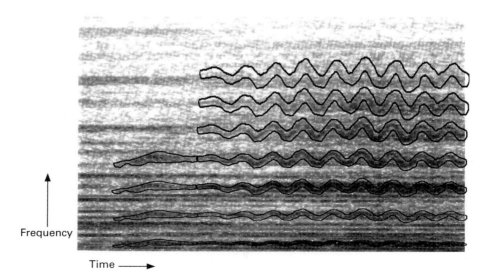

Figure 44.7 SpecDraw separation of vocals from orchestra. The vocal elements follow a common vibrato pattern.

AudioSculpt can perform a number of types of analysis, such as spectrum, spectrum envelope, fundamental frequency, partial tracking, chord sequences, and voiced/unvoiced analysis. For sound transformation it provides a break-point function editor that can be used for pitch change, time-base change, amplitude change, or filtering (figure 44.8).

One can also draw regions on top of the sonographic representation and apply filters that either boost or cut the selected region. A harmonic pencil lets one draw harmonics of a given fundamental line. Noise removal can be performed after an analysis of the *noise signature*. For advanced users, a command-line interface is also available.

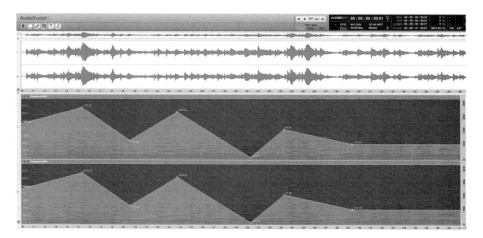

Figure 44.8   Breakpoint function drawn over the sonographic display in AudioSculpt.

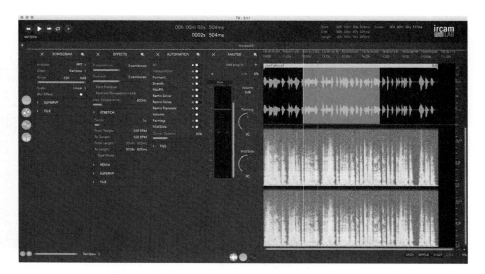

Figure 44.9   IrcamLab TS2 editor.

A more recent software product by IrcamLab called TS2 uses the same phase vocoder engine as AudioSculpt but applies a new interface (figure 44.9). While AudioSculpt has a broader range of scientific analysis functions, TS2 focuses on pitch-time changing effects.

Sonogram Spectrum Editing in Sound Editors

The sound editors Audacity and Adobe Audition both incorporate spectrum editing operations. To start in Audacity, one enables the spectrogram view. This corresponds to what we have called a sonographic representation of frequency on a time line.

One can draw a region in the spectrum and apply any plug-in effect to this region only, such as pitch shift, filtering, and so on (figure 44.10). This unique capability is quite powerful as a tool of sound transformation.

Audition has a spectral display and provides multiple tools for selecting and manipulating spectra (figure 44.11).

A special tool in Audition is an FFT filter (figure 44.12). This provides direct control of the amplitudes of a number of bands (e.g., 2,048) in the frequency domain. It can be used for precise equalization. One downside is increased real-time latency in comparison to a standard filter as described in chapter 28. Another is that its sharp response can introduce ringing effects that might not occur using a standard time-domain filter.

Sonogram-like Tracking Phase Vocoder Editors

Figure 44.13 shows a sonogram-like representation generated by the LemurEdit program (Holloway 1993). Notice the darkened region, which

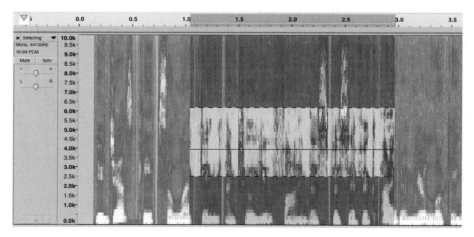

Figure 44.10 Spectral editing in Audacity. Defining a region of the spectrum for transformation. Any plug-in effect can be applied to the selected region

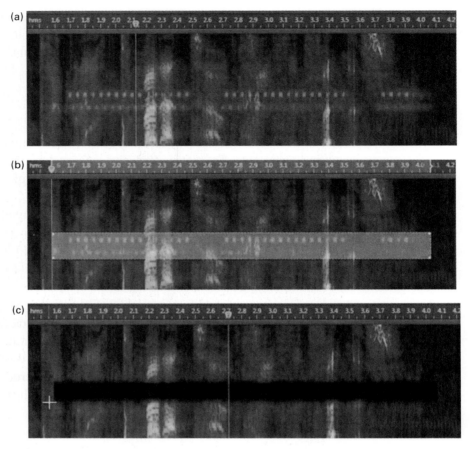

Figure 44.11   Using the spectral display in Audition to locate and remove telephone noise from a speech recording. (a) Zoomed-in image of telephone ring (the periodic dot pattern) mixed with speech. (b) Selection of telephone noise. (c) The result of deleting the telephone noise.

has been selected for editing. The analysis data displayed here was generated by the Lemur program (Walker and Fitz 1992), an implementation of a *tracking phase vocoder* (TPV), as described in chapter 37. A TPV follows or tracks the most prominent peaks in the spectrum over time. This approach is also called *sinusoidal modeling*.

Klingbeil (2005, 2009) implemented SPEAR, an intuitive spectral editor that starts from a TPV analysis (figure 44.14). The freeware app provides a palette of selection tools. After selecting a set of partial tracks, one can move them or transform them by pitch changing, time-base changing, frequency shifting, and frequency flipping (flips low frequencies to high, and vice versa). Radical transformations of sound are easy to achieve.

A related method, analysis, transformation, and synthesis (ATS) uses a sinusoidal-plus-critical-band noise model and psychoacoustic information

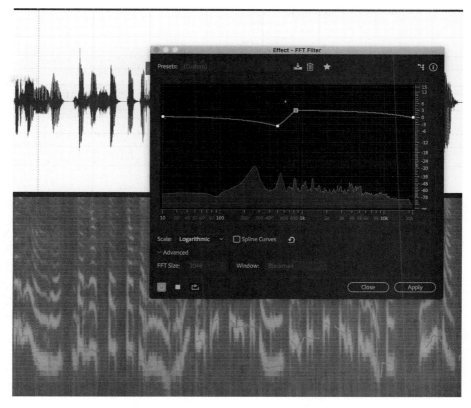

Figure 44.12 Audition FFT filter.

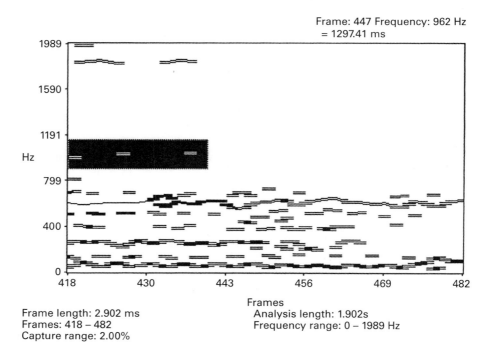

Frame: 447 Frequency: 962 Hz
= 1297.41 ms

Frame length: 2.902 ms   Analysis length: 1.902s
Frames: 418 – 482   Frequency range: 0 – 1989 Hz
Capture range: 2.00%

Figure 44.13 LemurEdit for editing tracking phase vocoder images.

(a)

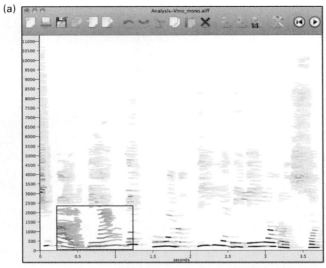

(b)

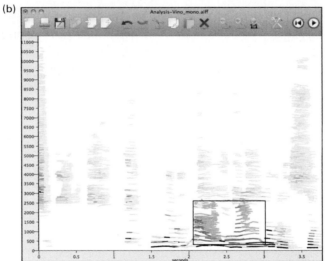

Figure 44.14   Spectrum editing using SPEAR. The audio is speech. The partials selected by the box in (a) are moved to a new time-frequency position in the spectrum in (b).

(Pampin 2004; Pampin et al. 2004). (See chapter 37 for a description.) ATSH is a sonographic editor based on ATS analysis (Di Liscia and Pampin 2003). ATSH provides tools for selecting a region and applying an envelope to the amplitude or frequency values of the region. The sound can also be stretched or shrunk in time or played backward.

SCATTER was an interactive app developed at UCSB for real-time sound transformation (figure 44.15). Whereas many editors in this chapter

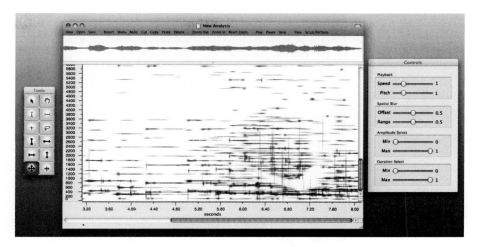

Figure 44.15 SCATTER app. The circular area with white space around it has been selected and moved.

are based on Fourier analysis, SCATTER's analysis used atomic decomposition (Sturm et al. 2009). Atomic decomposition can be seen as the analytical counterpart to granular synthesis. (See chapter 39.) SCATTER provided some of the same selection tools and transformations as SPEAR. One of its unique features was the ability to identify transients (short grains) versus sustained tones and to operate on them separately. A goal of SCATTER was to be able to spatialize (*scatter*) individual grains in space on the basis of their properties.

Repair and Restoration Editors

Certain editors focus on audio repair and restoration. For example, iZotope RX delivers a set of tools for this purpose, specifically de-click, de-clip, de-hum, and denoise. Figure 44.16 shows the screen of iZotope RX in denoise mode.

Steinberg's SpectraLayers Pro is bundled in a number of editors and DAWs including Cubase Pro. It features functions like de-clip, de-reverb, de-crackle, de-plosive, de-wind, denoise, de-bleed, and de-hum. It offers operations such as select transient, erase, amplify, clone, draw, and repair broken harmonics. SpectraLayers Pro automatically applies fades around graphical selections to smooth the results of subsequent edit operations.

Even utilitarian repair tools can be used to transform sounds creatively. Figure 44.17 shows how iZotope RX was used to poke a hole in a speech spectrum to create an exotic filtering effect.

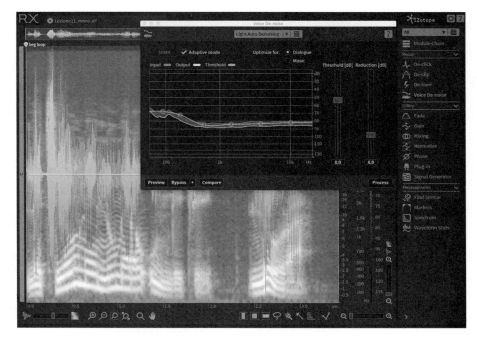

Figure 44.16 iZotope RX in denoise mode. The denoise control window is in front, displaying the spectral profile of the process. In this Light denoising operation, low-frequency noises are attenuated below −60 dB, and higher frequencies are attenuated below −80 dB.

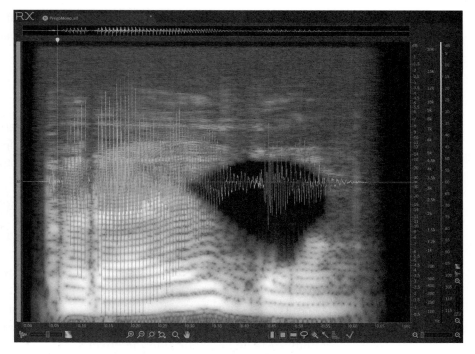

Figure 44.17 Using the iZoptope RX spectrum editor, one can poke a cavity in the middle of a speech sound.

Source Separation Editors

Another category of editors aims at *source separation* (unmixing or de-mixing), also discussed in chapter 35. Source separation identifies the spectral signature of voices and instruments and splits a mixed track into separate component tracks. A common goal is to separate a melody line such as a vocal from the rest of the song. Once separated, the melody can be remixed with a different accompaniment. Products include ReVoice Pro and VocALign (Synchro Arts), Stem Maker (Zynaptiq), Auto-Tune (Antares), Melodyne (Celemony), Trax, Xtrax Stems, and Instant Dialogue Cleaner (Audionamix).

These utilities perform pitch estimation based on spectrum analysis but combine this with sophisticated spectral pattern recognition algorithms, statistical methods, dynamic programming, and trained neural networks (Neubäcker 2011; Bloom, et al. 2010; Kohler 2000; Veneph et al. 2016; Cano et al. 2019). Automatic tools using recurrent neural networks extract the vocal melody with good results (Leglaive, Hennequin, and Badeau 2015). The recurrent aspect of the network allows the system to take both past and future temporal context into account to classify each input step.

Separation apps isolate notes by amplitude envelope detection and then separate related spectral components, such as vocal formants, which accompany that pitch. Once they have identified these components, the analyzed data can be used to transform and resynthesize individual notes as desired by the user. For example, some systems display a graphical pitch curve that can be refined with drawing and erasing tools.

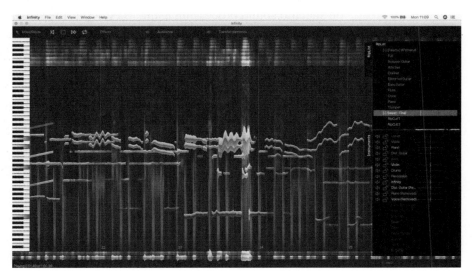

Figure 44.18   Hit'n'Mix Infinity editor.

The Interactive Source Separation Editor (ISSE) is notable because it is free, and the code is open source (Bryan, Mysore, and Wang 2014). It is designed around *interactive machine learning.* As a user selects and paints using different colors on a sonographic image, the system learns to associate these selections with separate sources. *Painting* in this case is essentially labeling. The core separation algorithm used in ISSE is based on *nonnegative matrix factorization* (NMF), a method that uses statistics to associate inputs to entries in a dictionary of spectrum patterns (Smaragdis and Brown 2003). The untrained NMF algorithm produces imperfect separation results. Common problems include bleed-through between sources and a loss of detail in a separated source. This it benefits from a process of iterative feedback involving a human user to refine the results.

In a similar spirit, RipX DeepRemix and DeepAudio (from Hit'n'Mix) uses the graphical interface of a painting program to let users manipulate individual instruments in a mixed audio file (figure 44.18). In particular, they let one manipulate pitch, duration, timbre, formant, and volume using either the editor display or scripts in the Python programming language. The RipX products are based on sinusoidal modeling (see chapter 37). Its Clone tools let one extract a property of one note (pitch, formant, timbre, volume, or panning) and apply it to another. However, to create realistic transformations requires trial-and-error experimentation (Vincent 2020).

Implementing a Sonographic Spectrum Editor

As mentioned in chapter 24, Jean-François Charles (2008) wrote a tutorial on spectral sound processing using Max, with Jitter for matrix computations. He explained the mechanics of working with sonographic data. Although the implementation details are specific to that platform, the basic principles are broadly applicable. The implementation is suitable for use in live performance. Gary Klingbeil's (2009) PhD dissertation on SPEAR is another resource for implementation details on spectrum editing. Finally, the ISSE application is open source: anyone can download and study the code (Bryan, Mysore, and Wang 2014).

45 *Common Music Notation Editors*

The Complexity of Music Notation

Music Printing and Editing: Background

   Mainframe-Based Music Editors
   Minicomputer-Based Music Editors
   Workstation-Based Editors
   Editors for Personal Computers

Rule-Based versus Graphics-Based Editors

Advantages of Computer-Based Music Editing and Printing

Functionality of CMN Editors

Music Font Resolution

Automatic Transcription from MIDI

   Practical Issues in Automatic Transcription

Custom Symbols and Integration with Graphics Programs

Browser-Based Notation Apps for Education

Exporting Notation Using Music XML

IEEE 1599 Music Representation Standard

Common music notation (CMN) is the standard music notation system originating in Europe in the early seventeenth century. In this chapter, we assume that the reader has basic familiarity with CMN. The software presented in this chapter is concerned with the traditional uses of notation: score editing, printing, and file export.

Notation languages have also emerged for interactive score generation live in concert. We address this direction in chapter 49 on composition languages. Because reading a score into a computer using a scanner with *optical music recognition* (OMR) software is an alternative to manual entry using a score input language, we also cover this briefly in chapter 49. The TENOR International Conference on Technologies for Music Notation and Representation presents advances in all of these areas.

The Complexity of Music Notation

CMN editors assist musicians with preparing scores and parts. Using a beginner's score editor, creating simple music notation is easy. By contrast, professional notation programs provide flexibility but require more study and practice. Becoming an expert in *music engraving* is a deep skill that is not generally taught in music schools. It can involve the use of graphic design apps and scripting in combination with CMN editors in order to solve complex notational problems.

Professional CMN editors such as Finale, Sibelius, Dorico, and Muse-Score have many of the same commands as text editors, such as cut, copy, and paste, but they work on notes, measures, parts, and systems of staves.

Music notation is much more complicated than text or mathematical notation. Roman alphabetic text (such as this) follows only a few syntactical rules; characters line up in a straight line; spaces or an occasional punctuation mark separate words. Mathematical notation is more complicated than unadorned text, but the simplicity of graphical mathematical notation editors proves that almost all mathematical expressions fall into one of about a dozen templates. Formulas typically fit on one line or simply carry across several lines. There is no need to precisely align several dozen lines on a large page, as one does in an orchestral score. Of course, the apparent simplicity of mathematical notation derives from its powers of abstraction; one can always compress a long expression into a single symbol.

Common music notation is less susceptible to abstraction, notwithstanding the presence of "macro instructions" such as *accelerando*. Apart from repeat signs such as *D.S.* (abbreviation for *dal segno*, meaning [go] "to the sign") music notation has no abstractions for time order.

In music, the separate parameters of a single event—pitch, rhythm, and amplitude—each divide into graduated scales with their own graphical symbols. When music symbols meet, they must change in a systematic way. For example, in a single chord, numerous elements—note heads, note stems, augmentation dots, flags, accidentals, and expressive markings—must make room for one another to form a meaningful chord representation. Arranging sequences of musical symbols properly involves many context-sensitive decisions. The spatial distance between successive notes varies with the duration of those notes. Stems, beams, and glissandi link notes; ties and slurs link phrases. The need to align vertically many staves in polyphonic music adds another level of constraints. These are only the most basic considerations; we have not mentioned artful or aesthetic aspects of score layout. Volumes are devoted to instruction in the practice of music engraving (Read 1969; Risatti 1975; Stone 1980; Boretz and Cone 1976; Dimpker 2013). Donald Byrd (2017) published *A Gallery of Interesting Music Notation* to illustrate challenges of music representation.

The complexity of music notation is reflected in the code base of professional notation programs. The source code of LilyPond, a scripting language for notation, exceeds one million lines written in nineteen languages (listed in the order of the number of lines, the languages are C++, Scheme, Python, MetaFont, shell script, TeX/LaTeX, XML, Autocuing, Emacs LISP, Make, Perl, C, HTML, CSS, Vim Script, Tcl, MetaPost, JavaScript, and PhP) (OpenHub 2019).

These complexities put into perspective the task consigned to notation editors. They explain why it is difficult to create an easy-to-use yet also full-featured CMN editor. The main way to cut down the complexity of an editor is to limit the complexity of the music. This is precisely what some products do. Entry-level music editors serve a useful purpose, but the range of the music that they can handle is restricted. For example, a simple editor might not allow a change of time signature within a piece. Thus a split exists between entry-level music editors and more professional music engraving programs.

Finally, in addition to the interactive notation editors described in this chapter is a world of *score input* or *music markup* languages (chapter 49). One of the most important is LilyPond ("The music typesetter"), a music engraving program devoted to producing high-quality sheet music (Nienhuys and Nieuwenhuizen 2003; LilyPond 2012). LilyPond aims to bring the aesthetics of traditionally engraved music to computer printouts. It is more similar to a document preparation system like LaTeX than graphical score editing software. That is, with LilyPond, one does not write music by dragging notes from a toolbar onto a score. One writes music by typing text. This text is compiled and produces engraved sheet music. Figure 45.1 gives a simple example showing text and rendered score.

```
\version "2.18.2"
{
c' e' g' e'
}
```

Figure 45.1   Lilypond text and score.

Music Printing and Editing: Background

Music written before the fifteenth century was scribed by hand. The introduction of movable-type printing in 1450 had a tremendous impact on the intellectual world. The output of books in the first fifty years after its discovery was greater than in the previous thousand years (Derry and Williams 1960). The first known printed music notation appeared in 1473, but it took a full century after Gutenberg's invention for the first collection of polyphonic music notation using movable type to appear. These were the volumes published by Ottaviano de Petrucci at Venice (Grout 1973). Around 1600, music notation evolved into the form known today as common music notation. After this, the practice of music printing did not vary much for a period of about 360 years.

In 1961 Lejaren Hiller and Robert Baker undertook the first experiments in music-printing programs at the University of Illinois, Urbana-Champaign. They used a modified Musicwriter typewriter for both input and output of notation symbols (Hiller and Baker 1965).

One of the first CMN editors based on computer graphics techniques was developed at the National Research Council (NRC) laboratory in Ottawa, Canada in the late 1960s (Pulfer 1971). Musicians entered notes, rests, and other musical symbols using a clavier and a "positioning wheel," similar in function to a mouse (figure 45.2). The NRC system also included a waveform editor and a simple sound synthesizer. These experiments tested the waters of music-editing technology, but it was only in the 1970s that practical systems emerged.

Mainframe-Based Music Editors

Pioneering music editors of the 1970s ran on the large mainframe computers of that era (figure 45.3). Musicians wrote scripts to enter music into Leland

Figure 45.2   One of the earliest graphical music notation editors, developed at the National Research Council, Canada, in the late 1960s (described in Pulfer 1971). Notice that the operator is using positional controllers rather than the alphanumeric keyboard to select and edit notes.

Smith's music printing program MS developed at Stanford University for a Digital Equipment Corporation (DEC) PDP-10 (Smith 1973). Each music symbol had a corresponding textual representation. Although it had a reputation of being difficult to learn, MS was a powerful music printing system from the standpoint of notational flexibility. (See examples in Roads 1985a.) In particular, it allowed musicians to create new symbols and customize score layout. These features were subsequently taken up in Smith's program SCORE and later in WinScore (Smith 1997). For years, WinScore was the choice of many international music publishers.

Donald Byrd's experimental SMUT (System for Music Translation) was a batch-oriented music printing program originally developed at Indiana University (Byrd 1974, 1977, 1984). Its strong suit was device independence.

Figure 45.3   Leland Smith, Center for Computer Research in Music and Acoustics, Stanford University, 1976.

(As a proof of its portability, Kimball Stickney once demonstrated a version of SMUT he had adapted to plot music notation on a tiny cash register printer interfaced to a large mainframe computer.)

Some of the first commercial music printing systems include Musicomp (Dal Molin 1978), La Ma de Guido (Barcelona), and Dataland's Scan-Note system (*Computer Music Journal* 1979) developed by Mogens Kjaer in Aarhus, Denmark (figure 45.4). Using a combination of manual and automatic methods, these large systems produced output that rivaled hand-engraved quality in many respects. Music publishers started using these services for score production in the late 1970s.

Minicomputer-Based Music Editors

By the late 1970s, a handful of research groups had implemented experimental interactive editors for minicomputers running the UNIX operating system environment. These included Ludwig (Reeves et al. 1979) and Scriva (Buxton 1979; Buxton et al. 1981) developed at the University of Toronto, and MIT's prototype Nedit (Wallraff 1979b). A major topic of research at the time was to find the best way to enter notes and rests—whether from a musical keyboard, menus and mouse, an alphanumeric keyboard command, or symbols manually scribbled with a pointing device. No best way for all circumstances has emerged; one can find all four ways in twenty-first-century music editors.

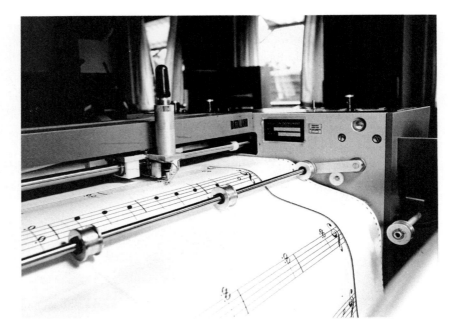

Figure 45.4   Dataland Scan-note system score printout on a large-format pen plotter (1978).

Early score editors suffered from severe limitations. They were implemented on slow and memory-deficient minicomputers. The programs ran in a time-sharing environment (i.e., multiple users per machine) using *vector display* screens. Vector displays draw objects as a series of connected lines: the more complicated the image, the slower the refresh rate. Refresh rates of less than 5 Hz were not uncommon. Today displays are based on the principle of *bit-mapped raster* display refreshed at constant rate of 60 Hz or higher. In a bit-mapped system, each dot (or *pixel*) on the screen maps to a word in a graphics memory.

Workstation-Based Editors

A new generation of more sophisticated score editors based on personal *work-station* computers appeared in the early 1980s. Workstation computers found in research labs were typically much more powerful than the personal comput-ers of that era. William Kornfeld's experimental MUZACS editor, imple-mented on a LISP Machine at the MIT Artificial Intelligence Laboratory, demonstrated in 1980 the power of interactive graphics in CMN editing.

The Mockingbird CMN editor, created at Xerox's Palo Alto Research Center (PARC), ran on a fast workstation in its day, the Xerox Dorado. The program's impressive graphical displays stunned musicians when it was demonstrated in 1981 (Maxwell and Ornstein 1983; Roads 1981b). Mockingbird was designed exclusively for piano notation (figure 45.5). In a typical session, the musician entered part of a piece by playing it on a musical keyboard. It was displayed in a form of piano-roll notation. The musician then edited the score using menu selection techniques to modify the graphical representation, adding measure lines, time signatures, key information, note stems, beams, and rests.

Figure 45.5   Example of music printing using the Mockingbird score editor.

The Xerox Mockingbird was a research project, never available commercially. By contrast, the Synclavier Music Engraving System (figure 45.6), developed at about the same time, offered high-quality music printing to those who could afford a Synclavier instrument, which cost tens of thousands of dollars (Talbot 1983).

Editors for Personal Computers

After pioneering CMN editors proved the viability of the concept, their features were incorporated into programs for personal computers. The first generation of music editors appeared in 1985, including such programs as Professional Composer, Score, Personal Composer, and Deluxe Music Construction Set. By 1988, a second wave of editors appeared, including the programs Finale and NoteWriter. These offered improved print quality, notational flexibility, and the ability to transcribe score data from a MIDI source.

Today we see mature and sophisticated editors like Finale, Sibelius, Dorico and MuseScore, as well as scripting languages like LilyPond in a broad field of over two hundred applications that produce common music notation.

Rule-Based versus Graphics-Based Editors

An important distinction between CMN editors is *rule based* versus *graphics based*. Rule-based editors like Finale understand rules of music notation. They keep track of the pitch and duration of notes, for example, enabling operations such as transposition, rhythmic error detection, automatic positioning of notes and other symbols, and playback of score via MIDI. The automatic decisions made by rule-based editors speed up the setting of conventional music.

By contrast, graphics-based editors treat music notation as a collection of graphic symbols to be arranged in any way the user wishes. Figure 45.7 depicts some of the symbols possible in NoteWriter (Hamel 1987, 1989). Although the score is not linked to a MIDI representation, the visual freedom of a graphical approach opens new possibilities for composers of new and experimental music.

This distinction between rule-based and graphics-based is not peculiar to music editors. Painting and drawing programs confront a similar *vector object* versus *bitmap* image dichotomy, and some programs provide separate tools for handling each domain.

Certain CMN editors can handle both types of symbols (Diener 1989; Roeder and Hamel 1989). These editors let users configure them, so that only

Figure 45.6 Score printed by the Synclavier Music Engraving System.

Figure 45.7   Music symbols and examples of the graphics-based notation editor NoteWriter.

the rules a user selects are applied. In addition, users can override automatic decisions. Nonstandard graphical notation can be inserted into the score.

Another approach is to use scripting tools such as LilyPond. LilyPond is aimed at latter-day music engravers, who are primarily concerned with notational quality. In such systems, the correctness and aesthetics of the notation is paramount (Hamel 1987, 1989; Müller and Giuletti 1987; Smith 1997; Nienhuys and Nieuwenhuizen 2003; LilyPond 2012). Because the focus is on notation, there is not necessarily a possibility for sound playback.

Many music professionals take a hybrid approach. They might create basic notational elements using a rule-based program like LilyPond or Sibelius and then export score fragments in a graphical format such as Portable Data Format (PDF) or Encapsulated PostScript (EPS) for final layout in a professional graphics design program like Adobe Illustrator. Such a combination provides design flexibility (Ingram 2001).

Advantages of Computer-Based Music Editing and Printing

All the benefits of text editors over typewriters and handwriting accrue to users of CMN editors. The computer memorizes score fragments, which can be edited at will and freely combined. Most CMN editors can take dictation from a MIDI instrument—an enormous time savings. Some offer graphical interfaces for guitar and bass fretboard, drum pads, and preset chord libraries.

Optical reading of scores provides another alternative (Wolman et al. 1992; Bellini, Bruno, and Nesi 2007). Some apps like StaffPad and MyScript (built into Presonus's Notion software) let users write on a tablet with stylus and perform automatic typesetting in real time (figure 45.8).

The output of a CMN editor, printed on a high-quality printer, is neater and easier to read than a handwritten manuscript. When plotted on a high-resolution printer, it rivals the quality of engraved scores. (This is not to deny the value of a hand-written score from a musicological perspective or at auction.)

CMN editors can format the same score in a variety of stave arrangements, such as full score, piano score, or as individual parts in a multipart score. The parts extracted by such software replace days of manual part-copying labor (figure 45.9).

When the score is prepared, many CMN editors can perform the score using MIDI instruments. As well as providing immediate sonic realization of musical ideas, this gives composers the opportunity to check notation

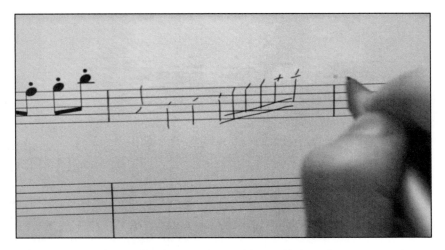

Figure 45.8   The StaffPad app turns writing with a stylus onscreen into typeset music notation. It also takes voice commands such as "add a piano."

accuracy. One can overlook a missing accidental on a page, for example, but its absence should be obvious when heard.

Functionality of CMN Editors

The functionality of interactive music notation editors can be divided into six classes of operations, explained in table 45.1: *setup, raw note entry, editing music data, text data entry, printing, and playback.* For a scripted editor like LilyPond, the effects would be equivalent, but the commands are text rather than mouse clicks.

Entering notes may be as simple as selecting a symbol from a menu (figure 45.10), playing on a music keyboard, drawing on a tablet, or typing an alphanumeric expression. The distinction between "raw note entry" and "editing music data" in table 45.1, however, indicates that note data is merely the starting point in preparing a finished score.

Music Font Resolution

The print quality of notation programs improved enormously in 1986 with the introduction of the PostScript music font Sonata, designed by Cleo Huggins of Adobe Systems. Hundreds of music fonts are now available (e.g., https://music-fonts.com/). PostScript fonts are *scalable.* This means that only

Figure 45.9 Notation editors provide easy extraction of parts from a full score. (a) Full score, *Symphony in G minor,* K. 550, W. A. Mozart (1788). (b) Extracted violin part.

Table 45.1   Functionality of Common Music Notation Editors

Setup

Set clef, time signature (possibly complex, such as $2 + 3/4$), and key signature

Set score layout on page (number of staves, adjust margins, page size)

Specify system bracket style and clefs

Raw note entry

Music symbol entry from alphanumeric keyboard, menus, special command keys, optical score reader, MIDI input device, or other MIDI source such as a sequencer file or algorithmic composition program

---

Editing music data

Cut, copy, paste of selected symbols, measures, and regions

Cut, copy, paste of selected items into a draw program for nonstandard scores

Edit note stems (up or down, no stems, stem between staves)

Edit beaming between notes, including tuplets

Edit ties, slurs, and phrase marks

Edit system breaks

Edit a voice or part alone and afterward remerge the voice with the full score

Number or label measures

Place chord symbols over staves

Adjust spacing (compress, expand, add or delete white space)

Edit the parameters of music symbols:

      Note heads—head type, x and y offset, dots, accents

      Note stems—offset and length

      Note flags—width and style

      Tremolo marks

      Note beams—width, slope, offset

      Ties—curvature, offsets, width

      Slurs—slope, offset, line width

Transpose pitches by clef, chromatically, diatonically, enharmonically, or by mode

Design custom symbols for unconventional scores

Zoom into the score to make fine adjustments on elements such as slurs; zoom out to adjust global layout

---

Text entry

Choose fonts

Enter title, lyrics, and expressive markings and annotations

Printing

Table 45.1   (continued)

Set characteristics of printing (reduction, printer type. etc.)

Print whole score

Print selected pages or selected regions

Extract and print a part alone

Playback

Play back selected region or voice at specified tempo and amplitude via MIDI

Adjust tuning for playback

Map dynamic markings to specific decibel levels

Map selected region to a software instrument (MIDI orchestration)

Open MIDI sequence editor within the score editor for fine adjustment of the playback parameters of individual voices (Dorico)

Figure 45.10   Default palette of tools in the Finale editor. On the left palette are the tools (from left to right) selection tool, zoom tool, handgrabber tool, staff tool, measure tool, key signature tool, time signature tool, simple note entry tool, speedy note entry tool, hyperscribe tool (sets up real-time MIDI input), tuplet tool, MIDI tool, smart shape tool (for slurs and other markings), expression tool, articulation tool, lyrics tool, chord tool, clef tool, repeat tool, note mover tool, resize tool, special tools (beaming, stemming, note positioning in a measure), text tool, page layout tool, ossia tool, and graphics tool. The right palette includes an eraser and various note options.

the outline of the font is stored in computer memory, as a set of mathematical curves that can be scaled to any size with minimum error. Thus the outline adjusts to the size and *resolution* of the device on which the font appears.

Resolution is often expressed in terms of *dots* or *pixels per inch* (dpi or ppi). On a display screen with a resolution less than 75 dpi, for example, certain symbols appear jagged. Modern screens have more than 200 dpi.

A test case for printer resolution is long and slightly angled note beams. For normal size music printing, high-resolution without "jaggies" (jagged edges in what should be smooth curved shapes) requires a printer capable of 1,200 dpi (Stickney 1987).

Automatic Transcription from MIDI

A timesaving feature of many CMN editors is *automatic transcription* of performed music. In the usual case, a musician performs on a MIDI keyboard along with a metronome generated by the notation program. But the note data can also come from other sources, including any MIDI controller or files in the standard MIDI file format. This includes the output of sequencers and algorithmic composition programs. Here we look at practical issues. Chapter 35 examines the technology behind automatic transcription from sound.

Practical Issues in Automatic Transcription

When a performer plays on a MIDI instrument, a microprocessor inside the instrument is transmitting control information such as "note C3 played at time 23:39:67 at velocity 90 on channel 1." The task of the transcription program is to segment this data into musical time units such as beats and measures and convert it into graphical commands for the display screen.

Human performance is not metrically perfect. Small deviations from constant note durations are typical. If the note data as performed is transcribed literally, the result is unreadable (figure 45.11). Thus the temporal *quantization factor* is an important setup parameter. The quantization factor sets the minimum note duration to be transcribed. This causes the program to ignore small variations in note and rest durations.

A reference beat is a necessity for accurate automatic music transcription. To allow flexibility, some programs let users tap their own beat along with the music. Transcription without a metronome source is a difficult problem for computers. In effect, the computer must "find the beat" and "tap its foot" to the rhythm while transcribing. For more on this research topic, see

Figure 45.11   When the quantization factor is a thirty-second note, a half note must last precisely as long as sixteen tied thirty-second notes, or it is transcribed incorrectly. This figure shows the transcription that results when the duration is only fifteen thirty-second notes long. If an entire performance is transcribed this way, the notation becomes unreadable.

chapter 35 (see also Rowe 1975; Chafe, Mont-Reynaud, and Rush 1982; Foster, Schloss, and Rockmore 1982; Piszczalski and Galler 1977; Piszczalski et al. 1981; Stautner 1983; Schloss 1985).

Even with a reference beat and a reasonable quantization factor, the result of automatic transcription inevitably requires manual editing (figure 45.12). Typical problems include colliding symbols, errors in rhythmic parsing, lack of recognition of key signature and meter changes, missing dynamic markings and slurs, and aesthetically poor justification (layout and spacing of measures, staves, and systems).

Custom Symbols and Integration with Graphics Programs

Most CMN editors let users import images from graphic design programs into the score; this could include custom symbols or unconventional score elements, such as icons representing electronic sounds on tape.

As mentioned previously, when the CMN editor cannot handle the graphical demands of a score, sometimes the best strategy is to use it only to prepare fragments of notation. The fragments can be exported in a scalable graphics format, such as EPS or PDF. In this case, the music notation can be scaled to fit whatever size is needed. The fragments can be arranged in a professional graphics program such as Adobe Illustrator.

Browser-Based Notation Apps for Education

Browser-based notation apps such as NoteFlight and Flat (among others) have advantages in music education settings. Students can bring their own laptop, tablet, or phone to class and everyone uses the same app. A single composition can be opened and edited in real time by multiple people using different devices at the same time. Students can form groups to analyze or compose

Figure 45.12 Difference between transcribed and final score, Felix Mendelssohn, *Six Songs Without Words,* Op. 19, no. 2. (a) Score as transcribed automatically by a notation program. (b) Final score as corrected.

scores online collaboratively. An online cloud database stores the history of the editing process.

Exporting Notation Using Music XML

XML (Extensible Markup Language) is a World Wide Web Consortium (W3C) standard for representing structured data in text, designed for ease of use over the Internet by a wide variety of applications. XML is a metamarkup language that lets designers and communities develop their own representation languages for different applications. XML balances simplicity and power in a way that has made it attractive to software developers. Because XML files are text files, users of XML files always have generic text-based tools available as a lowest common denominator. XML documents are represented in Unicode, providing support for international score exchange.

First proposed in 2000, MusicXML is an XML-based music notation interchange language (Good 2000, 2006). It represents common musical notation from the seventeenth century onward, including both classical and popular music. The language is designed to be extensible to future coverage of early music and less standard twentieth and twenty-first century scores. MusicXML is not intended to supersede other languages that are optimized for specific musical applications but rather to support sharing of musical data between applications.

Today, MusicXML is the universal standard file format for sheet music (see chapter 49). It is the recommended format for sharing sheet music between different notation editors, including MuseScore, Sibelius, Finale, Dorico, and more than two hundred others. (See https://www.musicxml.com.)

IEEE 1599 Music Representation Standard

Music information encoding often involves several distinct reference formats for audio, performance, music scores, and metadata. Some of these are formal standards, others represent de facto practices. Each deals with musical information only in a restricted sector and does not address all its aspects. The IEEE 1599 Music Representation standard addresses a need for the integration of the various dimensions of musical information in order to provide access to all these layers interactively. This makes it possible, for instance, to navigate score notation while listening to the corresponding audio (score following), to compare in real time different graphical representation as well as audio performances, and to interact in an environment with musical contents. IEEE 1599 encodes all music-related information in XML, a hierarchical, extensible, portable, and machine and human-readable language.

46 *Unconventional Score Editors*

Criticisms of Common Music Notation

Functions of Unconventional Score Editors

History of Unconventional Score Editors

Graphic Synthesis

Graphical Notation

Notation as Real-Time Visualization

Notation for Documentation and Analysis

Automatic Notation from Sound

Common music notation or CMN describes the majority of conventional Western music written between 1600 and the present day (chapter 45). However large this repertoire is, much notated music falls outside this scope. In order to enter, edit, or perform this music using a computer, specialized software editors are needed. An example would be an editor for medieval music notation (Crawford and Zeff 1983). Many editors support guitar tablature. Editors for non-European music systems (Indian, Chinese, Japanese, Indonesian, for example) require different sets of symbols and conventions (JapoScore 2020; Gujar-Kale 2020).

In the twentieth century, CMN evolved in many directions as composers expanded the art of notation. *Extended techniques* or unconventional ways of playing traditional instruments called for new notation practices (see Dimpker [2013] for a review).

Ultimately, however, musical imagination ranges beyond the precepts of CMN. John Cage's book *Notations* (1969), for example, contains score fragments by 269 composers, approximately one-third of whom did not use conventional staved notation. Also refer to Karkoschka (1966) and, more recently, Sauer (2009). As chapter 49 demonstrates, a note list in code such as Csound is a form of scripted score. Graphical scores for electronic music are important to its culture and history (figure 46.1). Thus, interactive editors open the door to new possibilities for expression and documentation. The TENOR International Conference on Technologies for Music Notation and Representation presents advances in this field.

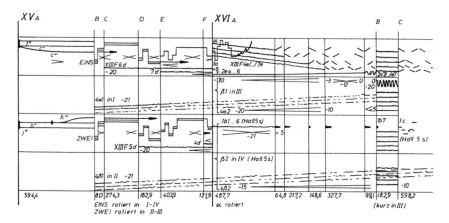

Figure 46.1 Example of unconventional music notation. Score excerpt from Karlheinz Stockhausen's *Kontakte* (1960) for electronic tape. Courtesy Stockhausen Verlag. http://www.karlheinzstockhausen.org.

Criticisms of Common Music Notation

Many musicians do not use CMN on a regular basis. The reasons follow:

CMN is biased toward pitch and duration of notes, to the detriment of other facets of music. Its pitch and time representations are limited to equal-tempered pitches (or offsets therefrom), fractional durations of a single geometric series (1/4, 1/8, 1/16, etc.), and pulsed rhythms. Refer to the critique in Stone (1963).

CMN has few provisions for the representation of timbre and does not represent spatial trajectories. The note concept is a single-event abstraction and does not account for the mutating multi-event sound complexes possible with computer music (e.g., granular streams and clouds). Synthesis parameters, for example, are difficult to represent in CMN; for example, multiple envelopes on sound parameters.

Competence in sight-reading takes years of study and practice. A CMN-based system excludes those who have not acquired this skill. By contrast, gestural and graphical notation can be intuitively understood without training.

CMN addresses only one level of musical form; it was not designed to represent an overview of high-level musical structure or form. In CMN, it is not possible to look below the level of a note to examine the details of the evolving sound structure.

Musicians who work with improvised music have little need of a strict notation system, except to document a recorded improvisation. Lead sheets use CMN for the melody and chord symbols for the harmony.

CMN is not necessary to edit much music data. The note lists of the Music *N* languages (e.g., Csound) are an obvious example. In a *digital audio workstation* (DAW), audio clips and MIDI sequence data can be edited without CMN.

CMN evolved to match conventional European concert performance practices. CMN serves as a framework for an interpreter working within an established tradition. In today's studios, however, the composer often plays the role of the interpreter. The expanded palette of sound and the changing performance possibilities of computer music prompt a need for new notation schemes. Along these lines, the Music Notation Project (http://musicnotation .org) aims to raise awareness of the disadvantages of CMN, to explore alternative music notation systems, and to provide resources for the wider consideration and use of these alternatives.

Functions of Unconventional Score Editors

Much of the repertoire of electronic music falls outside the scope of CMN. Traditional harmonic and rhythmic elements are usually stitched into a larger fabric of timbral and spatial development. In this context, an unconventional notation editor can play a number of roles. First, a musician may sketch out ideas graphically prior to or during the realization of a piece. Here sketching becomes a working medium of expression. Second, a musician may use a *graphical user interface* (GUI) to draw envelopes for parameters of sound synthesis. Third, a graphical representation made after the work is composed can serve as a reading score for documentation, to be used in study, analysis, and teaching. Finally, it is common to see a visualization along with electronic sound. The audience sees as well as hears *visual music* (Brougher et al. 2005; Abbado 2017).

In this chapter, we focus on the following five areas in which unconventional notation editors serve these roles:

- Graphic synthesis
- Graphical notation
- Notation as real-time visualization
- Notation for documentation and analysis
- Automatic notation from sound

We look at all these functions and editors that enable them. First, we glance at the history of unconventional score editors.

History of Unconventional Score Editors

One form of nonstandard music notation is graphic synthesis. Chapter 24 traces this history back to 1880. Here we begin with an early experiment in machine-aided transcription of electroacoustic music by Pierre Schaeffer, founder of the Groupe de Recherches Musicales (GRM) in Paris. In this case, a machine produced a written trace of amplitude versus time on sprocketed graph paper (Schaeffer and Moles 1952). This was transcribed by hand into more familiar notation. Schaeffer dubbed this experiment *notation concrète* (figure 46.2). Later he and colleagues engaged in a bold effort to classify all sounds according to their perceived properties (Schaeffer, Reibel, and Ferreyra 1967).

When it was introduced in 1978, Scriva, developed at the University of Toronto, was an advanced computer-based editor for unconventional music

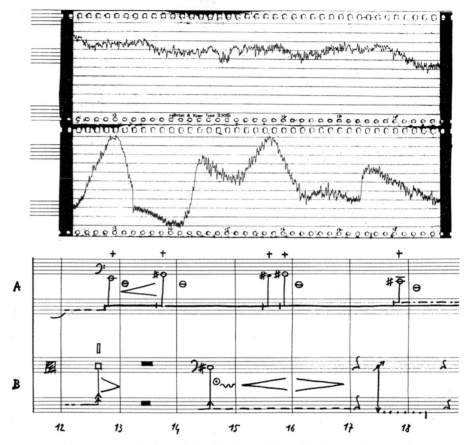

Figure 46.2   Extract of Pierre Schaeffer's machine-aided transcription of an étude of musique concrète. The upper curve is a Bathygram, an intensity versus-time trace. The lower portion shows a transcription into notation. (Courtesy of the Groupe de Recherches Musicales, Paris.)

notation (Buxton et al. 1978a; Buxton 1979; Buxton et al. 1981). Scriva permitted the following types of notation:

- CMN mode with or without staves
- Piano roll notation, with or without staves
- Envelope notation, showing each event's amplitude envelope, with or without staves
- Iconic notation, indicating the timbre of each event by icons

Scriva had various ways of letting users specify the scope of an editing operation such as cut, copy, paste, or modify. In the simplest technique, the user encircled notes using a hand-held pointer, as shown in figure 46.3. In the 1970s, Scriva was unique as a musician-friendly graphical user interface (GUI).

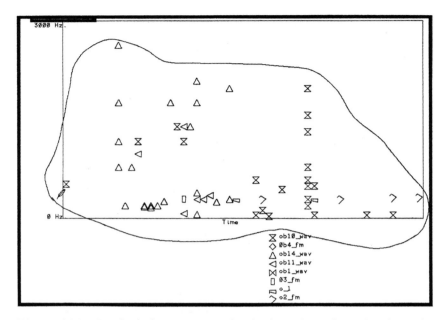

Figure 46.3   Iconic timbre representation in the scriva editor, showing a fragment of the composition that has been encircled in order to perform an operation on the entire group.

Graphic Synthesis

Graphic sound synthesis is an interactive approach based on drawing and image transformation. Graphic synthesis apps such as MetaSynth (Wenger and Spiegel 2010) or UPISketch (Bourotte and Kanach 2019) are visual editors in which user drawings can be organized on a time line. They provide paint boxes for sound images, with a variety of brushes and spray jets for applying sound color, as well as a multitude of implements for modifying sound images. Refer to chapter 24 on graphic synthesis.

Graphical Notation

Composers often sketch out ideas in graphical form. Delalande (2009) studied four hundred acousmatic compositions with working sketches on paper archived by the GRM. The sketches were heterogeneous; no single notational convention dominated. This demonstrates the challenge of developing a *computer-aided composition* (CAC) system with support for alternative notation.

Some CAC systems, such as PatchWork and OpenMusic, generate fragments of CMN but also support other elements. For example, a key feature of PatchWork was having both a CMN representation and also the patch that generated it (Agon et al. 1999). Besides CMN, OpenMusic allows elements such as rhythm trees, curves, arrays, text, mathematical functions, and pictures to be manipulated. A structure used for this is a *maquette,* a container for multiple musical objects (figure 46.4). Objects in a maquette can be manipulated according to temporal and graphical parameters. Thus to a certain extent, a maquette can be considered a patch (IRCAM 2018). Refer to Kuuskankare (2009) for a similar software package.

The Paris-based composer Horacio Vaggione has created intricate and detailed micro rhythmic figures using the program IRIN shown in figure 46.5, designed by Carlos Caires (2004, 2019). These examples of micromontage can be heard in pieces such as *24 Variations* (2002) and *Points critiques* (2011).

Decibel ScorePlayer enables network-synchronized scrolling of proportional color music scores and audio playback on multiple tablet computers (Hope, Wyatt, and Vickery 2015). It is designed to facilitate reading of scores featuring predominantly graphic notation in rehearsal and performance.

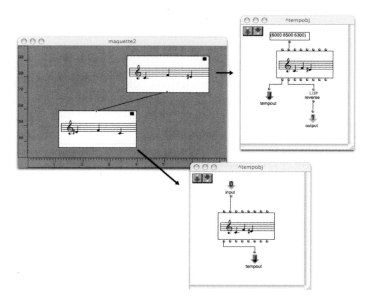

Figure 46.4   OpenMusic maquette is a container for musical objects. Each temporal box encloses a patch that produces a musical output. Some boxes can use data coming from other boxes by means of functional connections. In this example the pitches from a chord sequence are reversed and used in the second box. Another style of maquette can control sound synthesis.

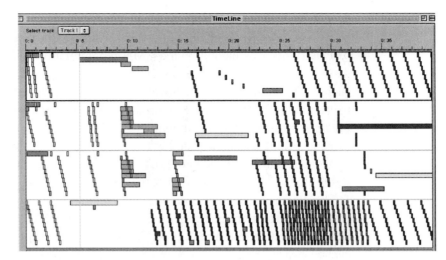

Figure 46.5   A 40-second excerpt of the score of Vaggione's *24 variations* (version 2), showing the four-track timeline designed with the IRIN program. Each rectangle represents a sound clip or sample. The vertical position of a sample within a track is not significant (i.e., it does not correspond to pitch). IRIN lets one encapsulate figures within a track and represents them as a single fragment, permitting one to build up mesostructure hierarchically.

Bach is a software package for computer-aided composition in Max (https://www.bachproject.net). The package implements both CMN and proportional music notation, with support for accidentals of arbitrary resolution, rhythmic trees, polymetric notation, MusicXML, and MIDI files. The graphic position of all notation elements can be queried so that reactive customized notation systems can be built (Agostino and Ghisi 2015).

Notation as Real-Time Visualization

The field of visual music is broad and has a long history, dating back to the *ocular harpsichord* (1725) of the monk Louis-Bertrand Castel (Abbado 2017). It can include everything from paintings inspired by music to scientific visualizations of sound (von Amelunxen, Appelt, and Weibel 2008; Brougher et al. 2005; Woolman 2000). Our interest here is focused on multimedia works that combine images and sound in real time. A prime example is the iconic *Poème électronique* (1958) with music by Edgard Varèse and visuals by Le Corbusier, created for the Philips Pavilion designed by Iannis Xenakis. Xenakis's famous sound and light spectacles, the Polytopes (figure 46.6), continued this tradition (Kanach 2008).

Figure 46.6　View looking upward of *Polytopy de Cluny* (1972), a sound and light spectacle by Iannis Xenakis. A regular grid of flash bulbs is visible with projections by multiple lasers creating geometrical forms above the heads of the audience.

We see echoes of this tradition in works like *Deep Web* (2016) by Christopher Bauder and Robert Henke (figure 46.7). In both the *Polytope de Cluny* and *Deep Web,* visuals were synchronized to sounds, but except for timing, there was no direct relationship between the visual and sonic patterns.

Another trend is works by composer-programmers in which a visual projection in real time is integral to the conception. In some cases, the imagery is a data visualization in which both music and visuals are driven by the same data set. In the 3D immersive audiovisual works by JoAnn Kuchera-Morin, what the audience sees could be described as a form of real-time notation (figure 46.8).

Juan Manuel Escalante explores unconventional notation as central to his artistic practice. He calls these code-generated animations *kinetic scores* (figure 46.9):

Movement introduces a different palette of narrative resources. The wide array of software tools we have today allows us to approach graphic scores in numerous ways, for example, by introducing movement to facilitate the reading and listening experience. . . . [The open-source software] Processing facilitates the generation of simple shapes such as lines, circles, and dots. This vector-based approach to drawing is parallel to the synthesized visual language of my hand-drawn diagrams. Such a similarity facilitates the transition from an analog diagram into a code-generated one. (Escalante 2020, 83)

Another term for this is *animated notation* (http://www.animatednotation .com).

Figure 46.7   Deep Web audiovisual kinetic installation by Christopher Bauder and Robert Henke installed at Kraftwerk, Berlin. Deep Web is an installation using twelve high-precision lasers and a matrix of 175 moving balloons to create a three-dimensional sculpture of lines and dots floating in space above the audience. The choreography is synced to a musical score played back in eight-channel surround sound.

Figure 46.8   JoAnn Kuchera-Morin on the bridge of the UCSB Allosphere at the control panel for her 2017 piece *PROBABLY/POSSIBLY?,* a collaboration with Luca Peliti, Lance Putnam, Dennis Adderton, Andres Cabrera, Kon Hyong Kim, Gustavo Rincon, Joseph Tilbian, Hannah Wolfe, Tim Wood, and Keehong Youn. The work is an interactive, immersive, visual and sound composition that tracks the probability currents and gradients of a hydrogen-like atom's electron in superposition, combining wave functions according to the time-dependent Schrödinger equation. The composition explores symmetry and changes in symmetry as a narrative in sound and image.

Figure 46.9   *The Generation of Maps* (2020) by Juan Manuel Escalante. In this audiovisual performance, a generative algorithm running on a laptop computer controls a modular synthesizer patch, shown in the lower part. The main section of the projection displays a code-generated grid. Each cell of the grid has two states, active or inactive. Inactive cells appear as X marks and do not influence the sound. Active cells appear as a combination of circles and lines moving in a clockwise direction at different speeds. Each active cell controls a trigger for an envelope in the modular patch. The projection offers an alternative visualization method on the right, rendering grid cells as horizontal lines in a single column. Each line has a small indicator that moves from left to right at different speeds. Once an indicator reaches the end, it sends a trigger signal to the synthesizer and resets itself, choosing a new speed value and a new starting position. The entire system resets itself randomly with new configurations of rows, columns, and different states for each iteration.

Notation for Documentation and Analysis

A traditional composer working with a DAW can improvise at a MIDI keyboard along with a metronome, knowing that the performance will be faithfully recorded and automatically transcribed into CMN. They can arrange audio clips and MIDI tracks on a time line. This is a form of score. The GUI of the DAW provides a front end to what is essentially a Music-*N* note list, which indicates the start time and duration of every clip and MIDI note. However, a

DAW file is not ideal as a reading score. To begin with, MIDI piano-roll notation lacks meta-information such as key and time signatures, accidentals, tuplet
ties, and so on. Second, audio waveforms are largely illegible. Only in limited
cases can a person identify a sound by its waveform. The global waveform of
most music is an amorphous blob, except for landmarks like silent passages
and contrasts between extremely loud and soft textures.

When notation is meant to serve as a reading score or documentation of an
electronic music composition, someone must analyze the music and turn it into
a graphic representation. Music analysis, even of conventional music, is fraught
with conceptual conundrums (Roads 2015). The analysis of electronic music
can be an especially daunting task, calling on solfège skills beyond those taught
in the conservatory (Schaeffer et al. 1967; Roy 2003; Delalande 2009). Even
assuming such skills, how to notate what one hears in the absence of a standard
representation? No ground truth exists. One must invent a conceptual framework. A visual language also needs to be invented, seemingly for each piece,
due to the heterogeneity of electronic music in its sounds, processes, and forms
(Emmerson and Landy 2016a, 2016b).

The composition *Stria* (1977) by John Chowning was the first work to derive
its sonic microstructure as well as its macrostructure from the ratio of the Golden
Section (Meneghini 2007). Thus it makes sense to visualize the unfolding in
time of the spectral components (figure 46.10) (Zattra 2020). Such a specific
representation may not be appropriate for another work.

Regular CMN editors can export notation fragments. Fragments can be rearranged and combined with other visual elements in a graphic design program
(e.g., Adobe Illustrator). New styles of notation can be created using drawing,
painting, and graphic design programs. Indeed, the artful integration of traditional notation, waveforms, spectrograms, new icons, and unusual graphics is
probably best handled by a professional graphic design program. Figure 46.11
is a page from the author's composition *Half-life* (1998) scored by notation
expert James Ingram (2001, 2002), which employed a variety of software tools.

A pioneering effort to integrate multiple tools in one software package is
Acousmographe, developed at the Groupe de Recherches Musicales by
Olivier Koechlin and Hughes Vinet (Bayle 1993). This software supports a
transcription of electroacoustic music starting from a spectrogram representation (figure 46.12). Acousmographe lets the user inscribe a library of color
graphic symbols onto a spectrogram. The spectrogram can then be removed,
condensing the display into a more readable and expressive form.

After Acousmographe have come a number of other interactive editors
with similar aims. Sonic Visualiser's stated goal is to be "the first program
you reach for when want to study a musical recording rather than simply
listen to it" (Cannam et al. 2010).

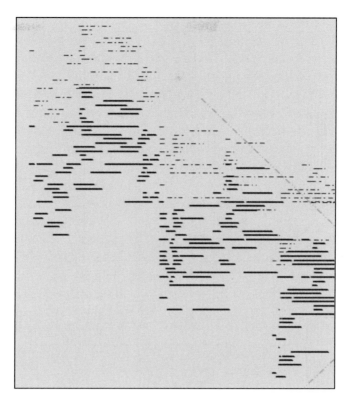

Figure 46.10   Visualization of the spectral components of *Stria* (1977) by John Chowning. From a graphic analysis by Laura Zattra (2020).

Sonic Visualiser has a familiar GUI setup, a set of visualization facilities, and plug-in support for automated analysis methods (figure 46.13). The app helps users assemble visual representations into custom documents. Visual representations include waveforms, spectrograms, time rulers, time instants, time values, notes, regions, boxes, text, images, and color 3D plots. The app includes methods for annotating audio with features such as beat times, using keyboard, mouse, or an attached MIDI device. Finally, it provides import and export for annotations in formats including Music Ontology RDF (http://musicontology.com) for use in linked data applications on the Semantic Web.

Tools for interactive aural analysis (TIAALS) enable users to develop interactive analyses in an environment integrating a sonogram and a chart maker (Clarke et al. 2013). The interface between the two workspaces—the sonogram and the chart—is a *palette* (figure 46.14). Users populate the palette with objects taken from the sonogram. One then moves elements from the palette to create a structured representation in the chart. Unlike sonogram objects, objects placed on the chart are visually abstract—a symbolic mode of representation.

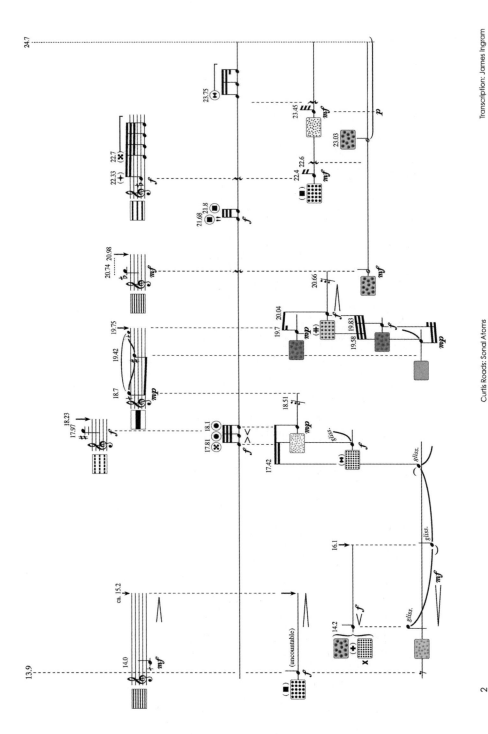

Figure 46.11 A page from the graphic score of *Half-life* (1998) by Curtis Roads. The score was realized by James Ingram.

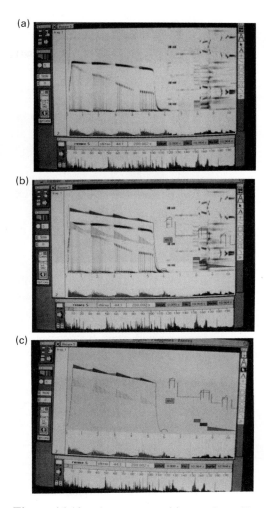

Figure 46.12   Acousmagraphic notation of *Rosace V* by François Bayle. Transcription realized by Dominique Besson. (a) Original sonogram of sound fragment. (b) Inscription of graphical symbols onto the sonogram, according to cues heard by the ear. (c) Final symbolic notation. (Courtesy of the Groupe de Recherches Musicales, Paris.)

The Aural Sonology Project provides another set of software tools. The stated objective of this project has been to "describe, transcribe and analyze music-as-heard." The project's concepts and analytical signs derive from Pierre Schaeffer's pioneering work (Schaeffer, Reibel, and Ferreyra 1967). An objective of the project has been to create a general methodology that makes it possible to analyze music in many styles and idioms with the same terms (Thoreson 2015).

Unlike the previously mentioned projects, eAnalyse and iAnalyse by Pierre Couprie supports video and image as well as audio files (Couprie

(a)   (b)

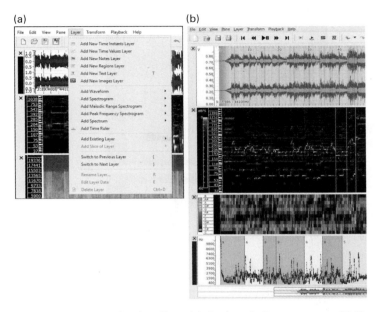

Figure 46.13   Sonic Visualiser. (a) Options in Layers menu. (b) Four visual displays. From top: waveform, spectrogram with peak frequencies highlighted, chromagram showing pitch distribution, and spectral centroid plot.

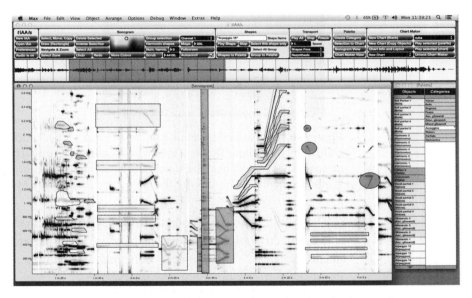

Figure 46.14   Screenshot of TIAALS software, showing the interactive sonogram and palette.

2016, 2018). These apps provide tools for creating analytic text and graphics for music study (figure 46.15). As a playback system, eAnalysis can navigate and compare different segments of a composition or play different tracks of a multitrack work. The image shown in figure 46.15 is but one example; the visual repertoire of eAnalyse and iAnalyse is diverse.

We should also mention interesting efforts to visualize Denis Smalley's *spectromorphology* model for analysis of electroacoustic music. Spectromorphology refers to the descriptive analysis of perceived shapes or morphologies in sound spectra over time (Smalley, 1986, 1997). Thoresen and Hedman (2007) and Manuella Blackburn (2011) created visual languages for describing spectromorphology types.

Automatic Notation from Sound

We have seen that several editors support manual annotation of waveforms and sonograms. Advances in sound analysis and machine learning raise the issue of *automatic transcription* from sound to symbolic notation. Chapters 34 through 39 present some of the difficult issues surrounding automatic transcription of traditional music into CMN. For obvious reasons, the transcription problem is more challenging in the absence of a standard notational framework for electronic music.

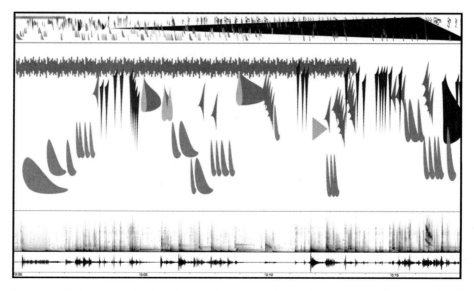

Figure 46.15   This eAnalyse image shows an extract of Pierre Couprie's analysis of the movement *Ondes croisées* from *De Natura Sonorum* (1975) by Bernard Parmegiani.

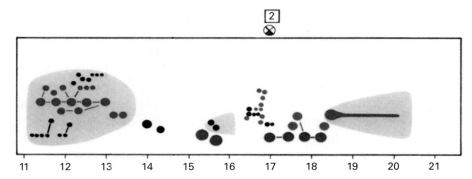

Figure 46.16 Ligeti's *Artikulation,* graphic score published by Schott Music. The circles indicate unfiltered impulses.

Spectrum analysis—plotting the time-frequency domain—is usually the starting point for automatic transcription (chapter 36). The pioneering EMPS system (Haus 1983) stands as one of the earliest attempts to transcribe automatically the sound of synthesized music into a reading score. Haus developed a graphic notation in which sounds in different registers appear as distinct symbols, and amplitudes are plotted as closely spaced histograms. The notation was somewhat similar to that used in the transcription of Gyorgy Ligeti's electronic music composition *Artikulation* (Ligeti and Wehinger 1970), shown in figure 46.16. *Artikulation* has been cited as a model for several editors mentioned in this chapter.

Klien, Grill, and Flexer (2012) studied automatic annotation of electronic music using *music information retrieval* (MIR) techniques. They adopted *spectromorphology* as a description model (Smalley 1986, 1997). Spectromorphology is a taxonomy of descriptors for sound shapes and structural functions of electronic music. As the authors point out, the task of automated structural discovery in electronic music is comparable to the same task performed on a mixture of environmental sounds. Indeed, fully automated transcription is not even a possibility due to the lack of a ground truth and the absence of semantic comprehension in computer models. Lack of ground truth means that there is no scientifically "correct" transcription; any such transcription involves interpretation. The study showed that MIR techniques can help a human analyst but that more research is needed to develop interactive tools.

Today machine learning is leading progress in automatic transcription (appendix A and chapter 35). It is a short conceptual step from training a machine learning system on data sets of traditional music and CMN, to training it on electronic music and a new form of graphic/symbolic notation. What is needed is the invention of this notation, which will no doubt be an ongoing endeavor.

47 *Instrument and Patch Editors*

Instrument Editors: Historical Background

Example of a Template Editor: FM8

Example of a Patch Editor: Max
> Basics of Max
> Message Boxes
> Control Objects versus Signal-Processing Objects
> A Waveform Generator Patch

Examples of Patch Editors: REAKTOR and Euro Reakt

Example of a Patch Editor: VCV Rack

Modular Patching within a DAW

Integrating Software and Eurorack Hardware

Instrument editors let users design and tune digital synthesizers. Interaction is mediated through a *graphical user interface* (GUI). Editors "open the hood" of a synthesizer, giving users access to the synthesis engine. Instrument editors fall into two major categories: *template editors* that let a musician tune the parameters of a fixed-function instrument, and *patch editors*—toolkits that let one design one's own synthesis instruments based on a collection of modules that can be freely interconnected into *patches*. The term *patch* derives from the patch cords in modular synthesizers that are used to connect modules. Patch editors or *patchers* are also called *visual programming languages* (VPLs). The earliest VPL was GRAIL—a remarkable flowchart interface—demonstrations of which can be seen online (Ellis, Heafner, and Sibley 1969).

A template editor gives access to a predefined synthesis engine. This means that the number of oscillators, envelope generators, filters, and other modules have been defined at the factory and cannot be changed. The way that these modules can be interconnected is also predefined.

A prime example of a template editor is Sound Quest's Midi Quest. This is a universal patch editor/librarian for hundreds of classic hardware instruments from Korg, Roland, Yamaha, Dave Smith Instruments, Kurzweil, Alesis, Waldorf, Kawai, Akai, and E-mu, among others (figure 47.1). Midi Quest lets users tune existing presets and make new ones. They can save the new preset to the instrument via a MIDI cable.

As we discuss further on, the GUIs of software synthesizers such as Native Instrument FM8 are essentially template editors. In this type of instrument, the capabilities are set by the manufacturer.

By contrast, using a patcher like Max, Pure Data, Reaktor, VCV Rack, or AudioMulch (figure 47.2), a musician can create as many modules as desired, up to the processing limits of the computer. Moreover, the modules can be interconnected in arbitrary ways. If a project needs to connect twenty-nine oscillators to seventeen filters, that is no problem. Patches can be encapsulated by embedding patches within patches. As with an analog synthesizer, it is the way things are connected, disconnected, and triggered that creates musical events.

Both template editors and patchers have their place. Template editors are easy to learn and use. Their GUIs are optimized for a specific synthesis method and interaction mode. They let musicians tune the parameters of a synthesis instrument while listening to the sound.

By contrast, mastering a patcher is a major commitment. Understanding someone else's patch can be a challenge. But unlike a template editor, a patcher enables rapid prototyping of new synthesis and interaction concepts. They let users design not just sounds but interactive composition systems (Winkler

Figure 47.1   Midi Quest editor for Roland D-50 Linear Synthesizer.

1998). Of course, one can also design an interactive system using a textual programming language (see chapters 48 and 49).

The distinction between template editor and patcher is not absolute. As we show, some template editors allow a limited amount of patching, such as routing modulation signals. Others offer a set of templates from which to choose. Finally, some patchers like OpenMusic or PWGL present an icon-based interface focused primarily on composition, not synthesis (see chapter 49).

Instrument Editors: Historical Background

The first generation of modular analog synthesizers provided a hands-on approach to designing and exploring synthesis patches. In analog synthesizers, each sound parameter requires a separate knob or switch, and each interconnection between modules requires a patch cord. For example, a Moog III synthesizer manufactured in the 1970s had about 150 rotary knobs and thirty-five switches. (The recent Moog System 55 is similar.) Dozens of patch cords might be used in a single patch. Although a hands-on approach

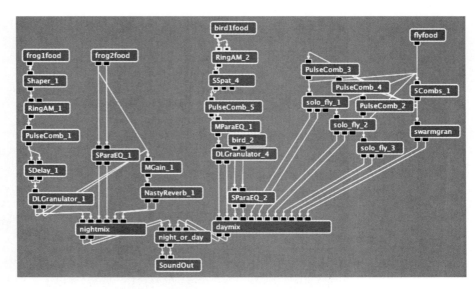

Figure 47.2   Granular synthesis patch in AudioMulch.

offered immediate access to all parameters, there was no way to save a patch other than by taking detailed notes. Repatching and retuning can take hours.

The modular toolkit concept was also embodied in the notion of the unit generator for the music synthesis languages Music III, IV, and V (Tenney 1963; Mathews 1969). Figures 5.4 and 8.2 present examples of Music V patches. Of course, Music V was a compiled text language. No real-time interaction was possible. One drew patch diagrams on paper as part of the design and documentation process. One could then translate the patch diagram into text.

Template editors let users design envelopes and waveforms onscreen. The earliest template editor for music was the Graphical Input (GRIN) system developed at Bell Telephone Laboratories (Mathews and Rosler 1968, 1969). Images drawn on a display screen with a light pen were compiled into envelope and waveform definitions for the Music IV sound synthesis language. Mathews and Rosler also used functions to control performance, such as curves for tempo. Another early application was graphical design of spatial paths in quadraphonic sound systems. John Chowning (1971) pioneered this use, which was also pursued by Moore (1983) and Loy (1985c).

The bit-mapped screen technology that we take for granted today was rare and expensive in the 1970s. However, several computer music laboratories had *vector graphics* screens, which used geometrical primitives such as points and lines to construct stick images. The Structured Sound Synthesis Project's (SSSP) pioneering Objed sound object editor was operational between 1978 and 1983 at the University of Toronto. Objed was one of the first programs to use interactive graphics in service of template editing (Buxton et al. 1982). To edit a frequency modulation instrument, for example, the musician could graphically manipulate all the waveforms and envelopes associated with the template (figure 47.3). A command to edit a waveform opened a window to a waveform editor. By moving a mouse, a musician could change other parameters by means of graphic potentiometers on the display screen.

Soon after the introduction of the MIDI protocol in 1983, Apple Macintosh and Microsoft Windows appeared with bit-mapped displays. Software-based GUI template editor/librarians for hardware synthesizers became widely available. Opcode Systems was a leader in this field. The early editors provided a GUI with which musicians could see waveforms and envelopes that were not displayed on the tiny character displays on the synthesizer itself. Editor/librarians manipulated MIDI *system exclusive data* (see chapter 51). That is, they

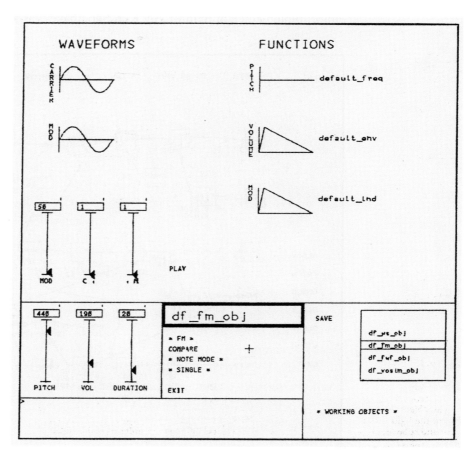

Figure 47.3   An early graphical user interface for sound synthesis, the Objed sound object editor.

edited a representation of the synthesizer's internal memory in the form of *bulk patch data*—the parameter settings of all the voices in the synthesizer. For example, all the editing information for the thirty-two-patch capacity of the legendary Yamaha DX7 FM synthesizer could be completely contained within its tiny 4,096 byte bulk patch memory.

One of the first graphical patchers was MITSYN developed by William Henke, a speech scientist at the Massachusetts Institute of Technology (Henke 1970). The MITSYN program was designed for scientific applications, but it was also used in music compositions. As shown in figure 47.4, a user could connect the output of a *pulse train generator* (which produces a buzzy sound like that of a human glottis) to a filter, in order to create a voice-like sound.

Oedit, a demonstration program developed at the MIT in the mid-1970s, borrowed ideas from MITSYN and was intended for music sound synthesis. Although not general enough to be called an instrument editor, the Reved editor implemented at Stanford by Ken Shoemake was similar in its interac-

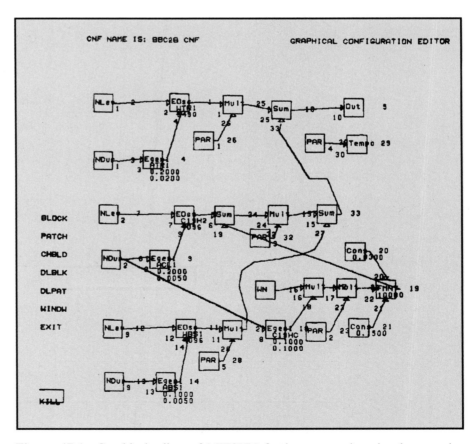

Figure 47.4 Graphical editor of MITSYN for interconnecting signal processing modules. The screen is typical of vector displays.

tion style to MITSYN. Reved let users patch together signal-processing modules such as comb and allpass filters to create reverberators.

A signal development was Max (originally called Patcher) by Miller Puckette (1988, 1991, 2002). Designed to process MIDI data for the control of synthesis hardware, it became a commercial product of Opcode Systems in 1989 and Cycling '74 in 1990. Max/MSP, introduced in 1997 added audio processing and the renamed Max is today widely used (Puckette and Zicarelli 1990; Puckette, Apel, and Zicarelli 1998; Cipriani and Giri 2010a, b). We look more at Max below.

Another notable patcher from this period was the GUI of the Fly30 real-time synthesis system (1990) developed at Rome's Centro di Ricerche Musicali (Lupone et al. 2020). Fly30 was used in numerous interactive performances by Laura Bianchini and Michelangelo Lupone.

Pure Data or Pd is an open source project by Miller Puckette (1996, 1997, 2007, 2017) that has many similarities with Max. Users interconnect objects in the manner of a modular synthesizer. A key design feature is the handling of asynchronous control information. Pd's messaging system sends asynchronous control information from one object to another. Audio computation is a separate synchronous system handled by objects that compute a block of samples at a time.

Clavia's Nord Modular synthesizer (1997–2003) gave users a graphical patching system that they could run on their computer (Clark 2003). Patches could be downloaded to the synthesizer, which could then be used without a computer.

Another notable example is the KYMA system developed by Carla Scaletti (1989a, 1989b, 2002, 2015), which continues to evolve. The KYMA graphical editor offers both template and patching options, and it works in conjunction with a custom hardware synthesizer.

Kronos is a more recent programming language for musical signal processing (Norilo 2012, 2015). Veneer is an experimental front-end patching system built on top of Kronos that works on mobile devices with touch interfaces (Norilo 2019). Finally we should mention Troikatronix Isadora, an audiovisual media playback system with a patching environment for setting up interactive performances. Isadora is used by multimedia artists such as Pamela Z, for example.

Example of a Template Editor: FM8

Template editors are easy to learn. A prime example is Native Instruments FM8, a software synthesizer that emulates the Yamaha DX7 hardware but

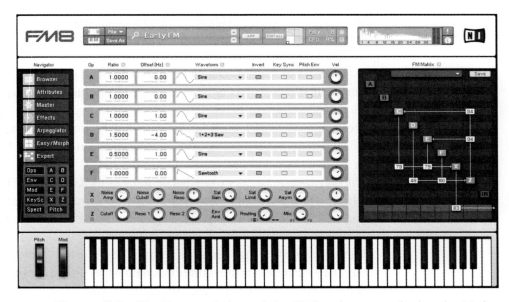

Figure 47.5 The Expert window of the FM8 software synthesizer by Native Instruments. Users can adjust waveforms, envelopes, and other settings. The panel on the right shows the synthesis circuit as a set of interconnected signal generators. This circuit can also be edited, within the constraints of the Yamaha FM architecture.

also offers enhancements like reverberation and other effects that were not on the original synthesizer. FM8 comes with hundreds of preset patches in the form of libraries. Most users will only tweak the presets, but FM8 provides an Expert window that gives access to the internals of a patch (figure 47.5). Notice the possibility of repatching modules in the subwindow on the right.

Example of a Patch Editor: Max

Max is a widely used graphical icon-based toolkit tailored for interactive performance of music and visuals (Puckette 1985, 1988, 2002; Puckette and Zicarelli 1990; Zicarelli 2002; Cipriani and Giri 2010a, b; Lyon 2012). Miller Puckette (2002) traced the early genesis of Max and analyzed its strengths and weaknesses. Max was designed for musicians, not computer scientists, and its wide use is proof of its utility.

Max can take input from MIDI, OSC, audio and video, as well as sensor data that has been previously converted to digital data by microcontrollers (such as Arduino or Rasperry Pi). MIDI and OSC are discussed in chapters 51 and 52. The output of a patch can be MIDI or OSC data, audio or video signals, or messages sent to applications running alongside Max.

Max has been used by thousands of musicians around the world in applications ranging over responsive instruments, interactive composition, art installations, and control of audio devices. An extension called Max for Live lets users embed the Max patching environment directly into Ableton Live. This enables the manipulation of MIDI, audio, OSC, and visuals by Max patch plug-ins. Another extension called Gen automatically converts visual patches into custom compiled Max objects.

Max provides access to multiple levels of control and computation on the same screen (Jette 2020). In particular, the inclusion of GUI objects means that one can embed a high-level control—such as a master slider controlling the volume of an entire patch—directly in the coding environment. Simultaneously, one can create intricate low-level patches to process MIDI data, as in Jean-Claude Risset's *Duet for One Pianist* (1989). Gen extends control to the level of individual samples.

In the rest of this section we present a condensed tutorial of patching in Max. A caveat is appropriate before we begin. In explaining Max patches, the cliché "One picture is worth a thousand words" applies. Even a simple patch requires a lengthy textual description if it is assumed that the reader is a novice, as we do here. Thus we must limit the presentation here to a basic example that illustrates general principles but does not expose the full power of the toolkit. Although simple, the patch has the advantage of showing how MIDI and audio processing can work together.

Basics of Max

The patch is a fundamental concept in Max: a graphical configuration of objects shown as boxes connected by patch cords. When a patch becomes too complicated on-screen, Max lets users collapse an entire patch into a single object. This greatly simplifies a patch's appearance, modularizes its functions, and provides a mechanism for arbitrarily complex nested patches.

A patch on-screen is in either *edit mode* or *run mode.* In edit mode, all the interconnections can be changed and new objects can be put in the window by selecting from an object palette. In run mode, the object palette disappears. The user cannot change the patch but can interact with it. The patch reacts to external events such as mouse clicks, keyboard tapping, MIDI messages, and sound input.

When objects receive a message or signal through their inlet, they can respond by sending a message or signal through their outlet. The data sent out by an object can be routed to a number of internal and external destinations via other Max objects. Max can output byte code, MIDI, OSC, sound and video matrices. The inlets and outlets appear as small dark half circles at the top and bottom of the object box.

Messages passed between objects contain numbers, symbols (strings), lists, or the symbol *bang*. The *bang* symbol is like a trigger; it is often used as a semaphore to start and stop processes. Knowing the order in which messages are sent is important for Max programming, but the example here does not require an exposition of this topic.

Message Boxes

Message boxes are ubiquitous in Max patches because they can send arbitrary messages to multiple destinations in a patch without patch cords. Thus a message box is a "wireless" message transmitter. Each message in a message box is separated by a semicolon. Look at the message boxes shown in the top left of figure 47.6, labeled On and Off. A message box assumes that its first message is to be sent directly out its outlet—if it is connected to another box by a patch cord. Because these message boxes are not connected directly to another box, the semicolon in the first line says "There is

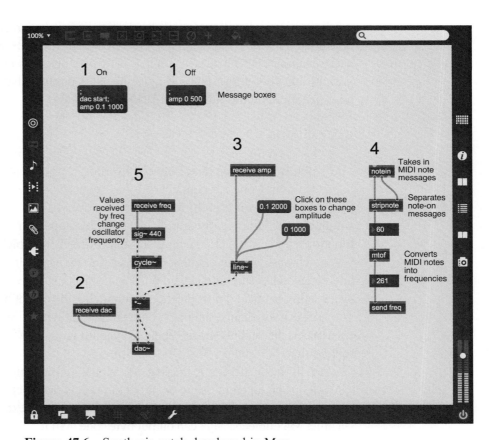

Figure 47.6   Synthesis patch developed in Max.

nothing to send out the outlet." The rest of the messages in the box are in the form

```
receive_object_name message;
```

The second line of text in the message box sends the message start to the receive object named dac (see label 2), which passes it immediately to the dac~ object. When the dac~ object receives a start message, it causes sound. The third line sends the message 0.1 100 to the receive object amp (see label 3). We will explain the meaning of this message in a moment.

Max sends messages to their destinations every time either *bang* or a message starting with a number is sent to the message box. Mouse-clicking on a message box in run mode is like sending it a bang. Now that we have explained the operation of message boxes, we can go on to a complete description of the Max patch.

Control Objects versus Signal-Processing Objects

Max includes signal processing objects that can generate and process signals in addition to the control objects that process messages. Whereas messages are triggered by external events (mouse clicks, MIDI notes, etc.), signals flow at a regular sampling rate through a Max patch.

The names of signal-processing objects end with the symbol tilde (~), such as cycle~, sig~, line~, adc~, and dac~. The sig~ object converts messages at control rate into signals that occur at the audio sampling rate. That is, it converts numerical messages into signals that the signal processing objects can understand. We present an example below.

A Waveform Generator Patch

Figure 47.6 depicts a simple signal-generating patch. Label 1 identifies the message boxes. As mentioned, the start message sent to the receive dac object at label 2 eventually causes the dac~ object to turn on the audio converters. At label 3, the receive object named amp picks up the arguments to be fed to a line~ object. The line~ object generates a straight line or ramp, which in this patch serves as a simple amplitude envelope for an oscillator cycle~. The arguments to line~ take the form

```
target_value duration
```

In the duration (in milliseconds) specified, line~ emits a ramp, starting at its current value and going to the specified target_value. When the patch begins, the initial value of line~ is 0, so the first message it receives tells it to go from

0 to 0.1 in 1000 ms, or 1 second. (The signals passed through Max are floating-point values in the range of−1.0 to 1.0.) After one second, the line~ object continues to emit a value of 0.1 until we send it a new message. The two other message boxes connected to the line~ object can be clicked in real time to change the amplitude of the oscillator. The box with the arguments 0 1000 causes the amplitude to drop to zero in one second. The other box causes it to go back up to 0.1 over a two-second period.

Now let us look at the MIDI processing part of the patch, labeled 4. The notein object receives MIDI messages from the computer's MIDI IN port and filters out everything except note-on and note-off messages. No patch cord or message box needs to be connected to a notein object, because it is connected to the MIDI IN port. A note-on message is MIDI's way of starting a note; the note-off ends it. (See chapter 51 for more on these messages.) The outlets of notein go to the stripnote object, which removes note-off messages and passes only the note-on messages. The output of stripnote is patched to a number box that displays the integer MIDI pitch value, which in figure 47.5 is 60 or MIDI middle C. From here the data passes to the mtof object, which converts a MIDI note number into a frequency value, shown in the number box below it as 261 Hz. The send object passes its input to the receive object named *freq,* labeled 5.

The frequency value coming out of the receive object is a control message. In order to be usable by a signal-processing object, it needs to be converted into a signal that is passed at the signal rate. The sig~ object performs this conversion. Notice the default value of 440 in the sig~ object. This is the frequency value that cycle~ uses to generate a waveform before the patch receives a MIDI note-on message. As soon as the patch receives a note-on message from the external world, the 440 initial value is overridden. Finally, the cycle~ object generates a cosine wave by default, accepting the frequency in its left inlet. After the multiplier object *~ scales the amplitude of the cosine, the signal splits into two, flowing out two output channels.

Examples of Patch Editors: REAKTOR and Euro Reakt

REAKTOR by Native Instruments is a modular signal processing laboratory in software. At a low level, REAKTOR is a visual programming environment based on basic modules connected by wires. A REAKTOR *instrument* can be a synthesizer, sequencer, effect, or other musical tool. It includes the internal structure, MIDI processing, panel (user interface), and snapshots (presets) associated with the tool. REAKTOR's factory library features dozens of instruments and effects: synthesizers, effects, sample players, and sequencers. User libraries add thousands more.

REAKTOR *blocks* emulate modules of a modular synthesizer. Each block is a separate instrument, allowing one to patch between multiple modules (figure 47.7). For example, Michael Hetrick's Euro Reakt is a collection of over one hundred blocks. This large collection focuses on aspects of modular synthesis that make it unique, including generative composition, multi-output effects, and flexible modulations. Example modules include a Buchla-style lowpass gate, wavefolder, probability router, drum voice, eight-way switch, complex envelope, frequency shifter, quadrature low-frequency oscillator, wavetable distortion, and Boolean logic calculators.

Example of a Patch Editor: VCV Rack

VCV Rack is a simulated Eurorack software synthesizer, originally developed by Andrew Belt and introduced in 2017. VCV Rack is open source, and the core software is free. The VCV Rack website features additional modules. The most notable free offering is a nearly complete set of Mutable Instruments

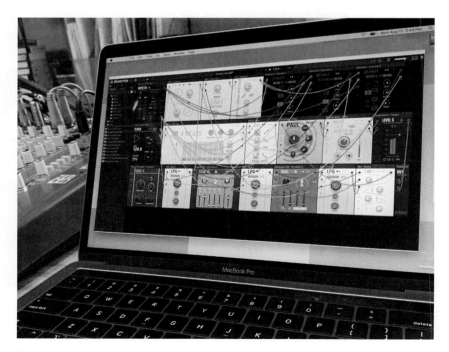

Figure 47.7   REAKTOR BLOCKS modular patcher.

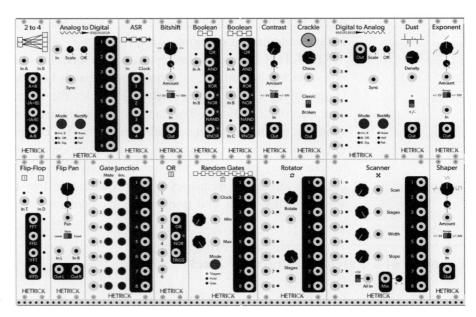

Figure 47.8   Hetrick modules in VCV Rack modular synthesizer.

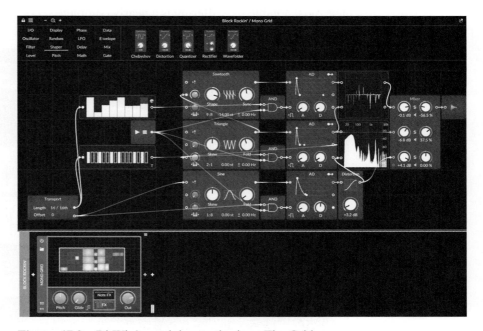

Figure 47.9   BitWig's modular synthesizer: The Grid.

modules, under the name Audible. Several dozen developers work on building and supporting additional modules, some free and some not.

Modular Patching within a DAW

All digital audio workstations host synthesizer plug-ins; some have patchable features. Some DAWS provide their own modular patching plug-ins. Apple's Environment provides a virtual view of a MIDI studio, giving the user patchable control over the MIDI setup. FL Studio has a Patcher tool for chaining instruments and effects. Reason provides a patchable rack and devices. Ableton Live has Max for Live, a development environment. BitWig features an integrated modular synthesizer called The Grid (figure 47.9).

Integrating Software and Eurorack Hardware

Modular hardware, especially Eurorack, is a part of many studios today. Thus it is important to have the possibility of connecting the laptop software world to the world of modular hardware. Integration of modular patching software with a Eurorack hardware synthesizer is straightforward. Certain audio interfaces, such as those made by Mark of the Unicorn (MOTU), permit DC control voltages (envelopes) as well as analog audio to be sent into and out of a computer. They can interface with a hardware module like the Expert Sleepers ES-8 to send and receive audio and control voltages on the Eurorack synthesizer.

48 *Languages for Sound Synthesis*

The world of programming languages for music is a constantly evolving lattice. For the purpose of this book we separate languages into two categories: sound synthesis (this chapter) and composition (chapter 49). We do this to simplify the presentation. In practice, music and its languages cross these boundaries.

This chapter focuses on text-based languages rather than on visual patchers like Pure Data, covered in chapter 47. Although the semantics of an FM instrument is the same in Pure Data and in a textual language like Nyquist (Dannenberg 2002, 2018), they present two different interface paradigms. Nishino and Nakatsu (2016) present a historical account of computer music systems including both textual languages and patchers. Joseph Tilbian (2018) made a detailed comparison of sound synthesis programming languages.

The languages on which we focus here are designed specifically for the task of sound synthesis and processing. However, they are not the only languages used to build music systems. General-purpose programming languages are in standard use in the audio and music industries for synthesis-related tasks. For example, most professional audio developers use the languages C and C++ to create apps and plug-ins. The MATLAB language was never designed for music. However, the research literature in computer music uses MATLAB to explicate synthesis and processing algorithms (Beltrán and Beltrán 2002; Zölzer 2011; Smith 2011). Another general-purpose language, Python, is commonly used for audio applications that involve machine learning.

General-purpose languages are aided by audio-specific software layers such as libraries, frameworks, and *application program interfaces* (APIs). These provide functions so that every developer does not have to rewrite a common operation such as reading a sound file. For example, professionals use the JUCE framework to create audio plug-ins and applications. Other libraries include AudioKit, RtAudio, RtMidi, PortAudio, and libsndfile.

Assessing Formal Languages

Formal programming languages written in text are a flexible means of controlling sound synthesis. As opposed to the closed world of canned software and hardware presets, formal languages liberate the potential of a music system. Any synthesis method or interface that can be imagined can be coded.

Formal languages lend precision to music specification because they require that musical ideas be stipulated explicitly in text. Herein lie both the advantage and disadvantage of formal language interaction with a computer music system. The advantage is that formalized instructions can yield a high degree of control. To create an imagined effect, composers need only specify it precisely. One can easily stipulate multithreaded musical structures that would be impossible to perform by human beings.

A textual expression can be much more efficient than gestural input. This is the case when a single command applies to a massive group of events or when a short script of commands replaces dozens of pointing and selecting gestures. The shell scripts of Unix-based operating systems such as MacOS and Linux are a typical example. Scripting languages were originally designed to automate tasks that were formerly executed one at a time by a human operator. Python, Perl, and Ruby are contemporary examples of general-purpose scripting languages.

The advantages of formal languages turn into a disadvantage when simple things must be coded in the same detail and with the same syntactic overhead as complicated things. For example, in a formal language without graphical support, envelope shapes that could be drawn on a screen in two seconds must be plotted out on paper by hand and transcribed into a list of numerical data to be typed. Thus some languages provide graphical tools for instrument design and waveform and envelope specification. Graphical aids for envelope design can be most helpful, because specifying curves in text is tedious and error-prone.

For rapid prototyping of an idea, many musicians feel that patchers, in which one interconnects graphical objects, are easier to use than a programming language (see chapter 47).

Some languages are interactive; one can type an individual statement and it is immediately executed. This has led to experimentation with *live coding*, which focuses on improvised interactive programming to create sound-and-image performances (Collins et al. 2003). We look at languages for live coding in chapter 49.

In many cases, it is easier to play a gesture rather than trying to type the code that would simulate the same gesture in a formal language. Gestural control is a naturally efficient means of achieving sonic expressiveness. Thus synthesis languages provide tools for integrating gestural controllers using MIDI or OSC (chapters 51 and 52).

Advantages and Disadvantages of Synthesis Languages

Synthesis languages retain three undeniable strong points:

1. An open modular toolkit approach to synthesis, in which each user can configure the kit for their own needs. The curious can experiment with new synthesis algorithms.

2. Arbitrarily complicated synthesis algorithms played by an arbitrary number of voices.

3. Precision: a composer can specify sonic events in extraordinarily fine numerical detail.

For each of these advantages is a corresponding disadvantage.

1. Toolkits imply a learning curve and obligate the musician to take up software engineering, including program debugging, code maintenance, and documentation.

2. Complicated synthesis algorithms may not be able to operate in real time, necessitating rendering to a sound file. They may not be amenable to gestural control due to too many variables.

3. Precision implies that the musician must specify masses of minutiae, possibly involving hundreds of parameter values for each second of sound.

In the rest of this chapter, we look at two categories of languages: classic unit generator languages that usually operate in non–real time, and languages for real-time synthesis. Chapter 8 introduces the basic principles of software synthesis and is a prerequisite to the discussion that follows.

Classic Unit Generator Languages

The classic synthesis languages based on the Music *N* model such as Csound (Boulanger 2000) assume that the composer creates a synthesis *orchestra* and a *score* that invokes the orchestra (figure 48.1). The *instruments* in the orchestra are modular patches in the form of text. This orchestra text declares interconnections between *unit generators* (UGs) and the input parameters. Each UG is a software module that emits audio or control signals such as envelopes. A UG can also take in signals and modify them. The synthesis compiler reads both the orchestra and the score, constructs a machine-level representation of the synthesis patches, and feeds them the data from the score. The final audio signal is rendered to a *sound file* for later playback. If the synthesis algorithm is efficient enough, the samples generated by the sound synthesis program could also be played in real time.

The UG concept allows great flexibility, because the output of a UG can be patched to the input of virtually any other UG. The most basic UGs are

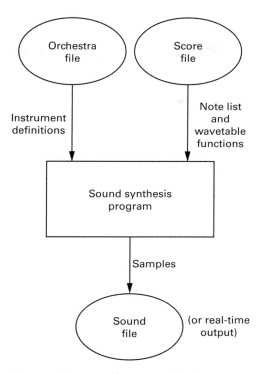

Figure 48.1   A software synthesis program takes in score and orchestra files and generates a sound sample file.

either signal generators (oscillators, noise generators, impulse generators, etc.) or signal modifiers (filters, delays, reverberators, spatializers, etc.). Other types of UGs include routines to handle sound file input/output and data coming from an input device.

The original unit generator language was the Music III language developed in 1960 by Max V. Mathews and his colleagues at Bell Telephone Laboratories. Since then, there have been numerous reworkings of this model, including Music IV, Music 4BF, Music V, Music 7, Music 11, MUS10, and so on. Table 48.1 lists Music *N* languages.

For historical reasons, one should cite the Music 4F language developed by Arthur Roberts (1966, 1969; Dumour 1993). Although it emulated the functionality of Max Mathews's Music IV program, it does not appear in table 48.1. Music 4F was not modular in structure; it was a single large instrument with many UGs controlled by many parameters.

The ubiquity of the UG concept has come into question in certain sound synthesis and analysis situations. We address this briefly at the end of this chapter.

Table 48.1 Text-based unit-generator synthesis languages

Program	Date introduced	Author(s)	Original host computer	Coding language	Location
Music III	1960	M. Mathews	IBM 7090	Assembler	Bell Laboratories, Murray Hill
Music IV	1963	M. Mathews J. Miller	IBM 7094	Macro assembler	Bell Laboratories, Murray Hill
Music IVB	1965	G. Winham H. Howe	IBM 7094	Macro assembler	Princeton University
MUS10	1966	J. Chowning D. Poole L. Smith	DEC PDP-10	Assembler	Stanford University
MUSIGOL (Music-Algol)	1966	D. MacInnes W. Wulf P. Davis	Burroughs 5500	Burroughs Algol	University of Virginia, Richmond
Music 4BF	1967	H. Howe G. Winham	IBM 360	Fortran II and BAL assembler	Princeton University
Music V	1968	M. Mathews J. Miller	GE 645	Fortran IV	Bell Laboratories, Murray Hill
Music 360	1969	B. Vercoe	IBM 360	BAL assembler	Princeton University
Music 7	1969	H. Howe	Xerox	Assembler XDS Sigma 7	Queens College CUNY
TEMPO	1970	J. Clough	IBM 360	BAL assembler	Oberlin Conservatory
B6700 (UCSD) Music V	1973	B. Leibig	Burroughs B6700	Fortran and Algol	University of California, San Diego
Music 11	1973	B. Vercoe S. Haflich R. Hale C. Howe	DEC PDP-11	Macro-11 assembler	MIT
MUSCMP	1978	Tovar	Foonly 2 (DEC PDP-10 clone)	FAIL assembler	Stanford University
Cmusic	1980	F. R. Moore D. G. Loy	DEC VAX-11	C	UCSD
MIX	1982	P. Lansky	IBM 370	IBM 360 assembler	Princeton University
Cmix	1984	P. Lansky	DEC PDP-11	C	Princeton University

Table 48.1 (continued)

Program	Date introduced	Author(s)	Original host computer	Coding language	Location
Music 4C	1985	S. Aurenz J. Beauchamp R. Maher C. Goudeseune	DEC VAX-11(later ported to other UNIX computers)	C	University of Illinois at Urbana-Champaign
Csound	1986	B. Vercoe R. Karstens	DEC VAX-11	C	MIT
Music 4C	1988	G. Gerrard	Apple Macintosh	C	University of Melbourne, Parkville
Common Lisp Music	1991	W. Schottstaedt	NeXT	Common Lisp	Stanford University
Music30	1991	J. Dashow	Texas Instr. TMS320C30	Assembler	Studio Sciadoni, Rome
Synthesis Toolkit	1995	P. Cook G. Scavone	Multiplatform	C, C++	Stanford and Princeton
SuperCollider	1996 / 2002	J. McCartney	Apple Macintosh	C, C++	University of Texas, Austin
Nyquist	1997	R. Dannenberg	LINUX	C++	Carnegie Mellon University
Faust	2002	Y. Orlarey	LINUX	C++	GRAME, Lyon
ChucK	2003	G. Wang	Multiplatform	C/C++	Princeton University
LuaAV	2010	G. Wakefield W. Smith C. Roberts	LINUX OSX	C/C++	UCSB
Kronos	2011	V. Norilo	Multiplatform	C++	University of the Arts Helsinki
AudioKit	2013	A. Prochazka	Multiplatform	Swift C, C++	https://AudioKitPro.com
Stride	2016	Joseph Tilbian Andres Cabrera	Multiplatform	C++	UCSB
SOUL	2018	J. Storer	Multiplatform	C++	ROLI

Scores and Orchestras

The classic UG languages encapsulate a score language and an orchestra language.

Score language

The score language serves two purposes:

1. It specifies the *note list:* the instrument names, start times, durations, and parameters of sonic events to be synthesized by the orchestra.
2. It defines the *function tables:* functions of time that are used as waveforms and envelopes by the instruments of the orchestra.

A typical line in a score file defines the parameters for one *note event.* Each note event enumerates the name of the instrument, starting time, duration, and other parameters that are specific to the instrument. Because the number and type of parameters are specific to each instrument, some note events may have more parameters than others.

The score can also include composition procedures (see the section on procedural composition languages), but in the simplest case it is simply a list of note events.

Orchestra language

The orchestra language is a toolkit for constructing instruments by interconnecting UGs. For example, one might specify that the output of an oscillator should be connected to the input of a filter. This is done by assigning the output of the oscillator to a *signal variable* and then using that signal variable in the input argument list of the filter.

Introduction to Music 0

For the purposes of explaining basic concepts of music languages, we present a simple imaginary language: Music 0. In the following example in the Music 0 language, the lines beginning with /* are comments. The symbol ← means "is assigned the value of."

```
/* wave freq amp.
signal1←osc f1 440.0 1000;
/* input cutoff_f dB
signal2←low_filter signal1 880 6;
```

The first line (after a comment line) specifies that the output of an oscillator osc is assigned (routed) to the signal variable *signal1*. On the second line (after a comment line) the value of *signal1,* at each sample period, flows to the input of the low_filter module.

Table 48.2 explains the syntax of Music 0 unit generators.

Interconnections between unit generators

It is easy to understand how interconnections between UGs are implemented in software. The synthesis language contains data structures that can be shared by more than one UG procedure. For two connected UGs osc and low_filter, the output of osc spills into an array that is common to both UGs. The low_filter UG reads the output value of osc from the array, thus making the connection (figure 48.2).

After the musician defines the score and orchestra, the synthesis compiler reads both files, generating samples that go to the output sound file. If the synthesis algorithm is efficient enough, the synthesis engine can generate sound directly through audio converters rather than writing a sound file.

The next two sections explain a simple orchestra and score in more detail.

Instrument Definition Example

This section presents a complete example of a simple instrument definition. Figure 48.3a depicts an instrument that uses an envelope generator to control the amplitude of a square wave oscillator. The output of the oscillator is lowpass filtered and then written to a sound file through the out UG.

Table 48.2　Syntax of Music 0 unit generators

Output		UG name	Argument 1	Argument 2	Argument 3
output_signal	←	envelope	*waveform number*	*duration*	*amplitude*
output_signal	←	osc	*waveform number*	*frequency*	*amplitude*
output_signal	←	low_ filter	input signal	cutoff	cutoff
				frequency	*slope in dB*
(Output is written to a sound file named in a dialog with the user)	out	input signal			

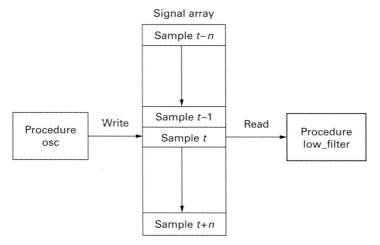

Figure 48.2 Connecting unit generators in software through shared data arrays in memory. The output of an osc UG is read as the input to a low_filter UG.

Figure 48.3b presents a text description of the same instrument, conforming to the Music 0 syntax.

In the text of figure 48.3b, the unit generator env_gen emits the control signal *env_signal*. The parameters of the unit generators can appear to their right as numbers, variable names (like the functions *f1* and *f2*), or names of *parameter fields* (*pfields* or columns in the score). Pfields begin with the letter *p,* as in *p3, p4,* etc. Function table *f1* holds the waveform for the envelope, and *f2* contains the oscillator waveform.

Score Definition Example

This section presents a simple score file that drives the instrument just defined. The score file contains two parts: function table definitions and the note list. Function tables contain waveforms that are fed to envelope generators and oscillators, as we showed in figure 48.3. The note list defines the start time, duration, and parameters of the notes.

Function table definition

Figure 48.4 shows a score file. The upper part consists of two function table definitions. Notice that the fourth arguments (line_segment and fourier) are *function generator types.* A *function generator* is a predefined algorithm that produces waveform functions. Music *N* languages typically provide a range of function generators. Some create waveforms by adding together sine

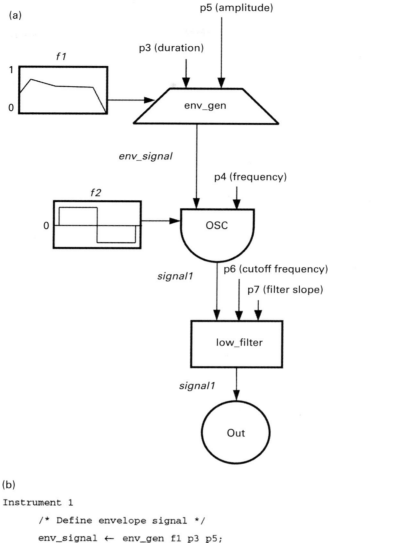

Figure 48.3   Orchestra language example. Definition of an instrument with an envelope for amplitude, an oscillator, and a lowpass filter. (a) Graphical representation. (b) Textual representation. The remarks surrounded by slash-asterisk ("/*" and "*/") are comments.

```
/*
Function definitions in the form:
Fname, start time, table size, function generator type, arguments
_____ */
f1 0  1024  line_segment  (0 0) (256 1) (512 .5) (768 .5) (1024 0);
f2 0  1024  fourier  11    (1 .4) (2 .3) (3 .05) (4 .06)  (5 .04)
                           (6 .04) (7 .03) (8 .04) (9 .02) (10 .03)
                           (11 .01);
```

/* Instr. ID	Start time	Dur.	Freq.	Amp.	Filt.cutoff frequency	Filter slope
p1	p2	p3	p4	p5	p6	p7

```
_____ */
i1        0    1.0    440.0   2000    4100        6;
i1      1.0    1.0    560.0   2000    3000        5;
i1      1.0    2.0    440.0   2000    2050        4;
i1      2.0    2.0    880.0  10000    9000;       3;
```

Figure 48.4 Score language example. A score corresponding to the instrument shown in figure 48.3. The score consists of two parts: the two function definitions at the top, followed by the note list at the bottom.

waves in various combinations, and others create waveforms out of line segments, exponentials, or polynomial functions.

Figure 48.5 explains the syntax of the line_segment and fourier function table definitions shown in figure 48.4.

Note list

The lower part of figure 48.4 presents a typical *note list* score format defining four notes for the instrument described in figure 48.3. Each note has several pfields, indicated in the score. The pfield layouts per note are as follows:

p1 Instrument number

p2 Start time in beats

p3 Duration in beats

p4 Fundamental frequency of oscillator

p5 Peak amplitude

p6 Filter cutoff frequency

p7 Filter slope in dB per octave

The lowpass filter attenuates spectral components above the cutoff frequency. The steepness of the attenuation is set by p7.

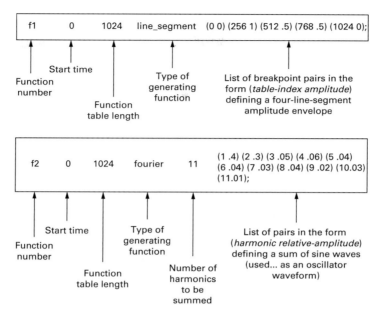

Figure 48.5   Syntax of the function table definitions of figure 48.4.

Alternative Score Representations

In Music N languages, the score is a flat (nonhierarchical) list of notes, mostly encoded as numbers. The note list is a precise means of specifying sound events, but the expressive weaknesses of note list score languages have been known for a long time (Haynes 1980). The main issues are the numerical orientation, rigid syntax, and a lack of higher-level structures (such as phrases, voices, clouds, streams, textures, gestures, and behaviors). In a complicated instrument with many parameters, the note list is unreadable as solfège, unlike a traditional score.

Some languages provide a more intuitive syntax. They allow the use of traditional musical terminology or a more flexible syntax. Instead of typing pitch in terms of frequency in hertz, for example, the composer can use a pitch-class and octave code, such as C4. *Score preprocessors* interpret these more intuitive specifications and convert them to a numerical note list before synthesis (Smith 1972; Fry 1980; Ames 1989b; De Poli and Vidolin 1984; Tochetti 1984; Jaffe 1989).

Another useful feature in a score language is *expression evaluation*— allowing computation within the score itself. In the simplest case we might want to specify that one parameter is a function of another parameter, as in the following: p8 = p7/2. With expressions in the score, composers can set a few global variables at the head of a score and let the language compiler calculate specific parameters on the basis of these settings. One can quickly try out variations of a score with such a facility. Music languages embedded in a general-purpose programming language make this easier.

Note lists represent only the lowest level of musical structure. The middle levels of structure, including phrases and voice interaction, are not addressed by note lists. To make a crescendo over a phrase, for example, it is necessary to specify the amplitudes of each of the individual notes in the phrase in relation to their point in the crescendo. Some compositional languages provide explicit constructs for phrases and voices (see chapter 49). These systems can generate output suitable for a synthesis program.

Chafe (1985) argued that the note list is inappropriate for the control of synthesis involving *physical modeling* of traditional instruments. (See chapter 18 for more on physical modeling.) Note lists consist of isolated event calls. On the other hand, physical models simulate the cause-and-effect chain of mechanical-acoustical events within a single instrument. This requires multiple parallel processes whose synchronization varies in different musical situations. For example, violin slurs (sliding from one note to the next) involve asynchrony between the two hands of a violinist.

Sound File Input

One of the most musically important applications of modern Music *N* languages is reading sound file input. Most languages provide a UG for reading in a sound file, such as the soundin operator of Csound. This means that arbitrary signal processing operations can be applied to sound files, such as filtering, re-enveloping, reverberation, or spatialization.

Sound file reading is triggered just like an oscillator, that is, by a note statement. By lining up a dozen overlapping note statements we can cross-fade a dozen sound files in a precise manner. Logically extrapolating from this point leads to complex, algorithmically controlled sound mixing processes, in which the note list is generated by a separate composition program. These capabilities have been exploited by composers such as Horacio Vaggione (1984). The Cmix language was developed expressly for the purpose of automated mixing (Lansky 1990).

Extensibility

One distinction between the various dialects of Music *N* is their degree of openness to user-written extensions. For example, Common Lisp Music is embedded in LISP, so all the data structures and control flow constructs of that language can be used in designing an instrument. By contrast, Music 11 was a closed system; it provided a limited set of data types and control constructs. Its code was written in assembler for a specific computer, the DEC PDP-11. Most other languages stand somewhere between these poles. For example, Music V was a closed system, but it provided hooks in Pass 1 and Pass 2 for user-written subroutines. SuperCollider can incorporate extensions written in C/C++ (Wilson, Cottle, and Collins 2011). Csound can also be extended and has been ported to mobile devices (Boulanger 2000; Lazzarini 2013, 2019).

Block versus Sample Computation

Music languages can be characterized as either *block-* or *sample-oriented.* A block-oriented compiler computes sound samples a *block* at a time, where a block is an arbitrary number of samples greater than one. Block computation is efficient because computer registers are loaded with synthesis parameter values just once for each block. By contrast, sample-oriented compilers are more flexible because every aspect of the computation can change for any sample, but they are less efficient because the setup time for each sample (such as loading registers with parameter values) requires more computation.

Among languages of the Music *N* family, Music IV, Music 4C, Common Lisp Music, and ChucK are sample-oriented, whereas Music V is block-oriented (Lazzarini 2013). Csound is also block-oriented because it updates synthesis parameters at a *control rate* set by the user. The control rate determines the block size. Too low a control rate leads to audio problems: clicks, zipper noise (caused by the staircase shape of the control function), and other artifacts. Increasing the control rate inevitably fixes these problems.

Several dialects of Music *N* can set variables on larger blocks, namely, at the beginning of each note. These variables are called *note initialization variables* (or *i*-variables), and they provide control from note to note. One application is to allow glissandi across separate note statements in the score by storing the pitch where the previous note left off, for example.

Languages for Real-Time Synthesis

Languages for real-time synthesis focus on gestural input rather than a prewritten note list to drive synthesis. They must respond to spontaneous—that is, asynchronous—events.

Real-Time Synthesis: Background

Slow computers and small memories constrained early attempts at real-time interaction. One solution was a hybrid approach: digital control of analog synthesis. The landmark music software system MUSYS developed at Electronic Music Studios (EMS), London, ran on a slow minicomputer with a total of 8K words of random-access memory (RAM). MUSYS was essentially a sequencer that controlled an analog synthesizer and tape recorder (Grogono 1984, 2011). The Canadian composer Martin Bartlett shoehorned his music control program for a KIM-1 microprocessor into a grand total of 1,152 bytes of RAM by using an analog synthesizer for sound output (Bartlett 1979).

Through the 1970s and beyond, computers had clock speeds in the low MHz range (current computers operate in the low GHz range). Real-time software synthesis was out of the question. Thus the focus turned to the design of high-speed hardware circuits controlled by a computer (Snell 1977a). When the early digital synthesizers were introduced in the 1970s, little was known about how to write usable software for them. Early commercial synthesizers, such as the New England Digital Synclavier, were based on a fixed-function hardware architecture (Alonso, Appleton, and Jones 1977). Fixed-function synthesizers are made up of dedicated components such as oscillators, filters, and envelope generators interconnected in a fixed configuration. A fixed-function architecture simplifies many difficult issues (because there is no repatching) and reduces the control problem to that of sequencing.

By contrast, a variable-function *digital signal processor* (DSP) contains a more flexible collection of functional units. This was characteristic of systems such as the IRCAM 4X and the Samson Box at Stanford University (Asta et al. 1980; Samson 1980, 1985; Loy 2013a, b). These systems let users interconnect or patch functional units via software. This flexibility allows the DSP to realize different synthesis and signal-processing tasks. It also adds to the complexity of the software and the musician's interface.

The problems of managing interactive control of a variable-function real-time synthesizer remained unresolved for some time. Attempts to control DSPs such as the 4A and 4B synthesizers at IRCAM ended with little more than a "learning experience" to show for it (Rolnick 1978). Part of the blame could be laid on an inadequate understanding of the communication demands between the host computer and the DSP. See Kaplan (1981) for an enlightening discussion of the issues involved in programming a commercial synthesizer in this primordial epoch.

Syter, developed at the Groupe de Recherches Musicales (GRM) in Paris is another early example of computer system attached to custom sound processing hardware (Allouis 1979; Allouis and Bernier 1982). Jean-Claude Risset created his masterwork *Sud* (1985) using the SYTER.

The Yamaha DX7 synthesizer was introduced at the same time as the MIDI protocol in 1983. It showed how MIDI could greatly simplify the problem of controlling a synthesizer.

The ambitious MARS workstation developed in Italy consisted of a computer and a circuit board for sound synthesis and processing. There were several versions with different hardware. The system was notable for its graphic programming environment for sound synthesis and performance control (Palmieri and Sapir 1992; Sapir 2002).

Control of Hardware Synthesizers

We can control a hardware synthesizer via its front panel, with an input device, or with a program that generates MIDI or OSC messages (figure 48.6). (MIDI and OSC are covered in chapters 51 and 52.) The usual type of data handled by a MIDI synthesizer is of the following three types:

1. Discrete note data (start time, stop time, channel number, etc.)

2. Continuous controller messages (equivalent to volume pedal changes, vibrato wheel, etc.)

3. Discrete program change messages (e.g., switch the timbre from *Voice 1: Piano* to *Voice 39: Choir*, etc.)

Another possibility is transmitting data in the form of *system exclusive* messages that set up the internal synthesis parameters particular to a specific synthesizer.

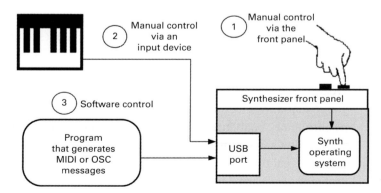

Figure 48.6   Three ways to control a MIDI device: via its front panel, with a MIDI input device, or with a program that generates MIDI or OSC messages.

OSC is a more open protocol. The types of messages sent can be customized to the specific capabilities of the synthesizer.

The operating systems MacOS, Windows, and Linux all provide support for MIDI. General-purpose programming languages talk to these services. Versions of many languages (Basic, C, C++, Java, Pascal, Lisp, Python, etc.) have been packaged with MIDI extensions. Music languages such as ChucK, Csound, Max, Pure Data, OpenMusic, and SuperCollider include built-in MIDI and OSC functions. For C++ developers, the JUCE audio development system by ROLI Limited supports both MIDI 2.0 and OSC.

Four Software Synthesis Languages

This section provides capsule overviews of four popular text-based software synthesis languages: Csound, ChucK, SuperCollider, and Faust. All can build real-time software synthesizers, letting users design their own instruments and modes of interactivity. Chapter 47 addresses patchers like Max and Pure Data.

Csound dates back to 1985 (Boulanger 2000; Lazzarini 2013; Zucco 2014). A classic UG language, Csound is built around the explicit separation of instruments and scores. Users design instruments by combining opcodes into patches. The instruments are then played by means of a separate score file, which includes a note list. Instruments can also receive MIDI data and external audio in real time. Csound has maintained backward compatibility and a syntax that is still related to one of the original Music N languages: Music 11. Over time, Csound has evolved into a programming library in which the synthesizer component can be embedded within a system written in another language (Lazzarini 2013). An interesting feature of Csound is the number of different front ends for it, from the traditional sequencer Blue to the CSoundQt (Cabrera 2011).

SuperCollider (SC) separates the language client (sclang) and the synthesis server (scsynth) (McCartney 2002; Cottle 2005; Wilson, Cottle, and Collins 2011). This separation is not strictly enforced in practice, however, as an SC orchestra can generate score events on its own. SC is an object-oriented language that draws inspiration from C++ and Smalltalk. SC is designed for live performance, enabling real-time execution of code blocks. The synthesis server allows new modules to be created, deleted, or repatched while playing sound in real time. Besides MIDI, commands can be received via the internet protocols TCP or UDP using OSC. SC also supports building graphical user interfaces (GUIs) out of widgets and attaching them to variables within one's code. Many people have developed additional libraries of extensions to the basic SC system, for example, Daniel Mayer (2019).

ChucK has a concise syntax to support its focus on live coding and real-time performance (Kapur et al 2015; Wang, Cook, and Salazar 2015). Used by a number of laptop orchestras, ChucK departs from the traditional block-processing approach, in which control signals are quantized to block sizes. ChucK processes audio one sample at a time, and the granularity of control signals or events can be controlled individually. ChucK is a strongly timed language and provides data types directly representing logical time and duration. The explicit control of the advance of logical time is part of the language specification. Logical time stands still until it is explicitly instructed to move forward. By such a design, ChucK provides simple and terse means to control timing behavior of a program with sample-rate accuracy in logical time. Chunity integrates ChucK within the Unity game engine (Atherton and Wang 2018).

Faust is a *meta-programming language* for digital signal processing (Gaudrain and Orlarey 2007; Orlarey, Fober, and Letz 2009; Fober, Orlarey, and Letz 2011). That is, Faust compiles its block diagram syntax to efficient code (C, C++, JAVA, etc.) that operates at the sample level. This is then compiled into binary code in various formats such as a stand-alone executable program, libraries, or plug-in for other computer music systems. Operating at the sample level makes it possible to realize one-sample feedback. Faust is a functional programming language with a concise syntax that can describe low-level block diagrams of DSP operations. Lazzarini (2017, 2019) used Faust as a description of audio algorithms.

Questioning the Unit Generator Paradigm

The modular UG concept has without doubt served its purpose. However, some have questioned the scope of the UG model. A question is: can any sound-processing algorithm, no matter how complex, be encapsulated in a UG? At what point does this abstraction hide valuable information? The question comes up the context of granular and other microsound synthesis techniques (Brandt 2008; Nishino, Osaka, and Nakatsu 2015; Norilo 2015, 2019). One issue is whether event scheduling should be incorporated into a UG, as it is in some Csound granular opcodes, for example.

The UG has also been questioned in the context of Fourier-based sound analysis systems. Here traditionally the goal was to hide the granularity underneath the mathematical abstraction of continuous sine waves. The *unit analyzer* of the ChucK language addresses this question by making individual frame and sample data accessible (Nishino, Osaka, and Nakatsu 2015; Wang, Cook, and Salazar 2015; Kapur et al. 2015). As an alternative, the Faust language builds UG functionality from simpler primitives (Orlarey et al. 2009). We refer readers to the cited papers for more on this philosophical topic.

Parallel Processing

Audio application developers face a limit on processing power because *central processing unit* (CPU) speeds have not increased significantly for many years. Some have turned to the power of parallel processing, using multiple cores, multiple computers, DSP chips, or *graphics processing units* (GPUs) to overcome this limitation. Asanovic et al. (2006) is an analysis of the state of parallel computing.

Both DSPs and GPUs can perform operations in parallel, which can greatly speed up certain processes. Audio applications of GPUs have included physical modeling, granular, and additive synthesis, for example. A downside of a DSP or GPU solution is increased dependency on specific hardware. If one does not have the right brand/model/version GPU, for example, one cannot benefit from code that has been optimized for it.

Popular parallel processing software packages include OpenCL, OpenMP, and CUDA. OpenCL (Open Computing Language) is a framework for writing programs that execute across heterogeneous platforms consisting of CPUs, GPUs, DSPs, and *field-programmable gate arrays* (FPGAs). OpenCL provides a standard API for parallel computing using task- and data-based parallelism.

OpenMP is a similar API that supports multicore parallel processing using C, C++, and FORTRAN on many platforms. It was used to add parallel processing to the Faust signal processing language (Orlarey, Fober, and Letz 2010).

Nvidia's CUDA (Compute Unified Device Architecture) is an API that enables software developers to use a GPU for audio applications. Coders in C and C++ can use CUDA as a software layer that gives access to the GPU's virtual instruction set and parallel computational elements.

49 *Languages for Composition*

Background: MUSICOMP

Score Input Languages

       Languages for Music Information Retrieval and Score Manipulation
       Impact of MIDI and Optical Scanning on Score Input Languages
       Encoded Scores and the Performance Problem

Procedural Composition Languages

Music Composition Languages Embedded in Programming Languages

Live Coding

Live Notation Languages

The domain of programming languages for composition is a complicated topic. We can break it into categories for the purpose of teaching, but in actuality the categories overlap. For example, chapters 45 and 48 look at some of the same systems but with different lenses.

In this chapter we look at several basic types of composition languages: score input languages, procedural composition languages, languages embedded in general-purpose languages, and live coding and live notation languages. Christopher Ariza (2005, 2007) lists one hundred composition languages and systems from 1966 to 2007.

Score input languages date to the early days of computer music, before the development of graphical notation editors. They were designed as a means to encode already-composed music scores for the purposes of analysis or sound synthesis. By contrast, procedural languages foster a generative or algorithmic approach to composition. That is, they generate musical events by stipulated procedures or rules.

Looking in detail, however, we see languages that serve both functions. For example, one can type a note list in the procedural language SuperCollider and one can use procedures in a score input language like Abjad. Languages like ChucK and SuperCollider are also fully functioning synthesis toolkits.

Background: MUSICOMP

The original music composition programming environment was the MUSICOMP library of assembly language subroutines developed by Robert Baker and Lejaren Hiller at the University of Illinois (Baker 1963; Hiller and Leal 1966; Hiller 1969). MUSICOMP ran on the ILLIAC I computer developed at the university (see figure 50.7).

The MUSICOMP library included functions for selecting items from a list according to a probability distribution, randomly shuffling items in a list, tone row manipulation, enforcing melodic rules, and coordination of rhythmic lines. As Baker put it,

MUSICOMP is a "facilitator" program. It presents no specific compositional logic itself, but is capable of being used with nearly any logic supplied by the user. (Baker 1963, p. i)

The alphanumeric output of MUSICOMP routines could be printed or formatted for input to sound synthesis programs. Hiller used the MUSICOMP routines to create a number of works for both traditional instruments and computer-generated sound, including his *Computer Cantata* (1963) for soprano, tape, and chamber ensemble, described in Hiller and Baker (1964).

Score Input Languages

Score input languages exist for the purpose of *data entry*. They enable a score written in *common music notation* (CMN) to be transcribed into an alphanumeric code for entry into a computer. Another term for a score input language is a *music markup* language.

Large music databases are being assembled, and score input languages are important tools in this process. It is likely that both music theory and musicology will evolve with increasing use of analytic toolkits for scores. These include script-based systems that could potentially be repurposed by composers for creative hacking and rehashed scores.

Dozens of score input languages have been implemented, aimed at different musical contingents. Pioneering languages like DARMS (Erickson 1975) and MUSTRAN (Wenker 1972) were developed for musicological purposes. Their goal was faithful transcription of the graphic symbols found in music scores into a computer, usually for the purpose of archiving or score analysis. Standard Music Description Language (SMDL), which was compliant with the international standard Extensible Markup Language (XML), was another effort along these lines (Newcomb and Goldfarb 1989; Newcomb 1991). A feature of these languages was their direct correspondence with the structures of CMN. They supported such constructs as measures, metrical rhythms, equal-tempered pitches and accidentals, slurs, ties, and simultaneous parts. In some cases they allowed the user to specify synthesis-related information such as envelopes and microtonal pitches. SCORE, for example, was appreciated for its musical flexibility (Smith 1972).

In recent times, Music XML has emerged as a standard for the interchange of scores between different notation apps (Good 2006, 2013; MakeMusic 2013). A simple example of Music XML is shown in figure 49.1. Although this appears somewhat complicated, it is easy to generate and parse algorithmically. Over two hundred programs that deal with music notation can read and write MusicXML.

Languages for Music Information Retrieval and Score Manipulation

Score input languages have emerged to support applications based on *music information retrieval* (MIR). One of the goals of MIR is the creation of large-scale collections of music materials in a variety of audio, symbolic, and metadata forms. These collections allow the music research community to perform many kinds of data-mining experiments for both musicological and commercial purposes. The most basic application of such systems is

```xml
<?xml version="1.0" encoding="UTF-8" standalone="no"?>
<!DOCTYPE score-partwise PUBLIC
    "-//Recordare//DTD MusicXML 3.1 Partwise//EN"
    "http://www.musicxml.org/dtds/partwise.dtd">
<score-partwise version="3.1">
  <part-list>
    <score-part id="P1">
      <part-name>Music</part-name>
    </score-part>
  </part-list>
  <part id="P1">
    <measure number="1">
      <attributes>
        <divisions>1</divisions>
        <key>
          <fifths>0</fifths>
        </key>
        <time>
          <beats>4</beats>
          <beat-type>4</beat-type>
        </time>
        <clef>
          <sign>G</sign>
          <line>2</line>
        </clef>
      </attributes>
      <note>
        <pitch>
          <step>C</step>
          <octave>4</octave>
        </pitch>
        <duration>4</duration>
        <type>whole</type>
      </note>
    </measure>
  </part>
</score-partwise>
```

Figure 49.1 A simple MusicXML example of a single measure with the note C. The first line is a header. Lines 2–4 declare a score with parts. DTD stands for document type definition, part of the Music XML standard. The <score-partwise> element is made up of parts, where each part is made up of measures. There is also a <score-timewise> option which is made up of measures, where each measure is made up of parts. The next lines consist of a header that lists the different musical parts in the score: one score-part, the required ID attribute for the score-part, and the required part-name element. Next, measure 1 is declared. Its attributes are listed. Then the pitch of the note C is defined, and its duration based on one division per quarter note. The <type> element tells us that this is notated as a whole note. The last four lines terminate the lexical scope of the nested elements.

searching for specific pieces of music based on properties such as the melody. These fit into the mold of *big data* analysis, involving massive amounts of information.

One example, focused on classical music, is the KernScores database (http://kern.ccarh.org), with over 100,000 encoded pieces encoded in the **kern format. KernScores is a text-based description for musical scores, and its primary purpose is for musical analysis using the Humdrum Toolkit (Huron 1999), a set of software tools for music research. A typical research question using this system would be, "In the music of Stravinsky, are dissonances more common in strong metric positions than in weak metric positions?" It is possible to pose queries based on the entire output of a composer's life and track trends.

By contrast, commercial MIR systems analyze the audio of tens of millions of songs in order to understand the relationship between songs and their fans. The goals include music recommendation, personalized playlists, internet broadcasting, enhancing interactive gaming, and product marketing.

Impact of MIDI and Optical Scanning on Score Input Languages

With MIDI-based sequencers and music printing packages the need for score input languages has decreased, because most music can be entered part by part, either by playing into a sequencer or by graphical editing with note lists, piano roll notation, or CMN menus. This is not to say that score input languages have been replaced by MIDI, because MIDI was not designed to read and write CMN symbols.

After early attempts to coax a computer to read music notation visually (Entwistle 1973; Prerau 1970, 1971; Pruslin 1966), a spectacular breakthrough was WABOT-2, the Tsukuba musical robot developed by Professor Sadamu Ohteru and a large team of graduate researchers at Waseda University, Tokyo. WABOT-2 read a single sheet of simple notation in about ten seconds while simultaneously planning all the motions needed to play it (Matsushima et al. 1985; Roads 1986c). Since that time, optical recognition of music has made great strides (Fujinaga, Alphonce, and Pennycook 1989; Fujinaga et al. 1991; Byrd and Simonsen 2015; Shatri and Fazekas 2020). The first commercial optical music recognition application, MIDISCAN (now SmartScore), was released in 1991 by Musitek Corporation. Today most commercial music notation editors support optical scanning as an option for score input.

Optical notation transcription is a pattern recognition problem, so it is no surprise that machine learning methods are now being applied to this task

(Calvo-Zaragoza and Rizo 2018; Shatri and Fazekas 2020). Refer to appendix A.

Encoded Scores and the Performance Problem

A score is an incomplete description of what will become a musical performance. Rote playback of a score typed in from a score input language often exhibits a wooden quality because performative gestures are not encoded. For example, in performance it is important to articulate the phrase structure of an encoded score by slight exaggerations of its time and amplitude profile. This can be achieved by having an explicit representation of phrase structure in the music specification language. Several of the composition languages discussed in the next section address phrasing directly.

In another approach, researchers have attempted to formalize performance rules in order to improve machine realizations (notably Sundberg, Askenfelt, and Frydén 1983; Clynes and Nettheim 1982; Clynes and Walker 1982; Friberg et al. 1991; Johnson 1991; Goebl et al. 2008). Such rules are dependent on the style of music being performed.

Procedural Composition Languages

Procedural composition languages go beyond the representation of traditional scores to support the unique possibilities of computer music. These include alternative tunings, multiple envelopes for control of timbre and spatial paths, voice interplay, performer interaction, and compositional algorithms. Procedural composition languages let composers specify music generatively. They represent the flow of music as a collection of interacting processes.

Most—but not all—composition languages mentioned in this chapter are also synthesis languages (chapter 48). Some are patch editors (chapter 45). However, the features that we highlight in this chapter relate to their ability to deal with the mesostructure of music: patterns and phrases.

Two advantages of representing a compositional process as a program stand out. First, compositional logic is made explicit, creating a system with a degree of formal consistency. Abstract formal unity in a composition is prized by some music theorists and composers. Second, rather than abdicating decision making to the computer, composers can use procedures to extend control over many more processes than they could manage with manual techniques. The following are a few examples of how algorithms can expand the scope of compositional decisions:

Controlling the microfrequency variations among the partials of a given tone

Sifting through massive amounts of data to select a specified sound or sound combination

Sending sounds on precise spatial paths computed according to composer-specified rules

Generating numerous variations quickly to provide the composer with many alternatives to a given sound or series of sounds

Realizing complex polyphonic textures that would otherwise be impossible to perform

Generating algorithmic music accompaniment in real time based on a performer's input

No standard language for procedural composition dominates the field. This is not surprising, because no two composers have exactly the same approach to composition. Table 49.1 lists examples of current procedural composition languages.

Most people would not describe a Music-*N* synthesis language like Csound as a vehicle for algorithmic composition. Yet several chapters in *The Csound Book* (Boulanger 2000) focus on its features for algorithmic control of sound synthesis. Indeed, the venerable Music V program had hooks for algorithmic composition in the form of its PLF routines (Mathews 1969).

Music Composition Languages Embedded in Programming Languages

Extensible languages enable the creation of a specialized *embedded language* written in terms of the original language. The advantage of this approach is that the facilities of the general language are always available to the sublanguage. A music composition language, for example, can always count on the general language for routines to handle utilitarian tasks common to all programs.

The extensible language LISP (and its cousin Scheme) has encouraged many embedded sublanguages over the years. For example, the composition languages MIDI-LISP (Boynton et al. 1986), FORMES (Rodet and Cointe 1984), Esquisse (Baisnée et al. 1988), PatchWork (Laurson and Duthen 1989; Barrière, Iovino, and Laurson 1991), Canon (Dannenberg 1989a), Flavors Band (Fry 1984), Symbolic Composer (Tonality Systems 1993), LISP Kernel (Rahn 1990), AC Toolbox (Berg 2003), and Common Music (Taube 1991) were all embedded in LISP. The more recent system Opusmodus (Morgan and Podrazik 2018; Podrazik 2020) is also LISP-based.

Table 49.1   Procedural composition languages

Language	References	Comments
Common Music	Taube (1991)	LISP-based. Run-time system for generating score files plus a pattern-oriented composing language.
Open Music	Agon (1998); Hirs and Gilmore (2009)	Incorporates music notation. Originally designed for spectral music composition, it has been extended into music theory and other areas.
Nyquist	Dannenberg (2002, 2018)	LISP-based. Combines synthesis with algorithmic composition.
SuperCollider	McCartney 1995, 1998, 2002	An environment and object-oriented programming language for real-time audio synthesis and algorithmic composition.
Max	Puckette and Zicarelli 1990; Puckette, Apel, and Zicarelli 1998; Cipriani and Giri 2010a,b	A modular visual patcher for music and multimedia. An application programming interface (API) allows third-party development of new routines (named *external objects*).
PureData (Pd)	Puckette 1996, 2017	A modular visual patcher for interactive computer music and multimedia. Open source. Graphics environment for multimedia (GEM) external and GridFlow matrix processing lets one create and manipulate video and graphics in real time.
ChucK	Kapur et al. (2015)	Combines sound synthesis and algorithmic composition. Arrays for data storage and functions for manipulating arrays to create patterns
JSyn	Burk (1998)	Modular synthesis API for Java. Incorporates the Java music specification language for algorithmic composition
jMusic	Sorenson and Brown (2000)	Computer-assisted composition in Java. Also used for instrument building, interactive performance, and music analysis.
JMSL	Didkovsky (2004)	Java-based implementation of the hierarchical music specification language.
AthenaCL	Ariza (2005)	Open source, object oriented, written in Python. Instrument libraries, pitch modeling tools, graphical outputs, and musical output in multiple formats.
SCAMP	Evanstein (2019)	Music specification language with multiple clocks running at different tempi allow for coordination of parallel structures.
OMN	Podrazik (2020); Morgan and Podrazik (2020)	A scripting language for musical events. It serves as the core of the Opusmodus composition system.

Although they rest on a LISP foundation, Patchwork and OpenMusic provide a patcher-style graphic interface (Assayag et al. 1999; Agon 1998). The result of an OpenMusic operation is usually displayed in common music notation. Libraries extend OpenMusic's functionality in various directions such as spectral music, music theory, music information retrieval, and sound synthesis.

The interpreted scripting language Python has spawned many custom embedded languages. Python has a design philosophy that emphasizes code readability. Rather than having all its functionality built into its core, Python was designed to be extensible. This compact modularity has made it popular as a means of adding scriptable interfaces to existing applications.

The unique KYMA sound design system developed by Carla Scaletti and Kurt Hebel is revolves around an interactive patcher made with the Smalltalk programming language (Scaletti 1989a, 1989b, 2002, 2015).

Many software synthesis languages can be instructed to call compositional procedures coded in general programming languages. Historical examples include Music V, through the previously mentioned PLF subroutines (Mathews 1969), the Cscore part of Cmusic (Moore 1982; 1990), and the Music 4C language (Beauchamp and Aurenz 1985; Gerrard 1989; Beauchamp 1992a). Because Cmusic and Music 4C were embedded in the C programming language, composers were free to use the resources of that language in specifying a composition. The MusicKit (Jaffe 1989; Smith 2009) could be used as a composition language for those versed in the Objective C language. SuperCollider and Max can be accelerated by coding custom functions in C/C++.

The Java Music Specification Language (JMSL) is a Java application programming interface (API) or library for music composition, interactive performance, and intelligent instrument design (Didkovsky 2004; Algomusic 2013). With JMSL, one can create stand-alone musical applications or deploy applets on the web.

Live Coding

Live coding is a branch of computer art. It involves the real-time coding of a sonic or multimedia experience. One or more programmers give a coding performance. Along with other possible visuals, the text of the code is often displayed as part of the experience.

Pioneers of live coding include Ron Kuivila, who coded in Forth onstage in the 1980s (Roads 1986a), and The Hub (Brown and Bischoff 2005). Nick

Collins, among others, advanced the philosophy and practice in the early 2000s (Collins 2003; Collins et al. 2003). The TOPLAP organization (toplap .org) formed in 2004 to promote live coding and gatherings such as Algoraves. Since that time, the number of languages supporting live coding has proliferated. Table 49.2 lists some of the main ones. Also refer to Wang, Cook, and Salazar (2015).

Although gestural control has replaced the stored Music N note list (chapter 48) in many performance situations, in live coding the performer specifies events by typing. The note list returns in this context, although a frequent strategy in live coding is to spawn algorithmic variations from an initial note list.

Live Notation Languages

A desire for real-time notation has emerged at the confluence of live coding, interactive composition with gestural controllers, and mixed ensembles combining instrumentalists and laptop artists. Roger Dannenberg's Temporal Programming Language (1996) pioneered the idea of real-time notation in performance.

Now that a large number of scores have been encoded into databases, compositional applications have appeared that are based on manipulating and remixing old scores (Winter 2012). Moreover, because a score can be generated from text, real-time algorithmic score generation has become a part of live performance (Barrett and Winter 2010). Facilitating such experiments are languages like Music21, a Python-based toolkit for computer-aided musicology (Cuthbert and Ariza 2010). Its musicological goals include the query of data sets of music. However, it also supports music notation scripting and music composition—both algorithmic and directly specified.

A related language is Abjad (Baca et al. 2015). Abjad helps composers build up complex pieces of music notation in an iterative way. Embedded in the Python programming language, composers can use Abjad to make systematic changes to the music as they work. Experiments with algorithmic input to Abjad have been tested in performance. Abjad generates score output using the LilyPond music notation package (Nienhuys and Nieuwenhuizen 2003).

MaxScore is a collection of software tools, the core of which was developed by Nick Didkovsky and Georg Hajdu (2008). An advantage of using MaxScore compared to other notation environments is its integration with the larger Max environment. This enables programmers to adapt MaxScore to specific needs. It can be controlled with Max messages and its output can be

Table 49.2 Live coding languages

ChucK	Kapur et al. 2015	Strongly timed, concurrent, and on-the-fly language
Extempore	Extempore 2020	Language designed to support cyberphysical programming; combines Scheme and xtlang; built-in synthesizers and drum machines
Fluxus	Griffiths 2010	Rapid prototyping, playing, and learning environment for graphics, sound, and games.
Impromptu	Brown and Sorensen 2007	Scheme (LISP) language environment for live coding graphics and sound.
ixi lang	Magnusson 2012	Embraces simplicity and constraints in design; used in teaching.
LiveCode	LiveCode 2020	Cross-platform rapid application development runtime environment and scripting language inspired by HyperCard.
Lua and LuaAV	Wakefield et al. 2010	Scripting language with simple syntax; used in many games.
Max	Puckette 1991	Graphical patcher for audiovisuals with large library of functions
Pharo	Pharo 2020	Dynamic and reflective language inspired by the programming language Smalltalk. Offers live coding features such as immediate object manipulation, live update, and hot recompiling.
Pure	Gräf 2009	Functional language that allows scheduling of Faust unit generators.
Pure Data	Puckette 1996	Open-source graphical patcher for audio and visual with large library of functions.
Scratch	Scratch 2020	Block-based visual programming language
Sonic Pi	Sonic Pi 2020	Based on the Ruby scripting language, with a SuperCollider synthesis engine.
SuperCollider	McCartney 2002	Dynamic object-oriented and functional programming language and synthesis server.
TidalCycles	McLean and Wiggins 2010	Live coding environment embedded in Haskell (a functional language), focused on the generation and manipulation of audible and visual patterns.
Wolfram Language	Wolfram Research 2020	Symbolic computation, functional programming, and rule-based programming.

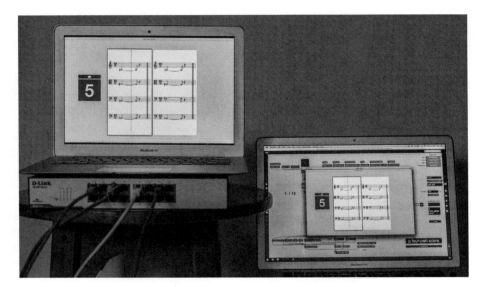

Figure 49.2   J. Branciforte's *0123* for low string quartet. In this work, a score is generated in real time using MaxScore (right screen) and displayed as scrolling notation on a performer's computer (left screen) via network connection (Branciforte 2017).

read by sound-generating patches for polyphonic and microtonal playback (figure 49.2).

INScore is an environment for the design of interactive music scores (Lepetit-Aimon et al. 2016). It allows arbitrary graphics to be used in the music representation. INScore supports CMN, described using Guido music notation or Music XML formats. The software environment has been extended to provided score level composition using a set of operators that take scores as arguments to compute new scores as output.

50 *Algorithmic Composition*

Background: Algorithmic Composition

      Brief History of Formal Processes in Music

      Automated Composition Machinery Prior to Electronic Computers

         Sequence control of composition

      Lejaren Hiller: Pioneer of Computer Music

      Other Pioneers of Algorithmic Music

Four Pioneering Composition Programs

      Stochastic Music Program

      Project 1

      POD

      AUTOBUSK

Strategies for Algorithmic Composition

Philosophical and Aesthetic Issues Posed by Algorithmic Methods

      Aesthetic Motivations

      Deterministic versus Stochastic Procedures

      Total Automation versus Interactive Composition

      All or Nothing: Batch Mode Interaction

      Interaction with Algorithms

      Combining Formal and Informal Strategies in Heuristic Algorithms

Assessment of Algorithmic Composition

Models of process are natural to musical thinking. As we listen, part of us drinks in the sensual experience of sound, while another part is constantly setting up expectations, and in so doing, constructing hypotheses of musical process. Many musical processes can be *formalized* into a symbolic representation. A *formal composition algorithm* is a generative engine for music creation; thus a computer can serve as a vehicle for musical ideas. As Stephen Wolfram (2002) observed in his book *A New Kind of Science,*

Just as the rules for any system can be viewed as corresponding to a program, so also its behavior can be viewed as corresponding to a computation. (5)

Hence musical behavior can be modeled by a computational process (Hiller and Isaacson 1959). We find compositional algorithms in the following assorted forms:

1. Interactive command languages for generation and transformation of musical data and control of musical processes, including live coding in performance
2. Musical extensions to traditional programming languages
3. Modular patching or programming environments designed for music
4. Self-contained automated composition apps

Chapters 47 and 49 covered categories 1, 2, and 3. This chapter surveys the history of algorithmic music and focuses on four historical apps from category 4. Then we list some common strategies used in algorithmic composition systems. Finally, we consider some aesthetic questions surrounding algorithmic composition.

In order to focus on original composition, we exclude systems that compose music in a known historical style. This includes, for example, programs that realize chorales in the style of J. S. Bach (for example, Ebcioglu 1988, 1992; Baroni et al. 1984; Hadjeres et al. 2017; Cope 1987, 1996, 2001, 2006, 2019; Huang et al. 2019a), compose in the style of Palestrina, Mozart, or Beethoven (Cope 2006), generate species counterpoint (Ebcioglu 1980; Schottstaedt 1989b; Gwee 2002), or produce music in the style of 12-tone chamber music (Bemman and Meredith 2018). Computers have been trained to generate conventional melodies, polyphony, and improvisations (Frieler et al. 2017; Krzyzaniak 2018; Déguernel et al. 2018; Huang et al. 2019b). Indeed a significant proportion of studies focus on improvisation in jazz styles (Fernández and Vico 2013). Other studies focused on electronic dance music and musical theater (Collins 2001; Collins 2008b; Eigenfeldt and Pasquier 2013; Collins 2016; Lopez-Serrano et al. 2018). The list of imitated genres will inevitably grow.

Because music styles can be reverse-engineered in innumerable ways, what is the meaning of using this or that algorithm? Certain simulations have specific musicological or scientific aims; they must be assessed according to those criteria. Pearce, Meredith, and Wiggins (2002), Ariza (2009), and Yang and Lerch (2020) examine epistemological challenges in evaluating generative music systems. We broach related issues at the end of this chapter.

Much effort in recent years has focused on *machine learning* (ML) (Collins 2012; Dean and McLean 2018; Fiebrink 2020; Ji, Luo, and Yang 2020; Cella 2020). Appendix A is an introduction to ML. For example, OpenAI's MuseNet is a generative music system that serves as a test application for the company's predictive language model. Google's WaveNet, a neural network technology originally developed for speech in Google Assistant, was applied to the automatic production of music (Deepmind 2016). When trained on recordings of classical piano music, WaveNet's output sounded like random clips of different classical piano pieces spliced together, with unpredictable shifts in note density and mood. The results are reminiscent of those obtained decades ago using a high-order Markov chain, with local note-to-note coherence but meandering phrase structure (Moorer 1972). Recent ML research uses an *attention model* that can reference its past output to derive long-term phrase structure (figure 50.1) (Huang et al. 2019b; Gururani, Sharma, and Lerch 2019). The composer Holly Herndon has applied ML in ways that intentionally expose the quirks of the algorithms (Herndon 2020).

Commercial apps for rule-based *style template* composition (e.g. Band in a Box, Orb Composer) generate popular songs. Users specify a piece by selecting stylistic elements from a menu (figure 50.2). Each style template is coded as a set of rules. Band in a Box offers Pop, Rock, Jazz, Blues, Funk, Americana, Country, Celtic, and World styles.

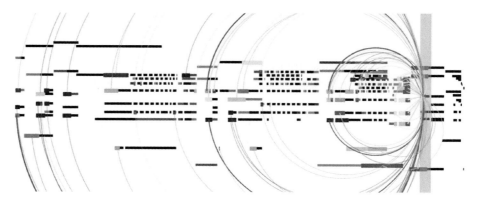

Figure 50.1   Still frame from an animation depicting self-reference in composition (Huang et al. 2019b). The score (left-to-right piano roll notation) was already composed. This visualization shows how current note patterns were derived from past material. The gray vertical bar at right is the musical now. The concentric circles to its left visualize its reach into the past. Gray notes are currently influencing the present. Refer to htpps://magenta.tensorflow.org/music-transformer.

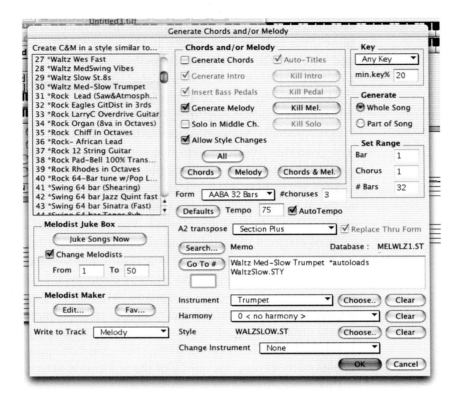

Figure 50.2   Screen image of Band-in-Box (PG Music), a program for composition and performance according to style templates. Given a list of chords, this program generates automatic accompaniment for bass, drums, piano, guitar, and strings according to rules formalized in a style template. The open menu lists some of the available styles.

Another approach to automation comes in the form of phrase-based sample libraries by companies like Sonokinetic. These let users mix and match thousands of precomposed phrases played by a real orchestra in well-known styles. Reams of orchestral music, suitable for any commercial purpose, can be generated by playing on a musical keyboard.

A new industry has emerged around artificial intelligence (AI) services for creating generic popular music, including Flow Machines, IBM Watson Beat, Google Magenta's NSynth Super, OpenAI's Jukebox, Jukedeck, Melodrive, Spotify's Creator Technology Research Lab, and Amper Music. This is the latest incarnation of a trend that started in the 1920s called Muzak, to provide licensed background music in elevators, business and dental offices, hotels, shopping malls, supermarkets, and restaurants.

By contrast, a lively experimental scene explores both generative image and sound (Matthews 2018; Burt 2018; Lewis 2009; Jette 2009; Fell and Gilmore 2013). A prime example is the audiovisual work of Lance Putnam (figure 50.3).

Figure 50.3   Still image from *Adrift* (2011) by Lance Putnam, a real-time audiovisual composition for multichannel audio and stereo projection systems, including virtual reality and 360° domes. *Adrift* is an audiovisual composition made for the UCSB AlloSphere 3D immersive environment. According to the artist, the goal of the work is to allow one to experience what it could be like to be inside a mathematical space embodied through unified visual and aural sensations. The underlying algorithm is a recursive matrix multiplication that generates a continuous sequence of coordinates. Adjusting the matrix coefficients produces an endless variety of both regular and complex patterns. The coordinates are graphed in space as oriented triangles and connected in sequence with light-like rays. Sound is generated by scanning along the rays and mapping the position information to the phases of several sine oscillators. The scanner voices are spatialized to produce an immersive sound field. The work interpolates from one parameter set to another, producing an evolving visual and sonic environment.

Background: Algorithmic Composition

The operating mechanism [of the Analytical Engine] . . . might act upon other things besides number, were objects found whose mutual fundamental relations could be expressed by those of the abstract science of operations, and which should be also susceptible of adaptations to the action of the operating notation and mechanism of the Engine. Supposing, for instance, that the fundamental relations of pitched sounds in the science of harmony and of musical composition were susceptible of such expression and adaptations, the Engine might compose and elaborate scientific pieces of music of any degree of complexity or extent.
—Ada Augusta, Countess of Lovelace, referring to Charles Babbage's mechanical computer, the Analytical Engine, 1842

Behind modern efforts in algorithmic composition is a long tradition of viewing music procedurally. A definitive history of this tradition has yet to be written. As an orientation to the subject, this section quickly scans developments in formal processes (software) and machinery (hardware) employed in algorithmic composition. This sets the historical context for the discussion of aesthetics that follows.

Brief History of Formal Processes in Music

Procedures for composition date back to ancient times. Around 1026, Guido d'Arezzo developed a formal technique for composing a melody to accompany a text (Kirchmeyer 1968). His scheme assigned a pitch to each vowel, so the melody varied according to the vowel content of the text. (See Loy [1989a] or Loy [2007] for more on this method.)

Compositional procedures based on numbers and ratios abound. An early exponent of this approach was Guillaume Dufay (1400–1474), who derived tempi for one of his motets from the proportions of a Florentine cathedral and used the ratio known as the *golden section* (1:1.618 . . .) in other works. Dufay also applied systematic procedures like *inversion* (make all positive intervals negative, and vice versa) and *retrograde* (reverse the order) to tone sequences centuries before they were expropriated by composers of *serial music* (Sandresky 1981).

Deployment of recurring rhythmic sequences shows up in the *isorhythmic* motets composed by G. Machaut and others in the period 1300–1450. The isorhythmic technique inserts a recurring rhythmic pattern into different melodic layers of a composition (figure 50.4).

The rounds, hockets, canons, fugues, and variations of traditional music are all examples of formalizable processes of repetition. (Pareyon [2011] is an interesting study of all manner of repetition or *self-similarity* in music processes.) Perhaps the most famous historical example of algorithmic composition is the *Musikalisches Würfelspiel* attributed to Mozart—a dice game for assembling minuets out of a set of prewritten measures of music (figure 50.5).

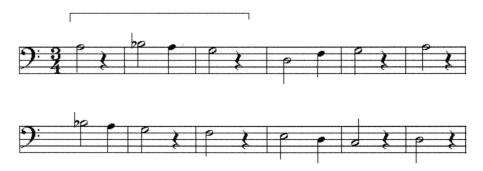

Figure 50.4   An example of the process of isorhythm in one voice.

Zahlentafel

1. Walzerteil

	I	II	III	IV	V	VI	VII	VIII
2	93	22	141	41	105	122	11	30
3	32	6	128	63	146	46	134	81
4	69	95	158	13	153	55	110	24
5	40	17	113	85	161	2	159	100
6	148	74	163	45	80	97	36	107
7	104	157	27	167	154	68	118	91
8	152	60	171	53	99	133	21	127
9	119	84	114	50	140	86	169	94
10	98	142	42	156	75	129	62	123
11	3	87	165	61	135	47	147	33
12	54	130	10	103	28	37	106	5

2. Walzerteil

	I	II	III	IV	V	VI	VII	VIII
2	70	121	26	9	112	49	109	14
3	117	39	126	56	174	18	116	83
4	66	139	15	132	73	58	145	79
5	90	176	7	34	67	160	52	170
6	25	143	64	125	76	136	1	93
7	138	71	150	29	101	162	23	151
8	16	155	57	175	43	168	89	172
9	120	88	48	166	51	115	72	111
10	65	77	19	82	137	38	149	8
11	102	4	31	164	144	59	173	78
12	35	20	108	92	12	124	44	131

Figure 50.5   Numeric tables from *Musikalisches Würfelspiel* (*Musical Dice Game*) by W. A. Mozart. (Edition by B. Schott's Söhne, Mainz.) The waltz is in two parts, represented by the two matrices. The Roman numerals over the eight columns of the refer to the eight phrases of each waltz, while the numerals in the rows to the left indicate the possible values of two dice when thrown. The numbers in the matrix point to measure numbers of musical phrases in another part of the score. Thus one throws the dice eight times to compose each phrase of each waltz.

The sequence of measures was determined by a set of dice throws. Hence this program incorporated an element of chance—a feature of many algorithmic programs to this day.

American businessmen marketed what could be called the first commercial music software. In 1822, Boston newspapers carried an advertisement for the Kaleidacousticon system—a deck of playing cards with instructions indicating how up to 214 million waltzes might be composed with the cards (Scholes 1975). A similar venture, dubbed the Quadrille Melodist, sold by Professor Clinton of the Royal Conservatory of Music, London, in 1865, was marketed as a practical aid to composition. This set of cards, notated with fragments of music notation, "enabled a pianist at a quadrille party (an early square dance) to keep the evening's pleasure going by means of a modest provision of 428 million quadrilles" (Scholes 1975).

In the twentieth century, the spread of scientific thinking led to the introduction of mathematical procedures for composition. These include serial and stochastic strategies, in which musical elements are manipulated according to set theory operations or probabilistic processes (Hiller and Isaacson 1959; Babbitt 1960, 1961; Gill 1963; Barbaud 1966, 1968; Zaripov 1960, 1969; Xenakis 1971, 1985, 1992; Austin 1992). Virtually any data set or mathematical formula can be turned into a music generator (Schillinger 1946; Clarke and Voss 1978; Pottier 2009). For surveys of formal models for composition, see Mihalic (2009), Loy (2007), and Nierhaus (2010).

Automated Composition Machinery Prior to Electronic Computers

The current proliferation of approaches to algorithmic composition is directly related to the spread of digital computers. However, we must not forget a long history of precomputer engines for musical ideas. Machinery for automated performance of music, such as mechanical carillons, goes back many centuries (Ord-Hume 1973; Buchner 1978). Machines for composition were less numerous than those for performance, but they were built. Composition machinery reflects available technology of the time. Gusts of wind powered the Aeolian harp and wind chimes–ancient devices for aleatoric, ambient composition that are still being made today. In 1660, Athanasius Kirchner designed his Arca Musirithmica (Musical Ark), a kind of composition game in a box (Prieberg 1975). A software emulation was shown in 2009 (Bumgardner 2009).

Dietrich Winkel's room-sized Componium, a mechanical contraption completed in 1821, produced variations on themes programmed into it (Lyr 1955; Buchner 1978). Years later, a large-scale mechanical machine similar to the Componium was exhibited in Vienna (Scholes 1970).

With the rise of electronics in the twentieth century came new possibilities for musical automation. Olson and Belar, inventors of the RCA synthesizers and pioneers of analog sequencing, also built an electromechanical composing machine around 1951 (Olson and Belar 1961; Hiller 1970). The primary innovation in the Olson and Belar machine was the automation of a probabilistic system of composition. Their machine used a pair of asynchronous bistable multivibrators (square wave generators) to generate random digits for a probabilistic pitch-and-rhythm-making circuit.

The appearance of "electronic brains," as computers were called in the 1950s, caught the public imagination. The promise of machine composition was the selling point of the battery powered GENIAC, shown in figure 50.6

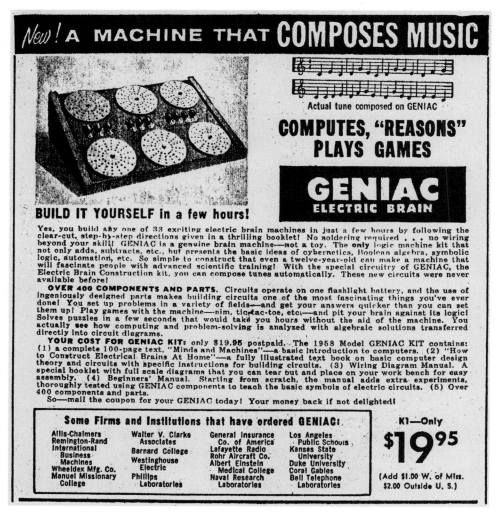

Figure 50.6   The GENIAC Electric Brain as advertised in a popular magazine in 1958.

(Sowa 1956). Advertisements touted the box as "A genuine brain machine—not a toy."

Sequence control of composition

The coupling of hardware logic for composition with sequence-controlled performance led to several one-of-a-kind systems. Some were developed after computers had already been invented but during a period when computers were still room-sized, expensive, and difficult to interface with other equipment. Sequence-controlled electronic music devices started to appear after the principle was demonstrated in the Coupleux-Givelet synthesizer prototype shown in 1929 (Prieberg 1963; Rhea 1972, 1984, U.S. Patent 1,957,392). The RCA Mark I and Mark II synthesizers used by Milton Babbitt were sequence-controlled synthesizers (Olson and Belar 1955; Olson 1967, 1991; Babbitt 1964).

The Barr and Stroud Solidac composing computer, installed in a retrofitted desk at the University of Glasgow in 1959, served as both an algorithmic composition engine and a sound generator (using a frequency divider circuit). Operating at a clock rate of 30 kHz (present computers operate at over 100,000 times this speed), the paper tape–reading Solidac ran a Dice-Music Master Programme that, according to its developers, could generate almost a billion Haydn-like trios.

An entirely different sort of beast, Raymond Scott's Electronium (early 1960s) was a large-scale composing machine programmed by knobs and switches (figure 50.7). (It is not to be confused with the Elektronium, a keyboard

Figure 50.7   Raymond Scott's Electronium composing machine, 1965.

instrument invented by the Hohner company in 1950 and used in a number of compositions by Stockhausen.) Scott would ask the Electronium to suggest a motive, which was then auditioned on a loudspeaker. When he heard a suitable motive, he actuated a switch that set the electrical relays and the drum memory of the Electronium in motion. The musical output of the system could be modified by means of knobs and switches, but not in a direct manner, because the response of the Electronium to these input controls was not entirely predictable. According to the inventor, Raymond Scott, "The Electronium is not played; it is guided" (Rhea 1984; Freff 1989; Manhattan Research, Inc. 2000).

In contrast to the custom-built Electronium, the Coordinated Electronic Music Studio (CEMS) at the State University of New York at Albany, set up by composer Joel Chadabe (1967), was assembled out of sequencer and synthesis modules made by the R. A. Moog Company. The Sal-Mar Construction (figure 50.8) developed by composer Salvatore Martirano and engineer Sergio Franco was designed to be performed live in concert (Martirano 1971). Although the Sal-Mar logic was digital, the machine did not contain a general-purpose computer. Like the Electronium, the Sal-Mar Construction was guided through an improvisation, rather than played in the virtuoso sense.

Lejaren Hiller: Pioneer of Computer Music

Lejaren Hiller (figure 50.9) laid much of the groundwork of modern computer music. Bored with the life of an industrial chemist, in which he received his doctorate and established an early career, Hiller turned his intellect to the muses in 1955, never looking back. Many "firsts" surround his name. He pioneered algorithmic composition with a computer. His book *Experimental Music* (Hiller and Isaacson 1959) documents these experiments. His research in digital sound synthesis by physical modeling is foundational (Hiller and Ruiz 1971). He was also a pioneer of music notation printing by computer (Hiller and Baker 1965). Acutely aware of the cultural significance of his era, he served as the earliest historian of computer music, contributing a seminal survey on "Music Composed with Computers" in 1970.

Hiller's core interest remained algorithmic composition. In the mid-1950s, the digital computer provided the ideal vehicle for his compositional visions (Hiller and Isaacson 1959; Hiller 1970, 1979, 1981). Computers were rare at the time he began his experiments. His early trials used an ILLIAC I computer constructed by engineers at the University of Illinois, Urbana-Champaign. The room-sized ILLIAC I computer contained a total of 1,024 words of memory. Coding in binary machine language (sequences of ones and zeros accepted directly by the computer), Hiller and his collaborator Isaacson created in 1956 the first computer-composed composition: *The Illiac Suite for String Quartet*—a landmark in the history of music. The

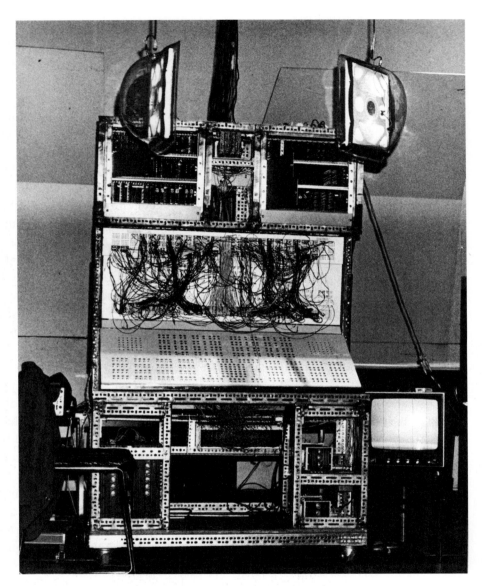

Figure 50.8   The Sal-Mar Construction (1971) set up for a concert.

Computer Cantata (1963) and *HPSCHD*, a collaboration with John Cage
(Hiller and Cage 1968; Austin 1992) followed. Outside the Illinois campus,
the impact of Hiller's experiments echoed worldwide (Hiller 1964).

Other Pioneers of Algorithmic Music

A handful of brave composers followed in the immediate wake of Hiller. These
include Herbert Brün and John Myhill (Urbana-Champaign), James Tenney (Bell

Figure 50.9   Lejaren Hiller and the ILLIAC computer as portrayed in *Scientific American* 1959. (Printed with permission of W. H. Freeman and Company.)

Laboratories, Murray Hill), Pierre Barbaud, Michel Phillipot, and Iannis Xenakis (Paris), and G. M. Koenig (Utrecht). While their computerized efforts came slightly later than Hiller's, in some cases they had already been composing according to formal procedures for some time. Xenakis's *Metastasis* for orchestra, for example, a piece composed according to stochastic formulas worked out by hand, was premiered in 1955—the same year Hiller began his computer experiments (Matossian 1987; Harley 2004)

In Los Angeles the orientation was commercial: *Push-Button Bertha* (1956), a pop song featuring lyrics by Hollywood tunesmith M. Klein and a melody excreted by a Burroughs Datatron computer (programmed by D. Bolitho), failed to storm the hit parade. Working in Moscow several years later, Rudolf Zaripov analyzed and then recomposed folk music using URAL computers made in the Soviet Union (Zaripov 1960, 1969; Hiller 1970).

Early British experiments in computer composition were realized outside of established musical institutions by D. Champernowne and S. Gill, a mathematical economist and a mathematician, respectively (Hiller 1970). (Incidentally, Champernowne was a colleague of Alan Turing at Cambridge University.) While Italian composers such as Luciano Berio and Luigi Nono were leaders in analog electronic music, computer music per se took time to establish roots in Italian soil. By 1970 Pietro Grossi and his colleagues in Pisa developed a hybrid computer system for composing original pieces and

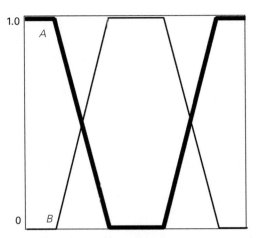

Figure 50.10   Graphical functions used to control compositional processes (after Mathews and Rosler 1969). The thick line is a scaling function for voice A; the thin line scales the influence of voice B. Notice that A dominates at first, then B enters, and then A returns to influence.

adulterating existing ones (Baruzzi, Grossi, and Milani 1975; Camilleri, Carreras, and Mayr 1987).

In the late 1960s, the first computer graphics terminals opened up the possibility of coupling algorithms to graphical interaction. Scientists such as Max Mathews at Bell Laboratories explored radical new possibilities offered by graphical control of composition and synthesis. These included experiments in which curves drawn on a computer screen controlled the degree of pitch and rhythm interpolation between two songs (Mathews and Rosler 1969). In figure 50.10, the two functions determine the relative influence of the notes of two songs over time.

Next, we look at four pioneering composition programs.

Four Pioneering Composition Programs

Many algorithmic composition programs have been written, but only a few have been used by more than one composer. Here we look briefly at four pioneering programs that have been used by others besides the original author: Iannis Xenakis's Stochastic Music Program (SMP), G. M. Koenig's Project 1, Barry Truax's POD programs, and Clarence Barlow's AUTO-BUSK program (Barlow 2001).

SMP and Project 1 originally generated a printed list of notes (represented alphanumerically) as their output. The note lists were meant to be transcribed into common music notation and played by traditional instruments. However, both programs were also connected to digital sound synthesis. The POD programs were designed from the beginning to be connected to a sound synthesis system, so the results were heard immediately. AUTOBUSK generated MIDI output so it could drive any compatible instrument.

Stochastic Music Program

With the aid of electronic computers, the composer becomes a sort of pilot: pressing buttons, introducing coordinates, and supervising the controls of a cosmic vessel sailing in the space of sound, across sonic constellations and galaxies that could formerly be glimpsed only in a distant dream.
—Iannis Xenakis, *Formalized Music,* 1971

The author of the Stochastic Music Program (SMP), the Paris-based composer Iannis Xenakis (figure 50.11), was a pioneer of algorithmic composition. His work in this domain was, however, only one of his many innovative achievements. An early version of the SMP program was published in his book (Xenakis 1971, 1992) as the Free Stochastic Music (FSM) program. The stochastic formulas in SMP were originally developed by scientists to describe the behavior of particles in gasses. By analogy, in Xenakis's view, a composition could be represented as a sequence of *clouds of sound,* with the particles corresponding to individual notes. (See Xenakis 1960, 1971, 1985, 1992 for a full discussion of the aesthetic ideas behind the program.)

Figure 50.11 Iannis Xenakis 1966. Getty Images.

SMP models a composition as a sequence of sections, each characterized by a duration and the density of notes within it. Figure 50.12 depicts the overall logic of the SMP program. The composer interacts with SMP by stipulating global attributes of the score and then executing the program. The global attributes include

1. Average duration of sections
2. Minimum and maximum density of notes in a section
3. Classification of instruments into *timbre classes*
4. Distribution of timbre classes as a function of density.
5. Probability for each instrument in a timbre class to play
6. Longest duration playable by each instrument

The SMP program helped create a number of important works in Xenakis's oeuvre, including *Eonta* (1964, Editions Salabert), for piano and brass, premiered by Yuji Takahashi on piano. The program was improved by the mathematician-composer John Myhill (1979). Donald Byrd connected SMP to the sound synthesis program Music V (Byrd 1977). The

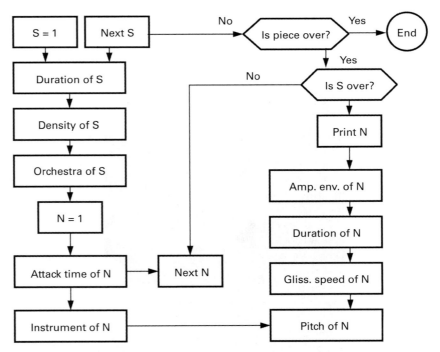

Legend: S = section, N = note in section

Figure 50.12   Overall logic of Xenakis's Stochastic Music Program.

SMP algorithms were adapted for real-time operation by Bokesoy and Pape (2003).

Project 1

Only very few composers may be inclined to schematize their work. But when out of sheer curiosity they try to compose with the aid of a computer, they are forced to do so . . . precisely because of the regulated combination of musical processes with results that cannot always be foreseen. These contacts between the composer and the musical material forcibly lead to reflection on the craft of composing and to the formulation of new musical theories.
—G. M. Koenig

Gottfried Michael Koenig (figure 50.13) created the Project 1 program at the Institute of Sonology, Utrecht, in 1970 (Laske 1979). Project 1 composes by applying seven *selection principles* to a database of five musical event *parameters:* instrument, rhythm, harmony, register, and dynamics.

In Project 1 the selection principles range from completely random (non-repetitive) to completely deterministic (repetitive). Between them, an intermediate principle combines randomness and determinism. It chooses at random from a set of elements without replacement of that element back into the set. Subsequent choices draw from a smaller set of elements until none are left to choose from. Then the cycle of choices can begin again. In

Figure 50.13   G. M. Koenig at the teletype of the Digital Equipment Corporation PDP-15 computer, Institute of Sonology, Utrecht, the Netherlands, 1971.

the most deterministic selection principle, the range of choices is constrained, causing much repetition.

The composer specified the following seed data to the program:

- A set of weightings for different sizes of chords
- The total number of events to be generated
- A set of tempi
- A random number that serves as a seed to stochastic procedures

The program then generated seven sections or "structures." Within a structure, each of the five parameters ran through the seven selection principles in a random order (figure 50.14). The results were printed out in the form of a note list. Later versions of the software could produce sound directly or generate MIDI note messages.

Project 1 produces variants of a given compositional structure embodied in the program. As Koenig stated: "I regard serial compositional technique as a special case of aleatoric compositional technique" (Koenig 1978a). Hence, the score generated by Project 1 obeys a logic of what Koenig has called "Serial music, Cologne style," with reference to the mixture of deterministic and aleatoric composition techniques explored by Koenig and other composers in the 1950s and 1960s (Koenig 1978b; 2018). The results of Project 1 can be heard in a number of Koenig's pieces including *Output* (1979).

Koenig developed another program called Project 2 that added more flexibility. With Project 2 the user could specify the selection principle to be used in generating values for a particular parameter in the output score (Koenig 1970b).

Koenig never considered Project 1 and Project 2 to be complete end-to-end composing systems. He celebrated the creative opportunities that could be taken when interpreting the numerical lists generated by his programs into scores for electronic and instrumental performance (Koenig 1979).

Project 1 has been rewritten in SuperCollider and is available from the composer's website, https://koenigproject.nl/. An English translation of his writings on composition was recently published, called *Process and Form* (Koenig 2018).

POD

While the SMP and Project 1 programs were designed mainly to generate scores for traditional instruments, Barry Truax's POD (Poisson distribution) programs were meant expressly for direct digital synthesis of sound (Truax 1975, 1977, 1985). POD replaced the traditional *note concept* used in SMP

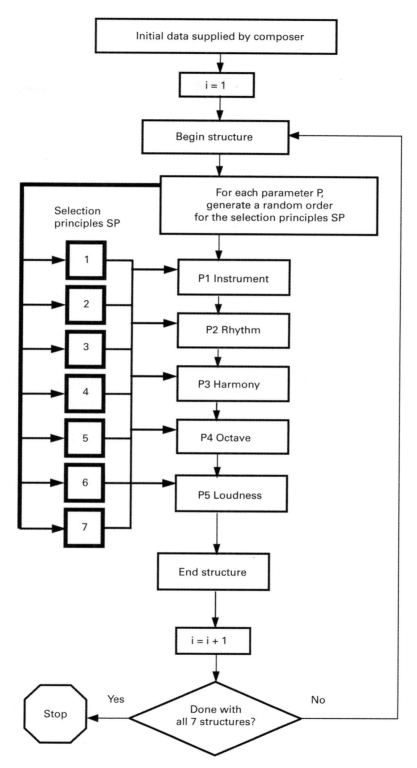

Figure 50.14 Program flow of Koenig's Project 1 program. The program generates seven structures, each of which applies the seven selection principles (SP) to each of the five parameters in a random order.

and Project 1 with the more general concept of *sound objects* (Schaeffer 1977, 2017). Truax (figure 50.15) began developing the first POD system as a student of Koenig at the Institute of Sonology at Utrecht in 1972. Over a period of several years he wrote new versions for different platforms.

Figure 50.16 shows the overall scheme of the POD programs, involving a mixture of human and machine decisions.

POD generated events within the bounds of *tendency masks*—frequency versus-time regions shown in figure 50.17. The distribution of events in time and frequency follows the Poisson distribution–a standard probability function. (For more on probability distributions in music, see Xenakis [1992] and Lorrain [1980].) The composer specifies the number of events within the tendency mask by adjusting the *event density* parameter.

In addition to sound objects, tendency masks, and densities, the composer also stipulated the selection principles (similar to those in Koenig's Project 1) to be employed in choosing sound objects to be placed in the mask. Once a synthesis score is generated, users can vary the performance of the score in a variety of ways, by changing the tempo, direction, degree of event overlap, envelope shape, and various synthesis variables.

Selection principles and tendency masks let composers work on a higher level of musical architecture than that of individual notes. "The composer is not only concerned with the nature of the individual sound event, but also with . . . larger groups of events, including entire compositional sections" (Truax 1975, p. ii).

Figure 50.15   Barry Truax lecturing, 1978. (Photograph by J. V. III.)

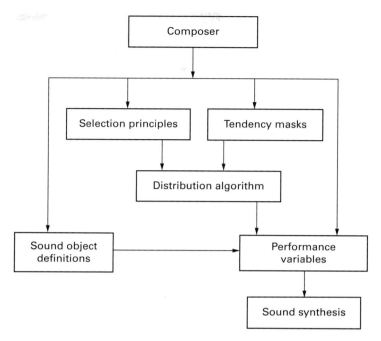

Figure 50.16   Overall plan of the POD system. The composer specifies the selection principles, tendency masks, performance variables, and sound object definitions. The distribution algorithm scatters sounds in time within the constraints specified by the composer. The result is synthesized by computer.

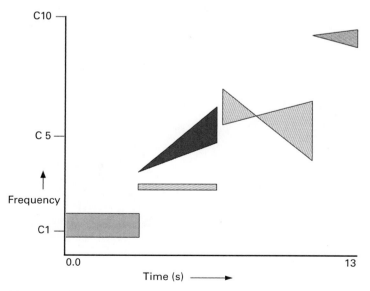

Figure 50.17   Tendency masks in a POD score. The fill patterns indicate different timbral settings.

Although POD's synthesis flexibility was limited, this can be explained by the fact that it was implemented on early computers that could not support a general-purpose synthesis system. The earliest implementation of POD generated sound in batch mode (non–real time). A later version, PODX, allowed quick interaction because the sound synthesis task was assigned to a real-time digital synthesizer. PODX was used to create works such as *Arras* (1980) and *Wave Edge* (1983, Wergo 2017-50, Mainz).

AUTOBUSK

AUTOBUSK is a real-time algorithmic composition program developed by Clarence Barlow (figure 50.18) (Barlow 2001). AUTOBUSK applies probabilistic methods to tonal and metrical principles that Barlow formalized while working on his monumental piano piece *Çoğluotobüsişletmesi* (1979), documented in Barlow (1980). AUTOBUSK has been used by Barlow and his many composition students ever since.

The first piece realized with AUTOBUSK was *Variazioni e un pianoforte meccanico* (1986). In this piece, often performed by Barlow himself, a pianist

Figure 50.18   Clarence Barlow (left) explaining his algorithms to another algorithmic composer, George Lewis, in 1985.

plays the opening bars of the *Arietta* from Beethoven's *Piano sonata op. 111* on a MIDI-controlled piano. The performance is gradually taken over by AUTOBUSK controlling the piano. The pianist eventually leaves the piano to play by itself, only to return at the end in order to conclude the piece.

AUTOBUSK was originally written in 1986 in the Pascal language for a custom-made computer running the Digital Research CP/M operating system. It was ported in 1987 to the popular Atari ST computer. It currently runs under Windows and MacOS using Atari emulators (figure 50.19). It has also been re-implemented by Georg Hajdu using Max and Ableton Live (Hajdu 2016).

Barlow's 2012 book *On Musiquantics* presents the composition theories behind AUTOBUSK. These theories explore the musical concepts of *harmonicity, metricity, tonicality,* and *eventfulness.* Harmonicity determines intervallic stability, in which the stability of intervals can be determined for any set of octave divisions. This idea can be applied to a complex 17-tone scale (which Barlow used for his piano piece *Otodeblu*) or to something as simple as a pentatonic scale. AUTOBUSK will calculate detailed pitch relationships of greatest harmonicity for any scale pattern. Metricity determines how a rhythmic stream will vary with respect to an original. Tonicality determines how close to a tonality a note sequence will remain. Eventfulness determines how often a note will occur. More specifically, it measures the number of notes per unit time (note density). It ranges from silence to saturation, where every available pulse in a given meter is attacked.

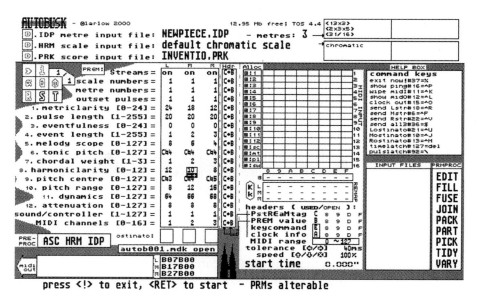

Figure 50.19   Screen image of Barlow's AUTOBUSK.

Strategies for Algorithmic Composition

Music can be generated in innumerable ways. Why choose one way over another? New algorithms are constantly being invented and incorporated into music systems. Many import concepts from scientific models of biology, mathematics, engineering, and computer science—and also linguistics (formal grammars) and machine learning.

Another class of generative algorithms take data sets and map them. Almost any data set can be mapped to sonic parameters: the moves of a chess game, the contour of skyscrapers, astronomical motions, climate variations, biological data, brain waves, and so on. These mappings can be direct (e.g., a pitch goes up when a number in the data set goes up) or arbitrarily complicated (Doornbusch 2002). Mapping data to sound inevitably crosses into the world of *sonification:* the auditory equivalent of data visualization (Hermann 2002).

Many survey papers and full-length book treatments cover generative strategies, and copious instructional material is available online. Articles by Ames (1987b), Langston (1989), Lorrain (1980), and Ariza (2007) summarize many techniques. Essl (2007) surveys multiple approaches from a musical point of view. Fernández and Vico (2013) have written a comprehensive survey with over 300 references. Tatar and Pasquier (2019) survey 78 generative music systems.

Classic books such as Xenakis (1992), Winsor (1987, 1990, 1991), Barbaud (1966, 1968), and Hiller and Isaacson (1959) survey various strategies and present example programs. Newer books include Barlow (2012), Cope (1996, 2006), Loy (2006), Taube (2005), Miranda and Biles (2007), Nierhaus (2010), Simoni and Dannenberg (2012), and Sandred (2017). Floreano and Mattiusi (2008) and Brownlee (2011) offer book-length treatments of biologically inspired algorithms. *The Oxford Handbook of Algorithmic Music* (2018) adds 650 pages to the discourse.

ML techniques, including neural networks, tend to dominate current research. Because this approach depends on training from an already existing database of compositions, most studies focus on re-creation of existing styles. However, one way that music evolves is by combining styles into a new hybrid. Thus historical styles could be used as a gene pool for new music.

A major line of research focuses on the convergence of mathematics and music (Winter 2019). Publications such as *Journal of Mathematics and Music,* conferences by the Society for Mathematics and Computation in Music, and scholarly books examine mathematical models for algorithmic composition (Benson 2007; Loy 2006, Fauvel, Flood, and Wilson 2003; Mazzola 2002; Mazzola, Mannone, and Pang 2016; Nierhaus 2010; Pottier 2009). Mathematics is a science of patterns, and music is an art of patterns. Their combination is clearly an open-ended enterprise (Andreatta 2009).

Beyond mathematical algorithms are idiosyncratic and heuristic methods such as those customized for each piece by Clarence Barlow (1980, 2012). A list of compositional algorithms could be extended as time goes on. Thus, rather than attempt to explicate each method in detail here, we provide table 50.1, which lists capsule descriptions of common strategies and references for further study.

For pedagogical reasons, we list each strategy separately, but clearly, in a composition one can combine different strategies. One algorithm, for example, could manage the microstructure of a piece, while a different algorithm determines the macrostructure. One algorithm could generate the beginning, another the end.

Philosophical and Aesthetic Issues Posed by Algorithmic Methods

This concluding section presents some philosophical and aesthetic issues raised by the use of algorithmic methods. We look at aesthetic motivations, the question of deterministic versus stochastic algorithms, total automation versus interactive composition, batch mode interaction, and combining formal and informal strategies in heuristic algorithms.

Aesthetic Motivations

What draws composers to generative methods? Generative methods are conceptually attractive. They offer the possibility of exploring novel musical processes and the creation of new musical structures according to freely invented strategies. One rationale for generative techniques is that they allow composers to reach beyond themselves (Berg 1979):

To hear that which could not be heard without the computer, to think that which could not be thought without the computer, and to learn that which could not be learned without the computer. The computer can allow a composer to write music that goes beyond that which she is already capable of. (355)

Romantic ideals can drive generative aesthetics, from purity of method to seductive metaphors of natural growth and evolution, life, and ecosystems. McCormack et al. (2009) likened generative composition to giving birth to a living organism:

Table 50.1   Common Strategies for Algorithmic Composition

Strategy	Capsule description	References
Set and group theory, combinatorics operations	Enumerations, permutations, combinations, rotations, partitions, series operations (invert, transpose, reverse), shuffling, sampling without replacement, and so on.	Loy 2006
Linked automata and transition networks	Finite-state automata in graph structures. Based on a given set of inputs, the automata have rules that determine the transition to the next state.	Nierhaus 2010; Cope 1996, 2001, 2006
Cellular automata	Systems of cellular automata are like linked automata systems. They have additional constraints, however, (1) the behavior of every automaton or cell is the same, and (2) the interconnection network between the automata is a symmetrical structure array or lattice that does not change over time as it may with ordinary linked automata. Fed with random inputs, complex behavior emerges as many automata interact locally and assemble themselves into hierarchies. Cellular automata can be extended by incorporating feedback from the past or by multilevel organization in which different rules apply at each level.	Beyls 1989; Millen 1990, 1992; Miranda and Biles 2007; Bilotta and Pantano 2010; Nierhaus 2010; Burraston 2006
Stochastic processes including Markov chains	A stochastic strategy implies the use of probability distributions. A probability distribution is a table that shows the likelihood of occurrence of one or more events. In a Markov chain model, the probability of the next event is conditional on previous events.	Xenakis 1992; Loy 2006; Nierhaus 2010; Taube 2005; Simoni and Dannenberg 2012
Fractal processes	Uses rules to generate self-similar nested patterns.	Mandelbrot 1977; Clarke and Voss 1978; Bolognesi 1983; Loy 2006
Chaotic systems	Deterministic algorithms that vary between stable and turbulent states as their parameters cross nonlinear thresholds.	Nierhaus 2010; Bidlack 1992; Di Scipio 1990; Gogins 1991
Genetic algorithms (GA) and artificial life models	GA imitates natural selection by producing new generations of candidates to solve a specific problem. A population is at first initiated randomly in a manner that depends on the problem to be solved. It is then evaluated for *fitness*. A number of individuals are selected by a procedure that most probably picks the best fitting candidates. A mating pool is formed of the chosen individuals. The algorithm stops when a chosen termination condition is fulfilled.	Burton and Vladimirova 1999; Miranda and Biles 2007; Tzimeas and Mangina 2009; Bilotta and Pantano 2010; Nierhaus 2010; Dahlstadt 2004
Translational methods	Translating information from an existing nonmusical medium into a new sound, also known as *data sonification*. The translation can be either rule-based or stochastic. An early example was Schillinger's mappings of curves like city skylines into music notation by quantization.	Schillinger 1946; Barlow 2012; Loy 2006

Table 50.1   (continued)

Strategy	Capsule description	References
Grammars and Lindenmeyer systems	Uses rules to generate strings based on a predefined grammar or set of rewriting rules.	Lidov and Gabura 1973; Bel and Kippen 1992; Nierhaus 2010
Generate-and-test or constrained search	1. Generate a parameter value at random from a repertoire of possible values. 2. Subject the random value to a series of tests (or searches) that determine valid values at that step of the process. 3. If the value passes all the tests, write the value as the output; otherwise generate a new random value and start again.	Miller, Galanter, and Pribram 1960; Newell and Simon 1972; Hiller 1970, 1981; Ames 1987a; Schottstaedt 1989a; Gill 1963
Process models	Models musical control flow. Transitions are represented as entities whose *firing* (transition) is based on the condition of a state variable (Petri nets) or calling a subroutine to generate the next phrase.	Smoliar 1967a, b, 1971; Haus 1984; Loy 2006; Hanappe 1999
Pattern matching and search	A composition program based on this method searches for instances of symbols in a database that match a general pattern specified by a composer.	Dashow 1989; Nierhaus 2010
Constraints	A simple constraint can be viewed as a network of devices connected by wires. Data values can flow along the wires, and computation is performed by the devices. A device computes only locally available information and places newly derived values on other locally attached wires. Computed values propagate in this way. Because variables are defined in several ways simultaneously (i.e., with respect to several different relationships among variables), constraints provide multiple viewpoints on the entities that they represent.	Sussman and Steele 1981; Levitt 1981, 1983, 1984; Henz, Lauer, and Zimmermann 1996; Sandred 2010; Anders and Miranda 2010
Expert systems	Expert systems can incorporate a large knowledge base of facts and rules and proceed by logical inference to generate an output. Another type of system employs *brute-force search:* trying all possible values at every stage and rating them on a statistical basis.	Nierhaus 2010; Cope 1996, 2001, 2006
Machine learning strategies, including neural networks (NN), also called connectionist models and deep learning	The NN paradigm consists of a large number of identical, interconnected processing elements. Each element receives a set of input activations in the form of a numerical vector. The strength of NNs is their ability to detect patterns through a training phase of being exposed to thousands of examples. (See appendix A.)	Rumelhart and McClelland 1986; Loy 1989b, 1989c, 2006; Dolson 1989a; Todd and Loy 1991; Nierhaus 2010; Huang et al. 2019a, b.
Music information, retrieval-based	Analyzing and extracting features from audio files to extract their content in the form of features. One can then navigate a database of analyzed files to find those with similar or different features as a composition strategy.	Humphrey, Turnbull, Collins (2013); Cella (2020); Sturm and Wiggins (2021)

Another mode [of composition] exists within which compositions generate and self-organize, shifting and oscillating, adapting, developing, and becoming whole: like an organism. (21)

When a composer frames her composition as the product of an elaborate technical process, this can make it seem more impressive. Some institutions (academia, research centers, journals, conferences, etc.) reward systematic approaches to composition.

An indisputable attraction of generative techniques is that they let composers control sonic processes on a level that would be impossible without algorithmic assistance. We see this in the control of processes like granulation, additive synthesis, frequency modulation, spatial upmixing, and live interactive performance (Collins 2003; Pottier 2009; Lewis 2000, 2009; Lorrain 2009). Rather than giving up control, a composer gains control over a domain that is difficult or impossible to manage without machine assistance. As John Chowning described his composition *Stria,* composed in 1978 (Roads 1985f),

It was the first time that I tried to use a high-level programming language to realize a composition in toto. . . . There were rules for the determining the details of the structure, from the microsound level up to the level of a phrase. In Stria, all frequency components are based on powers of the Golden Mean in the carrier:modulator ratios. So it is all very cohesive perceptually, even though it is inharmonic and sounds a little strange. But it does not take long, even for a naïve listener, to realize that even though it is strange, it is cohesive at a deep level. I believe this is because of the unified structure of spectral formation.

Deterministic versus Stochastic Procedures

The programs of Hiller and other pioneers of algorithmic composition contrasted two approaches: *deterministic* versus *stochastic* (or *probabilistic*) procedures. Deterministic procedures generate musical notes by carrying out a fixed but possibly complicated task that does not involve random selection. The variables supplied to a deterministic procedure are the seed data. The seed data may be a set of pitches, a musical phrase, or some constraints that the procedures must satisfy.

An example of a deterministic procedure would be a program to harmonize a chorale melody in the style of J. S. Bach. In this case, the seed is the melody. The rules of harmonization and voice leading, derived from a textbook, ensure that only certain chord sequences are legal. In more recent music, deterministic algorithms include Barlow's formulas for determining the dynamics of an attack at a given point in a given meter (Barlow 1980, 2012), and Ames's constrained search routines that generate counterpoint by applying a battery of tests on a set of alternative solutions—selecting one that best fits the specified constraints (Ames 1983).

Stochastic procedures, on the other hand, integrate random choice into the decision-making process. They generate musical events according to probability tables that weight the occurrence of certain events over others. These tables guarantee an overall trend, but the filigree of local events remains unpredictable. A basic stochastic generator produces a random number and compares it to values stored in a probability table. If the random number falls within a certain range of values in the probability table, the algorithm generates the event associated with that range.

Certain algorithms exhibit such mechanistic behavior that we can identify them by listening. Apart from simple cases, however, it is not possible to ascertain by listening whether a given fragment of music was generated by a stochastic or deterministic process. As Stephen Wolfram (2002) observed,

There seem to be many kinds of systems in which it is overwhelmingly easier to generate highly complex behavior than to recognize the origins of this behavior. (550)

Many generative algorithms are perceptually opaque. As Luciano Berio (2006, from lectures in 1993 and 1994) observed,

Today we can find examples of complete estrangement between the practical and sensory dimension and the conceptual one, between the work listened to and the process that generated it. (133)

Hence, the choice of algorithm is largely a matter of compositional philosophy and taste, influenced by cultural and technical fashions of the day.

Total Automation versus Interactive Composition

An early fear of automated composition was that it would replace human composers, just as recordings have replaced performing musicians in most venues. Decades after Hiller's highly publicized experiments, this has not occurred. Even so, the use of composition programs remains controversial. Writing a computer program for automated composition is a creative act. One the other hand, simply using a composition program written by someone else demands little creativity. Interaction is limited to supplying a small amount of seed data prior to execution of the program. The compositional strategy is fixed in the program, and the user merely reaps the harvest of notes. In its most extreme form, automated composition resembles a form of *found art*. The composer selects the output, and, in effect, signs and frames the work with a title and a performance medium.

One way to bypass the fixed strategy is to modify the program logic. In this case, a composer who is also a programmer retains overall responsibility.

Another departure from a fixed strategy is to revise the program's output. Early proponents of automated composition, notably Hiller and Barbaud, adhered to the doctrine that the output score generated by a composition program should not be edited by hand; rather, the program logic should be changed and run again. This doctrine stems from an aesthetic that values music that is formally consistent. Other composers feel there is nothing sacrilegious about modifying the output score of a composing program. Xenakis, in particular, rearranged and refined the raw data emitted by the SMP program. His oeuvre contains numerous examples of selection and rearrangement of program output (Roads 1973; Harley 2004).

All or Nothing: Batch Mode Interaction

Perhaps the most fundamental limitation of fully automated composition programs is the *batch* mode of interaction they impose on the composer. The term *batch* refers to the earliest computer systems that ran one program at a time; there was no interaction with the machine besides submitting a deck of punched paper cards for execution and picking up the printed output. No online editing could occur; all decisions had to be predetermined and encoded in the program and its input data.

In the batch mode of composition, the composer follows these steps:

1. Prepare and enter the input data.
2. Execute the program.
3. Accept or reject the output (usually an entire composition).

If we follow the batch doctrine and a single note or phrase is not to our taste, we must modify the program logic, recompile it, and generate another score. We cannot simply correct the offending events. In a batch approach to automated composition, the unit of composition and interaction is an entire score.

Interaction with Algorithms

By enriching an algorithmic system with interaction, we add flexibility that is missing from a batch approach. In so doing, we gain direct access to the different layers and time scales of compositional process. POD and AUTO-BUSK were designed to be interactive in the presence of sound. Another early example of real-time interactive algorithmic software is Music Mouse programmed by Laurie Spiegel (Spiegel 1986).

An interactive approach can allow us to choose which processes will be governed by algorithms versus those that will be handled by human interaction. The scope, degree, and mode of interaction is a compositional prerogative. This approach concurs with the "formal and informal" philosophy articulated by Horacio Vaggione (2003). He proposed a plurality of diverse tactics, both algorithmic and gestural, rather than handing over control to an autonomous bot that rules over all aspects of a composition:

The scope of interaction can vary from the small (a single parameter, an envelope, a sound, or individual grains), to the medium (a phrase, a voice, or a procedure), to the large (all notes or the entire compositional strategy). The degree of interaction can range from the intense real-time performance onstage, where there is no going back, to the reflective interaction experienced in a studio, where one can always stop and backtrack. Generated material can be treated as a kind of improvisation that can be freely edited.

Moreover we can choose the mode of interaction, from direct manual control of a synthesis parameter via a musical input device, to interaction with performance software, to iterative transformation, to live coding (Blackwell and Collins 2005; Roberts, Wakefield, and Wright 2015; Roberts 2016).

Combining Formal and Informal Strategies in Heuristic Algorithms

Music interacts in deep ways with consciousness, memory, and expectations of listeners (Huron 2006). Human beings respond intuitively to culturally context-dependent narrative impressions that are difficult to formalize: wit, irony, tension, surprise, virtuosity, humor, and clever twists and transitions. In general, formal methods do not address these types of narrative functions. The question is then: how to codify narrative functions based on human expectation? This is not obvious, but it seems unlikely to that it will emerge from a formula borrowed from an arbitrary branch of mathematics. Certain gifted people make inspired choices from myriad possibilities to create fascinating designs. This remains the strong suit of human talent.

To produce wondrous forms, perhaps what is needed is a hybrid formal/informal approach, combining the computational power of algorithmic control with the magical influence of heuristics. What is heuristic influence? Heuristics is the art of experience-based strategies for problem solving. As the mathematician Gregory Chaitin (2002) said of heuristic reasoning,

There is an empirical component in math: it is computation. You do calculations and see patterns and make conjectures. . . . But when you publish, normally you hide all of that and present it like a direct divine revelation. . . . Mathematics in the process of discovery is a little bit like physics, The way you discover something new is "quasi-empirical." . . . You have to learn the art of discovery and that is heuristic reasoning [or] inspired guesswork. (134)

The heuristic approach stands in contrast to brute-force computer models that enumerate and search millions of possibilities, then make choices based on statistics. Such an approach may succeed in the realm of fixed-rule games like checkers, chess, and Go, but has obvious limitations in the realm of art where rules are more fluid. In art, an inspired violation of the rules at the right moment is sometimes the correct gesture.

Heuristic methods include rules of thumb, educated guesses, intuitive judgments, and common sense—all based on experience. Heuristic methods are inevitably intertwined with an understanding of context, whether it be the state of a game, the state of a composition, or the state of a culture. Whereas certain pieces such as those of J. S. Bach have a timeless quality, other pieces have an impact precisely because they articulate a critical juncture in culture; *The Rite of Spring* (1913) of Stravinsky comes to mind.

Heuristic methods are compatible with formalization. However, in practice they implement tailor-made solutions that are domain-specific and context-dependent, rather than imported whole cloth from one area of study to another.

Most importantly, heuristic algorithms are tested by experiments and refined by human perceptual judgments. Xenakis used stochastic processes in a heuristic manner, sometimes modifying and rearranging the results to better suit the piece. Poetic license is the ultimate heuristic.

Assessment of Algorithmic Composition

Algorithmic toolkits for music, for example, Max and SuperCollider, are widespread (see chapter 49). Algorithmic procedures have also become part of digital audio workstations, including Max for Live projects, Logic's MIDI Scripter, and the tools for Reaper's MIDI editor.

Algorithmic tools can process more data in a shorter amount of time than would be possible by a human composer working alone. They let composers shift their attention from the tiniest details of composition (which are handled by the program, according to instructions specified or accepted by the composer) to concentrate on a higher level of abstraction. At this level, the composer manages the creation of a piece in terms of its formal architecture and process model.

Long ago, human beings learned that machines can easily outdo their human counterparts in certain tasks. Computers are superb at enumerating all possible solutions to a given set of constraints. This has led to optimal performance in well-defined tasks such as playing rule-based games. Google's AlphaZero can defeat all human players at Go, Chess, and Shogi (Silver et al. 2018). Trained by playing against itself millions of times, AlphaZero searches through all possible future moves and assigns a value to each move with respect to the goal and according to the rules. As we have argued, however, the decision-making powers of computers in aesthetic domains are severely limited.

With machine learning techniques, we can train a computer to imitate any style of music. The bigger challenge will always be to generate nonimitative original innovations. An effective music composition solves aesthetic problems posed by itself. What aesthetic problems are the most interesting? Only a talented composer possesses this critical cultural insight.

If composition were merely a parlor game, then the technical virtuosity of the machine would already have relegated human efforts to a sideshow. A machine can execute formal composition rules that are far more intricate than any human being could possibly manage. Like a sequencer that races through performances with superhuman speed and precision, the complex ratiocinations of machine composition inspire awe—up to a point. Excessive complexity, precision, or virtuosity for its own sake is a tiresome musical diet. The talent of composers who use algorithmic composition methods is reflected in their skill in managing the excesses of their occasionally self-indulgent software prodigies.

VII   Interconnections

51 *MIDI*

MIDI Then and Now

MIDI Communicates Control Data

Background: MIDI 1.0

Importance of MIDI

Musical Possibilities of MIDI

MIDI Hardware

> **MIDI Ports**
> **Daisy Chaining and MIDI Patchbays**
> **MIDI Computer Interfaces and USB-MIDI**
> **MIDI and Ethernet**

MIDI Channels

MIDI 1.0 Messages

> **MIDI's Representation of Pitch and Amplitude**
> **Status and Data Bytes**

MIDI 2.0

MIDI 2.0 Protocol
Universal MIDI Packet
MIDI 2.0 Message Formats
Per-Note Controllers
Jitter Reduction Timestamps
MIDI Capability Inquiry
  Protocol negotiation
  Profile configuration
  Property exchange

The Musical Instrument Digital Interface (MIDI) protocol has been described as

- An interconnection scheme between instruments and computers
- A set of guidelines for transferring data from one instrument to another
- A language for transmitting musical scores between computers and synthesizers

All these definitions capture an aspect of MIDI. MIDI was designed for real-time control of music devices. The MIDI specification stipulates a hardware interconnection scheme and a method for data communications (MIDI Association 1983; Loy 1985b; Moog 1986; Rothstein 1992). It also specifies a grammar for encoding musical performance information. MIDI information is packaged into *messages* sent from one device to another. For example, a message can specify the start time of a musical note, its pitch, and its initial amplitude.

Every MIDI device contains a microprocessor that interprets and generates MIDI data. Not every MIDI setup needs a separate computer; one can connect a MIDI keyboard to control a rackmount synthesizer, for example.

The relatively simple design of MIDI has led to its universal acceptance. A diverse electronic music industry has grown up as a direct effect of MIDI's success. The presence of a standard interface to synthesizers has led to a proliferation of new musical input devices—the physical controllers manipulated by performers.

Since MIDI was first proposed in 1983, it has undergone continuous amendment. At the same time, there has always been an awareness of fundamental limitations in MIDI as a representation of musical signals (Selfridge-Field 1997). In 2020, a new MIDI 2.0 specification was published (MIDI Association 2020; AMEI-MMA 2020b). It is backward compatible, so MIDI 1.0 remains a supported protocol. We present MIDI 2.0 at the end of this chapter.

Open Sound Control (OSC), presented in chapter 52, is an alternative to MIDI, but it is a different type of protocol. MIDI is a predefined language of communication. All MIDI devices speak the same language, so little in the way of setup is required of the user in most instances. By contrast, OSC involves more setup and programming. Once set up, however, OSC offers capabilities that go far beyond what MIDI 1.0 was designed to do. However, MIDI 2.0 has the potential to take on many of these capabilities.

The information in this chapter serves as an introduction. It is not meant to replace the official detailed MIDI specifications and the various addenda and supplements that have been added over time. For anyone developing MIDI hardware or software, these are essential documents. See the website of the MIDI Association, https://www.midi.org. Several detailed books on MIDI 1.0 are aimed at professionals, such as Lerhman and Tully (1993) and Guérin (2006). MIDI 2.0 is featured in Huber (2020). Video tutorials on MIDI abound online.

MIDI Then and Now

When MIDI was first introduced, it was used mainly to interconnect computers and synthesizer hardware via MIDI cables. Today many MIDI devices have USB ports and not MIDI ports. The bidirectional USB-MIDI standard eliminates one of the transmission limitations of the original MIDI standard by opening up the data flow to many more channels than MIDI's original sixteen (Ashour et al. 1999). (In general, a *MIDI channel* corresponds to an instrument timbre. So one might assign channel 1 to Piano and channel 2 to Organ.)

Moreover, many current applications of MIDI are software-only. A DAW such as Ableton Live, for example, transmits MIDI messages directly to software synthesizer plug-ins. This is done internally in software within the computer—no cables needed.

MIDI data can also be transmitted in real time via the internet, by local area network (Ethernet), and wirelessly by WiFi (e.g., GarageBand's JamSession mode for iOS). Thus in our discussion of MIDI in this chapter, we discuss both the original hardware setup with MIDI cables and MIDI ports, and modern setups. In sections in which we discuss the channel limitations and other aspects of cable-based MIDI systems, we refer specifically to *traditional setups*.

MIDI Communicates Control Data

Stepping back, we are reminded that there is nothing specific to music about MIDI. That is, it is not music that MIDI communicates. Rather, MIDI is a means of transmitting information about key presses, knob turnings, and joystick manipulations. What these transducers are controlling is almost secondary.
—William Buxton, "The Computer as Accompanist," 1986

Like the player piano rolls of yore, MIDI transmits control data as opposed to sound waveforms. This control data includes messages such as "Start a note event now," "Select a new patch now," or "Change volume now." A sequence of MIDI note messages defines a melody.

Sound timbre is not explicitly encoded in a MIDI 1.0 message. The choice of synthesis technique, envelopes, and signal-processing effects are left to the receiving device. This means that the same message sent to two different synthesizers can trigger greatly dissimilar sounds.

The General MIDI mode, added to the MIDI specification in 1990, provides a set of 128 preset timbre names. This adds a degree of timbre uniformity, primarily to commercial music applications, for a tiny subset of musical timbre space. Even so, a given timbre name (e.g., Piano [Bright Acoustic]) will not sound exactly the same on devices made by different companies, because each company uses its own samples.

Background: MIDI 1.0

Computer control of synthesizers began years before MIDI was conceived. These *hybrid systems* combined digital control of analog synthesizers. As figure 51.1 shows, the computer produced a stream of *control functions* (primarily amplitude and pitch envelopes) that were routed to a DAC channel by a *demultiplexer.* (A demultiplexer divides a high-speed digital stream into several slower streams.) The DAC converted the digital control functions into voltages fed to the control inputs of the synthesizer modules (like oscillators, filters, and amplifiers).

Pioneering hybrid synthesizers were the GROOVE system developed at Bell Telephone Laboratories in the early 1970s (Mathews and Moore 1970) and Edward Kobrin's HYBRID systems (Kobrin 1977). In both cases, all interface hardware was custom built, and the software protocols were specific to each system.

By the late 1970s, it became possible to use inexpensive microprocessors to control synthesizers. Hybrid synthesizers such as the Sequential Circuits Prophet-5 (1978) were marketed, but they could not communicate with each other (Vail 2000a). No standard way existed to synchronize the performance of one instrument with another.

This state of affairs prompted the creation of the MIDI protocol. The beginnings of MIDI date back to informal contacts between several American and Japanese synthesizer manufacturers in 1981. These led to broader communications between more companies in 1982 and the drafting of a specification for a digital music interface in 1983 by Dave Smith of Sequential. The first draft involved much collaboration between Smith and several companies, notably Roland and Oberheim (Smith 1984).

The first MIDI instruments, including the famous Yamaha DX7, were introduced into the market in early 1983. In August of that year, the MIDI 1.0 specification was published by a consortium of Japanese and American synthesizer manufacturers. The specification has been amended numerous times since. In 2013, Dave Smith and Ikutaro Kakehashi, founder of Roland

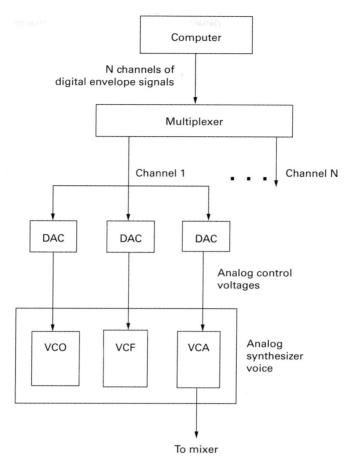

Figure 51.1   Hybrid control scheme. The computer generates digital envelopes that are routed via a multiplexer to several channels of DACs. The analog signals emitted by the DACs feed the control voltage inputs of the analog synthesizer modules. Here the audio output of a voltage-controlled oscillator (VCO) feeds into a voltage-controlled filter (VCF), which feeds into a voltage-controlled amplifier (VCA). A mixer combines the N synthesizer voices into a composite signal.

Corporation, were awarded a Technical Grammy for their work in establishing MIDI as an international standard.

Importance of MIDI

The importance of MIDI to musical culture cannot be overstated. Prior to the introduction of MIDI, computer music was practiced in a few academic and research centers around the world. Only a handful of synthesizer companies existed. MIDI led to a surge in research and development, creating a world-wide industry. At the same time, MIDI opened the doors of computer music to countless musicians around the globe.

Musical Possibilities of MIDI

A variety of musical possibilities emerge out of a system wired for MIDI, as follow:

1. MIDI separates the input device (for example, a musical keyboard) from the sound generator (synthesizer or sampler). Thus MIDI eliminates the need to have a separate input device for every synthesizer. If desired, a single input device can play many synthesizers.

2. The separation of control from synthesis means that any input device (breath controller, hornlike instrument, drum pad, guitar, etc.) can control a synthesizer. This has led to a wave of innovation in designing input devices (see chapter 40).

3. Software for interactive performance, algorithmic composition, score editing, and sequencing can be run on the computer with the results transmitted via MIDI to the synthesizer. In the opposite direction, scores, performances, voice tunings, or samples can be created on a synthesizer and transferred to the computer for editing or storage.

4. MIDI makes generic (i.e., device-independent) music software easier to develop. Generic music software runs on a personal computer and drives synthesizers manufactured by different companies. For example, generic music education software teaches music notation and fundamental concepts of music, regardless of the type of synthesizer or sampler used to illustrate these concepts.

5. MIDI makes targeted music software (i.e., software for a specific device) easier to develop by means of a common grammar of messages. Targeted music software includes *patch editor/librarian* programs that essentially replace the front panel of a synthesizer, sampler, or effects processor (see chapter 47). By pushing graphical buttons and adjusting the knobs on the screen image with a mouse, one can control the synthesizer as if one were manipulating its physical controls.

6. MIDI codes can be reinterpreted by devices other than synthesizers, such as audio effects units. This offers the possibility of real-time control of effects, such as changing the delay or reverberation time. MIDI can also synchronize synthesizers with media such as lighting systems. The standard

protocol for lighting systems is DMX and there are products that convert between the two.

7. Through MIDI, score and sequencer data can easily be exchanged between devices and apps made by different manufacturers.

MIDI Hardware

In this section we discuss both traditional MIDI hardware and more contemporary USB-MIDI. Traditional MIDI 1.0 hardware implements a simple protocol for the transmission and receipt of electronic signals. To best understand the hardware explanation, it is important to know the basic form of MIDI signals. MIDI messages transmitted between devices are sent in *serial binary form,* that is, as a series of pulses (bits) sent one at a time. Transmission occurs *asynchronously,* that is, whenever one device decides to send a message. This is usually when an event happens (for example, a musician presses a key on a musical keyboard).

The standard rate of transmission is 31,250 bits per second, derived arbitrarily by dividing the common clock frequency of 1.0 MHz by 32.

The hardware that handles these signals includes traditional MIDI ports and MIDI computer interfaces, the subjects of the next two sections.

MIDI Ports

A MIDI port on a device receives and transmits the messages. In the original MIDI standard, the MIDI port served as a connection point for a MIDI cable. As mentioned earlier, many devices today sport USB connectors, so the description here does not apply to them.

The traditional port consists of three connectors: IN, OUT, and THRU. These connectors are usually five-pin DIN jacks. (DIN denotes the German standards organization that designed the connectors.) The wiring of the jacks is specific to the MIDI standard; ordinary audio DIN cables are not designed to work in a MIDI system. In particular, the MIDI protocol wires two pins on the receiving (MIDI IN) port, and a third pin is connected to ground in the MIDI OUT port (figure 51.2). This allows the cable to shield without grounding problems over a span of up to 15 meters. Notice in figure 51.2 that pins 1 and 3 are never used.

The connectors are optically isolated (i.e., converted into optical signals at the endpoints) to prevent hum and interference from other electrical

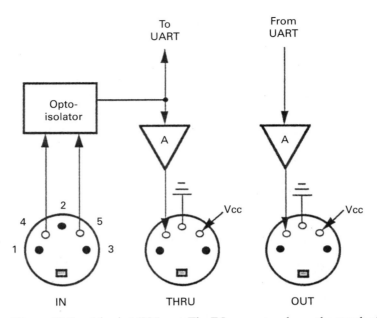

Figure 51.2   A basic MIDI port. The IN connector shows the standard pin numbering. The opto-isolator connected to the IN port consists of a light-emitting diode with its light output directed at a photocell, both enclosed in an opaque container. The MIDI signal pulses the light on and off, which switches the photocell on and off. The triangle labeled A is a buffer amplifier that boosts the signal before it is sent on to the next device. *Vcc* indicates a current source. The UART is explained in the text.

signals. Ultimately the signals are routed to a *universal asynchronous receiver/transmitter* (UART) chip.

The UART chip is the workhorse of the MIDI port. It assembles or *frames* the incoming bits into 10-bit packets, collecting the bits one at a time. The first bit always has a value of zero; the last bit has a value of 1. These are the start and stop bits that initiate and terminate a transmission. The UART discards the start and stop bits, leaving the contents: an 8-bit byte. The UART passes the byte to the microprocessor within the MIDI device (synthesizer, sampler, etc.) for decoding. Decoding the byte and acting on its contents takes a certain period of time; this latency depends on the speed of the microprocessor within the receiving MIDI device and is independent of MIDI transmission speed. (See the discussion in the section on limitations of MIDI.)

Electrically, MIDI is a *current loop,* which means it relies on switching current on and off, rather than switching voltage, to represent the logic levels. The *on* current is 5 mA, and this (counterintuitively) represents a binary value of 0. The *off* current represents a binary value of 1.

Daisy Chaining and MIDI Patchbays

The MIDI THRU port routes incoming data to another MIDI device. Specifically, the signal at the THRU output is a replica of the signal fed to the IN socket. A THRU port reamplifies the signal and passes it to the IN port of the next connected device. It is important to point out that THRU is not the same as an OUT jack. If you play on a keyboard synth, that MIDI information is transmitted to the OUT jack. It will not be sent to the THRU jack. THRU is merely an echo of the IN jack.

Interconnecting several devices using THRU jacks is called *daisy chaining.* Each device in the chain interprets the incoming messages; depending on the messages and their channels, each device may or may not respond to them.

In this way, MIDI devices can be daisy chained into a series of devices (figure 51.3a). Note that the daisy chain is a one-way (THRU-to-IN) connection. A reversal of the data path requires repatching the connections (figure 51.3b).

In practice, transmission losses (digital waveform distortions) can occur after more than two links. The opto-isolator smears the edges of the MIDI pulses (Penfold 1991). Smearing may lead to frame errors in daisy-chained MIDI transmissions, meaning that messages are garbled. The effect on the sound is random, depending on the type of messages being confused: missing or stuck notes, inappropriate messages, or other problems.

MIDI Computer Interfaces and USB-MIDI

The famous Atari ST computer of the 1980s had a dedicated five-pin MIDI port. Current computers do not. In olden times, on anything other than Atari ST, an external MIDI interface (which supports sixteen channels) could be attached to the serial or parallel port of a personal computer. In time, however, film composers found it desirable to have more than sixteen channels to support massed orchestral textures, so *multiport MIDI interfaces* were introduced. These allowed, for example, eight physical MIDI cables to be routed to many hardware devices. In Hollywood these were usually banks of rack-mount samplers. The MOTU Express 128 is a classic example of a multiport interface with eight MIDI IN jacks and eight MIDI OUT jacks supporting a total of 128 channels.

As more and more musical functionality migrated from hardware to software in the 1990s, the USB-MIDI protocol was introduced (Ashour et al. 1999). This provided the functionality of a bidirectional multiport MIDI interface on a single cable, allowing hundreds of internal software channels.

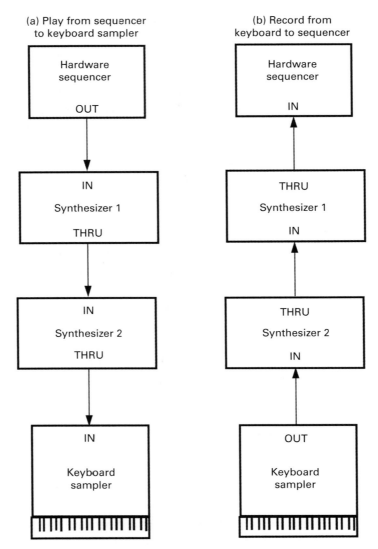

Figure 51.3 Daisy chaining MIDI devices with a MIDI THRU connector. (a) Playback from a hardware sequencer to two synthesizers and a sampler. (b) To reverse the chain, that is, to record from the keyboard sampler into the sequencer, requires repatching the chain. No additional MIDI data is contributed by the two intermediate synthesizers, although they may sound as the keyboard performer plays.

Even USB 1 transfers MIDI data hundreds of times faster than the original MIDI hardware specification.

Importantly, routing MIDI over a high-speed cable does not mean that the basic timing resolution of any MIDI channel is increased. For backward compatibility, the speed per channel remains as it always was: 31,250 bits per second. The main advantage of a high-speed interface is to serve as flexible multichannel MIDI interface with only a single cable to worry about, or in the case of wireless systems, no cable. As we discuss further on, the expansion of the number of channels enabled by USB-MIDI provides the technical support for MIDI Polyphonic Expression.

MIDI and Ethernet

USB connections are designed for short distances: the maximum cable length is fifteen meters. This can pose a problem onstage and in large studios. Another communications protocol, Ethernet, supports long cable runs (up to 100 meters). The length can be doubled by connecting an Ethernet switch (less than $20). After pioneering research on transmitting MIDI over Ethernet by Fober (1994), University of California computer scientists Lazarro and Warzynek (2004) presented a specification for transmitting MIDI over Ethernet called RTP-MIDI. This specification uses *real-time protocol* (RTP), an extensible transport mechanism for sending media streams over the internet. RTP is widely used for telephony and internet radio. RTP-MIDI is supported in all popular operating systems. Companies like iConnectivity offer hardware interfaces that accept Ethernet cables as well as USB-MIDI and traditional DIN-MIDI plugs.

MIDI Channels

A MIDI channel is an electronic address label that identifies a packet of digital information, specifying its ultimate destination. In a traditional hardware setup, all sixteen channels can be routed over one physical MIDI cable. Each receiving device needs to be set up beforehand to listen to one or more channels.

Each MIDI channel corresponds to a distinct stream of data. In the simplest case, each channel carries data for a particular part in a polyphonic score. For example, one channel might carry a snare drum part for a drum machine, while another channel plays a synthesizer voice. A multitimbral synthesizer that can play several voices with different timbres at once can handle several channels of MIDI data—one for each timbre. Hence, one way to orchestrate a composition is to assign different musical parts to the various MIDI channels (figure 51.4).

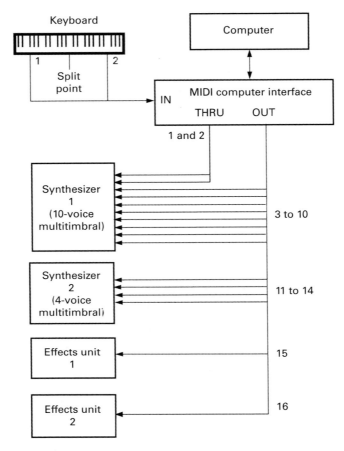

Figure 51.4   A logical (not physical) view of the MIDI channel mechanism. The keyboard output is split into two channels of information, 1 and 2. In order to record a keyboard performance these two channels are routed to the computer, which runs a sequencer program. In order to hear the performance, channels 1 and 2 are routed via the MIDI computer interface to Synthesizer 1. The computer is controlling two synthesizers and one effects unit and is taking in data from a keyboard. A total of twelve MIDI channels can be used at once in this configuration. Synthesizer 1 is a ten-voice multitimbral synthesizer, whereas Synthesizer 2 has four voices, and the effects units respond to one channel each.

MIDI 1.0 Messages

The MIDI 1.0 specification describes a language of messages sent from device to device. Most MIDI messages are asynchronous, meaning that they are sent when a change happens, such as when a key is pressed.

Expressions in the MIDI language are sequences of bits that can be parsed into 10-bit *words*. One or more words comprise a MIDI *message*. The first bit of a message is always 0, which is known as the *start bit*. Following the start bit are eight data bits (a byte), followed by a *stop bit* with a value of 1 (figure 51.5).

Most MIDI messages require two or three bytes, so the transmission rate over all sixteen channels MIDI is limited to 1,000 to 1,500 messages per second. The serial nature of the transmission means that there can be no such thing as two simultaneous notes. A chord is transmitted as a sequence of notes.

The messages to which a given MIDI devices responds are printed in its *MIDI implementation chart,* a document published by the manufacturer.

Table 51.1 lists a basic set of MIDI messages. In order to understand the definitions in the right column of table 51.1, it is helpful to know about the grammar of the MIDI protocol. This grammar includes the distinction between status and data bytes and the different categories of MIDI messages. Before explaining all this, however, let us take a moment to understand an important detail in the MIDI specification: its representation of a note's pitch and amplitude.

MIDI's Representation of Pitch and Amplitude

The first message documented in table 51.1 is the note-on message. This is MIDI's way of signaling the start of a sonic event. A note-on message contains a 7-bit field corresponding to a pitch value. Because $2^7 = 128$, the range extends over 128 pitches. The MIDI specification mandates that these pitches be equal-tempered, although they can be "bent" out of equal temperament by means of the pitch bend message (table 51.1). A problem with the pitch bend message is that it applies to all notes assigned to a channel. This makes it difficult to bend a single note in a chord (as is done on a pedal steel guitar, for example). MIDI Polyphonic Expression (MPE) provides a

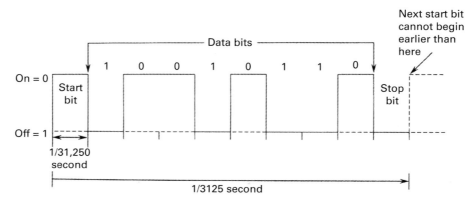

Figure 51.5   Format of a MIDI 1.0 message byte (after Lehrman and Tully 1993).

Table 51.1 MIDI messages (partial list)

Channel voice	Addressed to a specific MIDI channel
Note-on	If one plays a note on a keyboard, the synthesizer sounds the note and also sends a three-byte message through the MIDI OUT port. If we were to translate a message into words, it might say the following: Note event: on Channel 1 Key number 60 Velocity 122
Note-off	When the note is released, the keyboard sends another three-byte message: Note event: off Channel: 1 Pitch: 60 Velocity: 40 In lieu of a note-off message, some synthesizers transmit a note-on with a velocity of 0.
Channel pressure (multiple key aftertouch)	This conveys the average pressure applied to the keyboard from all notes being pressed down. The message contains two bytes: channel and channel pressure (0–127, with 127 as maximum pressure).
Polyphonic key pressure	This three-byte message transmits the finger pressure detected by the keyboard and indicates (1) channel, (2) key number of the note, and (3) key pressure.
Control change (CC)	Informs a receiving device that the position of a specific wheel, pedal or another continuous controller is changing. Sends a new three-byte (14-bit) message every time the controller changes. After the status byte, the first data byte indicates the controller number and the second data byte indicates the value. Controller number 6 (Data Entry), in conjunction with controller 96 (Data Increment), 97 (Data Decrement), 98 (Non-Registered Parameter Number LSB), 99 (Non-Registered Parameter Number MSB), 100 (Registered Parameter Number LSB), and 101 (Registered Parameter Number MSB), extend the number of controllers available. Parameter data is transferred by first selecting the parameter number to be edited using controllers 98 and 99 or 100 and 101, and then adjusting the data value for that parameter using controller number 6, 96, or 97. Registered and non-registered parameter numbers (RPN) and (NRPN) are typically used to send parameter data to a synthesizer in order to edit sound patches. Registered parameters have been assigned a particular function by manufacturers. Non-registered parameters have not been assigned specific functions.

Table 51.1 (continued)

Channel voice	Addressed to a specific MIDI channel
Pitch bend	This controller uses two data bytes, for 14 bits of resolution or 16,384 pitch divisions. One byte indicates coarse range, and the other indicates fine range. The range of pitch bend is set on the synthesizer or sampler. A pitch bend wheel that is turned slowly can generate thousands of pitch bend messages.
Program change	Program change messages contain a *channel select byte* and a *program select byte*. These cause the receiving device to switch its voice or patch to the designated program number. For example, a program change might tell a sampler on channel 4 to switch from a piano sound to an organ sound.
Bank select	Switches to the specified patch bank (up to 16,384 patch banks). This is useful for devices that support more than 128 patches, voices, or programs, because the usual program change message only allows 128 values.
Channel mode	Conveys the mode of a message. (See the description of modes below.)
Local/remote keyboard control	Breaks the connection between the keyboard and the sound engine of a synthesizer. In remote or local off mode, an instrument with sound generating capabilities transmits note messages out its MIDI OUT port but not to its internal synthesizer. The internal synthesizer can be controlled remotely via externally generated messages coming in to the MIDI IN port of the instrument.
All notes off	Emergency: turns off all notes.
Reset all controllers	Returns all controllers to their optimum initial status. For example, such a message would cause a vibrato wheel to be reset to 0 (no vibrato).
Mode select	Selects the MIDI mode.
System common	Sent to all units and all channels; these messages are designed to set sequencers to the proper piece and measure for playback.
Song position pointer (SPP)	SPP addresses a sequence in terms of a 14-bit quantity representing the number of "MIDI beats" that have occurred since the beginning of the song, where one MIDI beat = 1, and a sixteenth note = 6 clock pulses.
Song select	Selects one of 128 song files in a sequencer library.
Tune request	Initiates routines within an analog synthesizer to tune the oscillators. Not needed with digital synthesizers.
End system exclusive	Terminates a system exclusive message (see below).
Quarter frame	Used by instruments that transmit or receive MIDI Time Code (MTC). Each of the eight message variations acts as a timing pulse for the system and defines a unique location in SMPTE timecode. Eight quarter-frame messages completely define the SMPTE time (two each for hours, minutes, seconds, and frames).

(continued)

Table 51.1 (continued)

Channel voice	Addressed to a specific MIDI channel
System real time	Comprises clock messages and start and stop commands used by sequencers and drum machines to control other MIDI devices. Channel information is not transmitted.
MIDI clock	Used as a timing pulse by MIDI sequencers and drum machines. Transmitted 24 times per quarter note.
Start	Generated when a play or start button of a sequencer or drum machine is pushed. When received by a sequencer or drum machine, the sequence or pattern plays from the beginning.
Stop	Generated when the stop button on a sequencer or drum machine is pressed. Halts any sequencer or drum machine receiving it.
Continue	Generated when the continue button is pushed on a sequencer or drum machine. The device receiving it will play from the point where the last stop command was received.
Active sensing	Originally designed to prevent stuck notes that could occur if the MIDI connection were temporarily interrupted between the receipt of a note-on and a note-off message. Active sensing works by sending a message when there is no activity on the MIDI line. If the active sensing message ceases and there is no other activity on the line, then the slave turns off its sound generators to prevent stuck notes. Not often implemented.
System reset	When a device receives this message, it returns to its default settings.
System exclusive	Provided so that a manufacturer can send device-specific data; used to communicate sound parameters and to dump programs into a synthesizer or effects unit.
System exclusive (sysex)	Initiates a system exclusive transfer. This message transmits manufacturer's data that is not covered by other messages. The status byte indicates a sysex message. Next comes the manufacturer's number and following this a set of data bytes, such as the contents of a synthesizer's memory with all its parameter settings. Sysex is used to transmit bulk patch data—parameter settings derived by patch editing.
End of system exclusive	After sysex data has been sent the process ends with a one-byte end of system exclusive message or a reset message.
Device inquiry	Device inquiry transmits "Who are you?" The transmitting device seeks the manufacturer's ID, the instrument ID, and the software revision level of the receiving device.
Device ID	Transmits the requested identification data.

Note: Each shaded row heads a message type (left column) and its definition (right column). Beneath that type heading, the unshaded rows list (left) the name of a message of that type and (right) its description.

mechanism for individual note bending. MPE is described further along in the chapter.

The usual MIDI pitch range begins in the infrasonic octave with key numbers 0 to 12. This octave spans MIDI C0 (8.17 Hz) up to MIDI C1 (16.35 Hz). Key 60 represents MIDI C5 (261.63 Hz), which is MIDI middle C. In many music theory texts, middle C (261.63 Hz) is considered to be C4; thus the MIDI name for octaves is nonstandard. However, not all manufacturers conform to the pitch-naming scheme of MIDI. Some companies call key 60 C3, C4, or C5. The highest key, 127, represents MIDI G10 (12,543.89 Hz).

Most synthesizers let musicians alter the key-to-pitch mapping. In the simplest case, the synthesizer has a global tuning control that lets one shift the range by a logarithmic constant. For example, one could tune the synthesizer so that MIDI A5 (concert pitch) corresponded to 438 Hz or 442 Hz instead of 440 Hz.

In some synthesizers one can change the pitch mapping on a per-key basis, so that instead of responding in equal temperament, the synthesizer responds in a different scale. Unfortunately, some synthesizers limit the retuning to a one-octave span. That is, one can retune the twelve pitches of one octave only; the synthesizer simply repeats that tuning across all octaves in its pitch range. This makes it impossible to implement microtonal scales that include more than twelve notes per octave or that extend beyond an octave.

MIDI's representation of amplitude is encoded as a number from 0 to 127, usually derived from the note's velocity. The term *velocity* refers to the way that a MIDI keyboard detects how hard keys are played. If one presses hard on a key, the key's velocity from top to bottom is fast. MIDI synths generally interpret this to mean high amplitude. Pressing softly on a key, the velocity is slow, corresponding to low amplitude. But a MIDI device can be programmed to interpret the velocity value in whatever way one wants, mapping it to control brightness, for example, or filter bandwidth.

Status and Data Bytes

The stream of MIDI data divides into two types of bytes: *status* bytes and *data* bytes. A status byte begins with a 1 and identifies a particular function, such as note-on, note-off, pitch wheel change, and so on. A data byte begins with a 0 and provides the value associated with the status byte, such as the particular key and channel of a note-on message, how much the pitch wheel has changed, and so on.

For example, a note-on event message consists of three bytes (10010000 010000000 00010010). The first byte is the status. The first four bits (sometimes referred to as a *nibble*) of the status byte specify the function (in this case, note-on), and the last four bits specify the MIDI channel (0000 = channel 1).

Data bytes begin with a 0, leaving the remaining seven bits to carry the actual value of the data. This allows 128 different values (0 to 127), to be expressed in a single data byte. In a note-on message, for example, the first data byte expresses a key number (usually corresponding to pitch). Here the key value is 64, which by convention corresponds to 330 Hz. The remaining byte expresses the key velocity or amplitude.

Channel Messages

MIDI messages fall into two categories: *channel messages* and *system messages*. Channel messages target a specific channel. They are acted upon if the channel number associated with the message corresponds to an active channel of the receiving device. In contrast, system messages are received by all MIDI devices, regardless of the channel to which they are assigned.

Channel voice messages are the most common MIDI messages because they deal with note data. The note-on message, mentioned earlier, is a channel voice message. It transmits the timing and pitch of notes played, and their amplitude. Other channel voice messages communicate gestures such as manipulations of the pitch bend and modulation wheels and volume pedal.

Figure 51.6 depicts an example of music notation and its transcription into MIDI note messages.

Another category of channel voice message concerns *programs*, MIDI's term for a preset or patch. Generally, a *program change message* transmits an integer to a MIDI device that tells it to switch to another program. In a MIDI synthesizer, the message might select a preset such as "37: Bells." In an effects processor, it might select a preset such as "37: Large hall reverberation." The important point here is that the message sends an integer; it is up to the receiving device to interpret it.

System Messages

System common messages convey information such as "song selection" and "song position pointer." Another important category of system common messages are the *system exclusive (sysex)* messages. Sysex messages are reserved by each manufacturer for use with their products. By agreement, each manufacturer must publish an explanation of what its sysex codes do. A typical use of sysex is to transmit patches, envelope data, and other instrument-specific parameters.

System real time messages synchronize drum machines, sequencers, and other rhythm-oriented devices. They include clock messages (emitted at regular intervals) and start and stop commands for drum machines.

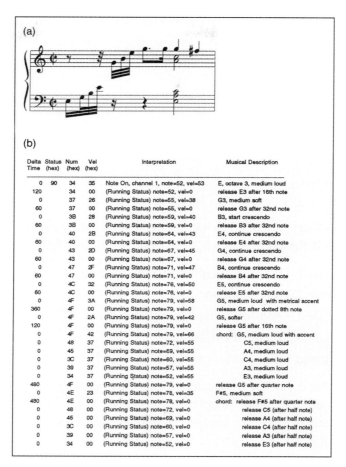

Figure 51.6 Score fragment and corresponding MIDI messages. (a) J. S. Bach: *Toccata* from *Partita VI, Clavierübung,* part 1, first measure. (b) Standard MIDI file corresponding to (a) with a resolution of 480 ticks per quarter note. *Delta time* means number of ticks since preceding event. Hex means hexadecimal coding. That is, each four-bit nibble is indicated by a number or letter 0, 1, 2, . . . 9, A, B, . . . F corresponding to a value from 0 to 15.

Running Status

The distinction between status bytes and data bytes makes possible a programming efficiency called *running status.* Running status trims MIDI data flow by cutting three-byte controller and note messages down to two bytes—a speed-up for controller and note messages. A musical implication of this is that chords sound more precise, because the individual notes (sent one after the other) are received in a shorter time period.

The process works as follows. Once a status byte has been received, the instrument maintains that command status until a different status byte is received. This means that a musician can play a burst of notes with one note-on status byte followed by pairs of data bytes (representing the note number and the velocity, respectively) for each note in a melody. A new status byte is sent only if a new type of command is required. Using this efficiency, software can turn off notes using note-on messages with velocity of zero (i.e., silence), rather than sending more status bytes in the form of note-off messages. Notice the use of running status in figure 51.6b.

MIDI Modes

Each device that sends and receives MIDI data interprets channel data according to the *mode* in which it is operating. The five defined modes are as follows:

Mode 1. Omni-on polyphonic (Omni mode)

Mode 2. Omni-on mono

Mode 3. Omni-off polyphonic (Poly mode)

Mode 4. Omni-off (Multi mode)

General MIDI mode

Most devices let one set the mode by pressing a sequence of buttons or by sending it a mode select message via MIDI. In practice, only modes 3, 4 and General MIDI are implemented today, so we omit descriptions of modes 1 and 2.

Mode 3 Poly

Poly is the default mode of most synthesizers. In Poly mode, different devices can be set to respond to different channels, so each device can act as a part in a multipart score. This is the most flexible mode, since individual channels can be turned on and off.

Poly mode tells each instrument to listen to one channel of information. Within that channel, the slave (or receiver) responds to as many different notes as it can. It is up to the user to specify the particular MIDI channel (1-16) on each of the MIDI devices. This is usually done by pressing a button on a device or selecting a channel number from a menu.

Mode 4 Multi

Multi mode supports multitimbral instruments that can play back more than one preset or program at a time. Each receives data from a different MIDI channel. Usually all available voices in the instrument are placed on consecutive MIDI channels, with the lowest one being the *base channel.* For example, an eight-voice instrument set on base channel 4 would have one voice assigned on each of channels 4, 5, 6, 7, 8, 9, 10, and 11. MIDI guitars use mode 4. Each of the six strings is set to a MIDI channel, and a voice on the receiving synthesizer is assigned to a guitar string timbre. Another application of Multi mode is pitch bend on individual notes in a polyphonic texture. (For an alternative solution to per-note pitch bend, see the description of MIDI Polyphonic Expression further on.)

General MIDI Mode and SoundFonts

The General MIDI (GM) mode, introduced in 1990, provides a standard MIDI setup (MIDI Association 2017). That is, devices equipped for GM respond to MIDI messages according to a standard mapping between channels, patches, and sound samples. The goal is that a sequence created on one MIDI system will be heard more or less the same on another MIDI system. This facilitates sharing of sequences between users (Jungleib 1995).

A GM-compatible device must be sixteen-part multitimbral and allow twenty-four-voice polyphony. The assignment of controllers is also standardized. Specifically, the synthesizer must respond to defined controllers such as velocity, channel pressure, and pitch bend messages as well as control change messages 1 (modulation), 7 (volume), 10 (pan), 11 (expression), 64 (sustain), 121 (reset all notes), and 123 (all notes off). It must also respond to pitch bend sensitivity, fine tuning, and coarse tuning parameters. (See the GM 2 specification for more details.)

GM assigns channels 1–9 and 11–16 to chromatic instrument sounds. Channel 10 is reserved for percussion, which includes forty-seven predefined percussion sounds assigned to different notes.

In addition, all 128 patches in GM are preassigned to specific sound categories based on traditional instruments or classic synthesizer sounds. For example, patch 3 is "Piano (Electric Grand)," patch 19 is "Organ (Rock)," patch 57 is "Trumpet," and so on.

General MIDI is simply a naming scheme and cannot guarantee that two different devices playing, for example, "4 Honky Tonk Piano," will sound identical. The goal of GM is similarity—not equivalence—in timbre. From a commercial standpoint, GM makes it possible to distribute musical arrangements that sound roughly the same on whichever instrument they are played, yet still allow for MIDI-based interaction.

In 1999, a standard called General MIDI 2 (GM 2) was introduced that increased the number of notes to thirty-two, allowed two percussion kits, offered spatial panning, and assigned controllers to parameters such as filter resonance and so on. (MIDI Association 2017). However, few products were offered with GM 2.

SoundFonts

The SoundFont standard was intended to "provide an extensible, portable, universal interchange format for wavetable synthesizer samples and articulation data" (SynthFont 2006). Unlike GM samples, which are cast in stone at the factory, the SoundFont standard creates a way for any musician to distribute a personal sound palette in a sharable format: SoundFont banks. A SoundFont bank can be likened to a custom GM sound set.

SoundFonts were invented in the 1990s era of personal computer sound cards. Although they have been superseded in many cases by the SFZ (.sfz) and Kontakt (.nki, .nkm) sampler formats, they are still supported by some synthesizers. Free or inexpensive SoundFont libraries are available on the Internet. The FluidSynth sound font synthesizer is available for Pd, Max, VLC media player, and the Denemo and MuseScore score editors (Flutists 2019).

In theory, a SoundFont-compatible synthesizer not only plays samples but also applies performance articulations such as an amplitude envelope or a lowpass filter, as well as panning, reverberation, and chorus. The "articulation data" previously mentioned controls these performance parameters and also defines pitch bend and vibrato ranges. In practice, however, few SoundFont synthesizers are fully compatible, so many SoundFonts are nothing more than short mono samples mapped to keys.

To create a sound font, one begins with samples in the .wav file format. The samples are transformed by a SoundFont editor into MIDI-controllable instruments in the .sf2 file format (a variation on the resource interchange file format [RIFF]). These instruments can be triggered by any MIDI note controller or sequencer. For a discussion of other sample formats, refer to chapter 9.

MIDI Control Change Messages

Up to this point we have discussed only one type of MIDI controller, a keyboard that generates note-on and note-off messages. For expressive performance, musicians want to use many types of controllers, such as foot pedals, faders, knobs, touch surfaces, ribbon controllers, modulation and pitch bend wheels, breath controllers, sustain foot switches, and joysticks. (See chapter 40.) Pitch bend wheels have their own category of channel voice messages (table 51.1) The rest of the controllers generate *control change* (CC) messages.

CC messages transmit real-time human performance gestures that shape the sound played by a receiving instrument. These messages can also be created in a DAW editor by drawing in an automation lane (see chapter 42). An example would be hand-drawn panning curves for a synthesizer plug-in.

This section presents a basic overview of MIDI 1.0 CC messages from a user perspective. The official MIDI documents present CC messages in much greater detail than is possible to provide here (MIDI Association 1983, 2019; Guérin 2006). MIDI 2.0, discussed further on, redesigned the controller scheme (Huber 2020).

A controller transmits a new CC message whenever its position changes, as rarely or frequently as the case may be. For example, a fader controlling the amount of reverberation would likely be set to a fixed position. A sustain pedal on-off switch might be tapped on occasional phrase boundaries.

By contrast, when a spring-loaded thumbwheel such as pitch bend is turned, the value is continuously changing, which generates a steady flow of message traffic. Figure 51.7, for example, shows messages sent by a pitch bend thumbwheel controller during one second to one channel.

Table 51.2 shows various categories of controller IDs. Certain controller IDs are predefined by certain manufacturers to affect a specific parameter. These predefined mappings are called the Registered Parameter Numbers

```
Channel 1        Note on at pitch 60 and velocity 107
Channel 1        Pitchbend change 13569
Channel 1        Pitchbend change 10837
Channel 1        Pitchbend change  8737
Channel 1        Pitchbend change  5418
Channel 1        Pitchbend change  3905
Channel 1        Pitchbend change  2393
Channel 1        Pitchbend change   376
Channel 1        Pitchbend change     0
Channel 1        Pitchbend change  1595
Channel 1        Pitchbend change  4410
Channel 1        Pitchbend change  6427
Channel 1        Pitchbend change  7939
Channel 1        Pitchbend change  9535
Channel 1        Pitchbend change 11130
Channel 1        Pitchbend change 13358
Channel 1        Pitchbend change 15375
Channel 1        Pitchbend change 16384
Channel 1        Note off at pitch 60 and velocity 64
```

Figure 51.7   Pitch bend messages generated by a one-semitone bend lasting one second.

Table 51.2 Control changes and mode changes

Control Changes and Mode Changes
Control Number (2nd Byte Value)

Decimal	Binary	Hex	Control Function	Value	Used As
				3rd Byte Value	
0	00000000	00	Bank Select	0–127	MSB
1	00000001	01	Modulation Wheel or Lever	0–127	MSB
2	00000010	02	Breath Controller	0–127	MSB
3	00000011	03	Undefined	0–127	MSB
4	00000100	04	Foot Controller	0–127	MSB
5	00000101	05	Portamento Time	0–127	MSB
6	00000110	06	Data Entry MSB	0–127	MSB
7	00000111	07	Channel Volume (formerly Main Volume)	0–127	MSB
8	00001000	08	Balance	0–127	MSB
9	00001001	09	Undefined	0–127	MSB
10	00001010	0A	Pan	0–127	MSB
11	00001011	0B	Expression Controller	0–127	MSB
12	00001100	0C	Effect Control 1	0–127	MSB
13	00001101	0D	Effect Control 2	0–127	MSB
14	00001110	0E	Undefined	0–127	MSB
15	00001111	0F	Undefined	0–127	MSB
16	00010000	10	General Purpose Controller 1	0–127	MSB
17	00010001	11	General Purpose Controller 2	0–127	MSB
18	00010010	12	General Purpose Controller 3	0–127	MSB
19	00010011	13	General Purpose Controller 4	0–127	MSB
20	00010100	14	Undefined	0–127	MSB
21	00010101	15	Undefined	0–127	MSB
22	00010110	16	Undefined	0–127	MSB
23	00010111	17	Undefined	0–127	MSB
24	00011000	18	Undefined	0–127	MSB
25	00011001	19	Undefined	0–127	MSB
26	00011010	1A	Undefined	0–127	MSB
27	00011011	1B	Undefined	0–127	MSB
28	00011100	1C	Undefined	0–127	MSB
29	00011101	1D	Undefined	0–127	MSB
30	00011110	1E	Undefined	0–127	MSB
31	00011111	1F	Undefined	0–127	MSB
32	00100000	20	LSB for Control 0 (Bank Select)	0–127	LSB

Table 51.2   (continued)

Control Changes and Mode Changes

Control Number (2nd Byte Value)				3rd Byte Value	
Decimal	Binary	Hex	Control Function	Value	Used As
34	00100010	22	LSB for Control 2 (Breath Controller)	0–127	LSB
35	00100011	23	LSB for Control 3 (Undefined)	0–127	LSB
36	00100100	24	LSB for Control 4 (Foot Controller)	0–127	LSB
37	00100101	25	LSB for Control 5 (Portamento Time)	0–127	LSB
38	00100110	26	LSB for Control 6 (Data Entry)	0–127	LSB
39	00100111	27	LSB for Control 7 (Channel Volume, formerly Main Volume)	0–127	LSB
40	00101000	28	LSB for Control 8 (Balance)	0–127	LSB
41	00101001	29	LSB for Control 9 (Undefined)	0–127	LSB
42	00101010	2A	LSB for Control 10 (Pan)	0–127	LSB
43	00101011	2B	LSB for Control 11 (Expression Controller)	0–127	LSB
44	00101100	2C	LSB for Control 12 (Effect control 1)	0–127	LSB
45	00101101	2D	LSB for Control 13 (Effect control 2)	0–127	LSB
46	00101110	2E	LSB for Control 14 (Undefined)	0–127	LSB
47	00101111	2F	LSB for Control 15 (Undefined)	0–127	LSB
48	00110000	30	LSB for Control 16 (General Purpose Controller 1)	0–127	LSB
49	00110001	31	LSB for Control 17 (General Purpose Controller 2)	0–127	LSB
50	00110010	32	LSB for Control 18 (General Purpose Controller 3)	0–127	LSB
51	00110011	33	LSB for Control 19 (General Purpose Controller 4)	0–127	LSB
52	00110100	34	LSB for Control 20 (Undefined)	0–127	LSB
53	00110101	35	LSB for Control 21 (Undefined)	0–127	LSB
54	00110110	36	LSB for Control 22 (Undefined)	0–127	LSB
55	00110111	37	LSB for Control 23 (Undefined)	0–127	LSB
56	00111000	38	LSB for Control 24 (Undefined)	0–127	LSB
57	00111001	39	LSB for Control 25 (Undefined)	0–127	LSB
58	00111010	3A	LSB for Control 26 (Undefined)	0–127	LSB
59	00111011	3B	LSB for Control 27 (Undefined)	0–127	LSB
60	00111100	3C	LSB for Control 28 (Undefined)	0–127	LSB
61	00111101	3D	LSB for Control 29 (Undefined)	0–127	LSB
62	00111110	3E	LSB for Control 30 (Undefined)	0–127	LSB

(continued)

Table 51.2   (continued)

Control Changes and Mode Changes

Control Number (2nd Byte Value)				3rd Byte Value	
Decimal	Binary	Hex	Control Function	Value	Used As
64	01000000	40	Damper Pedal on/off (Sustain)	≤63 off, ≥64 on	—
65	01000001	41	Portamento On/Off	≤63 off, ≥64 on	—
66	01000010	42	Sostenuto On/Off	≤63 off, ≥64 on	—
67	01000011	43	Soft Pedal On/Off	≤63 off, ≥64 on	—
68	01000100	44	Legato Footswitch	≤63 Normal, ≥64 Legato	—
69	01000101	45	Hold 2	≤63 off, ≥64 on	—
70	01000110	46	Sound Controller 1 (default: Sound Variation)	0–127	LSB
71	01000111	47	Sound Controller 2 (default: Timbre/ Harmonic Intensity)	0–127	LSB
72	01001000	48	Sound Controller 3 (default: Release Time)	0–127	LSB
73	01001001	49	Sound Controller 4 (default: Attack Time)	0–127	LSB
74	01001010	4A	Sound Controller 5 (default: Brightness)	0–127	LSB
75	01001011	4B	Sound Controller 6 (default: Decay Time—see MMA RP-021)	0–127	LSB
76	01001100	4C	Sound Controller 7 (default: Vibrato Rate—see MMA RP-021)	0–127	LSB
77	01001101	4D	Sound Controller 8 (default: Vibrato Depth—see MMA RP-021)	0–127	LSB
78	01001110	4E	Sound Controller 9 (default: Vibrato Delay—see MMA RP-021)	0–127	LSB
79	01001111	4F	Sound Controller 10 (default undefined—see MMA RP-021)	0–127	LSB
80	01010000	50	General Purpose Controller 5	0–127	LSB
81	01010001	51	General Purpose Controller 6	0–127	LSB
82	01010010	52	General Purpose Controller 7	0–127	LSB
83	01010011	53	General Purpose Controller 8	0–127	LSB
84	01010100	54	Portamento Control	0–127	LSB
85	01010101	55	Undefined	—	—
86	01010110	56	Undefined	—	—
87	01010111	57	Undefined	—	—
88	01011000	58	High Resolution Velocity Prefix	0–127	LSB

Table 51.2   (continued)

Control Changes and Mode Changes
Control Number (2nd Byte Value)

Decimal	Binary	Hex	Control Function	3rd Byte Value	
				Value	Used As
90	01011010	5A	Undefined	—	—
91	01011011	5B	Effects 1 Depth (default: Reverb Send Level - see MMA RP-023) (formerly External Effects Depth)	0–127	—
92	01011100	5C	Effects 2 Depth (formerly Tremolo Depth)	0–127	—
93	01011101	5D	Effects 3 Depth (default: Chorus Send Level - see MMA RP-023) (formerly Chorus Depth)	0–127	—
94	01011110	5E	Effects 4 Depth (formerly Celeste [Detune] Depth)	0–127	—
95	01011111	5F	Effects 5 Depth (formerly Phaser Depth)	0–127	—
96	01100000	60	Data Increment (Data Entry +1) (see MMA RP-018)	N/A	—
97	01100001	61	Data Decrement (Data Entry -1) (see MMA RP-018)	N/A	—
98	01100010	62	Non-Registered Parameter Number (NRPN) - LSB	0–127	LSB
99	01100011	63	Non-Registered Parameter Number (NRPN) - MSB	0–127	MSB
100	01100100	64	Registered Parameter Number (RPN) - LSB*	0–127	LSB
101	01100101	65	Registered Parameter Number (RPN) - MSB*	0–127	MSB
102	01100110	66	Undefined	—	—
103	01100111	67	Undefined	—	—
104	01101000	68	Undefined	—	—
105	01101001	69	Undefined	—	—
106	01101010	6A	Undefined	—	—
107	01101011	6B	Undefined	—	—
108	01101100	6C	Undefined	—	—
109	01101101	6D	Undefined	—	—
110	01101110	6E	Undefined	—	—
111	01101111	6F	Undefined	—	—
112	01110000	70	Undefined	—	—

(continued)

Table 51.2   (continued)

Control Changes and Mode Changes

Control Number (2nd Byte Value)				3rd Byte Value	
Decimal	Binary	Hex	Control Function	Value	Used As
114	01110010	72	Undefined	—	—
115	01110011	73	Undefined	—	—
116	01110100	74	Undefined	—	—
117	01110101	75	Undefined	—	—
118	01110110	76	Undefined	—	—
119	01110111	77	Undefined	—	—

Note: Controller numbers 120–127 are reserved for Channel Mode Messages, which rather than controlling sound parameters, affect the channel's operating mode. (See also table 51.1.)

120	01111000	78	[Channel Mode Message] All Sound Off	0	—
121	01111001	79	[Channel Mode Message] Reset All Controllers (See MMA RP-015)	0	—
122	01111010	7A	[Channel Mode Message] Local Control On/Off	0 off, 127 on	—
123	01111011	7B	[Channel Mode Message] All Notes Off	0	—
124	01111100	7C	[Channel Mode Message] Omni Mode Off (+ all notes off)	0	—
125	01111101	7D	[Channel Mode Message] Omni Mode On (+ all notes off)	0	—
126	01111110	7E	[Channel Mode Message] Mono Mode On (+ poly off, + all notes off)	Note: This equals the number of channels, or zero if the number of channels equals the number of voices in the receiver.	—
127	01111111	7F	[Channel Mode Message] Poly Mode On (+ mono off, +all notes off)	0	—

Note: A CC message consists of three bytes of information:

1. Controller status/MIDI channel number

2. Controller ID number

3. Controller value

(RPNs). Another group of CCs are the Non-Registered Parameter Numbers (NRPNs). NRPNs are not preassigned and are used for various functions by different manufacturers.

Controller IDs that are commonly implemented include the following:

CC 1 Modulation wheel

CC 4 Foot controller

CC 6 Data entry slider position

CC 7 Channel volume

CC 10 Channel pan

CC 11 Expression pedal

CC 64 Damper pedal (sustain switch)

Mapping Controllers to Instruments and MIDI Learn

Because there are many different possible input devices (see chapter 40) and many MIDI instruments (both software and hardware), the question arises, how are the mappings between controllers and instruments made?

Much depends on the specific software and hardware. Some companies bundle hardware controllers with software that already talks to the controllers: no configuration is required. For example, a prime feature of the Native Instruments Complete Control keyboard is its tight integration with Native Instruments plug-ins and DAWs like Ableton Live and Logic. Other companies offer similar bundles. This is a strong selling point to musicians who do not want to deal with the MIDI controller mapping problem.

With other controllers, it is left to the user to set up mappings. In general, one cannot assume that a given synthesizer will automatically respond to more than the most basic messages: note-on, pitch wheel, mod wheel, and volume.

One maps a controller to an instrument or effect parameter on the instrument or effect itself. For each parameter one wants to control, one might select a CC number from a menu associated with that parameter. Some instruments support MIDI Learn capability. With MIDI Learn (sometimes called MIDI Map) switched on, one selects the parameter one would like to control and then moves a slider or twists a knob to link it to that controller (figure 51.8).

Standard MIDI Files

The *standard MIDI files* (SMF) format was originally designed by David Oppenheim of Opcode Systems. The main use of SMF is the exchange of

Figure 51.8 MIDI Learn. The filter cutoff frequency in Ableton Live is mapped to a slider (top right) by enabling MIDI Learn. With MIDI Learn switched on, the user selected the parameter to be controlled (filter cutoff frequency knob at top left) and moved a slider on the hardware controller. This sets up a mapping.

sequence data created on different programs. SMF files can have the extension .smf or .mid.

An essential difference between SMF and MIDI real-time messages is that the data stored in SMF is *time stamped*. This means that every MIDI message has an associated time or position in the file, specified in *clock ticks* as a binary number between 8 and 32 bits. This number represents the time difference between the current event and the previous event. Time-stamping tells the program reading the data when the MIDI message is to be executed.

SMF files include a *header* and a variable number of tracks. The header indicates one of the following three types of files:

Type 0: A *single track* of MIDI information with possibly several channels of MIDI note data. This saves the entire composition in a single track.

Type 1: A *multitrack* MIDI file keeps the sequencer tracks separate.

Type 2: Data for *pattern-based programs* for storing a number of independent sequences or patterns in a single MIDI file. Type 2 files are also called *drum machine format*. They allow for any number of independent tracks, each with their own time signature and tempo that can change over time. Type 2 files are rarely supported.

Tempo changes or *tempo maps* are embedded within the single track of the Type 0 format. Type 1 files contain several simultaneous tracks that have the same instantaneous tempo and time signature. The tempo map is stored in the first track of the file. It stores the tempo for all subsequent tracks.

In addition to note data, MIDI sequencers also generate what SMF calls *meta-events*. These include specifications for tempo, time signature, key signature, sequence and track names, lyrics, cue points, score markers (rehearsal points), timing resolution, copyright notices, and sequencer-specific information (table 51.3)

Like the rest of the MIDI specification, the MIDI file format was designed for metered and equal-tempered songs, where each track is played by a single instrumental voice or patch.

Table 51.3   Meta-events in a MIDI files

Meta-events	Meta-events are stored in MIDI files. They are used for metadata such as track names, lyrics and cue points. These do not result in MIDI messages being sent but are still useful information. They are also used for control messages when read by a sequencer.
Text event	Annotates the track with arbitrary text.
Copyright notice	Inserts a copyright notice.
Sequence/track name	Names the sequence or track.
Instrument name	Describes the instrument(s) used on this track.
Lyric	Associates lyrics with a sequence.
Marker	Marks a significant point in the sequence (e.g., "Part 1").
End of track	Gives a track a clearly defined length, which is essential if it is looped or concatenated.
Set tempo	Sets tempo in microseconds per quarter note.
Time signature	Describes time signature.
Key signature	Describes key signature, expressed as the number of sharps or flats, and a major/minor flag.
Sequencer-specific meta-event	Supplies internal data. This is the MIDI-file equivalent of the system exclusive message. A manufacturer can incorporate sequencer-specific directives into a MIDI file using this event. For example, Apple's Logic program uses meta-events for various internal functions.

MIDI Timing

Most MIDI-controlled devices (synthesizers, effects units, etc.) operate in the ever-present *now*. Most MIDI messages are asynchronous: when a key is pressed, a message is sent. MIDI devices react. By contrast, hardware sequencers, DAWs, and drum machines are tempo-conscious. The MIDI protocol provides two ways to count time: MIDI clock messages and MIDI time code. The next sections briefly describe these techniques.

MIDI Clock

MIDI clock is a simple protocol used by MIDI devices that have a tempo setting or transport, including synthesizers with arpeggiators, drum machines, and DAWs. A typical application of MIDI clock would be a situation in which the tempo of a software sequencer controls the tempo of a hardware sequencer, or vice versa.

MIDI clock consists of a small set of command messages and one primary clock message: a simple "tick" (a one-byte system common message). The command messages correspond closely to the usual set of transport controls: start, stop, and continue. A locate message called a *song position pointer* (SPP) can be used for the leader to inform a follower that it should start or continue playback from a specific musical time. SPP messages are relatively coarse in time resolution: about one sixteenth note. MIDI clock tick messages do not have any timing or tempo information, they just indicate the passage of musical time. They happen at 24 times per beat.

Since MIDI clock measures time according to musical beats, the rate of timing messages depends on the tempo of the music. Thus MIDI clock is a *relative time* system. A clock message sent at 60 beats per minute occurs half as often as clock messages sent at 120 beats per minute.

MIDI clock can be transmitted over MIDI cables, between two software programs running on the same computer, or over a network connection between two computers. When two or more devices are synchronized using MIDI clock, one of them is always the leader. The leader generates the clock messages, and all the others are followers: they listen and synchronize their playback to match.

MIDI Time Code

Traditional film and video studios count time in a more precise way. They reference events by *absolute time* signals (measured in hours, minutes, seconds, and frames) written by a *SMPTE timecode generator*. Since matching sound to video and film is a common need, *MIDI time code* (MTC) was introduced as a way of converting SMPTE timecode into MIDI messages. MTC generates absolute time signals that synchronize SMPTE devices such as video and audio tape recorders with MIDI devices. Correlating two absolute times is much easier than trying to figure out which sixteenth note in which measure at what tempo corresponds to a given absolute time. Today MTC is seldom used, because audiovisual production can be handled within a single DAW or video editor app such as Adobe Premiere Pro, Apple Final Cut Pro, Avid Media Composer, or the like.

Limitations of MIDI 1.0

The MIDI 1.0 specification is a popular protocol, but it was not designed to solve all problems of intercommunication and representation in music. Anyone who works with MIDI 1.0 should be aware of its shortcomings as well as its capabilities. The shortcomings include bandwidth limitations, device and buffer latency, interconnection limitations, and music representation limitations (Loy 1985b; Moore 1988). Many of these issues are addressed by MIDI Polyphonic Expression and MIDI 2.0, discussed later.

Bandwidth Limitations

MIDI was designed around an inexpensive serial communications technology that was intended to cost around $5 per device to the manufacturer. A parallel connection would have been faster but would have cost more to implement. In 1983, it was thought that greater speed was not worth the added costs (Lehrman and Tully 1993).

As a result, the amount of control data that can be transmitted over a standard MIDI cable is limited to 31,250 bits per second (3,125 10-bit words). This is not fast enough to support performances with many different voices and multiple controllers. Neither does it support control of sound processes on a micro time scale.

By contrast, a standard communications protocol like Ethernet 1000BASE-T, which is built into inexpensive laptop computers, runs at 1 Gbit/s. This is 30,000 times faster than MIDI. Newer protocols are many times faster than this.

MIDI's initial sixteen-channel design limited the number of voices. The number of effective channels was increased with multiline interfaces, USB-MIDI, and DAWs with multiple software instrument plug-ins.

The bandwidth of a MIDI channel can be overwhelmed by a single player if heavy use is made of continuous controllers such as pitch bend and vibrato wheels, foot pedals, and breath controllers (Abbott 1984a; Moore 1988). This can occur because continuous controllers send out a continual stream of messages for as long as they are activated. Even a simple effect such as transmitting pitch bend messages to create a vibrato in a single voice consumes nearly the entire bandwidth of a MIDI channel (Moore 1988).

Data clogging (referred to as "MIDI choke") can also occur in playback of a moderately complex score. A typical cause is too much data occurring on a beat. Gaps and timing errors (manifesting as jerkiness) may be evident. Although in theory MIDI permits sixteen voices per cable, individual voices of a chord do not sound at the same time. This is caused by the serial nature of MIDI messages, in which the notes are sent one after the other.

Device and Buffer Latency

A certain delay in MIDI systems is extraneous to MIDI. Some devices are slow to respond, introducing latency. In older synthesizers this was due to the slowness of the microprocessor, but even in the latest software there are latency issues due to audio buffer sizes (discussed further on).

The response of a single oscillator to a note-on message may take as long as 7 ms (Marans 1991). Eight note-on messages to be played "simultaneously" sent to a multitimbral synthesizer (one oscillator per timbre) may take as long as 21 ms to be decoded. (Ideally it should take 8 ms, the time it takes for MIDI to transmit the eight note-on messages.) The delays increase dramatically when more oscillators per voice are used.

Audio buffer latency remains an issue that can affect modern MIDI systems. If the audio buffer size of a DAW is too large, the computer will not play sound until it has filled the buffer. This can be a problem in playing a software synthesizer using a MIDI controller. A keyboard player might hear a delay of a hundred milliseconds or more between the time a key is pressed and the sound is heard. Thus when recording, it is best to keep buffer sizes as small as possible. When playing back, one can increase the buffer size so that the computer has plenty of time to mix and process all the tracks without glitches and playback errors. Audio buffer sizes can be stipulated in the preferences menu of software synthesizer apps or DAW host.

Interconnection Limitations

The original MIDI interface specified that each direction of communication required a separate cable. This unidirectional bias resulted in a web of cables when several devices were interconnected. Part of the original argument for MIDI in 1983 as against a more sophisticated network like Ethernet was its low cost. The manufacturing cost is low for MIDI hardware in a single device. In practice, however, a traditional MIDI hardware setup with multiple synthesizers often requires a multiport MIDI interface costing hundreds of dollars.

Music Representation Limitations

A fundamental constraint of the MIDI specification is the concept of music embodied in its design. It was conceived for communicating real-time performances of popular songs as played on a musical keyboard. Digital synthesis and processing can take music far beyond this, but not always easily via MIDI.

Part of the problem is MIDI's lack of representation of timbre. By default, MIDI has no explicit control over the parameter envelopes controlling the synthesizer that plays the MIDI note messages. This is one of the reasons for the recognizable "canned" quality of many MIDI compositions in which every note has exactly the same timbre and envelope. To avoid this, one can assign synthesizer parameter envelopes to their own MIDI controller numbers, but this tedious work is rarely done.

MIDI 1.0's concept of pitch is limited. It was originally designed for equal-tempered pitches. It is possible to *bend* (detune) a pitch, but the MIDI pitch bend message is a global operation that applies to all notes on a channel. Tuning is not part of the MIDI specification.

MIDI note messages are a device-independent representation. This makes generic music software easier to develop, but it also means that any MIDI note list is incomplete—with few instructions as to orchestration. The same message sent to two different devices may produce a completely different sound. The channel mechanism, which is MIDI's method of separating individual lines of polyphony, says nothing about what instruments are assigned to those channels. The General MIDI mode has an arbitrary channel-to-instrument map, but it was designed for home entertainment and not for professional musicians. Even if General MIDI could guarantee identical timbres between devices, it would still represent only a tiny fraction of the timbres possible in computer music. SoundFonts (discussed previously) have their own limitations.

MIDI Polyphonic Expression (MPE)

MIDI Polyphonic Expression (MPE) enables per-note control of synthesis parameters. MPE came about with the rise of multidimensional controllers, such

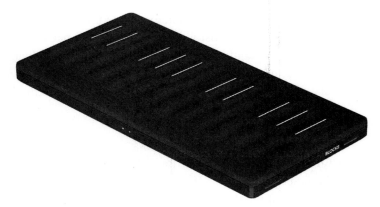

Figure 51.9   Roli Seaboard Block. This MPE keyboard is sensitive to the position of the fingers on the keys and allows individual pitch bend and other expressive gestures.

as the Roli Seaboard Block (figure 51.9). MPE enables multidimensional controllers to manipulate several parameters of every note within MPE-compatible software. An example of such software is the Presonus Studio 1 digital audio workstation, which provides automation lanes for MPE controller editing.

Most MPE controllers implement the following capabilities:

- Continuous pressure—a force exerted on a key continuously, not just aftertouch
- Horizontal movement, mostly used for polyphonic pitch bend or per-note vibrato
- Slide along the entire length of the keyboard from one chord to another
- Vertical movement—sliding a finger up and down a key, for crossfading between two timbres or adding reverberation to a note

In normal MIDI, messages such as pitch bend are applied to all notes being played on a single channel. In MPE, each note is assigned its own channel so that those messages can apply to each note individually. Thus MPE enables communication between expressive MIDI hardware controllers and software (Adam et al. 2015). Examples of MPE controllers include the Roli Seaboard Block, Expression E Touché, Linnstrument, Haken Audio Continuum, and Keith McMillen K-Board. The main tenets of MPE are as follows:

- When possible, every sounding note is temporarily assigned its own MIDI channel. This means pitch bend, aftertouch, and control-change messages can apply to that specific note only.
- MPE defines a message that is sent using Registered Parameter Number (RPN) 6 to establish a range of channels used for sending or receiving data. The message supports the division of the MIDI channel space into several

subspaces called *channel zones* (or just *zones*), allowing multitimbral playing using only one physical MIDI interface.

- When there are more active notes in a zone than available channels, notes share the channel. All notes continue to sound but are no longer uniquely controllable.

- To reduce MIDI traffic, each zone has a dedicated extra channel, called the Master Channel. In a single message it can convey common information to all channels in the zone. This includes Program Change messages, pedal data, and additional pitch bend.

The MPE specification also defines how to handle pitch bend, aftertouch, and control change messages in a uniform way for interoperability. MPE is supported by many digital audio workstations, MIDI controllers, and synthesizers. An example of MPE is Expression E's Arché violin, viola, and cello synthesizers. These combine an MPE software synthesizer with an MPE controller (figure 51.10). The MPE Collection from the same company combines a synthesizer engine with a library of sound presets that respond to any MPE controller.

Once it is recorded, editing MPE data can lead to glitches.

MIDI Programming Languages

MIDI applications can be written in any language. But the programmer who uses a language with libraries that support a MIDI device driver has a major head start. Libraries for the languages Python, Lisp, C++, and Java provide a

Figure 51.10   Playing the Expression E Arché software Cello with a keyboard for note selection (left) and the Touché MPE controller for articulation (right).

range of MIDI services through routines that access a MIDI device driver (De Furia and Scacciaferro 1988; Conger 1988, 1989; Boynton et al. 1986; Rahn 1990; Greenberg 1988; Oracle 2016). Myriad music-specific languages and patchers also support MIDI, including Max, Pure data, Nyquist, SuperCollider, ChucK, Common Music, and Faust among others.

MIDI 2.0

The MIDI 2.0 protocol specification was first published in 2020 (AMEI-MMA 2020b). It was motivated by a desire to enhance gestural expressivity. This mandated an expansion of the capabilities of MIDI to allow greater integration between software and new hardware controllers.

Technical improvements introduced by MIDI 2.0 include the possibility of better timing, bidirectional communication (as opposed to unidirectional in MIDI 1.0), and higher resolution in key velocity, key pressure, channel pressure, pitch bend, and control change. Higher resolution means greater precision, giving controls a "smooth, continuous, 'analog' feel" (MIDI Association 2020).

A stated goal of MIDI 2.0 is to allow precise control of the pitch of every note to better support nonwestern and non-equal-tempered scales, free intonation, note retuning, and time-varying pitch fluctuations.

Crucially, MIDI 2.0 does not stipulate a standard set of new features. What MIDI 2.0 defines is a way for manufacturers to add such features. Clearly, much depends on what manufacturers make with it over time. Thus our description here is limited to the protocol itself.

MIDI 2.0 Protocol

The MIDI 2.0 protocol was designed to be compatible with MIDI 1.0 (AMEI-MMA 2020b). Many basic MIDI 1.0 concepts such as notes and channels remain. Improvements include the following:

- MIDI 2.0 is transport agnostic. That is, MIDI 2.0 messages are not tied to any particular cable or connector.

- MIDI 2.0 packages both MIDI 1.0 and MIDI 2.0 messages in a single common container called *Universal MIDI Packet* (UMP) with improved resolution for several musical parameters.

- In MIDI 1.0, some common operations (e.g. bank select) required multiple MIDI messages. These are easier to process in MIDI 2.0 as they are implemented within a single unified message.

- New messages have been added, including system exclusive and mixed data set messages for transfer of large data sets, including non-MIDI data.

- MIDI 2.0 improves timing reliability. More data can be sent between devices, which lessens the chances of data bottlenecks that might cause delays. In addition, all MIDI messages can be tagged with precise timing information.

Universal MIDI Packet

Whereas MIDI 1.0 was initially tied to a specific hardware implementation, the new UMP message format makes it easier to implement MIDI 2.0 on any digital transport (such as USB or Ethernet). UMP packages both MIDI 1.0 and MIDI 2.0 messages in a single common container. The size of a UMP message can range from 32 to 128 bits. As the last ten entries shown in figure 51.11 indicate, a large space is reserved for new MIDI messages in the future.

The UMP format adds sixteen groups of sixteen channels to MIDI addressing. Therefore, a single connection using UMP carries up to sixteen sets of system messages and up to 256 channels.

UMP also adds a per-packet jitter reduction time-stamp mechanism in which a high-resolution absolute time stamp can be prepended to UMPs to improve timing accuracy.

MT	Packet Size	Description
0x0	32 bits	Utility Messages
0x1	32 bits	System Real Time and System Common Messages (except System Exclusive)
0x2	32 bits	MIDI 1.0 Channel Voice Messages
0x3	64 bits	Data Messages (including System Exclusive)
0x4	64 bits	MIDI 2.0 Channel Voice Messages
0x5	128 bits	Data Messages
0x6	32 bits	Reserved
0x7	32 bits	Reserved
0x8	64 bits	Reserved
0x9	64 bits	Reserved
0xA	64 bits	Reserved
0xB	96 bits	Reserved
0xC	96 bits	Reserved
0xD	128 bits	Reserved
0xE	128 bits	Reserved
0xF	128 bits	Reserved

Figure 51.11   MIDI 2.0 UMP messages. The first four bits specify the message type.

MIDI 2.0 Message Formats

Figure 51.12 shows the MIDI 2.0 format of two message types. The top shows the format of system real time and system common messages, which are 32 bits in length. The bottom shows how channel voice messages such as notes and control changes are contained in 64-bit packets; notice the 32-bit data field.

Figure 51.13 shows a note-on message. The velocity resolution of a note-on message is increased from 128 (7 bits) possible values in MIDI 1.0 to 65,536 (16 bits) in MIDI 2.0. The number of pitch values is still 128. However, new attribute type (8-bit) and attribute (16-bit) fields can be used to specify a microtonal pitch. In particular, note number is interpreted as an index into a pitch attribute for a note-on message. This allows a note to map to any pitch. The next section discusses per-note controllers.

In MIDI 1.0, some operations required multiple MIDI messages; for example, bank and program change, and creating and editing RPNs and NRPNs. MIDI 2.0 replaces RPN and NRPN compound messages with single messages to 16,384 *registered controllers* and 16,384 *assignable controllers* (figure 51.14). Controllers are organized into 128 banks, each bank having 128 controllers. Controllers support data values up to 32 bits in resolution.

Program change messages now incorporate bank select, which simplifies the process of selecting a new voice. A bank valid bit (B) determines whether a bank select is also performed along with a program change (figure 51.15).

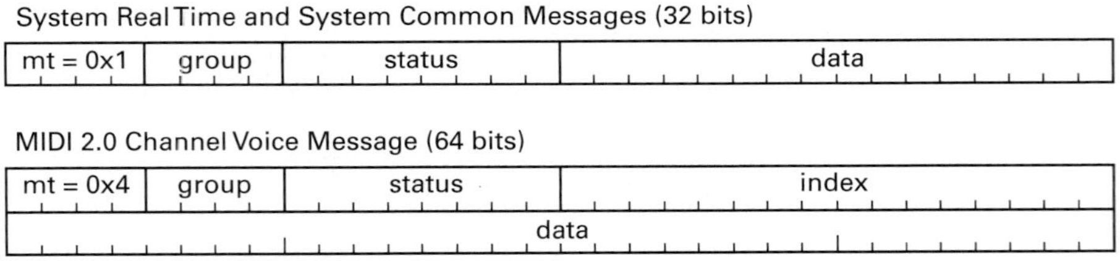

System Real Time and System Common Messages (32 bits)

mt = 0x1	group	status	data

MIDI 2.0 Channel Voice Message (64 bits)

mt = 0x4	group	status	index
data			

Figure 51.12   Format of MIDI 2.0 system real time and system common messages (top). Format of Channel voice messages such as notes and control changes (bottom).

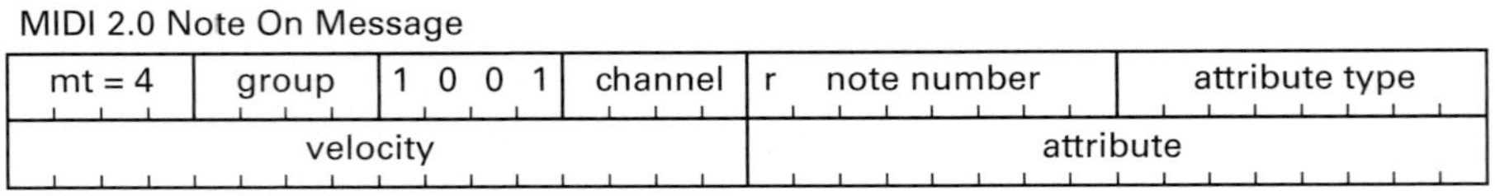

MIDI 2.0 Note On Message

mt = 4	group	1 0 0 1	channel	r	note number	attribute type
velocity				attribute		

Figure 51.13   Format of MIDI 2.0 note-on message.

MIDI 2.0 Registered Controller Message

mt = 4	group	0 0 1 0	channel	r	bank	r	index
data								

MIDI 2.0 Assignable Controller Message

mt = 4	group	0 0 1 1	channel	r	bank	r	index
data								

Figure 51.14   Format of MIDI 2.0 controller messages.

MIDI 2.0 Program Change Message

mt = 4	group	1 1 0 0	channel	reserved	option_flags	B
r program	reserved	r bank msb	r bank lsb		

Figure 51.15   Format of MIDI 2.0 program change message.

Per-Note Controllers

MIDI 2.0 introduces new messages for 256 registered per-note controllers and 256 assignable per-note controllers. Per-note control of envelopes from MIDI, for example, is a new feature. The registered per-note controllers have specific functions. Defined functions include modulation, breath, pitch, volume, balance, pan, expression, sound variation, timbre, release time, attack time, brightness, decay time, vibrato rate, vibrato depth, reverberation level, and chorus level.

The per-note pitch controller is especially significant. Registered per-note controller #3 is defined as Pitch 7.25. The message's 32-bit data field contains

- 7 bits: 128 semitones
- 25 bits: fractional pitch (i.e., fraction of one semitone).

Thus pitch is a 7.25 fixed-point unsigned integer. The 7-bit part shall be interpreted as if it were the pitch implied by the MIDI 1.0 note number in a 12-tone equal tempered scale with A = 440 Hz (note number 69). The 25-bit fractional part is a fraction of one semitone. Support for all 25 bits of fractional pitch resolution is not mandated. However, at least 9 bits is strongly recommended. Pitch bend and per-note pitch bend act as offsets from the pitch set by registered per-note controller #3.

Assignable Per-Note Controllers have no predefined function and are available for any device-specific or application-specific function. For details, refer to AMEI-MMA (2020b).

Jitter Reduction Timestamps

MIDI 2.0 allows devices to run their own timers so that messages can be time-stamped (like OSC, see chapter 52) in order to reduce timing jitter. With *jitter reduction* (JR) *time stamps,* one can mark multiple notes to play with identical timing. Indeed, all MIDI messages can be tagged with precise timing information, including MIDI clock messages.

MIDI Capability Inquiry

In developing MIDI 2.0, backward compatibility with MIDI 1.0 was a basic requirement. To protect backward compatibility in an environment with expanded features, devices need to confirm the capabilities of other connected devices. When two devices are connected to each other, they use MIDI 1.0 to confirm each other's capabilities before using expanded features. If both devices share support for the same expanded MIDI features, they can agree to use those features.

The protocol that protects backward capability is *MIDI Capability Inquiry* or MIDI-CI (AMEI-MMA 2020a). MIDI-CI separates older products from newer products. It provides a mechanism for two MIDI devices to understand what new capabilities are supported. MIDI-CI requires bidirectional communication. Once a MIDI-CI connection is established between devices, query and response messages define what capabilities each device has. MIDI-CI then negotiates to use features that are common between the devices. MIDI-CI provides test mechanisms when enabling new features. If a test fails, then devices fall back to using MIDI 1.0 for that feature.

MIDI-CI includes queries for three areas of expanded MIDI functionality: protocol negotiation, profile configuration, and property exchange (figure 51.16).

Protocol negotiation

Protocol negotiation defines how to decide to use MIDI 2.0 or MIDI 1.0. Devices that do not support MIDI 2.0 can continue to use MIDI 1.0. Once a MIDI 2.0 connection is established, all communication is via 32-bit Universal MIDI packets.

Profile configuration

The goal of *profile configuration* is seamless integration of software and hardware controllers. MIDI-CI allows devices to communicate their capabilities to each other. Devices can use that information to self-configure

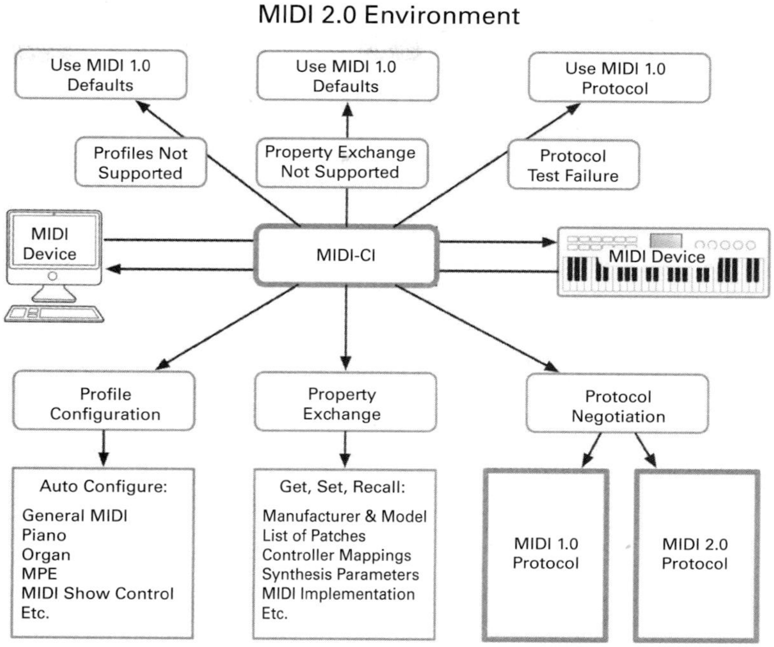

MIDI 2.0 Environment

Figure 51.16   MIDI 2.0 diagram (supplied by the MIDI Association).

their MIDI connections and related settings. Profiles enable intelligent auto-configuration. A profile is a defined set of rules for a how a MIDI receiver must respond to a chosen set of MIDI messages to achieve a particular purpose. For example, a piano profile might specify how a MIDI piano responds to sustain or note velocity, whereas an organ profile might specify an arrangement of drawbars.

Property exchange

Property exchange provides mechanisms to discover, get, and set device properties using MIDI-CI universal system exclusive messages. Property exchange enables devices to automap controllers, choose programs, change state, and provide visual editors to DAWs without prior knowledge of the device or special software. This kind of information was previously handled in the system exclusive messages of MIDI 1.0.

52 *Open Sound Control*

Curtis Roads and Matthew J. Wright

Comparing MIDI with OSC

Motivation for OSC

OSC Is an Open Protocol

OSC Messages and Bundles

Design of Message and Address Schemas

Overview of the OSC Protocol
>   **OSC Packets**
>   **OSC Messages**
>   **OSC Bundles**

A Simple OSC Example Using PureData and Csound

Assessment of OSC

A communications protocol defines the format and order of messages sent between *entities* (programs or devices), as well as actions taken on transmission and receipt of messages. Open Sound Control (OSC) is a communications protocol for sending data from one entity to another. Most musicians will encounter OSC in the context of higher-level languages or apps that handle low-level details.

This chapter presents the basic design philosophy of OSC and gives a simple example using communication between two software entities. For detailed information, refer to the OSC 1.0 specification (Open Sound Control 2021).

OSC was designed by Matthew Wright and Adrian Freed at the University of California, Berkeley's Center for New Music and Audio Technologies (CNMAT) (Wright and Freed 1997; Freed and Schweder 2009). Since its invention, OSC has achieved wide use in interactive music systems, robotics, video performance, distributed music systems, and interprocess communication (Wright 2005). OSC applications include real-time sound and media processing environments (installations), web interactivity tools, software synthesizers, and programming languages. For example, Mark of the Unicorn uses OSC to control their Audio Video Bridging (AVB) interfaces. Another application of OSC is controlling a sequencer such as Ableton Live from a mobile phone. The list of software and languages with support for OSC communication includes Ableton Live, Max, Faust (Fober, Orlarey, and Letz 2011), ChucK, PureData, Processing, Reaper, Stride, SuperCollider, and Csound, among others.

Note that an alternative to OSC is available for users of PureData (see chapter 47). The fast universal digital interface (FUDI) is a simple string-based networking protocol (Puckette 1997).

Comparing MIDI with OSC

To introduce OSC, let us compare it with MIDI (chapter 51), another communications protocol.

MIDI transmits a stream of standardized messages with predefined meanings. The syntax and semantics of MIDI messages are defined in the MIDI specification. MIDI assumes that music consists of notes that are turned on and off. Any program or synthesizer that understands MIDI note-on and note-off can talk to any other MIDI program or synthesizer. This makes it easy to set up a simple MIDI system in a home studio.

By contrast, messages in OSC are not predefined. For every OSC implementation, someone must define what specific messages mean and when those messages are sent.

MIDI provides a set of predefined addresses to which messages can be sent: *channels* and *controller numbers.*

By contrast, OSC implementors design their own address schemas according to the available capabilities. For two entities to work together, someone must configure them to send and receive meaningful messages.

Both MIDI and OSC transmit binary information. MIDI 1.0 handles integer numbers only. (MIDI 2.0 allows *mixed data set messages* that can encapsulate arbitrary-length data sets. It also allows for fractional numbers for specifying microtonal pitches; see chapter 51.)

By contrast, OSC messages can include integers, floating-point numbers, human-readable character strings, and arbitrary-length "blobs" of data.

MIDI hardware connectors include the classic 5-pin MIDI connector and USB.

By contrast, OSC has no hardware specification.

MIDI transmits information at a rate of 31,250 bits per second. The overall bit rate is faster using USB, but for backward compatibility the per-channel rate remains 31.25 kbits/s.

By contrast, OSC operates at speeds ranging to gigabits per second. This is because OSC can operate with a *network transport protocol* that moves the OSC-formatted messages from one entity to another via a network. Most use of OSC is via the internet's *User Datagram Protocol* (UDP). UDP is fast because it does not guarantee delivery of packets, but in practice it is reliable for musical applications on local area networks. For guaranteed delivery, OSC messages can also be sent over *Transmission Control Protocol* (TCP). As it is transport-independent, OSC can also be transmitted over serial connections such as USB, often with a microcontroller, or within a single computer as a means of communicating between or within apps.

According to internet protocol (IP), the end points of communication are called *ports.* Each entity with an IP address has 65,536 possible ports. Many network ports are reserved for predefined or *registered* functions, but other ports are allocated to temporary user processes, such as in OSC communication. Setting up an OSC communication via the internet requires a port number or handle (name) to be stipulated along with the receiver's host name or IP address.

At the hardware level, a classic MIDI 1.0 cable carries unidirectional communication. The sender is an unnamed hardware device with a MIDI OUT port that transmits electrical current down the cable. The receiver is an unnamed hardware device with a MIDI IN port. Changing the destination of MIDI messages requires a MIDI cable carrying those messages to be connected to another hardware device.

MIDI over USB provides more flexible routing. MIDI 2.0 is bidirectional and its Capability Inquiry lets devices identify themselves.

With OSC over a serial port (even a virtual one carried via USB) the situation is the same as MIDI: the sender and receiver are implicitly whatever entity is on each end of the connection. Over Ethernet or the internet, however, sender and receiver are identified (explained further on).

Motivation for OSC

OSC was designed for general-purpose high-speed communication between two hardware or software entities. OSC transmits human-readable parameter names such as /grain-density as well as integers and floating-point numbers.

Of course, an OSC communication grammar must be designed and programmed. Fortunately, support for OSC communication is built into many music systems, obviating the need for low-level coding.

A typical application of OSC is communication between a custom instrument controller and a custom sound synthesis patch for live performance. Indeed, the original motivation for OSC was the need for a high-speed networking protocol allowing a custom synthesizer with dozens of parameters running on one computer to be controlled in real time from another computer running a Max patch. This system had to integrate complex gestural inputs with interactive controllers via Ethernet. It was clear that MIDI's slow bit rate, limit of sixteen channels, simple note model, and lack of a representation for floating-point numbers could not be mapped to this setup.

OSC Is an Open Protocol

Open Sound Control is an open protocol. That is, it has no license requirements, does not require patented algorithms or protected intellectual property, and makes no strong assertions about how the format is to be used in applications (Schmeder, Freed, and Wessel 2010).

Unlike MIDI, which has a standard set of predefined messages that cause specific actions, OSC does not specify messages and actions. OSC has no predefined way to "play a note" or "increase the volume" or do any other specific thing. It is up to each implementation to design its own scheme made out of messages that are meaningful in the specific context of that implementation. This is a powerful feature of the protocol. It allows each implementer to use OSC in a customized way, specialized for a given task.

For example, if Jill writes a granular synthesizer that can receive OSC, Jill can design her own list of the features that can be controlled over OSC, her own names for these features, her own hierarchical arrangement of these names into an address space, her own rules for what arguments need to be provided along with each message, and her own conventions for the units of the parameters. Jill does not have to conform her implementation to someone else's idea of what a synthesizer should be able to do and how the features should be named.

This flexibility has a downside. Unlike the plug-and-play ease of most MIDI setups, OSC communication has to be designed and debugged for each system in which it is used. Jack could write another granular synthesizer with exactly the same parameters as Jill's but name them differently. A remote controller for Jack's program would need to be modified to talk to Jill's.

OSC Messages and Bundles

The OSC 1.0 specification defines a way of arranging sequences of 8-bit bytes to represent data such as numbers and text organized into *messages* and *bundles*, along with an addressing scheme that supports pattern matching and a timetag system (Open Sound Control 2002).

An OSC message consists of an *address* and *arguments*. An OSC message's address specifies what type of message it is; for example, setting the value of a certain parameter or triggering a particular behavior. The address can be any string of letters, numbers, and certain punctuation marks, always starting with a forward slash (/) character. For example, imagine a simple stereo synthesizer that produces only white noise, with the ability to start and stop the noise and to adjust the volume: it might accept only three OSC messages /start, /stop, and /volume.

The forward slash character in an OSC address has the same special meaning that it does in the internet's *Uniform Resource Locator* (URL) and Unix-style file paths: naming specific locations within a hierarchical tree structure. Imagine a stereo version of our white-noise-only synthesizer, with the same three controls but now with separate controls for left and right outputs, for a total of six possible messages. These messages could be /left/start, /left/stop, /left/volume, /right/start, /right/stop, and /right/volume. Figure 52.1 represents these as a hierarchical diagram.

OSC can carry MIDI-style data. For example, people often use MIDI note numbers in OSC. Moreover, devices that output MIDI (keyboards, foot pedals, and fader banks) are easy to incorporate because software tools for converting between MIDI and OSC are available.

Figure 52.1   An OSC message tree.

Design of Message and Address Schemas

Whereas MIDI provides a set of predefined messages, channels, and controller numbers, OSC encourages programmers to design their own communication schemas. Specifically, OSC lets them stipulate their own *address space* and *address schema*. The OSC address space is the set of all the OSC messages that are meaningful for a given sender or receiver. The address schema is an address space plus a specification of what each message means. So, /osc1/p-height is an address space, along with the specification "/p-height controls the pitch." When a receiver gets an OSC message, it dispatches a method or procedure corresponding to each address matching the message's address pattern.

In order that two programs entities, A and B, can talk to one another via OSC, the designer of an OSC communication scheme must do the following:

- Analyze the address schema that A sends.
- Specify exactly what A sends (what are its outputs?).
- Analyze the address schema that B receives.
- Specify exactly what B receives (what are its inputs?) and what it does in response.

A's *output namespace* defines every message that A can send. For example, if A is a potentiometer, it might generate a time series of measurements named /pot, scaled between 0 and 1.0.

Overview of the OSC Protocol

The following sections give a capsule overview of the OSC protocol.

OSC Packets

The basic unit of an OSC transmission is an *OSC packet*. Anything that sends an OSC packet is referred to as an *OSC sender*. Anything that receives an OSC packet is referred to as an *OSC receiver*. The size of an OSC packet is always a multiple of 4 bytes (i.e., 32 bits). The contents of an OSC packet must either be an OSC message or an OSC bundle (see below).

OSC Messages

An OSC message has the following general format:

`<address pattern> <type tag string> <arguments>`

The address pattern is a string that starts with a forward slash /, followed by a message routing or destination. OSC addresses follow a URL or directory tree structure, such as

`/voices/synth1/osc1/pitch`

The receiver's OSC address interpreter incorporates a pattern-matching language. Thus OSC messages can go to more than one destination and wildcard symbols such as ? (any character), * (any sequence of zero or more characters), characters inside brackets ([string] matches any character in the string), and comma-delimited lists of strings inside braces ({string1,string2}) allow a single sent message to match multiple destination address strings.

OSC supports the message argument data types shown in table 52.1.

These are the primary type tags. Refer to the OSC specification for special-purpose type tags.

OSC data use a *big-endian* byte order. In a big-endian system, the most significant value in the sequence is stored at the lowest storage address (i.e.,

Table 52.1   OSC Message Argument Data Types

int32	type tag string = i
float32	type tag string = f
OSC-timetag (64-bit int representing internet Network Time Protocol (NTP) timestamps: seconds and picoseconds since midnight on 1 January 1900)	type tag string = t
OSC-string (ASCII characters followed by a NULL and then padded with 0-to-3 additional NULL characters so that the total length in bytes is a multiple of 4)	type tag string = s
OSC-blob (32-bit byte count followed by that many bytes and then padded with zeros so that the total length in bytes is a multiple of 4)	type tag string = b

first). Big-endian is the most common format in data networking. For this reason, big-endian byte order is also referred to as *network byte order.*

OSC Bundles

An OSC bundle is a *timetag* plus any number of messages or sub-bundles. A timetag implies that there is a message scheduler on the receiving end that ensures that messages execute on time in spite of variable network delays. In typical practice, a bundle fits within a 64 kilobyte UDP packet.

When an OSC packet contains only a single message, the receiver should invoke the corresponding methods immediately. Otherwise a received packet contains a bundle, in which case the bundle's timetag determines when the corresponding methods should be invoked. If the time represented by the timetag is before or equal to the current time, the receiver should invoke the methods immediately (unless the OSC receiver is configured to discard messages that arrive too late). Otherwise the timetag represents a time in the future, and the receiver must store the bundle until the specified time and then invoke the appropriate methods (Schmeder and Freed 2008).

A Simple OSC Example Using PureData and Csound

All the major sound synthesis languages provide OSC support. This enables intercommunication between them. For example, Csound (Boulanger 2000) provides four OSC opcodes:

OSCinit—create a listening process for OSC messages at a stipulated port

OSClisten—listen for OSC messages sent to a predefined address path

OSCsend—send a message to other processes using the OSC protocol

OSCraw—listen for all OSC messages at a stipulated port

The following example is by Andres Cabrera (2010). It consists of a simple PureData (PD) patch to send OSC messages to a Csound instrument. In this case, the graphical interface of PD continuously sets the amplitude of a Csound instrument. (Note: This patch uses some nonstandard OSC external objects. In standard PD one would use oscparse, oscformat, netreceive and netsend objects.)

The PD patch to send messages is shown in figure 52.2. The sendOSC (external) object in the patch transmits OSC messages via the network after it receives a connect message specifying the host name ("localhost" or the same computer) and port number 9999.

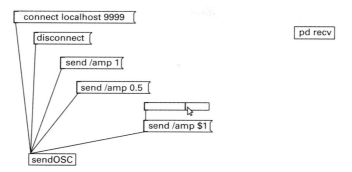

Figure 52.2   A simple PD patch used to send messages to Csound.

In Csound the first thing to do is initialize an OSC network port. This is done using the OSCinit (external) opcode, which starts an OSC listener thread by creating a *handle* or name that can be used to reference the port. The form of an OSCinit statement is

```
<handle>OSCinit <port>
```

Thus the statement

```
gioscl OSCinit 9999
```

sets the handle to giosc1 and the port number to 9999. (In Csound, a variable name starting with gi is a global initialization variable that is accessible by all instruments.)

The OSClisten opcode in the Csound instrument receives OSC messages. OSClisten has the following arguments:

```
kans OSClisten ihandle, idest, itype [, xdata1,
xdata2 . . .]
```

where *kans* is set to 1 if a new message was received, or 0 if not; *ihandle* contains the stipulated handle; *idest* is a string that is the message destination address; and *itype* is a string that indicates the types of the optional arguments that are to be read, which can contain the characters *c, d, f, h, i, and s,* which stand for character, double, float, 64-bit integer, 32-bit integer, and string, respectively. The remaining opcodes specify the Csound variables whose values will be updated by the argument values when this message is received.

The instrument that receives OSC messages is

```
instr 1
kamp init 0
kans OSClisten gioscl, "/amp", "f", kamp
aosc oscil kamp, 440, 1
outs aosc, aosc
endin
```

While this instrument is running it will listen for messages from the PD patch. Notice that the PD messages all send an */amp* floating-point value. Here *kamp* is the output of the OSClisten opcode. The audio oscillator oscil receives its amplitude from the *kamp* variable. The outs opcode sends the audio signal *aosc* to the stereo outputs.

Note that if PD and Csound were running on different machines, the PD patch would need to have an additional message box to connect the Csound machine with an internet address and port number.

For more OSC examples in Python, Csound, and FAUST, refer to Lazzarini (2017).

Assessment of OSC

Proposed by academic researchers, OSC has proven itself an effective means of designing flexible and high-speed communication for interactive performances and installations. Due to its utility in a wide range of applications, the OSC protocol, which was never registered formally by a standards body, is nonetheless supported in many commercial products.

Will OSC ever replace MIDI? This is unlikely. MIDI is supported by an industry consortium. MIDI 2.0 supports a message grammar that is largely unchanged from version 1.0 but supports more channels, more controllers, and finer control.

By contrast, OSC has been embraced by independent instrument builders and many companies for its flexibility in delivering custom solutions to various interactive systems. Refer to Schmeder, Freed, and Wessel (2010) for a guide to best practices for designing an OSC system.

Appendix A
Machine Learning

Bob L. T. Sturm with Curtis Roads

What Is Machine Learning?

How Do Machines Learn from Data?

A Toy Example of ML

Types of Machine Learning Algorithms

Fundamental Problems with Machine Learning

This appendix introduces *machine learning* (ML)–one branch of *artificial intelligence* (AI)–and explains its fundamentals. Research in ML studies how to make computers learn to perform specific tasks by leveraging data. Such methods are useful in a wide range of applications for which data is plentiful, e.g., detecting spam email, locating human faces in images, recognizing speech, and robotics and autonomous vehicles. The field of ML has grown greatly in recent years, in both research and application, due to a confluence of data availability, highly effective learning algorithms, widely accessible programming frameworks and computational resources—not to mention a considerable amount of hyperbole.

Pons (2018) presents a capsule history of neural networks and music. ML has been applied to a broad array of musical tasks. One task is sound synthesis (Donahue, MacAuley, and Puckette 2019; Engel et al. 2017; Engle et al. 2020; chapter 23) including virtual analog modeling (chapter 19). As an example, the composer Holly Herndon has used ML for vocal synthesis in performance with human singers (Herndon 2020).

ML methods are central to many types of analysis used in *music information retrieval*. These include audio source separation (chapter 44), pitch detection (chapter 34), tempo estimation (Böck et al. 2016), music segmentation (Nieto 2015), semantic tagging (Pons et al. 2018), and automatic transcription (chapter 35). ML can be effective in human gesture recognition (chapter 41). An example is Wekinator, a software tool that can translate body gestures for use in interactive systems without coding (Fiebrink and Cook 2010; Fiebrink 2020).

Another application is algorithmic composition (chapter 49). Early work by Todd (1989) generated a monophonic melody. Ji, Luo, and Yang (2020) presents a comprehensive survey of music generation by deep learning methods with over three hundred references. Cella (2020) recounts years of research trying to make sense of applying ML techniques to composition. A typical strategy is *style transfer* (Briot, Hadjeres, and Pachet 2020). Style transfer generates music that maximizes the *content similarity* to some initial score as well as the *style similarity* to a reference style. An example would be rendering a piece by J. S. Bach in the style of Duke Ellington.

What Is Machine Learning?

An *algorithm* specifies which actions a system should perform given some input and its current state. A simple example is provided by a vending machine, at which a person puts in money and specifies the item they want to purchase.

The algorithm used by the system consists of a series of IF-THEN statements. For example, IF the user selects an item that costs Y AND has inserted $X \geq Y$ amount of money (the *input*) AND the item is available AND the machine has enough change to return to the user (the *state*), THEN the machine delivers the item AND returns the difference X-Y (the *output*). Otherwise, IF the item is not available, OR the machine doesn't have enough change, then the machine returns X amount of money.

Such simple logic works well when the inputs and states of a system are limited and rules can be formally specified. However, there are many tasks that cannot be satisfactorily addressed by such an approach. A good example is speech recognition, which has enormous amounts of variation in, for example, the speaker, the acoustic environment, and the microphone. Another example is recognizing human faces in images, which has to be invariant to face orientation, number of people, personal characteristics, clothing, lighting and background, and so on. The complexity of such problems and the variation inherent to the observations cannot be satisfactorily addressed by manually-specified IF-THEN rules.

ML algorithms instead learn how to make predictions about the world from *training data sets*. An ML algorithm processes observations in training data sets many times and tunes its internal machinery to improve its ability to make inferences. For instance, in speech recognition, training data sets consist of audio recordings of spoken words or sentences paired with the text of what is spoken. The ML algorithm learns to connect the acoustic data with the textual representation. In face recognition, training data sets consist of images of people with locations of the faces. The ML algorithm learns what configuration of image pixels makes it similar to a face. For spam detection, training data sets consist of emails labeled "spam" or "not spam." The ML algorithm learns to identify combinations of words that makes an email suspicious.

The performance of ML algorithms can be measured in many ways, for example, error rate or accuracy, precision, false positive rate, and mean squared error. A general rule of thumb is that the more data an ML algorithm has that is representative of the problem domain, the better the performance one should expect from the trained system. The efforts of AI engineers in identifying and programming rules of behavior to address some task are thus devoted to collecting and labeling data and programming the machine to effectively process that data to learn its own rules. Importantly, ML leverages data to such an extent that the design and engineering of ML algorithms can be done without domain-specific expertise. For instance, developing a successful search engine for the WWW does not require engineers to be experts in all subjects appearing on the WWW. Developing a breast cancer screening system does not require engineers to be specialists in endocrinology. Developing speech recognition technology does not require engineers to be fluent in the speech being recognized. The ML algorithm is tasked to become the *expert* in these things through observing data. This is not without many caveats, as discussed further on. The ML engineer requires expertise in programming and access to computational resources and data. For the computer musician interested in exploring ML for music, these requirements are accessible, with many free tools readily available.

How Do Machines Learn from Data?

Suppose we wish to build ML systems that will operate in a world in which multiple kinds of music recordings exist. We want to build these systems to help us address some tasks. One task—let us call it *clustering*—is to organize a collection of music recordings by the kind of music in them. This entails inferring from a given collection of recordings how many different kinds of music there are, and then which recordings exemplify each kind. Another task called *classification* is to infer the kind of music in a given recording. This entails first knowing all the different kinds of music there are in this world and then choosing the appropriate one for a given recording. The first problem is harder than the second because more about the world must be hypothesized, that is, the number of different kinds of music and what distinguishes and identifies them. Both of these problems can be tackled with ML algorithms and data sets.

The classification problem is an example of *supervised learning*. In this case, the ML model learns to identify kinds of music by making predictions for a data set of recordings labeled by human beings. It is in the labeling that the model is trained in a supervised way.

The clustering problem, on the other hand, is an example of *unsupervised learning*. In this case, the ML algorithm infers the number of groups in an unlabeled data set and then criteria to discriminate between each group. There are a variety of objectives one can specify to tune such models, for instance, to reduce the number of clusters and/or to maximize distances between clusters. Supervised and unsupervised learning approaches can also be combined when engineering ML systems.

One major detail yet to be addressed here is how an ML model observes the world. If one wants to build an ML model for making inferences about music in a recording, it needs to somehow *perceive* the music. Let us say each audio recording from the world is 60 seconds and Compact Disc quality (two channels, 44.1 kHz sampling rate, 16-bit quantization). Should the ML model be fed the raw waveform of 5,292,000 16-bit numbers, or should it be given descriptions of the waveform, such as frequency content, rhythmic content, and timbral content? In the latter case, the raw audio is summarized by descriptive *features*. This process is called *feature extraction*: each music recording is summarized by quantities extracted from the waveform. These numerical features are the observations seen by an ML model.

Four simple features that can be computed from audio waveforms are the largest and smallest amplitudes, and the mean and variance of the amplitudes. Another feature could be the number of times the waveform changes polarity over some duration (*zero-crossing rate*). One might downsample a recording, keeping every hundredth sample. Features can be computed from the Fourier transform of an audio signal as well, such as spectral centroid, spectral flux, harmonicity, and pitch. Other features could include tempo estimates, envelope parameters, and so on. Features can describe entire waveforms or short segments (*frames*) of audio, for example, from every 100 ms. The number of possible features that can be extracted from an audio recording is large (Lerch 2012).

Which features should be used? The ML engineer must decide what characteristics are reliably computable and which of those are relevant for the task to be solved. One strategy to address this problem is by using expert knowledge to define features. This process is called *hand-engineering features*. An example of this could be a handwritten digit classifier, where from our knowledge of the shape of handwritten digits, we know that enclosed areas and line endings are structural characteristics that we can use in identification. Another approach is to compute several possible features and then automate the search for the ones that produce the best results. This is called *feature selection*. A more modern approach is to incorporate feature learning into the machine learning pipeline, but this requires large amounts of data.

A general rule of thumb is that the fewer features a ML model uses, the less training data it will need to reach its best possible performance. However, another rule of thumb is that reducing the number of features will generally produce ML models with worse performance. Hence, the ML engineer seeks the smallest number of the best features given the amount of training data available to train an ML model.

A Toy Example of ML

We now look at a specific example of building a ML system for music classification to make the above concepts clearer. Consider in the world there are two kinds of music, one named "kiki" and the other named "bouba," and that we have a data set consisting of two hundred labeled recordings of each. We want to build an ML system that can discriminate between these kinds. This will involve using supervised learning where the ML system learns by observing this labeled collection.

Our first engineering decision relates to how we will use our data set. We want not only to train the model but also to see how its training is proceeding by testing it. We thus need to split our data set into two pieces: one with which our models learn (training data set), and one with which we test it (*testing data set*). One approach is called *hold-out*: a percentage of the dataset is used for exploration and model training, and the rest is used to test the final ML models. Another strategy is *K-fold cross-validation*: the data set is split into K portions. Some portions are used to test, and the others are used to train. In our case, we use hold-out, with 50 percent of the recordings of each type of music selected at random for training and the rest kept separate for testing.

Our next task is to explore the training data set. In our case, with musical recordings, we will start by plotting some examples. The waveforms of two examples are shown in figure A.1. Just by looking at these waveforms some differences between them are apparent. We do not know if these differences hold in general, however. We would have to visually inspect many more examples to draw some possible hypotheses about differences.

Our next engineering decision concerns which features we will extract from each waveform. As a place to start, we will simply compute the zero-crossing rate for 100 ms contiguous audio frames. This means we will cut up the audio waveform into 100 ms segments and for each of those segments count the number of times the waveform changes sign. Figure A.2 shows zero-crossing rates for the two examples shown in figure A.1. Again, we see several differences between them. For instance, the zero-crossing rates extracted from the "kiki" example span a wider range (0–1775) than those extracted from the "bouba" example (0–610).

We compute the zero-crossing rates for all recordings in the training data set in the same way and then visualize these quantities for each class as a *histogram*. Figure A.3 shows the distributions of the zero-crossing rates extracted from the training data as a function of music type. We see from this that it is very rare to observe a 100 ms frame of "bouba" that has more than five hundred zero crossings.

This observation motivates a very simple classification rule for a given music recording: If it has any frames with a zero-crossing rate greater than five hundred, label it "kiki"; otherwise, label it "bouba." Applying this classification rule to the two hundred recordings of the testing data set and

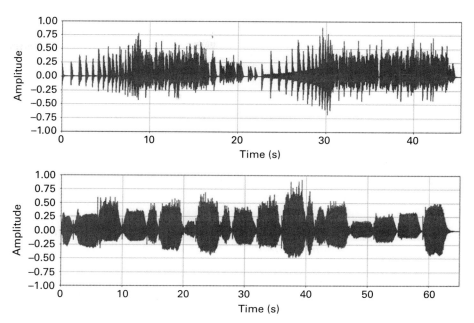

Figure A.1   Time-domain waveforms of two kind of music. Top: "Kiki." Bottom: "Bouba."

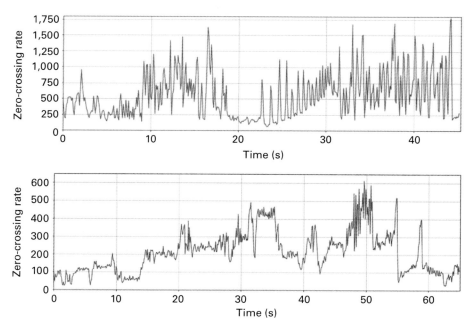

Figure A.2   Zero-crossing rates extracted from the two examples shown in figure A.1. Top: "Kiki," Bottom: "Bouba."

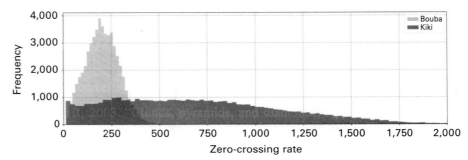

Figure A.3   Histogram of zero-crossing rates extracted from 100 ms frames of the two hundred recordings in the training data set.

tabulating the predicted class of each recording produces the following *confusion table*:

		Predicted	
		Kiki	*Bouba*
True	*Kiki*	100	0
	Bouba	21	79

This table summarizes the classifications resulting from this rule on the testing data. Of the one hundred "bouba" recordings, the system correctly classified 79 and incorrectly classified 21. All one hundred real "kiki" recordings are correctly classified. This basic classifier has done quite well.

If we increase the decision threshold from five hundred to one thousand, we obtain the following confusion table:

		Predicted	
		Kiki	*Bouba*
True	*Kiki*	100	0
	Bouba	0	100

This classifier obtains perfect predictions on the testing data set! This means that as long as this classifier has a full clean recording of music, we can expect its performance to be high. This changes, however, as the problem starts to become more complex.

What if the classifier is able to observe only a portion of a music recording? What if the classifier has to make a decision in real time about the kind of music being heard? We can simulate this by excerpting one second at random from each recording in the training data set, extracting its zero-crossing rates, and applying the same decision criterion using a threshold of one thousand. The results of one simulation using the testing data set are given in the following confusion table:

		Predicted	
		Kiki	*Bouba*
True	*Kiki*	53	47
	Bouba	0	100

The classifier is now correctly labeling all excerpts of "bouba," but it misidentifies almost half the excerpts of "Kiki". This can be explained by looking at the zero-crossing rates extracted from the "kiki" example shown in figure A.2. Most often the zero-crossing rates are below this threshold. We might solve this by decreasing the threshold, but then the classifier would begin to misidentify examples of "bouba."

What if the classifier is working with zero-crossing rates extracted from full recordings of music, but in a noisy environment? We can simulate this by adding white Gaussian noise to a recording and classifying it using the same decision criterion and threshold. At a high signal-to-noise power ratio of 60 dB, the resulting confusion table is

		Predicted	
		Kiki	*Bouba*
True	*Kiki*	100	0
	Bouba	82	18

If we reduce the SNR to 42 dB, then the classifier predicts everything to be "kiki." Clearly, then, the perfect performance of this simple classifier that we measured in ideal conditions is very fragile to a change in the conditions.

At this point the reader might be wondering how this is *machine* learning, because we formed the decision criterion of the classifier by looking at the distributions of our features and choosing a value that can separate the two classes in nonnoisy conditions. What we did manually in one dimension, machine learning does automatically in many dimensions—as long as the engineer can define what it is that makes a good decision criterion (e.g., large separation between classes or low prediction error).

Types of Machine Learning Algorithms

Perhaps the simplest type of supervised machine learning algorithm is the *nearest neighbor* classifier. In this case, the machine assumes that the local neighborhood of each training observation is a reliable indicator of class for any new observation. The engineer needs to define what a neighborhood is—for example, regions closest in Euclidean distance to single training observations. A different flavor is *K-nearest neighbor* classification, in which each neighborhood is defined by considering K training observations. Another kind of supervised machine learning algorithm assumes that observations are distributed according to some global function, the parameters of which are estimated from the training data. An example of this is fitting a line to data in some optimal way, for example, to minimize the mean squared error of prediction. There are many different supervised machine learning algorithms, but they can all be seen as a mixture of making assumptions about local structure and about global structure (Hastie, Tibshirani, and Friedman 2009).

When it comes to unsupervised machine learning, the task shifts to inferring relationships among observations in a data set. Two major classes of unsupervised ML algorithms are clustering and dimensionality reduction. An example of clustering is image segmentation, in which the pixels of a digital image are grouped together on the basis of the object they depict, such as a road, tree, building, or person. A classic clustering algorithm is *K-means*. In this case, the engineer decides there to be K clusters in a data set and the algorithm must work out which observations belong to which clusters. A probabilistic formulation of this is *Gaussian mixture models* (GMM). In the case of dimension reduction, the algorithm seeks to separate important features from noise and variation or to isolate the most critical information of each observation. Two dimension reduction algorithms are *principal component analysis (PCA)* and *multidimensional scaling*. A more recent example is *t-distributed stochastic neighborhood embedding* (tSNE).

Fundamental Problems with Machine Learning

Important fundamental problems with machine learning and its application merit discussion. The first problem to make clear is that discussion of ML and AI presents many pitfalls arising from *suitcase words* that contain many concepts that have to be unpacked. For example, the terms *learning, understanding, knowledge,* and *intelligence* are each pregnant with meanings that must be unpacked when used, especially in communications between engineers building systems and the general public. It is easy to apply these terms haphazardly and thereby unintentionally foster false expectations. As previously demonstrated, machine learning applies predefined statistical machinery tuned on training observations to draw inferences for unseen observations. In the case of nearest neighbor classification, this merely finds the numerically closest observation in the training data and adopts its label. If this mechanical process is called *learning* or *intelligence*, it is only in a shallow, nonhuman sense.

The second point to make clear is that machine learning derives its power from exploiting correlations in data. The statistical decision criteria formed by many machine learning methods ranging over data sets do not arise from understanding cause and effect between covariates in a data set but from correlations of variables. Machine learning is exceptionally powerful in cases in which data is plentiful, but the lack of an understanding of causation can result in major and unanticipated failures. However, there is a growing domain of research in which learning causal attributes in data is the objective. The confusion of correlation and causation can have harmful effects when such algorithms are applied to complex domains such as medical diagnostics, judicial recommendations, and financial matters. Although the application of ML to music data will likely not result in physical harm to people, there are still real harms that can result, for example, music recommendation biases, invalid copyright infringement restrictions, involuntary plagiarism, and banal or inane generative music (Holzapfel, Sturm and Coeckelbergh 2018; Sturm et al. 2019).

The third point to make clear is that however successful a machine learning model appears to be, one cannot conclude that it has learned to solve the task intended by the engineer (Sturm and Wiggins 2021). Training a model using a cleanly labeled data set of recorded music examples is not teaching it about music. Measuring how well a model reproduces the labels of a data set is not measuring its understanding of the concepts underlying the labels. To make this clear with reference to the "kiki-bouba" example above, one is not able to conclude from the perfect accuracy of the classifier that the system has learned about "kiki" music—neither how to identify it nor what distinguishes it from "bouba." What musical knowledge is exemplified by making a decision based on statistics of the zero-crossing rate of a time-domain waveform? We could in fact artificially reduce the zero-crossing rate of any "kiki" example by adding an offset to the entire waveform. The classifier would begin to mislabel all "kiki" examples and thus fail miserably if we didn't preprocess the data to remove such information.

Unfortunately, far too often in the engineering of music informatics system, success is claimed from evidence that provides no support (Sturm and Wiggins 2021). A specific example includes hundreds of papers in music genre recognition work. This is one of the most studied problems in the application of machine learning to music audio data: what is the *genre* of the audio excerpt. Over one hundred research papers have explored this problem with a particular data set of one thousand thirty-second excerpts. Many of the reported accuracies are over 80 percent. A deep analysis of this data set revealed it to have major problems, including repetition of data attributes, such as duplicated recordings or artists. If these structures are taken into consideration in the training and testing of ML models, the resulting accuracies drop precipitously to 40–50 percent. In one case, a ML system was discovered to be making its decisions based on information below 20 Hz (Rodríguez-Algarra, Sturm, and Maruri-Aguilar, 2016). Simply because a model has reproduced a correct answer does not imply that it is caused by using relevant criteria.

Echoing this theme, Cella (2020) described several years of experiences with deep learning techniques applied to composition. As a result of these experiences, he questioned the merit of obtaining good results without gaining useful knowledge. It boils down to the thorny question: what is the musical relevance of the learned features?

References

Abbado, A. 2017. *Visual Music Masters.* Milan: Skira.

Abbott, C. 1984a. "Letters." *IMA Bulletin* 1(3): 4.

Abbott, C. 1984b. "Efficient editing of digital sound on disk." *Journal of the Audio Engineering Society* 32(6): 394–402.

Abdallah, S. A., and M. D. Plumbley. 2006. "Unsupervised analysis of polyphonic music by sparse coding." *IEEE Transactions on Neural Networks* 17(1): 179–196.

Abelson, H., and G. Sussman. 1985. *Structure and Interpretation of Computer Programs.* Cambridge, MA: MIT Press.

Abesser, J., S. Balke, K. Frieler, M. Pfleider, and M. Müller. 2017. "Deep learning for walking bass transcription." In *Proceedings of the Conference on Semantic Audio, Erlangen.* New York: Audio Engineering Society.

Ableton. n.d. "Collision by Ableton." https://www.ableton.com/en/packs/collision/.

Adalbjörnsson, S. I. 2014. "Sparse modeling heuristics for parameter estimation: Applications in statistical signal processing." PhD thesis. Lund University.

Adam, C., G. Bevin, E. Eagan, A. Gaynes, L. Haken, C. Johanson, R. Jones, et al. 2015. *MPE: Proposed Specification.* Revision 1.25a. https://docs.google.com/document/d /1vpjxoPHw82X3xyNvE6_hsDeL86vloNQZC83NHD8edow/edit#heading=h .yll3e1clv7vt.

Adams, R. 1990. "An IC chip set for 20-bit A/D conversion." *Journal of the Audio Engineering Society* 38(6): 440–458.

Adler, A., V. Emiya, M. G. Jafari, M. Elad, R. Gribonval, and M. D. Plumbley. 2012. "Audio inpainting." *IEEE Transactions on Audio, Speech and Language Processing* 20(3): 922–932.

Adrien, J.-M. 1991. "The missing link: Modal synthesis." In *Representations of Musical Signals*, edited by G. De Poli, A. Piccialli, and C. Roads. Cambridge, MA: MIT Press, 269–297.

Adrien, J.-M., and X. Rodet. 1985. "Physical models of instruments, a modular approach, applications to strings." In *Proceedings of the 1985 International Computer Music Conference*, edited by B. Truax. San Francisco: International Computer Music Association, 85–89.

AES. 2009. "AES white paper: best practices in networked audio." *Journal of the Audio Engineering Society* 57(9): 729–741.

AES. 2019. "2018 AES International Conference on Immersive and Interactive Audio (March 2019)." *Journal of the Audio Engineering Society* 67(6): 452–458.

Agon, C. 1998. "OpenMusic: un langage visuel pour la composition musicale assistée par ordinateur." PhD diss. Université Paris. http://recherche.ircam.fr/equipes/repmus/Rapports/CarlosAgon98/index.html.

Agon, C., G. Assayag, M. Laurson, and C. Rueda. 1999. "Computer assisted composition at IRCAM: PatchWork and OpenMusic." *Computer Music Journal* 23(3): 59–72.

Agostini, A., and D. Ghisi. 2015. "A Max library for musical notation and computer-aided composition." *Computer Music Journal* 39(2): 11–27.

Aharon, M., M. Elad, and A. Bruckstein. 2006. "K-SVD: An algorithm for designing of overcomplete dictionaries for sparse representation." *IEEE Transactions on Signal Processing* 54(11): 4311–4322.

Ahrens, J., R. Rabenstein, and S. Spors. 2014. "Sound field synthesis for audio presentation." *Acoustics Today* 10(2): 15–25.

Alary, B., A. Politis, S. Schlecht, and V. Välimäki. 2019. "Directional feedback delay network." *Journal of the Audio Engineering Society* 67(10): 752–762.

Alford, A., S. Northrup, K. Kawamura, K.-W. Chan, and J. Barile. 1999. "Music playing robot." In *Proceedings of the 1999 International Conference on Field and Service Robotics*. World Academy of Science Engineering and Technology, 174–178.

Algomusic. 2013. "JMSL Overview." http://www.algomusic.com/jmsl/index.html.

Allen, J. B., and L. R. Rabiner. 1977. "A unified approach to short-time Fourier analysis and synthesis." *Proceedings of the IEEE* 65: 1558–1564.

Allen, P., and R. Dannenberg. 1990. "Tracking musical beats in real time." In *Proceedings of the 1990 International Computer Music Conference*, edited by S. Arnold and G. Hair. San Francisco: International Computer Music Association, 140–143.

Alles, H. 1980. "Music synthesis using real-time digital techniques." *Proceedings of the IEEE* 68(4): 436–449.

Alles, H., and G. Di Giugno. 1977. "The 4B: a one-card 64-channel digital synthesizer." *Computer Music Journal* 1(4): 7–9. Revised and updated version in C. Roads and J. Strawn, eds. 1985. *Foundations of Computer Music*. Cambridge, MA: MIT Press, 250–256.

Allouis, J.-F. 1979. "The use of high-speed microprocessors for sound synthesis." *Computer Music Journal* 3(1): 14–16. Reprinted in *Foundations of Computer Music*, edited by C. Roads and J. Strawn. 1985. Cambridge, MA: MIT Press, 281–288.

Allouis, J.-F., and J.-Y. Bernier. 1982. "The SYTER project: Sound processor design and software overview." In *Proceedings of the 1982 International Computer Music Conference*, edited by J. Strawn and T. Blum. San Francisco: International Computer Music Association, 232–240.

Alonso, S. 1973. "A computer terminal for music instruction." *Proceedings of the Acoustical Society of America*, 73.

Alonso, S., J. Appleton, and C. Jones. 1977. "A computer music system for every university: The Dartmouth College example." *Creative Computing* 3(2): 57–59.

Amatriain, X., J. Bonada, A. Loscos, J. Arcos, and V. Verfaille. 2003. "Content-based transformations." *Journal of New Music Research* 32(1): 95–114.

AMEI-MMA. 2020a. *MIDI Capability Inquiry (MIDI-CI) Bidirectional Negotiations for MIDI Devices*. https://www.midi.org.

AMEI-MMA. 2020b. *Universal MIDI Packet (UMP) Format and MIDI 2.0 Protocol*. https://www.midi.org.

Ames, C. 1983. "Stylistic automata in *Gradient*." *Computer Music Journal* 7(4): 45–56.

Ames, C. 1987a. "Automated composition in retrospect: 1956–1986." *Leonardo* 20(2): 169–186.

Ames, C. 1987b. "Tutorial on automated composition." In *Proceedings of the 1987 International Computer Music Conference*, edited by J. Beauchamp. San Francisco: International Computer Music Association, 1–8.

Ames, C. 1989a. "The Markov process as a compositional model: A survey and tutorial." *Leonardo* 22(2): 175–188.

Ames, C. 1989b. "Introduction to COMPOSE." Unpublished manuscript.

Amuedo, J. 1984. "Estimation of musical pitch when F[0] is large." In *Proceedings of the 1984 International Computer Music Conference, Paris, France*. San Francisco: International Computer Music Association.

Anders, T., and E. Miranda. 2010. "Constraint application with higher-order programming for modeling music theories." *Computer Music Journal* 34(2): 25–38.

Andersen, K. 1978. "A digital sound synthesizer keyboard." *Computer Music Journal* 2(3): 16–23.

Anderson, A. 2017. Wave Terrain Synthesizer. https://www.youtube.com/watch?v=OcYsbG8-z5M.

Anderson, A. 2018. WaveTerrainSynth. https://github.com/aaronaanderson.

Anderson, A. 2020. Personal communication.

Andreatta, M. 2009. "Calcul algébrique et calcul catégoriel en musique: Aspects théoriques et informatique." In *Le Calcul de la Musique: Composition Modèles et Outils*, edited by L. Pottier. Saint-Ètienne: Publications de l'Université de Saint-Ètienne, 429–477.

Applied Acoustic Systems. 2007. *Tassman User Manual.* Montréal: Applied Acoustic Systems.

Arfib, D. 1979. "Digital synthesis of complex spectra by means of multiplication of non-linear distorted sine waves." *Journal of the Audio Engineering Society* 27(10): 757–779.

Arfib, D. 1991. "Analysis, transformation, and resynthesis of musical sounds with the help of a time-frequency representation." In *Representations of Musical Signals*, edited by G. De Poli, A. Piccialli, and C. Roads. Cambridge, MA: MIT Press, 87–118.

Arfib, D., J.-M. Couturier, and L. Kessous. 2005. "Expressiveness and digital musical instrument design." *Journal of New Music Research* 34(1): 125–136.

Arfib, D., and N. Delprat. 1992. "Sound Mutations, a program to transform musical sounds." In *Proceedings of the 1992 International Computer Music Conference*, edited by A. Strange. San Francisco: International Computer Music Association, 442–443.

Arfib, D., F. Keiler, U. Zölzer, and V. Verfaille. 2011a. "Source-filter processing." In *DAFX: Digital Audio Effects*, 2nd ed., edited by U. Zölzer. Chichester, UK: John Wiley & Sons, 279–320.

Arfib, D., F. Keiler, U. Zölzer, V. Verfaille, and J. Bonada. 2011b. "Time-frequency processing." In *DAFX: Digital Audio Effects*, 2nd ed., edited by U. Zölzer. Chichester, UK: John Wiley & Sons, 219–278.

Ariza, C. 2005. "An open design for computer-aided algorithmic composition." PhD diss. New York University. Boca Raton, FL: Dissertation.com.

Ariza, C. 2007. "algorithmic.net: A Lexicon of Systems and Research in Computer-Aided Algorithmic Music Composition." http://www.flexatone.net.

Ariza, C. 2009. "The interrogator as critic: The Turing test and the evaluation of generative music systems." *Computer Music Journal* 33(2): 48–70.

Arnardottir, S., J. Abel, and J. Smith. 2008. "A digital model of the Echoplex tape delay." In *Proceedings of the 125th Audio Engineering Society Convention,* paper 7649. New York: Audio Engineering Society.

Aronson, I., and L. Tsimring. 2009. *Granular Patterns.* Oxford: Oxford University Press.

Arp. 1972. *Owner's Manual: The Arp Synthesizer Series 2500.* Needham, MA: Arp.

Asanovíc, K., R. Bodik, B. Catanzaro, J. Gebis, P. Husbands, K. Keutzer, D. Patterson, et al. 2006. *The Landscape of Parallel Computing Research: A View from Berkeley.* Technical Report No. UCB/EECS-2006–183. Electrical Engineering and Computer Sciences. Berkeley: University of California.

Ashour, G., B. Brackenridge, O. Tirosh, M. Kent, and G. Knapen. 1999. *Universal Serial Bus Device Class Definition for MIDI Devices.* https://www.midi.org/specifications/midi-transports-specifications/usb.

Ashton, A. 1971. "Electronics, music, and computers." PhD. diss. University of Utah, Computer Science Department.

Assayag, G., C. Rueda, M. Laurson, C. Agon, and O. Delerue. 1999. "Computer-assisted composition at IRCAM: From PatchWork to OpenMusic." *Computer Music Journal* 23(3): 59–72.

Asta, V., A. Chauveau, G. Di Giugno, and J. Kott. 1980. "The 4X: A real-time digital synthesis system." *Automazione e Strumentazione* 28(2): 119–133.

Atal, B. S. 2006. "The history of linear prediction." *IEEE Signal Processing Magazine* 23(2): 154–161.

Atal, B., and S. Hanauer. 1971. "Speech analysis and synthesis by linear prediction of the speech wave." *Journal of the Acoustical Society of America* 50(2): 637–655.

Atherton, J., and G. Wang. 2018. "Chunity: Integrated audiovisual programming in Unity." *Proceedings of the New Interfaces for Musical Expression Conference.* n.p.: New Interfaces for Musical Expression. https://chuck.stanford.edu/chunity.

Aucouturier, J.-J., and F. Pachet. 2006. "Jamming with plunderphonics: Interactive concatenative synthesis of music." *Journal of New Music Research* 32(1): 35–50.

Audio Engineering Society. 2008. "AES recommended practice for professional digital audio–Preferred sampling frequencies for applications employing pulse-code modulation." New York: Audio Engineering Society.

Austin, L. 1992. "An interview with John Cage and Lejaren Hiller." *Computer Music Journal* 16(4): 15–29. Reprinted from *Source: Music of the Avant-Garde* 2, no. 4 (1968), 11–19.

Avanzini, F., and R. Marogna. 2010. "A modular physically based approach to the sound synthesis of membrane percussion instruments." *IEEE Transactions on Audio, Speech, and Language Processing* 18(4): 891–902.

Avizienis, R., A. Freed, P. Kassakian, and D. Wessel. 2006. "A compact 120 independent element spherical loudspeaker array with programmable radiation patterns." In *Proceedings of the Audio Engineering Society 120th Convention*, paper no. 6783. New York: Audio Engineering Society.

Ayers, L., and A. Horner. 1999. "Modeling the Woodstock gamelan for synthesis." *Journal of the Audio Engineering Society* 47(10): 813–823.

Baalman, M. 2008. "On wave field synthesis and electro-acoustic music, with a particular focus on the reproduction of arbitrarily shaped sound sources." PhD diss. Technische Universitaet Berlin.

Babbitt, M. 1960. "Twelve-tone invariants as compositional determinants." *Musical Quarterly* 46: 246–259. Reprinted in *Problems in Modern Music*, edited by P. Lang, 1962. New York: Norton, 108–121.

Babbitt, M. 1961. "Set structure as a compositional determinant." *Journal of Music Theory* 5(2): 72–94. Reprinted in *Perspectives on Contemporary Music Theory*, edited by B. Boretz and E. Cone, 1972. New York: Norton, 129–147.

Babbitt, M. 1964. "An introduction to the RCA synthesizer." *Journal of Music Theory* 8(2): 251.

Bača, T., J. Oberholtzer, J. Treviño, and V. Adán. 2015. "Abjad: An Open-Software System For Formalized Score Control." In *Proceedings of the First International Conference on Technologies for Music Notation and Representation*. https://www.tenor-conference.org.

Backhaus, J. 1932. "Über die Bedeutung der Ausgleichsvorgänge in der Akustik." *Zeitschrift für technische Physik* 13(1): 31–46.

Backus, J. 1977. *The Acoustical Foundations of Music*. 2nd ed. New York: Norton.

Bader, R. 2005. *Computational Mechanics of the Classical Guitar*. Berlin: Springer.

Bader, R., ed. 2018. *Handbook of Systematic Musicology*. Cham, Switzerland: Springer.

Baffioni, C., F. Guerra, and L. T. Lalli. 1984. "The theory of stochastic processes and dynamic systems as a basis for models of musical structures." In *Musical Grammars and Computer Analysis*, edited by M. Baroni and L. Callegari. Florence: Leo Olschki Editore, 317–324.

Baggi, D. 1991. "Neurswing: An intelligent workbench for an investigation of swing in jazz." *IEEE Computer* 24(7): 60–64.

Baisnée, P.-F., J.-B. Barrière, M.-A. Dalbavie, J. Duthen, M. Lindberg, Y. Potard, and K. Saariaho. 1988. "Esquisse: A compositional environment." In *Proceedings of the 1988 International Computer Music Conference*, edited by C. Lischka and J. Fritsch. San Francisco: International Computer Music Association, and Cologne: Feedback Papers, 108–118.

Baker, R. 1963. *MUSICOMP: MUsic Simulator-Interpreter for COMpositional Procedures for the IBM 7090 Electronic Digital Computer*. Technical Report Number 9. Urbana: University of Illinois Experimental Music Studio.

Baldan, S., S. Monache, and D. Rocchesso. 2017. "The Sound Design Toolkit." *SoftwareX* 6: 255–260.

Ban, B., S. Zambon, and F. Fontana. 2010. "A modal-based real-time piano synthesizer." *IEEE Transactions on Audio, Speech, and Language Processing* 18(4): 809–821.

Banger, C., and B. Pennycook. 1983. "GCOMP: graphics control of mixing and processing." *Computer Music Journal* 7(4): 33–39.

Bank, B. 2006. "Physics-based sound synthesis of string instruments including geometric nonlinearities." PhD diss. Department of Measurement and Information Systems. Budapest University of Technology and Economics.

Bank, B., and J. Chabassier. 2019. "Model-based digital pianos." *IEEE Signal Processing Magazine* 36(1): 103–114.

Barbaud, P. 1966. *Initiation à la musique algorithmique.* Paris: Dunod.

Barbaud, P. 1968. *La musique, discipline scientifique.* Paris: Dunod.

Barbosa, A. 2008. *Displaced Soundscapes: Computer Supported Cooperative Work for Music Applications.* Saarbrucken: VDM.

Barbour, E. 1998. "The cool sound of tubes." *IEEE Spectrum* 35(8): 24–35.

Barlow, C. 1980. "Bus journey to parametron." *Feedback Papers*, 21–23.

Barlow, C. 1986. "Two essays on theory." *Computer Music Journal* 11(1): 44–60.

Barlow, C. 1989. Personal communication about the MIDIDESK environment.

Barlow, C. 2001. *AUTOBUSK: A Real-Time Pitch and Rhythm Generator.* Report number 44. University of Mainz, Musikinformatik & Medientechnik.

Barlow, C. 2012. *On Musiquantics.* Report number 51. University of Mainz, Musikinformatik and Medientechnik.

Baroni, M., R. Brunetti, L. Callegari, and C. Jacobini. 1984. "A grammar for melody: relationships between melody and harmony." In *Musical Grammars and Computer Analysis*, edited by M. Baroni and L. Callegari. Florence: Leo Olschki Editore, 201–218.

Barrett, G., and M. Winter. 2010. "LiveScore: Real-Time Notation in the Music of Harris Wulfson." *Contemporary Music Review* 29(1): 55–62.

Barrett, N. 2002. "Spatio-musical composition strategies." *Organised Sound* 7(3): 313–323.

Barrett, N. 2016. "A musical journey towards permanent high-density loudspeaker arrays." *Computer Music Journal* 40(4): 35–46.

Barrett, N., and M. Crispino. 2018. "The impact of 3-D sound spatialisation on listeners' understanding of human agency in acousmatic music." *Journal of New Music Research* 47(5): 1–17.

Barrière, J.-B. 1991. *Le timbre, métaphore pour la composition.* Paris: IRCAM and Cristian Bourgeois.

Barrière, J.-B., F. Iovino, and M. Laurson. 1991. "A new CHANT synthesizer in C and its control environment in Patchwork." In *Proceedings of the 1991 International Computer Music Conference*, edited by B. Alphonce and B. Pennycook. San Francisco: International Computer Music Association, 11–14.

Barrière, J.-B., Y. Potard, and P. F. Baisnée. 1985. "Models of continuity between synthesis and processing for the elaboration and control of timbre structure." In *Proceedings of the 1985 International Computer Music Conference*, edited by B. Truax. San Francisco: International Computer Music Association, 193–198.

Bartlett, M. 1979. "A microcomputer-controlled synthesis system for live performance." *Computer Music Journal* 3(1): 25–37. Revised and updated version in *Foundations of Computer Music*, edited by C. Roads and J. Strawn, 1985. Cambridge, MA: MIT Press, 539–550.

Baruzzi, G., P. Grossi, and M. Milani. 1975. *Musical Studies: Summary of Activity from 1969–1975*. Technical report 102. Pisa: Consiglio Nazionale delle Ricerche (CNUCE).

Bascou, C., and L. Pottier. 2005. "New sound decomposition method applied to granular synthesis." In *Proceedings of the 2005 International Computer Music Conference*. San Francisco: International Computer Music Association, 115–118.

Bass, S., and T. Goeddel. 1981. "The efficient digital implementation of subtractive music synthesis." *IEEE Micro* 1(3): 24–37.

Bastiaans, M. 1980. "Gabor's expansion of a signal into Gaussian elementary signals." *Proceedings of the IEEE* 68: 538–539.

Bastiaans, M. 1985. "On the sliding-window representation of signals." *IEEE Transactions on Acoustics, Speech, and Signal Processing* ASSP-33(4): 868–873.

Bastien, P. 2003. "Pitch shifting and voice transformation techniques." Victoria, BC: TC-Helicon Vocal Technologies.

Basu, S., I. Simon, D. Salesin, M. Agrawala, A. Sherwani, and C. Gibson. 2006. "Creating music via concatenative synthesis." U.S. Patent 7,737,354. Washington: US Patent Office.

Bate, J. 1990. "The effect of modulator phase on timbres in FM synthesis." *Computer Music Journal* 14(3): 38–45.

Battier, M. 1981. "Les tendances récentes des musiques electroacoustiques et l'environment informatique." Doctoral diss. Université Paris X.

Battier, M., ed. 2015. *TENOR 15: First International Conference on Technologies for Music Notation and Representation*. https://www.tenor-conference.org.

Bayle, F. 1989. "La musique acousmatique ou l'art des sons projetés." Paris: Encyclopedia Universalis.

Bayle, F. 1993. *Musique Acousmatique.* Paris: Institut National de l'Audiovisuel/ Groupe de Recherches Musicales et Buchet/Chastel.

Beauchamp, J. 1969. "A computer system for time-variant harmonic analysis and synthesis of musical tones." In *Music by Computers*, edited by H. von Foerster and J. Beauchamp. New York: Wiley.

Beauchamp, J. 1975. "Analysis and synthesis of cornet tones using nonlinear interharmonic relationships." *Journal of the Audio Engineering Society* 23(10): 718–795.

Beauchamp, J. 1979. "Brass-tone synthesis by spectrum evolution matching with nonlinear functions." *Computer Music Journal* 3(2): 35–43. Revised and updated version in *Foundations of Computer Music,* edited by C. Roads and J. Strawn, 1985. Cambridge, MA: MIT Press, 95–113.

Beauchamp, J. 1981. "Data reduction and resynthesis of connected solo passages using frequency, amplitude, and 'brightness' detection and the nonlinear synthesis technique." In *Proceedings of the 1981 International Computer Music Conference*, edited by San Francisco: International Computer Music Association, 316–323.

Beauchamp, J. 1992a. "Introduction to Music 4C (M4C)." Urbana-Champaign: Computer Music Project, School of Music, University of Illinois.

Beauchamp, J. 1992b. "Will the real FM equation please stand up?" Letters. *Computer Music Journal* 16(4): 6–7.

Beauchamp, J. 1993. "Unix workstation software for analysis, graphics, modification, and synthesis of musical sounds." Unpublished manuscript.

Beauchamp, J., and S. Aurenz. 1985. "New computer music facilities at the University of Illinois." In *Proceedings of the 1985 International Computer Music Conference*, edited by B. Truax. San Francisco: International Computer Music Association, 407–414.

Beauchamp, J., and A. Horner. 1992. "Extended nonlinear waveshaping analysis/ synthesis technique." In *Proceedings of the 1992 International Computer Music Conference*, edited by A. Strange. San Francisco: International Computer Music Association, 2–5.

Beauchamp, J., R. Maher, and R. Brown. 1993. "Detection of musical pitch from recorded solo performances." Unpublished manuscript.

Beeckman, I. (1604–1634) 1953. *Journal tenu par Isaac Beeckman de 1604 à 1634.* Four volumes. Edited by C. de Waard. The Hague: Martinus Nijhoff.

Begault, D. 1991. "Challenges to successful implementation of 3-D sound." *Journal of the Audio Engineering Society* 39(11): 864–870.

Beigel, M. 1979. "A digital 'phase shifter' for musical applications using the Bell Labs (Alles-Fischer) digital filter module." *Journal of the Audio Engineering Society* 27(9): 673–676.

Bel, B. 1992. "Music structures: interleaving the temporal and hierarchical aspects in music." In *Understanding Music with AI*, edited by M. Balaban, K. Ebcioglu, and O. Laske. Cambridge, MA and Menlo Park, CA: MIT Press and AAAI Press, 110–139.

Bel, B., and J. Kippen. 1992. "Bol processor grammars." In *Understanding Music with AI*, edited by M. Balaban, K. Ebcioglu, and O. Laske. Cambridge, MA and Menlo Park, CA: MIT Press and AAAI Press, 366–401.

Bellini, P., I. Bruno, and P. Nesi. 2007. "Assessing optical music recognition tools." *Computer Music Journal* 31(1): 63–93.

Bello, J., L. Duadet, S. Abdullas, C. Duxbury, M. Davies, and M. Sandler. 2005. "A tutorial on onset detection." *IEEE Transactions on Speech and Audio Processing* 13(5): 1035–1047.

Beltrán, J., and F. Beltrán. 2002. "MATLAB implementation of reverberation algorithms." *Journal of New Music Research* 31(2): 153–161.

Bemman, B., and D. Meredith. 2018. "Generating new musical works in the style of Milton Babbitt." *Computer Music Journal* 42(1): 60–79.

Benade, A. 1960. "The physics of wood winds." Reprinted in *The Physics of Music*, edited by C. M. Hutchins, 1978. San Francisco: Freeman, 34–43.

Benade, A. 1990. *Fundamentals of Musical Acoustics*. New York: Dover Publications. Originally published 1976.

Bencina, R. 2011. "Real-time audio programming 101: Time waits for nothing." http://www.rossbencina.com/code/real-time-audio-programming-101-time-waits-for-nothing.

Ben Daniel, M. 1983. "Automated transcription of music." BS thesis. MIT, Department of Electrical Engineering and Computer Science.

Benedict, R. 1976. *Electronics for Scientists and Engineers*. Englewood Cliffs, NJ: Prentice-Hall.

Benetos, E., S. Dixon, Z. Duan, and S. Ewart. 2019. "Automatic music transcription: An overview." *IEEE Signal Processing Magazine* 36(1): 20–30.

Benjamin, E., R. Lee, and A. Heller. 2006. "Localization in horizontal-only ambisonic systems." In *Proceedings of the 121st Convention of the Audio Engineering Society*. New York: Audio Engineering Society. http://www.ai.sri.com/ajh/ambisonics/BLaH1.pdf.

Bennett, G. 1981. "Singing synthesis in electronic music." In *Research Aspects of Singing*, edited by J. Sundberg. Publication 33. Stockholm: Royal Swedish Academy of Music, 34–50.

Bennett, G., and X. Rodet. 1989. "Synthesis of the singing voice." In *Current Directions in Computer Music Research*, edited by M. Mathews and J. Pierce. Cambridge, MA: MIT Press, 19–44.

Benson, D. 2007. *Music: A Mathematical Offering.* Cambridge: Cambridge University Press.

Beranek, L. 1949. *Acoustic Measurements.* New York: John Wiley & Sons.

Berdahl, E., and A. Kontogeorgakopoulos. 2013. "The FireFader: Simple, open-source, and reconfigurable haptic force-feedback for musicians." *Computer Music Journal* 37(1): 23–34.

Berg, H. 2019. *Henning Berg's Tango².* http://www.henning-berg.de.

Berg, P. 1975. "ASP—Automated synthesis program." Utrecht, Netherlands: Institute of Sonology.

Berg, P. 1978a. "PILE2—A description of the language." Utrecht, Netherlands: Institute of Sonology.

Berg, P. 1978b. *A User's Manual for SSP.* Utrecht, Netherlands: Institute of Sonology.

Berg, P. 1979. "PILE–A language for sound synthesis." *Computer Music Journal* 3(1): 30–41. Revised and updated version in *Foundations of Computer Music*, edited by C. Roads and J. Strawn, 1985. Cambridge, MA: MIT Press, 160–190.

Berg, P. 2009. "Composing sound structures with rules." *Contemporary Music Review* 28(1): 75–87.

Berg, J. 2016. "Tango²: Software for computer-human improvisation." In *Proceedings of 2016 New Interfaces for Musical Expression (NIME) Conference.* n.p.: New Interfaces for Music Expression. https://www.nime.org.

Berio, L. 2006. *Remembering the Future.* Cambridge, MA: Harvard University Press.

Berkhout, A. J. 1988. "A holographic approach to acoustic control." *Journal of the Audio Engineering Society* 36: 977–995.

Berkhout, A. J., D. de Vries, P. Vogel. 1993. "Acoustic control by wave field synthesis." *Journal of the Acoustical Society of America* 93(5): 2764–2779.

Berlioz, H., and R. Strauss. 1948. *Treatise on Orchestration.* New York: Edwin Kalmus, 416–417.

Bernardes, G. 2014. "Composing music by selection: Content-based algorithmic-assisted audio composition." PhD diss. Faculty of Engineering, University of Porto.

Bernardi, A., G.-P. Bugna, and G. De Poli. 1992. "Analysis of musical signals with chaos theory." In *Proceedings of the International Workshop on Models and Representations of Musical Signals*, edited by A. Piccialli. Naples: Università di Napoli Federico II, Dipartmento di Scienze Fisiche.

Bernardini, N. 1986. "Live electronics." In *Nuova Atlantide*, edited by R. Doati and A. Vidolin. Venice: La Biennale di Venezia, 61–77.

Bernardini, N., and P. Otto. 1989. "TRAILS: an interactive system for sound location." In *Proceedings of the 1989 International Computer Music Conference*, edited by T. Wells and D. Butler. San Francisco: International Computer Music Association, 29–33.

Berndt, A., S. Waloschek, and A. Hadjakos. 2016. "Hand gestures in music production." In *Proceedings of the 2016 International Computer Music Conference.* San Francisco: International Computer Music Association, 448–453.

Bernsee, S. 1999. "Time stretching and pitch shifting of audio signals–An overview." http://blogs.zynaptiq.com/bernsee/time-pitch-overview.

Bernstein, A., and E. D. Cooper. 1976. "The piecewise-linear technique of electronic music synthesis." *Journal of the Audio Engineering Society* 24(7/8): 446–454.

Bernstein, L. 1976. *The Unanswered Question.* Cambridge, MA: Harvard University Press.

Bertini, G., and P. Carossi. 1991. "Light baton: A system for conducting computer music performances." In *Proceedings of the International Workshop on Man-Machine Interaction in Live Performance.* Pisa: Computer Music Department of CNUCE/CNR, 1–8.

Beyls, P. 1988. "Introducing Oscar." In *Proceedings of the 1988 International Computer Music Conference*, edited by C. Lischka and J. Fritsch. San Francisco: International Computer Music Association, 219–230.

Beyls, P. 1989. "The musical universe of cellular automata." In *Proceedings of the 1989 International Computer Music Conference*, edited by T. Wells and D. Butler. San Francisco: International Computer Music Association, 34–41.

Beyls, P. 1991. Personal communication.

Bianchini, L., et al. 2019. "Augmented instruments at CRM–Centro Ricerche Musicali of Rome: Feed-Drum, SkinAct, WindBack and ResoFlute." *Proceedings of the International Computer Music Conference.* San Francisco: International Computer Music Association, 510–515.

Bidlack, R. 1992. "Chaotic systems as simple (but complex) compositional algorithms." *Computer Music Journal* 16(3): 33–47.

Bilbao, S. 2007. "A digital plate reverberation algorithm." *Journal of the Audio Engineering Society* 55(3): 135–144.

Bilbao, S. 2009a. "Direct simulation of reed wind instruments." *Computer Music Journal* 33(4): 43–55.

Bilbao, S. 2009b. *Numerical Sound Synthesis: Finite-Difference Schemas and Simulation in Musical Acoustics.* Chichester, UK: John Wiley & Sons.

Bilbao, S., C. Desvages, M. Ducceschi, B. Hamilton, R. Harrison-Harsley, A. Torin, and C. Webb. 2019. "Physical modeling, algorithms and sound synthesis: The NESS Project." *Computer Music Journal* 43(2–3): 15–30.

Bilbao, S., B. Hamilton, J. Botts, and L. Savioja. 2016. "Finite volume time domain room acoustics simulation under general impedance boundary conditions." *IEEE/ACM Transactions on Audio Speech and Language Processing* 24(1): 161–173.

Bilbao, S., and J. Parker. 2010. "A virtual model of spring reverberation." *IEEE Transactions on Audio, Speech, and Language Processing* 18(4): 799–808.

Bilbao, S., J. Perry, P. Graham, A. Gray, K. Kavoussanakis, G. Delap, T. Mudd, G. Sassoon, T. Wishart, and S. Young. 2019. "Large-scale physical modeling synthesis, parallel computing and musical experimentation: The NESS project in practice." *Computer Music Journal* 43(2–3): 31–47.

Bilbao, S., and A. Torin. 2015. "Numerical modeling and sound synthesis for articulated string/fretboard interactions." *Journal of the Audio Engineering Society* 63(5): 336–347.

Bilmes, J. 1993. "Techniques to foster drum machine expressivity." In *Proceedings of the 1993 International Computer Music Conference*, edited by S. Ohteru. San Francisco: International Computer Music Association, 276–283.

Bilotta, E., and E. Pantano. 2010. *Cellular Automata and Complex Systems: Methods for Modeling Biological Phenomena.* Hershey, NY: Medical Information Science Reference.

Bilsen, F. A. 1977. "Pitch of noise signals: evidence for a 'central' spectrum." *Journal of the Acoustical Society of America* 61: 150–161.

Bilsen, F., and R. Ritsma. 1969. "Repetition pitch and its implications for hearing theory." *Acustica* 22: 205–213.

Bird, J. 1982. *Percy Grainger.* South Melbourne: Sun Books.

Bischoff, J., R. Gold, and J. Horton. 1978. "A microcomputer-based network for live performance." *Computer Music Journal* 2(3): 24–29. Revised and updated version in *Foundations of Computer Music*, edited by C. Roads and J. Strawn, 1985. Cambridge, MA: MIT Press, 588–600.

Bjørn, K. 2017. *PUSH TURN MOVE: Interface Design in Electronic Music.* https://bjooks.com/.

Bjørn, K, and C. Meyer. 2018. *PATCH & TWEAK: Exploring Modular Synthesis.* https://bjooks.com/.

Black, H. 1953. *Modulation Theory.* New York: Van Nostrand-Reinhold.

Blackburn, M. 2011. "The visual sound-shapes of spectromorphology: An illustrative guide to composition." *Organised Sound* 16(1): 5–13.

Blackham, E. D. 1965. "The physics of the piano." *Scientific American* 235(12). Reprinted in *The Physics of Music*, edited by C. Hutchins, 1978. San Francisco: W. H. Freeman, 24–33.

Blackman, R., and J. Tukey. 1958. *The Measurement of Power Spectra.* New York: Dover.

Blackwell, A., and N. Collins. 2005. "The programming language as a musical instrument." In *Proceedings of 17th Psychology of Programming Interest Group.* https://citeseerx.ist.psu.edu/index.

Blake, W. 1986. *Mechanics of Flow-induced Sound and Vibration.* Two volumes. New York: Academic Press.

Blauert, J. 1983. *Spatial Hearing.* Cambridge, MA: MIT Press.

Blesser, B. 1978. "Digitization of audio." *Journal of the Audio Engineering Society* 26(10): 739–771.

Blesser, B. 2013. Quoted in J. Dattorro. 1997. "Effect design: Part 1: Reverberator and other filters." *Journal of the Audio Engineering Society* 45(9): 660–684.

Blesser, B., and J. Kates. 1978. "Digital processing in audio signals." In *Applications of Digital Signal Processing*, edited by A. V. Oppenheim. Englewood Cliffs, NJ: Prentice-Hall.

Blevis, E., M. Jenkins, and J. Glasgow. 1988. "Motivations, sources, and initial design ideas for CALM: A composition analysis/generation language for music." In *Workshop on Artificial Intelligence and Music, AAAI-88 Conference.* Menlo Park, CA: American Association for Artificial Intelligence.

Bloch, G., G. Assayag, O. Warusfel, and J. P. Jullien. 1992. "Spatializer: From room acoustics to virtual acoustics." In *Proceedings of the 1992 International Computer Music Conference*, edited by A. Strange. San Francisco: International Computer Music Association, 253–256.

Bloom, P. 1977. "Determination of monaural sensitivity changes due to the pinna by use of minimum audible field measurements in the lateral vertical plane." *Journal of the Acoustic Society of America* 61: 1264–1269.

Bloom, P. 2010. "Methods and apparatus for use in sound modification comparing time alignment data from sampled audio signals." U.S. Patent 7,825,321.

Blum, T. 1979. "Review of Herbert Brün: SAWDUST." *Computer Music Journal* 3(1): 6–7.

Blumensath, T., and M. E. Davies. 2006. "Sparse and shift-invariant representations of music." *IEEE Transactions on Audio, Speech and Language Processing* 14(1): 50–57.

Blumensath, T., and M. E. Davies. 2007. *On the Difference between Orthogonal Matching Pursuit and Orthogonal Least Squares.* Technical Report. Edinburgh: University of Edinburgh.

Blumensath, T., and M. E. Davies. 2008. "Gradient pursuits." *IEEE Transactions on Signal Processing* 56(6): 2370–2382.

Blumlein, A. 1933. "Improvements in and relating to sound-transmission, sound-recording, and sound-reproducing systems." British Patent 394,325. Reprinted in *Stereophonic Techniques: An Anthology*, by Audio Engineering Society, 1986. New York: Audio Engineering Society.

Boalch, D. 1956. *Makers of the Harpsichord and Clavichord, 1440–1840*. New York: Macmillan.

Bobrow, L., and M. Arbib. 1974. *Discrete Mathematics*. Philadelphia: W. B. Saunders.

Böck, S., F. Korzeniowski, J. Schlüter, F. Krebs, and G. Widmer. 2016. "madmom: A new Python audio and music signal processing library." In *Proceedings of the ACM International Conference on Multimedia*. New York: Association for Computing Machinery, 1174–1178.

Böcker, H.-D., and A. Mahling. 1988. "What's in a note?" In *Proceedings of the 1988 International Computer Music Conference*, edited by C. Lischka and J. Fritsch. San Francisco: International Computer Music Association, 166–173.

Bode, H. 1967. "The multiplier type ring modulator." *Electronic Music Review* 1.

Bode, H. 1974. "Apparatus for producing special audio effects utilizing phase shift techniques." U.S. Patent 3,800,088.

Bode, H. 1984. "History of electronic sound modification." *Journal of the Audio Engineering Society* 32(10): 730–739.

Bode, H., and R. Moog. 1972. "A highly-accurate frequency shifter for professional audio applications." *Journal of the Audio Engineering Society* 20(6): 453.

Bogards, N., A. Röbel, and X. Rodet. 2004. "Sound analysis and processing with Audiosculpt 2." In *Proceedings of the 2004 International Computer Music Conference*. San Francisco: International Computer Music Association, 462–465.

Boie, B., M. Mathews, and A. Schloss. 1989. "The Radio Drum as a synthesizer controller." In *Proceedings of the 1989 International Computer Music Conference*, edited by T. Wells and D. Butler. San Francisco: International Computer Music Association, 42–45.

Bokesoy, S., and G. Pape. 2003. "Stochos: software for real-time sound synthesis of stochastic music." *Computer Music Journal* 27(3): 33–43.

Bolognesi, T. 1983. "Automatic composition: experiments with self-similar music." *Computer Music Journal* 7(1): 25–36.

Bonada, J., and X. Serra. 2007. "Synthesis of the singing voice by performance sampling and spectral models." *IEEE Signal Processing Magazine* 24(2): 67–78.

Bonada, J., X. Serra, X. Amatriain, and A. Loscos. 2011. "Spectral processing." in *DAFX: Digital Audio Effect*, 2nd ed., edited by U. Zölzer. New York: Wiley, 393–445.

Bongers, B. 2000. "Physical interfaces in the electronic arts." In *Trends in Gestural Control of Music*, edited by M. Wanderley and M. Battier. CD-ROM. Paris: IRCAM.

Bongers, B., and Sensorband. 1998. "An Interview with Sensorband." *Computer Music Journal* 22(1): 13–24.

Boretz, B., and E. Cone, eds. 1976. *Perspectives on Notation and Performance*. New York: W. W. Norton.

Borgonovo, A., and G. Haus. 1984. "Musical sound synthesis by means of two-variable functions: Experimental criteria and results." In *Proceedings of the 1984 International Computer Music Conference*, edited by D. Wessel. San Francisco: International Computer Music Association, 35–42.

Borgonovo, A., and G. Haus. 1986. "Sound synthesis by means of two-variable functions: Experimental criteria and results." *Computer Music Journal* 10(4): 57–71.

Borin, G., G. De Poli, and A. Sarti. 1992. "Algorithms and structures for synthesis using physical models." *Computer Music Journal* 16(4): 30–42.

Borish, J. 1984. *Electronic Simulation of Auditorium Acoustics*. Department of Music Report STAN-M-18. Stanford, CA: Center for Computer Research in Music and Acoustics, Stanford University.

Bork, I. 1992. "Modal analysis of sound fields of musical instruments." Preprint 3243. In *Proceedings of the 92nd Convention of the Audio Engineering Society*. New York: Audio Engineering Society.

Borning, A. 1979. *Thinglab—A Constraint-Oriented Simulation Laboratory*. Technical Report SSL-79–3. Palo Alto, CA: Xerox Palo Alto Research Centers.

Bosi, M. 1990. "An interactive real-time system for the control of sound localization." *Computer Music Journal* 14(4): 59–64.

Bosi, M., and R. Goldberg. 2003. *Introduction to Digital Audio Coding and Standards*. Boston: Kluwer Academic.

Boulanger, R., ed. 2000. *The Csound Book*. Cambridge, MA: MIT Press.

Boulanger, R., and V. Lazzarini. 2011. *The Audio Programming Book*. Cambridge, MA: MIT Press.

Boulanger, R., P. Smaragdis, and J. Fitch. 2000. "Scanned synthesis: An introduction and demonstration of a new synthesis and signal processing technique." In *Proceedings of the International Computer Music Conference, Berlin*. San Francisco: International Computer Music Association, 372–375.

Boulez, P., and A. Gerzso. 1988. "Computers in music." *Scientific American* 258(4): 44–50.

Bourotte, R., and S. Kanach. 2019. "UPISketch: The UPIC idea and its current applications for initiating new audiences to music." *Organised Sound* 24(3): 252–260.

Boutillon, X. 1984. "Fonctionement des instruments à cordes libres. Approche mecanique, traitement du signal." Doctoral diss. Université de Paris Sud.

Bovermann, T., A. de Campo, H. Egermann, S.-I. Hardjowirogo, and S. Weinzierl, eds. 2017. *Musical Instruments in the 21st Century: Identities, Configurations, Practices.* Singapore: Springer.

Bowcott, P. 1989. "Cellular automata as a means of high level compositional control of granular synthesis." In *Proceedings of the 1989 International Computer Music Conference*, edited by T. Wells and D. Butler. San Francisco: International Computer Music Association, 55–57.

Bowen, B., and W. Brown. 1980. *VLSI Systems Design for Digital Signal Processing.* Reading, MA: Addison-Wesley.

Bowers, Q. D. 1972. *Encyclopedia of Automatic Musical Instruments.* New York: Vestal Press.

Boyd, S., and L. Vandenberghe. 2004. *Convex Optimization.* Cambridge: Cambridge University Press.

Boyer, F., and R. Kronland-Martinet. 1989. "Granular resynthesis and transformation of sounds through wavelet transform analysis." In *Proceedings of the 1989 International Computer Music Conference*, edited by T. Wells and T. Butler. San Francisco: International Computer Music Association, 51–54.

Boynton, L., P. Lavoie, Y. Orlarey, C. Rueda, and D. Wessel. 1986. "MIDI-Lisp, a Lisp-based music programming environment for the Macintosh." In *Proceedings of the 1986 International Computer Music Conference*, edited by P. Berg. San Francisco: International Computer Music Association, 183–186.

Braasch, J. 2018. "Convolution, Fourier analysis, cross-correlation, and their interrelationship." In *Handbook of Systematic Musicology*, edited by R. Bader. Cham, Switzerland: Springer, 273–284.

Braasch, J., N. Peters, and D. Valente. 2008. "A loudspeaker-based projection technique for spatial music application using virtual microphone control." *Computer Music Journal* 32(3): 55–71.

Braasch, J., J. Carter, S. Chabot, and J. Mathews. 2016. "An immersive teleconferencing system using spherical microphones and wave field synthesis." In *Proceedings of the 22nd International Congress on Acoustics.* http://www.ica2016.org.ar/ica2016proceedings/ica2016/ICA2016-0826.pdf.

Branciforte, J. 2017. "From the machine: realtime networked notation." *New Music Box.* nmbx.newmusicusa.org.

Brandao, M., and R. Nascimento. 1991. "A geometrical concordance device for sound synthesis." In *Proceedings of the 1991 International Computer Music Conference*, edited by B. Alphonce and B. Pennycook. San Francisco: International Computer Music Association, 412–415.

Brandt, E. 2008. *Temporal Type Constructors for Computer Music Programming.* PhD diss. Carnegie-Mellon University.

Brandtsegg, Ø., S. Saue, and T. Johansen. 2011. "Particle synthesis–A unified model for granular synthesis." In *Proceedings of the 2011 Linux Audio Conference.* https://linuxaudio.org/lac.html.

Brandtsegg, Ø., S. Saue, and V. Lazzarini. 2018. "Live convolution with time-varying filters." *Applied Sciences* 8. https://www.mdpi.com/journal/applsci.

Bressin, R., G. De Poli, and A. Vidolin. 1992. "Symbolic and sub-symbolic rules system for real-time performance." In *Proceedings of the 1992 International Computer Music Conference*, edited by A. Strange. San Francisco: International Computer Music Association, 211–214.

Bresson, J., and M. Stroppa. 2011. "The control of the CHANT synthesizer in Open-Music: Modeling continuous aspects in sound synthesis." In *Proceedings of the 2011 International Computer Music Conference.* San Francisco: International Computer Music Association, 332–337.

Bretan, M., and G. Weinberg. 2016. "A survey of robotic musicianship," *Communications of the ACM* 59(5): 100–109.

Brigham, O. 1974. *The Fast Fourier Transform.* Englewood Cliffs, NJ: Prentice Hall.

Brightman, T., and S. Crook. 1982. "Exploring practical speech I/O." *Mini-Micro Systems*, May: 291–304.

Brinkman, A. 1990. *Pascal Programs for Music Research.* Chicago: University of Chicago Press.

Briot, J.-P., G. Hadjeres, and F.-D. Pachet. 2020. *Deep Learning Techniques for Music Generation.* Cham, Switzerland: Springer.

Bristow, D. 1986. Personal communication.

Bristow-Johnson, R. 1995. "A detailed analysis of a time-domain formant-corrected pitch shifting algorithm." *Journal of the Audio Engineering Society* 43(5): 340–352.

Brixen, E. 2011. *Audio Metering: Measurements, Standards, and Practice.* 2nd ed. New York: Focal Press.

Brooks, F., A. Hopkins, P. Newmann, and W. Wright. 1957. "An experiment in musical composition." *Institute of Radio Engineers Transactions on Electronic Computers* EC-6(1): 175–182.

Brougher, K., J. Strick, A. Wiseman, and J. Zilczer. 2005. *Visual Music: Synaesthesia in Arts and Music Since 1900.* New York: Thames & Hudson.

Brown, A. 2005. "Extending dynamic stochastic synthesis." In *Proceedings of the 2005 International Computer Music Association.* San Francisco: International Computer Music Association.

Brown, A., and A. Sorensen. 2007. "Dynamic media arts programming in Impromptu." In *Proceedings of the 6th ACM SIGCHI Conference on Creativity and Cognition*. New York: Association for Computing Machinery, 245–246.

Brown, C., and J. Bischoff. 2005. "Computer network music bands: A history of the League of Automatic Music Composers and The Hub." In *At a Distance: Precursors to Art and Activism on the Internet*, edited by A. Chandler and N. Neumark. Cambridge, MA: MIT Press, 372–391.

Brown, F. 1977. "The language Scriptu." *Interface* 6: 9–28.

Brown, J., O. Houix, and S. McAdams. 2001. "Feature dependence in the automatic identification of musical woodwind instruments." *Journal of the Acoustical Society of America* 109(3): 1064–1072.

Brown, J., and M. Puckette. 1987. "Musical information from a narrowed autocorrelation function." Cambridge, MA: MIT Experimental Music Studio.

Brown, J., and M. Puckette. 1992. "An efficient algorithm for the calculation of a constant Q transform." *Journal of the Acoustical Society of America* 92(5): 2698–2701.

Brown, J., and M. Puckette. 1993. "A high resolution fundamental frequency determination based on phase changes of the Fourier transform." *Journal of the Acoustical Society of America* 94(2): 662–667.

Brownlee, J. 2011. *Clever Algorithms: Nature-Inspired Programming Recipes*. https://LuLu.com.

Brümmer, L. 2017. "Composition and perception of spatial audio." *Computer Music Journal* 41(1): 46–60.

Brümmer, L. 2020. Personal communication.

Brün, H. 1969. "*Infraudibles*." In *Music By Computers*, edited by H. Von Foerster and J. Beauchamp. New York: John Wiley & Sons, 117–121.

Bruyns, C. 2006. "Modal synthesis for arbitrarily shaped objects." *Computer Music Journal* 30(3): 22–37.

Bryan, N., G. Mysore, and G. Wang. 2014. "IEEE: An interactive source separation editor." In *Proceedings of CHI 2014*. New York: Association for Computing Machinery, 257–266.

Buchner, A. 1978. *Mechanical Musical Instruments*. Westport, CT: Greenwood Press.

Bumgardner, J. 2009. "Kircher's mechanical composer: A software implementation." In *Proceedings of Bridges 2009: Mathematics, Music, Art, Architecture, Culture*. https://krazydad.com/pubs/kircher_paper.pdf.

Burg, J. 1967. "Maximum entropy spectral analysis." In *Proceedings of the 37th Meeting of the Society of Exploration Geophysicists*. Houston: Society of Exploration Geophysicists.

Burk, P. 1998. "JSyn–A real-time synthesis API for Java." In *Proceedings of the 1998 International Computer Music Association.* San Francisco: International Computer Music Association.

Burns, E., and N. Viemeister. 1976. "Nonspectral pitch." *Journal of the Acoustical Society of America* 60: 863–869.

Burraston, D. 2006. "Generative music and cellular automata." PhD diss. Faculty of Information Technology, University of Technology.

Burt, W. 2018. "Thoughts on algorithmic practice." In *The Oxford Handbook of Algorithmic Music*, edited by R. Dean and A. McLean. Oxford: Oxford University Press, 520–528.

Burton, A., and T. Vladimirova. 1999. "Generation of musical sequences with genetic techniques." *Computer Music Journal* 23(4): 59–73.

Buser, P., and M. Imbert. 1992. *Audition.* Cambridge, MA: MIT Press.

Buxton, W. 1979. "The evolution of the SSSP score editing tools." *Computer Music Journal* 3(4): 14–25. Revised and updated version in *Foundations of Computer Music*, edited by C. Roads and J. Strawn, 1985. Cambridge, MA: MIT Press, 376–402.

Buxton, W. 1986. "The computer as accompanist." In *Human Factors in Computer Systems—CHI '86 Conference Proceedings*, edited by M. Mantei and P. Orbeton. New York: Association for Computing Machinery, 41–43.

Buxton, W., S. Patel, W. Reeves, and R. Baecker. 1981. "Scope in interactive score editors." *Computer Music Journal* 5(3). Reprinted in *The Music Machine*, edited by C. Roads, 1989. Cambridge, MA: MIT Press, 255–261.

Buxton, W., S. Patel, W. Reeves, and R. Baecker. 1982. "Objed and the design of timbral resources." *Computer Music Journal* 6(2): 32–44. Reprinted in *The Music Machine*, edited by C. Roads, 1989. Cambridge, MA: MIT Press, 263–275.

Buxton, W., E. A. Fogels, G. Fedorkow, L. Sasaki, and K. C. Smith. 1978a. "An introduction to the SSSP digital synthesizer." *Computer Music Journal* 2(4): 28–38. Revised and updated version in *Foundations of Computer Music*, edited by C. Roads and J. Strawn. Cambridge, MA: MIT Press, 206–224.

Buxton, W., W. Reeves, R. Baecker, and L. Mezei. 1978b. "The use of hierarchy and instance in a data structure for computer music." *Computer Music Journal* 2(4): 10–20. Revised and updated version in *Foundations of Computer Music*, edited by C. Roads and J. Strawn. Cambridge, MA: MIT Press, 443–466.

Byrd, D. 1974. "A system for music printing by computer." *Computers and the Humanities* 8(3): 161–172.

Byrd, D. 1977. "An integrated computer music software system." *Computer Music Journal* 1(2): 55–60.

Byrd, D. 1984. "Music notation by computer." PhD diss. Indiana University Department of Computer Science.

Byrd, D. 2017. *A Gallery of Interesting Music Notation.* https://homes.luddy.indiana .edu/donbyrd/InterestingMusicNotation.html.

Byrd, D., and M. Fingerhut. 2002. "The history of ISMIR—A short happy tale." *D-Lib Magazine* 8(11).

Byrd, D., and J. Simonsen. 2015. "Towards a standard testbed for optical music recognition: definitions, metrics, and page images." *Journal of New Music Research* 44(3): 169–195.

Cabrera, A. 2010. "Using OSC in Csound." Video. https://www.youtube.com/watch ?v=JX1C3TqP_9Y.

Cabrera, A. 2011. "Graphical user interfaces for audio programs using the Qt toolkit." In *The Audio Programming Book*, edited by R. Boulanger and V. Lazzarini. Cambridge, MA: MIT Press. DVD.

Cabrera, A. 2019. Personal communication.

Cabrera, A., and G. Kendall. 2013. "Multichannel control of spatial extent through sinusoidal partial modulation (SPM)." In *Proceedings of the 2013 International Computer Music Conference*. San Francisco: International Computer Music Association.

Cabrera, A., J. Kuchera-Morin, and C. Roads. 2016. "The evolution of spatial audio in the Allosphere." *Computer Music Journal* 40(4): 47–61.

Cáceres, J., and C. Chafe. 2010. "JackTrip: Under the hood of an engine for network audio." *Journal of New Music Research* 39(3): 183–187.

Cadoz, C. 2002. "The physical model as a metaphor for music creation." In *Proceedings of the 2002 International Computer Music Conference*. San Francisco: International Computer Music Association, 305–312.

Cadoz, C., L. Lisowski, and J.-L. Florens. 1990. "A modular feedback keyboard design." *Computer Music Journal* 14(2): 47–51.

Cadoz, C., A. Luciani, and J.-L. Florens. 1984. "Responsive input devices and sound synthesis by simulation of instrumental mechanisms." *Computer Music Journal* 8(3): 60–73.

Cadoz, C., A. Luciani, and J.-L. Florens. 1993. "CORDIS-ANIMA: A modeling and simulation system for sound and image synthesis—The general formalism." *Computer Music Journal* 17(1): 19–29.

Cadoz, C., A, Luciani, and J.-L. Florens. 2003. "Artistic creation and computer interactive multisensory simulation force feedback gesture transducers." In *Proceedings of the New Interfaces for Musical Expression (NIME) Conference*. n.p.: New Interfaces for Musical Expression, 235–246. https://www.nime.org.

Cafagna, V., and D. Vicinanza. 2002. "Audio synthesis by means of elliptic functions." In *Proceedings of the Second International Conference Creating and Understanding Music*. Salerno, Italy: University of Salerno.

Cage, J. 1937. "The future of music: Credo." In *Silence*, by J. Cage, 1961. Middletown, CT: Wesleyan University Press.

Cage, J. 1952. *Williams Mix*. New York: Edition Peters.

Cage, J. 1961. *Silence*. Middletown, CT: Wesleyan University Press.

Cage, J. 1969. *Notations*. New York: Something Else Press.

Cahill, T. 1897. U.S. Patents 580,035 (1897); 1,107,261 (1914); 1,213,803 (1917); 1,295,691 (1919). Patents for the telharmonium.

Caires, C. 2004. "IRIN: Micromontage in graphical sound editing and mixing tool." In *Proceedings of the 2004 International Computer Music Conference*. San Francisco: International Computer Music Association.

Caires, C. 2019. IRIN application program. https://irin.carloscaires.com.

Cakmakci, O., and J. Rolland. 2006. "Head-worn displays: a review." *IEEE Journal of Display Technology* 2(3): 199–216.

Calvet, O., R. Laurens, and J.-M. Adrien. 1990. "Modal synthesis: compilation of mechanical sub-structures and acoustical sub-systems." In *Proceedings of the 1990 International Computer Music Conference*, edited by S. Arnold and G. Hair. San Francisco: International Computer Music Association, 57–59.

Calvo-Zaragoza, J., and D. Rizo. 2018. "End-to-end neural optical music recognition of monophonic scores." *Applied Sciences* 8(4): 606.

Camilleri, L., F. Carreras, and A. Mayr, eds. 1987. *Pietro Grossi: Musica Senza Musicisti*. Florence: CNUCE/CNR.

Campbell, M., and C. Greated. 1987. *The Musician's Guide to Acoustics*. London: J. M. Dent and Sons.

Campbell, O., C. Roads, A. Cabrera, M. Wright, and Y. Vissel. 2016. "ADEPT: A framework for adaptive digital audio effects." In *Proceedings of the 2nd Audio Engineering Society Workshop on Intelligent Music Production*. London: Audio Engineering Society.

Camurri, A., C. Canepa, M. Frixione, C. Innocenti, C. Massucco, and R. Zaccaria. 1991. "A high-level system for music composition." In *Proceedings of the 1991 International Computer Music Conference*, edited by B. Alphonce and B. Pennycook. San Francisco: International Computer Music Association, 27–36.

Cann, R. 1978. "Speech analysis/synthesis for electronic vocal music." PhD diss. Princeton University Department of Music.

Cann, R. 1979–1980. "An analysis/synthesis tutorial." *Computer Music Journal* 3(3): 6–11; 3(4): 9–13; 4(1): 36–42. Reprinted in *Foundations of Computer Music*, edited by C. Roads and J. Strawn, 1985. Cambridge, MA: MIT Press, 114–144.

Cannam, C., C. Landone, and M. Sandler. 2010. "Sonic Visualiser: An open source application for viewing, analysing, and annotating music audio files." In *Proceed-*

ings of the ACM Multimedia 2010 International Conference. New York: Association for Computing Machinery. https://www.acm.org.

Cano, E., D. Fitzgerald, A. Liukus, M. Plumbley, and F. Stöter. 2019. "Musical source separation." *IEEE Signal Processing Magazine* 36(1): 31–40.

Cantor, D. 1971. "A computer program that accepts common music notation." *Computers and the Humanities* 6(2): 103–109.

Capps, S. 1992. "Sound editing system using control line for altering specified characteristic of adjacent segment of the stored waveform." U.S. Patent 5,151,998.

Carlos, W. 1986. "Tuning: At the crossroads." *Computer Music Journal* 11(1): 29–43.

Carlson, C. 2019. Borderlands Granular. http://www.borderlands-granular.com/app/.

Carlson, C., and G. Wang. 2012. "Borderlands: An audiovisual interface for granular synthesis." In *Proceedings of the New Interfaces for Musical Expression (NIME) Conference.* n.p.: New Interfaces for Musical Expression. https://www.nime.org.

Carpentier, T., M. Noisternig, and O. Warusfel. 2015. "Twenty years of IRCAM spat: Looking back, looking forward." In *Proceedings of the 2015 International Computer Music Conference.* San Francisco: International Computer Music Association, 270–277.

Carson, J. 1915. "Method and means for signaling with high-frequency waves." U.S. Patent 1,449,382.

Carson, J. 1922. "Notes on the theory of modulation." *Proceedings of the Institute of Radio Engineers* 10: 57–64.

Carterette, E., and M. Friedman, eds. 1978. *Handbook of Perception, Volume 4, Hearing.* New York: Academic Press.

Carvalho, R., and P. Smaragdis. 2017. "Towards end-to-end polyphonic music transcription: transforming music audio directly to a score." In *Proceedings of the 2017 IEEE Workshop on Applications of Signal Processing to Audio and Acoustics.* New York: IEEE.

Casey, M. 1996. "Multi-model estimation and classification as a basis for computational timbre understanding." Unpublished manuscript.

Casey, M. 2005. "Acoustic lexemes for organizing internet audio." *Contemporary Music Review* 24(6): 489–508.

Casey, M. 2010. MPEG-7 Multimedia Software Resources. http://mpeg7.doc.gold.ac.uk.

Casey, M., R. Veltkamp, M. Goto, M. Leman, C. Rhodes, and M. Slaney. 2008. "Content-based music information retrieval: Current directions and future challenges." *Proceedings of the IEEE* 96(4): 668–696.

Castagné, N., and C. Cadoz. 2002. "GENESIS: A friendly musician-oriented environment for mass-interaction physical modelling." In *Proceedings of the International*

Computer Music Conference. San Francisco: International Computer Music Association, 330–337.

Castine, P. 1993. "Whatever happened to CMAP for Macintosh? A status report." In *Proceedings of the 1993 International Computer Music Conference*, edited by S. Ohteru. San Francisco: International Computer Music Association, 360–362.

Cauchy, A. 1841. "Memoire sur diverse formules d'analyse." *Comptes Rendus Hebdomaires des Sciences de l'Academie des Sciences Paris* 12: 283–298.

Caux, J. 2013. *Almost Nothing with Luc Ferrari.* Berlin: Errant Bodies Press.

Cavaliere, S. 1991. "New generation architectures for music and sound processing." In *Representations of Musical Signals*, edited by G. De Poli, A. Piccialli, and C. Roads. Cambridge, MA: MIT Press, 391–412.

Cavaliere, S., G. Di Giugno, and E. Guarino. 1992. "MARS–The X20 device and the SM1000 board." In *Proceedings of the 1992 International Computer Music Conference*, edited by A. Strange. San Francisco: International Computer Music Association, 348–351.

Cavaliere, S., I. Ortosecco, and A. Piccialli. 1986. "Synthesis by formants: A new approach." In *Proceedings of the 1986 IEEE ASSP Workshop on Applications of Signal Processing to Audio and Acoustics.* New York: IEEE Acoustics, Speech, and Signal Processing Society.

Cavaliere, S., and A. Piccialli. 1997. "Granular synthesis of musical signals." In *Musical Signal Processing*, edited by C. Roads, S. Pope, A. Piccialli, and G. De Poli, 1997. Amsterdam: Swets & Zeitlinger, 155–186.

Cella, C.-E. 2020. "Music information retrieval and contemporary classical music: A successful failure." *Transactions of the International Society for Music Information Retrieval* 3(1): 126–136.

Cerruti, R., and G. Rodeghiero. 1983. "Comments on 'Musical sound synthesis by forward differences.'" *Journal of the Audio Engineering Society* 31(6): 446.

Chabassier, J. 2012. "Modélisation et simulation numérique d'un piano par modèles physiques." PhD diss. Ecole Polytechnique X.

Chabassier, J., A. Chaigne, and P. Joly. 2013. "Modeling and simulation of a grand piano." *Journal of the Acoustical Society of America* 134(1): 648–665.

Chabot, X. 1990. "Gesture interfaces and a software toolkit for performance with electronics." *Computer Music Journal* 14(2): 15–27.

Chabot, X., and L. Beauregard. 1984. "Control of a real-time sound processor by a traditional instrument." In *Proceedings of the 1984 International Computer Music Conference.* San Francisco: International Computer Music Association.

Chabot, X., R. Dannenberg, and G. Bloch. 1986. "A workstation in live performance: Composed improvisation." In *Proceedings of the 1986 International Computer Music*

Conference, edited by P. Berg. San Francisco: International Computer Music Association, 57–59.

Chadabe, J. 1967. "New approaches to analog studio design." *Perspectives of New Music* 6(1): 107–113.

Chadabe, J. 1984. "Interactive composing: An overview." *Computer Music Journal* 8(1): 22–27. Reprinted in *The Music Machine*, edited by C. Roads, 1989. Cambridge, MA: MIT Press, 143–148.

Chadabe, J. 1997. *Electric Sound: The Past and Promise of Electronic Music.* Upper Saddle River, NJ: Prentice Hall.

Chafe, C. 1985. "Control of bowed string synthesis from a physical model." Unpublished manuscript.

Chafe, C. 2009 "Tapping into the Internet as an acoustical/musical medium." *Contemporary Music Review* 28(4–5): 413–420.

Chafe, C., and D. Jaffe. 1986. "Source separation and note identification in polyphonic music." In *Proceedings of the International Conference on Acoustics, Speech and Signal Processing, Tokyo.* New York: IEEE.

Chafe, C., D. Jaffe, K. Kashima, B. Mont-Reynaud, and J. Smith. 1985. "Techniques for note identification in polyphonic music." In *Proceedings of the 1985 International Computer Music Conference*, edited by B. Truax. San Francisco: International Computer Music Association, 399–405.

Chafe, C., B. Mont-Reynaud, and L. Rush. 1982. "Toward an intelligent editor for digital audio: Recognition of musical concepts." *Computer Music Journal* 6(1): 30–41. Reprinted in *The Music Machine,* edited by C. Roads, 1989. Cambridge, MA: MIT Press, 537–548.

Chaitin, G. 1975. "Randomness and mathematical proof." *Scientific American* 232(5): 47–54.

Chaitin, G. 1998. *The Limits of Mathematics.* Singapore: Springer.

Chaitin, G. 2002. *Conversations with a Mathematician.* London: Springer.

Chamberlin, H., 1985. *Musical Applications of Microprocessors.* 2nd ed. Rochelle Park, NJ: Hayden Books.

Chan, S., and A. Horner. 1996. "Discrete summation synthesis of musical instrument tones using genetic algorithms." *Journal of the Audio Engineering Society* 44(7): 581–592.

Chang, J. 2011. "Composing noise." In *The Audio Programming Book*, edited by R. Boulanger, and V. Lazzarini, 2011. Cambridge, MA: MIT Press. DVD.

Chapuis, A., ed. 1955. *Histoire de la boîte à musique.* Lausanne, Switzerland: Edition Scriptar.

Charbonneau, G. R. 1981. "Timbre and the effects of three types of data reduction." *Computer Music Journal* 5(2): 10–19. Reprinted in *The Music Machine*, edited by C. Roads, 1989. Cambridge, MA: MIT Press, 521–530.

Charles, J.-F. 2008. "A tutorial on spectral sound processing using Max/MSP and Jitter." *Computer Music Journal* 32(3): 87–102.

Chavez, C. 1937. *Toward a New Music: Music and Electricity.* New York: W. W. Norton.

Chen, C. 2018. *Elements of Human Voice.* Singapore: World Scientific.

Chen, S. S., D. L. Donoho, and M. A. Saunders. 1998. "Atomic decomposition by basis pursuit." *SIAM Journal of the Science of Computation.* 20(1): 33–61.

Cheng, X., J. Hart, and J. Walker. 2009. "Time-frequency analysis of musical rhythm." *Notices of the American Mathematical Society* 56(3): 356–372.

Cherniakov, M. 2003. *An Introduction to Parametric Digital Filters and Oscillators.* New York: John Wiley & Sons.

Cherry, C. 1949. *Pulses and Transients in Communication Circuits.* London: Chapman and Hall.

Chion, M. 1982. *La musique électroacoustique.* Paris: Les Presses Universitaires de France.

Chion, M. 2009. *Film, A Sound Art.* New York: Columbia University Press.

Chirlian, P. 1971. *Electronic Circuits: Physical Principles, Analysis, and Design.* New York: McGraw-Hill.

Chowning, J. 1971. "The simulation of moving sound sources." *Journal of the Audio Engineering Society* 19: 2–6. Reprinted in *Computer Music Journal* 1(3): 48–52, 1977.

Chowning, J. 1973. "The synthesis of complex audio spectra by means of frequency modulation." *Journal of the Audio Engineering Society* 21(7): 526–534. Reprinted in *Foundations of Computer Music*, edited by C. Roads and J. Strawn, 1985. Cambridge, MA: MIT Press, 6–29.

Chowning, J. 1980. "Computer synthesis of the singing voice." In *Sound Generation in Winds, Strings, Computers*, edited by J. Sundberg and E. Jansson, 1980. Publication 29. Stockholm: Royal Swedish Academy of Music, 4–13.

Chowning, J. 1987. "FM is a universe of possibilities with a lot of surprises." *Yamaha* magazine advertisement.

Chowning, J. 1989. "Frequency modulation synthesis of the singing voice." In *Current Directions in Computer Music Research*, edited by M. Mathews and J. Pierce, 1989. Cambridge, MA: MIT Press, 57–63.

Chowning, J., and D. Bristow. 1986. *FM Theory and Applications.* Tokyo: Yamaha Music Foundation.

Chowning, J., and B. Mont-Reynaud. 1986. *Intelligent Analysis of Composite Acoustic Signals*. Department of Music Report STAN-M-36. Stanford, CA: Stanford University.

Chowning, J., J. Grey, L. Rush, and J. A. Moorer. 1974. *Computer Simulation of Music Instrument Tones in Reverberant Environments*. Department of Music Report STAN-M-2. Stanford, CA: Stanford University.

Christensen, M., and A. Jakobsson. 2009. *Multi-Pitch Estimation*. San Rafael, CA: Morgan & Claypool Publishers.

Christensen, M., and S. H. Jensen. 2007. "The cyclic matching pursuit and its application to audio modeling and coding." *Proceedings of the IEEE Asilomar Conference on Signals, Systems, and Computers*. New York: IEEE, 550–554.

Christensen, M., and B. L. Sturm. 2011. "A perceptually reweighted mixed-norm method for sparse approximation of audio signals," In *Proceedings of the IEEE Asilomar Conference on Signals, Systems, and Computers*. New York: IEEE, 575–579.

Christensen, O., and K. L. Christensen. 2005. *Approximation Theory: From Taylor Polynomials to Wavelets*. Boston: Birkhäuser.

Cipriani, A., and M. Giri. 2010a. *Electronic Music and Sound Design*. Rome: ContempoNet.

Cipriani, A., and M. Giri, 2010b. *Electronic Music and Sound Design Vol.2*. Rome: ContempoNet.

Civolani, M., and F. Fontana. 2008. "A nonlinear digital model of the EMS VC3 voltage-controlled filter." In *Proceedings of the 11th International Conference on Digital Audio Effects (DAFx-08), Espoo, Finland*. n.p.: DAFx, 35–42.

Clark, J. 2003. *Advanced Programming Techniques for Modular Synthesizers*. github.com/aolney/nord-modular-book.

Clark, M. 1959. "A new musical instrument." *Gravenser Blätter* 14: 110–123.

Clarke, E. 1987. "Levels of structure in the organization of musical time." *Contemporary Music Review* 2(1): 211–238.

Clarke, J., and R. Voss. 1978. "1/f noise in music: music from 1/f noise." *Journal of the Acoustical Society of America* 63(1): 258–263.

Clarke, M. 1990. "An FOF synthesis tutorial." In *Csound: A Manual for the Audio Processing System*, edited by B. Vercoe. Cambridge, MA: MIT Media Laboratory.

Clarke, M. 2000. "FOF and FOG synthesis in Csound." In *The Csound Book*, edited by R. Boulanger. Cambridge, MA: MIT Press, 293–306.

Clarke, M., F. Dufeu, and P. Manning. 2013. "Introducing TaCEM and the TIAALS Software." In *Proceedings of the 2013 International Computer Music Conference*, edited by A. Gardiner and A. Varano. San Francisco: International Computer Music Association, 47–53.

Clough, J. 1970. "TEMPO: a composer's programming language." *Perspectives of New Music* Fall/Winter: 113–125.

Clozier, C. 1997. "Composition-diffusion/interpretation in electroacoustic music." In *Proceedings of the International Academy of Electroacoustic Music.* Bourges, France: Institut Internationale de Musique Éléctroacoustique, 233–281.

Clozier, C. 2001. "The Gmebaphone concept and the Cybernéphone instrument." *Computer Music Journal* 25(4): 81–90.

Clynes, M., and N. Nettheim. 1982. "The living quality of music." In *Music, Mind, and Brain: The Neuropsychology of Music*, edited by M. Clynes. New York: Plenum, 47–82.

Clynes, M., and J. Walker. 1982. "Neurobiologic functions of rhythm, time, and pulse in music." In *Music, Mind, and Brain: The Neuropsychology of Music*, edited by M. Clynes. New York: Plenum, 47–82.

Cogan, R. 1984. *New Images of Musical Sound.* Cambridge, MA: Harvard University Press.

Cohen, H. 1984. *Quantifying Music.* Dordrecht, Netherlands: Reidel.

Cohen, L. 1989. "Time-frequency distributions—A review." *Proceedings of the IEEE* 77(7): 941–981.

Colburn, H., and N. Durlach. 1978. "Models of binaural interaction." In *Handbook of Perception, Volume 4*, edited by E. Carterette and M. Friedman. New York: Academic, 467–518.

Coleman, G., E. Maestre, and J. Bonada. 2010. "Augmenting sound mosaicing with descriptor-driven transformation." In *Proceedings of the COST-G6 International Conference on Digital Audio Effects (DAFx-10), Graz, Austria.* n.p.: DAFx, 1–4.

Collins, M. 1993. "Infinity: DSP sampling tools for Macintosh." *Sound on Sound* 9(1): 44–47.

Collins, N. 1991a. "Low brass: The evolution of trombone propelled electronics." *Leonardo Music Journal* 1(1): 41–44.

Collins, N. 1991b. "Cargo cult instruments." *Contemporary Music Review* 6: 73–84.

Collins, N. 2001. "Algorithmic composition methods for breakbeat science." In *Proceedings of Music Without Walls.* Leicester, UK: De Montfort University, 21–23.

Collins, N. 2002. "Relating superhuman virtuosity to human performance." In *Proceedings of MAXIS.* Sheffield, UK: Sheffield Hallam University. https://composerprogrammer.com/research.html.

Collins, N. 2003. "Generative music and laptop performance." *Contemporary Music Review* 22(4): 67–79.

Collins, N. 2007. "Audiovisual concatenative synthesis." In *Proceedings of the 2007 International Computer Music Conference*. San Francisco: International Computer Music Association, 389–392.

Collins, N. 2008a. "Errant sound synthesis." *Proceedings of the 2008 International Computer Music Conference*. San Francisco: International Computer Music Association.

Collins, N. 2008b. "Infno: Generating synth pop and electronic dance music on demand." *Proceedings of the 2008 International Computer Music Conference*. San Francisco: International Computer Music Association.

Collins, N. 2010. *Introduction to Computer Music*. West Sussex, UK: Wiley.

Collins, N. 2011. "Machine listening in SuperCollider." In *The SuperCollider Book*, edited by S. Wilson, D. Cottle, and N. Collins. Cambridge, MA: MIT Press, 439–461.

Collins, N. 2012. "Automatic composition of acousmatic music utilizing machine listening." *Computer Music Journal* 36(3): 8–23.

Collins, N. 2016. "A funny thing happened on the way to the formula: Algorithmic composition for musical theater." *Computer Music Journal* 40(3): 41–57.

Collins, N., A. McLean, J. Rohrhuber, and A. Ward. 2003. "Live coding techniques for laptop performance." *Organised Sound* 8(3): 321–330.

Collins, N., and B. L. Sturm. 2011. "Sound cross-synthesis and morphing using dictionary-based methods." In *Proceedings of the 2011 International Computer Music Conference*. San Francisco: International Computer Music Association, 595–601.

Colonel, J., C. Curro, and S. Keene. 2018. "Autoencoding neural networks as musical audio synthesizers." In *Proceedings of the 21st International Conference on Digital Audio Effects (DAFx-18)*. n.p.: DAFx. https://www.dafx.de.

Comajuncosas, J. 2000. 22. "Wave terrain synthesis with Csound." In *The Csound Book*, edited by R. Boulanger, 2000. Cambridge, MA: MIT Press. CD-ROM.

Comajuncosas, J., A. Barrachina, J. O'Connell, and E. Guaus. 2011. "Nuvolet: 3D gesture-driven collaborative audio mosaicing." In *Proceedings of the International Conference on New Interfaces for Musical Expression*. n.p.: New Interfaces for Musical Expression, 252–255. https://www.nime.org.

Composers Desktop Project. 2020. *CDP Documentation*. https://www.unstablesound.net/cdp.html.

Computer Music Journal. 1979. "Dataland's Scan-note system." *Computer Music Journal* 3(1): 60–61. (Product announcement.)

Computer Music Journal. 1980. "Marantz Pianocorder." *Computer Music Journal* 4(1): 89–90. (Product announcement.)

Computer Music Journal. 1984. "Key Concepts Notebender keyboard." *Computer Music Journal* 8(3): 92. (Product announcement.)

Computer Music Journal. 1989. "The Mandala—A music synthesizer played in a video performance." 13(1): 9.

Computer Music Journal. 1990. "Voice recognition: VoiceWaves MIDI for Apple Macintosh computers." *Computer Music Journal* 14(2): 92. (Product announcement.)

Computer Music Journal. 1993a. Special issue on music representation and scoring. 17(3).

Computer Music Journal. 1993b. Special issue on music representation and scoring. 17(4).

Conger, J. 1988. *C Programming for MIDI.* Redwood City, CA: M&T Books.

Conger, J. 1989. *MIDI Sequencing in C.* Redwood City, CA: M&T Books.

Coniglio, M. 1992. "Introduction to the Interactor language." In *Proceedings of the 1992 International Computer Music Conference,* edited by A. Strange. San Francisco: International Computer Music Association, 170–173.

Cook, P. 1991a. "Identification of control parameters in an articulatory vocal tract model, with applications to the synthesis of singing." PhD diss. Stanford University, Department of Electrical Engineering.

Cook, P. 1991b. "TBone: An interactive waveguide brass instrument synthesis workbench for the NeXT Machine." In *Proceedings of the 1991 International Computer Music Conference,* edited by B. Alphonce and B. Pennycook. San Francisco: International Computer Music Association, 297–299.

Cook, P. 1992. "A meta-wind-instrument physical model, and a meta-controller for real-time performance control." In *Proceedings of the 1992 International Computer Music Conference,* edited by A. Strange. San Francisco: International Computer Music Association, 273–276.

Cook, P. 1993. "SPASM: A real-time vocal tract physical model controller and Singer: The companion software synthesis system." *Computer Music Journal* 17(1): 30–44.

Cook, P. 1996. "Physically informed sonic modeling (PhISM): Percussive synthesis." In *Proceedings of the 1996 International Computer Music Conference,* edited by L. Ayers and A. Horner. San Francisco: International Computer Music Association, 228–231.

Cook, P. 1997. "Physically informed sonic modeling (PhISM): Synthesis of percussive sounds." *Computer Music Journal* 21(3): 38–49.

Cook, P. 2007. *Real Sound Synthesis for Interactive Applications.* Third corrected printing. Wellesley, MA: A K Peters.

Cook, P. 2017. "2001: Principles for designing computer music controllers." In *A NIME Reader: Fifteen Years of New Interfaces for Musical Expression,* edited by A. Jensenius and M. Lyons, 2017. Cham, Switzerland: Springer, 1–14.

Cooley, J., and J. Tukey. 1965. "An algorithm for the machine computation of complex Fourier series." *Mathematical Computation* 19: 297–301.

Cope, D. 1987. "An expert system for computer-assisted composition." *Computer Music Journal* 11(4): 30–46.

Cope, D. 1996. *Experiments in Musical Intelligence*. Middleton, WI: A-R Editions.

Cope, D. 2001. *Virtual Music: Computer Synthesis of Musical Style*. Cambridge, MA: MIT Press.

Cope, D. 2006. *Computer Models of Musical Creativity*. Cambridge, MA: MIT Press.

Cope, D. 2019. *5000 Emmy Bach chorales in MIDI format*. http://artsites.ucsc.edu /faculty/cope/new.html.

Corbett, I. 2012. "Los in translation: What data compression does to your music." *Sound on Sound* 27(4): 118–127.

Cottle, D. 2005. *Computer Music with Examples in SuperCollider 3*. http://rhoadley .net/courses/tech_resources/supercollider/tutorials/cottle/CMSC7105.pdf.

Couprie, P. 2016. "EAnalysis: Developing a sound-based music analytical tool." In *Expanding the Horizon of Electroacoustic Music Analysis*, edited by S. Emmerson and L. Landy. Cambridge: Cambridge University Press, 170–194.

Couprie, P. 2018. "Methods and tools for transcribing electroacoustic music." In *Proceedings of the International Conference on Technologies for Music Notation and Representation TENOR'18*. https://www.tenor-conference.org.

Crawford, D., and J. Zeef. 1983. "Gregory's Scribe: Inexpensive graphics for pre-1600 music notation." *Computer Music Journal* 7(1): 21–24.

Crawford, F. 1968. *Waves*. Berkeley Physics Course Volume 3. New York: McGraw-Hill.

Crochiere, R., and L. Rabiner. 1983. *Multirate Digital Signal Processing*. Englewood Cliffs, NJ: Prentice Hall.

Cuadra, P., A. Master, and C. Sapp. 2001. "Efficient pitch detection techniques for interactive music." In *Proceedings of the 2001 International Computer Music Conference*. San Francisco: International Computer Music Association.

Cuthbert, M., and C. Ariza, 2010. "music21: A toolkit for computer-aided musicology and symbolic music data." In *Proceedings of the International Symposium on Music Information Retrieval 11*, 637–642. n.p.: International Society for Music Information Retrieval. https://ismir2010.ismir.net/pdf-of-complete-proceedings/index .html.

Cutler, C. 1960. "Transmission systems employing quantization." U.S. Patent 2,927,962, filed in 1954.

Cuzzucoli, G., and V. Lombardo. 1999. "A physical model of the classical guitar, including the player's touch." *Computer Music Journal* 23(2): 52–69.

Dahlstadt, P. 2004. "Sounds unheard of: Evolutional algorithms as creative tools for the contemporary composer." PhD diss. School of Architecture. Chalmers University of Technology.

D'Allessandro, C., and X. Rodet. 1989. "Synthèse et analyse-synthèse par fonctions d'ondes formantiques." *Journal Acoustique* 2: 163–169.

Dal Molin, A. 1978. "A terminal for music manuscript input." *Computers and the Humanities* 12: 287–289.

Damskägg, E., L. Juvela, E. Thuillier, and V. Välimäki. 2019. "Deep learning for tube amplifier emulation." In *Proceedings of the IEEE International Conference on Acoustics, Speech, and Signal Processing.* New York: IEEE.

Daniélou, A. 1958. *Tableau Comparatif des Intervalles Musicaux.* Pondicherry, India: Institut Français d'Indologie.

Dannenberg, R. 1984. "An on-line algorithm for real-time accompaniment." In *Proceedings of the 1984 International Computer Music Conference*, edited by D. Wessel. San Francisco: International Computer Music Association, 193–198.

Dannenberg, R. 1989a. "The Canon score language." *Computer Music Journal* 13(1): 47–56.

Dannenberg, R. 1989b. "Real-time scheduling and computer accompaniment." In *Current Directions in Computer Music Research*, edited by M. V. Mathews and J. R. Pierce. Cambridge, MA: MIT Press, 225–261.

Dannenberg, R. 1996. "Extending music notation through programming." In *Computer Music in Context*, edited by Craig Harris, *Contemporary Music Review* 13(2): 63–76.

Dannenberg, R. 1998. "Interpolation error in waveform table lookup." In *Proceedings of the International Computer Music Conference.* San Francisco: International Computer Music Association, 240–243.

Dannenberg, R. 2002. "The implementation of Nyquist, a sound synthesis language." *Computer Music Journal* 21(3): 71–82.

Dannenberg, R. 2018. *Nyquist Reference Manual.* Version 3.10. http://www.cs.cmu.edu/~rbd/doc/nyquist/nyquistman.pdf.

Dannenberg, R., and K. Bookstein. 1991. "Practical aspects of a MIDI conducting system." In *Proceedings of the 1991 International Computer Music Conference*, edited by B. Alphonce and B. Pennycook. San Francisco: International Computer Music Association, 537–540.

Dannenberg, R., and B. Mont-Reynaud. 1987. "Following an improvisation in real time." In *Proceedings of the 1987 International Computer Music Conference*, edited by J. Beauchamp. San Francisco: International Computer Music Association, 241–247.

Dannenberg, R., and H. Mukaino. 1988. "New techniques for enhanced quality of computer accompaniment." In *Proceedings of the 1988 International Computer*

Music Conference, edited by C. Lischka and J. Fritsch. San Francisco: International Computer Music Association, 243–249.

Darter, T. 1979. "Dave Smith." In *The Art of Electronic Music*, edited by T. Darter and G. Armbruster, 1984. New York: Quill/Keyboard, 98–104.

Das, O., J. Smith, and C. Chafe. 2020. "Improved real-time monophonic pitch tracking with the extended complex Kalman filter." *Journal of the Audio Engineering Society* 68(1/2): 78–86.

Dashow, J. 1980. "Spectra as chords." *Computer Music Journal* 4(1): 43–52.

Dashow, J. 1987. "Looking into *Sequence Symbols*." *Perspectives of New Music* 25(1 and 2): 108–137.

Dashow, J. 1989. Personal communication.

Dattorro, J. 1997a. "Effect design: Part 1: Reverberator and other filters." *Journal of the Audio Engineering Society* 45(9): 660–684.

Dattorro, J. 1997b. "Effect design: Part 2: Delay line modulation and chorus." *Journal of the Audio Engineering Society* 45(10): 764–786.

Dattorro, J. 2002. "Effect design: Part 3: Oscillators: Sinusoidal and pseudonoise." *Journal of the Audio Engineering Society* 50(3): 115–146.

Daudet, L. 2006. "Sparse and structured decompositions of signals with the molecular matching pursuit." *IEEE Transactions on Audio, Speech and Language Processing* 14(5): 1808–1816.

D'Autilia, R., and F. Guerra. 1991. "Qualitative aspects of signal processing through dynamic neural networks." In *Representations of Musical Signals*, edited by G. De Poli, A. Piccialli, and C. Roads. Cambridge, MA: MIT Press, 447–462.

David, E., M. Mathews, and H. McDonald. 1958. "Description and results of experiments with speech using digital computer simulation." In *Proceedings of the National Electronics Conference*. Vol. IV. Chicago: National Electronics Conference, 766–775.

David, E., M. Mathews, and H. McDonald. 1959. "A high-speed data translator for computer simulation of speech and television devices." In *Proceedings of the Western Joint Computer Conference*. New York: Institute of Radio Engineers, 354–357.

Davies, H. 1996. "A history of sampling." *Organized Sound* 1(1): 3–11.

Davis, B., P. Gunckle, M. Kihira, K. Masato, and Q. Zheng. 2009. *Programmable Force-Feedback Keyboard*. ME 450 Winter 2009 Final Report. Department of Technical Engineering. Ann Arbor: University of Michigan.

Davis, G., S. Mallat, and M. Avellaneda. 1997. "Adaptive greedy approximations." *Journal of Constructive Approximations* 13(1): 57–98.

Dean, R., and A. McLean. 2018. *The Oxford Handbook of Algorithmic Music.* Oxford: Oxford University Press.

de Bruijn, W., T. Piccolo, and M. Boone. 1998. "Sound recording techniques for wave field synthesis and other multichannel sound systems." In *Proceedings of the 104th Convention of the Audio Engineering Society.* Preprint 4690 (P2–6). New York: Audio Engineering Society.

de Campo, A. 2011. "Microsound." In *The SuperCollider Book*, edited by S. Wilson, D. Cottle, and N. Collins. Cambridge, MA: MIT Press, 464–504.

de Cheveigné, A., and H. Kawahara. 2002. "YIN, a fundamental frequency estimator for speech and music." *Journal of the Acoustical Society of America* 111(4): 1917–1930.

Deepmind. 2016. "WaveNet: A generative model for raw audio." https://deepmind .com/blog/wavenet-generative-model-raw-audio.

Deer, J., P. Bloom, and D. Preis. 1985. "Perception of phase distortion in allpass filters." *Journal of the Audio Engineering Society* 33(10): 782–786.

De Furia, S., and J. Scacciaferro. 1988. *MIDI Programming for the Macintosh.* Redwood City, CA: M&T Books.

Déguernel, K., E. Vincent, and G. Assayag. 2018. "Probabilistic factor oracles for multidimensional machine improvisation." *Computer Music Journal* 42(2): 52–66.

de Heer, J., and K. Tazelaar. 2017. *From Harmony to Chaos: Le Corbusier, Varèse, Xenakis.* Amsterdam: Uitgeverij Duizend & Een.

de Jong, B. 2005. "The Freesound Project: A web community for free and open exchange of sounds." https://freesound.org/help/faq.

Delalande, F. 2009. "Pratiques et objectifs des transcriptions des musiques élec-troacoustiques." In *L'analyse musicale, une pratique et son histoire*, edited by R. Campos and N. Donin. Geneva: Droz, 131–156.

Deleflie, E., and G. Schiemer. 2009. "Spatial grains: Imbuing granular particles with spatial-domain information." *Proceedings of the Australasian Computer Music Conference.* Fitzroy, Australia: Australasian Computer Music Association.

Demoucron, M. 2008. "On the control of virtual violins: Physical modeling and control of bowed string instruments." Doctoral diss. Université Pierre et Marie Curie and Royal Institute of Technology.

Depalle, P. 1991. "Analyse, modèlisation et synthèse des sons basées sur le modèle source-filtre." Université du Maine, Faculté des sciences.

Depalle, P., and G. Poirot. 1991. "SVP: Phase vocodeur modulaire à deux canaux d'entrée." Paris: IRCAM.

De Poli, G. 1978. "Musica—Programme de codage de la musique." *Rapports IRCAM* 7/78. Paris: IRCAM.

De Poli, G. 1983. "A tutorial on digital sound synthesis techniques." *Computer Music Journal* 7(4): 8–26. Reprinted in *The Music Machine*, edited by C. Roads, 1989. Cambridge, MA: MIT Press, 429–447.

De Poli, G. 1984. "Frequency-dependent waveshaping." In *Proceedings of the 1984 International Computer Music Conference*, edited by W. Buxton, 1985. San Francisco: International Computer Music Association, 91–101.

De Poli, G., and A. Piccialli. 1991. "Pitch-synchronous granular synthesis." In *Representations of Musical Signals*. Cambridge, MA: MIT Press: 187–219.

De Poli, G., A. Piccialli, and C. Roads, eds. 1991. *Representations of Musical Signals*. Cambridge, MA: MIT Press.

De Poli, G., and A. Vidolin. 1984. "Music 5: manuale operativo." Padua, Italy: Centro di Sonologià Computazionale, Università di Padova.

De Prisco, R., P. Sabatino, G. Zaccagnino, and R. Zaccagnino. 2011. "A customizable recognizer for orchestral conducting gestures based on neural networks." In *Applications of Evolutionary Computation. EvoApplications*, edited by C. Di Chio et al. Lecture Notes in Computer Science 6625. Berlin: Springer, 254–263.

De Sanctis, G., and A. Sarti. 2010. "Virtual analog modeling in the wave-digital domain." *IEEE Transactions on Audio, Speech, and Language Processing* 18(4): 715–727.

Derry, T., and T. Williams. 1960. *A Short History of Technology*. Oxford: Oxford University Press.

Desain, P., and H. Honing. 1989. "Quantization of musical time: a connectionist approach." *Computer Music Journal* 13(3): 56–66. Reprinted in *Music and Connectionism*, edited by P. Todd and D. G. Loy, 1991. Cambridge, MA: MIT Press.

Desain, P., and H. Honing. 1992a. *Music, Mind, and Machine*. Amsterdam: Thesis.

Desain, P., and H. Honing. 1992b. "The quantization problem: traditional and connectionist approaches." In *Understanding Music with AI*, edited by M. Balaban, K. Ebcioglu, and O. Laske. Cambridge, MA and Menlo Park, CA: MIT Press and AAAI Press, 448–462.

Desain, P., and H. Honing. 1992c. "Time functions best as functions of multiple times." *Computer Music Journal* 16(2): 17–34.

Deslauriers, G., and C. Leider. 2009. "A bandlimited oscillator by frequency-domain synthesis for virtual analog applications." In *Proceedings of the 127th Audio Engineering Society Convention*. Paper number 7923. New York: Audio Engineering Society.

Devine, R. 2008. *The Electronic Music Manuscript*. Middleton, WI: Sony Creative Software.

Didkovsky, N. 2004. "Java Music Specification Language, v103 update." In *Proceedings of the 2004 International Computer Music Conference*. San Francisco: International Computer Music Association.

Didkovsky, N., and G. Hajdu. 2008. "MaxScore: Music notation in Max/MSP." In *Proceedings of the 2008 International Computer Music Conference*. San Francisco: International Computer Music Association.

Diener, G. 1989. "Nutation: Structural organization versus graphic generality in a common music notation package." In *Proceedings of the 1989 International Computer Music Conference*. San Francisco: International Computer Music Association.

Die Reihe. 1955. "Vol. 1. Elektronische Musik." Vienna: Universal Edition.

Dimpker, C. 2013. *Extended Notation: The Depiction of the Unconventional.* Vienna: LIT.

Ding, Y., and X. Qian. 1997. "Processing of musical tones using a combined quadratic polynomial phase sinusoid and residual (QUASAR) signal model." *Journal of the Audio Engineering Society* 45(7/8): 571–584.

Digital Signal Processing Committee. 1980. *Programs for Digital Signal Processing.* New York: IEEE Acoustics, Speech, and Signal Processing Society.

Dijkstra, E., 1976. *A Discipline of Programming.* Englewood Cliffs, NJ: Prentice Hall.

Di Liscia, O. 2013. "A Pure Data toolkit for real-time synthesis of ATS spectral data." In *Proceedings of the 2013 Linux Audio Conference.* Graz, Austria: Institute of Electronic Music. http://lac.linuxaudio.org/2013/papers/26.pdf.

Di Liscia, O., and J. Pampin. 2003. "Spectral analysis based synthesis and transformation of digital sound: The ATSH program." In *Proceedings of the IX Brazilian Symposium of Computer Music.* Minas Gerais, Brazil: NUCOM.

Disch, A., and U. Zölzer. 1999. "Modulation and delay-line-based digital audio effects." n.p.: DAFx, 5–8.

Di Scipio, A. 1990. "Composition by exploration of nonlinear dynamical systems." In *Proceedings of the 1990 International Computer Music Conference*, edited by S. Arnold and G. Hair. San Francisco: International Computer Music Association, 324–327.

Di Scipio, A. 1996. "Interactive composing with granular time-shifting of sound." *Proceedings of Journées d'Informatique Musicale.* http://jim.afim-asso.org/jim96 /actes/discipio/discipio.html.

Di Scipio, A. 1998. "Compositional models in Xenakis's electroacoustic music." *Perspectives of New Music* 36(2): 201–243.

Di Scipio, A. 1999. "Synthesis of environmental sound textures by iterated nonlinear functions." In *Proceedings of the Second COST G-6 Workshop on Digital Audio Effects (DAFx), Trondheim, Norway.* n.p.: DAFx.

Di Scipio, A. 2018. "Dwelling in the field of sonic relationships: Instrument and listening in an ecosystem of live electronics performance." In *Live Electronic Music*, edited by F. Sallis, V. Bertolani, J. Burle, and L. Zattra. London: Routledge, 17–45.

Di Scipio, A., and I. Prignano. 1996. "Synthesis by functional iterations: a revitalization on nonstandard synthesis." *Journal of New Music Research* 25: 31–46.

Distasi, R., M. Nappi, and S. Vitulano. 1992. "Automatic generation of MIDI files by optical reading of music scores." In *Proceedings of the International Workshop on Models and Representations of Musical Signals*, edited by A. Piccialli. Naples: Università di Napoli Federico II.

Dobson, R. 2011. "Audio plugins in C++." In *The Audio Programming Book*, edited by R. Boulanger and V. Lazzarini. Cambridge, MA: MIT Press. DVD.

Dodge, C. 1985. "*In Celebration:* The composition and its realization in synthetic speech." In *Composers and the Computer*, edited by C. Roads. Middleton, WI: A-R Editions.

Dodge, C. 1989. "On Speech Songs." In *Current Directions in Computer Music Research*, edited by M. Mathews and J. Pierce. Cambridge, MA: MIT Press, 9–17.

Dodge, C., and C. Jerse. 1985. *Computer Music.* New York: Schirmer.

Dolson, M. 1983. "A tracking phase vocoder and its use in the analysis of ensemble sounds." Ph.D. diss. California Institute of Technology.

Dolson, M. 1985. "Recent advances in musique concrète at CARL." In *Proceedings of the 1985 International Computer Music Conference*, edited by B. Truax. San Francisco: International Computer Music Association, 55–60.

Dolson, M. 1986. "The phase vocoder: A tutorial." *Computer Music Journal* 10(4): 14–27.

Dolson, M. 1989a. "Fourier-transform-based timbral manipulations." In *Current Directions in Computer Music Research*, edited by M. Mathews and J. R. Pierce. Cambridge, MA: MIT Press, 105–112.

Dolson, M. 1989b. "Machine tongues XII: neural networks." *Computer Music Journal* 13(3): 28–40.

Dolson, M., and R. Boulanger. 1985. "New directions in the musical use of resonators." Unpublished manuscript.

Donahue, C., J. MacAuley, and N. Puckette. 2019. "Adversarial audio synthesis." In Proceedings of the *International Conference on Learning Representations.* n.p.: OpenReview. https://openreview.net/forum?id=ByMVTsR5KQ.

Donoho, D. L., and X. Huo. 2001. "Uncertainty principles and ideal atomic decomposition."

Doornbusch, P. 2002. "A brief survey of mapping in algorithmic composition." In *Proceedings of the International Computer Music Conference.* San Francisco: International Computer Music Association, 205–210.

Doornbusch, P. 2005. *The Music of CSIRAC.* Melbourne: Common Ground.

Doppler, C. 1842. *Theorie des farbigen Lichtes der Doppelsterne.* Vienna: University of Vienna

Dorf, R. 1958. *Electronic Musical Instruments.* New York: Radiofile.

Dorfer, M., A. Artz, and G. Widmer. 2017. "Learning audio-sheet music correspondences for score identification and offline alignment." In *Proceedings of the International Society for Music Information Retrieval Conference.* n.p.: International Society for Music Information Retrieval, 115–122.

Dörfler, M., G. Velasco, A. Flexer, and V. Klien. 2010. "Sparse regression in time-frequency representations of complex audio." In *Proceedings of 7th Sound and Music Computing Conference.* Barcelona. https://www.researchgate.net/publication/268401607 _Sparse_Regression_in_Time-Frequency_Representations_of_Complex_Audio.

Douglas, A. 1968. *The Electronic Musical Instrument Manual.* 5th ed. New York: Pitman.

Douglas, A. 1973. *Electronic Music Production.* New York: Pitman.

Doval, B. and X. Rodet. 1993. "Fundamental frequency estimation and tracking using maximum likelihood harmonic matching and HMMs." In *Proceedings of the IEEE International Conference on Acoustics, Speech and Signal Processing.* New York: IEEE, 221–224.

Dowdy, R. 2014. "Pitch shifting with formants of the original signal." http://ses.library .usyd.edu.au/bitstream/handle/2123/10636/Written_Review_2_Pitch_Shifting_with _Formants_of_Original_Sound.pdf;jsessionid=E316682FE5AA857ABB350D40434 319C4?sequence=2.

Driessen, P., T. Darcie, and B. Pillay. 2011. "The effects of network delay on tempo in music performance." *Computer Music Journal* 35(1): 76–89.

Duan, Z., and E. Benetos. 2015. "Automatic music transcription." In *Proceedings of the 16th International Society for Music Information Retrieval Conference.* n.p.: International Society for Music Information Retrieval. http://c4dm.eecs.qmul .ac.uk/ismir15-amt-tutorial.

Dudley, H. 1936. "Synthesizing speech." *Bell Laboratories Record* December: 98–102.

Dudley, H. 1939a. "Remaking Speech." *Journal of the Acoustical Society of America* 11: 167–177.

Dudley, H. 1939b. "The vocoder." *Bell Laboratories Record* 17: 122–126.

Dudley, H. 1955. "Fundamentals of speech synthesis." *Journal of the Audio Engineering Society* 3(4): 170–185.

Dudley, H., and S. A. Watkins. 1939. "A synthetic speaker." *Journal of the Franklin Institute* 227: 739–764.

Duesenberry, J. 1990. "Understanding amplitude modulation." *Electronic Musician* 6(11): 56–65, 124.

Duffy, C. 1982. "Digital recording: the 3M system." *Studio Sound* 24(12): 30–32.

Dumour, E. 1993. "Interview with Arthur Roberts." *Computer Music Journal* 17(2): 17–23.

Duncan, A., and D. Rossum. 1988. "Fundamentals of pitch-shifting." Preprint 2714 (A-1). In *Proceedings of the 85th Convention of the Audio Engineering Society*. New York: Audio Engineering Society.

Durlach, N., and H. Colburn. 1978. "Binaural phenomena." In *Handbook of Perception, Volume 4*, edited by E. Carterette and M. Friedman. New York: Academic, 365–466.

Durrieu, J.-L., G. Richard, B. David, and C. Févotte. 2010. "Source/filter model for unsupervised main melody extraction from polyphonic audio signals." *IEEE Transactions on Audio, Speech, and Language Processing* 18(3): 564–575.

Dutilleux, H., A. Grossmann, and R. Kronland-Martinet. 1988. "Application of the wavelet transform to the analysis, transformation, and synthesis of musical sounds." Preprint 2727 (A-2). In *Proceedings of the 85th Convention of the Audio Engineering Society*. New York: Audio Engineering Society.

Dutilleux, P., K. Dempwolf, M. Holters, and U. Zölzer. 2011. "Nonlinear processing." In *DAFX: Digital Audio Effects*, 2nd ed., edited by U. Zölzer. Chichester, UK: John Wiley & Sons, 101–138.

Dutilleux, P., G. De Poli, A. von dem Knesebeck, and U. Zölzer. 2011. "Time-segment processing." In *DAFX: Digital Audio Effects*, 2nd ed., edited by U. Zölzer. Chichester, UK: John Wiley & Sons, 185–217.

Dutilleux, P., M. Holters, S. Disch, and U. Zölzer. 2011a. "Filters and delays." In *DAFX: Digital Audio Effects*, 2nd ed., edited by U. Zölzer. Chichester, UK: John Wiley & Sons, 47–81.

Dutilleux, P., M. Holters, S. Disch, and U. Zölzer. 2011b. "Modulators and demodulators." In *DAFX: Digital Audio Effects*, 2nd ed., edited by U. Zölzer. Chichester, UK: John Wiley & Sons, 83–99.

Dworak, P., and A. Parker. 1977. "Envelope control with an optical keyboard." In *Proceedings of the 1977 International Computer Music Conference*, edited by C. Roads, 1978. San Francisco: International Computer Music Association.

Eaglestone, B., and S. Oates. 1990. "Analytic tools for group additive synthesis." In *Proceedings of the 1990 International Computer Music Conference*, edited by S. Arnold and G. Hair. San Francisco: International Computer Music Association, 66–68.

Eaglestone, B., and A. Verschoor. 1991. "An intelligent music repository." In *Proceedings of the 1991 International Computer Music Conference*, edited by B. Alphonce and B. Pennycook. San Francisco: International Computer Music Association, 437–440.

Ebcioglu, K. 1980. "Computer counterpoint." In *Proceedings of the 1980 International Computer Music Conference*, edited by H. S. Howe Jr., 1980. San Francisco: International Computer Music Association.

Ebcioglu, K. 1988. "An expert system for harmonizing four-part chorales." *Computer Music Journal* 12(3): 43–51.

Ebcioglu, K. 1992. "An expert system for harmonic analysis of tonal music." In *Understanding Music with AI*, edited by M. Balaban, K. Ebcioglu, and O. Laske. Cambridge, MA and Menlo Park, California: MIT Press and AAAI Press, 294–333.

Eckel, G. 1990. "A signal editor for the IRCAM Musical Workstation." In *Proceedings of the 1990 International Computer Music Conference*, edited by S. Arnold and G. Hair. San Francisco: International Computer Music Association, 69–71.

Eckert, J. P. 1946. "Continuous variable input and output devices." In *The Moore School Lectures*, edited by M. Campbell-Kelly and M. Williams, 1985. Cambridge, MA: MIT Press, 393–423.

Edison, T. 1878. "Improvements in phonograph or speaking machines." U.S. Patent Number 200,521. Reprinted in *From Tin Foil to Stereo: Evolution of the Phonograph,* O. Read and W. Welch, 1976. Indianapolis: Howard Sams.

Eigenfeldt, A., and P. Pasquier. 2013. "Considering vertical and horizontal context in corpus-based generative electronic dance music." In *Proceedings of the International Conference on Computational Creativity*, 72–78. Sydney: Association for Computational Creativity.

Elad, M. 2010. *Sparse and Redundant Representations: From Theory to Applications in Signal and Image Processing*. New York: Springer.

Ellis, T., J. Heafner, and W. Sibley. "The GRAIL project: an experiment in man-machine communication." Memorandum RM-5999-ARPA. Santa Monica: Rand Corporation.

Elwell, K. 2020. Personal communication.

Emmerson, S., and L. Landy. 2016a. "The analysis of electroacoustic music: The differing needs of its genres and categories." In *Expanding the Horizon of Electroacoustic Music Analysis*, edited by S. Emmerson and L. Landy. Cambridge: Cambridge University Press, 8–28.

Emmerson, S., and L. Landy, eds. 2016b. *Expanding the Horizon of Electroacoustic Music Analysis*. Cambridge: Cambridge University Press.

Engel, J., K. Agrawal, S. Chen, I. Gulrajani, C. Donahue, and A. Roberts. 2019. "GANSynth: Adversarial neural audio synthesis." In *Proceedings of the International Conference on Learning Representations*. n.p.: OpenReview. https://openreview.net/forum?id=H1xQVn09FX.

Engel, J., L. Hantrakul, C. Gu, and A. Roberts. 2020. "DDSP: Differentiable digital signal processing." In *Proceedings of the International Conference on Learning Representations*. n.p.: OpenReview. https://openreview.net/forum?id=B1x1ma4tDr.

Engel, J., C. Resnick, A. Roberts, S. Dieleman, D. Eck, K. Simonyan, and M. Norouzi. 2017. "Neural audio synthesis of musical notes with WaveNet autoencoders." In *Pro-*

ceedings of the International Conference on Machine Learning, Vol. 70. New York: Association for Computing Machinery, 1068–1077.

Entwistle, J. 1973. "Visual perception and the analysis of music scores." BS thesis. MIT, Department of Humanities.

Erbe, T. 1992. *SoundHack User's Manual.* Oakland, CA: Mills College.

Erbe, T. 2014. "Designing the Erbe-Verb." Video of lecture in the Media Arts and Technology Seminar Series. University of California, Santa Barbara. https://www .youtube.com/watch?v=Il_qdtQKnqk. Slides at http://tre.ucsd.edu/wordpress/wp -content/uploads/2018/10/reverbtopo.pdf.

Erbe, T. 2015. "Building the Erbe-Verb: Extending the feedback delay network reverb for modular synthesizer use." In *Proceedings of the 2015 International Computer Music Conference.* San Francisco: International Computer Music Association, 262–265.

Erickson, R. 1975. "The DARMS project: A status report." *Computers and the Humanities* 7(2): 291–298.

Erkhut, C., V. Välimäki, M. Karjalainen, and H. Penttinen. 2008. "Physics-based sound synthesis." In *Sound to Sense—Sense to Sound: A State of the Art in Sound and Music Computing*, edited by P. Polotti and D. Rochesso, 2008. Berlin: Logos, 303–343.

Ernst, D. 1977. *The Evolution of Electronic Music.* New York: Schirmer Books.

Escalante, J.-M. 2020. "Diagrammatics: A theory of audiovisual notation." PhD diss. Media Arts and Technology, University of California.

Esqueda, F., H. Pöntynen, V. Välimäki, and J. Parker. 2017. "Virtual analog Buchla 259 wavefolder." In *Proceedings of the 20th International Conference on Digital Audio Effects (DAFx-17).* n.p.: DAFx, 192–199.

Essl, G. 2007. "Algorithmic composition." In *The Cambridge Companion to Electronic Music*, edited by N. Collins and J. d'Escrivan. Cambridge: Cambridge University Press, 107–125.

Essl, G., S. Sterafin, P. Cook, and J. O. Smith. 2004a. "Musical applications of banded waveguides." *Computer Music Journal* 28(2): 51–63.

Essl, G., S. Sterafin, P. Cook, and J. O. Smith. 2004b. "Theory of banded waveguides." *Computer Music Journal* 28(2): 37–50.

Evangelista, G. 1991. "Wavelet transforms that we can play." In *Representations of Musical Signals*, edited by G. De Poli, A. Piccialli, and C. Roads. Cambridge, MA: MIT Press, 119–136.

Evangelista, G. 1992. "Comb and multiplexed wavelet transforms and their applications to signal processing." Unpublished manuscript.

Evangelista, G. 1997. "Wavelet representations of musical signals." In *Musical Signal Processing*, edited by C. Roads et al. Abingdon, UK: Taylor & Francis, 127–153.

Evangelista, G. 2001. "Flexible wavelets for musical signal processing." *Journal of New Music Research* 30(1): 13–22.

Evangelista, G., 2011. "Time and frequency-warping musical signals." In *DAFX: Digital Audio Effects*, 2nd ed., edited by U. Zölzer. Chichester, UK: John Wiley & Sons, 447–472.

Evangelista, G. 2017. "Redressing warped wavelets and other similar warped time-something representations." In *Proceedings of the 20th International Conference on Digital Audio Effects (DAFx-17)*. n.p.: DAFx, 260–267.

Evangelista, G., and F. Eckerholm. 2010. "Player instrument interaction models for digital waveguide synthesis of guitar: touch and collisions." *IEEE Transactions on Audio Speech, and Language Processing* 18(4): 822–832.

Evangelista, G., S. Marchand, M. Plumbley, and E. Vincent. 2011. "Sound source separation." In *DAFX: Digital Audio Effects*, 2nd ed., edited by U. Zölzer. Chichester, UK: John Wiley & Sons, 551–588.

Evanstein, M. 2019. "SCAMP: A suite for composing algorithmic music in Python." In *Proceedings of the 2019 International Computer Music Conference*. San Francisco: International Computer Music Association.

Eventide. 2019. *Blackhole User Guide.* https://www.eventide.com.

Every, M., and J. Szymanski. 2006. "Separation of synchronous pitched notes by spectral filtering of harmonics." *IEEE Transactions on Audio, Speech, and Language Processing* 14(5): 1845–1856.

Ewert, S., B. Pardo, M. Muller, and M. Plumbley. 2014. "Score-informed source separation for musical audio recordings: An overview." *IEEE Signal Processing Magazine* 31(5): 116–124.

Extempore. 2020. "Extempore: An audiovisual live programming environment." https://extemporelang.github.io.

Factor, R., and S. Katz. 1972. "The digital audio delay line." *db Magazine* May: 18.

Fagen, M., ed. 1975. *A History of Engineering and Science in the Bell System: The Early Years (1875–1925)*. Murray Hill, NJ: Bell Telephone Laboratories.

Fairbanks, G., W. Everitt, and R. Jaeger. 1954. "Method for time or frequency compression-expansion of speech." *Institute of Radio Engineers Transactions on Audio* AV-2(1): 7–12.

Farina, A. 2000. "Simultaneous measurement of impulse response and distortion with a swept-sine technique." In *Proceedings of the Audio Engineering Society 110th Convention, Paris*. New York: Audio Engineering Society.

Farina, A. 2007. "Advancements in impulse response measurements by sine sweeps." In *Proceedings of the Audio Engineering Society 122nd Convention, Vienna*. New York: Audio Engineering Society.

Farina, A., and R. Ayalon. 2005. "Recording concert hall acoustics for posterity." In *Proceedings of the Audio Engineering Society 24th Conference on Multichannel Audio.* New York: Audio Engineering Society.

Farnell, A. 2010. *Designing Sound: Procedural Audio for Games and Film.* Cambridge, MA: MIT Press.

Faulkner, T. 2011. "Interview with Tony Faulkner." Video. https://www.youtube.com /watch?v=8uCcFlyJJ-w.

Fauvel, J., R. Flood, and R. Wilson, eds. 2003. *Music and Mathematics: From Pythagoras to Fractals.* Oxford: Oxford University Press.

Federkow, G., W. Buxton, and K. Smith. 1978. "A computer-controlled sound distribution system for performance of electroacoustic music." *Computer Music Journal* 2(3): 33–42.

Feichtinger, H., and T. Strohmer, eds. 1998. *Gabor Analysis and Algorithms.* Boston: Birkhäuser.

Fell, M., and J. Gilmore. 2013. "Composing with Process: Perspectives on generative and systems music." https://rwm.macba.cat/en/buscador/radio/etiquetas /componiendo-procesos-9840.

Fernández, J., and F. Vico. 2013. "AI methods in algorithmic composition: A comprehensive survey." *Journal of Artificial Intelligence Research* 48: 513–582.

Ferreira-Lopes, P. 2004. "Étude de modèles interactifs et d'interfaces de contrôle en temps réel pour la composition musicale." Doctoral diss. Université Paris 8.

Ferretti, E. 1965. "The computer as a tool for the creative musician." In *Computers for the Humanities.* New Haven: Yale University Press, 107–112.

Ferretti, E. 1966. "Exploration and organization of sound with the computer." *Journal of the Acoustical Society of America* 39(6): 1245.

Ferretti, E. 1975. "Sound synthesis by rule." In *Proceedings of the Second Annual Music Computation Conference*, edited by J. Beauchamp and J. Melby. Urbana: University of Illinois, 1–21.

Fiebrink, R. 2020. "Machine learning for musicians and artists." Online course. https://www.kadenze.com.

Fiebrink, R., and P. Cook. 2010. "The Wekinator: A System for Real-time, Interactive Machine Learning in Music." In *Proceedings of the Eleventh International Society for Music Information Retrieval Conference.* n.p.: International Society for Music Information Retrieval.

Fiebrink, R., and L. Sonami. 2020. "Reflections on eight years of instrument making using machine learning." In *Proceedings of the New Interfaces for Musical Expression (NIME 2020) Conference.* n.p.: New Interfaces for Musical Expression. https:// www.nime.org. Video presentation at https://vimeo.com/450616595.

Figueiredo, M., R. Nowak, and S. J. Wright. 2007. "Gradient projection for sparse reconstruction: Application to compressed sensing and other inverse problems." *IEEE Journal of Selected Topics in Signal Processing* 1(4): 586–597.

Fischer, V. 2020. "Case study: Performing band rehearsals on the Internet with Jamulus." https://llcon.sourceforge.io.

Fischman, R. 2003. "Clouds, pyramids, and diamonds: Applying Schrödinger's equation to granular synthesis and compositional structure." *Computer Music Journal* 27(2): 47–69.

Fitz, K., and L. Haken. 1996. "Sinusoidal modeling and manipulation using Lemur." *Computer Music Journal* 20(4): 44–59.

Fitz, K., L. Haken, S. Lefvert, C. Champion, and M. O'Donnell. 2003. "Cell-utes and flutter- tongued cats: Sound morphing using Loris and the reassigned bandwidth-enhanced model." *Computer Music Journal* 27(4): 47–65.

ffitch, J. 2000. "A look at random numbers, noise, and chaos with Csound." In *The Csound Book*, edited by R. Boulanger. Cambridge, MA: MIT Press, 321–338.

Five 12. 2014. *Numerology 4 Manual*. Albuquerque: Five 12.

Flanagan, J. L. 1972. *Speech Analysis, Synthesis, and Perception*. New York: Springer.

Flanagan, J. L., and R. Golden. 1966. "Phase vocoder." *Bell System Technical Journal* 45: 1493–1509.

Flanagan, J. L., et al. 1970. "Synthetic voices for computers." *IEEE Spectrum* 7(10): 22–45.

Fleming, J. A. 1919. *The Thermionic Valve and its Developments in Radiotelegraphy and Telephony*. London: The Wireless Press. Reprinted 2012. Miami: Hard Press.

Fletcher, H., E. Blackham, and D. Christensen. 1963. "Quality of organ tones." *Journal of the Acoustical Society of America* 35(3): 314–325.

Fletcher, H., E. Blackham, and R. Stratton. 1962. "Quality of piano tones." *Journal of the Acoustical Society of America* 34(6): 749–761.

Fletcher, N., and T. Rossing. 1991. *The Physics of Musical Instruments*. New York: Springer.

Floreano, D., and C. Mattiusi. 2008. *Bio-Inspired Artificial Intelligence: Theories, Methods, and Technologies*. Cambridge, MA: MIT Press.

Florens, J., and C. Cadoz. 1991. "The physical model: modeling and simulating the instrumental universe." In *Representations of Musical Signals*, edited by G. De Poli, A. Piccialli, and C. Roads. Cambridge, MA: MIT Press, 227–268.

FluidSynth. 2019. FluidSynth home page. https://www.fluidsynth.org.

Fober, D. 1994. "Real-time MIDI data flow on Ethernet and the software architecture of MidiShare." In *Proceedings of the International Computer Music Conference*. San Francisco: International Computer Music Association, 447–450.

Fober, D., Y. Orlarey, and S. Letz. 2011. "FAUST architecture design and OSC support." In *Proceedings of the 14th Conference on Digital Audio Effects (DAFx-11)*. n.p.: DAFx. https://www.dafx.de.

Fokker, A. 1975. *New Music with 31 Tones*. Bonn, Germany: Verlag für systematische Musikwissenschaft.

Fonseca, N. 2013. "3D particle systems for audio applications." In *Proceedings of the 16th Conference on Digital Audio Effects (DAFx-13)*. n.p.: DAFx. https://www.dafx.de.

Fontana, F. 2007. "Preserving the structure of the Moog VCF in the digital domain." In *Proceedings of the International Computer Music Conference*. San Francisco: International Computer Music Association, 291–294.

Fontana, F., and M. Civolani. 2010. "Modeling the EMS VCS3 voltage-controlled filter as a nonlinear filter network." *IEEE Transactions on Audio, Speech, amd Language Processing* 18(4): 760–762.

Focusrite. 2018. *Liquid Channel Factory Presets*. https://global.focusrite.com/mic-pres/liquid-channel/downloads.

Forgotten Futures. 2017. *The Ondioline: The Design and Development of an Electronic Musical Instrument*. New York: Forgotten Futures.

Foster, S., W. A. Schloss, and A. J. Rockmore. 1982. "Toward an intelligent editor fordigital audio: Signal processing methods." *Computer Music Journal* 6(1): 42–51. Reprinted in *The Music Machine*, edited by C. Roads, 1989. Cambridge, MA: MIT Press, 549–558.

Fourier, L. 1994. "Jean-Jacques Perrey and the Ondioline." *Computer Music Journal* 18(4): 18–25.

Framjee, P. F. 1958. *Text Book of Indian Music*. Hathras, India: Sakhi Prakashan.

Françoise, J. 2013. "Gesture–Sound mapping by demonstration in interactive music systems." In *Proceedings of the 21st ACM International Conference on Multimedia*. New York: Association for Computing Machinery, 1051–1054.

Franinovic, K., and S. Serafin, eds. 2013. *Sonic Interaction Design*. Cambridge, MA: MIT Press.

Franssen, N. 1973. "Tempered tone-scale generation from a single oscillator."*Journal of the Audio Engineering Society* 21(6): 457–460.

Freed, A. 1987. "MacMix: Recording, mixing, and signal processing on a personal computer." In *Music and Digital Technology*, edited by J. Strawn. New York: Audio Engineering Society, 158–162.

Freed, A., and M. Goldstein. 1988. "MacMix: Professional sound recording, editing, processing, and mixing software for the DYAXIS digital audio system." Menlo Park, CA: Studer Editech.

Freed, A., and A. Schmeder. 2009. "Features and Future of Open Sound Control version 1.1 for NIME." In *Proceedings of the New Interfaces for Musical Expression (NIME 2009) Conference*. n.p.: New Interfaces for Musical Expression. https://www.nime.org.

Freedman, M. D. 1965. "A technique for analysis of musical instrument tones." PhD diss. University of Illinois.

Freedman, M. D. 1967. "Analysis of musical instrument tones." *Journal of the Acoustical Society of America* 41: 793–806.

Freeman, J., and A. Troyer. 2011. "Collaborative textual improvisation in a laptop ensemble." *Computer Music Journal* 35(2): 8–21.

Freeman, W. J. 1991. "The physiology of perception." *Scientific American* 264(2): 78–87.

Freff, C. 1989. "Raymond Scott's Electronium (1965)." *Keyboard* 15(2): 50–56.

Frenette, J. 2000. "Reducing artificial reverberation algorithm requirements using time-varying feedback delay networks." MS thesis, Music Engineering Technology. University of Florida.

Friberg, A. 1991. "Generative rules for music performance: A formal description of a rule system." *Computer Music Journal* 15(2): 56–71.

Friberg, A., L., Frydèn, L. Bodin, and J. Sundberg. 1991. "Performance rules for computer-controlled contemporary keyboard music." *Computer Music Journal* 15(2): 49–55.

Friburg, A., and R. Bresin. 2008. "Real-time control of music performance." In *Sound to Sense—Sense to Sound: A State of the Art in Sound and Music Computing*, edited by P. Polotti and D. Rocchesso. 2008. Berlin: Logos, 279–302.

Frid, E. 2018. "Accessible digital musical instruments–A survey of inclusive instruments presented at the NIME, SMC and ICMC conferences." In *Proceedings of the 2018 International Computer Music Conference*. San Francisco: International Computer Music Association, 53–59.

Friedman, J. H., and J. W. Tukey. 1974. "A projection pursuit algorithm for exploratory data analysis." *IEEE Transactions on Computation* C-23(9): 881–890.

Frieler, K., J. Abesser, W. Zaddach, and B. Burkhard, eds. 2017. *Inside the Jazzomat. New Perspectives for Jazz Research*. Mainz, Germany: Schott Campus.

Fry, C. 1980. *YAMIL Reference Manual*. Cambridge, MA: The MIT Experimental Music Studio.

Fry, C. 1984. "Flavors Band: A language for specifying musical style." *Computer Music Journal* 8(4): 48–58. Reprinted in *The Music Machine*, edited by C. Roads, 1989. Cambridge, MA: MIT Press, 295–309.

Fry, C. 1992. "MidiVox Voice-to-MIDI converter." *Computer Music Journal* 16(1): 94–95.

Fujinaga, I., B. Alphonce, and B. Pennycook. 1989. "Issues in the design of an optical music recognition system." In *Proceedings of the 1989 International Computer Music Conference*, edited by T. Wells and D. Butler. San Francisco: International Computer Music Association, 113–116.

Fujinaga, I., B. Alphonce, B. Pennycook, and K. Hogan. 1991. "Optical character recognition: A progress report." In *Proceedings of the 1991 International Computer Music Conference*, edited by B. Alphonce and B. Pennycook. San Francisco: International Computer Music Association, 66–73.

Fulop, S., and K. Fitz. 2007. "Separation of components from impulses in reassigned spectrograms." *Journal of the Acoustical Society of America* 121(3): 1510–1518.

Gabor, D. 1946. "Theory of communication." *Journal of the Institute of Electrical Engineers* Part 3, 93: 429–457.

Gabor, D. 1947. *Acoustical Quanta and the Theory of Hearing. Nature* 159(1044): 591–594.

Gabor, D. 1952. *Lectures on Communication Theory*. Technical Report 238, Research Laboratory of Electronics. Cambridge, MA: MIT.

Gabrielli, L., S. Tomassetti, C. Zinato, and S. Squartini. 2017. "Introducing deep machine learning for parameter estimation in physical modelling." In *Proceedings of the International Conference on Digital Audio Effects (DAFx)*.n.p.: DAFx. https://www.dafx.de.

Gabrielsson, A. 1986. "Rhythm in music." In *Rhythm in Psychological, Linguistic, and Musical Processes*, edited by J. Evans and M. Clynes. Springfield, IL: Charles C. Thomas, 131–167.

Galas, T., and X. Rodet. 1990. "An improved cepstral method for deconvolution of source-filter systems with discrete spectra: Application to musical signals." In *Proceedings of the 1990 International Computer Music Conference*, edited by S. Arnold and G. Hair. San Francisco: International Computer Music Association, 82–84.

Gardner, T., and M. O. Magnasco. 2006. "Sparse time-frequency representations." *Proceedings of the National Academy of the Sciences* 103(16): 6094–6099.

Gardner, W. 1995. "Efficient convolution without input-output delay." *Journal of the Audio Engineering Society* 43(3): 127–136.

Garnett, G. 1987. "Modeling piano sound using waveguide digital filtering techniques." In *Proceedings of the 1987 International Computer Music Conference*, edited by J. Beauchamp. San Francisco: International Computer Music Association, 89–95.

Garnett, G. 1991. "Music, signals, and representations: A survey." In *Representations of Musical Signals*, edited by G. De Poli, A. Piccialli, and C. Roads. Cambridge, MA: MIT Press, 325–369.

Garnett, G., and B. Mont-Reynaud. 1988. "Hierarchical waveguide networks." In *Proceedings of the 1988 International Computer Music Conference*, edited by C. Lischka and J. Fritsch. San Francisco: International Computer Music Association, 297–312.

Garton, B. 1992. "Virtual performance modeling." In *Proceedings of the 1992 International Computer Music Conference*, edited by A. Strange. San Francisco: International Computer Music Association, 219–222.

Gaudrain, E., and Y. Orlarey. 2007. *A FAUST Tutorial.* http://www.grame.fr/pub /faust_tutorial.pdf.

Geiringer, K. 1945. *Musical Instruments.* London: George Allen and Unwin.

Gerhard, D. 2003. *Pitch Extraction and Fundamental Frequency: History and Current Techniques.* Technical Report TR-CS 2003–06. Department of Computer Science. University of Regina.

Gerrard, G. 1989. "Music 4C—A Macintosh version of Music4BF in C." Melbourne: Department of Music, University of Melbourne.

Gersho, A., and R. M. Grey. 1992. *Vector Quantization and Signal Compression.* Norwell, MA: Kluwer.

Gerzon, M. 1971. "Synthetic stereo reverberation: Part one." *Studio Sound* 13: 632–635.

Gerzon, M. 1972. "Synthetic stereo reverberation: Part two." *Studio Sound* 14: 24–28.

Gerzon, M. 1973. "Periphony: With-height sound reproduction." *Journal of the Audio Engineering Society* 21(3): 2–10.

Gerzon, M. 1977. "Design of ambisonic decoders for multi speaker surround sound." In *Proceedings of the 58th Audio Engineering Society Convention.* Audio Engineering Society: New York.

Gerzon, M. 1990. "Why do equalisers sound different?" *Studio Sound* 32(7): 58–65.

Gerzon, M. 1991. "Super-resolving short-term spectral analyzers." Preprint 3174 (T-5). In *Proceedings of the 91st Convention of the Audio Engineering Society.* New York: Audio Engineering Society.

Geslin, Y. 2002. "Digital sound and music transformation environments: A twenty-year experiment at the Groupe de Recherches Musicales." *Journal of New Music Research* 31(2): 99–107.

Ghent, E. 1967a. "The Coordinome in relation to electronic music." *Electronic Music Review* 1(1): 33–43.

Ghent, E. 1967b. "Programmed signals to performers." *Perspectives of New Music.* Reprinted in *Perspectives on Notation and Performance*, edited by B. Boretz and E. Cone. New York: W. W. Norton, 134–144.

Ghorbal, S., T. Auclair, C. Soladié, and R. Séguir. 2017. "Pinna morphological parameters influencing HTRF sets." In *Proceedings of the 20th International Conference on Digital Audio Effects (DAFx-17)*. n.p.: DAFx. https://dafx.de.

Gibson, J., T. Berger, A. Lookabaugh, R. Baker, and D. Lindberg. 1998. *Digital Compression for Multimedia: Principles and Standards.* Burlington, MA: Morgan Kaufman.

Gill, S. 1963. "A technique for the composition of music in a computer." *Computer Journal* 6(2): 29–31.

Gillespie, B. 1992. "Dynamical modeling of grand piano action." In *Proceedings of the 1992 International Computer Music Conference*, edited by A. Strange. San Francisco: International Computer Music Association, 77–80.

Gillespie, B., and M. Cutkowsky. 1992. "Dynamical model of the grand piano action." In *Proceedings of the 1992 International Computer Music Conference*. San Francisco: International Computer Music Association, 77–80.

Gillespie, B., B. Yu, R. Grijalva, and S. Awtar. 2011. "Characterizing the feel of the piano action." *Computer Music Journal* 35(1): 43–57.

Giordano, A. 2020. *Peppino Di Giugno: Macchine Digitali per la Musica in Tempo Reale.* Fontanarosa (AV), Italy: Edizioni Musicali Esarmonia.

Gish, W. 1978. "Analysis and synthesis of musical instrument tones." Preprint 1410. In *Proceedings of the 61st Convention of the Audio Engineering Society*. New York: Audio Engineering Society.

Gish, W. 1992. "Multistage signal analysis." In *Proceedings of the 1992 International Computer Music Conference*, edited by A. Strange. San Francisco: International Computer Music Association, 387–388.

Gjerdingen, R. 1988. "Shape and motion in the microstructure of song." *Music Perception* 6(1): 35–64.

Glaser, E., and D. Ruchkin. 1976. *Principles of Neurobiological Signal Analysis.* Orlando: Academic Press.

glui. 2020. "glui—25 years of custom technology for musicians and artists." http://www.glui.de/wp/.

Goebel, J., producer. 1995. *The historical CD of digital sound synthesis.* Computer Music Currents 13. Mainz, Germany: Wergo 2033. (Compact disc + 260-page booklet.)

Goebl, W., and B. Bresin. 2003. "Measurement and reproduction accuracy of computer-controlled grand pianos." *Journal of the Acoustical Society of America* 114(4): 2273–2283.

Goebl, W., S. Dixon, G. De Poli, A. Friberg, R. Bresin, and G. Widmer. 2008. "Sense in expressive music performance: Data acquisition, computational studies and models." In *Sound to Sense—Sense to Sound: A State of the Art in Sound and Music Computing*, edited by P. Polotti and D. Rocchesso. Berlin: Logos, 194–242.

Goeddel, T., and S. Bass. 1984. "High-quality synthesis of musical voices in discrete time." *IEEE Transactions on Acoustics, Speech, and Signal Processing* ASSP-32(3): 623–633.

Gogins, M. 1991. "Iterated function systems music." *Computer Music Journal* 15(1): 40–48.

Gold, B. 1962. "A computer program for pitch extraction." *Journal of the Acoustical Society of America* 34: 916.

Goldberg, D. 1989. *Genetic Algorithms in Search, Optimization, and Machine Learning.* Reading, MA: Addison-Wesley.

Goldstein, J. 1973. "An optimum processor theory for the central formation of the pitch of complex tones." *Journal of the Acoustical Society of America* 54(6): 1496–1516.

Gómez, E., A. Klapuri, and B. Meudic. "Melody description and extraction in the context of music content processing." *Journal of New Music Research* 32(1): 23–40.

Good, M. 2000. "Representing music using XML." Abstract for a poster session presented at the International Symposium on Music Information Retrieval (ISMIR), October 23–25, 2000, Plymouth, MA.

Good, M. 2006. "Music XML: Methodology and technical methods." https://wpmedia.musicxml.com/wp-content/uploads/2012/11/mainz2006-talk.pdf

Good, M. 2013. "Beyond PDF–Exchange and publish scores with MusicXML." Presented at the Frankfurt Musikmesse 2013. https://www.musicxml.com/publications/.

Goodwin, M. M. 1997. *Adaptive Signal Models: Theory, Algorithms, and Audio Applications*. PhD diss. University of California, Berkeley.

Goodwin, M. M., and M. Vetterli. 1999. "Matching pursuit and atomic signal models based on recursive filter banks." *IEEE Transactions on Signal Processing* 47, 1890–1902.

Gordon, J., and J. Grey. 1977. "Perception of spectral modifications on orchestral instrument tones." *Computer Music Journal* 2(1): 24–31.

Gordon, J., and J. Strawn. 1985. "An introduction to the phase vocoder". In *Digital Audio Signal Processing: An Anthology*, edited by J. Strawn. Middleton, WI: A-R Editions, 221–270.

Goto, M., and R. Dannenberg. 2019. "Music interfaces based on automatic signal analysis." *IEEE Signal Processing Magazine* 36(1): 74–81.

Goudard, V., and R. Muller. 2003. "Real-time plugin architectures." http://mdsp2.free.fr/ircam/pluginarch.pdf.

Gouyon, F., and S. Dixon. 2005. "A review of automatic rhythm description systems." *Computer Music Journal* 29(1) 34–54.

Gouyon, F., P. Herrera, E. Gómez, P. Cano, J. Bonada, A. Loscos, Z. Amatriain, and X. Serra. 2008. "Content processing of music audio signals." In *Sound to Sense—Sense to Sound: A State of the Art in Sound and Music Computing*, edited by P. Polotti and D. Rocchesso. Berlin: Logos, 83–160.

Gover, D., M. Jackson, and S. Schmitt. 2010. *REAKTOR PRISM Manual.* Berlin: Native Instruments.

Gräf, A. 2009. "Signal processing in the Pure programming language." *Linux Audio Conference.* https://lac.linuxaudio.org.

Graham-Knight, K., and G. Tzanetakis. 2015. "Adaptive music technology: history and future perspectives." In *Proceedings of the 2015 International Computer Music Conference.* San Francisco: International Computer Music Association, 416–419.

GRAME. 2017. "FAUST programming language." https://www.grame.fr/logiciels.

Grattan-Guinness, I. 1972. *Joseph Fourier: 1768–1830.* Cambridge, MA: MIT Press.

Greenberg, G. 1988. "Composing with performer objects." In *Proceedings of the 1988 International Computer Music Conference*, edited by C. Lischka and J. Fritsch. San Francisco: International Computer Music Association, 142–149.

Greiner, R., and D. Melton. 1991. "Observations on the audibility of acoustic polarity." Preprint 3170-(K-4). In *Proceedings of the 91st Convention of the Audio Engineering Society 1991 October 4–8, New York.* New York: Audio Engineering Society.

Grey, J. 1975. *An Exploration of Musical Timbre.* Report STAN-M-2. Stanford, CA: Stanford University Department of Music.

Grey, J. 1978. "Timbre discrimination in musical patterns." *Journal of the Acoustical Society of America* 64: 467–472.

Grey, J., and J. Gordon. 1978. "Perceptual effects of spectral modifications on musical timbres." *Journal of the Acoustical Society of America* 63: 1493–1500.

Gribonval, R. 1999. *Approximations Non-linéaires pour l'Analyse des Signaux Sonores.* PhD thesis. Université Paris-IX-Dauphine.

Gribonval, R. 2001. "Fast matching pursuit with a multiscale dictionary of Gaussian chirps." *IEEE Transactions on Signal Processing* 49(5): 994–1001.

Gribonval, R. 2002. "Sparse decomposition of stereo signals with matching pursuit and application to blind separation of more than two sources from a stereo mixture." In *Proceedings of the International Conference on Audio, Speech, and Signal Processing.* New York: IEEE, 3057–3060.

Gribonval, R., and E. Bacry. 2003. "Harmonic decompositions of audio signals with matching pursuit." *IEEE Transactions on Signal Processing* 51(1): 101–111.

Griesinger, D. 2000. Quoted in P. White. "David Griesinger (Lexicon): Creating reverb algorithms for surround sound." *Sound on Sound* 15(3).

Griesinger, D. 2014. "Long bio." http://www.davidgriesinger.com.

Griffiths, M., and P. Bloom. 1982. "A flexible digital sound-editing program for mini-computer systems." *Journal of the Audio Engineering Society* 30(3): 127–134.

Grogono, P. 1984. "Brief history of EMS." Unpublished manuscript.

Grogono, P. 2011. "Electronic Music Studios (London) Ltd." http://users.encs .concordia.ca/~grogono/Bio/ems.html. (Online source no longer available.)

Grossman, G. 1987. "Instruments, cybernetics, and music." In *Proceedings of the 1987 International Computer Music Conference*, edited by J. Beauchamp. San Francisco: International Computer Music Association, 212–219.

Grout, D. 1973. *A Short History of Western Music*. Revised edition. New York: W. W. Norton.

Guérin, R. 2006. *MIDI Power!* 2nd ed. Boston: Thomson Course Technology.

Guillaume, P. 2011. "Device for producing signals representative of sounds of a keyboard and string instrument." U.S. Patent 7,915,515 B2.

Gujar-Kale, P. 2020. *PhD Qualifying Examination Written Report*. Media Arts and Technology. Santa Barbara: University of California.

Gurevich, M. 2014. "Distributed control in a mechatronic musical instrument." In *Proceedings of the International Conference on New Instruments for Musical Expression (NIME)*. n.p.: New Interfaces for Music Expression, 487–490.

Gururani, S., M. Sharma, and A. Lerch. 2019. "An attention mechanism for musical instrument recognition." *20th International Society for Music Information Retrieval Conference*. n.p.: International Society for Music Information Retrieval.

Guttman, N. 1980. Personal communication.

Gwee, N. 2002. "Complexity and heuristics in rule-based algorithmic music composition." PhD diss. Department of Computer Science, Louisiana State University.

Habets, E. 2016. "Fifty years of reverberation reduction: From analog signal processing to machine learning." In *Proceedings of the AES 60th Conference on Dereverberation and Reverberation of Audio, Music, and Speech*. New York: Audio Engineering Society.

Habets, E., and P. Naylor. 2018. "Dereverberation." In *Audio Source Separation and Speech Enhancement*, edited by E. Vincent, T. Virtanen, and S. Gannot. New York: John Wiley & Sons, 317–343.

Hackbarth, B., N. Schnell, P. Esling, and D. Schwarz. 2013. "Composing morphology: concatenative synthesis as an intuitive medium for prescribing sound in time." *Contemporary Music Review* 32(1): 49–59.

Hacker, S. 2000. *MP3: The Definitive Guide.* Sebastopol, CA: O'Reilly.

Hadjeres, G., F. Pachet, and F. Nielson. 2017. "DeepBach: A steerable model for Bach chorales generation." In *Proceedings of the 34th International Conference on Machine Learning, Sydney.* New York: Association for Computing Machinery,

Haflich, S., and M. Burns. 1983. "Following a conductor: the engineering of an input device." In *Proceedings of the 1983 International Computer Music Conference, October 1983, Eastman School of Music, Rochester, NY.* San Francisco: International Computer Music Association.

Hajdu, G. 2016. "Resurrecting a dinosaur—The adaptation of Clarence Barlow's legacy software AUTOBUSK." In *Proceedings of the International Conference on Technologies for Music Notation and Representation.* https://www.tenor-conference.org.

Hall, H. 1937. "Sound analysis." *Journal of the Acoustical Society of America* 8: 257–262.

Haller, H. P. 1980. "Live-Elektronik." In *Teilton Schriftenreihe der Heinrich-Strobel-Stiftung des Südwestfunks.* Kassel, Germany: Barenreiter-Verlag, 41–46.

Hamel, K. 1987. "Issues in the design of a music notation system." In *Proceedings of the 1987 International Computer Music* Conference, edited by J. Beauchamp. San Francisco: International Computer Music Association, 325–332.

Hamel, K. 1989. "A design for music editing and printing software based on a notational syntax." *Perspectives of New Music* 27(1): 70–83.

Hamel, K., B. Pennycook, B. Ripley, and E. Blevis. 1987. "Composition Design System: a functional approach to composition." In *Proceedings of the 1987 International Computer Music Conference*, edited by J. Beauchamp. San Francisco: International Computer Music Association, 33–39.

Hamming, R. 1987. *Numerical Methods for Scientists and Engineers.* New York: Dover.

Hamming, R. 1989. *Digital Filters.* New York: Dover.

Hamon, C., E. Mouline, and F. Charpentier. 1989. "A diphone synthesis system based on time domain prosodic modifications of speech." In *Proceedings of the International Conference on Acoustics, Speech, and Signal Processing* (ICASSP). New York: IEEE, 238–241.

Hanappe, P. 1999. *Design and Implementation of an Integrated Environment for Music Composition and Synthesis.* Doctoral thesis. Paris: Université Paris 6.

Hanert, J. 1944. "Proposed system for producing chorus effect." U.S. Patent 2,498,367.

Hanert, J. 1945. "Electronic musical apparatus (L-C delay line with variable inductors for post source vibrato processing)." U.S. Patent 2,382, 413.

Hanert, J. 1946. "Manufactured system for producing chorus effect." U.S. Patent 2, 509,923.

Hansen, E. 1975. *A Table of Series and Products.* Englewood Cliffs, NJ: Prentice Hall.

Harada, T., A. Sato, S. Hashimoto, and S. Ohteru. 1992. "Real-time control of 3D space by gesture." In *Proceedings of the 1992 International Computer Music Conference,* edited by A. Strange. San Francisco: International Computer Music Association, 85–88.

Harley, A. 1998. "Spatiality of sound and stream segregation in twentieth century instrumental music." *Organised Sound* 3(2): 147–166.

Harley, J. 2004. *Xenakis: His Life in Music.* New York: Routledge.

Harris, F. 1978. "On the use of windows for harmonic analysis with the discrete Fourier transform." *Proceedings of the IEEE* 66(1): 51–83.

Hartman, W. H. 1978. "Flanging and phasers." *Journal of the Audio Engineering Society* 26(6): 439–443.

Hartmann, A. 2013. *Neuron VS: Neuron Software Synthesizer.* User manual. http://www.neuronsynth.com.

Harvey, J. 1981. "*Mortuos Plango, Vivos Voco:* A Realization at IRCAM." *Computer Music Journal* 5(4): 22–24.

Hastie, T., R. Tibshirani, and J. Friedman. 2009. *The Elements of Statistical Learning: Data Mining, Inference, and Prediction.* 2nd ed. Cham, Switzerland: Springer.

Hastings, C. 1978. "A recipe for homebrew ECL." *Computer Music Journal* 2(1): 48–59. Revised and updated version in *Foundations of Computer Music,* edited by C. Roads and J. Strawn, 1985. Cambridge, MA: MIT Press, 335–362.

Haus, G. 1983. "EMPS: A system for graphic transcription of electronic music scores." *Computer Music Journal* 7(3): 31–36.

Haus, G. 1984. *Elementi di Informatica Musicale.* Milan: Gruppo Editoriale Jackson.

Hauser, M. 1991. "Principles of oversampling A/D conversion." *Journal of the Audio Engineering Society* 39(1–2): 3–21.

Haynes, S. 1980. "The musician-machine interface in digital sound synthesis." *Computer Music Journal* 4(4): 23–44.

He, J., and Z. Fu. 2001. *Modal Analysis.* Woburn, MA: Butterworth-Heinemann.

Helmers, C. 1979. "Interfacing pneumatic player pianos." In *The Byte Book of Computer Music,* edited by C. Morgan. Peterborough, NH: Byte Books, 85–90.

Helmholtz, H. (1885) 1954. *The Sensations of Tone,* translated by A. Ellis. New York: Dover.

Helstrom, C. 1966. "An expansion of a signal in Gaussian elementary signals." *IEEE Transactions on Information Theory* IT-12: 81–82.

Henke, W. 1970. "Musical interactive tone synthesis system." Cambridge, MA: MIT.

Henz, M., S. Lauer, and D. Zimmermann. 1996. "COMPOzE—Intention-based Music Composition through Constraint Programming." In *Proceedings of the Eighth IEEE International Conference on Tools with Artificial Intelligence.* New York: IEEE.

Hermann, T. 2002. "Sonification for exploratory data analysis." PhD diss. Bielfeld University. pub.uni-bielefeld.de/person/11596.

Hermes, D. 1992. "Pitch analysis." In *Visual Representations of Speech Signals*, edited by M. Cooke and S. Beet. New York: John Wiley & Sons.

Herndon, H. 2020. Video keynote speech, Conference on Applications of Machine Learning in Audio. New York: Audio Engineering Society.

Hershey, S., S. Chaudhuri, D. Ellis, J. Gemmeke, A. Jansen, R. Moore, M. Plakal, D. Platt, R. Saurous, B. Seybold, et al. 2017. "CNN architectures for large-scale audio classification." In *Proceedings of the IEEE International Conference on Acoustics, Speech and Signal Processing (ICASSP).* New York: IEEE, 131–135

Hess, W. 1983. *Pitch Determination of Speech Signals: Algorithms and Devices.* Berlin: Springer.

Hetrick, M. 2016. "Modular understanding: A taxonomy and toolkit for designing modularity in audio software and hardware." PhD diss. Media Arts and Technology, University of California, Santa Barbara.

Hetrick, M. 2020. Personal communication.

Heusdens, R., R. Vafin, and W. B. Kleijn. 2002. "Sinusoidal modeling using psychoacoustic-adaptive matching pursuits." *IEEE Signal Processing Letters* 9(8): 262–265.

Hewlett, W., and E. Selfridge-Field. 1991. *Computing in Musicology.* Menlo Park, CA: Center for Computer Assisted Research in the Humanities.

Hiller, L. 1964, "Informationstheorie und Computermusik." *Darmstädter Beiträge zur Neuen Musik* 8. Mainz, Germany: Schott.

Hiller, L. 1969. "Some compositional techniques involving the use of computers." In *Music by Computers*, edited by H. Von Foerster and J. Beauchamp. New York: John Wiley & Sons, 71–83.

Hiller, L. 1970. "Music composed with computers—A historical survey." In *The Computer and Music*, edited by H. Lincoln. Ithaca, NY: Cornell University Press, 42–96.

Hiller, L. 1979. "Phrase structure in computer music." In *Proceedings of the 1978 International Computer Music Conference*, edited by C. Roads. Evanston, IL: Northwestern University Press, 192–213.

Hiller, L. 1981. "Composing with computers: A progress report." *Computer Music Journal* 5(4): 7–21. Reprinted in *The Music Machine*, edited by C. Roads, 1989. Cambridge, MA: MIT Press, 75–89.

Hiller, L., and R. Baker. 1964. "*Computer Cantata:* A study in compositional method." *Perspectives of New Music* 3: 62–90.

Hiller, L., and R. Baker. 1965. "Automated music printing." *Journal of Music Theory* 9: 129–150.

Hiller, L., and J. Beauchamp. 1967. *Review of Completed and Proposed Research on Analysis and Synthesis of Musical Sounds by Analog and Digital Techniques.* Technical Report 19. Urbana: University of Illinois Experimental Music Studio.

Hiller, L., and J. Cage. 1968. "HPSCHD: An interview by Larry Austin." *Source* 2(2): 10–19.

Hiller, L., J. Divilbiss, D. Barron, H. Brün, and E. Lin. 1966. *Operator's Manual for the CSX-1 Music Machine.* Technical Report 12. Urbana: University of Illinois Experimental Music Studio.

Hiller, L., and L. Isaacson. 1959. *Experimental Music.* New York: McGraw-Hill.

Hiller, L., and A. Leal. 1966. *Revised MUSICOMP Manual.* Technical Report 13. Urbana: University of Illinois Experimental Music Studio.

Hiller, L., and B. Levy. 1984. "General system theory as applied to music analysis—Part 1." In *Musical Grammars and Computer Analysis*, edited by M. Baroni and L. Callegari. Florence: Leo Olschki Editore, 295–316.

Hiller, L., and P. Ruiz. 1971. "Synthesizing sounds by solving the wave equation for vibrating objects." *Journal of the Audio Engineering Society* 19(7): 463–470, 542–551.

Hirs, R., and B. Gilmore, eds. 2009. *Contemporary Compositional Techniques and Open Music.* Paris: IRCAM.

Hirschman, S. 1991. "Digital waveguide modeling and simulation of reed woodwind instruments." Engineer thesis. Department of Electrical Engineering, Stanford University.

Hirschman, S., P. Cook, and J. Smith. 1991. "Digital waveguide modeling of reed woodwinds: An interactive development." In *Proceedings of the 1991 International Computer Music Conference*, edited by B. Alphonce and B. Pennycook. San Francisco: International Computer Music Association, 300–303.

Hoadley, R. 2015. "Semaphore: Cross-domain expressive mapping with live notation." In *Proceedings of the First International Conference on Technologies for Music Notation and Representation.* https://www.tenor-conference.org.

Hoffmann, P. 2000. "The new GENDYN program." *Computer Music Journal* 24(2): 31–38.

Holfelt, J., G. Csapo, N. Andersson, S. Zabetian, M. Castanieto, D. Overholt, S. Dahl, and C. Erkut. 2017. "Extraction, mapping, and evaluation of expressive acoustic features for adaptive digital audio effects." In *Proceedings of the 14th Sound and Music Computing Conference.* n.p.: Sound and Music Computing Network, 328–335. https://smcnetwork.org.

Hollerweger, F. 2006. "Periphonic sound spatialization in multi-user virtual environments." Master's thesis. Institute for Electronic Music.

Holloway, B. 1993. "LemurEdit: A graphical editing tool for Lemur analyses." Urbana-Champaign: CERL Sound Group, University of Illinois.

Holloway, B., and L. Haken. 1992. "A sinusoidal synthesis algorithm for generating transitions between notes." In *Proceedings of the 1992 International Computer Music Conference*, edited by A. Strange. San Francisco: International Computer Music Association, 14–17.

Holm, F. 1992. "Understanding FM implementations: A call for common standards." *Computer Music Journal* 16(1): 34–42.

Holm-Hudson, K. 1997. "Quotation and Context: Sampling and John Oswald's Plunderphonics." *Leonardo Music Journal* 7: 17–25.

Holtzman, S. 1980. "Non-uniform time-scale modification of speech." M. Sc. and E.E. thesis. Department of Electrical Engineering and Computer Science, MIT.

Holtzman, S. R. 1977. "A program for key determination." *Interface* 6: 29–56.

Holzapfel, A., B. Sturm, and M. Coeckelbergh. 2018. "Ethical dimensions of music information retrieval technology." *Transactions of the International Society of Music Information Retrieval* 1(1): 44–55.

Hope, C., A. Wyatt, and L. Vickery. 2015. "The Decibel Score Player–a digital tool for reading graphic notation." *Proceedings of the International Conference on Technologies for Music Notation and Representation TENOR'15.* https://www.tenor-conference.org.

Horiuchi, Y., and H. Tanaka. 1993. "A computer accompaniment system with independence." In *Proceedings of the 1993 International Computer Music Conference*, edited by S. Ohteru. San Francisco: International Computer Music Association, 418–420.

Horner, A., and J. Beauchamp. 1996. "Piecewise linear approximation of additive synthesis envelopes: A comparison of various methods." *Computer Music Journal* 20(2): 72–95.

Horner, A., J. Beauchamp, and L. Haken. 1992. "Wavetable and FM matching synthesis of musical instrument tones." In *Proceedings of the 1992 International Computer Music Conference*, edited by A. Strange. San Francisco: International Computer Music Association, 18–21.

Horner, A., J. Beauchamp, and L. Haken. 1993. "Methods for multiple wavetable synthesis of musical instrument tones." *Journal of the Audio Engineering Society* 41(5): 336–356.

Hou, S. 1969. "Review of modal synthesis techniques and a new approach." *Shock and Vibration Bulletin, US Naval Laboratories Proceedings* 40(4): 25–39.

Howard, D. 2017. "The Vocal Tract Organ: A new musical instrument using 3-D printed vocal tracts." *Journal of Voice* 32(6): 660–667.

Howard, D., and J. Angus. 2017. *Acoustics and Psychoacoustics.* 5th ed. New York: Routledge.

Howe, H. S., Jr. 1975. *Electronic Music Synthesis.* New York: Norton.

Huang, C., C. Hawthorne, A. Roberts, M. Dinculescu, J. Wexler, L. Hong, J. Howcraft. 2019a. "The Bach Doodle: Approachable music composition with machine learning at scale." In *Proceedings of the 20th International Society for Music Information Retrieval.* n.p.: International Society for Music Information Retrieval. http://archives.ismir.net/ismir2019/paper/000097.pdf.

Huang, C., A. Vaswani, J. Uszkoreit, N. Shazeer, I. Simon, C. Hawthorne, A. Dai, M. Hoffman, M. Dinulescu, and D. Eck. 2019b. "Music transformer: generating music with long-term structure." International Conference on Learning Representations. arxiv.org/abs/1809.04281.

Hub, The. 1989. *Computer Network Music.* ART 1002. Berkeley: Artifact Recordings (compact disc).

Huber, D. M. 2020. *The MIDI Manual: A Practical Guide to MIDI within Modern Music Production.* 4th ed. New York: Routledge.

Huber, P. J. 1985. "Projection pursuit." *The Annals of Statistics* 13(2): 435–475.

Humphrey, E., D. Turnbull, and T. Collins. 2013. "A brief review of creative MIR." *International Society for Music Information Retrieval Conference (ISMIR).* n.p.: International Society for Music Information Retrieval. http://ismir2013.ismir.net/wp-content/uploads/2014/02/lbd1.pdf.

Hung, Y.-N., and A. Lerch. 2020. "Multitask learning or instrument activation aware music source separation." *21st International Society for Music Information Retrieval Conference.* n.p.: International Society for Music Information Retrieval.

Hunt, A., and R. Kirk. 2000. "Mapping strategies for musical performance." In *Trends in Gestural Control of Music,* edited by M. Wanderley and M. Battier. CD-ROM, Paris: IRCAM.

Hunt, A., M. Wanderley, and M. Paradis. 2003. "The importance of parameter mapping in electronic instrument design." *Journal of New Music Research* 32(4): 429–440.

Huron, D. 1999. *Humdrum Toolkit User's Guide.* https://www.humdrum.org/Humdrum/guide.toc.html

Hurty, W., and M. Rubenstein. 1964. *Dynamics of Structures.* Englewood Cliffs, NJ: Prentice Hall.

Hush, D., et al. 1986. "An adaptive IIR structure for sinusoidal enhancement, frequency estimation, and detection." *IEEE Transactions on Acoustics, Speech, and Signal Processing* 34(6): 1380–1390.

Hutchins, B. 1973. "Experimental electronic music devices employing Walsh functions." *Journal of the Audio Engineering Society* 21(8): 640–645.

Hutchins, B. 1975. "Application of real-time Hadamard transform network to sound synthesis." *Journal of the Audio Engineering Society* 23: 558–562.

Hutchins, B. 1982–1988. Various tutorials, application notes, and code listings published in *Electronotes*. Ithaca, NY.

Hutchins, B. 1984. "Special issue D: A review of Fourier methods in signal processing and musical engineering." *Electronotes* 15 (155–160): 2.

Hutchins, B. 1986a. "Interpolation, decimation, and prediction of digital signals." *Electronotes* 15(164–167): 3–46.

Hutchins, B. 1986b. "Windows for signal processing." Application Note 292. Ithaca, NY: Electronotes.

Hutchins, B., and W. Ku. 1982. "A simple hardware pitch extractor." *Journal of the Audio Engineering Society* 30(3): 135–139.

Hutchins, B., D. Parola, and L. Ludwig. 1982. "A pitch extraction scheme based on Hilbert transformations." *Electronotes* 14(136).

Hutchins, C. 1978. *The Physics of Music.* San Francisco: W. H. Freeman.

Hybrid Management. 1984. "About the instrument." Garrison: Hybrid Management.

Ilmonen, T., and T. Takala. 1999. "Conductor following with artificial neural networks." In *Proceedings of the 1999 International Computer Music Conference.* San Francisco: International Computer Music Association, 367–370.

INA/GRM. 2019. GRM Tools software. Paris: Institut National de l'Audio-visuel/ Groupe de Recherches Musicales. https://inagrm.com/en.

Ingebretsen, R., and T. Stockham. 1984. "Random access editing of digital audio." *Journal of the Audio Engineering Society* 32.

Ingram, J. 2001. "Developing music with software tools." Presentation at the workshop on Contemporary Music Digital Publishing, Centro Tempo Reale, Florence, November 26, 2001. https://james-ingram-act-two.de.

Ingram, J. 2002. "Developing traditions of music notation and performance on the Web." Presented at Wedelmusic 2002, Fraunhofer Institute for Computer Graphics. https://james-ingram-act-two.de/writings/DevelopingTraditions/sonalAtoms/sonal AtomsPreface.html.

Inoue, W., S. Hashimoto, and S. Ohteru. 1993. "A computer music system for human singing." *Proceedings of the 1993 International Computer Music Conference.* San Francisco: International Computer Music Association, 150–153.

Insam, E. 1974. "Walsh functions in waveform synthesis." *Journal of the Audio Engineering Society* 22: 422–425.

Iovino, F. 1993. *Chant-PatchWork Manual.* Paris: IRCAM.

IRCAM. 2011. *Audiosculpt 3.0, guide rapide d'utilisation.* Paris: IRCAM.

IRCAM. 2018. *OpenMusic 6.6 User Manual.* https://support.ircam.fr/docs/om/om6 -manual/co/OM-User-Manual.html.

Irrlichtproject 2015. "Computer music in 1949?" http://irrlichtproject.blogspot.com /2015/11/computer-music-in-1949.html.

Ishibashi, M. 1987. "Electronic music instrument." U.S. Patent 4,658,691.

Iwamura, H., H. Hayashi, A. Miyashita, and T. Anazawa. 1973. "Pulse-code-modulation recording system." *Journal of the Audio Engineering Society* 21(7): 535–541.

Jaffe, D. 1987a. "Spectrum analysis tutorial, part 1: The discrete Fourier transform." *Computer Music Journal* 11(2): 9–24.

Jaffe, D. 1987b. "Spectrum analysis tutorial, part 2: properties and applications of the discrete Fourier transform." *Computer Music Journal* 11(3): 17–35.

Jaffe, D. 1989. "From the classical software synthesis note-list to the NeXT score-file." Redwood City, CA: NeXT Computer, Inc.

Jaffe, D., and J. Smith. 1983. "Extensions of the Karplus-Strong plucked string algorithm." *Computer Music Journal* 7(2): 56–69.

James, S. 2005. "Developing a flexible and expressive realtime polyphonic wave terrain synthesis instrument based on a visual and multidimensional methodology." Masters thesis. Edith Cowan University.

James, S. 2015. "Spectromorphology and spatiomorphology: Wave terrain synthesis as a framework for controlling timbre spatialisation in the frequency domain." PhD diss. Edith Cowan University.

Janer, J., M. Here, G. Roma, T. Fujishima, and N. Kojima. 2009. "Sound Object Classification for Symbolic Audio Mosaicing: A Proof-of-concept." *Proceedings of the Sound and Music Computing Conference.* n.p.: Sound and Music Computing Network, 297–302. https://smcnetwork.org.

Janse, P., and A. Kaizer. 1983. "Time-frequency distributions of loudspeakers: The application of the Wigner distribution." *Journal of the Audio Engineering Society* 31(4): 198–223.

Janse, P., and A. Kaizer. 1984. "The Wigner distribution: a valuable tool for investigating transient distortion." *Journal of the Audio Engineering Society* 32: 868–882.

JapoScore. 2020. *JapoScore Handbook.* https://fluteywinds.com/japoscore/handbook2 -5eng/.

Jehan, T. 2004. "Event-synchronous Mmusic analysis/synthesis." *Proceedings of the COST-G6 Conference on Digital Audio Effects.* n.p.: DAFx, 1–6.

Jehan, T. 2010. "Creating Music by Concatenative Synthesis." U.S. Patent 7,842,874 Washington: U.S. Patent Office.

Jenny, G. (1958) 2017. "L'Ondioline: Conception et réalisation." Paris: *Toute la radio.* Translated by ITC Global Translations, 2017. New York: Forgotten Futures.

Jensenius, A., and M. Lyons, eds. 2017. *A NIME Reader: Fifteen Years of New Interfaces for Musical Expression.* Cham, Switzerland: Springer.

Jette, C. 2009. "Decompartmental: conversing with Clarence Barlow." *Computer Music Journal* 33(4): 10–22.

Jette, C. 2020. Personal communication.

Ji, S., J. Luo, and X. Yang. 2020. "A comprehensive survey on deep music generation: Multi-level representations, algorithms, evaluations, and future directions." https://arxiv.org/pdf/2011.06801.pdf.

Johannsen, G., and T. M. Nakra. 2009. "Conductors' gestures and their mapping to sound synthesis." In *Musical Gestures: Sound, Movement, and Meaning,* edited by R. Godøy and M. Leman. New York: Routledge, 264–298.

Johns, I. 2017. "Net benefits: Everything you need to know about Ethernet audio." *Sound on Sound* 32(7).

Johnson, M. 1991. "Toward an expert system for expressive performance rules." *IEEE Computer* 24(7): 30–34.

Johnson, W., C. McHugh, H. Rice, and T. Rhea. 1970. "History of electronic music, part one." *Synthesis* 1.

Johnstone, B. 1994. "Wave of the future." *Wired* March: 50–63.

Jones, D., and T. Parks. 1988. "Generation and combination of grains for music synthesis." *Computer Music Journal* 12(2): 27–34.

Jones, K. 1981. "Compositional applications of stochastic processes." *Computer Music Journal* 5(2): 45–61. Reprinted in *The Music Machine,* edited by C. Roads, 1989. Cambridge, MA: MIT Press, 381–398.

Jones, R. 2020. "Humane design for organizing noises." Presented at virtual Media Arts & Technology (MAT) seminar. University of California, Santa Barbara.

Jordà, S. 2007. "Interactivity and live computer music." In *The Cambridge Companion to Electronic Music,* edited by N. Collins and J. d'Escrivan. Cambridge: Cambridge University Press, 89–107.

Jot, J.-M., and A. Chaigne. 1991. "Digital delay networks for designing artificial reverberators." In *Proceedings of the 90th Convention of the Audio Engineering Society.* Paris, France. Preprint 3030.

Jot, J.-M., and A. Chaigne. 1996. "Method and system for artificial spatialization of digital audio signals," U.S. Patent 5,491,754.

Jungleib, S. 1995. *General MIDI*. Middleton, WI: A-R Editions.

Justice, J. 1979. "Analytic signal processing in music computation." *IEEE Transactions on Acoustics, Speech, and Signal Processing* ASSP-27(6): 670–684.

Kaegi, W. 1967. *Was Ist Elektronisches Musik?* Zürich: Orell Füssli Verlag.

Kaegi, W. 1973. "A minimum description of the linguistic sign repertoire (part 1)." *Interface* 2: 141–156.

Kaegi, W. 1974. "A minimum description of the linguistic sign repertoire (part 2)." *Interface* 3: 137–158.

Kaegi, W., and S. Tempelaars. 1978. "VOSIM—A new sound synthesis system." *Journal of the Audio Engineering Society* 26(6): 418–426.

Kadis, J. 2012. *The Science of Sound Recording*. Oxford: Focal Press.

Kaiser, J. 1963. "Design methods for sampled data filters." *Proceedings of the First Annual Allerton Conference on Circuit Systems Theory*. Reprinted in *Digital Signal Processing*, edited by L. Rabiner and C. Rader, 1972. New York: IEEE Press, 20–34.

Kalchbrenner, N., E. Elsen, K. Simonyan, S. Noury, N. Casagrande, E. Lockhart, F. Stimberg, A. Oord, S. Dieleman, and K. Kavukcuoglu. 2018. "Efficient neural audio synthesis." *Proceedings of the 35th International Conference on Machine Learning* PMLR 80: 2410–2419.

Kanach, S. 2008. "The Polytopes." In *Music and Architecture by Iannis Xenakis*. Hillsdale, New York: Pendragon Press, 198–279.

Kaplan, S. J. 1981. "Developing a commercial digital sound synthesizer." *Computer Music Journal* 5(3): 62–73. Reprinted in *The Music Machine*, edited by C. Roads, 1989. Cambridge, MA: MIT Press, 611–622.

Kapur, A. 2005. "History of robotic musical instruments." *Proceedings of the 2005 International Computer Music Conference*. San Francisco: International Computer Music Association, 21–28.

Kapur, A., P. Cook, S. Salazar, and G. Wang. 2015. *Programming for Musicians and Digital Artists: Creating Music with ChucK*. Shelter Island, NY: Manning.

Kapur, A., M. Darling, D. Diakopoulos, J. Murphy, J. Hochenbaum, O. Vallis, and C. Bahn. 2011. "The machine orchestra: an ensemble of human laptop performers and robotic musical instruments." *Computer Music Journal* 35(4): 49–63.

Kareer, S., and S. Basu. 2018. "Musical polyphony estimation." Convention e-Brief 484. Presented at the 144th Convention of the Audio Engineering Society. New York: Audio Engineering Society.

Karjalainen, M., and H. Järveläinen. 2007. "c." In *Proceedings of the Audio Engineering Society 30th International Conference on Intelligent Audio Environments.* New York: Audio Engineering Society. users.spa.aalto.fi/mak/PUB/AES_Jarvelainen _velvet.pdf.

Karjalainen, M., U. Laine, T. Laakso, and V. Välimäki. 1991. "Transmission-line modeling and real-time synthesis of string and wind instruments." In *Proceedings of the 1991 International Computer Music Conference*, edited by B. Alphonce and B. Pennycook. San Francisco: International Computer Music Association, 293–296.

Karkoschka, E. 1966. *Das Schriftbild der Neuen Musik.* Celle, Germany: Moeck.

Karpen, R. 2000. "Csound's phase vocoder and extensions." In *The Music Machine*, edited by C. Roads, 1989. Cambridge, MA: MIT Press, 541–560.

Karplus, K., and A. Strong. 1983. "Digital synthesis of plucked string and drum timbres." *Computer Music Journal* 7(2): 43–55. Reprinted in *The Music Machine*, edited by C. Roads, 1989. Cambridge, MA: MIT Press, 467–480.

Kashino, K., and H. Tanaka. 1993. "A sound source separation system with the ability of automatic tone modeling." In *Proceedings of the 1993 International Computer Music Conference*, edited by S. Ohteru. San Francisco: International Computer Music Association, 248–255.

Katayose, H., and S. Inokuchi. 1990. "The Kansei Music System '90." In *Proceedings of the 1990 International Computer Music Conference*, edited by S. Arnold and G. Hair. San Francisco: International Computer Music Association, 309–311.

Katz, B. 2002. *Mastering Audio: The Art and the Science.* Burlington, MA: Focal Press.

Kay, S., and S. Marple. 1981. "Spectrum analysis—A modern perspective." *Proceedings of the Institute of Electrical and Electronics Engineers* 69(11): 1380–1419.

Keane, D., G. Smecca, and K. Wood. 1990. "The MIDI Baton II." In *Proceedings of the 1990 International Computer Music Conference*, edited by S. Arnold and G. Hair. San Francisco: International Computer Music Association.

Keefe, D. 1992. "Physical modeling of wind instruments." *Computer Music Journal* 16(4): 57–73.

Keislar, D. 1987. "History and principles of microtonal keyboards." *Computer Music Journal* 11(1): 18–28.

Keller, A. 1981. "Early hi-fi and stereo recording at Bell Laboratories (1931–1932)." *Journal of the Audio Engineering Society* 29(4): 274–280.

Keller, D., and B. Truax. 1998. "Ecologically-based granular synthesis." In *Proceedings of the 1998 International Computer Music Conference*, edited by M. Simoni. San Francisco: International Computer Music Association, 117–120.

Kelly, J., and C. Lochbaum. 1962. "Speech synthesis." In *Proceedings of the Fourth International Congress on Acoustics*, Paper G42, 1–4.

Kemp, M. 2000. "Dynamic convolution." http://www.sintefex.com/docs/appnotes /dynaconv.pdf.

Kendall, G. 1995a. "A 3-D sound primer: Directional hearing and stereo reproduction." *Computer Music Journal* 19(4): 23–46.

Kendall, G. 1995b. "The decorrelation of audio signals and its impact on spatial imagery." *Computer Music Journal* 19(4): 71–87.

Kendall, G. 2010. "Spatial perception and cognition in multichannel audio for electroacoustic music." *Organised Sound* 15(3): 228–238.

Kendall, G., C. Haworth, and R. Cadiz. 2014. "Sound synthesis with auditory distortion products." *Computer Music Journal* 38(4): 5–23.

Kendall, G., and W. Martens. 1984. "Simulating the cues of spatial hearing in natural environments." In *Proceedings of the 1984 International Computer Music Conference*, edited by D. Wessel, 1984. San Francisco: International Computer Music Association, 111–125.

Kendall, G., W. Martens, and S. Decker. 1989. "Spatial reverberation: discussion and demonstration." In *Current Directions in Computer Music Research*, edited by M. Mathews and J. R. Pierce. 1989. Cambridge, MA: MIT Press, 65–87.

Kendall, G., W. Martens, D. Freed, D. Ludwig, and R. Karstens. 1986. "Spatial processing software at Northwestern Computer Music." In *Proceedings of the 1986 International Computer Music Conference*, edited by P. Berg. San Francisco: International Computer Music Association, 285–292.

Kereliuk, C. 2012. "Sparse and structured atomic modeling of audio." PhD diss. McGill University.

Kereliuk, C., and P. Depalle. 2011. "Sparse atomic modeling of audio: A review." In *Proceedings of Digital Audio Effects*. Paris, 81–92.

Kereliuk, C., and P. Depalle. 2013. "Analysis/Synthesis Using Time-Varying Windows and Chirped Atoms." In *Proceedings of Digital Audio Effects*. Maynooth, Ireland, 1–6.

Kersten, S., and H. Purwins. 2012. "Sparse Decomposition, Clustering and Noise for Fire Texture Sound Re-Synthesis." *Proceedings of Digital Audio Effects*. York, UK, 1–5.

Kim, J., J. Salamon, P. Li, and J. Bello. 2018. "CREPE: a convolutional representation for pitch estimation." *Proceedings of IEEE International Conference on Audio, Speech, and Signal Processing.*

Kirchmeyer, H. 1968. "On the historical constitution of a rationalistic music." *Die Reihe* 8: 11–24. English edition.

Klapuri, A. 2004. "Automatic music transcription as we know it today." *Journal of New Music Research* 33(3): 269–282.

Klapuri, A. 2008. "Multipitch analysis of polyphonic music and speech signals using an auditory model." *IEEE Transactions on Audio, Speech, and Language Processing* 16(2): 255–266.

Klapuri. A., and M. Davy, eds. 2006. *Signal Processing Methods for Music Transcription.* New York: Springer.

Klapuri, A., A. Eronen, and J. Astola. 2005. "Analysis of the meter of acoustic musical signals." *IEEE Transactions on Audio, Speech and Language Processing* 14(1): 342–355.

Kleczkowski, P. 1989. "Group additive synthesis." *Computer Music Journal* 13(1): 12–20.

Kleimola, J., P. Pekonen, J. Penttinen, and V. Välimäki. 2009. "Sound synthesis using an allpass filter chain with audio-rate coefficient modulation." In *Proceedings of the 10th International Conference on Digital Audio Effects (DAFx-10).* n.p.: DAFx, 1–8. http://dafx10.iem.at/proceedings.

Kleimola, J., V. Lazzarini, J. Timoney, and V. Välimäki. 2011. "Feedback amplitude modulation synthesis." *Eurasip Journal on Advances in Signal Processing 2011*: 1–18.

Klien, V., T. Grill, and A. Flexer. 2012. "On automated annotation of acousmatic music." *Journal of New Music Research* 41(2): 153–173.

Klingbeil, M. 2005. "Software for spectral analysis, editing, and synthesis." In *Proceedings of the 2005 International Computer Music Conference.* San Francisco: International Computer Music Association, 107–110.

Klingbeil, M. 2009. "Spectral analysis, editing, and resynthesis: Methods and applications." DMA diss. Columbia University.

Knapp, B. R., and H. Lustad. 1990. "A bioelectric controller for computer music applications." *Computer Music Journal* 14(1): 42–47.

Knowlton, P. 1971. "Interactive communication and display of keyboard music." PhD diss. Department of Computer Science, University of Utah.

Knowlton, P. 1972. "Capture and display of keyboard music." *Datamation* 5.

Knuth, D. 1973a. *The Art of Computer Programming, Vol. 1: Fundamental Algorithms.* 2nd ed. Reading, MA: Addison-Wesley.

Knuth, D. 1973b. *The Art of Computer Programming, Vol. 3: Sorting and Searching.* Reading, MA: Addison-Wesley.

Knuth, D. 1974. "Structured programming with goto statements." *ACM Computing Surveys* 6: 260–301.

Knuth, D. 1981. *The Art of Computer Programming, Vol. 2: Seminumerical Algorithms.* 2nd ed. Reading, MA: Addison-Wesley.

Kobrin, E. 1977. *Computer in performance.* Berlin: DAAD.

Koenig, G. M. 1957. *Essay.* Composition for electronic sounds. Score. Vienna: Universal Edition.

Koenig, G. M. 1959. "Studium im Studio." *Die Reihe* 5.

Koenig, G. M. 1962. "Commentary." *Die Reihe* 8.

Koenig, G. M. 1970a. "Project 1: A programme for musical composition." *Electronic Music Reports* 2: 32–44. (Reprinted 1977. Amsterdam: Swets and Zeitlinger.)

Koenig, G. M. 1970b. "Project 2: A programme for musical composition." *Electronic Music Reports* 3: 1–16. (Reprinted 1977. Amsterdam: Swets and Zeitlinger.)

Koenig, G. M. 1978a. "Description of the Project 1 programme." Utrecht, Netherlands: Institute of Sonology.

Koenig, G. M. 1978b. Lecture at the Institute of Sonology, Netherlands, August.

Koenig, G. M. 1979. "Protocol." *Sonological Reports* 4. Utrecht, Netherlands: Institute of Sonology.

Koenig, G. M. 2018. *Process and Form: Selected Writings on Music.* Edited by K. Tazelaar. Hofheim, Germany: Wolke.

Koenig, R. 1899. Articles in *Annalen der Physik* 69: 626–660, 721–738. (Cited in Miller 1916, 1935.)

Koenig, W., H. K. Dunn, and L. Y. Lacy. 1946. "The sound spectrograph." *Journal of the Acoustical Society of America* 18: 19–49.

Kohler, J. 2000. "System and method for automatically detecting a set of fundamental frequencies simultaneously present in an audio signal." U.S. Patent No. 6,140,568.

Kornfeld, W. 1980. "Everything you always wanted to know about MUZACS but were afraid to grovel through the code to find out." Lecture. Cambridge, MA: MIT Artificial Intelligence Laboratory.

Kostelanetz, R., ed. 1970. *John Cage.* New York: Praeger.

Kowalski, M., and A. Glassner. 1982. "The N.Y.I.T. digital sound editor." *Computer Music Journal* 6(1): 66–73.

Kramer, G., R. Moog, and A. Peevers. 1989. "The Hybrid: A music performance system." In *Proceedings of the 1989 International Computer Music Conference,* edited by T. Wells and D. Butler. San Francisco: International Computer Music Association, 155–159.

Kronland-Martinet, R. 1988. "The wavelet transform for the analysis, synthesis, and processing of speech and music sounds." *Computer Music Journal* 12(4): 11–20.

Kronland-Martinet, R., and A. Grossmann. 1991. "Application of time-frequency and time-scale methods (wavelet transforms) to the analysis, synthesis and transformation of natural sounds." In *Representations of Musical Signals*, edited by G. De Poli, A. Piccialli, and C. Roads. Cambridge, MA: MIT Press, 45–85.

Krstulovic, S., and R. Gribonval. 2006. "MPTK: Matching pursuit made tractable," *Proceedings of the International Conference on Audio, Speech, and Signal Processing.* New York: IEEE. 496–499.

Krzyzaniak, M. 2018. "Interactive learning of timbral rhythms for percussion robots." *Computer Music Journal* 42(2): 35–51.

Kuhn, W. 1990. "A real-time pitch recognition algorithm for music applications." *Computer Music Journal* 14(3): 60–71.

Kussmaul, C. 1991. "Applications of the wavelet transform at the level of pitch contour." In *Proceedings of the 1991 International Computer Music Conference*, edited by B. Alphonce and B. Pennycook. San Francisco: International Computer Music Association, 483–486.

Kuuskankare, M. 2009. "ENP: a system for contemporary music notation." *Contemporary Music Review* 28(2): 221–235.

Lachartre, N. 1969. "Les musiques artificielles." *Diagrammes du monde* 146: 1–96.

Lagadec, R. 1983. "Digital sampling frequency conversion." In *Digital Audio*, edited by B. Blesser, B. Locanthi, and T. Stockham. New York: Audio Engineering Society, 90–96.

Lagadec, R., and D. Pelloni. 1983. "Signal enhancement via digital signal processing." Preprint 2037 (G-6). In *Proceedings of the 74th Convention of the Audio Engineering Society*. New York: Audio Engineering Society.

Laitinen, M., S. Disch, and V. Pulkki. 2013. "Sensitivity of human hearing to changes of phase spectrum." *Journal of the Audio Engineering Society* 61(11): 860–877.

Lane, J. 1990. "Pitch detection using a tunable IIR filter." *Computer Music Journal* 14(3): 46–59.

Lane, J., D. Hoory, E. Martinez, and P. Wang. 1997. "Modeling analog synthesis with DSPs." *Computer Music Journal* 21(4): 23–41.

Langston, P. 1989. "Six techniques for algorithmic composition (extended abstract)." In *Proceedings of the 1989 International Computer Music Conference*, edited by T. Wells and D. Butler. San Francisco: International Computer Music Association, 164–167.

Lansky, P. 1987. "Linear prediction: the hard but interesting way to do things." In *Proceedings of the Fifth International Conference: Music and Digital Technology*, edited by J. Strawn. New York: Audio Engineering Society.

Lansky, P. 1990. "The architecture and musical logic of Cmix." In *Proceedings of the 1990 International Computer Music Conference*, edited by S. Arnold and G. Hair. San Francisco: International Computer Music Association, 91–94.

Lansky, P., and K. Steiglitz. 1981. "Synthesis of timbral families by warped linear prediction." *Computer Music Journal* 5(3): 45–49. Reprinted in *The Music Machine*, edited by C. Roads, 1989. Cambridge, MA: MIT Press, 531–536.

Laroche, J. 1989a. "Etude d'une système d'analyse et de synthèse utilisant la méthode de Prony: application aux instrument de musique de type percussif." Doctoral thesis. Ecole Nationale Supérieure des Télécommunications.

Laroche, J. 1989b. "A new analysis/synthesis system based on the use of Prony's method. Application to heavily damped percussive sounds." In *Proceedings of the International Conference on Acoustics, Speech, and Signal Processing*. New York: Institute of Electrical and Electronics Engineers.

Laroche, J. 1998. "Using resonant filters for the synthesis of time-varying sinusoids." In *Proceedings of the 105th Convention of the Audio Engineering Society*. Preprint 4782. San Francisco.

Laroche, J. 2000. "Synthesis of sinusoids via non-overlapping inverse Fourier transform." *IEEE Transactions on Speech and Signal Processing* 8(4): 471–477.

Laroche, J. 2003. "Efficient tempo and beat tracking in audio recordings." *Journal of the Audio Engineering Society* 51(4): 226–233.

Laroche, J., and M. Dolson. 1999. "New phase vocoder techniques for pitch-shifting, harmonizing, and other exotic effects." In *Proceedings of the IEEE Workshop on Applications of Signal Processing to Audio and Acoustics*. New York: IEEE, 91–94.

Laroche, J., and X. Rodet. 1989. "The use of Prony's method for the analysis of musical sounds: applications to percussive sounds." In *Proceedings of the 1989 International Computer Music Conference*, edited by T. Wells and D. Butler. San Francisco: International Computer Music Association, 168–171.

Laske, O. 1979. "Compositional theory in Koenig's Project One and Project Two." *Computer Music Journal* 5(4): 54–65. Reprinted in *The Music Machine*, edited by C. Roads, 1989. Cambridge, MA: MIT Press, 119–130.

Lassfolk, K. 1996. "Simulation of electron tube audio circuits." In *Proceedings of the 1996 International Computer Music Conference*, edited by D. Rossiter. San Francisco: International Computer Music Association, 222–223.

Laurson, M., and J. Duthen. 1989. "PatchWork, a graphical language in PreForm." In *Proceedings of the 1989 International Computer Music Conference*, edited by T. Wells and D. Butler. San Francisco: International Computer Music Association, 172–175.

Laurson, M., C. Erkut, V. Välimäki, and M. Kuushankare. 2001. "Methods for modeling realistic playing in acoustic guitar synthesis." *Computer Music Journal* 25(3): 38–49.

Layzer, A. 1971. "Some idiosyncratic aspects of computer synthesized sound." In *Proceedings of the Sixth ASUC Conference*. New York: American Society of University Composers, 27–39.

Lazarro, J., and J. Wawrzynek. 2004. "RTP payload format for MIDI." In *Proceedings of the 117th Convention of the Audio Engineering Society, San Francisco*. New York: Audio Engineering Society.

Lazzarini, V. 2011a. "Programming the phase vocoder." In *The Audio Programming Book*, edited by R. Boulanger and V. Lazzarini. Cambridge, MA: MIT Press, 557–580.

Lazzarini, V. 2011b. "Soundfiles, soundfile formats and libsndfile." In *The Audio Programming Book*, edited by R. Boulanger and V. Lazzarini. Cambridge, MA: MIT Press, 739–770.

Lazzarini, V. 2011c. "The STFT and spectral processing." In *The Audio Programming Book*, edited by R. Boulanger and V. Lazzarini. Cambridge, MA: MIT Press, 539–556.

Lazzarini, V. 2011d. "Time-domain audio processing." In *The Audio Programming Book*, edited by R. Boulanger and V. Lazzarini. Cambridge, MA: MIT Press, 463–518.

Lazzarini, V. 2013. "The development of computer music programming systems." *Journal of New Music Research* 42(1): 97–110.

Lazzarini, V. 2017. *Computer Music Instruments I: Foundations, Design, and Development*. Cham, Switzerland: Springer.

Lazzarini, V. 2019. *Computer Music Instruments II: Real-time and Object-oriented Audio*. Cham, Switzerland: Springer.

Lazzarini, V., and J. Timoney. 2010. "New perspectives on distortion synthesis for virtual analog oscillators." *Computer Music Journal* 34(1): 28–40.

Lazzarini, V., and J. Timoney. 2013. "Synthesis of resonance by nonlinear distortion methods." *Computer Music Journal* 37(1): 35–43.

Lazzarini, V., S. Yi, J. ffitch, J. Heitz, O. Brandtsegg, and I. McCurdy. 2016. *Csound: A Sound and Music Computing System*. Cham, Switzerland: Springer.

Lazzarini, V., J. Timoney, and T. Lysaght. 2007. "Adaptive FM synthesis." In *Proceedings of the 10th International Conference on Digital Audio Effects (DAFx-07)*. Bordeaux, France, 21–26.

LeBrun, M. 1977. "A derivation of the spectrum of FM with a complex modulating wave." *Computer Music Journal* 1(4): 51–52. Reprinted in *Foundations of Computer Music*, edited by C. Roads and J. Strawn, 1985. Cambridge, MA: MIT Press, 65–67.

LeBrun, M. 1979. "Digital waveshaping synthesis." *Journal of the Audio Engineering Society* 27(4): 250–266.

Lee, C., A. Horner, and J. Beauchamp. 2012. "Discrimination of musical instrument tones resynthesized with piecewise-linear approximated harmonic amplitude envelopes." *Journal of the Audio Engineering Society* 60(11): 899–912.

Lee, F. 1972. "Time compression and expansion of speech by the sampling method." *Journal of the Audio Engineering Society* 20(9): 738–742.

Lee, M., G. Garnett, and D. Wessel. 1992. "An adaptive conductor follower." In *Proceedings of the 1992 International Computer Music Conference*, edited by A. Strange. San Francisco: International Computer Music Association, 454–455.

Leglaive, S., R. Hennequin, and R. Badeau. 2015. "Singing voice detection with deep recurrent neural networks." In *Proceedings of the 40th International Conference on Acoustics, Speech and Signal Processing (ICASSP)*. New York: IEEE, 121–125.

Le Grice, M. 1978. *Abstract Film and Beyond.* Cambridge, MA: MIT Press.

Leibig, B. 1974. "Documentation on Music V for the Burroughs B6700 computer." La Jolla: Department of Music, University of California, San Diego.

Leichtentritt, H. 1934. "Mechanical music in olden times." *Musical Quarterly* 20: 15–26.

Leman, M. 2016. *The Expressive Moment: How Interaction (with Music) Shapes Human Empowerment.* Cambridge, MA: MIT Press.

Lemouton, S. 1993. "CHANT-Macintosh." Unpublished manuscript.

Lent, K., R. Pinkston, and P. Silsbee. 1989. "Accelerando: a real-time general-purpose computer music system." *Computer Music Journal* 13(4): 54–64.

Leonard, J., N. Castagné, C. Cadoz, and J.-L. Florens. 2013. "A modeller-simulator for instrumental playing of virtual musical instruments." In *Proceedings of the 2013 International Conference on Digital Audio Effects (DAFx-13)*. n.p.: DAFx. https://www.dafx.de.

Lepetit-Aimon, G., D. Fober, Y. Orlarey, and S. Letz. 2016. "INScore expressions to compose symbolic scores." In *Proceedings of the International Conference on Technologies for Music Notation and Representation TENOR'16*, edited by R. Hoadley, C. Nash, and D. Fober. https://www.tenor-conference.org.

Lerch, A. 2012. *An Introduction to Audio Content Analysis.* Hoboken, NJ: John Wiley & Sons.

Lerdahl, F., and R. Jackendoff. 1983. *A Generative Theory of Tonal Music.* Cambridge, MA: MIT Press.

Lehrman, P., and T. Tully. 1993. *MIDI for Professionals.* New York: Amsco.

Lesbros, V. 1993. *Phonogramme.* Computer program.

Lesbros, V. 1999. "Phonograms, Elastic Couplings, and Trajectories." *Computer Music Journal* 23(2): 70–79.

Leslie, D. 1949. "Rotatable tremulant sound producer." U.S. Patent 2,489,653.

Leslie, D. 1952. "Apparatus for imposing vibrato on sound." U.S. Patent 2,622,693.

Leveau, P., E. Vincent, G. Richard, and L. Daudet. 2008. "Instrument-specific harmonic atoms for mid-level music representation." *IEEE Transactions on Audio, Speech and Language Processing* 16(1): 116–128.

Levin, T. Y. 2003. "'Tones from out of nowhere': Rudolf Pfenninger and the archaeology of synthetic sound." *Grey Room* 12: 32–79.

Levitt, D. 1981. *A Melody Description System for Jazz Improvisation.* M.S. Thesis. Cambridge, MA: Artificial Intelligence Laboratory.

Levitt, D. 1983. "Learning music by imitating." Unpublished manuscript.

Levitt, D. 1984. "Machine tongues X: constraint languages." *Computer Music Journal* 8(1): 9–21.

Lewicki, M. S. 2002. "Efficient coding of natural sounds." *Nature Neuroscience* 5(4): 356–363.

Lewis, G. 2000. "Too many notes: complexity and culture in Voyager." *Leonardo Music Journal* 10: 33–39.

Lewis, G. 2007. "The virtual discourses of Pamela Z." *Journal of the Society for American Music* 1(1): 57–77.

Lewis, G. 2009. "Interactivity and improvisation." In *The Oxford Handbook of Computer Music*, edited by R. Dean. Oxford: Oxford University Press, 457–466.

Lewis, J. P. 1989. "Algorithms for music composition by neural nets: Improved CBR paradigms." In *Proceedings of the 1989 International Computer Music Conference*, edited by T. Wells and D. Butler. San Francisco: International Computer Music Association, 180–183.

Li, Z., N. Kovachki, K. Azizzadenesheli, B. Liu, K. Bhattacharya, A. Stuart, and A. Anandkumar. 2020. "Fourier neural operator for parametric partial differential equations." Submitted to *2021 International Conference on Learning Representations.* http://arxiv.org/pdf/2010.08895.pdf.

Licata, T., ed. 2002. *Electroacoustic Music: Analytical Perspectives.* Westport, CT: Greenwood Press.

Licklider, J. C. R. 1950. "Intelligibility of amplitude-dichotomized time quantized speech waves." *Journal of the Acoustical Society of America* 22: 820–823.

Licklider, J. 1951. "A duplex theory of pitch perception." *Experimentia* 7: 128–133.

Licklider, J. 1959. "Three auditory theories." In *Psychology: A Study of Science, Volume 1*, edited by S. Koch. New York: McGraw-Hill, 41–144.

Lidov, D., and J. Gabura. 1973. "A melody-writing algorithm using a formal language model." *Computers and the Humanities* 4(3–4): 138–148.

Ligeti, G., and R. Wehinger. 1970. *Artikulation.* Mainz, Germany: Schott.

LilyPond. 2012. *LilyPond: Essay on Automated Music Engraving.* lilypond.org.

Lindemann, E. 2001. "Musical synthesizer capable of expressive phrasing." U.S. Patent 6,316,710.

Lindemann, E. 2007. "Music synthesis with reconstructive phrase modeling." *IEEE Signal Processing Magazine* 24(2): 80–91.

Lindemann, E. 2009. *Synful Orchestra User's Guide.* https://www.synful.com.

Lindemann, E., F. Dechelle, B. Smith, and M. Starkier. 1991. "The architecture of the IRCAM musical workstation." *Computer Music Journal* 15(3): 41–49.

Lindroos, N., H. Penttinen, and V. Välimäki. 2011. "Parametric electric guitar synthesis." *Computer Music Journal* 35(3): 18–27.

Lindsay, A. T., A. P. Parkes, and R. A. Fitzgerald. 2003. "Descriptor-driven context-sensitive effects." *Proceedings of the COST-G6 International Conference on Digital Audio Effects.* London, 350–353.

Link, B. 1992. "A real-time waveguide toolkit." In *Proceedings of the 1992 International Computer Music Conference*, edited by A. Strange. San Francisco: International Computer Music Association, 396–397.

Link, D. 2007. "There must be an angel: On the beginnings of the arithmetics of rays." In *Variantology 2*, edited by S. Zielinski. Cologne: Walter Koenig, 15–42.

Linster, C. 1992. "On analyzing and representing musical rhythm." In *Understanding Music with AI*, edited by M. Balaban, K. Ebcioglu, and O. Laske. Cambridge, MA and Menlo Park, CA: MIT Press and AAAI Press, 415–427.

Lipshitz, S., R. Wannamaker, and J. Vanderkooy. 1992. "Quantization and dither: A theoretical survey." *Journal of the Audio Engineering Society* 40(5): 355–375.

Liski, J., and V. Välimäki. 2017. "The quest for the best graphic equalizer." In *Proceedings of the International Conference on Digital Audio Effects, DAFx.* n.p.: DAFx. https://www.dafx.de.

Liskov, B., et al. 1979. *CLU Reference Manual.* TR-225. Cambridge, MA: Laboratory for Computer Science, MIT.

LiveCode. 2020. "Develop apps yourself." https://livecode.com/.

Livingston, J. 2006. "Time-scale modification of audio signals using the dual-tree complex wavelet transform." Thesis, MS in Engineering. University of Texas.

Loescher, F. A. 1959. "The active loudspeaker." *Gravesaner Blätter* 14: 7–9.

Loescher, F. A. 1960. "The problem of the secondary electro-acoustical transducers." *Gravensaner Blätter* 18: 53–60.

Lohner, H. 1986. "The UPIC system: a user's report." *Computer Music Journal* 10(4): 42–49. Reprinted 1987 in *Musik-Konzepte* 54/55: 71–82.

Longuet-Higgins, H. C. 1976. "The perception of melodies." *Nature* 263: 646–653. Reprinted in *Mental Processes*, by H. C. Longuet-Higgens, 1987. Cambridge, MA: MIT Press.

Longuet-Higgins, H. C. 1987. *Mental Processes.* Cambridge, MA: MIT Press.

Longuet-Higgins, H. C., and C. S. Lee. 1983. "The rhythmic interpretation of monophonic music." In *Studies in Musical Performance* 39, edited by J. Sundberg, 1983. Stockholm: Royal Swedish Academy of Music, 7–26.

Lopez-Lezcano, F. 2016. "Searching for the GRAIL." *Computer Music Journal* 40(4): 91–103.

López-Serrano, P., M. Davies, J. Hockman, C. Dittmar, and M. Müller. 2018. "Break-informed audio decomposition for interactive redrumming." In *Proceedings of the International Society of Music Information Retrieval Conference, Paris, France.* n.p.: International Society for Music Information Retrieval.

Lorrain, D. 1980. "A panoply of stochastic 'cannons.'" *Computer Music Journal* 4(1): 53–81. Reprinted in *The Music Machine*, edited by C. Roads, 1989. Cambridge, MA: MIT Press, 351–379.

Lorrain, D. 2009. "Interpolations." In *Le calcul de la music: composition, modèles et outils*, edited by L. Pottier. Saint-Étienne, France: Publications de l'université de Saint-Étienne, 367–400.

Losano, M. 1990. *Storie de Automi.* Turin, Italy: Einaudi.

Lossius, T., P. Baltazar, and T. de la Hogue. 2009. "DBAP–Distance-based amplitude panning." In *Proceedings of the 2009 International Computer Music Conference.* San Francisco: International Computer Music Association.

Loughlin, P., L. Atlas, and J. Pitton. 1992. "Advanced time-frequency representations for speech processing." In *Visual Representations of Speech Signals*, edited by M. Cooke and S. Beet. New York: J. Wiley.

Lowe, B., and R. Currie. 1989. "Digidesign's Sound Accelerator: Lessons lived and learned." *Computer Music Journal* 13(1): 36–46.

Loy, D. G. 1981. "Notes on the implementation of MUSBOX: A compiler for the Systems Concepts Digital Synthesizer." *Computer Music Journal* 5(1): 34–50. Reprinted in *The Music Machine*, edited by C. Roads, 1989. Cambridge, MA: MIT Press, 333–350.

Loy, D. G. 1985a. "About AUDIUM: A conversation with Stanley Shaff." *Computer Music Journal* 9(2): 41–48.

Loy, D. G. 1985b. "Musicians make a standard: The MIDI phenomenon." *Computer Music Journal* 9(4): 8–26. Reprinted in *The Music Machine*, edited by C. Roads, 1989. Cambridge, MA: MIT Press, 181–198.

Loy, D. G. 1985c. "Sndpth: A program to interactively create/edit sound trajectories." Unpublished.

Loy, D. G. 1986. "Player." Technical memorandum. La Jolla: Center for Music Experiment, University of California, San Diego.

Loy, D. G. 1987. "On the scheduling of multiple parallel processors executing synchronously." In *Proceedings of the 1987 International Computer Music Conference*, edited by J. Beauchamp. San Francisco: International Computer Music Association, 117–124.

Loy, D. G. 1989a. "Composing with computers—A survey of some compositional formalisms and music programming languages." In *Current Directions in Computer Music Research*, edited by M. Mathews and J. R. Pierce. Cambridge, MA: MIT Press, 292–396.

Loy, D. G., ed. 1989b. Special issue on neural nets and connectionism 1. *Computer Music Journal* 13(3).

Loy, D. G., ed. 1989c. Special issue on neural nets and connectionism 2. *Computer Music Journal* 13(4).

Loy, D. G. 2006. *Musimathics: The Mathematical Foundations of Music.* Volume 1. Cambridge, MA: MIT Press.

Loy, D. G. 2007. *Musimathics: The Mathematical Foundations of Music.* Volume 2. Cambridge, MA: MIT Press.

Loy, D. G. 2013a. "Life and times of the Samson Box." *Computer Music Journal* 37(3): 26–48.

Loy, D. G. 2013b. "The Systems Concepts Digital Synthesizer: An architectural retrospective." *Computer Music Journal* 37(3): 49–67.

Loy, D. G., and C. Abbott. 1985. "Programming languages for computer music." *ACM Computing Surveys* 17(2): 235–266.

Luce, D. 1963. "Physical correlates of nonpercussive instrument tones." Sc.D. diss. Department of Physics, MIT.

Lucretius. (55) 1951. *The Nature of the Universe.* Translated by R. Latham. Harmondsworth, UK: Penguin Books.

Lukin, A., and J. Todd. 2006. "Adaptive time-frequency resolution for analysis and processing of audio." Presented at the 120th Convention of the Audio Engineering Society. New York: Audio Engineering Society. https://www.aes.org/e-lib/browse.cfm?elib=13521.

Lundén, P., and T. Ungvary 1991. "MacSonogram: A programme to produce large scale sonograms for musical purposes." In *Proceedings of the 1991 International Computer Music Conference*, edited by B. Alphonce and B. Pennycook. San Francisco: International Computer Music Association, 554–554C.

Lupone, M., L. Bianchini, S. Lanzalone, and A. Gabriele. 2020. "Research at Rome's Centro Ricerche Musicali on interactive and adaptive installations and on augmented instruments." *Computer Music Journal* 44(2/3): 133–158.

Lynch, H., and R. Sazdov. 2017. "A perceptual investigation into spatialization techniques used in multichannel electroacoustic music for envelopment and engulfment." *Computer Music Journal* 41(1): 13–33.

Lyon, E. 2012. *Designing Audio Objects for Max/MSP and Pd.* Middleton, WI: A-R Editions.

Lyon, E., ed. 2016. Special issue on "High density loudspeaker arrays, part 1." *Computer Music Journal* 40(4).

Lyon, E., ed. 2017. Special issue on "High density loudspeaker arrays, part 2." *Computer Music Journal* 41(1).

Lyon, E., T. Caulkins, D. Blount, I. Bukvic, C. Nichols, M. Roan, and T. Upthegrove. 2016. "Genesis of the Cube: the design and deployment of an HDLA-based performance and research facility." *Computer Music Journal* 40(4): 62–78.

Lyon, R., A. Katsiamis, and E. Drakakis. 2010. "History and future of auditory filter models." In *Proceedings of 2010 IEEE International Symposium on Circuits and Systems.* New York: IEEE.

Lyon, R., and L. Dyer. 1986. "Experiments with a computational model of the cochlea." In *Proceedings of the International Conference on Acoustics, Speech, and Signal Processing, Tokyo.* New York: IEEE, 1975–1978.

Lyon, R., M. Rehn, S. Bengio, T. C. Walters, and G. Chechik. 2010. "Sound retrieval and ranking using sparse auditory representations." *Neural Computation* 22(9): 2390–2416.

Lyr, R. 1955. "Une merveille de mécanisme: le Componium de T. N. Winkel." In *Histoire de la boîte à musique*, edited by A. Chapuis. Lausanne, Switzerland: Edition Scriptar.

MacCallum, J., M. Goodheart, and A. Freed. 2015. "Antony: A reimagining." In *Proceedings of the 2015 International Computer Music Conference.* San Francisco: International Computer Music Association, 342–345.

Maestre, E., M. Blaauw, J. Bonada, E. Guaus, and A. Pérez. 2010. "Statistical modeling of bowing control applied to violin sound synthesis." *IEEE Transactions on Audio, Speech, and Language Processing* 18(4): 855–871.

Maestre, E., R. Ramírez, S. Kersten, and X. Serra. 2009. "Expressive concatenative synthesis by reusing samples from real performance recordings." *Computer Music Journal* 33(4): 23–42.

Magnusson, T. 2012. ixilang. https://github.com/thormagnusson/ixilang.

Maher, R. 1990. "Evaluation of a method for separating digitized duet signals." *Journal of the Audio Engineering Society* 38(12): 956–979.

Maher, R. 1992. "On the nature of granulation noise in uniform quantization systems." *Journal of the Audio Engineering Society* 40(1/2): 12–20.

Maher, R., and J. Beauchamp. 1990. "An investigation of vocal vibrato for synthesis." *Applied Acoustics* 30: 219–245.

Maillard, B. 1976. "Sur la modulation de fréquence." *Cahiers recherche/musique* 3: 179–204.

Make. 2019. https://makezine.com.

MakeMusic. 2013. "What is Music XML?" https://www.makemusic.com/press-room/brand-assets/musicxml/.

Makhoul, J. 1975. "Linear prediction: a tutorial review." *Proceedings of the Institute for Electrical and Electronic Engineers* 63: 561–580.

Maldonado, G. 2011. "Working with audio streams." In *The Audio Programming Book*, edited by R. Boulanger and V. Lazzarini. Cambridge, MA: MIT Press, 329–381.

Malham, D. 1998. "Approaches to spatialisation." *Organized Sound* 3(2): 167–178.

Malham, D. 2003. "Space in Music–Music in Space." PhD diss. University of York.

Malham, D., and A. Myatt. 1995. "3-D sound spatialisation using Ambisonic techniques." *Computer Music Journal* 19(4): 58–70.

Malinowski, S. 2015. "The Conductor Program–Computer-mediated musical performance." https://www.musanim.com/Tapper.

Mallat, S. 1989. "A theory of multiresolution signal decomposition: the wavelet representation." *IEEE Transactions on Pattern Analysis and Machine Intelligence* 11(7): 674–693.

Mallat, S. 2009. *A Wavelet Tour of Signal Processing: The Sparse Way*. Amsterdam: Academic Press, Elsevier.

Mallat, S., and Z. Zhang. 1993. "Matching pursuits with time-frequency dictionaries." *IEEE Transactions on Signal Processing* 41(12): 3397–3415.

Mandelbrot, B. 1977. *Fractals: Form, Chance, and Dimension.* San Francisco: W. H. Freeman.

Manhattan Research, Inc. 2000. *New Plastic Sounds and Electronic Abstractions Composed and Performed by Raymond Scott.* Book + compact disc. Holland: Basta Music.

Manjunath, B. S., P. Salembier, and T. Sikora, eds. 2002. *Multimedia Content Description Interface.* New York: Wiley.

Manning, P. 2013. *Electronic and Computer Music*. 4th ed. Oxford: Oxford University Press.

Mansour, H. 2016. "The bowed string and its playability: Theory, simulation and analysis." PhD diss. Department of Music Research, McGill University.

Manthey, M. 1978. "The Egg: A purely digital real time polyphonic sound synthesizer." *Computer Music Journal* 2(2): 32–37.

Manthey, M. 1979. "Real-time sound synthesis: A software microcosm." PhD dissertation. State Department of Computer Science, University of New York at Buffalo.

Manzagol, P.-A., T. Bertine-Mahieux, and D. Eck. 2008. "On the use of sparse time-relative auditory codes for music." *Proceedings of the International Society on Music Information Retrieval*. Philadelphia, 603–608.

Marans, M. 1991. "Timing is everything." *Keyboard* 17(12): 94–103.

Marino, G., J.-M. Raczinski, and M.-H. Serra. 1990. "The new UPIC system." In *Proceedings of the 1990 International Computer Music Conference*, edited by S. Arnold and G. Hair. San Francisco: International Computer Music Association, 249–252.

Marino, G., M.-H. Serra, and J.-M. Raczinski. 1993. "The UPIC system, origins and innovations." *Perspectives of New Music* 31(1): 258–269.

Markel, J. 1972. "Digital inverse filtering—A new tool for formant trajectory tracking." *IEEE Transactions on Audio and Acoustics* Vol. AU-20(5): 367–377.

Markel, J., and A. Gray, Jr. 1976. *Linear Prediction of Speech*. New York: Springer.

Markowitz, J. 1989. *Triumphs and Trials of an Organ Builder*. Macungie, PA: Allen Organ Company.

Marlen, W. 1966. "Duration and frequency alteration." *Journal of the Audio Engineering Society* 14(2): 132–139.

Marple, S. 1987. *Digital Spectral Analysis*. Englewood Cliffs, NJ: Prentice Hall.

Martinez, J., ed. 2004. "MPEG-7 overview." *IEEE Multimedia* 9: 83–93.

Martirano, S. 1971. "An electronic music instrument which combines the composing process with performance in real time." Progress Report 1. Department of Music. Urbana: University of Illinois.

Maserati, T. 2014. "Tony Maserati on Multiband Compression for Vocals." https://www.waves.com/vocal-multiband-compression-with-c4.

Massie, D. 1986. "A survey of looping algorithms for sampled data musical instruments." In *Final Program of the IEEE Acoustic, Speech, and Signal Processing Workshop on Applications of Signal Processing to Audio and Acoustics*. New York: IEEE.

Massie, D., and V. Stonick. 1992. "The musical intrigue of pole-zero pairs." In *Proceedings of the 1992 International Computer Music Conference*, edited by A. Strange. San Francisco: International Computer Music Association, 22–25.

Mathews, M. 1969. *The Technology of Computer Music*. Cambridge, MA: MIT Press.

Mathews, M. 1989. "The conductor program and mechanical baton." In *Current Directions in Computer Music Research*, edited by M. Mathews and J. R. Pierce. Cambridge, MA: MIT Press, 263–282.

Mathews, M., and C. Abbott. 1980. "The sequential drum." *Computer Music Journal* 4(4): 45–59.

Mathews, M., and J. Miller. 1963. *Music IV Programmer's Manual.* Murray Hill, NJ: Bell Telephone Laboratories.

Mathews, M., J. Miller, and E. David, Jr. 1961. "Pitch synchronous analysis of voiced sounds." *Journal of the Acoustical Society of America* 33: 179–186.

Mathews, M., and F. R. Moore. 1970. "GROOVE—A program to compose, store, and edit functions of time." *Communications of the Association for Computing Machinery* 13(12): 715–721.

Mathews, M., and L. Rosler. 1968. "Graphical language for the scores of computer-generated sounds." *Perspectives of New Music* 6(2): 92–118.

Mathews, M., and L. Rosler. 1969. "Graphical language for the scores of computer-generated sounds." In *Music by Computers*, edited by H. von Foerster and J. Beauchamp. New York: John Wiley & Sons, 84–114.

Mathworks, The. 1999. *Signal Processing Toolbox User's Guide.* Natick, MA: Mathworks.

Matossian, N. 1987. *Xenakis.* New York: Taplinger.

Matsushima, T., T. Harada, I. Sonomoto, K. Kanamori, A. Uesugi, Y. Nimura, S. Hashimoto, and S. Ohteru. 1985. "Automated recognition system for musical score—The visual system of WABOT-2." *Bulletin of Science and Engineering Research Laboratory, Waseda University* 112: 25–52.

Matthews, K. 2018. "Beyond me." In *The Oxford Handbook of Algorithmic Music*, edited by R. Dean and A. McLean. Oxford: Oxford University Press, 503–506.

Mauchly, J. 1982. "Merging event lists in real time." In *Proceedings of the Second Symposium on Small Computers in the Arts, 15–17 October 1982, Philadelphia.* Los Angeles: IEEE Computer Society, 23–28.

Maxwell, J., and S. Ornstein. 1983. "Mockingbird: A composer's amanuensis." Technical Report CSL-83-2. Palo Alto, CA: Xerox.

Mayer, A. 1878. *Sound.* New York: D. Appleton.

Mayer, D. 2019. *miSCellaneous: A library of SuperCollider extensions 2009–2019.* Software documentation. https://github.com/dkmayer/miSCellaneous_lib.

Mazzola, G. 2018. *The Topos of Music.* 2nd ed. Cham, Switzerland: Springer.

Mazzola, G., M. Mannone, and Y. Pang. 2016. *Cool Math for Hot Music: A First Introduction to Mathematics for Music Theorists.* Cham, Switzerland: Springer.

McAdams, S. 1982. "Spectral fusion and the creation of auditory images." In *Music, Mind, and Brain: The Neuropsychology of Music*, edited by M. Clynes. New York: Plenum, 279–298.

McAdams, S. 1987. "Music: a science of mind?" *Contemporary Music Review* 2(1): 1–61.

McAdams, S., and A. Bregman. 1979. "Hearing musical streams." *Computer Music Journal* 3(4): 26–44. Reprinted in *Foundations of Computer Music*, edited by C. Roads and J. Strawn, 1985. Cambridge, MA: MIT Press, 658–698.

McAulay, R., and T. Quatieri. 1986. "Speech analysis/synthesis based on a sinusoidal representation." *IEEE Transactions on Acoustics, Speech, and Signal Processing* ASSP-34: 744–754.

McCartney, J. 1990. Synth-O-Matic version 0.06 software.

McCartney, J. 1994. Synth-O-Matic version 0.45 software.

McCartney, J. 1995. SuperCollider version 1 software.

McCartney, J. 1997. Personal communication.

McCartney, J. 1998. SuperCollider version 2 software.

McCartney, J. 2002. "Rethinking the Computer Music Language: SuperCollider." *Computer Music Journal* 26(4): 61–68.

McLaren, N., and R. Lewis. 1948. "Synthetic sound on film." *Journal of the Society of Motion Pitcture Engineers* 50: 233–247.

McLean, A., and G. Wiggins. 2010. "Tidal–Pattern language for live coding of music." *Proceedings Sound and Music Computing.* https://www.researchgate.net/publication/261134964_Tidal_-_Pattern_Language_for_the_Live_Coding_of_Music.

McClellan, J., T. Parks, and L. Rabiner. 1973. "A computer program for designing optimal FIR linear phase digital filters." *IEEE Transactions on Audio and Electro-acoustics* AU-21: 506–526.

McCormack, J., A. Eldridge, A. Dorin, and P. McIlwain. 2009. "Generative algorithms for making music: emergence, evolution, and ecosystems." In *The Oxford Handbook of Computer Music*, edited by R. Dean. Oxford: Oxford University Press, 355–379.

McGee, R. 2015. "Scanning spaces: New paradigms for spatial sonification and synthesis." PhD diss. Media Arts and Technology, University of California, Santa Barbara.

McGee, R. 2018. Personal communication.

McGill, J. F. 1985. "Digital recording and reproduction: An introduction." In *Digital Audio Engineering: An Anthology*, edited by John Strawn. Middleton, WI: A-R Editions, 1–28.

McIntyre, M., R. Schumacher, and J. Woodhouse. 1983. "On the oscillations of musical instruments." *Journal of the Acoustical Society of America* 74(5): 1325–1345.

McLaren, N. 1948. "Synthetic sound on film." *Journal of the Society of Motion Picture Engineers* March: 233–247.

McLellan, J., R. Schafer, and M. Yoder. 2003. *Signal Processing First.* Upper Saddle River, NJ: Prentice Hall.

McLeod, P., and G. Wyvill. 2005. "A smarter way to find pitch." In *Proceedings of the 2005 International Computer Music Conference.* San Francisco: International Computer Music Association, 138–141.

McLeran, A., C. Roads, B. Sturm, and J. Shynk. 2008. "Granular sound spatialization using dictionary-based methods." In *Proceedings of the Sound and Music Computer Conference.* n.p.: Sound and Music Computing Network. http://smc.afim -asso.org.

McMillen, K. 2015. "Granular synthesis: An introduction." https://www.keithmcmillen .com. (Online source no longer available.)

McNally, G. 1984. "Dynamic range control of digital audio signals." *Journal of the Audio Engineering Society* 32(5): 316–327.

McNally, G., et al. 1985. "Digital audio editing." Preprint 2214(B-2). Presented at the 77th Audio Engineering Society Convention, March 5–8, 1985, Hamburg. New York: Audio Engineering Society.

McPherson, A. 2015. "Buttons, handles and keys: Advances in continuous-control keyboard instruments." *Computer Music Journal* 39(2): 28–46.

Meddis, R., M. Hewitt, and T. Schackleton. 1990. "Implementation details of a computation model of the inner hair-cell/auditory-nerve synapse." *Journal of the Acoustical Society of America* 87: 1813–1816.

Médigue, G. 2020. "The early days of the UPIC." In *From Xenakis's UPIC to Graphical Notation Today,* edited by P. Weibel, S. Kanach, and L. Brümmer. Karlsruhe, Germany: ZKM, 118–141. https://zkm.de/de/from-xenakiss-upic-to-graphic -notation-today.

Melchior, V. 2019. "High resolution audio: a history and perspective." *Journal of the Audio Engineering Society* 67(5): 246–257.

Mellinger, S. 1991. "Event formation and separation in musical sound." PhD diss. Center for Computer Research in Music and Acoustics, Department of Music, Stanford University.

Mendel, J. 1991. "Tutorial on higher-order statistics (spectra) in signal processing and system theory: Theoretical results and some applications." *Proceedings of the IEEE* 79(3): 278–305.

Menenghini, M. 2007. "An analysis of the compositional technique in John Chowning's *Stria.*" *Computer Music Journal* 31(3): 26–37.

Mermelstein, P. 1976. "Distance measures for speech recognition, psychological and instrumental." In *Pattern Recognition and Artificial Intelligence*, edited by C. Chen. New York: Academic, 374–388.

Meyer, E., and G. Buchmann. 1931. "Die Klangspektren der Musikinstrumente." *Sïtzungsberichte der Preussischen Akademie der Wissenschaften.* Berlin: Verlag der Akademie der Wissenschaften/Walter de Gruyter, 735–778.

Meyer, F., and H. Zimmermann. 2006. *Edgard Varèse: Composer, Sound Sculptor, Visionary.* Basel: Paul Sacher Foundation.

Meyer, J. 1984. "Time correction of anti-aliasing filters used in digital audio systems." *Journal of the Audio Engineering Society* 32(3): 132–137.

Meyer Sound Laboratories. 2020. "UPM UltraCompact Loudspeakers." https://meyersound.com/product/upm.

Meyer, Y. 1993. *Wavelets: Algorithms and Applications.* Philadelphia: Society for Industrial and Applied Mathematics.

Meyer-Eppler, W. 1955. "Statistic and psychologic problems of sound." *Die Reihe* 1: 55–61 (English edition).

Meyer-Eppler, W. 1959. *Grundlagen und Aufwendungen der Informationstheorie.* Berlin: Springer.

Mian, A., and G. Tisato. 1984. "Sound structuring techniques using parameters derived from a voice analysis/synthesis system." In *Proceedings of the 1984 International Computer Music Conference*, edited by D. Wessel. San Francisco: International Computer Music Association.

MIDI Association. 1983. "MIDI musical instrument digital interface specification 1.0." Los Angeles: International MIDI Association.

MIDI Association. 2017. *General MIDI 2 (GM2).* https://www.midi.org/specifications /item/general-midi-2.

MIDI Association. 2019. "Control Change Messages." https://www.midi.org /specifications-old/item/table-3-control-change-messages-data-bytes-2.

MIDI Association. 2020. "MIDI 2.0 Specification Overview." https://www.midi.org.

Mihalic, M. 2009. "Modèles et données extra-musicale: etude de leur incidence dans le processus compositionnel." In *Le calcule la music: composition modèles et outils*, edited by L. Pottier. Saint-Étienne, France: Publications de l'université de Saint-Étienne, 23–162.

Mikelson, H. 2000a. "Mathematical modeling with Csound: From waveguides to chaos." In *The Csound Book*, edited by R. Boulanger. Cambridge, MA: MIT Press, 369–388.

Mikelson, H. 2000b. "Terrain mapping synthesis." In *The Csound Book*, edited by R. Boulanger. Cambridge, MA: MIT Press. CD-ROM.

Millen, D. 1990. "Cellular automata music." In *Proceedings of the 1990 International Computer Music Conference*, edited by S. Arnold and G. Hair. San Francisco: International Computer Music Association, 314–316.

Millen, D. 1992. "Generation of formal patterns for music composition by means of cellular automata." In *Proceedings of the 1992 International Computer Music Conference*, edited by A. Strange. San Francisco: International Computer Music Association, 398–399.

Miller, B., D. Scarborough, and J. Jones. 1992. "On the perception of meter." In *Understanding Music with AI*, edited by M. Balaban, K. Ebcioglu, and O. Laske. Cambridge, MA and Menlo Park, CA: MIT Press and AAAI Press, 429–447.

Miller, D. C. 1916. *The Science of Musical Sounds*. New York: MacMillan.

Miller, D. C. 1935. *Anecdotal History of the Science of Sound*. New York: MacMillan.

Miller, G., E. Galanter, and K. Pribram. 1960. *Plans and the Structure of Behavior*. New York: Holt.

Miller, N. 1973. "Filtering of singing voice signal from noise by synthesis." PhD diss. Department of Electrical Engineering, University of Utah.

Milne, S. 1980. "A digital sound editor." BSc thesis. Department of Electrical Engineering and Computer Science, MIT.

Mintz, D. 2007. "Toward Timbral Synthesis: A new method for synthesizing sound based on timbre description schemes." MS thesis. Media Arts and Technology, University of California, Santa Barbara.

Miranda, E., and J. Biles, eds. 2007. *Evolutionary Computer Music*. London: Springer.

Miranda, E., and M. Wanderley. 2006. *New Digital Musical Instruments: Control and Interaction Beyond the Keyboard*. Middleton, WI: A-R Editions.

Mitra, S. 2006. *Digital Signal Processing: A Computer-Based Approach*. 3rd ed. New York: McGraw-Hill.

Mitre, A., M. Queiroz, and R. Faria. 2006. "Accurate and efficient fundamental frequency determination from precise partial estimates." In *Proceedings of the 4th Congress of the Audio Engineering Society, Brasil*. New York: Audio Engineering Society.

Mitsuhashi, Y. 1980. "Waveshape parameter modulation in producing complex spectra." *Journal of the Audio Engineering Society* 28(12): 879–895.

Mitsuhashi, Y. 1982a. "Audio signal synthesis by functions of two variables." *Journal of the Audio Engineering Society* 30(10): 701–706.

Mitsuhashi, Y. 1982b. "Musical sound synthesis by forward differences." *Journal of the Audio Engineering Society* 30(1/2): 2–9.

Mitsuhashi, Y. 1982c. "Piecewise interpolation technique for audio signal synthesis." *Journal of the Audio Engineering Society* 30(4): 192–202.

Miyama, C., G. Dipper, and L. Brümmer. 2015. "Zirkonium MK III—a toolkit for spatial composition." *Journal of the Japanese Society for Sonic Arts* 7(3): 54–59.

Moles, A. 1968. *Information Theory and Esthetic Perception.* Urbana: University of Illinois Press.

Monro, G. 1995. "Fractal interpolation waveforms." *Computer Music Journal* 19(1): 88–98.

Mont-Reynaud, B. 1985a. *The bounded-Q Approach to Time-Varying Spectral Analysis.* Technical Report STAN-M-28. Stanford, CA: Stanford University Department of Music.

Mont-Reynaud, B. 1985b. "Problem-solving strategies in a music transcription system." In *Proceedings of the International Joint Conference on Artificial Intelligence, Los Angeles.* Los Altos, CA: Morgan-Kaufmann, 915–918.

Mont-Reynaud, B., and M. Goldstein. 1985. "On finding rhythmic patterns in musical lines." In *Proceedings of the 1985 International Computer Music Conference*, edited by B. Truax. San Francisco: International Computer Music Association, 391–397.

Moog, R. 1965. "Voltage-controlled electronic music modules." *Journal of the Audio Engineering Society* 13(3): 200–206.

Moog, R. 1986. "MIDI: Musical Instrument Digital Interface." *Journal of the Audio Engineering Society* 34(5): 394–404.

Moog, R. 1987. "Position and force sensors and their application to keyboards and related performance devices." In *Proceedings of the AES 5th International Conference: Music and Digital Technology*, edited by J. Strawn. New York: Audio Engineering Society, 173–184.

Moog, R., and T. Rhea. 1990. "Evolution of the keyboard interface: The Bösendorfer 290 SE recording piano and the Moog multiply-touch-sensitive keyboards." *Computer Music Journal* 14(2): 52–60.

Moon, F. 1987. *Chaotic Vibrations: An Introduction for Applied Scientists and Engineers.* New York: Wiley.

Moore, F. R. 1977. "Table lookup noise for sinusoidal digital oscillators." *Computer Music Journal* 1(2): 26–29. Reprinted in *Foundations of Computer Music*, edited by C. Roads and J. Strawn, 1985. Cambridge, MA: MIT Press, 326–334.

Moore, F. R. 1978a. "An introduction to the mathematics of digital signal processing. Part 1: Algebra, trigonometry, and the most beautiful formula in mathematics." *Computer Music Journal* 2(1): 38–47. Reprinted in *Digital Audio Signal Processing: An Anthology*, edited by J. Strawn, 1985. Middleton, WI: A-R Editions.

Moore, F. R. 1978b. "An introduction to the mathematics of digital signal processing. Part 2: Sampling, transforms, and digital filtering." *Computer Music Journal*

2(2): 38–60. Reprinted in *Digital Audio Signal Processing: An Anthology*, edited by J. Strawn, 1985. Middleton, WI: A-R Editions.

Moore, F. R. 1982. "The computer audio research laboratory at UCSD." *Computer Music Journal* 6(1): 18–29.

Moore, F. R. 1983. "A general model for spatial processing of sounds." *Computer Music Journal* 7(3): 6–15. Reprinted in *The Music Machine*, edited by C. Roads, 1989. Cambridge, MA: MIT Press, 559–568.

Moore, F. R. 1985. "The FRMBox—A modular digital music synthesizer." In *Digital Audio Signal Processing: An Anthology*, edited by J. Strawn. Middleton, WI: A-R Editions.

Moore, F. R. 1988. "The dysfunctions of MIDI." *Computer Music Journal* 12(1): 19–28.

Moore, F. R. 1990. *Elements of Computer Music.* Englewood Cliffs, NJ: Prentice Hall.

Moore, F. R., and G. Loy. 1982. "Essays about computer music." La Jolla: Center for Music Experiment, University of California, San Diego.

Moorer, J. A. 1972. "Music and computer composition." *Communications of the ACM* 15(2): 104–113.

Moorer, J. A. 1973. "The optimum comb method of pitch period analysis of continuous digitized speech." AIM-207. Stanford, CA: Stanford Artificial Intelligence Laboratory.

Moorer, J. A. 1975. "On the segmentation and analysis of continuous musical sound." STAN-M-3. Stanford, CA: Stanford University Department of Music.

Moorer, J. A. 1976. "The synthesis of complex audio spectra by means of discrete summation formulas." *Journal of the Audio Engineering Society* 24: 717–724.

Moorer, J. A. 1977. "Signal processing aspects of computer music." *Proceeding of the IEEE* 65(8): 1108–1137. Reprinted in *Computer Music Journal* 1(1): 4–37 and in *Digital Audio Signal Processing: An Anthology*, edited by J. M. Strawn, 1985. Middleton, WI: A-R Editions.

Moorer, J. A. 1978. "The use of the phase vocoder in computer music applications." *Journal of the Audio Engineering Society* 26(1/2): 42–45.

Moorer, J. A. 1979a. "About this reverberation business." *Computer Music Journal* 3(2): 13–28. Reprinted in *Foundations of Computer Music*, edited by C. Roads and J. Strawn, 1985. Cambridge, MA: MIT Press, 605–639.

Moorer, J. A. 1979b. "The digital coding of high-quality musical sound." *Journal of the Audio Engineering Society* 27(9): 657–666.

Moorer, J. A. 1979c. "The use of linear prediction of speech in computer music applications." *Journal of the Audio Engineering Society* 27(3): 134–140.

Moorer, J. A. 1981a. "General spectral transformations for digital filters." *IEEE Transactions on Acoustics, Speech, and Signal Processing* ASSP-29(5): 1092–1094.

Moorer, J. A. 1981b. "Synthesizers I have known and loved." *Computer Music Journal* 5(1): 4–12. Reprinted in *The Music Machine*, edited by C. Roads, 1989. Cambridge, MA: MIT Press, 589–598.

Moorer, J. A. 1983a. "The audio signal processor: The next step in digital audio." In *Digital Audio*, edited by B. Blesser, B. Locanthi, and T. Stockham, 1983. New York: Audio Engineering Society, 205–215.

Moorer, J. A. 1983b. "The manifold joys of conformal mapping: Applications to digital filtering in the studio." *Journal of the Audio Engineering Society* 31(11): 826–841.

Moorer, J. A. 1996. "Breaking the sound barrier: Mastering at 96 kHz and beyond." Preprint 4357. In *Proceeding of the 101st Audio Engineering Society Convention, Los Angeles*. New York: Audio Engineering Society.

Moorer, J. A. 2019. Lecture at the Center for Research in Electronic Art Technology (CREATE), University of California, Santa Barbara, June 1, 2019.

Moorer, J. A., and M. Berger. 1986. "Linear phase bandsplitting: theory and applications." *Journal of the Audio Engineering Society* 34(3): 143–152.

Moorer, J. A., A. Chauveau, C. Abbott, P. Eastty, and J. Lawson. 1979. "The 4C machine." *Computer Music Journal* 3(3): 16–24. Revised and updated version in *Foundations of Computer Music*, edited by C. Roads and J. Strawn, 1985. Cambridge, MA: MIT Press, 261–280.

Moorer, J. A., J. Grey, and J. Snell. 1977a. "Lexicon of analyzed tones. Part 1: A violin tone." *Computer Music Journal* 1(2): 39–45.

Moorer, J. A., J. Grey, and J. Strawn. 1977b. "Lexicon of analyzed tones. Part 2: Clarinet and oboe." *Computer Music Journal* 1(3): 12–29.

Moorer, J. A., J. Grey, and J. Strawn. 1978. "Lexicon of analyzed tones. Part 3: Trumpet." *Computer Music Journal* 2(2): 23–31.

Morawska-Büngler, M. 1988. *Schwingende Elektronen.* Cologne: P. J. Tonger.

Morgan, N., and J. Podrazik. 2020. *Guide Rapide: Introduction à Opusmodus.* Translated by S. Boussuge. https://opusmodus.com.

Morita, H., S. Hashimoto, and S. Ohteru. 1991. "A computer music system that follows a human conductor." *IEEE Computer* 24(7): 44–53.

Morrill, D. 1977. "Trumpet algorithms for computer composition." *Computer Music Journal* 1(1): 46–52. Reprinted in *Foundations of Computer Music*, edited by C. Roads and J. Strawn, 1985. Cambridge, MA: MIT Press, 30–44.

Morrill, D. 1981a. "The dynamic aspects of trumpet phrases." *Rapports IRCAM* 33/81. Paris: IRCAM.

Morrill, D. 1981b. "Loudspeakers and performers: Some problems and proposals." *Computer Music Journal* 5(4): 25–29. Reprinted in *The Music Machine*, edited by C. Roads, 1989. Cambridge, MA: MIT Press, 95–99.

Morrison, J., and J.-M. Adrien. 1991. "Control mechanisms in the MOSAIC synthesis program." In *Proceedings of the 1991 International Computer Music Conference*, edited by B. Alphonce and B. Pennycook. San Francisco: International Computer Music Association, 19–22.

Morrison, J., and D. Waxman. 1991. *MOSAIC 3.0.* Paris: IRCAM.

Morse, P. 1936. *Vibration and Sound.* Woodbury, NY: American Institute of Physics.

Mozart, W. A. 1770. *Musikalische Würfelspiele*, K. 294D. Catalog number 4474. Mainz, Germany: Schott.

Müller, G., and R. Giuletti. 1987. "High quality music notation: interactive editing and input by piano keyboard." In *Proceedings of the 1987 International Computer Music Conference*, edited by J. Beauchamp and S. Tipei. San Francisco: International Computer Music Association, 333–340.

Müller, M. 2015. *Fundamentals of Music Processing: Audio Analysis, Algorithms, Applications.* Chur, Switzerland: Springer Nature.

Müller, M., A. Artz, S. Balke, M. Dorfer, and G. Widmer. 2019. "Cross-model music retrieval and applications." *IEEE Signal Processing Magazine* 36(1): 52–62.

Müller, M., D. Ellis, A. Klapuri, and G. Richard. 2011. "Signal processing for music analysis." *IEEE Journal on Selected Topics in Signal Processing* 5(6): 1088–1110.

Müller, M., M. Goto, and M. Schedl. 2012. *Multimodal Music Processing.* Saarbrücken, Germany: Dagstuhl.

Müller, S., and P. Massarani. 2001. "Transfer function measurements with sweeps." *Journal of the Audio Engineering Society* 49(6): 443–471.

Mumma, G. 1975. "Live-electronic music." In *The Development and Practice of Electronic Music*, edited by J. Appleton and R. Perera. Englewood Cliffs, NJ: Prentice Hall, 286–335.

Murail, T. 1991. "Spectres et Lutins." In *L'Itineraire*, edited by D. Cohen-Levinas, 1991. Paris: La Revue Musicale.

Murphy, D., A. Kelloniemi, J. Mullen, and S. Shelley. 2007. "Acoustic modeling using the digital waveguide mesh." *IEEE Signal Processing Magazine* 24(2): 55–66.

Musicus, B. 1984. "Optimal frequency-warped short time analysis/synthesis." Unpublished manuscript.

Musicus, B., J. Stautner, and J. Anderson. 1984. *Optimal Least Squares Short Time Analysis/Synthesis.* Technical report. Cambridge, MA: Research Laboratory of Electronics, Massachusetts Institute of Technology.

Myhill, J. 1979. "Some simplifications and improvements in the stochastic music program." In *Proceedings of the 1978 International Computer Music Conference*, edited by C. Roads. Evanston, IL: Northwestern University Press, 272–317.

Nahin, P. 1996. *The Science of Radio.* New York: American Institute of Physics.

Najnudel, J., T. Hélie, and D. Roze. 2019. "Simulation of the ondes martenot ribbon-controlled oscillator using energy-balanced modeling of nonlinear time-varying electronic compositions." *Journal of the Audio Engineering Society* 67(12): 961–971.

Nakajima, H., T. Doi, J. Fukuda, and A. Iga. 1983. *Digital Audio Technology.* Blue Bell, PA: Tab Books.

Nakajima, H., T. Doi, Y. Tsuchiya, and A. Iga. 1978. "A new PCM system as an adapter of digital audio tape recorders." Preprint 1352. In *Proceedings of the 60th Convention.* New York: Audio Engineering Society.

Nakra, T., Y. Ivanov, P. Smaragdis, and C. Ault. 2009. "The UBS virtual maestro: an interactive conducting system." In *Proceedings of the 9th International Conference on New Interfaces for Musical Expression, Pittsburgh.* n.p.: New Interfaces for Musical Expression. https://www.nime.org.

Nakra, T. M. 2000. "Inside the Conductor's Jacket: Analysis, interpretation, and musical synthesis of expressive gesture." PhD diss. MIT.

Nam, J., V. Välimäki, J. Abel, and J. O. Smith. 2010. "Efficient antialiasing oscillator algorithms using low-order fractional delay filters." *IEEE Transactions on Audio, Speech, and Language Processing* 18(4): 773–785.

Nawab, S., T. Quatieri, and J. Lim. 1983. "Signal reconstruction from short-time Fourier transform magnitude." *IEEE Transactions on Acoustics, Speech, and Signal Processing* ASSP-31(4): 986–998.

Naylor, P., and N. Gaubitch. 2010. *Speech Dereverberation.* London: Springer.

Needham, J., W. Ling, and K. Girdwood Robinson. 1962. *Science and Civilisation in China. Volume 4: Physics and Physical Technology.* Cambridge: Cambridge University Press.

Negyesy, J., and L. Ray. 1989. "Zivatar: a performance system." In *Current Directions in Computer Music Research*, edited by M. V. Mathews and J. R. Pierce. Cambridge, MA: MIT Press, 283–289.

Nelson, G. 1989. "Algorithmic approaches to interactive composition." In *Proceedings of the 1989 International Computer Music Conference*, edited by T. Wells and D. Butler. San Francisco: International Computer Music Association, 219–222.

Nelson, G. 1991. "Gary Lee Nelson: A concert of new works for computers, synthesizers, and MIDI Horn." Program notes.

Nelson, J. 2000. "Understanding and using Csound's GEN routines." In *The Csound Book*, edited by R. Boulanger. Cambridge, MA: MIT Press, 65–97.

Nercessian, S., and A. Lukin. 2019. "Speech dereverberation using recurrent neural networks." In *Proceedings of the International Conference on Digital Audio Effects, DAFx.* n.p.: DAFx. https://www.dafx.de.

Neubäcker, P. 2011. "Sound-object oriented analysis and note-object oriented processing of polyphonic sound recordings." U.S. Patent 8,022,286.

Neukom, M. 2013. *Signals, Systems, and Sound Synthesis.* Berlin: Peter Lang.

Neve, R. 1992. "Rupert Neve of Amek replies." *Studio Sound* 34(3): 21–22.

Newcomb, S. "Standards. Standard Music Description Language Complies with Hypermedia Standard." *IEEE Computer* 24/7 (July 1991): 76–79.

Newcomb, S., and C. Goldfarb. 1989. "X3V1.8M/SD-6 Journal of Development, Standard Music Description Language (SMDL), Part One: Objectives and Methodology." San Francisco: International Computer Music Association.

Newell, A., and H. Simon. 1972. *Human Problem Solving.* Englewood Cliffs, NJ: Prentice-Hall.

Newmarch, J. 2017. *Linux Audio Programming.* New York: Apress/Springer.

Nichols, C. 2002. "The vBow: a virtual violin bow controller for mapping gesture to synthesis with haptic feedback." *Organised Sound* 7(2): 215–220.

Nienhuys, H., and J. Nieuwenhuizen. 2003. "LilyPond: A system for automated music engraving." In *Proceedings of the XIV Colloquium on Musical Informatics (XIV CIM 2003).* Firenze, Italy: Italian Computer Music Association (AIMI).

Nierhaus, G. 2010. *Algorithmic Composition: Paradigms of Automated Music Generation.* Vienna: Springer.

Nieto, O. 2015. "Discovering structure in music: Automatic approaches and perceptual evaluations." PhD diss. New York University.

Nii, H., E. Feigenbaum, J. Anton, and A. Rockmore. 1982. "Signal-to-symbol transformation: HASP/SIAM case study." *AI Magazine* 3(2): 25–35.

Nikias, C., and M. Raghuveer. 1987. "Bispectrum estimation: a digital signal processing framework." *Proceedings of the IEEE* 75(5): 869–891.

Nishino, H., and R. Nakatsu. 2016. "Computer music languages and systems: The synergy between technology and creativity." In *Handbook of Digital Games and Entertainment Technologies*, edited by R. Nakatsu et al. Singapore: Springer, 1–49.

Nishino, H., N. Osaka, and R. Nakatsu. 2015. "The microsound synthesis framework in the LC computer music programming language." *Computer Music Journal* 39(4): 49–79.

Noike, K., N. Takiguchi, T. Nose, Y. Kotani, and H. Nisimura. 1993. In *Proceedings of the 1993 International Computer Music Conference*, edited by S. Ohteru. San Francisco: International Computer Music Association, 363–365.

Noll, A. M. 1967. "Cepstrum pitch determination." *Journal of the Acoustical Society of America* 41(2): 23.

Nolte, D. 2020. "The fall and rise of the Doppler effect." *Physics Today* 73(3): 30–35.

Norilo, V. 2012. "Visualization of signals and algorithms in Kronos." In *Proceedings of the International Conference on Digital Audio Effects, DAFx.* n.p.: DAFx. https://www.dafx.de.

Norilo, V. 2015. "Kronos: a declarative metaprogramming language for digital signal processing." *Computer Music Journal* 39(4): 30–48.

Norilo, V. 2019. "Veneer: visual and touch-based programming for sound." In *Proceedings of the International Conference on Digital Audio Effects, DAFx.* n.p.: DAFx. https://www.dafx.de.

Norris, M. 2013. "SPIN/DRIFT: A real-time spatialized granular synthesis algorithm with particle system physics and behaviours." In *Proceedings of the International Computer Music Conference.* San Francisco: International Computer Music Association.

Nugraha, A., A. Liutkus, and E. Vincent. 2016. "Multichannel audio source separation with deep neural networks." *IEEE/ACM Transactions on Audio, Speech, Language Processing* 24(9): 1652–1664.

Nussbaumer, H. 1981. *Fast Fourier Transform and Convolution Algorithms.* New York: Springer.

Nuttall, A. 1981. "Some windows with very good sidelobe behavior." *IEEE Transactions on Acoustics, Speech, and Signal Processing* ASSP-29(1): 84–91.

Nyquist, H. 1928. "Certain topics in telegraph transmission theory." *Transactions of the American Institute of Electrical Engineers* 47: 617–644.

Oboe, R. 2006. "A multi-instrument force-feedback keyboard." *Computer Music Journal* 30(3): 38–52.

Ohta, H., H. Akita, M. Ohtari, S. Ishicado, and M. Yamane. 1993. "The development of an automatic bagpipe-playing device." In *Proceedings of the 1993 International Computer Music Conference*, edited by S. Ohteru. San Francisco: International Computer Music Association, 430–431.

Old Colony Sound Labs. 2004. Catalog of analog electronics books. https://www.audioXpress.com.

Olive, J. 1977. "Rule synthesis of speech from dyadic units." *Proceedings of the 1977 IEEE Conference on Acoustics, Speech, and Signal Processing.* New York: IEEE, 568–570.

Oliveira, J.-P., and R. Radna. 2021. SpaceControl. Unpublished software application. University of California, Santa Barbara.

Oliveros, P., S. Weaver, J. Pitcher, J. Braasch, and C. Chafe. 2009. "Telematic music–Six perspectives." *Leonardo Music Journal* 19. Online supplement.

Olson, H. 1967. *Music, Physics, and Engineering.* 2nd ed. New York: Dover.

Olson, H. 1991. *Acoustical Engineering.* Philadelphia: Professional Audio Journals. Reprint of 1957 edition.

Olson, H., and H. Belar. 1955. "Electronic music synthesizer." *Journal of the Acoustical Society of America* 27(5): 595.

Olson, H., and H. Belar. 1961. "Aid to music composition system employing a random probability system." *Journal of the Acoustic Society of America* 33: 1163–1170.

O'Modhrain, S. 2011. "A framework for the evaluation of digital musical instruments." *Computer Music Journal* 35(1): 28–42.

Oohashi, T., E. Nishina, Y. Fuwamoto, and N. Kawai. 1993. "On the mechanism of hypersonic effect." In *Proceedings of the 1993 International Computer Music Conference*, edited by S. Ohteru. San Francisco: International Computer Music Association, 432–434.

Oohashi, T., E. Nishina, N. Kawai, Y. Fuwamoto, and H. Imai. 1991. "High frequency sound above the audible range affects brain electric activity and sound perception." Preprint 3207(W-1). In *Proceedings of the 91st Convention of the Audio Engineering Society*. New York: Audio Engineering Society.

OpenHub. 2019. "GNU LilyPond Music Typesetter." https://www.openhub.net/p/lilypond/analyses/latest/languages_summary.

Open Sound Control. 2021. *Open Sound Control 1.0 Specification.* https://opensoundcontrol.stanford.edu/.

Oppenheim, A., and R. Schafer. 1975. *Digital Signal Processing.* Englewood Cliffs, NJ: Prentice Hall.

Oppenheim, A., and A. Willsky. 1983. *Signals and Systems.* Englewood Cliffs, NJ: Prentice Hall.

Oracle. 2016. *Synthesizing Sound.* https://docs.oracle.com/javase/tutorial/sound/MIDI-synth.html.

Oram, D. 1972. *An Individual Note: Of Music, Sound and Electronics.* London: Galliard.

Ord-Hume, A. W. J. G. 1973. *Clockwork Music.* New York: Crown.

Ord-Hume, A. W. J. G. 1984. *Pianola: The History of the Self-playing Piano.* London: George Allen and Unwin.

Orio, N. 2006. "Music Retrieval: A Tutorial and Review." *Foundations and Trends in Information Retrieval* 1(1):1–90. dx.doi.org/10.1561/1500000002.

Orlarey, Y., D. Fober, and S. Letz. 2009. "Faust: An efficient functional approach to DSP programming." In *New Computational Paradigms for Music*, edited by G. Assayag and A. Gerszo. Paris: Delatour, 65–97.

Orlarey, Y., S. Letz, and D. Fober. 2010. "Automatic parallelization of audio applications with Faust." In *Proceedings of the 10ème Congrès Français d'Acoustique.* http://hal.archives-ouvertes.fr/hal-00537188/document.

Orton, R., A. Hunt, and R. Kirk. 1991. "Graphical control of granular synthesis using cellular automata and the Freehand program." In *Proceedings of the 1991 International Computer Music Conference*, edited by B. Alphonce and B. Pennycook. San Francisco: International Computer Music Association, 416–418.

Oswald, J. 2001. *69plunderphonics69* (audio compact discs). Seeland Records 515.

Otis, A., G. Grossman, and J. Cuomo. 1968. *Four Sound-Processing Programs for the Illiac II Computer and D/A Converter.* Experimental Music Studios Technical Report Number 14. Urbana: University of Illinois.

Overholt, D. 2005. "The Overtone Violin." In *Proceedings of the 2005 International Computer Music Conference.* San Francisco: International Computer Music Association.

Ozerov, A., A. Liutkus, and G. Richard. 2014. "A tutorial on informed source separation." In *Proceedings of the IEEE International Conference on Acoustics, Speech, and Signal Processing (ICASSP).* New York: IEEE.

Ozzola, V., G. Melzi, and A. Corghi. 1984. "Experiments in stochastic approximation of musical language." In *Musical Grammars and Computer Analysis*, edited by M. Baroni and L. Callegari. Florence: Leo Olschki Editore, 325–327.

Pachet, F. 2003. "The Continuator: musical interaction with style." *Journal of New Music Research* 32(3): 333–341.

Paiva, R., T. Mendes, and A. Cardoso. 2006. "Melody detection in polyphonic musical signals exploiting perceptual rules, note salience and melodic smoothness." *Computer Music Journal* 30(4): 80–98.

Paiva, R., J. Pakarinen, and V. Välimäki. 2012. "Acoustics and modeling of pickups." *Journal of the Audio Engineering Society* 60(10): 768–782.

Paladin, A., and D. Rocchesso. 1992. "Towards a generalized model of one-dimensional musical instruments." In *Proceedings of the International Workshop on Models and Representations of Musical Signals*, edited by A. Piccialli. Naples: Università di Napoli Federico II.

Palmieri, G., and S. Sapir. 1992. "MARS: Musical applications." In *Proceedings of the 1992 International Computer Music Conference.* San Francisco: International Computer Music Association, 352–353.

Pampin, J. 2004. "ATS: A system for sound analysis transformation and synthesis based on a sinusoidal plus critical-band noise model and psychoacoustics." In *Proceedings of the 2004 International Computer Music Conference.* San Francisco: International Computer Music Association.

Pampin, J., O. Di Liscio, W. Moss, and A. Norman. 2004. "ATS user interfaces." In *Proceedings of the 2004 International Computer Music Conference.* San Francisco: International Computer Music Association.

Pape, G. 1992. "Some musical possibilities of the new UPIC system." Massy, France: Les Ateliers UPIC.

Pape, G. 2020. "Composing with sound at Les Ateliers UPIC." In *From Xenakis's UPIC to Graphic Notation Today,* edited by P. Weibel, S. Kanach, and L. Brümmer. Karlsruhe, Germany: ZKM, 187–197. https://zkm.de/de/from-xenakiss-upic-to-graphic-notation-today.

Paradiso, J. 1997. "Electronic music: new ways to play." *IEEE Spectrum* 34(12): 18–30.

Paradiso, J., C. Schmandt, K. Vega, C. Kao, R. Kleinberger, X. Liu, J. Qi, A. Roseway, A. Yetisen, J. Steimle, and M. Weigel. 2016. "UnderWare: Aesthetic, expressive, and functional on-Skin technologies." https://www.media.mit.edu/people/joep/publications.

Pardo, B., Z. Rafil, and Z. Duan. 2018. "Audio source separation in a musical context." In *Handbook of Systematic Musicology,* edited by R. Bader. Cham, Switzerland: Springer, 285–298.

Pareyon, G. 2011. *On Musical Self-Similarity.* Helsinki: Acta Semiotica Fennica XXXIX.

Parker, J. 2011. "A simple digital model of the diode-based ring modulator." In *Proceedings of the 14th International Conference on Digital Audio Effects (DAFx-11), Paris, France.* n.p.: DAFx. https://www.dafx.de.

Parker, J., and S. Bilbao. 2009. "Spring reverberation: a physical perspective." In *Proceedings of the 12th International Conference on Digital Audio Effects (DAFx-09).* n.p.: DAFx. https://www.dafx.de.

Parker, J., and S. D'Angelo. 2013. "A digital model of the Buchla lowpass gate." In *Proceedings of the 16th Digital Audio Effects Conference.* n.p.: DAFx. https://www.dafx.de.

Parmenter, J. 2011. "The Unit Generator." In *The SuperCollider Book,* edited by S. Wilson, D. Cottle, and N. Collins. Cambridge, MA: MIT Press, 55–80.

Pati, Y., R. Rezaiifar, and P. Krishnaprasad. 1993. "Orthogonal matching pursuit: Recursive function approximation with applications to wavelet decomposition." In *Proceedings of the Asilomar Conference on Signals, Systems, and Computers.* New York: IEEE, 40–44.

Pearce, M., D. Meredith, and G. Wiggins. 2002. "Motivations and methodologies for automation of the compositional process." *Musicae Scientiae* 6(2): 119–147.

Peavey. 2016. *ReValver 4 User Guide.* Meridian, MS: Peavey Electronics Corporation.

Peel, T., V. Emiya, L. Ralaivola, and S. Anthoine. 2012. "Matching pursuit with stochastic selection." In *Proceedings of the European Signal Processing Conference.* n.p.: European Association for Signal Processing, 1–5.

Peeters, G. 2004. "A large set of audio features for sound description (similarity and classification) in the CIUDADO project." http://recherche.ircam.fr/anasyn/peeters /ARTICLES/Peeters_2003_cuidadoaudiofeatures.pdf.

Penfold, R. 1991. *Advanced MIDI User's Guide.* Tonbridge, UK: PC Publishing.

Peters, N., T. Lossius, and J. Schacher. 2013. "The Spatial Sound Description Format: Principles, specifications, and examples." *Computer Music Journal* 37(1): 11–22.

Petersen, T. L. 1975. "Vocal tract modulation of instrumental sounds by digital filtering." In *Proceedings of the Second Annual Music Computation Conference*, edited by J. Beauchamp and J. Melby. Part 1. Urbana: University of Illinois, 33–41.

Petersen, T. L. 1980. *Acoustic Signal Processing in the Context of a Perceptual Model.* Technical Report UTEC-CSc-80–113. Salt Lake City: University of Utah, Department of Computer Science.

Peterson, G., and H. Barney. 1952. "Control methods used in a study of the vowels." *Journal of the Acoustical Society of America* 24: 175–184.

Petersen, T. L., and S. Boll. 1983. "Critical band analysis-synthesis." *IEEE Proceedings on Acoustics, Speech, and Signal Processing* ASSP-31(3): 656–663.

Peterson, G., W. Wang, and E. Sivertsen. 1958. "Segmentation techniques in speech synthesis." *Journal of the Acoustical Society of America* 30: 739–742.

Pfeifle, F. 2017. "Real-time physical model of a Wurlitzer and Rhodes electric piano." In *Proceedings of the 20th International Conference on Digital Audio Effects (DAFx-17),* 17–24. n.p.: DAFx. https://www.dafx.de.

Pharo. 2020. https://pharo.org.

Piaget, J., and B. Inhelder. 1967. *The Child's Conception of Space.* New York: W. W. Norton.

Piccialli, A., S. Cavaliere, I. Ortosecco, and P. Basile. 1992. "Modifications of natural sounds using a pitch synchronous technique." In *Proceedings of the International Workshop on Models and Representations of Musical Signals*, edited by A. Piccialli. Napoli: Università di Napoli Federico II.

Pielemeier, W., G. Wakefield, and M. Simoni. 1996. "Time-frequency analysis of musical signals." *Proceedings of the IEEE* 84(9): 1216–1230.

Pierce, A. 1994. *Acoustics: An Introduction to its Physical Principles and Applications.* Woodbury, NY: Acoustical Society of America.

Pietruszweski, M. 2019. "Digital instrument as an artifact." In *From Xenakis's UPIC to Graphic Notation Today*, edited by P. Weibel, S. Kanach, and L. Brümmer.

Karlsruhe, Germany: ZKM. https://zkm.de/de/from-xenakiss-upic-to-graphic-notation -today, 9–21.

Pinch, T., and F. Trocco. 2002. *Analog Days*. Cambridge, MA: Harvard University Press.

Pirkle, W. 2015. *Designing Software Synthesizer Plugins in C++*. Burlington, MA: Focal Press.

Pirkle, W. 2019. *Designing Audio Effect Plugins in C++*. 2nd ed. Burlington, MA: Focal Press.

Piszczalski, M., and B. Galler. 1977. "Automatic music transcription." *Computer Music Journal* 1(4): 24–31.

Piszczalski, M., B. Galler, R. Bossemeyer, and F. Looft. 1981. "Performed music: analysis, synthesis, and display by computer." *Journal of the Audio Engineering Society* 21(1/2): 38–46.

Placencia, J., J. Murphy, and D. Carnegie. 2019. "Survey of hardware and software design approaches for mechatronic chordophones." *Computer Music Journal* 43(1): 38–58.

Plomp, R. 1976. *Aspects of Tone Sensation*. London: Academic Press.

Plumbley, M., T. Blumensath, L. Daudet, R. Gribonval, and M. Davies. 2009. "Sparse representations in audio and music: from coding to source separation." *Proceedings of the IEEE* 98(6): 995–1005.

Podrazik, J. 2020. "OMN the language." https://opusmodus.com/forums/tutorials/.

Poepel, C., and R. Dannenberg. 2005. "Audio signal driven sound synthesis." In *Proceedings of the International Computer Music Conference*. San Francisco: International Computer Music Association, 391–394.

Pohlmann, K. 1989a. *The Compact Disc: A Handbook of Theory and Use*. Middleton, WI: A-R Editions.

Pohlmann, K. 1989b. *Principles of Digital Audio*. Indianapolis: Howard Sams.

Pohlmann, K. 2010. *Principles of Digital Audio*. 6th ed. New York: McGraw-Hill.

Polansky, L., and T. Erbe. 1996. "Spectral mutation in SoundHack." *Computer Music Journal* 20(1): 92–101.

Pollock, I., and J. Pickett. 1957. "Cocktail party effect." *Journal of the Acoustical Society of America* 29: 1262.

Polotti, P. 2003. "Fractal additive synthesis: Spectral modeling of sound for low rate coding of high quality audio." Lausanne, Switzerland: École Polytechnique Fédérale de Lausanne.

Polotti, P., and G. Evangelista. 2001. "Fractal additive synthesis via harmonic-band wavelets." *Computer Music Journal* 25(3): 22–37.

Polotti, P., and D. Rocchesso, eds. 2008. *Sound to Sense—Sense to Sound: A State of the Art in Sound and Music Computing.* Berlin: Logos Verlag.

Pompei, F. J. 1999. "The use of airborne ultrasonics for generating audible sound beams." *Journal of the Audio Engineering Society* 47(9): 726–731.

Pons, J. 2018. "Neural networks for music: a journey through its history." https://towardsdatascience.com/neural-networks-for-music-a-journey-through-its-history-91f93c3459fb.

Pons, J., O. Nieto, M. Prockup, E. Schmidt, A. Ehmann, and X. Serra. 2018. "End-to-end learning for music audio tagging at scale." In *Proceedings of the International Society for Music Information Retrieval.* n.p.: International Society for Music Information Retrieval. https://ismir.net.

Portnoff, M. 1976. "Implementation of the digital phase vocoder using the fast Fourier transform." *IEEE Transactions on Acoustics, Speech and Signal Processing* 24(3): 243–248.

Portnoff, M. 1978. "Time-scale modification of speech based on short-time Fourier analysis." ScD diss. Cambridge, MA: Department of Electrical Engineering and Computer Science, MIT.

Portnoff, M. 1980. "Time-frequency representation of digital signals and systems based on short-time Fourier analysis." *IEEE Transactions on Acoustics, Speech, and Signal Processing* ASSP-28: 55–69.

Potard, Y., P. F. Baisnée, and J.-B. Barrière. 1986. "Experimenting with models of resonance produced by a new technique for the analysis of impulsive sounds." In *Proceedings of the 1986 International Computer Music Conference,* edited by P. Berg. San Francisco: International Computer Music Association, 269–274.

Potard, Y., P. F. Baisnée, and J.-B. Barrière. 1991. "Méthodologie de synthèse du timbre: l'exemple des modèles de résonance." In *Le timbre, métaphore pour la composition,* edited by J.-B. Barrière. Paris: IRCAM and Cristian Bourgeois, 135–163.

Potter, C., and D. Teaney. 1980. "Sonic transliteration applied to descriptive music notation." In *Proceedings of the 1980 International Computer Music Conference,* edited by H. S. Howe, Jr. San Francisco: International Computer Music Association, 138–144.

Potter, R. 1946. Article on visible speech. *Bell Laboratories Record* 24(1): 7.

Pottier, L., ed. 2009. *Le Calcul de la Musique: Composition, Modèles, et Outils.* Saint-Étienne, France: Publications de l'Université de Saint-Étienne.

Poynting, J., and J. Thomson. 1900. *Sound.* 2nd ed. London: Charles Griffin.

Präzlich, Z., R. Bittner, A. Liutkus, and M. Müller. 2015. "Kernal additive model for interference reduction in multi-channel music recordings." In *Proceedings of the IEEE International Conferemnce on Audio, Speech, and Signal Processing.* New York: IEEE, 584–588.

Preis, D. 1982. "Phase distortion and phase equalization in audio signal processing—A tutorial review." *Journal of the Audio Engineering Society* 30(11): 774–794.

Preis, D., and P. Bloom. 1983. "Perception of phase distortion in anti-alias filters." Preprint 2008 (H-3). In *Proceedings of the 74th Convention of the Audio Engineering Society, October 8–12*. New York: Audio Engineering Society.

Preis, D., and V. Georgopoulos. 1999. "Wigner distribution representation and analysis of audio signals: an illustrated tutorial review." *Journal of the Audio Engineering Society* 47(12): 1043–1053.

Preis, D., F. Hlawatsch, P. Bloom, and J. Deer. 1987. "Wigner distribution analysis of filters with perceptible phase distortion." *Journal of the Audio Engineering Society* 35(12): 1004–1012.

Prerau, D. 1970. "Computer pattern recognition of standard engraved music notation." PhD diss. Department of Electrical Engineering, MIT.

Prerau, D. 1971. "Computer pattern recognition of printed music." In *Proceedings of the Fall Joint Computer Conference*. Montvale, NJ: AFIPS Press.

Press, W., B. Flannery, S. Teukolsky, and W. Vetterling. 1988. *Numerical Recipes in C*. Cambridge: Cambridge University Press.

Prieberg, F. 1975. *Musica ex machina*. Italian edition. Turin, Italy: Giulio Einaudi Editore.

Prony, G. R. B. de, 1795. "Essai expérimentale et analytique." *Paris Journal de l'Ecole Polytechnique* 1(2): 24–76.

Průša, Z., and N. Holighaus. 2017. "Phase vocoder done right." In *Proceedings of the 25th European Signal Processing Conference*. n.p.: European Association for Signal Processing. http://www.eurasip.org/Proceedings/Eusipco/Eusipco2017/papers/1570343436.pdf.

Pruslin, D. 1966. "Automatic recognition of sheet music." ScD diss. Department of Electrical Engineering, MIT.

Puckette, M. 1985. "A real-time music performance system." Cambridge, MA: MIT Experimental Music Studio.

Puckette, M. 1988. "The Patcher." In *Proceedings of the 1988 International Computer Music Conference*, edited by C. Lischka and J. Fritsch. San Francisco: International Computer Music Association, and Cologne: Feedback Papers, 420–429.

Puckette, M. 1991. "Combining event and signal processing in the MAX graphical programming environment." *Computer Music Journal* 15(3): 68–77.

Puckette, M. 1995. "Formant-based audio synthesis using nonlinear distortion." *Journal of the Audio Engineering Society* 43(1/2): 40–47.

Puckette, M. 1996. "Pure Data." In *Proceedings of the International Computer Music Conference*. San Francisco: International Computer Music Association, 269–272.

Puckette, M. 1997. "Pure Data: recent progress." *Proceedings of the Third Intercollege Computer Music Festival, Tokyo*, 1–4.

Puckette, M. 2002. "Max at seventeen." *Computer Music Journal* 26(4): 31–43.

Puckette, M. 2007. *The Theory and Techniques of Electronic Music.* Singapore: World Scientific.

Puckette, M. 2011. "Infuriating nonlinear reverberator." In *Proceedings of the 2011 International Computer Music Conference.* San Francisco: International Computer Music Association.

Puckette, M. 2017. *Pure Data documentation.* http://puredata.info/docs/manuals/pd.

Puckette, M. 2020. *QuackTrip documentation.* msp.ucsd.edu/tools/quacktrip/.

Puckette, M., T. Apel, and D. Zicarelli. 1998. "Real-time audio analysis tools for Pd and MSP." *Proceedings of the 1998 International Computer Music Conference.* San Francisco: International Computer Music Association.

Puckette, M., and C. Lippe. 1992. "Score following in practice." In *Proceedings of the 1992* International *Computer Music Conference*, edited by A. Strange. San Francisco: International Computer Music Association, 182–185.

Puckette, M., and D. Zicarelli. 1990. *MAX–An Interactive Graphical Programming Environment.* Menlo Park, CA: Opcode Systems.

Pulfer, J. K. 1971. "Man-machine interaction in creative applications." *International Journal of Man-Machine Studies* 3: 1–11.

Pulkki, V. 1997. "Virtual sound source positioning using vector base amplitude panning." *Journal of the Audio Engineering Society* 45(6): 456–466.

Pulkki, V., T. Lokki, and D. Rocchesso. 2011. "Spatial effects." In *DAFX: Digital Audio Effects*, edited by U. Zölzer. 2nd ed. Chichester, UK: John Wiley & Sons, 139–183.

Putnam, L. 2015. "Echo shaping using sums of damped complex sinusoids." *Computer Music Journal* 39(2): 67–76.

Quatieri, T., and R. McAulay. 1986. "Speech transformations based on a sinusoidal model." *IEEE Transactions on Acoustics, Speech, and Signal Processing* ASSP-34: 1449–1464.

Quian, S., and D. Chen "Discrete Gabor transform." *IEEE Transactions on Signal Processing* 41(7): 2429–2438.

Rabenstein, R., T. Koch, and C. Popp. 2010. "Tubular bells: a physical and algorithmic model." *IEEE Transactions on Audio, Speech, and Signal Processing* 18(4): 881.

Rabenstein, R., and S. Petrausch. 2008. "Block-based physical modeling with applications in musical acoustics." *International Journal of Applied Mathematics and Computer Science* 18(3): 295–305.

Rabenstein, R., S. Petrausch, A. Sarti, G. DeSanctius, C. Erkhut, and M. Karjalainen. 2007. "Blocked-based physical modeling for digital sound synthesis." *Signal Processing Magazine* 24(2): 42–54.

Rabiner, L. 1977. "On the use of autocorrelation analysis for pitch detection." *IEEE Transactions on Acoustics, Speech, and Signal Processing* ASSP-25(1).

Rabiner, L. 1983. "Digital techniques for changing the sampling rate of a signal." In *Digital Audio*, edited by B. Blesser, B. Locanthi, and T. Stockham. New York: Audio Engineering Society, 79–89.

Rabiner, L., M. Cheng, A. Rosenberg, and M. McGonegal. 1976. "A comparitive performance study of several pitch detection algorithms." *IEEE Transactions on Acoustics, Speech, and Signal Processing* ASSP-24(5).

Rabiner, L., J. Cooley, H. Helms, L. Jackson, J. Kaiser, C. Rader, R. Schafer, K. Steiglitz, and C. Weinstein. 1972. "Terminology in digital signal processing." *IEEE Transactions on Audio and Acoustics* AU-20: 322–337.

Rabiner, L., and B. Gold. 1975. *Theory and Applications of Digital Signal Processing*. Englewood Cliffs, NJ: Prentice Hall.

Rabiner, L., and R. Schafer. 2011. *Theory and Applications of Digital Speech Processing*. Englewood Cliffs, NJ: Prentice Hall.

Raczinski, J.-M., and G. Marino. 1988. "A real time synthesis unit." In *Proceedings of the 1988 International Computer Music Conference*, edited by C. Lischka and J. Fritsch. San Francisco: International Computer Music Association, 90–100.

Raczinski, J.-M., G. Marino, and M.-H. Serra. 1991. "New UPIC system demonstration." In *Proceedings of the 1991 International Computer Music Conference*, edited by B. Alphonce and B. Pennycook. San Francisco: International Computer Music Association, 567–570.

Raes, G. 2012. "Autosax." https://logosfoundation.org.

Raffel, C., and J. O. Smith. 2010. "Practical modeling of bucket brigade device circuits." In *Proceedings of the 13th International Conference on Digital Audio Effects (DAFx-10)*. n.p.: DAFx, 50–56. https://www.dafx.de.

Raffensperger, P. 2012. "Toward a wave guide digital filter model of the Fairchild 670 limiter." In *Proceedings of the 15th Conference on Digital Audio Effects*. n.p.: DAFx, 50–56. https://www.dafx.de.

Rahn, J. 1990. "The Lisp kernel: A portable software environment for composition." *Computer Music Journal* 14(4): 42–58.

Ramakrishnan, C. 2009. "Zirkonium: non-invasive software for sound spatialisation." *Organized Sound* 14(3): 268–276.

Rao, K., and P. Yip. 1990. *Discrete Cosine Transform: Algorithms, Advantages, Applications*. Boston: Academic Press.

Raphael, C. 2008. "A classifier-based approach to score-guided source separation of musical audio." *Computer Music Journal* 32(1): 51–59.

Raphael, C. 2009. "Current directions with musical minus one." In *Proceedings of the 2009 Conference on Sound and Music Computing.* n.p.: Sound and Music Computing Network, 71–76. http://smc.afim-asso.org.

Rauhala, J., M. Laurson, V. Välimäki, H. Lehtonen, and V. Norilo. 2008. "A parametric piano synthesizer." *Computer Music Journal* 32(4): 17–30.

Ravelli, E., G. Richard, and L. Daudet. 2008. "Union of MDCT bases for audio coding." *IEEE Transactions on Audio, Speech and Language Processing* 16(8): 1361–1372.

Ravelli, E., G. Richard, and L. Daudet. 2010. "Audio signal representations for indexing in the transform domain." *IEEE Transactions on Audio, Speech and Language Processing* 18(3): 434–446.

Rayleigh, J. (1894) 1945. *The Theory of Sound.* Reprint. New York: Dover.

Read, G. 1969. *Music Notation.* New York: Crescendo.

Read, O., and W. Welch. 1976. *From Tin Foil to Stereo: Evolution of the Phonograph.* Indianapolis: Howard Sams.

Reeves, A. 1938. "Electric signal system." British Patent 535,860. U.S. Patent 2,272,070 (1942).

Reeves, W. 1983. "Particle systems—A technique for modeling a class of fuzzy objects." *ACM Transactions on Graphics* 2(2): 359–376.

Reeves, W., et al. 1979. "Ludwig: An example of interactive computer graphics in a score editor." In *Proceedings of the 1978 International Computer Music Conference,* edited by C. Roads. Evanston, IL: Northwestern University Press.

Reich, S. 1974. *Writings About Music.* Halifax and New York: Nova Scotia College of Art and Design Press and New York University Press.

Reiss, J. 2008. "Understanding sigma-delta modulation: The solved and unsolved issues." *Journal of the Audio Engineering Society* 56(1/2): 49–64.

Reiss, J., and Ø. Brandtsegg. 2018. "Applications of cross-adaptive audio effects: Automatic mixing, live performance and everything in between." *Frontiers in the Digital Humanities* 5(17).

Reveillon, F. 1994. Personal communication.

Rhea, T. 1972. "The evolution of electronic musical instruments in the United States." PhD dissertation. George Peabody College for Teachers.

Rhea, T. 1977. "Electronic Perspectives: Photoelectric acoustic-sound instruments." *Contemporary Keyboard* October: 62.

Rhea, T. 1984. "The history of electronic musical instruments." In *The Art of Electronic Music*, edited by T. Darter. New York: Quill, 1–63.

Rhys, P. 2016. "Smart interfaces for granular synthesis by fractal organization." *Computer Music Journal* 40(3): 58–67.

Rich, R. 1988. "Blank Software Alchemy sample editing software." *Music Technology* May. http://www.muzines.co.uk/articles/blank-software-alchemy/2264.

Risatti, H. 1975. *New Music Vocabulary.* Urbana: University of Illinois Press.

Risberg, J. 1982. "Non-linear estimation of FM synthesis parameters." Unpublished manuscript.

Risset, J.-C. 1966. "Computer study of trumpet tones." Murray Hill, NJ: Bell Telephone Laboratories.

Risset, J.-C. 1969. "Catalog of computer-synthesized sound." Murray Hill, NJ: Bell Telephone Laboratories. Reprinted in *The historical CD of digital sound synthesis*, produced by J. Goebel, 1995. Computer Music Currents 13. Mainz, Germany: Wergo 2033. (Compact disc + 260-page booklet.)

Risset, J.-C. 1985a. "Computer music experiments: 1964—." *Computer Music Journal* 9(1): 11–18. Reprinted in *The Music Machine*, edited by C. Roads, 1989. Cambridge, MA: MIT Press, 67–74.

Risset, J.-C. 1985b. "Digital techniques and sound structure in music." In *Composers and the Computer*, edited by C. Roads. Middleton, WI: A-R Editions, 113–138.

Risset, J.-C. 1991. "Timbre analysis by synthesis: representations, imitations, and variants for musical composition." In *Representations of Musical Signals*, edited by G. De Poli, A. Piccialli, and C. Roads. Cambridge, MA: MIT Press, 7–43.

Risset, J.-C. 2000. "Time and digital music." In *International Academy of Electroacoustic Music 2000*, edited by F. Barrière and C. Clozier. Bourges, France: Institut de Musique Electroacoustique de Bourges.

Risset, J.-C., and M. Mathews. 1969. "Analysis of musical instrument tones." *Physics Today* 22(2): 23–40.

Risset, J.-C., and D. Wessel. 1982. "Exploration of timbre by analysis and synthesis." In *Psychology of Music*, edited by D. Deutsch. Orlando: Academic Press.

Ristow, J. 1993. "Audiotechnology in Berlin to 1943: Optical sound." Preprint 3487 (H2–8). In *Proceedings of the 94th Audio Engineering Society Convention, 1993 March, Berlin*. New York: Audio Engineering Society.

Ritter, M., and A. Aska. 2014. "Leap Motion as expressive interface." In *Proceedings of the 2014 International Computer Music Conference.* San Francisco: International Computer Music Association, 659–662.

Roads, C. 1973. "Analysis of the composition *ST/10* and the computer program Free Stochastic Music by Iannis Xenakis." Unpublished manuscript.

Roads, C. 1978a. "An interview with Gottfried Michael Koenig." *Computer Music Journal* 2(3): 11–15. Reprinted in *Foundations of Computer Music*, edited by C. Roads and J. Strawn, 1985. Cambridge, MA: MIT Press, 568–580.

Roads, C. 1978b. "Automated granular synthesis of sound." *Computer Music Journal* 2(2): 61–62. Revised version published as "Granular synthesis of sound" in *Foundations of Computer Music*, edited by C. Roads and J. Strawn, 1985. Cambridge, MA: MIT Press, 145–159.

Roads, C. 1978c. *Composing Grammars.* San Francisco: International Computer Music Association.

Roads, C. 1979. "A tutorial on non-linear distortion or waveshaping." *Computer Music Journal* 3(2): 29–34. Revised version in *Foundations of Computer Music*, edited by C. Roads and J. Strawn, 1985. Cambridge, MA: MIT Press.

Roads, C. 1980. "Interview with Max Mathews." *Computer Music Journal* 4(4): 15–22. Reprinted in *The Music Machine*, edited by C. Roads, 1989. Cambridge, MA: MIT Press, 5–12.

Roads, C. 1981a. "An intelligent composer's assistant." Unpublished manuscript.

Roads, C. 1981b. "A note on music printing by computer." *Computer Music Journal* 5(3): 57–59. Reprinted in *The Music Machine*, edited by C. Roads, 1989. Cambridge, MA: MIT Press, 239–242.

Roads, C. 1982. "A conversation with James A. Moorer." *Computer Music Journal* 6(4):10–21. Reprinted in *The Music Machine*, edited by C. Roads, 1989. Cambridge, MA: MIT Press, 13–24.

Roads, C. 1983. "Interactive orchestration based on score analysis." In *Proceedings of the 1982 International Computer Music Conference*, edited by J. Strawn and T. Blum. San Francisco: International Computer Music Association, 703–717.

Roads, C. 1984. "An overview of music representations." In *Musical Grammars and Computer Analysis*, edited by M. Baroni and L. Callegari. Florence: Leo Olschki Editore, 7–37.

Roads, C., ed. 1985a. *Composers and the Computer*. Middleton, WI: A-R Editions.

Roads, C. 1985b. "Grammars as representations for music." In *Foundations of Computer Music*, edited by C. Roads and J. Strawn, 1985. Cambridge, MA: MIT Press, 403–442.

Roads, C. 1985c. "Granular synthesis of sound." In *Foundations of Computer Music*, edited by C. Roads and J. Strawn, 1985. Cambridge, MA: MIT Press, 145–159.

Roads, C. 1985d. "Improvisation with George Lewis." In *Composers and the Computer*, edited by C. Roads. Middleton, WI: A-R Editions, 75–87.

Roads, C. 1985e. "Interview with James Dashow." In *Composers and the Computer*, edited by C. Roads. Middleton, WI: A-R Editions, 27–45.

Roads, C. 1985f. "John Chowning on composition." In *Composers and the Computer*, edited by C. Roads. Middleton, WI: A-R Editions, 17–26.

Roads, C. 1985g. "The realization of nscor." In *Composers and the Computer*, edited by C. Roads. Middleton, WI: A-R Editions, 140–168.

Roads, C. 1985h. "Research in music and artificial intelligence: a survey." *ACM Computing Surveys* 17(2): 163–190. Reprinted as "Richerche sulla musica e l'intelligenza artificiale" in *Nuova Atlantide*, edited by A. Vidolin and R. Doati, 1986. Venice: La Biennale di Venezia, 121–147. Reprinted in the Japanese computer journal *bit* (Tokyo), 1987.

Roads, C. 1986a. "The second STEIM symposium on interactive composition in live electronic music." *Computer Music Journal* 10(2): 44–50.

Roads, C. 1986b. "Symposium on composition." *Computer Music Journal* 10(1): 40–63.

Roads, C. 1986c. "The Tsukuba musical robot." *Computer Music Journal* 10(2): 39–43.

Roads, C. 1987. "Experiences with computer-assisted composition." Translated as "Esperienze di composizione assistata da calculatore" in *I Profili del Suono*, edited by S. Tamburini and M. Bagella. Rome: Musica Verticale and Galzeramo, 173–196.

Roads, C., ed. 1989. *The Music Machine*. Cambridge, MA: MIT Press.

Roads, C. 1991. "Asynchronous granular synthesis." In *Representations of Musical Signals*, edited by G. De Poli, A. Piccialli, and C. Roads. Cambridge, MA: MIT Press, 143–185.

Roads, C. 1992. "Musical applications of advanced signal representations." Presented at the International Workshop on Models and Representations of Musical Signals, Capri, Italy, October 1992.

Roads, C. 1993a. "Musical sound transformation by convolution." In *Proceedings of the 1993 International Computer Music Conference*, edited by S. Ohteru. San Francisco: International Computer Music Association, 102–109.

Roads, C. 1993b. "Organization of *Clang-tint*." In *Proceedings of the 1993 International Computer Music Conference*, edited by S. Ohteru. San Francisco: International Computer Music Association, 346–348.

Roads, C. 1996a. *The Computer Music Tutorial*. Cambridge, MA: The MIT Press.

Roads, C. 1996b. "Early electronic instruments: Time line 1899–1950." *Computer Music Journal* 20(3): 20–23.

Roads, C. 1997. "Sound transformation by convolution." In *Musical Signal Processing*, edited by C. Roads et al., 1997. London: Routledge, 411–438.

Roads, C. 1998. *L'audionumérique.* Translated by J. de Reydellet. Paris: Dunod.

Roads, C. 1999. "Time scales of musical structure." In *Actes V. Académie Internationale de Musique Électroacoustique*, edited by F. Barrière and G. Bennett. Bourges, France: Editions Mnemosyne.

Roads, C. 2001a. *Microsound.* Cambridge, MA: MIT Press.

Roads, C. 2001b. "Sound composition with pulsars." *Journal of the Audio Engineering Society* 49(3): 134–147.

Roads, C. 2004. *POINT LINE CLOUD.* Compact disc and digital video disc. San Francisco: Asphodel. Reissued 2019. Milan: Presto!?

Roads, C. 2005. "The art of articulation: The electroacoustic music of Horacio Vaggione." *Contemporary Music Review* 24(4/5): 295–309.

Roads, C. 2007. *L'audionumérique: Musique et informatique.* 2nd rev. ed. Translated by J. de Reydellet. Paris: Dunod.

Roads, C. 2012. "Grains, forms, and formalization." In *Xenakis Matters*, edited by S. Kanach. Hillsdale, NY: Pendragon, 385–410.

Roads, C. 2015. *Composing Electronic Music: A New Aesthetic.* New York: Oxford University Press.

Roads, C. 2016. *L'audionumérique: Musique et informatique.* 3rd rev. ed. Translated by J. de Reydellet. Paris: Dunod.

Roads, C., and J. Alexander. 1995. *CloudGenerator Manual.* Distributed with the app CloudGenerator. http://www.create.ucsb.edu.

Roads, C., S. Pope, A. Piccialli, and G. De Poli, eds. 1997. *Musical Signal Processing.* London: Routledge, 411–438.

Roads, C., J. Kilgore, and R. Duplessis. 2020. *EmissionControl2 Manual.* Distributed with the app EmissionControl 2. https://www.curtisroads.net.

Roads, C., and J. Strawn, eds. 1985. *Foundations of Computer Music.* Cambridge, MA: MIT Press.

Röbel, A. 2008. "Frequency-slope estimation and its application to parameter estimation for non-stationary sinusoidal models." *Computer Music Journal* 32(2): 68–79.

Roberts, A. 1966. "An ALL-FORTRAN music generating computer program." *Journal of the Audio Engineering Society* 14: 17–20.

Roberts, A. 1969. "Some new developments in computer-generated music." In *Music by Computers*, edited by H. Von Foerster and J. Beauchamp. New York: John Wiley & Sons, 63–68.

Roberts, C. 2016. "Code as information and code as spectacle." *International Journal of Performance Arts and Digital Media* 12(2): 201–206.

Roberts, C., and T. Höllerer, 2011. "Composition for conductor and audience: new uses for mobile devices in the concert hall." In *Proceedings of the User Interface*

Software and Technology Conference (UIST). New York: Association for Computing Machinery, 65–66.

Roberts, C., G. Wakefield, and M. Wright. 2015. "Designing musical instruments for the browser." *Computer Music Journal* 39(1): 27–40.

Robinson, E. 1982. "A historical perspective of spectrum estimation." *Proceedings of the Institute of Electrical and Electronics Engineers* 70(9): 885–907.

Robjohns, H. 2013. "Parallel compression: the real benefits." *Sound on Sound* 28(2). https://www.soundonsound.com/techniques/parallel-compression.

Robjohns, H. 2018. "Tascam ML32D A-D/D-A Converter." *Sound On Sound* 33(12): 34–36.

Rocchesso, D. 1997. "Maximally diffusive yet efficient feedback delay networks for artificial reverberation" *IEEE Signal Processing Letters* 4(9): 252–255.

Rocchesso, D. 2000. "Fractionally-addressed delay lines." *IEEE Transactions on Speech and Audio Processing* 8(6): 717–727.

Rocchesso, D., and J. O. Smith. 1997. "Circulant and elliptic feedback delay networks for artificial reverberation." *IEEE Transactions on Speech and Audio Processing* 5(1): 51–63.

Rocchesso, D., and J. Smith. 2003. "Generalized digital waveguide networks." *IEEE Transactions on Speech and Audio Processing* 11(3): 242–254.

Rodet, X. 1980. "Time-domain formant-wave-function synthesis." In *Spoken Language Generation and Understanding*, edited by J. G. Simon. Dordrecht, Netherlands: Reidel. Reprinted in *Computer Music Journal* 8(3): 9–14. 1984.

Rodet, X. 1986. Personal communication.

Rodet, X. 1992. "Nonlinear oscillator models of musical instrument excitation." In *Proceedings of the 1992 International Computer Music Conference*, edited by A. Strange. San Francisco: International Computer Music Association, 412–413.

Rodet, X., and G. Bennett. 1980. "Synthese de la voix chantee par ordinateur." In *Conferences des journees d'etudes 1980*. Paris: Festival International du Son, 73–91.

Rodet, X., and P. Cointe. 1984. "FORMES: composition and scheduling of processes." *Computer Music Journal* 8(3): 32–50. Reprinted in *The Music Machine*, edited by C. Roads, 1989. Cambridge, MA: MIT Press, 405–426.

Rodet, X., and J. Delatre. 1979. "Time-domain speech synthesis by rules using a flexible and fast signal management system." In *Proceedings of the IEEE International Conference on Acoustics, Speech, and Signal Processing, Washington, DC, 2–4 April.* New York: IEEE, 895–898.

Rodet, X., and P. Depalle. 1992. "A new additive synthesis method using inverse Fourier transform and spectral envelopes." In *Proceedings of the 1992 International*

Computer Music Conference, edited by A. Strange. San Francisco: International Computer Music Association, 410–411.

Rodet, X., P. Depalle, and G. Poirot. 1988. "Diphone sound synthesis based on spectral envelopes and harmonic/noise excitation functions." In *Proceedings of the 1988 International Computer Music Conference*, edited by C. Lischka and J. Fritsch. San Francisco: International Computer Music Association, 313–321.

Rodet, X., Y. Potard, and J.-B. Barrière. 1984. "The CHANT project: From synthesis of the singing voice to synthesis in general." *Computer Music Journal* 8(3): 15–31. Reprinted in *The Music Machine*, edited by C. Roads, 1989. Cambridge, MA: MIT Press, 449–466.

Rodet, X., and C. Santamarina. 1975. "Synthèse, sur un miniordinateur, du signal vocale dans la representation amplitude-temps." *Actes des sixiemes journees d'etude su la parole du GALF, Toulouse*. Paris: GALF, 364–371.

Rodgers, C. A. P. 1981. "Pinna transformations and sound reproduction." *Journal of the Audio Engineering Society* 29(4): 226–234.

Rodríguez-Algarra, F., B. Sturm, and H. Maruri-Aguilar. 2016. "Analysing scattering-based music content analysis systems: Where's the music?" In *Proceedings of ISMIR Conference*. n.p.: International Society for Music Information Retrieval. https://ismir.net.

Roeder, J., and K. Hamel. 1989. "A general-purpose object-oriented system for musical graphics." In *Proceedings of the 1989 International Computer Music Conference*, edited by T. Wells and D. Butler. San Francisco: International Computer Music Association, 260–263.

Rogers, G. 1987. "Console design and MIDI." *Studio Sound* 29(2): 42–44.

Rolnick, N. 1978. "A composer's notes on the development and implementation of software for a digital synthesizer." *Computer Music Journal* 2(2): 13–22. Reprinted in *Foundations of Computer Music*, edited by C. Roads and J. Strawn, 1985. Cambridge, MA: MIT Press, 467–490.

Romblom, D. 2004. Personal communication.

Rosao, C. 2012. "Onset detection in music signals." PhD diss. Dept. of Information Science and Technology, Instituto Universário de Lisboa.

Rosenthal, D. 1988. "A model of the process of listening to simple rhythms." In *Proceedings of the 1988 International Computer Music Conference*, edited by C. Lischka and J. Fritsch. San Francisco: International Computer Music Association, 189–197.

Rosenthal, D. 1992. "Emulation of human rhythm perception." *Computer Music Journal* 16(1): 64–76.

Rossing, T., and N. Fletcher. 1983. "Nonlinear vibrations in plates and gongs." *Journal of the Acoustical Society of America* 73(1): 345–351.

Rossum, D. 1992. "Making digital filters sound 'analog.'" In *Proceedings of the 1992 International Computer Music Conference*, edited by A. Strange. San Francisco: International Computer Music Association, 30–33.

Rothstein, J. 1992. *MIDI: A Comprehensive Introduction.* Middleton, WI: A-R Editions.

Rottondi, C., C. Chafe, C. Allochio, and A. Sarti. 2016. "An overview of networked music performance technologies." *IEEE Access* 4: 8823–8842.

Rowe, N. 1975. "Machine perception of musical rhythm." BS thesis. MIT Department of Electrical Engineering, MIT.

Rowe, R. 1992a. *Interactive Music Systems.* Cambridge, MA: MIT Press.

Rowe, R. 1992b. "Machine listening and composing with Cypher." *Computer Music Journal* 16(1): 43–63.

Rowe, R. 2001. *Machine Musicianship.* Cambridge, MA: MIT Press.

Rowe, R. 2005. "Real time and unreal time: Expression in distributed performance." *Journal of New Music Research* 34(1): 87–95.

Roy, S. 2003. *L'analyse des musiques élecroacoustiques.* Paris: L'Harmattan.

Rozenberg, M. 1979. "Microcomputer-controlled sound processing using Walsh functions." *Computer Music Journal* 3(1): 42–47.

Rubine, D., and P. McAvinney. 1990. "Programmable finger-tracking instrument controller." *Computer Music Journal* 14(1): 26–41.

Ruiz, P. 1970. "A technique for simulating the vibrations of strings with a digital computer." MM thesis. University of Illinois School of Music.

Rumelhart, D., and J. McClelland. 1986. *Parallel Distributed Processing.* 2 vols. Cambridge, MA: MIT Press.

Rumsey, F. 2001. *Spatial Audio.* Oxford: Focal Press.

Rumsey, F. 2009. "Searching, analyzing, and recommending audio content." *Journal of the Audio Engineering Society* 57(3): 166–169.

Rumsey, F. 2019. "Making audio networking easier." *Journal of the Audio Engineering Society* 67(3): 144–147.

Russ, M. 1993. "MIDI timing delays: Software and hardware thrus." *Sound on Sound* 8(3): 94–98.

Russolo, L. (1916) 1986. *The Art of Noises.* Translated by B. Brown. New York: Pendragon.

Ryan, J. 1991. "Some remarks on musical instrument design at STEIM." *Contemporary Music Review* 6(1): 3–17.

Ryynänen, M., and A. Klapuri. 2008. "Automatic transcription of melody, bass lines, and chords in polyphonic music." *Computer Music Journal* 32(3): 72–86.

Sabine, W. 1922. *Collected Papers on Acoustics.* Reprinted 1964. New York: Dover.

Samson, P. 1980. "A general-purpose synthesizer." *Journal of the Audio Engineering Society* 28(3): 106–113.

Samson, P. 1985. "Architectural issues in the design of the Systems Concepts Digital Synthesizer." In *Digital Audio Engineering: An Anthology*, edited by J. Strawn. Middleton, WI: A-R Editions, 61–94.

Sandel, L. 1989. "Graphical compiler for Music V." Padua: Centro di Sonologià Computazionale, Università di Padova.

Sandell, G., and W. Martens. 1992. "Prototyping and interpolation of multiple musical timbres using principle components-based analysis." In *Proceedings of the 1992 International Computer Music Conference*, edited by A. Strange. San Francisco: International Computer Music Association, 34–37.

Sandred, O. 2010. "PWMC, a constraint-solving system for generating musical scores." *Computer Music Journal* 34(2): 8–24.

Sandred, O. 2017. *The Musical Fundamentals of Computer Assisted Composition.* Winnipeg: Audiospective Media.

Sandresky, M. 1981. "The golden section in three Byzantine motets of Dufay." *Journal of Music Theory* 25(2).

Sancristoforo, G. 2020. *Substantia User Manual.* https://www.giorgiosancristoforo.net.

Santacruz, J., L. Tardon, I. Barbancho, and A. Barbancho. 2016. "Spectral envelope transformation in singing voice for advanced pitch shifting." *Applied Sciences* 6: 368.

Sapir, S. 2002. "Gestural control of digital audio environments." *Journal of New Music Research* 31(2): 119–129.

Savioja, L., and U. Svensson. 2015. "Overview of geometrical room modeling techniques." *Journal of the Acoustical Society of America* 138: 708–730.

Savioja, L., V. Välimäki, and J. Smith. 2011. "Audio signal processing using graphics processing units." *Journal of the Audio Engineering Society* 59(1/2): 3–19.

Sauer, T. 2009. *Notations 21.* New York: Mark Batty.

Sayood, K. 2000. *Introduction to Data Compression.* Burlington, MA: Morgan Kaufmann.

Scaletti, C. 1989a. "Composing sound objects in KYMA." *Perspectives of New Music* 27(1): 42–69.

Scaletti, C. 1989b. "The Kyma/Platypus computer music workstation." *Computer Music Journal* 13(2): 23–38. Updated version in *The Well Tempered Object*, edited by S. Pope, 1991. Cambridge, MA: MIT Press, 119–140.

Scaletti, C. 2002. "Computer music languages, Kyma, and the future." *Computer Music Journal* 26(4): 69–82.

Scaletti, C. 2015. "Looking back, looking forward: a keynote address for the 2015 International Computer Music Conference." *Computer Music Journal* 40(1): 10–24.

Scandalis, P., J. Smith, and N. Porcaro. 2015. "Physically modeled musical instruments on mobile devices." http://www.moforte.com/wp-content/uploads/2015/05/CCRMA-presentation-better1.pdf.

Scavone, G. 2018. "Delay-lines and digital waveguides." In *Handbook of Systematic Musicology*, edited by R. Bader. Cham, Switzerland: Springer, 259–272.

Schaefer, R. 1970. "Electronic tone production by nonlinear waveshaping." *Journal of the Audio Engineering Society* 18(4): 413–417.

Schaeffer, J., N. Burch, Y. Björnsson, A. Kishimoto, M. Müller, R. Lake, P. Lu, and S. Sutphen. 2007. "Checkers is solved." *Science* 317(5844): 1518–1522.

Schaeffer, P. 1977. *Traité des Objets Musicaux.* 2nd ed. Paris: Editions du Seuil.

Schaeffer, P. 2017. *Treatise on Musical Objects.* Translated by Christine North and John Dack. Berkeley: University of California Press.

Schaeffer, P., and A. Moles. 1952. *À la Recherche d'une Musique Concrète.* Paris: Editions du Seuil.

Schaeffer, P., G. Reibel, and B. Ferreyra. 1967. *Trois microsillons d'exemples sonores de G. Reibel et Beatriz Ferreyra illustrant le Traité des Objets Sonores et présentés par l'auteur.* Paris: Éditions du Seuil. Re-released on compact disc in 1998 as *Solfège de l'objet sonore.* With translation in English and Spanish. Paris: INA-GRM.

Schafer, R., and L. Rabiner. 1970. "System for automatic formant analysis of voiced speech." *Journal of the Acoustical Society of America* 47(2): 634.

Schafer, R., and L. Rabiner. 1973a. "Design and simulation of a speech analysis-synthesis system based on short-time Fourier analysis." *IEEE Transactions on Audio and Electroacoustics* AU-21: 165–174.

Schafer, R., and L. Rabiner 1973b. "A digital signal processing approach to interpolation." *Proceedings of the IEEE* 61(6): 692–702.

Scharf, B. 1961. "Complex sounds and critical bands." *Psychological Bulletin* 58: 205–217.

Scharf, B. 1970. "Critical bands." In *Foundations of Modern Auditory Theory*, edited by J. Tobias. Orlando: Academic Press.

Scheirer, D. 2000. "Music-listening systems." PhD diss. Media Arts and Sciences, MIT.

Scherpenisse, J. 1977. "Digital control in electronic music studios." *Interface* 6: 73–80.

Schillinger, J. 1946. *The Schillinger System of Musical Composition.* New York: Carl Fischer. Reprinted 1978. New York: Da Capo Press.

Schissler, C., and D. Manocha. 2011. "Gsound: interactive sound propagation for games." *Proceedings of the AES 41st Conference: Audio for Games.* New York: Audio Engineering Society.

Schloss, W. 1985. *On the Automatic Transcription of Percussive Music—From Acoustic Signal to High-Level Analysis.* Report STAN-M-27. Stanford, CA: Stanford University Department of Music.

Schmeder, A., and A. Freed. 2008. "Implementation and applications of Open Sound Control timestamps." In *Proceedings of the International Computer Music Conference.* San Francisco: International Computer Music Association, 655–658.

Schmeder, A., A. Freed, and D. Wessel. 2010. "Best practices for Open Sound Control." In *Proceedings of the Linux Audio Conference, Utrecht, The Netherlands, 2010.* https://linuxaudio.org/lac.html.

Scholes, P. 1975. *The Oxford Companion to Music.* London: Oxford University Press.

Schörkhuber, C., and A. Klapuri. 2010. "Constant-Q transform toolbox for music processing." *Proceedings of the 2010 Sound and Music Computing Conference.* n.p.: Sound and Music Computing Network. https://smcnetwork.org.

Schottstaedt, W. 1977. "The simulation of natural instrument tones using frequency modulation with a complex modulation wave." *Computer Music Journal* 1(4): 46–50. Reprinted in *Foundations of Computer Music*, edited by C. Roads and J. Strawn, 1985. Cambridge, MA: MIT Press, 54–64.

Schottstaedt, W. 1983. "Pla—a composer's idea of a language." *Computer Music Journal* 7(1): 11–20. Reprinted in *The Music Machine*, edited by C. Roads, 1989. Cambridge, MA: MIT Press, 285–294.

Schottstaedt, W. 1989a. "Automatic counterpoint." In *Current Directions in Computer Music Research*, edited by M. Mathews and J. R. Pierce, 1989. Cambridge, MA: MIT Press, 225–262.

Schottstaedt, W. 1989b. "A computer music language." In *Current Directions in Computer Music Research*, edited by M. Mathews and J. R. Pierce, 1989. Cambridge, MA: MIT Press, 215–224.

Schottstaedt, W. 1991. "Common Lisp Music." Stanford, CA: Center for Computer Research in Music and Acoustics, Stanford University.

Schottstaedt, W. 2009. "An introduction to FM." https://ccrma.stanford.edu/software/snd/snd/fm.html.

Schroeder, M. 1959. "Improvement of acoustic feedback stability in public address systems." *Journal of the Acoustical Society of America* 31(6): 851–852.

Schroeder, M. 1961. "Improved quasi-stereophony and colorless artificial reverberation." *Journal of the Acoustical Society of America* 33: 1061.

Schroeder, M. 1962. "Natural sounding artificial reverberation." *Journal of the Audio Engineering Society* 10(3): 219–223.

Schroeder, M. 1966. "Vocoders: analysis and synthesis of speech." *Proceedings of the IEEE* 54: 720–734.

Schroeder, M. 1970. "Digital simulation of sound transmission in reverberant spaces." *Journal of the Acoustical Society of America* 47(2): 424–431.

Schroeder, M., and B. S. Atal. 1962. "Generalized short-time power spectra and autocorrelation functions." *Journal of the Acoustical Society of America* 34: 1679–1683.

Schroeder, M., and B. S. Atal. 1985. "Code-excited linear prediction (CELP): high-quality speech at very low bit rates." In *Proceedings of the IEEE International Conference on Acoustics, Speech, and Signal Processing* 10. New York: IEEE, 937–940.

Schroeder, M. R., and B. F. Logan. 1961. "Colorless artificial reverberation." *Journal of the Audio Engineering Society* 9(3): 192–197.

Schwarz, D. 2004. "Data-driven Concatenative Sound Synthesis." Thèse de doctorat. Université Paris 6 (Pierre et Marie Curie).

Schwarz, D. 2006. "Concatenative Sound Synthesis: The Early Years." *Journal of New Music Research* 35(1): 3–22.

Schwarz, D. 2007. "Corpus-based Concatenative Synthesis." *IEEE Signal Processing Magazine* 24(2): 92–104.

Schwarz, D. 2011. "State of the Art in Sound Texture Synthesis." *Proceedings of the COST-G6 International Conference on Digital Audio Effects*. Paris, 221–231.

Schwarz, D., G. Beller, B. Verbrugghe, and S. Britton. 2006. "Real-time Corpus-based Concatenative Synthesis with CataRT." *Proceedings of the COST-G6 International Conference on Digital Audio Effects*. n.p.: DAFx, 279–282. https://www.dafx.de.

Schwarz, D., R. Cahen, and S. Britton. 2008. "Principles and Applications of Interactive Corpus-based Concatenative Synthesis." In *Proceedings Journées d'Informatique Musicale*. n.p.: Association Francophone d'Infomatique Musical (AFIM).

Schwartz, R., J. Klovstad, J. Makhoul, D. Klatt, and V. Zac. 1979. "Diphone synthesis for phonetic coding." In *Proceedings of the IEEE Acoustics, Speech and Signal Processing Conference*. New York: IEEE, 891–894.

Schwede, G. 1983. "An algorithm and architecture for constant-Q spectrum analysis." In *Proceedings of the International Conference on Acoustics, Speech, and Signal Processing*. New York: IEEE.

Scientific American. 1987. "Fourier transformation." *Scientific American* 257(1): 27–28.

Scratch. 2020. "#ScratchAtHome." https://sip.scratch.mit.edu.

Secor, G. 1975. "Specifications of the Motorola Scalatron." *Xenharmonikon* 2(2).

Seeger, C. 1951. "An instantaneous music notator." *Journal of the International Folk Music Society* 3: 103–107.

Sekiguchi, K., R. Amemiya, and H. Kubota. 1993. "The development of an automatic drum-playing robot." In *Proceedings of the 1993 International Computer Music Conference*, edited by S. Ohteru. San Francisco: International Computer Music Association, 428–429.

Selfridge-Field, E., ed. 1997. *Beyond MIDI.* Cambridge, MA: MIT Press, 252–280.

Serafin, S., and A. De Götzen. 2009. "An enactive approach to the preservation of musical instruments reconstructing Russolo's Intonarumori." *Journal of New Music Research* 38(3): 231–239.

Serafin, S., C. Erkut, J. Kojs, N. Nilsson, and R. Nordahl. 2016. "Virtual reality musical instruments: state of the art, design principles, and future directions." *Computer Music Journal* 40(3): 22–40.

Serra, M.-H. 1992. "Stochastic composition and stochastic timbre: GENDY3 by Iannis Xenakis." Paris: Centre d'Etudes de Mathematiques et Automatiques Musicale.

Serra, M.-H. 1997. "Introducing the phase vocoder." In *Musical Signal Processing*, edited by C. Roads et al., 1997. London: Routledge, 31–90.

Serra, M.-H., D. Rubine, and R. Dannenberg. 1990. "Analysis and synthesis of tones by spectral interpolation." *Journal of the Audio Engineering Society* 38(3): 111–128.

Serra, X. 1989. "A system for sound analysis/transformation/synthesis based on a deterministic plus stochastic decomposition." Stanford, CA: Center for Computer Research in Music and Acoustics, Department of Music, Stanford University.

Serra, X. 1997. "Musical sound modeling with sinusoids plus noise." In *Musical Signal Processing*, edited by C. Roads, S. Pope, A. Piccialli, and G. De Poli. London: Routledge, 91–122.

Serra, X., M. Magas, E. Benetos, M. Chudy, S. Dixon, A. Flexer, E. Gómez, F. Gouyon, P. Herrera, S. Jordà, O. Paytuvi, G. Peeters, J. Schlüter, H. Vinet, and G. Widmer. 2013. *Roadmap for Music Information Research.* Creative Commons. http://www.mires.cc.

Serra, X., and J. Smith. 1990. "Spectral modeling synthesis: a sound analysis/synthesis system based on a deterministic plus stochastic decomposition." *Computer Music Journal* 14(4): 12–24.

Sethares, W. 2019. "A phase vocoder in MATLAB." https://sethares.engr.wisc.edu/vocoders/phasevocoder.html.

SFZ. 2019. "Welcome to SFZFormat.com!" http://sfzformat.com.

Shannon, C. 1948. "A mathematical theory of communication." *Bell System Technical Journal* 27.

Shannon, C., and W. Weaver. 1949. *The Mathematical Theory of Communication.* Urbana: University of Illinois Press.

Shatri, E., and G. Fazekas. 2020. "Optical music recognition: State of the art and major challenges." In *Proceedings of the International Conference on Technologies for Music Notation and Representation.* https://www.tenor-conference.org.

Shensa, M. 1992. "The discrete wavelet transform: wedding the à trous and Mallat algorithms." *IEEE Transactions on Signal Processing* 40(10): 2464–2482.

Shpak, D. 1992. "Analytic design of biquadratic filter sections for parametric filters." *Journal of the Audio Engineering Society* 40(11): 876–885.

Siedenburg, K., and M. Dörfler. 2011. "Structured sparsity for audio signals." *Proceedings of Digital Audio Effects.* Paris, 1–4.

Silver, A. L. L. 1957. "Equal beating chromatic scale." *Journal of the Acoustical Society of America* 29: 476–481.

Silver, D., T. Hubert, J. Schrittwieser, I. Antonoglou, M. Lai, A. Guez, M. Lanctot, L. Sifre. D. Kumaran, T. Graepel, et al. 2018. "A general reinforcement learning algorithm that masters chess, shogi, and Go through self-play." *Science* 362(6419): 1140–1144.

Simon, I., S. Basu, D. Salesin, and M. Agrawala, 2005. "Audio analogies: creating new music from an existing performance by concatenative synthesis." In *Proceedings of the International Computer Music Conference.* San Francisco: International Computer Music Association, 65–72.

Simoni, M. 1995. "A survey of gender issues related to computer music and strategies for change." In *Proceedings of the 1995 International Computer Music Conference.* San Francisco: International Computer Music Association, 13–18.

Simoni, M. 2003. *Algorithmic Composition: A Gentle Introduction to Music Composition Using Common LISP and Common Music.* https://quod.lib.umich.edu/s /spobooks/bbv9810.0001.001/1:1/—algorithmic-composition-a-gentle-introduction -to-music?rgn=div1;view=fulltext.

Simoni, M., ed. 2006. *Analytical Methods of Electroacoustic Music.* New York: Routledge.

Simoni, M., and R. Dannenberg. 2012. *Algorithmic Composition: A Guide to Composing Music with Nyquist.* Ann Arbor: University of Michigan Press.

Singleton, R. 1967. "A method for computing the fast Fourier transform with auxiliary memory and limited high-speed storage." *IEEE Transactions on Audio and Electroacoustics* AU-15(2): 91–98.

Slaney, M., D. Naar, and R. F. Lyon. 1994. "Auditory model inversion for sound separation." *Proceedings of the IEEE International Conference on Audio Speech, and Signal Procressing.* Volume II: 77–80.

Slaney, M., and R. Lyon. 1991a. *Apple Hearing Demo Reel.* Apple Computer Technical Report 25. Cupertino, CA: Apple Corporate Library.

Slaney, M., and R. Lyon. 1991b. "Visualizing sound with auditory correlograms." Submitted to the *Journal of the Acoustical Society of America.*

Slaney, M., and R. Lyon. 1992. "On the importance of time—A temporal representation of sound." In *Visual Representations of Speech Signals*, edited by M. Cooke and S. Beet. New York: John Wiley.

Slater, D. 1998. "Chaotic sound synthesis." *Computer Music Journal* 22(2): 12–19.

Smalley, D. 1986. "Spectro-morphology and structuring processes." In *The Language of Electroacoustic Music*, edited by S. Emmerson. New York: Harwood Academic.

Smalley, D. 1991. "Spatial experience in electro-acoustic music." In *L'espace du son*, edited by F. Dhomont. Ohain, Belgium: Musiques et Recherches, 123–126.

Smalley, D. 1997. "Spectromorphology: explaining sound shapes." *Organised Sound* 2(2): 107–126.

Smalley, D. 2007. "Space-form and the acousmatic image." *Organised Sound* 12(1): 35–58.

Smallwood, S., P. Cook, D. Trueman, and L. McIntyre. 2017. "2009: A history of hemispherical speakers at Princeton, plus a DIY guide." Originally presented at NIME 2009, here with additional commentary. In *A NIME Reader: Fifteen Years of New Interfaces for Musical Expression*, edited by A. Jensenius and M. Lyons. Cham, Switzerland: Springer, 353–372.

Smaragdis, P., and J. Brown. 2003. "Non-negative matrix factorization for polyphonic transcription." *IEEE Workshop on Applications of Signal Processing to Audio and Acoustics,* 177–180.

SMC. 2012. "Sound and music computing roadmap: Challenges and strategies." https://smcnetwork.org/roadmap.

Smirnov, A. 2013. *Sound in Z: Experiments in Sound and Electronic Music in Early 20th Century Russia.* London: Koenig Books.

Smirnov, A. 2020. "UPIC's precursors." In *From Xenakis's UPIC to Graphic Notation Today*, edited by P. Weibel, S. Kanach, and L. Brümmer. Karlsruhe, Germany: ZKM, 97–114. https://zkm.de/de/from-xenakiss-upic-to-graphic-notation-today.

Smith, D. 1984. Interviewed in D. Milano. 1984. "Turmoil in MIDI land." *Keyboard* 10(6): 42–63.

Smith, E., and M. S. Lewicki. 2005a. "Efficient auditory coding." *Nature* 439(23): 978–982.

Smith, E., and M. S. Lewicki. 2005b. "Efficient coding of time-relative structure using spikes." *Neural Computation* 17(1): 19–45.

Smith, J. O. 1981. "Digital signal processing committee, IEEE ASSP: Programs for digital signal processing." *Computer Music Journal* 5(2): 62–65.

Smith, J. O. 1982. "Synthesis of bowed strings." In *Proceedings of the 1982 International Computer Music Conference*, edited by J. Strawn and T. Blum. San Francisco: International Computer Music Association, 308–340.

Smith, J. O. 1983. "Techniques for digital filter design and system identification with application to the violin." PhD diss. Technical Report STAN-M-14. Stanford University Department of Music.

Smith, J. O. 1985a. "Fundamentals of digital filter theory." *Computer Music Journal* 9(3):13–23. Reprinted in *The Music Machine*, edited by C. Roads, 1989. Cambridge, MA: MIT Press, 509–520.

Smith, J. O. 1985b. "Introduction to digital filter theory." In *Digital Audio Signal Processing: An Anthology*, edited by J. Strawn. Middleton, WI: A-R Editions, 69–135.

Smith, J. O. 1985c. "A new approach to reverberation using closed waveguide networks." In *Proceedings of the 1985 International Computer Music Conference*, edited by B. Truax. San Francisco: International Computer Music Association, 47–53.

Smith, J. O. 1986. "Efficient simulation of the reed-bore mechanism and bow-string interactions." In *Proceedings of the 1986 International Computer Music Conference*, edited by P. Berg. San Francisco: International Computer Music Association, 275–279.

Smith, J. O. 1987a. *Musical Applications of Digital Waveguides*. Technical Report STAN-M-39. Stanford, CA: Stanford University Department of Music.

Smith, J. O. 1987b. "Waveguide filter tutorial." In *Proceedings of the 1987 International Computer Music Conference*, edited by J. Beauchamp. San Francisco: International Computer Music Association, 9–16.

Smith, J. O. 1991a. "Viewpoints on the history of digital synthesis." In *Proceedings of the 1991 International Computer Music Conference*, edited by B. Alphonce and B. Pennycook. San Francisco: International Computer Music Association, 1–10.

Smith, J. O. 1991b. "Waveguide simulation of non-cylindrical acoustic tubes." In *Proceedings of the 1991 International Computer Music Conference*, edited by B. Alphonce and B. Pennycook. San Francisco: International Computer Music Conference, 304–307.

Smith, J. O. 1992. "Physical modeling using digital waveguides." *Computer Music Journal* 16(4): 74–91.

Smith, J. O. 1993. "Efficient synthesis of stringed musical instruments." In *Proceedings of the 1993 International Computer Music Conference*, edited by S. Ohteru. San Francisco: International Computer Music Conference, 64–71.

Smith, J. O. 2003. "Four-pole tunable lowpass/bandpass filters." https://ccrma.stanford .edu/~jos/filters.

Smith, J. 2004. "Virtual acoustic musical instruments: review and update." *Journal of New Music Research* 33(3): 283–304.

Smith, J. 2007a. *Introduction to Digital Filters with Audio Applications.* https://ccrma .stanford.edu/~jos.

Smith, J. 2007b. *Mathematics of the Discrete Fourier Transform (DFT), with Audio Applications.* 2nd ed. n.p.: W3K Publishing. https://ccrma.stanford.edu/~jos.

Smith, J. 2010. *Physical Audio Signal Processing.* n.p.: W3K Publishing. https://ccrma .stanford.edu/~jos.

Smith, J. 2011. *Spectral Audio Signal Processing.* n.p.: W3K Publishing. https://ccrma .stanford.edu/~jos.

Smith, J. 2012. "FFT versus direct convolution." https://ccrma.stanford.edu/~jos/sasp /FFT_versus_Direct_Convolution.html.

Smith, J. 2013. "Audio signal processing in FAUST." https://ccrma.stanford.edu /~jos/aspf.

Smith, J. 2018. "MUS420/EE367A, Lecture 3: Artificial reverberation and spatialization." https://ccrma.stanford.edu/~jos/Reverb.

Smith, J. O., and P. Cook. 1992. "The second-order digital waveguide oscillator." In *Proceedings of the International Computer Music Conference.* San Francisco: International Computer Music Association, 150–153.

Smith, J. O., S. Serafin, J. Abel, and D. Berners. 2002. "Doppler simulation and the Leslie." In *Proceedings of the Fifth International Conference on Digital Audio Effects (DAFx-02).* n.p.: DAFx, 13–20. https://www.dafx.de.

Smith, J. O., and X. Serra. 1987. "An analysis/synthesis program for non-harmonic sounds based on a sinusoidal representation." In *Proceedings of the 1987 International Computer Music Conference.* International Computer Music Association: San Francisco, 290–297.

Smith, L. C. 1972. "SCORE—A musician's approach to computer music." *Journal of the Audio Engineering Society* 20(1): 7–14.

Smith, L. C. 1973. "Editing and printing music by computer." *Journal of Music Theory* 9: 129–150.

Smith, L. C. 1997. "SCORE." In *Beyond MIDI:The Handbook of Musical Codes,* E. Selfridge-Field. Cambridge, MA: MIT Press, 252–280.

Smith, L. M. 1996. "Modelling rhythm perception by continuous time-frequency analysis." In *Proceedings of the 1996 International Computer Music Conference.* San Francisco: International Computer Music Conference, 392–395.

Smith, L. M. 2009. "The MusicKit V5.6.2." http://musickit.sourceforge.net.

Smith, L. M., and H. Honing. 2008. "Time-frequency representation of musical rhythm by continuous wavelets." *Journal of Mathematics and Music* 2(2): 81–97.

Smoliar, S. 1967a. "Euterpe: A computer language for the expression of musical ideas." A. I. Memo 129. Cambridge, MA: Artificial Intelligence Laboratory, MIT.

Smoliar, S. 1967b. "Euterpe-Lisp: A Lisp System with Music Output." A. I. Memo 141. Cambridge, MA: Artificial Intelligence Laboratory, MIT.

Smoliar, S. 1971. "A Parallel Processing Model of Musical Structures." A. I. Technical Report AI-TR-90. Cambridge, MA: Artificial Intelligence Laboratory, MIT.

Smyth, T., and J. O. Smith. 2001. "Applications of bioacoustics in physical modeling and the creation of new musical instruments." In *Proceedings of the International Symposium on Musical Acoustics*.

Snell, J. 1977a. "Design of a digital oscillator that will generate up to 256 low-distortion sine waves in real time." *Computer Music Journal* 1(2): 4–25. Revised and updated version in *Foundations of Computer Music*, edited by C. Roads and J. Strawn, 1985. Cambridge, MA: MIT Press, 289–325.

Snell, J. 1977b. "High-speed multiplication." *Computer Music Journal* 1(1): 38–45.

Snell, J. 1983. "Sensors for playing computer music with expression." In *Proceedings of the 1983 International Computer Music Conference*. San Francisco: International Computer Music Association, 114–127.

Sofer, D. S. 2022. *Sex Sounds: Vectors of Difference in Electronic Music*. Cambridge, MA: MIT Press.

Solis, J., K. Chida, K. Taniguchi, S. Hashimoto, K. Suefuji, and A. Takanishi. 2006. "The Waseda flutist robot WF-4RII in comparison with a professional flutist." *Computer Music Journal* 30(4): 12–27.

Solis, J., and K. Ng, eds. 2011. *Musical Robots and Interactive Multimodal Systems*. Berlin: Springer.

Sonami, L. 2006. "On my work." *Contemporary Music Review* 25(5/6): 613–614.

Sonic Pi. 2020. "Sonic Pi: Welcome to the future of music." https://sonic-pi.net.

Sorensen, A., and A. Brown. 2000. "Introducing jmusic." *Proceedings of the Australasian Computer Music Conference*. Brisbane: Australasian Computer Music Association, 68–76.

Sousa, J. P. 1906. "The menace of mechanical music." *Appleton's Magazine* September: 278–284. Reprinted with an introduction by C. Roads in *Computer Music Journal* 17(1): 12–13, 1993.

Sowa, J. 1956. *A Machine to Compose Music*. Instruction manual for GENIAC. New Haven, CT: Oliver Garfield Company.

Spek, L. 2009. "Xenakis Dynamic Stochastic Synthesis. Gendyn core cell." https://www.native-instruments.com. (See Native Instruments User Library for Reaktor.)

Spiegel, L. 1986. *The Music Mouse Manual.* http://musicmouse.com/mm_manual/mouse_manual.html.

Springer, A. 1955. "Ein akusticher Zeitregler." *Gravesaner Blätter* 1: 32–37.

Stahnke, W. 1981. "Method and apparatus for measuring the dynamics of a piano performance." U.S. Patent 4,307,648.

Stahnke, W. 2009. "About Us." http://www.live-performance.com/about.html.

Stan, G., J. J. Embrechts, and D. Archambeau. 2002. "Comparison of different impulse response measurement techniques." *Journal of the Audio Engineering Society* 50(4): 249–262.

Stanek, J. 1979. "Exploration of concurrent digital sound synthesis on a prototype data-driven machine." MS thesis. Department of Computer Science, University of Utah.

Starke, P. 1972. *Abstract Automata.* Amsterdam: North-Holland.

Stautner, J. 1983. "Analysis and synthesis of music using the auditory transform." MS thesis. Department of Electrical Engineering and Computer Science, MIT.

Stautner, J., and M. Puckette. 1982. "Designing multi-channel reverberators." *Computer Music Journal* 6(1): 62–65.

Steiglitz, K. 1996. *A Digital Signal Processing Primer: With Applications to Digital Audio and Computer Music.* Menlo Park, CA: Addison-Wesley.

Stevens, K., and G. Fant. 1953. "An electrical analog of the vocal tract." *Journal of the Acoustical Society of America* 25: 734–742.

Steward, J. 1922. "An electrical analogue of the vocal organs." *Nature* 110: 311–312.

Stickney, K. 1987. "Computer tools for engraving-quality music notation." In *Music and Digital Technology*, edited by J. Strawn. New York: Audio Engineering Society.

Stilson, T., and J. O. Smith. 1996. "Alias-free digital synthesis of classic analog waveforms." In *Proceedings of the 1996 International Computer Music Conference.* San Francisco: International Computer Music Association, 332–335.

Stockham, T. 1966. "High-speed convolution and correlation." In *Spring Joint Computer Conference, AFIPS Conference Proceedings* 28: 229–233.

Stockham, T. 1969. "High-speed convolution and convolution with applications to digital filtering." In *Digital Processing of Signals*, edited by B. Gold and C. Rader. New York: McGraw-Hill, 203–232.

Stockham, T., T. Cannon, and R. Ingebretsen. 1975. "Blind deconvolution through digital signal processing." *Proceedings of the IEEE* 63: 267–270.

Stockhausen, K. 1955. "Actualia." *Die Reihe* 1.

Stockhausen, K. 1956. Program notes for *Gesang der Jünglinge.* Reprinted in K. Stockhausen. 1992. *Elektronische Musik 1952–1960.* Booklet with compact disc. Kürten, Germany: Stockhausen-Verlag, 135–136.

Stockhausen, K. 1957. ". . . how time passes . . ." *Die Reihe* 3: 10–43. English edition 1959. Reprinted as ". . . wie die Zeit vergeht . . ." in *Texte zur elektronischen und instrumentalen Musik,* Band 1, K. Stockhausen, 1963. Cologne: DuMont Schauberg, 99–139.

Stockhausen, K. 1958. "Musik im Raum." Reprinted in *Texte zur elektronischen und instrumentalen Musik,* Band 1, K. Stockhausen, 1963. Cologne: DuMont Schauberg, 152–175.

Stockhausen, K. 1961. "Two lectures." *Die Reihe* 5. English edition. Bryn Mawr, PA: Theodore Presser Company, 59–82.

Stockhausen, K. 1963. "Die Einheit der musikalischen Zeit." In *Texte zur elektronischen und instrumentalen Musik,* Band 1, K. Stockhausen, 1963. Cologne: DuMont Schauberg, 211–221. Reprinted as "The concept of unity in electronic music," translated by E. Barkin, in *Perspectives on Contemporary Music Theory,* edited by B. Boretz and E. Cone, 1972. New York: Norton, 129–147.

Stockhausen, K. 1964. "Elektronische Studien I und II." In *Texte zu eigenen Werken zur Kunst Anderer.* Cologne: DuMont Schauberg.

Stockhausen, K. 1968. *Kontakte.* Score number UE 13678. London: Universal Edition.

Stockhausen, K. 1971a. "Osaka-Projekt." In *Texte zur Musik 1963–1970.* Cologne: DuMont Schauberg, 153–187.

Stockhausen, K. 1971b. *Texte zur Musik 1963–1970,* Band 3. Cologne: DuMont Schauberg.

Stockhausen, K. 1978. *Texte zur Musik 1970–1977,* Band 4. Cologne: DuMont Schauberg.

Stone, K. 1963. "Problems and methods of notation." *Perspectives of New Music.* Reprinted in *Perspectives on Notation and Performance,* edited by B. Boretz and E. Cone, 1976. New York: Norton, 9–31.

Stone, K. 1980. *Music Notation in the Twentieth Century.* New York: W. W. Norton.

Storer, J. 2018. "SOUL announcement." Talk at Audio Developer conference. www.youtube.com/watch?v=-GhleKNaPdk.

Strang, G. 1989. "Wavelets and dilation equations: a brief introduction." *SIAM Review* 31(4): 614–627.

Strange, A. 1983. *Electronic Music: Systems, Techniques, Controls.* 2nd ed. Dubuque, IA: W. C. Brown.

Strauss, L. 1960. *Wave Generation and Shaping.* New York: McGraw-Hill.

Strawn, J. M. 1980. "Approximation and syntactic analysis of amplitude and frequency functions for digital sound synthesis." *Computer Music Journal* 4(3): 3–24.

Strawn, J. M., ed. 1985a. *Digital Audio Engineering: An Anthology.* Middleton, WI: A-R Editions.

Strawn, J. M., ed.1985b. *Digital Audio Signal Processing: An Anthology.* Middleton, WI: A-R Editions.

Strawn, J. M. 1985c. "Modelling musical transitions." PhD diss. Department of Music, Stanford University.

Strawn, J. M. 1987a. "Analysis and synthesis of musical transitions using the discrete short-time Fourier transform." *Journal of the Audio Engineering Society* 35(1/2): 3–14.

Strawn, J. M. 1987b. "Editing time-varying spectra." *Journal of the Audio Engineering Society* 35(5): 337–352.

Strawn, J. M. 1988. "Implementing table lookup oscillators for music with the Motorola DSP56000 family." Preprint 2716 (-6). In *Proceedings of the 85th Convention of the Audio Engineering Society, Los Angeles.* New York: Audio Engineering Society.

Streicher, R., and W. Dooley. 1978. "Basic stereo microphone perspectives—A review." *Journal of the Audio Engineering Society* 33(7/8): 548–556. Reprinted in *Stereophonic Techniques: An Anthology*, Audio Engineering Society, 1986. New York: Audio Engineering Society.

Stuart, J., and P. Craven. 2019. "The gentle art of dithering." *Journal of the Audio Engineering Society* 67(5): 278–299.

Sturm, B. 2006a. "Adaptive concatenative sound synthesis and its application to micromontage composition," *Computer Music Journal* 30(4): 44–66.

Sturm, B. 2006b. "Concatenative sound synthesis and intellectual property: An analysis of the legal issues surrounding the synthesis of novel sounds from copyright-protected work." *Journal of New Music Research* 35(1): 23–33.

Sturm, B. L. 2009. "Sparse Approximation and Atomic Decomposition: Considering Atom Interactions in Evaluating and Building Signal Representations." PhD thesis. University of California, Santa Barbara.

Sturm, B. L. 2014. "The state of the art ten years after a state of the art: Future research in music information retrieval." *Journal of New Music Research* 43(2): 147–172.

Sturm, B. 2018. Personal communication.

Sturm, B. L., and M. Christensen. 2010. "Cyclic matching pursuit with multiscale time-frequency dictionaries." In *Proceedings of the Asilomar Conference on Signals, Systems, and Computers.* New York: IEEE, 581–585.

Sturm, B., M. Iglesias, O. Ben-Tal, M. Miron, and E. Gomez. 2019. "Artificial intelligence and music: open questions of copyright law and engineering praxis." *MDPI Arts* 8(3): 115.

Sturm, B. L., L. Daudet, and C. Roads. 2006. "Pitch-shifting audio signals using sparse atomic approximations." In *Proceedings of the ACM Workshop on Audio and Music Computation in Multimedia*. New York: Association for Computing Machinery, 45–52.

Sturm, B. L., J. J. Shynk, L. Daudet, and C. Roads. 2008. "Dark energy in sparse atomic estimations." *IEEE Transactions on Audio, Speech and Language Processing* 16(3): 671–676.

Sturm, B. L., C. Roads, A. McLeran, and J. J. Shynk. 2009. "Analysis, visualization, and transformation of audio signals using dictionary-based methods." *Journal of New Music Research* 38: 325–341.

Sturm, B. L., and J. J. Shynk. 2010. "Sparse approximation and the pursuit of meaningful signal models with interference adaptation." *IEEE Transactions on Audio, Speech and Language Processing* 18(3): 461–472.

Sturm, B., and G. Wiggins. 2021. "The mismeasure of music: On computerised music listening and analysis." In *Oxford Handbook of Music and Corpus Studies*. New York: Oxford University Press.

Suen, C. 1970. "Derivation of harmonic equations in nonlinear circuits." *Journal of the Audio Engineering Society* 18(6): 675–676.

Sullivan, C. 1990. "Extending the Karplus-Strong plucked-string algorithm to synthesize electric guitar timbres with disortion and feedback." *Computer Music Journal* 14(3): 26–37.

Sundberg, J. 1972. "A perceptual function of the 'singing formant.'" In *Speech Transmission Lab Quarterly Progress and Status Report 1972*. Stockholm: KTH, 2–3, 61–63.

Sundberg, J., A. Askenfelt, and L. Frydén. 1983. "Musical performance: A synthesis-by-rule approach." *Computer Music Journal* 7(1): 37–43. Reprinted in *The Music Machine*, edited by C. Roads, 1989. Cambridge, MA: MIT Press, 693–699.

Surges, G., T. Smyth, and M. Puckette. 2016. "Generative audio systems using power-preserving all-pass filters." *Computer Music Journal* 40(1): 54–69.

Sussman, G., and G. Steele. 1981. "Constraints: a language for expressing almost-hierarchical descriptions." Memo 502A. Cambridge, MA: MIT Artificial Intelligence Laboratory. Reprinted in *Artificial Intelligence* 14: 1–39.

Suzuki, H. 1987. "Modal analysis of a hammer-string interaction." *Journal of the Acoustical Society of America* 82(4): 1145–1151.

Suzuki, Y. 2018. "Z Machines." https://yurisuzuki.com/design-studio/z-machines.

Swami, A., J. Mendel, and C. Nikias. 2001. *High-Order Spectrum Analysis Toolbox: For Use with MATLAB. User's Guide Version 2*. Boca Raton, FL: United Signals and Systems. http://labcit.ligo.caltech.edu/~rana/mat/HOSA/HOSA.PDF.

SynthFont. 2006. "SoundFont Technical Specification." Version 2.04. http://www.synthfont.com/sfspec24.pdf.

Szilas, N., and C. Cadoz. 1993. "Physical models that learn." In *Proceedings of the 1993 International Computer Music Conference*, edited by S. Ohteru. San Francisco: International Computer Music Conference, 72–75.

Tadokoro, Y., and T. Higishi. 1978. "Discrete Fourier transform computation via the Walsh transform." *IEEE Transactions on Acoustics, Speech and Signal Processing* ASSP-26(3): 236–240.

Tahiroğlu, K. 2021. "Ever-shifting roles in building, composing and performing with digital musical instruments." *Journal of New Music Research* 50(2): 117–120.

Talambirus, R. 1985. "Limitations on the dynamic range of digitized audio." In *Digital Audio Engineering: An Anthology*, edited by J. Strawn. Middleton, WI: A-R Editions, 29–60.

Talbot, A. 1983. "Finished musical scores from the keyboard: an expansion of the composer's creativity." In *Proceedings of the 1983 ACM Conference on Computers*. New York: Association for Computing Machinery, 234–239.

Tanaka, A. 1999. "Network audio performance and installation." In *Proceedings of the 1999 International Computer Music Conference*. San Francisco: International Computer Music Association, 519–522.

Tanaka, A. 2009. "Sensor-based instruments and interactive music." In *The Oxford Handbook of Computer Music*, edited by R. Dean. Oxford: Oxford University Press, 233–257.

Tarr, E. 2019. *Hack Audio: An Introduction to Computer Programming and Digital Signal Processing in MATLAB*. New York: Routledge.

Tatar, K., and P. Pasquier. 2019. "Musical agents: A typology and state of the art towards musical metacreation." *Journal of New Music Research* 48(1): 56–105.

Taube, H. 1991. "Common Music: a music composition language in Common Lisp and CLOS." *Computer Music Journal* 15(2): 21–32.

Taube, H. 2005. *Notes from the Metalevel: Introduction to Computer Composition*. London: Taylor and Francis.

Taylor, P. 2009. *Text-to-Speech Synthesis*. Cambridge: Cambridge University Press.

Tazelaar, K. 2013. *On the Threshold of Beauty: Philips and the Origins of Electronic Music in the Netherlands 1925–1965*. Rotterdam: V2_Publishing.

TC Helicon. 2018. *VoiceLive Rack User's Manual Version 1.0.* https://www.tc -helicon.com.

Tellman, E., L. Haken, and B. Holloway. 1995. "Timbre morphing of sounds with unequal numbers of features." *Journal of the Audio Engineering Society* 43(9): 678–689.

Tempelaars, S. 1976. "The VOSIM oscillator." Presented at the 1976 International Computer Music Conference, MIT, Cambridge, MA, October 28–31. San Francisco: International Computer Music Association.

Tempelaars, S. 1977. *Sound Signal Processing.* Translated by Ruth Koenig. Utrecht, Netherlands: Institute of Sonology.

Tenney, J. 1963. "Sound generation by means of a digital computer." *Journal of Music Theory* 7: 24–70.

Tenney, J. 1965. "The physical correlates of timbre." *Gravesaner Blätter* 26: 103–109.

Tenney, J. 1969. "Computer music experiments: 1961–64." *Electronic Music Reports* 1: 23–60.

Terhardt, E. 1982. "Algorithm for extraction of pitch and pitch salience from complex tonal signals." *Journal of the Acoustical Society of America* 71(3): 679.

Thall, D. 2005. "Experiments in sound granulation and spatialization for immersive environments." Poster at Interactive Digital Multimedia IGERT Annual Research Review. Santa Barbara: University of California.

Thall, D. 2019. Personal communication.

Thibault, B., and S. Gresham-Lancaster. 1992. "Songlines.DEM." In *Proceedings of the 1992 International Computer Music Conference, San Jose.* San Francisco: International Computer Music Association, 465–466.

Thibault, B., and S. Gresham-Lancaster. 1997. "Experiences in Digital Terrain: Using Digital Elevation Models for Music and Interactive Multimedia." *Leonardo Music Journal* 7: 11–15.

Thibodeau, J., and M. Wanderley. 2013. "Trumpet augmentation and technological symbiosis." *Computer Music Journal* 37(3): 12–25.

Thoreson, L. 2015. *Emergent Musical Forms: Aural Explorations.* Studies in Music from the University of Western Ontario, vol. 24. London, Ontario: University of Western Ontario.

Thoresen, L., and A. Hedman. (2007) "Spectromorphological analysis of sound objects: an adaptation of Pierre Schaeffer's typomorphology." *Organised Sound* 12(2): 129–141.

Thorington, H. 2005. "Breaking out: The trip back." *Contemporary Music Review* 24(6): 445–458.

Thuillier, E., O. Lähdeoja, and V. Välimäki. 2019. "Feedback control in an actuated acoustic guitar using frequency shifting." *Journal of the Audio Engineering Society* 67(6): 373–381.

Tibshirani, R. 1996. "Regression shrinkage and selection via the LASSO." *Journal of the Royal Statistical Society. Series B* 58(1): 267–288.

Tilbian, J. 2018. "Stride: A language for sound synthesis, processing, and interaction design." PhD diss. Media Arts and Technology, University of California, Santa Barbara.

Tjepkema, S. 1981. *A Bibliography of Computer Music.* Iowa City: University of Iowa Press.

Tobenfeld, E. 1984. "A general-purpose sequencer for MIDI synthesizers." *Computer Music Journal* 8(4): 43–54.

Tochetti, G. 1984. *Un preprocessore per il compilatore Music 5.* Padua, Italy: Universita di Padova, Centro di Sonologia Computazionale.

Todd, N. 1993. "Wavelet analysis of rhythm in expressive musical performance." In *Proceedings of the 1993 International Computer Music Conference,* edited by S. Ohteru.. San Francisco: International Computer Music Association, 264–267.

Todd, P. 1989. "A connectionist approach to algorithmic composition." *Computer Music Journal* 13(4): 27–43.

Todd, P., and D. G. Loy, eds. 1991. *Music and Connectionism.* Cambridge, MA: MIT Press.

Tomisawa, N. 1981. "Tone production method for an electronic music instrument." U.S. Patent 4,249,447.

Tonality Systems. 1993. *Symbolic Composer.* (Documentation and program.) Wakefield, UK: Tonality Systems.

Topper, T., and B. Wills. 1987. "The computer simulation of piano mechanisms." *International Journal of Modeling and Simulation* 7(4): 135–139.

Torchia, R., and C. Lippe. 2004. "Techniques for multi-channel real-time spatial distribution using frequency-domain processing." In *Proceedings of the 2004 Conference on New Interfaces for Musical Expression (NIME).* n.p.: New Interfaces for Musical Expression. https://www.nime.orghttps://www.nime.org.

Tosic, I., and P. Frossard. 2011. "Dictionary learning: What is the right representation for my signal?" *IEEE Signal Processing Magazine* 28(2): 27–38.

Tovar, J., and L. Smith. 1977. *MUS10 Manual.* Stanford, CA: Center for Computer Research in Music and Acoustics, Stanford University.

Trautmann, L., and R. Rabenstein. 2003. *Digital Sound Synthesis by Physical Modeling Using the Functional Transformation Method.* New York: Kluwer/Academic.

Trieb, M. 1996. *Space Calculated in Seconds: The Philips Pavilion, Le Corbusier, Edgard Varèse.* Princeton, NJ: Princeton University Press.

Tropp, J. 2004. "Greed is good: algorithmic results for sparse approximation." *IEEE Transactions on Information Theory* 50(10): 2231–2242.

Truax, B. 1975. "The computer composition—Sound synthesis programs POD4, POD5, and POD6." *Sonological Reports Number 2.* Utrecht, Netherlands: Institute of Sonology.

Truax, B. 1977. "The POD system of interactive composition programs." *Computer Music Journal* 1(3): 30–39.

Truax, B. 1985. "The PODX system: interactive compositional software for the DMX-1000." *Computer Music Journal* 9(1): 29–38.

Truax, B. 1987. "Real-time granulation of sampled sound with the DMX-1000." In *Proceedings of the 1987 International Computer Music Conference*, edited by J. Beauchamp. San Francisco: International Computer Music Association, 138–145.

Truax, B. 1988. "Real-time granular synthesis with a digital signal processing computer." *Computer Music Journal* 12(2): 14–26.

Truax, B. 1990a. "Composing with real-time granular sound." *Perspectives of New Music* 28(2): 120–134.

Truax, B. 1990b. "Time-shifting of sampled sound with a real-time granulation technique." In *Proceedings of the 1990 International Computer Music Conference*, S. Arnold and G. Hair. San Francisco: International Computer Music Association, 104–107.

Trueman, D., P. Cook, S. Smallwood, and G. Wang. 2006. "PLORK: The Princeton Laptop Orchestra." In *Proceedings of the 2006 International Computer Music Conference.* San Francisco: International Computer Music Association, 443–450.

Tsingos, N. 2009. "Pre-computing geometry-based reverberation effects for games." In *Proceedings of the Audio Engineering Society 35th International Conference.* New York: Audio Engineering Society.

Tyndall, J. 1875. *Sound.* 3rd ed. Akron, OH: Werner.

Tzimeas, D., and E. Mangina, 2009. "Dynamic techniques for genetic algorithm-based music systems." *Computer Music Journal* 33(3): 45–60.

Tzinis, E., S. Wisdom, J. Hershey, A. Jansen, and D. Ellis. 2020. "Improving universal sound separation using sound classification." In *Proceedings of the IEEE International Conference on Acoustics, Speech, and Signal Processing.* New York: IEEE.

U&I Software. 2021. "Getting started with MetaSynth Creative Toolbox." https://uisoftware.com.

Umbert, M., J. Bonada, M. Goto, T. Nakano, and J. Sundberg. 2015. "Expression control in singing voice synthesis: features, approaches, evaluation, and challenges." *IEEE Signal Processing Magazine* 32(6): 55–73.

Unfiltered Audio. 2016. *G8 Online Manual.* https://www.unfilteredaudio.com.

Usher, A. P. 1954. *A History of Mechanical Inventions.* Cambridge, MA: Harvard University Press. Reprinted 1988. New York: Dover.

Ussachevsky, V. 1958. "Musical timbre by means of the 'Klangumwandler.'" Preprint No. 65. In *Proceedings of the 10th Annual Meeting of the Audio Engineering Society.* New York: Audio Engineering Society.

Vaggione, H. 1984. "The making of *Octuor.*" *Computer Music Journal* 8(2): 48–54.

Vaggione, H. 2003. "Composition musicale et moyens informatique: questions d'approche." In *Formel-Informel: Musique-Philosophie*, edited by M. Solomos, A. Soulez, and H. Vaggione. Paris: L'Harmattan, 91–116.

Vail, M. 1993. "The E-mu Emulator." *Keyboard* 19(1): 108–111.

Vail, M. 2000a. "Sequential Circuits Prophet-5: Defining the future of poly-synths." In *Vintage Synthesizer*s, 2nd ed., edited by M. Vail. San Francisco: Miller Freeman Books, 173–177.

Vail, M., ed. 2000b. *Vintage Synthesizers.* 2nd ed. San Francisco: Miller Freeman Books.

Vail, M. 2014. *The Synthesizer.* New York: Oxford University Press.

Valentino, R. 1986. "Le altre elettroniche." In *Nuova Atlantide*, edited by R. Doati and A. Vidolin, 1986. Venice: La Biennale di Venezia, 77–101.

Valhalla. 2011. *Valhalla Shimmer Manual.* https:valhalladsp.com/2011/01/24/valhalla shimmer-the-manual.

Välimäki, V. 2005. "Discrete-time synthesis of the sawtooth waveform with reduced aliasing." *IEEE Signal Processing Letters* 12(3): 214–217.

Välimäki, V., S. Bilbao, J. O. Smith, J. Abel, J. Pakarinen, and D. Berners. 2011. "Virtual analog effects." In *DAFX: Digital Audio Effects*, 2nd ed., edited by U. Zölzer. Chichester, UK: John Wiley & Sons, 473–522.

Välimäki, V., B. Holm-Rasmussen, B. Alary, and H.-M. Lehtonen. 2017. "Late reverberation synthesis using filtered velvet noise." *Applied Sciences* 7(5). Article number 483.

Välimäki, V., and A. Huovilainen. 2006. "Oscillator and filter algorithms for virtual analog synthesis." *Computer Music Journal* 30(2): 19–31.

Välimäki, V., and A. Huovilainen. 2007. "Antialiasing oscillators in subtractive synthesis." *IEEE Signal Processing Magazine* 24(2): 116–125.

Välimäki, V., J. Parker, and J. Abel. 2010. "Parametric spring reverberation effect." *Journal of the Audio Engineering Society* 58(7/8): 547–562.

Välimäki, V., J. Parker, L. Savioja, J. Smith, and J. Abel. 2012. "Fifty years of artificial reverberation." *IEEE Transactions on Audio, Speech, and Language Processing* 20(5): 1421–1448.

Välimäki, V., H. Penttinen, J. Knif, M. Laurson, and C. Erkut. 2006. "Discrete-time modeling of musical instruments." *Reports on Progress in Physics* 69(1): 1–78.

van de Plassche, R. 1983. "Dynamic element matching puts trimless converters on chip." *Electronics* 16 June 1983.

van de Plassche, R., and E. Dijkmans. 1983. "A monolithic 16-bit d/a conversion system for digital audio." In *Digital Audio*, edited by B. Blesser, B. Locanthi, and T. Stockham. New York: Audio Engineering Society, 54–60.

Vanderkooy, J., and S. Lipschitz. 1984. "Resolution below the least significant bit in digital systems with dither." *Journal of the Audio Engineering Society* 32(3): 106–113.

van der Pol, B. 1930. "Frequency modulation." *Proceedings of the Institute of Radio Engineers* 18: 1194–1205.

Van Duyne, S., and J. Smith. 1993. "Physical modeling with a 2-D digital waveguide mesh." In *Proceedings of the 1993 International Computer Music Conference*, edited by S. Ohteru. San Francisco: International Computer Music Association, 40–47.

Vaneph, A., E. McNeil, F. Rigaud, and R. Silva. 2016. "An automated source separation technology and its practical applications." Convention e-Brief 278. In *Proceedings of the 140th Convention of the Audio Engineering Society*. New York: Audio Engineering Society.

Van Nort, D., P. Oliveros, and J. Braasch. 2013. "Electro/acoustic improvisation and deeply listening machines." *Journal of New Music Research* 42(4): 303–324.

Varèse, E. (1920) 1970. Quotation from G. Charbonnier. 1970. *Entretiens avec Varèse.* Paris: Editions Pierre Belfond.

Varèse, E. 1936. "Nouveaux instruments et nouvelle musique." In *Edgar Varèse: Écrits*, edited by L. Hirbour. Paris: Christian Bourgois Éditeur, 90–93.

Varèse, E. 1971. "The liberation of sound." In *Perspectives on American Composers*, edited by B. Boretz and E. Cone. New York: Norton, 26–34.

Venkataramani, S., C. Subakan, and P. Smaragdis. 2017. "Neural network alternatives to convolutive audio models for source separation." In *Proceedings of the IEEE International Workshop on Machine Learning for Signal Processing*. http://arxiv.org/pdf/1709.07908.

Vercoe, B. 1984. "The synthetic performer in the context of live performance." In *Proceedings of the 1984 International Computer Music Conference, Paris.* San Francisco: International Computer Music Association.

Verfaille, V., M. Holters, and U. Zölzer. 2011. "Introduction." In *Digital Audio Effects*, 2nd ed., edited by U. Zölzer. Chichester, UK: John Wiley & Sons, 1–46.

Verge, P. 1996. "Physical modeling of aeroacoustic sources in flute-like instruments." In *Proceedings of the 1996 International Computer Music Conference.* San Francisco: International Computer Music Association, 5–8.

Verplank, B., M. Mathews, and R. Shaw. 2000. "Scanned synthesis." http://www.billverplank.com/ScannedSynthesis.PDF.

Vetterli, M. 1992. "Wavelets and filter banks: theory and design." *IEEE Transactions on Signal Processing* 40(9): 2207–2233.

Vidolin, A. 1993. Personal communication.

Villeneuve, J., C. Cadoz, and N. Castagné. 2015. "Visual representation in GENESIS as a tool for physical modeling, sound synthesis and musical composition." *Proceedings of the International Conference on New Interfaces for Musical Expression.* n.p.: New Interfaces for Musical Expression.

Vincent, E., T. Virtanen, and S. Gannot. 2018. *Audio Source Separation and Speech Enhancement.* New York: John Wiley & Sons.

Vincent, R. 2020. "Hit'n'Mix Infinity." Review in *Sound on Sound* 35(1): 52–58.

Visell, Y., R. Murray-Smith, S. Brewster, and J. Williamson. "Continuous auditory and tactile interaction design." 2013. In *Sonic Interaction Design*, edited by K. Franinovic and S. Serafin. Cambridge, MA: MIT Press, 77–124.

Voelkel, A. 1985. "A cost-effective input processor pitch-detector for electronic violin." In *Proceedings of the 1985 International Computer Music Conference*, edited by B. Truax. San Francisco: International Computer Music Association, 15–18.

Volonnino, B. 1984. *Programmi per la sintisi del suono tramite distortione non lineare dipendente dalla frequenza.* Padua, Italy: Centro di Sonologià Computazionale, Università di Padova.

von Amelunxen, H., D. Appelt, and P. Weibel. 2008. *Notation: Kalkül und Form in den Künsten.* Berlin: Academie der Künst, Karlsruhe: Zentrum für Kunst und Medientechnologie.

Von Foerster, H., and J. Beauchamp, eds. 1969. *Music by Computers.* New York: Wiley.

Von Kempelen, W. 1791. *The Mechanism of Human Speech.* http://www.coli.uni-saarland.de/~trouvain/Kempelen-Web_2017_07_31.pdf.

Von Neumann, J. 1951. "The general and logical theory of automata." In *The World of Mathematics*, edited by E. Newmann. New York: Simon and Schuster, 2070–2098.

Vorländer, M. 2008. *Auralization: Fundamentals of Acoustics, Modelling, Simulation, Algorithms and Acoustic Virtual Reality.* Berlin: Springer.

Vorländer, M. 2018. "Room acoustics—fundamentals and computer simulation." In *Handbook of Systematic Musicology*, edited by R. Bader. Cham, Switzerland: Springer, 197–215.

Waisvisz, M. 1985. "The Hands, a set of remote MIDI controllers." In *Proceedings of the 1985 International Computer Music Conference*, edited by B. Truax. San Francisco: International Computer Music Association, 313–318.

Wakefield, G., W. Smith, and C. Roberts. 2010. "LuaAV: extensibility and heterogeneity for audiovisual computing." *Proceedings of the Linux Audio Conference.* Utrecht, Netherlands.

Wakefield, G., and G. Taylor. 2022. *Generating Sound & Organizing Time: Thinking with gen~.* Walnut, CA: Cycling '74.

Walker, B., and K. Fitz. 1992. *Lemur Manual.* Urbana: CERL Sound Group, University of Illinois.

Wallraff, D. 1979a. "The DMX-1000 signal processing computer." *Computer Music Journal* 3(4): 44–49. Revised and updated version in *Foundations of Computer Music*, edited by C. Roads and J. Strawn, 1985. Cambridge, MA: MIT Press, 54–60.

Wallraff, D. 1979b. "Nedit—Graphical editor for musical scores." In *Proceedings of the 1978 International Computer Music Conference*, edited by C. Roads. Evanston, IL: Northwestern University Press, 410–429.

Walsh, J. 1923. "A closed set of orthonormal functions." *American Journal of Mathematics* 45: 5–24.

Wanderley, M., and M. Battier, eds. 2000. *Trends in Gestural Control of Music.* CD-ROM. Paris: IRCAM.

Wang, G., P. Cook, and S. Salazar. 2015. "ChucK: A strongly timed computer music language." *Computer Music Journal* 39(4): 10–29.

Wan Rosli, M. H. 2016. "Spatiotemporal granulation." PhD diss. Media Arts and Technology, University of California, Santa Barbara.

Warnock, R. 1976. "Longitudinal digital recording of audio." Preprint 1169. New York: Audio Engineering Society.

Waschka, R., and A. Kurepa. 1989. "Using fractals in timbre construction: an exploratory study." In *Proceedings of the 1989 International Computer Music Conference*, edited by T. Wells and D. Butler. San Francisco: International Computer Music Association, 332–335.

Wayne, W. C., Jr. 1961. "Audio modulation system (choral tone modulator)." U.S. Patent 3,004,460.

Weaver, D. 1956. "A third method of generation and detection of single-sideband signals." *Proceedings of the IRE* 44(12): 1703–1705.

Webb, C., and S. Bilbao. 2011. "Computing room acoustics with CUDA—3D FDTD schemes with boundary losses and viscosity." In *Proceedings of the 2011 IEEE International Conference on Acoustics, Speech and Signal Processing (ICASSP)*. New York: IEEE, 317–320.

Wegel, R., and C. Lane. 1924. "The auditory masking of one pure tone by another and its probable relation to the dynamics of the inner ear." *Physics Review* 23: 266–285.

Weibel, P., S. Kanach, and L. Brümmer, eds. 2020. *From Xenakis's UPIC to Graphic Notation Today*. Karlsruhe, Germany: ZKM. https://zkm.de/de/from-xenakiss-upic -to-graphic-notation-today.

Weidenaar, R. 1991. "The alternators of the Telharmonium, 1906." In *Proceedings of the 1991 International Computer Music Conference*, edited by B. Alphonce and B. Pennycook. San Francisco: International Computer Music Association, 311–314.

Weinberg, G., and S. Gan. 2001. "The squeezables: toward an expressive and interdependent multi-player musical instrument." *Computer Music Journal* 25(2): 37–45.

Weinreich, G. 1983. "Violin sound synthesis from first principles." *Journal of the Acoustical Society of America* 74: 1S52.

Weiss-Stauffacher, H., with R. Bruhin. 1976. *The Marvelous World of Music Machines*. Tokyo: Kodansha International.

Wells, T. 1981. *The Technique of Electronic Music*. New York: Schirmer.

Wendt, F., G. Sharma, M. Frank, F. Zotter, and R. Höldrich. 2017. "Perception of spatial sound phenomena created by an icosahedral loudspeaker." *Computer Music Journal* 41(1): 76–88.

Wenger, E., and E. Spiegel. 2010. *MetaSynth 5 User Guide and Reference*. Redwood City, CA: U&I Software.

Wenker, J. 1972. "MUSTRAN II—An extended music translator." *Computers and the Humanities* 7(2).

Wessel, D. 1979. "Timbre space as a musical control structure." *Computer Music Journal* 3(2): 45–52. Reprinted in *Foundations of Computer Music*, edited by C. Roads and J. Strawn, 1985. Cambridge, MA: MIT Press, 640–657.

Wessel, D. 1991. "Improvisation with highly interactive real-time performance systems." In *Proceedings of the 1991 International Computer Music Conference*, edited by B. Alphonce and B. Pennycook. San Francisco: Computer Music Association, 344–347.

Wessel, D., D. Bristow, and Z. Settel. 1987. "Control of phrasing and articulation in synthesis." In *Proceedings of the 1987 International Computer Music Conference*, edited by J. Beauchamp. San Francisco: International Computer Music Association, 108–116.

Wessel, D., R. Felciano, A. Freed, and J. Wawryznek. 1989. "The Center for New Music and Audio Technologies." In *Proceedings of the 1989 International Computer*

Music Conference, edited by T. Wells and D. Butler. San Francisco: International Computer Music Association, 336–339.

Wessel, D., and M. Wright. 2002. "Problems and prospects for intimate musical control of computers." *Computer Music Journal* 26(3): 11–22.

Whitfield, I. 1978. "The neural code." In *Handbook of Perception, Volume 4*, edited by E. Carterette and M. Friedman, 1983. Orlando: Academic Press, 163–183.

Widmer, G., S. Dixon, P. Knees, E. Pampalk, and T. Pohle. 2008. "From sound to sense via feature extraction and machine learning deriving high-level descriptors for characterizing music." In *Sound to Sense, Sense to Sound: A State of the Art in Sound and Music Computing*, edited by P. Polotti and D. Rocchesso. Berlin: Logos, 161–194.

Widrow, B., and M. Lehr. 1990. "30 years of adaptive neural networks: Perceptron, madaline, and backpropagation." *Proceedings of the IEEE* 78(9): 1415–1442.

Wiener, N. 1930. "Generalized harmonic analysis." *Acta Mathematica* 55: 117–258.

Wiener, N. 1964. "Spatial-temporal continuity, quantum theory, and music." In *The Concepts of Space and Time*, edited by M. Capek. 1975. Boston: D. Reidel.

Wiggins, B. 2004. "An Investigation into the real-time manipulation and control of three-dimensional sound fields." PhD thesis. University of Derby.

Wigner, E. 1932. "On the quantum correction for thermodynamic equilibrium." *Physical Review* 40: 749–759.

Wilber, S. 2013. "Entropy analysis and system design for quantum random number generators in CMOS integrated circuits." http://comscire.com/files/whitepaper/Pure_Quantum_White_Paper.pdf.

Wilkinson, S., P. Freeman, P. Gotcher, M. Jeffrey, and C. Johnson. 1989. *Turbosynth User's Manual*. Menlo Park, CA: Digidesign.

Wilmering, T., T. Rehaag, and A. Dupke. 2012. "Pulsar Synthesis Revisited: Considerations for a MIDI Controlled Synthesiser." In *Proceedings of the Ninth International Symposium on Computer Music Modelling and Retrieval (CMMR 2012)*. London: Queen Mary University of London. http://cmmr2012.eecs.qmul.ac.uk/sites/cmmr2012.eecs.qmul.ac.uk/files/pdf/papers/cmmr2012_submission_121.pdf.

Wilson, S., D. Cottle, and N. Collins, eds. 2011. *The SuperCollider Book*. Cambridge, MA: MIT Press.

Winckel, F. 1967. *Music, Sound, and Sensation*. New York: Dover Publications.

Winham, G. 1966. *The Reference Manual for Music 4B*. Princeton, NJ: Princeton University Music Department.

Winkler, T. 1998. *Composing Interactive Music: Techniques and Ideas Using Max*. Cambridge, MA: MIT Press.

Winograd, T. 1968. "Linguistics and the computer analysis of tonal harmony." *Journal of Music Theory* 12(1): 2–49.

Winsor, P. 1987. *Computer-Assisted Music Composition.* Princeton, NJ: Petrocelli Books.

Winsor, P. 1990. *Computer Composer's Toolbox.* New York: TAB Books.

Winsor, P. 1991. *Computer Music in C.* New York: TAB Books.

Winter, M. 2019. "A few more thoughts about Leibniz: the prediction of harmonic distance in harmonic space (with text to preliminary thoughts)." *MusMat: Brazilian Journal of Music and Mathematics* 3: 79–92.

Wishart, T. 1988. "The composition of Vox-5." *Computer Music Journal* 12(4): 21–27.

Wishart, T. 1994. *Audible Design.* Oxfordshire, UK: Orpheus the Pantomime.

Winter, M. 2012. Personal communication.

Wold, E. 1987. "Nonlinear parameter estimation of acoustic models." PhD diss. Report Number UCB/CSD 87/354. Department of Electrical Engineering and Computer Science, University of California, Berkeley.

Wolfram, S. 2002. *A New Kind of Science.* Champaign, IL: Wolfram Media.

Wolfram Research. 2020. *Wolfram Language and System Documentation Center.* https://reference.wolfram.com/language.

Wolman, A., J. Choi, S. Asgharzadeh, and J. Kahana. 1992. "Recognition of handwritten music notation." In *Proceedings of the 1992 International Computer Music Conference*, edited by A. Strange. San Francisco: International Computer Music Association, 125–127.

Wood, A. 1940. *Acoustics.* London: Blackie and Sons.

Wood, P. 1991. "Recollections with John Robinson Pierce." *Computer Music Journal* 15(4): 17–28.

Woodhouse, J. 1992. "Physical modeling of bowed strings." *Computer Music Journal* 16(4): 43–56.

Woolman, M. 2000. *Sonic Graphics: Seeing Sound.* London: Thames and Hudson.

Woszczyk, W., and F. Toole. 1983. "A subjective comparison of five analog and digital tape recorders." Preprint 2033 (H-8). In *Proceedings of the 74th Convention, 8–12 October 1983.* New York: Audio Engineering Society.

Wright, M. 2005. "Open Sound Control: An enabling technology for musical networking." *Organized Sound* 10(3): 193–200.

Wright, M. 2008. "The shape of an instant: Measuring and modeling perceptual attack time with probability density functions (if a tree falls in the forest, when did 57 people hear it make a sound?)." PhD diss. Department of Music, Stanford University.

Wright, M., J. Beauchamp, K. Fitz, X. Rodet, A. Röble, X. Serra, and G. Wakefield. 2000. "Analysis/synthesis comparison." *Organised Sound* 5(3): 173–189.

Wright, M., A. Chaudhary, A. Freed, S. Khoury, and D. Wessel. 1999. "Audio applications of the Sound Description Interchange Format Standard." Preprint #5032. In *Proceedings of the Audio Engineering Society 107th Convention*. New York: Audio Engineering Society.

Wright, M., and A. Freed. 1997. "Open sound control: A new protocol for communicating with sound synthesizers." In *Proceedings of the 1997 International Computer Music Conference*. San Francisco: International Computer Music Association.

Wu, A. 2017. "SuperSampler: A new polyphonic concatenative sampler synthesizer in supercollider for sound motive creating, live coding, and improvisation." In *Proceedings of the 2017 International Computer Music Conference*. San Francisco: International Computer Music Association.

Wu, C.-W., C. Dittmar, C. Southall, R. Vogl, G. Widmer, J. Hockman, M. Müller, and A. Lerch. 2018. "A review of automatic drum transcription." *IEEE/ACM Transactions on Audio, Speech, and Language Processing* 26(9): 1457–1483.

Xambó, A. 2018. "Who are the women authors in NIME?–Improving gender balance in NIME research." *Proceedings of the 2018 New Interfaces for Musical Expression (NIME) Conference*. n.p.: New Interfaces for Musical Expression. https://www.nime.org.

Xenakis, I. 1960. "Elements of stochastic music." *Gravesaner Blätter* 18: 84–105.

Xenakis, I. 1971. *Formalized Music*. Bloomington: Indiana University Press.

Xenakis, I. 1985. "Music composition treks." In *Composers and the Computer*, by C. Roads. Middleton, WI: A-R Editions, 171–192.

Xenakis, I. 1992. *Formalized Music*. Revised ed. Stuyvesant, NY: Pendragon Press.

Xin C. 1987. Personal communication.

Xiph. 2015. xiph.org/flac.

Yadegari, S. 2003. "Chaotic signal synthesis with real-time control: Solving differential equations in PD, Max/MSP and Jmax." In *Proceedings of the Sixth Conference on Digital Audio Effects (DAFx-03), London*. n.p.: DAFx. http://yadegari.org/publications.

Yamaha. 1993. Marketing literature for the VL1 synthesizer. Buena Park, CA: Yamaha.

Yang, L., and A. Lerch. 2020. "On the evaulation of generative models in music." *Neural Computing and Applications* 32(2): 4773–4784.

Yeh, D. 2012. "Automated physical modeling of nonlinear audio circuits for real-time audio effects—Part II: BJT and vacuum tube examples." *IEEE Transactions on Audio, Speech, and Language Processing* 20(4): 1207–1216.

Yeh, D., J. Abel, A. Vladirimescu, and J. O. Smith. 2008. "Numerical methods for simulation of guitar distortion circuits." *Computer Music Journal* 32(2): 23–42.

Yeh, D., J. Abel, and J. O. Smith. 2010. "Automated physical modeling of nonlinear audio circuits for real-time audio effects—Part I: Theoretical development." *IEEE Transactions on Audio, Speech, and Language Processing* 18(4): 728–737.

Yerkes, K. 2018. Personal communication.

Yeston, M. 1976. *The Stratification of Musical Rhythm.* New Haven, CT: Yale University Press.

Young, G. 1985. *Hugh LeCaine: Pioneer in electronic music instrument design, compositions and demonstrations 1948–1972.* Long-play phonograph recording. Toronto: JWD Music.

Young, G. 1989. *The Sackbut Blues.* Ottawa: National Museum of Science and Technology.

Yunik, M., M. Borys, and G. W. Swift. 1985. "A digital flute." *Computer Music Journal* 9(2): 49–52.

Zabetian, S. 2018. "Extensions to dynamic wave terrain synthesis for multidimensional polyphonic expression." MS thesis. Aalbog University Copenhagen.

Zaripov, R. 1960. "An algorithmic descriiption of the music composing process." *Doklady Academiia Nauk* SSSR 132: 1283. English translation in *Automation Express* 3: 17.

Zaripov, R. 1969. "Cyberbetics and music." *Perspectives of New Music* 7(2): 115–154. Translation by J. Russell of *Kibernetika i Muzyka* (1963).

Zattra, L. 2020. "Analyse de *Stria* de John Chowning." https://brahms.ircam.fr /analyses/Stria.

Zaunschirm, M., J. Reiss, and A. Klapuri. 2012. "A sub-band approach to modification of musical transients." *Computer Music Journal* 36(2): 23–36.

Zicarelli, D. 2002. "How I learned to love a program that does nothing." *Computer Music Journal* 26(4): 44–51.

Zils, A., and F. Pachet. 2001. "Musical Mosaicing." In *Proceedings of the COST-G6 International Conference on Digital Audio Effects.* n.p.: DAFx, 1–6. https://www .dafx.de.

Zivanovic, M., A. Röbel, and X. Rodet. 2008. "Adaptive threshold determination for spectral peak classification." *Computer Music Journal* 32(2): 57–67.

Zölzer, U., ed. 2011. *DAFX: Digital Audio Effects.* 2nd ed. New York: Wiley.

Zotter, F., and M. Frank. 2019. *Ambisonics: A Practical 3D Audio Theory for Recording, Studio Production, Sound Reinforcement, and Virtual Reality.* Chur, Switzerland: Springer.

Zotter, F., M. Zaunschirm, M. Frank, and M. Kronlacher. 2017. "A beamformer to play with wall reflections: The icosahedral loudspeaker." *Computer Music Journal* 41(3): 50–68.

Zucco, G. 2014. *Inside Csound.* Torino, Italy: Giancarlo Zedde.

Zwicker, E. 1961. "Subdivision of the audible frequency range into critical bands." *Journal of the Acoustical Society of America* 33(2): 248.

Index